A Global Encyclopedia of Historical Writing

GARLAND REFERENCE LIBRARY OF THE HUMANITIES (VOL. 1809)

A Global Encyclopedia of Historical Writing

Volume I
A–J

Editor
D.R. Woolf

Managing Editor
Kathryn M. Brammall

Editorial Assistant
Greg Bak

Advisory Editors
Peter Burke
John Flint
Georg G. Iggers
Donald R. Kelley
F.J. Levy
D.L. McMullen
Peter Novick
Karen Offen
Anthony Reid
Kenneth Sacks
Judith P. Zinsser

GARLAND PUBLISHING, INC.
A member of the Taylor & Francis Group
New York & London, 1998

Library of Congress Cataloging-in-Publication Data

A global encyclopedia of historical writing / editor, D.R. Woolf ;
managing editor, Kathryn M. Brammall ; editorial assistant, Greg Bak
; advisory editors, Peter Burke . . . [et al.].
        v.   cm. — (Garland reference library of the humanities ; vol.
1809)
        Includes bibliographical references and index.
        ISBN 0-8153-1514-7 (v. 1 : alk. paper)
        1. Historiography.   2. Historians.   I. Woolf, D. R. (Daniel R.)
II. Series.
        D13.G47   1998
        907'.2—dc21   97-42982
                                                                                    CIP

Cover art: Antique map, World / Seutter 1730
Cover design: Lawrence Wolfson Design, New York

Printed on acid-free, 250-year-life paper
Manufactured in the United States of America

In memory of my grandparents

Contents

Volume I

ix   Acknowledgments

xi   Introduction and Editorial Conventions

xix   Contributors

xxxiv   About the Editor

1   The Encyclopedia

Volume II

499   The Encyclopedia

993   General Index

Acknowledgments

In any scholarly enterprise, one is likely to run up debts well in excess of the credits created by the final product. In a reference work such as this, these obligations are even weightier. I am very grateful to the authors for having agreed to supply entries and for having countenanced my frequent requests for changes or further information, and in proving patient with the sometimes nagging correspondence that is an editor's lot. The advisory editors played an important role both in reviewing and criticizing the contents of the entry list and in suggesting potential authors for many of the articles. They served an even more valuable function in reviewing for accuracy, style, and clarity, the draft entries that were submitted and, in some instances, supplying additional text. A number of them also agreed, late in the process, to write entries in their own areas. Many scholars outside the advisory board also contributed considerable time and effort in reading draft entries: it is my pleasure to acknowledge under this category the assistance of Tessa Morris-Suzuki, Anthony Seldon, D.S. Chandler, B.J.C. McKercher, Susan A. Eacker, Susanne DeBerry Cox, Ian Mabbett, Ellen Nore, Bertrum MacDonald, and Robert Stacey. Reuven Amitai-Preiss and John Lee offered advice on the standardization of transliteration and use of diacritics in the Arabic and Korean entries, respectively. I wish also to thank for their assistance in varying capacities my colleagues in the School of Historical Studies at the Institute for Advanced Study (1996–97), in particular Deborah Klimburg-Salter and Richard Sharpe, and the Institute's associate librarian, Marcia Tucker, for assistance with innumerable eleventh-hour bibliographical queries. Tom Gieryn, Diane Vaughan, Martina Kessel, Margaret Rossiter, Fernando Cervantes and Don Kelley all provided intellectual stimulation during the same period in Princeton.

At Garland, Gary Kuris, who first suggested that I undertake this book early in 1993, has been a patient and thoughtful publisher, always willing to discuss ideas for shaping and reshaping its structure; he proved an invaluable guide, moreover, to the various challenges involved in assembling a multi-authored work. Elizabeth Manus and Marianne Lown were of considerable assistance in administrative matters; Jason Goldfarb and Chuck Bartelt offered useful advice on computational matters connected with the publishing process. Helga McCue oversaw final production with great care. Fred Leventhal of Boston University and Peter N. Stearns of Carnegie Mellon, both recent editors of similar Garland encyclopedias on different subjects, were encouraging as to this project and offered early and wise advice on its execution.

My debt to members of the Dalhousie community is, if possible, even greater. Cathy Lunn of University Computing and Information Services provided prompt and patient answers to a seemingly endless variety of software problems in 1994 and 1995. Laura Adams of the Financial Services Department and Tina Jones, administrative secretary for the History Department, undertook oversight of the financial records of the project. Tina Jones again, and graduate secretary Mary Wyman-Leblanc, were also extremely helpful in other, nonhistoriographical capacities, not least because the preparation of this book was virtually coterminous with my term as chair of the graduate program of my department. Lola Doucet undertook a great deal of typing and retyping, as well as some bibliographical checking and querying the clarity of certain entries from the viewpoint of the intelligent undergraduate reader; David Adams and Deborah Osmond also assisted in the last two categories. Greg Bak, currently a doctoral candidate working with me on seventeenth-century English history, proved a model editorial assistant, seeing to it that documents were properly filed and that correspondence was processed and answered promptly. Dr. Kathryn Brammall, now a member of the History Department at Truman State University in Kirksville, Missouri, occupied his position in the first year and a half of the project, and eventually assumed, as managing editor, overall administrative coordination in association with Mr. Bak. Both have proved endlessly patient, methodical, and insightful, and have made constructive suggestions of their own that have proved indispensable in finishing the project on schedule. Without their help, and sense of humor, the book simply could not have been done. Various other graduate students in the department assisted in other ways, in particular Krista Kesselring, Jennifer Morawiecki, Lorraine Gallant, Ruth McClelland-Nugent, Keith Robinson, Edward Michalik, Peter Twohig, and Laurie Gagnier. I would also like to thank members of various editions of my honors and graduate seminar on historiography (and in particular the class of 1995–96 who acted as guinea pigs for sample entries) for having convinced me, sometimes unintentionally, of the need for such a work and the importance of making it as global as possible. Other students in other classes have also provided valuable ideas on historiographical matters, as have student groups elsewhere; I think in particular of the Northeastern Illinois (Chicago) and Eastern Illinois (Charleston) chapters of the Phi Alpha Theta Honor Society, who kindly invited me to address their respective annual meetings in 1996 on matters connected to the book; I am pleased also to acknowledge the gracious hospitality of Zachary Schiffman, Newton Key, and Robert Bucholz on these two occasions.

A number of Dalhousie colleagues have assisted in various ways by commenting on draft entries, providing answers to queries, and in some instances even writing a number of entries. It is impossible to name them all, but I particularly wish to single out, in no particular order, Norman Pereira, Hubert Morgan, Ronald Tetreault, Jack Crowley, Michael Cross, Lawrence Stokes, Stephen Brooke, Philip Zachernuk, Jane Parpart, Shirley Tillotson, and Cynthia Neville. John O'Brien, chair of the History Department, took a considerable interest in the project, as did Graham Taylor, formerly the chair and now dean of the Faculty of Arts and Social Sciences (who graciously donated his own departmental office to provide the home for the project that my own tiny office could not afford). Jane Arscott provided early encouragement, and advice on how to make the work more global and inclusive than it might otherwise have been. A number of friends and family members unconnected with the project were pillars of strength and sources of good humor: among the former, Marian Binkley, Norman and Linda Pereira, Lisa Profitt, Denise and Natan Nevo, and, especially, Lesley Barnes; among the latter, my parents, my brother, and, last but not least, my three children, Sarah, Samuel, and David.

To all of the above, and especially to the authors, is owed any of the credit for this book.

D.R. Woolf, Halifax
September 30, 1997

Introduction and Editorial Conventions

"It should be known that history is a discipline that has a great number of approaches."

—*Ibn Khaldūn, from the introduction to the* Muḳaddima

History does not make itself. It is constructed by men and women, living at specific times, who wish to understand a period or episode in the past, and to describe it for contemporary (and often future) readers. From Herodotus to our own era, historians have served a variety of related functions: sages, diplomats, priests, teachers, prophets, politicians, poets, and ladies and gentlemen of leisure; only in the last hundred years or so have they been a distinctive profession, within and outside an academic setting. But what distinguishes them as *historians* has been their effort to mediate between the raw evidence of the past, recent or remote, and an audience that is itself imagined in the process of writing, long before the history is actually read. Thus Thucydides thought of his famous *History of the Peloponnesian War* as a work not just for his own contemporaries, but for the ages, and the disgraced Han historian Sima Qian submitted to castration rather than commit suicide, so that he could finish his own *Shiji* (China's first comprehensive history of the then known past) and redeem his reputation in the future. Other historians have written with the aim of correcting errors created or perpetuated by their predecessors: Thucydides, again, had this in mind in fifth-century Athens; nearly two millennia further on, in the late fourteenth century, Ibn Khaldūn opened his famous *Muḳaddima* with an attack on the accuracy of earlier Muslim scholars such as the tenth-century historian Mas'ūdī.

Just as historians have fulfilled different roles, so has the craft they practice. At various times history has been seen as a branch of rhetoric or literature (as in the Renaissance); it has been contained in poetic form, as in the Homeric epics, or in memorable and entertaining prose such as the Scandinavian sagas that began in the twelfth century A.D., and the Japanese *Rekishi Monogatari* (historical tales) of the eleventh to fourteenth centuries. At other times, history has been reconceptualized as a branch of law, or of philosophy, and even of science. It has proved far too pliable and resilient to remain confined for long within a single disciplinary box.

Although the great nineteenth-century German historian Leopold von Ranke aspired to recount the past *wie es eigentlich gewesen* (as it actually—or essentially—happened), students and teachers have been aware virtually since the time of the Greeks that history is an imperfect craft and the historian subject to error, misinterpretation, or short-sightedness. Each age, as Ranke himself knew, rewrites the past in the light of new knowledge, and with different concerns; the questions asked of the documents and artifacts that provide the source for most history similarly change from age to age, and culture to culture, making the answers offered by historians very different. It is probably true that there has never been complete accord between two historians, even those exactly contemporary and living in the same nation. At various times, efforts have been made to minimize the possibilities of error: the ancient Chinese approach of basing a single Standard History (*Zhengshi*) of a former dynasty on materials compiled by that dynasty and then suppressed by the next offered one approach to the establishment of a univocal interpretation of the past. There have been similar attempts made in the West, for instance during the Renaissance, and under modern totalitarianisms of the Right and Left, to ensure that a single version of the past, generally favorable to the ruler or government of the time, has achieved official status, and that dissenting versions have been suppressed. Other regimes throughout the world have employed degrees of censorship to ensure the hegemony of one particular view of history, and in some instances continue to do so. We are apt to dismiss, from a liberal present, the notion that history ought to be ideologically driven; nevertheless, it is a fact that history has *always* been influenced, to a greater or lesser degree, by external forces operating on the historian, be they governmental, religious, material, or simply careerist. Nor is relative freedom to enquire and write likely to ensure the triumph of an objective history as the "last word" on its subject. In fact, nothing could be further from the case. Beginning with the ancients, continuing on through the Middle Ages and the Renaissance, through the Enlightenment, and down to the modern era of the "professional," historians have written and rewritten the canons of proper historical method countless times. What seemed an appropriate method for several centuries of scholars employed in the Chinese Imperial bureaucracy would have seemed alien to their contemporaries in Rome or, later, in the Middle Ages. The methods of Renaissance philologists such as the fifteenth-century Italian, Lorenzo Valla, often praised by modern historians for their "anticipation" of modern methods of textual criticism, were designed around the reconstruction of ancient wisdom, not the discovery of new facts.

Issues of method, accuracy, and validity of interpretation are first and foremost the concern of historians, but they have a direct bearing on readers as well. The modern nonacademic purchaser of a history book is generally more interested in what actually happened than in the method or style of its telling. She or he probably looks to a history, in the first instance, to discover a concrete "fact" such as the number of dead at Gettysburg or the date of a Zulu uprising; alternatively, the casual reader may simply wish to be entertained by a historian who is speaking, through the book itself, to that reader in as authoritative a manner as possible. Given this, most nonacademic readers of history are likely to find discussions of method and interpretation dull, arcane, and frustrating.

Yet such questions can surely not be ignored if a reader is to engage in a dialogue with the historian, to evaluate critically what is being read and make informed judgments. In the past century and a half there has been an ongoing debate concerning the degree to which history either fulfills or falls short of the standards of objectivity and precision set by the natural, and especially the physical sciences. This is a question to which there exists no unequivocal answer. There are historians who have seen and continue to see history as a "science, nothing more and nothing less," such as the Cambridge ancient historian J.B. Bury at the start of the twentieth century, or the nineteenth-century champion of positivism Auguste Comte, or the latter-day exponents of quantification from the French-based Annales school, to American cliometricians. There are, in equal supply, others who have seen history as happily unscientific, defending its status as a literary art (for instance Bury's younger contemporary, G.M. Trevelyan), wherein the historian imposes on the bare, atomic facts of history so high a degree of imaginative interpretation and colorful, persuasive language as to make any pretense to scientific objectivity meaningless. This book does not seek to resolve that age-old division but to present many examples of both types of view.

Students and general readers may also be troubled by the degree to which interpretation, ideology, and even outright mendacity have intervened to produce accounts of history that have been found defective, even by contemporaries. It is certainly true that not every history written in the past, nor every school that has for a time reigned over Clio's dominion, remains useful today as a guide to "what actually happened," and even the great historians of the late nineteenth and early twentieth centuries are, with a few exceptions, read less for information on the episodes they covered than for evidence of the mentality of their *own* age. No one would seriously suggest that Thomas Babington Macaulay is the authority on the reign of James II, or that Alexis de Tocqueville's study of the Old Regime is definitive, but both historians continue to be read because they wrote compelling prose and because they tell us much about the nineteenth century's attitude to the past. In earlier periods, this division is less clearcut: there are many chronicles from Europe and Asia, some of which were based on sources no longer extant, that have become the "primary" source for their subject.

But the process of criticism and correction is now an intrinsic structural feature of historical writing, just as methodological innovation coupled with the occasional return to what some historians, such as the late Sir Geoffrey Elton, regard as "essentials" of good scholarship, is an ongoing feature of scholarly research. Historians do not write in a vacuum consisting merely of themselves and their primary sources. Accounts of the past written tomorrow will be guided by those published today, even when they come to radically different views; similarly, the history writing of the late twentieth century has built on not one but a variety of traditions going back many hundreds of years, traditions that have taken different shapes on six continents. The encyclopedia explores the richness, not the rigidity, of historiography. It aims to illustrate both the obvious point that interest in the past is not solely a preserve of modernity, and also the fact—regrettably less evident to Western eyes—that it has not been the monopoly of European and American cultures. There is no single monograph embracing the historical writing of all ages *and* all nations; such a book would be extremely difficult to write for a historian unfamiliar with a vast number of national histories, cultural conventions, and languages. A multiauthored encyclopedia, precisely because it draws on experts from different countries and with different training and perspectives, offers one way of filling that gap.

This is, then, a book about history in the sense of the practice of writing about the past, not a book about the past itself. A term commonly used to describe the art—or science—of history writing is "historiography." This is a word that undergraduates, graduate students, and even their professors, often come to dread—the editor has experienced the anxiety of several generations of students at his own university, and recalls from undergraduate days his own mystification (and the beginning of a long-standing interest). While most of the contributors to this book might agree that "historiography" is not a term that should be feared, it is most certainly one that is often misunderstood, because it is used in a number of different ways. And, since it is also a word repeated at length in the following pages, particularly where national traditions of historical writing are concerned, it requires some explanation here.

Generally speaking, "historiography" (from the Latin *historiographus,* writer of history, and ultimately from an earlier Greek root) is used in three distinct senses: (1) to describe writing about the past in general, as, for instance, in Ernst Breisach's very useful recent survey of Western historical writing, entitled *Historiography: Ancient, Medieval, & Modern;* (2) to describe the current and recent state of writing about a particular period, person, or topic in the past, for instance, "the historiography of the fall of Rome" or "the historiography of the Spanish Civil War" or "the historiography of the Tang dynasty." Undergraduate and especially beginning graduate students are often given "historiographic" assignments that involve reviewing the state of debate on a particular issue, or in assessing the merits of two or more different historians' arguments; (3) as shorthand for a class on historical method(s) or on the logic of historical enquiry.

This encyclopedia is intended to provide points of departure for readers curious about historiography in all three senses. It presents the greatest names in European and North American historical writing, past and present, many of whom will be familiar to readers already; it also includes a variety of historians previously excluded from general accounts, such as women and authors from non-Western cultures. It presents old forms of writing about the past, such as sagas and chronicles, modern "schools" such as the progressives and the Annales, and the latest developments from psychohistory to cultural history, from cliometrics to women's history and postmodernism. Through all this, the aim of the editor and advisory editors has been to provide a guide, not a set of Confucian canons. The book prescribes no "correct" or uniform method, and offers no argument that one particular approach or interpretation is more valid than others—although individual authors have been encouraged to indicate points on which historians they have described have been praised or faulted and to indicate what is living and what is dead in older examples of historical writing. To be less pluralist than this would have been to defeat the aims of the book, and the preference of the editor has been to take all due care to avoid clear error, but otherwise to encourage multiple approaches. While the selection of topics is therefore a personal one, resting with the advisory board and, ultimately, with the editor, authors are responsible for the accuracy in fact and interpretation of their individual articles.

Coverage

Articles in this book fall into three broad categories: (1) brief biographical entries on individual historians or sometimes individual works and genres of historiography associated with no particular author or with multiple authors; (2) longer surveys of national or regional historiographies, sometimes contained in more than one entry (as for instance in the case of China, England, and Japan), but more typically in a single entry; and (3) topical articles on certain concepts, approaches, or themes in historiography, for instance Philosophy of History, Counterfactuals, the Industrial Revolution, Class, Marxism, and so on.

Although this work is global in scope, it is a two-volume reference tool rather than an exhaustive multivolume compilation on the order of the *Encyclopedia Britannica*. In order to represent the widest possible range of historiographical topics, subdisciplines, conceptual categories, national historiographies, and, finally, individual historians, and to do so within the space allotted, it has been essential to make the work representative rather than comprehensive.

Two types of exclusion have been made. (1) With certain exceptions, such as the Historiography of the French Revolution, the Holocaust, or the Industrial Revolution, whence the issues raised have spilled into other branches of historical writing, we have not endeavored to provide historiographical essays on every subject controverted among historians; this could easily have expanded two volumes into twenty. (2) Individual historians have been selected carefully and with the overall aims of the volume in mind. Making the final choice of whom to put in and whom to leave out proved a considerable challenge. Since this is an encyclopedia of historical writing, and not a biographical dictionary of historians, certain principles of selection have been followed. We have endeavored to include most if not absolutely all of the recognized "greats" in various languages: Herodotus, Tacitus, Sima Qian, Guicciardini, Michelet, Macaulay (Catharine *and* Thomas), Ranke, and Beard (Charles *and* Mary), but also a host of historians of undeniable importance to their fields but with a somewhat lower "name recognition" factor. The inclusion of little-known Chinese historians at the expense of greater space that might have been allotted to Livy, Matthew Paris, or Carl Becker is intended to correct a Western bias in most comparable textbooks and dictionaries on historical writing without ignoring the usual cast of characters found in such works, from Thucydides to Toynbee. A number of early female historians whose quantity of published scholarly work is relatively small have been included, often in preference to contemporary male historians who are better known; this kind of "affirmative action" principle would seem justified by recent investigations, such as those by Bonnie Smith and Natalie Zemon Davis, into the hurdles that stood in the way of women interested in the past until relatively recent times. Finally, under this second rubric of exclusion, the decision was reached at an early stage to commission entries on only a handful of still-living historians. Our selection here will not be to every taste: in general we opted to include living historians (including a few who died during the preparation of the work, such as Edward Thompson, Merle Curti, Maruyama Masao, Richard Cobb, Georges Duby, George Rudé, and Geoffrey Elton) and certain nonhistorians (such as the anthropologist Clifford Geertz) who have had a broad impact on the discipline outside their particular field of interest, and with little reference to the *quantity* of their work. Readers who find their own favorite living historian without a home in this book should bear this in mind.

Editorial Conventions
1. Arrangement of articles

Articles are either biographical or topical and are arranged alphabetically by the first word of the surname: thus Ma Huan precedes Ma Su, and both precede Mabillon and Maruyama. Accents and apostrophes do not figure in alphabetization and can be regarded as silent for those purposes. In the case of Arabic historians, the form most commonly recognized is used (thus Ibn ʿAʾidh, Muḥammad), with a historian's more formal name, if different, following; all Arabic or Islamic historians whose proper name is generally preceded by "Ibn" are grouped together under Ibn ("son of") for ease of reference: this is in keeping with the practice of standard works in Islam such as the revised *Encyclopedia of Islam*. The prefix "al-" is *not* counted as a word for alphabetical sequence, also in keeping with standard practice.

Topical articles (for instance: Microhistory; Medicine, Historiography of; Women's History, Indian and Pakistani) begin with their heading and are followed immediately by a brief definition before the main body of the entry begins. Many large topics (for instance, Japanese Historiography and Chinese Historiography) have been broken down into two or more articles both to reflect the richness of a field and to allow for the subspecializations of contributors.

Biographical articles begin with surname, given names, generally without initials (H.J. Habakkuk, and R.H. Tawney are thus listed, respectively, as Habakkuk, Hrothgar John and Tawney, Richard Henry), with maiden name for women if different from publishing name, and dates of birth and death, which are A.D. except where noted as B.C. (The use of Christian reckoning of years rather than "B.C.E." and "C.E.," which might appear to violate our global aims, is a compromise made in the interests of ease of reference.) For a number of historians, in particular those in antiquity or the Middle Ages, the date of birth and/or death remains either unclear or controverted. These dates are noted with a "ca." meaning "about"; in some cases, they are noted with two dates separated by a /, as in the case of Livy, where two alternative dates, 59 and 64 B.C., are variously accepted. If little is known about an author other than what he or she wrote, then the dates are given as a "fl.," that is, "flourished." Historians still alive as of December 1, 1997, are listed as (b. 1915). In the case of topical entries, especially those concerned with national historiographies (for instance, Spanish Historiography, Polish Historiography) dates for individual historians who are incidentally or illustratively mentioned, many of whom do not have distinct entries of their own, generally appear in the body of the entry.

Chinese, Korean, and Japanese names appear with the family name first followed *without a comma* by the given name: this is well-known and common practice for Chinese and Korean, but in the case of Japanese, Western journalistic practice has tended to invert the name order according to North American usage, a practice that we have not followed: thus the entry on Ōtsuka Hisao denotes a historian whose surname is Ōtsuka. Occasional exceptions, mainly historians whose names appear Western-style on their English-language publications, are indexed *with* commas to avoid confusion.

2. Transliteration and Translation

Arabic, Persian, and Islamic-world proper names, for which many renderings are possible, normally follow the conventions of the revised or "new" edition of *The Encyclopedia of Islam* (which as of 1996 had only reached the letter "S"). Russian names are transliterated according to U.S. Library of Congress principles but without diacritical marks, except where a recognized English version is known: thus, we use Kliuchevskii, not Klyuchevsky, and Pokrovskii, not Pokrovsky, but we retain Trotsky; M-I. Rostovzeff is listed under the more commonly-used spelling "Rostovtzeff."

Chinese names and words are rendered according to the pinyin system, which has supplanted the older Wade-Giles system as the standard protocol for transliteration: Mao Tse-tung should be looked for under Mao Zedong. In most cases, a cross-reference has been rendered in the volume directing the reader to the correct heading. (This is necessary in part because most library cataloging systems continue to employ the Wade-Giles form). Certain exceptions to this rule apply for historians with established Western names, such as Confucius, whose Chinese name was either Kong Qiu or Kong Zi (Master Kong). The names of Chinese historians publishing in Western languages, and the titles of books originally issued in those languages, follow the actual spelling of the author or title, whether Wade-Giles or pinyin.

Korean words and names are more problematic, as no system has yet achieved dominance, and romanization practices vary; we have chosen the McCune-Reischauer system, although often providing alternative spellings of a word or name and leaving personal names hyphenated.

Although the encyclopedia is global in scope and should, it is hoped, be of use to any interested reader around the world, it is nonetheless presented in American English and in such a way that readers who are exclusively anglophone can make use of it. We have therefore adopted the sometimes cumbersome and typographically ugly practice of furnishing in square brackets [ ] a literal English translation of foreign titles, whether in familiar Western languages like Spanish or German, Latin or modern Greek, or in non-Western and often transliterated tongues like Chinese and Vietnamese. These bracketed translations are deliberately kept in Roman rather than Italic type to avoid misleading a reader into thinking that an English edition of the work exists. Where such a translated edition does, in fact, exist (as for instance in the case of most works by Carlo Ginzburg or Fernand Braudel), the original title is given in the main entry but the translated editions are listed under "Texts" (see *Bibliographies* below). Bracketed translations are generally given at the first mention of a title, either in the main body of the entry or in the bibliography; they are not repeated in the bibliographical section if given earlier.

3. Accents and diacriticals

It is the intention of the editors to be as accurate as possible in rendering names and words in languages other than English and especially in alphabets or writing systems (such as Arabic and Chinese, respectively) other than Roman. In the case of Japanese, names are commonly spelled in the media either without any diacritics or with a circumflex over the "o" or "u." We have adopted the practice of using a macron (a bar over the "o" or "u"), which is closer to the Japanese rendering. In Arabic, the mark ' denotes a diacritic ('ayn) often written with an inward facing single quotation mark; ' denotes a quite distinct diacritic (hamza) often written as a superscripted, *backward* facing "c." As with transliteration we have kept as close as possible to the conventions of the *Encyclopedia of Islam* (new edition, 1960–). Indian names and words are also heavily accented, especially those from earlier periods, but these marks have normally been discarded for entries on modern India and modern Indian historians, in keeping with current scholarly practice on the subcontinent. In the case of Arabic, Persian, and Indian names or words other than proper names (e.g., Safavid dynasty) we have not adopted full diacritics but kept to familiar English usage; Mamlūk, however, is rendered with a bar over the "u." Western-language titles of books are not adjusted but are as they appear in bibliographical records.

4. Cross-Referencing and Indexing

The reader will find a comprehensive index of every name or concept mentioned in the book, but in the interests of economy we have not provided full internal cross-referencing of all articles. Topical entries are, however, cross-referenced to related topical entries by means of a *See also* at the conclusion of the entry, after the contributor's name. The reader should note that items mentioned herein may denote a *series* of suggested entries rather than a single one, as in the case of "Women's History," an enormous category that has been broken down by geographical region. We have not normally provided cross-referencing for entries on individuals, although a few exceptions have been made where two such entries are so closely related as to render an explicit cross-reference to the other desirable: thus, Thucydides and Herodotus are mutually cross-referenced.

5. Bibliographies

Each entry is followed by the contributor's name, by cross-references, if any, and then by two bibliographical sections called "Texts" and "References," respectively. "Texts" are those works *by* a particular author or classic works on a topic. "References" are works for further reading *about* an author (such as a biography or historiographical study) or secondary works *about* a topic (monographs, historiographical journal articles, and sometimes bibliographies). Collections of correspondence and autobiographies by historians have been included where they bear on the historian's views on history (in such instances under "Texts") or if they contain substantial biographical information about him or her (in which case they have fallen, somewhat arbitrarily, under "References").

In the case of biographical entries, both "Texts" and "References" are given. In rare instances where no accessible edition exists of a nonetheless important historian, or where a historian's work is known from other sources but is itself no longer extant, a notation explaining the absence has been provided. Some biographical entries, in particular those on historians still living or only recently deceased, lack a "References" section, signifying that in the judgment of the entry's author and the editor no significant body of published work has yet been written *about* that historian.

In the case of topical entries, the practice varies according to the nature and scope of the entry itself. Virtually all topical entries are followed by a list of "References," which should *not* be taken as including every work or author mentioned in the entry. These lists also vary considerably in length, with some relatively new subdisciplines granted greater latitude than more established branches of the discipline. In some instances, a topical entry will also have a list of "Texts" before the "References," signifying sample editions of works mentioned in the article that are typical for the topic but, again, do not amount to a comprehensive list of the works discussed or referred to therein.

One important caveat should be noted in the selection of both titles and editions of those titles for mention in the bibliographical sections. Since this is an encyclopedia in the first instance and neither a biographical dictionary nor a critical bibliography, no entry, biographical or otherwise, has an *exhaustive* bibliography. Rather, the author and editorial staff have selected a few works (generally books but in some instances seminal journal articles) by the historian under study for inclusion under "Texts." Although dates of initial publication, where known, are given in the main body of most entries, the "Texts" section deliberately departs from this practice and instead lists that edition (or reliable translation if available) that in the editor's judgment is most widely available. Where a modern critical or collected edition is established as definitive, this information is given in lieu of repeating individual titles.

Names of publishers are rendered as they appear in title pages (or transliterated along the lines referred to above). Names of cities of publication, however, are given in modern English forms: thus The Hague, not 's-Gravenhage; Florence, not Firenze, and so on.

Contributors

Guido Abbattista
Dipartimento di Storia
Università di Torino

Emma C. Alexander
Trinity College
Cambridge University

Guy S. Alitto
Department of History
University of Chicago

J.D. Alsop
Department of History
McMaster University
Hamilton, ON

Donald Altschiller
Mugar Memorial Library
Boston University

Jorge M. dos Santos Alves
Amadora, Portugal

Reuven Amitai-Preiss
Institute of Asian and African Studies
Faculty of Humanities
Hebrew University of Jerusalem

Josef Anderle
Department of History
University of North Carolina
Chapel Hill

Alfred J. Andrea
Department of History
University of Vermont

David F. Appleby
Department of History
US Naval Academy
Annapolis, MD

Ian W. Archer
Keble College
Oxford

David Armitage
Department of History
Columbia University

Christopher Pratt Atwood
Department of Central Eurasian Studies
Indiana University
Bloomington

Michael Arthur Aung-Thwin
Asian Studies, University of Hawaii
Honolulu

Greg Bak
Department of History
Dalhousie University

Michel Balivet
Departement des Études Islamiques de
    l'université de Provence
Centre des Lettres et Sciences Humaines
Université de Provence (Aix-Marseille I)

John W. Barker
Department of History
University of Wisconsin
Madison

Scot Barmé
Division of Pacific and Southeast Asian History
Research School of Pacific and Asian Studies
Australian National University
Canberra

Robin B. Barnes
Department of History
Davidson College
Davidson, NC

Andrew E. Barshay
Department of History
University of California
Berkeley

Kenneth Bartlett
Victoria College
University of Toronto

Barrett L. Beer
Department of History
Kent State University

Christopher M. Bellitto
Institute of Religious Studies and St. Joseph's
    Seminary
Dunwoodie

Jerry H. Bentley
Department of History
University of Hawaii
Manoa

Barry Bergdoll
Department of Art History
Columbia University

Pradip Bhaumik
Department of History
University of Minnesota

Rusty Bittermann
Department of History
University College of Cape Breton
Sydney, NS

Jeremy Black
Department of History
University of Exeter

Corinne Blake
Department of History
Rowan College of New Jersey

G.R. Blue
Department of History
University of Victoria
Victoria, BC

Mark E. Blum
Department of History
University of Louisville

James Borchert
Department of History
Cleveland State University

D.A. Brading
Centre of Latin-American Studies
Cambridge University

Kathryn M. Brammall
Department of History
Truman State University
Kirksville, MO

David Braybrooke
Department of Government
University of Texas
Austin

Warren Breckman
Department of History
University of Pennsylvania

Ernst Breisach
Department of History
Western Michigan University
Kalamazoo

Francis J. Bremer
Department of History
Millersville University
Millersville, PA

Robin Brooks
Department of History
San Jose State University

Susan E. Brown
Department of History
University of Prince Edward Island

John S. Brownlee
Department of East Asian Studies
University of Toronto

Anthony Brundage
Department of History
California State Polytechnic University
Pomona

Lawrence M. Bryant
Department of History
California State University
Chico

Paul Budra
Department of English
Simon Fraser University
Burnaby, BC

Paul M. Buhle
American Civilization
Brown University

Glenn Burgess
Department of History
University of Hull

Peter Burke
Emmanuel College
Cambridge University

Valerie Burton
Department of History
Memorial University of Newfoundland
St. John's

Louis P. Cain
Department of Economics
Loyola University Chicago, and
Department of Economics
Northwestern University

Ian Caldwell
Centre for Southeast Asian Studies
University of Hull

A.J. Carlson
Department of History
Austin College
Sherman, TX

Fernando Cervantes
Department of Hispanic, Portuguese and Latin
  American Studies
University of Bristol

Henry Y.S. Chan
Department of History
Moorhead State University
Moorhead, MN

John Chance
Department of Anthropology
Arizona State University
Tempe

David Chandler
Monash Asia Institute, Centre of Southeast
  Asian Studies
Monash University
Clayton, Australia

Chun-shu Chang
Department of History
University of Michigan

Mark W. Chavalas
Department of History
University of Wisconsin, La Crosse

W.K. Cheng
Department of History
Hofstra University

Michael Childs
Department of History
Bishop's University
Lennoxville, QC

Leslie Choquette
Department of History
Assumption College

Y.M. Choueiri
Arabic and Islamic Studies
University of Exeter

J.R. Christianson
Department of History
Luther College

Elizabeth S. Cohen
Department of History
York University
Toronto

H. Floris Cohen
University of Twente
Netherlands

Thomas V. Cohen
Department of History
York University
Toronto

Franck Collard
Université de Reims
France

Alon Confino
Corcoran Department of History
University of Virginia

William J. Connell
Department of History
Rutgers University

N.J. Cooke
Southeast Asian Studies Programme
National University of Singapore

Ian Copland
Centre for South Asian Studies
Monash University
Clayton, Australia

William S. Cormack
Department of History
Queen's University
Kingston, ON

Helen Creese
Department of Asian Languages and Studies
University of Queensland
St. Lucia, Australia

Don M. Cregier
Department of History
University of Prince Edward Island

Robert Cribb
Nordic Institute of Asian Studies
Copenhagen, Denmark

E. David Cronon
Department of History
University of Wisconsin
Madison

C.M.D. Crowder
Department of History
Queen's University
Kingston, ON

Denis Cryle
Department of History
The University of Central Queensland
Australia

Thomas H. Curran
University of King's College
Halifax, NS

Kenneth R. Curtis
Department of History
California State University
Long Beach, CA

J. Dainauskas
Lithuanian Research and Studies Center
Chicago, IL

David P. Daniel
Slovak Academic Information Agency, Service
Center for the Third Sector (SAIA-SCTS)
Bratislava, Slovakia

Gloria Davies
Asian Languages and Studies
Monash University

Antoon de Baets
Department of History
University of Groningen

Judith Boyce DeMark
Department of History
Northern Michigan University

R. Detrez
Brussels, Belgium

Toby L. Ditz
Department of History
Johns Hopkins University

Ewa Domańska
Institute of History
Adam Mickiewicz University
Poznan, Poland

B. Dooley
History and Social Studies
Harvard University

Carol Doyon
Département d'Histoire de l'Art
Université du Québec à Montréal

Michael R. Drompp
Department of History
Rhodes College
Memphis, TN

Dennis Dworkin
Department of History
University of Nevada
Reno

Ian Dyck
Department of History
Simon Fraser University
Burnaby, BC

Carville Earle
Department of Geography
Louisiana State University
Baton Rouge

Bonnie Effros
Department of Historical Studies
Southern Illinois University
Edwardsville

Amikam Elad
Institute of Asian and African Studies,
    Faculty of Humanities
Hebrew University of Jerusalem

George M. Enteen
Department of History
Penn State University

Adele Ernstrom
Department of Art History
Bishop's University
Lennoxville, QC

Raymond Evans
Department of History
University of Queensland
St. Lucia
Australia

David M. Fahey
Department of History
Miami University
Oxford, OH

Toyin Falola
Department of History
University of Texas
Austin

James R. Farr
Department of History
Purdue University
West Lafayette, IN

M.R. Fernando
History Section
School of Humanities
University Sains Malaysia
Penang, Malaysia

Albert Feuerwerker
Department of History and Center for Chinese
    Studies
University of Michigan

Sheila ffolliott
Department of Art and Art History
George Mason University
Fairfax, VA

Paul A. Fideler
Department of History and Humanities
Lesley College
Cambridge, MA

William E. Fischer Jr.
Department of History
University of Ottawa
Ottawa, ON

Carney T. Fisher
Centre for Asian Studies
University of Adelaide
Adelaide, Australia

H.J. Fisher
Department of History, School of Oriental and
    African Studies
University of London

Richard Fowler
St John's College
Oxford

R.M. Frakes
Department of History
Clarion University of Pennsylvania
Clarion, PA

James Friguglietti
Department of History
Montana State University
Billings

Ronald H. Fritze
Department of History
Lamar University
Beaumont, TX

Thomas Fuchs
Historisches Institut, Neuere
    Geschichte II
Justus-Liebig-Universität Giessen
Giessen, Germany

Takashi Fujii
Department of Economics
Niigata University
Niigata, Japan

Laurie J. Gagnier
Department of History
Dalhousie University

Lorraine Gallant
Department of History
Dalhousie University

Ralph F. Gallucci
Department of History
University of Central Arkansas
Conway, AR

Ian Germani
Department of History
University of Regina
Regina, SK

G.H. Gerrits
Department of History
Acadia University
Wolfville, NS

Dianne D. Glave
African-American Studies Department
Loyola Marymount University
Los Angeles, CA

Elisabeth G. Gleason
Department of History
University of San Francisco

Andrew Colin Gow
Department of History and Classics
University of Alberta

Devorah Greenberg
Department of History
Simon Fraser University
Burnaby, BC

Martin Greig
Department of History
University of Toronto

Paul F. Grendler
Department of History
University of Toronto

Elizabeth V. Haigh
Department of History
Saint Mary's University
Halifax, NS

P.K. Hämäläinen
Department of History
University of Wisconsin
Madison

Grant R. Hardy
Department of History
University of North Carolina
Asheville

Carol E. Harrison
Department of History
Auburn University
Auburn, AL

Louis-Georges Harvey
Department of History
Bishop's University
Lennoxville, QC

David Henige
Memorial Library
University of Wisconsin
Madison

Philip Hicks
Humanistic Studies
Saint Mary's College
Notre Dame, IN

Mark David Higbee
Department of History
Eastern Michigan University

Thomas P. Hillman
Ocean Grove, NJ

John R. Hinde
Nanaimo, BC

Bernard Hirschhorn
Formerly of Bernard Baruch College
City University of New York

Elizabeth Hitz
Department of History
University of Wisconsin
Milwaukee

Mack P. Holt
Department of History
George Mason University
Fairfax, VA

Tze-ki Hon
Department of History
State University of New York
Geneseo

K.R. Howe
Department of History
Massey University
Palmerston North, New Zealand

J. Donald Hughes
Department of History
University of Denver

Andrew J. Hull
Wellcome Unit for the History of Medicine
University of Glasgow

Janet E. Hunter
Department of Economic History
London School of Economics and
    Political Science
University of London

John O. Hunwick
Department of History
Northwestern University

Patrick Hutton
Department of History
University of Vermont

Mahmood Ibrahim
Department of History
California State Polytechnic University
Pomona

Georg G. Iggers
Department of History
State University of New York
Buffalo

Kris Inwood
Department of Economics
University of Guelph
Guelph, ON

A. Hamish Ion
Department of History
Royal Military College of Canada
Kingston, ON

Edmund E. Jacobitti
Department of Historical Studies
Southern Illinois University
Edwardsville

Ellen Jacobs
Départemente d'Histoire
Université du Québec à Montréal

Jennifer W. Jay
Department of History and Classics
University of Alberta

Jenny Jochens
Department of History
Towson State University
Towson, MD

Patrick Jory
Research School of Pacific Studies
Australian National University
Canberra

Stephen Kalberg
Department of Sociology
Boston University

Fujiya Kawashima
Department of History
Bowling Green University
Bowling Green, OH

Harvey J. Kaye
Center for History and Social Change
University of Wisconsin
Green Bay

Linda Kealey
Department of History
Memorial University of Newfoundland
St. John's, NF

Ralph Keen
School of Religion
University of Iowa

Thomas Keirstead
Department of History
State University of New York
Buffalo

Donald R. Kelley
Department of History
Rutgers University

Krista Kesselring
Department of History
Queen's University at Kingston, ON

James Edward Ketelaar
Department of History
University of Chicago

Newton E. Key
Department of History
Eastern Illinois University
Charleston

Tarif Khalidi
Department of History
American University
Beirut

Mehrdad Kia
Department of History
University of Montana
Missoula

Colin Kidd
Department of Scottish History and Literature
University of Glasgow

Minjae Kim
Seoul, South Korea

Paschalis M. Kitromilides
Department of Political Science and Public
    Administration
University of Athens
Greece

John M. Kleeberg
American Numismatic Society
New York, NY

Nathaniel Knight
Department of History
University of New Hampshire

E. Ulrich Kratz
School of Oriental and African Studies
University of London

Maura Lafferty
Pontifical Institute for Medieval Studies
Toronto, ON

John F. Laffey
Department of History
Concordia University
Montreal

Siobhan Lambert Hurley
School of Oriental and African Studies
University of London

John Langdon
Department of History and Classics
University of Alberta

Klaus Larres
Department of Politics
Queen's University of Belfast

John Lee
Department of History
Saint Mary's University
Halifax, NS

James A. Leith
Department of History
Queen's University
Kingston, ON

S. Lemny
Alfortville, France

David Levine
Ontario Institute for Studies in Education
Toronto, ON

F.J. Levy
Department of History
University of Washington

Thomas T. Lewis
Department of History
Mount Senario College
Ladysmith, WI

Li Tana
Department of History and Politics
University of Wollongong
Australia

Felice Lifshitz
Department of History
Florida International University
Miami

Yuet Keung Lo
Asian Studies
Grinnell College
Grinnell, Iowa

Roger D. Long
Department of History and Philosophy
Eastern Michigan University
Ypsilanti

Chris F.G. Lorenz
Vakgroep Geschiedenis, Faculteit der Letteren
Vrije Universiteit
Amsterdam, Netherlands

Morris F. Low
Division of Pacific and Asian History
Research School of Pacific and Asian Studies
Australian National University
Canberra

Ben Lowe
Department of History
Florida Atlantic University
Boca Raton

Colin Mackerras
Key Centre for Asian Languages and Studies
Griffith University
Nathan, Australia

Christine MacLeod
Department of Historical Studies
University of Bristol

Russell M. Magnaghi
Department of History
Northern Michigan University

Juan M. Maiguashca
Department of History
York University
Toronto

Thomas Maissen
Fachbereich Geschichtswissenschaften
Universitat Potsdam

Rohan Maitzen
Department of English
Dalhousie University

Michael Marrus
Department of History
University of Toronto

Jim Masselos
Department of History
University of Sydney
Australia

John Austin Matzko
Department of History
Bob Jones University
Greenville, SC

Thomas F. Mayer
Department of History
Augustana College
Rock Island, IL

Mary G. Mazur
Center for East Asian Studies
University of Chicago

Joseph M. McCarthy
Department of Education and Human Services
Suffolk University
Beacon Hill, MA

Ruth McClelland-Nugent
Department of History
Dalhousie University

John F. McClymer
Department of History
Assumption College
Worcester, MA

Adriana A.N. McCrea
Department of History
Dalhousie University

William McCuaig
Department of History
Erindale College
University of Toronto

E. Ann McDougall
Department of History and Classics
University of Alberta

James Edward McGoldrick
Department of History
Cedarville College
Cedarville, OH

Barbara A. McGowan
Department of History
Ripon College
Ripon, WI

J.J.N. McGurk
Department of History
Liverpool Institute of Higher Education
Liverpool, England

Shawn McHale
Department of History
George Washington University
Washington, D.C.

C.T. McIntire
Trinity College
University of Toronto

Rafael Medoff
Monsey, NY

James V. Mehl
Department of History
Missouri Western State College

Charles Melville
Faculty of Oriental Studies
Cambridge University

Jennifer Melville
Ontario Institute for Studies in Education
Toronto, ON

Edward Michalik
Department of History
Dalhousie University

Raymond A. Mohl
Department of History
Florida Atlantic University

Robin J. Moore
School of Humanities
Flinders University
Bedford Park, Australia

Tina Weil Moore
Department of History
Arizona State University

Jennifer A. Morawiecki
Graduate Research Centre in the Humanities
University of Sussex

Ian Morris
Departments of Classics and History
Stanford University

Tessa Morris-Suzuki
Research School of Pacific Studies
Australian National University
Canberra

Edward Muir
Department of History
Northwestern University

S.N. Mukherjee
Centre for Indian Studies
School of Asian Studies
University of Sydney
Sydney, Australia

Rhoads Murphey
Centre for Byzantine, Ottoman and Modern
  Greek Studies
University of Birmingham

Janaki Nair
Madras Institute of Development Studies
Madras, India

Elliot Neaman
Department of History
University of San Francisco

Cynthia J. Neville
Department of History
Dalhousie University

James P. Niessen
University Library
Texas Tech University
Lubbock

Myron C. Noonkester
Department of History
William Carey College

Byron J. Nordstrom
Department of History
Gustavus Adolphus College
Saint Peter, MN

Ellen Nore
Department of Historical Studies
Southern Illinois University
Edwardsville

H.T. Norris
School of Oriental and African Studies
University of London

Mohamed Lahbib Nouhi
Department of History and Classics
University of Alberta

Ebere Nwaubani
Department of History
University of Colorado
Boulder

Apollos Nwauwa
Department of History
Rhode Island College

Robert A. Nye
Department of History
Oregon State University

Bruce R. O'Brien
Department of History
Mary Washington College
Fredericksburg, VA

Elvy Setterqvist O'Brien
Williamstown, MA

John T. O'Brien
Department of History
Dalhousie University

Karen O'Brien
School of English Studies, Communication and
  Philosophy
Cardiff University of Wales

Nilo Odalia
São Paulo, Brazil

Onaiwu Wilson Ogbomo
Department of History
Allegheny College
Meadville, PA

Clare O'Halloran
Department of History
University College
Cork, Ireland

Kevin J. O'Keefe
Department of History
Stetson University
DeLand, FL

Ignacio Olábarri
Departamento de Historia
Universidad de Navarra
Pamplona, Spain

William O. Oldson
Department of History
Florida State University

Jens E. Olesen
Ernst-Moritz-Arndt-Universität
Historisches Institut
Greifswald, Germany

David J. Olson
North Carolina Division of Archives
  and History
North Carolina State Archives
Raleigh, NC

Claudia Orange
Dictionary of New Zealand Biography
Department of Internal Affairs
Wellington, New Zealand

Jane L. Parpart
Department of History
Dalhousie University

Ross Evans Paulson
Department of History
Augustana College
Rock Island, IL

Jolanta T. Pękacz
Department of History and Classics
University of Alberta

Carlos Pérez
Department of Humanities
University of New England
Biddeford, Maine

Barbara Bennett Peterson
Department of History
University of Hawaii

Stuart O. Pierson
Department of History
Memorial University of Newfoundand

Andrejs Plakans
Department of History
Iowa State University

Carl Pletsch
Department of History
University of Colorado
Denver

Attila Pók
Institute of History
Academy of Sciences
Budapest

Roy Porter
Wellcome Institute for the History of Medicine
London

Alison Prentice
Department of History and Philosophy of
    Education
Ontario Institute for Studies in Education

Laurence W. Preston
Department of Asian Studies
University of British Columbia

Stanislao G. Pugliese
Department of History
Hofstra University

Mary C. Quilty
St. Kilda
Victoria, Australia

T.K. Rabb
Department of History
Princeton University

J. Rackauskas
Lithuanian Research and Studies Center
Chicago

Eugene L. Rasor
Department of History
Emory and Henry College
Emory, VA

Toivo U. Raun
Department of Central Eurasian Studies
Indiana University

Anthony Reid
Research School of Pacific Studies
Australian National University
Canberra

Dennis Reinhartz
Department of History
University of Texas
Arlington

Barry Riccio
Department of History
Eastern Illinois University

R.C. Richardson
Department of History and Archaeology
King Alfred's College of Higher Education
Winchester, England

Melvin Richter
Department of Political Science
Graduate School and Hunter College
City University of New York

Harry Ritter
Department of History
Western Washington University

Claire C. Robertson
Department of Women's Studies
Ohio State University

Neil G. Robertson
University of King's College
Halifax, NS

Chase Robinson
The Oriental Institute
Oxford University

Keith Robinson
School of Journalism
Carleton University

Stuart Robson
Asian Studies
Monash University

John B. Roney
Department of History
Sacred Heart University
Fairfield, CT

Renato Rosaldo
Department of Anthropology
Stanford University

Catherine Rubincam
Department of Classics
Erindale College
University of Toronto

Rochelle Goldberg Ruthchild
Vermont College
Norwich University

Kenneth Sacks
Faculty of Arts and Sciences
Brown University

Michael Sage
Department of Classics
University of Cincinnati

Teruko Saito
Department of Southeast Asian Studies
Tokyo University of Foreign Studies
Tokyo

J.H.M. Salmon
Department of History
Bryn Mawr College

Loren J. Samons II
Department of Classical Studies
Boston University

Lionel J. Sanders
Department of Classics
Concordia University
Montreal

T. Sanders
United States Naval Academy
Annapolis, MD

Monica Sandor
Department of History
Queen's University
Kingston, ON

Pierre Savard
Department of History
University of Ottawa

Elizabeth D. Schafer
Loachapoka, AL

Zachary S. Schiffman
Department of History
Northeastern Illinois University

David P. Schweitzer
Department of History
Wilfrid Laurier University
Waterloo, ON

Karl W. Schweizer
Department of Social Science and
    Policy Studies
New Jersey Institute of Technology

Patricia Seed
Department of History
Rice University

Robert M. Seltzer
Jewish Studies Social Program
Department of History
Hunter College
City University of New York

Hootan Shambayati
Department of Political Science and Public
    Administration
Bilkent University
Ankara, Turkey

Shao Dongfang
Department of Chinese Studies
National University of Singapore

Anita Shelton
Department of History
Eastern Illinois University

Nikki Shepardson
Department of History
Rutgers University

Michael Shermer
Core Program in Liberal Arts
Occidental College
Los Angeles

Gordon Shrimpton
Department of Classics
University of Victoria
Victoria, BC

Joseph M. Siracusa
Department of History
University of Queensland
Brisbane, Australia

Arthur J. Slavin
Division of Humanities
University of Louisville
Louisville, KY

Bonnie G. Smith
Department of History
Rutgers University

John David Smith
Department of History
North Carolina State University
Raleigh

Kerry E. Spiers
Department of History
University of Louisville
Louisville, KY

Graham Squires
Japanese Section
Department of Modern Languages
Newcastle University
Newcastle, Australia

Robert Stallaerts
Heusden
Belgium

Timothy J. Stapleton
Department of History
University of Fort Hare
Alice, South Africa

Peter N. Stearns
Department of History
Carnegie Mellon University

Stephen A. Stertz
Department of History
Kean College
Union, NJ

John W. Storey
Department of History
Lamar University
Beaumont, TX

Susan Mosher Stuard
Department of History
Haverford College
Haverford, PA

Susan A. Stussy
Library Director
Madonna University
Livonia, MI

Walter A. Sutton
Department of History
Lamar University
Beaumont, TX

Hiroshi Takayama
Faculty of Letters
University of Tokyo

Charles Tandy
Ria University Institute for Advanced Study
Palo Alto, CA

Tao Tien-yi
Department of History
University of Hawaii
Manoa

Graham D. Taylor
Department of History
Dalhousie University

M. Brook Taylor
Department of History
Mount Saint Vincent University
Halifax, NS

Nicholas Terpstra
Department of History
Luther College
University of Regina

Romila Thapar
Department of History
Jawaharlal Nehru University
New Delhi

Nellie L. Thompson
New York, NY

William Thorpe
ASTEC
University of South Australia

Barbara Sher Tinsley
Los Gatos, CA

Norman Tobias
Division of Humanities
New Jersey Institute of Technology

Jo Tollebeek
Department of History
University of Groningen
Netherlands

Luís Reis Torgal
Instituto de História e Teoria das Ideias
Faculdade de Letras
Universidade de Coimbra, Portugal

Rosemary Gray Trott
Research School of Pacific Studies
Australian National University
Canberra

Aviezer Tucker
Palacký University
Olomouc, Czech Republic

Judith E. Tucker
Department of History
Georgetown University

Veronika Tuckerová
Votobia Publishing House
Olomouc, Czech Republic

Peter L. Twohig
Department of History
Dalhousie University

Paul J. Vanderwood
Department of History
San Diego State University

George L. Vásquez
Department of History
San Jose State University

Bruce L. Venarde
Department of History
University of Pittsburgh

Georgi Verbeeck
Department of Modern History
University of Leuven
Belgium

M. Vessey
Department of English
University of British Columbia
Vancouver, BC

Diane Villemaire
Department of History
University of Vermont

Richard A. Voeltz
Department of History
Cameron University
Lawton, OK

Geoff Wade
Centre of Asian Studies
University of Hong Kong

William T. Walker
Department of Humanities
Philadelphia College of Pharmacy and
Science

Q. Edward Wang
Department of History
Rowan College of New Jersey
Glassboro, NJ

Somkiat Wanthana
Faculty of Social Sciences
Kasetsart University
Bangkok, Thailand

Georges Whalen
Toronto, ON

Leigh Whaley
Department of History
Acadia University
Wolfville, NS

John Whelpton
Hong Kong

Thomas E. Willey
Department of History
McMaster University

George S. Williamson
Sewanee, TN

Samuel Williamson
Department of Economics
Miami University
Oxford, OH

Edward M. Wise
Wayne State University Law School
Detroit, MI

Christine Woodhead
Centre for Middle Eastern and Islamic Studies
University of Durham

Damon L. Woods
Department of History
University of California
Irvine

D.R. Woolf
Department of History
Dalhousie University

David K. Wyatt
Department of History
Cornell University

Shoucheng Yan
Department of Asian Languages
Victoria University of Wellington
New Zealand

Joseph Frederick Zacek
Department of History
State University of New York
Albany

P.S. Zachernuk
Department of History
Dalhousie University

T.C. Price Zimmermann
Department of History
Davidson College
Davidson, NC

Judith P. Zinsser
Department of History
Miami University
Oxford, OH

Melinda Zook
Department of History
Purdue University
West Lafayette, IN

About the Editor

D.R. Woolf was born in England in 1958 and raised in Winnipeg, Canada. He received his B.A. from Queen's University in Kingston, and his D.Phil. from Oxford University. He has taught at Queen's University, Bishop's University and, since 1987, Dalhousie University, where he is professor of history and associate dean of graduate studies. He has held research fellowships at the Folger Shakespeare Library, the Harry Ransom Humanities Research Center, and the Institute for Advanced Study. His major publications include *The Idea of History in Early Stuart England* (1990) and two coedited volumes, *Public Duty and Private Conscience in Seventeenth-Century England* (1993) and *The Rhetorics of Life-Writing in Early Modern Europe* (1995). He is also the author of a number of articles on aspects of early modern historiography in journals such as *Past and Present, Journal of the History of Ideas, Renaissance Quarterly,* and *The American Historical Review.* He is currently at work on a book on English historical culture from the sixteenth to the early eighteenth century. He lives in Halifax, Nova Scotia, with his three children.

A Global Encyclopedia of Historical Writing

Volume I
A–J

Abu'l-Faḍl ʿAllāmī (1551–1602)

Historian and ideologue of the Mughal emperor Akbar the Great. Abu'l-Faḍl was born in Agra and received his education from his father, an eminent if controversial religious scholar. Abu'l-Faḍl was presented to Akbar in 1574 and thereafter rapidly became a close friend and confidant of the emperor. He helped to develop the theoretical basis for Akbar's claim to divinely sanctioned authority, and promoted his view of Mughal India as a multiconfessional imperial society. This ideological stance pervades his major work, the *Akbar-nāma* [Book of Akbar], which contains an annalistic record of Akbar's reign to 1602 preceded by an account of his ancestors and spiritual genealogy. The third section of this work, entitled *Āʾīn-i Akbarī* [The Customs of Akbar], provides a detailed description of Akbar's religious views, the household administration, court ceremonials, coinage, official ranks and salaries, and revenue administration, as well as literary and intellectual life. Abu'l-Faḍl was murdered at the instigation of Akbar's heir, the future Jahāngīr.

Charles Melville

Texts

Āʾīn-i Akbarī. Persian text ed. H. Blochmann; trans. H. Blochmann and H.S. Jarrett. 2 vols. Calcutta: Asiatic Society of Bengal, 1867–1877. Second (revised) edition. Ed. D.C. Phillott with annotations by Sir Jadu-Nath Sarkar. 3 vols. Calcutta: Asiatic Society of Bengal, 1927–1949.

Akbar-nāma. Persian text ed. Ahmad ʿAli and Maulawi ʿAbdur-Rahim. 3 vols in 2. Calcutta: Asiatic Society of Bengal, 1873–1887. Trans. H. Beveridge. 3 vols. Calcutta: Asiatic Society of Bengal, 1897–1921.

References

Richards, J.F. "The Formulation of Imperial Authority under Akbar and Jahangir." In *Kingship and Authority in South Asia,* ed. J.F. Richards. Madison: University of Wisconsin, 1978, 252–285.

Siddiqi, N.A. "Shaikh Abul Fazl." In *Historians of Medieval India,* ed. Mohibbul Hasan, Meerut: Meenakshi Prakashan, 1968. 123–141.

Acciaiuoli, Donato (1429–1478)

Renaissance humanist historian. Active in the small circle of patrician humanists who perpetuated the values of civic humanism in Medici-dominated Florence, Acciaiuoli held administrative posts in the city and territory of Florence and was its ambassador to courts in Italy and beyond. Some commentators see him as a living exponent of civic humanism, others as an example of its decline into a quiescent and more purely intellectual pursuit. As a proponent of Greek studies, Acciaiuoli translated Plutarch's *Lives* of Demetrius and Alcibiades into Italian and prepared commentaries on Aristotle's *Politics, Physics, De Anima,* and *Ethics.* His historical work consisted of biographies and translations that promoted the responsibility of philosophically trained rulers and citizens to secure liberty, establish justice, promote learning and culture, and pursue virtue. These were the themes of a variety of works: a *Life of Charlemagne* presented to the French king Louis XI upon his coronation in 1461, lives of Scipio and Hannibal closely based on Plutarch, and a translation into Italian of Leonardo Bruni's twelve-volume *History of Florence,* which, starting in 1473, went into five editions and was the only readily accessible version of that work until Bruni's Latin original was published in 1610.

Nicholas Terpstra

Texts

Istoria della casa de gli Ubaldini [History of the House of Ubaldini]. Florence: Bartolommeo Sermartelli, 1588.

Istoria fiorentina. Trans. Leonardo Bruni. Venice: Jacobus Rubeus, 1476.

Vita Caroli Magni [Life of Charlemagne]. Rome: Ulrich Han, 1471.

References

Cochrane, Eric. *Historians and Historiography in the Italian Renaissance.* Chicago: University of Chicago Press, 1981, 33.

Dizionario biografico degli Italiani. Ed. A.M. Ghisalberti. Rome: Istituto della Enciclopedia italiana, 1960– , I, 80–82.

Ganz, Margery. "The Humanist As Citizen: Donato di Neri Acciaiuoli, 1428 [*sic*]–1478." Ph.D. dissertation, Syracuse University, 1979.

Garin, Eugenio. *Portraits from the Quattrocento.* Trans. Victor A. Velen and Elizabeth Velen. New York: Harper and Row, 1972.

Acsády, Ignác (né Adler) (1845–1906)

Hungarian historian. The son of a landowner of eastern Hungary, Ignác Adler studied law at the University of Budapest. After graduating in 1869 he worked as a journalist, adopting the surname Acsády. His articles, mainly published between 1870 and 1888, identified him as an advocate of liberal reforms. Acsády began historical research in the 1870s, seeking to illuminate the antecedents of contemporary issues in Austro-Hungarian relations and society. His portrayal of life in late-seventeenth-century Hungary (1886) was influenced by the English historian Thomas Babington Macaulay, while his examination of the economy under Ferdinand I (1888) emulated the work of his older contemporary Wilhelm Roscher (1817–1894). For his pioneering research in fiscal archives, Acsády became a corresponding member of the Hungarian Academy in 1888, but he never obtained a teaching position. His chief historical syntheses, a national history (1903–1904) and a very influential history of Hungarian serfdom (1906), were widely criticized for their unfavorable portrayal of the landed establishment.

James P. Niessen

Texts

A magyar birodalom története. [The History of the Hungarian Empire in Two Volumes]. 2 vols. Budapest: Athenaeum, 1903–1904.

A magyar jobbágyság története [The History of Hungarian Serfdom]. Budapest: Politzer, 1906.

Magyarország Budavár visszafoglalásának korában [Hungary in the Age of the Retaking of Buda Castle]. Budapest: Méhner, 1886.

Magyarország pénzügyei I. Ferdinánd uralkodása alatt. 1526–1564 [Monetary Affairs of Hungary under the Reign of Ferdinand I. 1526–1564]. Budapest: Athenaeum, 1888.

Széchy Mária, 1610–1679. Budapest: Méhner, 1885.

References

Gunst, Péter. *Acsády Ignác történetírása* [The History Writing of Ignác Acsády]. Budapest: Akadémiai, 1961.

Acton, Lord John Emerich Edward Dalberg (1834–1902)

English historian and moralist. Acton was born in Naples and educated in England and Munich, where his intellect was shaped by his university tutor, Döllinger. The earlier part of his life was taken up with the religious tensions of the century, and as a liberal Catholic he edited and contributed to a number of Catholic journals. He served in Parliament and was ennobled in 1869. He helped found the *English Historical Review* and was appointed Regius professor of modern history at Cambridge University near the end of his life. At the same time, he flung himself into the enormous task of preparing the first volumes of the *Cambridge Modern History,* an effort which wore down his health. Despite an unrivaled knowledge of the contents of European archives, Acton published no historical books during his lifetime: his work appeared posthumously and consisted of previously published journal articles. He was preoccupied with the history of liberty, but a proposed definitive book on the topic was never written. His main concerns were the abuse of power (by church and state) and the motives of historians, whose main duty he saw as passing moral judgment on the work of men and nations, a view which led to quarrels with his contemporaries. Acton was considered one of the leading historians of his age and greatly elevated the study of history at Cambridge.

David R. Schweitzer

Texts

Essays in the Liberal Interpretation of History. Chicago: University of Chicago Press, 1967.

Essays on Church and State. Ed. Douglas Woodruff. London: Hollis and Carter, 1952.

Lectures on Modern History. New York: Meridian, 1961.

References

Butterfield, Herbert. *Man on His Past.* Cambridge, Eng.: Cambridge University Press, 1969.

Himmelfarb, Gertrude. *Lord Acton: A Study in Conscience and Politics.* Chicago: University of Chicago Press, 1962.

Tulloch, Hugh. *Acton.* New York: St. Martin's Press, 1988.

Adam of Bremen (d. 1081/1085)

Saxon chronicler. The personal history of Adam is impossible to ascertain except that he arrived in Bremen between May 1066 and April 1067. His chronicle of the archbishops of Hamburg–Bremen memorializes, in particular, Adalbert, archbishop and intimate of the Salian emperors Henry III and IV. This work expresses a view of life on the northern edge of Christendom during the reforms of the eleventh century. In addition, Adam is a source for understanding the extension of geographical knowledge at the time.

Kerry E. Spiers

Texts

Hamburgische Kirchengeschichte. Ed. B. Schmeidler; revised by S. Steinberg. Leipzig: Dyk, 1926.

History of the Archbishops of Hamburg–Bremen. Trans. F. Tschan. New York: Columbia University Press, 1959.

References

Smalley, Beryl. *Historians in the Middle Ages.* London: Thames and Hudson, 1974.

Adams, Henry (1838–1918)

American historian, novelist, and philosopher. Born in Boston, a descendant of two presidents, Adams attended Harvard College (1854–1858) and served as private secretary to his father (1860–1868). Briefly a reform journalist and editor, he taught history at Harvard (1870–1877) and wrote a political narrative of the Jefferson–Madison era. The work is notable for its clear prose, high standards of accuracy, and shrewd sense of the psychology of power, however, critics have noted Adams's subtle use of irony against Jefferson. Adams turned to cultural studies in *Mont Saint Michel and Chartres* (1904) and *The Education of Henry Adams* (1907), which contrasted the organic stasis of medieval society (based on religious faith) with the mechanical dynamic of modern society (based on scientific beliefs). He attempted to articulate a scientific philosophy of history (based on an analogy with thermodynamics), but current interpreters regard him more as a literary figure than as a philosopher of history.

Ross E. Paulson

Texts

History of the United States of America during the Administrations of Thomas Jefferson and James Madison. New York: Library of America, 1986.

Novels, Mont Saint Michel and The Education. New York: Library of America, 1983.

References

Contosta, David R. *Henry Adams and the American Experiment.* Boston: Little, Brown, 1980.

Adams, Herbert Baxter (1850–1901)

American historian and educator. Adams was born in Shutesbury, Massachusetts. A graduate (1872) of Amherst College, he studied history and political science under mentor Johann Bluntschli at Heidelberg University (Germany) from 1874 to 1876. Adams's association with Johns Hopkins University began in 1876 and lasted until his premature death at Amherst, Massachusetts. A leading figure in historical studies, Adams used his graduate seminar, based upon the German model, to inculcate the scientific approach in an entire generation of historians. Although Adams selected an overarching motto of History Is Past Politics and Politics Present History for the seminar, his interests were considerably broader. As a product of his times and training, much of Adams's inquiry focused upon the theory of Teutonism. Yet he remained dedicated to the concept of *Kulturgeschichte* and supported wide-ranging graduate research. More importantly, Adams was a driving force in the professionalization of history in the United States. He began a historical studies series, actively sought the advancement of American higher education, and served as secretary of the nascent American Historical Association from 1884–1900.

William E. Fischer Jr.

Texts

The Germanic Origin of New England Towns. Baltimore, MD: N. Murray/Johns Hopkins University, 1882.

Methods of Historical Study. Baltimore, MD: N. Murray/Johns Hopkins University, 1884.

Thomas Jefferson and the University of Virginia: With Authorized Sketches of Hampden-Sydney, Randolph-Macon, Emory-Henry, Roanoke, and *Richmond Colleges, Washington and Lee University, and Virginia Military Institute.* Washington, DC: Government Printing Office, 1888.

Work among Workingwomen in Baltimore: A Social Study. Baltimore, MD: J. Murphy, 1889.

References

Cunningham, Raymond J. "Is History Past Politics? Herbert Baxter Adams As Precursor of the 'New History.'" *History Teacher* 9 (1976): 244–257.

———. "The German Historical World of Herbert Baxter Adams: 1874–1876." *Journal of American History* 68 (1981): 261–275.

Holt, W. Stull, ed. *Historical Scholarship in the United States, 1876–1901: As Revealed in the Correspondence of Herbert B. Adams.* Baltimore, MD: Johns Hopkins University Press, 1938.

Adelung, Johann Christoph (1732–1806)

Popular philosopher, publicist, and historian. Adelung was an important representative of the German Enlightenment in the second half of the eighteenth century. He studied theology at Halle before going to Leipzig in 1765, and finally to Dresden in 1787, where he served as court librarian. Enormously productive, Adelung edited, translated, and wrote on a wide range of topics. Among his many scholarly interests were linguistics, geology, and geography. In addition, he published extensively in history, his works stressing the rational and progressive nature of human cultural development. His *Versuch einer Geschichte der Cultur des menschlichen Geschlechts* [Attempt at a History of the Culture of Mankind] (1782), continued the tradition of cultural history, which questioned the one-dimensional quality of much political history. Adelung sought a more balanced approach through the incorporation of intellectual and material culture, which possessed its own characteristics unique to the age.

John R. Hinde

Texts

Geschichte der menschlichen Narrheit [History of Human Folly]. 7 vols. Leipzig: Weygand, 1785–1789.

Versuch einer Geschichte der Cultur des menschlichen Geschlechts. Leipzig: C.G. Hertel, 1782.

References

Bahner, Werner, ed. *Sprache und Kulturentwicklung im Blickfeld der deutschen Spätaufklärung: Der Beitrag Johann Christoph Adelungs* [Language
and the Development of Culture from the Perspective of the Late German Enlightenment: The Contribution of Johann Christoph Adelung]. East Berlin: Akademie-Verlag, 1984.

Aduarte, Diego de, O.P. (ca. 1570–1636)

Spanish friar and historian. Born in Zaragoza, Aduarte entered the Dominican order at age sixteen. He joined the Dominican mission to the Philippines in 1594 and arrived the next year. Six months later, Aduarte joined the ill-fated Spanish expedition to Cambodia. After many difficulties and a long illness, he returned to Manila in 1597. Two years later, having returned to China, Aduarte was himself imprisoned for a time. He returned to Spain in 1603 on matters concerning his order. Together with additional friars, he returned to the Philippines in 1606, but in the following year was sent back to Spain, where he remained until 1628. Aduarte returned to the Philippines one last time with another group of mendicants. Elected prior of the convent in Manila, he was later made bishop of Nueva Segovia. Aduarte wrote an institutional history of the Dominicans entitled *Historia de la provincia del Sancto Rosario de la Orden de Predicadores en Philippinas, Iapon, y China* [History of the Province of St. Rosario of the Order of Preachers in the Philippines, Japan, and China]. This was completed by Domingo Gonzalez, a fellow Dominican, and published in Manila three years after Aduarte's death. It was written to persuade friars in Spain to volunteer for duty in the Philippines, Japan, and China. Thus the work contains details of martyrdom and hagiographical biographies of various Dominicans. Aduarte's *Historia* is valuable to the historian not only for its material regarding the work of the Dominicans in the Philippines but also for its accounts of Aduarte's experiences in Cambodia and China.

Damon L. Woods

Texts

Blair, Emma Helen, and James Robertson. *The Philippine Islands, 1493–1803,* vols. 30–32 [translation of selections from the *Historia*]. 55 vols. Cleveland, OH: Arthur H. Clark, 1903–1909.

An Eyewitness Account of the Cambodian Expedition by Diego Aduarte. Manila: Historical Conservation Society, 1988.

Historia de la Provincia del Santo Rosario de la Orden de Predicadores en Filipinas, Japon, y China [por] Diego de Aduarte. 2 vols.

Madrid: Consejo Superior de Investigaciones Cientificas, 1962–1963.

References

C.R. Boxer. "Some Aspects of Spanish Historical Writing on the Philippines." In *Historians of South East Asia,* ed. D.G.E. Hall. London: Oxford University Press, 1961, 200–212.

Ady, Cecelia Mary (1881–1958)

English historian. Ady was born in Edgcote, Northamptonshire, the daughter of the art historian Julia Cartwright and her husband, Henry Ady, a clergyman. She took a degree in history in 1903, one of the first women awarded a degree at Oxford. She was tutor in modern history at St. Hugh's College, Oxford, from 1909 to 1923, later returning as research fellow until her retirement in 1951. Ady explored the political operation of ruling Renaissance families in studies of the Sforza of Milan (1907) and Bentivoglio of Bologna (1937). To such analyses she joined attention to cultural modes, viewing the quattrocento as a privileged moment that had allowed for the expression of artistic, literary, and ethical ideals.

Adele Ernstrom

Texts

The Bentivoglio of Bologna: A Study in Despotism. London: Oxford University Press, 1937.

A History of Milan under the Sforza. Ed. E. Armstrong. New York: Puttnam, 1907.

Lorenzo dei Medici and Renaissance Italy. London: English Universities Press, 1955.

Pius II (Aeneas Silvius Piccolomini): The Humanist Pope. London: Methuen, 1913.

References

Jacob, E.F., ed. *Italian Renaissance Studies: A Tribute to the Late Cecilia [sic] M. Ady.* London: Faber & Faber, 1960.

African Historiography—Chronicles

Chronicles in the familiar style, that is, a chronological, year-by-year narration of the past were compiled in Africa at least as early as the sixteenth century, when a chronicle tradition took hold in Ethiopia. Several accounts in Amharic survive detailing the lives and activities of the Ethiopian rulers, particularly their struggles against Islam. At almost the same time, two histories *(Ta'rīkh as-Sudan* and *Ta'rīkh al-Fattash)* of the area around Timbuktu were compiled in Arabic. These accounts remain the best available sources for the time and area covered.

This was a brief flowering, however, and, with the exception of histories in Arabic of Sinnar in the Sudan and Gonja in modern Ghana, the chronicle virtually disappeared from the continent for several centuries. The genre, however, was reborn toward the end of the nineteenth century under a markedly different guise. About this time there began to be written accounts of particular ethnic groups and states, composed by newly literate members of the society and designed to emulate the historiographical traditions of the colonizers in hopes of benefiting in the rearrangement of political and economic power that was underway. Of these the most influential were the works of Samuel Johnson, C.C. Reindorf, Apolo Kagwa, J.H. Soga, and J.U. Egharevba.

The earliest of these accounts was Samuel Johnson's *History of the Yoruba,* completed in the 1890s. Johnson was himself a Yoruba and a cleric of the Church Missionary Society. Basing himself on the rich oral traditions of the Yoruba, as well as the records of Arabic and European travelers in the area, Johnson attempted to offer a synopsis of the origins and later development of the Yoruba from (by his account) the eleventh or twelfth century to his own time. In this he stressed the historical preeminence of Oyo, one of the many Yoruba kingdoms.

Carl Christian Reindorf, like Johnson, was an African Protestant clergyman, in this case from the coastal area of modern Ghana. His *A History of the Gold Coast and Asante* was published in 1895, just as the British were poised to conquer Asante and create the forerunner of the modern state of Ghana. More than Johnson or any of the other authors mentioned here, Reindorf based his account on almost equal measures of oral and written data; for the latter he could rely on printed sources extending back to the fifteenth century.

Apolo Kagwa's background was different— he was chief minister of Buganda for over thirty years—but otherwise his intent and effect were much the same. Relying more fully on oral sources, Kagwa rendered an account, *The Kings of Buganda* (1901), that pictured an ancient and militant kingdom, preeminent by both descent and success, which by the time of the arrival of the Europeans had imposed its control over much of what became the Uganda protectorate. He was remarkably successful. To this day, Buganda remains the preeminent subpolity of the modern country of Uganda, thanks in large part to British colonial support.

John H. Soga, a Xhosa missionary and son of a missionary, also wrote his *The South-Eastern Bantu* (1930) with the purpose of testifying to the antiquity and authority of his own people, who were once the leading group in the area but who, through fission and the rise of the Zulu and British, had sunk into virtually dependent status. Jacob Egharevba, a native of Benin in southern Nigeria, once the most powerful state in the area, published *A Short History of Benin* in 1934. Egharevba wrote the work at a time when the office of *oba*, or paramount chief, was in danger of being eclipsed as a result of threatened reorganization.

These African chronicles, and others like them, had much in common. None transcended the ethnic boundaries of the authors; indeed, they were designed to aggrandize particular groups at the expense of deprecating or ignoring others. Furthermore, they share much in their approach. Each author was greatly influenced by biblical teachings and sought to connect the origins of his group, either directly or indirectly, with biblical testimony. Each work contains unique information, but all except Kagwa's drew heavily from European sources, making it difficult to distinguish material based on local oral tradition from that learned from outside. Each author had roughly the same purpose—to persuade the new colonial overlords that the group in question had long-established rights to renewed authority. The success of each work—all have gone through several printings—has rendered them canonical; competing accounts produced by contemporary writers have tended to be overlooked by modern historians.

This success accounts perhaps for the persistence of this genre. Similar works are still being produced in many African societies, particularly among the Mande, the Yoruba, and the Akan.

David Henige

See also AFRICAN HISTORIOGRAPHY—NORTH AFRICA (MAGHREB); AFRICAN HISTORIOGRAPHY—SUB-SAHARAN; CHRONICLES, MEDIEVAL; SOUTH AFRICAN HISTORIOGRAPHY.

References

Law, Robin. "Early Yoruba Historiography." *History in Africa* 3 (1976): 69–89.

Twaddle, Michael. "On Ganda Historiography." *History in Africa* 1 (1974): 85–100.

Usuanlele, U., and T. Falola. "The Scholarship of Jacob Egharevba of Benin." *History in Africa* 21 (1994): 303–318.

African Historiography—North Africa (Maghreb)

The concept *Maghrib* (occident, setting, as in setting sun), is itself a product of history. Arab authors of the Middle Ages contrasted it with *M'shreq* (orient, rising). They used *djazirat al-maghrib* (the island of the Maghrib), to refer to the region east of Tripolitania and north of the desert frontier with the country of the "Blacks." *Aqsa* (extreme), *awsat* (middle), and *adna* (near) distinguished the three regions that provided the base for national (later nationalist) historiographies. The peoples of the Maghrib, known variously in history as *Lybiens, Numides, Maures,* and *Africans,* were *Baraber* or *Barbar* to Arab authors. From the thirteenth century, Europeans derived the term *Berberia* to refer to North Africa itself. *Barbary* continued to refer to the states stretching from the Atlantic to Tripolitania. It was French nineteenth-century colonial historiography that equated the expressions Africa *du nord, mineure, septentrionale,* and even *blanche* with the medieval Maghrib (*Maghreb* in French). The vagaries of colonial expansion determined the region's ultimate geographical frontiers, those of French North Africa. In 1922, the influential Evariste Lévi-Provençal resurrected its medieval Arab meaning with the concept *occident musulman*. For him it designated a wider geographical region (including Andalusia), but most importantly, it was the cultural domain of "Western Islam," a concept adopted by many contemporary historians. Recent politics has generated the idea of *al-Maghrib al-Kabir*—formerly French North Africa, Libya, and Mauritania—officially represented in the Maghreb Arab Union. Whether this latest metamorphosis will find a place in Maghrebian historiography has yet to be seen.

The Precolonial or "Traditional" Era, Pre-1830

At the time of the fall of the Almohade empire (thirteenth century), histories were largely locally centered accounts of events and dynasties. Following oriental tradition, they tended to be narrative chronologies, genealogies, or biographies (usually hagiographic, of saints, kings, and learned men). Writers' interests were provincial, reflecting their urban intellectual and social background. Ibn Khaldūn (1332–1406), a historian whose thinking and works reflected the larger historical and sociological realities of the medieval Maghreb, was a notable exception. Pressures felt by Maghrebian societies facing European incursions from the sixteenth century stimulated scholarship conscious of a wider reality. By the nineteenth century, a generation of scholars emerged who combined learned Muslim traditions with the emerging discipline of history. "History," however, figured in formal Maghrebian education only recently. The traditional essentials continued to exert influence over

Maghrebian historiography well into the twentieth century, even as the training and themes specific to French colonial education shaped new generations.

The Colonial Era, 1830–1954

The French taking of the Ottoman Regencies of Algiers in 1830 and Tunis in 1881, followed by the colonization of Morocco in 1912, initiated a colonial era that left an indelible imprint on Maghrebian historiography. Starting in 1856, with the founding of the *Revue Africaine* at the University of Algiers, the occupation became a theme exploited to personify France as the "liberator from the Turks" and bearer of Christian civilization. With the *Revue* as their principal venue, scholars whose research generated a virtual *École d'Alger* tended to justify the expansion of France's empire and the pacification of the empire's peoples. An influential school of ancient history (a field curiously undeveloped by Maghrebian historians, with some Tunisian exceptions), was developed under Stephane Gsell. Based on Greco-Roman writings and archaeology, it subtly presented French colonization as a successor to Rome. A more realistic political analysis of the occupation of Algiers was produced in the 1920s, but the idea that it marked a victory over barbarism persisted in numerous publications of corsair exploits and Christian slave memoirs. Similarly, the nineteenth-century European observation that the Barbary Coast was characterized by political anarchy and Berber dissidence provided evidence with which *École* historians constructed a model contrasting European state-building with Maghrebian political regression. Geography (favoring economic and technological backwardness), the destructive impact of the eleventh-century Hilalian invasions, the generic inability of nomads to construct states (echoing Ibn Khaldūn), and the inherent resistance of Berbers were all invoked as explanations. The problem was in part articulated as the *bled el-makhzen* (the territory of the state) versus the *bled es-siba* (the territory of dissidence). By 1930, a century of literature had established French colonization as "progressive"; the centenary decade that followed celebrated that illusion, marking the most prolific era of the *École d'Alger*. Charles-André Julien's critical *Histoire de l'Afrique du Nord* (1931) was the notable exception. Though now regarded as having been a seminal work, its liberal perspective won it few contemporary admirers.

World War II was not a major historiographical watershed, but it generated questions about the social and economic impact of colonialism, which began to be reflected in historical writing. While political themes continued to dominate, histories of major urban centers appeared as did publications of source materials at the national level. And not to be overlooked was the continuing significance of *Hesperis*, a key journal established in Rabat in 1921 (published as *Hesperis-Tamuda* starting in 1960).

The Era of Decolonization 1956–1970

Throughout Africa, 1956–1970 was an era of decolonization and the creation of nations. This continental reality was mirrored in Maghrebian historiography, which sought to "decolonize" itself. The Hilalian invasion was central to debates throughout the 1960s. Nationalists argued that the "destructive invasion model" gave credence to French colonialism. Several French scholars supported the revisionists in pointing to problems with sources, alternative explanations for economic decline, the need to understand better the behavior of pastoral societies, and the lack of sufficient archaeological research. The respective roles of Christians and corsairs in the early modern Mediterranean economy were subjects of serious research (most notably by Fernand Braudel); the image of the "uncivilized Barbary" finally faded from publication. The most lively debates revisited the question of Maghrebian states. Marxist theories informed approaches to the question of precolonial nations (as defined by consciousness). The earlier *bled al-makhzen / bled es-siba* dichotomy was reformulated in terms of "modes of production"; *bled es-siba* was debated as a feudal social organization that slowed development of the economy and national collectivity. Maghrebian historians wrestled with the intellectual and cultural legacies of the African colonial experience. But they also had to deal with the identities of the Arab and Islamic worlds to which they belonged. This tension was articulated in the debate over the meaning of *Maghreb,* which was for many a colonial creation, reinforced by anticolonialist struggles and perpetuated by neocolonialist historians.

An ambivalence about who should write history and how they should write it soon became apparent: scientific appreciation for rigorous methodology and extensive use of documentation was often cited, but, simultaneously, emotional admiration for the writers who had "lived" their research was also evident. This was especially true of work on Algeria. The war of 1954–1962 brought independence but not national unity. It produced disappointed colonialists, passionate activists, radical Marxists, and disillusioned nationalists, each of whom was concerned with some variant of the question: Was "French Algeria" ever a reality that could (or should) have endured? The postwar exodus of both French and French-Algerians gave particular poignancy to the revisionists' discussion of colonial mistakes and the search for a postcolonial identity.

The emergence of "national" history was not limited to Algeria. French theses, increasingly reflecting the influence of the Annales school as well as that of other disciplines (like psychology, sociology, and literature each of which developed subfields in colonialism), began to appear on each of the Maghrebian countries. American and British anthropologists crossed French academic frontiers bringing with them new fieldwork methodologies, models (tribal segmentation in particular), and interests in religious culture (*shaikhs* and saints). The emergent historiography was one increasingly sensitive to social and economic issues and reflective of interdisciplinary approaches.

The Era of Disillusionment, 1970–1979
The handful of French and Maghrebian universities interested in the Maghreb in 1960 had become a network of institutes in Europe (notably Italy), Britain, and America a decade later. These centers (the *Centre de Recherches et d'Études sur les Sociétés Méditerranéennes* or CRESM in Aix-en-Provence being key) sponsored colloquia, published proceedings, and established academic journals. The latter included CRESM's *Annuaire de l'Afrique du Nord* (1962) and *Revue de l'Occident Musulman et de la Méditerranée* (Aix-en-Provence, 1966), replacing *Revue Africaine,* which ceased publication; *Revue d'Histoire et de Civilisation du Maghreb* (Algiers, 1966); and *Revue d'Histoire Maghrebine* (Tunis, 1974). The institutes also trained growing numbers of students, many Maghrebian.

The drive to decolonize scholarship continued. The economic realities of the 1970s determined that "underdevelopment" was central to all academic (including historical) debate. Marxian paradigms dominated, elevating economic history in general, and discussion of the precolonial state continued. Universality versus (Maghrebian) specificity in state formation, the validity of the *bled el-makhzen / bled es-siba* dichotomy, and the role (if any) that the "Arab versus Berber" question should play were all issues generating passion and publications. Historians and social scientists scrutinized imperialism, thereby raising further theoretical and concrete debate. Could, for instance, the Maghrebian developmental process be articulated in the same terms as that of the European?

The most penetrating and passionate writing challenged a range of questions: the meaning of the Maghreb, the "usability" of historical evidence, the definition of national consciousness, the essence of the postcolonial "Arab-Muslim," and the nature of decolonization itself. A principal scholar was Abdallah Laroui (*L'histoire du Maghreb, un essai de synthèse,* 1970). For Laroui, Islam had allowed for the development of a certain autonomy and tentative unity; an "imperial" Maghreb had existed between the ninth and fourteenth centuries. Thereafter followed stagnation, disintegration, and colonialism—the continuing cultural reality. For Laroui and others of his generation, only a more profound exploration of "Maghrebian Islam" could lead to meaningful decolonization and nationalism.

National differences in historiographical emphasis reflected political peculiarities. In independent Morocco, interest in the precolonial state and society continued, aided by the exceptional work of American and British anthropologists. Nationalists argued for the existence of a "Moroccan nation" from at least the sixteenth century, attributing its disintegration not to the colonialists' "dichotomies" (of power and ethnicity) but to the process of European penetration. In Tunisia, debates about opposition and resistance to colonial rule produced work of a quality and vigor without equal. Tunisian scholars also led in research on trade unionist, working-class, and social history in general. In Algeria, more objective analyses of the war appeared, as historians penetrated myths perpetrated by both sides. But memoirs of journalists, politicians, and soldiers (including Algerians who fought alongside the French and vice versa) appeared together with them, ensuring that passion pertained even as "history" emerged. Attention turned, also, to the socialist revolution. Unique among the Maghrebian experiences, this was failing, and as historians sought explanations, Algerian historiography embarked on a new era.

New Directions? 1980–1995
The "modes of production" and "underdevelopment" paradigms have increasingly become the domain of economists and sociologists. The impassioned debate over the Maghreb as a framework of analysis has had an impact. Research in the social sciences suggests that Maghrebian intellectuals are situating themselves increasingly within "Arab" and "Islamic" scholarship; subjects defined as "Maghrebian" tend to correspond with those of current concern to French scholars (such as historical demography and migration). Concomitantly,

Maghrebian history per se seems to be declining relative to disciplines perceived as more "pertinent" to contemporary postcolonialist issues.

National interests are increasingly pronounced. In the early 1980s, new work on imperialism and resistance gave renewed impetus to precolonial and colonial history. In Morocco, the 1975 "Green March" to reclaim the former Spanish Sahara ignited local resistance; the state's continuing preoccupation with the issue has strongly influenced research. Contemporary politics has also rejuvenated writing on the "Berber question." The Algerian experience is interrelated. By 1980, the cleavages in Algerian society, suppressed in the name of independence, had resurfaced in the context of the failing revolution. Islamic fundamentalist and Berberist sensibilities were affronted by the postcolonial reality. As of the middle of 1997, an Algerian civil war (a second war of independence?) continues, underscoring the all too tragic relevance of historical inquiry.

Conclusions

Historians responded to the changes wrought by colonialism, decolonization, and independence with the same questions and debates that were generated elsewhere in Africa, but reference to that continental scholarship is conspicuously absent in Maghrebian historiography. While imported models elevating economic and social history were very influential during the 1970s, recent directions suggest a limited long-term impact. Adherents of Marxism and the Annales school continue to have a voice, and religious and cultural history remain informed by trends in Western anthropology. But the evolution of social history, which elsewhere has brought forward women and feminism; race, class, and gender theory; the issue of cultural appropriation; and experiments with new methodologies and source materials has had negligible influence. Finally, English-speakers interested in the Maghreb should be aware that the view afforded them by the existing historiography is a very limited one: the bulk of the published works remains French, and the majority of recent research (as reflected in Maghrebian memoirs and theses) is in Arabic.

E. Ann McDougall and Mohamed Lahbib Nouhi

See also AFRICAN HISTORIOGRAPHY, SUB-SAHARAN; SOUTH AFRICAN HISTORIOGRAPHY.

References

Abun-nasr, Jamil M. *A History of the Maghrib.* Cambridge, Eng.: Cambridge University Press, 1971.

Braudel, Fernand. *The Mediterranean and the Mediterranean World in the Age of Philip II.* Trans. Siân Reynolds. New York: Harper and Row, 1972.

Gsell, Stephane. *Histoire ancienne de l'Afrique du Nord* [Early History of North Africa]. 8 vols. Paris: Hachette, 1913–1928.

Ibn Khaldūn. *Histoire des Berbères et des dynasties musulmanes de l'Afrique septentrionale* [History of the Berbers and the Muslim Dynasties of North Africa]. Trans. G. de Slane (into French). 4 vols. Algiers: 1852–1856.

Julien, Charles-André. *History of North Africa from the Arab Conquest to 1830.* Ed. and rev. (1952) R. Le Tourneau; trans. John Petrie; ed. C.C. Stewart. London: Routledge and Kegan Paul, 1970.

Laroui, Abdallah. *The History of the Maghrib: An Interpretive Essay.* Trans. Ralph Manheim. Princeton, NJ: Princeton University Press, 1977.

Lévi-Provençal, Evariste. *Historiens des Chorfas* [Historians of Chorfas]. Casablanca: Editions Afrique-Orient, 1991.

Le Maghreb en 2000 titres: ecrits et lectures sur le Maghreb. Casablanca: Foundation du Roi Abdul-Aziz; Paris: Institut du Monde Arabe, 1991.

Valensi, Lucette. *On the Eve of Colonialism: North Africa before the French Conquest, 1790–1830.* Trans. Kenneth J. Perkins. New York: Africana Publishing, 1977.

African Historiography—Sub-Saharan

Historical writing in and about the sub-Saharan region of Africa, not including South Africa. African historiography, as a modern academic project, was conceived in the womb of colonialism. As a cultural agenda, colonialism did much to debase indigenous African culture. However, colonialism was to generate a nationalism in Africa that made the understanding of the past relevant to the challenges of the time and the future. In Europe, colonialism was a glorious moment in the history of expansion, one that required integration into national and international histories. After 1940, colonialism began to crumble, providing Africans with the opportunity to assert themselves. At the same time, Europe itself began to decline, providing the opportunity to question the Eurocentric conception of history. Thus, both within and outside Africa, the past of Africa needed to be understood, although the motivation was, and still is, very different. The two forces—of nationalism in Africa and concerns for "overseas history" in Europe—crystallized after World War II, a period that marked the last phase of colonial rule. The academic study of Africa began slowly in the 1940s, gained world attention in the 1950s, reached a peak in the 1960s, flourished in the 1970s, and has begun to decline since the 1980s.

The forces that created the discipline were to shape its contents and orientations for a long time. In Europe and many other places outside of Africa, the concerns were to analyze the colonial systems, the varieties of encounters between the West and Africa, and the institutions and structures (political, social, and economic) of non-Europeans. Some works that derived from this were Eurocentric: they assigned little credit to Africans for the evolution of civilization, condemned them as people without a history, made the European expansion in Africa the very core of African history, and reduced the entire African experience to one of violence and migrations. The thesis was both simple and crude: Africans were backward and contacts with the superior Europeans stimulated growth.

There are more positive things to be said, however, and not every scholar was condescending. Paying attention to Africans became popular, at least in many academic circles, with the School of Oriental and African Studies in London pioneering the teaching at the university level in 1948. Colonial civil servants had to be trained in languages and history if only to govern better. An increasing number of students demanded courses on Africa, leading to more graduate training and recruitment of faculty. There was a group of scholars interested in a wide range of subjects, from those traditional ones like the military and kingship to new ones like social systems. The study of African history also spread to the United States and other countries where it expanded rapidly. Many scholars were to distinguish themselves as pioneers, including J.D. Fage, R. Oliver, Catherine Coquery-Vidrovitch, and Jan Vansina. Influential journals were established, doctoral students graduated, and enduring works of research and synthesis, like the *Cambridge History of Africa,* have been published since 1960.

In Africa itself, the initial concerns of its early scholars, now equipped with Western education and models of history, were to correct misleading errors created by outsiders, provide enormous evidence on ancient civilizations and successful kingdoms, discuss the varieties of African reactions to the European incursions since the fifteenth century, and create a new curriculum for schools that put Africa at the center of world history. Regarding themselves

as victims of European prejudice and racism, Africans who had been condemned as "people without history" quickly seized the initiative to show that they had a history. Vindicating the past became an obsession, one that had to be done rather quickly and forcefully. But it was an exercise that required sanitization: not only would Eurocentric errors be corrected, no dirty linen would be washed in public. They were able to demonstrate that Africans had always practiced history, in such forms as oral traditions, and had preserved it, even through writings in hieroglyphics or Arabic. Chroniclers had emerged among them, like Samuel Johnson of the Yoruba, who used foreign languages to write. Traditions of historical consciousness were very deep, leaving a rich legacy of data that today's historians can profit from. Following the leads in traditions and chronicles and imitating popular themes in European history, African historians researched a wide range of issues, mainly political. Often the orientation was anticolonial or simply nationalistic. The celebration of this orientation is the eight-volume study by UNESCO entitled the *General History of Africa* and such well-known figures as B. Ogot, K. Dike, and J.F.A. Ajayi bear witness to the creation of a robust nationalist historiography.

The topics, issues, ethnic groups, countries, periods, and controversies became so numerous as to make African historiography appear unwieldy. But this is only so on the surface. For one thing, while there is no consensus on how to study Africa, there is a lot of borrowing of "universalist" ideologies and models that have been applied to the continent. Thus, such popular models as modernization, dependency, Marxism, modes of production, etc. have been extended to the study of Africa in a way that connects the continent to mainstream scholarship. Moreover, Africa is part of a "colonial world," that convenient label; and because of its underdevelopment, part of the "Third World," yet another label. Both labels have always served to provide cohesion to the field, legitimating courses in schools, textbooks, film documentaries, and novels. African historiography also became an "area approach" to the study of history. History as a discipline can be enriched and broadened by studying this "area." As an "area approach," it involves the understanding of the "other," that is, to "other" people based in the West. Thus, from the very beginning, the rationale of understanding "different civilizations" and integrating them into one's own has defined Africa to the rest of the world. Irrespective of the theme, topic, and period, "Africanists" are united by their ability to understand another language, people, and culture. Another factor adding coherence is that, from the very beginning, there was a consensus on methodology: African history has to be unraveled by relying on a multiplicity of sources—oral, written, archaeological, linguistic, etc. Indeed, one of its principal contributions to historical scholarship is the great refinement and use of oral traditions as sources. Thus, the discipline acquires the characteristic of being interdisciplinary, one which involves the collaboration and cooperation of different specialists.

African historiography has changed a good deal from its early days. One significant change arose from the need to assess the performance of African states after independence. For most of the 1960s, critical debate centered on the role of the West in the development process. This connected with a previous anticolonial tradition, with modernization paradigms, and with a rising Marxist and dependency scholarship popularized by Walter Rodney and Immanuel Wallerstein. If the confrontation in the early years pitted the so-called African nationalists against the so-called colonialists, that in the 1960s and 1970s was between the Right and the Left. Previous data was reinterpreted, the role of history in nation building came to the forefront, and increasing attention was paid to contemporary issues.

Yet another significant change was the diversification of themes and issues after the mid-1960s, including resistance, slavery, gender, population, and religion. Most of the themes in other continents have their parallels in Africa. African history became highly professionalized, and rigid boundaries emerged to distinguish specialists by ideologies, themes, and region. Whereas one person could read all the new books about Africa in the 1950s, this was no longer so in the 1970s.

Since the 1980s, most of the changes in historiography have been connected with the economic decline of the continent and its marginalization in world politics. Publications of books and journals have diminished, interest in Africa has declined in many Western universities, and intellectual production in Africa is difficult because of limited resources.

African historiography is very much alive. The discipline enjoys a recognition beyond dispute, its methodologies have been tested, and its contribution to the broad discipline of history is widely acknowledged. The challenge is now to seek the means to overcome its decline. In Africa, the commitment of the populace to Western education is strong, with history at the core of the humanities. Beyond Africa, there are constituencies that continue to work hard to sustain interest. New publications reflect contemporary concerns about the continent, against the background of the decline of ideologies and the fall of the Soviet Union. Precolonial histories are being revisited to shed evidence on social and cultural issues. Colonial regimes are being contrasted with the post-independence countries, revising assumptions about the state and critiquing indigenous leadership. The notion of an inherited nation-state is being questioned, to evaluate the relevance of European political ideas and institutions. Historians relate the past to the present to seek explanations for the persistence of cultures as well as current economic and political troubles. While themes and issues that are specific to Africa remain dominant fields of inquiry, new ranges of possibilities are being created by those who connect the continent with comparative and theoretical works, with the mainstream scholarship in the various disciplines, and with the new trend of postmodernism.

Toyin Falola

See also AFRICAN HISTORIOGRAPHY—NORTH AFRICA (MAGHREB); SOUTH AFRICAN HISTORIOGRAPHY.

Texts

The Cambridge History of Africa. 8 vols. Cambridge, Eng.: Cambridge University Press, 1985.

Davidson, Basil. *The Black Man's Burden: Africa and the Curse of the Nation State.* London: James Currey, 1992.

Oliver, Roland. *The African Experience: Major Themes in African History from Earliest Times to the Present.* New York: Harper Collins, 1991.

Rodney, Walter. *How Europe Underdeveloped Africa.* London: Bogle-L'Ouverture Publications, 1972.

UNESCO. *General History of Africa.* Vols. 1–8. Paris and London: UNESCO & Heinemann, 1981–1993.

References

Falola, Toyin. *African Historiography: Essays in Honour of J.F. Ade Ajayi.* London: Longman, 1993.

Fyfe, C., ed., *African Studies since 1945: A Tribute to Basil Davidson.* London: Longman, 1976.

Jewsiewicki, B., and D. Newbury, eds. *African Historiographies: What History for Which Africa?* Beverly Hills, CA: Sage, 1986.

Africanus, Julius (fl. late second—middle third century A.D.)

Christian philosopher and chronographer. There is scant evidence, and hence, much scholarly controversy regarding the life of Africanus. He probably came from Palestine and traveled widely throughout the Roman Empire. He went on an embassy for the city of Emmaus ca. 220 to the emperor Elagabalus. Africanus wrote several works: epistles on biblical interpretations; the *Chronography* (in five books), which synthesized pagan and Christian history; and the *Kestoi,* which was probably an encyclopedic hodgepodge. Of these, two epistles are extant; the other works are preserved as fragments in the works of later authors. The *Chronography* is the most important. It has traditionally been regarded as a major historical source for Eusebius of Caesarea, although recently doubts have been raised about this connection.

R.M. Frakes

References

Croke, Brian. "The Origins of the Christian World Chronicle." In *History and Historians in Late Antiquity,* ed. Brian Croke and Alanna Emmett. Sydney and New York: Pergamon, 1983, 116–131.

Mosshamer, A. *The Chronicle of Eusebius and Greek Chronographic Tradition.* Lewisburg, PA, and London: Bucknell University Press and Associated University Press, 1979.

Thee, Francis C.R. *Julius Africanus and the Early Christian View of Magic.* Tübingen, Germany: J.C.B. Mohr, 1984.

Ajayi, Jacob Festus Ade (b. 1929)

Nigerian historian, educator, and university administrator. Ajayi was born in Ikole-Ekiti, Ondo state, in what is now Nigeria and graduated in 1946 from the famous Igbobi College in Lagos. He then attended Yaba Higher College, University College Ibadan, University College Leicester, and the University of London. Following his doctoral work at the University of London, he returned home in October 1958 to join the faculty of the Department of History, University of Ibadan. This was two years before Nigeria's independence and at a time when Africans were struggling to rid the continent of European colonial domination.

Alongside the struggle for political independence, emergent African intellectuals were in the process of establishing the significance of the study of African history as a discipline. Ajayi and Kenneth Onwuka Dike, another pioneering African historian, launched a crusade that maintained Africans had a history long before European intrusion. They both established that oral tradition was important in the reconstruction of that past. One of Ajayi's contributions to the development of African historiography was the inauguration of the Ibadan History Series in 1965 with his book *Christian Missions in Nigeria, 1841–1891: The Making of a New Elite.* The ideas and views expressed in the series (of which he was the general editor) gave rise to what is today known in scholarly circles as the Ibadan history school.

Over the years, while his scholarship has focused on understanding the nature of the forces at work in nineteenth- and twentieth-century Africa, Ajayi has also emphasized the continuity of African institutions and identity in the process of change on the continent. It is along these lines that he once asserted that "in any long-term historical view of African history, European rule becomes just another episode. . . . Colonialism must be seen not as a complete departure from the African past, but as one episode in the continuous flow of African history." His writings have also examined such issues as the historiography of African history, culture, education, nation building, and national integration and the role of the university in the process of national development. In collaboration with Dike and his other contemporaries at Ibadan, Ajayi brought about a major shift in the focus of the History Department's curriculum. Of particular note was the change from a focus on European activities in Africa to the development of courses that examined the contributions of Africans to African historical experience.

As a leading member of the first generation of Africa's academic historians, Ajayi has also made his mark in the training of younger scholars. The hallmark of his teaching career has been to encourage in his students the development of a critical mind. As some of his former students noted at his reception of the African Studies Association of the United States' Distinguished Africanist Award in 1993, Ajayi's stature as an eminent scholar and teacher is not in doubt. According to one of them, "Ajayi stimulates his students to question stereotypes and to be original in interpretation. He welcomes criticisms in the best traditions of historical scholarship."

Ajayi is first and foremost a writer and teacher, but he has also contributed to the development of education in Africa through various administrative and academic positions. For this work he has been accorded such honors as the Nigerian National Merit Award (1986), the vice presidency of the

Association of African Universities (1970–1980), and the chairmanships of the International African Institute (1975–1987) and the Governing Council of the United Nations University (1976–1977).

Onaiwu Wilson Ogbomo

Texts

Africa in the Nineteenth Century until the 1880s. Jordin Hill, Oxford: Heinemann; Berkeley: University of California Press; Paris: Unesco, 1989.

Christian Missions in Nigeria, 1841–1891: The Making of a New Elite. London: Longmans, 1965.

Ed., with Bashir Ikara. *Evolution of Political Culture in Nigeria.* Ibadan, Nigeria: University Press, 1985.

Ed., with M. Crowder. *A History of West Africa.* Third ed. Burnt Mill, Harlow, Essex, England: Longman, 1985.

Ed., with Ian Espie. *A Thousand Years of West African History.* Rev. ed. London: Nelson, 1969.

With Adu Boahen and Michael Tidy. *Topics in West African History.* Second ed. Burnt Mill, Harlow, Essex, England: Longman, 1986.

With Robert Smith. *Yoruba Warfare in the Nineteenth Century.* Second ed. Cambridge, England: Cambridge University Press in association with the Institute of African Studies, University of Ibadan, 1971.

References

Falola, Toyin. *African Historiography: Essays in Honour of Jacob Ade Ajayi.* London: Longman, 1993.

Ikime, Obaro. "Citation on Professor J.F. Ade Ajayi." In *History and the Nation and Other Addresses* by J.F. Ade Ajayi. Ibadan, Nigeria: Spectrum Books Ltd., 1991.

Akiga [Akighirga] Sai (1898–1959)

African traditional historian. Akiga (more correctly Akighirga) Sai was a member of the Tiv, an ethnic group in Nigeria. In 1911, European missionaries brought Christianity to his village. Encouraged by his father, Akiga quickly embraced the new religion, became an evangelist, and served much of Tivland. He edited a Tiv newsletter and was for five years a member of the Northern Nigeria House of Assembly. Worried that the old Tiv order was fast disappearing, Akiga sought to collect and preserve in writing as much of it as he could.

The result was *Akiga's Story,* a penetrating account, based on oral sources, of Tiv history and institutions. The subjects it covered include Tiv origins, sociopolitical organization, agricultural practices, belief systems, rites of passage, gender relations, disease and medicine, a wide range of ethnographic practices, and the people's initial responses to the arrival of Europeans. For many, *Akiga's Story* remains the starting point for study of the Tiv. Rupert East translated part of a massive manuscript prepared in Tiv by Akiga and first published it in 1939. This edition was reprinted in 1965. In 1952, Paul Bohannan found the manuscript in safekeeping at the Dutch Reformed Church mission in Mkar, Nigeria, and developed part of it into his subsequent article entitled "The 'Descent' of the Tiv from Ibenda Hill."

Ebere Nwaubani

Texts

Akiga's Story: The Tiv Tribe As Seen by One of Its Members. Ed. and trans. Rupert East. London: Oxford University Press, 1939.

Bohannan, Paul. "The 'Descent' of the Tiv from Ibenda Hill." *Africa* 24 (1954): 295–310.

References

East, Rupert. "Introduction." In *Akiga's Story,* ed. and trans. Rupert East. London: Oxford University Press, 1939.

Alciato [Alciati], Andrea (1492–1550)

Milanese humanist lawyer. Born into an influential family, Alciato received a humanist education in Milan and studied law at the universities of Pavia and Bologna. As a professor in Avignon, Bourges, and Pavia, he became, together with Guillaume Budé, the renowned founder of the *mos gallicus,* the historical school of Roman law. Analyzing its tradition with unusual philological skill and historical insight, Alciato decisively influenced younger lawyers in France, who would then focus on legal and institutional history. Another lasting success was Alciato's explanation of allegories and symbols (*Emblemata,* 1531), often translated and reprinted more than 170 times. Written before his legal career, Alciato's properly historical works are less well known: an unpublished *Monumentorum veterumque inscriptionum collectanea* [Collection of Ancient Inscriptions], judged by Theodor Mommsen to be the foundation of epigraphy, and a history of Milan from its beginnings to Valentinian, published in 1625. In 1517, Alciato's *Annotationes* accompanied an edition of Tacitus;

several times reprinted as *Encomium historiae,* they exalt Tacitus above the then more popular Livy, anticipating the late-sixteenth-century vogue for the former among readers of Roman history.

Thomas Maissen

Texts

Opera omnia. 4 vols. Basel, Switzerland: Thomas Guarinus, 1582.
Rerum patriae libri IV. Milan: I.B. Bidellium, 1625.

References

Heckscher, William S. *The Princeton Alciati Companion.* New York: Garland, 1989.
Kelley, Donald R. *Foundations of Modern Historical Scholarship.* New York: Columbia University Press, 1970.

Âlî, Mustafa (1541–1600)

Ottoman historian. The son of a prosperous Muslim merchant of Gallipoli, Âlî was highly educated in the Ottoman theological-legal tradition before choosing the parallel careers of bureaucrat and man of letters. After several years as private secretary to leading provincial governors, he held a series of middle-ranking posts in the state financial bureaucracy, culminating in 1599 and 1600 in a more senior appointment as district governor and trustee of Jeddah on the Red Sea coast, where he died shortly after his arrival. Âlî's fifty or more literary works—in particular, the relevant section of his principal work, *Künhü 'l-ahbar* [Essence of History]—are invaluable sources for late-sixteenth-century Ottoman political and social history. A man of generally frustrated ambition, vehement opinions, and a lively prose style, Âlî contributed significantly to the dominant notion of Ottoman "decline" after the reign of Suleiman the Magnificent and is regarded as the outstanding Ottoman historian of his time.

Christine Woodhead

Texts

Künhü 'l-ahbar. 5 vols. Istanbul: n.p., 1861–1869.
Menakib-i hünerveran [Artists' Lives and Achievements]. Ed. Ibnülemin Mahmud Kemal [Inal]. Istanbul: Türk Tarih Encümeni, 1926.
Meva'idu 'n-nefa'is fi kava'idi'l-mecalis [Tables of Delicacies in Social Etiquette]. Ed. M.C. Baysun. Istanbul: n.p., 1956.
Mustafa 'Âlî's Counsel for Sultans of 1581 [Nushat us-selatin]. Ed. and trans. Andreas Tietze. 2 vols. Vienna: Österreichische Akademie der Wissenschaften, 1978–1982.

Mustafa 'Âlî's Description of Cairo of 1599. Ed. and trans. Andreas Tietze. Vienna: Österreichische Akademie der Wissenschaften, 1975.
Mustafa 'Âlî's Fursatname: Edition und Bearbeitung einer Quelle zur Geschichte des persischen Feldzugs unter Sinan Paşa 1580– 1581 [Mustafa 'Âlî's *Fursatname:* An Edition of and Revisions to a Source for the History of the Persian Campaigns under Sinan Paşa]. Ed. Rana von Mende. Berlin: Klaus Schwarz Verlag, 1989.

References

Fleischer, C.H. *Bureaucrat and Intellectual in the Ottoman Empire: The Historian Mustafa Âlî (1541–1600).* Princeton, NJ: Princeton University Press, 1986.
Schmidt, J. *Pure Water for Thirsty Muslims: A Study of Mustafā 'Âlî of Gallipoli's Künhü 'l-ahbār.* Leiden: Het Oosters Instituut, 1991.

Alison, Archibald (1792–1867)

Scottish historian. Alison studied at Edinburgh University, where he absorbed the historical culture of the Scottish Enlightenment. A practicing lawyer, he spent the greater part of his career as sheriff of Lanarkshire and was created baronet in 1852. He remained a Tory throughout his life, contributing copious articles to the Tory *Blackwood's Magazine.* In spite of his opposition to both electoral reform and Catholic emancipation, his writings show him to have been a man of an amiable and tolerant cast. Alison's major achievement, the *History of Europe from the Commencement of the French Revolution to the Restoration of the Bourbons* (1833–1842), was a popular work that went through ten (frequently revised) editions in the author's lifetime. It was the first scholarly attempt at a complete history of the French Revolution. Its "main design," as Alison explained in his *Autobiography* (1883), "is to illustrate the danger of revolutions." The story of the revolution is set in a broad context (Alison's reach extends to Poland and the Americas) and narrated with some fluency. Alison's method draws upon traditional Scottish providential history: human vice, including both the "fateful pride" of the aristocracy, who caused the revolution, and the violence of the revolutionaries are ultimately instrumental to God's larger purpose. Yet Alison's work is also wedded to a conjectural history of liberty, derived from his Scottish Enlightenment predecessors; the "convulsion" of the French Revolution is part of the European transition from feudalism and despotism to a more liberal modernity. The continuation of this history was entitled a *History of Europe from the Fall of Napoleon in 1815 to . . . 1852* (1853–1859). Alison also wrote biographies of Marlborough (1847, 1852) and Castlereagh (1861).

Karen O'Brien

Texts

History of Europe from the Commencement of the French Revolution to the Restoration of the Bourbons. Ninth ed. London: W. Blackwood, 1853.
History of Europe from the Fall of Napoleon in 1815 to the Accession of Louis Napoleon in 1852. 8 vols. Edinburgh: W. Blackwood, 1854–1859.
Some Account of My Life and Writings: An Autobiography. 2 vols. Edinburgh: W. Blackwood, 1883.

References

Ben-Israel, Hedva. *English Historians on the French Revolution.* Cambridge, Eng.: Cambridge University Press, 1968.

Altamira y Crevea, Rafael (1866–1951)

Spanish historian, jurist, and pedagogue. Altamira is remembered primarily as the historian of the generation of 1898—those Spanish intellectuals who came to maturity in the aftermath of the Spanish–American War—who taught that regeneration would come through education and the study of history. He published a collection of patriotic addresses in 1902 entitled *Psicología del pueblo español* [Psychology of the Spanish People]. In these he stressed that the defeat of Spain in 1898 was not an isolated incident but the culmination of a long-term process and that Spaniards needed to dig deep into their past to discover and rekindle the essence of the Spanish genius in order to ensure the country's political and moral regeneration. To this end he wrote his four-volume *Historia de España y de la civilización española* [A History of Spanish Civilization] (1900–1911). Altamira's nonlegal historical works were not specialized monographs but popular syntheses. His "internal" history dealt with many aspects of civilization, not only with political and military history. Altamira held several important positions, including the chair of American political institutions at the University of Madrid, the general directorship of primary education, and a regular seat on the Permanent Court of International Justice.

George L. Vásquez

Texts

A History of Spanish Civilization. Ed. and trans. P. Volkov. New York: Biblo and Tannen, 1968.
Psicología del pueblo español. Second ed. Barcelona: Editorial Minerva, 1918.

References

Fagg, John E. "Rafael Altamira (1866–1951)." In *Essays in Modern European Historiography,* ed. S. William Halperin. Chicago: University of Chicago Press, 1970, 3–21.
Malagón Barceló, Javier. *Rafael Altamira y Crevea: el historiador y el hombre* [Rafael Altamira y Crevea: The Historian and the Man]. Mexico City: Universidad Nacional Autónoma de México, Institutio de Investigaciones Históricas, 1971.
Vásquez, George L. "Altamira: Historian of the Generation of 1898." *Mediterranean Studies* 5 (1995): 85–100.

American Historiography

An overview of the writing of history in the United States from colonial times to the late twentieth century and of developments within and outside the historical profession since the late nineteenth century.

As with most modern nations that originated as colonial offshoots of European powers, historical writing in the North American colonies—excluding indigenous traditions and oral tales—began as a variant of travel literature, designed less to commemorate the past than to describe for readers in the mother country the flora and fauna of the new territories and to provide some sense of the customs of their peoples. The first English writer to compose a "history" in the sense of a more-or-less true story about the recent past was the explorer John Smith (1579–1631), in his *A True Relation* (1608) and later in his *General History of Virginia, New England, and the Summer Isles* (1624), a work modeled on contemporary English accounts of European peoples such as the Ottoman Turks. Apart from its apology for Smith's own actions, the latter work is most famous in popular lore for the story of Pocahontas, which was added to subsequent editions. It also provided the first account of an early American settlement and the lives of its colonists, albeit one presented as a colorful epic so as to lure more settlers from England.

Further north, in the very different religious climate of New England after 1620, history developed a distinctive providentialist strain that has never entirely disappeared from America's account of its past. There, early historians were influenced by such English books as the Protestant martyrologist John Foxe's *Acts and Monuments* (1583) and the explorer Sir Walter Ralegh's *History of the World* (1614), both of which conveyed a strong sense of the active role of the divine in human affairs. New England colonists composed histories relating the settlement of these rugged territories, interpreting the near-miraculous deliverance of the Mayflower migrants from hunger and cold as a sign of God's will that a godly community be established in "New" England. Among the notable works in this genre, from the original Plymouth colony and later the wider Massachusetts Bay area, are William Bradford's (1590–1657) *History of Plymouth Plantation* (first published 1856) and William Hubbard's (1621–1704) *General History of New England to 1630* (first published 1815). In 1676, Increase Mather (1639–1723) authored a *Brief History of the War with the Indians in New England* (1676), perhaps the first example of American military history writing, although cast in providentialist terms. His son, Cotton Mather (1663–1728), also wrote history but turned his attention away from the original settlement ventures and refocused it on Massachusetts's more recent growth into a godly, reborn society of "saints."

English historiography continued to exercise a strong stylistic influence on its New World offspring up to and including the Revolutionary Era, although historians often wrote from a distinctively colonial standpoint. Thus Robert Beverley (1675–1716) composed his 1705 *History of Virginia* both to correct factual errors in English accounts and to provide a colonist's perspective on the first century of settlement in Virginia. An even more strongly independent sense of the past can be found in William Stith's (1689–1755) unfinished history of Virginia up to 1624 (1747), a work that recounted the struggles of colonists against unscrupulous or corrupt royal governors and that aspired in its relating of facts to imitate the contemporary standards of European scholarship. Other colonies also had their historians, such as Rhode Island's John Callender (1706–1748) and Connecticut's Benjamin Trumbull (1735–1820). An overall picture of the colonial experiment was contributed by the Boston physician William Douglass (1691–1752) in his *Summary View, Historical and Political, of the British Settlements in North America* (1747–1750). The last history to be written in the colonial period was,

perhaps appropriately, the work of the last civil governor of Massachusetts before the revolution, Thomas Hutchinson (1711–1780), who completed his multivolume history of the Bay Colony while in exile.

With the American Revolution came a more concerted effort to provide a distinctive past for the new nation, one that emphasized its long tradition of independence from Britain (and its imperial rival France) while retaining a respect for certain Old World customs and laws. Mercy Otis Warren (1728–1814), the first notable female historian produced by the United States, wrote a strongly republican account of the Revolution favorable to democratic sentiments and critical of the elitist tendencies among leaders such as John Adams (who had also suggested that women were ill-suited to the writing of history). Living in an era that would soon produce the more radical French Revolution, Warren was not alone in seeing the successful revolt of the thirteen colonies in apocalyptic terms, marking the beginning of a new republican world order. Other important historians of the Revolutionary and early republican periods included David Ramsay (1749–1815), who wrote a sympathetic treatment of the Revolution itself, and Noah Webster (1758–1843). Finally, biographies of founding fathers such as Washington became a popular dish in the American literary diet, most famously in the celebratory 1800 life of the first president by Mason Locke Weems (1759–1825) and the multivolume *Life and Writings of Washington* by Jared Sparks (1789–1866).

The nineteenth century is seen, in many accounts of the development of historical writing, as a kind of "Golden Age of Historiography" in the sense that it produced a great many classic historical works that remain highly readable today and because the last decades of the century witnessed the beginnings of professionalization of the historical discipline. These achievements had some severe limitations—the works themselves were on a narrower range of topics than is the case today, and the "profession" was socially highly exclusionary until relatively recent times. It is important, too, to recognize that nineteenth-century developments would not have been possible had there not arisen an intense public thirst for history in the early decades of the century, measurable in the numbers of middle-class publications (such as magazines) that included some historical articles, reviews, and sometimes serialized versions of full-length books; in historical novels such as those by James Fenimore Cooper; in the beginnings of local archives and state historical societies devoted to preserving and disseminating historical materials; and, in some places, in a vigorous interest in family history. A recent scholar, George Callcott, has pointed out that 36 percent of the best-selling books in the United States from 1800 to 1860 were historical, as compared with a figure around 15 percent before 1800 and again after 1860. Moreover, by mid century, history was firmly established as a major subject in the curriculum of public schools—though not, yet, of the colleges. The earliest textbook on American history, John McCulloch's (1754–1824) *Introduction to the History of America* (1787), was published during the Revolution, and a flood of such works appeared between 1820 and 1850, including Peter Parley's (a pseudonym for Samuel Griswold Goodrich [1793–1860]) *A Pictorial History of the United States* (1845) and Emma Hart Willard's (1787–1870) *History of the United States* (1828), both of which were immensely successful. World history, too, found a place in the curriculum, especially Greek and Roman history, which was still studied principally as a source of political and philosophical wisdom. By 1860 there existed more than one hundred textbook surveys of world history. Curiously, the most popular author on world history was not an American but the eighteenth-century English novelist and historian Oliver Goldsmith.

This popularization of the past applied, of course, to readers rather than writers. So far as the latter were concerned, history remained firmly the province of the gentleman of leisure at least until the Civil War. History was taught at the older colleges, such as Harvard and Yale, but rarely as a distinct subject, and the great wave of history department building lay ahead in the last quarter of the century. The greatest American historians of the period from 1800 to 1860, often broadly referred to as the Romantic historians, were nonprofessionals, men of independent means or government position rather than academics, albeit a great number of them had been educated at Harvard and came from the same Boston Brahmin class. They also had extraordinary literary ability, comparable to British authors such as Sir Walter Scott (who was widely read in America and was a direct influence on novelists like Cooper as well as on historians) and Thomas Babington Macaulay.

The Romantic historians' vision of the past was shaped by a sense of nationhood and of national and racial character, by firm moral convictions, by a belief in progress, and by a continuing faith in the active involvement of God in history. Among these nineteenth-century Americans, William Prescott (1796–1859), John Lothrop Motley (1814–1877), and Francis Parkman (1823–1893) are especially noteworthy: the first for his gripping histories of early modern Spain and its conquests of Mexico and Peru; the second for his history of an earlier nation born in religious and commercial revolution, the Dutch Republic; and the last for his celebration of the American frontier. (Prescott and Parkman were also remarkable in having been nearly blind through most of their active lives.) Another historian, less successful in his own time because of his utilitarian distaste for colonial religious zeal and his repudiation of the high literary style then in fashion, was Richard Hildreth (1805–1865), author of a six-volume *History of the United States of America* (1849–1852). Although he has never achieved the stature of his famous contemporaries, Hildreth nevertheless deserves to be considered among the great historians of the mid-nineteenth century; his skeptical treatment of the motives of those who framed the Constitution was an early expression of the economic interpretation of American history that would be revived sixty years later by Charles A. Beard.

By far the outstanding historian of his age, however, in both his personal longevity and his stature among his international peers was George Bancroft (1800–1891), a Jacksonian democrat whom the great German historian Leopold von Ranke (1795–1886) considered a worthy contemporary. Bancroft taught very briefly at Harvard but spent most of his years in the U.S. diplomatic service; this allowed him access to foreign archives hitherto inaccessible to American scholars and exposed him to a number of prestigious European, especially German, historians. He was among the very first American students to obtain a Ph.D. in Germany (at Göttingen in 1818), thereby anticipating by half a century the great flood of apprentice historians who would be sent to Germany for quick doctorates in the 1860s and 1870s. Bancroft's masterpiece is the *History of the United States from the Discovery of the American Continent to the Present,* a work published over several decades in ten volumes, the last of which appeared in 1874 and, contrary to its title, reached only the year 1782.

Despite his own brief Germanic training, Bancroft, like the rest of his generation of American historians, tended to use archives (and the footnotes that represented their contents) to fill in gaps in narratives already largely written, rather than beginning with the documents and writing only after all of these had been mastered. But by the year Bancroft's last volume appeared, it was already behind the times historiographically. In the second half of the century, the influence of

Baconian inductive philosophy, French Comtian positivism (as mediated by the English historian H.T. Buckle), Scottish "common-sense," and Darwinian evolutionary theory had created an environment suitable to the development of what many contemporaries considered a more "scientific" approach. Above all this stood the towering Germanic idol, Leopold von Ranke. His concept of a systematic and critical, document-based historiography taught by master historians to their postgraduate apprentices in a formal seminar setting with an archival component—fell on receptive American ears and ensured that German-style historical training would quickly catch on in the United States. As early as 1857, Andrew D. White (1832–1918) had introduced such a system to the University of Michigan, where he was that institution's first professor of history.

In the wake of the Civil War and Reconstruction and the opening of several new universities such as Johns Hopkins (founded 1876), a whole generation of bright American college graduates was sent to Germany to study at the feet of, or at least in the orbit of, Ranke and his students. In fact, very few of them were actually exposed to Ranke himself, studying instead under second- and third-generation Rankean disciples, such as the influential Hermann Eduard von Holst (1841–1904), who would later emigrate from Freiburg to the University of Chicago. American graduates came back, as a result, with a narrow understanding of the historian's role and methods, beginning with a naive and even misguided sense of the German master's theories respecting the objectivity and meaning of history: Ranke's famous dictum about describing the past *wie es eigentlich gewesen,* which probably meant more accurately "as it *essentially* happened," was rendered, too literally, into "as it *actually* happened." Secondly, American students overseas absorbed little of the post-Rankean, antipositivist Germanic thought of the last part of the century, expressed by thinkers such as Wilhelm Dilthey, Wilhelm Windelband, and Heinrich Rickert. By the time those German authors had achieved prominence, the stream of students going abroad had been reduced to a trickle, as most began remaining in the newer American graduate programs. Finally, the hot-house atmosphere of the German "seminar" was a thoroughly male and middle-class bastion that set itself apart from the less research-oriented, rather more accessible domain of the public lecture; this too would have implications for the course of American historical writing over the next century.

This training in history as a discipline, and an abiding confidence in the capacity of properly executed research to produce nearly absolute knowledge about the past, was not especially important in producing major historical works; the German doctorate of the time was not a formidable piece of research, and many of its graduates ended up as primarily teachers rather than writers. It was, however, of enormous importance in helping to produce a kind of cult of "objectivity" in the study of the past. The "objectivity question" has remained a common theme in American methodological discussions for over a century, though some recent scholars, such as Ernst Breisach, have downplayed its significance.

In 1884, the American Historical Association (AHA) was founded as a national body dedicated to the writing and teaching of history, under the initial leadership of Herbert Baxter Adams (1850–1901) of Johns Hopkins; within a quarter of a century it would have nearly three thousand members. In 1895, under the nominal direction and eventually formal sponsorship of the AHA, the *American Historical Review* was established as the primary vehicle for the presentation of scholarly research in periodical form and as a venue for discussions of methodology. In its early days, under Adams's leadership and influence, the AHA was an inclusive body that embraced academic and non-academic, professional and amateur. Thus the early growth of the "profession" of history in the last part of the nineteenth century did not immediately have an impact on the prominence and status of the extra-academic historical writer. This is amply demonstrated by the successful historical careers of Henry Adams (1838–1918), who was briefly a Harvard academic and student of Anglo-Saxon history, but who spent most of his career as an independent man of letters; James Ford Rhodes (1848–1927), the first great historian of the Civil War; and Henry Charles Lea (1825–1909), a publisher and political activist turned self-taught historian, who produced several scholarly and well-written histories of European religious persecution.

Those days did not long continue. A watershed was reached with the rise to influence of Herbert B. Adams's first graduate student, J. Franklin Jameson (1859–1937) of Brown University—a pupil who was critical of his former master. Jameson, who became president of the AHA in 1907, was a devoted champion of "scientific history" and an opponent of "amateurism." In addition to being a formidable educator himself and a voluminous writer, (although he himself published relatively little), Jameson used his influence within the AHA to turn it into the haven of professionals—which meant university-based historians. As editor of the *Review,* he also had an enormous impact on the selection of articles for publication and on the appointment of book reviewers.

The hegemony of Jameson and his supporters is often seen as a triumph of scientific history over history as a literary form, of rigorous training and Germanic *Quellenkritik* (source criticism) over haphazard reading in the sources, but it came at the cost of a rift among the practitioners of history that has never entirely healed. The so-called amateurs (who still enjoyed a broader audience for their books than most academics) together with many academics who objected to the elitism and Northeastern dominance of the AHA, turned instead to organizations such as the Mississippi Valley Historical Association (founded 1907, the forerunner of the modern Organization of American Historians) and the Southern Historical Association (founded 1934), both of which quickly established their own journals.

A second consequence of Jameson's influence was the use of the issue of "objectivity" to stifle rather than to promote debate and criticism, on the assumption that collegial relations within the profession were of greater importance than the advancement of partisan or radically innovative points of view. This atmosphere of amiable collegiality, in which academic historians were assumed to agree on most points of substance and method, and perhaps to take issue with each other only on points of detail, proved too artificial to maintain for very long. It was challenged at two distinct points in the twentieth century: just before, during, and after World War I by Progressivism and then its peculiar offspring Relativism; and again in the 1960s, more decisively, by the emergence of social history, women's history, radical history, Black history, and a variety of other approaches to the past.

At the end of the nineteenth century, with the trend toward professionalism well under way, American historians were beginning to make an international reputation for themselves in a variety of areas. The direct German influence on historical training, already declining by the 1890s, had largely dried up even before World War I made pro-German sympathies politically dangerous, and the major historians of this period were as often as not home-grown. Charles Homer Haskins (1870–1937) of Harvard, a medievalist, and James Henry Breasted (1865–1935) of Chicago, an Egyptologist, are two prominent examples.

In American historiography, the immediate heirs of figures like H.B. Adams and J.F. Jameson were, first of all, two different "schools" of history. The first, a group of historians sometimes referred to collectively as the "Imperial school," was led by Herbert Levi Osgood (1855–1918), Charles McLean Andrews (1863–1943), and Andrews's student George Louis Beer (1872–1920). These historians paid particular attention to the early colonial period and to America's place within the British imperial system; they were thus "revisionist" in the sense of questioning the roots of America's distinctiveness. One should also mention the related contributions of Albert Bushnell Hart (1854–1943), an Americanist who, like Henry Adams and H.B. Adams, saw the roots of American institutions in Anglo-Saxon history (what is usually called the "Germanist" thesis); Hart also edited the multivolume *American Nation* series, which was an attempt to present an overview of American history on "scientific principles," with each volume penned by a noted authority on his period.

The second influential school of thought was initiated by Columbia's William A. Dunning (1857–1922), who led a revisionist attack on Unionist views of slavery and Reconstruction. Dunning and his followers were considerably harsher on abolitionists and "agitators" than on slaveholders, and they saw Reconstruction as an unmitigated catastrophe owing largely to Northern errors and greed. Dunning himself shared with the Imperial school a desire to demonstrate the continuity of American institutions, and he also wished to diminish sectional mistrust by providing a less negative view of Southern history than the prevailing "Yankee" interpretation had allowed. Both Dunning and many of his students, such as Ulrich B. Phillips (1877–1934), also shared in the growing postwar racism that regarded black Americans as an inferior race for whom slavery may have been better than freedom. Phillips went further, contrasting the economic failure of slavery by 1860 with the necessity, as he saw it, of its retention as an instrument of racial control. It is worth noting that his views were not shared by all Southern historians. The Virginian William B. Hesseltine (1902–1963), who spent most of his career in the North, was a one-time socialist and persistent critic of the racist interpretation of Southern history from the 1930s on.

Outside both the Imperial and Dunning schools of American history lay yet another group, including both Americanists and Europeanists, that would achieve prominence in the period before and after World War I and would have a considerable impact on the course of historical writing and thinking about the aims of history. This group—"school" in this instance would be misleading—consisted of a number of scholars based, like William A. Dunning, at Columbia University, who were connected with or had studied under Holst's former Freiburg pupil, James Harvey Robinson (1863–1936). They are often referred to collectively under the rubric of "New History" (and associated with a book by that name which Robinson published in 1912), which overlaps with the slightly later and broader movement known as "Progressive History."

The New Historians emerged alongside the so-called pragmatic revolt, a thorough revaluation of the status of and methods for discovering truth that occurred in other fields such as philosophy, while similar criticisms of traditional historiography were being mounted by Henri Berr (and, slightly later, the early Annales school) in France and by Karl Lamprecht in Germany. The idea of a "new" history attracted a number of scholars interested in subjects other than American history: Robinson himself, a modern Europeanist; historian and political scientist James Thomson Shotwell (1874–1965); authority on medieval science and magic Lynn Thorndike (1882–1965); and, most important, student of English history turned Americanist Charles Austin Beard (1874–1948), who joined Columbia's teaching staff in 1904.

Under Robinson's and Beard's leadership from about 1900 to America's entry into World War I, the New Historians initiated a revolt against the preoccupation of "scientific history" with matters of high politics. They advocated greater attention to everyday life, to the relationship between ideas and their environment, to social conflict, to economic forces, and to current problems. The earliest published signpost to their views was Robinson's and Beard's jointly written two-volume textbook *The Development of Modern Europe* (1907–1908), subtitled "An Introduction to the Study of Current History." The New Historians were thus to some degree both the descendants of such Enlightenment figures as Vico and Voltaire and the direct ancestors of modern social history, though there was nothing inherently radical in their program. Indeed, much of this had already been advocated by a late Victorian English historian, John Richard Green (1837–1883). It had also been anticipated by nineteenth-century American cultural historians such as the former English professor Moses Coit Tyler (1835–1900); by the

intellectual historian Edward Eggleston (1837–1902), perhaps the first to coin the term "New History" as early as 1900; by the historian of "the people" John Bach McMaster (1852–1932); and, most recently, by Frederick Jackson Turner (1861–1932) in the 1890s.

The Progressive historians included most of the Robinson circle as well as the Wisconsin-based Turner, whose essays on the importance of the frontier in American history and on the contribution of sectional rivalry to major American events such as the Revolution and the Civil War have remained in dispute to this day. The Progressives also included two other formidable and unconventional figures. The first was a literary historian and English professor, Vernon Louis Parrington (1871–1929), the author of *Main Currents of American Thought* (two vols., 1927–1930; a third volume was never completed). In the wake of World War I and of what he saw as a decline in American values in the industrial age, Parrington was, unlike many of his contemporaries, a Progressive who was himself highly skeptical toward the idea of "progress" in history. Although he certainly saw in the past genuine periods of economic and social progress, Parrington also observed the achievements of these periods retarded or negated by deeply rooted forces of reaction such as irrationality, superstition, and dogma. This same skepticism could be found in Cornell's Carl Lotus Becker (1873–1945), who was a former student of Turner and perhaps the most searching American thinker of his time on historiographical matters. Along with his contemporary Beard, Becker would eventually move from Progressivism to its 1930s variant, Relativism. It was Becker, like Parrington an intellectual rather than a social historian, who first made popular the term "climate of opinion," a centerpiece of his 1932 book *The Heavenly City of the Eighteenth Century Philosophers*.

By far the most energetic member of both groups was Beard. Over the course of his lengthy career, he stirred up one controversy after another. Although he gave up his academic post in 1917 in protest against restrictions on academic freedom at Columbia (and was followed by his colleague Robinson two months later), he continued to exercise extraordinary influence for at least two more decades, and both he and Robinson were early, if only temporary, members of the New School for Social Research, founded in 1919. Beard's most famous book from his Columbia years, *An Economic Interpretation of the Constitution of the United States* (1913), together with its sequel, *Economic Origins of Jeffersonian Democracy* (1915) aroused great fury for suggesting that the founding fathers of the country had, in drawing up the federal Constitution, been motivated by property interests rather than disinterested republican spirit. This was not in itself a new idea, but Beard's clearly expressed view that this had constrained democracy rather than carefully nurturing its slow growth made him a number of enemies—not for the last time in his life. On leaving Columbia, he devoted most of his time to a variety of public and professional activities and to writing. He would go on to produce a number of monographs and textbooks, including the best-selling work, coauthored with Mary Ritter Beard, *The Rise of American Civilization* (1927).

Despite Beard's premature abandonment of the academy, he managed in a relatively short time to teach many of the next generation of interwar historians, of whom Arthur M. Schlesinger (1888–1965) and Harry Elmer Barnes (1889–1968) may serve as examples. A student of the colonial era, Schlesinger was perhaps the most farsighted and inclusive champion of social history among the Progressives. His sensitivity to the conditions of daily life of the common man and woman far outstripped the class interpretation of his mentor, and he brought these views to a wide audience as coeditor of the successful *History of American Life* series. Barnes, in contrast, was a more prolific but less subtle and ultimately less influential historian. A firm proponent of history's alliance with the social sciences he was, like Beard himself, a born polemicist. In the 1920s, he provoked the most serious academic controversy of the decade with his revisionist skepticism toward Germany's war guilt (*The Genesis of the World War* [1926]). Barnes was also nearly unique among his peers in being conversant with current French historiography, in particular the Annales school of Marc Bloch and Lucien Febvre.

Both the New Historians and the Progressive historians faced the difficult problem of reconciling their wish that history be, on the one hand, less academically detached and more focused on promoting social change, and that it be, on the other, made more rather than less scientific through an alliance with the new social sciences such as sociology, psychology, and anthropology. Few were really "leftist" in any meaningful sense; some flirted with socialism but none, not even Beard (who used the word "class" to mean little more than "group"), was a Marxist, and others, such as Turner, remained socially quite conservative. Their commitment to social change now looks rather pale in the wake of the radicalism of

the 1960s and the more recent postmodernist and feminist challenges to historiographical conservatism. And their attempt to balance activism with "objectivity" in its old sense was, it would seem, bound to failure, particularly as they were mainly in agreement with the scientific historians on the issue of the reliability of certain historical facts and on the need for a rigorous method free of "literature." They shared, at least for a time, the scientific historians' positivist faith in the establishment and improvement of knowledge in history and other fields. But despite these inherent contradictions, the Progressives were, through their writings and their control of a number of major academic programs, a critical force in the development of the profession up to the late 1930s.

By that time, however, Progressive history had long outlived the Progressive era. The buoyancy of the 1920s had faded in the swathe of social destruction cut by the Great Depression, while the certainty of the natural sciences had itself been undermined by the theory of relativity and by such new scientific terms as "uncertainty principle" and "indeterminacy." Out of all this came a serious insurgence within the ranks of the Progressives, one that appeared to threaten the very foundations of historical research as it had been understood in the prewar period. This was Relativism, and it was advanced most coherently by Beard and Becker, with occasional contributions from others such as Barnes, who had now become a journalist, and Robinson, who died in 1936.

Beard's contribution to the Relativist position, once again influenced by German thought (in particular that of Karl Heussi and Theodor Lessing) came in the form of a presidential address, "Written History As an Act of Faith" (*American Historical Review,* 39 [1934]) and, a year later in a famous essay, "That Noble Dream?" (*American Historical Review,* 41 [1935]). In these two pieces, Beard owned up to a belief that no absolute "scientific" objectivity in history was attainable, that ideology and social status invariably played a part in even the most "disinterested" scholarship, and that every age remakes its own past in the process of making its present. But he refused to yield the belief that social activism was still possible within these constraints and thereby managed to put a happy face on his version of Relativism.

Beard's conversion to Relativism appears to have occurred suddenly, with its implications not always fully worked out in his writings. In contrast, Becker's arguments had been developing since the early 1920s and were, when fully articulated, both more subtle and more frightening. In his famous lecture entitled "Everyman His Own Historian," he drew attention to the need to make history relevant to the ordinary citizen (a New History theme). History, he suggested, was ultimately little more than a "myth," albeit a useful one, and every individual made and remade his or her own history according to present circumstances and in the light of new knowledge; ultimately, the discipline could never be a science. Becker also largely repudiated the idea of progress in history, his skepticism fueled by his reading of Italian historical thinker Benedetto Croce's writings. In a way, Relativism in Becker's formulation also signified a growing if as yet unspoken strain between history and the social sciences. This had been discernible since the mid-1920s under the impact of writings by Sigmund Freud, Vilfredo Pareto, Karl Mannheim, and others of a nonpositivist bent and of the repudiation by disciplines like sociology of the sort of grand speculation on laws and general development that had excited the Progressives in the first place. As Ernst Breisach has put it, "the rhetoric of an alliance with the social sciences stayed intact, while the reality of such an alliance became more and more distant."

Relativism was intrinsically neither right- nor left-leaning, but in the context of Nazism and Stalinism, it appeared morally irresponsible to some observers. Even Becker, who died just at the end of World War II, had struggled in the early 1940s to reconcile his doubts with the need to defend liberal democracy. Victory in the war produced a new sense of national optimism as the United States emerged as the West's leading power (something the aging Beard found increasingly odious), but it also generated the Cold War and McCarthyism. During the late 1940s and the 1950s, a number of historians were dismissed from their positions for ties, real or alleged, to the Communist Party; others began to move to the right. Progressive history, even in its Relativist phase, had dominated historiography since World War I, but it now lost its place at the head of the profession. Beard's own enormous influence, so potent in the 1920s and 1930s, had largely dissipated by the time of his death in 1948.

At the same time, the ethnic and social makeup of the profession changed profoundly. Hitherto, history professors had been drawn mainly from the upper-middle classes and had generally been white American Protestants. Now, more recent immigrants and their sons began to enter the profession in larger numbers. Although anti-Semitism continued to play a role in the hiring process at most history departments, Jews began to achieve prominence as historians. As Peter Novick (1988) points out, however, they gained this place by fitting into the historical establishment rather than changing it. The acculturation of Jewish-American historians (including a number of prewar refugees from Hitler's Germany) into the mainstream stands in marked contrast to the more separatist inclinations of some women historians and of minorities such as African-Americans in the 1960s and after.

Challenges to the Progressivist view came from various quarters. As early as the 1920s and 1930s, the Harvard historian Samuel Eliot Morison (1887–1976) and the Harvard English professor Perry Miller (1905–1963), had shown a strong sympathy for seventeenth-century Puritanism. They had thus been able to present a more favorable view of the early New England period than could be found in the Progressives, who had seen it largely as an age of superstition and dogma. Morison and Miller had each studied closely the role of ideas in American history and, largely, though not entirely, eschewed the environmental materialism that marked the works of Beard and Parrington in particular. At about the same time, a philosopher at Johns Hopkins University, Arthur O. Lovejoy (1873–1962), had successfully turned the history of ideas back to the content of those ideas themselves; in 1940 he founded the *Journal of the History of Ideas,* which remains today a leading journal of intellectual history.

The most formidable challenge, however, awaited the end of World War II. From the late 1940s into the mid-1960s, there arose what has been called the "Consensus school," or, perhaps more accurately, "Counter-Progressive" historiography. The leading figures of this line of thought were Louis Hartz (1919–1986), Richard Hofstadter (1916–1970), and Daniel Boorstin (b. 1914). Like the Progressives themselves, Consensus was less a school than a tendency—significantly, none of its putative adherents identified themselves as such. There is a great distance between Boorstin's patriotic conservatism, which downplays the role of ideology and theory, and Hofstadter's and Hartz's more skeptical pluralism. Some recent works have pointed out both the mutual incompatibility of some of the Consensus historians' views and the fact that they retained many of the liberal values of the Progressives—Hartz's most famous book is indeed a study of *The Liberal Tradition in America* (1955).

On the whole, however, the Consensus historians did agree on two essential points that set them apart from the Progressives. Firstly, they rejected the Progressives' focus on environmental influences on politics (while remaining sympathetic to the interaction between external forces and ideas) in favor of renewed attention to the motives of individuals. Secondly, the Consensus historians argued against the long-standing Turneresque thinking that America had been forged by conflict between competing sections, north and south, east and west, or urban and rural. Instead, they saw a continuity of American interest in which such rivalries as occurred were submerged in the pursuit of common goals, in the spirit of what Hofstadter called "comity." Boorstin in particular—who had briefly been a member of the Communist Party in the late 1930s—appeared to echo the providentialism of seventeenth-century historians in his pronouncements of the destiny and distinctiveness of the Americans, though he did not believe that the United States had a "mission" to impose its values and institutions on the world. In the Consensus view, a calamity such as the Civil War was less the example of serious sectional division that it had long been understood to be, than it was a crucible for the American dream: a crisis that the nation had weathered and emerged from with greater unity.

A major problem facing the Consensus historians was how to integrate the South into their vision of a unified heritage and continuity of tradition; this, it will be recalled, was an old problem dating back to the Dunning–Phillips revisionism of the beginning of the century. Aside from the related but separate issues of race and slavery, the South's apparent maintenance of a rural society seemed to set it apart from the industrial and urban experience of the North since 1865. The boldest answer to this came not from the Consensus historians themselves but from the influential C. Vann Woodward (b. 1908) of Yale, whose prizewinning study, *Origins of the New South* (1951), debunked much of the mythology of Southern conservatism in the postbellum period and demonstrated how the South had in fact been influenced by Northern institutions, including industrial capitalism. Woodward, together with David M. Potter (1910–1971), was among the scholars most responsible for making Southern history, first established by writers such as Hesseltine in the 1930s, a distinctive and prominent field in the 1950s and 1960s. Potter himself was among a number of historians in the 1950s who began to be concerned with matters of national identity that had not been seriously controverted since the era of H.B. Adams and A.B. Hart. Potter's *People of Plenty: Economic Abundance and the American Character* (1954) was a brilliant essay on the entirety of the American experience that attributed American success in avoiding the evils of totalitarianism or violent popular uprising to a continuous high level of economic well-being and consistent progress. Although more properly considered "cultural" rather than "intellectual" history, Potter's work in some ways echoed Hartz's own ascription of the same political stability to the absence of any European-style *ancien régime* and to the continued influence—in daily life as well as in theory—of the political and economic principles of liberty and personal security derived from the seventeenth-century English philosopher John Locke.

The hegemony of the Consensus historians in the historiography of the United States was short-lived and by no means all-encompassing. The Progressive tradition had not entirely vanished with Beard, for it remained alive during the 1950s in the work of such historians as Arthur M. Schlesinger Jr. (b. 1917) and Merle Curti (1897–1996). Schlesinger *fils* was the author of a seminal work on *The Age of Jackson* (1945) that built on Turner's ideas but took greater account of the role of the urbanized industrial classes. Curti, one of Turner's last pupils (and his successor at Wisconsin), produced in his *The Growth of American Thought* (1943) a more sophisticated, inclusive, and detached history of American culture than that previously provided by Parrington. Moreover, among the critics of the Progressives, Hoftstadter himself had contributed much to a sympathetic appreciation of their work (Beard's in particular) in a series of books, notably *The Age of Reform* (1955) and, near the premature end of his life, *The Progressive Historians* (1968).

Many of the ideals of Progressivism would be revived, in more radical form, in the repudiation of Consensus thought by the New Left historians of the 1960s and early 1970s. With the end of the Eisenhower era came the Kennedy and Johnson administrations, complete with a repudiation of 1950s conservatism, the Great Society, Johnson's "War on Poverty," the civil rights movement, and, above all, Vietnam. A serious challenge to the historiographical mainstream was mounted by a number of radical historians such as Staughton Lynd (b. 1929), Howard Zinn (b. 1922), Gabriel Kolko (b. 1932), Herbert Gutman (1928–1985), and William Appleman Williams (1921–1990). One of their number, Jesse Lemisch (b. 1936) has become famous for having popularized the phrase "history from the bottom up" to denote social history that focused on the masses rather than on institutions and leaders. (It is important to note in passing that not every radical historian shared Lemisch's faith in "bottom up" history—Eugene D. Genovese (b. 1930), for one, saw it as overly present-minded and no more complete than "top-down" history.) These historians were strongly influenced by the British historian E.P. Thompson's (1924–1993) *The Making of the English Working Class* (1963); like Thompson, and unlike their New History ancestors half a century earlier, nearly all wrote from a Marxist or neo-Marxist perspective. Several of the radicals, although not all, were Communists or Communist sympathizers (a few, like Herbert Aptheker and Philip S. Foner, had long-standing Communist associations going back to the 1940s). This was in marked contrast to Thompson himself and other British Marxists like Christopher Hill (b. 1912), both of whom had left the British Communist Party after the Soviet Union's suppression of the Hungarian revolt in 1956.

Some of these radicals began to focus on ethnic and racial minorities, especially African-Americans. Discussion of the black experience in America had for a century been largely defined by the historiography of the Civil War and of slavery. White historians such as William A. Dunning, Ulrich B. Phillips and, more recently, Kenneth M. Stampp (b. 1912), David M. Potter, Herbert Aptheker (b. 1915), and Stanley Elkins (b. 1925) had argued about the moral, mental, and economic consequences of slavery for both whites and blacks before and after Emancipation and about the success or failure of Reconstruction. There had also been a number of distinguished African-American historians, most importantly W.E.B. Du Bois (1868–1963) and Carter G. Woodson (1875–1950), and an early, important periodical, *The Journal of Negro History,* founded in 1916. The advent as a distinct field of what for a time was (and in some circles still is) called "Black History" is a complicated phenomenon, not least because three distinctive groups were involved over and above the students of slavery. First, there were established African-American scholars such as John Hope Franklin (b. 1915), who saw themselves as historians who happened to be black rather than Black Historians. Then, there were liberal-left white historians such as Gutman, Genovese, and August Meier (b. 1923) who worked on issues such as slavery and postwar black labor from both a social and a political-economic standpoint, often (as in Gutman's case) emphasizing multiple local studies as the key to understanding national problems. Both these groups, however, ran into the hostility of a younger generation of African-American historians who disliked Franklin's brand of integrationism and distrusted white liberals, whom they deemed racially and often economically, unqualified to be students of the black experience. Since the advent of Black History, the older historical image of African-Americans, slave and free, as victims has receded in the face of work emphasizing past black solidarity, activism, and self-discipline in the face of adversity. Black History is now offered in a majority of midsized and larger college history departments, white and black, and the subdiscipline has produced an impressive list of accomplished historians of African-American descent, such as John Blassingame, Nathan Huggins (1927–1989), Vincent Harding, Thomas C. Holt, Barbara J. Fields, and Nell Painter.

A similar phenomenon originating in the 1960s and 1970s, which has continued today, is the growth of women's history. This has often although not always been linked with the wider social and intellectual movement of feminism. There had been female historians in America since the time of Mercy Otis Warren, and the AHA in its early days had made efforts to include them in its ranks. During the period up to the end of World War II, women constituted a small but significant component of the profession, with scholars such as Lucy Maynard Salmon (1853–1927), Elizabeth Donnan (1883–1955), and Margaret Judson (1899–1991) acquiring positions of some influence at universities. Others had made significant contributions from outside academe, such as Mary Ritter Beard (1876–1958), a sometime collaborator with her husband Charles, and a pioneering women's historian in her own right. Much of the early female contribution to academic historiography came in economic history, which lay outside the mainstream of political historiography—the only woman elected to the AHA presidency prior to 1987 was, perhaps significantly, the medieval economic historian Nellie Neilson (1873–1947), in 1943. Moreover, the percentage of women taking Ph.D.'s and going on to enter the profession declined alarmingly in the 1940s and 1950s, during the Consensus period, and only began to recover in the mid-1960s. As with Black History, women's history began as a "separate-but-equal" exercise, devoted to showing the contribution of women to the American mainstream but also expanding into areas such as social history and the history of the family. The risk inherent in this exercise was that it tended to ghettoize the study of women's experience within one isolated corner of the discipline. The tendency since the mid-1980s has been toward reintegrating women's history into the mainstream—or indeed, changing the mainstream's direction—by focusing on "gender," the ways in which women's and men's lives have been determined by socially constructed gender identities (as opposed to biological sex), and by pointing out how history itself has been gendered. American women historians working not only on American history but also on European and world history have taken the lead in this direction: a few of the most notable contributors include Carroll Smith-Rosenberg, Nancy F. Cott, Elaine Tyler May, Linda K. Kerber, Joan Wallach Scott, and Joan Kelly-Gadol (1928–1982). Scott and Gerda Lerner (b. 1920), an Austrian-born scholar, have been especially influential as theorists of women's history. Women's history in the United States has also expanded its subject area beyond principally white middle-class women (such as the suffragists) and now includes women of color, other ethnic minorities, and men and women of different sexual orientations. In alliance with other disciplines such as sociology, economics, and anthropology, American-based women's/gender historians are now increasingly also looking beyond the confines of the West to Africa, Asia, and Latin America.

The current New Left version of radical history from the Johnson era, has, since the early 1980s, been rather less potent as a major, distinguishable force (although there are still radical historians), as the advent of Reaganite conservatism and an end to the New Deal–Great Society tradition has made the past two decades less socially activist. Yet American historiography at the end of the twentieth century remains highly pluralist, in spite of recent suggestions for the need for a new and all-embracing "grand narrative" accessible to a wider public—a call that to some degree echoes criticisms of academic history by Woodrow Wilson and others at the birth of New History. The enormous wave of university expansion in the 1960s created new positions in history departments. Although many larger departments are now shrinking in size in an era of sustained fiscal restraint, most still offer a variety of courses in areas well beyond the traditional American or European history taught up to 1960: urban history and the history of Native North Americans are two prominent examples within the American field. Globalization has similarly bestowed prominence on a new generation of American Asianists, Islamists, and Africanists, who are studying underdeveloped nations and the cultures of the Pacific Rim (and often describe themselves as "comparative historians"). World history in particular, as practiced, for example, by William H. McNeill and Philip D. Curtin, is a major growth area of the last decade and now has its own journal. Public history—devoted to bringing history outside the academe in the form of museums, national parks, and other publicly funded institutions and to harmonizing academic history with the popular traditions of the past that have long existed—has become an important element within the profession; it is now a field in its own right rather than simply a place for history Ph.D.'s without university positions to turn by default. The rise of public history has been driven since the mid-1980s by a renewed popular interest in the past, as evidenced by such forms as historical reenactments of famous events, displays at highway rest stops, cartoons (even if highly inaccurate, as in the case of recent Disney films), documentaries such as those by filmmaker Ken Burns, a cable television History Channel, and Internet Web and discussion sites. The degree of public engagement with the past can be seen in occurrences such as the controversy over the content of the Smithsonian Institution's Enola Gay and atomic bomb exhibit in 1995, in which revisionist interpretations of the necessity of dropping the atomic bomb on Hiroshima in 1945 came directly into conflict with received views, the latter strongly supported by veterans and other groups.

In comparison, historiography within the more traditional walls of the academy, remains, for the most part, a scholarly pursuit often at a considerable remove from the historical tastes of the book-buying public; although a few academic books of the last decade or so have had wider commercial success, the nonacademic popular survey continues to outsell it: the educated amateur Civil War "buff" will likely be more familiar with Ken Burns and Bruce Catton than with Ulrich B. Phillips or Robert William Fogel and Stanley Engerman (two major proponents of American-style new economic history, or "cliometrics"). The continued draw of military and political history in the commercial book market has indeed maintained a crucial niche for the nonacademic historian, as sales of books by writers like Barbara Tuchman, Shelby Foote, and William L. Shirer illustrate.

On the other hand, in part because of response to public interests and political trends but also because of the vast expansion of the profession since the 1960s, a wider net is now being cast even by highly traditional institutions like the AHA: a comparison of the programs of any recent AHA meeting and that of the association's meetings in the late 1940s illustrates the greater breadth of subject matter being researched and also the lack of dominance of any single interpretation.

A word, finally, should be said on the theoretical underpinnings of all these recent changes. American historians are fonder than those of any other Western nation of writing about their own discipline in a fashion that makes little use of the philosophy of history (in sharp contrast to the French or the Germans). It is no accident that most of the major surveys of Western historiography published this century have emanated from American-based Europeanists such as Harry Elmer Barnes, James T. Shotwell, James Westfall Thompson, and, most recently, Ernst Breisach, while émigrés like Felix Gilbert, Georg G. Iggers, and Leonard Krieger have made the study of past historiography one of their principal areas of interest. On the other hand, there remains a long-standing Anglo-inspired hostility to "theory" as such, as illustrated by the lack of sophistication in most responses to Beard and Becker's relativism and later in the general rejection of an "analytical philosophy of history" by the profession in the 1960s. Attempts to apply to the disciplines of history the "paradigm shift" model of scientific change developed by Thomas S. Kuhn (b. 1922) in his 1962 *The Structure of Scientific Revolutions* have inspired considerable discussion but have had relatively little impact on actual historical writing. Even the most reflective American scholars tend to prefer a commonsense philosophy, borrowed from such philosophers as the Englishman R.G. Collingwood (1889–1943) and the Canadian philosopher W.H. Dray (b. 1921) to the speculation of German and French critics, although the United States is home to the major international philosophy of history journal, *History and Theory*, which was established in 1960.

Having never experienced a profound *Methodenstreit* of the sort that occurred in Germany at the end of the nineteenth century, professors teaching mandatory undergraduate and graduate classes in historiography are less likely to adopt radical positions on the status of history (and its similarity to literature and philosophy of history, as argued by Hayden White, or its resemblance to the natural sciences, as put by Carl Hempel) than they are to teach a "no-nonsense" set of methods whose pedigree goes back to the original cult of Rankeanism and French positivism in the second half of the nineteenth century. Historiography course reading lists, especially those developed by current senior faculty members are more likely to include G.R. Elton's *Practice of History,* David H. Fischer's *Historian's Fallacies,* and perhaps Collingwood's *Idea of History* than they are to include Hegel, Foucault, Heidegger, or White; this is, however, becoming noticeably less true as younger scholars begin to take faculty positions.

By the same token, various attempts since the age of New History to tie the cart of history to various nonhistorical horses have met with a mixed reception, even when emanating from scholars as distinguished as David M. Potter, a historian of the Civil War who strongly advocated a new entente with economics and psychology, or William L. Langer (1896–1977), a Europeanist who in 1957 urged the AHA to pay closer attention to psychology. The cool reaction in many segments of the profession to such "scientific" inquiries as psychohistory and cliometrics may serve as an illustration of this resistance. Still, the love–hate relation between history and the social sciences, temporarily resolved in the 1950s and 1960s in favor of the autonomy of history, has in recent years produced a more cautious alliance between American historians, such as the Europeanists Robert Darnton and Natalie Zemon Davis, and the sort of anthropologically inspired historiography long practiced by the French Annales school; the American anthropologist Clifford Geertz has been especially influential in this connection. A branch of historiography in the United States that has made particular use of social techniques is urban history.

D.R. Woolf

See also ANNALES SCHOOL; COMPARATIVE HISTORY; FAMILY HISTORY (COMPARATIVE); IMMIGRATION, HISTORIOGRAPHY OF UNITED STATES; IMPERIAL SCHOOL OF AMERICAN HISTORY; NEW HISTORY; PROGRESSIVE HISTORY; PUBLIC HISTORY; RADICAL HISTORY; RELATIVISM; SLAVERY; SOCIAL HISTORY; URBAN HISTORY; WOMEN'S HISTORY—NORTH AMERICAN; WORLD HISTORY.

References

Breisach, Ernst. *American Progressive History: An Experiment in Modernization.* Chicago: University of Chicago Press, 1993.

Callcott, George H. *History in the United States 1800–1860: Its Practice and Purpose.* Baltimore, MD: Johns Hopkins University Press, 1970.

Hall, H. Lark. *V.L. Parrington: Through the Avenue of Art.* Kent, OH: Kent State University Press, 1994.

Higham, John. *History: Professional Scholarship in America.* Rev. ed. Baltimore, MD: Johns Hopkins University Press, 1983.

Hofstadter, Richard. *The Progressive Historians.* Chicago: University of Chicago Press, 1968.

Kammen, Michael, ed. *The Past before Us: Contemporary Historical Writing in the United States.* Ithaca, NY: Cornell University Press, 1980.

Linenthal, Edward T., and Tom Engelhardt, eds. *History Wars: the Enola Gay and Other Battles for the American Past.* New York: Metropolitan Books, 1996.

Meier, August, and Elliott Rudwick. *Black History and the Historical Profession: 1915–1980.* Urbana: University of Illinois Press, 1986.

Novick, Peter. *That Noble Dream: The "Objectivity Question" and the American Historical Profession.* Cambridge, Eng.: Cambridge University Press, 1988.

Pole, J.R. *Paths to the American Past.* New York: Oxford University Press, 1979.

Scott, Joan W. "American Women Historians, 1884–1984." In her *Gender and the Politics of History.* New York: Columbia University Press, 1988, 178–198.

Skotheim, Robert Allen. *American Intellectual Histories and Historians.* Princeton, NJ: Princeton University Press, 1966.

Sternsher, Bernard. *Consensus, Conflict, and American Historians.* Bloomington: Indiana University Press, 1975.

Strout, Cushing. *The Pragmatic Revolt in American History: Carl Becker and Charles Beard.* New Haven, CT: Yale University Press, 1958.

Tyrrell, Ian. *The Absent Marx: Class Analysis and Liberal History in Twentieth-Century America.* New York: Greenwood Press, 1986.

Van Zandt, Roland. *The Metaphysical Foundations of American History.* The Hague: Mouton, 1959.

Zinsser, Judith P. *History and Feminism: A Glass Half Full.* New York: Twayne, 1993.

Ammianus Marcellinus (ca. 330–400)

Roman soldier and historian. Born somewhere in the eastern, Greek-speaking part of the Roman Empire, Ammianus had a distinguished career in the Roman army, rising by 353 to the rank of imperial staff officer under Emperor Constantius (337–361). He also served under Julian "the Apostate" (361–363), whom he accompanied on that emperor's ill-starred Persian campaign. His admiration for Julian was great if not unbounded, although he did not share the emperor's hostility toward the Christians despite his own professed paganism. The details of Ammianus's later life are unknown. His history of the Roman Empire ends after the battle of Adrianople (378), but it is thought that he lived into the early 390s, when the work was almost certainly published. This history, in thirty-one books, begins where Tacitus's *Annals* ends (although the books covering the period before 353 are lost). While concerning himself primarily with military and political affairs, digressions of various types pervade his history and provide important information on ancient science, social life at Rome, and barbarian groups such as the Huns. His style is eclectic, difficult, and highly infused with quotation and allusion to earlier Latin stylists, whom he admired more than emulated. He also includes occasional accounts of his own adventures written in the first person, a technique notable for its reflection of an autobiographical tendency of the fourth century more fully developed by Libanius and St. Augustine.

Loren J. Samons II

Texts

Histories. Trans. J.C. Rolfe. 3 vols. Cambridge, MA: Loeb, 1963–1972.
The Later Roman Empire. Trans. W. Hamilton. London: Penguin, 1986.

References

Fornara, C.W. "Studies in Ammianus Marcellinus." *Historia* 41 (1992): 328–344; 420–438.
Matthews, J. *The Roman Empire of Ammianus Marcellinus.* Baltimore, MD: Johns Hopkins University Press, 1989.
Thompson, E.A. *The Historical Work of Ammianus Marcellinus.* Oxford: Oxford University Press, 1947.

Ammirato, Scipione (1531–1601)

Italian courtier, historian, political theorist, and genealogist. Born in Lecce, Ammirato had already shown his capacities as a genealogist, mostly in Naples, when, in 1569, he was engaged by Grand Duke Cosimo I of Tuscany as an official historiographer. In Florence, Ammirato became one of the leading anti-Machiavellians with his *Discorsi sopra Cornelio Tacito* [Discourses about Tacitus] (1594); he died there soon after the publication of the first part of the *Istorie Fiorentine* [Florentine Histories] (1600). His disciple Scipione Ammirato Jr., published the complete work with some additions of his own in 1641 and 1647. Based on the accurate study of its predecessors, thorough research in the archives, and a sound judgment, it was to become the definitive history of Florence for more than two centuries. Ammirato was the first historian explicitly to exclude the legends about Florence's origins from its history. He considered the times in which he lived to be the climax of a process leading to the union of Tuscany, a deed performed by Florence and the Medici dukes.

Thomas Maissen

Texts

Istorie Fiorentine. Ed. Luciano Scarabelli. Turin: Nuova biblioteca popolare, class 2, 1853.

References

Cochrane, Eric. *Florence in the Forgotten Centuries 1527–1800.* Chicago and London: University of Chicago Press, 1973, 93–161.

———. *Historians and Historiography in the Italian Renaissance.* Chicago: University of Chicago Press, 1981, 284–292.

An Chŏng-Bok (1712–1791)

Korean scholar and historian. An held minor government positions and was a tutor of the crown prince. His principal work, *Tongsa Kangmok* [The Main Currents of Korean History] (1778), is considered one of the two major general histories of Korea written before the later nineteenth century. Like his mentor, Yi Ik, he explored *sirhak* (practical learning) and emphasized the importance of historical geography, historical criticism, and the practical applications of history. An lamented that the Koreans had traditionally treated their country's history as a mere subsidiary of Chinese history. This was one of the main reasons that he wrote a general history of Korea. In *Tongsa Kangmok* he suggested a structure of Korean history based on the legitimacy and morality of dynasties, not their strength. An corrected many errors of sources, reorganized the early historical geography of Korea, and argued that Manchuria and northeastern China had been a part of Korea's early kingdoms, as Yi Ik had earlier insisted.

Minjae Kim

Texts

Kugyŏk Tongsa Kangmok. Trans. into Korean. Ed. Minjok Munhwa Ch'ujinhoe. 10 vols. Seoul: Minjok Munhwa Ch'ujinhoe, 1977–1980.
Sunam Chŏnjip [Works]. 4 vols. Seoul: Yogang Chulpansa, 1984.

References

Shim Woojun. *Sunam An Chŏng-bok Yŏnku* [Studies on An Chŏng-bok]. Seoul: Iljisa, 1985.

Anachronism

Deriving from the Greek *ana* (up, backwards) and *chronos* (time), designates a confusion in order of time, especially the mistake of placing an event, attitude, or circumstance *too early* (as in Shakespeare's reference to a chiming clock in *Julius Caesar*). In history the error arises most significantly in the guise of "presentism" or "present-mindedness," the impropriety of depicting past phenomena in terms of present values, assumptions, or interpretive categories. The "sense of anachronism"—that is, heightened awareness that the past may differ fundamentally from the present—is today considered a defining feature of advanced historical consciousness. Although awareness of anachronism may have existed in various degrees throughout history, it is evidently only recently that a regularized sense of its special importance has arisen. Among signs of a heightened sense of anachronism was the rise of the doctrine of historical "individuality" among early-nineteenth-century German scholars—that is, the notion that historical phenomena must be understood according to their unique, time-and-place-specific principles of origin and development. Thus Leopold von Ranke proclaimed each epoch "immediate to God." Ranke and his like-minded contemporaries sought to avoid anachronism by establishing sympathy with the past through immersion in historical records. Two early-twentieth-century works drew added attention to the problem of historiographical anachronism: Herbert Butterfield's *The Whig Interpretation of History* (1931) and Friedrich Meinecke's *Die Entstehung des Historismus* ["Historism" or more commonly "Historicism"] (1936). Meinecke celebrated the rise of Ranke's approach, while Butterfield indicted the "Whig" school that explained all British history from the standpoint of prevailing Protestant and liberal values. The ascription of present categories to earlier periods is now regularly deplored as a violation of the past's alien integrity. Yet despite its importance for historical understanding, the problem of anachronism has not been the object of extensive theoretical reflection, and warnings against methodological anachronism seldom extend much beyond simple injunction. While some form of the nineteenth century's doctrine of sympathy is probably still held by many historians, that notion is now frequently considered untenable, and the inherently "present-centered" starting point of historical knowing remains problematic; that is, how can historians, who inevitably belong to some present, in the mere act of conceiving and constituting their research, possibly avoid imposing present categories on the past in some degree?

Harry Ritter

See also WHIG INTERPRETATION OF HISTORY.

References
Ashplant, T.G., and Adrian Wilson. "Present-Centred History and the Problem of Historical Knowledge." *Historical Journal* 31 (1988): 253–274.

Lowenthal, David. *The Past Is a Foreign Country.* Cambridge, Eng.: Cambridge University Press, 1985.

Annales School

A group of reform-minded French historians who published their work in the journal originally entitled *Annales d'histoire économique et sociale.* This journal was founded at the University of Strasbourg in 1929 by Marc Bloch (1886–1944) and Lucien Febvre (1878–1956). In 1946 the journal was renamed *Annales: économies, sociétés, civilisations,* marking a greater coherence in vision, namely the aim to create a new encompassing history—*histoire totale*—to replace the highly compartmentalized historical study that, these reformers argued, had characterized French work in the field since the late nineteenth century.

Success was sudden and unforeseen, a signal, perhaps, that these historians rightly diagnosed that the discipline of history had reached a state of crisis and had failed to account adequately for the disaster-ridden first half of the twentieth century. Traditional histories, particularly the detailed diplomatic studies that Febvre derided, suddenly appeared to be outdated exercises that were irrelevant to people caught in the throes of two world wars and an interwar depression.

Earlier, in the late 1930s, Annales school historians had stormed Paris and had become the *sixième section* (sixth section) of the *École des hautes études,* the centrally funded institute for study of the social sciences. Their fame grew with the war years, and their *rapprochement* with the social sciences, geography, and economics in particular achieved for history a dominant role among the social sciences in France, a position unparalleled in other Western countries.

Three men contributed to the swift success of Annales school history, Bloch, Febvre, and their most promising follower, Fernand Braudel (1902–1985). Bloch advocated a comparative method rather than a search for the origins of modern states in the study of the remote medieval past. His *Société féodale* [Feudal Society], published in 1940, brought general acceptance of the view that Europe, rather than France, England, and Germany was the proper unit of study for medieval historians. Bloch established the issue of slavery's demise as a distinguishing feature of the medieval world. His death at the hands of the Nazis while a member of the French Resistance brought him posthumous fame that further increased dissemination of his ideas.

Febvre, a scholar of the French Renaissance, established his reputation through book reviews, articles, and scholarly talks, which amounted to both a blueprint and a credo for the "New History" as the reform-minded saw it. His justifiably famous *Problème d'incroyance au XVIᵉ siècle* [The Problem of Unbelief in the Sixteenth Century] (1942), which began as a book review of Abel Lefranc's biography of the sixteenth-century poet François Rabelais, burst the confines of that format and became an exposition on the danger of anachronism, the importance of establishing context for ideas of all kinds, and the necessity of analysis of the vocabulary and grammar of an era. Febvre argued that without the semantic "tools" to describe a universe outside a Christian context sixteenth-century thinkers were bound to a Christian cosmology against which they might rail but that they could not, as yet, replace.

As a prisoner of war in Lübeck during World War II, Fernand Braudel produced notebook after notebook of history text, which he sent to Lucien Febvre, who was living in retirement in Franche Comté. These notebooks, composed from memories of his archival studies completed in the 1930s (Braudel claims to have been the first scholar to employ film—according to him, taken with an ordinary camera—for archival research) became the monumental two-volume study, *La Méditerranée et le monde méditerrranéen à l'époque de Philippe II* [The Mediterranean in the Age of Philip II], which appeared in 1949. Braudel went on to produce a trilogy under the general title of *Civilisation matérielle, économie et capitalism: XVᵉ–XVIIIᵉ siècle* [Civilization and Capitalism from the Fifteenth to the Eighteenth Centuries], of which all volumes have been translated into English. In their vast sweep of time and distance, their rejection of events and great men as the simple causes of historical change, and their grasp of detail, Braudel's histories approached the ideal of *histoire totale.*

Bloch's and Febvre's original idea—to reject narrowly conceived political and diplomatic studies—brought them to a search for the *mentalité* of earlier ages. In time, under the influence of Braudel and his colleagues, *mentalité* was transformed into a *structure,* that is, a controlling pattern of thought or an ingrained habit of interacting with environmental or economic and social factors. Both typically were unacknowledged and therefore unquestioned. This sense of *structure* was expanded and came to encompass those characteristic and enduring features of an age whose sum might be defined as *histoire totale.* The social structures spoken of by Marc Bloch and the mental structures stressed by Lucien Febvre lost some consequence in the search for economic structures during the decades when Braudel dominated the scholarship of the *sixième section.* However, all three founders of the Annales school considered conditions of material life and economic trends consequential and were deeply influenced by the social geography of Vidal de la Blache and the price studies of the economist François Simiand. Indeed the price fluctuations that Simiand charted from 1500 onward led Braudel to punctuate the long-term secular trend he identified in his "long" sixteenth century (mid-fifteenth century to early seventeenth century) with phases such as rises and declines in prices, population, popular unrest, warfare, and a host of other trends. He paid particular attention to *conjonctures* (conjunctures); that is, moments when diversely phased peaks or troughs intersected in consequential fashion. For all the myriad details, often codified into tables, that this approach entailed, Annales school historians strove for clarity of expression and employed a straightforward narrative prose for the elucidation of their vast schemes of *histoire totale.* They avoided employing a theory-laden exposition.

In the years after World War II, Annales school history grew in popularity and influence. S.E.V.P.E.N., their publishing organ, issued hundreds of volumes and many thousands of pages from the hands of Annales school historians. Pierre Chaunu's *Seville et l'Atlantique* (1955–1959) reached Volume VIII before beginning an in-depth analysis of the gathered evidence. Pierre Goubert completed his exhaustive analysis of Beauvais; Jean Claude Schmitt produced a cultural history of St. Guinefort, a holy greyhound who has been the center of a cult since the thirteenth century. Among the brilliant group of French scholars working in the Annales tradition, Emmanuel Le Roy Ladurie stands out because his *Montaillou, village occitan de 1294 à 1324* (1975), designed as an ethnographic report based upon inquisition testimony, became a best-seller in France.

Perhaps more important, Annales historians forged alliances with foreign scholars during the postwar years (and indeed, even before World War II, when the link with the Belgian historian Henry Pirenne was particularly fertile). First, close neighbors, such as Charles Verlinden from Belgium and Gino Luzzatto and Carlo Cipolla from Italy, joined forces; then, through his wartime prison contacts Braudel introduced Poles such as Marian Małowist to his seminars in Paris. Seminars took on the role of international conferences producing new interpretations. Through comparative study of prices and other long-term factors Annales seminars charted the sixteenth-century deviation of a poorer Eastern Europe from the more developed commercially successful Western European economies. Consequently, Annales school history is often equated with the history of the early modern world and the emergence of a global network of capitalist trading relationships. Historians working in this tradition emphasized the cost of development to the human community, both in the Atlantic societies that were the beneficiaries of early capitalist trading networks and, more devastatingly, in the communities tied to the West by trade.

Annales school historians continued to offer an intellectual home to European scholars willing to practice "history with a French accent." Hungarians, Czechs, Yugoslavs, and Francophile Canadians joined their Annales colleagues, producing cooperative projects that represented alternatives to the increasing Anglo-American dominance of the social sciences. During the Cold War years, Annales historians established a rapprochement with historians from the USSR, and *Annales* was among the few journals to publish Russian historians (in translation) in the West. Febvre had been particularly critical of the deterministic features of Marxist theory; the alliances forged by Eastern bloc historians with the Annales school thereby marked a move away from rigid Marxist interpretation, an opening of sorts to a theoretically based but less rigidly construed history.

During this period, the Annales school came to stand for a new attitude toward history. Daily life and routines became important considerations. The masses, more than individuals, received attention, and trends as well as conjunctures predominated over a history focused on events. Indeed focus on events was criticized as a distraction that had kept historians from coming to terms with history that was "written at a deeper level." Above all, Annales school history was about limits. Fernand Braudel said:

"Let us also assume that man's whole life is restricted by an upper limit, always difficult to reach and still more difficult to cross. This boundary between possibility and impossibility is established for every period (even our own). [Before the eighteenth century] man was locked in an economic condition that reflected the human condition. . . . Whatever he did, he could not step over a certain line—and this line was always drawn close to him. He did not even reach it most of the time. That was possible only for individuals, groups, or civilizations peculiarly favored by circumstances. Those who succeeded usually did so ruthlessly at the expense of others. For this advance, though always limited, required an infinite number of victims." (*Capitalism and Material Life,* New York: Harper, 1967, pp. ix, xiv.)

If the use of film was an early Annales technical breakthrough, the application of computers to historical study was the great achievement of the 1970s. Christiane Klapisch-Zuber, in collaboration with the American medievalist David Herlihy, entered the data of an early European census, the *Catasto* of 1427 for the city of Florence and for Tuscany, into computers and produced the monumental *Tuscans et leurs familles* [Tuscans and their Families] in 1977. The 1970s also saw the translation of numerous Annales histories into the English language. French historians visited the United States and began to communicate with historians writing in English, who in turn visited France. This served to spread Annales influence even wider.

The intense interest in gender shown by Klapisch-Zuber means that Annales is no longer concerned with "man" alone. To an extent, her work and that of others working in the Annales tradition through the 1980s modifies an approach sometimes characterized as "history without people" because the masses given such prominence by Annales had appeared to some critics to be undifferentiated and somewhat out of focus. Annales historians are currently known for their interest in new directions in history and their integration of new knowledge into the understanding of *histoire totale.*

Cross-Atlantic contacts suggest that the Annales approach has become influential in American historiography. Indeed in the 1980s and 1990s, the "new" history of Annales has entered the mainstream of historical study so thoroughly that Annales no longer constitutes a distinct school

of history. Today, Annales signifies a concern with the historical consequence of routine features of daily life, with mentalities and the long term, with structure and conjuncture, and with total history. Many outside France—for example, Carlo Ginzburg in Italy and Robert Darnton in the United States—claim to be followers of Annales. Both Jean-François Bergier, who now teaches in Zurich, and Immanuel Wallerstein, of the Braudel Institute at SUNY, Binghamton, claim descent from the Annales school, widening its influence further.

Susan Mosher Stuard

See also COMPUTERS AND HISTORIOGRAPHY; FILM AND HISTORY; MENTALITIES; RURAL HISTORY; SERIAL HISTORY; SOCIAL HISTORY.

Texts

Bloch, Marc. *Feudal Society.* Trans. L.A. Manyon. Chicago: University of Chicago Press, 1962.

Braudel, Fernand. *The Mediterranean in the Age of Philip II.* Trans. Sîan Reynolds (from second French edition). New York: Harper, 1976.

Febvre, Lucien. *The Problem of Unbelief in the Sixteenth Century.* Trans. Beatrice Gottlieb. Cambridge, MA: Harvard University Press, 1982.

Herlihy, David, and Christian Klapische-Zuber. *Tuscans and Their Families.* New Haven, CT: Yale University Press, 1985.

Le Roy Ladurie, Emmanuel. *Montaillou, Promised Land of Error.* Trans. Barbara Bray. New York: Harper, 1979.

References

Burke, Peter. *The French Historical Revolution: The Annales School, 1929–1989.* Stanford, CA: Stanford University Press, 1990.

Recherche historique en France de 1940 à 1965. Ed. Comité des Sciences Historiques. Paris: Editions du Centre National de la Recherche scientifique, 1965.

Stoianovich, Traian. *French Historical Method: The Annales Paradigm.* Ithaca, NY: Cornell University Press, 1976.

Annius of Viterbo

See NANNI, GIOVANNI

Anthropology and History

In recent decades, anthropology has had a widening influence on historical practice. Since the 1970s, historians have often turned to it for inspiration.

In these same years, anthropology, increasingly, has looked to history for data and techniques. Several intellectual currents have encouraged this convergence of disciplines. Some social historians, reacting against the vogue for quantification, which often seems to flatten the past because it requires sufficient sameness in the phenomena counted to permit statistics, have turned toward anthropology as a model for exploring the texture and individuality of bygone cultures. Others have looked to anthropology for tools to explore the lives of hitherto forgotten people on the margins of societies or below the conspicuous, literate elites. Other scholars, inspired by the growth of world system theory, have turned to anthropology for analysis of the reciprocal relations between peripheral cultures and economies and a powerful, distant center. At the same time, cross-cutting all these interests, area studies, which are interdisciplinary investigations, often of the non-European, more sparsely documented parts of the globe, perforce have turned to anthropology for method, for interpretation, and for data.

Meanwhile, anthropology has rehistoricized its own outlook. While late nineteenth-century anthropology had often entertained historical evolutionism of a Darwinian cast, the classic work of Bronislaw Malinowski and his imitators of the 1920s and 1930s tended rather to a static analysis of "primitive" and timeless societies, as yet untouched by European "history." More recently, anthropologists prefer to see even the most remote societies as evolving. The conceptualization of a rapidly shrinking planet and the concomitant transformation of even seemingly pristine cultures have impelled current anthropology back into historical reasoning. Furthermore, Marxism, always historical, has induced numbers of anthropologists, some of whom focus on large, complex societies or interpret the entire world as a single economic system, to study change through time. At the same time, anthropology, evermore self-reflective, has turned to the intellectual, institutional, and social history of its own science.

Anthropology is far from unitary, and its several divisions vary in their contribution to history. The parts that have most touched historians are the cultural, social, and political–economic approaches, at once separate and interwoven. Other distinctions of which anthropologists are acutely aware also divide their discipline: between the participant observer in the field and the book-bound cross-culturalist; between synchronic analysis, which analyzes one past or present time, and diachronic analysis, which traces development

through time; between work on isolated cultures and the study of small units in complex, often urban worlds; between micro- and macro-subjects; among evolutionary, diffusionist, functionalist, structuralist, and post-structuralist textual explanations of phenomena. There are overarching debates, such as the eternal Marx/Weber tussle over the priority of material necessity or of culture in the shaping of human activities, or, cross-cutting that, the argument over the relative force of rules or processes in shaping human actions. Far more than historians, anthropologists position themselves with an eye to such theoretical distinctions. Nevertheless, even though not all anthropologists ever take to the field, the ideal of the participant observer gives the discipline a notional unity that shapes its sense of self and its definition of its problems and that sharply distinguishes it from archive-bound history, for which all but the most recent past is too dead to visit and interview.

Anthropology has served history in many ways. It has helped to broaden the scope of historical study, both by example and by method. Anthropology has left a mark, as history, for reasons of its own, evermore has taken up work on forgotten folk, marginal and subaltern, for many of whom the written record is at best spotty. Among them are those non-European societies that Eric Wolf, with ironic intent, calls "peoples without history." Anthropology has also justified and promoted many subjects for inquiry: gossip, magic, healing, gift-giving, rites of passage, and other formal and informal rituals of consecrating and desecrating, of honoring and shaming, of conflict and reconciliation. The field asks about family, kinship, inheritance, and matrimonial strategies and likewise friendship, patronage and clientage, factions and coalitions, disputes, negotiations and settlements, feuding and peacemaking, not to mention social control, the social division of space, and social memory. It also investigates the exchanges between periphery and center, colonization, dependency, and cultural appropriation. The familiarity of many of these topics illustrates just how energetically historians have embraced the matter of anthropology.

At the same time, anthropology has enriched the historian's conceptual vocabulary. On the social–cultural side, Clifford Geertz's championing of exhaustive "thick description" and seasoned "local knowledge," and his elaboration of Claude Lévi-Strauss's idea of an underlying "structure" that patterns every aspect of cultural expression are now common coin. Bourdieu's notion of "habitus," semiautonomous, semiacculturated behavior, and his vocabulary of agency are making rapid headway among those uneasy with the apolitical determinism of Geertzian structuralism. The textual self-consciousness of Clifford, Marcus, and Rosaldo, who question anthropology's "poetics" and who explore their field as performance, has reinforced similar self-skepticism among some historians. Meanwhile, political economy has offered modes for the analysis of the interaction between capitalism and other systems of exchange. The countercurrent, the historicizing of anthropology, is probably more a matter of practices of research than of concepts, for history, overall, is the less fecund source of theories.

Anthropology and history have retained very different attitudes toward data and the validation of argument. Their quite distinct habits of citation illustrate this divergence. Adhering to social science conventions, anthropologists break the flow of prose with parenthetical references to authors and dates of publication. Historians, who cling to the literary origins of their craft, leave their sentences uncluttered with internal breaks. Anthropological footnotes themselves, to historians' eyes, often seem cryptic, for they tend to refer the reader to other published works and to say little about how the scholar established facts. Historical footnotes, by contrast, very often lead the reader to the source of data, either in print, or in an archive, or in some other well-described source. This difference in citation habits bespeaks divergent attitudes toward authority and toward truth. The raw data of much anthropology are the fieldwork of the practitioner, experience which no one can replicate or print. Most anthropologists' notebooks remain unpublished, first, because informants deserve confidentiality, and second, because field notes' very idiosyncrasy obscures their meaning. Thus, anthropology, unlike history, must authenticate perceptions which none can repeat. Reports of fieldwork try to escape arbitrary subjectivism and to gain cachet by invoking what anthropology calls "theory," breaking their texts to cite both the work of other scholars and the hermeneutics practiced by one or another substantial faction in their profession. Much such "theory" is only heuristic, guiding interpretation rather than offering firm predictive or explanatory power. Anthropologists often marvel at how little theory historians flaunt and at how fact-bound the discipline seems. Historians, who, fortunately, can cite documents at least notionally in the public domain, are not rarely content to offer up past data, rescued from time's oblivion, as if it were unproblematic. Historians prefer the illusion of transparency: "If you do not believe me, go see for yourself," say their footnotes, which nevertheless assume that only a highly trained fellow scholar who could decode such papers would ever wish to look. Such archival reconstruction often seems less thorny to historians than does ethnographic fieldwork to many anthropologists, who thus invoke theory to counter all the subjective ambiguities of culture shock.

This difference between the two disciplines may be narrowing as authorial self-consciousness spreads among historians. A vogue for literary textual studies, invading both disciplines and urging alertness to the language of scholarship, has sped this convergence. Anthropology's oxymoronic "participant-observer," at once in and out, cannot avoid Heisenbergian disturbance of the object of study. Also, a pervasive guilty doubt has besieged postcolonial anthropology, a realization, that which once seemed benign—objective science—was in fact overweening intrusion and culture-bound, exploitative misreading. Such qualms do not haunt all historians. Almost never participants in what they study, they seldom worry about having disturbed it. Only some apologize for appropriating their subjects. Few scholars of Mesopotamian demography, Capetian coinage, Ming infantry tactics, or Bismarckian foreign policy feel like intruders or thieves of someone else's heritage. On the other hand, historians using oral records, and those who study race, gender, or recently colonial places, like the anthropologists, do more often wrestle with their consciences, as well as with the living claimants to proprietorship of the cultures under investigation. Most important, an acute sense that the investigator must interpret a world at best only half accessible, now current among anthropologists, has helped to sharpen historians' awareness of the profound gap between then and now, of how the past is indeed a foreign country. Both disciplines are thus learning better to detect and to respect what cultural studies call "alterity," otherness.

The rich exchange between the two disciplines is likely to go on. Among historians, anthropology has inspired very innovative work, on, for instance, the impact of Mediterranean honor culture upon ancient Greek sexuality, on medieval Icelandic feuds or French gestures of supplication, on indigenous Mexican attitudes to land, or on early-modern African appropriation of European language and religion in coastal trading zones. While some areas of inquiry, especially social and cultural history, show the clearest imprint of anthropology, the mode is spreading. Political history, increasingly, ponders the power of ritual. The history of science has begun to look at the exchange of

A

specimens as a form of gift-giving and to interpret science as symbolic performance. There is room for considerable exploration in areas where historians have yet much to use anthropology: the arts, philosophy and speculative thought, modern organizations such as the university, the military, big business, labor unions, and political parties. On some of these topics, anthropologists have already made their own forays into the past. Meanwhile, they continue to absorb history's interest in temporal argument and its skills in finding and interpreting the documentary evidence of particular times and places.

Thus, the two disciplines have entered an era of rapprochement, mutual curiosity, and lively trade. Exchange of ideas, however, has not brought in its train acculturation or assimilation; the two sciences remain distinct and slightly wary of one another. As can happen between symbiotic disciplines, practitioners often accuse one another of uncritical borrowing. Anthropologists at times bemoan the haste with which historians adopt their tools and wield them with unpracticed hands, taking their theoretical abstractions out of context. Historians meanwhile find that, invoking history, some anthropologists caricature Clio's enterprise by oversimplifying or reifying it or abuse it by naive use of documents. Institutions have not merged; thus, anthropologists and historians seldom hire one another, sit on one another's tenure cases, adjudge one another's manuscripts and grant applications. On the other hand, the internal political economy of area studies of course encourages a more robust intellectual exchange, for academic goods—ideas, rhetorics, resources, cash and tokens of prestige—flow along "force fields" of academic power. Also, practitioners do regularly encounter one another at interdisciplinary conferences or on the pages of journals such as *Annales: E.S.C., Journal of Interdisciplinary History,* and *Comparative Studies in Society and History.* For all the contact, there is as yet no sign that either discipline is about to establish hegemony over the other.

Elizabeth S. Cohen and Thomas V. Cohen

See also CULTURAL HISTORY; INTERDISCIPLINARY HISTORY; MENTALITIES; MICROHISTORY; SOCIAL HISTORY; SOCIOLOGY AND HISTORY.

Texts

Burke, Peter. *The Historical Anthropology of Early Modern Italy.* Cambridge, Eng.: Cambridge University Press,1987.

Cohen, David. *Law, Sexuality and Society: The Enforcement of Morals in Classical Athens.*
Cambridge, Eng., and New York: Cambridge University Press, 1991.

Fentress, James, and Chris Wickham. *Social Memory.* Oxford and Cambridge, MA: Blackwell, 1992.

Lockhart, James. *The Nahuas after the Conquest: A Social and Cultural History of the Indians of Central Mexico, Sixteenth through Eighteenth Centuries.* Stanford, CA: Stanford University Press, 1992.

Miller, William I. *Bloodtaking and Peacemaking: Feud, Law and Society in Saga Iceland.* Chicago: University of Chicago Press, 1990.

Muir, Edward. *Mad Blood Stirring: Vendetta and Factions in Friuli during the Renaissance.* Baltimore, MD: Johns Hopkins University Press, 1993.

Thornton, John. *Africa and Africans in the Making of the Atlantic World, 1400–1680.* Cambridge, Eng.: Cambridge University Press, 1992.

Wolf, Eric. *Europe and the People without History.* Berkeley, Los Angeles, London: University of California Press, 1982.

References

Clifford, James, and George E. Marcus, eds. *Writing Culture: The Poetics and Politics of Ethnography.* Berkeley, Los Angeles, London: The University of California Press, 1986.

Comaroff, Jean, and John Comaroff. *Ethnography and the Historical Imagination.* Boulder, San Francisco, Oxford: Westview, 1992.

Geertz, Clifford. *The Interpretation of Cultures.* New York: Basic Books, 1973.

Rogers, Nicholas. "The Anthropological Turn in Social History." In *Approaching the Past,* ed. Philip H. Gulliver and Marilyn Silverman. New York: Columbia University Press, 1992, 325–368.

Antiquarianism

The study of artifacts and materials of the past; secondarily, the love of old objects. Sometimes distinguished from history, antiquarianism is an approach to the study of the past emphasizing the collection of materials about some chosen subject. Such a collection would most likely be systematic, but the organization might well be quite loose. The antiquarian differs from the historian in that the latter tells a story in chronological order, while the former may avoid both story and chronology. The historian is commonly concerned with using his story to influence the behavior of his readers, usually for moral purposes, sometimes for political, and so adopts all the resources of rhetoric to tell it well. The antiquary, not bound in this fashion and so prepared to abandon stylistic elegance, feels less compunction about encumbering his work with a wide variety of documents.

According to the account of antiquarianism in Arnaldo Momigliano's seminal article, the heyday of the antiquarians lasted from the seventeenth century to the early nineteenth century. However, as was so often the case, the writers of the seventeenth century leaned on their humanist predecessors (for instance, the fifteenth-century historian and topographer Flavio Biondo), and these in turn imitated the works of the ancients, Diodorus Siculus, Dionysius of Halicarnassus, and especially the enormously learned Roman scholar, Marcus Terentius Varro (who himself had borrowed from earlier Greek writers, including Aristotle). Most of Varro's writings have vanished, but enough survive, either directly or through quotations by his successors (especially St. Augustine), to enable us to develop a clear idea of his method. Varro, according to his contemporary, Cicero, taught the Romans who they were and whence they came, so that they need no longer walk as strangers in their own city. He did so by investigating the age of the city, the calendar, the rules governing priests, household discipline, and the like—"the names, kinds, functions, and origins of everything divine and human."

When, in the fifteenth century, the Italians turned once more to Rome for instruction, Varro provided a model. His influence could be perceived most clearly in the writings of Flavio Biondo (1388–1463). Biondo's *Roma Instaurata* (1446) described the topography of ancient Rome, using as evidence not only the writings of the Romans but also the materials turned up by Biondo's incessant walking about the city. *Italia Illustrata* (1453) extended the method of his first book to the whole country. Biondo divided Italy into its original regions; on his visits, he rode the old Roman roads, sometimes using an early version of "field archaeology" to find them; and everywhere, he sought out the ruins of ancient Rome. Then, in *Roma Triumphans* (1459), he reconstructed the public and private life of the city. Biondo, however, was more than a proto-archaeologist: he used literary evidence, and he recorded the relics of medieval Italy as well as ancient. In the process, Biondo reconstructed the mixture of history and geography that Ptolemy had called "chorography." Chorography was to become one of the antiquarians' favorite types of writing. In Germany, Conrad Celtis (1459–1508) modeled his *Germania Illustrata* on Biondo; in England, William Camden (1551–1623) did the same with *Britannia* (1586). With all these authors, as with Varro, their literary ancestor, patriotic motives were strong: such books not only portrayed a country unified by a common ancestry but also showed how that past played itself out in the present.

Britannia set the English fashion for several centuries to come. The center of Camden's work was the Roman province; the English counties were organized into groups roughly following the geographic location of the British tribes encountered by the invading Romans. Within these subdivisions, Camden traveled along the rivers, then spread his investigation out into the countryside. At each significant stop, Camden traced the history of the location from Roman times to the present. To the volume as a whole, Camden prefaced a series of essays on British, Roman, Saxon, and Norman Britain. To accomplish all this, Camden made use of an extremely wide variety of evidence. The history of placenames (which required that he learn Anglo-Saxon and Welsh) was supplemented by medieval charters, town records, chronicles, and genealogy. Along with this literary evidence, Camden used archaeological materials. He rode along the Roman roads, working out the identity of the ancient way stations as he went. Roman and British coins provided data for the physical appearance of rulers; together with the evidence provided by inscriptions, the coins also showed the extent of the Roman penetration of the island. In all this, Camden was scrupulous in keeping antiquarianism separate from history: *Britannia,* though it contained many small histories, was *not* a chronological account of the history of England, or even of the Roman province. Where Camden had been assisted by predecessors like William Lambarde (1536–1601), author of *The Perambulation of Kent* (1576), and by the loan of the manuscripts of John Leland (ca. 1506–1552), the English proto-antiquarian, he now received help from a network of friends. Especially after the first publication of *Britannia,* drawings of inscriptions came to him from all over the island, and it was this sort of information in particular that fueled the growth of the book from the small octavo of 1586 to the substantial, and heavily illustrated, folio of 1607. In addition, this epigraphical material was forwarded to Janus Gruter, an antiquarian who served as Palatine librarian in Heidelberg, as England's contribution to his mammoth (and wonderfully indexed) collection of Roman inscriptions from all over Europe.

It was no accident that the initial publication of *Britannia* coincided with the founding of the first Society of Antiquaries, a group of lawyers, genealogists, and historians centered in London. For twenty years, these men met to discuss such subjects as the history of English coinage, the age of castles, the antiquity of parliament, and the history and nature of various royal offices like that of the earl marshal. The meetings of the society served to propagate the new antiquarian methods; they also brought to light many new documents, as the members competed to display their discoveries. Such activity, however, was not altogether disengaged from politics, and King James I's hint of disapproval closed down the meetings; they were not to be revived until the early eighteenth century. Nevertheless, antiquarian activity continued unabated, most especially in the countryside. Half a century after Camden, a minor gentleman and antiquary named John Layer could propose to himself an account of his county of Cambridgeshire that entailed a reading of all the Roman and British historians, a diligent search of legal records, a run through all the public and private libraries of the kingdom including a search for rolls, deeds, and descents, perusal of the records of the towns, and an examination of inscriptions, monuments, and the like all over the shire. Layer did not, in fact, complete his ambitious project, but he made a good start; and his plan bears more than a slight resemblance to that of the mammoth, modern *Victoria History of the Counties of England*, also still incomplete.

Parallels to the English experience could be found on the Continent, particularly in France and Italy, not least because seventeenth-century antiquarianism (like seventeenth-century science) was conducted by groups of scholars linked by correspondence. Books were passed around, as was information about the sources—in particular, the *material* sources—on which they were based. In part, this resulted from the characteristically humanist veneration of the Greek and Roman classics, from the conviction that the great historians of the past could only be corrected in detail, not superseded. This forced the antiquarians to concentrate on the history of institutions, of provinces (like *Britannia*), of coinage, and the like. The material data made it possible to go beyond the ancients but, in addition, its very materiality was seen as an antidote to the prevailing skepticism of the age. Where historical narratives might have been forged, or at least altered, coins, inscriptions, ruined buildings, and the Roman roads themselves preserved the past in a form whose very substan-

tiality served as a guarantee of reliability. So, too, did the unadorned style of the work of the antiquarians, its very lack of structure, which ran visibly counter to the rhetoric and tendentiousness of the historians.

The "hard" evidence of the antiquarians did much to preserve the subject of history from the corrosives of the radical skeptics, but documents, pictures of artifacts and maps, surrounded by detailed analysis, hardly made for easy or entertaining reading. More importantly, antiquarian writing did not provide either the moral or the political guidance that ordinary readers expected of political history, though it did help engender both local and national patriotism. In England, all this could be seen in the period around 1700. Local antiquarianism flourished in the wake of William Dugdale's *Antiquities of Warwickshire* and John Aubrey's more archaeological *Wiltshire;* a group of writers provided histories of specific political institutions; Thomas Hearne edited volume after volume of chronicles, with elaborate annotation; Edmund Gibson (1669–1748) produced a new, collaborative edition of Camden's *Britannia,* encapsulating all the local studies of the previous century; and William Nicolson (1655–1727) provided an essential reference work, *The English Historical Library,* listing all the sources for British history. By the second decade of the eighteenth century, the antiquarians were organizing once more. New archaeological work, such as John Horsley's (1685–1732) *Britannia Romana; or, the Roman Antiquities of Britain* (1732) or the various explorations of William Stukeley (1687–1765) continued to be published. Nevertheless, despite the Society of Antiquaries' receipt of a royal charter (1751), English antiquarianism was gradually becoming marginalized, and the meetings of the new society began to take on a faintly ludicrous air. Too much attention was paid to details, or even to "wonders," too little to any overarching concept of where all this material was to lead. Bolingbroke's dictum that history was philosophy teaching by example was generally accepted—and did not apply to the antiquarian enterprise. Nor did the philosophical history of the eighteenth century have much use for the antiquarian model.

But by this time, the center of antiquarian activities had once more shifted to the Continent. Dom Jean Mabillon (1632–1707) put the study of charters on a firm foundation. A series of writers, French, Italian, and German, culminating in Bernard de Montfaucon (1655–1741), amplified the study of Greek and Roman antiquities, while

Ludovico Muratori (1672–1750) assembled an enormous collection of material for the study of medieval Italy. The tradition continued in the long series of stately volumes published by the French Academy of Inscriptions, for which Edward Gibbon was glad to pay the substantial sum of twenty pounds. And it was Gibbon's *Decline and Fall of the Roman Empire* (1776–1788) that once more united the endeavors of the antiquarian and the narrative historian.

From the end of the eighteenth century, however, the territory of the antiquarian came under increasing assault. Some of the philosophical historians, like Voltaire and Herder, gradually incorporated social history into their writings. The new historians of Rome, following on from B.G. Niebuhr (1776–1831), concentrated their attentions on the history of ancient institutions, thus absorbing what had been an antiquarian specialty. Moreover, the antiquarians' careful accumulation, and *testing,* of evidence gradually became the norm for all workers on historical subjects. In addition to these substantive matters, however, antiquarianism came under increasing pressure from the academization of history and archaeology. Even nationalism, to which the collections of the antiquarians had formerly made so large a contribution, passed into the hands of the professionals in the universities or in the offices of governmental publication societies like the German *Monumenta Germaniae Historica.* Gradually, antiquarianism became a haven for the amateur, perhaps a cleric with a good university degree who whiled away his leisure time by writing an account of his parish, based on a careful study of the available sources, but disconnected from the concerns of the world of professional scholars. By the twentieth century, as the burgeoning university history departments gradually took over the local history societies, even that last refuge vanished. The word "antiquarian," which had once denoted the practitioner of a subject that was nonliterary, untraditional, and highly analytical in its handling of evidence, ended by becoming synonymous with foolish accumulation and muddle-headedness.

F.J. Levy

References

Haskell, Francis. *History and Its Images.* New Haven, CT: Yale University Press, 1993.

Levine, Philippa. *The Amateur and the Professional.* Cambridge, Eng.: Cambridge University Press, 1986.

Momigliano, Arnaldo D. "Ancient History and the Antiquarian." *Journal of the Warburg*

and Courtauld Institutes 13 (1950): 285–315. Reprinted in his *Studies in Historiography.* New York: Harper & Row, 1966, 1–39.

Rawson, Elizabeth. *Intellectual Life in the Late Roman Empire.* Baltimore, MD: Johns Hopkins University Press, 1985, 233–249.

Weiss, Roberto. *The Renaissance Discovery of Classical Antiquity.* Oxford: Basil Blackwell, 1969.

Apes [or Apess], William (fl. 1798–ca. 1836)

Pequot historian and advocate. Born in 1798 to a father whose maternal ancestors were Pequot and probably to a Pequot mother, Apes was indentured at the age of six, but received some education as a servant to various Euro-American families. Converted to evangelical Christianity at Methodist revivals, he fled servitude and acted as drummer boy for a militia unit during the War of 1812. After the war and travels in Canada, he became an itinerant preacher to groups of Native and African Americans living in New York and New England. The date of his death is uncertain. In 1829, he published his autobiography, *A Son of the Forest,* describing his acceptance of Christianity in the manner of many such nineteenth-century autobiographies. Having become a preacher to the Pequots during the final decade of his known life, he presented Christ as a person of color and preached on the outrages practiced against Indian peoples of New England. In 1835, as a participant-observer, he published documents on the Mashpees' successful revolt (1833) against white authority in their village. Apes's *Eulogy on King Philip* (1836) portrayed the Native American leader as a noble resister against violent, mendacious pilgrims, as a hero comparable to George Washington fighting for his country.

Ellen Nore

Texts

On Our Own Ground: The Complete Writings of William Apes, a Pequot. Ed. Barry O'Connell. Amherst: University of Massachusetts Press, 1992.

References

McQuaid, Kim. "William Apes, a Pequot: An Indian Reformer in the Jackson Era." *New England Quarterly* 50 (1977): 605–625.

O'Connell, Barry. "Introduction." In *On Our Own Ground: The Complete Writings of William Apes, a Pequot.* Amherst: University of Massachusetts Press, 1992, xiii–lxxvii.

Appian [Appianus Alexandrinus] (ca. 90–ca. 165)

Greek historian and official. Appian was born in Alexandria, participated in the suppression of the Jewish rebellion of A.D. 116, held local office in Alexandria and then a legal position in Rome, finally becoming imperial procurator. He wrote a now-lost autobiography and a *Romaica* [Roman History] of twenty-four books of which eleven survive entirely (or virtually so) and six exist as fragments. The work is an account of Rome's wars, including the civil wars, from archaic times to the reign of Trajan, arranged geographically rather than chronologically. Books 13–17, dealing with the civil wars in the late republic, contain substantial amounts of information unavailable elsewhere, derived from lost works probably including Polybius's lost books.

Stephen A. Stertz

Texts

Appian's Roman History. Trans. H. White. 4 vols. Cambridge, MA: Harvard University Press, 1961–1964.

References

Gabba, E. *Appiano e la storia delle guerre civile* [Appian and the History of the Civil Wars]. Florence: La Nuova Italia, 1956.

Arabic Historiography

A vast and rich topic extending from the rise of Islam in the seventh century A.D. down to the present time. It is generally divided into three broad periods: classical, medieval, and modern. Early Arabic historiography was closely bound up with the emergence of Islam and its subsequent expansion as a dynamic religion. The beginnings of Arabic history writing are thus rooted in the career of the Prophet Muḥammad (ca. 610–632); the subsequent Arabian conquests of Syria, Iraq, Iran, and Egypt; and the struggle for power within the newly formed Islamic community.

It is generally accepted that the career of Muḥammad, particularly his military engagements after his migration from Mecca to Medina in 622, was the first theme to receive extensive treatment as a subject of historical and political interest. The earliest compilations are said to have been collected from eyewitnesses (often based on a chain of transmitters or *isnad*) and some written records. 'Urwah ibn al-Zubayr (d. 712) is credited with inaugurating this particular genre, but whose work has only survived in the form of quotations cited by later historians. The pioneering narratives of al-Zubayr were supplemented and arranged in precise chronological sequences by Muḥammad ibn Muslim ibn Shihab al-Zuhrī (d. 742). Once again, only fragments of his works have survived in later chronicles.

In addition to the Prophet's career and expeditions, known in Arabic as *maghāzī,* individual events were recorded following the initial conquests and the removal of the imperial capital from Medina to Damascus in 661. These individual events, such as battles, acts of assassination, and the election of a new caliph, were often accompanied by genealogical accounts depicting the accomplishments of certain tribal groups and their entitlement to war booty and land grants in the newly conquered territories.

The formative period of classical Arabic historiography is considered by a number of scholars to consist of three interdependent schools: western Arabian, Syrian, and Iraqi. The first was distinguished by its pious and religious approach, the second flourished under the Umayyad dynasty (661–750), having as its focus politico-military affairs and biographies of ancient kings, and the third, based in the garrison towns of Kufa and Basrah, was primarily tribal in its subject matter or thematic treatment. However, this regional specialization has been criticized for its geographical determinism and its negligence of a common frame of reference that underpinned all early Arabic chronicles.

The representatives of the Medinan school, and whose works are still extant, include Muḥammad ibn Isḥak (d. 761), the biographer of the Prophet, and Muḥammad ibn 'Umar al-Wāḳidī (d. 823). The Syrian school produced 'Awana Ibn al-Ḥakam (d. 764) who is credited with a biography, which is now lost, of the first Umayyad Caliph Mu'awiya (661–680), and Muḥammad ibn 'Abd Allah al-Azdī (fl. ca. 805), who wrote a history of the Arab conquest of Syria. The Iraqi school was represented by Sayf ibn 'Umar (d. 796) and Luṭ ibn Yaḥya Abū Mikhnaf (d. 774). Although the latter authored more than thirty books, and the former is credited with two chronicles, only fragments of their works have survived, thanks to the methodological approach of al-Ṭabarī (d. 923) in his universal chronicle, *Ta'rīkh al-rusul wa al-muluk* [History of Prophets and Kings]. The massive work of Muḥammad ibn Jarir al-Ṭabarī represented the culmination of early Arabic historiography, and his methodology combined approaches of the earlier historians Ibn Isḥāḳ, Muḥammad ibn 'Umar al-Wāḳidī (d. 823), and al-Balādhurī (d. 892).

The ninth and tenth centuries were the golden age of Arabic historiography. It was in these two centuries that a galaxy of historians composed chronicles that echoed the flourishing studies of culture, literature, and philosophy. They were consequently universalistic in scope and humanistic in approach. Their universality was related to the notion of Islam as being the culmination of all religions, whereas the formative period of Islamic society (622–660) was judged to be the apogee of perfection. Hence, almost all histories began with the creation of the world, depicted the various beliefs of its inhabitants, and singled out those nations that had developed state institutions and conducted their affairs according to a set of standard laws. In other words, world history formed in Arabic historiography the background and the prelude to the emergence of Islam as both a religion and a state. In this sense, the universalistic character of history writing became wedded to a vision of humanism that encompassed cultures that were often alien to Islam or Arab values. The works of al-Dīnawarī (d. 895), al-Ya'qūbī (d. 897), and al-Mas'ūdī (d. 957) stand out as the best representatives of this trend.

The invasions of the Crusaders and the Mongols between the eleventh and thirteenth centuries, coupled with the rise of militaristic dynasties, often of Turkic origin, marked the onset of the medieval period in Islamic culture and historiography. This trend was further accentuated by the destruction of the Caliphate in 1258. Arabic historiography began as a result to assume a formal and official approach with an ever-narrowing focus. Although universal histories continued to be written, such as *al-Kamil* by Ibn al-Athīr (d. 1232), most chronicles were confined to annalistic (that is, entries arranged by years) narration of contemporary events dealing with the career of a prominent Sultan or the policies of a particular dynasty.

Alongside this trend, which reached its climax under the Mamlūk Sultanate (1250–1517), there developed the art of compiling dictionaries and biographies dealing with men and women according to rank, station, and profession.

It was toward the end of this period that a number of authors produced works devoted exclusively to the methodology and purpose of history. One such was the essay on historical method by al-Kafiyajī (d. 1474). A more extended version, culled from all available Arabic sources was penned by al-Sakhawī (d. 1497). Nevertheless the *Mukaddima* (prolegomenon) of Ibn Khaldūn (d. 1406) stands out as one of the most original medieval treatises on historical methodology.

Between the death of Ibn Khaldūn and the dawn of the modern age, Arabic historiography became more and more a disjointed recording of daily events, compiled and arranged in the familiar annalistic style. These chronicles often read like the pages of a modern newspaper whereby disparate and unrelated occurrences, be they political, economic, social, or natural, are faithfully jotted down. The absence of direct commentary or causal explanations did not, however, deter these chroniclers from stating their political and social preferences in a long preface or introduction.

Nevertheless, these intervening centuries (1500–1800) did witness the birth of local schools of historiography as well as the emergence of a nascent patriotic sense of the past. These tendencies were most strongly pronounced in countries that enjoyed virtual independence from the Ottoman state or had managed to wrest a large degree of autonomy from the imperial court in Istanbul. Hence, the Moroccan, Tunisian, Egyptian, and Lebanese Arab identities began to figure more prominently in chronicles written in the eighteenth century. A century later, almost all Arab countries could count on native historians to chronicle the eventful turning points of their present or recent past.

However, the modern period of Arabic historiography did not become fully entrenched until the second half of the nineteenth century. Thus, modernity arrived as a result of two interdependent factors: Ottoman reforms and European expansionism. These twin movements led to the rise of a modern Arab intelligentsia and the establishment of history as a valuable patriotic instrument and a separate discipline. Thenceforth, Arabic historiography became part of a wider program of political reform and national regeneration. Whereas in the medieval period history was valued for its usefulness in teaching correct political conduct, it was tied in its modern incarnation to the idea of performing one's duty in the service of the fatherland. Moreover, ancient civilizations ceased to be mere preludes to the full glory of Islam and were rendered living links in the unfolding events of one's own country. Thus the old annalistic or dynastic style gave way to a continuous sequence of narration centered on a particular national territory.

One of the first historians to foster this new approach was the Egyptian religious scholar Rifa'a Rafi' al-Ṭahṭāwī (1801–1873). Apart from translating French historical works into Arabic, he published in 1868 and 1869 a history of ancient Egypt, depicting it as a well-defined fatherland with a clear territorial and political unity. He was followed by two Syrian historians, Ilyās Maṭar (1857–1910) and Jurjī Yannī (1856–1941), each of whom wrote a history of his own country in 1874 and 1881, respectively. This modern trend, initially confined to Egypt, Syria, and Tunisia, soon spread into other Arab countries by the first half of the twentieth century.

In its initial phase, modern Arabic historiography was practiced by amateur historians who were at the same time journalists, administrators, teachers, lawyers, and medical doctors. Furthermore, they exhibited a tendency to rely on secondary European sources, paying perfunctory attention to unpublished documents or archival material. It was during its second phase (1920–1990) that modern Arabic historiography became fully professionalized both in research techniques and in methodological approaches. Practiced and taught by historians who were trained in European and North American universities, Arabic historiography has been finally integrated into the mainstream of a worldwide phenomenon.

This professional historiography was pioneered by Asad Rustum (1897–1965) in Lebanon and Syria, Shafiq Ghurbāl (1894–1961) and Muḥammad Ṣabrī (1894–1984) in Egypt, and 'Abd al-'Azīz al-Dūrī (b. 1919) in Iraq. These historians, together with numerous colleagues in the Arab world, were the first to use unpublished documents, both native and foreign, in order to offer an original interpretation of their societies' history. With the exception of al-Dūrī, who paid close attention to social and economic questions, they relished the narration of political, military, and diplomatic events, while adhering to an evolutionary or biological model in their methodological interpretations.

By the 1960s and 1970s social and economic issues claimed the attention of a third generation of modern Arab historians. Their contributions were largely the result of radical changes in the structures of a number of Arab countries (Egypt, Syria, Iraq, Algeria, Tunisia, and the Sudan).

These three phases did not coincide in their emergence or development in all Arab countries. This is the case in particular of the Arabian peninsula, whose historians have not yet emerged from the second phase.

Y.M. Choueiri

See also PERSIAN HISTORIOGRAPHY; WOMEN'S HISTORY, ISLAMIC.

References

Abou-El-Haj, R.A. "The Social Uses of the Past: Recent Arab Historiography of Ottoman Rule." *International Journal of Middle East Studies* 14 (1982): 185–201.

Cahen, Claude. "L'historiographie Arabe: Des origines au VII's. H." *Arabica* 33 (1986), 133–198.

Chejne, A.G. "The Concept of History in the Modern Arab World." *Studies in Islam* 4 (1967): 1–31.

Choueiri, Youssef M. *Arab History and the Nation-State: A Study in Modern Arab Historiography.* London, New York: Routledge, 1989.

Crabbs, J.A. *The Writing of History in Nineteenth Century Egypt: A Study in National Transformation.* Cairo: The American University in Cairo; Detroit, MI: Wayne State University Press, 1984.

Duri, A.A. *The Rise of Historical Writing among the Arabs.* Ed. and trans. Lawrence I. Conrad. Princeton, NJ: Princeton University Press, 1983.

Khalidi, Tarif. *Arabic Historical Thought in the Classical Period.* Cambridge, Eng.: Cambridge University Press, 1994.

Noth, Albrecht. *The Early Arabic Historical Tradition: A Source-Critical Study.* Trans. Michael Bonner. Princeton, NJ: The Darwin Press, 1994.

Rosenthal, Franz. *A History of Muslim Historiography.* Second ed. Leiden: E.J. Brill, 1968.

Arai Hakuseki (1657–1726)

Japanese Confucian scholar, historian, and statesman. Arai entered service to the Tokugawa family in 1694 when he became a tutor to Tokugawa Tsunatoyo, who later became the sixth Tokugawa shōgun, Ienobu. During Ienobu's reign (1709–1712) and continuing through the seventh shōgun Ietsugu's reign (1713–1716), Arai served as a key advisor to both the shōguns and to the Tokugawa government as a whole. He was responsible for significant revisions in laws related to local administration and the governing of the military clans as well as for important reforms regarding currency and foreign trade. While many of his reforms were continued by the powerful eighth shōgun, Yoshimune (r. 1716–1745), Arai's most radical attempt at restructuring the Tokugawa system met with limited success and was later discontinued by Yoshimune. Arai sought to have the shōgun called the "nation's king" *(kokuō)*, and rather than continue the military bureaucracy, he attempted to revise the ranks, titles, and formal state ceremonies to reflect Confucian models. These modifications would have, in effect, eliminated the role of the emperor in favor of an exclusive sovereignty residing in the new position of shōgun *qua* king and were not widely accepted.

The basis for Arai's specific recommendations regarding policy and politics was a thorough study of and reflection upon history and historiography. He wrote histories of the great military houses (*Hankanpu*, 1702) and the ancient records of earliest Japan (*Koshitsū*, 1716). In addition, he wrote a history of Japan itself, *Tokushi yoron* (1712–1724), as well as an interpretation of western (that is, European) lands, *Seiyō kibun* (1715). Late in life he also composed several essays on the interpretation and meanings of history *(Shigi)*, most of which are no longer extant, as he attempted to situate Japanese history in the broader context of East Asian and world history.

James Edward Ketelaar

Texts

Arai Hakuseki zenshū [Complete Works]. 6 vols. Tokyo: Kokusho Kankōkai, 1905–1907.
Lessons from History: Arai Haukseki's Tokushi Yoron. Trans. Joyce Ackroyd. St. Lucia, Australia: University of Queensland Press, 1982.
Told Round a Brushwood Fire. Trans. Joyce Ackroyd. Tokyo: University of Tokyo Press, 1979.

References

Nakai, Kate Wildman. *Shogunal Politics: Arai Hakuseki and the Premises of Tokugawa Rule.* Cambridge, MA: Harvard University Press, 1988.

Arbaleste du Plessis-Mornay, Charlotte d' (1550–1606)

French biographer. Married to Jean de Pas, seigneur of Feuquères, and widowed at nineteen (1569), she was herself a Huguenot (French Protestant) and had to flee the St. Bartholomew Day's massacre of 1572 with her small daughter. At Sedan, Philippe Mornay, of Plessis Marly, was attracted by her "sharp wit and solid judgement"; they married in (1575). Arbaleste kept an accurate journal that became the first volume of her husband's *Memoirs*. In the words of the historian Henri Hauser, she "never let fanaticism color her judgments," despite her and her husband's strong religious views. Charlotte's journal, begun in 1584, continued until the death of the couple's only son in

1605. It covered Mornay's childhood, education and early travels, and periods of diplomatic service in England, the low countries, and Navarre, as well as numerous family matters. But it also contained detailed accounts of the wider context provided by the massacre of 1572 (of which her account has been called by Raoul Patry among the most "moving"); the religious war of 1575–1577; the wars with the Catholic League; and Henri IV's accession. Mornay's *Memoirs* covered the years from 1610 until his death (1623). They were continued in 1647 by David Licques, using Arbaleste's unedited manuscript, and were completed by the Mornay children's tutor, Jean Daillé.

Barbara Sher Tinsley

Texts

Mémoires de Mme. Duplessis-Mornay. Vol. I. In *Mémoires et correspondances de Duplessis-Mornay* [Memoirs and Correspondence of Duplessis-Mornay] (1824–1825). Geneva: Slatkine Reprints, 1969.

References

Crump, Lucy Hill. *A Huguenot Family in the XVI Century; The Memoirs of Philippe De Mornay.* London: George Routledge & Sons, 1926.
Patry, Raoul. *Philippe du Plessis-Mornay: Un Huguenot Homme d'Etat* [A Huguenot Statesman]. Paris: Librairie Fishbacher, 1933.

Archaeology

Through much of the Middle Ages, European kings collected Roman art primarily to justify their own power by creating an image of their own continuity from the Roman Empire. This kind of approach to archaeology remained important until at least the eighteenth century, when two new forces became important. The first was the idea of renewing modern art through inspiration from ancient examples, which was very much in Lord Elgin's mind when he removed the Parthenon sculptures from the Acropolis of Athens at the end of the century. Within this framework, nonclassical archaeology attracted little attention. Prehistoric monuments held little interest outside the local residents and a few folklorists, although there were notable exceptions, such as William Stukeley, who investigated Stonehenge, Avebury, and Silbury Hill in the 1750s.

The second approach was stimulated by Enlightenment ideas. Napoleon's expedition to Egypt in 1798 and 1799 was arguably a turning point. He took a massive staff of antiquarians and surveyors, who recorded Egyptian monuments and inscriptions. Meanwhile, at the opposite end of Europe, similarly important developments were under way. In 1816 Christian Thomsen, invited to produce a catalog for the Danish National Museum of Antiquity, hit on the idea of organizing the prehistoric material into three ages of stone, bronze, and iron, based partly on stylistic trends. Sven Nilsson of Lund linked these ideas to Enlightenment concerns with social evolution in the 1830s, and in the 1840s Jens Worsaae, the first professor of archaeology at the University of Copenhagen, confirmed Thomsen's scheme by stratigraphic excavations. Worsaae argued that serious prehistoric archaeology developed in Scandinavia faster than in other European nations because the Danes lacked Roman remains, preventing them from falling into mere antiquarianism.

Similar factors perhaps affected early developments in North America. John Stephens's discovery of lost Mayan cities in the 1840s suggested that America had a past as glorious as Europe's, and European settlers were equally struck by the large mounds they found in the Mississippi and Ohio valleys. Some argued that these had been built by Native Americans who had since degenerated, but the more popular theory was that they belonged to a vanished white race which had been destroyed by invading savages.

Self-styled professionals, like Worsaae, took over archaeology in the mid- and late-nineteenth century. Darwin's theories were influential in encouraging evolutionary models and a longer timescale, and geological analogies further encouraged rigorous stratigraphic work. Prehistoric archaeology grew in significance, although the classical fields, in which artistic concerns still dominated, remained the most prestigious. Some sites, such as Pompeii or Bath, had been dug into since the mid-eighteenth century, but fieldwork was conducted at a much lower standard than in contemporary prehistoric archaeology. Stratigraphic recording only began at Pompeii in 1860, with the arrival of Giuseppe Fiorelli. Heinrich Schliemann's work at Troy and Mycenae, beginning in 1870, was also very important. Schliemann was very much a romantic amateur, but his finds dispelled current skepticism about Homer's stories of the Trojan War, and forced classicists to accept that archaeology could be a tool in historical research. His methods were primitive, but were quickly refined by others to document an unimagined Bronze Age civilization as well as to explore later sites like Olympia. However, classical archaeology has continued to be linked more strongly to artistic connoisseurship than to history.

Early in the twentieth century, prehistoric archaeology was generally treated, on Schliemann's model, as an extension of political history into the distant past. Racial theories were popular, with particular material culture groups being identified with "peoples," whose migrations were traced in the diffusion of cultural traits. This approach reached its high point in Gustaf Kossinna's "settlement archaeology." It began to fall out of favor after 1945, because of its associations with fascism, but remained strong in some subfields until at least the 1970s.

The most important development since the professionalization of archaeology in the 1870s began in the 1960s, with a widespread rejection of these models in North America and western Europe. Stigmatizing history as particularist, the self-styled new (or processual) archaeologists advocated an ecological, quantitative, and functionalist approach that would lead to general laws of culture rather than to the accumulation of specific details about the past. Lewis Binford argued that archaeology was anthropology rather than history and should proceed by hypothetico-deductive methods, with archaeologists proposing lawlike generalizations that could then be tested against the finds.

By the mid-1970s this position had become orthodox in English-language prehistory, although in other national traditions and in classical, medieval, and industrial archaeology it had less impact. But a reaction began in Britain in the early 1980s, in which a postprocessual school, led by Ian Hodder, claimed that the processual position took a naive view of history, ignoring human agency and intention and reducing all the past to sameness. Hodder advocated a more historical approach, recognizing that all material culture is implicated in the production and manipulation of symbolic codes and must be understood in semiotic terms. Hodder was particularly influenced by R.G. Collingwood and argued that archaeological understanding consisted primarily of re-creating the thoughts of people living in the past. Postprocessualists have been much influenced by poststructuralist literary theory, and their work in the 1990s tends to emphasize the plurality of readings of the past, both among participants situated in the past and among archaeologists in the present. This has brought archaeology closer to the interests of contemporary cultural historians, especially those concerned with material culture, but has also generated charges of relativism and nihilism from other archaeologists. Archaeology is currently a very fragmented field.

Ian Morris

See also PREHISTORY.

References

Binford, Lewis. *An Archaeological Perspective.* New York: Academic Press, 1972.

Hodder, Ian. *Theory and Practice in Archaeology.* London: Routledge, 1993.

Trigger, Bruce. *A History of Archaeological Thought.* Cambridge, Eng.: Cambridge University Press, 1989.

Architecture and History

The use of architecture as historical evidence in European historical writing. Monuments being in large measure inspired by an individual or a society's concern for posterity, the correlation between architecture and history predates textual chronicles in most societies. Thucydides, in his *History of the Peloponnesian War* (I.x.2) realized both the potential and the pitfalls of architecture as historical evidence in his remark that were Sparta to be sacked posterity would never gauge its importance from its remains, "but if the same misfortune were to overtake Athens, the power of the city, from its visible remains, would seem to have been twice as great as it is."

Beginning in the fifteenth century, the problem of cultural decline preoccupied Renaissance antiquarians and historians alike as they correlated the relationship of the visible decline of quality of the arts and architecture in late antiquity with the fall of Rome itself, pointing to the possibility of architecture to provide clues to cycles of historical development. Likewise, Giorgio Vasari, in his *Le Vite de'più eccellenti architetti, pittori, et scultori italiani* [Lives of the Most Eminent Italian Architects, Painters, and Sculptors] (1550), maintained that the architecture of the Goths and the Lombards was a direct reflection of the barbarous quality of their civilizations.

Not until the modern period would architecture's value for history be premised upon a more specific correlation between architecture and society than simply as a record of greatness. In the late seventeenth century, French and Italian antiquarians began to collect and classify images of buildings as historical artifacts in their own right, rather than as confirmation of textual evidence or as supports for inscriptions. In the circle of the Abbé Bernard Montfaucon and his Benedectine followers of the congregation of St. Maur, as well as in the work of the Italians Giovanni Guistiono Ciampini and Ludovico Antonio Muratori, who claimed that "everything concerning customs, religion, clothes, buildings" was properly part of history, visual and textual evidence were given equal weight. Engraved plates as much as text composed his *L'Antiquité expliquée et représentée en figures* [Antiquity Explained and Illustrated] (1719), and *Les Monumens de la Monarchie françoise qui comprennent l'Histoire de la France* [Monuments of the French Monarchy Which Encompass the History of France] (1729–1733), in which Montfaucon implied that the evolution of artistic style itself be counted a historical fact.

From the mid-eighteenth to the late nineteenth century architectural practice evolved in tandem with archaeological research and with history, Giambattista Vico's "new science." The polemical exchanges between the "Greeks" and the "Romans," unleashed by the explorations of the English artists James Stuart and Nicholas Revett (*The Antiquities of Athens,* vol. 1, 1762) and the French architect Julien David Leroy (*Les Ruines des plus monuments de la Grèce considérées du coté de l'Histoire et de l'Architecture* [Ruins of the Most Beautiful Monuments of Greece Considered in Light of History and of Architecture] (1758) to document Greek architecture at first hand and to draw sharp distinctions with later Roman styles, opened a period in which aesthetic debate was framed in historical terms, and theories of the evolution of architectural style were formulated. Leroy's efforts to develop a historical chronology of Greek architecture paralleled Johann Joachim Winckelmann's theories in his seminal *Gedanken über die Nachahmung der Griechischen Werke in der Malherei und Bildhauerkunst* [Reflections on the Imitation of Greek Works in Painting and Sculpture] (1755) of the intimate relationship between the excellence of Periclean art and the Greek climate, political system, and social attitudes of Athenian society, a view much inspired by Montesquieu's writings. This notion of architecture as an index of society was to dominate architectural history for more than a century. In 1772 Goethe claimed that Gothic architecture was a direct reflection of Germanness. He was inspired no doubt by Herder's claims that "as men live and think, so they build and inhabit," a nationalistic extension of Winckelmann's earlier arguments that quickly found vigorous competition in rival claims for the Frenchness and Englishness of Gothic architecture and the great movement of antiquarian research spearheaded by English antiquarians both at home and in northern France. For the next fifty years nationalism was deeply invested in historical debates on the origins and progress of Gothic architecture and the possible influence of earlier and foreign cultures, particularly Byzantium, on its achievements.

By careful chronological arrangement of sculptural and architectural fragments confiscated from churches and aristocratic residences and spanning the twelfth to eighteenth centuries, Alexandre Lenoir, in his Musée des Monuments Français, founded in 1793, converted French revolutionary vandalism into a moving spectacle of the relationship between the evolution of artistic style and the history of France and inspired a whole generation of Romantic historians before the museum was disbanded in 1816. François Guizot, Augustin Thierry, and Jules Michelet all acknowledged its impact and paid homage to Lenoir's work by according architecture a central place in the sweeping narratives in which they sought to explain the rise of modern French institutions, most particularly Michelet in his *Introduction à l'Histoire Universelle* [Introduction to Universal History] (1831). Guizot and Thierry's work in turn helped frame the most important architectural histories of the early nineteenth century, including those of E.E. Viollet-le-Duc, who explained Gothic architecture as the product of the gradual emancipation of lay culture and a spirit of inquiry in the communes of the later Middle Ages. As the contemporary critic and champion of the young historicists at the École des Beaux-Arts Hippolyte Fortoul noted in 1841, "L'architecture est la véritable écriture des peuples." Most influential was to be Guizot's creation, during his period as government minister of the interior, of parallel historical commissions on national monuments, one to preserve and publish textual documents, the other to research the architectural heritage of France and to establish criteria for its restoration and preservation by the state.

In England the great narrative tradition of Macaulay was paralleled in John Ruskin's *The Stones of Venice* (1851–1853), a stirring reading of the rise and fall of the Venetian republic as recorded in the architectural forms and decorations of the city, tracing at once the interactions of the most diverse historical influences and the essence of Venetian character and genius. Given further support from the 1820s by the place of architecture in systems of philosophical history, notably those expounded by G.W.F. Hegel in Berlin and the Saint-Simonians in Paris, among others, an intimate link between historical progress and the evolution of architectural style became commonplace by the mid-nineteenth century. Although the study of stylistic change remained central to most theories of art and architectural history advanced in the nineteenth century, increasingly the German tradition, inspired by the work of Karl Schaase, Gottfried Semper, and others, sought to understand art as a domain with its own history and dynamic of development.

In recent decades increased interchanges of methods and concerns has created new bridges between the investigations of historians and those of architectural historians, particularly those concerned with the social history of architecture, issues of patronage, and the use of architecture to craft personal power or national identity and those investigating the history of the very institutions of architecture.

Barry Bergdoll

See also ART AS HISTORICAL EVIDENCE.

References

Bergdoll, Barry. *Léon Vaudoyer: Historicism in the Age of Industry.* New York: The Architectural History Foundation, 1994.

Haskell, Francis. *History and Its Images, Art and the Interpretation of the Past.* New Haven, CT: Yale University Press, 1993.

Lowenthal, David. *The Past Is a Foreign Country.* Cambridge, Eng., and New York: Cambridge University Press, 1985.

Nora, Pierre, ed. *Les lieux de mémoire, II: La Nation* [The Places of Memory, vol. II: The Nation]. Paris: Gallimard, 1986.

Watkin, David. *The Rise of Architectural History.* London: The Architectural Press, 1980.

Archives

Organized body of records produced by a public, semi-public, institutional, business, or private entity in the transaction of its affairs. They are also the place where such records are kept. An operating organization responsible for preserving such records is frequently referred to as "the archives."

Since ancient times, humanity has always needed archives. Beginning with the invention of writing in ancient Sumeria, records were stored in places for future reference. These repositories were crude archives. In such places as Ur, ca. 2100 B.C., active archives of clay tablets existed. Archaeologists have found more than 400,000 such tablets in the ancient mideast. In pharonic Egypt the written record was often placed on papyrus (a crude paperlike surface) and wood. As a result, much of the record was lost with the deterioration of these materials. In Greece only the papyrus and wood of the Metroon (the city archives of Athens) were kept archivally and few survived. Thus, most of what we know of ancient Greece is from literary sources.

The wood tablets of the early Roman archives of the republican period did not fare much better. Though few survive, it is clear from other sources that active archives existed. At the terminus of the Roman forum stood the Great Tabularium, an imposing structure that served one purpose—to house archival records. A significant staff of "quaestors" administered the collection. Similarly, an extensive records program existed in the Roman occupation of Egypt—especially in Alexandria where the "Bibliotheke" functioned as a central archival repository. In imperial Rome the writing surface changed to papyrus and the tabularium continued to function for the emperors as it had for the republic. Perhaps the crowning achievement of the Roman period was the establishment in the third to fourth century A.D. of the papal archives. This institution—which exists to this day—is the one extant bridge between the archives of the ancient world and those of modern times.

The decentralization of the medieval period can, of course, be seen in the means of record keeping. Archives of this period were generally restricted to incoming materials of a financial or legal aspect. As the monarchs of the period traveled with their courts and generally had no permanent home, the records were often kept in a safe place, such as that provided by the church. The scarcity of writing surfaces (often animal hides) and the limited level of literacy accentuated the value of records, and the intricate lumination of such items by monks of the high Middle Ages grew from this. Toward the end of the Middle Ages, the gradual consolidation of power in the monarchies of Europe and the end of the monarch's peripatetic lifestyle resulted in the slow rise of a bureaucracy and, consequently, the creation and storage of records. The final link to modern archives was the invention of modern paper in the thirteenth century. Throughout the early modern era, the increasingly centralized regimes in Italy, France, the British monarchies, Spain, and many German principalities paid increasing attention to organizing their archival facilities, often hiring leading scholars to manage them. The former puritan polemicist, William Prynne, for example, was retained by England's King Charles II in the 1660s to put the records in the Tower of London, then in a chaotic state, into greater order. Two major works of French scholarship, Etienne Pasquier's *Recherches de la France* (final version, 1621) and Jean du Tillet's *Receuil des roys de France* [Collection of the Kings of France] (published posthumously in 1577 and 1578) were a direct result of greater interest of governments in their own repositories.

The tumult of the French Revolution of the late eighteenth century marked the dawn of the era of modern archives. There were four important developments for archives in these events. First, archives became an organic part of the government with the creation of the *Archives Nationales* in 1789. Second, there was an acknowledgment of the state's responsibility for records. Third, the concept of accessibility to records as right became evident in the concept of the "public record." Finally, the fourth great result of these events was the formulation of the first theories for the administration of modern archives—especially the important principle of *Respect des Fonds* and the closely related concept of records provenance. These concepts have at their root the belief that the organic arrangement from which a group of records emerges has a significance and that records should be kept in their original arrangement to the extent possible. They also imply that records from one agency should not be intermingled with those of another.

Soon the archival developments in France were being emulated in other European states. In England public records offices developed in the early nineteenth century with the foundation of the Public Record Office and with the establishment of the Historical Manuscripts Commission, whose members' series of *Reports* on private archives provided printed calendars (summaries) of centuries of family muniments, well before the advent of the English county record office system. In Sweden, the archives evolved from the chancery and into the "Riksarkiv" where they were preserved. The function evolved similarly in Prussia (in the Privy State Archives). In Russia, developments awaited the revolution of the early twentieth century. The Dutch—having evolved the archival function similarly—were also instrumental in the development of modern principles of archival administration in about 1840.

In the United States there was discussion of the need for a national archival program from the early federal period, but not much happened until the early twentieth century, when programs for public records developed first in the states (Alabama, Mississippi, and North Carolina); the

National Archives of the United States was not established until 1934.

The profession of archivist has developed along with national archival endeavors. By the mid-twentieth century, national and international societies of archivists had begun and were thriving. Locations for archival programs also spread from governments and to college and university campuses, especially in the period after World War II. Many of the university archives were merged with collections of private manuscripts, and the two fields of archives and historical manuscripts administration gradually came closer together. Programs for the education of archivists based in university environments also developed.

Perhaps the most significant professional development in the period since World War II has been the development of techniques for the orderly disposition and transfer of records (either to archives or for the disposal of the records). This field, Records Management, has enabled archivists to address vast volumes of records and seek only the relatively small amount with archival value. These appraisal techniques liberate archivists from the passive role of receptor of records and make them an integral part of an active records program. However, the archivist's and record manager's activities have grown more distinct and have varying educational requirements for entry. As the archival profession has extended itself into the Third World, the records of emerging nations have received archival care, often with consultative assistance from established programs in the West. Many nations in Africa, Latin America, and Asia have established programs in this way.

Techniques for the preservation of paper records have become increasingly sophisticated and well articulated over time. A basic consideration for the care of records is the environment in which the records are stored. Usually this means a storage temperature of 68 degrees Fahrenheit (22 degrees Celsius) with humidity at near 50 percent. The acidity of the paper itself is a crucial factor in the overall preservation of the paper. As paper became mass produced in the industrial revolution, paper quality suffered, and high acid and lignin contents became common. Therefore, the usual approach to preservation entails the deacidification of the paper, at times its encapsulation in inert mylar, and its storage in acid neutral filing environments and proper environmental conditions.

The development of new technologies in the later twentieth century has had numerous affects upon the administration of archives. On the one hand, this technology makes possible the loading of information into various national and international databases and available electronically. This spreads information literally worldwide. However the increasing use of this technology is also problematic for archivists as it means that yet another format for records must be preserved—electronic records. Much discussion and debate is occurring in the profession as it looks to providing archival care for electronic records. From clay tablet to computer disk—archivists have thus struggled over time to preserve the records of contemporary generations for later ones.

David J. Olson

See also MUSEUMS; PUBLIC HISTORY.

References
Clanchy, M.T. *From Memory to Written Record: England, 1066–1307.* London: Edward Arnold, 1979.
Daniels, M., and T. Walch. *A Modern Archives Reader: Basic Readings on Archival Theory and Practice.* Washington, DC: National Archives and Records Administration, 1984.
Dearstyne, Bruce W. *The Archival Enterprise: Modern Archival Principles, Practices, and Management Techniques.* Chicago: American Library Association, 1993.
Dollar, Charles M. *Archival Theory and Information Technologies: The Impact of Information Technologies on Archival Principles and Methods.* Ed. Oddo Bucci. Ancona, Italy: University of Macerata, 1992.
Posner, Ernst. *Archives in the Ancient World.* Cambridge, MA: Harvard University Press, 1972.

Ariès, Philippe (1914–1984)
Pioneering French historian in the history of mentalities in the 1960s and 1970s. Although he studied to be a historian, Ariès spent much of his early career outside academe, during which period, he wrote some of his most creative works. In 1978 his achievements were recognized when, near the end of his life, he was given an appointment at the *École des Hautes Études en science sociales.* Ariès is known especially for two research projects: the first dealing with the history of changing attitudes toward family and childhood (1960); the second tracing stages in the evolution of attitudes toward death and dying in Western society (1977). Each work is famous for a key thesis: the former for Ariès's argument that the idea of childhood as a preparatory stage for adult life was not conceived until the early

modern era; the latter, for his contention that commemoration as an expression of public mourning for personal loved ones is a recent historical phenomenon. In both works, Ariès traced the emergence of the modern temper in Western culture, with its stress on personal development and affection in human relationships. But he considered such trends in light of the countervailing power of customs and tacit understandings that favor social obligation, deference to authority, and respect for tradition, which, he argued, have never completely lost their hold upon popular culture.

Scholars associate Ariès with the new cultural history that developed in France in the 1960s as an alternative to political history. But his scholarly work must be appreciated in light of his family's royalist heritage and his personal sympathies for traditionalism. From adolescence into middle age he promoted royalist political causes. From a political standpoint, his historical scholarship in his mature years represented an indirect appeal to a more erudite audience in behalf of these same causes, for his work idealizes traditionalist values no longer politically viable but still powerful in their sentimental appeal.

Ariès also made important contributions to historiography. His history of French historiography (1954) was prescient in identifying coming trends in historical writing. Precisely because he worked apart from the academic milieu until late in life, he pursued his own lines of inquiry. Despite criticisms for the shortcomings of his ambitious scholarly projects, he today enjoys the respect of historians for opening new historical vistas on neglected topics dealing with basic human attitudes toward everyday life.

Patrick Hutton

Texts

Centuries of Childhood. Trans. Robert Baldick. New York: Random House, 1962.
Essais de mémoire [Essays on Memory]. Ed. Roger Chartier. Paris: Seuil, 1993.
Un Historien du dimanche [A Weekend Historian]. Ed. Michel Winock. Paris: Seuil, 1982.
The Hour of Our Death. Trans. Helen Weaver. New York: Knopf, 1981.
Le Temps de l'histoire [The Time of History]. Paris: Seuil, 1986.

References

Hutton, Patrick. *History As an Art of Memory.* Hanover, NH: University Press of New England, 1993.

Arrian [Lucius Flavianus Arrianus] (ca. 85–ca. 175)

Greek historian and official. Arrian was born in Bithynis, studied under the Stoic Epictetus, and, as governor of Cappadocia, defeated a barbarian invasion in A.D. 134. His works include a tract on India, a history of the successors of Alexander (surviving in fragments), as well as a history of Alexander the Great's expedition, the *Anabasis* [Upcountry Voyage] based on such contemporary sources as Ptolemy I. His style is plain, and any bias, owing to his sources, favors Alexander.

Stephen A. Stertz

Texts

History of Alexander. Trans. P.A. Brunt. 2 vols. Cambridge, MA: Harvard University Press, 1976–1983.

References

Bosworth, A.B. *From Arrian to Alexander: Studies in Historical Interpretation.* Oxford: Clarendon Press, 1988.
———. *A Historical Commentary on Arrian's History of Alexander.* Vol. I. Oxford: Clarendon Press, 1980.
Stadter, P.A. *Arrian of Nicomedia.* Chapel Hill: University of North Carolina Press, 1980.

Ars Historica

Literally, "Art of History." From the late fifteenth century to the early seventeenth the *ars historica* constituted a specific literary genre concerned with the nature and purpose of history. The Neapolitan historian Giovanni Pontano provided the first example with his dialogue *Actius: On Poetic Numbers and the Law of History,* written in 1499. Among the last of such treatises were *On the Method and Order of Reading Histories,* composed in 1623 by the first Camden professor of history at Oxford University, Degory Wheare, and *Ars historica ,* published by the Dutch scholar, Gerhard Voss or Vossius in the same year. A collection of sixteen Renaissance *artes historicae,* together with two classical models (*A Judgment on the History of Thucydides* by Dionysius of Halicarnassus, and *How to Write History* by Lucian of Samosata) were published by Johann Wolf at Basel in 1579 under the title *Artis historicae penus* [A Treasury of the Historical Art].

The theme of the *ars historica* was taken from the dictum of Dionysius of Halicarnassus: "History is philosophy teaching by examples." Its practitioners elaborated on pronouncements about history made by Stoic rhetoricians of the last decades of the Roman republic and the early years of the empire. The most famous was Cicero's definition of history in *De oratore* as "the witness of the times, the light of truth, the force of memory, the mistress of life, and the messenger of antiquity." As the mistress or guide to life, history played its exemplary role by providing vicarious experience. Seneca and Quintilian discoursed on the nature of examples and precepts derived from, or supported by, history. Moral lessons often had less to do with ideal good than with Stoic prudence in private and public life. To be useful in this context an example had to be true, and Cicero had insisted that "the light of truth" required the historian to eschew falsehood, to tell the whole truth, and to avoid prejudice. Tacitus had said that true history must be written "without anger or affection," and Lucian had set down standards of impartiality. Over three hundred years before Lucian, Polybius had developed criteria for acceptable historical evidence, and at the same time stressed the need to explain in terms of cause and effect.

These ancient sources were expatiated upon by Renaissance authors of *artes historicae,* who offered summations and criticisms of actual historians and regurgitated each other's comments. The tensions within the genre appeared most clearly in Francesco Patrizi's (Patrizzi) *Della historia diece dialoghi* [Ten Dialogues on History] (1560), which questioned the reliability of history and even the exemplar theory. However, Patrizi also introduced the idea of history as scientific explanation, a theme developed in terms of comparative generalization in Jean Bodin's *Methodus ad facilem historiarum cognitionem* [Method for the Easy Comprehension of History] (1566). In the seventeenth century, the ties of the *ars historica* with classical rhetoric began to weaken, while the mutually opposed trends of skepticism or "pyrrhonism" and erudition for its own sake created an intellectual climate in which it no longer flourished.

J.H.M. Salmon

See also RENAISSANCE, HISTORIOGRAPHY DURING.

References

Cochrane, Eric. *Historians and Historiography in the Italian Renaissance.* Chicago: University of Chicago Press, 1981, 479–487.

Cotroneo, Girolamo. *I trattatisti dell' "Ars historica"* [Tracts on the Art of History]. Naples: Giannini, 1971.

Nadel, George H. "Philosophy of History before Historicism." In *Studies in the Philosophy of History,* ed. Nadel. New York: Harper and Row, 1965, 49–73.

Reynolds, Beatrice. "Shifting Currents in Historical Criticism." *Journal of the History of Ideas* 14 (1953): 471–492.

Spini, Giorgio "Historiography: The Art of History in the Italian Counter-Reformation." In *The Late Italian Renaissance, 1525–1630,* ed. Eric Cochrane. New York: Harper and Row, 1970, 91–133.

Wickenden, Nicholas. *G.J. Vossius and the Humanist Concept of History.* Assen, Netherlands: Van Gorcum, 1993.

Witschi-Bernz, Astrid. *Bibliography of Works in the Philosophy of History, 1500–1800.* History and Theory, Beiheft 12. Middletown, CT: Wesleyan University Press, 1972.

Art As Historical Evidence

There are several valid approaches to art history; here we are interested only in how the general historian can use art as another source of evidence. Most art historians have concentrated on the succession of styles that has marked Western art from the Middle Ages to the present, analyzing them from a predominantly aesthetic point of view. A historian, however, can use these changes in style as clues to wider social and cultural developments. For instance, up until the late fourteenth and fifteenth centuries, figures still appeared flat and were shown against a solid background, giving them a timeless quality. By the mid-fifteenth century, especially in Italy, figures appeared more rounded and appeared to move about in a three-dimensional space, making the painting seem an extension of our own world of space and time. This seems to reinforce the argument that the Renaissance was an age of greater individualism and secularism.

Subsequent styles also provide evidence of shifting outlooks. In the sixteenth century, mannerism, with its sinuous lines and visual distortions, seems to reflect the anxieties of an age of instability and religious upheaval. In the seventeenth century, baroque, with its flamboyant expression and illusion of motion, seems to have expressed a period when powerful national monarchs were flexing their muscles and the church was reasserting itself. In the eighteenth century, rococo, with its fluid lines, pastel colors, and playful themes seems to have captured the spirit of the aristocracy of the age. In the later eighteenth century the emergence of neoclassicism, with its sculptured figures, bold colors, and heroic scenes appears to have responded to a growing demand for a more serious art conveying didactic messages to the public. It was a style that would prove useful to the art ministers of the old regime, the French revolutionaries, Napoleon, and other rulers.

Even the proliferation of styles from the nineteenth century onward—impressionism, fauvism, cubism, futurism, constructivism, expressionism, surrealism, pop art, minimalism, and so on—may provide clues to deeper changes in our civilization. Individualism seems to have been carried to an extreme as artists in liberal regimes rejected all constraints. Their art seems also to suggest an insatiable desire for novelty. At the same time, the proliferation of styles suggests that we have lost any sense of central values and symbols around which the community can unite. Above all, nonrepresentational art seems to express a lack of faith in the "reality" we see, an art symptomatic of the age of relativity, quantum theory, and indeterminacy.

Even apart from the interpretation of styles, the historian can use art to cast light on the general history of civilization. For instance, art can provide invaluable information about material history before the advent of still photography or moving pictures. We can glean a great deal of information about the clothing, the housing, the furniture, the food, the eating utensils, children's games, the means of production, the modes of transportation, and other aspects of daily life in a particular society at a given period. To give one example, Fernand Braudel, the great French historian of material life, studied all the paintings in Christian art of people eating—the Last Supper, the Wedding at Cana, Herod's Feast, and so on—to find out when the fork first appeared on the table.

The historian can also discover in art the world-outlook and social attitudes of people in different periods and cultures. A Gothic cathedral can be analyzed from a purely aesthetic or architectural point of view, however such a building was also an encyclopedia in stone, providing a synthesis of the view of creation, of nature, of history, and of human destiny held by the builders. At the same time, the thousands of stone carvings and hundreds of square meters of windows include, not only religious scenes from the Old and New Testaments, but images of contemporary peasants, craftsmen, and traders. At Chartres, even money-changers were given a place in the stained glass. Or, to cite an example from Asian civilization, traditional Chinese paintings reveal eloquently the view of nature, of humans' place in it, and the role of the sexes held by the Mandarin class that

dominated China until the end of the series of imperial dynasties that ruled China until the Revolution of 1911.

Feminist historians have made an important contribution by teaching us how to look for evidence of attitudes toward gender relations in various periods and cultures, especially in group portraits. The way the male head of the family is placed in relation to his wife or children is often very significant. This is true, not just in Western art, but in Asian art as well. In traditional Chinese art, for instance, when a sage or a poet is shown, usually in contemplation of nature, the individual is invariably male. Women are almost never shown in the company of men but are shown sequestered, with upper-class women often being represented under the guard of eunuchs. After 1949, the Communists changed the way in which women were depicted, showing them in active roles, as guerrillas, teachers, workers, engineers, and researchers. But if women were now portrayed doing traditional male chores, men were never shown performing traditional female roles of caring for children or preparing meals. Moreover, in Chinese communist art one must look for other images that are missing. Women seldom appear among the top leaders of the Party or government unless they have been married to one of them.

Historians have been especially interested recently in those movements and regimes that have consciously tried to communicate a religious or political message to the public. The idea of art as propaganda is of course very old, going back to ancient Egypt, Periclean Athens, Augustan Rome, and the medieval Church. Then rulers from the Middle Ages onward sought to have themselves and their ancestors shown in a favorable light. In this respect, the evolution of the court portrait in the Renaissance and the early modern period is especially revealing. The flattery of the ruler through art reached its climax with kings such as Philip II of Spain, Charles I of England, and Louis XIV of France. Peter Burke has recently shown how imagery in paintings, engravings, medals, coins, and statues in public places played a major role in the "fabrication" of the Sun King. In the eighteenth century, the *Encyclopédistes* and philosophies proposed that arts should be redirected to teach domestic morality and public virtue. The French revolutionaries took up this idea, attempting to steer art toward scenes of civic virtue, revolutionary heroism, and the major events of the revolution.

Modern revolutionary and totalitarian regimes have likewise sought to mobilize art for their purposes. In the Soviet Union the Party and the government suppressed avant-garde art in the 1930s, enforcing a new orthodoxy called socialist realism. This was "realistic" in two senses: it was representational; and it supposedly portrayed the real course of history according to Marxist-Leninism. This enforced program gave rise to a flood of art portraying growing class-consciousness before 1917, the events of the Bolshevik revolution, the leadership of Lenin, the building of the new communist society, the happy Soviet life, and the beneficence of Stalin. Meanwhile, in Germany, the Nazis condemned modern art as individualistic, international, Jewish, and unintelligible. In place of this "degenerate" art, the Nazis promoted genre painting that idealized German landscape, rural life, and traditional values. At the same time, they promoted idealized images of Hitler and other party leaders, heroic members of the armed forces, and pictures and statues of ideal Nordic men and women. These revolutionary and totalitarian regimes cannot be understood without some attention to what they attempted through art.

Architecture is especially revealing to the general historian. Various regimes have sought to impress their importance on the minds of the masses by erecting large monuments and public buildings such as churches, palaces, legislatures, and triumphal arches or columns. Such regimes have sought simultaneously to educate the masses with the current ideology by covering such structures with symbols, allegorical figures, low reliefs of historical events, and statues of famous individuals. "The walls must speak," declared a French revolutionary leader. Moreover, many regimes have created huge assembly halls, outdoor stadiums, and rallying grounds for public ceremonies. Also such regimes have tried to demonstrate their concern for the welfare of the masses by providing useful facilities—athletic centers, libraries, art galleries, public promenades, and so on. Finally, in so-called free societies great corporations display their power in huge stores, shopping centers, head offices, and factories.

James A. Leith

See also ARCHITECTURE AND HISTORY; FILM AND HISTORY; PHOTOGRAPHS, HISTORICAL ANALYSIS OF.

References
Bown, Matthew C. *Art under Stalin.* Oxford: Phaidon, 1991.
Burke, Peter. *The Fabrication of Louis XIV.* New Haven, CT: Yale University Press, 1992.
Hinz, Berthold. *Art in the Third Reich.* New York: Pantheon Books, 1974.
Laing, Ellen J. *The Winking Owl: Art in the People's Republic of China.* Berkeley: University of California Press, 1988.
Leith, James A. *The Idea of Art As Propaganda in France 1750–1799: A Study in the History of Ideas.* Toronto: University of Toronto Press, 1965.
Mâle, Emile. *The Gothic Image.* New York: Harper, 1958.
Strong, Roy. *Van Dyck, Charles I on Horseback.* London: Penguin, 1972.

Asaka Tampaku (1656–1737)

Japanese historian. Employed from 1670 in the service of Tokugawa Mitsukuni (1628–1700), lord of Mito, Asaka played a major role in completing the *Dai Nihon shi* [The Great History of Japan], a history of Japan in the Chinese standard history style, sponsored by his lord. Asaka wrote, in particular, comments on each section that were published separately and enjoyed a wide circulation.

John Lee

Texts
Dai Nihon shi ronsan [Comments on the Great History of Japan]. In *Kinsei shiron shū* [Early Modern Treatises on History]. Tokyo: Iwanami Shoten, 1974, 11–319.

References
Beasley, W.G., and E.G. Pulleyblank, eds. *Historians of China and Japan.* London: Oxford University Press, 1961.

Ashley, Sir William James (1860–1927)

British economic historian. Born in London, Ashley studied history at Balliol College, Oxford, where Arnold Toynbee first interested him in economic history. Ashley became professor of political economy and constitutional history at the University of Toronto, and in 1892 was appointed to the world's first chair of economic history at Harvard. He later became professor of commerce at the new University of Birmingham. Like his older contemporary, William Cunningham, Ashley was a historical, empirical economist who campaigned against the deductive, theoretical version of economics being standardized at Cambridge. He followed the younger German historical school (especially Schmoller) in taking an evolutionary view of society's development; stressing the importance of economic and social factors in shaping both institutions and economic theory;

and in believing that the economist should be active in devising social reform programs expanding the role of the state. His key historical works were *An Introduction to English Economic History and Theory* (1888–1893), which rejected the applicability of contemporary economic theory to the past and instead described past economic organization, and *The Economic Organisation of England* (1914), a much praised introduction to English economic history. His work was largely a synthesis of existing (especially German) scholarship, partly because being abroad kept him from the primary sources and partly because he became increasingly active in social and political issues, especially tariff reform and labor problems, often serving as an expert adviser to the government.

Andrew J. Hull

Texts

The Economic Organisation of England: An Outline History. London: Longmans, Green, 1914.
An Introduction to English Economic History and Theory. 2 vols. London: Rivington's, 1888–1893.
Surveys, Historic and Economic. London: Longmans, Green, 1900.

References

Kadish, A. *Historians, Economists and Economic History.* London and New York: Routledge, 1989.
Koot, Gerard M. *English Historical Economics, 1870–1926.* Cambridge, Eng.: Cambridge University Press, 1987.
Maloney, John. *Marshall, Orthodoxy and the Professionalisation of Economics.* Cambridge, Eng.: Cambridge University Press, 1985.
Wood, J.C. *British Economists and the Empire.* London: Croom Helm, 1983.

Ashton, Thomas Southcliffe (1889–1968)

English economic historian. Educated at Manchester University in history and political economy, Ashton later taught public finance and monetary history at the same institution before holding the chair of economic history at the London School of Economics. Ashton is regarded as one of the greatest historians of the industrial revolution in England. His most enduring works are his original and penetrating general surveys, *The Industrial Revolution* (1948) and *An Economic History of England in the Eighteenth Century* (1955). In the debate about the standard of living of the English masses during the industrial revolution, Ashton maintained that economic conditions did not deteriorate during that period. Not industrialism and capitalism, but obsolete laws and organization, economic fluctuations, shortage of capital, and the Napoleonic wars were responsible, in his view, for the commoners' misery. A liberal of the Manchester school, Ashton was a lifetime advocate of the application of the methods of economics in historical analyses of economic phenomena.

Pradip Bhaumik

Texts

An Economic History of England in the Eighteenth Century. London: Methuen, 1955.
The Industrial Revolution. London: Oxford University Press, 1948.

References

Sayers, R.S. "Thomas Southcliffe Ashton, 1889–1968." *Proceedings of the British Academy* 56 (1970): 263–281.

Asser (d. 908/909)

Medieval biographer. Asser was educated, tonsured, and ordained at St. David's monastery in Wales. In about 885 he met King Alfred the Great of Wessex, who came to value Asser's learning and eventually made him abbot of several monasteries, also appointing him bishop of Sherborne. Asser's Latin prose work, now known as *The Life of King Alfred* (893), is the most important narrative source on Alfred's reign and the earliest biography of an Anglo-Saxon ruler. Asser turned to the *Anglo-Saxon Chronicle* for some of his material, and to Einhard's *Life of Charlemagne* for a literary pattern. Yet Einhard's robust and aggressive Charlemagne offered an imperfect model for Asser, whose own subject, Alfred, suffered chronic ill health and whose political situation was precarious. The centrality of suffering and endurance in Asser's royal image is reminiscent of the conception of pastoral leadership expressed in the works of Pope Gregory I, which Asser knew, and is rooted in the Christian sacrificial tradition. Despite its limited circulation, *The Life of King Alfred* had a substantial influence on English royal biography during the Middle Ages and Renaissance.

David F. Appleby

Texts

Alfred the Great: Asser's "Life of King Alfred" and Other Contemporary Sources. Ed. and trans. Simon Keynes and Michael Lapidge. New York: Penguin Books, 1983.

References

Campbell, James. "Asser's Life of Alfred." In *The Inheritance of Historiography, 350–900,* ed. Christopher Holdsworth and T.P. Wiseman. Exeter, Eng.: University of Exeter Press, 1986, 115–135.

Atlases—Historical

Atlases that at any one time depict the geography of the world in earlier periods; to be distinguished from "historic" atlases (old works that depict the then contemporary world). The "pre-history" of the historical atlas was a long one, for the characteristic works of that genre were preceded by others that are less easy to define, notably individual maps depicting the Holy Land at the time of Christ, or the classical world, such as the map of ancient Greece produced by the Venetian cartographer Ferdinando Bertelli in 1563. Such maps would not have been regarded as historical in the same way as they are today. Without exactly being contemporary, their contents made up so large a part of people's intellectual baggage as to give them a distinctly contemporary tincture.

The first known historical atlas, the *Parergon* of Abraham Ortell (Ortelius), was published in Antwerp in 1579, initially as part of his general atlas, but from 1624 as a separate work. The *Parergon* was followed by a number of other works. They shared a common subject: the world of the Bible and the classics. Knowledge of this world was seen as a vital aspect of genteel education, and there was a growing sense that a cartographic perspective was important to this process.

The notion that maps might not only aid understanding but also add a new dimension to it was an important development in early modern European cartography. This led in the eighteenth century to a growing interest in mapping the postclassical world. Works appeared that included maps of medieval Europe, although the classical world remained the dominant theme and many historical atlases sought to go no further.

In the early nineteenth century, atlases that were primarily not classical/biblical started to appear in numbers. The *Atlas Historique, Généalogique, Chronologique et Géographique* [Historical, Genealogical, Chronological and Geographical Atlas] (Paris, 1803–1804) of Lesage (Marie Joseph Emmanuel Auguste Dieudonné de Las Cases, marquis de la Caussade) was one such: its circulation was immense. The *Atlas und Tabellen zur Übersicht der Geschichte aller Europäischen Länder und Staaten* by Christian Kruse [Atlas and Tables for an Overview of the History of All European Countries and States] (Halle, 1834) was an influential work that omitted antiquity. An even more influential work was the *Historisch-geographischer Hand-Atlas zur Geschichte der Staaten Europas von Anfang des Mittelalters bis auf die neuste Zeit* [A Historical and Geographical Atlas on the History of the States of Europe from the Beginning of the Middle Ages to Recent Times] (Gotha, 1846), by Karl von Spruner. An atlas depicting the development of Europe primarily from the perspective of the growth and interaction of its states, as was, and still is, the common pattern, Spruner's book was influential because of his rigor and insistence on sound sources.

Within fifty years, the historical atlas was to be established firmly on the European scene. The establishment of mass national schooling and the growth of academic history at the university level created a pedagogic demand for such works, while the development of a general book-reading public was also important. The growth of nation-states was both cause and consequence of mentalities that were more focused on the nation, and this extended to the past, for past greatness and pretensions were crucial components of national myths, and the continuity of present and past was stressed. Furthermore, reliable maps became easier to provide and to publish. Most of the world had been mapped, color printing became easier, and the production of historical atlases created a fund of information for further works.

In the twentieth century, the agenda became broader as compilers sought to show both what were seen as the forces underlying political history and other aspects of history. The former led initially to an emphasis on physical geography that responded to the environmentalism of the period. Since World War II, the agenda of historical atlases has greatly changed. There is now far more nonpolitical history and a much less Eurocentric approach. Whereas late-nineteenth-century historical atlases frequently closed their map section with a world map depicting the European colonial empires, it is now more common to close with a map showing the state of the world incorporating socioeconomic indicators. In addition, many specialized works, often on very detailed subjects, have appeared.

Changes in content have reflected shifts in academic interest and knowledge; a broader range in the nature of historical study, at both the academic and popular level; the development of less national, indeed less Eurocentric, attitudes; developments in cartographic methods; and the role of the marketing strategies of publishers.

Historical atlases are aimed at many different markets, from classrooms to coffee tables. A typology can be offered stressing the distinctions between atlases meant essentially for reference and those for teaching, and between general and particular works, but there is a considerable amount of overlap, as well as similar issues of mappability and depiction. Technological change continues to be important. Computers rapidly construct spatial information systems containing diverse interrelated layers of data, instead of the paper map with its essentially static character. It is possible that eventually many atlases will be generated and stored digitally and presented differently for the particular requirements of individual users: an atlas will be more clearly a database.

Mental maps have never been a constant, and it is wrong to treat historical cartography as a largely inconsequential sideline, as is all too often the case. Instead, historical atlases offer an important tool to understanding both past scholarship and modern scholarship on the past. Maps are thus simultaneously both "texts" and significant teaching and research tools.

Jeremy Black

See also GEOGRAPHY—HISTORICAL; IMMIGRATION, HISTORIOGRAPHY OF UNITED STATES; WORLD HISTORY.

References

Black, Jeremy. "Historical Atlases." *Historical Journal* 37 (1994): 643–667.
———. *Maps and History: Constructing Images of the Past*. London and New Haven, CT: Yale University Press, 1996.
Dörflinger, Johannes. "Geschichtskarte, Geschichtsatlas [Historical Maps, Historical Atlas]." In *Lexikon zur Geschichte der Kartographie von den Anfängen bis zum ersten Weltkreig* [Lexicon on the History of Cartography from Its Origins to World War I], ed. I. Kretschmer et al. 2 vols. Vienna: Deuticke, 1986, I, 265–268.
Goffart, Walter. "The Map of the Barbarian Invasions: A Preliminary Report." *Nottingham Medieval Studies* 32 (1988): 49–64.
Wolf, Armin. "Das Bild der europäischen Geschichte in Geschichtsatlanten verschiedener Länder [The Depiction of European History in the Historical Atlases of Various Countries]." *Internationales Jahrbuch für Geschichts- und Geographieunterricht* 13 (1970–1971): 64–101.

Augustine, Saint (354–430)

Bishop of Hippo and influential father of the early Christian church. Augustine was born at Thagaste, North Africa. He received a classical education and then taught rhetoric, first at Rome and then at Milan, where he converted to Christianity in 387. In 388 he returned to Africa and became a monk. In 395 he became the bishop of Hippo. Augustine's theory of history was formulated largely in the *City of God* (413–427), written in reaction to the fall of Rome to the Visigoths in 410, an event that shook Christian faith in human progress under Christian rule. Augustine rejects any idea of progress within the secular "earthly city" and stresses instead the "heavenly city," the salvation of individuals over time. Following earlier theologians, Augustine rejects pagan concepts of an eternal universe, cyclically renewed, in favor of a history modeled on the Bible, in which the universe began with Creation and followed a linear history, developing along a course determined by God, ending with the Last Judgment. The center upon which all history hinges, in his view, is Christ. In a formulation with a lasting impact on medieval historiography, Augustine divides history into six ages (Adam to the Flood, the Flood to Abraham, Abraham to David, David to the Babylonian Captivity, the Babylonian Captivity to the Birth of Christ, the Birth of Christ to the Second Coming), parallel to the six days of Creation. Although this Christian conception of history was anticipated by earlier theologians, Augustine's outline of history, supplemented by his disciple Orosius in a work called *Seven Books of History against the Pagans* (417), became very influential throughout the Middle Ages. Another of Augustine's works, his *Confessions,* later became a model for spiritual autobiography.

Maura K. Lafferty

Texts

The City of God by Saint Augustine. Trans. Marcus Dods. New York: Modern Library, 1993.

References

Markus, R.A. *Speculum: History and Society in the Theology of St. Augustine.* Cambridge, Eng.: Cambridge University Press, 1970.
Pelikan, Jaroslav. *The Mystery of Continuity: Time and History, Memory and Eternity in the Thought of St. Augustine.* Charlottesville: University Press of Virginia, 1986.

Aulard, Alphonse (1849–1928)

French historian of the French revolution. Aulard sprang from a conservative background. His father, a devout Catholic, was a philosopher and state school inspector. Born in Montbron (Charente), Aulard received an excellent education in provincial and Parisian schools. While attending the École Normale Supérieure (1867–1870) he demonstrated strong republican and anticlerical feelings. He served courageously during the Franco-Prussian War before entering the teaching profession. Aulard, who earned his doctorate in 1877 for a dissertation on the Italian poet Giacomo Leopardi, became interested in studying revolutionary orators. In 1886 his scholarship earned him a post teaching history at the Sorbonne, where he remained until retirement in 1922. Sympathetic to the revolution, Aulard nonetheless considered himself a "scientific" historian who emphasized the search for unpublished archival sources and their rigorous criticism. He produced numerous works concerning the political and religious history of the revolution as well as editing several important collections of revolutionary documents. Aulard's considerable output and university teaching helped put the study of the period on a scholarly basis.

James Friguglietti

Texts

The French Revolution: A Political History. 4 vols. Trans. Bernard Miall. New York: Charles Scribner's Sons, 1910.

References

Belloni, Georges. *Aulard historien de la Révolution française* [Aulard, Historian of the French Revolution]. Paris: Presses Universitaires de France, 1949.

Australian Historiography

Writings about Australian history since 1788. A society with a relatively short European history—a little more than two centuries of continental occupation—can logically be assumed to have produced an even shorter historiography. In Australia's case, this abbreviated past may also be wedded to the peculiar nature of its national origins in order to help explain its slow and fitful beginnings in compiling a sustained historical record. To its white immigrants, the Australian environment was viewed, paradoxically, as either quaint and peculiar or monotonous and devoid of interest. Possessing no "historic ruins" in the European sense, it was judged historically empty, thus ignoring the rich human past it contained of more than two hundred thriving aboriginal societies of great antiquity. Societies lacking "civilization," however, were also seen to lack history, and aboriginal people's alleged "primitivism and savagery" precluded any effective participation in the overall Australian story. Furthermore, the ravages they experienced during the onslaught of settler colonialism encouraged a further bout of white historical reticence.

Although some early historians during the era of sustained conflict (most notably, James Bonwick and John West, researching the dramatic fate of Tasmanian aboriginal societies) wrote openly of violent frontier interactions, by the later nineteenth century, evasion, subterfuge, and myopia had replaced candor in the general avoidance of such racial themes. Racial conflict and oppression, whether of Aborigines, Asians, or Pacific Islanders, became largely a forbidden topic and was linked, as a "twin shame," to another great unspoken—convictism. The threat of a convict genealogy seemed to hang like Damocles's sword over many a free colonist's head. The year 1888 was commemorated as a colonial centenary, yet convict origins went largely unmentioned. Both the character of the felons and the tyrannies of the system that transported and punished them were rejected as "loathsome and moral leprosy." Ironically, however, the intensely bureaucratic, surveillance-oriented nature of convict society ensured that it became one of the most intricately documented societies on earth—rich grist for later historians with less pressing qualms to inhibit them. Similarly, as aboriginal social remnants fell under increasing European official control, especially during the twentieth century, they too became a people as heavily processed—and thus documented—as the convicts had been.

A range of disparate historical observations nevertheless infused the journals of the earliest white administrators and interspersed the political accounts of prominent participants in colonial affairs. Such participant–observer approaches were necessarily based upon personal experience, reminiscences, and the testimony of compatriots—in effect, the pioneering of oral history in Australia—rather than intense manuscript or archival research. Though often capable literary efforts, there is much of the unstructured hobbyist, amateur, or antiquarian about them. In invariably avoiding the harsh and sordid, they presented the colonies as the place for a fresh start. Their stolid narratives lauded orderly progress, whether political progress toward self-government, democracy, or federation, or material progress toward general affluence and social success. Novelists, journalists, politicians, and public servants all contributed their congratulatory tomes on "the precocity of development," and there were only a few, such as Marcus Clarke, G.W. Rusden, or Charles White who pursued colorful—though worrisome—countervailing themes like convict beginnings, aboriginal destruction, or bushranging.

For the most part the colonial past unfolded uninspiringly as "a mere record of commerce and cricket, of wool and wickets," interspersed with such acceptable male heroes as explorers and pioneer graziers. These men were seen as prime exemplars of the imperial type—"a British race at work"—and white Australia's brief tale was boosted by attaching it humbly to the grand saga of the "mother country" and its magnificent empire. The early Australian story, then, was immersed in the imperial achievements of triumphant "transplanted Britons," its own indigenous fragility and shallowness hedged around for the most part by a sense of inferiority and apology.

The slow but escalating professionalization of the discipline from the late nineteenth century inherited many of these thematic preoccupations—a concentration upon outback environments, masculine achievement in a far corner of the empire, the virtues of "British stock," a preoccupation with optimism and progress, and an avoidance of racial, class, or gender conflict issues. Yet to these themes academics in the history departments of the new universities brought enhanced codification, the disciplines of contextualization and cautious primary research, and improved critical analysis, as well as a sense of "scientific objectivity." Such vaunted objectivity nevertheless remained something of a chimera. G.A. Wood, who began the introduction of academic methodology into Australian historical study during the 1880s, also commented in 1921, "The study of history and the practice of patriotism are very closely related." Whether it was C.E.W. Bean or Ernest Scott lauding Australian patriotic endeavor on warfronts or homefronts; Wood himself, S.H. Roberts, or Margaret Kiddle praising British explorers or pastoralists; or C.V. Portus and Keith Hancock extolling the hardy, egalitarian virtues of "independent Austral Britons," these official and professional historians all possessed a dominant verisimilitude in their historical productions—a shared paradigm of liberal patriotism and a whiggish account of inexorable national advance stimulated by the capital achievements and sacrifices of outstanding (and invariably male) individuals.

Only the odd account, such as Eris O'Brien's *The Foundation of Australia* (1938) introduced a note of pique and protest, as he dealt sympathetically with convicts as victimized British workers, more sinned against by tyrannous British officialdom than sinning.

For the most part, the dazzling synoptic statements of Hancock's *Australia* (1930) held sway, exercising a mesmeric hold over the profession until well into the 1960s. The historical profession itself remained small and its published output limited. There were few controversies, little specialization, and no discernible, contesting historical "schools." No historical journal appeared until 1940. Amateurs continued to outnumber professionals until after World War II. Australian history was not consistently taught to undergraduates until 1946, and the first doctorate in the subject was not granted until the following year. A year later, the first historical research unit was established at the Australian National University.

The ideology of liberalism, therefore, ruled over a small empire, but it additionally has presided over the longest period of Australian historical production—for it sustained not only the liberal patriots but also inspired many of the labor, radical nationalist, and sociologically influenced historians of the 1950s and 1960s. Labor history, however, already had a long local pedigree, stretching forward from John Norton's edited omnibus, *History of Capital and Labour in All Lands and Ages* (1888). It was written originally mainly by activists—trade union leaders, left-wing politicians, and bureaucrats—achieving intellectual respectability in 1923 with Vere Gordon Childe's eviscerating *How Labour Governs*. From the late 1930s, the Marxist civil libertarian, Brian Fitzpatrick, provided it with lasting scholarly substance from outside the academies in a series of inspiring studies, posing British capital against an organized Australian working class and presenting Australian history as one of colonial dependency and unequal class struggle, with the state weighing in on the side of the rich.

Yet the leftist-inspired historians (roughly grouped as radical nationalists) who followed Fitzpatrick in the cold war climate of the 1950s were as much influenced by traditional liberalism as they were by Marxism. Like the liberal patriots, they told an optimistic story about a resourceful and egalitarian Australian people, imbued with mateship and distrusting authority—values molded by a unique environment. Like the liberals, they, too, depicted Australian labor as the political party of initiative and Australian history as one of working-class progress toward increasing social

A

rights. Themes of racism and sexism were eschewed, and their conception of class was vague and unfocused. Instead, the working class, especially its rural component, and the Australian nation were readily conflated. Class, community, and nation were telescoped, as mateship led on unproblematically to socialism and nationalism. The national essence—its supposed unitary culture—was located therefore in the naturally formed mores of the "down-to-earth Australian worker." Capital, interlinked with British imperialism and elite culture, was largely ignored. Russel Ward's highly influential *The Australian Legend* (1958) was the main purveyor of this proletarian mystique, but he was later joined by Ian Turner and Geoffrey Serle in their search for the constituent elements of Australian culture. Turner, too, along with Robin Gollan, continued to unfold Fitzpatrick's class analysis, albeit in a somewhat lopsided manner, privileging workers and ignoring detailed capitalist profiles. Together these historians (along with others) helped weld labor history into a consolidated, institutional form, founding the Australian Society for the Study of Labor History with its own journal in 1961–1962.

Yet, whereas radical nationalists differed from liberal patriots and those preceding them by according Australian genius indigenous rather than British roots, one iconoclastic historian, Charles Manning Hope Clark, was to begin, from the mid-1950s, a questioning of the entire whiggish tenor of Australian history, together with its emphasis on material development, its "comforters" of British stewardship or Australian mateship, and its avoidance of conflict and pessimism or of the struggles for transcendent human values. His protean and controversial *History of Australia,* produced in six massive volumes between 1962 and 1987, however, tends to parallel rather than direct subsequent historiographical developments. It presents a unique vision, epic, literary, enigmatic, and magisterially flawed, owing its inspiration more to Virgil's *Aeneid,* the King James Bible, Milton, Dostoevsky, and Thomas Hardy rather than to any established Western historiographical or theoretical traditions.

Clark's maverick questioning of established historical modes, however, began to breach the liberal dam in Australian historical studies. As the 1960s unfolded, several conservative historians launched a limited counteroffensive against the rural, labor-oriented influences dominating research, while other sociologically minded investigators, such as Ken Inglis, Geoffrey Blainey, and Geoffrey Bolton, began tentatively to introduce more systematic social analysis of a neo-Weberian kind. Such theoretical intrusions, modest and cautious as they were, paved the way for the New Left and new social historians who followed.

Developing in an era of prolonged social, political, and moral tumult, New Left historians, such as Humphrey McQueen, Terry Irving, and Stuart Macintyre, attacked most of the ruling premises of Australian history—its antitheoretical mode, its empiricist faith in "facts," and its emphasis on unity, tranquillity, and progress. Mostly, they attacked the radical nationalists (now dubbed the "Old Left") for their naive faith in mateship's transformative powers and their lack of class analysis. The celebrated connection between Australian nationalism and its workers was especially pilloried in McQueen's *A New Britannia* (1970), where nationalism was execrated as militaristic and racist and the working class as conservative and petit-bourgeois.

A group of race relations historians now began to expose long-concealed horrors of colonial "settlement" as these had impinged upon Aborigines and other non-Europeans, as well as the ways in which such peoples had resisted these impositions. Feminist historians, smarting at the monumental omission of approximately half the national population from the record by virtually all their predecessors, whether male or female, began to delineate women's social roles before turning more systematically to the sterner operations of patriarchy. A range of social historians also began to explore a variety of themes only previously whispered about—poverty, criminality, insanity, generational relations, ethnic relations, social and ideological division and violence, the colonists' devastating environmental impact, and others. As a plethora of underprivileged and disempowered groups surfaced for the first time historiographically, Australian histories were written without obligatory "happy endings" and themes of conflict and pessimism superseded those of harmony and buoyancy.

Such critical studies met with a resounding revisionist backlash in the 1980s, however, as a coterie of newer historians attempted to establish that humanity, variety, and choice existed on Australian frontiers; that convictism could provide opportunity alongside oppression; that Australian families could be companionate as well as crippling; that Australian capitalism was often "civilized" as well as exploitative; and that even the depression of the 1930s had its ennobling side. In confronting the studied pessimism of the preceding generation, and influenced by prevailing philosophical tenets of economic rationalism, these historians emphasize agency, opportunity, achievement, and conciliation, tending to return the overall interpretive framework to its previously deeply rutted and largely sanguine historiographical track. While this battle between pessimists and optimists remains enjoined, however, a group of cultural studies historians, strongly influenced by European poststructuralism and postmodernism, threaten to derail the historical cart entirely by essentially denying that history's very "texts"—that is, its purported tools for excavating the outlines of the past—cannot be taken to reveal any underlying social or economic reality. By manipulating cultural surfaces rather than probing substantive social forms, such culturalists severely question history's purported quest to delineate past material realities with some pretension toward accuracy and precision.

If nineteenth-century historians depicted Australian colonists as "transplanted Britons" and liberal patriots hopefully saw the citizens of the new Commonwealth as "independent Austral" ones, then historians like Fitzpatrick and Clark began to reveal an obverse side to the national romance with the British connection, which New Left and other 1970s researchers systematically detailed. But in the process, these latter historians also deconstructed and fragmented that unitary sense of nation that the radical nationalists had coveted as the creation of ordinary Australian people, and that splintered, destabilizing sense at present prevails, as conflict and conciliation historians, sunny optimists and determined pessimists, culturalists and materialists, continue to tussle interpretively over the possible sense and meaning of it all.

Raymond Evans

See also EUROCENTRISM IN THE WRITING AND TEACHING OF HISTORY; NEW ZEALAND HISTORIOGRAPHY; PACIFIC ISLANDS HISTORIOGRAPHY.

References

Fletcher, B.H. *Australian History in New South Wales 1888–1938.* Kensington: New South Wales University Press, 1993.

Irving, T., ed. *Challenges to Labour History.* Kensington: New South Wales University Press, 1994.

Macintyre, S. "The Writing of Australian History." In *Australians: A Guide to Sources,* ed. D.H. Borchardt and V. Crittenden. Broadway, NSW: Fairfax, Syme and Weldon, 1987, 1–29.

Osborne, G., and W.F. Mandle, eds. *New History: Studying Australia Today.* Sydney and Boston: Allen and Unwin, 1982.

Pascoe, R. *The Manufacture of Australian History.* Melbourne: Oxford University Press, 1979.

Autobiography

Form of historical writing in which an individual narrates the story of his or her own life. Autobiographies have most often appeared as prose epistles, written or told orally, but claims have been made for funereal inscriptions, poems, novels, musical compositions, and film. Autobiography has furnished ground for philosophical debates very similar to those that have accompanied the practice of history in general.

Historians writing in the Western tradition have valued autobiography as something between a primary and a secondary source of information about past events. Supplementing impersonal official records and other material traces of the past, curious researchers have looked to autobiographers for inside views of affairs of state, everyday life and times during a particular period, or, depending on the degree of authorial self-revelation, single personalities. Since the mid-twentieth century, autobiography has emerged as a "genre" within literary studies. It has been the subject of a large critical literature that has distinguished among goals pursued by autobiographers of different eras and diverse circumstances. Many autobiographers in the Western tradition recorded, as did Saint Augustine and numerous later Puritan writers, the circumstances of their conversion to Christianity. Others, such as Jean Jacques Rousseau, appeared in passionate response to critics, or proposed to analyze, as did Henry Adams, individual alienation. In contrast to most males, numerous women have seen themselves as neither heroic nor representative of their times but instead, as outsiders. As history has become more democratic and inclusive, critical attention increasingly has turned to the autobiographical expressions of those marginalized by structures of power, such as enslaved persons, other groups of poor, and ordinary people, as well as to the lives told by women, immigrants, subjects of racist and colonial policies, aboriginal peoples, and Native and African Americans.

During the twentieth century, as historians began to question the "objective" nature of their enterprise, they came to view history as always in some sense the creation of a particular author, picking and choosing, arranging and linking traces deemed "significant" into an argument about what happened in the past. Autobiography, the product of the same sorts of choices, though confined to a single life, came also to be viewed as problematic, as less than an accurate record of a single person's experience, as subject, like the writing of larger history, to frames of reference dictated by the society in and cultural moment during which the author lived. Thus, some have argued that all history is a form of autobiography, while others have argued that autobiography is always a social construction.

As with history, the epistomological foundations of the autobiographical enterprise have been shaken by interdisciplinary critics of objective theories of knowledge. Memory does not simply contain pure chunks of the past waiting to be brought out and stated as historical knowledge. "Retrieval," Jerome Brunner notes, "must be steered to the appropriate storage 'address' by some sort of program." Despite the strong tradition of romantic individualism in Western culture after the eighteenth century, these critics argue that individual experience recapitulated represents not a person but a society. From society, not from inner resources, the individual gains language, experience, and opportunities, so that autobiography represents a social as much as an individual fabrication. Language and culture determine the structure of memory, the metaphors employed, and the attribution of significance to what is related. Thus, autobiography is a revised edition of one's life, a fiction informed by a teleological process of applying to events the patterns giving coherence to the present.

Following this logic, deconstructionists have attempted to destroy the notion of autobiography as a form of individual history by reducing the subject to the text. "[T]he question of autobiographical truth is in some sense no question at all," writes W.R. Buck, "since the identity that the text seeks to represent is originally constituted as fiction." If there is only the text and present discourse, there can be no "historical" understanding of the autobiographer and thus of major concerns of historians: class, gender, power, religion—everything that constitutes societies. History becomes impossible. Unwilling to accept either the solipsism of subjective romantic individualism, which emphasizes the uniqueness of every person, or the solipsism of being alone with an alien and fictional text, the historian wishing to continue must develop an unverifiable faith in common human experiences as a basis for communication.

Historians aware of the epistomological problems posed for autobiography and for all history may yet approach their work through several strategies. First, texts can be read for what they omit and distort as well as for what they say on the surface. Secondly, historians may adopt the hermeneutical position of Wilhelm Dilthey, who took the knowing subject as the point of reference for historical knowledge. Unlike empiricists or positivists who expect to discover events and facts existing outside of the knowing subject, the hermeneuticist stresses autobiographical reflection by the historian. Knowledge of human affairs emerges from self-knowledge: "The first condition of the possibility of historical studies is that I myself am a historical being—that he who *studies* history is the same as he who *makes* history." Reflecting autobiographically, historians will understand the historic relations in which their lives are grounded. Such autobiographical knowledge is not only individual and subjective but also linguistic. As Dilthey wrote, "every single individual is at the same time a point of intersection for structures that permeate individuals, exist through them, but extend beyond their lives." Historians' interpretations then move beyond the autobiographical to operate as the self-knowledge of particular societies at particular times.

Ellen Nore

See also BIOGRAPHY; MICROHISTORY.

References

Bruner, Jerome. *Acts of Meaning*. Cambridge, MA: Harvard University Press, 1990.

Bruss, Elizabeth. *Autobiographical Acts: The Changing Situation of a Literary Genre*. Baltimore and London: Johns Hopkins University Press, 1976.

Buck, William R. "Reading Autobiography." *Genre* 13 (1980): 477–498.

Dilthey, Wilhelm. *Meaning in History: Wilhelm Dilthey's Thoughts on History and Society*. Trans. H.P. Rickman. London: Allen and Unwin, 1961.

Eakin, Paul John, ed. *American Autobiography: Retrospect and Prospect*. Madison: University of Wisconsin Press, 1991.

Folkenflik, Robert, ed. *The Culture of Autobiography: Constructions of Self-Representation*. Stanford, CA: Stanford University Press, 1993.

Gusdorf, Georges. "Conditions and Limits of Autobiography." Trans. James Olney. In *Autobiography: Essays Theoretical and Critical*, ed. James Olney. Princeton, NJ: Princeton University Press, 1980, 28–48.

Jelinek, Estelle C. *The Tradition of Women's Autobiography: From Antiquity to the Present*. Boston: Twayne, 1986.

Lejeune, Philippe. *On Autobiography*. Ed. Paul John Eakin; trans. Katherine Leary. Minneapolis: University of Minnesota Press, 1989.

Murphy, John. "The Voice of Memory: History, Autobiography and Oral Memory." *Historical Studies* 22 (1986): 157–175.

Olney, James. *Studies in Autobiography*. New York and London: Oxford University Press, 1988.

Spengemann, William C. *The Forms of Autobiography: Episodes in the History of a Literary Genre.* New Haven, CT, and London: Yale University Press, 1980.

Stanley, Liz. *The Auto/biographical I.* Manchester, Eng.: Manchester University Press, 1992.

Steedman, Carolyn. "History and Autobiography: Different Pasts." In *Past Tenses: Essays on Writing Autobiography and History,* ed. Steedman. London: Rivers Oram Press, 1992, 41–50.

Sturrock, John. *The Language of Autobiography: Studies in the First Person Singular.* Cambridge, Eng.: Cambridge University Press, 1993.

Aventinus (1477–1534)

German historian. Aventinus was the name taken by the humanist and historian, Johann Thurmair, who was born at Abensberg (Latin *Aventinum*). He studied at Ingolstadt, Vienna (under Conrad Celtis), Cracow, and Paris. In 1507 he returned to Ingolstadt and entered ducal service, first as tutor (1508/1509) to the younger sons of Albrecht the Wise and, from 1517, as court historian. Between 1519 and 1522 he composed the work that established his reputation, the *Annales ducum Boiariae.* A German version, the *Bayrische Chronik,* dates from the period 1522 to 1533. The *Annales* are a history of Bavaria from the earliest times to 1460, set against the general background of European history. Aventinus anticipated many trends in German history writing; he made extensive use of documentary sources and evinced a strong sympathy for the empire in its many encounters with the papacy. Imprisoned in 1528 for Protestant leanings, Aventinus was released owing to the intervention of powerful friends. The first edition of the *Annales* was published under ducal censorship in 1554 and thus lacked many passages. A complete German version appeared at Frankfurt in 1566, and Nicolas Cisner brought out an unabridged Latin version at Basel in 1580. Aventinus, sometimes called the "Bavarian Herodotus," exercised considerable influence on German history writing by providing a model for *Landesgeschichte* as a distinct and respectable specialty.

Andrew Colin Gow

Texts

J. Thurmair, genannt Aventinus: Sämmtliche Werke [Collected Works of Aventinus]. 6 vols. Munich: Königliche Bayerische Akademie der Wissenschaften, 1880–1906.

References

Strauss, G. *Historian in Age of Crisis: The Life and Work of Johann Aventinus, 1477–1534.* Cambridge, MA: Harvard University Press, 1963.

al-ʿAynī, Badr al-Dīn (1361–1451)

Historian and religious scholar of north Syrian origin, who early in his career moved to Cairo where he held many civil and religious positions. He became the companion of several sultans and has been described as "a perfect courtier." Al-ʿAynī was the author of a voluminous chronicle of the Mamlūk period, *ʿIqd al-jumān,* which has only recently begun to be published in a systematic way. It is not surprising, then, that this work has been less known (and used) than the chronicle of al-ʿAynī's famous contemporary and rival, al-Maqrīzī. Al-ʿAynī's work, however, is in general superior not only to that of al-Maqrīzī's, but for early Mamlūk history, as D.P. Little writes, it "surpasses, indeed, all other sources, published or not, in the amount of original material which it contains." Al-ʿAynī cites, almost invariably by name, large sections from the works of earlier Mamlūk historians, some of which are now lost. Al-ʿAynī also composed a work on poetics and a commentary on al-Bukhārī's collection of traditions about Muḥammad.

Reuven Amitai-Preiss

Texts

ʿIqd al-jumān fī taʾrīkh ahl al-zamān [Events for 1250–1307]. Ed. M.M. Amīn. 4 vols. Cairo: Al-Hayʾa al-Miṣriyya al-ʿĀmma lil-Kitāb, 1987–1990.

ʿIqd al-jumān fī taʾrīkh ahl al-zamān [Events for 1409–1446]. Ed. ʿA-R. al-Ṭanṭāwī al-Qarmūṭ. 2 vols. Vol. 1, Cairo: al-Zuhrāʾ lil-Iʿlām al-ʿArabī, 1985; vol. 2, Cairo: Maṭbaʿa ʿAlāʾ, 1989.

Recueil des historiens des croisades. Historiens orientaux [Selections Relating to the Crusades]. Vol. 2. Paris: Imprimerie nationale 1872–1906, 181–250.

References

Little, D.P. *An Introduction to Mamlūk Historiography.* Wiesbaden: Franz Steiner Verlag, 1970, 80–87.

Marçais, W. "Al-ʿAynī." *Encyclopaedia of Islam.* Second ed. Vol. 1. Leiden: E.J. Brill, 1960, 790–791.

B

Babad

Genre of works in (classical modern) Javanese. These are always in verse-form and have clear connections with history. A large number are extant, the most famous being the extensive *Babad Tanah Jawi* [Chronicle of the Land of Java], which takes the history of Java from mythological beginnings up to the late eighteenth century. The core of a Babad is the foundation-story of the kingdom and an account of the descent of its rulers from a powerful ancestor. Capitals have been moved from time to time, and the dynastic line disrupted, so these texts serve to explain and legitimize. In particular they function to describe the House of Mataram and its troubled relations with the Dutch East India Company. There is a subcategory of Babad texts that deals with one particular incident or personality, such as the *Babad Dipanagara*, relating Prince Dipanagara's struggle against Dutch imperialism in the Java War (1825–1830). By comparison with colonial archives, historians have shown that much in the Babads is factual, while taking account of their Javanese viewpoint.

Stuart Robson

See also DEŚAWARNANA; PARARATON.

References

Ras, J.J. "The Babad Tanah Jawi and Its Reliability: Questions of Content, Structure, and Function." In *Cultural Contact and Textual Interpretation,* ed. C.D. Grijns and S.O. Robson. Verhandelingen van het Koninklijk Instituut voor Taal-, Land- en Volkenkunde, vol. 115. Dordrecht, Netherlands, and Cinnaminson, NJ: Foris Publications, 1986, 246–273.

Bābur, Ẓahīr al-Dīn [Ẓahiru'd-din Muḥammad Bābur] (1483–1530)

Founder of the Mughal dynasty in India and author of autobiographical history of his times. A descendant of Timur and Genghis Khan (Chingiz Khān), Bābur was born in 1483 in Farghānā (present-day Afghanistan). He inherited the throne in 1494, commencing his career as one of the foremost invaders of his time. Unable to triumph over the powerful Uzbek forces of Shaybānī Khān, Bābur directed his attention to the east, capturing Kabul in 1504, then expanding into India. The decisive battle occurred in April 1526, when he defeated the much larger army of Sultan Ibrāhīm Lodī at Pānipāt. He was declared emperor of Hindustan, a title that he held until his death. Throughout his life, Bābur kept detailed notes of his activities, recording both military tactics and personal impressions. These rough diary jottings were the basis of his autobiography, *Bāburnāma,* which was written during his last years in India (1526–1530). Though there are significant gaps in the manuscript, the memoirs provide an accurate account of Bābur's life from 1494 to 1530, as well as a thorough description of Indian society and customs during his reign.

Siobhan Lambert Hurley

Texts

The Baburnama: Memoirs of Babur, Prince and Emperor. Ed. and trans. Wheeler M. Thaxton. Oxford, Eng.: Oxford University Press for Smithsonian Institution, 1996.
Divān-i-Pādishāh. In "A Collection of Poems by the Emperor Babur." Ed. E. Denison Russ. *Journal and Proceedings of the Asiatic Society of Bengal* 6 (1910).
Memoirs of Zehir-ed-Din Muhammed Babur.

Trans. John Leyden and William Erskine; revised by Lucas King. 2 vols. London and New York: Oxford University Press, 1921.

References

Hasan, Mohibbul. *Babur: Founder of the Mughal Empire in India.* New Delhi: Manohar Publications, 1985.

Richards, John F. *The Mughal Empire.* Cambridge, Eng.: Cambridge University Press, 1993.

Bachofen, Johann Jakob (1815–1887)

Swiss legal historian, classical philologist, and philosopher of history. Bachofen, born in Basel, was descended from a wealthy upper-class family. After his philological studies he turned to the study of law under the influence of Friedrich Karl von Savigny and earned his doctorate at Göttingen with a dissertation on Roman civil courts. In 1841 he became a professor of Roman jurisprudence at the University of Basel. Bachofen formulated several theses that later became important for historiography. In his renowned work *Das Mutterrecht* [The Mother Right] (1861), he claimed that in the beginnings of the human civilization there existed a right of the mother that in the course of history had been driven out by patriarchy. As opposed to the critical notion of historiography, he formulated a program for the interpretation of myths to describe the preliterate, oral, and "mother right" stages, which are found at the beginnings of civilization. Myth, in Bachofen's view, reflects the religious and historical archetypes of the human race. His interpretation is valuable for its explanation and illustration of historical processes in prehistoric times. His views of the "mother right" and his interpretation of myths led to a philosophy of history with a dualistic character. Bachofen's work had an impact on cultural sociology and ethnology, but was largely ignored in historiography. His romantic philosophy of history and interpretation of myths, and his speculative methods, were considered retrograde by the standards of the critical historiography of the nineteenth century.

Thomas Fuchs

Texts

Johann Jakob Bachofens Gesammelte Werke [Complete Works of Bachofen]. Ed. K. Meuli. 10 vols. Basel: Benno Schwabe, 1943–1967.

Myth, Religion and Mother Right: Selected Writings of J.J. Bachofen. Trans. R. Manheim. Second ed. Princeton, NJ: Princeton University Press, 1992.

References

Cesana, A. *Johann Jakob Bachofens Geschichtsdeutung: Eine Untersuchung ihrer geschichtsphilosophischen Voraussetzungen* [Bachofen's Interpretation of History: An Examination of the Premises of His Philosophy of History]. Basel: Birkhäuser Verlag, 1983.

Gossman, L. *Orpheus Philologus: Bachofen versus Mommsen on the Study of Antiquity.* Philadelphia, PA: The American Philosophical Society, 1983.

Bacon, Francis, Viscount St. Alban (1561–1626)

English statesman, philosopher, and historian. Born in London, Bacon was trained as a lawyer and enjoyed a long but controversial political career, although he was soon renowned chiefly for his ambitious scheme to reform the state of learning. In *The Advancement of Learning* (1605), he had bemoaned the shortcomings of contemporary knowledge and commenced its repair by surveying its various areas and assessing their needs. "History" played a crucial part in the "Great Instauration" of knowledge that he projected: for Bacon, history (both in the ancient sense of an "inventory" and as a record of past events) was the sum of human experience and thus one of the main branches of knowledge. Adopting a scheme borrowed in part from French theorists such as Jean Bodin, he divided history into a number of subcategories, discussed their parameters, and appealed for the application of a systematic method that would provide a precise and unquestionable record of the past while simultaneously serving as a stimulus for future action. His one completed political history, *The Reign of King Henry VII* (1622) was a *tour de force* in characterization. Intended as advice for Prince Charles, heir to the throne, it also embodied Bacon's belief that history was the preserve not of scholars but of statesmen. He admired Tacitus and Machiavelli as models in history writing and political analysis; in spite of its factual inaccuracies, his portrait of Henry VII has remained highly influential in interpretations of that king's reign.

Adriana A.N. McCrea

Texts

The History of the Reign of King Henry the Seventh. Ed. F.J. Levy. Indianapolis, IN: Bobbs-Merrill, 1972.

Letters and Life of Francis Bacon. Ed. J. Spedding. 7

vols. London: Longman, Green, Longman, and Roberts, 1861–1874.

Works of Francis Bacon. Ed. J. Spedding, R.L. Ellis, and D.D. Heath. 7 vols. London: Longmans, 1857–1861.

References

Marwil, Jonathan. *The Trials of Counsel: Francis Bacon in 1621.* Detroit, MI: Wayne State University Press, 1976.

Woolf, D.R. *The Idea of History in Early Stuart England: Erudition, Ideology, and "The Light of Truth" from the Accession of James I to the Civil War.* Toronto: University of Toronto Press, 1990.

Wormald, B.H.G. *Francis Bacon.* Cambridge, Eng.: Cambridge University Press, 1992.

Bader, Clarisse (1840–1902)

Orientalist and historian of women's history. Bader was born in Strasbourg and, at the age of twenty, conceived the idea of writing a history of women in ancient societies. In 1864 she published *La Femme dans l'Inde antique* [Women in Ancient India]. It was her most famous work and earned her membership in the Société Asiatique de Paris; it was reprinted in India in 1964. The remainder of the larger project was realized by volumes on Biblical, Greek, Roman, and French women of her time published between 1866 and 1883. Bader has been labeled as an Orientalist and her work superseded by those working from original texts. However, these criticisms belie her important recognition of the lacunae in the scholarly literature regarding women in ancient history that she strove to fill.

Emma C. Alexander

Texts

La femme française dans les temps moderne. Second ed. Paris: E. Perrin, 1885.

La femme romaine. Second ed. Paris: Didier, 1877.

Women in Ancient India: Moral and Literary Studies. Trans. Mary E.R. Martin. London: Routledge and Kegan Paul, 1925.

References

Chakravarti, Uma. "Whatever Happened to the Vedic Dasi? Orientalism, Nationalism, and a Script for the Past." In *Recasting Women: Essays in Indian Colonial History,* ed. K. Sangari and S. Vaid. New Brunswick, NJ: Rutgers University Press, 1990, 27–87.

Bailyn, Bernard (b. 1922)

American intellectual historian. A prolific writer on the colonial history of the United States, Bailyn graduated from Williams College in 1945. He studied with Oscar Handlin at Harvard, earning his M.A. in 1947, and a Ph.D. in 1953. He has been a faculty member at Harvard since that time. His writing has centered on the political and social aspects of colonial history, and he has garnered many prizes, including a National Book Award for history (for his 1974 work, *The Ordeal of Thomas Hutchinson*) and the Jefferson Medal of the American Philosophical Society (1993). He served as president of the American Historical Association in 1981. Bailyn's early work studied colonial economic history, resulting in a book on *The New England Merchants in the Seventeenth Century* (1955). He then turned to the intellectual history of early America, collecting and editing a series of *The Pamphlets of the American Revolution* (1965). He expanded his introduction to this collection into his most famous book, *The Ideological Origins of the American Revolution* (1967), which was awarded both the Bancroft and Pulitzer prizes. An influential work that put the ideas of the revolutionaries within their social and political context, it also lent considerable impetus to the revival of intellectual history in the United States. More recently, Bailyn has returned to his earlier interests in social history, chronicling the settlement of the colonies in his *Peopling of British North America* (1986).

Susan A. Stussy

Texts

Et al. *The Great Republic: A History of the American People.* Fourth ed. Lexington, MA: D.C. Heath, 1992.

The Ideological Origins of the American Revolution. Enlarged ed. Cambridge, MA: Belknap Press of Harvard University Press, 1992.

The New England Merchants in the Seventeenth Century. Cambridge, MA: Harvard University Press, 1955.

The Ordeal of Thomas Hutchinson. Cambridge, MA: Harvard University Press, 1974.

Ed., with Jane N. Garrett. *The Pamphlets of the American Revolution, 1750–1776.* Cambridge, MA: Belknap Press of Harvard University Press, 1965.

The Peopling of British North America: An Introduction. New York: Knopf, 1986.

Voyagers to the West: A Passage in the Peopling of America on the Eve of the Revolution. New York: Knopf, 1986.

B

Bainton, Roland Herbert (1894–1984)

American church historian. Bainton was born in Ilkeston, Derbyshire, England, the son of a Congregational minister whose memory he would later honor with a biography (*Pilgrim's Parson,* 1958). Bainton's classical education gave him a life-long commitment to languages. His B.A. degree in classics from Whitman College was followed by a B.D. from Yale Divinity School (1917) and a Ph.D. (1921), also from Yale. Bainton's pacifism earlier had led to service with a Quaker Red Cross unit in France and a passion for the history of religious liberty and toleration. These themes dominated his forty-two year scholarly career at Yale from 1920 until 1962. Bainton believed that the Renaissance interest in non-Christian religions, critical inquiry, and "the religions of the spirit" had created the sixteenth-century climate for Erasmus and for major reformers, such as Luther, Castellio, and Ochino. Major works on each of these figures would establish Bainton's reputation as the defining biographer of the Protestant Reformation. He popularized the term "left wing reformation," first coined by Harold Bender (a concept now criticized by the polygenesis view of Anabaptism). In a sense, Bainton "discovered" the Anabaptists for the twentieth century. His sketches brought the Reformation to life for generations of Yale students and millions of readers of his thirty-eight books.

A.J. Carlson

Texts

Erasmus of Christendom. New York: Scribner, 1969.
Here I Stand: A Life of Martin Luther. New York: Scribner, 1950.
The Travail of Religious Liberty. Philadelphia, PA: Westminster, 1951.
Women of the Reformation. 3 vols. Minneapolis, MN: Augsburg, 1971-1977.

References

Reformation Studies: Sixteen Essays in Honor of Roland H. Bainton. Ed. Franklin H. Littell. Richmond, VA: John Knox Press, 1962.
Simpler, Steven H. *Roland H. Bainton: An Examination of His Reformation Historiography.* Lewiston, NY: Edwin Mellen Press, 1985.

Bakhrushin, Sergei Vladimirovich (1882–1950)

Russian historian of the early modern period. Bakhrushin studied at Moscow University under V.O. Kliuchevskii and taught there from 1909 throughout the remainder of his life. In 1939 Bakhrushin was made a corresponding member of the All-Union Academy of Sciences and, in 1943, a full member of the Academy of Pedagogical Sciences. After the Revolution of 1905, Bakhrushin became an active member of the Constitutional Democratic Party. Like many historians trained before the October Revolution, he suffered vituperation in the late 1920s and early 1930s and then arrest and a brief incarceration. He is best known for his studies of the colonization of Siberia and Central Asia, but also wrote studies of the formation of an internal market in seventeenth-century Muscovy and a biography of Ivan IV. He was active in discussions about the nature of the Russian historical process. Not only his findings, but his historiographical work, source analysis, and geographical studies remain important.

George Enteen

Texts

Nauchnye trudy [Scholarly Works]. 4 vols. Moscow: Akademiia Nauk, 1952–1959.

References

Dubrovskii, A.M. *S.V. Bakhrushin i ego vremia* [S.V. Bakhrushin and His Time]. Moscow: Russian University of Friendship of Peoples, 1992.

al-Balādhurī, Aḥmad ibn Yaḥyā (d. ca. 892)

Arabic-Islamic historian and genealogist. Little is known of al-Balādhurī's life except that he seems to have spent most of it in Baghdad, where he was a government bureaucrat. His reputation rests principally on two works. The *Futūḥ al-Buldān* [Conquest of the Regions] is a comprehensive history of the Arabic-Islamic conquests of the seventh century, arranged by conquered regions. It is a fundamental source for information on the early conquests and is based in large part on the transmitted traditions of the original conquerors. The *Ansāb al-Ashrāf* [Genealogies of Notables] is a vast history (not yet completely edited) of the Arabic-Islamic elite, arranged according to the families of notables and thus mainly biographical and anecdotal in form. This work is also of fundamental importance regarding the first three centuries of Arab-Islamic history. Al-Balādhurī is, on the whole, an accurate historian who preserved contrasting accounts of events but often expressed his own preferences in terse and authoritative comments, reflecting perhaps the attention to detail and bureaucratic thoroughness of the 'Abbāsid regime that he served.

Tarif Khalidi

Texts

Ansāb al-Ashrāf. Vol. 1. Ed. M. Hamidullah. Cairo: Dar al-Maʿarif, 1959. Vol. 3, ed. A.A. Duri. Wiesbaden: Franz Steiner Verlag, 1978. Vol. 4/1. Ed. I. Abbas. Wiesbaden: Franz Steiner Verlag, 1979.

Futūḥ al-Buldān. Ed. M.J. de Goeje. Leiden: Brill, 1866. Trans. P.K. Hitti and F.C. Murgotten as *The Origins of the Islamic State.* 2 vols. New York: Columbia University, 1916–1924.

References

Duri, A.A. *The Rise of Historical Writing among the Arabs.* Ed. and trans. Lawrence I. Conrad. Princeton, NJ: Princeton University Press, 1983.

Khalidi, Tarif. *Arabic Historical Thought in the Classical Period.* Cambridge, Eng.: Cambridge University Press, 1994.

Rosenthal, Franz. *A History of Muslim Historiography.* Second ed. Leiden: E.J. Brill, 1968.

Balazs, Etienne (1905–1963)

Hungarian-born French sinologist. Balazs's interests in Taoism and Buddhism, acquired during his philosophical studies at the University of Berlin, evolved into his concentration on Chinese history under the direction of Otto Franke. Active in the anti-fascist movement, Balazs fled to southern France. Balazs pioneered the economic history of the Tang period. After World War II, he taught at the Sorbonne but died before he could finish compiling his monumental historiographical work, *A Sung Bibliography.* This project was completed by his colleagues and published in 1978. In it, Balazs analyzed a wide range of primary sources, in particular those concerned with intellectual history, thereby documenting a pivotal dynasty that had been neglected by many Chinese historians. In addition to translating Chinese sources, Balazs studied institutional developments and legal history. Balazs criticized traditional sinologists who focused on antiquity and omitted cultural history. Themes in his several books included the conflict between destructive, authoritarian bureaucracies and struggling creative thinkers. His two-volume *Études sur la société et l'économie de la Chine médiévale* [Studies on the Society and Economy of Medieval China] (1953–1954), in which he examined the Sui Dynasty, earned him accolades as an outstanding scholar of Chinese history.

Elizabeth D. Schafer

Texts

Et al. *Aspects de la Chine: Langue, histoire, religions, philosophie, litterature,arts* [Aspects of China: Language, History, Religions, Philosophy, Literature, and Arts]. Paris, Presses Universitaires de France, 1959.

Chinese Civilization and Bureaucracy: Variations on a Theme. Ed. Arthur F. Wright; trans. Hope M. Wright. New Haven, CT: Yale University Press, 1964.

And Henri Maspero. *Histoire et Institutions de la Chine Ancienne: Des Origines au XIIᵉ Siècle Après J.-C.* [History of Institutions in Ancient China: From the Beginnings to the Twelfth Century A.D.]. Revised by Paul Demieville. Paris: Presses Universitaires de France, 1967.

Trans. *Le Traité economique du Souei-chou.* [The Economic Treatise of the Sui Dynasty]. Leiden: E.J. Brill, 1953.

Trans. *Le Traité juridique du Souei-chou.* [The Judicial Treatise of the Sui Dynasty]. Leiden: E.J. Brill, 1954.

References

Aubin, Francoise, ed. *Études Song: In Memoriam Etienne Balazs* [Song Studies in Memory of Etienne Balazs]. Paris: Mouton, 1970.

Balbín, Bohuslav (1621–1688)

Czech historian, encyclopedist, poet, dramatist, pedagogue, and hagiographer. A Jesuit priest, Balbín studied philosophy and theology in Prague. His teaching appointments allowed him to examine primary sources of Czech history from geographically diverse regions. The publication of his Czech history, *Epitome historica rerum Bohemicarum seu Historiae Boleslaviensis* [Epitome of the History of the Bohemians], was temporarily prevented in 1669, for being nationalistic and anti-monarchistic. As punishment Balbín was sent to Klatovy, where he wrote in 1672–1673 his most famous work in favor of the Czech language, *Dissertatio apologetica pro lingua Slavonica, praecipue Bohemica* [Apology for the Slavonic Language, Especially Bohemian]. In 1676 he was allowed to return to Prague, where he was protected by aristocratic friends; and in the following year, his political fortunes having improved, the publication of his *Epitome* was finally permitted. In 1679, Balbín began to publish his *Miscellanea historica regni Bohemiae* [Historical Miscellany of the Kingdom of Bohemia], the first encyclopedia of Czech national geography and history, dealing with Czech nature, settlements, habits, language, national dress, saints, religious orders and churches, history of religious and secular leaders, artists and scientists, a history of Prague's Charles university, civil and military administration, and genealogy. Balbín is considered to have had greater heuristic than critical talent in his interpretation of sources, but he collected and saved much material. His "patriotic" preservation of Czech culture and history, and his defense of the Czech language, made later, nineteenth-century Czech nationalists view Balbín as a precursor.

Veronika Tuckerová

Texts

Epitome historica rerum Bohemicarum seu Historiae Boleslaviensis. 3 parts in one. Prague: Johann Hampel, 1673–1677.
Historia de ducibus ac regibus Bohemiae [History of the Dukes and Kings of Bohemia]. Old Prague: Archepiscopal Press/S. Clement and J.N. Fitzsky, 1735.

Bale, John (1495–1563)

English historian, polemicist, and cleric. Bale was born into a poor Suffolk family. Educated by the Carmelites at Norwich, he entered their order, continued his studies at Cambridge, and graduated bachelor of divinity in 1529. He developed an early interest in monastic history (particularly Carmelite), which shifted its emphasis as he converted to Protestantism in the early 1530s; at about the same time, he became acquainted with the antiquarian John Leland. Forced into exile during the antiheretical reaction of the last years of King Henry VIII, Bale returned under the Protestant Edward VI and became bishop of Ossory in Ireland. Under the Catholic Mary I, he again fled to the Continent but returned under Elizabeth as a prebendary of Canterbury where he died in 1563. In spite of his Protestant bias, Bale made three contributions to historical writing. First, his polemical ecclesiastical histories, such as *The Actes of Englysh Votaryes* (1546) and his accounts of the fifteenth-century Lollard, Sir John Oldcastle, and the Henrician martyr, Anne Askew, helped to inspire the greatest English martyrologist, John Foxe. Second, his bio-bibliographies of medieval English writers: *Illustrium Maiores Britanniae Scriptorium Summarium* [Summary of the Most Famous Writers of Great Britain] (1548) and *Illustrium Maiories Britanniae Scriptorium Catalogus* [Catalog of the Most Famous Writers of Great Britain] (1557), along with his manuscript *Index Britanniae Scriptorium* [Index or Guide to British Writers]

greatly aided the work of later scholars. Finally, his play *King Johan,* on the resistance to papal "tyranny" of the thirteenth-century English King John, reversed the previously negative image of that monarch while also pioneering the history play; Bale's drama provides the transition between the medieval interludes of his own youth and the fully developed history plays of Elizabeth's reign, most notably Shakespeare's, which eventually would have a potent influence on English perceptions of the past.

Ronald H. Fritze

Texts

Index Britanniae Scriptorium. Ed. R.L. Poole and Mary Bateson. Oxford: Oxford University Press, 1902.
King Johan. Ed. Barry B. Adams. San Marino, CA: Huntington Library, 1969.

References

Fairfield, Leslie P. *John Bale: Mythmaker for the English Reformation.* West Lafayette, IN: Purdue University Press, 1976.
Harris, Jesse W. *John Bale: A Study in the Minor Literature of the Reformation.* Urbana: University of Illinois Press, 1940.

Balinese Historiography

Historical traditions of the island of Bali, Indonesia. The Balinese recognize a wide variety of sources and traditions as historical. Most are concerned with origins and seek to explain present social and ritual relationships. Bali has a rich literary tradition and a wealth of textual historiographical materials, but the Balinese representation of the past also encompasses oral traditions and finds expression in performing and dramatic arts, the ownership of artifacts such as inscriptions, weapons, and *lontar* manuscripts that are historically significant, and ritual obligations centered on temple networks that link communities in the past with the present.

Balinese textual sources deal with three main periods: the ancient history of the island, the origins and history of the unified Balinese realm of Gèlgèl, and the period after 1700 when Bali comprised a number of independent kingdoms. Much of the island's ancient history is couched in mythical terms. Textual representations of the early history of Bali are recorded in works such as the *Usana Bali* and *Usana Jawa.* Other sources for the ancient history of Bali include archaeological remains, inscriptions *(prasasti),* monuments, and oral traditions surrounding specific locales and illustrious ancestors.

The core historical text for the Gèlgèl period is the *Babad Dalem* [Chronicle of Kings]. It was probably written in the early eighteenth century and records the conquest of Bali by Majapahit and the establishment and rule of the Gèlgèl dynasty. Most extant Balinese sources trace the historical origins of Bali back only as far as this period, and both oral and written sources are closely linked to pre-Islamic Javanese traditions, such as the *Deśawarṇana* (or *Nāgarakṛtāgama*) and *Pararaton*. The *Babad Dalem* documents the arrival in Bali of the ancestors of most of the island's ruling and priestly families, and later historical writings draw on *Babad Dalem* traditions for their origins.

Critical events such as wars, important state rituals, natural disasters, and personal concerns are recorded in commemorations *(pangeling-eling)* or short notes attached to copies of literary and religious texts. These commemorations serve as an aid to remembering the past. Royal edicts *(paswara)* and village regulations *(awig-awig)* also form part of the Balinese record of the past.

Historical writing in Bali received added impetus with the arrival of the Dutch in the nineteenth century, with the proliferation of dynastic chronicles *(babad)* and genealogies *(silsilah)*, ideally updated with each new generation, poetical works *(geguritan, kidung)* relating specific events, and particularly metrical poems, called *uug* or *rereg*, detailing the destruction of the ruling houses of Bali in the nineteenth century. The twentieth century has seen an increasing number of official histories of Bali written in the national language, Indonesian.

Helen Creese

See also BABAD; *DEŚAWARṆANA;* INDONESIAN HISTORIOGRAPHY—MODERN; *PARARATON.*

Texts

Babad Buleleng: A Balinese Dynastic Genealogy. Ed. P.J. Worsely. The Hague: Martinus Nijhoff, 1972.

Babad Dalem. Ed. I Wayan Warna et al. Denpasar, Indonesia: Dinas Pendidikan dan Kebudayaan, Propinsi Daerah Tingkat I Bali, 1986.

References

Hinzler, H. "The Usana Bali As a Source of History." In *Papers of the Fourth Indonesian-Dutch History Conference 1983,* vol. 2, ed. Taufik Abdullah. Yogyakarta, Indonesia: Gajah Mada Press, 1986, 124–162.

Vickers, A. "Balinese Texts and Historiography." *History and Theory* 29 (1990): 158–178.

Ban Gu [Pan Ku] (A.D. 32–92)

Chinese poet and historian. Ban Gu, the son of the scholar Ban Biao, originally intended to finish his father's continuation of Sima Qian's *Shiji* [Historical Records], but in the end he compiled the *Hanshu* [History of the Former Han], a complete history of the former Han dynasty from 209 B.C. to A.D. 25. Although early on he was denounced and imprisoned for writing an illegal, private history, when the emperor read a draft he allowed Ban to continue, granting him imperial sponsorship and access to the archives. Later Ban was jailed again because of his association with a rebellious general, and he died in prison. After his death, his sister Ban Zhao completed the *Hanshu.* The organization and early narratives of the *Hanshu* were adapted from the *Shiji,* and Ban's work contains twelve annals (on emperors), eight chronological tables, ten treatises, and seventy biographical chapters (almost all of which cover more than one individual). Ban's most important innovations include a treatise on bibliography (listing all extant texts in the archives) and another on penal law. Ban's viewpoint is thoroughly Confucian, and his *Hanshu* set the pattern for later standard histories.

Grant Hardy

Texts

Courtier and Commoner in Ancient China: Selections from the History of the Former Han by Pan Ku. Trans. Burton Watson. New York: Columbia University Press, 1974.

History of the Former Han Dynasty. Trans. Homer H. Dubs. 3 vols. Baltimore, MD: Waverly Press, 1938–1955, translation of *Hanshu* chapters 1–12, 99 only.

References

Van Der Sprenkel, O.B. *Pan Piao, Pan Ku, and the Han History.* Canberra: Australian University Centre of Oriental Studies, 1964.

Ban Zhao [Pan Chao] (A.D. 49–120)

Early woman historian of China. Ban Zhao was born late in the western Han dynasty in Shaanxi province, becoming part of eastern Han court life when her father Ban Biao was invited to court by Emperor Guang Wu and was commissioned to write the *Hanshu* [History of the Han Dynasty]. Ban Zhao married Cao Shou, and they had two sons and two daughters. Her father died in A.D. 54, before completing *Hanshu,* and the project passed initially to her older brother, Ban Gu [Pan Ku] who died in A.D. 92 (and under whose name it generally appears), leaving its ultimate completion to Ban Zhao who quickly gained the emperor's confidence and access to the Imperial Library. She completed the Eight Tables, genealogical charts spanning two hundred years, which included the emperor's genealogy on his mother's side and the empress's families. She edited the entire manuscript, adding facts, polishing style, checking original sources and documents, and included a treatise on astronomy, which illustrated that she was a mathematician as well as a true scholar. Her work using the "annals-and-biographies" style became the model and prototype for all subsequent standard Chinese dynastic histories. As completed by Ban Zhao, the *Hanshu* provided the basis for the idea that each new dynasty had the duty of continuing the record of preceding dynasties, because it was accepted as a "standard" history of the western (Former) Han. Ban Zhao also taught members of the court in the Imperial Library, and was so respected that Empress Deng styled her *Cao Dagu* (Learned or Gifted One). In addition to the famed *Hanshu*, Ban Zhao also wrote *Nu Chien* [Lessons for Women], which set the standard for womanly conduct and virtues in early China.

Barbara Bennett Peterson

Texts

Ban Gu. *The History of the Former Han Dynasty.* Ed. and trans. Homer H. Dubs with Jen T'ai and P'an Lo-chi. Baltimore, MD: Waverly Press, 1938.

The Chinese Book of Etiquette and Conduct for Women and Girls. Trans. S.L. Baldwin. New York: Eaton and Mains, 1900.

References

Swann, Nancy Lee. *Pan Chao: Foremost Woman Scholar of China.* New York: Russell and Russell, 1968.

Bancroft, George (1800–1891)

American historian and statesman. Born in Worcester, Massachusetts, George Bancroft graduated from Harvard in 1817 and obtained a doctorate from the University of Göttingen in 1820. While in Europe, he met Hegel in Berlin, Alexander von Humboldt in Paris, and Lord Byron in London. Returning to the United States in 1822, he taught for a year at Harvard. From 1823 to 1831 he operated Round Hill School for boys at Northampton. In 1837 President James K. Polk named him secretary of Navy, a post he held until late 1846, when he became the country's minister

to Great Britain, where he stayed until 1849. In 1867 President Andrew Johnson sent him as minister to Berlin, where he was retained until 1874; he died in Washington, D.C. His brilliance notwithstanding, Bancroft had been a poor teacher at both Harvard and Round Hill. His talents lay in writing, and in the early 1830s he began his *History of the United States from the Discovery of the American Continent to the Present.* The first three volumes, which appeared successively in 1834, 1837, and 1840, dealt with colonization. Upon returning home from London in 1849, he devoted himself almost exclusively to writing, and by 1867 he had produced six more volumes covering the revolutionary era. Published in 1874, the tenth and last volume took the story to 1782, falling short of Bancroft's original intention of writing "to the present." An additional two volumes on the *History of the Formation of the Constitution of the United States* were released in 1882. In his writing, Bancroft reflected the spirit of nineteenth-century Jacksonian America. Seeing in the United States the unfolding of democracy, his heroes were men like Roger Williams, Sam Adams, and Andrew Jackson. With a rhetorical flourish he summarized the "villainy" of the foes of freedom, as in: "The history of our colonization is the history of the crimes of Europe."

John W. Storey

Texts

History of the American Revolution. London: Richard Bentley, 1852.

History of the Colonization of the United States. 3 vols. Boston: Little, Brown, 1838–1857.

History of the Formation of the Constitution of the United States. 2 vols. New York: D. Appleton, 1882.

References

Nye, Russel B. *George Bancroft: Brahmin Rebel.* New York: Knopf, 1944.

Barbour, John, Archdeacon of Aberdeen (d. 1395)

Scottish historical poet. The author of a genealogy of the Stuart kings of Scotland (now lost), Barbour is best known for his heroic poem *The Bruce,* written between 1375 and 1377. Composed in the vernacular Scots, the work describes the struggle by the Scottish king, Robert I, to win independence for his kingdom from Edward I of England. It is regarded by modern critics as one of the earliest representations of "nationalist" literature in western Europe, distinct from and superior to many contemporary chronicles, which aim chiefly to extol the chivalric values of the period. Barbour based his account in large part on oral sources, some of these the stories of eyewitnesses, and is noted in particular for the accuracy of his detail and the vividness of his descriptions of battles and campaigns. Later medieval chroniclers, including Blind Harry, Fordun, and Wyntoun drew extensively on its contents. *The Bruce* remains an authoritative source for the history of the Scottish war of independence.

Cynthia J. Neville

Texts
Barbour's Bruce: A Fredome Is a Noble Thing! Ed. Matthew P. McDiarmid and James A.C. Stevenson. 3 vols. Edinburgh: Scottish Text Society, 1980–1985.

References
Ebin, Lois A. "John Barbour's Bruce: Poetry, History, and Propaganda." *Studies in Scottish Literature* 9 (1972): 218–242.

Barkan, Ömer Lütfi (ca. 1903–1979)
Turkish economic historian. Born in Edirne, Turkey, Barkan was trained at the University of Istanbul and the University of Strasbourg. After earning his doctorate from the University of Istanbul in 1939, he taught Ottoman economic history in Istanbul and Strasbourg, as well as in a number of European and American universities. Barkan's extensive publications, based on documentary evidence from the Ottoman archives such as tax and population registers, provided new perspectives on economic, material, and social developments in the Ottoman empire. He published pioneering works on subjects such as the Ottoman land tenure system and administrative law, the colonization of conquered land in the fifteenth and sixteenth centuries, and the construction of the Sulaymaniye mosque in Istanbul. He also published numerous documents, including law codes from different provinces, budgets, and demographic information.

Corinne Blake

Texts
"The Price Revolution of the 16th Century: A Turning Point in the Economic History of the Middle East." *International Journal of Middle Eastern Studies* 6 (1975): 3–28.
"Research on the Ottoman Fiscal Surveys." In *Studies in the Middle East,* ed. Michael Cook. London: School of Oriental and African Studies, 1970.
XV. ve XVI. Asirlarda Osmanli Imparatorlugunda Zirai Ekonominin Hukuki ve Mali Esaslari: Kanunlar [The Legal and Financial Bases of Agricultural Economics in the Ottoman Empire in the Fifteenth and Sixteenth Centuries: Laws]. Istanbul: Edebiyat Fakültesi Türkiyat Enstitüsü Ayinlarindan, 1943.

References
Mantran, Robert, ed. *Mémorial Ömer Lutfi Barkan.* Paris: Librairie d'Amérique et d'Orient Adrien Maisonneuve, 1980.

Barnes, Harry Elmer (1889–1968)
Twentieth-century American historian and sociologist. Barnes was the "odd man out" of the historical profession in his generation. Immensely learned and energetic, Barnes published numerous works on intellectual and cultural history, political theory, criminology, diplomacy, and historiography. He was an early and enthusiastic partisan of the New History, believing that history at its best was a vehicle for social reform. Barnes is best remembered for his polemical works on American diplomacy. His name, in fact, is synonymous with revisionism. Although a full-throated supporter of World War I, by the early 1920s Barnes was writing (and promoting) books critical of that conflict. When another world war loomed, Barnes could only see World War I *redivivus* and consequently sponsored a new round of revisionist studies. Most of these had a decidedly right-wing cast, even though Barnes himself was a man of the Left. (Barnes's strictures against the early cold war would in fact anticipate some of the themes of 1960s New Left revisionists.) And the "devil theory of war" advanced in these works did not fit well with Barnes's own philosophical determinism. In part because of his *ad hominem* style and in part because of the wide support for World War II within the intellectual community, Barnes's star lost its luster; his postwar support of Holocaust revisionists further damaged his reputation.

Barry Riccio

Texts
The Genesis of the World War: An Introduction to the Problem of War Guilt. New York: Alfred A. Knopf, 1929.
A History of Historical Writing. Second ed. New York: Dover Publications, 1962.
An Intellectual and Cultural History of the Western World. 3 vols. New York: Dover Publications, 1965.

The New History and the Social Studies. New York: Century, 1925.

References

Cohen, Warren I. *The American Revisionists.* Chicago: University of Chicago Press, 1967.

Goddard, Arthur, ed. *Harry Elmer Barnes, Learned Crusader: The New History in Action.* Colorado Springs, CO: Ralph Myles Press, 1968.

Novick, Peter. *That Noble Dream: The "Objectivity Question" and the American Historical Profession.* Cambridge, Eng.: Cambridge University Press, 1988.

Turnbaugh, Roy C. "Harry Elmer Barnes: The Quest for Truth and Justice." Ph.D. dissertation, University of Illinois at Urbana–Champaign, 1977.

Baron, Hans (1900–1988)

German emigré historian of the Renaissance. One of the most influential of the scholars to emigrate to the United States in the 1930s, Baron is best known for his thesis concerning the role of Florentine civic humanism in the history of republican thought. Baron was trained at the University of Leipzig by Ernst Troeltsch, Walter Goetz, and Friedrich Meinecke. After initial studies on northern humanism and the Reformation, he took up research on the Italian Renaissance. What Baron called "civic humanism" (from the German *Bürgerhumanismus*) consisted of a synthesis of the civic tradition of the Italian communes with an awakened interest in the political and moral philosophy and the traditions of historical writing of the republics of classical antiquity. In his most famous work, *The Crisis of the Early Italian Renaissance,* Baron argued that Florentine resistance to the imperialist designs of Giangaleazzo Visconti of Milan in the years 1400 to 1402 provided the specific circumstances for the transformation of literary humanism into a vehicle for Florentine civic ideology. Baron's civic humanists included Leonardo Bruni, Giannozzo Manetti, and Matteo Palmieri. Elaboration of his theory led Baron to further significant readings of the works of Petrarch, Coluccio Salutati, and Niccolo Machiavelli. Baron's papers were left to Duke University.

William J. Connell

Texts

The Crisis of the Early Italian Renaissance: Civic Humanism and Republican Liberty in an Age of Classicism and Tyranny. 2 vols. Princeton, NJ: Princeton University Press, 1955. Revised one-volume edition, Princeton, NJ: Princeton University Press, 1966.

In Search of Florentine Civic Humanism: Essays on the Transition from Medieval to Modern Thought. 2 vols. Princeton, NJ: Princeton University Press, 1988.

References

Fubini, Riccardo. "Renaissance Historian: The Career of Hans Baron." *Journal of Modern History* 64 (1992): 541–574.

Hankins, James. "The 'Baron Thesis' after Forty Years." *Journal of the History of Ideas* 56 (1995): 309–338.

Molho, Anthony, and John Tedeschi, eds. *Renaissance Studies in Honor of Hans Baron.* DeKalb: Northern Illinois University Press, 1971, lxxiii–lxxxvii (bibliography of the writings of Hans Baron.)

Baron, Salo Wittmayer (1895–1989)

Jewish historian. Born in Galicia, Baron was educated at the University of Vienna, where he earned doctorates in philosophy, political science, and law. Emigrating to the United States in 1926, he soon joined the faculty of Columbia University, where he held the first chair in Jewish history to be established at an American university. His monumental study, *A Social and Religious History of the Jews,* was the most comprehensive contemporary study of Jewish history. Baron rejected what he called "the lachrymose conception of Jewish history," once a common feature of Jewish historiography (for instance, the works of Heinrich Graetz), which emphasized Jewish suffering rather than Jewish survival and creativity. Baron placed Jewish history in the broader context of world history, focusing on the cross-fertilization between Jewish society and its non-Jewish neighbors. Master of a wide array of disciplines and languages, he authored the first significant study, in English, of Russian Jewry, *The Russian Jew under Tsars and Soviets.* His vast bibliography also included several important edited works in American Jewish history, notably *The Jews of the United States, 1790–1940: A Documentary History* and *Steeled by Adversity.* Baron played a seminal role in organizations devoted to Jewish scholarship, serving as president of the American Academy of Jewish Research, the Conference on Jewish Social Studies, and the American Jewish Historical Society.

Rafael Medoff

Texts

And Joseph L. Blau, eds. *The Jews of the United States, 1790–1940: A Documentary History.* 3 vols. New York: Columbia University Press, 1963.

Modern Nationalism and Religion. New York: Harper, 1947.

The Russian Jew under Tsars and Soviets. Second ed. New York: Macmillan, 1976.

A Social and Religious History of the Jews. 18 vols. New York: Columbia University Press, 1952–1983.

Steeled by Adversity: Essays and Addresses on American Jewish Life. Ed. Jeannette M. Baron. Philadelphia, PA: Jewish Publication Society of America, 1971.

References

Hertzberg, Arthur, and Leon Feldman, eds. *History and Jewish Historians: Essays and Addresses.* Philadelphia, PA: Jewish Publication Society of America, 1964.

Yerushalmi, Yosef H. *Zakhor: Jewish History and Jewish Memory.* Seattle: University of Washington Press, 1982.

Baronio, Cesare [Caesar Baronius] (1538–1607)

Italian ecclesiastical historian during the Counter Reformation. A cardinal, Vatican librarian, and head of the Oratorian Order, Baronio was first introduced to historical studies by Guglielmo Sirleto. His interest in the history of the Catholic Church and the political activities of the papacy was first manifested in his 1583 revision and correction of the *Martyrologium romanorum* [Roman Martyrologies]. He is best known for his *Annales Ecclesiastici* [Ecclesiastical Annals], the massive twelve-volume response to the *Magdeburg Centuries*. The Protestant authors of the *Centuries* had chronicled the growth of antiapostolic innovations throughout the history of the institutional church. Baronio, with the help of the entire Roman scholarly community, endeavored to rebut these claims with a study based firmly on the best antiquarian, historical, philological, and documentary evidence. His purpose was to demonstrate that all the central doctrines that the Roman church held as orthodox in the sixteenth century had been so regarded since the first century. Methodologically, Baronio distinguished between the composition of histories, which described contemporaneous events, and the writing of annals, which related past events—hence his adoption of the latter title

for his work. His insistence on truth and accuracy, though not always infallible, led him to question, or even ignore, some cherished apocrypha, and, despite the criticism of Protestant scholars such as Isaac Casaubon, the work was grudgingly admired for its erudition even by opponents of Catholicism. The *Annales* proved immensely successful: by 1756 the book had reached its twenty-first edition and had been emended, expanded, abridged, and translated into French, Italian, Polish, and German.

Krista Kesselring

Texts

Annales Ecclesiastici. Rome: Ex Typographia Vaticana, 1588–1607.

References

Cochrane, Eric. "Caesar Baronius and the Counter-reformation." *Catholic Historical Review* 67 (1980): 53–58.

———. *Historians and Historiography in the Italian Renaissance.* Chicago: University of Chicago Press, 1981.

Jedin, Hubert. *Kardinal Caesar Baronius: der Anfang der katholischen Kirchengeschichtsschreibung im 16. Jahrhundert* [Cardinal Caesar Baronius: The Beginnings of Catholic Ecclesiastical Historiography in the Sixteenth Century]. Münster: Aschendorff, 1978.

Pullapilly, Cyriac K. *Caesar Baronius, Counter-Reformation Historian.* Notre Dame, IN: University of Notre Dame Press, 1975.

Barraclough, Geoffrey (1908–1984)

English medieval and modern historian. Barraclough was born in Yorkshire. After receiving his degree at Oriel College, Oxford, his postgraduate studies led him to Rome and expertise in the thirteenth-century papacy. He taught first at Merton College, Oxford, and then at St. John's College, Cambridge, serving in the Royal Air Force during World War II. After 1945 he became professor of medieval history at the University of Liverpool and, in 1956, succeeded Arnold Toynbee as Stevenson Research Professor at the Royal Institute of International Affairs. Later appointments took him to the University of California, Brandeis University, and, finally, back to Oxford as Chichele Professor (1970–1974); his last major post was the senior editorship of the *Times Atlas of the World.* Barraclough's earliest interest, in the thirteenth century, resulted in two still-cited books, *Public Notaries and the Papal Curia* (1934) and *Papal*

Provisions (1935). Two further books, *The Medieval Papacy* (1968) and *The Origins of Modern Germany* (1946), provide excellent introductions to their respective subjects. The latter, widely regarded as Barraclough's finest work, is especially good on post-Carolingian Germany. After the war he developed an interest in English history and wrote several works on medieval Cheshire. Then, however, there began a major shift in his interest from medieval to contemporary history, an action that puzzled numbers of professional colleagues and to which some reacted critically. In 1955 he published *History in a Changing World* (1955), a year before he succeeded Toynbee in the Stevenson chair. After leaving that post in 1962 he produced several important works, the best known of which was his thought-provoking *Introduction to Contemporary History* (1964).

Kerry E. Spiers

Texts

History in a Changing World. Oxford: Blackwell, 1955.
Introduction to Contemporary History. London: C.A. Watts, 1964.
The Medieval Papacy. New York: Harcourt, Brace, 1972.
The Origins of Modern Germany. New York: Paragon, 1979.
Papal Provisions. Oxford: Blackwell, 1935.
Public Notaries and the Papal Curia. London: Macmillan, 1934.

References

Dewar, Kenneth C. "Geoffrey Barraclough: From Historicism to Historical Science." *Historian* 56 (1994): 449–464.

Barros, João de (ca. 1496–1570)

Portuguese historian, grammarian, philosopher, and pedagogue. Born in Viseu, Barros began serving in the Portuguese court while still young, beginning his career as treasurer of the *Casa da Índia,* where he became *Feitor* [Administrator] (1533–1567). Erudition and versatility mark the vast range of known works making him one of the most famous humanist figures of the Portuguese Renaissance. He gained repute in several fields including grammar: *Gramática da Lingua Portuguesa* [Grammar of the Portuguese Language] (1540). Nevertheless, lasting fame came with *Ásia,* commonly called *Décadas da Ásia* (1552–1553), a wide-ranging synthesis of the history, geography, ethnography, and socioeconomics of the Portuguese

in the Orient with information on Asian societies, a work that made him the outstanding ideologue of sixteenth-century Portuguese expansion.

Jorge M. dos Santos Alves

Texts

Ásia: Dos feitos que os Portugueses fizeram no descobrimento e conquista dos Mares e Terras do Oriente [Asia: On Deeds Done by the Portuguese in the Discovery and Conquest of the Seas and Lands of Asia]. Ed. Hernâni Cidade. Sixth ed. Lisbon: Agência Geral das Colonias, 1945–1946.

References

Andrade, A. Banha de. *João de Barros: Historiador do Pensamento Humanista Português de Quinhentos* [João de Barros: Historian of Portuguese Humanist Thought of the Sixteenth Century]. Lisbon: Academia Portuguesa da História, 1980.
Boxer, C.R. *João de Barros: Portuguese Humanist and Historian of Asia.* New Delhi: Concept Publishing Company, 1981.

Barruel, Augustin (1741–1820)

French priest, historian, and Counter-Revolutionary theorist. Born in Villeneuve-de-Berg into a family of Languedoc nobility, Barruel entered the Society of Jesus. Following the Jesuits' expulsion from France, he traveled abroad before returning to edit the *Journal ecclésiastique* and to denounce the philosophies as enemies of religion. Barruel opposed the revolution from the beginning, writing tracts against the Civil Constitution of the Clergy and the Constitution of 1791. He fled to England in 1792, where he wrote his principal work, but returned to give Bonaparte qualified support. While Barruel argued initially that the revolution represented divine punishment, his *Mémoires pour servir à l'histoire du jacobinisme* (1798) assert that it was the outcome of a vast conspiracy by philosophies and freemasonry. He separates this into three interwoven plots against Christianity, monarchy, and the social order involving leading figures of the eighteenth century. Despite absurd claims and weak scholarship, Barruel's conspiracy thesis had tremendous influence on those hostile to the revolution.

William S. Cormack

Texts

The History of the Clergy during the French Revolution. Dublin: P. Wogan et al., 1794.

Mémoires pour servir à l'histoire du jacobinisme. 2 vols. Vouillé, France: Diffusion de la Pensée Française, 1974.

References

Godechot, Jacques. *The Counter-Revolution: Doctrine and Action, 1789–1804.* Trans. Salvator Attanasio. Princeton, NJ: Princeton University Press, 1981.

Basadre, Jorge (1903–1980)

Peru's greatest twentieth-century historian, Basadre was also a teacher and government official. He served twice as the director of the Biblioteca Nacional and as minister of public education. His major historiographical work, *Historia de la República del Perú* [History of the Republic of Peru], was published originally in 1939 and is now available in its seventh revised edition (1983) in eleven volumes. This general history, used as the basic reference work for all students of Peruvian history, traces the fortunes of republican Peru from 1822 until 1933. Another major work is the accompanying three-volume collection of bibliographical sources published in 1971 entitled *Introducción a las bases documentales para la historia de la República del Perú con algunas reflexiones* [Introduction to the Sources for the History of the Republic of Peru, with Some Reflections]. Basadre, alone among the Peruvian historians of his generation (who generally preferred Incaic and colonial history), chose to write about the modern period of Peruvian history. His *Historia* was unusual as it considered economic, social, and cultural questions as well as political ones. Basadre projected an optimistic overview of Peruvian history, emphasizing education as the means for improving the life of the majority of Peruvians.

George L. Vásquez

Texts

Historia de la República del Perú. 17 vols. Lima: Editorial Universitaria, 1968–1970.
Introducción a las bases documentales para la historia de la República del Perú con algunas reflexiones. 3 vols. Lima: Ediciones P.L. Villanueva, 1971.

References

Davies, Thomas M., Jr. "Jorge Basadre (1903–1980)." *Hispanic American Historical Review* 61 (1981): 84–86.
Pacheco Velez, César. "Jorge Basadre." *Revista de historia de América* 92 (1982): 195–213.

Basham, Arthur Llewellyn (1914–1986)

English-born historian of India. Basham was born in Loughton (Essex) into a family that had some Indian associations. His first publication, however, in 1935, was a collection of poems entitled *Proem,* followed by a novel, *The Golden Furrow* (1939). His exploration of literature led to an interest in Sanskrit, which he studied for his B.A. Honours degree (1941), having won a scholarship to the School of Oriental and African Studies (SOAS), University of London. He spent the period of World War II as a conscientious objector. His Ph.D. thesis, published in 1951 as *History and Doctrine of the Ājīvikas,* concerned a religious sect contemporary with the early Buddhists and Jainas, but which did not survive. Having been appointed lecturer in the ancient history of south Asia at SOAS in 1948, he was promoted in 1957 to the professorship. He took up a chair at the Australian National University in 1965, from which he retired in 1979.

In 1954 Basham published *The Wonder That Was India,* as part of a series on the ancient world. Departing from earlier colonial studies and providing a more sensitive and integrated understanding of early Indian society and culture, it rapidly became the standard text for students and for the general reader interested in the pre-Islamic history of India. It remains an exceptional work of synthesis covering every aspect of the civilization of ancient south Asia. A collection of papers was published as *Studies in Indian History and Culture* (1964) and his Heras Memorial Lectures as *Aspects of Ancient Indian Culture* (1966). Basham edited *Papers on the Date of Kaniṣka* (1968), *The Civilisations of Monsoon Asia* (1974), and *A Cultural History of India* (1975). His transcripts for a series of lectures sponsored by the American Council of Learned Societies were published posthumously as *Origin and Development of Classical Hinduism.* In his understanding of Indian history, Basham drew on his extensive scholarship and his empathy for an ancient culture. Many of his insights, placed unostentatiously in the text, converted the text into a thought-provoking essay. His liberalism was demonstrated in his willingness to argue the merits of even those interpretations of Indian history to which he did not subscribe. Moving away from the domination of dynastic history and replacing it with a preference for cultural and religious history, he anticipated in the process some of the new dimensions of the postcolonial study of ancient Indian history.

Romila Thapar

Texts

Aspects of Ancient Indian Culture. New York: Asia Publishing House, 1966.

Ed. *A Cultural History of India.* Oxford: Clarendon Press, 1975.

History and Doctrine of the Ājīvikas: A Vanished Indian Religion. London: Luzac, 1951.

The Origins and Development of Classical Hinduism. Ed. Kenneth G. Zysk. Boston: Beacon Press, 1989.

Ed. *Papers on the Date of Kaniṣka.* Oriental monograph series, no. 4. Canberra: Australian National University Centre of Oriental Studies, 1968.

Studies in Indian History and Culture. Calcutta: Sambodhi Publications, 1964.

The Wonder That Was India. Third ed. London: Sidgwick & Jackson, 1967.

Basin, Thomas (1412–1490)

French bishop and historian. Basin was one of eight sons of a prosperous grocer of Caudebec in Normandy. He received a master of arts degree from the University of Paris and the licentiate in canon law from Louvain. Through the patronage of Cardinal Branda Castiglioni's family, Basin became professor of canon law at the University of Caen and bishop of Lisieux in 1447. Because of Louis XI's enmity, he resigned the post in 1474 and wrote about the problems of the Anglo-French wars in his *History of Charles VII* and *History of Louis XI*. He died in Utrecht. His writings were highly personal accounts of his own time, based on experiences, memories, reports of others, and rumors. In conception, more than in Latin style, they were close to the new civic historiography of the Italian humanists that Basin knew and admired. His political focus clearly rejected the French chronicler and courtier traditions that emphasized descriptive details and narratives of deeds. Basin's histories contributed to Louis XI's enduring historical image as a tyrant.

Lawrence M. Bryant

Texts

Histoire de Charles VII. Ed. and trans. C. Samaran. 2 vols. Paris: Societé d'edition "Les Belles Lettres," 1933–1944.

Histoire de Louis XI. Ed. and trans. C. Samaran. 3 vols. Paris: Societé d'edition "Les Belles Lettres," 1963–1972.

References

Archambault, Paul. *Seven French Chroniclers.* Syracuse, NY: Syracuse University Press, 1974.

Guenée, Bernard. *Between Church and State: The Lives of Four French Prelates in the Late Middle Ages.* Trans. Arthur Goldhammer. Chicago and London: University of Chicago Press, 1991.

Basque Historiography

Historical writing by and about the Basque people. A people without a state, the Basques live in what was known in the nineteenth century as the "Basque provinces" (Vizcaya [Biscay], Guipúzcoa, and Alava) and in the kingdom of Navarre, all of which were integrated into the crown of Castile by the early sixteenth century, even though they retained their right to self-government *(Fueros)* until the nineteenth century; they also occupied the western Pyrenees within French Aquitaine. Since the late nineteenth century onward a nationalist movement has gained much ground in those parts of the Basque territories that came under Spanish rule and has been calling for a state *(Euskadi)* encompassing the entire Basque people; it has achieved from the Spanish state, though not the French, a considerable degree of self-government.

The later Middle Ages saw the writing of the first chronicles of the kingdom in Navarre by Garci López de Roncesvalles (d. ca. 1438), the Prince of Viana, and, in Vizcaya, the universal chronicle of Lope García de Salazar (1399–1476). These show no awareness of a Basque national identity. In the sixteenth century, however, a series of historical myths arose in the provinces, which were upheld until the nineteenth century. The fundamental aim of these was to reinforce the belief in the historical sovereignty of the provinces and thereby defend their *Fueros*. According to these myths, which are comparable to national myths debated by historians elsewhere in Europe during the sixteenth century, the "Cantabrians," led by Tubal, a grandson of Noah, had been the first inhabitants of Spain; they had never been conquered by any other people and had been integrated into the crown of Castile only by agreement. Among the main supporters of these ideas were Andrés de Poza (1537–1595), Esteban de Garibay (1533–1599) Gabriel de Henao (1612–1704), and Manuel de Larramendi (1690–1766). Navarrese national historiography, meanwhile, was consolidated during these centuries by the kingdom's official chroniclers, José de Moret (1615–1687), Francisco de Aleson (1635–1715), and Pablo Miguel de Elizondo (1670–1728), while the Béarnais historian Arnaud d'Oihenart (1592–1667) published the first general history of the Basques (1638). It would not be until the beginning of the nineteenth century, in 1818, that the Biscayan Juan Antonio de Zamácola would publish the second one.

Between 1770 and 1880, the attacks launched by the Spanish state on the *Fueros* exacerbated the polemical and political character of Basque historiography and favored the survival of the old myths, even though the interpretation of Basque history as a means of defending the *Fueros* was conducted alike by traditionalists, such as Pedro Novia de Salcedo (1790–1865), the French viscount Charles of Belsunce, and Arístides de Artiñano (1840–1911), and liberals, such as Pablo de Gorosábel (1803–1868), Fidel de Sagarmínaga (1830–1894), and José Yanguas y Miranda (1782–1863). At the same time, a romanticism shared by representatives of a wide variety of political opinions created new myths of a proto-nationalist nature. After the abolition of the *Fueros* and their replacement by decentralized administrative regimes both in Navarre (1839–1841) and in the provinces (1876–1878), the disruption of traditional Basque society by a rapid process of modernization, initiated in Vizcaya, fostered the emergence of the nationalist movement whose founder, Sabino Arana (1865–1903), built his ideas on an interpretation of Basque history that owed much to myth, both old and new. A different formulation of Basque nationalism, based on Navarrese history, was developed by Arturo Campión (1854–1937). From that time until the present, Basque historical writing has reflected a tension between two nationalisms, the Basque on the one hand, and the Spanish or French on the other.

Since 1960, an academic historiography has grown up which can find antecedents as far back as the late nineteenth century and which is largely in opposition to the historical theses of Basque nationalism. This period has, however, also seen the appearance of Basque historiography in the Basque language, *euskera,* for which the only important precedent is the nineteenth-century writer Juan Ignacio de Iztueta (1767–1845).

Ignacio Olábarri

See also SPANISH HISTORIOGRAPHY.

Texts

Crónica de Garci López de Roncesvalles. Ed. C. Orcástegui. Pamplona, Spain: Ediciones Universidad de Navarra, 1977.
García de Salazar, Lope. *Las Bienandanzas e Fortunas* . . [.The Successes and Fortunes]. Ed. A. Rodríguez-Herrero. 4 vols. Bilbao, Spain: Diputación de Vizcaya, 1967.
Henao, Gabriel de. *Averiguaciones de las antigüedades de Cantabria* [Researches into the Antiquities of Cantabria]. Salamanca, Spain: García, 1689.
Moret, José de. *Anales del Reino de Navarra* [Annals of the Kingdom of Navarre]. Ed. S. Herreros. 4 vols. (to date). Pamplona, Spain: Government of Navarre, 1987–.
Oihenart, Arnaud d'. *Notitia utriusque Vasconiae tum Ibericae tum Aquitanicae* [Description of Iberian and Aquitainian Vasconia]. Paris: Cramoissy, 1638.

References

Goyhenetche, Jean. *Les Basques et leur histoire* [The Basques and Their History]. Bayonne, France: Elkar, 1993.
Sánchez-Prieto, Juan María. *El imaginario vasco* [The Imaginary Basque]. Barcelona: EIUNSA, 1993.

Bateson, Mary (1865–1906)

English medieval historian. A representative of the first wave of Englishwomen to have a university career, virtually her whole career was spent at Cambridge, where she became a fellow of Newnham College. Her reputation rests chiefly on studies of the English medieval borough; in these studies, her mentor, patron, and friend was F.W. Maitland, who influenced in particular the two volumes in which Bateson examined borough customs as a branch of English law. The range of her production was unusually wide: editions of the poems of a minor fifteenth century bureaucrat; documents reflecting the Elizabethan church settlement; and letters illuminating political alignments in George III's reign. With R.L. Poole, Bateson revised a standard guide to medieval authors. She published a catalog of the library of a late-medieval English monastery. At the time of her unexpectedly early death, she had been appointed an editor of the *Cambridge Medieval History,* had contributed a chapter on early French settlements in America to the *Cambridge Modern History,* and had written a general text on feudal England. This last work is unusual in emphasizing social and intellectual history within a series of volumes usually directed to political history. Her many articles mirror her great range.

C.M.D. Crowder

Texts

Borough Customs. 2 vols. Publications of the Selden Society, 18, 21. London: B. Quaritch, 1904–1906.

The Cambridge Gild Records. Cambridge, Eng.: Cambridge Antiquarian Society, 1903.

The Charters of the Borough of Cambridge. Cambridge, Eng.: Cambridge University Press, 1901.

Records of the Borough of Leicester. 3 vols. London: C.J. Clay, 1899–1905.

Bayhaḳī, Abu'l-Faḍl Muḥammad (995–1077)

Secretary and historian at the Ghaznavid (Persian) court. Bayhaḳī was born in the Sabzavar region of eastern Iran and after studying in Nishapur entered the service of Maḥmūd of Ghazna. He became head of the secretariat around 1050, but shortly afterwards fell from favor and was imprisoned; he appears to have retired after his release in 1052 and dedicated himself to writing his great history of the Ghaznavid dynasty. The *Ta'rīḵ-i Bayhaḳī* [History of Bayhaḳī] comprised thirty volumes, of which only the bulk of volumes 5 through 10 survive, covering the years 1030–1041, of the reign of Sultan Mas'ūd; these were written in 1059. A few other parts are preserved in quotations by later authors. The work is not only a masterpiece of early Persian prose literature, but also a penetrating, balanced, scrupulous, and multifaceted history of his times.

Charles Melville

Texts

Ta'rīḵ-i Mas'ūdī (Bayhaḳī). Ed. 'A.-A. Fayyaz. Mashhad, Iran: Mashhad University Press 1971.

References

Humphries, R. Stephen. *Islamic History: A Framework for Enquiry.* London: I.B. Tauris, 1991, chap. 5.

Savory, R.M. "Abu'l-Fazl Bayhaqi As an Historiographer." In *Yad-nama-yi Abu'l-Faḍl Bayhaḳī* [Commemoration Volume on Abu'l-Fazl Bayhaqi], ed. Jalal Matini. Mashhad, Iran: 1971, 84–128.

Waldman, Marilyn Robinson. *Toward a Theory of Historical Narrative: A Case Study in Perso-Islamicate Historiography.* Columbus: Ohio State University Press, 1980.

Bayle, Pierre (1647–1706)

French philosopher. Born in Carlat (in southern France), Bayle, a Huguenot, left the Protestant Academy of Sedan at its closure in 1681 to accept a professorship in Rotterdam, which he lost for political reasons in 1693. Bayle's early works reveal him as an embarrassing advocate of tolerance and a skeptic against all kinds of dogma, traditional authority, and superstition. His antiquarian interest, profound erudition, and subversive satire resulted in the biographical *Dictionnaire historique et critique* [Historical and Critical Dictionary] (1695–1697, revised and extended until Bayle's death). Every entry consists of a short account of life and deeds, followed by Bayle's often extensive critical discussion of controversial sources and interpretations. The *Dictionnaire* was reprinted ten times until 1760 and translated into different languages. Bayle's critical rationalism inspired the *Encyclopédie* as well as the historical thinking of Voltaire, Hume, and Gibbon.

Thomas Maissen

Texts

The Dictionary Historical and Critical. New York, London: Garland, 1984. Facsimile of the London: Knapton, 1734, edition.

Historical and Critical Dictionary: Selections. Trans. Richard H. Popkin. Indianapolis, New York, Kansas City: Macmillan, 1965.

References

Whelan, Ruth. *The Anatomy of Superstition: A Study of the Historical Theory and Practice of Pierre Bayle.* Oxford: Voltaire Foundation, 1989.

Beard, Charles Austin (1874–1948)

American historian, political scientist, and activist. Raised in rural Indiana, the son of a wealthy landowning family of Quaker ancestry, Beard graduated from DePauw University (1898) and then spent several years in England, studying at Oxford University, participating in worker-education programs, and helping to found what became Ruskin College, Oxford. In England, he and his wife, Mary Ritter Beard, gained a profound understanding of the changes wrought by industrialization and began a lifelong career emphasizing both critical scholarship and active participation in efforts at social reform. After completing his doctorate (1904) in political science at Columbia University, Beard taught there until he resigned in 1917, as a protest against the university's dismissal of faculty who had criticized the U.S. involvement in World War I. For the rest of his life, although he published copiously and served as president of both the American Political Science Association (1926) and the American Historical Association (1933), he remained an independent scholar, reformer, and sometime international consultant, unaffiliated with any university on a regular basis.

At Columbia, Beard and James Harvey Robinson encouraged a New History, which, in contrast to the Rankean goal of re-creating the past as it actually had been, sought to connect history more closely with current events. Between 1904 and 1917, Beard published his most famous book, *An Economic Interpretation of the Constitution of the United States* (1913), and its companion, *Economic Origins of Jeffersonian Democracy* (1915), both of which attempted to demonstrate that practical motives, rather than abstract theories of government, weighed most heavily in the constitutional politics of the founding fathers. Activists of his own time, Beard hoped, would learn from studying deeds of the founders that a Constitution designed by wealthy men of the eighteenth century needed to be adjusted to the demands of a restless would-be democracy of the twentieth. In 1927, Charles and Mary Beard published the best-known of numerous collaborative works, *The Rise of American Civilization,* written for a broad public as an attempt to create a common history for a society of diverse peoples. With others, notably Carl Becker, Beard came to doubt that history could ever be objective. Thus, he titled one of his most controversial discussions of this proposition "Written History As an Act of Faith" (1933). During the 1930s, in *The Open Door at Home* (1934), *The Idea of National Interest* (1934), and *Giddy Minds and Foreign Quarrels: An Estimate of American Foreign Policy* (1939) Beard directed attention to the need for national planning and to the connections between foreign and domestic policy. Although strongly antifascist, Beard questioned the need for American intervention in World War II, particularly President Franklin Roosevelt's refusal to educate the public directly on the need for intervention. His last books, *American Foreign Policy in the Making, 1932–1940* (1946) and *President Roosevelt and the Coming of War, 1941: A Study in Appearances and Realities* (1948), while vigorously attacked by supporters of presidential power during the 1950s, anticipated criticism of the "imperial Presidency" that emerged in the 1960s.

Ellen Nore

Texts

American Foreign Policy in the Making, 1932–1940. New York: Macmillan, 1946.

An Economic Interpretation of the Constitution of the United States. New York: Macmillan, 1913.

Economic Origins of Jeffersonian Democracy. New York: Macmillan, 1915.

Giddy Minds and Foreign Quarrels. New York: Macmillan, 1939.

The Idea of National Interest: An Analytical Study of American Foreign Policy. New York: Macmillan, 1934.

The Open Door at Home: A Trial Philosophy of National Interest. New York: Macmillan, 1934.

President Roosevelt and the Coming of War, 1941. New York: Macmillan, 1948.

The Rise of American Civilization. 2 vols. New York: Macmillan, 1927.

"Written History As an Act of Faith." *American Historical Review* 39 (1934): 219–231.

References

Nore, Ellen. *Charles A. Beard: An Intellectual Biography.* Carbondale: Southern Illinois University Press, 1983.

Novick, Peter. *That Noble Dream: The "Objectivity Question" and the American Historical Profession.* Cambridge, Eng., and New York: Cambridge University Press, 1988.

Beard, Mary Ritter (1876–1958)

Historian of the United States and of women. Born in Indianapolis, Mary Ritter graduated from DePauw University in 1897 and married her lifelong partner, Charles A. Beard, in 1900. With her husband, she lived in England for two years, developing a strong interest in progressive social reform, and later traveled extensively in Europe and the Far East. After a brief period of study at Columbia University (1902), she held no academic post, but participated, before 1914, in the Women's Trade Union League and edited *The Woman Voter,* a suffragist newspaper. During the interwar years, she lobbied unsuccessfully for a World Center for Women's Archives. Beard focused early in her career on writing history that included both men and women. Her *Women's Work in Municipalities* (1915) surveyed women's part in urban reform. Beginning in the 1920s, the Beards coauthored a number of books, most notably *The Rise of American Civilization* (1927) and its sequels, all of which stressed cultural themes and women's activities along with men's. Always emphasizing women's public rather than purely domestic roles, Mary Beard's *On Understanding Women* (1931) presented a woman-centered view of European civilization, while *America through Women's Eyes* (1933) documented "the share of women in the development of American society." Both anticipated themes developed in *Women As*

Force in History (1946), in which she argued that women, rather than being victims, had always been active agents in the building of human societies.

Ellen Nore

Texts

(Ed.) *America through Women's Eyes.* New York: Macmillan, 1933.

On Understanding Women. New York: Longmans, Green, 1931.

The Rise of American Civilization. 2 Vols. New York: Macmillan, 1927.

Woman As Force in History. New York: Macmillan, 1946.

Women's Work in Municipalities. New York: D. Appleton, 1915.

References

Cott, Nancy F. *A Woman Making History: Mary Ritter Beard through Her Letters.* New Haven, CT, and London: Yale University Press, 1991.

Lebsock, Suzanne. "Reading Mary Beard." *Reviews in American History* 17 (1989): 324–339.

Beccadelli, Antonio (called "Il Panormita") (1394–1471)

Renaissance Italian historian. As his cognomen, "il Panormita," indicates, Beccadelli was a native of Palermo. His contemporary notoriety rested largely on his *Hermaphroditus* (1425), a collection of elegant Latin epigrammatic verses, many of them salacious, which won him appointment as court poet to the duke of Milan. From 1434 until his death he served the Aragonese kings of Naples in various important offices. His *De dictis et factis Alphonsi regis* [Deeds and Sayings of King Alfonso] (composed 1455) was intended to imitate Xenophon's *Memorabilia.* His unfinished *Liber rerum gestarum Ferdinandi regis* [Book of the Deeds of King Ferdinand], covers King Ferdinand's (Italian: Ferrante) early years. Both are episodic, uncritical, and not highly regarded as history, but provided models for later Renaissance biographers.

T.C. Price Zimmermann

Texts

Alfonsi V. regis dicta ac facta. Pisa, Italy: Gregorio de Gente, 1485.

Liber rerum gestarum Ferdinandi regis. Ed. G. Resta. Palermo, Italy: Centro di studí filologici e linguistici siciliani, 1968.

References

Bentley, Jerry H. *Politics and Culture in Renaissance Naples.* Princeton, NJ: Princeton University Press, 1987, 84–100.

Cochrane, Eric. *Historians and Historiography in the Italian Renaissance.* Chicago: University of Chicago Press, 1981, 144–150.

Becker, Carl Lotus (1873–1945)

American historian. One of the most distinguished scholars in the fields of both American and European history, Carl Becker was born in Black Hawk county, Iowa. His early life centered on the agricultural life of a small German-American community and the traditions and values of the Methodist church and the Republican party. At Cornell College in Iowa and especially at the University of Wisconsin, Becker rejected many of these values and developed a lifelong interest in the rationalist thinkers of the Enlightenment. Most of his graduate work was done at Wisconsin, where he came under the influence of Charles Homer Haskins, the prominent medievalist, and Frederick Jackson Turner, the noted historian of the frontier. From these mentors, he learned much about the teaching and writing of history. Turner especially emphasized the necessity of questioning inherited ideas and the need for each generation to rewrite history. Upon receiving his Ph.D. from Wisconsin, Becker taught at several institutions before beginning his long career at Cornell, retiring in 1941. Becker was a versatile and prolific author whose writings reshaped historians' understanding of major topics and issues. His early study of provincial politics in eighteenth-century New York propounded the thesis of a "dual revolution" in the conflict between the colonies and the mother country. Becker argued that, in addition to the rebellion against Great Britain, an internal struggle also took place reflecting divisions in New York between upper and lower classes. This "Becker thesis" has subsequently been extended to the other colonies. Another of his writings, *The Declaration of Independence* (1922), contained a remarkable historical analysis of that document and has endured as a classic of American intellectual history. In European history, his reputation rests heavily on *The Heavenly City of the Eighteenth-Century Philosophers,* his provocative interpretation of prerevolutionary French intellectuals. Becker maintained that the philosophes were not as modern as historians had supposed and that the Enlightenment owed much to the "Heavenly City" of medieval theologians.

As a scholar, Carl Becker is somewhat difficult to categorize and, throughout his career, he strongly resisted being labeled as any particular kind of historian. Whether writing about America or Europe, he was concerned with ideas, climates of opinion, and trends of thought. In a sense, he was a twentieth-century "philosophe." History, for him, was not a matter of fact but rather a never-ending reinterpretation of the past to suit the needs of the present. Like James Harvey Robinson and the other "New Historians" of the early years of the century, Becker maintained that history should be useful. In his search for the meaning of history, he became identified, more than any of his contemporaries, with the idea of historical relativism. As early as 1919, he questioned the idea of "hard facts" and argued that the "truths" of history were true only for a time and should serve particular needs of each generation. During the postwar period, the historical community became more receptive to Becker's thinking, and in 1931 he delivered what became known as a landmark address in the history of historical thought in the United States. His presidential address before the American Historical Association, "Everyman His Own Historian," was a bold and articulate avowal of the relativity of historical knowledge. Becker insisted that historians, while continuing to use scientific methods in gathering and organizing data, must adapt their scholarship to the needs and interests of "Mr. Everyman," the broad general public. Concluding that history could be considered "a useful myth," Becker advised: "Let not the harmless, necessary word 'myth' put us out of countenance." Many in the historical profession, however, were put "out of countenance," and the debate over the "objectivity question" has continued to the present time.

Kevin J. O'Keefe

Texts

Beginnings of the American People. New York : Houghton Mifflin, 1915.

The Declaration of Independence, a Study in the History of Political Ideas. New York: Harcourt, Brace, 1922.

Detachment and the Writing of History: Essays and Letters of Carl L. Becker. Ed. P.L. Snyder. Ithaca, NY: Cornell University Press, 1958.

The Heavenly City of the Eighteenth-Century Philosophers. New Haven, CT: Yale University Press, 1932.

References

Novick, Peter. *That Noble Dream: The "Objectivity Question" and the American Historical Profession.* Cambridge, Eng.: Cambridge University Press, 1988.

Rockwood, Raymond O., ed. *Carl Becker's Heavenly City Revisited.* Ithaca, NY: Cornell University Press, 1958.

Smith, Charlotte. *Carl Becker: On History and the Climate of Opinion.* Carbondale: Southern Illinois University Press, 1973.

Strout, Cushing. *The Pragmatic Revolt in American History: Carl Becker and Charles Beard.* New Haven, CT: Yale University Press, 1958.

Wilkins, B.T. *Carl Becker.* Cambridge, MA: MIT Press, 1961.

Bede, the Venerable (ca. 672–735)

English Benedictine monk, teacher, and chronicler. The father of English history, Bede entered the monastery at Wearmouth at about age 7 and shortly thereafter moved to nearby Jarrow. Ordained deacon at the young age of 19, and priest at 30, Bede was not well-traveled but benefited from the monastery's extensive library and frequent visitors. His groundbreaking achievement in writing history is the *Historia ecclesiastica gentis Anglorum* [Ecclesiastical History of the English People], completed in 731. It combined church history with British events (which he considered inseparable) and traced how orthodox Christianity grew in Britain, came under Rome's authority, and rooted out Pelagian heresy while unifying diverse Anglo-Saxon cultures. The central source for information concerning Augustine's British and Aidan's Irish missions, Bede also wrote to provide moral examples. Besides introducing the method of dating historical events and marking time from Jesus' birth, he wrote a world history, biographies of abbots and saints, prayers, textbooks for his monastic students, poems, scriptural commentaries, and sermons.

Christopher M. Bellitto

Texts

Bede's Ecclesiastical History of the English People. Ed. Bertram Colgrave and R.A.B. Mynors. Oxford: Clarendon Press, 1969.

References

Bonner, Gerald, ed. *Famulus Christi: Essays in Commemoration of the Thirteenth Centenary of the Birth of the Venerable Bede.* London: SPCK, 1976.

Begriffsgeschichte

The history of concepts, or conceptual history. *Begriffsgeschichte* is an emerging genre, which is becoming increasingly international in its scope. Since about 1960, German scholars have developed distinctive methods for writing the history of concepts. Applied to France as well as to Germany, their work has set new standards for historical study of the distinctive vocabularies of political, social, and philosophical languages. The questions addressed by conceptual historians, and the methods they apply systematically to previously unexplored sources, differ as much from the earlier German styles of Hegel, Dilthey, and Meinecke as from those of more recent writers in English, such as A.O. Lovejoy, J.G.A. Pocock, and Quentin Skinner. National histories of political and social concepts in the Netherlands, Hungary, and modern China are being prepared, while there is a growing interest in such studies in Italy, Denmark, Finland, and Sweden.

Begriffsgeschichte is used here as a generic term to designate three sets of scholarly practices. All have chosen concepts as units of analysis, thus distinguishing *Begriffsgeschichte* from alternative methods focusing on other topics: individual authors, texts, schools, traditions, persisting problems, forms of argument, styles of thought, discourses, ideologies. Three multivolume works, each with its own distinctive program, have been the principal sites of *Begriffsgeschichte: Basic Concepts in German Political and Social Language; A Dictionary of Philosophy on Historical Principles; A Handbook of Basic Political and Social Concepts in France, 1680–1820*. Reinhart Koselleck provided the theory for the first, Joachim Ritter for the second, Rolf Reichardt for the third.

Begriffsgeschichte treats political language neither as autonomous discourse, nor as the product of ideology, social structure, or elite manipulation. Although conceptual historians agree that the field of human action is defined by language, with the exception of historians of philosophy, they place concept formation and use within historical contexts. By surveying systematically the conceptual vocabularies of political and social discourses, this genre traces how the great modern revolutions have been conceptualized in sharply contested forms by competing political and social formations, groups, and classes, as well as by individual thinkers. Combining intellectual with social history, historians of concepts track linguistically the advent, mentalities, and effects of modernity. Once the different national conceptual histories have been completed, a genuinely comparative study of

political and social vocabularies will be possible. This would contrast the diverse forms in which major changes in politics and society were conceptualized from the sixteenth to the twentieth centuries in different societies. For concepts in part directed, and in part registered, experiences such as the accelerated rate of change; democratization of social structures; increasing access to participation in politics; the change from a predominantly agrarian to a commercial and then to an industrial economy; and the proliferation of ideologies.

The quality to date of the major projects in *Begriffsgeschichte* now set the standard for rigorous historical study of the specialized vocabularies of political and social theory, as well as of philosophy. Because of these advances, analogous large-scale histories of key concepts in aesthetics, rhetoric, and theology are under way. But the greatest remaining lacuna in our knowledge of language and culture is the absence of any in-depth study of the distinctive forms, cultural and linguistic, as well as political and social, of the principal conceptual categories developed in English-speaking societies.

Melvin Richter

See also IDEAS, HISTORY OF; KOSELLECK, REINHART.

References
Brunner, Otto, Werner Conze, and Reinhart Koselleck, eds. *Geschichtliche Grundbegriffe: Historisches Lexikon zur Politisch-Sozialer Sprache in Deutschland* [Historical Concepts: A Historical Lexicon of German Political and Social Thought]. 7 vols. to date. Stuttgart: Klett-Cotta, 1972– .

Lehmann, Hartmut, and Melvin Richter, eds. *Begriffsgeschichte*. German Historical Institute (Washington, DC). Occasional Paper. New York and Oxford: Berg Publishers, 1996.

Reichardt, Rolf, and Eberhard Schmitt, in collaboration with Gerd van den Heuvel and Annette Hofer, eds. *Handbuch politisch-sozialer Grundbegriffe in Frankreich, 1680–1820* [Handbook of Political and Social Concepts in France, 1680–1820]. 10 vols. to date. Munich: R. Oldenbourg Verlag, 1985– .

Richter, Melvin. *The History of Political and Social Concepts: A Critical Introduction.* New York: Oxford University Press, 1996.

Ritter, Joachim, and Karlfried Gründer, eds. *Historisches Wörterbuch der Philosophie* [Historical Dictionary of Philosophy]. 7 vols. to date. Basel/Stuttgart: Schwabe & Co., 1971– .

Bél, Matthias [Hungarian: Mátyás; Slovak: Matej] (1684–1749)

Hungarian or Slovak historian. Born in Upper Hungary (today's Slovakia), Bél studied at various schools of this region before taking his degree in theology from the University of Halle in 1708. He taught in Besztercebánya (Banská Bystrica) until 1714, then became rector of the school in Pozsony (Bratislava) and Lutheran pastor of this town in 1719. Though claimed today by both Hungarians and Slovaks, he was essentially a *Hungarus* (identifying himself with his country rather than with any single ethnic group): teaching, writing, and preaching in Latin, German, and Hungarian. He helped found the first Austrian learned society and was a member of various other societies. Bél wrote extensively on classical, Hungarian, German, and Slavic philology. His greatest contributions to historiography were the organization of a project for the economic, ethnographic, and historical description of the counties of Hungary, the *Notitia Hungariae novae historico-geographica* [Historical and Geographical Remarks on the New Hungary], of which he published five volumes and left several others in manuscript, and the publication of twelve early accounts of the history of Hungary, the *Adparatus ad historiam Hungariae* [Introduction to the History of Hungary].

James P. Niessen

Texts

Adparatus ad historiam Hungariae. 2 vols. Posonius, Slovakia (then Hungary): Royer, 1735–1746.
Notitia Hungariae novae historico-geographica. 2 vols. Vienna: Ghelen, 1735–1742.

References

Belák, Blažej. *Matej Bél, 1684–1749: Vyberová personalná bibliografia k 300. storociu narodenia Mateja Bela* [Bibliography of Bél Studies]. V Martine, Slovakia: Matica slovenská, 1984.
Hungáriábol Magyarország felé [From Hungary to Hungary]. Ed. Andor Tarnai. Budapest: Szépirodalmi, 1984.
Pavalek, Juraj, ed. *Listy Mateja Bela* [Correspondence of Bél]. V Martine, Slovakia: Matica slovenská, 1990.

Belgian Historiography

Historiography of the Belgian state, founded 1830, and its historical antecedents. The key problem of Belgian historiography is that of the most suitable geographical framework. Belgium has few natural borders and an ethnically heterogeneous population. Moreover, during its tumultuous history prior to 1830, Belgium was, in part or whole, and for longer or shorter terms, part of the territory of various European superpowers. Many historians endeavored to project Belgium's unity in that past. Others opted for wider demarcations (for example, the Great-Dutch and the All-Dutch models) or smaller ones (the regional models in Dutch-speaking Flanders and French-speaking Wallonia). Depending on the framework chosen, the historical periods, episodes, and protagonists selected as antecedents differed widely. Frequently, the search for either ancient glory and freedom, or eternal oppression and dark ages, made historiography teleological.

The first traces of historical consciousness among the inhabitants of the present Belgian territory stem from the seventh century. Until the end of the eighteenth century, historiography was rich and diverse, but remained mainly particularistic, serving church, city, or region and, occasionally, the reigning dynasty. Milestones along the way were the mastery of the medieval chronicler Sigebert of Gembloux (1030–1112), and the erudition of the Jesuits Jean Bolland (1596–1665) and Daniel Papebroch (1628–1714).

The "Belgian-national" model emerged fifty years before independence. The Austrian Netherlands developed its own identity and the Académie Impériale et Royale des Sciences et Belles-Lettres (founded 1772) gave the initial impetus to "nationalize" the past. This new tradition survived every change of government. Beginning in 1830, the national historical awareness of the young state received a tremendous impulse. Driven by romantic and patriotic ideas, a generation of autodidacts produced a flood of national histories. This development was encouraged by the young government, for example through the establishment of the Commission Royale d'Histoire (1834), which published chronicles and other sources. Louis-Prosper Gachard (1800–1885) was the moving spirit behind the organization of the Belgian archives. Around 1875 two developments caused a mutation. The tension between church and state discredited the historiography by turning it into a weapon in the polemics between liberals and catholics. At the same time, historiography was professionalized, initially by Godefroid Kurth (1847–1916), who introduced the German system of historical seminars. A scientific infrastructure of professional journals, research centers, and source publications was set up (partly derived from older traditions) and historiography gradually fell into the hands of university professors. The 1890 Higher Education Act confirmed this development. Belgian-national historiography culminated in the *Histoire de Belgique* (1900–1932) by Henri Pirenne (1862–1935). To Pirenne, Belgium's identity was reflected in the economic and cultural unity that, all along, had supposedly connected the Belgians in peaceful mutual understanding at Europe's crossroad. He broke down the monopoly of the political, institutional, and religious histories and gave a place to socioeconomic and urban history. He was of international influence. After Pirenne, the Belgian-national approach revived in the apologetic historiography of Belgian Congo (ending suddenly with decolonization in 1960). There, in the colonial field, the Belgian-national approach probably persisted longest.

Beginning in the 1920s, the Dutch historian Pieter Geyl (1887–1966) attacked Pirenne's panoramic vision with a "Great-Dutch" *(Groot-Nederlandse)* approach. His model was mainly built upon the linguistic affinity between the Netherlands and Flanders, but it never gained widespread support. Nevertheless, it formed the preamble to an "All-Dutch" *(Algemeen-Nederlandse)* approach, emphasizing the episodes of common Belgian and Dutch history, such as the Burgundian-Habsburg empires of the fifteenth and sixteenth century. The collaboration of Belgian and Dutch historians resulted in the multivolume *Algemene Geschiedenis der Nederlanden* [General History of the Low Countries] (1949–1958; revised edition 1977–1983). This is a major work, though it treats Belgian and Dutch developments separately rather than comparatively. Neither was the All-Dutch concept genuinely supported by Belgium's French-speaking historians. All the same, this approach remains authoritative today, despite the emergence of other models.

A revived political awareness of the Flemish and Walloon movements after 1900 lay at the outset of the regional models. According to one theory, losers have a strong historical consciousness: within the national context, many Flemings felt like losers in the first half of the century, and many Walloons have felt likewise in the second half. Perhaps this partly explains why the first full-fledged history of Flanders was published in 1936 and its Walloon counterpart only in 1973. The federalization of the Belgian state (1963–1993) certainly intensified these tendencies. The regional models managed to avoid, definitely after 1945, extreme interpretations. Today they are powerful, but their success cannot match that of the Belgian-national model after 1830.

Belgian history education abandoned the Belgian-national framework only around 1960, and even then it did not embrace the regional models, but tried instead to broaden the horizons to European and general history. Between 1970 and 1990 the subject went through three serious crises, when it was cut back and nearly banned from secondary school curricula. Did the state turn away from history education when it no longer could or would serve as its legitimization?

Whatever geographical framework has been fashionable, two constants should be noticed. First, there has always been a very active local historiography. Attached to the oldest traditions, it has never slackened and continues to flourish today. Secondly, for more than a century, Catholics, liberals, socialists, and other ideological families have developed vertical networks of political parties, trade unions, schools, newspapers, clubs, and societies. Many historians have been active in writing the history of their own network or "pillar" (Dutch: *zuil*). During the decade from 1975 to 1985, however, these networks began to break down. This process of "depillarization" *(ontzuiling)* engendered a feeling of discontinuity that led the several pillars to establish their archives and historical research centers.

Nobody can overlook the enormous historiographical production: the annual bibliography contained a total of 51,656 titles between 1958 and 1987. The number of historical journals increased from 107 in 1961 to 310 in 1983. Around 1960, Belgium counted forty-eight circles for local history, folklore, and archaeology, in 1980 there were 433. After 1945, the best Belgian historiography joined in with the interdisciplinary methods propagated by the Annales historians, the cliometricians, and other historical schools. The work of scholars such as Jan Dhondt (1915–1972), Léopold Genicot (1914–1995), Jean Stengers (b. 1922), Herman Van der Wee (b. 1928), and Jan Vansina (b. 1929), to name but a few, has attracted attention far beyond the country's borders. Leading Belgian historians, however, often differ in their appraisal of actual Belgian historiography. Their arguments can support both an increase or decrease of public interest in history (for instance, the thriving of local history versus the recent assault on history education). Neither do they agree on the question of whether Belgian historiography is sufficiently open to innovations from abroad or suffers from isolationism. (Complaints about the lack of foreign attention to Belgian historiography are, however, nearly unanimous.) Furthermore, Belgian historiography is often characterized as highly erudite—the product of a 350-year-old tradition strengthened by nineteenth-century empiricism. Connected to this erudite outlook, three further observations can be made: there is a tendency to strong—some say overdone—specialization embodied in numerous research centers; there is a lack of discussion across regional and ideological borders and a strong aversion to theory; and, finally, there exists a need for sensible historical popularization (this last partially explains the crises in the educational field and the problems of public image being experienced by the history profession).

In the meantime, the key problem of the geographical framework remains unsolved. It cannot be predicted whether the All-Dutch model will be gradually refined, or whether it will be replaced by new models, assuming, for example, that a suitable geographical framework does not exist or is larger than presumed. The pursuit of a widely accepted, plausible overview of Belgian history is still considered the most important task of Belgian historians.

Antoon de Baets

References

Genicot, Léopold, ed. *Vingt ans de recherche historique en Belgique 1969–1988* [Twenty Years of Historical Research in Belgium, 1969–1988]. Brussels: Gemeentekrediet, 1990.

Hasquin, Hervé, ed. "Histoire et historiens depuis 1830 en Belgique" [History and Historians in Belgium since 1830]. *Revue de l'Université de Bruxelles* 1–2 (1981): 3–234.

Stengers, Jean. "Belgian Historiography since 1945." In *Reappraisals in Overseas History: Essays on Post-war Historiography about European Expansion,* ed. Pieter C. Emmer and Henk L. Wesseling. Leiden: Leiden University Press, 1979, 161–181.

Tollebeek, Jo. *De ijkmeesters: opstellen over de geschiedschrijving in Nederland en België* [The Masters of the Standard: Essays on the Historiography in the Netherlands and Belgium]. Amsterdam: Bert Bakker, 1994.

Van Uytven, Raymond, et al. "De geschiedschrijving in de Nederlanden" [Historiography of the Low Countries]. In *Algemene Geschiedenis der Nederlanden XII* [General History of the Low Countries], ed. Jan Arthur van Houtte et al. Zeist, Netherlands: De Haan and Antwerp, Belgium: Standaard, 1958, 440–487; 509–512.

Below, Georg von (1858–1927)

German historian. Below received his university training in Königsberg and Bonn and did his doctorate (1883) in Berlin under Moriz Ritter, who asked him to create a compilation of the files of the Jülich and Berg Landtag; this appeared in two volumes published in 1895 and 1907, respectively. After he had habilitated (1896) in Marburg, he became professor extraordinarius at Königsberg University. In 1891 he was appointed to a chair in Münster, and then to chairs at Marburg and Tübingen, before moving finally to Freiburg, where he remained until 1924. From 1903 he was coeditor of the *Vierteljahrsschrift für Wirtschafts- und Sozialgeschichte* [Quarterly Journal of Economic and Social History] and, from 1910, of Germany's leading historical journal, the *Historische Zeitschrift.* At the Bavarian Academy of Sciences he supervised the publication of the *Städtechroniken* (town chronicles) and the *Jahrbücher des deutschen Reiches* [Yearbooks of the German Empire]. Together with Friedrich Meinecke he edited the *Handbuch der mittelalterlichen und neueren Geschichte* [Handbook of Medieval and Modern History]. Below defined the state as the real subject of the historian and, as a result, considered himself a political historian. He always viewed constitutional and social history from the point of view of state action. He spoke out harshly against cultural history and the developing discipline of sociology, and against the idea that there were "laws" of historical causation; and throughout his work, he emphasized individual action as a force in history. Below demanded a strict critical-historical method and advocated the borrowing of analytical terms from jurisprudence. In his major work *Der deutsche Staat des Mittelalters: Ein Grundriss der deutschen Verfassungsgeschichte* [The German State in the Middle Ages: An Outline of German Constitutional History] (1914), he allocated the medieval state the public-legal character of his own time as opposed to Otto von Gierke's private-law interpretations. In *Die deutsche Geschichtschreibung von den deutschen Befreiungskriegen an bis zu unseren Tagen* [German Historical Writing from the German Wars of Liberation to Our Own Day] (1916) he emphasized the importance of romanticism in the development of nineteenth-century historiography. Below is regarded as one of the most influential but also pugnacious and aggressive historians of the Wilhelminian age. With his attacks on Karl Lamprecht in 1893, he set off the so-called Methodenstreit, or Lamprecht controversy. After 1907, Below became increasingly active in politics and, during World War I, agitated against democratic reform plans. Following the German defeat he vehemently propagated the "Dolchstosslegende" and inveighed against democracy. His narrow notion of historiography, combined with his tendency to lean heavily on tradition, ensured that his work had relatively little impact on later generations of historians.

Thomas Fuchs

Texts

Der deutsche Staat des Mittelalters: Ein Grundriss der deutschen Verfassungsgeschichte. Leipzig: Quelle und Meyer, 1914.

Die deutsche Geschichtschreibung von den Befreiungskriegen an bis zu unsern Tagen. Munich and Berlin: R. Oldenbourg, 1924.

Probleme der Wirtschaftsgeschichte: Eine Einführung in das Studium der Wirtschaftsgeschichte [The Problem of Economic History: An Introduction to the Study of Economic History]. Second ed. Tübingen, Germany: J.C.B. Mohr (Paul Siebeck), 1926.

References

Iggers, Georg G. *The German Conception of History: The National Tradition of Historical Thought from Herder to the Present.* Second ed. Middletown, CT: Wesleyan University Press, 1983.

Oexle, O.G. "Ein politischer Historiker: Georg von Below" [A Political Historian: Georg von Below]. In *Deutsche Geschichtswissenschaft um 1900* [German Historical Thought around 1900], ed. N. Hammerstein. Stuttgart: Steiner-Verlag Wiesbaden, 1988, 283–312.

Benjamin, Walter Benedix Schönflies (1892–1940)

German social philosopher and literary critic. Born into a well-to-do Jewish family in Berlin, Benjamin studied philosophy from 1912 to 1919 in Freiburg im Breisgau, Berlin, Munich, and finally Bern, where he graduated with a thesis entitled *Der Begriff der Kunstkritik in der deutschen Romantik* [The Idea of Art Criticism in German Romanticism]. From 1920 to 1933 he lived in Berlin, traveling to Moscow, Paris, and Ibiza. Thereafter he lived mainly in Paris until the outbreak of World War II. Hoping to emigrate to the United States he fled to Port-Bou, a Spanish border town, where he committed suicide in September 1940. Benjamin's thought was influenced by writers as various as Goethe, Baudelaire, Kafka,

and Brecht, as well as by Jewish mysticism. His numerous essays, some collected in *Illuminations* (1969), argue for a Marxist humanism mixed with cabalistic views of history. He described mass society and the rise of fascism as the culmination of bourgeois cultural degradation: art in his view had ceased to instruct and had become merely a source of personal satisfaction. Benjamin also contended, however, that art inspired by communism could yet prove the means to overcoming the anomie of the masses. Benjamin's work has had renewed impact on cultural history in recent years, having been influential in current postmodern examinations of art and literature.

Elvy Setterqvist O'Brien

Texts

The Correspondence of Walter Benjamin, 1910–1940. Ed. Gershom Scholem and Theodor W. Adorno; trans. Manfred R. Jacobson and Evelyn M. Jacobson. Chicago: University of Chicago Press, 1994.

Illuminations. Ed. Hannah Arendt; trans. Harry Zohn. New York: Schocken Books, 1969.

References

Witte, Bernd. *Walter Benjamin: An Intellectual Biography.* Trans. James Rolleston. Detroit, MI: Wayne State University Press, 1991.

Wolin, Richard. *Walter Benjamin: An Aesthetic of Redemption.* New York: Columbia University Press, 1982.

Berlin, Sir Isaiah (1909–1997)

British historian of ideas, philosopher, and liberal political theorist. Born in Riga, Latvia, Berlin emigrated as a child to Britain. Apart from diplomatic service in Washington and Moscow (1941–1946) and occasional visiting professorships, he spent all his life at Oxford University. In the history of ideas, Berlin used the skills of an analytical philosopher to produce lucid explications of ideas against their intellectual background. In his intellectual biography of Karl Marx, Berlin contextualized Marx's ideas, thereby situating Marx as a humanist thinker. Berlin's studies of prerevolutionary Russian thinkers include classics of the history of ideas such as "The Hedgehog and the Fox" (on Tolstoy) and "Fathers and Sons" (on the generation gap in pre-revolutionary Russia). Berlin examined the arguments about the destiny of Russian history between Slavophiles and westernizers, revolutionaries, and reformers. He also explored the philosophies of the Enlightenment and their alternatives in the counter-enlightenment, romanticism, nationalism, and a distinctive thinker such as Giambattista Vico (to whose rediscovery as a philosopher of the humanities and the social sciences he contributed). A committed Zionist, Berlin also wrote on Jewish and Israeli issues and personalities.

Berlin participated in the creation of twentieth-century Oxford philosophy, under the influence of logical-positivism. He attacked the idea of historical inevitability as leading to denial of human responsibility and freedom, the foundations of morality, and he berated the idea of scientific historiography as missing the essence of historiography in commonsensical understanding of the concrete, based on professional experience. Berlin's criticisms were directed mostly at the Marxist versions of historical inevitability and science, but did not address more sophisticated, non-Marxist, versions of these positions.

Aviezer Tucker

Texts

Against the Current: Essays in the History of Ideas. Ed. Henry Hardy. Oxford: Clarendon Press, 1991.

The Age of Enlightenment: The Eighteenth-Century Philosophers. Boston: Houghton-Mifflin, 1956.

Concepts and Categories. London: Hogarth Press, 1978.

The Crooked Timber of Humanity: Chapters in the History of Ideas. London: John Murray, 1990.

Four Essays on Liberty. London: Oxford University Press, 1969.

Karl Marx: His Life and Environment. Fourth ed. Oxford: Oxford University Press, 1978.

The Magus of the North: J.G. Hannan and the Origins of Modern Irrationalism. London: John Murray, 1993.

Russian Thinkers. London: Hogarth Press, 1978.

Vico and Herder. London: Hogarth Press, 1976.

Berossus (fl. 300 b.c.)

Babylonian priest and chronologer. Berossus, who wrote the *Babyloniaca* (which is no longer extant), likely received a scribal education in Sumero-Akkadian literature. The work was abridged by polyhistors into two distinct sections (the histories of Babylonia and Assyria), excerpts of which survive in Josephus (*Contra Apion* 1:12–21) and Eusebius (*Chronica* I). Josephus states that the

Babyloniaca was dedicated to Antiochus I to provide the king a history of the land he ruled. Berossus apparently did not write history in the Greek sense, but a general introduction to Babylonian culture. The book became an ideal for ensuing attempts by Hellenized non-Greeks to export their culture to the Greeks.

Mark W. Chavalas

Texts

Burstein, Stanley M. *The Babyloniaca of Berossus.* Malibu, CA: Undena Publications, 1978.

References

Drews, R. "The Babylonian Chronicles and Berossus." *Iraq* 37 (1975): 39–55.

Schnabel, P. *Berossus und die babylonisch-hellenistiche Literatur* [Berossus and Babylonian-Hellenic Literature]. Second ed. Hildesheim, Germany: Georg Olms, 1968.

Berr, Henri (1863–1954)

French philosopher of history. After serving for some time as a professor of rhetoric at different provincial lycées, Berr began teaching French literature at the Lycée Henri IV, where he would stay until his retirement in 1926. He remains best known for his efforts to construct a scientific philosophy of history. Berr criticized traditional nineteenth-century empiricism and positivism (well known to contemporaries in a famous manual of historical writing by Charles-Victor Langlois and Charles Seignobos) and believed that historians were in a position to make the new scientific synthetic stage of knowledge possible. He called for historians and philosophers to work together and criticized the growing trend toward academic specialization. To further his goals, in 1900 Berr founded the *Revue de synthèse historique.* The new journal attracted contributions from some of the leading scholars of the day, such as Emile Durkheim and Karl Lamprecht, and the editorial services of two younger scholars, Marc Bloch and Lucien Febvre. After World War I, Berr continued his search for a *synthèse historique* and worked closely with the producers of the mammoth *Evolution de l'humanité* series, writing nearly three-quarters of the introductions to its hundred volumes. After his retirement, Berr directed the Centre International de Synthèse in Paris. Though many of his contemporaries ignored his calls for change and integration, Berr is now counted, along with

Bloch and Febvre, as having laid the foundations upon which the Annales school was constructed.

Krista Kesselring

Texts

L'histoire traditionnelle et la synthèse historique. Paris: Alcan, 1921.

References

Delorme, S. "Henri Berr." *Osiris* 10 (1951): 5–9.
Siegel, M. "Henri Berr's *Revue de Synthèse Historique.*" *History and Theory* 9 (1970): 322–334.

Berry, Mary (1763–1852)

English historian and literary figure. Berry was born in Yorkshire, England, and died in London at the age of 89. Neither she nor her sister Agnes ever married. Both young women were close friends with the writer Horace Walpole in his later years. Upon his death, Walpole left to them the home in which the two sisters lived, along with a financial settlement. He bequeathed all his printed works and manuscripts jointly to Mary, her sister, and their father, Robert Berry. Mary Berry's literary career began with this bequest because she became one of the editors of a five-volume edition of Walpole's works, which was published in 1798. In 1819, her first individual work appeared as an edited collection of letters of English women entitled *Some Account of the Life of Rachel Wriothesley, Lady Russell.* This work was well received, and she was encouraged to focus on social history. Berry is most well known for her two-volume social history of Europe, *A Comparative View of the Social Life of England and France* (1828–1831).

Judith Boyce DeMark

Texts

A Comparative View of the Social Life of England and France, from the Restoration of Charles the Second to the French Revolution. 2 vols. London: Longman, Rees, Orme, Brown and Green, 1828–1831.
Some Account of the Life of Rachael Wriothesley, Lady Russell. London: Strahan and Spottiswoode, 1819.
Ed. *The Works of Horatio Walpole, Earl of Orford.* 5 vols. London: G.G. and J. Robinson and J. Edwards, 1798.

References

Stenton, Doris Mary. *The English Woman in History.* London: George Allen & Unwin, Ltd., 1957.

Bhandarkar, Sir Ramkrishna Gopal, (1837–1925)

Indian Sanskritist, educationist, and social reformer who was a pioneer in applying Western methods of scholarship to the study of Sanskrit and the ancient history of India. In addition to being a historian he produced important works on the Sanskrit and Prakrit languages, religion, and philosophy. He became the first Wilson Philological Lecturer (1877), Indian professor of Sanskrit at Deccan College, Poona (1882), and vice-chancellor of Bombay University (1893–1895). He was appointed to the Viceroy's Legislative Council (1903) and served on the Bombay Legislative Council (1904–1908). The author of "The Early History of the Deccan" (1884) and *A Peep into the Early History of India* (1900), the Bhandarkar Oriental Research Institute was inaugurated on his eightieth birthday in 1917. The main thrust of his studies was with "what happened" in ancient India rather than "why." The *Collected Works* (1927–1933) in four volumes contain his writings.

Roger D. Long

Texts

The Critical, Comparative and Historical Method of Inquiry As Applied to Sanskrit Scholarship and Philology and Indian Archaeology. Bombay: Free Church, 1888.
"The Early History of the Deccan Down to the Mahomedan Conquest." In the *Collected Works of Sir R.G. Bhandarkar,* vol. 3, ed. Narayan Bapuji Utgikar. Poona: Bhandarkar Oriental Research Institute, 1927, 1–198.
A Peep into the Early History of India. Second ed. Varanasi: Bharatiya Publishing House, 1978.

References

Dandekar, R.N. *Ramkrishna Gopal Bhandarkar As an Indologist.* Poona: Bhandarkar Oriental Research Institute, 1976.

Bibliography—Historical

The listing of historical works or sources in a systematic manner; an important ancillary discipline in historical research. Derived from the Greek words, *biblion* (book) and *graphein* (to write), the term "bibliography" literally refers to the writing of books. The *Oxford English Dictionary* defines bibliography as a "list of the books of a particular author, printer, or country, or of those dealing with any particular theme." While bibliographies are generally considered an invention of the printing age, the listing of books has ancient origins. In the second century B.C., the prolific Greek physician Galen wrote *De propriis libris liber,* a classified arrangement of his writings. In later centuries, many bibliographies were included in biographical works. The *Ecclesiastical History of Britain* written by the Venerable Bede, an Anglo-Saxon historian and theologian of the seventh century A.D., was considered the first bibliography appended to a book other than a biography.

The father of modern bibliography, Johann Trithem or Trithemius (1462–1516), compiled lists for scholars and clerics containing author and title information and arranged in chronological order. In 1545, Conrad Gesner (1516–1565) published the first universal bibliography comprising 12,000 books written in Latin, Greek, and Hebrew. At about the same time, antiquaries such as John Leland and John Bale in England were busily compiling lists of (and helping to preserve) the historical manuscripts held by the dissolved monastic orders. Specialized bibliographies in history began appearing in the seventeenth century, including works with such titles as *Bibliotheca historica* (1620), *Bibliographica historica* (1685), and the three-volume *English, Scottish, and Irish Historical Libraries* (1696–1699) compiled by the English bishop William Nicolson (1655–1727).

Bibliographies became a major source for academic research in specific subject disciplines during the nineteenth and early twentieth centuries. In the United States, the Boston Public Library and the John Crerar Library in Chicago published bibliographies on a variety of subjects, including history. In the field of British history, the Royal Historical Society of Great Britain along with the American Historical Association has published the serial *Bibliography of British History. The Harvard Guide to American History* is a major reference bibliography for students and scholars of this subject.

First published in 1931, the *American Historical Association's Guide to Historical Literature*—now in its third edition (1995)—is an evaluative bibliographical source of primarily English-language works on world history. *Historical Abstracts,* published by ABC-Clio, is the preeminent annotated index for journal articles covering world history since the middle of the fifteenth century; *America: History and Life,* its companion volume, covers U.S. and Canadian history.

Edited for the International Committee of Historical Sciences, *The International Bibliography of Historical Sciences* is an annual, unannotated bibliography covering events from prehistory to modern times. A topical guide, *International Medieval Bibliography,* covers the whole range of medieval studies, culled from scholarly journals. Some journals, such as the *American Historical Review,* the *Journal of American History,* and the *English Historical Review* are major sources for recent bibliographical information. Notable specialized bibliographies also include the *International Bibliography of Jewish History and Thought, International African Bibliography,* and *Historiography: An Annotated Bibliography of Journal Articles, Books and Dissertations.* Other important topical, regional, and specialized historical guides are listed in Theodore Besterman's *A World Bibliography of Bibliographies.*

The Association for the Bibliography of History, founded in 1978, is composed of historians and librarians and aims to promote and publish historical bibliographies; it meets regularly during the annual conference of the American Historical Association. Cosponsored by the American Historical Association and the National Endowment for the Humanities, the Belmont conference, held in Elkridge, Maryland, in May 1967, was a major symposium for historians, archivists, and librarians to discuss the current state of bibliographical services in history. Since that conference, computers have revolutionized access to historical sources: CD-ROMs, on-line catalogs, and the Internet now allow scholars and students to locate quickly journal articles, books, and occasionally the full text of historical documents.

Donald Altschiller

See also ARCHIVES; MUSEUMS.

References

Besterman, Theodore. *The Beginnings of Systematic Bibliography.* Second ed. New York: Burt Franklin, 1968.
Harmon, Robert B. *Elements of Bibliography.* Metuchen, NJ: Scarecrow Press, 1989.
Perman, Dagmar H., ed. *Bibliography and the Historian.* Santa Barbara, CA: CLIO, 1968.

Bichurin, Nikita Iakovlevich (1777–1852)

Russian orientalist and sinologist. Born in Kazan province, Bichurin studied theology and took holy orders. In 1807 he headed an ecclesiastical mission to China where he remained for fourteen years translating works on history and geography into Russian. Having become an opponent of colonialism, he returned home where he worked for the Asian Department of the Ministry of Foreign Affairs.

Emperor Nicholas I refused his request to be released from his religious vows. In 1830 he traveled to the Trans-Baikal region, returning with a mass of Tibetan and Mongol material. While there, he organized a school in Kiakhta for the Chinese language and published a Chinese grammar. He donated his entire library and manuscript collection to the Kazan Academy. Bichurin was the first notable Russian oriental scholar, and he wrote extensively on the history, geography, and culture of people of China, Central Asia, Mongolia, and the Far East. Today he is criticized for idealizing the early history and the legal and sociopolitical structure of China.

Elizabeth V. Haigh

Texts

Sobranie svedenii o narodakh, obitavshikh v srednei Azii v drevnie vremenia [Collection of Materials about the Nations Inhabiting Central Asia in Ancient Times]. 3 vols. Moscow: Akademia Nauk, USSR, 1950–1953.

Sobranie svedenii po istorecheskoi geografii vostochnoi i seredinnoi Azii [Collection of Materials on the Historical Geography of Eastern and Central Asia]. Moscow: Geograficheska obschestva, USSR, 1960.

Bickerman, Elias Joseph (1897–1981)

Russian-American historian. Bickerman was born in Kishinev in 1897; after military service, he studied at the universities of St. Petersburg (Petrograd) and Berlin. He held academic posts at Berlin and Paris, emigrated to New York in 1942, where he taught at the New School for Social Research, the Jewish Theological Seminary, and Columbia University, and retired in 1967. His principal areas of interest lay in Jewish and Christian history during late antiquity. Major publications include his Berlin dissertation (1926) *Das Edikt des Kaisers Caracalla in P. Giss. 40* [The Edict of the Emperor Caracalla in Papyrus Giss. 40] and his study of the period in Jewish history from the fifth to first centuries before the Christian era, *From Ezra to the Last of the Maccabees*.

Stephen A. Stertz

Texts

Chronology of the Ancient World. Second ed. London: Thames and Hudson, 1980.

Das Edikt des Kaisers Caracalla in P. Giss. 40 [The Edict of the Emperor Caracalla in Papyrus Giss. 40]. Berlin: Collignon, 1926.

Four Strange Books of the Bible. New York: Schocken Books, 1984.

From Ezra to the Last of the Maccabees: Foundations of Post-Biblical Judaism. New York: Schocken Books, 1962.

The God of the Maccabees: Studies on the Meaning and Origin of the Maccabean Revolt. Trans. Horst R. Moehring. Leiden: E.J. Brill, 1979.

The Jews in the Greek Age. Cambridge, MA: Harvard University Press, 1988.

References

Smith, Morton. "Elias J. Bickerman." *Gnomon* 54 (1982): 223–224.

Bidyalankar, Mritunjaya (ca. 1762–1819)

Indian historian. The author of *Rajavali* [History of Kings] in Bengali, Bidyalankar was "Chief Pundit" of the Fort William College (1801–1816) and of the Supreme Court (1816–1819), Calcutta. A formidable Sanskrit scholar, he opposed Rammohun Roy's (1772–1834) reforms, but spoke against the practice of widow-burning. His book *Rajavali* (1808) deals with the history of India from the earliest times to the British occupation. Unreliable for historical detail—it is largely based on legends, myths, and rumors—it nevertheless provides a connected account of the Indian past, composed in a simple style and with remarkable narrative ease.

S.N. Mukherjee

Texts

Mrityunjaya Granthavali. Ed. Brajendranath Bandyopadhaya [Banerjee]. Calcutta: Ranjan Publishing House, 1939.

References

Bandyopadhaya [Banerjee], Brajendranath, et al., eds. *Sahitya Sadhak Charitmala.* 12 vols. Calcutta: Bangiya-Sahitya-Parishat, 1943–1977, vol. 1., 1952.

Biography

A reconstruction of a historical person's life. Many historians have regarded history and biography as separate genres of literature, but the majority have probably considered biography to be "a branch of history." The myriad forms of biography are now classified according to the writer's approach or the subject's field of interest, such as political biography, literary biography, intellectual biography, fictionalized biography, psychobiography, and autobiography. The term "historical biography" is commonly used to refer to well-researched accounts that minimize private life and give special emphasis to the subject's social role. Traditionally, biographers have often taken liberty with historical data, based on the assumption that one of their purposes is to teach moral lessons by means of example. Biographies per se can be distinguished from the "biographical approach to history," John J. Neale's term to refer to historical accounts that emphasize the roles and contributions of many individuals.

Although the term "biography" was not commonly used until the seventeenth century, the germ of the enterprise can be found in oral traditions about folk heroes, as well as references to individuals in tombs and monuments in all ancient civilizations. Early works of literature, including Homer and the Old Testament, emphasized the actions of legendary persons who presumably lived in the past, although without any attempt to separate myth from events as they "really happened." With the emergence of Greek humanism after the fifth century B.C., writers of a skeptical disposition tried to present factual accounts of individual lives. Although Herodotus and Thucydides were only interested in individuals when they contributed to the welfare of the state, they did include microbiographies and character sketches as a part of their narrative, always with the assumption that individuals had at least marginal influence on what occurred. Accounts of the life and death of Socrates by Plato and Xenophon can be considered as examples of didactic biography. Although Xenophon's *Cyropaedia* is often called the first detailed biography, it might also be classified as a historical novel, because of the author's lack of interest in separating truth from fiction. Early in the second century A.D., Plutarch, Suetonius, and Tacitus did much to popularize the craft of biography. Plutarch's great work, *The Parallel Lives of Noble Grecians and Romans* (ca. 110), was so influential that Plutarch is often called "the father of biography." While trying to separate historical fact from legend, he explained that his purpose was "not to write histories, but lives," for he assumed that the former dealt only with objective accounts of public events such as wars, not with private lives and character. Suetonius's *Lives of the Caesars* (c. 120), although gossipy and often uncritical, encouraged a closer association between history and biography.

In Europe during the Middle Ages, the majority of biographies were hagiographies, or credulous lives of saints that concentrated on miracles and piety. Yet a number of lively and useful accounts were written, including Einhard's *Life of Charlemagne,* Eadmer's *Life of St. Anselm,* and Jean de Joinville's *Life of St. Louis IX.* With the Renaissance (c. 1350–1600), a secular worldview and critical use of sources became increasingly prevalent, but invented dialogues and didactic intentions remained common. Important biographers of the period included Giorgio Vasari, Leonardo Bruni, Thomas More, and George Cavendish. Jean Bodin's analysis of the types of history in *Methodus ad facilem historiarum cognitionem* [Method for the Easy Understanding of History] (1566) distinguished between "universal history" and "particularistic history," using the latter term to refer to "a single people" or "a single person."

During the seventeenth century, the English writers Izaak Walton and John Aubrey popularized the use of informality and intimacy, especially in works about poets and men of letters. In the eighteenth century, interesting biographies by Voltaire, Conyers Middleton, William Robertson, and Samuel Johnson attracted much attention, but the most influential work was James Boswell's *Life of Samuel Johnson LL.D.* (1791), an account notable for its detailed use of Johnson's writings and conversations to develop a complex portrait of the man. The early nineteenth century, with its romantic glorification of heroic individuals, was especially conducive to the writing of biography. Thomas Carlyle, biographer of Oliver Cromwell (1845) and Frederick the Great (1858–1865), became the spokesman for the view that "great men" were the dominant forces in history. Leopold von Ranke emphasized the historic role of individuals almost to the same degree. Countless biographers of the century, especially in England, produced examples of the "life-and-times" of public men, often detailed, uncritical, and filled with pages of original documents. One of the century's greatest achievements was England's *Dictionary of National Biography* (1885–1900), of which Sir Leslie Stephen was the principal editor.

The twentieth century has been a golden age of biography, with thousands of works illustrating extreme diversity in content and approach. The "debunking" tradition, encouraged by Lytton Strachey's *Eminent Victorians* (1918), attracted countless imitators, and following the publication of Erik Erikson's *Young Man Luther* (1958), there were numerous applications of psychoanalytical theories in order to interpret the personalities and motivations of persons of the past, with much controversy about the method. Some historians followed the example of Charles Beard and Sir Lewis Namier in writing "collective biography," or prosopography. Others, like Douglas Freeman, Dumas Malone, and Arthur Link, modified the life-and-time approach by utilizing exhaustive research, critical methods, and readable style. Many professional historians, especially proponents of social history and the Annales school, have tended to disparage biography, but most concede that individual persons sometimes have an impact on the course of events, that the study of an individual can give insight into the culture of a period and that the readers find the study of individuals to be inherently fascinating.

Thomas T. Lewis

See also AUTOBIOGRAPHY; HAGIOGRAPHY; MARTYROLOGY; PROSOPOGRAPHY; PSYCHOHISTORY.

References

Bowen, Catherine Drinker. *Biography: The Craft and the Calling.* Boston: Little, Brown, 1969.
Garraty, John. *The Nature of Biography.* New York: Alfred Knopf, 1957.
Iles, Teresa, ed. *All Sides of the Subject: Women and Biography.* New York: Teachers College Press, 1992.
The Rhetorics of Life-Writing in Early Modern Europe, ed. T.F. Mayer and D.R. Woolf. Ann Arbor: University of Michigan Press, 1995.
Momigliano, Arnaldo. *The Development of Greek Biography.* Cambridge, MA: Harvard University Press, 1993.
Oates, Stephen, ed. *Biography As High Adventure: Life-Writers Speak on Their Art.* Amherst: University of Massachusetts Press, 1986.

Biondo, Flavio (1392–1463)

Italian Renaissance antiquarian, and the first modern historian of the Middle Ages. Born at Forlì, Biondo was a lay secretary in the papal curia and later sought patrons to support his writing. The full title of his major historical work, conventionally referred to as the *Decades* because of its organization into units of ten books, is *Historiarum ab Inclinatione Romani Imperii Decades* [History since the Decline of the Roman Empire]. Completed in 1453 and first printed in 1483, it begins with the sack of Rome in 410 and treats the following thousand years as a unit—what we call the Middle Ages. Biondo was the first humanist to study medieval history objectively and methodically and the first to recognize the end of the ancient empire and the birth of new political forms out of its ruin; in so doing he essentially created the modern periodization of European historical time. In the final part of the work he covers contemporary Italian history from 1410 to 1441. Biondo was not immediately influential in Italy because most historians in succeeding generations concentrated on the histories of particular cities and regions. His true heirs were Carlo Sigonio and, more remotely, Edward Gibbon.

William McCuaig

Texts

Historiarum ab Inclinatione Romani Imperii Decades. In the standard edition of Biondo's collected works: *De Roma triumphante . . . [etc].* Basel: Froben, 1531.
Scritti inediti e rari di Biondi Flavio [Unpublished and Rare Writings]. Ed. Bartolomeo Nogara. Rome: Tipografia poliglotta Vaticana, 1927.

al-Bīrūnī, Abu'l-Rayḥān Muḥammad (973–ca. 1050)

Muslim scientist and polymath. Al-Bīrūnī was a native of Khwarazm, south of the Aral Sea. Apart from brief travels in northern Iran, he lived there until 1017, when he was taken to Ghazna by the conqueror Sultan Maḥmūd. Attached to the latter's court, he accompanied several Ghaznavid campaigns into northern India. Of his enormous scientific output (some 180 works), two are of historiographical importance: the *K·al-Āthār al-Bākiya 'an al-Kurūn al-Khāliya* [Chronology of Ancient Nations], probably completed in A.D. 1000, and the *Kitāb taḥqīq ma li'l-Hind* [Book Confirming Things Indian], completed in 1030. The former addresses ancient eras and calendrical problems. The latter largely concerns Indian philosophy and religious beliefs but is valuable also for information on geography, Hindu eras, and cultural history, including full accounts of Hindu ritual practices.

Charles Melville

Texts

Kitāb al-Āthār al-baqiya 'an al-kurūn al-Khāliya [The Surviving Traces of Past Ages]. Arabic text ed. C.E. Sachau. Leipzig: Brockhaus, 1878. Trans. C.E. Sachau as *The Chronology of Ancient Nations.* London: Oriental Translation Fund, 1879.
Kitāb taḥqīq mā li'l-Hind. Arabic text ed. C.E. Sachau. London: Trubner 1887. Trans. C.E. Sachau as *Alberuni's India.* 2 vols. London: Trubner, 1888.

References

The Commemoration Volume of Biruni International Congress Tehran, B: English and French Papers. Tehran: 1976.

Khan, M.S. "Al-Biruni and the Political History of India." *Oriens* 25–26 (1976): 86–115.

Said, H.M., ed. *Al-Biruni Commemorative Volume.* Karachi, Pakistan: Hamdard Academy, 1979, 141–315.

Yarshater, E. and D. Bishop, eds. *Biruni Symposium.* New York: Columbia University, Iran Center, 1976.

Bizzarri [Bizari], Pietro (1525–after 1586)

Italian historian of ambiguous religious allegiance, though inclined to Protestantism, who lived most of his adult life in England, Germany, and the Spanish Netherlands. His histories are journalistic accounts concentrating on recent and current events in Europe and Asia and have the value of reportage. His history of Genoa failed to win him the recompense he hoped for from the city and was placed on the Index of Forbidden Books in 1590.

William McCuaig

Texts

Cyprium bellum inter Venetos et Selymum Turcarum imperatorem gestum [The War Waged between the Venetians and the Turkish Emperor Suleiman for Cyprus]. Basel: Henricpetri, 1573.

Historia della guerra fatta in Ungheria dall' 'invittissimo Imperatore de' Christiani contra quello de' Turchi [History of the War Waged in Hungary by the Unconquered Christian Emperor against the Turkish Emperor]. Lyon, France: Rovillius, 1568.

Rerum Persicarum historia [History of the Deeds of the Persians]. Antwerp: Plantin, 1583.

Senatus populique Genuensis rerum domi forisque gestarum historiae [History of the Domestic and Foreign Deeds of the Senate and People of Genoa]. Antwerp: Plantin, 1579.

References

Cochrane, Eric. *Historians and Historiography in the Italian Renaissance.* Chicago: University of Chicago Press, 1981, 244–245; 355–356.

Bloch, Marc (1886–1944)

French historian of medieval Europe. Bloch was born in Lyon on July 6, 1886, and was descended from a Jewish family of eastern France. He received his historical training at the École Normale Supérieure, where his father Gustave taught ancient history. Bloch chose to become a medievalist, and, largely due to the influence of Emile Durkheim, he became a sharp critic of traditional political history. It was at the University of Strasbourg that he established his historical reputation and, in 1920, first met his colleague and collaborator, Lucien Febvre. At Strasbourg, Bloch and Febvre established their new approach to history and founded their own historical journal, *Annales.* This new history stressed that historians had to pay closer attention to other social sciences, such as psychology, economics, sociology, and anthropology, as well as to humanistic disciplines such as linguistics, art history, and philosophy. In short, Bloch wanted to broaden and widen the historian's horizons and move beyond the traditional, narrow focus on diplomatic and military history. Bloch and Febvre had already attracted a small number of enthusiasts and followers when Bloch left Strasbourg in 1936 to accept the chair of economic history at the Sorbonne in Paris, itself a sign of his distinction. World War II cut short Bloch's career, however, and he had no hesitation in joining the French resistance after the collapse of the Third Republic. Captured by the Vichy government, Bloch was shot by the Germans along with a number of other prisoners of war on June 16, 1944, in Lyon, his birthplace—less than two weeks after the Allied landings in Normandy.

Bloch's first major historical work, *The Royal Touch* (1924), was a prime example of the kind of history he and Febvre sought to create. Although his other major books, *French Rural History* (1931) and *Feudal Society* (1939) were equally innovative and still command a wide readership, *The Royal Touch* is probably Bloch's most important work, and in the opinion of some is one of the great historical works of the twentieth century. It deals with the popular belief, current in both France and England from the Middle Ages to the late eighteenth century, that kings had the power to cure the skin disease known as scrofula merely by touching its victims. The book also focuses on the ritualistic manner in which French and English kings actually touched the sick for this very purpose, usually just after their consecration and coronation. This book differed sharply from more traditional historical writing in at least three distinct ways. First, Bloch did not focus on a specific king or a particular historical period, but chose to look at a longer view encompassing both the Middle Ages and early modern periods—he thereby anticipated the *longue durée* [long duration] favored by later Annales school historians such as Fernand Braudel. Second, the book was a major contribution to "religious psychology" and the history of "mentalities." That is, Bloch was more

B

fascinated by what people believed about royal power rather than whether kings actually could heal with their royal touch. In this regard, *The Royal Touch* has provided a model for modern cultural history concerns with popular and elite mentalities. Thirdly and finally, by comparing England and France Bloch's book became a pioneering example of comparative history. All these things made Bloch's history of monarchy very different from the traditional studies of medieval political history. Bloch's reflections on the duties and proper methods of the historian were published posthumously in an *Apologie pour l'histoire,* later translated under the somewhat misleading title, *The Historian's Craft.*

Mack P. Holt

Texts

Feudal Society. Trans. L.A. Manyon. 2 vols. London: Routledge, 1961.

French Rural History: An Essay on Its Basic Characteristics. Trans. Janet Sondheimer. London: Routledge, 1966.

The Historian's Craft. Trans. P. Putnam. Manchester, England: Manchester University Press, 1954.

The Royal Touch. Trans. J.E. Anderson. New York: Dorset Press, 1989.

References

Burke, Peter. *The French Historical Revolution: The Annales School, 1929–89.* Stanford, CA: Stanford University Press, 1990.

Fink, Carole. *Marc Bloch: A Life in History.* Cambridge, Eng.: Cambridge University Press, 1989.

Boahen, Albert Adu (b. 1932)

Ghanaian historian, author, educationalist, and statesman. Boahen received his B.A. with honors in history from London University as a student at the new University College at Legon, which became the independent University of Ghana, where he later became the first African professor of history. He earned his doctorate from the School of Oriental and African Studies of London University in 1959. He became president of the Historical Society of Ghana in 1966 and was appointed president of the UNESCO African history project in 1983. He has held visiting fellowships at the Australian National, Columbia, Cornell, and Johns Hopkins universities. He retired from the University of Ghana in 1990 and holds the title of professor emeritus from that

institution. Boahen is one of the first generation of African historians to gain international recognition, having published nine scholarly books and more than two dozen articles. He began his scholarly career at a time when Hugh Trevor-Roper, Regius professor of history at Oxford, could publicly announce that Africa had no history worth studying. His first book, *Britain, the Sahara and the Western Sudan, 1728–1861,* published in 1964, adopted an African perspective to the analysis of British activities. Boahen was in no sense an "ivory tower" historian, but became famous for the way he could interpret new historical perspectives in the age of African independence and nationalism to a wider audience. His essays, *Topics in West African History,* published in 1966, originated as a series of radio talks, in simple language that brilliantly conveyed the complexities of historical research. This soon gained widespread use in schools and colleges throughout Ghana, Nigeria, and Sierra Leone. He continued to cooperate with Nigerian and other colleagues to produce new textbooks for use in schools and colleges. His success in this effort was crowned in 1975 with the publication of the joint work, with J.B. Webster, *The Revolutionary Years: West Africa since 1800,* a synthesis of then current scholarship that became the basic textbook used in the final school years and early university studies in English-speaking African schools, as well as overseas. It was fitting therefore that Boahen should be appointed editor of UNESCO's *History of Africa,* Vol. 7, *Africa under Colonial Domination, 1880–1935,* published in 1985, a wide-ranging work of thirty chapters, using interdisciplinary techniques and adopting regional, continental, and international perspectives.

Apollos O. Nwauwa

Texts

African Perspectives on Colonialism. Baltimore, MD: Johns Hopkins University Press, 1987.

Britain, the Sahara and the Western Sudan, 1728–1861. London: Oxford University Press, 1964.

With J.B. Webster. *The Revolutionary Years: West Africa since 1800.* London: Longman, 1975.

Topics in West African History. London: Longman, 1966.

Ed. *UNESCO History of Africa.* Vol 7. *Africa under Colonial Domination, 1880–1935.* London: Heinemann Educational Books; Berkeley : University of California Press, 1985.

Bobrzyński, Michał (1849–1935)

Historian of Poland's legal and political systems; representative of the so-called Cracow school of history (together with J. Szujski and W. Kalinka); political activist in Galicia. Bobrzyński was born in Cracow and studied there and in Germany. In 1877 he became professor of the history of law at Jagiellonian University and by 1878 was a member of the Polish Academy of Sciences and Arts. Bobrzyński's reputation rests primarily on *Dzieje Polski w zarysie* [An Outline of the History of Poland] (1879), which presented a sober, even severe, evaluation of Polish political history. Bobrzyński regarded anarchy, "golden freedom," and lack of a strong government in the latter half of the eighteenth century as the primary reasons for the collapse of the Polish state. Past experience proved, for Bobrzyński, the necessity for a strong government in contemporary Poland. For this reason Bobrzyński was active with the Cracow conservatists *(stańczycy),* leading the party and holding offices in the Galician Diet, the Austrian State Council, and the National School Council in Galicia. His greatest political success came between 1908 and 1913, during which time he was governor of Galicia.

Jolanta T. Pękacz

Texts

Dzieje Polski w zarysie. 2 vols. Warsaw: Gebethner i Wolff, 1887–1890.
Szkice i studia historyczne [Historical Studies and Essays]. Cracow: Krakowska Spółka Wydawnicza, 1922.
Wskrzeszenie państwa polskiego [The Restoration of the Polish state]. 2 vols. Cracow: Krakowska Spółka Wydawnicza, 1920–1925.
Z moich pamiętników [From My Memoirs]. ed. J. Galos. Wrocław: Zakład Narodowy im. Ossolińskich, 1957.

References

Bartel, Wojciech M. "Michał Bobrzyński 1849–1935." In *Spór o krakowską szkołę historyczną* [The Controversy over the Cracow School of Historiography], ed. C. Bobińska and J. Wyrozumski. Cracow: Wydawnictwo Literackie, 1972, 145–189.
Demkovych-Dobrians'kyi, Mykhailo. *Potots'kyi i Bobzhyns'kyi tsisars'ki namisnyky Halychyny 1903–1913* [Potocki and Bobrzynki, the Tsarist Governors of Galicia 1903–1913]. Rym: Ukraons'kyi katolyts'kyi universytet Sv. Klymenta Papy, 1987.

Hetnal, Adam A. "Bobrzyński—Historian and Statesman." *Polish Review* 30 (1985): 99–103.
Łazuga, Waldemar. *Michał Bobrzyński: Myśl historyczna a działalność społeczna* [Michał Bobrzynski: Historical Thought and Political Activity]. Warsaw: PWN, 1982.

Bock, Gisela (b. 1942)

German social theorist and gender historian. Bock was born in Karlsruhe, Germany. She attended the University of Freiburg and received a doctorate from the Free University of Berlin. Bock has been a professor at the Technical University in Berlin and the University of Bielefeld. She was a Kennedy fellow at the Center for European Studies at Harvard University. As director of the European Culture Research Centre at the European University Institute in Florence, she developed historiographical symposiums. Bock's focus on international women's history has won her scholarly acclaim. Her critical examinations of women and racism in modern society have been published in *Zwangssterilisation im Nationalsozialismus: Studien zur Rassenpolitik und Frauenpolitik* [Compulsory Sterilization in National Socialism: Studies in the Politics of Race and Sex] (1986), and *Beyond Equality and Difference: Citizenship, Feminist Policies and Female Subjectivity,* edited with Susan James (1992). Bock's seminal article, "Women's History and Gender History," in *Gender and History* (1989), outlined her theories about incorporating female experiences and gender relations into historiography.

Elizabeth D. Schafer

Texts

Ed. with Quentin Skinner and Maurizio Viroli. *Machiavelli and Republicanism.* Cambridge, Eng.: Cambridge University Press, 1990.
Ed. with Pat Thane. *Maternity and Gender Policies: Women and the Rise of the European Welfare States, 1880–1950s.* New York: Routledge, 1991.
Thomas Campanella. Tübingen, Germany: Niemeyer, 1974.
Zwangssterilisation im Nationalsozialismus: Studien zur Rassenpolitik und Frauenpolitik. Opladen, Germany: Westdeutscher Verlag, 1986.

References

Offen, Karen, Ruth Roach Pierson, and Jane Rendall, eds. *Writing Women's History: International Perspectives.* Bloomington: Indiana University Press, 1991.

Bodin, Jean (1529/30–1596)

French historian and jurisconsult. Born in Angers, Bodin practiced and taught law in Toulouse until the 1560s when he held various royal offices. He was a deputy to the Estates General at Blois in 1576 and an adherent to the Holy League in the 1590s. Bodin's most significant historiographical work is the *Methodus ad facilem historiarum cognitionem* [Method for the Easy Comprehension of History] (1566), a handbook on how to read history. Schooled in legal humanism, Bodin reconstructed juristic science based on universal law, which in turn served as the basis for the ideal state. The essence of universal law lay in the past and could be isolated by comparison of historical states, the best of which the jurist/historian could then select as a model for the present. To organize the refractory mass of material, Bodin devised a method of criticism that directly influenced eighteenth-century historians and, indirectly, those of the twentieth century. Rather than read historical sources as literary models, as Renaissance humanists had advocated, Bodin considered them as evidence. Inspired by skepticism, he was the first historian to question sources for bias by assuming that an author's interests affect his commitment to truthfulness. Therefore, he concluded, historians must consider evidence from various sources and must present balanced accounts.

James R. Farr

See also ARS HISTORICA.

Texts

Method for the Easy Comprehension of History. Trans. Beatrice Reynolds. New York: Columbia University Press, 1945.
The Six Books of a Commonweale. Ed. K.D. McRae. Cambridge, MA: Harvard University Press, 1962.

References

Franklin, Julian H. *Jean Bodin and the Sixteenth-Century Revolution in the Methodology of Law and History.* New York: Columbia University Press, 1963.

Boece, Hector (ca. 1470–1536)

Scottish humanist and historian [name also spelled Bois, Boys, or, in Latin, Boethius]. Boece was born into a family of Dundee burgesses. Moving to the University of Paris, he became friends with Erasmus and graduated M.A. in 1494. He taught at Montaigu College until 1497 when William Elphinstone, bishop of Aberdeen, invited him to teach at the new University of Aberdeen where he became the first principal in 1505 and remained until his death. Boece published two historical works: *Murthlancensium et Aberdonensium Episcoporum Vitae* [Lives of the Bishops of Aberdeen] (1522) and the *Scotorum Historiae* [Histories of the Scots] (1526). The first work was derived from the second and was a tribute to his patron, Elphinstone. In the second work, Boece used Livy as his model for a comprehensive history of Scotland, which was the first to be aimed at European readers. The English chronicler Raphael Holinshed incorporated it into his *Chronicles* later in the century. Later historians have denigrated the work because Boece included considerable mythological and supernatural material and relied on some chronicles that later proved to be forgeries, but it is reliable for the late medieval period.

Ronald H. Fritze

Texts

The Chronicles of Scotland by Hector Boece. Ed. R.W. Chambers and E.C. Batho. Edinburgh: Scottish Text Society, 1938–1941.
Murthlancensium et Aberdonensium Episcoporum Vitae. Ed. J. Moir. Aberdeen: New Spalding Club, 1894.

References

Quatercentenary of the Death of Hector Boece. Ed. W.D. Simpson. Aberdeen: University of Aberdeen Press, 1937.

Boethius, Anicius Manlius Torquatus Severinus (ca. 480–524/526)

Philosopher, poet, and statesman. Born into a Roman senatorial family, Boethius held a variety of high civil offices from 510 to 523, when he was unjustly arrested for treason. Following a torture-filled imprisonment, he was executed at an unknown date. During imprisonment, Boethius composed *The Consolation of Philosophy.* Combining Neoplatonic thought and Christian doctrine, this work proclaims faith in the beneficent direction of human history under divine providence. Instructed by Lady Philosophy, Boethius learns that, despite the randomness of the Wheel of Fortune, one can find peace and perfect happiness by rejecting the distractions of transitory worldly fortune and choosing God. Upon making this free choice, one perceives that all that is, was, and will be is under God's guidance. *The Consolation of Philosophy's* impact on medieval Europe's historiographical vision was profound, inasmuch as it affirmed that human history is rational and divinely directed. Consequently, it was one of the most widely copied and read treatises in the postclassical West, and it was one of the first Latin classics translated into a European vernacular tongue. Anglo-Saxon, German, French, English, and Italian translations appeared between the ninth and fourteenth centuries.

Alfred J. Andrea

Texts

The Consolation of Philosophy. Trans. Richard H. Green. Indianapolis, IN: The Library of Liberal Arts, 1962.

The Consolation of Philosophy. Trans. V.E. Watts. Harmondsworth, Eng.: Penguin, 1969.

References

Gibson, Margaret T., ed. *Boethius: His Life, Thought and Influence.* Oxford: Basil Blackwell, 1981.

Pickering, Frederick P. *Augustinus oder Boethius? Geschichts-schreibung und epische Dichtung im Mittelalter-und in der Neuzeit.* 2 vols. Berlin: E. Schmidt, 1967–1976.

Bolingbroke, Henry St. John, Viscount (1678–1751)

English politician and philosopher. St. John was born at Lydiard Tregoze in Wiltshire, became a Tory member of Parliament and minister under Queen Anne, and was compelled to leave England after the Tory electoral defeat in 1715. He lived in exile in France until 1744, but frequently visited England for private as well as political purposes, attempting to organize an opposition or "country" party against the administration of Sir Robert Walpole. Bolingbroke's historical writings originated from his political-ideological and philosophical interests rather than from a scholarly attitude. In his *Remarks on the History of England*— originally published as essays in *The Craftsman*, 1730–1731—and in the *Dissertation upon Parties*, printed in the same journal in 1733–1734, he offered a complete outline of the political and constitutional history of England from the ancient Britons to his own time. He represented British history as a permanent struggle between the spirit of liberty and the spirit of tyranny, insisting upon the necessity of a political opposition to contrast the modern forms of political corruption that he believed were now threatening traditional English liberties. In this account lies his claim to the authorship of one of the earliest and most

popular versions of what Herbert Butterfield has famously called the "Whig interpretation of history." Bolingbroke's *Letters on the Study and Use of History* was written in 1735 and published in 1752, developing themes suggested in the *Substance of Some Letters to M. de Pouilly* (1720). They convey, in epistolary form, his reflections, very much in the humanist tradition, on the superiority of political and diplomatic history for the training of statesmen and politicians. Bolingbroke's view of history as "philosophy teaching by examples" was inspired by a strong disdain for mere antiquarianism, but it was coupled with a deep skepticism about the possibility of attaining sound historical knowledge, especially of ancient times. This "pyrrhonism," following a pattern of Enlightenment historical criticism also associated with Pierre Bayle and, later, with Voltaire, led Bolingbroke to doubt the veracity of the Bible and even its value as a historical document.

Guido Abbattista

Texts

Bolingbroke's Historical Writings. Ed. Isaac Kramnick. Chicago: University of Chicago Press, 1972.

The Works. 4 vols. New York: A.M. Kelley, 1967.

References

Butterfield, Herbert. *The Englishman and His History.* Cambridge, Eng.: Cambridge University Press, 1944.

Kramnick, Isaac. *Bolingbroke and His Circle: The Politics of Nostalgia in the Age of Walpole.* Ithaca, NY and London: Cornell University Press, 1992.

Kramnick, Isaac. "Introduction." In *Bolingbroke's Historical Writings,* ed. Kramnick. Chicago: University of Chicago Press, 1972.

Bollandists and Maurists

Belgian Jesuit and French Benedictine scholarly organizations, respectively, which initiated communal efforts to edit medieval Christian manuscripts. The Bollandist undertaking was conceived by Héribert Rosweyde (d. 1629), a Jesuit who in 1603 acquired sponsorship to edit extant Belgian saints' *Lives.* After his death, Jean Bolland (d. 1665) broadened the Antwerp project's scope to saints in historical sources and martyrological entries. Thus began the Bollandist publication of *Acta Sanctorum* [Deeds of the Saints] (1643). Bolland and Godefroid Henschenius (d. 1681), succeeded by Daniel von Papenbroeck or Papebroch (d. 1714), completed volumes comprising January to early June. Work proceeded steadily until the suppression of the Jesuits (1773), when the Bollandists found monastic quarters. In 1794 French armies devastated the Bollandist collections, temporarily bringing publication to a halt. The Bollandists were revived in 1837 in Brussels. Under Charles de Smedt (d. 1911), Bollandist work regained momentum, and with the scholarship of Hippolyte Delehaye (d. 1941) and Paul Grosjean (d. 1964), among others, they made significant progress toward completion of the *Acta*. The Bollandists continue their labors, having at present completed the *propylaeum* for the month of December.

Although the Bollandists had no formal methodology, their critical work on original manuscripts constituted a vast improvement over existing editions. In the format devised by Henschenius, each entry included a biography, a discussion of chronological issues and historical context, as well as the correction of errors of previous editions. The Bollandist effort to identify saints whose veracity could not be confirmed, however, was not always well received. Papebroch's suspicion of the historicity of Benedictine manuscripts provoked Jean Mabillon's (d. 1707) brilliant defense in *De re diplomatica* [Regarding Diplomatic] (1681). Likewise, Papebroch's questioning of the authenticity of Carmelite hagiographical traditions led to a twenty-year denunciation of the *Acta* by the Spanish Inquisition (1695). Under De Smedt, modern critical methodology was first applied to Bollandist editions. Moreover, in 1882, the group founded *Analecta Bollandiana* [Bollandist Analects], a journal publishing hagiographical research, and soon afterwards a monographical series *Subsidia Hagiographica* [Hagiographical Aids]. Through his *Les légendes hagiographiques* [The Hagiographical Legends] (1905), Delehaye successfully encouraged the study of saints' lives among a larger academic community.

In contrast, the Benedictine Congregation of Saint-Maur was founded in France in 1618, modeled after monastic houses under the authority of Saint-Vanne at Verdun (Lorraine). Led by Grégoire Tarrisse (d. 1648), the Maurists established headquarters at Saint-Germain-des-Prés. Under Luc d'Achery (d. 1685), they acquired the library collection central to their scholarship. Only the most erudite members of the congregation such as Thierry Ruinart (d. 1709), Jacques Bouillart (d. 1726), Edmond Martène (d. 1739), Bernard de Montfaucon (d. 1741), and Michel-Toussaint Chrétien Du Plessis (d. 1764), were awarded places at Saint-Germain-des-Prés, and there they devoted themselves to composing textual editions and historical works. By the time of the French Revolution, Maurist houses were 193 in number, and the library of Saint-Germain contained close to fifty thousand printed books and seven thousand manuscripts. Despite demands for reform in 1754, 1763, and 1766, the monks' requests to limit religious obligations of scholars went unanswered. Meanwhile, many Maurists found similar employment at the Cabinet des Chartes, created in 1762. In 1790, revolutionaries liquidated Saint-Germain-des-Prés, bringing an end to Maurist scholarship.

Maurist energies centered on assembling manuscripts of provincial and local monastic history; their greatest contributions lay in the development of paleographical methodology rather than in critical analysis of their documents' contents. They produced improved editions of the church fathers and Benedictine leaders based upon the original manuscripts, such as the series of the *Acta Sanctorum Ordinis Sancti Benedicti* [Deeds of the Saints of the Order of St. Benedict] (1668–1701) inaugurated by Mabillon, and the Maurist edition of the works of Saint Augustine (1679–1700). Following Spanish condemnation of Bollandist works in 1695, however, the Maurists turned to less controversial pursuits, such as the biographies of all church office holders of France in the series *Gallia Christiana* [Christian Gaul] (1716–1785). In *Recueil des historiens des Gaules et de la France* [Account of the Historians of the Gauls and of France] (1737–1786), directed by Martin Bouquet (d. 1754), Maurists entered into the long-standing historical debate over the origins of the French monarchy. By 1788, the Cabinet des Chartes had taken over responsibility for both of these endeavors.

Bonnie Effros

See also MABILLON; MONTFAUCON.

Texts

Acta Sanctorum. Ed. Jean Carnandet. 69 vols. Paris: V. Palmé, 1863–1940.

Analecta Bollandiana. Brussels: Société des Bollandistes, 1882–present.

Bibliotheca hagiographica Graeca [Greek Hagiographical Catalog]. Brussels: Société des Bollandistes, 1957.

Bibliotheca hagiographica latina antiquae et mediae aetatis [Antique and Medieval Latin Hagiographical Catalog]. 3 vols. Brussels: Société des Bollandistes, 1954.

Bibliotheca hagiographica orientalis [Oriental Hagiographical Catalog]. Brussels: Société des Bollandistes, 1954.

Bouquet, Martin, et al. *Recueil des historiens des Gaules et de la France.* Ed. Léopold Delisle. 24 vols. Farnborough, Eng.: Gregg, 1967–1968.

Delehaye, Hippolyte. *The Legends of the Saints. An Introduction to Hagiography.* Trans. Donald Attwater. New York: Fordham University Press, 1962.

Gallia Christiana. 13 vols. Farnborough, Eng.: Gregg, 1970.

Mabillon, Jean. *De re diplomatica Libri VI.* Rome: Bibliopola, 1965.

Rosweyde, Héribert. *Fasti sanctorum quorum vitae in Belgicis bibliothecis manuscriptae* [A List of Saints Whose Manuscript Lives Are in Belgian Libraries]. Antwerp: Plantin, 1607.

Sancti Aurelii Augustini Hipponensis Operum tomus primus [-tomus decimus] [The Works of St. Aurelius Augustinus of Hippo Volumes One to Ten]. Revised ed. 11 vols. Paris: Gaume Fratres, 1835–1839.

References

Barret-Kriegel, Blandine. *Les académies de l'histoire* [The Academies of History]. Paris: Presses Universitaires de France, 1988.

Chaussy, Yves. *Les Bénédictins de Saint-Maur* [The Benedictines of Saint-Maur]. 2 vols. Paris: Études Augustiniennes, 1989.

Delehaye, Hippolyte. *The Work of the Bollandists through Three Centuries, 1615–1915.* Princeton, NJ: Princeton University Press, 1922.

Edelman, Nathan. *Attitudes of Seventeenth Century France toward the Middle Ages.* New York: King's Crown Press, 1946.

Knowles, David. *Great Historical Enterprises: Problems in Monastic History.* London: Thomas Nelson and Sons, Ltd., 1963.

Tassin, René-Prosper. *Histoire littéraire de la Congrégation de Saint-Maur* [Literary History of the Congregation of Saint-Maur]. Paris: Chez Humblot, Libraire, 1770.

Bolton, Herbert Eugene (1870–1953)

U.S. historian. Born in Wisconsin, Bolton was a student of Frederick Jackson Turner at the University of Wisconsin and of John B. McMaster at the University of Pennsylvania, where he received his Ph.D. (1899). Both men influenced the future direction of Bolton's research. At the University of Texas (1901–1909), he pioneered the study of the Spanish borderlands and what is now known as ethnohistory. Later, at the University of California

(1911–1940), he developed comparative colonial history and produced with Thomas Marshall *The Colonization of North America, 1492–1783* (1920). A year later he published his classic book, *The Spanish Borderlands.* He also pioneered the history of the Americas, which was first taught in 1919 and published an elaborate syllabus titled *History of the Americas* (1928). In 1932 he presented his concept of the Americas in a presidential address, "The Epic of Greater America," to the American Historical Association. This new approach to hemispheric history proved popular in the United States and Canada until the 1970s. He was also chair of the history department at California and director of the Bancroft Library. He published numerous articles and books on borderlands topics, always stressing the value of archival material. Although the Spanish borderlands remains a popular subject, the history of the Americas remains dormant as a concept in the United States.

Russell M. Magnaghi

Texts

And T.M. Marshall. *The Colonization of North America, 1492–1783.* New York: Macmillan, 1920.

The Hasinai: Southern Caddoans As Seen by the Earliest Europeans. Ed. R.M. Magnaghi. Norman: University of Oklahoma Press, 1987.

History of the Americas. Boston: Ginn and Company, 1928.

The Spanish Borderlands. New Haven, CT: Yale University Press, 1921.

Wider Horizons of American History. New York: Appleton-Century Co., 1939.

References

Bannon, J.F., ed. *Bolton and the Spanish Borderlands.* Norman: University of Oklahoma Press, 1964.

Bannon, J.F. *Herbert Eugene Bolton: The Historian and the Man.* Tucson: University of Arizona Press, 1978.

Hanke, Lewis, ed. *Do the Americas Have a Common History? A Critique of the Bolton Theory.* New York: Alfred A. Knopf, 1964.

Book, History of the

Branch of sociocultural history dedicated to the study of the book's production and diffusion in past societies. As an area of specialization the history of the book may be seen as an amalgam of subgenres that evolved separately within distinct historiographical traditions. In addition, the field incorporates both theoretical and methodological insights gained from other disciplines—cultural anthropology, descriptive and textual bibliography, and library science among others. Robert Darnton provides one of the better definitions of the field in its modern incarnation, stating that the history of the book is that of a communications circuit which "runs from the author to the publisher, the printer, the shipper, the bookseller and the reader."

In broad terms, the historiographical evolution of the field can be divided into two distinct traditions. The first is the primarily Anglo-American tradition of descriptive and textual bibliography, the study of the production of books. Scholars associated with descriptive bibliography manifested a primarily physical concern for the book, compiling scrupulously detailed lists of titles and their various editions. The links between this tradition and the evolving science of library cataloging are obvious, and many of the great early works of descriptive bibliography were in fact produced for and by libraries. The more historical of the bibliographers also demonstrated a limited concern for the diffusion of books. In the American tradition, for example, it became popular to examine early colonial records to establish the presence of certain titles in either private collections, the inventories of booksellers, or the catalogs of colonial libraries. Alternatively, such studies could be used to establish which titles were being printed or, most often, reprinted in America. Indeed, such works as George Littlefield's *Early Boston Booksellers, 1642–1711* (1900) marked the evolution of the American tradition of book history and continue to influence it even today. Textual bibliographers, working within a more literary framework, were concerned primarily with establishing the integrity of texts and tracing their genealogy through subsequent editions. In their quest to compile definitive editions of important works these scholars made significant contributions to the history of publishing. For the most part, however, it is only recently that the Anglo-American tradition has concerned itself with the social diffusion of books.

That evolution is to a large extent a reflection of the significant impact of the second of the main trends in the historiographical evolution of the history of the book, the French tradition of *histoire du livre*. Although the term means literally "history of the book," it is used, even in English, to denote an approach that is distinctly more sociological than that of the bibliographers. *Histoire du livre* is usually traced back to the seminal work of Lucien Febvre and Henri-Jean Martin,

L'Apparition du livre [The Coming of the Book], first published in 1958. Febvre and Martin called for a serious reconsideration of the book's social impact, and, conversely, of the social forces influencing its production. In so doing they pioneered a new approach to the problem of the social diffusion of knowledge relying on records documenting all aspects of the book's life cycle and founded a historical subdiscipline that was to become both complex and wide-ranging. Through the 1960s and 1970s French *historiens du livre* such as Roger Chartier, Michel Marion, and, indeed, Martin himself, produced impressive research dealing mostly with the *Ancien Régime* drawing on such varied sources as the records of government censors, postmortem inventories, and the inventories of both private and public libraries.

Histoire du livre, then, shifted attention from the book as cultural artifact to the book as a communications medium. In making this transition the genre's practitioners consciously moved beyond the book's historical significance in textual or material terms to a consideration of its interaction with the social context. In this sense, Robert Darnton's *The Business of Enlightenment* was a study of the famous *Encyclopédie* which, while not neglecting the importance of the work to the Western intellectual tradition, sought rather to examine how it was distributed and consequently to determine who in French society had enjoyed privileged access to new and potentially subversive ideas. Book historians need not, however, begin with a title or even a series of titles, but rather can simply establish patterns of book ownership within the population. This was the case of Michel Marion's work, based on a study of postmortem inventories drawn from French records for the first half of the eighteenth century. His study established that book ownership remained relatively rare and that those individuals who owned books tended to favor works of either a historical or theological nature. These two examples illustrate the alternative perspective offered by *histoire du livre* and its emphasis on reconstructing social networks used for the diffusion of print in past societies.

Growing out of these basic preoccupations, the genre has branched out in many directions over the past twenty years. The approaches taken by historians of the book have been adapted to the temporal and geographic particularities of the societies they studied. In the case of newly literate societies, the book's appearance initiated a shift from oral to written traditions and empowered new groups within a literate elite. Indeed, as Rhyss Isaac has shown, the very possession of a book conferred social authority to its owner in societies with low rates of literacy such as early Virginia. In these cases the study of book history integrated approaches associated with cultural anthropology. Even where books and reading were more common the possession of knowledge was still closely linked to their ownership, although in this case the size of an individual's library and his affiliation to a literate elite were measures of both erudition and social status. Tracing the networks of book distribution and establishing the linkages between the members of a literate elite brought book historians back to the sources once valued by the bibliographers: booksellers' inventories, publishing records, and estate inventories. Newer works such as Richard Brown's *Knowledge Is Power,* a study of the literate elite in New England from the late eighteenth to the mid-nineteenth century, simply approached these sources from a social perspective.

As historians of the book approached the threshold of the nineteenth century, they were met with a far more complex situation. In the first half of the century literacy rates increased in most Western societies, and the nature of reading itself evolved. This era was marked by the continued rise of the novel and by a general decline in the production costs of printed material. Reading became consumption, and both the supply and the diffusion of published material increased dramatically. The networks diffusing the book grew to an international scale in response to growing demand. Circulating libraries, which emerged almost everywhere in the early-nineteenth century, provided a new solution to the problem of diffusing print through society. These libraries, most often the creation of middle-class philanthropy, offered new opportunities and challenges to the historian of the book. Here the genre branched out to yet another discipline, in this case that of library history.

Although most library history to the late 1970s was primarily institutional in nature, the impact of book history forced a new consideration of the social role of early libraries. Once again the French had innovated with early studies of circulating libraries and the famous *cabinets de lecture.* In the American context early circulating libraries, or social libraries as they became known, were studied both for their role in early nineteenth-century American associational life and as important sources of literary culture in the emerging urban societies of antebellum America. At one level these studies revealed the importance of the book to early nineteenth-century urban elites as a means of refashioning the cultural landscape of their towns in accordance with their own value systems.

More detailed analysis of the diffusion of books through these institutions has also demonstrated the different functions of the library for the various social groups making use of its collection.

As many of the previous examples indicate, the methods and approaches associated with *histoire du livre* have been favorably received in the United States. The adoption of these methods was very much a conscious effort, sponsored largely by the American Antiquarian Society (AAS) which invited French practitioners to share their insights with American scholars. The society's *Proceedings* through the early 1980s contain many good methodological and historiographical discussions on the topic, and the AAS continues to promote the history of the book. The genre also remains popular in France and in French Canada, where it is at the forefront of sociocultural history.

Louis-Georges Harvey

Texts

Brown, Richard. *Knowledge Is Power.* Oxford: Oxford University Press, 1989.

Darnton, Robert. *The Business of Enlightenment: A Publishing History of the Encyclopédie.* Cambridge, MA: Belknap Press, 1979.

Febvre, Lucien, and Henri-Jean Martin. *The Coming of the Book: The Impact of Printing 1450–1800.* Ed. Geoffrey Nowell-Smith and David Wootton; trans. David Gerard. London: New Left Books, 1976.

Isaac, Rhys. "Books and the Social Authority of Learning: The Case of Mid-Eighteenth Century Virginia." In *Printing and Society in Early America,* ed. William Joyce et. al. Worcester, MA: American Antiquarian Society, 1983, 229–249.

Littlefield, George. *Early Boston Booksellers, 1642–1711.* New York: Burt Franklin, 1969.

Marion, Michel. *Recherches sur les bibliothèque privées à Paris au milieu du XVIIè siècle.* Paris: Bibliothèque nationale, 1978.

References

Darnton, Robert. "What Is the History of Books?" In *Books and Society in History,* ed. K.E. Carpenter. New York: Bowker, 1983, 3–26.

Boorstin, Daniel Joseph (b. 1914)

American historian and teacher. A major voice in the field of American history, Boorstin began his academic career at Harvard (A.B., 1934) and earned additional degrees at Oxford and Yale. His interest and training in law led to the publication

B

of his first book, *The Mysterious Science of Law* (1941), an essay on Blackstone's commentaries. His distinguished teaching career includes a long tenure at the University of Chicago (1944–1969) and a number of posts abroad, including one at the University of Paris, where he was the first incumbent of the chair of American History in 1961–1962. Boorstin also served as the director and senior historian of the National Museum of History and Technology in the Smithsonian (1969–1975), as Librarian of Congress (1975–1987), and as Librarian of Congress Emeritus after 1987.

Boorstin's writings are prolific and influential. Works such as *The Americans: The National Experience* (1965, Francis Parkman Prize) and *The Americans: The Democratic Experience* (1973, Pulitzer Prize) firmly established him as a defender of both American exceptionalism and American consensus. He argues that New World circumstances and settlers' ingenuity were the primary factors in shaping English America. He suggests that intellectual movements such as the American Enlightenment were ultimately unimportant in the formation of the American Revolution, prompting disagreement from fellow Consensus historian Bernard Bailyn. He has also been challenged by social historians such as Francis Jennings for the noninclusive and sometimes impressionistic nature of his work. In more recent years, Boorstin has turned to broader questions of history and historiography in works such as *The Republic of Technology* (1978), *Hidden History* (1987), and *Cleopatra's Nose* (1994).

Ruth McClelland-Nugent

Texts

The Americans: The Colonial Experience. New York: Vintage Books, 1958.

The Americans: The Democratic Experience. New York: Random House, 1973.

The Americans: The National Experience. New York: Vintage Books, 1965.

Cleopatra's Nose: Essays on the Unexpected, ed. Ruth F. Boorstin. New York: Random House, 1994.

The Creators. New York: Random House, 1992.

The Discoverers. New York: Random House, 1983.

Hidden History. New York: Harper and Row, 1987.

The Mysterious Science of Law. Cambridge, MA: Harvard University Press, 1941.

The Republic of Technology. New York: Harper and Row, 1978.

References

Higham, John. *History: Professional Scholarship in America.* Rev. ed. Baltimore, MD: Johns Hopkins University Press, 1983.

Novick, Peter. *That Noble Dream: The "Objectivity Question" and the American Historical Profession.* Cambridge, Eng.: Cambridge University press, 1988.

Pole, J.R. "Daniel J. Boorstin." In his *Paths to the American Past.* New York: Oxford University Press, 1979, 299–334.

Sternsher, Bernard. *Consensus, Conflict, and American Historians.* Bloomington: Indiana University Press, 1975.

Bortolotti, Franca Pieroni (1925–1985)

Italian feminist historian. Professor of the history of political parties and movements at the University of Siena and actively involved in the political and cultural life of Florence, Bortolotti pioneered the field of women's history in Italy. A lifelong member of the Italian Communist Party, she participated in the antifascist resistance and contributed to the revitalization of the University of Florence after World War II. Influenced by Gaetano Salvemini and Delio Cantimori, she produced work on the women's movement in Italy in *Alle origine del movimento femminile in Italia, 1848–1892* [Origins of the Feminist Movement in Italy, 1848–1892] (1963) and on an early Italian feminist in *Anna Maria Mozzoni: La liberazione della donna* [Anna Maria Mozzoni: The Liberation of a Woman] (1975). Her later research led to an interest in the relationship between feminism and pacifism, the results of which were published as *La donna, la pace, L'Europa, L'Associazione Internazionale delle Donne dalle origini alla prima guerra mondiale* [Woman, Peace, Europe: The International Association of Women from Its Origins to World War I] (1985). These works established her as the founder of women's history in Italy. Although her work was often met with skepticism on the part of older historians, she left a profound influence on a generation of younger scholars, mostly women. For Bortolotti, the status of women was crucial in assessing the true character of democracy.

Stanislao G. Pugliese

Texts

Femminismo e partiti politici in Italia (1919–1926) [Feminism and Political Parties in Italy]. Rome: Editori Riuniti, 1978.

Socialismo e questioni femminile [Socialism and the Woman Question]. Milan: Marzotta, 1974.

Sul movimento politico delle donne. Ed. Annarita Buttafuoco. Rome: Utopia, 1987.

References

Di Cori, Paola. "Women's History in Italy." In *Writing Women's History: International Perspectives,* ed. Karen Offen, Ruth Roach Pierson, and Jane Rendall. London: Macmillan, 1991, 443–456.

Bossuet, Jacques-Bénigne (1627–1704)

French bishop, pamphleteer, preacher, and historian. Bossuet was born of middle-class parents in Dijon. Trained locally by Jesuits, Bossuet studied in Paris (1642–1652), receiving his doctorate in theology in 1652. His appointment as archdeacon in Metz (1652) led to his first published work, *Réfutation du Catéchisme* of the reformed pastor Paul Ferry in 1655. That year also began Bossuet's reputation as a preacher ("le plus grand prédicateur du Grand Siècle") with numerous published *oraisons funèbres* (funeral orations) over three decades, leading to the bishopric of Condom (1669) and of Meaux (1681). Later controversies with Fénelon on quietism and with Richard Simon on biblical criticism diminished Bossuet's critical reputation for modern scholars but improved his contemporary popularity. Interest in Bossuet for historians rests in his tenure as tutor to the Dauphin (1670–1680). Bossuet's studies resulted in his monumental *Discours sur l'Histoire Universelle depuis la Création du Monde jusqu'à Charlemagne* [Discourse on Universal History from the Creation to Charlemagne] (1681) which he conceived in twelve "epochs" blending the history of the East with Europe: " . . . the deeds of men and the will of God." His *Abrégé de l'Histoire de France* [Concise History of France] (1675) was designed to instruct the Dauphin in the "incidental hazards of kingship," and his *Histoire des Variations des Églises protestantes* [History of the Differences among the Protestant Churches] (1691) confronts "interior history" in the manner of St. Augustine.

A.J. Carlson

Texts

Correspondance de Bossuet. Ed. C. Urbain and E. Lévèsque. 15 vols. Paris: Hachette, 1909–1925.

Discourse on Universal History. Ed. Orest Ranum; trans. Elborg Forster. Chicago: University of Chicago Press, 1976.

Œuvres complètes de Bossuet [Complete Works]. Ed. J.-P. Migne. 11 vols. Paris: J.-P. Migne, 1865–1875.

References

Goyet, Thérèse, *L'Humanisme de Bossuet* [The Humanism of Bossuet]. 2 vols. Paris: Klincksieck, 1965.

Meyer, Jean. *Bossuet.* Paris: Plon, 1993.

Richardt, Aimé. *Bossuet.* Paris: Ozoir-la-Ferriere, 1992.

Terstegge, Georgiana. *Providence As Idée Maîtresse in the Works of Bossuet (Theme and Stylistic Motif).* New York: AMS Press, 1970.

Bracciolini, Poggio (1380–1459)

Renaissance humanist historian. One of the first generation of Florentine humanists, he spent most of his career as a layman with the papal curia. This brought him to the Council of Constance (1414–1418), and the opportunity to search the libraries of St. Gallen and Cluny for classical manuscripts. His celebrated discoveries of works by Cicero, Quintilian, Vitruvius, and others significantly stimulated humanist cultural and historical scholarship. From 1423 to 1452 he worked in the Roman curia and wrote on a wide range of subjects, from obscene and satirical stories to moral philosophy. *De varietate fortunae* [Of the Mutability of Fortune] (ca. 1448) expressed the characteristic humanist view that history unfolded as the interplay of human effort and fate. Returning to Florence as its chancellor in 1453, Poggio began an unfinished *Historia fiorentina* [Florentine History] on the thematic model of Sallust, covering the city's wars from 1350 to 1455. Its emphasis on civilian morale and praise for diplomacy over battle demonstrated an appreciation of human factors that could counter fickle *fortuna.* The frequent, if inconsistent, moral judgments emphasized individual behavior rather than public policy.

Nicholas Terpstra

Texts

Opera Omnia. 4 vols. Turin, Italy: Erasmo, 1964–1969.

References

Cochrane, Eric. *Historians and Historiography in the Italian Renaissance.* Chicago: University of Chicago Press, 1981, 28–29.

Struever, Nancy. *The Language of History in the Renaissance.* Princeton, NJ: Princeton University Press, 1970.

Wilcox, Donald J. *The Development of Florentine Humanist Historiography in the Fifteenth Century.* Cambridge, MA: Harvard University Press, 1969.

B

Brady, Robert (d. 1700)

English historian and physician. Brady was born in Norfolk and studied at Caius College, Cambridge, of which he became master in 1660. He was appointed Regius professor of physics at Cambridge University and on two occasions in the 1680s represented the university in the House of Commons. He was Physician in Ordinary to both Charles II and James II. It is, however, as a historian that Brady is best remembered, a role that was facilitated by his appointment as Keeper of the Records at the Tower of London. Brady's particular field was the history of English feudalism, which he entered into with a blend of scholarship and partisanship. His scholarship, based on careful scrutiny of the available sources, was demonstrated in his depiction of the close linkage between changes in landholding in England and the law and by his rejection of claims concerning the "ancient constitution" of the Anglo-Saxons. The Normans, he insisted, had introduced the feudal state. Brady's approving account of feudalism was developed in his *Introduction to the Old English History* (1684) and in his *Complete History of England* (2 vols. 1685–1700). By the time he published his *Historical Treatise of Cities and Burghs* (1690), Brady was already falling into eclipse in the changed political circumstances following the 1688 revolution.

R.C. Richardson

Texts

A Complete History of England. 2 vols. London: Samuel Lowndes, 1685–1700.

An Introduction to the Old English History. London: Samuel Lowndes, 1684.

References

Douglas, D.C. *English Scholars, 1660–1730.* Second ed. London: Eyre and Spottiswoode, 1951.

Pocock, J.G.A. *The Ancient Constitution and the Feudal Law.* Second ed. Cambridge, Eng.: Cambridge University Press, 1987.

Brătianu, Gheorghe I. (1898–1953)

Romanian historian. Born in Ruginoasa (in the district of Iasi), he was the son of Princess Maria Moruzi and of Ion I.C. Brătianu, a Romanian prime minister. After studying in Iasi and then in Paris, he obtained a doctorate in history at the Sorbonne in 1929. He was appointed a professor of world history at the University of Iasi (1924–1940) and then at Bucharest (1940–1947). In collaboration with younger historians, he edited the *Revista istorică română* [Romanian Historical Journal], which is generally considered to have been the organ of a "new historical school" in Romania. Active in politics as a leader of the liberal dissidents, he was jailed by the communist regime and died a prisoner in Sighet.

Brătianu had an international reputation during his life, and his work proved of interest to members of the French Annales school. His major field was world history, with a special interest in the economic and political history of Eastern Europe and the Byzantine empire. His Paris dissertation *Recherches sur le commerce génois dans la mer Noire au XIIIᵉ siècle* [Research on Genoese Commerce in the Black Sea during the Thirteenth Century] (1929) remained for some time the essential study of its subject. In 1937, he invited a number of great historians to join him in producing *Une nouvelle histoire de l'Europe au Moyen Age* [A New History of Europe in the Middle Ages], a work that was to be written from an Eastern European perspective, but his plans failed to be realized. Brătianu's masterpiece in world history is the book *La mer Noir: Des origines à la conquête ottomane* [The Black Sea: From Its Origins to the Ottoman Conquest], which was published in 1969, sixteen years after his death and outside Romania, where publication of his work was for a long time forbidden by the government. Like Fernand Braudel, in his *La Méditérranée,* Brătianu provided a synthesis of all the cultures and civilizations that had developed in the Black Sea region from antiquity up to the fifteenth century.

Brătianu also wrote a number of studies of Romanian history. The most important of these, *Une énigme et un miracle historique: Le peuple roumain* [An Enigma and a Historical Miracle: The Romanian People] (1937), defends the thesis that the Romanian people had occupied their land from earliest times without any major historical rupture. In *Origines et formation de l'unité roumaine* [The Origins and Formation of Romanian Unity] (1943) he examined the historical unity of Romanians living in Moldavia, Wallachia, and Transylvania, the countries that constituted modern Romania. While always the good patriot, Brătianu nevertheless maintained in these studies his modern critical views on historical writing and practiced a rigorously scientific analysis of his sources. His book *Tradiția istorică despre întemeierea statelor românești,* published in 1945, is not only an important study of the foundation of Romanian states in the early Middle Ages, but also an analysis of the value of historical tradition.

S. Lemny

Texts

Actes des notaires génois de Péra et de Caffa de la fin du treizième siècle (1281–1290) [Acts of Genoese Notaries from Péra and Caffa at the End of the Thirteenth Century]. Bucharest: Cultura Nationala, 1927.

Une énigme et un miracle historique: Le peuple roumain. Second ed. Bucharest: n.p., 1942.

Éudes byzantines d'histoire economique et sociale [Studies in Byzantine Social and Economic History]. Paris: Libraire orientaliste Paul Geuthner, 1938.

La mer Noire: Des origines à la conquête ottomane. Munich, Germany: Societas academica Dacoromana, 1969.

Napoléon III et les nationalités [Napoleon III and the Nationalities]. Paris: E. Droz; Bucharest: Fundaţia pentru literatură şi artă "Regele Carol II," 1934.

"Une nouvelle histoire de l'Europe au Moyen Age: La fin du monde antique et le triomphe de l'Orient." *Revue belge de philologie et d'histoire* [Belgian Review of Philology and History] 18 (1939): 252–266.

Origines et formation de l'unité roumaine. Bucharest: Institut d'histoire universelle "N. Iorga," 1943.

Recherches sur le commerce génois dans la mer Noire au XIIIe siècle. Paris: P. Geuthner, 1929.

Tradiţia istorică despre întemeierea statelor româneşti. Ed. V. Râpeanu. Bucharest: Eminescu, 1980.

References

Lewis, Archibald R. "Review of *La mer noire.*" *American Historical Review* 77 (1972): 809–810.

Spinei, Victor, ed. *Confluenţe istoriografice româneşti si europene. 90 de ani de la naşterea istoricului Gheorghe I. Brătianu* [Romanian and European Historiographical Trends in Honor of the Ninetieth Anniversary of the Birth of Gheorghe I. Brătianu]. Iasi: Universitatea "Al. I. Cuza," 1988.

Turdeanu, E. "L'oeuvre de G.I. Brătianu" [The Works of G.I. Brătianu]. *Revue des études roumaines* [Review of Romanian Studies] 7–8 (1961): 137–152.

Braudel, Fernand (1902–1985)

French historian. Among the most influential historians of the twentieth century, Braudel received the *agrégation d'histoire* in 1922 and was appointed to the lycée de Constantine in Algeria.

He subsequently served as professor of history at the University of Sao Paolo in Brazil in 1935, and in the École Pratique des Hautes Études [EPHE], IVe section, in 1937. As a prisoner of war from July 1940 until May 1943, Braudel drafted from memory his thesis, *La Méditerranée et le monde méditerranéen à l'époque de Philippe II,* which he completed in 1947. In 1948 he served as Secrétaire of the École Pratique des Hautes Études, VIe section, under Lucien Febvre's presidency, thus bringing Braudel into official association with the influential journal *Annales: Economies, sociétés, civilisations,* which had been created by Febvre and Marc Bloch before the war. In 1949, Braudel was elected to the Collège de France. He served as president of the VIe section of the EPHE from 1956 to 1972, and was director of *Annales* from 1957 to 1969. In 1984 he was elected to the Académie Française.

Among Braudel's chief contributions to historical writing were his thesis on the Mediterranean world and the later trilogy, *Civilisation matérielle, économie et capitalisme, XVe–XVIIIe siècle* (1967). These works embody his fundamental historiographical concerns, including a commitment to interdisciplinary methods—*histoire globale* or *totale* ("total history"). They also argued for a tripartite schema of temporality that distinguished among *l'histoire evènementielle* [the short-term history of human-made events]; *conjonctures* or medium-term changes in the economy and society; and the very slow changes to ecological systems of what he called the *longue durée.* His books are also noticeable for their long-term analysis of capitalist world economies. Braudel was committed to opening the historical discipline to the social sciences. As president of the VIe section and director of the *Annales,* he extended the interdisciplinary program of Bloch and Febvre, while in his own work he incorporated especially the discipline of geography. For Braudel, history was thoroughly rooted in geography, which conditions the capacity of human endeavor. Indeed, Braudel saw geography as so determinative of history that humanity is "decentered" in his works and the historical significance of human voluntarism expressed in short-lived events *(l'histoire evènementielle)* is minimized. Placing the consideration of the significance of space and its extension at the beginning of historical analysis was consistent with Braudel's commitment to *histoire globale,* a concept in which "everything is connected" in nonlinear fashion. It also logically informed his schema of tripartite temporality, devised as a counterweight to the ahistorical structuralism, derived from sociology, that had also influenced his earlier thought. Braudel employed these concepts to analyze spatial configurations—first, the Mediterranean, and then the world. Braudel explored the relations between material life, markets, and capitalism, concluding that integrated and self-sustained regional economies (world economies), like that of the Mediterranean in the sixteenth century or the global capitalistic economy of the twentieth century, are always hierarchized among nations. There is always an economic center of the world with peripheral zones spatially radiating from it. The center sits at the apex of the hierarchy, and the peripheral nations descend from it and possess proportionately less wealth and power.

Braudel's impact on modern historiography has been enormous. Few historians have attempted *histoire totale,* and his tripartite temporal schema has attracted few direct followers. But "Braudelian" concepts of analysis of world economies are employed by many economic historians, not least by those associated with the Fernand Braudel Center, a research institute dedicated to the analysis of capitalist world economies and the World Economy. Perhaps Braudel's greatest legacy to historiography, however, is his commitment to interdisciplinarity. The social sciences have become a mainstay of contemporary historiography in no small measure owing to his influence.

James R. Farr

Texts

Civilization and Capitalism, 15th–18th Century. Trans. Siân Reynolds. 3 vols. New York: Harper and Row, 1981–1984.
The Mediterranean and the Mediterranean World in the Age of Philip II. Trans. Siân Reynolds. New York: Harper and Row, 1972.
On History. Trans. Sarah Matthews. Chicago: University of Chicago Press, 1980.

References

Aymard, Maurice, et al. *Lire Braudel* [Reading Braudel]. Paris: Le Découverte, 1988.
Burke, Peter. *The French Historical Revolution: The Annales School, 1929–1989.* Stanford, CA: Stanford University Press, 1990.

Braun, Lily (1865–1916)

German feminist historian. Born in Halberstadt, Braun, a pioneering feminist considered radical during her lifetime, was the oldest child in a noble family. The daughter of a Prussian army captain, she became disillusioned by aristocratic, unwritten social codes. She rebelled, joining the German Social Democratic Party and protesting against patriarchy, capitalism, and the exploitation of women. She was twice married, first to the philosopher Georg Gizicky, then to the socialist Heinrich Stammte. Her varied roles as wife, mother, and feminist strained her health, and she collapsed on a Berlin street, dying soon afterward. Braun's most famous and controversial work was *Die Frauenfrage, ihre geschichtliche Entwicklung und ihre wirtschaftliche Seite* [The Woman Question, Her Historical Development and Her Economic Side] (1901). A study of women workers, this book won instant acclaim, being translated and printed in at least twenty editions. Considered a basic text for socialist feminism, it detailed the oppression of female workers. Braun anticipated the feminist movement of the late twentieth century, posing crucial questions and ideas. Her political peers criticized her, however, for giving feminism higher priority than working-class issues and forced Braun to leave the Social Democratic Party. Braun continued her radical feminist work, although many feminists criticized her for emphasizing femininity and motherhood and remaining in an unhappy marriage.

Elizabeth D. Schafer

Texts

Die Frauenfrage, ihre geschichtliche Entwicklung und ihre wirtschaftliche Seite. Leipzig: S. Hirzel, 1901.
Gesammelte Werke [Complete Works]. 5 vols. Berlin: H. Klemm, 1923.
Memoiren einer Sozialistin [Memoirs of a Socialist]. Ed. M.M. Kramme. Berlin: Dietz, 1985.
Selected Writings on Feminism and Society. Ed. and trans. Alfred G. Meyer. Bloomington: Indiana University Press, 1987.

References

Meyer, Alfred G. *The Feminism and Socialism of Lily Braun.* Bloomington: Indiana University Press, 1985.

Brazilian Historiography

Historical writing, principally in Portuguese, about Brazil from colonial times to the modern day. The circumstances of the Portuguese colonization of Brazil were in general extremely unfavorable for the creation of cultural life. Between the sixteenth century and the end of the eighteenth century, intellectual activity was rare in a situation where the principal objective of most men was to acquire wealth quickly and return to Portugal. The exceptions to this bleak trend principally consisted of the efforts of priests and a few other well-educated men to make known in Europe the characteristics of a new land possessed of indigenous inhabitants, flora, fauna, and climatic conditions that appeared exotic to Old World readers. For these reasons it is not surprising to see such early commentators as Frei Vicente do Salvador and Rocha Pita describing the country in a laudatory manner rather than writing genuine historical works. Nevertheless, the colonial period still managed to produce a number of outstanding books concerned with actual conditions in the colony, written by authors such as Gabriel Soares de Sousa, Fernão Cardim, and Ambrósio Fernandes Brandão, who each described the daily life of its inhabitants in detail.

The achievement of independence in September 1822 brought an abrupt end to the intellectual apathy of the former colony. New sentiments arose, together with new political problems, such as the construction of a nation and a strong state, and the transformation of people belonging to three different ethnic groups into Brazilian citizens of an undifferentiated mass. Consequently, the hour of history and of historians had at last arrived, together with the urgent need for a general history of Brazil made by and for Brazilians. Early efforts in this regard were unpromising: the first books about Brazilian history to be published have only their poor quality in common and did not rival the historical writing by foreigners.

The foundation of the Instituto Histórico e Geográfico Brasileiro (IHGB; Brazilian Historical and Geographical Institute) in 1838, however, brought about a fundamental improvement of this situation. The institute's major preoccupation was to develop both a program and a methodology for a proper Brazilian history. In 1840, Januário da Cunha Barbosa, then president of the IHGB, decided to hold a competition on the issue, How to write Brazilian history. The winner of the contest was the German naturalist Karl Friedrich Philip von Martius. His submission generated a number of basic principles that would eventually serve as guidelines for later Brazilian historians. Some of these ideas were the need to remember that not one but three distinct ethnic groups had contributed to the formation of Brazilian society, the related need for serious study of Indian society, and the necessity of studying Portuguese colonization within a global context while remaining aware of its peculiarities. Martius also paid attention to the importance of the Jesuits and to the place of social conditions in the development of the colony.

It soon proved necessary, for political reasons, to demonstrate that a civilized society was possible in the tropics, and historians were expected to provide the evidence for this. One of the first to do so was Francisco Adolfo de Varnhagen. Often called the "father of Brazilian history," Varnhagen was certainly the first Brazilian to write a general history of the country based upon exhaustive research in Brazilian and European archives. His *História Geral do Brasil* [General History of Brazil] virtually became the "official" history of Brazil; it would long remain obligatory reading for professional historians, their students, and, indeed, all who had an interest in the country's past. There was a negative side, however, to the success of Varnhagen's history. In a sense, he single-handedly channeled Brazilian historiography into a conservative mainstream. As his later critic João Capistrano de Abreu would remark using a different metaphor, Varnhagen put Brazilian history in iron chains.

In many ways, Capistrano de Abreu, the greatest Brazilian historian of the early twentieth century, was just the opposite of Varnhagen. Critical, brilliant, and an indefatigable researcher, his sole objective was to create a "scientific" history along European lines. Utterly uninterested in using history to construct a nation or a state, he was preoccupied exclusively with the reconstruction of the Brazilian past according to Ranke's principle *wie es eigentlich gewesen*—"the past as it essentially happened." Capistrano was an innovator who developed fresh approaches to Brazilian history, including new methods for the study of Indian society and of the development of the Brazilian hinterland; the best of his many books was *Capítulos de História Colonial* [Chapters in Colonial History].

From the end of the nineteenth century to the 1930s a number of historians and social scientists made further contributions, but they were often concerned with the same problems that had been treated by Varnhagen. Other than the work of Capistrano himself, the most striking historiographical development during this period was the activity of a number of historians interested in literature, such as José Verissimo and Silvio Romero.

Oliveira Vianna, a very important and influential conservative thinker, provides a link of sorts between the nineteenth and twentieth centuries. The old historical questions remained, but the solutions, and their political implications, were quite different. As it had been for Varnhagen, Vianna's major problem was how to construct a socially unified nation; the instrument he favored was a corporate state. These views translated into

B

a novel reading of the Brazilian past that remains influential even today. But the greatest innovation in Brazilian historiography came in the 1930s with the work of three historians in particular: Gilberto Freyre, Caio Prado Júnior, and Sérgio Buarque de Hollanda. The publication of Freyre's *Casa Grande e Senzala* was a major intellectual event. Both his interpretation of the history of Brazilian society and the types of sources he used were new; in a way, he was an early predecessor of French *Nouvelle Histoire* in the Annales mold.

An eclectic interpretation of Brazilian society, leavened with a slight marxist influence, also proved a new and far-reaching development at the same period. In Brazil, the marxist interpretation of history found its greatest representative in Caio Prado Júnior. Prado reinterpreted Portuguese expansion in particular, and European colonization in general, as a global process that had a single clear objective, namely the primitive accumulation of capital. Brazilian society of the nineteenth century was, in Prado's view, the product of a Portuguese colonization founded on commercial capitalism, indifferent to the needs and aspirations of women and men but highly sensitive to products and merchandise.

Sergio Buarque de Holanda's *Raízes do Brasil* [Roots of Brazil] rewrote Brazilian cultural history, and he is properly counted with Prado and Freyre as a trinity of modern historians who, as José Honório Rodrigues has pointed out, caused a fundamental break in the development of Brazilian historiography by introducing new analytical methods and fresh perspectives. But it is also necessary to put José Honório Rodrigues among the pioneers, as the first Brazilian historian to concern himself with a history of Brazilian historiography.

The other great event of the 1930s was the foundation of the University of São Paulo (USP) and the National College (Faculty) in Rio de Janeiro. With these two institutions there came the professionalization of the social sciences, including history, and further significant modifications in methodology, generally in the direction of scientific history. The traditional panoramic views of Brazilian history were replaced by more specific problems of colonization, empire, and the new republic. In the period since then there have been further efforts to modernize Brazilian historiography, along lines developed in Europe and especially in France. The presence of intellectuals like Fernand Braudel, Claude Lévi-Strauss, Roger Bastide, Paul

Arbousse-Bastide, Giles Granger, Claude Lefort, Jean Glennisson, and many others at USP for more than two decades made possible the creation of strong departments of history, sociology, and philosophy. The end result was the education of several generations of historians who, together with sociologists, political scientists, economists, and philosophers, have kept Brazilian historiography current. This ongoing process of historiographical renovation is no longer restricted to São Paulo and Rio de Janeiro, but has evolved into a national movement, with first-class schools for the training of historians now operating in Porto Alegre (Rio Grande do Sul), Curitiba (Paranà), Belo Horizonte (Minas Gerais), Salvador (Bahia), and Recife (Pernambuco).

Nilo Odalia

See also LATIN AMERICAN HISTORIOGRAPHY; MEXICAN HISTORIOGRAPHY; SPANISH HISTORIOGRAPHY.

References

Burns, E. Bradford. *Perspectives on Brazilian History.* New York: Columbia University, 1967.
Fringer, Katherine. "The Contribution of Capistrano de Abreu to Brazilian Historiography." *Journal of Inter-American Studies* 13 (1971): 258–278.
Rodrigues, José Honório. *Teoria da historia do Brasil: Introdução metodologica* [The Idea of History in Brazil: Methodological Introduction]. Third ed. São Paulo: Companhia editora nacional, 1969.

Breysig, Kurt (1866–1940)

German historian, sociologist, and philosopher of history. Breysig, who was born in Posen (Poznan), studied law at the University of Berlin before turning to history under the influence of Heinrich von Treitschke. In 1888 he earned his doctorate, under the supervision of Gustav von Schmoller, with a study of Brandenburgian history; he habilitated in 1892 under Schmoller and Treitschke. In 1896 he became professor extraordinarius at Berlin and in 1923 attained one of the first chairs in sociology to be established in Prussia. In 1925, with the sponsorship of Werner Sombart, Breysig was admitted as a full member of the Deutsche Gesellschaft für Soziologie (German Society for Sociology). Politically, Breysig turned from a National-Prussian conservative into a critic of the empire and eventually a supporter of the Weimar Republic.

Initially a historian of Prussia, Breysig evolved into a sociologist and a philosopher of world history. Until 1896 he worked within the tradition of Treitschke's Prussian Nationalist history and Schmoller's more recently established historical school of economics, producing seminal studies on the financial history of Brandenburg. After that year, he embarked on his *Kulturgeschichte der Neuzeit* [Cultural History of the Modern Age] and wrote his important *Der Stufenbau und die Gesetze der Weltgeschichte* [The Structure and Laws of World History], a work intended to establish a comparative European social history. In the 1920s Breysig, who believed in the gradual development of humanity toward greater unity, turned his attention to sociology and philosophy of history, paying special attention to questions of social psychology. His interest in the history of humanity led naturally to universal history, for which he formulated a comprehensive sociological theory. Breysig's interest in universal history can be seen in his major work, *Die Geschichte der Menschheit* [History of Humanity] (1936–1940). In *Vom Sein und Erkennen geschichtlicher Dinge* [On the Nature of History] (1935/1944) he formulated his theory of a developmental history of mankind; his sociological system would be posthumously reconstructed in *Gesellschaftslehre, Geschichtslehre* [Social Teachings, Historical Teachings] (1958). Breysig's cultural-historical program was largely rejected by the historians of his own time, and his influence on modern historiography has diminished considerably.

Thomas Fuchs

Texts

Die Geschichte der Menschheit. Second ed. 5 vols. Berlin: W. de Gruyter, 1955.
Gesellschaftslehre, Geschichtslehre. Berlin: W. de Gruyter, 1958.
Kulturgeschichte der Neuzeit. 2 vols. Berlin: G. Bondi, 1900–1901.
Der Stufenbau und die Gesetze der Weltgeschichte. Second ed. Stuttgart and Berlin: J.G. Cotta'sche Buchhandlung Nachfolger, 1927.
Vom geschichtlichen Werden: Umrisse einer zukünftigen Geschichtslehre [On Historical Development: Sketch for a Future Study of History]. 3 vols. Stuttgart and Berlin: J.G. Cotta'sche Buchhandlung Nachfolger, 1925–1928.

References

Barnes, Harry Elmer. *A History of Historical Writing.* Second ed. New York: Dover Publications, 1962.

Vom Brocke, B. *Kurt Breysig: Geschichtswissenschaft zwischen Historismus und Soziologie* [Kurt Breysig: Historical Scholarship between Historicism and Sociology]. Lübeck and Hamburg: Matthiesen, 1971.

Bridenbaugh, Carl (1903–1992)

American historian of the colonial period. Born in Philadelphia, Bridenbaugh earned a bachelor's degree at Dartmouth College and graduate degrees from Harvard University. He taught at the Massachusetts Institute of Technology and the University of California, Berkeley, before becoming professor of American history at Brown University. Bridenbaugh was an organizer and first director of the Institute of Early American History. Based in Williamsburg, Virginia, the institute remains the major organization in the United States dedicated to the furtherance of study, research, and publication about early American history. It supports the *William and Mary Quarterly,* considered one of the finest historical journals in the United States. Bridenbaugh specialized in the colonial American field with a particular emphasis on social history. His *Vexed and Troubled Englishmen* (1968) gave detailed insight into the everyday life of those ordinary people who came to North America in the early seventeenth century. In an earlier work, *Cities in the Wilderness* (1938), Bridenbaugh argued that the colonial city exercised a far more significant influence on the life of early America than historians had previously recognized. These and his other books garnered Bridenbaugh many awards, and in 1962, he was elected president of the American Historical Association.

Kevin J. O'Keefe

Texts

Cities in Revolt: Urban Life in America, 1743–1776. New York: Knopf, 1955.
Cities in the Wilderness: The First Century of Urban Life in America, 1625–1742. Second ed. New York: Knopf, 1955.
Mitre and Sceptre: Transatlantic Faiths, Ideas, Personalities and Politics, 1689–1776. New York: Oxford University Press, 1962.
And Roberta Bridenbaugh. *No Peace beyond the Line: The English in the Caribbean, 1624–1690.* New York: Oxford University Press, 1972.
Vexed and Troubled Englishmen, 1590–1642. New York: Oxford University Press, 1968.

Brinton, Clarence Crane (1898–1968)

American historian of Europe. Brinton was born in Winsted, Connecticut. He earned his B.A. at Harvard (1919) and his Ph.D. at Oxford (1923), where he had been a Rhodes scholar. In 1920 he began his long teaching career at Harvard, where in his later life he was a senior fellow (1939–1964). During World War II he worked for the Office of Strategic Services (1942–1945). Brinton was primarily interested in the history of European ideas. One of his major areas of study was the French Revolution, about which he wrote several of his best books, for example *The Jacobins* (1930). He was also interested in European intellectual history and particularly the Enlightenment and the nineteenth century. Two of his best-known books are *The Anatomy of Revolution* (1938), an excellent comparative study of several revolutions, and *A Decade of Revolution* (1934), a volume about the 1790s included in the popular series *The Rise of Modern Europe*. A prolific author of widely used textbooks and a superb stylist who appealed both to academic and popular audiences, Brinton was an optimistic liberal who believed in the power of human reason and of democratic society.

Walter A. Sutton

Texts

The Americans and the French. Cambridge, MA: Harvard University Press, 1968.
The Anatomy of Revolution. Rev. ed. New York: Prentice-Hall, 1965.
A Decade of Revolution, 1789–1799. New York: Harper and Brothers, 1934.
A History of Western Morals. New York: Harcourt, Brace, 1959.
The Jacobins: An Essay in the New History. New York: MacMillan, 1930.
The Lives of Talleyrand. New York: W.W. Norton, 1936.

Briquet, Marguerite-Ursule-Fortunée Bernier (1782–1825)

French biographer. Briquet was born at Niort. She married Louis-Hilaire-Alexandre Briquet, a historian of that city. She began her literary career writing poems published in *L'Almanach des muses,* while also authoring pamphlets and articles for the *Bibliothèque française.* Briquet's most important work was *Dictionnaire Historique, littéraire et bibliographique des Françaises et des étrangères naturalisées en France* [Historical, Literary and Bibliographical Dictionary of Frenchwomen and Foreigners Naturalized in France] (1804). Briquet's tome was a pioneering history of women. Although dedicated to Napoleon, this text included sketches of a variety of prominent, contemporary French women, including revolutionary heroines, salonières, writers, and political leaders. Differing from male versions of history, Briquet portrayed women as creative individuals in an encyclopedic trend promoting the biographical study of "great women" pursued by her literary peers, Mary Betham, Mary Pilkington, and Mary Hays. Briquet's work inspired nineteenth-century women intellectuals by providing them role models and stimulated biographical scholarship and the emergence of gender history.

Elizabeth D. Schafer

Texts

Dictionnaire Historique, littéraire et bibliographique des Françaises et des étrangères naturalisées en France. Paris: Gille, 1804.

References

Offen, Karen. "The Beginnings of 'Scientific' Women's History in France 1830–1848." *Proceedings of the 11th Annual Meeting of the Western Society for French History* 11 (1984): 255–271.
Smith, Bonnie G. "The Contribution of Women to Modern Historiography in Great Britain, France, and the United States, 1750–1940." *American Historical Review* 89 (1984): 709–732.

Browne, Edward Granville (1862–1926)

British historian of Persia. Despite his formal training as a medical doctor, Browne is best known as an Iranologist. He began his studies of the "orient" by studying Turkish, and later Arabic and Persian, at Cambridge University. His 1877 trip to Iran resulted in his celebrated *A Year amongst the Persians* (1893). In 1902 he became Sir Thomas Adams Professor of Arabic at Pembroke College, Cambridge, a position that he held until his death. The most important and best known of his many works is *A Literary History of Persia,* published in four volumes between 1900 and 1924 and covering Iranian history and literature from the medieval period to the 1920s. His interest in and sympathy for the constitutional movement in Iran produced *The Persian Revolution of 1905–1909* (1910) along with a number of shorter writings. Browne also wrote about the Babi and Bahai religions.

Hootan Shambayati

Texts

Account of a Rare Manuscript History of the Seljuqs. Hertford, Eng.: S. Austin, 1906.

Brief Narrative of Recent Events in Persia. London: Luzac, 1909.

Ed. *A Catalogue of the Persian Manuscripts in the Library of the University of Cambridge.* Cambridge, Eng.: Cambridge University Press, 1896.

A History of Persian Literature in Modern Times: A.D. 1500–1924. Cambridge, Eng.: Cambridge University Press, 1930.

Ed. *Kitab-I Nuqtatul-Kaf, Being the Earliest History of the Babis Compiled by Hajji Mirza Jani of Kashan between the Years A.D. 1850 and 1852.* Leiden: E.J. Brill; London: Luzac, 1910.

A Literary History of Persia. 4 vols. London: Fisher Unwin, 1900–1924.

The Persian Revolution of 1905–1909. Cambridge, Eng.: Cambridge University Press, 1910.

A Year amongst the Persians: Impressions As to the Life, Character, & Thought of the People of Persia, Received during Twelve Months' Residence in That Country in the Years 1887–1888. London: A. and C. Black, 1893.

References

Arnold, T.W., and Reynold A. Nicholson. *A Volume of Oriental Studies Presented to Edward G. Browne on His 60th Birthday (7 February 1922).* Cambridge, Eng.: Cambridge University Press, 1922.

Balyuzi, H.M. *Edward Granville Browne and the Baha'i Faith.* London: George Ronald, 1970.

Browne, E.G., and Reynold Nicholson. *A Descriptive Catalogue of the Oriental Mss. Belonging to the Late E.G. Browne, by Edward G. Browne, Completed & Edited with a Memoir of the Author and a Bibliography of His Writings.* Cambridge, Eng.: Cambridge University Press, 1932.

Bruni, Leonardo (1370–1444)

Renaissance Italian scholar and bureaucrat; the first great humanist historian of the Renaissance. Born in Arezzo, where he received his early schooling and training in Latin, Bruni moved to Florence for his university studies, pursuing a traditional curriculum in civil jurisprudence. He writes in his memoirs that in 1398 he stopped studying law in order to learn Greek with the Byzantine scholar Manuel Chrysoloras. Bruni was a close friend of Florentine chancellor Coluccio Salutati and of others in the city's circle of humanists. In 1405 he obtained a job in Rome, as apostolic secretary, on the recommendation of another humanist, Poggio Bracciolini. In 1410 he was named chancellor of Florence, but in 1411 he returned to papal service, leaving only in 1415, when he again took up residence in Florence. He was chosen Florentine chancellor for the second time in 1427, retaining the position until his death. Bruni was married to a Florentine, and he became a Florentine citizen, amassing a considerable estate. (Fellow humanists thought him avaricious.) More than a state functionary, Bruni played a considerable role in the group of citizens that controlled Florence unofficially in the 1430s and 1440s. His many works include translations and commentaries of writings by Aristotle and Plato; biographies of Aristotle, Cicero, Dante, and Petrarch; two dialogues; numerous orations; a memoir, the *Commentarius rerum suo tempore gestarum* [Commentary on Events in His Own Time]; and early treatments of Xenophon, Polybius, and Procopius.

Bruni's masterpiece is his *Historiarum Florentini Populi Libri XII* [History of the Florentine People in Twelve Books], a history of Florence from its founding down to 1402. Once considered (as by Hans Baron) a paean to the liberal values of Florentine republicanism, Bruni's *Histories* are now generally read (following Riccardo Fubini) as an expression of a statist ideology that developed in Florence in the wake of territorial expansion and the consolidation of an oligarchic regime. Influenced by (and sometimes responding to) Sallust, Livy, and Tacitus among the Roman historians, Bruni was also one of the first of the Italian humanists with sufficient Greek to read Thucydides. As Thucydides rejected the evidence of Homer, so Bruni disagreed with Dante about the early history of Florence. Sources for more recent times included Florentine chronicles, state papers, and even the private papers of leading Florentine families. Speeches in the *Histories,* some of them transcribed or paraphrased from contemporary records, were used as vehicles to explain historical events. The work circulated widely in an Italian translation by Donato Acciaiuoli, first published in 1473 in Venice. Bruni's *Histories* were an important source for Niccolò Machiavelli, who mentioned (and criticized) his predecessor in the *proemio* to his own *Florentine Histories.*

William J. Connell

Texts

Commentarius rerum suo tempore gestarum. Ed. C. Di Pierro. In *Rerum Italicarum Scriptores.* Second ed., vol. 19. Bologna: S. Lapi, 1926.

Historiarum Florentini Populi Libri XII. Ed.
Emilio Santini. In *Rerum Italicarum Scrip-
tures.* Second ed., vol. 19, part 3. Città di
Castello: S. Lapi, 1927.
The Humanism of Leonardo Bruni: Selected Texts.
Trans. Gordon Griffith, James Hankins,
and David Thompson. Binghamton, NY:
MRTS, 1987.
Humanistisch-philosophische Schriften. Ed.
Hans Baron. Leipzig and Berlin: Teubner,
1928.

References

Baron, Hans. *In Search of Florentine Civic Hu-
manism.* 2 vols. Princeton, NJ: Princeton
University Press, 1988, vol. 1, 24–93.
Cochrane, Eric. *Historians and Historiography in
the Italian Renaissance.* Chicago: University
of Chicago Press, 1981.
Fubini, Riccardo. "Osservazioni sopra gli
Historiarum Florentini Populi Libri XII di
Leonardo Bruni" [Observations on Bruni's
*History of the Florentine People in Twelve
Books*]. In *Studi di storia medioevale e
moderna per Ernesto Sestan* [Studies in Me-
dieval and Modern History for Ernesto
Sestan]. Florence: Olschki, 1980, vol. 1,
403–448.
Ullman, Berthold L. "Leonardo Bruni and Hu-
manistic Historiography." In his *Studies in
the Italian Renaissance.* Rome: Edizioni di
Storia e Letteratura, 1955.
Viti, Paolo, ed. *Leonardo Bruni cancelliere della
repubblica di Firenze.* Florence: Olschki,
1990.
Wilcox, Donald J. *The Development of Florentine
Humanist Historiography in the Fifteenth
Century.* Cambridge, MA: Harvard University Press, 1969.

Brunner, Heinrich (1840–1915)

Austrian legal historian. Brunner studied law
from 1858 to 1862 in Vienna, and after 1860 at the
Institut für österreichische Geschichtsforschung
of Theodor Sickel. In 1864 he earned a doctorate in Vienna for *Landeshoheit und Immunität
unter den Babenbergern,* his major contribution to
medieval legal history. After further study under
Georg Waitz in Göttingen in 1864 he habilitated
the following year in Vienna. In 1866 he became
professor extraordinarius in Lemberg, and professor ordinarius in 1867. In 1870 he moved to
the University of Prague, and subsequently to
Strasbourg (1872) and Berlin (1873). From 1912

he was member of the Prussian Upper Chamber.
Brunner is regarded as the most prominent German-speaking legal historian of his time and as a
major founder of historical German jurisprudence. He dedicated himself especially to researching Germanic legal history, in particular
the Frankish law. He became well known with
Die Entstehung der Schwurgerichte [Origins of the
Jury] (1872). His most important work, however, is the two-volume *Deutsche Rechtsgeschichte*
[German Legal History] (1887–1892), a monumental systematic handbook of the Frankish-
Germanic age. This work permanently influenced
research on this subject. His *Grundzüge der
deutschen Rechtsgeschichte* [Foundations of German Legal History] (1901) was a general textbook of legal history. Besides these works, Brunner
published numerous essays concerned with the
criticism of the sources of the Franconian legal
tradition. His use of documents as sources for
legal history was essential for the development of
his subject.

Thomas Fuchs

Texts

*Abhandlungen zur Rechtsgeschichte: Gesammelte
Aufsätze* [Essays on Legal History]. Ed. K.
Rauch. 2 vols. Weimar: Hermann Böhlaus
Nachfolger, 1931; reprint Leipzig: Zentral-
Antiquariat der DDR, 1965.
Deutsche Rechtsgeschichte. Ed. C. Freiherr von
Schwerin. Second ed. 2 vols. Munich and
Leipzig: Duncker & Humblot, 1906–1928.
Die Entstehung der Schwurgerichte. Aalen:
Scientia Verlag, 1967.
*Forschungen zur Geschichte des deutschen und
fränkischen Rechts: Gesammelte Aufsätze*
[Research on the History of German and
Frankish Law: Collected Essays].
Stuttgart: J.G. Cotta'sche Buchhandlung
Nachfolger, 1894.
Grundzüge der deutschen Rechtsgeschichte
[Foundations of German Legal History].
Munich and Leipzig: Duncker &
Humblot, 1901.
The Sources of the Law of England. Trans. W.
Hastie. Edinburgh: T. & T. Clark, 1888.

References

Mitteis, H. *Vom Lebenswert der Rechtsgeschichte.*
Weimar: Hermann Böhlaus Nachfolger,
1947.
Stutz, U. "Heinrich Brunner." In *Zeitschrift der
Savigny-Stiftung für Rechtsgeschichte.
Germanistische Abteilung* 36 (1915): ix–lv.

Brunner, Otto (1898–1982)

Austrian historian. After serving in World War I, Brunner studied history and geography from 1921 to 1922 at the Institut für österreichische Geschichtsforschung and took his doctorate under Oswald Redlich with a study of *Österreich und die Walachei während des Türkenkrieges von 1683–1699* [Austria and Wallachia during the Turkish Wars, 1683–1699]. From 1923 he worked as an archivist in Vienna and habilitated in 1929 with a study of the history of Viennese finances. In 1931 he became an adjunct professor; and in 1940 he attained a chair in Vienna. From 1942 to 1945 he directed the Institut für österreichische Geschichtsforschung. After World War II he was dismissed because of his attitude toward the National Socialism, though in 1954 he again obtained a chair in Hamburg, assuming emeritus status in 1966. Together with Werner Conze and Reinhard Koselleck he edited the historical encyclopedia *Geschichtliche Grundbegriffe*. In his article on *Feudalismus*, written for the encyclopedia, he argues that all scientific opinions are conditioned by history and by the history of the sciences. Brunner is regarded as one of the forerunners of a modern social and concept history. He first became famous with his 1939 book *Land und Herrschaft*, in which Brunner attempted a better understanding of medieval constitutional reality by introducing a terminology that corresponded to the sources: he saw the terms "Land" and "Herrschaft" (lordship) as central concepts of medieval history. After World War II *Adeliges Landleben und europäischer Geist* (1949) was published, a work that reestablished his reputation. Using the example of the life of an Austrian nobleman he illustrated the mental world and the ethos of the premodern aristocracy. Brunner borrowed from Conze the concept of "structural history" for his picture of a European social history, in order to describe the relationship of modern and premodern historical processes through a general view of social, conceptual, and scientific history. Politically, Brunner's ideas were close to the antiliberal thought of Carl Schmitt. Though his views became more moderate after the war, he saw the liberal state under the rule of law as subject to history, and thus explained its subordination by National Socialism.

Thomas Fuchs

Texts

Adeliges Landleben und europäischer Geist: Leben und Werk Wolf Helmhards von Hohberg 1612–1688 [Noble Life and the European Spirit: The Life and Work of W.H. von Hohberg]. Salzburg: Otto Müller, 1949.

Land and Lordship: Structures of Governance in Medieval Austria. Trans. H. Kaminsky and J. Van Horn Melton (from the fourth, rev. ed.). Philadelphia: University of Pennsylvania Press, 1992.

Neue Wege der Verfassungs- und Sozialgeschichte. [New Directions in Constitutional and Social History]. Second ed. Göttingen: Vandenhoeck & Ruprecht, 1968.

References

"Introduction." In *Land and Lordship: Structures of Governance in Medieval Austria* by Otto Brunner, trans. Kaminsky and Melton. Philadelphia: University of Pennsylvania Press, 1992.

Melton, J.V.H. "From Folk History to Structural History: Otto Brunner (1898–1982) and the Radical-Conservative Roots of German Social History." In *Paths of Continuity: Central European Historiography from the 1930s to the 1950s,* ed. H. Lehmann and J.V.H. Melton. Washington, DC: German Historical Institute; Cambridge, Eng. and New York: Cambridge University Press, 1994, 263–292.

Buckle, Henry Thomas (1821–1862)

English historian. Born in London, Buckle attended private school, and his father bequeathed him sufficient income to pursue a life of reading and study. He traveled throughout Europe acquiring mastery of a number of languages before returning to London. After enjoying a decade of acclaim as a scholar, he died while journeying through the Middle East. Much of his short life was spent as a recluse until the publication of his two-volume *History of Civilization in England* (1857–1861) made him famous virtually overnight. Buckle called for the construction of history on sounder methodological footings and advocated the interpretation of historical development according to universal laws. Despite its title, the work is really not about English civilization. The first volume provided a general introduction to the physical and intellectual factors governing history, veiled within the general premise that the emergence of civilization coincided with the overthrow of religion. The second volume was a study of Scotland and Spain, two countries that apparently shared a devotion to superstition and bigotry. Buckle attempted to determine whether the actions of people are governed by fixed natural laws or by chance and the supernatural. Darwin thought the work clever and the enthusiastic interest shown by Huxley, Thackeray, John Stuart Mill, and others brought the author instant popularity in the literary world. The second volume, published a year before he died, brought similar praise, and his work was popular in Europe and America for a generation after his death. Later historians criticized him for being too opinionated and for failing to sufficiently distinguish between statements of universal law on one hand, and assertions of trends and tendencies on the other, while his useful insights on the development of modern thought were largely unsubstantiated by verifiable theory. Acton wrote two scathing attacks on the *History,* and it was dismissed by Leslie Stephen in the *Dictionary of National Biography.*

David R. Schweitzer

Texts

History of Civilization in England. 2 vols. London: J.W. Parker and Son, 1857–1861.
Miscellaneous and Posthumous Works of Henry Thomas Buckle. 3 vols. London: Longmans, Green, 1872.

References

Hanham, H.J. *Buckle on Scotland and the Scotch Intellect.* Chicago: University of Chicago Press, 1970.
Robertson, J.M. *Buckle and His Critics: A Study in Sociology.* London: Swan Sonnenschein, 1895.
St. Aubyn, Giles. *A Victorian Eminence: The Life and Works of Henry Thomas Buckle.* London: Barrie, 1958.

Budé, Guillaume (1468–1540)

French humanist, legal scholar, and philologist. Budé was born in Paris, the son of a major chancellery official and courtier. For three years, he attended the University of Orleans. At the age of twenty-three, he began a program of self-instruction and became conspicuous among scholars and public servants of his age. His wife, Roberte Le Lyeur, aided him in his scholarship. He was well respected at the royal court, in the Parliament of Paris, in the Parisian *Hôtel de la Ville* (where he was *prévôt des marchants*), and among humanists. Francis I placed him in charge of organizing the royal library at Fontainebleau, and Budé apparently persuaded the king to found a "trilingual" college at Paris—the predecessor to the *Collège*

Royal, now the *Collège de France.* He remained in the Catholic Church but, after his death, his wife and sons supported the reformed religion and moved to Geneva. Tagged the "prodigy of France" by Erasmus, Budé was acclaimed for his imaginative and wide-ranging study of Greek and Roman coinage, weights and measures, *De Asse* [The As and Its Parts] (1514; revised edition 1532). Besides advancing Hellenic studies, his *Annotations on the Pandects* brought the philological method to dominance in the study of Roman law and helped to identify legal humanism as a force for administrative and political reform. He also applied non-literary and archaeological sources to a program for "the restitution and perpetuation of antiquity," as he wrote in his *De l'Institution du prince* [The Institution of the Prince]. He saw antiquity as the source for an impressive, and essentially French-sponsored, revival of learning and civilization. Budé turned to the problem of the incompatibility of Christianity and *bonae litterae* in *The Passage from Hellenism to Christianity* (1529).

Lawrence M. Bryant

Texts

Annotationes . . . in quatuor & viginti Pandectarum libros. Paris: Robert Estienne, 1535.
De Asse et partibus ejus libri quinque. Paris: Venundantur in aedibus Ascensianus, 1514.
De l'Institution du prince. In *Le Prince dans la France des XVIe et XVIIe siècles,* C. Bontems et al. Paris: *C.N.R.S.,* 1966.
Le passage de l'hellenisme au christianisme. Ed. and trans. M. de la Garanderie and G.F. Penham (into French). Paris: Les Belles Lettres, 1993.

References

Kelley, Donald R. *Foundations of Modern Historical Scholarship: Language, Law, and History in the French Renaissance.* New York: Columbia University Press, 1970.
McNeil, D.O. *Guillaume Budé and Humanism in the Reign of Francis I.* Geneva: Librairie Droz, 1975.

Bugis and Makasar (Sulawesi) Historiography

A tradition of history writing in precolonial South Sulawesi, notably in a "state chronicle" form. Bugis and Makasar historical traditions have much in common and may be discussed together. Historical texts make up a sizable portion of the surviving writings and reflect a deep interest in the past among the former ruling elites of lowland South Sulawesi.

Bugis and Makasar historical texts may be divided into source materials and historiographical literature. Source material comprises diaries, treaties, legal records, correspondence, king lists, and genealogies. Historiographical literature comprises court chronicles and short accounts of single subjects in the form of notes or a narrative. Chronicles and narratives are called *attoriolong* (Makasar, *pattorioloang*), "that which concerns people of the past." There are also poems in the *tolo'* meter that are woven around historical individuals and events.

Bugis historical sources date from around 1400, this being the date of the development of writing in South Sulawesi. The Bugis-Makasar script, a near-syllabary, is modeled on a South Sumatran script and is ultimately derived from India. Writing was originally on long strips of palm leaf but was replaced after 1600 by imported European paper, bound into books. Makasar historical sources are fewer than Bugis and date from the development of the Old Makasar script in the first half of the sixteenth century. From the eighteenth century the Bugis-Makasar script has been used to write both languages. One of the first uses of writing in Bugis-speaking areas was the recording of genealogies for the purpose of marriage alliances. Important genealogies are headed by a *tomanurung* (a heavenly descended being) or a *totompo'* (a being who arose from the underworld) or both. These supernatural beings account for the origin of status, which in theory was always ascriptive and legitimized political authority. Genealogies record the transmission, through women, of status, and thus the right to rule: the kingdom of Gowa alone developed a patrilineal transmission of office. The wide distribution of genealogies among the upper classes and their apparent veracity, as witnessed by the ability to cross-reference individuals in different genealogies, enable the construction of a historical chronology for the period before 1600, for which there are few European sources. Second in importance to the genealogies are the court diaries, which belong mostly to the seventeenth century and provide precise dates for the events they record.

From the seventeenth century onward, there is abundant supporting evidence for Bugis historical records in credible European sources. The same century saw the development of the chronicle, a form of historical writing that was probably stimulated by European models (one chancellor of Makasar had a library of European books) although an early version of the Sejarah Melayu may also have been known in Makasar. A chronicle is in essence a history of the ruling of a particular kingdom. The succession of its rulers is set out, and historical events are located within their reigns. The chronicles are written in a terse, matter-of-fact style, and supernatural events are generally found only at their beginnings; the author of the *Chronicle of Bone* carefully distances himself from these by use of the words *gare'* ("so the story goes") and *riasengngi* ("it is said"). The names of a few remembered rulers before 1400 are found in the early parts of some chronicles and genealogies. There is clear evidence of a rigorous selection process, and most chronicles are quite short: that of Bone, the most powerful Bugis kingdom, contains just seventeen manuscript pages. Chronicles contain no dates (the use of dates in diaries suggests that this was a stylistic convention) but their chronology, which is by time distance (days, months, years) and reign-lengths, is remarkably accurate. Their authors are unknown but had access to court archives and were unafraid to state the truth plainly: one ruler is described as lacking intelligence and possessing a bad temper.

The other form of historiographical writing, short texts in narrative or note form dealing with a single subject, does not represent such a distinct genre as the chronicles, and historicity has to be established on an individual basis. Many narrative texts are evidently of oral origin and some are plainly legends. Nevertheless, short texts are more numerous than the chronicles and in time may yield much useful information on South Sulawesi's past, as well its historical traditions.

Traditional historical forms survived until the twentieth century but have since been replaced in all but the most remote regions by modern historical forms originating in Europe.

Ian Caldwell

References

Abidin, Andi Zainal. *Wajo Abad XV-XVI* [Wajo in the Fifteenth and Sixteenth Centuries]. Bandung: Penerbit Alumni, 1985.

Noorduyn, J. "Some Aspects of Makassar-Buginese Historiography." In *Historians of South-East Asia,* ed. D.G.E. Hall. London: Oxford University Press, 1961.

Bujak, Franciszek (1875–1953)

Social and economic historian of medieval and modern Poland. Born in Maszkienice near Cracow, Bujak held posts at Jagiellonian University in Cracow (1909–1918, 1946–1952), at Warsaw University (1919–1921), and Lwów University (1921–1942). He was a member of the Polish

Academy of Sciences and Letters from 1919 and president of the Polish Historical Society between 1932 and 1934 and again from 1936 to 1937. Bujak, along with J. Rutkowski, established Polish economic history as a separate area of study. In 1925 he initiated a series "Badania Dziejów Społecznych i Gospodarczych" [Research on Social and Economic History] and was the editor of "Roczniki Dziejów Społecznych i Gospodarczych" [Yearbooks of Social and Economic History] from 1931 to 1950. Bujak's work dealt with problems of rural settlement, elemental plagues, and historical and geographical questions. In addition, he initiated research on social and economic monographs of villages and posited economic weakness as one cause of the successive partitions of Poland since the eighteenth century.

Jolanta T. Pękacz

Texts

Studia geograficzno-historyczne [Geographical and Historical Studies]. Cracow: W.L. Anczyc i Spólka, 1925.
Studia historyczno-społeczne [Historical and Social Studies]. Lwów: Zakład Narodowy im. Ossolinskich, 1924.
Wybór pism [A Selection of Writings]. Ed. Helena Madurowicz-Urbańska. 2 vols. Warsaw: PWN, 1976.

References

Grabski, Andrzej F. "Franciszek Bujak and Economic History: A Discussion of His Methodological Views." *Studia Historicae Oeconomicae* 16 (1981): 3–27.
Madurowicz-Urbańska, Helena. "Der Beginn des Sozial- und Wirtschaftsgeschichtlichen Faches in Polen: Die Schule von Franciszek Bujak (1875–1953) [The Beginning of Social and Economic History in Poland: The School of Franciszek Bujak]." *Virteljahrschrift für Sozial- und Wirtschaftsgeschichte* 75 (1988): 483–502.
Shelton, Anita Krystyna. *The Democratic Idea in Polish History and Historiography: Franciszek Bujak (1875–1953).* Boulder, CO: East European Monographs, no. 267; New York: Distributed by Columbia University Press, 1989.

Bulgarian Historiography

Historical writing of the Bulgarian people. Apart from medieval annals, chronicles, biographies, and compilations of sources in Byzantine religious style, there was no Bulgarian historical writing until the completion of the *Slavo-Bulgarian History* by Father Paisiy of Hilandar (1722–1773) in 1762, which marked the beginning of the romantic period in Bulgarian historiography. To Paisiy, historiography was a means of nation building, and for about a century, historiography was to remain subservient to the promotion of national independence. Father Spiridon (ca. 1750–1815), Hristaki Pavlovich (1804–1848), Dobri Voynikov (1833–1878), Georgi S. Rakovski (1821–1867), Gavril Krûstevich (1817–1898), and others glorified the Bulgarian past, resorting to distortions, deliberate omissions, and highly imaginative additions whenever these served their goal. The Slavic affiliation of the Bulgarians was emphasized as Russia was conceived as a potential liberator from the "Turkish yoke"; at the same time (and quite contradictorily), Bulgarians were ascribed to an ancient (Macedonian, Scythian) or Hunnic origin, which was expected to make the nation more venerable. Foreign histories of Bulgaria—like the Ukrainian Yuriy Venelin's hagiographic *Ancient and Contemporary Bulgarians* (1819–1840)—were welcomed to the extent they affirmed the image of the past the Bulgarians had created for themselves. The Bulgarian national-revival historians, who most successfully met the requirements of their patriotic readers, were actually amateurs —journalists, writers, schoolteachers, and the like; the deserving professional historian, Spiridon Palauzov (1818–1872), a Bulgarian who spent his life in Russia, was considerably less popular because of his objectivity and critical-mindedness. Marin Drinov (1838–1906), another professional "realistic" historian with a similar biography, was more influential thanks to his social and political activities.

After the establishment of an autonomous principality in 1878 and the 1888–1889 establishment of the Sofia High School (which eventually developed into the Sofia University), Bulgarian historiography came to be practiced, owing to the lack of available experts, predominantly by philologists like Aleksandûr Teodorov-Balan (1859–1959), Ivan Shishmanov (1862–1928), and others. It was Vasil Zlatarski (1866–1935), a medievalist trained at Saint Petersburg and Berlin, who consolidated Bulgarian academic historiography after his 1906 appointment as a professor of history at Sofia. Although Zlatarski considered collecting sources and facts as the main task of Bulgarian historiography for the time being, he successfully synthesized the knowledge he had accumulated in his monumental *History of the Bulgarian State in the Middle Ages* (1918–1940). After his death in 1935, Zlatarski was succeeded by

Petûr Nikov (1884–1938), a Byzantinist trained at Munich and Vienna, who was originally mainly interested in thirteenth- and fourteenth-century Bulgarian history. His *The National Revival of the Bulgarian People* (1929), which dealt, however, with the nineteeth-century Bulgarian struggle for a national church, is still a standard work.

In the same period, philologists continued making essential contributions to Bulgarian historiography. Yordan Ivanov (1872–1947) did research on the Middle Ages in Macedonia; Mihail Arnaudov (1878–1978) wrote a number of penetrating, though sometimes rather hagiographic, biographies of figures of the national liberation movement. Bulgarian church history was given attention by historians with a theological background, such as Ivan Snegarov (1883–1971). The newly founded Faculty of Law produced a number of specialists in the history of Bulgarian state institutions, legislation, and diplomacy. The first studies in Bulgarian economic history, often written by authors with a Marxist background, also appeared in the 1920s. Nikov, who died in 1938, only three years after his appointment, was succeeded by Petûr Mutafchiev (1883–1843), another Byzantinist and an archaeologist. Mutafchiev was also a fierce nationalist who seems to have broken with the tradition of neutrality and objectivity established by Zlatarski and Nikov. Mutafchiev was the first Bulgarian historian who tried to unveil, in a philosophical way, the deeper sense of Bulgarian history in the framework of the whole of medieval Europe. Mutafchiev's successor, Ivan Duychev (1907–1977), who held the chair of Bulgarian, Byzantine, and Balkan history from 1943 to 1945, was the last of Bulgaria's classical medievalists. His authority increased in the decades after the war, although in 1947, three years after the Communist takeover of September 1944, Duychev's chair was given to Aleksandûr Burmov, a confirmed Marxist who gradually enlarged his field of interest from the Middle Ages to the nineteenth century.

The postwar period witnessed an impressive boom of historiography in Bulgaria, owing to the rapid development of education in general and to the particular importance Marxism attributes to history. The Sofia University history department was divided into a number of specialized chairs, according to the different periods in Bulgarian history. Relatively more attention was now paid to the national-revival period and especially to the history of the Bulgarian kingdom (1878–1944). The Marxist interpretation of history was meticulously followed, although with a declining degree of dogmatism throughout the years. The history of the Bulgarian labor movement, linked to the history of industrialization and proletarization, became a separate subject; a special chair for the history of the Bulgarian Communist Party was created. In the spirit of the nineteenth century and striving for an impressive national pedigree, research into Thracian history, officially encouraged, achieved remarkable successes (Hristo Danov, Aleksandûr Fol). Medieval phenomena like the heresy of the Bogomils received special attention (Dimitûr Angelov). For the first time, serious research was done on the demographic, social, and cultural situation of the Bulgarian people under Ottoman rule (for instance by Bistra Tsvetkova, Vera Mutafchieva, and Nikolai Todorov), though often with a barely concealed anti-Turkish bias (Petûr Petrov). Considerable attention was paid to the problems of the formation of the Bulgarian nation in the nineteenth century (Hristo Gandev, Dimitûr Kosev), its cultural development (Nikolay Genchev), the April uprising in 1876 (Tsenko Genov), the great figures of the national liberation movement (Ivan Undzhiev, Krumka Sharova), and Macedonia as a Bulgarian *irredenta*. Monarchical Bulgaria also attracted the attention of many prominent historians (Ilcho Dimitrov, Andrey Pantev), a particular issue being the alleged "first antifascist uprising" in September 1923 and the partisan movement during World War II. Bulgarian publications on the history of the Communist period are abundant, but should be consulted with caution. As a rule, postwar Bulgarian historiography of modern times overemphasized the role of the Communist Party, gave a one-sidedly positive picture of all things Russian and Soviet, and was overtly biased in regard to the "Macedonian question." Apart from Byzantium (Dimitûr Angelov) and the Balkans (Nikolai Todorov, Strashimir Dimitrov), there was little interest in foreign history. A monumental achievement of Bulgarian postwar historiography, showing all its merits and shortcomings, is the *History of Bulgaria,* published by the Academy of Sciences. Seven of the projected fourteen volumes have now appeared, covering the period from prehistory to 1903.

During the recent post-Communist years a number of exciting historical studies have been published that had either been previously forbidden or that now attempt to correct the earlier distortions of Communist historiography. In addition, there has been a revival of amateur historiography, often with an outspoken nationalist tendency. Some professional and internationally respected historians have paid tribute to nationalism too, focusing on the Macedonian question and on the alleged Turkish threat. Other historians (Vera Mutafchieva, Antonina Zhelyazkova), however, have tried to give a more realistic picture of the Ottoman period.

R. Detrez

References

Grozdanova, Elena. "Contemporary Bulgarian Historiography (1971–1980) on the Impact of Ottoman Rule on the Development of the Bulgarian People during the Period from the 15th through the 18th Century." *Bulgarian Historical Review* 9 (1981): 68–85.

Petrovich, Michael B. "The Romantic Period of Bulgarian Historiography: From Paisii to Drinov." In *Bulgaria Past and Present: Studies in History, Literature, Economics, Music, Sociology, Folklore and Linguistics. Proceedings of the Second International Conference on Bulgarian Studies, Druzhba, Varna, June 13–17, 1978,* ed. Dimitur Kosev. Sofia: Bulgarian Academy of Sciences, 1982: 128–137.

Pundeff, Marin. "Bulgaria's Academic Historiography." In *Bulgaria Past and Present: Studies in History, Literature, Economics, Music, Sociology, Folklore and Linguistics. Proceedings of the First International Conference on Bulgarian Studies, University of Wisconsin, Madison, May 3–5, 1975,* ed. Thomas Butler. Columbus, OH: American Association for the Advancement of Slavic Studies, 1976, 91–98.

Todorova, Maria. "Historiography of the Countries of Eastern Europe: Bulgaria." *American Historical Review* 97 (1992): 1105–1117.

Burckhardt, Jacob (1818–1897)

Swiss historian of the Renaissance and one of the most influential of European cultural historians. After a brief, unsatisfactory time of theological study in his birthplace of Basel, Burckhardt turned to history, studying for four years in Berlin under Leopold von Ranke, Franz Kugler, and Johann Droysen. He returned to Basel in 1843 and in 1846 went to Italy to immerse himself in culture and separate himself from the political turmoil consuming Switzerland. In 1852 his *The Age of Constantine the Great* appeared, followed in 1854 by his *Cicerone*. In 1855 Burckhardt was appointed to a professorial chair at the University of Zurich. Three years later he accepted a chair at Basel and would later become a professor of both history (to 1885) and art history (to 1893). He stopped writing for publication after 1867, preferring to share his ideas only with his students and friends. Three books of his lectures were published posthumously: *History of Greek Culture* (1898); *Reflections on History* (1905); and *Historical Fragments* (1929). *Recollections of Rubens* (1898), the only work on an individual artist that he published, also appeared posthumously at Burckhardt's request.

Burckhardt's *The Civilization of the Renaissance in Italy* (1860), is his most well-known work. In it Burckhardt examined the unique circumstances in politics, ideas, and religion that contributed to the development of the idea of an individual self. The lack of a strong central power resulted in the development of despots, whose reigns marked the beginning of man seeing himself as an individual. Without the oppression of a strong central power, the arts began to flourish. Creativity was valued, and knowledge became a means to power. While exploring religious questions, Burckhardt drew a parallel to his own time, believing that the circumstances of the Italian Renaissance most closely resembled his own. He hoped for a renaissance in the late nineteenth century but doubted it would occur.

Burckhardt became extremely pessimistic about the future of European culture. He viewed the rise of the military state, industrialism, and democracy as heralding the destruction of the culture he had devoted his life to exploring. He theorized that three forces determined society. Two, the state and religion, remained constant, while culture, the third, developed spontaneously when neither state nor religion could suppress individual expression. Mass democracy did not allow the development of the individual, and the military state suppressed individual thought. Industrialization only aided the masses and the military to subsume completely individual conscience.

Thomas F. Mayer

Texts
The Age of Constantine the Great. Trans. Moses Hadas. New York: Pantheon, 1964.
The Civilization of the Renaissance in Italy. Trans. S.G.C. Middlemore. Oxford: Oxford University Press, 1938.
History of Greek Culture. Trans. Palmer Hilty. New York: Ungar, 1963.
Recollections of Rubens. Ed. H. Gerson and trans. Mary Hottinger. New York: Phaidon, 1950.
Reflections on History. Trans. M.D. Hottinger. London: George Allen and Unwin, 1943.

References

Gilbert, Felix. *History: Politics or Culture? Reflections on Ranke and Burckhardt.* Princeton, NJ: Princeton University Press, 1990.

Mommsen, Wolfgang J. "Jacob Burckhardt—Defender of Culture and Prophet of Doom." *Government and Opposition* 18 (1983): 458–475.

Rusen, J. "Jacob Burckhardt: Political Standpoint and Historical Insight on the Border of Post-Modernism." *History and Theory* 24 (1985): 235–246.

White, Hayden. *Metahistory: The Historical Imagination in Nineteenth-Century Europe.* Baltimore, MD: Johns Hopkins University Press, 1973.

Burke, Edmund (1729–1797)

Anglo-Irish statesman, orator, and historian. Edmund Burke was born in Dublin, Ireland, and graduated from Trinity College in 1748. In 1750 he began to study law in London but then turned to writing literary and political history. First elected to Parliament in 1765, he increasingly influenced the Rockingham faction of the Whig party for a quarter of a century. After a long parliamentary career ending in 1794, Burke retired in Beaconsfield where he died. Burke's conservatism, which should be understood within the context of his own times, was rooted in his convictions that man existed solely as a member of civil society, that human reason was limited, and that the historical past impacted on man and society. He revered institutions founded on prescription: the state, the British unwritten constitution, church, aristocracy, property. But he believed that gradual reform to improve society was necessary to conserve past gains. Burke's first published work, *A Vindication of Natural Society* (1756) was a short essay defending subordination and hierarchy. His pamphlet, *Thoughts on the Cause of the Present Discontents* (1770), a defense of party government, illustrated his opposition to uncontrolled, arbitrary power, which was evidenced also in his attachment to the English Revolution of 1688. Among causes he championed in the political field was the effort to resolve the British–American dispute, in his *Speech on American Taxation* (1774) and *Speech on American Conciliation with the American Colonies* (1775). Burke's *Reflections on the Revolution in France* (1790), his propagandistic and most influential work—immediately successful literarily and politically—assailed the radical reforms of the National Assembly. In *Letters on a Regicide Peace* (1796), Burke wanted the foreign war to overthrow Jacobin rule continued. Burke's ideas appealed to modern conservatives but those of a liberal persuasion interpreted them differently.

Bernard Hirschhorn

Texts

Burke's Politics: Selected Writings and Speeches of Edmund Burke on Reform, Revolution and War. Ed. Ross J.S. Hoffman and Paul Levack. New York: A.A. Knopf, 1949.

Reflections on the Revolution in France. Ed. J.G.A. Pocock. Indianapolis, IN: Hackett, 1987.

References

O'Brien, Conor Cruise. *The Great Melody: A Thematic Biography and Commented Anthology of Edmund Burke.* London: Sinclair-Stevenson, 1992.

Ritchie, Daniel E., ed. *Edmund Burke: Appraisals and Applications.* New Brunswick, NJ: Transaction Publishers, 1990.

Wilkins, Burleigh Taylor. *The Problem of Burke's Political Philosophy.* Oxford: Clarendon Press, 1967.

Burmese Historiography—Chronicles (Yazawin)

If historiography is understood primarily as the *writing* of history, and if history is defined mainly as *events* (of the past), then on one level, Burma's chronicles can indeed be considered part of its historiography. On another level, however, the purpose, content, methodology, and concept of history and historiography in Burma's chronicles are more than a written chronicling of events. To be sure, they *do* record events, pay close attention to dates, and describe what some in the discipline might consider history in a narrower, traditional sense. But the chronicles are also rich repositories for extracting the basic structural and conceptual principles underlying Burmese society, often using history to illustrate "the truth" about those principles.

They accomplish this by invariably including the context in which history occurs: the institutions and beliefs that influence the individuals that make events, which in turn make history. In addition, their source of information is derived from oral as well as other genres of literature not strictly defined as historical. Their methodology, moreover, incorporates the use of literary devices (myths, prophecies, omens, and didactic dialogue similar to Herodotus's "speeches"), which are assumed to be as "true" as actual historical events, around which they are woven. These "literary devices" speak to issues of self-validation, address beliefs about the Burmese conceptual system (including the cosmos and its origins, time, change, and continuity), and raise questions concerning power, legitimacy, and leadership.

Thus, if history can be defined more broadly to include patterns of development, forms of political action, types of social behavior, and ways of thinking about the world, and if the writing and conceptualization of that history imply no preconceptions about the linear and progressive nature of change (or being obsessed with change itself), then the Burmese chronicles can be included in the genre of scholarship that we think of today as historiography and history.

The Burmese term *yazawin,* taken from the Sanskrit *rajavamsa,* is often glossed over as "chronicle" but literally means "genealogy of kings." And the "chronicles" are indeed about that: a record of events generated by and about kings and their royal families. Burma, however, has other "histories," called *thamaing,* which are considered neither chronicles, nor concerned with royalty. (In fact, the word for "history" itself, in Burmese, is *thamaing*). These are socioeconomic and demographic records of towns, cities, temples, villages, irrigation works, and the like. And although they are not normally called chronicles, because they do fit the definition of historiography, any discussion of the subject should not be limited to *yazawin* alone.

Most extant Burmese chronicles found today are copies: hardly one original has been shown unequivocally to have survived. Yet, because there is a long tradition of preserving manuscripts deemed sacred (for Burmese writing itself is thought to be the Buddha's script), and since copying such manuscripts gives one merit (which is of paramount concern in Burmese society), and because Burma has been a highly literate society (a result of monastic education required of all young males), many contemporary or near-contemporary copies of original manuscripts have survived. Of these, about six *yazawin* are accepted by scholars as "standard," representing what Burmese society believes to be the truth about its royal past.

The general consensus among scholars is that the earliest extant chronicle is the *Yazawinkyaw* [the Celebrated Chronicle of Kings], written by Shin Thilawuntha in 1520. He was a highly respected monk, known for his literary genius in dealing with both secular and religious subjects. In this work, he explicitly referred to earlier *yazawin* that he used, although he did not cite them by name. His concept of history, as implicitly revealed

by his concerns and not by any explicit statement, is essentially a religious one: the religious past is the legitimator of the religious present. His purpose for writing the *Yazawinkyaw* was to link Burma's royalty to Prince Siddhartha's family (hence, to the Buddha) and the Burmese *sangha* (Buddhist church) to the origins of the Buddhist *sangha* in India and thenceforth in Sri Lanka, thereby validating the Burmese state and Burmese Buddhist society as it existed during his time.

Although the *Yazawinkyaw* is considered the oldest extant chronicle found today, the *Yaza Mu Haung* [Ancient Actions of Kings] by Zambu Kungya, a tutor of the crown prince in the latter half of the fourteenth century, is even older. However, the latter is not as well known and is not technically considered a chronicle. Another work called *Zatatawbon Yazawin* [The Chronicle of Royal Horoscopes], whose original author is not known with any certainty, may also have been written earlier than the *Yazawinkyaw.* But since subsequent authors added to it information belonging to the seventeenth century, it is usually considered to be later than the *Yazawinkyaw.* As its name suggests, the work includes diagrams of horoscopes belonging to Burmese royalty along with their cosmologically significant numeric information. It also provides a chronological list of kings that go back to the Buddha, as well as another of known historical kings of Burma that is extremely accurate. Furthermore, the work contains important demographic information, such as the number of fighting men that provided military and other service and the specific towns and villages in the kingdom from which they were recruited. Towns and cities that were "freed" from such corvée obligations are also mentioned. A formulaic list of what the Burmese considered to have been the country's ethnic groups can be found. In addition, a short but important narrative account is included that casts considerable light on the chronology of events and individuals in early Burmese history.

In the first quarter of the eighteenth century, during the reign of King Taninganwe of the Second Ava dynasty (1714–1733), an individual by the name of U Kala wrote the *Mahayazawingyi* [The Great Chronicle of Kings]. The son of a rich man (perhaps of Indian background, hence the name U Kala or "Mr. Indian"), his work appears to be the first comprehensive chronicle written by a single author, in a genre that became the standard for subsequent chroniclers, which modern scholars have come to regard as representative of the Burmese chronicle. It is certainly a genealogy of kings: their births and deaths, their children, their queens, their works of merit, and their achievements, both secular and religious. But it is more than that. Although the text follows a chronological sequence based on the births and deaths of kings, his criterion for organizing Burmese history is location. That is, each dynasty was named not after its founder but its capital city; hence, the Pagan dynasty, Ava dynasty, Toungoo dynasty, Second Ava dynasty, and the Konbaung dynasty, categories we still use today. Thus, the criterion for organizing history and identifying ruling dynasties was sacred location. That was important to him because Burmese capital cities were believed to have received the all important Buddha prophecy, thereby legitimating them, their founders, and their successors. The chronicle also describes events dealing with neighboring individuals and countries, provides details of court life and rituals such as royal coronations, speaks on military strategy and war, and supplies socioeconomic information of numerous kinds.

Myanma Yazawinthit [The New Chronicle of Myanma], written in the late eighteenth century by a minister under King Bodawpaya of the next, Konbaung dynasty, follows U Kala's organizational and periodizing scheme as well as general subject matter. It is in many respects a copy, sometimes verbatim, of U Kala's work. But it is more critical of sources, dates, and events that are not confirmed by epigraphy. As the official in charge of verifying the bona fides of religious property in the kingdom, Twinthin was given the authority to collect and/or copy all donative stone inscriptions, the ultimate proof of clear title to religious lands and labor. He thus compared the information found on the stone, usually contemporary to the event it described, with that in U Kala's chronicle, making changes where necessary. He was also a scholar who knew his literature: poetry, ballads, songs, religious and secular treatises. Yet, his purpose for writing history was not much different from that of his predecessors and successors: it was to legitimate the political, social, and religious status quo. However, the title of his history reveals a most important, though subtle change in his perception of what he was writing about; the term *Myanma Yazawinthit* meant a "new history of Myanma" (or Burma), and was not simply a chronicle of its kings. *Yazawin,* in other words, no longer meant to him a simple "genealogy of kings" but also a history of the Myanma people and/or nation-state.

But Twinthin's "modern" perspective was not perpetuated by his successors. Instead, the older meaning of *yazawin* was resurrected by the authors of the next standard chronicle, the *Hmannan*

Mahayazawindawgyi (The Great Royal Chronicle of the Glass Palace). Compiled by a group of appointed learned scholars ostensibly to correct U Kala's work, they nevertheless followed his organizational and thematic schema, if not much of the content, while for the most part (if not totally), ignored Twinthin's work. In many places, the *Hmannan* is a verbatim copy of U Kala's work, whose purpose and much of its content had remained unchanged (with the exception of Twinthin's corrections) since at least Shin Thilawuntha's *Yazawinkyaw* of 1520. The *Hmannan* was also officially called *Pahtama Yazawindawgyi* [The First Royal Chronicle] but it is much better known by scholars and the public as the *Hmannan.*

In A.D. 1867, King Mindon, of the same dynasty and a successor of King Bagyidaw who had commissioned the *Hmannan,* ordered another group of scholars to continue the "First Chronicle" and bring it up to date. The first part, in seven volumes, ended with the year 1854, and the second, in three volumes, with 1869. These two parts were together combined and named *Dutiya Yazawindawgyi* [The Second Royal Chronicle]: that is, the second one to be commissioned by a king. After the British formally annexed Burma in 1886, another group of scholars—presumably on their own initiative—continued the narrative of the "Second Chronicle" to the year 1885, the date Mandalay fell to the British, ending the thousand-year-old Burmese monarchy.

The compilers adopted the main features of their predecessors, even though they had been in contact with Westerners for at least a quarter of a century by then. Indeed, it was a time of social and political anxiety, as Burma was effectively landlocked. The Second Anglo-Burmese War of 1852 had given Great Britain Lower Burma, sealing off Burma from its coasts: its main cultural and intellectual "window" to the outside world, and of course, also its source of trade revenues, upon which the state depended to supplement its largely agricultural economy. From the perspectives of the authors of the "Second Chronicle," the world was falling apart all around them, and one of the few things left that they could do to control that downward spiral was to preserve the integrity of *yazawin* writing—which they did.

The "Second Chronicle" was updated by one of its authors, U Tin, and published in 1922 as the *Konbaungset Mahayazawindawgyi* [The Great Royal Chronicle of the Konbaung Dynasty]. It is the last chronicle to be written in the traditional manner. Interestingly, the narrative begins not with the Buddha this time, but with A.D. 1752 when

King Alaunghpaya founded the Konbaung dynasty. True, he was still linked to Mahasammata, the first king of the world in Hindu-Buddhist mythology, whose lineage produced Siddhartha, who later became the Buddha. Nonetheless, this was a subtle change that seemed to reassert the primary purpose of writing *yazawin,* focusing on the dynastic components of Burmese history. He must have felt compelled to tell the end of the story regarding the final dynasty to rule Burma and did so by choosing to terminate his narrative at 1916, when King Thibaw, the last king, died while in British-forced exile in India. In the end, then, from the earliest to the most recent chronicle, the main criterion for writing *yazawin* retained its literal meaning: "genealogy of kings."

All these major chronicles have been published in Burmese; yet none has been translated into English in its entirety. It is also extremely difficult to determine if the published versions are based on the originals. As several copies of these manuscripts were made almost immediately by scribes desiring merit, one is not certain if the published version is really a contemporary copy or the original itself. It is difficult to assess with any certainty if the originals themselves survived the three days of burning and looting of Mandalay in 1885 during the British conquest. There are manuscripts of chronicles in the British Library and the National Library in Rangoon, but a precise and thorough document exegesis has not yet been carried out to determine if any of the published versions were actually taken from their originals or from copies.

In all of these chronicles, the purpose for writing history was to "set the record straight" from a particular perspective; that is, to be historically, religiously, socially, ideologically, and politically "correct." They were also written to teach lessons, usually of a moral kind, and for that function, dialogues, along with prophetic and symbolic occurrences were inserted at appropriate times and places in the text. These literary devices marked, and were clues to, what were considered important values in Burmese culture. Thus, history was not written for its own sake, or to distinguish myth from empirical fact, and certainly not to demonstrate and document "the idea of progress" in linear time.

Michael Arthur Aung-Thwin

Texts

Hmannan Mahayazawindawgyi [The Great Royal Chronicle of the Glass Palace]. Ed. Daw Pwa Khin and U Hla Maung. 3 vols. Rangoon, Burma: Pyi Kyi Mandaing Press, 1967.

U Kala. *Mahayazawingyi* [The Great Chronicle of Kings]. Ed. Saya Pwa. 3 vols. Rangoon, Burma: Hanthawaddy Press, 1960.

Konbaungset Mahayazawindawgyi [The Great Royal Chronicle of the Konbaung Dynasty]. Ed. U Maung Maung Tin. 3 vols. Rangoon, Burma: Laytimandaing Press, 1968.

Maha Shin Thilawuntha. *Yazawinkyaw* [The Celebrated Chronicle of Kings]. Ed. Pe Maung Tin. Rangoon, Burma: Hanthawaddy Press, 1965.

Maha Shin Thilawuntha (attribution uncertain). *Zatatawbon Yazawin* [The Chronicle of Royal Horoscopes]. Ed. U Hla Tin. Rangoon, Burma: Ministry of Union Culture, 1960.

Twinthintaikwun Mahasithu. *Twinthin Myanma Yazawinthit* [The New Chronicle of Myanma]. Rangoon, Burma: Mingala Printing Press, 1968.

References

Aung-Thwin, Michael. "Prophecies, Omens, and Dialogue, Tools of the Trade in Burmese Historiography." In *Moral Order and the Question of Change: Essays on Southeast Asian Thought,* ed. David K. Wyatt and Alexander Woodside. Southeast Asia Studies Monograph Series, no. 24. New Haven, CT: Yale University Southeast Asia Program, 1982, 78–103.

The Glass Palace Chronicle of the Kings of Burma. Trans. Pe Maung Tin. Rangoon, Burma: Rangoon University Press, 1923, Introduction.

Lieberman, Victor. "How Reliable Is U Kala's Burmese Chronicle? Some New Comparisons." *Journal of Southeast Asian Studies* 17 (1986): 236–255.

Pannacami. *Sasanavamsa.* Trans. Bimala Churn Law. London: Pali Text Society, 1952.

Shin Sandalinka. *The Maniyadanabon of Shin Sandalinka.* Trans. L.E. Bagshawe. Southeast Asia Program Data Papers, no. 115. Ithaca, NY: Cornell University Southeast Asia Program, 1981.

"Slapat Rajawan Datow Smin Ron." Trans. R. Halliday. *Journal of the Burma Research Society* 13 (1923): 1–249.

Tet Htoot. "The Nature of the Burmese Chronicles." In *Historians of South East Asia,* ed. D.G.E. Hall. London: Oxford University Press, 1961, 50–62.

Than Tun. "Historiography of Burma." *Shiroku* 9 (1976): 1–22.

Burnet, Gilbert (1643–1715)

Scottish theologian and historian. Burnet was born in Edinburgh and educated at Aberdeen. After five years as professor of divinity at Glasgow, he moved to London in 1674. He retired to the Continent in 1683, returning during the Glorious Revolution as William of Orange's chaplain. In 1689 he was appointed bishop of Salisbury. He died in London. Although the author of dozens of books and pamphlets, Burnet is best remembered for two monumental historical works. His three-volume *History of the Reformation of the Church of England* (1679–1714) was the first attempt to write an account of the English Reformation from authentic sources. It was also unabashedly Protestant in sympathies and written to counter Catholics who do "confidently disparage our Reformation." Composed between 1683 and 1713, the two-volume *History of My Own Time* (1723–1724 and 1733–1734) was originally intended as a memoir, but, inspired by the French historian Jacques-Auguste De Thou's *Historia sui Temporis* and the earl of Clarendon's *History of the Rebellion,* Burnet transformed it into a full-scale historical work that remains a valuable source.

Martin Greig

Texts

Bishop Burnet's History of His Own Time. 6 vols. Oxford: Clarendon Press, 1823.
History of the Reformation. Ed. N. Pocock. 7 vols. Oxford: Clarendon Press, 1865.

References

Clarke, T.E.S., and H.C. Foxcroft. *A Life of Bishop Burnet.* Cambridge, Eng.: Cambridge University, 1907.
MacGillivray, Royce. *Restoration Historians and the English Civil War.* The Hague: Martinus Nijhoff, 1974, 185–196.

Burnet, Thomas (ca. 1635–1715)

English theologian and historian. Burnet was born in Yorkshire and educated at Cambridge, where he became a fellow of Christ's College in 1657, remaining there until 1685, when he was appointed master of the Charterhouse. He also held an appointment as royal chaplain-in-ordinary to William III and for a time was considered a serious candidate for a bishopric, until the controversy over his views of the age and creation of the earth erupted. Burnet is best known for *Telluris Theoria Sacra* (Latin, 2 vols. 1681–1689; English version, *The Theory of the Earth,* 1689) and *Archaeologiae*

Philosophicae (Latin and English, 1692), both written in response to the opponents of the Royal Society who argued that the "new science" neglected Revelation in favor of nature. Burnet instead insisted that the "new science" could be used to deepen revealed knowledge about nature. He sought to combine the metaphors of time's arrow and time's cycle into a unified view of history that was both linear in its narrative yet cyclical in its overall framework. In God's great "Tragicomedy of the World" the history of both humanity and the earth paralleled one another in a progression from the Fall and the Flood back to the original paradise of Eden. Burnet's books were published during a period in which New World discoveries and the unearthing of ancient fossils were occasioning increasing doubts across Europe as to the veracity of the Bible as a historical source and speculation that the world might in fact be considerably older than asserted in Scripture. Although his own imaginative, and erroneous, interpretation of the development of the earth now seems peculiar, it was an important exercise in pre-Lyellian geological and historical thought.

Martin Greig

Texts

Archaeologiae Philosophicae; or, The Ancient Doctrine Concerning the Originals of Things. London: E. Curll, 1729.
The Sacred Theory of the Earth. Ed. Basil Willey. London: Centaur Press, 1965.

References

Gould, Stephen Jay. *Time's Arrow, Time's Cycle.* Cambridge, MA: Harvard University Press, 1987.
Tuveson, Ernest Lee. *Millennium and Utopia.* Berkeley and Los Angeles: University of California Press, 1949.

Burtt, Edwin Arthur (1892–1989)

Philosopher of the history of religion and the history of science. The center of Burtt's philosophical interest was the quest for a reconciliation between modern scientific thinking, with its emphasis on Cartesian duality and mathematical logic, and the greater dimensions of human rational experience, defined as philosophy and religion. Burtt thought that theological dogmatism and the psychological need for certainty in a hostile environment were impediments to the formulation of a new philosophy of mind. He recommended the critical historical analysis of the fundamental presuppositions of the world's major idea systems, including modern science, the various schools of modern philosophy, and the world religions as a necessary first step toward a new epistemology. Burtt recognized the limitations of logical positivism long before his contemporaries did and was convinced that extensive historical analysis of that philosophy as well as other idea systems would reveal them to be little more than objectifications of the mood of an age, fitful and temporary. Any new scientific cosmology as well as global understanding and world peace depend on our successful search for a new philosophy of mind.

Diane Villemaire

Texts

In Search of Philosophic Understanding. New York: New American Library, 1965.

Man Seeks the Divine: A Study in the History and Comparison of Religions. New York: Harper, 1957.

The Metaphysical Foundations of Modern Physical Science: A Historical and Critical Essay. London: Kegan Paul, Trench, Trubner & Co., 1924.

Religion in an Age of Science. Ed. John Herman Randall. New York: Frederick A. Stokes Co., 1929.

Texts

The Ancient Greek Historians. London: Macmillan, 1909.

A History of Freedom of Thought. Second ed. London: Oxford University Press, 1952.

A History of Greece to the Death of Alexander the Great. Fourth ed. London: Macmillan, 1975.

A History of the Eastern Roman Empire from the Fall of Irene to the Accession of Basil I (A.D. 802–867). London: Macmillan, 1912.

A History of the Later Roman Empire from Arcadius to Irene (A.D. 395 to A.D. 800). London: Macmillan, 1889.

History of the Later Roman Empire from the Death of Theodosius I to the Death of Justinian (A.D. 395–A.D. 565). London: Macmillan, 1923.

The Idea of Progress: An Inquiry into Its Origins and Growth. London: Macmillan, 1920.

Selected Essays of J.B. Bury. Ed. Harold Temperley. Cambridge, Eng.: Cambridge University Press, 1930.

References

Lewis, Scott M. "Unity and Continuity: J.B. Bury's Philosophy of History in the Development of Byzantine Studies." *Orientalia Christiana Periodica* 59 (1993): 483–506.

Bury, John Bagnell (1861–1927)

British historian. Bury was born in county Monaghan, Ireland, and studied at Trinity College, Dublin, holding academic posts there and (from 1902) at Cambridge. He was both a classicist and a Byzantinist and, for much of his career, a strong believer in nineteenth-century ideas of rationalism and progress. According to Bury history must follow the methods of the natural sciences, stressing the exact determination of facts, rather than functioning as a branch of literature. Bury denied that there was a "Byzantine Empire" separate from the later Roman Empire, insisting on continuity. Among his best-known works are Bury's edition, with commentary, of Gibbon's *Decline and Fall of the Roman Empire* (1896–1900), his *History of Greece to the Death of Alexander the Great* (1900), and *The Ancient Greek Historians* (London, 1909). His interests extended beyond classical and Byzantine history, and he also produced a *History of Freedom of Thought* (1914) and a celebrated study of *The Idea of Progress* (1920).

Stephen A. Stertz

Business History

Subfield of economic and social history concerned with the study of the origins and development of particular commercial enterprises, mainly since the early modern era, and with the impact on global development of such factors as entrepreneurship and managerialism. Histories of businesses and people in business have proliferated since the beginning of the Industrial Revolution, reflecting wide variations in quality and perspectives. Enterprises have commissioned their own histories—the earliest of these was a German iron manufacturer in 1825—generally uncritical of their patrons; and since the era of the English Victorian journalist Samuel Smiles there have been numerous biographies of "industrial statesmen," equally celebratory in tone. On the other side have ranged critics of business who thrived around the beginning of the twentieth century and again during the Great Depression, emphasizing the predatory character of capitalist "robber barons" and the devastating effects of their actions on their competitors, workers, and communities.

Business history as an academic field, however, is of more recent vintage, an offshoot of economic history although not exclusively focused on the economic aspects of the subject. As in many other fields of history, German archivists and scholars laid the groundwork for the systematic study of business enterprises. In the early 1900s, German chambers of commerce established regional industrial archives *(Wirtschaftsarchiv)*, emulated by several large firms such as the steelmaker, Krupp, and the electrical manufacturer, Siemens. In 1906 Richard Ehrenberg produced a history of Siemens based on intensive research in the company's records.

Among the most influential of German figures was Werner Sombart (1863–1941), an economic historian influenced by Marx who, however, was dissatisfied with what he perceived as the overly theoretical and ahistorical tendencies of both classical economists and Marxists. The author of *Der Bourgeois* (1913) and of a multivolume study entitled *Der moderne Kapitalismus* (1915), Sombart devoted much of his career, from the 1880s to the 1930s, to exploring what he termed the "spirit of capitalism" as a cultural rather than solely economic phenomenon. He emphasized the emergence of a distinctive cast of mind among European businessmen in the sixteenth and seventeenth centuries, characterized by acquisitiveness, individualism, and economic rationality. Focusing on the psychological traits of business people, Sombart identified the role of the individual entrepreneur as an agent of historical change in the capitalist system. Although later scholars challenged Sombart's research methods and conclusions, his conceptual influence was substantial.

Perhaps not surprisingly, the field of business history flourished most successfully in the United States. In 1926 the Harvard Business School appointed Canadian-born Norman S.B. Gras (1884–1956) as its first professor of business history. An economic historian by training, Gras expended much effort seeking to establish business history as a distinct academic field and to clarify its boundaries. Gras focused on the internal arrangements and practices of business enterprises, encompassing the evolution of instruments of credit and exchange, accounting and administration, marketing and production. This emphasis on business administration and the history of individual firms was particularly congruent with the orientation of the Harvard Business School toward training corporate managers through intensive "case studies."

Gras and his associates produced a formidable array of "case histories" of primarily American companies over the next several decades, most notably a multivolume history of Standard Oil of New Jersey, commissioned by the company but conducted by an independent Business History Foundation established by Gras in 1948. Gras also encouraged the development of the Baker Library at Harvard as a major repository of business archives and promoted an association of business historians and a journal. (This last is now the *Business History Review,* one of three major journals in the field, the others being the American publication *Business and Economic History* and the British journal *Business History*). While Gras's achievements helped to establish business history as a legitimate field of academic study, the focus on business "case studies" encountered criticism in some quarters as obsessively empirical and isolated from the mainstream of historical inquiry.

During the 1940s another group of scholars at Harvard adopted a different approach, more oriented toward theoretical conclusions. Inspired by the work of the Austrian economist Joseph Schumpeter who, like Sombart, emphasized the role of entrepreneurship in generating economic change, Arthur H. Cole and his colleagues set up a Research Center in Entrepreneurial History that undertook to define the concept and encouraged comparative and cross-cultural studies and linkages with the social sciences. The center proved to be short-lived, closing down in 1958, and its practitioners acknowledged intellectual frustration in developing "entrepreneurial history" as a coherent field of analysis. Nevertheless, the center had carried business history several steps beyond the empirical preoccupations of the case-study approach.

By the 1960s some economists, such as Edith Penrose and J.K. Galbraith, recognized that the emergence of big business required modification of the ideas of classical economics regarding the relationship of the individual firm to the market. Their work formed a backdrop to the development of the "organizational school" of business historians, the most notable representative of which is Alfred D. Chandler Jr., whose work focused on the advent of "managerial capitalism" in the nineteenth and twentieth centuries. Chandler and his colleagues drew substantially on the tradition of company histories but coupled this research approach with intensive analysis of the changes in financing, marketing, production, and administrative organization that accompanied the growth of large corporate enterprises: the "visible hand" of management complemented, if it did not supplant, the "invisible hand" of the market.

The organizational historians, like the entrepreneurial historians, also adopted a comparative approach that both reflected and contributed to conceptual advances in the social sciences and in social and economic history. Ultimately their research and conclusions extended well beyond the realm of business to embrace large-scale institutions in the public as well as private sector.

By the 1980s the organizational approach to business history had expanded beyond its American base to the study of business evolution in Europe, Japan, and the emerging industrializing countries and to the rise of multinational enterprises. More recently, some scholars have explored areas that did not figure prominently into the perspective of the organizational school, such as the persistence of small businesses and "family capitalism" and the impact of changing business structures on the relations of management and labor. But the "organizational synthesis" of Chandler and his associates still constitutes the dominant conceptual paradigm within which most business historians proceed.

Graham D. Taylor

See also CLIOMETRICS; ECONOMIC HISTORY.

References

Braudel, Fernand. *Civilization and Capitalism, 15th to 18th Century.* Trans. Sian Reynolds. 3 vols. New York: Harper & Row 1979–1984.

Chandler, Alfred D., Jr. *Scale and Scope: The Dynamics of Industrial Capitalism.* Cambridge, MA: Belknap Press, 1990.

———. *Strategy and Structure: Chapters in the History of Industrial Enterprise.* Boston: M.I.T. Press, 1962.

———. *The Visible Hand: The Managerial Revolution in American Business.* Cambridge, MA: Belknap Press, 1977.

———. and Herman Daems, eds. *Managerial Hierarchies: Comparative Perspectives on the Rise of the Modern Industrial Enterprise.* Cambridge, MA: Harvard University Press 1980.

Cochran, Thomas C. *Business in American Life: A History.* New York: McGraw-Hill, 1972.

Cole, Arthur H. *Business Enterprise in Its Social Setting.* Cambridge, MA: Harvard University Press, 1959.

Gras, N.S.B. *Business and Capitalism: An Introduction to Business History.* New York: F.S. Crofts & Co. 1939; reprint, New York: A.M. Kelley, 1971.

Miller, William, ed. *Men in Business: Essays in the History of Entrepreneurship.* Cambridge, MA: Harvard University Press, 1952.

Sombart, Werner. *The Quintessence of Capitalism: A Study of the History and Psychology of the Business Man.* Trans. Mortimer Epstein. New York: H. Fertig, 1967.

———. *Der moderne Kapitalismus.* 3 vols. Berlin: Duncker & Humblot, 1928–1955.

Butterfield, Sir Herbert (1900–1979)

British historian and religious thinker. Butterfield was born in Oxenhope in Yorkshire, England. He was educated at the Trade and Grammar School, Keighley, and entered Peterhouse, Cambridge, as a history scholar in 1919; in 1923 the college elected him a fellow. Butterfield took up the chair of modern history in 1944 and in 1963 became Regius professor of history. He was master of Peterhouse from 1955 to 1968, president of the Historical Association (1955–1958) and vice-chancellor of Cambridge University (1955–1968). Butterfield's life work centered on four major themes: the history of historiography, the reconfiguration of British history, Christianity and history, and the theory of international relations. The first reached its culmination in *The Whig Interpretation of History* (1931) and *Man on His Past* (1955), works in which he analyzed the recurrent obstacles to historical understanding and emphasized the importance of imagination, flexibility, and creative insight in any meaningful reconstruction of the past. In relation to the second, Butterfield produced *George III, Lord North and the People* (1949) and *George III and the Historians* (1956), both influential in changing the understanding of constitutional developments in Hanoverian Britain. His views as a religious thinker were embodied in his widely read *Christianity and History* (1949) and *Christianity in European History* (1951), which transcended mere "technical history" in their emphasis on the interplay between human personality, intentions, and the workings of providence in historical events. The ramification of Christian principles for international relations was addressed in *History and Human Relations* (1952) and *International Conflict in the Twentieth Century* (1960). Butterfield also launched the study of the history of science in *The Origins of Modern Science* (1949), perhaps his most successful work, which guided history into new channels, introduced scientists to historical scholarship, and stimulated research on the subject in England and America. A wide-ranging historian with great imaginative power and insight, Butterfield reflected more deeply than any contemporary Briton on the nature of history and historical knowledge and was indefatigable in his defense of history as the highest form of human culture. In this he made his most lasting and important contribution.

Karl Schweizer

Texts

Christianity and History. London: G. Bell, 1949.
Christianity in European History. London and New York: Oxford University Press, 1951.
George III and the Historians. London: Collins, 1957.
George III, Lord North and the People, 1779–80. London: Bell, 1949.
History and Human Relations. New York: Macmillan, 1952.
International Conflict in the Twentieth Century: A Christian View. New York: Harper, 1960.
Man on His Past: The Study of the History of Historical Scholarship. Cambridge, Eng.: Cambridge University Press, 1955.
The Origins of History. Ed. A. Watson. New York: Basic Books, 1981.
The Origins of Modern Science. Revised ed. New York: Free Press, 1965.
The Whig Interpretation of History. New York: AMS Press, 1978.

References

Coll, Alberto R. *The Wisdom of Statecraft: Sir Herbert Butterfield and the Philosophy of International Politics.* Durham, NC: Duke University Press, 1985.
Elliott, J.H., and H.G. Koenigsberger, eds. *The Diversity of History: Essays in Honour of Sir Herbert Butterfield.* London: Routledge and Kegan Paul, 1970.

Byzantine Historiography

As a leading category of literature, the writing of Greek historical narrative was a rich and significant part of the classical tradition inherited and extended by the Byzantine Empire that, as the direct continuation of the Roman Empire refocused in the eastern end of the Mediterranean world, is generally reckoned as extending from Constantine the Great's rebuilding of ancient Byzantium as his new capital, Constantinople, in the early fourth century up to its capture by the Ottoman Turks in 1453.

Following distinctions made by some Byzantine authors themselves, it has become conventional to recognize two separate categories of writing: the formal, more stylistically pretentious "history" proper and the less cultivated, more annalistic "chronicle" (often further identified with monkish authorship, though that stereotype is by no means consistently correct). That simplistic division has come under increasing challenge in recent years, but might still be retained, with caution, for some simple purposes of classification. In addition, the first category can, for a certain period of time, be subdivided into the histories written by secular men of learning on one hand and the distinct genre of "church history" on the other. These categories assume further importance because writers within them often took up where predecessors left off, in conscious efforts to maintain continuities of coverage.

The early Byzantine centuries witnessed a strenuous effort by educated writers to maintain the traditions of Greek historical writing based on standards and models set by Herodotus, Thucydides, and Polybius. The surviving texts are scanty or often fragmentary (as is the case, for instance, with the writings of Priskos of Panion in the fifth century, who left us accounts of the empire's dealings with Attila the Hun). An inevitable preoccupation was with the disasters suffered by the empire in the age of the barbarian attacks, as juxtaposed with the internal triumph of Christianity over paganism. Paganism retained much support among intellectuals and became a polemic issue for many serious historians. Such was the case with Zosimus (Greek: Zosimos) who, though he lived in the late fifth and early sixth centuries, has left us a strongly pro-pagan account of the fourth century.

In addition to partisan agendas, conservative intellectuals disliked writing about anything not known to their ancient models. Accordingly, early Byzantine historians, even though presumably or manifestly Christians themselves, chose to avoid or restrict discussion of the vital religious life, ecclesiastical politics, and theological controversies of their day. This was notably true of the main historian of the age of Justinian I (527–565), Procopius (Prokopios) of Caesarea, whose remarkable, if complex, writings have won him a reputation as the last of the major writers in the great historical tradition of classical antiquity. Although lesser figures, his sixth-century continuators, Agathias and Menander Protector, are important adjuncts.

Meanwhile, however, the need to fill in the missing Christian dimension prompted the early creation of the genre known as church history, which not only dealt with the religious life of an era but also traced the workings of Christ and his message through historical events. This genre was effectively created in the early third century by Eusebius (Eusebios) of Caesarea, the confidant of Constantine the Great. It was continued into the fifth century by the historians Socrates and Sozomenus (Sozomenos) and through the sixth century by Evagrius (Evagrios).

While the line of literary historians wore out by the early seventh century, with Theophylakt Symokatta, the idiom of the chronicle came into full maturity with the works of John Malalas in the sixth century and of John of Antioch and the so-called "Easter Chronicle" *(Chronikon paschale)* of the early seventh. The utter dearth of literary history during the next three centuries makes us particularly dependent upon the major chronicle of Theophanes Confessor, writing in the early ninth century. Supplementing his major chronicle is one by the patriarch Nicephorus (Nikephoros) of the same period, followed by chronicles of George Hamartolos and further successors in the later ninth and tenth centuries.

Thanks to the intellectual revivals of the ninth and tenth centuries, and the encouragement of the scholar-emperor Constantine VII Porphyrogenitos, historical writing in the scholarly tradition was resumed by the likes of Joseph Genesios and Leo the Deacon, followed in the eleventh century by Michael Attaleiates and Nikephoros Bryennios. Their histories are supplemented by the chroniclers Symeon Magister, Leo Grammatikos, and John Skylitzes. A particularly special plateau was reached in the eleventh century with the courtier, scholar, and politician, Michael Psellus (Psellos), whose highly egocentric memoir of court life still makes vivid reading.

The epoch from the late eleventh to early thirteenth century, ruled mainly by the Komnenian dynasty, witnessed a particularly brilliant period of historiography that is dominated by two commanding figures. At the outset came the dynastic founder's daughter, the princess Anna Comnena (Anna Komnene) whose colorful history of her father's reign arguably establishes her as the only great female writer of history until our century. At the other end is the fussy but powerful Niketas Choniates, who traced the empire's skid from the last Komnenoi to the catastrophic capture of Constantinople by the Fourth Crusade in 1204. In between stands the lesser historian John Kinnamos (Cinnamus), while chroniclers of this epoch include Michael Glykas and such quite ambitious writers as George Kedrenos and John Zonaras.

The revival of intellectual as well as political life, by the Laskarid emperors of Nicaea and then by the Palaiologan dynasty restored in Constantinople in 1261, produced a lively flowering of new historical writers, begun by the Laskarid politician and scholar George Akropolites, extended into the next century by the polymath George Pachymeres, and brought to a peak in the mid-fourteenth century by the memoirist-emperor John VI Cantacuzenos (Kantakouzenos) and the scholar-theologian Nicephorus (Nikephoros) Gregoras. Following a serious lapse of nearly seventy-five years, one last burst of historical writing attended the epoch of Byzantium's final collapse, represented by the mid-fifteenth-century writers Doukas, Laonikos Chalkokondyles, George Sphrantzes (Phrantzes), and Kritoboulos of Imbros.

The Byzantine historiographic tradition also includes brief accounts of disasters or crises: Eustathios of Thessaloniki on the Norman sack of that city in 1185; John Kananos on the Turkish attack on Constantinople in 1422; and John Anagnostes on the Turkish capture of Thessaloniki in 1430. Moreover, the Greek tradition beyond the Byzantine Empire itself is represented by fifteenth-century chroniclers such as Michael Panaretos on the separatist empire of Trebizond or Leontios Machairas and George Boustronios on the Lusignan realm of Cyprus.

Different ages prompted varying preoccupations through some eleven centuries of literary tradition, but the consistency of that tradition is remarkable. Chroniclers were more specific in their data, whereas the more ambitious historians preferred grander literary constructions to mere information. But all recognized a linear concept of time and understood serious principles of causality. As the Christian mentality became fully consolidated, the role of divine providence was accepted as a comprehensive force, but this was also understood by more sophisticated writers as in tension with human initiatives, represented by the ancient principle of *Tyche,* or chance. Byzantine historical writers never shied away from strong biases or partisan stances. Nevertheless, especially the more sophisticated of them were aware that they were writing in a grand tradition and upholding high responsibilities of scholarly technique and critical judgment—all on a level rarely matched in other quarters of the Western world until well through the Middle Ages.

John W. Barker

See also CHRONICLES, MEDIEVAL; CRUSADES, HISTORIES OF THE; ECCLESIASTICAL HISTORY; GREEK HISTORIOGRAPHY—ANCIENT; GREEK HISTORIOGRAPHY—MODERN; HAGIOGRAPHY.

Texts

Agathias. *The Histories.* Trans. J.D. Frendo. Berlin and New York: de Gruyter, 1975.

Anonymous. *Chronicon Paschale, 284–628 A.D.* Trans. Michael and Mary Whitby. Liverpool, Eng.: Liverpool University Press, 1989.

Doukas. *Decline and Fall of Byzantium to the Ottoman Turks [Historia Turco-Byzantina].* Trans. Harry J. Magoulias. Detroit, MI: Wayne State University Press, 1975.

Eusebius (Eusebios) of Caesarea. *The History of the Church.* Trans. G.A. Williamson. Baltimore, MD: Penguin Books, 1965.

Eustathios of Thessaloniki. *The Capture of Thessaloniki.* Trans. John R. Melville Jones. Canberra: Australian Association for Byzantine Studies, 1988.

Evagrius (Evagrios). *A History of the Church from A.D. 431 to A.D. 594.* Trans. E. Walford. London: Bohn's Ecclesiastical Library, 1851.

Comnena [Komnene], Anna. *Alexiad.* Trans. E.R.A. Sewter. Harmondsworth and New York: Penguin Books, 1969.

Kinnamos, John. *Deeds of John and Manuel Komnenus.* Trans. Charles M. Brand. New York: Columbia University Press, 1976.

Kritovoulos, Michael. *History of Mehmed the Conqueror.* Trans. C.T. Riggs. Princeton, NJ: Princeton University Press, 1954.

Malalas, John. *Chronicle.* Trans. Elizabeth Jeffreys, Michael Jeffreys, Roger Scott, et al. Melbourne: Australian Association for Byzantine Studies, 1986.

Nicephorus (Nikephoros) Patriarch of Constantinople. *Short History.* Ed. and trans. Cyril Mango. Washington, DC: Dumbarton Oaks, 1990.

Niketas Choniates. *Annals (O City of Byzantium).* Trans. Harry J. Magoulias. Detroit, MI: Wayne State University Press, 1984.

Procopius (Prokopios) of Caesarea. [Complete Works]. Ed. and trans. H.B. Dewing and Glanville Downey. 7 vols. London and New York: Loeb Classical Library, 1914–1940.

———.[Selected passages]. Trans. Averil Cameron. New York: Washington Square Press, 1967.

———. *Secret History.* Trans. G.A. Williamson. Baltimore, MD: Penguin Books, 1966.

Psellus (Psellos), Michael. *Fourteen Byzantine Rulers* [Chronographía]. Trans. E.R.A. Sewter. Harmondsworth and New York: Penguin Books, 1966.

Sphrantzes (Phrantzes). *The Fall of the Byzantine Empire* [Chronicon minus]. Trans. Marios Philippides. Amherst, MA: University of Massachusetts Press, 1980.

Theophanes. *Chronicle* [for years 602–813 only]. Trans. Harry Turtledove. Philadelphia, PA: University of Pennsylvania Press, 1982.

Theophylact Simocatta. *History.* Trans. Michael and Mary Whitby. Oxford: Clarendon Press, 1986.

Zosimus (Zosimos). *New History.* Trans. Ronald T. Ridley. Canberra: Australian Association for Byzantine Studies, 1982.

References

Scott, Roger. "The Classical Tradition in Byzantine Historiography." In *Byzantium and the Classical Tradition,* ed. Margaret Mullett and Roger Scott. Birmingham: University of Birmingham Centre for Byzantine Studies, 1981, 61–74.

See also articles on individual authors, and on "Chronology" and "Historiography" in *The Oxford Dictionary of Byzantium.* 3 vols. Oxford: Clarendon Press, 1991.

C

Cadière, Léopold (1869–1955)

Missionary, historian, linguist, and religious ethnographer of Vietnam. From 1892 until his death, Cadière mainly lived among ordinary Vietnamese near Hue. Alone among the French scholars of the Ecole française d'Extrême-orient, Cadière's personal knowledge of popular Vietnamese consciousness transformed his scrupulous research into an exacting written resource, making his work a valuable introduction to late traditional Vietnam. As long-serving editor of the *Bulletin des Amis du Vieux Hué,* he also published many useful descriptive materials ranging from translated inscriptions to early travelers' accounts.

N.J. Cooke

Texts

Croyances et pratiques religieuses des Vietnamiens.
3 vols. Saigon, Vietnam: École française d'Extrême-Orient, 1955–1957.

Caesar, Gaius Julius [Iulius] (102/100–44 B.C.)

Roman statesman, general, author, and dictator. Born into a patrician family that claimed descent from Venus and Aeneas, early in his career Caesar attached himself to the partisans of Marius (to whom he was related by marriage), opponents of the reactionary dictator Lucius Sulla (d. 78 B.C.). He later formed the so-called First Triumvirate with Pompeius and Crassus in 60 B.C., and these three virtually controlled Roman politics until Crassus's death in 53, after which a breach developed between the remaining two members. During the period 58 B.C. to 50 B.C. Caesar campaigned against the Gauls and invaded the island of Britain in 55 and 54. Meanwhile Pompeius consolidated his power in Rome, ultimately joining his former enemies in an alliance against Caesar. Crossing the Rubicon River in January of 49 B.C., Caesar began a civil war that continued after Pompeius's death in 48 and the famous suicide of Cato in 46 until Caesar finally found himself unopposed in the field by 45 B.C. Having revived the ancient office of dictator he ruled until his assassination by a group of sixty conspirators led by Brutus and Cassius on the Ides of March, 44 B.C. Caesar was considered a great man of letters even in his own lifetime and was ranked as the second greatest orator in Rome after Cicero. His works included at least one long poem, a political pamphlet called the *Anti-Cato,* and the commentaries on the Gallic and civil wars, which are still extant. Such commentaries were not history proper, but were rather considered useful sources for "full-dress" history. However, Caesar employed many techniques of the historian, writing in the third person, inserting occasional digressions on peoples or locations, and even rare use of direct speech. In fact, some considered his work insusceptible of improvement by historians. Stylistically Caesar preferred short, pellucid sentences that emphasized rapidity over Ciceronian periodic balance. His works have remained influential for both military and literary figures, from Napoleon to T.E. Lawrence.

Loren J. Samons II

Texts

The Civil Wars. Trans. A.G. Peskett. Cambridge, MA: Loeb, 1914.
The Gallic War. Trans. H.J. Edwards. Cambridge, MA: Loeb, 1917.

References

Adcock, F.E. *Caesar As Man of Letters.* Cambridge, Eng.: Cambridge University Press, 1956.

Dorey, T.A. *The Latin Historians.* New York: Basic Books, 1966, 65–84.

Gelzer, M. *Caesar, Politician and Statesman.* Trans. P. Needham. Cambridge, MA: Harvard University Press, 1968.

Caetani, Leone (1869–1935)

Italian Orientalist and politician. Born in Rome to one of the oldest and most prominent noble families in Italy, Caetani began to learn Arabic, Hebrew, Persian, and other eastern languages at an early age. He earned his doctorate from the University of Rome in 1891, then traveled extensively throughout the Middle East and southeast Asia, collecting hundreds of manuscripts about Islamic history. A socialist, he served in the Italian Parliament from 1909 to 1913. In 1905, Caetani published the first volume of his masterpiece, *Annali dell'Islam,* a history of Islam intended to serve as a comprehensive guide to Islamic source material from the time of the prophet Muḥammad (d. 632) to 1517. At the time of his death, Caetani, in collaboration with other European orientalists, had completed ten volumes of the *Annali* covering the history of early Islam to 661. This ground-breaking work included translations of numerous Arabic chronicles and an analysis of their diverse perspectives on pivotal events, as well as Caetani's own ideas about the rise of Islam.

Corinne Blake

Texts

Annali dell'Islam. Milan: University Hoepli, 1905–1926.

"The Development of Mohammad's Personality." *Muslim World* 4 (1914): 353–364.

References

Hasan, Reyazul. "Prince Leone Caetani—a Great Italian Orientalist (1869–1935)." *Hamdard Islamicus* 5 (1982): 45–81.

Caffaro of Genoa (1080/81–1166)

Genoese statesman and chronicler (name also spelled Cafaro, Caffarus, or Caschifelone). Caffaro's family served in the court of the archbishop of Genoa, and Caffaro held numerous public offices in that city, including those of admiral, magistrate, ambassador, and state consul. In 1099 he joined the Genoese fleet on crusade to the Holy Land. He participated in the capture of Caesarea, recorded in his *De liberatione civitatum Orientis* [On the Liberation of the Cities of the East]. In part an eyewitness account, this work provides many details,

not known from other sources, about the Genoese role in the First Crusade. In 1146–1148 he took part in the campaign to liberate Spain from the Muslims, which is recorded in his *Ystoria captionis Almarie et Turtuose* [History of the Capture of Almaria and Tortosa]. In retirement from 1152, Caffaro completed the crusade chronicles and the annals of Genoa he had been writing throughout his life. The *Annales Ianuae* [Annals of Genoa] cover the history of the city from 1099 to 1163, and toward the end of his life, the Genoese consuls gave them official recognition. Though his memory was at times unreliable, and his early narratives highly succinct, the work is a valuable source on a long and crucial period in the development of the commune. The later portions, written when he was a well-regarded statesman, are peppered with his moral, religious, and political beliefs.

Monica Sandor

Texts

Annales Ianuae and *De liberatione civitatum Orientis liber.* Ed. G.H. Pertz. *Monumenta Germaniae Historica. Scriptorum,* 18. Hanover and Leipzig, Ger.: Hahnsche Buchhandlung, 1863, 11–48.

De liberatione civitatum Orientis and *Ystoria captionis Almarie et Turtuose.* Ed. P. Riant. In *Recueil des Historiens des Croisades. Occidentaux,* V. Paris: Académie des Inscriptions et Belles Lettres, 1895, 47–73.

Annali genovesi di Caffaro e de' suoi continuatori dal MXCCIX al MCCXCIII. Ed. L.T. Belgrano and C. Imperiale de Sant'Angelo. In *Fonti Per la Storia d'Italia,* 11. Rome: Istituto Storico Italiano, 1890, 3–124.

References

Face, Richard D. "Secular History in Twelfth-Century Italy: Caffaro of Genoa." *Journal of Medieval History* 6 (1980): 169–184.

Imperiale di Sant'Angelo, C. *Caffaro e i suoi tempi* [Caffaro and His Times]. Turin, Italy: Roux, 1894.

Petti Balbi, Giovanna. *Caffaro e la cronachistica genovese* [Caffaro and Genoese Chronicle-Writing]. Genoa, Italy: Tilgher, 1982.

Vaughan, Richard. "The Past in the Middle Ages." *Journal of Medieval History* 12 (1986): 1–14.

Vitale, V. "Le fonti della storia medievale genovese [The Sources of Medieval Genoese History]." In *Storia di Genova,* ed. M.M. Martini. Milan, Italy: A. Garzanti, 1941, vol. II, pp. 314–334.

Cahen, Claude (1909–1991)

French historian, specializing in medieval Islam (in Arab countries, Turkey, and Persia) and the Crusades. Cahen was born in Paris and entered the École Normale Supérieure in 1928. In 1931 he graduated from the École Nationale des Langues Orientales, with studies in Turkish and Arabic languages, and the following year passed the Agrégation d'Histoire. During the ensuing years he was a teacher in Amiens, Rouen, then Paris, and traveled widely to do his research. In 1940 he wrote a very important doctoral thesis titled: *La Syrie du Nord à l'époque des Croisades* [Northern Syria in the Age of the Crusades]. During World War II, he was a prisoner for five years. After the war, he started teaching again at Strasbourg University, where he remained until 1959, and then at the Sorbonne, in the departments of history and Arabic, where he finished his career. As well as being a member of the Académie des Inscriptions et Belles-Lettres from 1973, he was chairman of the Société Asiatique and was made Chevalier de la Légion d'Honneur. He died at Savigny-sur-Orge. Cahen was able to pursue a very wide range of interests in the history of the medieval Middle East owing to his knowledge of the primary languages of the area. One may distinguish several main directions in his research. He systematically used sources very little exploited but very useful for the study of history in the medieval Muslim world (for example, treaties on taxes, laws, or mathematics). This allowed him to make a highly precise analysis of the economic life, social structures, and institutions in Anatolia, Syria, and Egypt. At the same time, Cahen also produced original scholarship on the history of the Rûm Seldjuks and the different Turkish Beyliks in Asia Minor. He eventually completely revised the historical interpretation of the Crusades by the means of a close comparison of European, Byzantine, and Arabic. Thanks to his wide purview, Cahen not only opened fields of research that had been studied only little or at least very schismatically before him, but also developed innovative approaches to comparative studies in Islamology, Turkology, and Byzantinology, and to the history of relations between the different peoples of the Mediterranean and Middle East during the Middle Ages.

M. Balivet

Texts

Introduction à l'histoire de l'orient musulman médiéval (VIIᵉ–XVᵉ siècle): Méthodologie et éléments de bibliographie [Introduction to the History of the Medieval Muslim Orient from the Seventh to the Fifteenth Century]. Paris: Librairie d'Amérique et d'Orient 1982.

L'Islam. Paris: Bordas, 1970–.

Orient et Occident au temps des Croisades [East and West at the Time of the Crusades]. Paris: Aubier, 1983.

Pre-Ottoman Turkey: A General Survey of the Material and Spiritual Culture and History Circa 1071–1330. Trans. J. Jones-Williams (from the French manuscript). London, Sidgwick & Jackson, 1968. (New French edition: *La Turquie pré-ottomane.* Istanbul: L'Institut francais d'études anatoliennes d'Istanbul, 1988).

La Syrie du nord à l'époque des croisades et la principauté franque d'Antioche [Northern Syria in the Age of the Crusades and the French Kingdom of Antioch]. Paris: P. Geuthner, 1940.

"Turkish Invasion: The Selchukids." In *A History of the Crusades,* vol. I, ed. K.M. Setton. Philadelphia: University of Pennsylvania Press, 1958.

"The Turks in Iran and Anatolia before the Mongol Invasions." In *A History of the Crusades,* vol. II, ed. K.M. Setton. Philadelphia: University of Pennsylvania Press, 1962.

Cai Meibiao [Ts'ai Mei-piao] (b. 1928)

Chinese historian. Born in Tianjin, Cai Meibiao completed his undergraduate courses at Nankai University in 1949 and a graduate program at Beijing University in 1952. Since 1953 he has been a research fellow at the Institute of Modern History at the Chinese Academy of Sciences. Cai has made important scholarly contributions in three areas. The first of these is his compilation of a general history of China: the highly regarded ten-volume *Zhongguo tongshi* [A General History of China] (1994), coauthored with Fan Wenlan and others, used Marxist class structures to introduce thousands of Chinese students to the breadth of Chinese history. Cai's second major contribution has been in the area of research in Mongolian language and Yuan dynasty history—his outstanding studies of such topics as the status of the Yuan dynasty in Chinese history have made an indelible impression on the thinking and writing of many leading scholars in these fields. Finally, Cai has investigated the history of earthquakes in China and was the editor in chief of *Zhongguo dizhen lishi ziliao huibian* [Sources of Earthquakes in Chinese

History] (1983–1987), which received high critical praise and remains the only significant modern study of earthquakes in Chinese history.

Shao Dongfang

Texts

Basibazi yu Yuandai hanyu [Pagspa Characters' Relation with Chinese Language in the Yuan Dynasty]. Beijing: Kexue chubanshe, 1960.
Yuandai baihuabei jilu [Yuan Epitaphs in Vernacular Language]. Beijing: Kexue chubanshe, 1955.
Ed. *Zhongguo dizhen lishi ziliao huibian*. Beijing: Kexue chubanshe, 1983–1987.
Et al. *Zhongguo tongshi*. 10 vols. Beijing: Renmin chubanshe, 1994.

References

Feuerwerker, Albert, ed. *History in Communist China*. Cambridge, MA: M.I.T. Press, 1968.

Cam, Helen Maud (1885–1968)

English historian of the Middle Ages. Born in Abingdon, Cam received a first-class B.A. from the University of London. She subsequently became a fellow of Girton College, Cambridge, and Radcliffe professor of history at Harvard. She was the first woman to deliver the Raleigh Lecture before the British Academy and was also the first female member of the Selden Society, but her name will always be associated with a knowledge of local records, particularly the hundred rolls. Of her collected studies, *Liberties and Communities in Medieval England* (1944) emphasizes the relevance of administrative practice and topography, while *Law Finders and Law Makers in Medieval England* (1962) analyzes the legal culture of medieval communities and pays tribute to Cam's predecessors. Though Cam admired the work of William Stubbs, F.W. Maitland, and Paul Vinogradoff, she countered their emphasis upon central encroachments in the localities with a recognition of the resiliency of customary institutions.

Myron C. Noonkester

Texts

England before Elizabeth. New York: Harper, 1960.
The Hundred and the Hundred Rolls. London: Methuen, 1930.
Law Finders and Law Makers in Medieval England. Fairfield, NJ: A.M. Kelley, 1979.
Liberties and Communities in Medieval England: Collected Studies in Local Administration and Topography. Cambridge, Eng.: Cambridge University Press, 1944.

References

Album Helen Maud Cam. Louvain, Belgium: Publications Universitaires de Louvain, 1960.

Cambodian Historiography

Historical writing by and principally about the Cambodian nation. Although Cambodia has a long and complex history, and Cambodians have been literate in their own language for over fifteen hundred years, the art of historiography developed fairly late under colonial influence and in response to ideas imported from the West. Despite its lengthy literate tradition, printing reached Cambodia under the French Protectorate (1863–1954), along with secular, subject-oriented education. History was a far less prestigious subject in Cambodia than it was in neighboring Vietnam. Historical texts, of which few had survived the turmoil of the eighteenth and nineteenth centuries, did not form part of the Buddhist-oriented monastic educational system, where texts on other subjects were generated, studied, and preserved.

National history in Cambodia was always conceived in royal terms, while the histories of foreign countries have attracted little attention. Historians worked for the court and wrote about the king's activities. Historical texts were items of regalia rather than documents to be perused outside the palace. There is some evidence that chronicle texts (Cambodian *pangsavatar*) were compiled and stored in medieval Cambodia, in the Ankorean period (ca. 800–ca. 1420), but these texts, inscribed on perishable materials, have not survived. Indeed, no extant historical texts can be dated earlier than the late eighteenth century, and nearly all of these date from the colonial era. To be sure, texts were copied from earlier ones and contain data about earlier periods; but contemporary chronicles, and other documents relating to earlier periods, are not available for study. Cambodia's *histoire événementielle,* or a detailed social history, cannot therefore be written. Moreover, documents of the sort so often found in China or medieval Europe (for instance court and tax records, wills, personal memoirs, popular literature, and so on) are also very scantily represented in the body of historical documents that has come down to us.

French scholars in the colonial era, confronting this terra incognita and the monumental evidence of earlier Cambodian greatness, worked hard to decipher pre-Angkorean and Angkorean stone inscriptions. They also drew on traveler's tales, foreign chronicles, and any documents they could find to reconstruct the chronology of the Angkorean era. European scholars, led by George Coedès made a gift to the Cambodian people of their forgotten history, but Cambodians failed to share their excitement or their labor. Cambodian history was taught only cursorily in Cambodian schools. There was no university in Cambodia until the 1950s. Because history was thought to be a royal monopoly, no indigenous scholars were attracted toward the discipline before Cambodia's independence.

Cambodian disinterest in "accurate" history, as conceived and presented by Western scholars predated the colonial era, when *pangasvatar* did not circulate widely, although the deeds of kings and princes, usually mythological or from other countries, entered Cambodian folklore. A study of the chronicles themselves reveals that historical accuracy was less important to those who compiled them than presenting a text that could be considered as an item of regalia, which contained pleasing and heroic stories about "the past." Indeed, Michael Vickery has argued persuasively that Cambodian chronicles dealing with events earlier than the mid-sixteenth century tend to be factually unreliable, and in some cases "Cambodian" chronicles have been copied verbatim, with a few names changed, from Thai-language chronicles of Thai history.

Vickery's findings point to a serious gap in Cambodian historiography, only partially filled by French scholarship. If chronicle texts are not valuable sources for events prior to 1500, it seems unlikely that our knowledge of Angkorean political history, or of its mysterious fifteenth-century collapse, can be expanded beyond what we learn from stone inscriptions. There is much to be done, using Khmer-language inscriptions, to uncover Angkorean social structure and the evolution of bureaucratic titles. But the gaps in political history persist.

A more verifiable tradition of historiography within the *pangasvatar* tradition appears to have caught hold in Cambodia between the late sixteenth century and 1700. The chronicle for this period is rich in detail, much of which can be verified from Thai and European accounts. This portion of the definitive 1934 chronicle text (the *Tiounn Chronicle*) has been translated into French by Mak Phoeun. Chronicles dealing with the eighteenth century have yet to be studied in detail, while those of the half century preceding the French Protectorate are fragmented but verifiable from other sources.

Cambodian chronicles concentrate on a given king's activities, laid end to end in chronological form, without explanation, analysis, or documentation. Occasional stretches of dialogue may well be imaginary, and seem to respond to wishful thinking. Similarly, some descriptions of military engagements seem to have been written primarily to entertain. The texts differ sharply from their counterparts in Vietnam, where a long and vigorous historiographical tradition, backed up by an archival tradition, was in effect.

The French introduced to Cambodia the European academic disciplines and procedures, such as mapping, but the teaching of Cambodian history was not given high priority in colonial schools, aside from passing references to the Angkor as reconstituted by French savants. Postcolonial historiography was also moribund and an edition of the *Tiounn Chronicle,* prepared in the palace in 1928–1934, was not published until 1969.

Cambodians studying abroad after World War II, on the other hand, were occasionally drawn toward Marxism-Leninism and adopted Marxian schemata of Cambodian history, progressing from primitive communism through feudalism to capitalism—categories that failed to fit what was known about the trajectory of Cambodian history.

When the Cambodian Communists came to power in 1975, publishing and education stopped, and a spokesman proclaimed that "2000 years of history" had ended. In fact, the Cambodian Communists, or Khmer Rouge, proposed a new reading of Cambodian history, whereby it was seen as a long struggle of the poor against injustice and foreigners, culminating in the Khmer Rouge seizure of power. These views of history played down the royal dimension. They remained in place under the Vietnamese Protectorate that followed (1979–1989), when texts emphasized Cambodia's abiding friendship with Vietnam, something not perceptible to earlier or subsequent scholars.

In the 1990s, Cambodian history is ripe for reassessment, but the task of integrating Angkorean grandeur, as communicated by the French, and the chaotic squalor of the Khmer Rouge era, as experienced by everyone over 30, presents daunting obstacles to coherence.

David Chandler

See also THAI HISTORIOGRAPHY—CHRONICLES; THAI HISTORIOGRAPHY—MODERN; *TIOUNN CHRONICLE;* VIETNAMESE HISTORIOGRAPHY.

Texts

Chroniques royales du Cambodge (de 1417 à 1595). Trans. Khin Sok. Paris: EFEO, 1988.

Chroniques royales du Cambodge (de 1594 à 1677). Trans. Mak Phoeun. Paris: EFEO, 1981.

Sut, Eng. *Akkasar mahaboros khmer* [Documents about Cambodian Heroes]. Phnom Penh, Cambodia: Ly Sa, 1969.

References

Chandler, David P. *A History of Cambodia*. Third ed. Boulder, CO: Westview Press, 1996.

———. "Seeing Red: Khmer Rouge Perceptions of Cambodian History." In *Revolution and Its Aftermath in Kampuchea: Eight Essays,* ed. David Chandler and Ben Kiernan. Southeast Asian Studies Monograph Series. New Haven, CT: Yale University, 1983.

Jacques, Claude. "Nouvelles directions pour l'étude de l'histoire du pays Khmer [New Directions for the Study of Cambodia]." *Asie du Sud-est et monde insulindien* 13 (1982): 39–57.

Vickery, Michael. *Cambodia after Angkor: Chronicular Evidence from the Fifteenth and Sixteenth Centuries*. Ann Arbor, MI: University Microfilms, 1979.

———. "The Composition and Transmission of the Ayudhya and Cambodian Chronicles." In *Perceptions of the Past in Southeast Asia,* ed. David Marr and Anthony Reid. Singapore: Heinemann Educational Books, 1979, 130–154.

Camden, William (1551–1623)

Historian and antiquarian. William Camden was born in London, the son of the painter Samson and his wife Elizabeth. After attending Oxford University, he taught at Westminster School from 1575 to 1597, when he became Clarenceux King-at-Arms (a heraldic appointment) through the patronage of the courtier Sir Fulke Greville. From that position Camden continued his historical and antiquarian studies and his courtly connections, including his friendship with Sir Robert Cotton, a major collector of manuscripts, a relationship that continued until Camden's death. Camden published three major works during his lifetime. *Britannia* (1586), his best-known book, heavily utilized the researches of John Leland. Written in Latin, it was aimed at a scholarly Continental audience and was basically an antiquarian topography of Roman Britain based on the *Antonine Itinerary*. Five more expanded editions appeared by 1607 and an English translation in 1610, with major reedited versions appearing in 1695 and 1789. It was to prove the single most important influence on public interest in antiquarian remains. A shorter book, the *Remains of a Greater Worke, Concerning Britaine* (1605) was a philological study of the English language and place-names. Camden's last great work was a narrative history, the *Annales rerum Anglicarum et Hibernicarum regnante Elizabetha* [Annals of England and Ireland in the Reign of Elizabeth] (1615–1627). It was based on primary sources provided to Camden by Cotton and by the crown and used Polybius and Tacitus as models. Camden's writings helped to promote the growth of scholarly antiquarianism and objective history while implicitly undermining popular belief in the legendary British past of Brutus and King Arthur.

Ronald H. Fritze

Texts

Camden's Britannia. Ed. Edmund Gibson. London: A. Swalle and A. and J. Churchil, 1695.

The History of . . . Princess Elizabeth. Ed. Wallace T. McCaffrey. Chicago: University of Chicago Press, 1970.

Remains Concerning Britain. Ed. R.D. Dunn. Toronto: University of Toronto Press, 1984.

References

Levy, F.J. *Tudor Historical Thought*. San Marino, CA: Huntington Library, 1967.

Woolf, D.R. *The Idea of History in Early Stuart England*. Toronto: University of Toronto Press, 1990.

Canadian Historiography

Historical writing in the English language relating to Canada, from the colonial period to the present. Prior to Canada's confederation in 1867, life was lived on two scales, the local and the imperial: the former a consequence of geographic diversity and distance, the latter of common empire. The tension between the two scales drove public affairs, and men of public affairs turned to the past in search of lessons with which to influence the present and shape the future. The best of these works, for example John Stewart's *An Account of Prince Edward Island* (1806) and Thomas Chandler Haliburton's *An Historical and Statistical Account of Nova-Scotia* (1829), reconciled distinctive colonial identities with continuing imperial loyalty. This was not always easy, particularly for the English-language historians of the predominantly

French-speaking colony of Lower Canada (Quebec), such as Robert Christie, and for historians in the American-influenced inland colony of Upper Canada (Ontario), such as Robert Gourlay.

Britain's adoption of a free-trade policy and the granting of responsible government to the self-governing colonies of British North America in the 1840s loosened the ties of the empire. The expansionist energies of the two Canadian colonies filled the vacuum and began the process of fashioning a new intermediate, national scale of experience. Again historical precedents were harnessed in part as justification, and such works as John McMullen's *The History of Canada* (1855) legitimized confederation even before the event. Initially, central Canadian historians ran up against conceits as strong as their own in the other colonies, especially in Nova Scotia, where the archivist Thomas Beamish Akins and historian Beamish Murdoch defended a distinctive identity. The achievement of confederation in 1867, however, rendered such alternatives parochial at best, divisive at worst. The fact that Canada's first generation of national historians, such as William Kingsford, were intolerant of competing loyalties should not disguise the extent to which they were themselves little more than central Canadians in masquerade.

When history emerged as a discipline in central Canada's English-language universities in the 1890s, the first professionals, like their amateur predecessors, had the future of the new nation in mind. As Canada progressed toward greater levels of political freedom within the empire, historians fashioned a liberal line of descent and proffered it to the world as an example of national accommodation, most notably in two multiauthored series, *The Makers of Canada* (20 vols.; Toronto, 1903–1908) and *Canada and Its Provinces* (23 vols.; Toronto, 1913–1917). This process of constitutional evolution was, however, open-ended and ambiguous. To Britannic idealists such as George MacKinnon Wrong, it showed the way toward an empire based on equal partnership and cooperation. To others, such as Oscar Douglas Skelton, it was a path toward independence. In this, historians reflected contemporary disagreement over the future alignment of the country.

The sombre Canadian experience of World War I ultimately proved fatal to the cause of a strong imperial connection. As the nation moved toward the effective independence granted by the Statute of Westminster in 1931, historians shifted their attention from the ties of the empire to those of its continent. British precedents were replaced by American examples and the tracing of fine points of constitutional law, by an examination of underlying social, economic, and geographic structures. The American Progressive historians, such as Charles Beard and Frederick Jackson Turner, were particularly influential: Frank Underhill, for example, combined the class analysis of Beard with the wit of muckraking journalists to debunk the idealism of earlier constitutional historians; and Arthur R.M. Lower exploited Turner's frontier thesis in an effort to find a national soul in the northern forests. More significant for the long term were the decisions of Canadian students to turn to American rather than British universities for graduate degrees in history.

As influential as American sources were, the most important work of the interwar period, indeed of any period in English-Canadian historiography, was not derivative. In 1930 the political economist Harold Adams Innis published *The Fur Trade in Canada*. The underlying assumption of the study was that colonial economies are distinctive and require their own theory of development. It was Innis's thesis that patterns of colonial economic, institutional, and cultural growth were intimately related to the exploitation of staple commodities. When Innis applied the staples thesis to the Canadian fur trade, his startling conclusion was that the natural lines of development ran east–west rather than north–south, that the nation "emerged not in spite of geography but because of it."

Innis's findings became more important as Canadians began to suspect that American domination was a greater threat to national development than British imperialism had ever been. Donald Grant Creighton exploited Innis's insights to construct his own Laurentian thesis in *The Commercial Empire of the St. Lawrence, 1760–1850* (1937), which focused on the St. Lawrence River system as the unifying backbone of the nation. This vision was brought to life with unrivaled artistry in his two-volume biography of Canada's first prime minister, *John A. Macdonald* (1952–1955). This work was complemented by J.M.S. Careless's biography, also in two volumes, of Macdonald's arch rival, *George Brown of "The Globe"* (1959–1963), which once again emphasized the British roots of Canadian politics, metropolitanism over frontierism. The publication of these works also heralded a return by historians to more traditional political narratives and biographies.

Inevitably there was a reaction to the centralizing nationalism of Canadian historiography and its preoccupation with politics. The social and political ferment of the 1960s, especially the growth of the new nationalism among French Canadians in Quebec, coupled with the proliferation of graduate schools outside central Canada drew attention to the "limited identities" of region, class, gender, ethnicity, and the like. New methodologies, often drawn from the social sciences, were employed to fashion a much more complex and detailed picture of the Canadian past. The results defy neat categories, synthesis, or even harmony. Regionally, the history of the Canadian west and north has been well served by W.L. Morton, Morris Zaslow, and, more recently, Gerald Friesen, while the history of the Atlantic region dates its revival to the founding, in 1971, of the journal *Acadiensis* in Fredericton, New Brunswick, the work of E.R. Forbes being particularly important. As for Quebec, historians such as Ramsay Cook, Michael Behiels, and Allan Greer have pressed beyond the old stereotypes and drawn French Canada into the mainstream of English-Canadian historiography. Ontario, too, now is studied as a region rather than the nation writ large, a transition highlighted in the monographs of the Ontario Historical Studies Series (1971–). Leaders in Canadian working-class history are Greg Kealey and Bryan D. Palmer; in the history of gender, Sylvia Van Kirk and Joy Parr; in the history of Native peoples, Bruce G. Trigger and Olive P. Dickason; and in ethnic studies, James W. St. G. Walker—although such categories do not do justice to the richness of their work.

The failure of the new history to produce an acceptable synthesis and its increasing abstraction from the general reading public has itself inspired a reaction. This reaction is also in part a consequence of Canada's constitutional debates of the 1980s, centered on the threat of Quebec separatism, provincial fragmentation, and the politics of group rights. Jack Granatstein, Michael Bliss, and David Bercuson, in particular have reasserted the preeminence of national politics and the viability of Canadian liberalism. They have also demonstrated a striking ability to write on serious topics in a publicly accessible way. In this they meet the challenge of a new breed of nonacademic popular historians in Canada—such as Pierre Berton, Peter C. Newman, and Sandra Gwyn—whose works sell remarkably well. The present result is a vibrant historiography, if also one difficult to comprehend.

M. Brook Taylor

See also QUÉBÉCOIS HISTORIOGRAPHY.

References

Berger, Carl. *The Writing of Canadian History: Aspects of English-Canadian Historical Writing since 1900.* Second ed. Toronto: University of Toronto Press, 1986.

Owram, Doug, ed. *Canadian History: A Reader's Guide,* vol. 2: *Confederation to the Present.* Toronto: University of Toronto Press, 1994.

Taylor, M. Brook. *Promoters, Patriots, and Partisans: Historiography in Nineteenth-Century English Canada.* Toronto: University of Toronto Press, 1989.

——, ed. *Canadian History: A Reader's Guide,* vol. 1: *Beginnings to Confederation.* Toronto: University of Toronto Press, 1994.

Cantacuzenos, John VI (1295–1383)

Byzantine emperor and historian. After serving under Andronicus II and Andronicus III, Cantacuzenos became regent for John V in 1341. Conflict with John's mother, Anne of Savoy, the patriarch John Kalekas, and Alexios Apokaukos provoked John's usurpation of the imperial title at Didymochtheion. A six-year civil war was ended with Cantacuzenos's entry into Constantinople and assumption of joint rule with John V in 1347. Following crises on both domestic and foreign fronts, Cantacuzenos abdicated in 1354 and spent his remaining years as the monk Joasaph in Constantinople, a respected and influential figure, occasionally involved in political life, though generally absorbed in writing activity. While Cantacuzenos wrote polemics against Jews, Moslems, and anti-Hesychasts, his most significant work was his *History* in four books, concentrating upon the period 1320 to 1356. Written in a direct, classicizing style, Cantacuzenos's work is fundamentally apologetic in thrust, seeking to exonerate Cantacuzenos himself of usurpation and to excuse his disastrous alliance with the Ottomans, which in effect initiated Turkish infiltration into Europe.

Lionel J. Sanders

Texts

Historiarum libri IV [Four Books of History]. Ed. Ludwig Schopen. 3 vols. Bonn: Corpus Scriptorum Historiae Byzantinae, 1828–1832, vols. 4–6.

The History of John Kantakouzenos (Book I). Ed. and trans. R.H. Trone. Ph.D. thesis, Catholic University of America, 1979.

Ioannes Kantacuzenos. Ed. A. Cerile. *Corpus Fontium Historiae Byzantinae* (forthcoming).

References

Nicol, D.M. *The Byzantine Family of Kantakouzenos (Cantacouzenos) ca. 1100–1460*. Washington, DC: Dumbarton Oaks, 1968, 35–103.

Cantemir, Dimitrie (1673–1723)

Romanian historian, scientist, and Prince of Moldavia. Cantemir was born in Silişteni in Moldavia. He was educated in Iaşi and completed his studies in Constantinople, where he would live for twenty-two years. Like his father, he was a prince of Moldavia for a short time (November 1710–July 1711) under Ottoman suzerainty. He allied himself with Peter the Great in a war against the Ottoman empire and was defeated at the battle of Stănileşti on the Pruth, whereupon he fled to Russia to spend the rest of his days. Cantemir had an encyclopedic mind, was fluent in several languages, and wrote on a wide range of fields including history, philosophy, religion, and musicology. His most important literary work was *Istoria ieroglifică* [Hieroglyphical History], a hermetic writing composed in a baroque style, which presents the struggle for power between warring aristocratic parties. His preeminent calling, however, was history. His first venture in this discipline was the *Descriptio Moldaviae*, a description of Moldavia written for the Berlin Academy, of which he became a member in 1714. His international reputation, however, rests largely on his *History of the Growth and Decay of the Ottoman Empire,* written in Latin and translated into English, French, and German after his death. The originality of this book lies in its author's profound knowledge of Ottoman life and culture, uniquely insightful owing to his own experience of having lived in Constantinople. The work reflects Cantemir's adherence to a cyclical view of history, arguing that the Ottoman empire's period of expansion would inevitably be followed by a decline. Cantemir also wrote *Hronicul vechimei a romano-moldo-vlahilor* [Chronicle of Moldavians, Romanians, and Wallachians], the first critical history of the Romanian people and a work that upheld the unity and Roman origins of the Romanian people. Initially circulated only in manuscript (in which form the historian Petru Maior would use it a century later), it was first published in the nineteenth century.

S. Lemny

Texts

Beschreibung der Moldau [A Description of Moldavia]. Bucharest: Kriterion, 1973.

Dimitrie Cantemir, Historian of South East Europe and Oriental Civilisations. In *Extracts from the History of the Ottoman Empire,* ed. Alexandru Duţu and Paul Cernovodeanu. Bucharest: Association internationale d'études du sud-est européen, 1973.

The History of the Growth and Decay of the Othman Empire. Trans. N. Tindal. 2 vols. London: J.J. and P. Knapton, 1734–1735.

Hronicul vechimei a romano-moldo-vlahilor. Ed. Stela Toma. Bucharest: Editura Albatros, 1981.

Opere complete [Complete Works]. Ed. Virgil Cândea. 9 vols. published to date. Bucharest: Editura Academiei Republicii Socialiste Romania, 1974–.

References

Cândea, Virgil. *Dimitrie Cantemir, 1673–1723.* Bucharest: Editura Enciclopedică Română, 1973.

Gheorghiu, Mihnea. "Demeter Cantemir's Cultural and Political Horizons." *Dacoromania* 2 (1974): 5–11.

Iliescu, Victor. "Demeter Cantemir As a Problem of the Romanian Spirituality." *Dacoromania* 2 (1974): 43–56.

Panaitescu, P.P. *Dimitrie Cantemir: Viaţă şi opera* [Dimitrie Cantemir: His Life and Work]. Bucharest: Editura Academiei Republicii Populare Romîne, 1958.

Zub, Al. "Early-Enlightenment and Causality in Dimitrie Cantemir." In *Enlightenment and Romanian Society,* ed. Pompiliu Teodor. Cluj-Napoca: Dacia, 1980, 168–180.

Cantimori, Delio (1904–1966)

Italian historian. His most famous book, *Eretici italiani del Cinquecento: Ricerche storiche* [Italian Heretics of the Sixteenth Century: Historical Investigations] (1939; new edition 1992) remains a standard work. Heretics in his specific sense were figures rooted in Italian humanism who became champions of toleration, religious freedom, the dignity of the individual as thinker—in short, precursors of modern liberal thought. Although Cantimori subsequently wrote about democratic and utopian Enlightenment thinkers and his university courses testify to a broad interest in the history of ideas, his main fields of inquiry remained the sixteenth century and historical methodology. He mistrusted general principles as points of departure for historical work and was committed to structuring arguments on the basis of meticulously examined texts. His most important works include essays published posthumously as *Storici e storia: Metodo, caratteristiche e significato del lavoro storico* [Historians and History: Methods, Character and Significance of Historiographical Work] (1971), and *Umanesimo e religione nel Rinascimento* [Humanism and Religion during the Renaissance] (1975). His last book, *Prospettive di storia ereticale italiana del Cinquecento* [Perspectives on the History of Sixteenth-Century Italian Heresy] (1960), in addition to establishing a chronology of Italian nonconformist thought, shows that he planned a grand synthesis of Italian religious and political history of the early modern period.

Elisabeth G. Gleason

Texts
Eretici italiani del Cinquecento e altri scritti. Ricerche storiche. Florence: Sansoni, 1939. New edition, ed. Adriano Prosperi. Turin: Einaudi, 1992.
Prospettive di storia ereticale italiana del Cinquecento. Bari, Italy: Laterza, 1960.
Storici e storia: Metodo, caratteristiche e significato del lavoro storico. Second ed. Turin: Einaudi, 1971.
Umanesimo e religione nel Rinascimento. Turin: Einaudi, 1975.

References
Cochrane, Eric, and John Tedeschi. "Delio Cantimori: Historian (1904–1966)." *Journal of Modern History* 39 (1967): 438–445.
Miccoli, Giovanni. *Delio Cantimori.* Turin: Einaudi, 1970.

Capgrave, John (1393–1464)
English theologian, historian, and Augustinian friar. Ordained in 1417 or 1418 and educated at Cambridge, Capgrave served as provost of his order in England and later as prior of the Lynn monastery. He authored *Lives* for Saints Norbert (1440), Katherine (1445), Augustine (ca. 1451), and Gilbert (1451), as well as numerous biblical commentaries. Capgrave's most historical works were his *De illustribus Henricis* [The Illustrious Henries] (ca. 1447) and his *Chronicle of England to A.D. 1417* (ca. 1462). His writings became known chiefly through the works of John Leland (*Commentarii de scriptoribus Britanniae* [Commentaries on British Writers], ca. 1533–1538) and of John Bale (*Illustrium Maioris Britanniae scriptorum* [Illustrious Writers of Great Britain], 1549). Bale particularly approved Capgrave's criticisms of corrupt prelates.

Ruth McClelland-Nugent

Texts
The Life of St. Norbert by John Capgrave, O.E.S.A. (1393–1464). Ed. Cyril Lawrence Smetana, O.S.A. Toronto: Pontifical Institute of Medieval Studies, 1977.
John Capgrave's Abbreuiacion of Cronicles. Ed. Peter J. Lucas. Oxford: Oxford University Press, 1983.
John Capgrave's Lives of St. Augustine and St. Gilbert of Sempringham, and a Sermon. London: Early English Text Society, 1910.

References
Seymour, M.C. "The Manuscripts of John Capgrave's English Works." *Scriptorium* 40 (1986): 248–255.
Winstead, Karen A. "Piety, Politics and Social Commentary in Capgrave's *Life of St. Katherine.*" *Medievalia et humanistica* 17 (1991): 59–80.

Capistrano de Abreu, João (1853–1927)
Brazilian historian. Capistrano studied in Fortaleza and Recife prior to working in journalism and at the Biblioteca Nacional in Rio de Janeiro. In 1883 he attained the chair in Brazilian history at the Colégio de Pedro II. Although influenced by positivism and Darwinism, he nevertheless became a follower of German historicism. Although he never wrote a full-length study, he is best remembered for two innovative essays: *Os Caminhos Antigos e o Povamento do Brasil* [Old Roads and the Populating of Brazil] (1889) and *Capítulos de História Colonial* [Chapters of Colonial History] (1907). Regarded as "the most lucid conscience of Brazilian historiography," Capistrano's contribution was fourfold: he stressed the importance of the *sertão* (backlands) over coastal settlements; he provided the first rational periodization of Brazilian history; he demonstrated the value of social and economic history over political and diplomatic studies; and he listed the problems that future Brazilian historians should investigate. His thesis, maintaining the importance of the frontier in the shaping of national character, predated the American historian Frederick Jackson Turner's famous address by four years and played a role of comparable importance in Brazilian historiography.

George Vásquez

Texts

Os Caminhos Antigos e o Povamento do Brasil. Rio de Janeiro: Edição da Sociedade Capistrano de Abreu, Livraria Briguiet, 1930.

Capítulos de História Colonial, 1500–1800. Sixth edition, ed. José Honorio Rodrigues. Rio de Janeiro: Civilização Brasileira, 1976.

O Descobrimento do Brasil e seu Desenvolvimento no Sécolo XVI [The Discovery of Brazil and Its Development in the Sixteenth Century]. Rio de Janeiro: G. Leuzinger, 1883.

References

Câmara, José Aurelio Saraiva. *Capistrano de Abreu.* Rio de Janeiro: Libraria J. Olympio Editôra, 1969.

Fringer, Katherine. "The Contribution of Capistrano de Abreu to Brazilian Historiography." *Journal of Inter-American Studies* 13 (1971): 258–278.

Rodrigues, José Honório. "Capistrano and Brazilian Historiography." In *Perspectives on Brazilian History,* ed. E. Bradford Burns. New York: Columbia University Press, 1967, 156–180.

Capitalism

Capitalism as an economic and social formation is universally acknowledged as having first developed in Europe. However, there have been heated debates about its historical origins revealing diverse understandings about what it is precisely, and exactly how, when, and where in Europe it actually began. These diverse understandings fall into three groups: a particular "spirit of livelihood"; commerce, or the market economy; and a historically specific mode of production.

Capitalism as a particular "spirit" is most closely associated with the work of German economic historian and sociologist Max Weber, who defined it as "the pursuit of profit, forever renewed profit by means of continuous rational capitalistic enterprise." Weber located the historical origins of modern capitalism in the Protestant Reformation, specifically, in the entrepreneurial activities of English Puritans and European Calvinists who, believing in predestination, devoted themselves to their livelihoods in hopes that their commercial successes might be a sign that they were truly among God's elect.

Capitalism understood as commerce, or the market economy, is found in the *The Wealth of Nations* by the eighteenth-century Scottish political-economist, Adam Smith, especially; but a major historical argument was made by the early-twentieth-century Belgian medievalist Henri Pirenne, who contended that capitalism commenced among a class of "merchant adventurers" in the twelfth century with "long-range trading and the spirit of big business." While Pirenne's historical thesis is not widely accepted, the idea of capitalism as commerce and a market economy is probably the most widely accepted understanding of it in the disciplines of economics and economic history.

Capitalism as a mode of production is derived from the work of Karl Marx who saw history as a process of class struggle determined by historically specific social relations of exploitation and oppression. The three major class-structured modes of production have been ancient slavery (master/slave), medieval feudalism (lord/peasant), and modern capitalism (capitalist/worker); and, whereas capitalism had developed out of feudalism, so, too, socialism (a classless society) would develop out of capitalism. According to Marx, capitalism originated in sixteenth-century England with the primitive accumulation of capital, the enclosure of agricultural lands and the *proletarianization* of the English peasantry, creating a new and even more revolutionary class relationship between a propertied bourgeoisie and propertyless proletarians.

These different understandings of capitalism contributed to important critical debates about the "transition from feudalism to capitalism" first instigated by the work of British Marxist economic historian Maurice Dobb and renewed by the studies of American historian Robert Brenner, American sociologist Immanuel Wallerstein, and British historical sociologist Perry Anderson.

Harvey J. Kaye

See also CLASS; MARXISM; REVOLUTION.

Texts

Anderson, Perry. *Lineages of the Absolutist State.* London: Verso, 1974.

———. *Passages from Antiquity to Feudalism.* London: Verso, 1974.

Aston, T.H., and C.H.E. Philpin, eds. *The Brenner Debate.* Cambridge, Eng.: Cambridge University Press, 1985.

Dobb, Maurice. *Studies in the Development of Capitalism.* London: Routledge, 1947.

Hilton, R.H., et al. *The Transition from Feudalism to Capitalism.* London: Verso, 1976.

Marx, Karl. *Capital: Volume One.* Trans. B. Fowkes. London: New Left Books, 1976.

Marx, Karl, and Friedrich Engels. *The Communist Manifesto.* Ed. F.L. Bender. New York: W.W. Norton, 1988.

Pirenne, Henri. *A History of Europe.* Trans. B. Miall. Garden City, NY: Doubleday, 1958.

Smith, Adam. *The Wealth of Nations.* Ed. A. Skinner. London: Penguin Books, 1970.

Wallerstein, Immanuel. *The Modern World System.* New York: Academic Press, 1974.

Weber, Max. *The Protestant Ethic and the Spirit of Capitalism.* Trans. T. Parsons. London: Unwin, 1930.

References

Holton, R.J. *The Transition from Feudalism to Capitalism.* London: Macmillan, 1985.

Kaye, Harvey J. *The British Marxist Historians.* Cambridge, Eng.: Polity Press, 1984.

Carion [Nägelin], Johann (1499–ca. 1538)

German chronicler. Educated at Tübingen, Carion learned his trade under the mathematician and astronomer Johannes Stoeffler and came into contact with his later collaborator, Philip Melanchthon. In 1522, Carion became court astronomer to Elector Joachim I of Brandenburg. His prediction of a great flood in Berlin in 1524 reflected a contemporary apocalyptic-astronomical panic in Germany. In addition to making astrological calendars or "Practica" (for example, at Nuremberg in 1531) and prognostications, Carion advised the elector and, after 1527, Duke Albrecht of Prussia. In 1535, Carion was awarded a doctorate; he died a year or so later, apparently from the effects of alcohol abuse. As a historian, Carion is known for a short world history or *Chronicon,* originally written in German, a work that owed as much to Melanchthon's subsequent revision and chronological table as to Carion's ability. Melanchthon saw this work through the press at Wittenberg in 1532. The *Chronicon* was a popular favorite that was reprinted many times and translated into numerous languages (for instance, Latin, in 1538).

Andrew Colin Gow

Texts

Chronicon Carionis. Halle, Germany: M. Niemayer, 1898.

The thre [sic] *bokes of cronicles.* Trans. Walter Lynne. London: J. Day, 1550.

References

Furst, Dietmar, and Jürgen Hamel. *Johann Carion (1499–1537).* Berlin, Germany: Archenhold-Sternwarte-Berlin-Treptow, 1988.

Carlyle, Thomas (1795–1881)

Scottish essayist, historian, and prophet. After a strict Calvinist upbringing in Dumfriesshire, Carlyle studied at Edinburgh University. He read deeply in German literature and philosophy and gradually lost the faith of his childhood. He established himself in Scottish literary circles before moving to London in 1834. *The French Revolution: A History* (1837, revised 1857) gained him a reputation as a historian of a prophetic and moral cast. Numerous extended essays on both historical and contemporary themes followed, among them *Chartism* (1839), *On Heroes and Hero-Worship* (1841), and *Past and Present* (1843). Their unflinching exposure of the spiritual bankruptcy of industrial society, the moral failure of the ruling class, and the sufferings of the masses gained him enormous prestige as a cultural commentator and social prophet. Never a democrat, the harsh authoritarianism of his later writings alienated contemporary and future audiences. Carlyle's first and greatest history, *The French Revolution* is more noted for the quality of its vision and style than for its scholarly originality. Carlyle draws upon his Calvinist heritage and presents the French Revolution as a series of horrors visited upon a society that had turned its back on the divine. The work also embodies a distinctively German transcendentalist sense of history as a mysterious process incompletely accessible to the prophetic imagination. It is structured as a series of dark, symbolic pageants, themselves shadows of a deeper reality that the historian struggles to identify and name. Carlyle's vivid and experimental style presents a challenge to the decorum of conventional history and, paradoxically, conveys both the immediacy and the inscrutability of history. Carlyle produced a scholarly and still useful edition of Oliver Cromwell's *Letters and Speeches* in (1845). The primary material is connected by long narrative sections, which largely succeeded in their aim of restoring Cromwell's reputation as a Puritan hero. Carlyle's declining years were occupied by another study of a Protestant leader, the *History of Frederick the Great* (1858–1865). This is a monumental but unbalanced work, with powerful descriptions of battle scenes and long, stale royal genealogies. Frederick makes an awkward and unattractive hero, and Carlyle's praise of Prussian military authoritarianism has found little favor with his readers.

Karen O'Brien

Texts

Letters and Speeches of Oliver Cromwell, with Elucidations by Thomas Carlyle. Ed. S.C. Lomas. 3 vols. London: Methuen, 1904.

The French Revolution: A History. Ed. K.J. Fielding and David Sorensen. Oxford: World's Classics, 1989.

History of Frederick the Great. Ed. and abrid. John Clive. Chicago: Chicago University Press, 1969.

References

Ben-Israel, Hedva. *English Historians on the French Revolution.* Cambridge, Eng.: Cambridge University Press, 1968.

Rosenberg, John D. *Carlyle and the Burden of History.* Oxford: Clarendon Press, 1985.

Carr, Edward Hallett (1892–1982)

British diplomat and historian. Carr was a graduate of Trinity College, Cambridge. During his early adulthood, he worked for the British Foreign Office (1916–1936), holding several positions of responsibility; he received the Order of the Commander of British Empire for his work at the Paris Peace Conference in 1919. Like many intellectuals of his generation, he was a Marxist, and, during his service in Riga, Latvia, he began to study Russian culture and history. The results were the superior biographies of Marx and others, which he published in the 1930s. From 1936 to 1947 he was professor of international relations at the University College of Wales, Aberystwyth. He served as an assistant editor of *The Times* from 1941 to 1945, exercising influence on its editorial policies. He became a senior fellow of Trinity College, Cambridge, in 1955. He wrote about a number of European topics, but in 1944 he began his life's work, *A History of Soviet Russia* (1954–1978), taking thirty-three years to complete it. The volumes deal with the Bolshevik revolution, Lenin, and Stalin's early years. Together, they constitute a classic. At the same time he produced several works on the Comintern: *Twilight of the Comintern* (1982) and the posthumously published *The Comintern and the Spanish Civil War* (1984).

Walter A. Sutton

Texts

The Comintern and the Spanish Civil War. Ed. Tamara Deutscher. London: Macmillan, 1984.

A History of Soviet Russia: Foundations of a Planned Economy. 3 vols. in 5 parts. New York: Macmillan, 1969–1978.

A History of Soviet Russia: Socialism in One Country. 4 vols. New York: Macmillan, 1958–1964.

A History of Soviet Russia: The Bolshevik Revolution. 3 vols. London: Macmillan, 1950–1953.

A History of Soviet Russia: The Interregnum, 1923–24. London: Macmillan, 1954.

The Twenty Years Crisis. Second ed. London: Macmillan, 1981.

Twilight of the Comintern. New York and Basingstoke, Eng.: Macmillan, 1982.

What Is History? Second edition, ed. R.W. Davies. London: Macmillan, 1986.

References

Abramsky, C., with B.J. Williams. *Essays in Honour of E.H. Carr.* Hamden, CT: Archon, 1974.

Davies, R.W. "Edward Hallett Carr, 1892–1982." *Proceedings of the British Academy* 69 (1983): 473–511.

Cartwright, Julia (1851–1924)

English novelist, biographer, and writer on art. Julia Cartwright was born to a landed family in Edgcote, Northamptonshire, and educated at home. While publishing novels anonymously, she also became known as a biographer and writer on the art of the Italian Renaissance. In 1880 Cartwright married a clergyman, Henry Ady; their daughter was the historian Cecelia Ady. Cartwright wrote for a wide public. In works such as her 1895 monograph on Raphael, she reworked commonplace events that made the artist a hero within a vividly characterized historical setting. She also corrected many erroneous traditions through her archival scholarship. Her lives of Isabella and Beatrice d'Este established these figures' importance for Renaissance historiography.

Adele Ernstrom

Texts

Beatrice d'Este, Duchess of Milan. London: J.M. Dent, 1899.

Isabella d'Este, Marchioness of Mantua, 1474–1539: A Study of the Renaissance. Second ed. 2 vols. New York: E.P. Dutton, 1903.

Italian Gardens of the Renaissance and Other Studies. New York: Scribner's, 1914.

The Painters of Florence from the Thirteenth to the Sixteenth Century. New York: E.P. Dutton, 1901.

Raphael in Rome. London: Seeley; New York: Macmillan, 1895.

C

References

Emanuel, Angela. "Introduction." In *A Bright Remembrance: The Diaries of Julia Cartwright 1851–1924,* ed. Angela Emanuel. London: Weidenfeld and Nicolson, 1989.

———. "Julia Cartwright and Bernard Berenson." *Apollo* (October 1984): 273–277.

Cassiodorus [Flavius Maximus Aurelius Cassiodorus Senator] (ca. 487–ca. 580)

Roman official, statesman, and historian. Cassiodorus was born in Bruttium and served as prefect of Italy under Theoderic from 533 to 537. Some time after 550, he founded the monastery of Vivarium in Calabria, where he died ca. 580. In addition to religious work, Cassiodorus wrote a *Historia Tripartita* [Tripartite History], a rearrangement in Latin of three Greek church histories, the *Chronology* of Roman and world history from the Creation to A.D. 519, a collection of his official correspondence, entitled *Variae [Varia],* and a *History of the Goths* which survives only in the abridgment of Jordanes.

Stephen A. Stertz

Texts

Cassiodori Opera [Works]. In *Patrologia Latina,* ed. J.-P. Migne. Vols. 69–70. Paris: J.-P. Migne, 1847.

The Gothic History of Jordanes in English Version, ed. C.C. Mierow. New York: Barnes and Noble, 1960.

The Letters of Cassiodorus. Trans. T. Hodgkin. London: H. Frowde, 1886.

Variae. Ed. T. Mommsen. In *Monumenta Germaniae Historica, Auctores Antiquissimi* [Monumental Works of Germanic History, Most Ancient Authors], vol. 12. Berlin: Weidmann, 1894.

References

Atti della Settimana di studi su Flavio Magno Aurelio Cassiodoro. Ed. S. Leanza. Soveria Mennelli, Italy: Rubbettino, 1986.

O'Donnell, J.J. *Cassiodorus.* Berkeley: University of California Press, 1979.

Castro, Américo (1885–1972)

Brazilian-born Spanish historian. Castro was born in Cantaglo, Brazil, but in 1889 his family returned to Granada, Spain. In 1904, he attended the University of Granada, eventually receiving a degree in arts and letters. In 1910, Castro joined the faculty of the Center for Historical Studies and in the following year received his doctorate from the University of Madrid. From 1915 to 1936, he was a professor at the University of Madrid. The publication of *El pensamiento de Cervantes* [The Ideas of Cervantes] (1925) established him as an expert on Miguel de Cervantes, the author of *Don Quixote,* by placing Cervantes within the European humanistic tradition. In 1936, the Spanish Civil War interrupted Castro's career and drove him into exile in the United States, where he became a faculty member at Princeton University, remaining there until his retirement in 1953; he would return to Madrid in 1969, three years before his death. Castro's move to the United States took his historical interests in a new direction, and in 1948 he published his most celebrated work, *España en su historia: Cristianos, moros y judios* [Spain in Its History: Christians, Muslims, and Jews], a major contribution to modern Spanish historiography that broke with his own former ideas on Spanish civilization. Together with various later books in which he further developed his views on the cultural development of modern Spain, *España en su historia* not only considered the role of the Islamic occupation of the Iberian peninsula in creating Spain's unique historical construction, but also that of the Jews and New Christians. Castro rejected the traditional view that modern Spanish identity was the end result of a Christian mainstream and thereby recast the history of his country to include the contributions, social and cultural, of Jewish and Moorish Spaniards who had been previously marginalized in Spanish historiography, and who had been reintegrated into a new Spanish collectivity in the centuries after the reconquest.

Carlos Pérez

Texts

España en su historia: Cristianos, moros y judios. Second ed. Barcelona: Editorial Critica, 1983.

An Idea of History: Selected Essays of Américo Castro. Ed. and trans. Stephen Gilman and Edmund L. King. Columbus: Ohio State University Press, 1977.

El pensamiento de Cervantes. Second ed. Barcelona: Editorial Critica, 1987.

The Spaniards: An Introduction to Their History. Trans. Willard F. King and Selma Margaretten. Berkeley: University of California Press, 1985.

The Structure of Spanish History. Trans. Edmund L. King. Princeton, NJ: Princeton University Press, 1954.

References

Burcia, José Rubia, and Selma Margaretten, eds. *Américo Castro and the Meaning of Spanish Civilization.* Berkeley: University of California Press, 1976.

Hornik, M.P., ed. *Collected Studies in Honor of Américo Castro's Eightieth Year.* Second ed. Oxford: Lincombe Lodge Research Library, 1975.

Surtz, Ronald E., Jaime Ferran, and Daniel P. Testa, eds. *Américo Castro: The Impact of His Thought: Essays to Mark the Centenary of His Birth.* Madison, WI: Hispanic Seminary of Medieval Studies, 1988.

Catalan Historiography

The historical writing of the principality of Catalonia, which came into being under Charlemagne's "Spanish March," and which is written in the romance language of the area; including the historiography, also written in Catalan, of the kingdoms of Majorca and Valencia. In 1137 the principality was united with the Kingdom of Aragon under the head of the sovereign, but kept its own charters *(fueros);* Majorca and Valencia, which James I conquered from the Moors in 1229 and 1238, respectively, were brought under the Crown of Aragon following the "confederate" model of the Catalan-Aragonese union. Catalonia's *fueros* were lost during the War of Succession (1701–1714), but in the mid-nineteenth century a strong nationalist sentiment arose in Catalonia, which is still evident in Catalan historiography today.

The first important work of Catalan historiography is the chronicle of the counts of Barcelona and kings of Aragon, started in the eleventh century, the definitive version of which, written in Latin and Catalan, dates from the fourteenth century. James I (1213–1276) dictated his memoirs of his reign in another notable chronicle. During the fourteenth century, when the crown of Aragon enjoyed a period of outstanding achievement, three classics of Catalan historiography were published which, with that of James I, are usually called the "Four Great Chronicles": Bernat Desclot's superbly written chronicle narrating the great deeds of Peter III the Great (r. 1276–1285), the conqueror of Sicily; Ramón Muntaner's (1265–1336) masterpiece, a re-creation of "national" history covering the period from 1204 to 1327, as well as a personal account of Catalan-Aragonese victories in the eastern Mediterranean against the Byzantines, the Turks, and the French; and, finally, the denominated chronicle of Peter IV the Ceremonious (1336–1387), in which Bernat Descoll helped the king to describe, in masterly fashion, court intrigues, town life, and popular uprisings.

In the fifteenth century, Alfonso V (1416–1458) established his court at Naples, attracting humanists such as Lorenzo Valla to immortalize the glories of his reign. After the crowns of Aragon and Castile were united in the person of the monarch in 1474, the time-honored Castilian desire for Spanish unity did not prevent Catalonia from preserving its national consciousness and continuing its own historiographical tradition. In the seventeenth century, the Portuguese Francisco Manuel de Melo (1611–1676) published a history of the Catalan revolt against Castile, and Francisco de Moncada (1586–1635) recorded the glories of Catalonia's past in the eastern Mediterranean; but the last historiographical works in Catalan until the nineteenth century were those of Jeroni Pujades (1568–1635). From the seventeenth to the nineteenth century most Catalan historians wrote their works in Spanish. During this period, however, one can discern a sense of Catalonian difference in the *Fénix de Cataluña* (1683), the main work of Narciso Feliu de la Peña; in the historian of the Church Jaime Caresmar (1717–1791); in the historian of the Catalan economy, Antonio de Capmany (1742–1813); and the archivist Próspero de Bofarull y Mascaró (1777–1859).

The suppression of the *fueros* in the War of Succession proved a decisive event in the history of Catalonia. During the eighteenth century, in which the Catholic monarchy reestablished itself, the new situation seemed to be accepted without tensions; but when problems in Spanish unity reemerged, the Catalans also gradually returned to their special national tradition. The cultural *Renaixença* (Renaissance), which was born in the 1830s, and its political counterpart, *catalanisme,* which took shape some fifty years later, gave rise to a historiography, written generally in Catalan and deeply influenced by romanticism. This includes the works of Manuel Milá i Fontanals (1818–1884), Antonio Rubió i Lluch (1856–1937), Josep Puig i Cadafalch (1867–1952), Antoni Rovira i Virgili (1882–1949), and Ferrán Valls i Taberner (1888–1956). In a similar vein is the work of Ferrán Soldevila (1894–1971), but a new stage of Catalan historiography began when, in the first third of the twentieth century, Antonio de la Torre (1878–1966) and Pedro Bosch Gimpera (1891–1974) placed great emphasis on modernizing the historian's work in line with achievements elsewhere in Europe during the previous century.

One of the effects of the Francoist dictatorship of the mid-1930s to mid-1970s within intellectual circles was that historians—those in Spain and those in exile alike—had to face questions that were still closely connected with the romanticism of an earlier era. Among these was the weighing-up of the respective strengths of the centripetal and centrifugal elements in the Iberian peninsula in the course of its history, a question that gave rise to a fierce debate between the Castilian school of Ramon Menéndez Pidal (1869–1968) and Claudio Sánchez Albornoz (1893–1984) and the Catalans Pedro Bosch Gimpera and Jaime Vicens Vives (1910–1960).

From the 1950s onward, Vicens Vives and Pierre Vilar (b. 1906) introduced Annales school and Marxist perspectives to Catalan historiography, which is divided today between historians who believe that it is impossible to write from a position of "national neutrality" and others who consider that dogmatic nationalism is incompatible with rigorous historical scholarship.

Ignacio Olábarri

Texts

Capmany, Antonio de. *Memorias históricas sobre la marina, comercio y artes de la ciudad de Barcelona.* Ed. G. Giralt and C. Batlle. Barcelona: Cámara Oficial de Comercio y Navegación, 1963.

Moncada, Francisco de. *Expedición de los catalanes y aragoneses contra turcos y griegos.* Ed. Samuel Gili y Gaya. Madrid: Espasa-Calpe, 1954.

Les Quatre Grans Cròniques [The Four Great Chronicles]. Ed. M. Coll i Alentorn and F. Soldevila. Barcelona: Ed. Selecta, 1971.

References

Nadal, J. et al. *La historiografia catalana, balanç i perspectives* [Catalan Historiography: Balance and Perspectives]. Girona, Spain: Cercle d'Estudis Històrics, 1990.

Causation

The relationship between two events such that the first brings about the second. Causation is a primitive fundamental notion. It is impossible to define, analyze, or reduce causation to a combination of sufficient and necessary conditions, to governing laws, or anything else, only to classify its kinds. The philosophy of history discusses the meanings, kinds, legitimacy, and justifications of causation in historiography.

Until a generation ago, causation *was* expressed as a subjunctive: *if* the cause did not occur, *then* neither would the effect. "Strict causation" specified all the sufficient and necessary conditions to bring about an event and justified this assignment, although it was recognized that historiographic causation cannot be "strict."

R.G. Collingwood differentiated historiographic *comprehension* from natural science *causation.* According to him, in order to preserve free will, the actions of free, conscious, and rational agents should be explained by reasons and motives that may remain without effect, rather than by sufficient or necessary causes. Michael Oakeshott agreed with Collingwood about the inappropriateness of causation to historiography. There are no scientific causes, "the minimum conditions required to account for any example of an observed result" in historiography because it is impossible in history to isolate one cause from another or cause from effect; instead, historians explain by detailed description.

Still, it was recognized that it is impossible to have historiography without causation, that pure, noncausal language is impossible. Later developments in the philosophy of science have also demonstrated that "strict" causation is rarely practiced in the natural sciences. Michael Scriven has held that there is a continuum between cause and effect, wherein "effect" may be an aspect of the "cause," happening at the same time and physically identical. Similarly, Maurice Mandelbaum showed how cause and effect may be aspects of a single process. The historian is neither willing nor able to suggest sufficient conditions, only necessary contingency. "Cause is one of several alternative factors the presence of one (any one) of which is necessary in order that a set of conditions actually present be sufficient for the effect" (Scriven 1966, p. 249). The historian brings evidence that: the cause was present; that on other occasions it demonstrated clearly its capacity to produce an effect of the sort under study; and that there is no evidence that the cause did not operate, and no alternative causes were present. Historians compile lists of possible causes, using their privileged experience, *verstehen* (sympathetic understanding) of history and human nature, and training. They then eliminate possible alternative causes to the one they favor. Scriven did not explain the nature and reliability of the "privileged knowledge" of historians or how it can be objectively ascertained, nor did he account for different historians compiling different lists according to their different theoretical backgrounds. As C.B. McCullagh pointed out, the list of causes may be incomplete, or there may be unknown factors and "overdetermination" when more than one factor on the list is sufficient to bring the effect under the circumstances.

Mandelbaum holds that different kinds of causation operate in general historiography of social processes and in specific historiographies of fields such as culture or technology. Explaining a process brings to light the particular series of events out of which it is composed or the connections between structures within it. At the background there are "loose generalizations" that perform heuristic functions, suggesting where to find the connections between parts of a whole process. Description and explanation, how and why, tend to coalesce. In special histories, causation consists of contextualization, accounting for changes through outside influences. Some types of historiographic causation may be misleading, for example, the inference of causal connection from qualitative correspondence (similarity).

Historians often distinguish "causes," from "conditions." Philosophers have questioned the criteria for this distinction, since from a neutral point of view there are only conditions. Collingwood, however, showed that in practical science, causes, unlike conditions, can be humanly manipulated. For example, the *cause* of the fire was a lit cigarette, but the presence of oxygen and combustible materials were necessary *conditions.* Causes are relative and anthropomorphist tools to manage the environment. But since the past is over, in history there are no manipulable causes. H.L.A. Hart and A.M. Honoré suggested that causes, unlike conditions, are abnormal or voluntary. Still, exceptions to their rule have been found, and "normality" has proved difficult to define. W.H. Dray suggested instead a subjective criterion of moral responsibility. He analyzed the historiography of the causes of the American Civil War and of World War II and discovered that assignment of causes depended on which side the historian wished to blame for the war.

Gradually, an agreement has emerged that causes are differentiated from conditions according to a *comparison* or *contrast* situation in which events of the same types as the conditions are present, but not "the cause," and an event of the same type as the result to be explained is absent. The added factor in relation to the comparison situation is the cause. For example, why was printing invented in northern Europe rather than in Italy? The *conditions* for the invention of printing may be identical in the comparison situation (Italy) and northern Europe; the *causes* are exclusively northern European. Explanations are relative but

not subjective. McCullagh added contextually dependent stipulation of types of factors sought in a causal explanation, for example motivational, physical, proximate, or remote causes.

Another question that arises is how to weigh the importance of causes. Some philosophers claim it parallels the distinction between causes and conditions. McCullagh claims that causes are weighed by asking the following questions: how would the effect have changed had a cause not been present; by how much did the event become more probable or possible by the cause; and when human agency is involved, who is responsible?

More recent studies have compared the conflicting assignments of causes by different historians, discovering the important influence of different and conflicting interpretations of theoretical backgrounds, revealing the incommensurability and unconfirmability of historiographic causal accounts.

Aviezer Tucker

See also COLLIGATION; COLLINGWOOD, ROBIN GEORGE; COUNTERFACTUALS; DETERMINISM; DRAY, WILLIAM H.; LOGIC AND HISTORICAL ENQUIRY; PHILOSOPHY OF HISTORY, ANALYTIC.

References

Hart, H.L.A., and A.M. Honoré. *Causation in the Law.* Oxford: Oxford University Press, 1959.

Mandelbaum, Maurice. *The Anatomy of Historical Knowledge.* Baltimore, MD: Johns Hopkins University Press, 1977.

McCullagh, C. Behan. *Justifying Historical Descriptions.* Cambridge, Eng.: Cambridge University Press, 1984.

Miller, Richard W. *Fact and Method: Explanation, Confirmation and Reality in the Natural and the Social Sciences.* Princeton, NJ: Princeton University Press, 1987.

Scriven, Michael. "Causes, Connections and Conditions in History." In *Philosophical Analysis and History,* ed. W.H. Dray. New York: Harper and Row, 1966, 238–264.

Cavendish, Margaret, Duchess of Newcastle (1624?–1674)

Biographer. Cavendish was the youngest of eight children of Thomas Lucas, an Essex gentleman. She left England as a maid of honor to the queen in 1644 and waited out the civil wars and Interregnum on the Continent, marrying William Cavendish while in exile. After the Restoration she returned to England. Cavendish wrote in a variety of genres, including philosophical and "scientific" musings, poetry, and plays. She is noteworthy as an early female writer who wrote on a number of "masculine" topics, publishing her writings under her own name in self-confessed pursuit of fame. In 1667 *The Life of William Cavendish Duke of Newcastle* was published, making Cavendish one of the first women to write political biography. It is upon this work that her reputation as an historian rests. The *Life* includes an account of her husband's role in the civil war as a commander of Royalist forces in the north and his subsequent exile. While the work combines elements of martial and political history, Cavendish's willingness to distort historical fact in order to glorify her husband devalues the biography as a history of the civil wars and Restoration. Nonetheless, it is of enduring significance as a carefully constructed portrait of a perfect Restoration-era aristocrat.

Greg Bak

Texts
The Life of William Cavendish Duke of Newcastle. Ed. C.H. Firth. London: Routledge, 1906.

References
Grant, Douglas. *Margaret the First.* Toronto: University of Toronto Press, 1957.
Mendelson, Sarah Heller. *The Mental World of Stuart Women: Three Studies.* Amherst: University of Massachusetts Press, 1987, chap. 1.
Smith, Hilda L. *Reason's Disciples: Seventeenth-Century English Feminists.* Urbana and Chicago: University of Illinois Press, 1982.

Celalzade, Mustafa Çelebi (ca. 1490–1567)
Ottoman historian and state chancellor. Born around 1490 into a well-educated Ottoman legal family, Celalzade began his bureaucratic career in 1516 as a scribe in the imperial council and by 1525 had risen to chief clerk. From 1534 to 1557 (and again in 1566–67), he held the highest nonmilitary administrative office of state, that of *nişancı,* head of the chancery. As a historian he is known chiefly for his *Tabakat ül-Memalik ve Derecat ül-Mesalik* [Levels of the Dominions and Grades of the Professions], perhaps the most authoritative and influential contemporary history in Ottoman Turkish of the reign of Suleiman the Magnificent, developed from close personal knowledge of state affairs. His *Selimname* [History of Selim I] (1512–1520) is a comparatively late and short work, apparently designed to clear Selim I of the charge of having brought about the deposition and death of his father Bayezid II (r. 1481–1512).

Christine Woodhead

Texts
Geschichte Sultan Süleyman Kānūnīs von 1520 bis 1557, oder Tabakat ül-Memalik ve Derecat ül-Mesalik von Celalzade Mustafa genannt Koca Nişancı [The History of Sultan Suleiman Kānūnīs, or the Tabakat by Mustafa Celalzade]. Facsimile ed. with introduction by Petra Kappert. Wiesbaden, Germany: Otto Harrassowitz, 1981.
Selimname. Ed. and trans. A. Uğur and M. Çuhadar (into modern Turkish). Ankara: Turkish Ministry of Culture, 1990.

References
Kerslake, Celia J. "The Selim-name of Celal-zade Mustafa Çelebi As a Historical Source." *Turcica* (Paris) 9.2–10 (1978): 39–51.

Cen Zhongmian [Tsen Chung-mien] (1885–1961)
Chinese historian and geographer. Born to a family of rice merchants in Shunde county, Guangdong province, Cen Zhongmian initially trained and worked in tax revenues in Beijing. Self-educated in historical research, his spare-time excursions developed into a full-fledged career at the age of forty. His most productive years occurred between 1937 and 1948, when he was a research scholar in Academia Sinica and moved several times with the institute during the war years. From 1949 until his death, he returned to his native province and taught Sui, Tang, and Mongol history at Zhongshan University in Guangzhou. With a publication list of nineteen monographs and about 200 articles, Cen Zhongmian is best known as a specialist in medieval China from 400–900, and a generalist in inscriptions, historical geography, military science, institutional history, and Sino–Turkish relations. Among his notable works are *Sui Tang shi* [History of the Sui and Tang], which since its publication has been used as a university text at Chinese and Hong Kong universities. Cen Zhongmian's works are extensively consulted both inside and outside China, but none has been translated into Western languages.

Jennifer W. Jay

Texts

Cen Zhongmian shixue lunwen ji [Cen Zhongmian's Essays in Historiography]. Beijing: Zhonghua shuju, 1990.

Sui Tang shi [History of the Sui and Tang Dynasties]. Hong Kong: Wenchang shuju, 1960.

Censorship and Historical Writing

Systematic control of the content or exchange of information and ideas concerning the past imposed by, or with the connivance of, the ruling power. Censorship of history is always accompanied by historical propaganda: the systematic manipulation of information concerning the past by, or with the connivance of, the authorities. From time immemorial, rulers have tried to manipulate the past, discipline historians, and control collective memory. The Chinese emperor Qin Shihuangdi ordered a large-scale burning of historical works and had possibly hundreds of intellectuals executed in an attempt to eliminate tradition and its guardians (213 B.C.). After the death of each Inca, his successor decided what the official history was to be; the greatest of them, Pachacuti, invented a divine origin for the Inca to support his prestige and justify his regime, and declared treason any dissident historical view (1434). Various other early-modern examples can be added to the list, since few historians between the Renaissance and the eighteenth century enjoyed anything approaching complete freedom of expression and since the development of the printing press (and substantial growth in the readership of history after the Renaissance) magnified the potential offense to a ruler or regime. Thus, for instance, the Florentine statesman Francesco Guicciardini's *History of Italy* was censored after his death by ecclesiastical authorities between 1561 and 1564. The English courtier and historian Fulke Greville, planning to write a biography of Elizabeth I, was denied access to government documents because the queen's leading minister did not like Greville's political and religious views—and even William Camden, who was granted access to these materials a few years later for his own *Annales* of the queen's reign (1615–1628), had to tread very carefully, commenting on the dangers of doing "contemporary history." Only a few decades previously, in 1586, the famous *Chronicles* of England, Scotland, and Ireland assembled by Raphael Holinshed were called in by England's privy council and several pages were expurgated from it. In seventeenth-century France, the church and the crown made serious efforts to prevent the publication of works putting "scandalous" or "libertine" cases, such as the possibility of the Franks having descended not from the Trojan refugees (as held in long-venerated myths) but from the same ancestry as the Germans. These are but a few illustrations, and one should not make the mistake of assuming that the days of that kind of censorship are long gone: as recently as 1931 Stalin called disloyal historians "archive rats."

Although the severity of censorship and propaganda varies enormously, usually two domains are watched more closely, as the above examples suggest: contemporary history (because the witnesses are still alive) and popular history (because of its reach). As the English historian and politician Sir Walter Ralegh observed in his 1614 *History of the World,* in connection with contemporary history, those who follow truth too near the heels "are likely to have their teeth struck out." The aim of censoring regimes is to purge historiography in order to make it a tool of the ideology justifying the rulers' position of power. This monopolization of the past has usually forced historians to make a choice: some of them collaborate actively on the official historical propaganda, others yield to the pressure and employ self-censorship, while a third group is submitted to direct censorship and sometimes punishment. The last group includes the professionally or physically persecuted historians as well as the historians who carry on their work underground or abroad. The results of censorship are often ambiguous. The Chinese book-burning, for example, did hamper the development of historiography, not only because much information was destroyed, but also because it provided an excuse to future scholars to falsify ancient texts. At the same time, however, it caused an immense arousal of historical consciousness: Han scholars tried to recover and edit whatever texts remained, and a cult of books developed. Thus did the aim of censorship defeat itself.

The transition to democracy, as it has occurred at different times in different parts of the world, tends to enable the development of an independent historiography. The task is difficult and includes demystifying the falsified historiography, replacing compromised historians, and keeping alive the memory of the period of censorship and atrocities. And even in democratic societies historians should remain alert: in spite of the fact that censorship is not supposed to exist in those societies, there is often still an official interpretation of history to be reckoned with. Exceptional provisions in archive laws and Freedom of

Information Acts may restrict or close off the access to information. Unofficial groups (for instance, religious institutions, ethnic groups, and political parties) may also put considerable pressure on historians. The dominance of one particular interpretation of a period or problem (what the historian of science Thomas Kuhn would call a "paradigm") may make it difficult for historians who dissent from that view to secure funding for their research or to find employment.

Censorship of history is an obvious abuse, but not a simple problem. It gives rise to many questions. Does censored history reach the public via alternative channels (such as literature or theater)? What is the relationship between censorship, self-censorship, (induced) taboos, and (organized) amnesia? Does historical consciousness increase or diminish in times of censorship? How legitimate is historical propaganda both by the authorities and by the opposition? At what point do the selection of facts and inherent biases to which all historians are subject exceed the limits of intentional falsification and deception?

These questions are an indirect reflection of the ethical principles to which historians in democratic societies aspire. There is a broad consensus on the fundamental rights and duties that constitute academic freedom: freedom of information (for research) and freedom of expression (for publishing and teaching) both for historians and their critics, and the duty to use a critical method and aim for the truth. The historians' Ciceronian oath is "Never say something false, never withhold something true." Beyond this, opinions differ with regard to the issues at stake, for example whether political commitment or moral judgments are permitted, or what the margins are in the interpretation of research results. Neither is there unanimity on the question of whether the right to memory and history should be enforced through a tribunal: should those who abuse history (for example, by denying the Holocaust and other testified crimes) be brought before the court? Are historians entitled to demand inspection of documents or, conversely, to protect their sources?

In the preface of a book by the persecuted historian Maina wa Kinyatti, the Kenyan author Ngũgĩ wa Thiong'o gave an outline of the debate on censorship and ethics when he asked himself: "Why is history subversive?" and replied: "History is subversive, because truth is."

Antoon de Baets

References

Ferro, Marc. *L'histoire sous surveillance: Science et conscience de l'histoire* [History under Surveillance: Historical Craft and Consciousness]. Paris: Calmann-Lévy, 1985.

Grosser, Alfred. *Le crime et la mémoire* [Crime and Memory]. Paris: Flammarion, 1989.

Index on Censorship. Special issues 1985, no. 6; 1986, no. 2; 1995, no. 3.

Lewis, Bernard. *History Remembered, Recovered, Invented.* Princeton, NJ: Princeton University Press, 1975.

Scammell, Michael. "Censorship and Its History: A Personal View." In *The Article 19 World Report 1988: Information, Freedom and Censorship,* ed. Kevin Boyle. New York: Times Books; London: Longman, 1988, 1–18.

Central Asian Historiography

The peoples of Central Asia, most of whom have traditionally followed a nomadic or seminomadic way of life, have left comparatively few historical records. There are no native written sources from many of Central Asia's most well known early peoples such as the Scythians, Xiongnu, Kushans, Avars, and Huns. The earliest writing that can be regarded as historical in nature took the form of epigraphic stone monuments, the oldest of which date to approximately the eighth century A.D. and are associated with early Turkic-speaking peoples such as the Türks (Chinese: Tujue), Uighurs, and Kirghiz. Most of these have been found in modern Mongolia and Siberia. Until the creation of the Mongol Empire in the thirteenth century, such monuments constituted the only significant record of native Inner Asian historiography, although there exists a much larger body of historical writing about these peoples, composed by historians of neighboring civilizations (Chinese, Persian, Arab, Greek, Russian, and so forth) and by travelers to the region.

The Islamification of the Turkic peoples of Central Asia (Western Inner Asia), which had begun prior to the Mongol era, brought them into contact with Islamic (Arab-Persian) traditions of historiography; some pre-Mongol, as well as virtually all post-Mongol, Turkic historiography reflects that influence. The earliest histories written for the Islamified Turkic states were generally produced in Persian; it was only in the fifteenth century that a Turkic literary language, Chaghatay (which, like Persian, employed the Arabic script), came to be used to write Central Asian history. The post-Mongol period saw the creation of many works of Turkic history, including regional histories (such as the two histories by Abu'l-Ghāzī Bahādur Khān, seventeenth-century ruler of Khiva), genealogies, and memoirs (such as the *Bābur-nāma*, a description of the life of the famed Mughal conqueror). It is sometimes difficult to distinguish between literature and history in these; convention allowed historians to include poetry within their accounts, and many works of "literature" were in fact poetic descriptions of actual events. In addition, Turkic peoples continued to write down (and transmit orally) native epic tales as well; the line between these and history is not always clear.

In the modern era, Central Asia was absorbed by the Russian and Qing empires—a process that was completed in the nineteenth century. In Western Central Asia, under the rule of the Russian czars, large numbers of historical works were nevertheless produced during the late nineteenth and early twentieth centuries. These were written primarily in Chaghatay Turkic or Persian by court historians and included chronologies and regional histories, as well as some works that were broader in scope, such as the 1915 *Turkistan ta'rikhi* [History of Turkistan], written in Chaghatay, which focuses on Khokand but also describes events in neighboring regions such as Khiva and Bukhara. In keeping with tradition, most of these works were written at least partly in verse.

The Russian and Qing territories of Central Asia (with the exception of Mongolia) were largely inherited by the Soviet Union and the People's Republic of China. Under those regimes, the writing of national histories among Central Asian peoples sometimes flourished and sometimes was discouraged; those works that were written were generally required to conform to Marxist interpretations that suited the central governments in Moscow and Beijing. Since the dissolution of the Soviet Union, nationalism in Central Asia has increased, which may lead to the reconsideration of Central Asian history by its own writers.

Michael R. Drompp

See also MONGOLIAN HISTORIOGRAPHY.

Texts

Aboul-Ghâzi Bèhadour Khân. *Histoire des Mogols et des Tatares par Aboul-Ghâzi Bèhadour Khân* [History of the Mongols and Tartars]. Ed. and trans. Baron Petr I. Desmaisons. 2 vols. Amsterdam: Philo, 1970.

Bābur, Ẓahiru'd-din Muḥammad. *Bābur-nāma (Memoirs of Bābur), Translated from the Original Turki Text of Ẓahiru'd-din Muḥammad Bābur Pādshāh Ghāzī*. Trans. Annette Susannah Beveridge. E.J.W. Gibb Memorial Series, no. 1. New Delhi: Oriental Books Reprint Corp., 1979.

Mirza Muhammad Haidar, Dughlát. *A History of the Moghuls of Central Asia, Being the Tarikh-i Rashidi of Mirza Muhammad Haidar, Dughlát*. Ed. N. Elias and trans. E. Dennison Ross. New York: Barnes and Noble, 1972.

Tekin, Talât. *A Grammar of Orkhon Turkic*. Uralic and Altaic Series, vol. 69. Bloomington: Indiana University Press, 1968.

References

Bombaci, Alessio. *Histoire de la littérature turque* [History of Turkish Literature]. Trans. I. Mélikoff. Paris: Librairie C. Klincksieck, 1968.

Grousset, René. *The Empire of the Steppes: A History of Central Asia*. Trans. Naomi Walford. New Brunswick, NJ: Rutgers University Press, 1970.

Chabod, Federico (1901–1960)

Italian historian. Chabod's work demonstrates the engaged scholar viewing the past in light of contemporary challenges. His ideal of a critical liberalism pursued through the challenges of particularism, nationalism, and authoritarianism emerged in a large number of works produced on the place of early modern Italy in European thought and politics (dealing chiefly with Machiavelli, Milan, the Renaissance and Reformation in Italy, and Charles V). He also wrote extensively on modern Italy's response to unification and fascism, opposing the latter both as a scholar and, during the war, as an underground partisan. In method and philosophy, he sought the liberal balance between opposing forces. Chabod believed that necessity and power constantly threatened human freedom; the preservation of that freedom might require skillful accommodation of both, but no determinism relieved nations and individuals of their ability and responsibility to create a free society. The historian was to address universal questions through specialized studies, but could not let the expression of values descend into ideology or polemic.

Nicholas Terpstra

Texts

A History of Italian Fascism. Trans. Muriel Grindrod. London: Weidenfeld and Nicolson, 1963.

Italian Foreign Policy: The Statecraft of the Founders. Trans. William McCuaig. Princeton, NJ: Princeton University Press, 1996.

Lezioni di metodo storico [Readings on Historical Method]. Ed. Luigi Firpo. New ed. Rome and Bari: Editori Laterza, 1988.

Machiavelli and the Renaissance. Trans. David Moore. New York : Harper & Row, 1965.

References

Dizionario biografico degli Italiani. Ed. Alberto M. Ghisalberti. Rome: Istituto della Enciclopedia italiana, 1960– , vol. 24, 344–351.

Vigezzi, Brunello, ed. *Federico Chabod e la "Nuova Storiografia" Italiana dal Primo al Secondo Dopoguerra, 1919–1950* [Federico Chabod and Italian "New History" from the End of World War I to 1950]. Milan: Jaca Books, 1984.

Chalkokondyles, Laonikos (ca. 1423–ca. 1490)

Byzantine historian. Chalkokondyles was born in Athens, studied at the court of Mistra in the Peloponnesus (under Gemistus Plethon, the philosopher), and lived in the Aegean region; little else is known of his life. He wrote a history in ten books, covering the period from 1298 to 1463 and completed in the 1480s. This work is remarkable for its emphasis on the rise of the Turkish Empire and reveals direct familiarity with Ottoman documentary sources, including records of the sultan's secretaries; it thereby provides an account of the Byzantine Empire's fall from the perspectives of both sides, together with evidence on the history of early Turkish institutions.

Stephen A. Stertz

Texts

Laonici Chalcocondylae Atheniensis Historiarum libri decem [Ten Books of History] (Corpus scriptorum historiae byzantinae). Bonn: Weber, 1843.

References

Wifstrand, Albert. *Laonikos Chalkokondyles, der letzte Athener: Ein Vortrag.* [Laonikos Chalkokondyles, the Last Athenian: A Study]. Lund, Sweden: Gleerup, 1972.

Chamorro, Pedro Joaquin (1891–1952)

Nicaraguan historian. His country's foremost historian, and scion of one of its most prominent families, Chamorro was also a distinguished educator, diplomat, politician, and journalist. He is best remembered for founding and running Nicaragua's premier newspaper, *La Prensa,* in 1928 and for his persecution under Somoza. An enlightened defender of *hispanidad*—praise for Spanish values, including Catholicism—he was nevertheless a dedicated Nicaraguan nationalist, a strong believer in the balance of church and state, and an untiring advocate of freedom of the press. Chamorro wrote traditional narrative history that evaluated and extolled the impact of the Spanish legacy on Central American culture and society. His best-known works include: *El último filibustero* [The Last Filibuster] (1933), which deals with the abortive filibustering expedition by the American adventurer, William Walker, in 1856; and *Historia de la federación de la América Central, 1823–1840* [History of the Central American Federation, 1823–1840] (1951), a study of the political evolution of early-nineteenth-century Central America. It is still used as a standard reference work because of its valuable documentary appendix, assembled in both Europe and the New World.

George L. Vásquez

Texts

Historia de la federación de la América Central, 1823–1840. Madrid: Ediciones Cultura Hispánica, 1951.

El último filibustero. Managua, Nicaragua: Tip. Alemana de Carlos Henberger y Cía., 1933.

References

Mejía Sánchez, Ernesto. "Pedro Joaquín Chamorro." *Revista de Historia de América* 34 (1952): 545–548.

Chang Hsüeh-ch'eng
See ZHANG XUECHENG.

Chang Ping-lin
See ZHANG BINGLIN.

Chao I
See ZHAO YI.

Chaos Theory and History

Scientific and mathematical theory with implications for contemporary historiography. The analysis of physical and biological systems through models and mathematics of chaos theory and nonlinear dynamics rose to prominence in the 1980s. Countless authors, most notably Ilya Prigogine, made glancing references to applications of this new paradigm to the social and historical sciences, but with few results until the early 1990s. Psychologists examining brain activity, economists tracking stock price movements, military strategists assessing the outbreak and outcome of wars, sociologists modeling the rise of cities, literary critics, and many others found nonlinear dynamics refreshingly stimulating in reevaluating (and often restructuring) old theories and creating new ones. Modeling the past was an inevitable extension of this trend, and theorizing on the new historiography soon followed, with the terms of the debate outlined from 1990 to 1993 by Charles Dyke, George Reisch, Donald McCloskey, and Michael Shermer. A strong critique to this extension was formulated by Paul Roth and Thomas Ryckman, who, along with Reisch and Shermer, participated in an American Historical Association conference session in January 1994, and a Forum exchange of papers in *History and Theory* (vol. 34, no. 1, 1995).

The subject of "the chaos of history" is now enjoying a healthy exchange of ideas from all sides. Theoretical models have been proposed, critiqued, and modified. Specific historical examples have been presented to demonstrate that history is, at least at times, nonlinear in nature. History may be interpreted as present human action projected into the past. One way to prove that history is chaotic is to show that past social movements and historical events express nonlinear dynamics in a manner similar to those of the present. This has been done by A.M. Saperstein and Alan Beyerchen in examining the nonlinear nature of war, by W. Brian Arthur and Philip Anderson in modeling the economy, and by Michael Shermer in comparing the witch crazes of the sixteenth and seventeenth centuries to their modern twentieth-century descendants of mass hysterias, moral panics, and social movements such as sexual abuse accusations.

While much debate remains over the details of how and when history is chaotic, there is little doubt that, within certain parameters, history shows sensitive dependence on initial conditions, is subject to frequent bifurcations, demonstrates self-organized criticality, and finds itself in negative and positive feedback loops driven by information exchange within the system. These characteristics have long been known to historians under a different language: for instance, the interaction of predictable laws of nature and unpredictable chance events discussed by physicists corresponds to the amalgamation of historical forces and the contingencies and accidents of history narrated by historians. The "butterfly effect" of sensitive dependence in physical systems has its correlate to the old military saw "for the want of a horseshoe nail the kingdom was lost"; and the self-organization and bifurcation of storms and avalanches is not unlike that of social movements that are born, grow, hit a critical peak, and collapse. Historians and scientists have much to learn from one another about how systems change over time, since these universal principles apply to all systems—physical, biological, and social.

Michael Shermer

References

Anderson, Philip W., Kenneth J. Arrow, and David Pines, eds. *The Economy As an Evolving Complex System.* Reading, MA: Addison-Wesley, 1988.

Arthur, W. Brian. "Positive Feedbacks in the Economy." *Scientific American* (Feb. 1990): 92–99.

Beyerchen, Alan. "Clausewitz, Nonlinearity, and the Unpredictability of War," *International Security* 17 (1992/93): 59–90.

Hayles, N. Katherine. *Chaos Bound: Orderly Disorder in Contemporary Literature and Science.* Ithaca, NY: Cornell University Press, 1990.

Kauffman, Stuart A. *Origins of Order.* New York: Oxford University Press, 1992.

McCloskey, Donald. "History, Differential Equations, and the Problem of Narration." *History and Theory* 30 (1991): 21–36.

Prigogine, I., and I. Stengers. *Order Out of Chaos.* New York: Bantam, 1984.

Reisch, George. "Chaos, History, and Narrative." *History and Theory* 30 (1991): 1–20.

Saperstein, A.M. "Chaos—A Model for the Outbreak of War." *Nature* 309 (1984): 303–305.

Shermer, Michael. "The Chaos of History: On a Chaotic Model That Represents the Role of Contingency and Necessity in Historical Sequences." *Nonlinear Science Today* 2 (1993): 1–13.

Chastellain, Georges (1405–1475)

Chronicler and poet-historiographer of the Burgundian court. Chastellain was born of a noble father near the city of Alost in eastern Flanders and attended the University of Louvain. In 1433, he fought in the armies of Philip the Good, duke of Burgundy, afterward traveling to France to enter the service of Pierre de Brèze in Poitou. From 1466 until his death, he resided at the Burgundian court. In 1457, he was commanded to keep a chronicle of the times. Duke Charles the Bold made him a member of the Order of the Golden Fleece, the Burgundian court's highest honor, in 1473. His many poems, moral works, and occasional pieces are in the grave, pompous, convoluted, and allegorical Burgundian style that Johan Huizinga saw as representative of the waning Middle Ages. Along with his *Chronicles,* they are good sources to both the sentiments and events of the time. In particular, the *Chronicles* give first-hand descriptions of events and insightful portrayals of major political figures. They begin with the fall of Constantinople in 1453. They pretend to universal coverage, but the greater and valuable parts of the work are his accounts of events that he witnessed in person or knew through direct reports.

Lawrence M. Bryant

Texts

Oeuvres de Georges Chastellain. Ed. H. Kervyn de Lettenhove. Brussels: F. Heussner et al., 1863–1866.

References

Archambault, Paul J. *Seven French Chroniclers.* Syracuse, NY: Syracuse University Press, 1974.

Delclos, Jean-Claude. *Le Témoignage de Georges Chastellain: Historiographe de Philippe le Bon et de Charles le Téméraire* [The Testimony of Georges Chastellain, Historiographer to Philip the Good and Charles the Bold]. Geneva: Librairie Droz, 1980.

Guenée, Bernard. "Histoire et chronique: Nouvelles réflexions sur les genres historiques au Moyen Age" [History and Chronicle: New Reflections on Historical Genres in the Middle Ages]. In *La Chronique et l'histoire au Moyen Age,* ed. D. Poiron. Paris: Presses de l'Université de Paris-Sorbonne, 1984, 3–12.

Chastenay-Lanty, Louise-Marie-Victorine, Comtesse de (1771–1835)

French historical and literary writer. Chastenay-Lanty was born at Château d'Essarois to a noble family and received a religious education. She accompanied her father, Gérard-Louis-Gui de Chastenay-Lanty, to Versailles when he was elected to the Estates General and embraced his liberal ideas and "republican frenzy." Repulsed by the violence of the French Revolution, however, Chastenay modified her opinions and chronicled her revolutionary experiences. At the time of her death at Châtillon-sur-Seine, Chastenay was writing a manuscript about early Christian Europe. The aristocratic Chastenay began her literary career by translating into French Oliver Goldsmith's *Le Village abandonné* [The Abandoned Village] (1797) and Anne Radcliffe's *Les Mystères d'Udolphe* [The Mysteries of Udolphe] (1797). She compared the condition of women in different cultures in her highly regarded historical tomes, including the four-volume *Du Génie des peuples anciens* [The Genius of the Ancient Peoples] (1808). Befriended by Napoleon, Chastenay began writing her memoirs in 1810, describing contemporary French figures and intellectual and social life. She has been most praised for her description of the Terror in Rouen where she fled with her family to escape persecution.

Elizabeth D. Schafer

Texts

Les chevaliers normands en Italie et en Sicile [The Norman Knights in Italy and Sicily]. Paris: Maradan, 1816.

Memoires de Madame de Chastenay, 1771–1815 [Memoirs of Madame Chastenay]. Ed. A. Roserot. 2 vols. Paris: E. Plon, Nourrit, 1896–1897.

Du Génie des peuples anciens. Paris: Maradan, 1808.

References

Lapérouse, G. *Mme la comtesse Victorine de Chastenay.* Châtillon-sur-Seine: G. Rodet 1855.

Yalom, Marilyn. *Blood Sisters: The French Revolution in Women's Memory.* New York: Basic Books, 1993.

Chateaubriand, François Auguste René, Vicomte de (1768–1848)

French romantic historian. Chateaubriand was the leading French novelist and historian living in exile during the French Revolution. He represents the conservative tendencies in early romanticism, the British counterpart of which can be found in Burke and Coleridge. In 1797 he condemned the excesses of the revolution in his *Essai historique, politique et morale sur les révolutions* [Historical, Political, and Moral Essay Concerning Revolutions]. He pointed to a parallel between the French and English revolutions: as Charles I was beheaded, Louis XVI was guillotined; as monarchy had returned to England, so, too, it would soon return to France. His thesis was that each nation must follow its natural development based on its fundamental morals and customs. Institutions must follow this progression; revolutions were only a beautiful dream. In empowering and glorifying the masses, the revolution destroyed the very essence of France, the Church. In his popular *Le Génie du christianisme* (1802) Chateaubriand revived an interest in the medieval church, and through an extremely vivid and sentimental style he demonstrated the drama of history while drawing attention to its colorful personalities. Like Walter Scott, Chateaubriand inspired the next generation of romantic writers and is often called the founder of French romanticism.

John B. Roney

Texts

The Genius of Christianity. New York: Fertig, 1975
The Martyrs. Ed. and trans. O.W. Wright. New York: Fertig, 1976.

References

Barbéris, Pierre. *Chateaubriand: Une réaction au monde moderne.* Paris: Librairie Larousse, 1976.
Evans, Joan. *Chateaubriand: A Biography.* London: Macmillan, 1939.
Painter, George Duncan. *Chateaubriand: A Biography.* London: Chatto and Windus, 1977.

Chaudhuri, Sashi Bhusan (1905–1983)

Indian historian. Chaudhuri was born in Agartala (Tripura) and educated at the Scottish Church College, Calcutta, and Dacca University. He taught at M.C. College, Sylhet, Dacca University, and Presidency College, Callege. He served as editor of the *Gazetteers of India* (1958–1960), as professor of history, head of the department of history (1960–1971), and then vice-chancellor at Burdwan University (1971–1973). In his early career he worked on ancient India but then turned to popular discontent with British rule during the revolt of 1857. Contrary to the established canon of the time as argued by his mentor Ramesh Chandra Majumdar, Chaudhuri suggested that there had been a great deal of popular opposition to British rule.

Roger D. Long

Texts

Civil Disturbances during the British Rule in India, 1765–1857. Calcutta: World Press, 1955.
Civil Rebellion in the Indian Mutinies (1857–59). Calcutta: World Press, 1957.
English Historical Writings on the Indian Mutiny. Calcutta: World Press, 1979.
Theories of the Indian Mutiny, 1857–59: A Study of the Views of an Eminent Historian on the Subject. Calcutta: World Press, 1965.

References

Stokes, Eric. *The Peasant and the Raj: Studies in Agrarian Society and Peasant Rebellion in Colonial India.* Cambridge, Eng.: Cambridge University Press, 1978.

Chaunu, Pierre René (b. 1923)

French quantitative and structural historian. Chaunu was born in 1923 in Belleville and educated at the Sorbonne, where he was taught by Fernand Braudel while preparing for his aggregation. It was Braudel's "New History" of societies and civilizations, stressing the *longue durée* (very long spans of time), that determined Chaunu's methodology. Chaunu spent the years from 1948 to 1951, researching the economic and demographic history of Latin America. He taught briefly at schools in provincial France before preparing a doctorate at the Centre National de la Recherche Scientifique (CNRS) on Seville and the Atlantic. While a professor at the University of Caen from 1959 to 1970, he was founder and director of the Centre de Recherche d'Histoire Quantitative. In 1970, he became professor of modern history at the Sorbonne and since 1980, has been a member of the history section of the Scientific Council at the CNRS. Chaunu's most significant history is the multivolume *Seville et l'Atlantique (1504–1650)* [Seville and the Atlantic, 1504–1650] (1955–1959) written in collaboration with his wife, Huguette. In it, he examined the historical dimensions of demography and the extensive trade links in the Atlantic. His subsequent works deal with subjects as varied as the Reformation, attitudes to death in early modern Paris, and crises in Western civilization. Chaunu's history is concerned primarily with spatial and economic systems of the early modern world, historical demography, and quantitative research. He is not interested in the past for its own sake, but rather as a mechanism for understanding the present. A pioneer in demographic history and quantitative methods, Chaunu invented

the concept of the cultural and economic "time series" *(histoire sérielle),* or developmental cycles.
Leigh Whaley

Texts
European Expansion in the Later Middle Ages. Trans. Katharine Bertram. Amsterdam: North Holland Publishing Company, 1979.
Histoire quantitative, histoire sérielle [Quantitative History, Serial History]. Paris: A. Colin, 1978.
Seville et l'Atlantique (1504–1650). 12 vols. Paris: A. Colin, 1955–1959.

References
Bardet, Jean Pierre, and Madeleine Foisils, eds. *La vie, la mort, la foi, le temps: Mélanges offerts à Pierre Chaunu* [Life, Death, Faith, and Time: Essays in Honor of Pierre Chaunu]. Paris: Presses universitaires de France, 1993.
Quillot, Roland. "Le vitalisme historique de Pierre Chaunu [The Historical Vitalism of Pierre Chaunu]." *Esprit* 6 (1982): 286–297.

Chen Shou [Ch'en Shou] (A.D. 233–297)
Chinese historian. A minor courtier of the kingdom of Shu, Chen Shou later served in the court of Jin (A.D. 265–420). In a private capacity he compiled the *Sanguo zhi* [The Records of Three Kingdoms], a history of the kingdoms of Wei (190–265), Shu (190–264), and Wu (190–280). The value of his work was greatly enhanced by Pei Songzhi's (372–451) commentary, which was prepared under imperial commission in the early fifth century.
Henry Y.S. Chan

Texts
Sanguo zhi [Records of Three Kingdoms]. Beijing: Zhonghua shuju, 1959.

References
De Crespigny, Rafe. *The Records of the Three Kingdoms.* Canberra: The Australian National University Press, 1970.

Chen Yinke [Chen Yin Ko; Tschen Yinkoh] (1890–1969)
Historian of Chinese Buddhism, Tang institutions, and Ming and Qing culture. Born into a literary family in Jiangxi, Chen received a thorough training in traditional learning during childhood. In 1902 he began two decades of study abroad, acquiring a number of languages including Sanskrit and Pali. Returning to China, he quickly developed into one of the most sophisticated scholars of Chinese Buddhist texts. During the Sino–Japanese War, Chen became blind; but blindness did not prevent him from writing two important studies on Tang institutions, elucidating the connections among family, clan, and politics. Partly in response to the cultural iconoclasm of the 1920s and 1930s, he consistently stressed the historical continuity of China's traditions, notwithstanding its borrowing from other cultures. After 1949 Chen broke new ground by combining history with poetry. His last writings demonstrate how history can benefit from incorporating poetry as a source of evidence and how poetry in turn can be enriched when understood historically.
Tze-ki Hon

Texts
Chen Yin-ko wen chi [Works of Chen Yinke]. 5 vols., each in multiple tomes. Shanghai: Shanghai guchi chubanshe, 1980–1982.
"Han Yu and the Tang Novel." *Harvard Journal of Asiatic Studies* 1 (1936): 39–43.

References
Wechsler, Howard. "Factionalism in Early Tang Government." In *Perspectives on the Tang,* ed. Arthur Wright and Denis Twitchett. New Haven, CT: Yale University Press, 1973, 87–120.

Chen Yuan [Chen Yüan] (1880–1971)
Modern Chinese historian of the Yuan dynasty and Chinese religion. Born in Xinhui, in Guangdong province, Chen graduated from medical school in 1910, but turned to historical research in 1913. From 1929 he headed Beijing's Furen University, a Catholic institution. During World War II, he remained at Furen, under Japanese occupation. In 1952, Chen became president of Beijing Normal University, the successor institution to Furen University. He participated in the Communist land reform campaign in 1951, but did little active research after 1949. In a nationalist era, Chen was one of the few continuators of the rich Qing tradition of Inner Asian research, although his later works focused on Buddhist and Daoist studies. Chen also made major contributions in the field of textual criticism and chronology.
Christopher Pratt Atwood

Texts

Shixue lunwen ji [Collected Historical Articles].
    Beijing: Beijing Normal University Press,
    1981.
*Western and Central Asians in China under the
    Mongols.* Trans. Ch'ien Hsing-hai and L.
    Carrington Goodrich. Los Angeles: Univer-
    sity of California Press, 1966.
"Wu Yü-shan." Trans. Eugene Feifel.
    Monumenta Serica 3 (1938): 130–170.

References

Zhou Kangxie ed. *Chen Yuan xiansheng
    jinniannian shixue lunji* [Collected His-
    torical Essays of Chen Yuan's Last Twenty
    Years]. Hong Kong: Ch'ung-wen Book-
    store, 1971.

Cheng Chiao
See ZHENG QIAO.

Cheney, Edward Potts (1861–1947)

American historian of England and educator.
Cheyney was born in Wallingford, Pennsylvania.
He graduated from the University of Pennsylvania
in 1884 and devoted himself to teaching at that
university as a professor of English history. From
1909 to 1933 he was the chairman of the American Historical Association's Committee on the
Bibliography of Modern British History. In 1929
he was appointed the first holder of the Henry C.
Lea professorship in medieval history at the University of Pennsylvania, the position from which
he retired in 1934. Cheyney's writing consisted
chiefly of historical narrative combined with description. Following the publication of several articles on thirteenth- and fourteenth-century England, he began to write textbooks, believing that
therein lay the most important contribution professional historians could make toward the improvement of the teaching of history and the promotion of popular education. His interest in the
Industrial Revolution in England resulted in his
well-illustrated text, *An Introduction to the Industrial and Social History of England* (1901). In
that book Cheyney raised the question of the
"condition of the people" and concluded that the
climate for real change to improve the lives of
the exploited lower classes did not seriously develop until the second half of the nineteenth and
early twentieth centuries. Personally committed to
what he called "industrial democracy" as a means
to protect the working classes from the hazards of

modern industrial life, Cheyney noted that the
brief period between 1906 and 1914 had witnessed the most intense and significant activity
in social reform. His other textbook, *A Short
History of England* (1904), which was revised
and reissued a number of times, offered an account of significant events in the nation's long
and varied past. Eager to provide students with
documentary materials, he also edited *Readings in English History Drawn from the Original
Sources, Intended to Illustrate a Short History of
England* (1908).

Cheyney's own research interests centered
on sixteenth- and nineteenth-century England,
his concentration on economic and social history arising from his concerns for the masses.
Turning to the Tudor period, he published in
two volumes *A History of England, from the
Defeat of the Armada to the Death of Elizabeth*
(1914–1926). On the later period, he published
*Modern English Reform, from Individualism to
Socialism* (1931), a book based on his lectures
that drew attention to the rise of the working
classes and their ability to influence the course
of social and political reforms through the suffrage and pressure. In this work Cheyney lauded
England's approach to reform, through legislation rather than revolution.

Bernard Hirschhorn

Texts

The Dawn of a New Era, 1250–1453. New York
    and London: Harper & Brothers, 1936.
*European Background of American History, 1300–
    1600.* New York: F. Ungar, 1966.
*A History of England, from the Defeat of the Ar-
    mada to the Death of Elizabeth.* 2 vols. New
    York: Longmans, 1914–1926.
*An Introduction to the Industrial and Social His-
    tory of England.* New York: Macmillan,
    1901.
*Modern English Reform, from Individualism to
    Socialism.* Philadelphia: University of Penn-
    sylvania Press, 1931.
Ed. *Readings in English History Drawn from the
    Original Sources, Intended to Illustrate a
    Short History of England.* New ed. Boston:
    Ginn, 1935.
A Short History of England. Boston: Ginn &
    Company, 1904.

References

Lingelbach, William E., ed. *Portrait of an Histo-
    rian: Edward Potts Cheyney.* Philadelphia:
    University of Pennsylvania Press, 1935.

Ch'ien Mu

See QIAN MU.

Ch'ien Ta-sin

See QIAN DAXIN.

Child, Lydia Maria Francis (1802–1880)

American author and social reformer. Child was born in Medford, Massachusetts, the youngest offspring of a prosperous baker. She was educated at local dame schools and female seminaries, briefly taught school, and in 1822 published her first novel. Incredibly prolific, Child quickly assumed editorship of a children's magazine, wrote a fictional account of the American Revolution, and published a best-selling book on household management. In the late 1820s, Child who by then had married reformer Richard Child became heavily involved in both the abolitionist movement and the defense of Indian rights. To support these causes, she wrote *The First Settlers of New England,* an account of that region's Indians, and *An Appeal in Favor of That Class of Americans Called Africans* (1833), a history of slavery and a condemnation of racism. Child then turned her attention to women's rights, publishing a two-volume history of the condition of women, which called for full equality between the sexes. During the 1840s, Child edited an antislavery periodical. Her next major historical effort was a three-volume treatise, *The Progress of Religious Ideas through Successive Ages,* which argued in favor of the Unitarian view that human progress had more to do with religious thought than revealed dogma. At the beginning of the Civil War, Child made her most lasting contribution to historiography when she edited the recollections of former slave, Harriet Jacobs, and published them as *Incidents in the Life of a Slave Girl.*

Barbara A. McGowan

Texts

An Appeal in Favor of That Class of Americans Called Africans. New York: Arno Press, 1968.

The First Settlers of New England. Boston: Munroe and Francis, 1829.

The History of the Condition of Women in Various Ages and Nations. Boston: Otis, Broaders and Co., 1835.

Ed. with Jean F. Yellin. *Incidents in the Life of a Slave Girl.* Cambridge, MA: Harvard University Press, 1987.

The Progress of Religious Ideas through Successive Ages. New York: C.S. Francis and Co., 1855.

The Rebels; or Boston, before the Revolution. Boston: Cummings, Hilliard, 1825.

References

Osborne, William S. *Lydia Maria Child.* Boston: Twayne, 1980.

Chinese Historical Thought—Ancient to Ming

Speculation on and discussion of the past and of the proper purpose and scope of various forms of historical writing.

Historical consciousness and thought has been a major component in all Chinese philosophical discourse since the Golden Age of Philosophers in the sixth to third centuries B.C. But the earliest roots of Chinese historical thought and consciousness go back even further, to the eleventh century B.C., when China's earliest classics, such as *The Book of Change, The Book of History,* and *The Book of Songs,* began to take their definitive forms. These canons expounded the view that history was the discernible pattern of past human conduct and served as a guide for human action. Such historical thought was based on a profound understanding of natural law, according to which the universe is in constant change and human beings must also change every day in order both to survive and to grow stronger. This was the prevailing belief of the time. It was also this belief that produced the dialectic interpretation of all process of change in the universe: a thesis would produce an antithesis and then a synthesis. For example, a life that just begins also begins the process of its ending, and the final ending is the birth of a new life. History, to the Chinese of the eleventh century B.C., is a process of change that recorded the process of the change of human life and activities. One must learn from history to improve one's life in the world of change: thus was history portrayed in the world of the most ancient Chinese canons.

Historical thought became more diverse and wide-ranging during China's Golden Age of Philosophers, ca. 600–222 B.C. In this period of tremendous socioeconomic, political, and cultural changes, the great thinkers considered the effect of history on men's view of life. Confucius [Kong Qiu] (551–479 B.C.) saw the moral function of history and its usefulness to mankind. Mencius [Meng Ke] (371–289 B.C.), too, recognized the moral importance of historical writing, but he also held that the pattern of history as a whole was cyclical rather than progressive. The Daoists, for their part, doubted that history had any meaning or any use, seeing it simply as a record of the decline of human freedom and individualism. In contrast, Mo Di (fl. 479–438 B.C.), the founder of Mohism, held that history reflected the progress of human civilization in social order and political stability. Mo Di believed that human society progressed in the complex manner of a developing "social contract" between the "great man" and the masses. The Legalists, such as Han Fei (280–233 B.C.), believed that human history was always in linear progress, and voiced the view that the past had no value for humankind. The great philosophers of this period also considered whether history had a purpose, or the existence of a prime mover behind human destiny. Both Confucianists and Mohists argued for the profound purpose of history, but the Daoists, the Legalists, and Xun Qing (fl. 298–238 B.C.) questioned the validity and sensibility of such a view. Human history, they believed, was a natural process, and there could not be a grand divine design behind human affairs.

Sima Qian (145–86 B.C.), the father of Chinese historiography, advanced the most comprehensive system of historical thought. Through his imaginative and original thinking, he set forth his views of history in his immortal *Shiji* [Historical Records] in 130 books (that is, chapters). History as past, according to Sima Qian, is the creative process of the interaction among human beings in accordance with the will of a supreme divine force; in a larger sense, civilization was created in this process. History, as a literary text, is the record of past events, big and small, and the story of all those persons who stand out through their special achievements and unique skills. History is written, on this view, to advise, educate, and admonish the present world and the living. Therefore, the duty of a historian is not only to record but to evaluate and judge human affairs as well as to discern the will of the supreme divine mover and the pattern of history. To achieve this goal, Sima Qian devised a special format for the writing of history consisting of five parts: Imperial Annals (*benji* or *ji*), biographies (*liezhuan* or *zhuan*), tables (*biao*), hereditary houses (*shijia*), and monographs (*shu*). He also emphasized that writing history is more than recording the facts; it is a lively, creative undertaking. The historian not only writes history, but *creates* history through his powers of imagination and his freedom to interpret and to add interesting details. Sima Qian is important in the history of Chinese historical thought

because he defined the nature and purpose of history, expounded the dimension and function of historical knowledge, explored the scope of historiography, and emphasized the unity of history and literature—the creative and imaginative aspect of history writing.

Sima Qian defined the historian's craft in an age of grand philosophical synthesis, the period of the Han dynasty (202 B.C.–A.D. 220). His craft became the standard way of compiling and writing history (*zhengshi*), and his model was followed not only by the great Han historian Ban Gu (32–92), author of the *Hanshu* [History of the Former Han Dynasty], but also by later historians.

The historians and thinkers of the next age, the Middle Imperial Period (220–960), followed Sima Qian's craft in writing and thinking about history. But they also placed new emphasis on certain issues in their thought about history and in their search for its meaning. Xun Xu (fl. late third century) and Li Chong (fl. early fourth century) undertook to define the territory of history. They divided all human writings (both published and unpublished) into four categories: classics, history, philosophy, and literature; and in history, they included all written works on the human past. As their fourfold classification of writings henceforth became the standard system in China, their definition of the territory of history was also followed by later historians and scholars. In the search for the nature, meaning, and pattern of history, some historians and thinkers of this period considered social change to be the focus for examining the moving forces in the historical process—to understand history was, in short, to discern the forces of change at work in human society. To others, however, the lives of individuals, contained in biographies, became of central concern; for this group, the center of history was man himself. In general, the relationship between fate and free will, and the role of the "great man" versus the commoner in making history provided another focus for the historiographical and intellectual pursuits of a variety of historians and philosophers. Liu Yiqing (403–444), Han Yu (768–824), and Liu Zongyuan (773–819) were the leading voices raising these questions. Still others made the idea of progress versus the force of tradition the central concern of their historical thought. The great Liu Zhiji (661–721) of the Tang dynasty (618–907), author of the great classic on historical criticism *Shitong* [Generalities on History], was one such writer in this last category. Some historians believed that the key to understanding the historical process was through the structure and evolution

C

of the governmental organization and administration, and through related social and economic matters. Du You (735–812) was the representative voice and best-known advocate of this view. His monumental *Tongdian* [Comprehensive Institutes], in 200 chapters, established a format and style for institutional history. The work is divided into nine sections: the economic system, civil service examinations, the official system, rites, music, the military system, the legal system, political geography, and border affairs; and in each the period covered extends from the earliest historical times (traditionally the third millennium B.C.) down to A.D. 755.

The Song (Sung) dynasty (960–1279) was an age of economic prosperity and military crisis. The Chinese empire was constantly being pressed by non-Chinese peoples, the Tanguts, the Khitans, the Jurchens, and the Mongols, and Song China's primary concern was how to deal with one military crisis after another. The need for reform and revitalization provided a continuing theme among Song statesmen, who were in traditional China also among the leading thinkers and historians.

In such a national context, historical thought during Song times returned to the earliest and most fundamental Chinese conception of history: namely, the practical use of history. Leading Song historians and thinkers such as Wang Qinruo (962–1025), Yang Yi (947–1020), Song Qi (998–1061), Ouyang Xiu (1007–1072), Sima Guang (1019–1086), Lu You (1125–1210), Zhu Xi (1130–1200), Lü Zuqian (1137–1181), and Tang Zhongyu (1138–1188), all held that history is the most essential guide to statecraft and that both institutions and the intelligent individual should consult history in planning successful action. History, as they all proceeded to elaborate in their various forms of discourse, shows the merits and demerits of past institutions, the scope and operation of social forces, the role of ideas in various social and political processes, the diversity of the human conscience, models of behavior, the myriad facets of human affairs and natural environment, and the place of social change in general and progress in particular. History was thus conceived of not just as a mirror of the past, but as guidebook for the active citizen and statesman. Moreover, these scholars also insisted that writing history and compiling historical records were both a necessary and a noble responsibility for the intellectual, whose primary pursuit in life was to serve the state and the people and to lead the common people in the right direction. As for the type of history that could best serve the purpose of history so defined, two schools stood out as the most influential. One focused on examining history by a special period (such as the history of only one dynasty) or through a special subject (such as the history of political systems), and the other insisted on looking upon history as a continuous stream—thereby the importance of writing general history that was comprehensive in subject coverage and that covered a *longue durée* in time span. Among the representative works of the former were the *Xin Tang shu* [A New History of the Tang Dynasty, 618–907], in 225 chapters, by Ouyang Xiu and Song Qi and *Lida Zhidu Xiangshuo* [A Comprehensive History of the Administrative Systems Throughout the Ages], in 13 chapters, by Lü Zuqian. Zheng Qiao's *Tongzhi* [General Treatise] was the best-known work of the school of comprehensive general history. Competed in 1161, it was modeled after Sima Qian's *Shiji,* in six major sections divided into 200 chapters: imperial annals, biographies, hereditary houses, chronological tables, records of independent kingdoms, and monographs. The period covered extends from earliest historical times down to the end of the Tang dynasty in A.D. 907. Zheng Qiao also held that in making history useful the historian must write it with a strict adherence to objectivity and let the facts speak for themselves. He took issue with those who believed that history had a divine purpose and that writing history was making a moral judgment.

Since history was given such an immense function in directing human affairs, some Song scholars, such as Zhu Xi and Lu You, began to see the power of history as the power to influence and teach. They argued accordingly that history should be written with a sense of enormous responsibility and with strong moral and political correctness. It should be seen as a divine design to uphold the eternal justice in all human affairs. In doing so, they were going back to the ideas of both Sima Qian and even Confucius. In the end, however, they also held that the writing of history is a matter of creative choice and is thus a subjective, not objective, intellectual undertaking. In history, a thinker finds his intellectual autonomy and power, beyond and above any mundane human concerns and political restrictions. It is no wonder then that more than 1,300 historical works were written during the Song period.

Ming (1368–1644) historians inherited the Song tradition while developing it in new directions. First, like the Song writers, they recognized the power of history and went on to assert its equivalent status to the great Confucian classics in directing human affairs; they advanced the theory that the classics were actually originally all historical works *(Liujing jieshi)* and that history writing from the very beginning of Chinese intellectual tradition had wielded an extraordinary degree of influence. Wang Shizhen (1526–1590) first advanced this thesis in his *Yanzhou shanren sibu gao* [Treatises on Classics, History, and Literature] (1576), which was elaborated by his contemporary, Li Zhi (1527–1602) in his *Fenshu* [Collected Works] (1590). As expressed by these late Ming writers, the theory would become a central feature of Chinese intellectual discourse during the early Qing period in the eighteenth century, particularly in the writings of Zhang Xuecheng (1738–1801), as in his *Wenshi tongyi* [General Meaning of Literature and History, 1772–1800]. Secondly, the Ming historians picked up on one stream of Song thought by moving the individual more decisively to the center of their historical thought. History was made by man and should take biography, the story of man, as its central task. More interestingly, history could be the moving story of an individual's struggle to survive and to achieve. Thus history was really the story of the human spirit, from its most pitiful weakness to its most incredible strength, and the story of each man's struggle for survival in the face of national, social, or personal crisis.

Late Ming China was a time of national and political crisis, social breakdown, economic uprooting, and great intellectual change. That context provided the golden opportunity for such historians as Li Zhi, Zhang Dai (1597–1684), and Zha Jizuo (1601–1676), to write their new history, with the story of man as the main focus of their work. Late Ming was an age of intellectual revolution, and the new view in historical thought was in keeping with the spirit of this revolution. The Ming historians gave history a canonical status among the literary genres and made the life story of man, rather than the state, society, or heaven, its central subject.

From the Zhou dynasty in the eleventh century B.C. to the late Ming in the seventeenth century A.D., Chinese historical thought had thus shifted in its concerns away from the State and society toward an appreciation of the individual, the hallmark elsewhere in the world of a nascent historicism. As China entered the modern age in the seventeenth century, so did Chinese historical thought.

Chun-shu Chang

See also CHINESE HISTORIOGRAPHY—CHRONICLE/ ANNAL FORM HISTORIES; COMMENTARIES; GENERAL HISTORIES; LOCAL GAZETTEERS; STANDARD HISTORIES, ETC.; CHINESE HISTORIOGRAPHY— MODERN (POST-MING) AND COMMUNIST.

References

Beasley, W.G., and E.G. Pulleyblank, eds. *Historians of China and Japan.* London: Oxford University Press, 1961.

Chang, Chun-shu, and Shelley Hsueh-lun Chang. *Crisis and Transformation in Seventeenth-Century China: Society, Culture, and Modernity.* Ann Arbor: University of Michigan Press, 1992.

Chang, Shelley Hsueh-lun. *History and Legend: Ideas and Images in the Ming Historical Novels.* Ann Arbor: University of Michigan Press, 1990.

Gardner, Charles S. *Chinese Traditional Historiography.* Second ed. Cambridge, MA: Harvard University Press, 1961.

Twitchett, D.C. *The Writing of Official History under the T'ang.* Cambridge, Eng. and New York: Cambridge University Press, 1992.

Chinese Historiography—Chronicle/Annal Form Histories *(Biannian Shi)*

A type of historical writing in which information is divided into discrete time periods and arranged in strict chronological order. The earliest extant Chinese chronicle is the *Chunqiu* [Spring and Autumn Annals], a terse history of the state of Lu from 722 to 481 B.C. (its dating by season gave rise to its quaint name). Because this text was considered to have been edited by Confucius, scholars searched for hidden moral judgments in its dry notices of deaths, ritual observances, and wars and eventually the chronicle form was associated with sageliness to the extent that several nonchronological, philosophical works borrowed the title "Chunqiu."

Early historians recognized the advantages of annals, namely their comprehensiveness and their clear presentation of chronological relationships, but their disadvantage was that extended narratives were difficult to follow since they were divided into yearly installments and mixed with other narrative fragments. The Standard Histories, beginning with Sima Qian's *Shiji* [Historical Records] (ca. 90 B.C.), overcame this difficulty by balancing an annalistic section with a series of biographies that covered the same time period. Nevertheless, chronicles continued to be written, as when Xun Yue rearranged the most important passages of Ban Gu's *Hanshu* [History of the Han] into a year-by-year chronicle, the *Hanji* [Record of the Han] (A.D. 200).

The greatest of Chinese chronicles is the *Zizhi tongjian* [Comprehensive Mirror for Aid in Government] (1085) by the Song historian Sima Guang, which continued the Spring and Autumn Annals, and recounted Chinese history from 403 B.C. to A.D. 959 (from the Warring States period to the Later Zhou, one of the short-lived Five Dynasties of the tenth century). One advantage that it had over its predecessor, however, was a commentary by the author explaining his sources and editorial decisions. Another important example of chronicle form history is the Veritable Records—detailed accounts of the emperor's and government's daily activities that were used as sources for annals sections of the Standard Histories.

Grant Hardy

See also BAN GU; CHINESE HISTORIOGRAPHY—STANDARD HISTORIES *(ZHENGSHI)*; CONFUCIUS; SIMA GUANG [SSU-MA KUANG]; SIMA QIAN [SSU-MA CH'IEN].

References

Franke, Wolfgang. "Historical Writing during the Ming." In *The Cambridge History of China*. Vol. 7, *The Ming Dynasty*, ed. Frederick W. Mote and Denis Twitchett. Cambridge, Eng.: Cambridge University Press, 1988, 736–760.

Van der Loon, P. "The Ancient Chinese Chronicles and the Growth of Historical Ideals." In *Historians of China and Japan*, ed. W.G. Beasley and E.G. Pulleyblank. London: Oxford University Press, 1961, 25–30.

Chinese Historiography—Commentaries

Form of historical writing, including the sub-categories of *shiping* (theoretical study of historiography), *shilun* (critical remarks on historical events and figures), and *shikao* (evidential research on historical writings).

Concomitant with developments in Chinese historical writing during and after the Tang dynasty, there emerged theoretical works on historiography, the most important of which are Liu Zhiji's (661–721) *Shitong*, Zheng Qiao's (1104–1162) "General Introduction" to the *Tongzhi*, and Zhang Xuecheng's (1738–1801) *Wenshi tongyi*. Therein the methods, scope, and conceptions of historiography are extensively discussed.

Ever since the writing of the *Zuozhuan* and the *Shiji*, Chinese historians had tended to derive moral insights from history, which were usually expressed in the "prefaces and comments" to the dynastic and general histories. With the rise of neo-Confucianism, historians became more interested in historical lessons, which they regarded as an aid not only in statesmanship but also in ethical cultivation. So from this "prefaces and comments" genre there developed such works of *shilun* as Hu Yin's (1098–1156) *Dushi guanjian* and Wang Fuzhi's (1619–1692) *Du Tongjian lun*—the former being principally concerned with morality and the latter addressing both Confucian moral politics and practical statecraft.

Because of the great number and variety of historical writings in China, the assessment, selection, and organization of source materials was of frequent concern to historians. Sima Guang, for instance, composed the *kaoyi* commentary to his *Comprehensive Mirror for Aid in Government* to compare variant statements in his sources and to explain his reasons for selecting some over others. In the Qing period, historians at large took a more critical view of historical texts. Many of them adopted the then highly developed methodology of the School of Evidential Research (which emphasized positive, factual knowledge, rather than metaphysical discussion, of the Confucian classics) in their historical studies. A number of notable *shikao* works appeared—represented by Qian Daxin's (1728–1804) *Nianershi kaoyi*, Wang Mingsheng's (1722–1798) *Shiqishi shangque*, and Zhao Yi's (1727–1814) *Nianershi zhaji*—which applied inductive, empirical methods of textual scholarship to historiography.

Shoucheng Yan

Texts

Cui Shu. *Kaoxin lu* [A Record of Beliefs Investigated]. In *Cui Dongbi yishu* [Collected Works of Cui Shu], ed. Gu Jiegang. Shanghai: Yadong tushuguan, 1936.

Liang Yusheng. *Shiji zhiyi* [Notes on Doubtful Points in the *Records of the Grand Historian*]. Beijing: Zhonghua shuju, 1981.

Liu Zhiji. *Shitong* [General Study of Historiography]. In *Sibu congkan chubian*. Shanghai: Shangwu yinshuguan, 1919–1922.

Qian Daxin. *Nianershi kaoyi* [An Inquiry into Discrepancies among the Twenty-Two Standard Histories]. In *Congshu jicheng chubian*. Shanghai: Shangwu yinshuguan, 1935–1937.

Sima Guang. *Zizhi tongjian kaoyi* [An Inquiry into Discrepancies in (the Source Materials of) the *Comprehensive Mirror*]. In *Sibu congkan chubian*. Shanghai: Shangwu yinshuguan, 1919–1922.

Wang Fuzhi. *Du Tongjian lun* [Remarks on Reading the *Comprehensive Mirror*]. Beijing: Zhonghua shuju, 1975.

———. *Song lun* [Remarks on Song (History)]. Beijing: Zhonghua shuju, 1964.

Wang Mingsheng. *Shiqishi shangque* [Deliberations on the Seventeen Standard Histories]. In *Congshu jicheng chubian*. Shanghai: Shangwu yinshuguan, 1935–1937.

Zhang Xuecheng. *Wenshi tongyi* [General Principles of Literature and History]. Beijing: Zhonghua shuju, 1961.

Zhao Yi. *Nianershi zhaji* [Notes on the Twenty-Two Standard Histories]. Beijing: Zhonghua shuju, 1963.

Zheng Qiao. *Tongzhi ershilue* [The Twenty Treatises in the *Comprehensive Historical Record*]. In *Sibu beiyao*. Shanghai: Zhonghua shuju, 1936.

References

Liu Yizheng. *Guoshi yaoyi* [The Essential Principles of Chinese Historiography]. Taibei: Taiwan Zhonghua shuju, 1957.

Zhang Shunhui. *Zhongguo gudai shiji juyao* [An Introduction to Important Premodern Chinese Historical Works]. Wuhan: Hubei renmin chubanshe, 1980.

Chinese Historiography—General Histories (*tongshi, [t'ung-shih]* premodern and imperial)

General, comprehensive, or universal histories of China written in chronicle form or as a chronological narrative. In contrast to the dynastic histories, which focus on one dynasty, general histories are characterized by a broader perspective featuring the rise and fall of dynasties and the succession of regimes. General histories are limited in vision by regarding the history of China not only merely as the central thread, but the entirety, of the history of the world. This controlling vision is evident in the author's frequent interjections of personal interpretations of events or personalities.

The chronological or annalistic presentation of China through the dynasties is embraced by the two most important general histories, Sima Qian's *Shiji* [Historical Records], written in 90 B.C., and Sima Guang's *Zizhi tongjian* [Comprehensive Mirror As an Aid to Government], completed in 1085.

The *Shiji* relates the history of China from the legendary period to the second century B.C. in five sections: basic-annals, chronological tables, treatises, hereditary houses, and biographies. Although written as a private work and a general history, *Shiji* became known as the first of the twenty-five (or, counted differently, twenty-six) dynastic or Standard Histories of China.

Sima Guang's *Zizhi tongjian* [Comprehensive Mirror As an Aid to Government] is written in the basic annals format and presents a chronological history of China from 403 B.C. to A.D. 959. The *Tongjian* inspired companion volumes of general history and produced sequels that continued the chronological narrative to the later periods. One example is Bi Yuan's *Xu Zizhi tongjian* [Continuation of the Comprehensive Mirror], written in the eighteenth century. The category of general histories sometimes includes institutional histories, or the histories of institutions extending across the dynasties. One example is the *Wenxian tongkao* [General Study of the Literary Remains].

Jennifer W. Jay

See also CHINESE HISTORIOGRAPHY—MODERN GENERAL HISTORIES.

Texts

Shiji. Beijing: Zhonghua shuju, 1959.

Zizhi tongjian. Taibei, Taiwan: Guoxue jiben congshu, 1971.

References

Beasley, W.G., and E.G. Pulleyblank, eds. *Historians of China and Japan*. London: Oxford University Press, 1961.

De Crespigny, Rafe. "Universal Histories." In *Essays on the Sources for Chinese History,* ed. Donald Leslie, Colin Mackerras, and Wang Gungwu. Canberra: Australian National University Press, 1973, 64–70.

Chinese Historiography—Histories of Illegitimate Dynasties (*wei shi*)

A term employed by Chinese historians to refer to histories written in and of illegitimate dynasties. During the late years of the Eastern Jin dynasty (317–420), there were many short-lived small kingdoms set up by various warlords. They called themselves kings and emperors and ordered historians to write the histories of their short-lived dynasties. It was in Ruan Xiaoxu's *Qi lu* [Seven Records] that the term *wei shi* was first coined with reference to such histories. Ruan (479–536) was a great bibliographer in the Southern Liang dynasty (502–557). The term, sometimes written as *bashi* (histories of usurpers), also appears in both the *Jiu Tangshu* [Old Tang History] and the *Xiu Tangshu* [New Tang History], as well as in most works written in the Song dynasty (960–1279). However from the Song dynasty onward, the meaning of the *wei shi* began to attain a broad connotation. It refers not only to any histories that deal with illegitimate dynasties that existed in the fifth and sixth centuries—prior to the unification of the Sui dynasty (581–618)—but also to those in the tenth century when China was once again split among several regional ruling dynasties (including the Ten Kingdoms of the period 907–979).

Q. Edward Wang

Texts

No texts of *wei shi* survive.

References

Han Yu-shan. *Elements of Chinese Historiography.* Hollywood, CA: W.M. Hawley, 1955, 41–42.

Chinese Historiography—Histories of Institutions *(zhi guan)*

Form of historical writing that deals with a variety of official titles used in one or several dynasties. It was often included, categorized in the *Zhi* (Record), in the *Zhengshi* (Standard Histories), or in the histories of institutions such as the *Tongdian, Tongzhi,* and *Tongkao,* written by Du You, Zheng Qiao, and Ma Duanlin, respectively. During the Qing dynasty (1644–1911), it began to be composed as an independent reference book. In the Qianlong years (1736–1795), for example, the emperor ordered historians to compile a seventy-two-volume *Lidai zhiguan biao* [A Table of the Official Titles in All Dynasties], which compares and contrasts the official titles among different dynasties. Some other works of the kind were also completed in the period, such as the *Sanguo zhiguan biao* [A Table of the Official Titles in the Three Kingdoms], which supplies the knowledge that was otherwise unavailable from the Standard Histories of the time.

Q. Edward Wang

See also CHINESE HISTORIOGRAPHY—STANDARD HISTORIES *(ZHENGSHI).*

References

Han Yu-shan. *Elements of Chinese Historiography.* Hollywood, CA: W.M. Hawley, 1955, 59–76.

de Crespigny, Rafe. "Universal Histories." In *Essays on the Sources for Chinese History,* ed. Donald D. Leslie, Colin Mackerras, and Wang Gungwu. Canberra: Australian National University Press, 1973, 64–70.

Chinese Historiography—Local Gazetteers *(Fangzhi)*

Genre of Chinese historical writing focusing on a particular place. Sometimes called local histories, these compilations of heterogeneous information about a particular administrative jurisdiction (province, prefecture, or county) are a unique product of Chinese civilization for which there is no exact Western equivalent. Prior to the twentieth century, their fundamental purpose was to provide information on a locale for the governing officials. The latter always were posted in a province different from their home and in what was tantamount to a foreign society. The gazetteer was to serve them as a vade mecum.

The *Fangzhi* geographical scope is a fixed administrative unit, and the range of material extends to all phenomena within the area; it is precisely this that makes it different from both Western and other Chinese books. Drawn from government records, genealogies, stone steeles, literary collections, random notes, local surveys, and oral interviews, the *Fangzhi* provides data, past and present, on natural history, ethnography, economy, mythology, and even meteorology, as well as the biographies and administrative and political narratives that Western local histories include.

There are between nine and ten thousand different editions of *Fangzhi* stored in libraries in China and around the world. Their fundamental features, format, and contents have not varied greatly over time since the tenth century. They are still being produced, the latest editions emerging from the late 1980s through the 1990s.

Guy Alitto

References

Ai Kai [Guy Alitto]. "Zhongguo fangzhi yu Xifang difangshi de bijiao" [A Comparison of the Chinese Local Gazetteer and Western Local Histories]. *Hanxue yanjiu* [Sinological Studies] 3 (1985): 59–71.

Lai Xinxia. *Zhongguo difangzhi zonglan 1949–1987* [A Survey of Chinese Local Gazetteers, 1949–1987]. Hofei: Huangshan Press, 1988.

Wei Deng. *Fangzhixue* [Local Gazetteers]. Shanghai: Fudan University Press, 1993.

Xue Hong. *Zhongguo fangzhixue gailun* [An Introduction to Chinese Local Gazetteers]. Haerbin: Heilongjiang Provincial Press, 1984.

Chinese Historiography—Manchu

Chinese historical writing in the Manchu language. The Manchu language as a vehicle for Chinese historiography dates from the seventeenth century, and especially from the time when the Manchus conquered China and established the Qing dynasty (1644–1911). There are some archival materials from the preconquest period. For the early Qing, abundant court material survives.

In nature these Manchu historical sources are very similar to Chinese counterparts. Indeed, the largest single category consists of documents that exist both in Chinese and Manchu and, sometimes, Mongolian as well. Examples are the veritable records (*shilu* in Chinese, *yargiyan qooli* in Manchu), which form the basic records of the imperial reigns of China, whether of the Manchu or earlier dynasties, and the basic annals (*benji* in Chinese, *da xergen-i bitxe* in Manchu). Other documents of historical value to survive in both languages are collections of Qing law and imperial edicts, such as the imperial admonitions (*shengxun* in Chinese, *enduringge tačixiyan* in Manchu) of the first ten reigns.

There is also extensive documentation in Manchu for which no Chinese translations are available. Examples of literature in the Manchu language, including poetry and proverbs, survive from as late as the nineteenth century, although it is not possible to make attributions to authors. They are worth the historian's notice for what they reveal about Manchu society, thought and poetic feeling, including attitudes toward fate, and the nature and animals of the steppe territory, which had been their home before the conquest and to some extent remained so afterward.

Translation of official documents into Manchu was discontinued during the course of the Qing dynasty. The Manchu language has gradually gone out of use, with the result that almost all Manchus nowadays speak only Chinese. The Manchu script survives only in a small community of Xibe people who live just outside the city of Yining, capital of Yili in the far northwest of China.

For the earliest period of Qing history, Manchu sources can provide information lacking in Chinese writings. Where a document exists in both languages, knowledge of both languages helps toward understanding. As the Manchus became increasingly assimilated into the people they had conquered, so their historiography also tended to blend into Chinese.

Colin Mackerras

See also MONGOLIAN HISTORIOGRAPHY.

References

Bartlett, Beatrice. "Books of Revelations: The Importance of the Manchu Language Archival Record Books for Research on Ch'ing History." *Late Imperial China* 6.2 (1985): 25–36.

Fletcher, Joseph. "Manchu Sources." In *Essays on the Sources for Chinese History,* ed. Donald D. Leslie, Colin Mackerras, and Wang Gungwu. Canberra: Australian National University Press, 1973, 141–146.

Weiers, Michael, and Giovanni Stary, eds. *Florilegia Manjurica in Memoriam Walter Fuchs.* Wiesbaden, Ger.: Otto Harrassowitz, 1982.

Chinese Historiography—Miscellanea (*Biji* [Pi-chi])

Chinese anthologies, notebooks, travelogues, or collections of random jottings and anecdotes that belong to the area of unofficial or private historiography. Outside regular duties, historians, scholars, essayists, and poets wrote notebook collections known as *yeshi, bieshi* (unofficial histories), and *zaji* (miscellaneous records) on a variety of topics ranging from historical trivia and hearsay to profound analyses and social criticism. An opinion of the moment or the result of meticulous research can both be found in discussions of archaeological excavations, historical and political marginalia, autobiographical and biographical observations, freakish occurrences, local customs, arts, poetry and poetics, and mere gossip.

These anthologies, written or compiled from the fifth century up to the present time, number in the tens of thousands. Many of these are included in *congshu* [collectanea] editions. Diverse in content, uneven in reliability, and sometimes bordering between fact and fiction, the works supplement the official histories and are particularly useful for the construction of social history. Often these notebooks were passed from one generation to the next, then compiled, published, and circulated among friends and colleagues.

Owing to the sheer bulk of this genre, a comprehensive index of the entries in all these collections is not available, although limited indices of about two hundred collections exist. Both traditional and modern historians must read through entire collections to find relevant entries. Many *biji* sources are cited in Chinese historical research, but only two collections, as listed below, have been translated into English.

Jennifer W. Jay

See also CHINESE HISTORIOGRAPHY—LOCAL GAZETTEERS; CHINESE HISTORIOGRAPHY—STANDARD HISTORIES.

Texts

Ding Quanjing. *Songren yishi huibian* [A Compilation of Anecdotes of Song Personalities]. Trans. Chu Djang and Janice C. Djang. Taibei, Taiwan: Taibei Paper Manufactory Press, 1989.

Liu Yiqing. *Shishuo xinyu* [A New Account of Tales of the World]. Trans. Richard B. Mather. Minneapolis: University of Minnesota Press, 1976.

References

Hervouet, Yves, ed. *A Sung Bibliography.* Hong Kong: Chinese University of Hong Kong Press, 1978, 92–116; 279–318.

Nienhauser, William H., Jr. et al. *The Indiana Companion to Traditional Chinese Literature.* Bloomington: Indiana University Press, 1986, 650–652.

Chinese Historiography—Modern General Histories (twentieth-century *tongshi*)

New genre of Chinese historical writing, created to provide narratives of the past promoting cultural and national identity. Influenced by Liang Qichao and Zhang Taiyan, the theory of the new general history combined Chinese values and Western historiographic developments. In 1902, publication of Liang's *Xin shixue* [New History] stimulated discussion of the histories needed for the future in the Qing dynasty crisis and the country's confrontation with Western imperialism. The conception of this history stressed cause and effect, evolutionary change, and the experience of all the people in society, not merely dynastic events and leaders. Zhang Taiyan recommended the study of general history textbooks in educational institutions to strengthen the nation.

The emergence of modern general history in China was influenced by European cultural history and social psychology and the New History taught by James Harvey Robinson at Columbia University. The historian He Bingsong, who was one of Robinson's students, translated Robinson's *The New History* into Chinese in 1925 and wrote about the conception of general history in *Tongshi xinyi* [The New Principles of General History], his adaptation into Chinese of Charles Seignobos's *La Méthode Historique aux Sciences Sociales* (1928). The Chinese histories utilized recently discovered historical sources: bronze and bone inscriptions and archaeological artifacts and previously unused sources like local documents, private collections, and early fiction.

One of the very earliest general histories, by Xia Zengyou (an associate of Liang Qichao), was the *Zhongguo gudai shi* [Ancient History of China], published in 1904. Xia stressed change and discontinuity in China's history. A new view of China as a particular state in a region of the world was presented by Gu Jiegang in *Ben guo shi* [The History of China] (1924), a middle school textbook. Gu made evolutionary change a central theme and placed the ethnic groups, who had strengthened and enriched Chinese culture, in the center of the historical narrative. The *Zhongguo zhexueshi dagang, shangchuan* [Outline of the History of Chinese Philosophy] by Hu Shi (1919), another former Columbia University student, also influenced later histories. In the general histories published in the 1930s and 1940s, the themes of change and connecting links among events, and the broadened view of society, were fundamental. General histories by Deng Zhicheng, Zhang Yinlin, Zhou Gucheng, Qian Mu, Jian Bozan, and Fan Wenlan had the dual purpose of establishing a new theoretical basis for Chinese historiography and providing textbooks that used the past to foster national identity.

Mary G. Mazur

See also CHINESE HISTORIOGRAPHY—GENERAL HISTORIES (PREMODERN AND IMPERIAL), CHINESE HISTORIOGRAPHY—MODERN (POST-MING) AND COMMUNIST; NEW HISTORY.

Texts

Liang Qichao. "Xin shixue [The New Historiography]." In *Yinbing shi heji,wenji* [Collected Works and Essays from the Ice-Drinker's Studio]. Shanghai: Zhonghua bookstore, 1936.

Zhang Binglin. "Ai Qing shi [Lament for Qing History]." *Qiu shu* 59 (1984): 156–162.

References

Duara, Prasenjit. *Rescuing History from the Nation: Questioning Narratives of Modern China.* Chicago: University of Chicago Press, 1995.

Laitinen, Kauko. *Chinese Nationalism in the Late Qing Dynasty: Zhang Binglin As an Anti-Manchu Propagandist.* London: Curzon Press, 1990.

Tang Xiaobing. "Writing a History of Modernity: A Study of the Historical Consciousness of Liang Ch'i-ch'ao." Ph.D. dissertation, Duke University, Durham, NC, 1991.

Chinese Historiography—Modern (post-Ming) and Communist

Survey of historical writing in China since the mid-seventeenth century.

The Qing Dynasty, 1644–1911.

Chinese historiography changed little during the Qing dynasty. As during the Ming dynasty, Qing period "official" history was still in the hands of the government bureaucracy. The forms and formats of documentation upon which it relied remained much the same as in the preceding centuries. The Qing court followed Ming precedents in compilation of "Collected Institutions" *(Huidian),* "Veritable Records" *(Shilu),* and "Universal Statutes" *(Tongdian)* and assembled the usual "Standard History" *(Zhengshi)* for the previous dynasty (the *Mingshi,* completed in 1739). The Qing also sponsored colossal compendium projects, which literally sought to edit and reproduce everything of significance ever written. The *Siku chuanshu* [Complete Library of the Four Treasures], referring to the classics, history, philosophy, and literature was compiled in the 1780s. Yet another example of the increased scale of traditional forms was the abundance of local histories (*fangzhi* or "gazetteers") throughout the Qing; today more than five thousand Qing editions of *Fangzhi* for individual counties, prefectures, and provinces provide a treasure-trove for modern socioeconomic historians. Another form of historical research-cum-documentation that became widespread during the Qing was the "Notebook" (*suibi* or *biji*), the subjects of these random scholarly jottings being primarily historical.

In content, however, much had changed. The decline and fall of the Ming gave rise to an "intellectualist" reaction to the introspective moral tradition of neo-Confucianism, together with a new concern with the technical and institutional management of problems of state and society *(Jingshi).* Some historians now speak of a profound change of consciousness among the literati, from the ontological to the ontic, constituting a fundamental transition in China's intellectual history. These vigorous new intellectual impulses produced a quasi-historicism in several scholars, notably the three Ming loyalists Huang Zongxi (1610–1695), Wang Fuzhi (1619–1692), and Gu Yanwu (1613–1682). Although by the twentieth century these three had come to be regarded primarily as proto-nationalist opponents of imperial despotism and bureaucratic centralization, they were also legitimate historians. They all emphasized careful textual research based on wide-ranging evidence, adopted a critical attitude toward sources, and argued for expedient change relative to the age.

Huang's monumental intellectual history of the Ming, *Mingru xuean,* sought to link neo-Confucian philosophy and the deterioration of the Ming with a peculiarly meticulous objectivity. In his *Du Tongjian lun* [On reading the Universal Mirror] and *Song Lun* [On the Song Dynasty], Wang argued the hypothesis that historically China had been powerful against the barbarians when the provinces were stronger against the central government, and in the process disclaimed the influence of fate, preternatural powers, or mysticism in history; each age had its own characteristics and needs. Gu, an innovator in research methodology, could be considered the founder of the school of empirical research. His principles, exemplified in his prodigious work *Rizhilu* [Record of Daily Knowledge], were the critical and extensive use of evidence and the refining of textual criticism. From his efforts evolved the school of empirical research, which was to dominate Chinese historiography until the twentieth century. The three argued for a kind of historicist relativism, but this remained in tension with their abiding faith in the trans-historical, universal character of the Way *(Dao)* of the sages.

The same can be said of Zhang Xuecheng (1738–1801), who asserted the primacy of history over both philosophy and mere philology, and claimed that history, although a matter of fact, embodied the basic norms of humanity. He also called for greater attention to local history, both in earnestness and in technique. Possibly the upsurge of *Fangzhi* owed something to his stimulus.

The intellectual trend known as the school of empirical research (also known as the school of "Han learning" *[Hanxue]* and "evidentiary research" *[kanzheng]*) not only developed critical philology to extreme sophistication, but also stimulated the development of the auxiliary disciplines of history, such as epigraphy, archaeology, and bibliography. Its systematically skeptical stance toward texts was exemplified by such scholars as Yan Ruozhu (1636–1704) who proved that a part of the *Shujing* [Classic of History] was a forgery. The work of these scholars played a part in the twentieth-century revolution in Chinese historical thinking, often thought to be a mere matter of Western influence. By the end of the nineteenth century, foreign imperialism had demonstrated all too clearly the incapacities of traditional Chinese scholarship and indeed the incapacities of total worldview that had rested on the assumption of China's politico-cultural supremacy.

In historiography, the landmark statement for radical reform was made by Liang Qichao (1873–1929), the most influential Chinese intellectual during the first two decades of this century. In 1902, Liang published several pronouncements on a "new historiography," which clearly revealed the impact of the concept of evolution, especially in Social Darwinist and Spencerian forms. It also showed the impact on Liang of Robert Mackenzie's paean to progress, *The History of the Nineteenth Century,* which had been widely read throughout China. In Liang's formulation of a new Chinese historiography there can be identified several principles that were to remain fundamental to Chinese historiography in this century. The first was an assumption of unilinear progress, with the nation-state as the dominant historical subject; a primary purpose of Liang's new history was to serve Chinese national consciousness and the Chinese nation-state. Secondly, history was to serve as a guide for present action for the public and the polity, a Baedeker for nationalistic reformers. Thirdly, the scope and direction of history must be the people and the society of the nation rather than the monarch. Liang also roundly criticized traditional Chinese historiography while praising that of the West.

In 1904, Liang's fellow reformer and friend, Xia Zengyu, published the first general history of China *Zuixin shixue Zhongguo lishi jiaokeshu* (Shangwu chubanshe, 1904). Intended as a basic textbook, this work clearly reflected Liang's principles. In format, periodization, and style, however, Xia followed Naka Michiyo's *Shina tongshi* [General History of China] (Tokyo, 1888–1890), the first Japanese Western-style history of China. In history as well as other areas of intellectual work, Chinese intellectuals often learned Western concepts and methods through Japan.

The Republic 1912–1949

In the following decade, a Western-style school system was gradually established throughout China, and students went to the West and Japan for advanced study in various academic fields. The process continued through the establishment of a republic in 1912. Led in the main by these returned students, the iconoclastic New Culture and May Fourth movements (1915–1927) intensified both the influence of Western historiography and nationalism. James Harvey Robinson of Columbia University proved an especially strong influence from abroad. His New History expanded the subject matter of history to include all aspects of human life and stressed the use of all the social sciences in the study of history.

By the late 1920s, the discipline of Chinese archaeology was firmly established, and its members proceeded to do spectacular work in prehistory and ancient history. Especially noteworthy was the discovery of Peking Man (1929) and the Anyang excavations of remains of Shang dynasty (1766?–1122? B.C.) royal tombs, which not only proved the existence of that dynasty, but tended to confirm many of the ancient texts that had been held suspect by contemporary professional historians.

The most eminent of these, and one of the most iconoclastic skeptics toward ancient texts, was Gu Jiegang (1895–1980), whose critically analytic *Gushibian* [Discussion of Ancient History] (1926–1941) fundamentally reevaluated China's traditional history and methodology. Gu stressed China's multiethnic, multicultural nature and its popular culture and broader society at the expense of dynasties and heroes. He was so emphatic in his debunking of the myth of a Golden Antiquity of Sage Kings, in fact, that in 1928 the ministry of education deemed Gu's writings unsuited for reading by students.

Although sociologically inclined, Gu was not a typical historian of the times, in that he was neither intensely nationalistic nor a Marxist. By the late 1920s, various shades of Marxism predominated in academia and among littérateurs. With the tenuous conclusion of the Nationalist Party's Northern Expedition to unite China (1928), many intellectuals again looked to history as a guide for present action, but this time they framed their inquiry in Marxist categories. The desire among intellectuals to establish the historical stage at which China had arrived led to the most intense historiographical debates of the early twentieth century, the "Social History Controversy" (ca. 1930–1937). Dozens of participants, relying almost solely on historical materialist terms and premises, concerned themselves with the periodization of China's long past. Almost none of the parties involved was a Communist, but they shared with the Communist Party a faith in "Science," and many historians viewed Marxism as social science par excellence. Throughout the debate, both the actual facts of Chinese socioeconomic history and the concepts of historical materialism were recklessly contorted in attempts to fit China's past into a European procrustean bed. A "consensus by default" was reached whereby the bulk of Chinese history (roughly the two millennia prior to 1840) was consigned to "feudalism." After the establishment of the People's Republic of China in 1949, this conclusion became official orthodoxy.

Through the late 1920s and 1930s, however, the academic discipline of history developed rapidly. Several universities built world-class departments, professional journals were founded, and specialized monographs were published. In 1928, the Nationalist government established a central research academy, the Academia Sinica. Its Institute of History and Philology, headed by the historian Fu Sinian (1896–1950), published a highly respected *Bulletin* and other special publications of high quality.

Like so much that was hopeful in China during the 1930s, however, the historical profession and academia in general were devastated by the Japanese invasion and occupation (1937–1945) and the Communist–Nationalist civil war (1946–1949). Most universities and academic institutions migrated to western China, where they continued to function. Historical scholarship and historical publications continued, albeit greatly diminished. Several general histories of China by Marxists (Zhou Gucheng, Fan Wenlan) and the non-Marxists (Qian Mu) were published and widely read.

The People's Republic 1949–Present

During the first few years after the founding of the People's Republic, Soviet academic books and historical scholarship became models for emulation. Research establishments and universities were based on Soviet models. Soviet historical scholarship was held up as the ideal for emulation. History textbooks were often direct translations of Russian ones. Scholarship and politics had always been intimately connected in China, but during the PRC era the relationship moved to an unprecedented level of intensity. The spring of 1951 saw the first of many campaigns to indoctrinate the intellectuals in the tenets of Marxism–Leninism

and the thought of Mao Zedong. This "thought-reform" process was not limited to historians or even academics, but historians were prominent targets because the Chinese Communist Party considered ideologically correct historical studies as a crucial factor in its legitimization. The new history would have one purpose—to make the Party's seizure of power and progression toward Communism seem inevitable. Within those limits, historians could argue diverse positions on a controversial subject, at least until the Party mandated unanimity.

The required levels of conformity varied over time; campaigns to tighten ideological conformity were followed by periods of relaxation. The most destructive to the historical profession (as well as to intellectuals in general) was the 1958 Anti-Rightist campaign, during which many senior historians were attacked. This kind of pressure drove historians toward inoffensive compendiums of historical sources or to safer antiquarian topics, but the Party continued to demand both discipline and spontaneity, and forced historians to participate in various controversies and address particular topics. Through the 1950s and 1960s the most important topics were peasant rebellions, the origins of capitalism in China, foreign imperialism, and, of course, the inevitable and interminable problem of periodization.

The single most important topic was the peasant rebellion, as it was the most striking evidence of class struggle in Chinese history. Class struggle was in turn the theoretical touchstone in the ideological remolding of the Chinese people. Another subject on which historians expended much effort was the search for Ming and Qing period "sprouts of capitalism." During its two-thousand-year "feudal period," Chinese society should have been evolving, however slowly, in accordance with the Marxist normative stages of societal development, therefore a search was launched (when the Party allowed it) to find "sprouts" of capitalism and bourgeois thought. On the other side of the question, such discoveries would partially exculpate the malevolent imperialist aggressors' heinous transformation of China into a "semicolonial, semifeudal" condition. These controversies were most often "concluded" by a high Party leader's public (and sometimes random) remark.

Senior historians often were less committed to Party orthodoxy than the younger scholars, but everyone employed the same formulas and quotations in their work, however perfunctorily. Even the usual cant, however, could not save historians from the Cultural Revolution, launched in 1966 by an attack on the respected senior historian Wu Han (1909–1960). During this cataclysmic upheaval, historians' work, and sometimes they themselves, were destroyed, their institutions dismantled, and their very raison d'être invalidated.

In 1979, the Party inaugurated a gradual reconstruction of academia. The self-imposed academic isolation of China ended, and thereafter historians were sent to the West for further study. By the late 1980s, thousands of history students and scholars were in history departments abroad, hundreds of history books had been translated into Chinese, dozens of international academic exchanges and contacts had been established, and myriad foreign historiographical constructions explored. Older historians, perhaps through a combination of trepidation and habit, tended to retain orthodox modes of analysis and expression, while younger ones tended to be more adventuresome.

Another period of severe repression followed the massacre of demonstrators at Tiananmen Square in June 1989. Party secretaries in academic institutions called upon historians to write and teach only Marxist–Leninist history, but in a few years, the situation had evolved back to that of the late 1980s. Today, although Party historiographical orthodoxy remains dominant on the surface, and still dictates educational historical curricula, at the centers of historical research and among advanced researchers historiographical heterogeneity predominates.

Guy Alitto

See also CHINESE HISTORICAL THOUGHT—ANCIENT TO MING.

Texts

Huang Zongxi. *Mingru xuean* [Studies of Ming Confucianists]. Beijing: Zhonghua shuju, 1985.

Ku Jiegang et al. *Gushibian* [Debates on Ancient History]. 7 vols. Beijing and Shanghai: Zhicheng yinshuguan, 1926–1941.

Ku Yanwu. *Ruzhilu* [Record of Knowledge Gained Day by Day]. Taibei, Taiwan: Pingping chubanshe, 1974.

Liang Qichao. "Xin shixue [The New Historiography]." In *Yinbing shi heji,wenji* [Collected Works and Essays from the Ice-Drinker's Studio]. Shanghai: Zhonghua bookstore, 1936, 4, 9.

Mackenzie, Robert. *The History of the Nineteenth Century.* London: Thomas Nelson and Sons, 1880.

Mingshi [History of the Ming Dynasty]. Ed. Zhang Tingyu et al. n.p. 1739.

Wang Fu-chih. *Chuan-shan chuan shu* [Collected works of Wang Fuzhi]. Changsha: Yuelu Publishing, 1988.

Xia Zengyou. *Zuixin shixue Zhongguo lishi jiaokeshu* [Chinese History Textbook Based on the Newest Historiography]. Shanghai: Shangwu chubanshe, 1904. Republished as *Zhongguo gudai shi* [History of Ancient China]. Shanghai: Shangwu Publishing, 1933.

References

Beasley, W.G., and E.G. Pulleyblank, eds. *Historians of China and Japan.* London: Oxford University Press, 1961.

Chang Meng-lun. *Zhonguguo shixue shi* [History of Chinese Historiography]. Lanzhou: Gansu People's Provincial Press, 1983–1986.

Elman, Benjamin A. *From Philosophy to Philology: Intellectual and Social Aspects of Change in Late Imperial China.* Cambridge, MA: Harvard University Council on East Asian Studies, 1984.

Feuerwerker, Albert, ed. *History in Communist China.* Cambridge, MA: MIT Press, 1968.

Nivison, David S. *The Life and Thought of Chang Hsueh-ch'eng (1738–1801).* Stanford, CA: Stanford University Press, 1966.

Schneider, Laurence A. *Ku Chieh-kang and China's New History: Nationalism and the Quest for Alternative Traditions.* Berkeley: University of California Press, 1971.

Yin Da, ed. *Zhongguo shixue fazhan shi* [History of the Development of Chinese Historiography]. Zhengzhou: Zhongzhou Press, 1985.

Chinese Historiography—Records of the Beginnings and Ends of Events *(Jishi Benmuo [chi-shih pen-mo])*

One of the three major types of traditional Chinese historiography, this developed chronologically somewhat later than the chronicle or the Standard History; the first work produced in this style was the *Tongjian jishi benmo (T'ung-chien chi-shih pen-mo)* [Beginnings and Ends of the Events in the Comprehensive Mirror] by Yuan Shu (1131–1205), which was published in 1174. Works in this style were seldom original, generally amounting to the rearrangement of existing works whose contents were reorganized chronologically on the basis of the course of major events. Nevertheless, in its highlighting of cause-and-effect, the genre as a whole signified an advance in Chinese historical consciousness. Many

Chinese critics of historical writing indeed hailed it as an ideal way to write history. The *Jishi Benmuo* style was especially popular during the Ming (1368–1644) and the Qing (Ch'ing) (1644–1911), and a number of works were produced. Noteworthy among them are the *Songshi jishi benmuo (Sung-shih chi-shih pen-mo)* [Beginnings and Ends of the Events of the History of the Song] by Feng Qiyuan (Feng Ch'i-yuan) and Chen Bangzhan (Ch'en Pang-chan), the *Yuanshi jishi benmuo (Yuan-shih chi-shih pen-mo)* [Beginnings and Ends of the Events in the History of the Yuan] by Chen Bangzhan, and the *Mingshi jishi benmuo (Ming-shih chi-shih pen-mo)* [Beginnings and Ends of the Events in the History of the Ming] by Gu Yingtai (Ku Ing-t'ai).

John Lee

See also CHINESE HISTORIOGRAPHY—CHRONICLE/ ANNAL FORM HISTORIES; CHINESE HISTORIOGRAPHY— STANDARD HISTORIES.

References

Beasley, W.G., and E.G. Pulleyblank, eds. *Historians of China and Japan.* London: Oxford University Press, 1961.

Han Yu-shan. *Elements of Chinese Historiography.* Hollywood, CA: W.M. Hawley, 1955.

Chinese Historiography—Standard Histories (*Zhengshi*)

Set of twenty-six texts that constitute the official history of China, dynasty by dynasty; also known as dynastic histories. In general, each dynasty demonstrated its receipt of Heaven's Mandate by writing the history of its predecessor. The earliest in the series, the *Shiji* [Historical Records] by Sima Qian (ca. 90 B.C.), was a universal history that recounted Chinese history from its legendary beginnings to Sima's own day and was undertaken as a private enterprise, but thereafter most Standard Histories focused on single dynasties and received official sponsorship. From the Tang dynasty on, they were compiled by large government bureaus. Eventually twenty-five works were accepted into the Standard Histories, and the completion of the *Draft History of Qing* in 1927 (and a competing Taiwanese version of 1962) brought the total to twenty-six. The time periods covered by these texts range from twenty-four years (Northern Zhou dynasty) to 319 years (Song dynasty), and the works themselves vary from thirty-six chapters (*History of Chen*) to 536 chapters (*Draft History of Qing*). All together, they cover Chinese history from 841 B.C.

to A.D. 1911, and in the uniform *Zhonghua shuju* edition, they comprise nearly 100,000 pages.

The Standard Histories share a common form, adapted from the *Shiji* and known as *jizhuan ti* (annals–biographies form). Each history begins with a section of annals that provides a year-by-year account of the emperors, and this is balanced by a series of biographies that covers the same time period, but focuses on individuals. Although most of the information in the Standard Histories was copied from earlier sources, almost every chapter concludes with a few paragraphs of personal comment by the compilers. In addition, eleven of the histories include chronological tables, and nineteen include treatises on subjects such as ritual, the calendar, astronomy, natural omens, penal law, fiscal law, administrative geography, and official posts. Biographies make up over half of the chapters in the Standard Histories, and together they provide information on some fifty thousand individuals. Frequently several biographies are grouped into a single thematic chapter devoted to Confucian scholars, loyal officials, chaste widows, and so on.

While early Standard Histories were the work of individuals or families, from the Tang dynasty on they were generally the product of the Bureau of Historiography. These court-appointed historians not only compiled the history of the preceding dynasty, they also kept the records that would eventually become the primary sources for the standard history of their own time. Both a Court Diary and an Administrative Record were edited at the end of each reign into a Veritable Record *[shilu]*, which was used as the basis for the annals section of the next Standard History. However, the production of the Standard Histories was not always smooth. In some cases rival compilations competed for official status, records were lost or destroyed, and political turmoil resulted in long delays. For instance, the present *History of Jin* was commissioned by an emperor some 225 years after the end of that dynasty, and the *New History of Yuan* was completed in 1920, about 550 years after the original *History of Yuan* was hastily compiled in a single year at the beginning of the Ming dynasty (the Tang, Five Dynasties, and Yuan each have two histories included among the Standard Histories).

The Standard Histories are based on "mandate of heaven" theories, which assumed the ideal of a unified China under one heaven-sanctioned emperor. History was conceived as a cyclical series of dynasties, each founded by a strong, virtuous hero-rebel who overthrew his corrupt predecessor and gained heaven's approval. Unfortunately,

Chinese history is not so simple, and when the Standard Histories divide the past into discrete segments, they often distort the record. Naturally, they magnify the faults of the previous dynasty and give scant attention to trends and factors that continued through dynastic breaks. Their focus is resolutely on the court, so much so that it is often difficult to distinguish regional patterns, and historians were forced to decide just who held the mandate during periods when China was divided among several rival regimes.

The Standard Histories have been criticized for their cut-and-paste format; sparse, moralistic analysis; stereotyped figures; omission of social history; and Confucian biases (for example, they slight eunuchs, barbarians, and popular religious movements); and some have questioned the ability of the bureau historians to escape political pressure as they collected information about contemporary people and policy disputes. Yet despite their limitations, the Standard Histories remain our primary source for the study of imperial China. They provide a continuous and extensive account of China, and when checked against independent sources, their information is usually accurate, at least with regard to what their compilers chose to include. In addition, several of the histories are regarded as masterpieces of Chinese prose, and their style has been imitated by Chinese scholars into the twentieth century.

Grant R. Hardy

See also BAN GU; CHINESE HISTORIOGRAPHY—CHRONICLE/ANNAL FORM HISTORIES; SIMA QIAN.

Texts

Frankel, H.H. *Catalogue of Translations from the Chinese Dynastic Histories for the Period 220–960.* Berkeley: University of California Press, 1957.

References

Leslie, Donald D., Colin Mackerras, and Wang Gungwu, eds. *Essays on the Sources for Chinese History.* Canberra: Australian National University Press, 1973, 42–63.
Twitchett, Denis. *The Writing of Official History under the T'ang.* Cambridge, Eng.: Cambridge University Press, 1992.
Yang Lien-sheng. "The Organization of Chinese Official Historiography: Principles and Methods of the Standard Histories from the T'ang through the Ming Dynasty." In *Historians of China and Japan,* ed. W.G. Beasley and E.G. Pulleyblank. London: Oxford University Press, 1961, 44–59.

Ch'oe Nam-sŏn (1890–1957)

Korean scholar, journalist, publisher, and historian. He briefly studied in Japan, returned to Korea to run a printing company, and published the first Korean modern magazine, *Sonyŏn* [The Youth] (1908). He drafted the Korean Declaration of Independence (1919), which led to his imprisonment for about two years. In his later career, however, he tended to support Japanese rule of Korea: he became a member of writers for *Chosŏnsa* [History of Korea], which had been designed to justify Japanese colonialism. After independence (1945) he was prosecuted and was found guilty of betraying the country. In *Tankun Ron* [Discussions on Tankun] (1926) and in *Asi Chosŏn* [The Dawning of Korean History] (1926) he comprehensively explored history, folklore, religion, and historical geography. He reproduced many Korean classics to preserve the "Chosŏn spirit" and compiled and edited old poems. Most of all, he is recognized as the first modern Korean scholar to have made a serious study of Korean folklore. Among his theses, he maintained that the Baekdu mountain, where Tankun (the founder of the Korean nation) resided, was the true historical center of east Asian culture.

Minjae Kim

Texts

Asi Chosŏn. Kyŏngsŏng: Tongyang Sŏwŏn, 1927.
Chosŏn Yŏksa [History of Korea]. Seoul: Dongmyŏngsa, 1931.

References

Song Ch'an-ho. *Hankuk Hyŏndae Inmul Saron* [Biographical History of Modern Korea]. Seoul: Han'gilsa, 1984.

Chŏng Inbo (1892–1950)

Korean scholar, historian, journalist, and patriot. Under the Japanese colonial regime Chŏng Inbo participated in the underground independence movement and experienced imprisonment. He held academic positions until his abduction by the North Korean army during the Korean War (1950). Historiographically, he was the heir to Sin Ch'ae-ho's earlier nationalist interpretation of Korean history, and by his own admission, he studied history in order to rectify perceived distortions of Korean history by pro-Japanese scholars. Chŏng advanced the study of *sirhak* (practical learning), and the comprehensive study of all aspects of Korean culture can be said virtually to have begun with him. He subscribed to an idealist philosophy of history wherein "Soul" was the prime moving force of history; the discovery of their inherent "soul," through study of the past, could permit Koreans to maintain a sense of identity even at a time when they had lost their independence. In his major work, *Chosŏnsa Yŏn'gu* [Studies on the History of Korea] (1946), he argued that Tankun, mythic founder of the first Korean state, was a real historical figure, that Korea had not been a Chinese or Japanese colony in its early history, and that the territory of the early Korean states had included Manchuria.

Minjae Kim

Texts

Chosŏnsa Yŏn'gu. 2 vols. Seoul: Seoul Sinmunsa, 1946–1947.

References

Hong Isŏp. "Chŏng Inbo Ron [Studies on Chŏng Inbo]." In *Hankuksaŭi Pangbŏp.* Seoul: Tamgudang, 1962.

Chŏng In-ji (1396–1478)

Korean historian and scholar. Chŏng flourished during the reign of King Sejong (1418–1450), probably the greatest of the Yi dynasty monarchs, under whom the neo-Confucian Korean bureaucratic state and culture reached a pinnacle. In 1420 King Sejong reestablished the Chiphyŏnjŏn (Royal Academy of Scholarship), Chŏng being one of its most distinguished leaders. Possibly its greatest achievement, in which Chŏng was closely involved, was the invention of the Korean script called *han'gul,* originating in 1443 and still universally used among Koreans. Chŏng was the chief compiler of the *Koryŏsa* [History of Koryŏ], completed in 1451. It is a detailed history of the Koryŏ kingdom (918–1392), written in the Confucian Chinese style complete with court annals, monographs on such topics as astronomy, geography, the rites, music, chronological tables, and numerous biographies of prominent men, with the whole being organized in strict chronological fashion and designed to establish the official account of the preceding dynasty as well as promote Confucian orthodoxy. It represents the peak of the "annals-and-biography" style of historical scholarship in Korea. In 1955 a photographic reprint of a woodblock version was published by Yonsei University.

Colin Mackerras

Texts

No easily accessible edition of Chŏng's works exists.

Chŏng Yagyong [Chŏng Ta-san] (1762–1836)

Korean historian, geographer, and encyclopedist. Chŏng Yagyong passed the civil service examination in 1738, but his career suffered because of the embracing by some of his family members of the banned Roman Catholic faith. Banished between 1801 and 1818, he subsequently retired from active life. Among the most influential of the Korean intellectuals of the nineteenth century, Chŏng made major contributions to institutional history and to historical geography. His trilogy of institutional history, *Kyŏngse yup'yo* [Testament on Managing the World], *Mongmin simsŏ* [Essentials of Governing People], and *Hŭmhŭm sinsŏ* [A New Treatise on Punishments], addressed, respectively, central government, local government, and criminal justice. His chief achievement in historical geography was *Abang kang'yŏk ko* [The History of the Boundaries of Our Country].

John Lee

Texts

Chŏng Yag-yong chakp'umjip [Collected Works]. Py'ŏngyang, N. Korea: Munye Ch'ulpansa, 1990–.
Kugyŏk Tasan simunjip [Selections]. Seoul: Minjok Munhwa Ch'ujinhoe, 1982.

References

Kwahagwŏn Chŏrhak Yŏnguso. *Chŏng Ta-san yŏngu* [Studies on Chŏng Ta-san]. Seoul: Hanmadang, 1989.

Christianity, Views of History in

Understandings of both history and historical inquiry that Christians derive from the ultimate meaning they find in Jesus of Nazareth (ca. 4 B.C.–A.D. 30), whom they call the Christ, mediated by their belonging to the community of his followers known as the Christian church. Christianity engenders intense historical consciousness and multiple attachments to history, connections that even the most other-worldly and intellectually abstract Christians cannot sever without removing themselves from the religion. Christians take their spiritual nourishment above all from certain events in the life of Jesus, especially his birth in Bethlehem in Judea to Mary of the lineage of King David of Israel, his death by crucifixion under the rule of Rome in Jerusalem, and his burial and resurrection. They learn of Jesus from early works of Christian historiography, created within the first Christian communities: the Gospels according to

Matthew, Mark, Luke, and John, and the Acts of the Apostles. Christians have created many diverse and even opposing views of history during the first two millennia of the Christian era, yet their views have certain features in common. They generate these views primarily within their worship and secondarily within their theological discussions and their historical writings.

Their views of history are epitomized by the name Jesus Christ, the primal Christian creed, and an interpretation of history. By this name Christians connect him with the history of ancient Israel, proclaim him to be the anointed one, the long-awaited Messiah, and disclose the meaning of history, which they find in his coming for the salvation of the world. In their liturgy they announce the mystery of faith with a sweeping review of his life—past, present, and future: "Christ has died, Christ is risen, Christ will come again." In the Nicene and the Apostles' creeds, their two most widely used symbols of the faith, whose structure marks the Trinity, they rehearse a sacred world history. They begin with God's creation of the heavens and the earth, proceed to the life of Jesus, continue with the appearance of the Holy Spirit, followed by the church, and culminate in the future return of Jesus, the resurrection of the faithful, and life everlasting. They recite repeatedly the prayer of Jesus, known as the Lord's Prayer, which construes history as the fulfillment of creaturely needs, the overcoming of sin, and the coming of the kingdom of God. Through baptism and the Eucharist, also called the Mass and the Lord's Supper, the two universally accepted sacraments in the church, they identify with and reenact the death and resurrection of Jesus. They gather as communities especially on Sunday, the day representing the resurrection of Jesus and the creation of the world. They reexperience the life of Jesus within the annual liturgical cycle of the church. They read aloud the Scriptures of the Old and New Testament and elaborate upon them in sermons, art, and songs. The Scriptures tell of events in many cultures covering at least two thousand years, recount history as the medium of sin and salvation, disclose the acts of God in history, and represent humans as historical agents who are called to live their lives in love of God and neighbor. Such worship behooves Christians to interpret history at each hearing of Scripture, within each Eucharist and baptism, with each confession of faith, in each sermon.

By these means Christians unfold a view of history that is both linear and cyclical. They envision history as irreversibly ongoing from the beginning in creation to the fall into sin, the redemption found in Jesus Christ, and the end at the revelation of the new heavens and the new earth. They find the meaning of history in the incarnation of God in Jesus Christ and the coming of the commonwealth of God. But they also disclose history as recurrent in that the perfection of creation at the beginning returns to the perfection of re-creation at the end, and the first advent of Jesus yields to his return at the end of history. This great cycle converts the world from the Garden of Eden into the New Jerusalem. Throughout history renewal follows disintegration, healing occurs repeatedly, restoration results from repentance and forgiveness, and Christians annually and on sacramental occasions recapitulate the life of Jesus and retell the story of their salvation. Gradually Christians devised a calendar, reckoning time at first A.D. *(anno domini)* from the birth of Jesus and later B.C. (before Christ). As Western societies came to dominate much of the world during the last five hundred years, Christian ways of viewing history, including the Christian calendar, became pervasive.

Nurtured by their worship, writers arose easily over the ages wherever Christian communities were found around the globe—India, Ethiopia, Armenia, France, Russia, Papua–New Guinea, Canada, and elsewhere—to construct histories stimulated by the Christian references. A vast and diverse tradition of Christian historiography emerged that, in the aggregate, included a focus not only on ecclesiastical history, but on political, intellectual, and social history as well. The histories displayed common features of a Christian view of historical inquiry. They honored the specificity of events and appreciated details. They connected their particular histories to universal history and nurtured a sense of the whole. They expressed heightened awareness of human sin and salvation and good and evil. They freely intermingled the acts of God and human deeds and referred to both divine and human agency in their historical explanations. They respected human freedom to will and act, even as they acknowledged the limits imposed on human actions by circumstances, the nature of reality, and God's sovereign providence. They disclosed the meaning of history.

Since World War II in particular, a renewal of Christian views of history has influenced the church, intellectual discourse, and historical study. Christians who are also historians came to regard their work as a vocation through which they serve the church and the world, while admitting their own limited competences and refusing to absolutize anything within creation. Their histories continued to bear the traditional features of a Christian view of historical inquiry, except for at least one striking change. The Christian character of the histories became entirely implicit as the historians removed from the history books all explicit references to God's action and the historians' own Christian theology. These references passed into a distinct and parallel literature containing reflections by historians on history and theology. In the histories themselves, the historians replaced the references to God with explicit acknowledgment of the validity of human spirituality, faith, and religion in history. Instead of explanations that included divine agency, they restricted themselves to the human and natural factors involved. These they elaborated, displaying a preference for multifactoral explanations rather than monocausal ones, and honoring the complexity, diversity, and interaction of human beings as well as of the natural world. Readers could tell that the histories were informed by a Christian view of history either by paying close attention to the emphases and omissions in the text in comparison with other approaches, or by seeking the historian's explicit views elsewhere.

C.T. McIntire

See also CHRONICLES; ECCLESIASTICAL HISTORY; JUDAISM; TIME.

Texts

The Holy Bible. New Revised Standard Version. New York: Oxford University Press, 1989.
Leith, John H., ed. *Creeds of the Churches.* Chicago: Aldine, 1963.
McIntire, C.T., ed. *God, History, and Historians.* New York: Oxford University Press, 1977.
———— and Ronald Wells, eds. *History and Historical Understanding.* Grand Rapids, MI: W.B. Eerdmans, 1984.
Thompson, Bard, ed. *Liturgies of the Western Church.* New York: New American Library, 1974.

References

Breisach, Ernst. *Historiography: Ancient, Medieval, and Modern.* Second ed. Chicago: University of Chicago Press, 1994.
Butterfield, Herbert, *The Origins of History.* New York: Basic Books, 1981.

Christine de Pizan (1363–ca. 1434)

French woman of letters. The daughter of a university professor of astrology, she was born in Venice and moved to France in 1368 after her father secured an appointment at the French royal court. After her father and husband both died, Christine was left to care for her three children, her mother, and a niece. She turned to writing to support her household, producing poetry, an autobiography, a biography of King Charles V of France, and various treatises on morality, government, and military strategy. In 1403 she published a world history in verse, *Livre de la Mutacion de Fortune* [Book of the Change of Fortune]. Her 1405 *Livre de la Cité des Dames* [Book of the City of Ladies], imagined conversations with historically famous women. Wide reading in French and Italian, including translations from classical languages, nourished both her historical understanding and her prose style.

Joseph M. McCarthy

Texts

The Book of the City of Ladies. Trans. Earl Jeffrey Richards. New York: Persea Books, 1982.
Le Livre de la Mutacion de Fortune, par Christine de Pisan. Ed. S. Solente. 4 vols. Paris: Société des anciens textes français, 1959–1968.

Reference

Willard, Charity Cannon. *Christine de Pizan: Her Life and Work.* New York: Persea Books, 1984.

Chronicles, African

See AFRICAN HISTORIOGRAPHY—CHRONICLES.

Chronicles, Ancient (prehellenic)

A set of mostly Babylonian and Assyrian texts in fragmentary condition whose main series begins in the mid-eighth century B.C. and continues until the early third century B.C. Other specialized and isolated examples may date as early as the tenth century B.C.

Extant chronicles can best be characterized as records of events written in the third person and ordering events by their chronology. In general, they do not offer explanations for their factual entries and provide little sense of continuity of the events they describe. The major Babylonian series can be divided into two groups; the Early Babylonian and Late Babylonian; the division is made at 539 B.C., the year of the Persian conquest of Babylon. The first series is related by unusual and specific vocabulary, though the structure of their introductory and transitional phraseology shows that they form a single group with the Late Babylonian chronicles, which are in essence a continuation of the earlier texts. The main series begins with the reign of the Babylonian king Nabunasir (747–734 B.C.). The reasons for the commencement of the series at this time are not totally clear but may be connected to a greater interest in events. This reign marked the beginning of the keeping of more precise astronomical records in the form of "Astronomical Diaries" that may have served as a source for the chronicles. The diaries cover one-half of a year, divided into months, and contain short notices of military affairs, political events, and market prices, as well as astronomical and meteorological observations. The chronicles are related in form to other Babylonian historical genres such as date lists, king lists, and eponym lists. It is often difficult to draw a firm dividing line. It may be the combination of the king-list form with the information available from the "Astronomical Diaries" that lies behind the development of the chronicle form in Babylonia and Assyria. Unfortunately, the five Assyrian chronicles extant are in such a fragmentary condition that they can provide little help in tracing the tradition in the north. In any case the chronicles are a form of local history, limited with rare exceptions to events either in Babylonia or of immediate importance to the inhabitants.

In addition to the main series, there exist a number of more specialized chronicles. The "Religious Chronicle" begins in the late eleventh century and continues to the mid-tenth. It focuses on interruptions in the celebration of the Akitu or Babylonian New Year's festival and various unusual events such as the entry of wild animals into Babylon. The "Weidner Chronicle," which covers the last half of the third millennium focuses on the relation between the chief Babylonian god, Marduk, and various kings. A further unusual feature of this document is the use of direct speech, which is wholly atypical of the chronicle form.

In addition to chronicles that focus on religious affairs, several are clearly political in nature. The "Esarhaddon Chronicle" covering the events of that Assyrian king's reign (680–669 B.C.) reworks the events recorded in the main Babylonian series to present Esarhaddon's kingship in a favorable light. This may be connected with his restoration of Babylon. More unusual is the "Synchronistic Chronicle," a strongly biased account of relations between the kings of Assyria and Babylonia from the first half of the fifteenth century B.C. until the end of the eighth century B.C. It is divided into sections covering an Assyrian king and his Babylonian contemporary and omitting kings who had no involvement in Babylonia. It is

a justification of Assyrian supremacy achieved by an arbitrary selection of facts and the invention of a fictitious boundary used to cast the Babylonians as transgressors. The chronicles that lie outside of the main series lack the objectivity and accuracy characteristic of it, but do show a greater readiness to use more varied source material such as historical epic and omen collections.

The chronicles are arranged by king, with individual entries subdivided by regnal years. Often the length of the reign is noted. Some chronicles name the place of burial. Within each regnal year these chronicles give the month and the precise day of the event noted. The material for the most part consists of a simple statement about military campaigns, references to internal political happenings, religious affairs, and events of court history that focus on the king and the royal family. The tone is remarkably objective and military defeats and other Babylonian failures are related impartially. It is a remarkable exception to the general tendency in the ancient Near East to use historical material for propagandistic purposes, despite the fact that the king and his court stand at the center of these texts.

The Mesopotamian achievement in this area is striking. No other Near Eastern culture independently produced a comparable genre.

Michael M. Sage

Texts

Grayson, A.K., ed. *Assyrian and Babylonian Chronicles.* Locust Valley, NY: J.J. Augustin, 1975.

Smith, Sidney, ed. *Babylonian Historical Texts Relating to the Capture and Downfall of Babylon.* London: Methuen, 1924.

References

Dentan, R.C., ed. *The Idea of History in the Ancient Near East.* New Haven, CT: Yale University Press, 1955.

Grayson, A.K. "Assyria and Babylonia." *Orientalia* 49 (1980): 140–189.

Van Seters, J. *In Search of History.* New Haven, CT: Yale University Press, 1983.

Chronicles, Medieval

Typical historical records of the millennium or so that separates the recognizable histories of the late Roman Empire from those of the Renaissance. In that long period chronicles were written throughout Europe, and they appeared in many forms, from simple annals to sequential narratives in which events are connected and explained.

The annal is a plain, factual statement. In an oral culture it stood somewhat as a charter stood to the transfer of property that it recorded. Beside the action itself, it had little significance; but it served as a memorial for a later time. The distinction between annal, chronicle, and history has been likened to the ore, the refined metal, and the finished ornament, and the sixth to the thirteenth centuries shows a rough progress in the sophistication of medieval historical writing. Not that it was uniform: for already in the first half of the eighth century Bede wrote his *Ecclesiastical History of the English People* in Northumbria at the geographical margin of the civilized world. It was Bede, in this and his purely chronological works, who caused the reckoning of time before and after Christ's incarnation to be generally accepted.

As a record of past events, chronicles have their place beside the other kinds of evidence that constitute history for a modern reader. Even in the simplest entry the chronicler selects and so may influence historical interpretation more than collections of charters and the mounting tide of administrative records. These and biographies are not included in these comments. Chroniclers sometimes formed their narratives around the careers of secular or religious rulers, separately or in sequence; many accepted miracles unquestioningly; but biographies, with their roots in classical models as well as hagiography, are rare in the medieval period and form a separate genre.

From A.D. 450 to 1200, when literacy in Europe was exceptional, chronicles were written by monks for monks. For most of that time all monasteries in western Christendom, except the Irish, followed the Rule of St. Benedict, and the Irish monks too had their own tradition of annals. The earliest annals appeared in the Easter tables of liturgical books as isolated records that identified different years: the death of a leading figure, a natural phenomenon, a political disaster. Easter being a moveable feast governed by the lunar calendar, these tables were essential to orderly prayer in Western christendom. The annal, therefore, is connected with the inevitable attention that Benedictines were required to give to the passage of time in the unceasing round of their daily offices. It provided here and there a point of reference.

In the course of centuries annals became more dense as entries became more frequent and more complete. By ca. 1000, the typical monastic chronicle may not be very different from the rarer thematic and consecutive histories that had been written in the centuries since the fall of Rome in

the west, such as those by Bede or Gregory of Tours or Liudprand of Cremona. All the Germanic invaders of Rome, Goths, Sueves, Vandals, Franks, Lombards, Anglo-Saxons, and Saxons remaining in Germany, had been provided with one or more representative chronicles grown out of annals, and later the Slavs to their east were similarly served. Except for being written in the vernacular and not Latin, the *Anglo-Saxon Chronicle* is typical. Fostered by the West Saxon dynasty from the time of Alfred, it appeared in different versions from Winchester and Canterbury and also from Worcester and York, beyond Wessex's border. Eventually a single edition continued to be written until 1154 by the monks of Peterborough. While there was no general reading public for the *Anglo-Saxon Chronicle* and its like, it nevertheless promoted the reputation of the people or the kingdom, just as later the crusading chronicles advertised the glory to be won in the Holy Land.

The impact of feudal order in principalities under firmer rule, reforms in papacy and church, restored trade and revitalized towns, the leaven of cathedral schools, and, finally, the beginning of universities combined between 1000 and 1200 to consolidate both the quality and the number of chronicles. For the most part they still originated in monasteries; but by the close of those two centuries secular clerks had begun to contribute. The Anglo-Norman kingdom was particularly productive of well-informed and reflective chronicles. Orderic Vitalis working in Normandy and William of Malmesbury in England both wrote reliable political narratives of their times as parts of a larger coverage. Both men were of mixed heritage and both were monks. Earlier, the Conquest itself had been described by the Normans, William of Poitiers, and William of Jumièges; later English chroniclers like William of Newburgh and the seculars, Henry of Huntingdon, Ralph de Diceto, and Roger of Howden (Roger de Hoveden) continued to provide a rich historical record, which persisted through the thirteenth century. Fewer, but equally competent, writers provided the history of the German Empire, particularly for the War of Investitures, and of the expanding Capetian monarchy.

Once sequential narrative replaced unconnected annals, a typical monastic chronicle began with the creation of the world and aimed to continue to the present. This was natural in a culture grounded on the Bible and its providential dispensation. A chronicler's narrative had independent value only for his own time and his own place. For earlier periods existing accounts were appropriated without acknowledgment. This expressed monkish

C

modesty: respect for the authority of the past and its records, and the instinct for anonymity in the face of such a legacy. Authorship also was often collective, passed down the years through a succession of continuators. Even the sequence of chronicles from the abbey of St. Alban, close to London, which began at creation and provided first-hand reports on John's reign to Henry VI's, has periods of anonymous authorship in its long tradition. Even the most opinionated of these writers, Roger of Wendover, Matthew Paris, and Thomas Walsingham, still took the calendar year as the unit of their narrative. At the abbey of Saint-Denis, just outside Paris, a sequence of chronicling monks served effectively, and sometimes by name, as historiographers royal. Because of their location, both St. Alban and Saint-Denis had ready access to royal officials, and these chronicles regularly incorporated official documents into their story. Other convents obtained them more casually as the royal administration itself, or a representative, moved through the country. As a result of their close association with the court, the chronicles from Saint-Denis enhanced the reputation of the king's government, from Abbot Suger's *Life of Louis the Fat* (Louis VI) to the accounts of the reigns of Louis IX, his son, and his grandson by Guillaume de Nangis. The prejudices of the St. Alban writers were just as obvious and, finally, just as influential (they provided the remote ground for the later Whig tradition in modern English historiography): but they took the side of the baronial critics of John and Henry III, or of Richard II a century later. They blamed their rulers for the cost of bad advice, often from foreigners, whether in the government of the realm or the church; and in the fourteenth century rebellious serfs and unlicensed preachers spreading heresy incurred their criticism.

Monks did not dominate historical writing in all regions before A.D. 1200. In the Byzantine Empire a tradition of lay persons writing history continued from the mature, frequently Waspish observations of Procopius on the politics of Justinian to the memorial of her father's reign by Anna Comnena at the time of the First Crusade. During that eastern pilgrimage feudal crusaders were infected by that independent lay outlook: there was no available model for them to follow in recording those distant events, and crusading chronicles were often written by laymen.

In the 1140s Otto, bishop of Freising, returned from the Second Crusade and wrote a world chronicle, *The History of Two Cities*. Like others of its kind, it offered the story of the providential ordering of time in six historical ages from Adam to the Second Coming, the last naturally being incomplete. Otto's world was likewise under the dispensation of the last of the four kingdoms prescribed in the prophecies of the Book of Daniel: this had always been understood to be Rome, although the German Empire now presided over its government, succeeding the Byzantines and the Franks. This framework originated with Augustine and had been popularized by Orosius in the fifth century. In worldly terms, Otto's interpretation of history was bound to generate an outlook that was apocalyptic and pessimistic. His book, it seems, attracted little attention at the time, except that it was read by Emperor Frederick I, his nephew; and Frederick asked him to write an official history of his ongoing reign.

Otto's historical work is significant for, as a close relative of emperors, educated in Paris, Cistercian monk and bishop, as well as author, his career represents a watershed in medieval historiography, connected to the changes between 1000 and 1200 already noted. The historical detachment of the cloister began to give place to histories by men with greater involvement in current affairs; and knowledge of history began to spread to wider circles, eventually touching laymen. Monasteries continued to produce chronicles: St. Alban and Saint-Denis were only leaders among hundreds from Compostella to Kiev; but the remote and recent past increasingly appealed to an audience in the secular world. In the second quarter of the fourteenth century a monk of Chester, Ranulf Higden, also wrote a world history, compiled like the others from sources available in his convent's library. His *Polychronicon* served as an encyclopedia of the past and included a valuable survey of the geography of Britain. In this case the large number of surviving manuscripts, mainly but not wholly from religious and academic institutions, suggests that Ranulf's compilation was highly regarded in late-medieval England. As the basis for continuing chronicles of current events elsewhere in England it claimed the field, apart from the established tradition at St. Alban's and among a new form of historical writing, town chronicles. The latter appeared all over Europe: the best show the merchant pride of Florence, say, Nuremberg or Novgorod as well as London in the late Middle Ages. Chivalric histories recording the Hundred Years War mirror another social group prominent in the period. Froissart, a knight from Hainault, was the author of the most celebrated of them. A group of his successors at the stylish Burgundian court recorded the ambitions of that rising polity; and national pride appears in each of Bower's *Scotichronicon,* the *Brut* in England and in the French *Grandes Chroniques.* Chronicles of war were natural vehicles for expressing the differences of peoples. Official newsletters helped to consolidate self-conscious popular attitudes. The sequence of lives of Henry V, for example, whether contemporary or written after his death, show the stereotypes of Anglo-French relations, which lasted well beyond the fifteenth century. In some of the productions of the fourteenth and fifteenth centuries their annalistic origins still show and some retain the traditional Latin; but opinionated history written in the vernacular is offered by the best of them in the modern manner.

C.M.D. Crowder

See also BYZANTINE HISTORIOGRAPHY; CRUSADES; ECCLESIASTICAL HISTORY; HAGIOGRAPHY; MARTYROLOGY.

References

Gransden, Antonia. *Historical Writing in England.* 2 vols. Ithaca, NY: Cornell University Press, 1974–1982.
Hay, Denys. *Annalists and Historians.* London: Methuen, 1977.
Partner, Nancy F. *Serious Entertainments: The Writing of History in Twelfth-Century England.* Chicago: University of Chicago Press, 1977.
Smalley, Beryl. *Historians in the Middle Ages.* London: Thames and Hudson, 1974.
Spiegel, Gabrielle M. *The Chronicle Tradition of Saint-Denis: A Survey.* Brookline, MA: Classical Folio Editions, 1978.
———. *Romancing the Past.* Berkeley: University of California Press, 1993.
Sterns, Indrikis. *The Greater Medieval Historians: An Interpretation and a Bibliography,* Washington, DC: University Press of America, 1981.
Taylor, John R. *The Use of Medieval Chronicles.* London: The Historical Association, 1965.

Chu Hsi

See ZHU XI.

Ch'üan Tsu-wang

See QUAN ZUWANG.

Churchill, Sir Winston Spencer (1874–1965)

English political leader, journalist, and historian. Churchill was born at Blenheim palace, the son of Lord Randolph Churchill, a Victorian politician. During his political career he served in many cabinet positions: president of the Board of Trade (1908–1911), home secretary (1910–1911), first lord of the admiralty (1911–1915), chancellor of the duchy of Lancaster (1915), secretary for war (1919–1921), and colonial secretary (1921–1922). One of the few opponents to appeasement, he was virtually a political outcast during the 1930s, but Neville Chamberlain made him first lord of the admiralty in 1939. He is best known for his staunch leadership and magnificent oratory as prime minister (1940–1945) during World War II, and he served again in that office from 1951 to 1955. In his early life Churchill was a popular journalist who wrote of his experiences in Africa in the 1890s. Later he produced fine biographical works: *Lord Randolph Churchill* (1906) about his father and *Marlborough* (1933–1936) about his famous ancestor. His lengthy memoirs, *The World Crisis* (1923–1931) and *The Second World War* (1948–1953) are important but opinionated sources. In addition to his history of World War II, he is most famous for *A History of the English Speaking Peoples* (1956–1958), a popular work for which he won the Nobel Prize for literature. Although its account of Britain's growth and expansion abroad was derivative from much older accounts, Churchill's highly readable style and personal reputation gave it new life for thousands of nonacademic readers and has given it a "classic" status among twentieth-century popular histories.

Walter A. Sutton

Texts

A History of the English Speaking Peoples. 4 vols. London: Cassell, 1956–1958.
Lord Randolph Churchill. 2 vols. London and New York: Macmillan, 1906.
Marlborough: His Life and Times. 4 vols. London: G.G. Harrap, 1933–1936.
The Second World War. 6 vols. London and Boston: Houghton Mifflin, 1948–1953.

References

Broad, C. Lewis. *Winston Churchill.* 2 vols. New York: Hawthorn, 1958–1963.
Gilbert, Martin. *Churchill: A Life.* New York: Holt, 1991.

C

Clapham, Sir John Harold (1873–1946)

English historian, university professor, and administrator. Clapham was born in Manchester. In 1892, he entered King's College, Cambridge, was elected a fellow in 1898 and, for the next four years, studied history under Lord Acton and economics under Alfred Marshall. Their influence led him to work on eighteenth- and nineteenth-century English economic history, a neglected field of study. Visiting Yorkshire manufacturing towns to gain first-hand knowledge of wool manufacturing and trade, he published *The Woollen and Worsted Industries* (1907), his first important book. He wrote it at Leeds University where in 1902 he became a professor of economics. In 1908, he returned to King's College as dean and assistant tutor in history, becoming the first professor of economic history (1928–1938) and vice-provost (1933–1943). His writing reflected his interest in putting more history into economics and connecting this economic history with the political, social, and literary life of a nation. For three decades, his lectures on the economic history of England won the praise of Cambridge undergraduates. Clapham also lectured on France and Germany—indeed his interest was in all of western European economic history—which he turned into a book, *The Economic Development of France and Germany, 1815–1914* (1921). It focused on economic forces operating as a result of the century of peace following the Napoleonic wars. These forces, as Clapham pointed out, were also evidenced in the rest of western Europe. Clapham's major work was *An Economic History of Modern Britain,* and it established him as a major historian of the Industrial Revolution. Volume one (1926) was subtitled *The Early Railway Age, 1820–1850;* volume two (1932) concerned *Free Trade and Steel, 1850–1886;* and volume three (1938) studied *Machines and National Rivalries, 1887–1914.*

Bernard Hirschhorn

Texts

The Bank of England: A History. 2 vols. Cambridge, Eng.: Cambridge University Press, 1944.

A Concise Economic History of Britain, from the Earliest Times to 1750. Cambridge, Eng.: Cambridge University Press, 1949.

An Economic History of Modern Britain. 3 vols. Cambridge, Eng.: Cambridge University Press, 1926–1938.

References

"Bibliography of Sir John Clapham." *Cambridge Historical Journal* 7 (1946): 205–206.

The Council of King's College. *Sir John Harold Clapham 1873–1946: A Memoir.* Cambridge, Eng.: Cambridge University Press, 1949, 7–28.

Postan, M.M. "Sir John Clapham." *Economic History Review* 16 (1946): 56–59.

Clarendon, Edward Hyde, Earl of (1609–1674)

English historian and statesman. Hyde was educated at Magdalen Hall, Oxford, trained as a lawyer, and prospered in that profession. He entered Parliament in 1640, took part in the chorus of criticism directed against Charles I, and was involved in the impeachment of the earl of Strafford. Firmly on the king's side, however, by the outbreak of the civil war in 1642 he remained a devoted constitutional Royalist and served Charles II no less faithfully than he had his father before him. Created earl of Clarendon in 1661 and made Lord Chancellor, he fell from office and royal favor in 1667 and, taken as the scapegoat for England's failure in the war against the Dutch, was exiled. He died, still under banishment, in Rouen in 1674. Clarendon's fame as a historian outstrips that which he temporarily enjoyed as a statesman, and his *History of the Rebellion and Civil Wars in England,* the classic Royalist account of the mid-century upheavals, was published posthumously in 1702 to 1704. "A majestic patchwork," in the words of H.R. Trevor-Roper, Clarendon's *History* was a conflation of an earlier work written in the 1640s for the private instruction of Charles I and a later, self-justifying autobiography, written in exile.

R.C. Richardson

Texts

History of the Rebellion and Civil Wars in England. Ed. W.D. Macray, 6 vols., Oxford: Clarendon Press, 1888.

References

Brownley, Martine Watson. *Clarendon and the Rhetoric of Historical Form.* Philadelphia: University of Pennsylvania Press, 1985.

Hutton, Ronald. "Clarendon's History of the Rebellion." *English Historical Review* 97 (1982): 70–88.

Richardson, R.C. *The Debate on the English Revolution Revisited.* London: Routledge, 1988.

Wormald, B.H.G., *Clarendon: Politics, Historiography and Religion, 1640–1660.* London and Chicago: Chicago University Press, 1976.

Clark, Alice (1874–1934)

British historian of early modern English women. A worker in her family's shoe factory and politically active as a suffragist, Clark wrote the first detailed study that took seriously the issues of work, family, and economic opportunities as they related to women's lives in the years preceding the Industrial Revolution. While holding the Mrs. George B. Shaw Scholarship at the London School of Economics she published her only book, *Working Life of Women in the Seventeenth Century* in 1919; after finishing it, Clark devoted the rest of her life to relief work for the Society of Friends. Employing a wide range of sources, *Working Life* crosses class and geographical boundaries to present a full picture of how changes from domestic work to larger-scale industry constricted employment opportunities for women, reduced the value of their productive capacity, and excluded them from participating in England's burgeoning capitalist economy. Clark's original thesis was one of the earliest scholarly challenges to traditional historiography, which had not regarded gender as a category of historical analysis or which had assumed that capitalist innovations had benefited all the English people during these years. While current research has expanded on Clark's book by focusing more on how ideas about women's work and occupational status were constructed within a broader cultural milieu, her pioneering conclusions have remained essentially intact and are still a touchstone for further inquiry.

Ben Lowe

Texts

Working Life of Women in the Seventeenth Century. London: Routledge, 1982.

References

Amussen, Susan Dwyer. *An Ordered Society: Gender and Class in Early Modern England.* Oxford and New York: Basil Blackwell, 1988.
Wiesner, Merry. *Working Women in Renaissance Germany.* New Brunswick, NJ: Rutgers University Press, 1986.

Clark, (Charles) Manning (Hope) (1915–1991)

Australian historian. Born in Sydney, Clark was educated at the University of Melbourne and Oxford University. In 1946 he taught Australian history at the University of Melbourne; in 1949 he became professor of history at Canberra University College. In 1972 he attained the first chair in Australian history, at the Australian National University, Canberra. There, in 1975, he became a library fellow until the end of his working life. Clark's major study *A History of Australia* spanned a period from several centuries prior to British colonization in 1788, until the 1930s. This, together with documentary collections, autobiographies, articles, and public statements elaborated Clark's vision of Australia's past. Placing him in Australia's historiography is not straightforward. Unlike most Australian historians, Clark saw the historian's need to understand the human condition. Steeped in Idealist thought, Christianity, and European and Australian literature, Clark emphasized the working out in the Australian context, through sometimes titanic individuals, of key European systems of thought—Enlightenment, Protestantism, and Catholicism. A firm Australian nationalist, Clark increasingly interpreted Australian history as an anticolonial cultural and political struggle against British philistinism. Such interpretations, and his prolific output, made Clark Australia's best-known and perhaps most controversial historian.

William Thorpe

Texts

A History of Australia. 6 volumes. Carlton: Melbourne University Press, 1962–1987.
Select Documents in Australian History 1788–1850. Sydney: Angus and Robertson, 1950.
A Short History of Australia. New York: New American Library, 1963.

References

Bourke, H. "History As Revelation: The Problem of Manning Clark." *Journal of Historical Geography* 9 (1983): 196–199.
Bridge, C., ed. *Manning Clark—Essays on His Place in History.* Carlton: Melbourne University Press, 1994.
Clark, C.M.H. "Writing *A History of Australia.*" *Australian Historical Studies* 23 (1988): 168–170.
Clark, M. *A Historian's Apprenticeship.* Carlton: Melbourne University Press, 1992.
Crawford, R.M., M. Clark, and G. Blainey. *Making History.* New York: Penguin, 1985.
Holt, S. *Manning Clark and Australian History 1915–1963.* St. Lucia: University of Queensland Press, 1982.
Inglis, K.S. "Charles Manning Hope Clark 1915–1991." *Academy of the Social Sciences in Australia, Annual Report.* Canberra: Academy of the Social Sciences in Australia, 1991.

Lechte, J. *Politics and the Writing of Australian History: An Introduction to a Structural Study.* Melbourne, Australia: Melbourne University Political Science Department, 1979.

Pascoe, R. *The Manufacture of Australian History.* Melbourne: Oxford University Press, 1979.

Class

Social, economic, and cultural historians have deployed the categories of class, class relations, and class conflict in their work with great effect, especially since the 1960s. Yet their theoretical understanding of class is rooted in the classical social theories of the nineteenth and early twentieth century, particularly those of Karl Marx and Max Weber. Marx and Weber's perspectives on class, like their views on society and history more generally, were notably different. Where Marx viewed class and class struggle as being intrinsic to an overall philosophy of history, Weber rejected philosophies of history altogether. For Marx, class relations—unequal relationships that resulted from the control of a ruling class over the means of production—broadly shaped the nature of a given society, including the consciousness of oppressed groups within it. For Weber, classes were derived from market (as opposed to productive) relationships, their consciousness was not so nearly affected by structural determinants, and "status" rather than "class" was typically a better guide to group behavior. Yet if Marx and Weber approached class from different vantage points, they also shared a set of common assumptions. They believed that "class" in modern capitalist societies played a pivotal role. And more importantly, their thinking about class was dualistic: they distinguished between objective or structural relations and the subjective or group-related activities resulting from them. In *The Eighteenth Brumaire,* Marx made the distinction between "class-in-itself" (objective relations) and "class-for-itself" (subjective response). He argued that the French peasantry, though objectively a "class-in-itself," had not developed the requisite collective consciousness that a "class-for-itself" entailed.

In the two decades following World War II, this dualistic view of class became dominant in the social sciences, notably because of the influence of American structural-functionalist sociology. Within historical writing, E.P. Thompson, a cultural Marxist historian opposed to this school of thought, was responsible for the most widely influential account of class and class relations. In *The Making of the English Working Class* (1963), Thompson argued that classes were neither structures nor concrete things: they were "historical," changed over time, and developed their consciousness in relation to other groups. Class consciousness was not simply (as orthodox Marxists believed) the inevitable result of the logic of productive relations: it was the result of how such relations were handled in cultural terms as embodied in traditions, values, and institutions. Thompson's understanding of class as a historical and cultural process was extended in a series of memorable studies of eighteenth-century English plebeian culture written in the 1970s and collected in *Customs in Common* (1991). He challenged the idea that the structure and consciousness of a class were separable and insisted that the conflict between unequal social groups—or class struggle—was primary. In an article from 1978, Thompson argued, "Classes do not exist as separate entities, look around, find an enemy class, and then start to struggle . . . they identify points of antagonistic interest, they commence to struggle around these issues and in the process of struggling they discover themselves. . . ." (p. 149)

Thompson's theoretical reflections on class relations and his historical recovery of the working-class experience in England played a pivotal role in shaping the new social history of the 1960s and 1970s and helped to overcome the artificial dualism of the classical view. Yet ironically Thompson's work also helped to reproduce this dualism, since despite his emphasis on history, experience, and process he also accepted Marx's (if not orthodox Marxists') privileging of the social relations of production in the making of class culture. Indeed, it has been only since the late 1970s that the classical model has begun to be seriously questioned. A complex array of forces—economic, political, social, and cultural—contributed to create the context in which this rethinking flourished, but two stand out. First, economic globalization, the emerging perception of a postmodern world, and the decline of the traditional working class and its movements posed difficult challenges for social theorists and historians. Using approaches labeled as postmodern and/or post-structuralist that were rooted in linguistic or cultural perspectives, they questioned not only the image of society derived from classical social theory and social history but also the categories that made the image possible, particularly the notion of class. To cite one instance, the labor historian William Sewell believes that the classical model's intent was to explain the emergence of proletarian labor in the nineteenth century and needed rethinking in light of the more complex forms of labor manifest in the recent past. In his view, labor history, and the class-based model associated with it, had been founded on the arbitrary assumption that economic determinants were purely material and thus more real than political, ideological, and cultural ones. He called for a new theoretical vocabulary—a "postmaterialist rhetoric" in labor history. Secondly, the spreading influence of feminism and the work of feminist historians helped to undermine a model of society that tended to sweep the connection between class and gender under the table and emphasized the public sphere of men at the expense of the more private and domestic world connected (particularly in the nineteenth century) with women. Here Catherine Hall and Leonore Davidoff's *Family Fortunes* (1984), a study of the English middle classes in the first half of the nineteenth century, and Hall's own *White, Male and Middle-Class: Explorations in Feminist History* (1992) helped break new ground by suggesting that the class experience itself was gendered, that masculine and feminine identities are defined in relation to each other, and that they make sense only when placed in a whole social, economic, and cultural world in which class played a central part.

Two developments have been cited here that have contributed to the conceptual unraveling of the classical model of class. But in practice they have not always acted separately, as recent work on the Chartist movement of the nineteenth century makes clear. In a major reevaluation of Chartism, *The Languages of Class* (1984), Gareth Stedman Jones challenged the prevailing notion that its origins and decline were a consequence of social and economic transformation. According to Stedman Jones, this view ignored the active role played by language and ideology in the making of class consciousness: the Chartist worldview was derived from an older tradition of political discourse predating these changes. While sympathetic to Stedman Jones's cultural and linguistic approach, the American feminist historian Joan Scott believed that he had inverted rather than overthrown the classical model, treating language "as a vehicle for communicating ideas rather than a system of meaning or a process of signification." If Stedman Jones had followed his own position to its logical conclusion, Scott argued, he would have analyzed the discursively related systems—class, gender, and the family—which constructed Chartist identity.

Taken together, the critical approaches in historiography discussed here contributed to challenging the classical view of class. As labor practices have been transformed and cultural identity has become more complex, both the image of reality that it sought to describe and the theoretical tools that produced that image have proved highly problematic. Recent work inspired by contemporary social theory has begun to produce new understandings of both past and present.

Dennis Dworkin

See also CAPITALISM; FEMINISM; GENDER; MARXISM; POSTMODERNISM; SOCIAL HISTORY.

Texts

Jones, Gareth Stedman. The Language of Class. Cambridge, Eng.: Cambridge University Press, 1983.

Joyce, Patrick, ed. *Class.* Oxford: Oxford University Press, 1995.

References

Calvert, Peter. *The Concept of Class: An Historical Introduction.* New York: St. Martin's Press, 1982.

Thompson, E.P. "Eighteenth-Century English Society: Class Struggle Without Class." Social History, 3 (1978): 133–165.

Clavijero [Clavigero], Francisco Javier (1731–1787)

Mexican historian. Clavijero, one of the main figures of the Mexican Enlightenment, was born in Veracruz, Mexico, and attended the College of San Jeronimo and the Seminary of San Ignacio in Puebla. In 1748, after joining the Society of Jesus, he studied at the College of San Pedro and San Pablo, Mexico City. Subsequently, he was named prefect of the College of San Ildefonso. In Mexico City, while teaching at the College of San Gregorio, he studied the ancient Mexican codices. In 1767, the expulsion of the Jesuits disrupted his intellectual activities. Exiled to Italy, nostalgia for his home stimulated his desire to investigate and write about Mexico's past. He wrote his monumental work, *Historia Antigua de Mexico* [Ancient History of Mexico] in Spanish, but published it in Italian as the four-volume *Storia Antica del Messico* in 1780–1781. The *Storia* traces the development of Mexican Indian civilization from the pre-Aztec period to the Spanish conquest. One of the most serious works on this topic to be written during this period, it contributed to a new appreciation of Mexico's Indian past. Subsequently, Clavijero wrote the *Disertaciones sobre la tierra, los animales y los habitantes de Mexico* [Dissertations on the Land, Animals, and People of Mexico] to counteract the rising anti-American works of certain European writers. In 1782, he published a treatise on Mexico's Virgin of Guadalupe. He died in Bologna, leaving behind many unedited and unpublished works; among these, his *Historia de la California* [History of (Lower) California] was published by Clavijero's brother.

Carlos Pérez

Texts

Historia Antigua de Mexico. 4 vols. Mexico City, Mexico: Editorial Porrua, 1945.

The History of Mexico. Ed. Burton Feldman. New York: Garland, 1979.

The History of Lower California. Ed. and trans. Sara E. Lake and A.A. Gray. Stanford, CA: Stanford University Press, 1937.

References

Ronan, Charles E. *Francisco Javier Clavigero, S.J. (1731–1787), Figure of the Mexican Enlightenment: His Life and Works.* Chicago: Loyola University Press, 1977.

Cliometrics

The application of economic theory and quantitative techniques to describe and explain history. The word "cliometrics" joins "Clio" to the suffix "metrics" taken from econometrics. While traditional economic historians are more interested in describing what happened, cliometricians are more interested in why something took place; they are apt to offer deductive inferences as part of their explanation. It should be noted that, for many years, the field was known as the "new economic history." Among practitioners, the "new economic history" was jokingly referred to as "cliometrics." As "new" became increasingly less applicable, the joke became the name.

While practitioners of the "new economic history" were quick to note their work was a continuation of what had gone before, those in the field during the late 1950s and early 1960s recognized a change. Economic historians had called for the increased use of theoretical and quantitative tools from the start, but it was not until the mid-1950s that a group of young economic historians entered the field intent on using such techniques to analyze historical questions. In addition, as Alex Field (1987) noted, the rapid success cliometricians enjoyed was helped by external factors that included the general change in the demand for economists and the demographics of the time. The postwar period was one of rising educational aspirations and enrollments.

Before World War II, questions about the causes of economic growth and the development of economic institutions were integral parts of economic history. During the postwar period, economic theory began crowding out what came to be called institutional economics. Keynesian theorists defined economic growth as an increase in output per capita and explained growth with mathematical models involving factors of production and saving rates. The question of what caused industrialization in the past evolved into how to encourage industrialization in the present and how to help less developed countries.

An equally important factor was the development of computers that enabled cliometricians to analyze large data sets that historians had regarded as unusable, uninteresting, or irrelevant for describing the past. Hughes and Reiter (1958) is methodologically noteworthy as the first published paper in economic history to use computers. In 1957 the Economic History Association and the National Bureau of Economic Research (NBER) Conference on Income and Wealth held joint sessions. Two methodological papers were presented that drew little attention at the time, but clearly denote the differences. W.W. Rostow (1957) asked, "Are we to conclude, then, that of the nature of their professions the economic theorist and the economic historian are doomed to work different sides of a street so wide that it is hardly worth shouting across?" John Meyer and Alfred Conrad (1957) called for the tools of scientific inference to be applied to economic historiography, "one can encompass deterministic or systematic factors and unique or unsystematic factors within a single and also consistent model."

A sustained controversy over methodology soon developed. Fritz Redlich (1968) defined much of cliometric work to be antihistorical research and called its practitioners "counterfactualists." He did not dismiss the work, but classified it as social science and not history. If theory was the master of the research, it was not history to Redlich.

Within economics departments, economic history has come to be regarded as another applied field of economics; it is no longer one of the three legs of Joseph Schumpeter's stool. Yet cliometricians must learn the tools of history, geography, demography, languages, and so forth, that broadened their predecessors; this in addition to being able to talk the language of their economist colleagues. Older economic historians were never expected to run regressions, but were supposed to "know the story" of the past. The cliometrician is expected to do both—know the past and be able to model and test explanations about it. If the model is sloppy, the economists are critical, and, if the history is inadequate, the historians are. To do both well is labor intensive.

With a few notable exceptions, most American cliometricians studied with three men or their students: Douglass North, Simon Kuznets, and Alexander Gerschenkron. The latter two did not regard themselves as cliometricians. Kuznets (Johns Hopkins and Harvard) influenced a generation of scholars to seek better measures of historical economic variables that explain economic growth. Both North (University of Washington and Washington University) and Gerschenkron (Harvard) had active workshops where rigorous economic hypotheses of historical events were heatedly debated. Others who had a significant influence were William Parker (Yale), Moses Abramovitz (Stanford), Harold Williamson (Northwestern), and even Walter Rostow (MIT and Texas).

The primary outlet for cliometric work has been *Explorations in Economic History*. In 1955 John Meyer took over *Explorations in Entrepreneurial History*, an outlet of Harvard's Entrepreneurial Research Center. In 1963, after a hiatus of three years, the first issue of *Explorations in Entrepreneurial History* (Second series) appeared with Ralph Andreano as editor. The name was changed to its present form in 1970. North and Parker became coeditors of *The Journal of Economic History*, the journal of the Economic History Association, in 1960. They held those posts through 1966 and were responsible for cliometric techniques being accepted by the field.

Meyer and Conrad presented a second paper at the aforementioned 1957 conference, "The Economics of Slavery in the Antebellum South," which drew considerable attention. While their conclusions basically seconded those of historian Kenneth Stampp (1956), their methods were regarded as revolutionary. Rather than examine the motives of slaveholders directly or review the accounts of particular plantations, they approached the subject as an investment problem: Was it worth making an investment in a capital asset that has a depreciation rate, maintenance costs, and a probability of becoming obsolete? They looked at historical data on cotton yields, the average life span of slaves, prices of inputs and output, and concluded that owning slaves was a sensible investment. For the next twenty years, a flood of cliometric work culminating in controversy over Fogel and Engerman's *Time on the Cross* (1974) was aimed at the economics of slavery. The controversy emanated from many directions. Some cliometricians took aim at its assumptions, theoretical models, and the representativeness of the data used; others felt that it was inappropriate to look at the institution of slavery through a quantitative lens.

Cliometricians have followed several avenues. With the advent of the computer, it became possible to answer the question of how much. Instead of comments such as "vital factors" or "it is difficult to exaggerate the importance of," cliometricians were deflating metaphors with better numbers. Statements such as, There were exactly 1,945 steamships, or, The profit was from 8 to 12 percent, took the romance out of history and supplied concrete, almost "scientific," answers.

In addition to finding better numbers, cliometricians were able to infer numbers that could not be found. For example, in order to understand if the South was self-sufficient in food before the Civil War, it proved necessary to know at what weight hogs were being slaughtered. Since such records were not available, information on feeding habits was used to compute indirectly how much hogs could have weighed. Further, in the absence of a large sample of accounting books from nineteenth-century midwestern farmers, the question of whether it was profitable to buy a reaper was approached by looking at the relative cost of hand- versus machine-harvesting on a hypothetical average-sized farm.

Cliometricians began using economic and accounting theory to change the focus of arguments that have raged in history for years. The search for more definitive answers often began with a simple rephrasing of the question. In some cases, controversies have been widened rather than resolved, but the argument has become more rigorous. One of the more important innovations of early cliometric work was the application of neoclassical microeconomic theory. As North (1965) pointed out, in all the debates about the burden of the Navigation Acts, a cliometrician was the first to consider what the elasticities of demand may have been.

Cliometricians became masters at the use of the counterfactual hypothesis, as Redlich noted. A counterfactual is an attempt to measure the significance of an event by pretending it never happened, then asking how the world would have been different. Robert Fogel concluded that, had the railroad not existed, the U.S. economy could have produced almost the same output with the use of canals and wagons. Others have used this technique to measure the cost of the Civil War, the costs and benefits to the American colonies of remaining part of the British Empire, and the impact of New Deal fiscal policies.

As the toolbox of economists has grown, so has the application of theoretical and quantitative techniques to historical questions. The possibility of market imperfections has been used to explain agricultural organization in the postbellum U.S. South and in twentieth-century China. The theory of efficiency wages has been applied to the dynamics of nineteenth- and twentieth-century labor markets. Translog production functions have been applied to the question of the relative labor-saving bias of technology between the United States and Britain. General equilibrium models have been applied to a large number of questions ranging from how income distribution changed in both the United States and Britain to who bore the burden of the Corn Laws. Game theory, information costs, and contract theory have revolutionized our study of economic institutions. The historical records of weight and heights have been used to create a biological measure of the standard of living. Finally, new insights into the explanation of long-term growth within and between countries, as well as into the causes of the Great Depression, have been gained from the application of new macroeconomic theories.

This short summary necessarily omits many topics. Williamson (1991) presents a history of cliometrics and is the primary resource for this essay. Interested readers are also referred to Donald N. McCloskey and George K. Hersh Jr. (1990). Other sources with extensive bibliographies are Nicholas Crafts (1987), Alex Field (1987), Donald McCloskey (1987), or the recent edition of any economic history textbook that prominently features cliometric research. Among the latter are Atack and Passell (1994), Hughes and Cain (1993), and Walton and Rockoff (1994).

In 1993, the Nobel Prize in Economics was awarded to Robert Fogel and Douglass North "for having renewed research in economic history." The announcement noted, "They were pioneers in the branch of economic history that has been called the 'new economic history,' or Cliometrics." At the American Economic Association luncheon in their honor, Claudia Goldin (1995) said, "Economic history is not a quaint field, but a highly relevant one. What then is this Cliometrics? Cliometrics is not just the use of historical data or the study of old institutions. It is, instead, a rigorous examination of history as a piece of cloth extending seamlessly from the past to the present."

Samuel Williamson and Louis Cain

See also BUSINESS HISTORY; COMPUTERS AND HISTORIOGRAPHY; COUNTERFACTUALS; ECONOMIC HISTORY.

References

Atack, Jeremy, and Peter Passell. *A New Economic View of American History.* Second ed. New York: W.W. Norton, 1994.

Conrad, Alfred H., and John R. Meyer. "The Economics of Slavery in the Ante Bellum South." *Journal of Political Economy* 66 (1958): 94–130.

Crafts, N.F.R. "Cliometrics, 1971–1986: A Survey." *Journal of Applied Econometrics* 2 (1987): 171–192.

Field, Alexander J. "The Future of Economic History." In *The Future of Economic History,* ed. Alexander J. Field. Boston: Kluwer-Nijhoff, 1987.

Fogel, Robert W., and Stanley Engerman. *Time on the Cross: The Economics of American Negro Slavery.* Boston: Little, Brown, 1974.

Goldin, Claudia. "On Cliometrics and the 1993 Nobel Award in Economics," *The Newsletter of the Cliometric Society* 10, no. 1 (1995).

Hughes, Jonathan R.T., and Louis P. Cain. *American Economic History.* Fourth ed. New York: HarperCollins, 1993.

Hughes, Jonathan R.T., and Stanley Reiter. "The First 1,945 British Steamships." *American Statistical Journal* 3, no. 282 (1958): 360–381; reprinted in *Purdue Faculty Papers in Economic History.* Homewood, IL: Richard D. Irwin, 1967.

McCloskey, Donald N. *Econometric History,* London: Macmillan, 1987.

———, and George K. Hersh Jr. *A Bibliography of Historical Economics to 1980.* Cambridge, Eng. and New York: Cambridge University Press, 1990.

Meyer, John R., and Alfred H. Conrad. "Economic Theory, Statistical Inference, and Economic History." *Journal of Economic History* 17 (1957): 524–544.

North, Douglas C. "The State of Economic History." *American Economic Review* 55 (1965): 86–98.

Redlich, Fritz. "Potentialities and Pitfalls in Economic History." *Explorations in Entrepreneurial History,* Second series 6 (1968): 93–108.

Rostow, W.W. "The Interrelation of Theory and Economic History." *Journal of Economic History* 17 (1957): 509–523.

Stampp, Kenneth. *The Peculiar Institution: Slavery in the Ante-Bellum South.* New York: Alfred A. Knopf, 1956.

Walton, Gary M., and Hugh Rockoff. *History of the American Economy.* Seventh ed. Fort Worth: The Dryden Press, 1994.

Williamson, Samuel H. "The History of Cliometrics." In *The Vital One: Essays in Honor of Jonathan R.T. Hughes,* ed. Joel Mokyr. Greenwich, CT: JAI Press, 1991.

Cobb, Richard (1917–1996)

Historian of the French Revolution. Born in Essex in 1917, Cobb grew up in Tunbridge Wells and was educated at Shrewsbury and Oxford. Cobb first visited France in 1935 and lived there for nine years following World War II. Subsequently, he occupied university posts at Aberystwyth, Manchester, and Leeds, before returning to Oxford in 1962. He retired in 1984. Cobb's most important work was his study of the *armées révolutionnaires* (1961), civilian armies of militant revolutionaries that served as instruments of the Terror in 1793–1794. Although it complemented the studies of the popular movement being done by Albert Soboul and George Rudé, Cobb's work was distinguished by its emphasis upon individual biographies and upon the regional diversity of the popular movement. These characteristics became more accentuated in later works. In *The Police and the People* (1970), Cobb insisted upon the narrowness of vision and anarchic character of the popular movement. In *Reactions to the French Revolution* (1972) Cobb's preoccupation with evoking the individual experience led him to consider people on the margins of society for whom the Revolution itself had little relevance. While abjuring any particular methodology, Cobb's writing was based upon extensive archival investigation, an awareness of the importance of geographical environment, and an imaginative reconstruction of individual and collective mentalities.

Ian Germani

Texts

Paris and Its Provinces, 1792–1802. London: Oxford University Press, 1975.

The People's Armies. Trans. Marianne Elliott. New Haven, CT: Yale University Press, 1987.

The Police and the People: French Popular Protest 1789–1820. Oxford: Clarendon Press, 1970.

Reactions to the French Revolution. London: Oxford University Press, 1972.

References

Lyons, Martyn. "Cobb and the Historians." In *Beyond the Terror: Essays in French Regional and Social History, 1794–1815,* ed. Gwynne Lewis and Colin Lucas. Cambridge: Cambridge University Press, 1983.

C

Cobban, Alfred (1901–1968)

Historian of modern France. Cobban was born and grew up in London and studied at Cambridge. His first professional appointments were at Cambridge (as research fellow) and then Newcastle, but he returned to his native city in 1937 and spent the rest of his career at University College, London. Alfred Cobban's most widely read books are his three-volume *A History of Modern France* (1957–1965) and *The Social Interpretation of the French Revolution* (1964). The latter represented a wide-ranging attack upon the orthodox or Marxian interpretation of the French Revolution. Criticizing the orthodox historians for forcing historical facts to fit a predetermined theory, Cobban sought to demonstrate that the Revolution, far from representing a triumph for bourgeois capitalism, was in fact a reaction against capitalism. Cobban's book effectively launched the modern debate on the origins of the French Revolution, as "revisionist" historians answered his call for a more empirical approach to the subject. Only slightly less provocative were Cobban's works on intellectual history. In his study of the Enlightenment he opposed the widely held view that the Revolution was the fruit of Enlightenment philosophy by arguing that the Revolution had betrayed the liberal values that Cobban admiringly regarded as essential to the spirit of the Enlightenment.

Ian Germani

Texts

Aspects of the French Revolution. New York: G. Braziller, 1968.

A History of Modern France. 3 vols. Harmondsworth, Eng.: Penguin, 1965.

Rousseau and the Modern State. Second ed. Hamden, CT: Archon, 1964.

The Social Interpretation of the French Revolution. Cambridge, Eng.: Cambridge University Press, 1964.

References

Behrens, C.B.A. "Professor Cobban and His Critics." *Historical Journal* 9 (1966): 236–241.

Bosher, J.F. "Alfred Cobban's View of the Enlightenment." In *The Modernity of the Eighteenth Century,* ed. Louis T. Milic. London: Case Western Reserve University Press, 1971.
———. ed. *French Government and Society, 1500–1850: Essays in Memory of Alfred Cobban.* London: Athlone Press, 1983.

Cobbett, William (1763–1835)

English journalist, historian, and political reformer. Born in Farnham, Surrey, the son of a publican and small farmer, Cobbett spent six years in the British army before moving to the United States in 1792, where, under the pen name of Peter Porcupine, he rose to fame as an anti-Jacobin journalist. In 1800 he returned to England, establishing the weekly *Political Register* (1802–1835), which soon began to promote parliamentary reform, universal manhood suffrage, and improved living standards for the laboring poor. Historical allusions are frequent in Cobbett's writings, and he was strongly critical of those historians, principally David Hume, whom he accused of ignoring social matters and of adhering to a model of linear progress. It was Cobbett's view that England had passed into social, economic, and political decline after the Protestant Reformation, though he did look upon the eighteenth century as a "golden age" for English agricultural workers. He believed that his regressive view of English history was confirmed by traditional ballads and folk memory. On occasion Cobbett argued that history should be written soon after the age to which it relates, and he practiced this himself by writing a history of the times of King George IV.

Ian Dyck

Texts

Political Register. 89 vols. London: R. Bagshaw et al., 1802–1835.
History of the Protestant "Reformation" in England and Ireland. 2 vols. New York: D. and J. Sadlier, 1834.
History of the Regency and Reign of King George the Fourth. 2 vols. London: Mills, Jowett, and Mills, for W. Cobbett, 1830–1834.

References

Dyck, Ian. *William Cobbett and Rural Popular Culture.* Cambridge, Eng.: Cambridge University Press, 1992.
Spater, G. *William Cobbett: The Poor Man's Friend.* 2 vols. Cambridge, Eng.: Cambridge University Press, 1982.

Cochran, Thomas Childs (b. 1902)

American historian of business. Cochran was born in Brooklyn, New York. He attended New York and Columbia universities and received his Ph.D. from the University of Pennsylvania in 1930. He began his career as a professor of history at New York University, and in 1950 he moved to the University of Pennsylvania at Philadelphia where he remained until his retirement in 1972. He received an honorary law degree and after his retirement was named professor emeritus. Cochran served as president of the Organization of American Historians (1966–1967) and the American Historical Association (1972). He was Thomas Lee Bailey professor at the University of North Carolina, Charlotte (1973–1975). Cochran is considered a founder of modern business history. He is the author of numerous works on business and social history published from 1932 to 1981. His first major business history, *The Age of Enterprise: A Social History of America,* was coauthored with William Miller in 1942. Cochran is also well known for his history of the Pabst Brewing Company and for the study of cross-cultural businesses, in particular the history of business and entrepreneurship in Latin America. The results of his scholarship were published in such works as *The Pabst Brewing Company: The History of an American Business* (1948) and *The Puerto Rican Businessman: A Study in Cultural Change* (1959).

Judith Boyce DeMark

Texts

And William Miller. *The Age of Enterprise: A Social History of Industrial America.* Revised ed. New York: Harper, 1961.
Basic History of American Business. Princeton, NJ: Van Nostrand, 1959.
And Ruben E. Reina. *Capitalism in Argentine Culture: A Study of Torcuato Di Tella and S.I.A.M.* Philadelphia: University of Pennsylvania Press, 1971.
Challenges to American Values: Society, Business, and Religion. New York: Oxford University Press, 1985.
The Pabst Brewing Company: The History of an American Business. New York: New York University Press, 1948.
The Puerto Rican Businessman: A Study in Cultural Change. Philadelphia: University of Pennsylvania Press, 1959.
Social Change in America: The Twentieth Century. New York: Harper & Row, 1972.

References

Sharlin, Harold Issadore, ed. *Business and Its Environment: Essays for Thomas C. Cochran.* Westport, CT: Greenwood Press, 1983.

Codera y Zaidín, Francisco (1836–1917)

Spanish Arabist and medieval historian. Codera taught Arabic at the University of Madrid; as a member of the Real Academia de la Historia, he was on the committee responsible for writing Spain's *Diccionario biográfico* [Biographical Dictionary]. He published his monumental work, *Tratado de numismática arábigo-española* [Treatise on Arabic-Spanish Numismatics], in 1879. The first of ten volumes of his *Biblioteca Arábico-Hispana* [Arabic-Hispanic Library], a collection of original source materials on Muslim Spain, appeared three years later. He also prepared an Arabic grammar, and assembled and restored numerous Arabic codices, insuring that the Escorial Library would have the largest collection of Arabic manuscripts in Spain; he compiled a bibliography of historiographical sources of primary importance for Spanish Arabists; and he built up a school of specialists on Muslim Spain, helping them to interpret Arabic manuscripts and classify medieval coins. He wrote several monographs on Islamic Spain, including *Decadencia y desaparición de los almorávides en España* [Decline and Disappearance of the Almoravides in Spain] (1899).

George L. Vásquez

Texts

Biblioteca Arábico-Hispana. 10 vols. (varying imprints) Madrid: Rojas; Madrid: Romero; and Zaragoza: Comas, 1882–1895.
Decadencia y desaparición de los almorávides en España. Zaragoza: Tipografía de Comas Hermanos, 1899.
Tratado de numismática arábigo-española. Madrid: M. Murillo, 1979.

References

Saavedra, Eduardo. "Prólogo: Estudios de erudición oriental [Prologue: Studies on Oriental Learning]." In *Homenaje á D. Francisco Cordera, en su jubilación del profesorado* [Essays in Honor of Don Francisco Codera on His Retirement]. Zaragoza: M. Escar, 1904.

Coedès, George (1886–1969)

French historian and epigrapher, concerned with early Southeast Asia and particularly with precolonial Cambodia, the so-called Angkorean civilization (ca. 802–ca. A.D. 1430). Born and educated in Paris, Coedès published a learned article dealing with a seventh-century Cambodian inscription when he was only eighteen. He joined the École Française d'Extrême Orient in Hanoi in 1911. Aside from a stretch in the 1920s as director of the Thai national library, Coedès remained at the École until his retirement in 1947. Returning to France, he remained active as a scholar until his death. Over the years, he published some three hundred major works, including a seminal history of Indianized Southeast Asia (1964) and a magisterial edition of Cambodian inscriptions (1937–1966). Coedès was largely responsible for sorting out the six-hundred-year-long chronology of Angkorean history—a reconstruction complicated by the fact that inscriptions and other sources took the chronology for granted without stating it openly. Coedès also offered many insights into such issues as Indianization, the relationship between religion and politics, and Angkorean kingship. His monumental corpus was based on superb linguistic skills and fastidious analysis, set off by a generous, imaginative spirit that enabled him to stand back and observe precolonial Southeast Asia as holistically as the available sources allowed.

David Chandler

Texts

Ed. *Les inscriptions du Cambodge.* 8 vols. Hanoi and Paris: EFEO, 1937–1966.
The Indianized States of Southeast Asia. Honolulu: East-West Press, 1968.
Articles sur le Cambodge. 2 vols. Paris: EFEO, 1988–1992.

References

D.G.E. Hall, ed. *Historians of South East Asia.* London: Oxford University Press, 1961.

Colin, Francisco (1592–1660)

Spanish Jesuit historian. From a prominent Catalan family, Colin entered the Society of Jesus in 1607. He was sent to the Philippines and arrived in 1626. When the Jesuits attempted to establish missions in Formosa and Jolo, Colin was assigned to the task. These efforts failed and Colin remained in Manila, where he occupied a chair in the Jesuit college. In 1634, Colin was sent to the new mission of Mindoro but he returned to Manila three years later as rector of the college and two years later was made provincial of the Jesuits in the Philippines. The latter part of his life was spent in literary work, among other activities. Colin's most significant literary work was the institutional history of the Jesuits in the Philippines, entitled: *Labor evangélica* [Evangelical Work]. It was published in Madrid three years after his death. While it was principally written (as with other histories of the Mendicant Orders) to inform and encourage their European supporters, as well as to justify their continuing presence in the Philippines, his work contains valuable material regarding the peoples of the Philippines, including descriptions of different aspects of life of the indigenous population.

Damon L. Woods

Texts

Labor evangélica: Ministerios apostolicos de los obreros de la Compañia de Jesús. Ed. Pablo Pastells, S.J. 3 vols. Barcelona: Henrich y compania, 1900–1902.

References

Boxer, C.R. "Some Aspects of Spanish Historical Writing on the Philippines." In *Historians of South East Asia,* ed. D.G.E. Hall. London: Oxford University Press, 1961.

Blair, Emma Helen, and James Robertson, eds. *The Philippine Islands, 1493–1803.* 55 vols. Cleveland, OH: A.H. Clark, 1903–1909, vol. 27.

Colligation

Explaining known particular historical actions by relating and synthesizing them into a single entity as parts into a directing whole that is greater than the sum of its parts. Colligation explains by adding something to previous knowledge of historical actions, making them parts of a conceptual framework, for example, particular actions at the end of 1989 in eastern Europe may be explained as parts of the collapse of the Soviet Empire, a greater whole than the sum of demonstrations, changes of government, and so on.

William Whewell introduced the term in 1840, referring to the binding together of facts by concepts to create general terms. W.H. Walsh held that colligation explained through a teleology: "dominant ideas" make intelligible separate actions, e.g., as a "movement," or a "policy." W.H. Dray explicated colligation as reorganization and synthesis of events under a classifying general concept, pattern, metaphor, or analogy that explains. Colligation was brought as an alternative "humanistic" model of historiographic explanation of *what?* to Hempel's "covering law," explaining *why?* Positivists like Carl Hempel dismissed colligation as no explanation at all, holding it to be based on confused or bad logic. Yet, if colligation is understood as fitting actions to a theoretical conceptual framework, it may still be reconcilable with positivism.

Aviezer Tucker

See also CAUSATION; PHILOSOPHY OF HISTORY, ANALYTIC.

References

Cebik, L.B. "Colligation and the Writing of History." *The Monist* 53 (1969): 40–57.

Collingwood, Robin George (1889–1943)

British idealist philosopher, archaeologist, and historian. The son of a landscape painter and author, Collingwood was born in Cartmel Fell, Lancashire, and educated at Rugby and Oxford, where he became a tutor in philosophy in 1912. His range of interests was broad, extending from metaphysics, epistemology, and aesthetics to field work in the archaeology of Roman Britain. As an archaeologist and historian he published more than one hundred articles and three books: *Roman Britain* (1923), *The Archaeology of Roman Britain* (1930), and the first part of *Roman Britain and the English Settlements* (1936), volume one of the *Oxford History of England.* His chief philosophical works are: *Speculum Mentis* (1924); *Outlines of a Philosophy of Art* (1925); *An Essay on Philosophical Method* (1933); *The Principles of Art* (1938); *An Essay on Metaphysics* (1940); *The New Leviathan* (1942); and (most important for historiography) the posthumous and fragmentary *The Idea of History* (1946). Collingwood's theory of historical knowledge, which he described in a 1928 letter to Benedetto Croce as "my chief task in philosophy," was the linchpin of the comprehensive philosophy he sought to create, based on his conception of the unity of human experience. It builds on the work of such idealist philosophers as Wilhelm Dilthey and Croce and bears the special stamp of his work as an archaeologist, which required the exercise of synthetic imagination to bring order to disparate and often fragmentary artifacts and inscriptions. This led him to argue that history is at bottom the study of thought and that the historian's method consists essentially in reenacting the ideas and intentions of people in the past—a British variation on the nineteenth-century German doctrines of *Verstehen* and *Einfühlung.* To this end, he developed an explicit concept of the "historical imagination," based on the mind's constructive power to constitute artifacts as evidence and to bridge gaps between these items of evidence to form a continuous picture of the past. Collingwood thus extended the neo-idealist defense of historical understanding as an autonomous mode of inquiry, distinct from natural science. While the notion of "reenactment" has sometimes been dismissed as fanciful and unempirical, and though some of his own work in Roman history stretches the evidence too far, Collingwood was widely admired among mid-twentieth-century English-language historians, a fact reflected in E.H. Carr's reference to him as the "only British thinker in the present century who has made a serious contribution to the philosophy of history." Such respect derived largely from the way his defense of the autonomy of historical understanding could be used to justify history as a unique and epistemically licit mode of inquiry in the ongoing debate over the nature of explanation in the natural and cultural sciences. More recently, Collingwood's conception of the historical imagination has influenced constructionist and narrativist approaches to the nature of historical understanding, which stress history's relationship to modes of storytelling and suggest that the past to which historical accounts refer may be as much "constructed" as it is "real."

Harry Ritter

Texts

The Idea of History. Revised edition, ed. Jan van der Dussen. Oxford: Clarendon Press, 1993.

References

Dray, William H. *History As Re-enactment: R.G. Collingwood's Idea of History.* Oxford: Clarendon Press, 1995.
Johnston, William M. *The Formative Years of R.G. Collingwood.* The Hague: Martinus Nijhoff, 1967.
Mink, Louis O. *Mind, History, and Dialectic: The Philosophy of R.G. Collingwood.* Bloomington: Indiana University Press, 1969.

Colmeiro, Manuel (1818–1894)

Spanish jurist, legal and economic historian. Colmeiro, who taught political–legal systems at the University of Madrid, also had an active public career: he sat in the Cortes (1865 and after); he served as inspector general of public instruction (1874); and he was appointed to the Spanish Supreme Court (1881). He revolutionized the juridical study of social, administrative, and political institutions by examining them in their historical context as opposed to simply interpreting legal codes textually. His legal publications, used as

textbooks in Spain, include *Derecho administrativo español* [Administrative Spanish Law] (1850) and *Elementos de derecho político y administrativo de España* [Elements of Spanish Political and Administrative Law] (1858). His historical works dealt almost exclusively with economic history, especially with the *arbitristas* or economic reformers and political economy treatise writers of sixteenth- and seventeenth-century Spain. These included *Historia de la economía política en España* [History of Political Economy in Spain] (1863) and *Biblioteca de los economistas españoles de los siglos XVI, XVII y XVIII* [The Library of Spanish Economists of the Sixteenth, Seventeenth, and Eighteenth Centuries] (1880).

George L. Vásquez

Texts

Biblioteca de los economistas españoles de los siglos XVI, XVII y XVIII. Madrid: Memorias de la Academia de Ciencias Morales y Políticas, 1880.
Derecho administrativo español. 2 vols. Madrid: Librerías de D. Angel Calleja, ed., 1850.
Elementos de derecho político y administrativo de España. Madrid: F. Martínez García, 1858.
Historia de la economía política en España. 2 vols. Madrid: Cipriano López, 1863.

References

Torres Campos, Manuel. *Bibliografía española contemporánea del derecho y de la política* [Contemporary Spanish Bibliography of Law and Politics, 1800–1880]. Madrid: Imp. de Fortanet, 1883.

Commynes, Philippe de (1447–1511)

French royal counselor and historian. Commynes's father, Colard van den Clyte, was of a newly ennobled family and died young; his son took his name from an ancient fief belonging to the uncle who raised him. After 1464 Commynes rose rapidly to the office of chamberlain under Charles the Bold, who became duke of Burgundy in 1467. In 1471, Commynes left Burgundy and entered the service of Louis XI of France. He became a royal favorite and enjoyed great wealth and influence. He survived the retributions that followed Louis XI's death in 1483, but intrigues resulted in his imprisonment in 1487. After 1491, with brief exceptions, he remained in royal service for the rest of his life. During his fall from favor, Commynes began his *Memoirs* as notes for a friend who planned to write a humanist-style Latin life of the dead king. By 1491, however, Commynes had turned the recollections into his six books of *Memoirs,* with two more books completed by 1498. Commynes's history was an eyewitness account of the relentless pursuit of power, and he emphasized the usefulness of its lessons as well as the role of divine providence in the final course of events. Sixteenth-century Europeans, including the Emperor Charles V, praised the *Memoirs* both as a practical guide to politics, and as a trustworthy record of events. Commynes departed from the facts to sustain his narrative and to support his biases, but such lapses are outweighed by his naive frankness and freedom from stifling official and courtly conventions of his milieu, and by his determination to show men's roles and motives in shaping the outcome of events.

Lawrence M. Bryant

Texts

Mémoires. Ed. J. Calmette with G. Durville. 3 vols. Paris: H. Champion, 1924–1925.

References

Archambault, Paul. *Seven French Chroniclers: Witnesses to History.* Syracuse, NY: Syracuse University Press, 1974.

Dufournet, Jean. *Études sur Philippe de Commynes.* Paris: H. Champion, 1975.

Kinser, Samuel. "Introduction" to *The Memoirs of Philippe de Commynes.* Ed. S. Kinser and trans. Isabelle Cazeaux. 2 vols. Columbia: University of South Carolina Press, 1969–1973.

Comnena, Anna (1083–ca. 1153/4)

Byzantine princess and historian. Anna Comnena was born in Constantinople, the eldest daughter of the Emperor Alexius I. In 1118, she plotted to put her husband Nicephorus Bryennius on the throne, but failed and was forced to retire to a convent, where she spent the rest of her days. After 1148, she wrote the *Alexiad,* essentially a long panegyric to her father, but an important source for ninth- and tenth-century Byzantine history, including wars and international relations. The work provides vivid psychological portraits but includes partisan distortions and chronological inconsistencies.

Stephen A. Stertz

Texts

The Alexiad of Anna Comnena. Trans. E.R.A. Sewter. Baltimore, MD: Penguin, 1969.

References

Buckler, G. *Anna Comnena: A Study.* London: Oxford University Press, 1929.

Compagni, Dino (ca. 1246–1324)

Florentine merchant, politician, and historian. A White Guelf, Compagni served as a prior until forced to resign after the victory of the Blacks in 1301. His *Cronica fiorentina* [Chronicle of Florence] (1310–1312) explains the factional strife *(discordia)* in his hometown as an almost inevitable series of fractures, as every winning party immediately splits up into two new factions. It describes the different conflicts of Florence from 1280 to 1312, with its climax 1300/01, and ends with the Italian journey of Emperor Henry VII. The latter gave Compagni new, though vain expectations of a White revenge and thus inspired his book. The *Cronica* was barely read until first published by Muratori in 1726; its authenticity, questioned in the nineteenth century, has since been confirmed.

Thomas Maissen

Texts

Chronicle of Florence. Ed. and trans. Daniel E. Bornstein. Philadelphia: University of Pennsylvania Press, 1986.

References

Bornstein, Daniel E. "Introduction." In *Chronicle of Florence.*

Comparative History

The practice of comparing historical entities, structures, processes, and so on, especially those of an economic, social, sociocultural, or political nature and of medium- or long-term duration. Also, a broad category of historical writing, examples of which can be found in various cultures, though it has been produced particularly in the modern West and by intellectuals influenced by it. Assessing the genuineness of documents, judging the reliability of existing scholarship, ascertaining the significance of facts and issues, such activities necessarily make the historian's craft a comparative one. However, "comparative history" as a particular genre of historical analysis is constituted more narrowly by the practice of interpreting two or more historical objects with explicit reference to one another. In this sense it involves constructing substantive comparisons for the purpose of establishing the similarities and/or differences among distinct historical objects.

The drawing of contrastive comparisons between peoples was established in the early historical literatures of various early societies. Medieval and early-modern European authors commonly explained existing nations in terms of genealogical derivations from ancient ancestors, particularly the biblical patriarchs. European expansion from the late fifteenth century resulted in encounters with societies that demonstrated the diversity of human manners and institutions and also posed problems to biblically derived interpretations of world history. Seventeenth-century work on comparative chronology was an important step toward the emergence of the historical consciousness of the Enlightenment. The works of Gerard and Isaac Vossius and of Isaac de La Peyrère, like those of Voltaire and Montesquieu, illustrate that controversies in both these periods over differential historical development were framed by disputes concerning the rightness or otherwise of existing institutions, practices, and beliefs. In turn, the ideas of progress and historical stages as developed by Turgot, Adam Smith, and Condorcet were founded on comparative readings of history and provided a theoretical framework for assessing the levels of development of different societies. Such ideas were remolded along organicist lines by the romantics, while Hegel and Ranke fitted them into their conceptions of history as divine emanation. Implicitly or explicitly these comparative concepts have operationally shaped much subsequent historical thinking.

In the nineteenth century, three distinct approaches to comparative history were elaborated under the mantles of sociological positivism, historical materialism, and Aryanism, associated respectively with the names of Comte, Marx, and Gobineau. Inspired by comparative anatomy into thinking that the diverse stages of human development could be found reproduced in the contemporary variety of the world's peoples, Comte held that scientific reconstruction of human history could be achieved through systematic historical and ethnographical comparison. Drawing on the Enlightenment's "four-stages" theory, Marx and Engels elaborated a conception of history as progressing through five or six modes of production in terms of which societies could be analyzed. They used this framework both for interpreting successive societies and for conceiving political strategies for change; and they have been followed in this by others in the Marxist tradition. Finally, the doctrines of white race superiority that proliferated in the nineteenth and early twentieth centuries were buttressed by a comparative historical literature that interpreted particular nations, civilizations, and world history generally, in terms of the dissemination of purportedly racial characteristics.

The German *Methodenstreit* late in the century brought to light a variety of differences over philosophical, political, and methodological issues between these approaches and the document-oriented history cultivated in the universities, and revealed widespread distrust of systematic comparativism among academic historians. The early twentieth century nonetheless saw renewed commitment to pursue systematic comparative history among certain academic historians including Henri Pirenne and especially Max Weber, whose influence (like Marx's) has continued to be felt through the century. In the interwar period, the works of Oswald Spengler and Arnold J. Toynbee made the comparative study of civilizations a topic of public prominence. In the same period the early members of the Annales group, particularly Marc Bloch, laid the basis for what was to become a fruitful and long-lasting program of thorough-going comparative research, of which Braudel's work remains perhaps the best-known example. Postwar Annales studies formed part of a broader movement among economic and social historians toward comparative research, much of it based on the collection and systematic analysis of vast amounts of quantitative data illustrative of long-term trends. Comparative political history flourished anew in the postwar period, and research into the comparative history of science saw the beginnings of systematic study of non-European traditions. The flowering of comparative studies since 1945 seems to have been stimulated in part by globalization and the pressing issues of postcolonial development.

As a type of scholarship, "comparative history" is probably best identified as an existing corpus of writings rather than by any clearly defined method. Much of this literature is focused on problems and themes. Among the more prominent of these are the rise and fall of civilizations, the role of religions in society, the family, capitalism, industrialization, economic development, women's place in society, feudalism, nationalism, democratization and the obstacles to it, slavery, colonialism, the frontier, bureaucracy, business cycles, and economic trends.

Certain characteristic conceptual and procedural aspects of comparative history, however, can be noted. The selection of the units of comparison is a central issue. Though it is often done spontaneously and according to "common sense," making an appropriate and fruitful selection poses one of comparative history's greatest challenges. The historian involved in constructing a comparison has recourse, at least implicitly, to classificatory

C

abstractions (nations, feudalism, exchange, Nature) in order to match units that are of the same order and thus appropriate for comparison. However, common classificatory terms are often theoretically problematic and sometimes group items of quite different orders. Such problems of categorization constitute a pitfall for anyone undertaking comparisons; on the other hand, systematic reflection on the terms of comparison can lead to valuable conceptual insights.

Conceptual "modeling" is a procedure common both to the social sciences and to comparative history. It can be defined as the hypothetical identification of the essential components of a process or structure and specification of their relations. The analysis of data in terms of such models and the testing of the models against available information have proved to be powerful tools of analysis. Such models (and "ideal-types") can provide valuable frameworks for constructing historical comparisons. The notion of "functional equivalents" adapted from anthropology can serve as a useful tool in the construction of historical comparisons. However, reification, ethnocentrism, the imputation of false "essences" and simplistic assumptions of continuous development between apparently similar phenomena are all important conceptual pitfalls to be avoided.

B.H. Slicher van Bath identifies several types of historical comparisons. He points out, for example, that comparisons can be constructed in which either time or space, or both, are variables. *Synchronic* comparisons are those in which the objects analyzed are chosen from roughly the same time, while *diachronic* comparisons are carried out on an entity or entities in different periods. Alternatively, a spatially homogenous comparison is one in which different periods or aspects of a given geographical unit are compared, whereas a spatially differentiated study compares different geographical units. He also elaborates a functional typology of comparisons distinguished according to the result that each is intended to achieve. Such types include: *generalizing* comparisons, in which similar objects are compared for the purpose of defining an abstract or general category; *philosophical* or *paradigmatic* comparisons, in which broad comparisons are made in order to establish a universal (such as human nature); *individualizing* comparisons, in which comparison serves as the basis for establishing the specificity of an object; *analogical* comparison, in which an assumption of formal similarity within a class of objects provides a basis for clarifying a previously unknown aspect of one of them; *synthetic* comparisons, in which

comparison of various particular known entities is used as the basis for defining an unknown (as in historical linguistics) or for throwing light on a higher-order totality; and *quantitative* comparisons, in which quantitative data are compared in order to clarify patterns, similarities, and differences.

Modern economic historians contrast economic *structures,* or relatively stable features of a given society, with *processes,* or patterns of change, which may be further distinguished into cyclical processes, like business cycles, and open processes, like industrialization. Though not necessarily exclusive, these distinctions are useful for constructing symmetrical comparisons.

It is probably fair to expect that a historical comparison will be more solid the fewer the number of variables involved and the fewer the differences between the units compared. However, solidity is not the only aim of scholarship. Those who consider quality of insight and the stimulation of further inquiry as more important are likely to prefer complex and artful comparisons. Other important factors determining the value of a comparison might therefore be the significance of the subject, the relative completeness of information in the area of comparison, and the skill of the researcher.

G.R. Blue

See also ANNALES SCHOOL; ENVIRONMENTAL HISTORY—WORLD; ESSENTIALISM; EUROCENTRISM; GENEALOGY; GERMAN HISTORICAL THOUGHT; MARXISM AND HISTORIOGRAPHY; NATIONALISM; PHILOSOPHY OF HISTORY—SUBSTANTIVE; SOCIOLOGY AND HISTORY; WORLD HISTORY.

Texts

Anderson, Benedict. *Imagined Communities.* London: Verso, 1991.

Bairoch, Paul. *Cities and Economic Development: From the Dawn of History to the Present.* Trans. C. Braider. Chicago: University of Chicago Press, 1988.

Bloch, Marc. *Feudal Society.* Trans. L.A. Manyon. London and New York: Routledge, 1989.

Braudel, Fernand. *The Perspective of the World.* Vol. 3 of his *Civilization and Capitalism, 15th–18th Century.* London: Collins; New York: Harper & Row, 1984.

Burke, Peter. *Venice and Amsterdam: A Study of Seventeenth Century Elites.* Second ed. Cambridge, MA: Polity, 1994.

Curtin, Philip D. *Cross-Cultural Trade in World History.* Cambridge, Eng.: Cambridge University Press, 1984.

Davidson, Basil. *The Black Man's Burden: Africa and the Curse of the Nation-State*. London: James Currey, 1992.

Hobsbawm, E.J. *Nations and Nationalism since 1780: Programme, Myth, Reality*. Cambridge, Eng.: Cambridge University Press, 1990.

Jones, E.L. *The European Miracle: Environments, Economies and Geopolitics in the History of Europe and Asia*. Cambridge, Eng.: Cambridge University Press, 1987.

Kennedy, Paul. *The Rise and Fall of Great Empires*. New York: Random House, 1987.

McNeill, William. *Polyethnicity and National Unity in World History*. Toronto: University of Toronto Press, 1986.

Moore, Barrington. *Social Origins of Dictatorship and Democracy: Lord and Peasant in the Making of the Modern World*. Boston: Beacon, 1966.

Needham, Joseph. *The Grand Titration: Science and Society in East and West*. London: Allen & Unwin; Toronto: University of Toronto Press, 1969.

Rozman, Gilbert, ed. *The East Asian Region: Confucian Heritage and Its Modern Adaptation*. Princeton, NJ: Princeton University Press, 1991.

Slicher van Bath, B.H. *The Agrarian History of Western Europe, A.D. 500–1850*. London: Edward Arnold, 1963.

Teggart, Frederick J. *Theory and Processes of History*. Berkeley and Los Angeles: University of California Press, 1962.

Weber, Max. *Economy and Society: An Outline of Interpretive Sociology*. 2 vols. Berkeley, Los Angeles, and London: University of California Press, 1978.

Wolf, Eric. *Europe and the People without History*. Berkeley and Los Angeles: University of California Press, 1982.

References

Burke, Peter. *History and Social Theory*. Ithaca, NY: Cornell University Press, 1992, 22–33.

Slicher van Bath, Bernard. *Geschiedenis: Theorie en praktijk* [History: Theory and Practice]. Utrecht and Antwerp: Spectrum, 1978, 26–33; 142–153.

Veyne, Paul. *Writing History: Essay on Epistemology*. Trans. Mina Moore-Rinvolucri. Middletown, CT: Wesleyan University Press, 1984.

Wallerstein, Immanuel. *Unthinking Social Science: The Limits of Nineteenth-Century Paradigms*. Cambridge, Eng.: Polity, 1991, 7–22; 41–50; 237–256.

C

Computers and Historiography

The use of computers in the research, writing, and teaching of history. Few technological innovations since the advent of the printing press in the fifteenth century can have had so enormous and rapid an impact on historiography as the computer. The earliest applications of computer technology to the study of the past came almost exclusively in the area of quantitative history. As mainframe computers became increasingly available at larger universities in the late 1950s and 1960s, economic and social historians were the first to put them to use in storing and analyzing large quantities of data. What was once known as new economic history, and remains popularly known as cliometrics, became intimately linked with the computer, since the complex mathematical operations (such as regression analysis) that are the hallmark of that approach to historical evidence were rendered far easier through machine-assisted analysis. Other successful early ventures in computer-assisted quantification concerned legislative behavior, as tracked by William O. Aydelotte for Britain and by a number of historians for the United States. Collective biography or prosopography, of the kind once tackled, in Lewis Namier's day, by hand, also proved highly suited to the computer, as evidenced in the 1959 study of *Massachusetts Shipping, 1697–1714* by Bernard and Lotte Bailyn.

In the 1960s and 1970s, social historians, too, began to discover the use of the computer for storing and retrieving records of birth, marriage and death, social status, and geographical or economic mobility. A good example of the application of computational technology to a single large archival document containing both demographic and economic data is the study of the Florentine *catasto* (taxation records) of 1427, carried out by David Herlihy and Christiane Klapisch-Zuber and published as *Les Toscans et leurs familles* (1978). A quite different instance, this one examining a series of English parochial records over a period of more than three centuries, is provided by the work of E.A. Wrigley, R.S. Schofield, and their associates in the Cambridge Group for the History of Population and Social Structure, a project that culminated in Wrigley and Schofield's massive *The Population History of England and Wales, 1541–1871* (1981).

At this stage in its existence, several constraints limited the exploitation of the computer. The first was cost. In order to use a computer at all, a researcher generally needed to be affiliated with a university or large research center; current on-line access via modem (a device for allowing computers to "talk" to one another over telephone lines) or ethernet (a direct or "hard-wired" connection between a personal computer and a remote "host" mainframe that provides a communications "backbone") has been a relatively recent development. A second constraint was technical: early computers were large, clumsy, and slow by modern standards, and they required a considerably greater degree of familiarity with programming than do their current successors. As recently as the late 1970s, programs and data sets had to be encoded, then converted to keypunch cards and input in that manner; and the memory of the largest mainframe in 1960 or even 1970, paltry by the standard of today's personal computers, obliged the researcher to write programs that were often long and cumbersome. Faced with such problems, it is scarcely surprising that many scholars engaged in quantitative analysis continued for a long time to use more traditional methods, collecting data on file cards and manually sorting them, rather than investing considerable time and effort, not to mention expense, in converting their materials into machine-readable form.

The advent of the microcomputer (also often called the personal computer or "PC") in the late 1970s, and its massive growth in the 1980s, combined with much faster and smarter mainframes and mini-mainframes, and with the development of software packages for both data collection and statistical analysis, is what really brought the computer from the periphery into the center of historical research. By the early 1980s, the old punch cards had largely disappeared from view, replaced by direct-input video-terminals. And even the most novice researcher, now freed from the need to master FORTRAN, Cobal, and similar early programming languages, now had available on a mainframe (and accessible from his or her office or home via modem) such tools as the popular Statistical Package for the Social Sciences (SPSS) first developed at Stanford University, and the more powerful (but less widely favored by many historians) Statistical Analysis System (SAS). Both packages are still widely used, though they have been supplemented by PC versions of themselves, and by smaller, simpler programs designed around particular types of task, whether straightforward counting and cross-tabulation, or more sophisticated statistical analysis such as chi-squares, correlations, and regressions. Many of the straightforward counting exercises that, a decade ago, had to be done with SPSS (and a generation ago programmed from scratch in FORTRAN), can now

be done through PC spreadsheet programs like the popular Lotus 1–2–3, while data can be collected and resorted rapidly on databases such as D-Base. Other popular programmes for the PC include Systat and NSDstat+. It has also become much easier to relate statistics compiled on one subject, for instance, census materials, to those on another, such as crime or health, through the use of relational databases. Use of database programs has been rendered easier by the development of what amounts to an international standard for querying databases, in the form of the Structured Query Language (SQL).

The enormous progress in personal computer technology, which in the past five years has seen the rapid rise and equally rapid decline of the first generation of PCs and their replacement by fast, high-RAM machines capable of storing and processing large quantities of data, has thus diminished though not eliminated the need for individual scholars to rely on the university mainframe, which for many users has become simply a "server" or "host" for electronic communications. A measure of the change in little over ten years can be given in the experience of most contributors to and many readers of this book. The author of the present article, as recently as 1987, had to rely on an IBM mainframe to conduct a quantitative analysis (using SAS) of biographical data on eight hundred English historical writers of the sixteenth, seventeenth, and eighteenth centuries, converting the results into more readable graphic and tabular format with the aid of a personal computer with a twenty-megabyte hard disk with no graphical user interface (gui). The random access memory on the personal computer on which the present article was written now exceeds the total hard disk storage capacity of the author's first PC.

A number of specialized journals have sprung up over the past two or three decades in order to promote and discuss the use of computers in historical research. The *Journal of Interdisciplinary History* and *Journal of Family History* are only two examples of scholarly periodicals that frequently contain articles using computer-intensive historical analysis. A journal concerned with the application of computers to various humanistic disciplines, *Computers and the Humanities,* has been published in New York since 1966. Of more specific relevance to the historian, *Historical Methods* (continuing the older *Historical Methods Newsletter,* 1967–1977) has since 1978 become well known as a forum for articles developing and refining the statistical and methodological techniques used on historical data, as has the newer journal *History and Computing*, published in Britain since 1989 (several articles from which appear in the "References" section below). Other periodicals with a computational orientation include *Computers in Genealogy, Computers and the Social Sciences, Computers and the Humanities,* and the *Social Science Microcomputer Review.* More traditional intellectual history journals such as the *Journal of the History of Ideas* have also begun regularly to publish work in the quantitative analysis of political and philosophical texts.

Over the years, a number of authors have contributed useful manuals on the application of computers to research in history and other humanistic or social scientific disciplines, though a mark of the speed of change in hardware and software during recent years has been how quickly these works are rendered obsolete. Notable pioneering (if now largely outdated) contributions to this genre include Susan Hockey's *A Guide to Computer Applications in the Humanities* (1980) and Edward Shorter's *The Historian and the Computer* (1971), which goes back to the era of encoded cards, machine rooms, and the then "new" IBM 029 keypunch. More recent works, written since the advent of the PC and the Internet, have begun to multiply, but these, too, are still rapidly dated by changes in technology.

As the above reference to the *Journal of the History of Ideas* suggests, economic and social history have long since ceased to be the only subdisciplines in which the computer has had an impact on scholarship (as opposed to pedagogy or communications). In fact, despite the 1970s prophecy by the *Annaliste* Emmanuel Le Roy Ladurie that all historians would soon be "programmers" or cease to be historians, the use of computers to provide complex regressions and other statistical forms of analysis has remained a small (and shrinking, in comparison with growth elsewhere) area of computer applications in historiography. The real growth has in fact occurred in other historical subdisciplines, and, as suggested above, in cybernetically assisted historical communications.

A number of universities began, a decade or so ago, to use computers in the study of more traditional humanistic problems, in particular for the philological analysis of texts. As traditional history of ideas began to be rivaled in the 1960s—under the influence of linguistics and structuralism—by a curiosity about the vocabulary, syntax, and structure of specific literary and historical texts, a further use was found for the computer. It was now possible to store a document such as the U.S. Constitution, or the French Declaration of the Rights of Man and Citizen, on a computer and, using specially designed software, analyze the authors' choices of words and phrases. At institutions such as Arizona State University, centers grew up devoted to the storing of the works of particular authors and the quantitative analysis of their texts. The University of Kansas provides in "Carrie" a full-text electronic library of authors in western and many non-Western languages. The ARTFL project at the University of Chicago, to provide another example, contains an enormous number of archived French literary, historical, and political texts, and other major universities in France, the United Kingdom, Canada, Australia, and Japan have developed similar collections. Optical scanners, primitive and slow in the 1980s, and still far from foolproof, are increasingly providing a shortcut to inputting large texts, though they do not remove the need for scrupulous proofreading and have yet to reach the sophistication necessary to handle most manuscripts and premodern typefaces (something that may soon change).

Computers have now also drastically reduced the distances separating scholars from archives, libraries, and one another. The development and meteoric growth of the Internet, in existence since the mid-1960s but only in full flight from the early 1990s, has made it possible for scholars remote from these textual archives (or from other mainframes storing economic and social datasets) to find databases and textbases through easy-to-use "gophering" and to transfer these sets to their local mainframe, or even download them to their personal computer, via a File Transfer Protocol (FTP). A doctoral student in rural Nova Scotia wanting to analyze Shakespeare's plays for their use of the term "monster" and "monstrosity" (and cognate terms) would a few years ago have had to rely on a concordance, or sheer reading; it is now possible, through the Internet, to search for archived text and then, once it has been found, do a word search generating the results in seconds.

A less esoteric but no less important development is the ability of historians to "converse" virtually with colleagues on the other side of the planet and to send one another text, with minimum delay. The administration and editing of this encyclopedia, with over two hundred contributors scattered over five continents, was rendered incomparably more manageable and faster through electronic mail. Electronic mail discussion groups, enabled by a local "Listserv" facility, allow scholars in a particular subfield to communicate with those doing similar work, post queries relating to teaching and research, and discuss literature in their area.

There are other ways, in which the computer is redrawing the boundaries and shape of the historical field. As printing costs continue to rise and university library budgets, hard hit in the fiscally conservative 1990s, continue to shrink, severe limits have been placed on the growth of publication, particularly in the form of scholarly periodicals. The Internet, combined with readily available (and regularly updatable) CD-ROMs for such expensive hardcover reference sources as *Historical Abstracts* and the *Social Sciences Citation Index* has made it possible—many may think too easy—for reference librarians to cut subscriptions to these volumes and replace them with target-article document-delivery services. Clearly this has both advantages and disadvantages: the scholar or student who has a peripheral interest in a particular article or book and who does not have free access to remote-delivery documents, may think twice before ordering a specific title once found easily on the shelf; and, to some degree, the replacement of "real" books and articles with single-ordered photocopies and on-line text has removed the serendipitous aspect of library research whereby one could "cruise" a bookshelf looking for one title and find several others of relevance shelved nearby. On the other hand, the use of Internet library searching (usually through a gopher or similar search program) and of hypertext to provide electronic links between one topic and another, especially on the fast-growing World Wide Web sector of the Internet, still makes it possible for the researcher reading about one topic to find "pointers" to others of potential interest; but scanning the bookshelf and searching the "net" should still be seen as complementary rather than mutually exclusive secondary research techniques. Numerous bibliographies are available on the Web or via FTP, for instance that compiled by the Association for History and Computing.

Publishers of books and articles have for hundreds of years played a critical role in the communication of historical knowledge, and it is at the publisher's end of the scholarly process that one finds additional evidence of the use of computers in a variety of ways. Many journals have, for instance, been obliged as much by fiscal restraint as positive inclination to make use of the new technologies. Authors are now routinely asked to supply text on disk that can then be typeset using cheaper desktop publishing programs which cost a fraction of traditional composing methods and are more easily revisable. The Internet, via FTP, and still more the Web, have allowed existing journals to precirculate new articles to subscribers months before they actually appear in print and to make tables of contents of back issues available to potential subscribers. Perhaps most strikingly, new journals are arising that eschew the print medium altogether, instead offering their articles and reviews in electronic format alone on a Web homepage. Academic orthodoxy has been slow to accept this latest cybernetic wrinkle—one is reminded of the hostility to print expressed by late-fifteenth- and sixteenth-century humanists who saw that device as a vulgarization of knowledge. Those who set up new journals in electronic format find it necessary repeatedly to assert that an article published electronically can be of the same intellectual quality as one printed in black and white on paper. In order to encourage authors to submit their work to such journals, it is necessary to ensure that comparable standards of academic peer-reviewing are maintained and that the Internet does not simply become a promiscuous vehicle for the random-issuing of second-rate knowledge and poor or intellectually vapid writing. Academic assessment authorities, such as deans and tenure committees, are only now beginning to develop protocols for the evaluation of electronically published scholarship.

Finally, the computer is having a lasting impact on historical pedagogy. Whereas courses on "historical methodology" used to be compulsory, shudder-inducing classes, often dreaded alike by the undergraduate and graduate students forced to take them and the faculty obliged to teach captive audiences, most undergraduates in Western countries now have at least a rudimentary degree of computer literacy. Simulation packages and interactive software have been developed by scholars with expertise in particular areas (the U.S. Civil War; the Age of Louis XIV; the Renaissance) that allow the student to grasp historical concepts by playing with them on-line, to experiment electronically with different historical outcomes, and to search a range of available topics with far greater freedom than even the best-indexed conventional textbook can permit. Professors can download high-resolution color images from remote servers such as the Louvre, the Vatican Library, or the Library of Congress, and show them to students on-screen in lectures, as a supplement to or even replacement for conventional slide projection. Assignments requiring students to find materials in remote libraries over the Internet, or to hand in a list of URLs (Universal Resource Locators, essentially Web homepage addresses) on relevant topics, are becoming commonplace even in junior-level classes, though still resisted by many academics, who are by no means always in the older, precomputer generation. Many scholars have expressed cautions about the impact of the new technology on historical pedagogy, and some of these are well founded: the reliance of students on spellchecking and grammatical programs rather than dictionaries has rapidly proved to be a mixed blessing, and it is not clear whether such compositional tools may not yet prove more of a curse than a cure, diminishing still further the basic level of linguistic competence by "downloading" the responsibility for good writing on to the machine.

Computers need to be viewed as the servants of Clio, not as her master. The full implications of the new technology on the discipline are scarcely capable of anticipation even in the latter half of the 1990s. But as the millennium draws to a close, it is plain that the computer is here to stay and that the work of the historian in a variety of fields and at every level of sophistication can be aided by its proper and intellectually responsible exploitation.

D.R. Woolf

See also CLIOMETRICS; DEMOGRAPHY—HISTORICAL; FAMILY HISTORY (COMPARATIVE); FAMILY RECONSTITUTION; IDEAS, HISTORY OF; INTERDISCIPLINARY HISTORY; SOCIAL HISTORY.

Texts

Aydelotte, William O., Allan G. Bogue, and Robert William Fogel, eds. *The Dimensions of Quantitative Research in History.* Princeton, NJ: Princeton University Press, 1972.

Bailyn, Bernard, and Lotte Bailyn. *Massachusetts Shipping, 1697–1714: A Statistical Study.* Cambridge, MA: Harvard University Press, 1959.

Floud, Roderick. *An Introduction to Quantitative Methods for Historians.* Second ed. London: Methuen, 1979.

Herlihy, David, and Christiane Klapisch-Zuber. *Tuscans and Their Families: A Study of the Florentine Catasto of 1427.* New Haven, CT: Yale University Press, 1985.

Hockey, Susan. *A Guide to Computer Applications in the Humanities.* London: Duckworth, 1980.

Shorter, Edward. *The Historian and the Computer: A Practical Guide.* Englewood Cliffs, NJ: Prentice-Hall, 1971.

Wrigley, E.A., and R.S. Schofield. *The Population History of England and Wales, 1541–1871.* Cambridge, Eng.: Cambridge University Press, 1981.

References

Butler, C. "Integrating Computing into the History Curriculum." *History and Computing* 5 (1993): 199–203.

Genet, Jean-Philippe, and Antonio Zampolli, eds. *Computers and the Humanities.* Brookfield, VT: Ashgate Publishing, 1992.

Greenstein, Daniel I. *A Historian's Guide to Computing.* Oxford and New York: Oxford University Press, 1994.

Hitchcock, Tim. "'She's Gotta Have I.T.': Teaching Information Technology to Undergraduate History Students." *History and Computing* 5 (1993): 193–198.

Horik, René van. "Recent Progress in the Automatic Reading of Printed Historical Documents." *History and Computing* 5 (1993): 68–73.

Igartua, José E. "The Computer and the Historian's Work." *History and Computing* 3 (1991): 73–83.

Jonassen, David H., et al., eds. *Designing Hypermedia for Learning.* Berlin and New York: Springer-Verlag, 1990.

McMichael, Andrew, Michael O'Malley, and Roy Rosenzweig. "Historians and the Web: A Guide." AHA *Perspectives* 34.1 (Jan. 1996): 11–15.

Schick, James B.M. *Teaching History with a Computer: A Complete Guide for College Professors.* Chicago, IL: Lyceum Books, 1990.

Thorvaldson, Gunnar. "Making Historical Sources Machine Readable: Some Experiences with Optical Character Recognition." *History and Computing* 5 (1993): 74–81.

Tibbo, Helen R. *Abstracting, Information Retrieval and the Humanities: Providing Access to Historical Literature.* Chicago and London: American Library Association, 1993.

Turk, Christopher, ed. *Humanities Research Using Computers.* London: Chapman & Hall; New York: Van Nostrand Reinhold, 1991.

Condorcet, Marquis de (Marie-Jean-Antoine-Nicolas de Caritat) (1743–1794)

French *philosophe* and historical thinker. Condorcet was born in Picardy, the son of a military officer, and educated at the Collège de Navarre. As a young mathematician he was admitted to the Academy of Sciences in 1769, thereby entering the circles of the *philosophes*. He became secretary of the academy in 1776 and a member of the French Academy in 1782. Under the influence of Turgot, the controller-general to King Louis

XVI, he became a passionate propagandist for the natural rights of man, liberal economics, and anticlericalism. Bound to reason and rationality, Condorcet promoted a new social theory, which can be seen in the title of his *Essay on the Application of Mathematics to the Theory of Decision-Making*. During the French Revolutionary "Terror" Condorcet was arrested and imprisoned for his outspoken support for the ousted Girondins; he died soon after, apparently by his own hand. He never finished his great historical work, but left only the introduction, *Sketch for a Historical Picture of the Progress of the Human Mind*. According to this work, all of history should be seen as the product of human action, rather than divine intervention. Infinite human progress was possible, Condorcet theorized, if rational political policies and science could be universally accepted.

John B. Roney

Texts

Condorcet: Selected Writings. Ed. Keith Michael Baker. Indianapolis, IN: Bobbs-Merrill, 1976.
Sketch for a Historical Picture of the Progress of the Human Mind. Westport, CT: Greenwood Press, 1979.
Condorcet: Foundations of Social Choice and Political Theory. Ed. and trans. Iain McLean and Fiona Hewitt. Brookfield, VT: Elgar, 1994.

References

Keith Michael Baker. *Condorcet, from Natural Philosophy to Social Mathematics*. Chicago: University of Chicago Press, 1975.

Confucius [Kong Qiu; Kong Zi] (551–479 B.C.)
Chinese sage and compiler of the *Chunqiu*. Confucius is the most influential and revered philosopher in Chinese history. He has also been considered a great historian, mainly for his alleged authorship of the canon *Chunqiu* [Spring and Autumn Annals], one of the five most revered Confucian Classics in traditional times. Modern scholars have questioned the authenticity of this ascribed authorship, but also believe that Confucius might have indeed compiled a *Chunqiu* that differed in some ways from the current text of the book. The latter view seems most reasonable to this author. The basic structure of the two texts also should be very similar.

The *Chunqiu* is a chronicle of ancient China (mainly the northern state of Lu) from 722 to 481 B.C. It contains certain views on the pattern of history and on the moral function of history—that

is, how history should be used to praise the good and to blame the bad (the principle of *bao-bian*). History is considered a book of judgment on political and social actions. Certain historiographical principles were also established in compiling this book. On the philosophical side, the author of *Chunqiu* held that history had a purpose and the will of Heaven should be observed in writing about it; he also believed that writing history was not an objective pursuit but a subjective intellectual undertaking.

The *Chunqiu* was the first historical work in Chinese history privately compiled by an individual (rather than the product of official endeavor like much subsequent Chinese historiography). It also laid down the basic structure of the style of chronicles in the history of Chinese historiography. Confucius was the earliest Chinese thinker to periodize Chinese history in ancient times. He also edited some earlier historical works for his students to read, but this has been a subject of continuing intellectual debate since the Han dynasty (202 B.C.–A.D. 220).

Chun-shu Chang

Texts

The Ch'un Ts'ew. Trans. James Legge. Hong Kong: Hong Kong University Press, 1960.

References

Creel, H.G. *Confucius and the Chinese Way*. New York: Harper Torchbooks, 1960.
Chang, Chun-shu. *The Making of China: Main Themes in Premodern Chinese History*. Englewood Cliffs, NJ: Prentice-Hall, 1975.

Contarini, Nicolò (1553–1631)
Historian of Venice, politician, and doge (duke). Contarini was born in Venice into a patrician family and educated at the University of Padua. He served the republic in many important offices both in Venice and the Terraferma empire. He was a strong supporter of Venetian independence from the Holy See, a position he shared with his friend and fellow historian, Paolo Sarpi. Contarini's political career culminated in his election as doge in 1630, the year before his death. In 1620 Contarini was chosen official historian of the republic. He prepared for his *Historie venetiane* [Venetian Histories] by searching through state records, believing that truth should be the only objective of historians, not the praise of the powerful or mere stylistic elegance. The history reflects his pride in Venice, its institutions, history, and nobility; it

equally illustrates his concern over its recent economic and military decline. Contarini's history was left unfinished at his death. Venice's ruling body, the Council of Ten, decided not to print it because it contained still-sensitive material. Only excerpts of it have been printed to date.

Kenneth Bartlett

Texts

See appendix to Cozzi, *Il Doge Nicolo Contarini,* below.

References

Cochrane, Eric. *Historians and Historiography in the Italian Renaissance.* Chicago: University of Chicago Press, 1981, 238.

Cozzi, Gaetano. *Il Doge Nicolo Contarini: Ricerche sul patriziato veneziano agli inizi del seicento* [The Doge Nicolo Contarini: Research on the Venetian Patriciate at the Beginning of the Seventeenth Century]. Venice: Istituto per la collaborazione culturale, 1958.

Contingency

One of the forms of the debate over causation. There are two major definitions of contingency, both dependent on a preceding definition of chance. The first takes chance to mean the unpredictable intersection of two independent causal series, and contingency to indicate that some events are not determined, but can be affected in unpredictable ways, most often by human agency. The second definition is much simpler, and collapses contingency into chance taken as an occurrence to which we cannot assign a cause. Thus the first definition treats contingency as an inherent property of the universe, while the second regards it as merely a manifestation of the limitations of our knowledge.

Aristotle (384 B.C.–322 B.C.) set the terms of the discussion in his works treating modal, or three-valued logic, *On Interpretation* and *Categories.* He used the example of a sea battle, which must either happen or not tomorrow, but at the same time "it is not necessary for a sea-battle to take place tomorrow, nor for one not to take place." That is, the law of the excluded middle (that a contradiction necessarily means that one of two things cannot be true) does not apply to future events. Whatever has already happened is necessary in that it cannot now be otherwise than it is, but what has not yet happened is not determined in the same way; it is contingent. Elsewhere, Aristotle apparently repudiated the idea

of contingency, putting its appearance down to our failure to discover the real causes behind an event. Yet at the same time, he also tried to leave room for human will, which seems to mean that he endorsed the first definition presented above. Aristotle thus represented both of the major positions on contingency.

Christian thinkers were centrally concerned with the problem of free will and evil, but only a few of them returned to Aristotle's discussion. Most important in its transmission was the work of the Roman patrician Boethius (480–524). He coined the Latin word *contingentia* in his translation of *On Interpretation* to denote those things that are possible. More important, Boethius wrote a commentary on the work, in which he developed his own definition of contingent events as those that "equally are or are not" in the future, that is, the future is in large measure indeterminate. In the Middle Ages, discussion largely turned on the role of God's foreknowledge in causing future contingent events. It concluded with William of Ockham (ca. 1285–ca. 1347) denying contingency altogether.

By the end of the fourteenth century the framework of the idea was largely set among theologians and philosophers, and the word "contingency" had entered, or was about to, most western European vernaculars. Thereafter until about 1750 the term was almost exclusively used by logicians. Antoine Augustin Cournot (1801–1877) was the first philosopher to take up the idea of contingency and apply it to historical causation. His *An Essay on the Foundations of our Knowledge,* together with the fuller treatment in his *Traité de l'enchainement des idées fondamentales dans les sciences et dans l'histoire* [Treatise on the Sequence of Fundamental Ideas in the Sciences and History] (1861), drew a distinction between scientific and historical knowledge and worked with an essentially epistemological definition of contingency. Science, the superior form of knowledge, seeks general laws, and history enters only when science runs up against facts it cannot explain, the contingent. There are not many of these, and they form the only object of historical study. By the time Cournot was done, history had virtually vanished as a discipline, just as he hoped that contingencies, such as races, could eventually be eliminated. J.B. Bury (1861–1927), the first working historian to discuss contingency, took over Cournot's ideas almost in their totality, especially in his essay "Cleopatra's Nose" (1916), although by the time of *The Idea of Progress* (1920) he was prepared to allow a somewhat larger role for contingency.

In the twentieth century, discussion of contingency has been largely confined to Anglo-French historians, and while debates over determinism continue largely unabated among both historians and philosophers, the term has largely disappeared. The majority of historians have followed Cournot's lead and tried to get rid of contingency, right down to the second edition of William H. Dray (b. 1921), *Philosophy of History* (pp. 128 ff.). The influential idealist philosopher and historian R.G. Collingwood (1889–1943) scoffed in his *Idea of History* (p. 151) at Bury's idea of contingency as marking "the final collapse of his thought" and W.B. Gallie (b. 1912) developed the idea of history as a followable story as a means largely to remove contingency. On the other side, Raymond Aron's (1905–1983) *Introduction to the Philosophy of History,* proceeding from a critique of Cournot, argued for contingency as a fundamental aspect of both the universe and historical analysis, while Gordon Leff's (b. 1926) *History and Social Theory* put forward a thoroughly voluntarist view of human agency in history and the centrality of contingency. As Leff summed up, "historical events are in response to circumstances which although not of men's own choosing are largely of their own making."

Thomas F. Mayer

See also CAUSATION; CHAOS THEORY AND HISTORY; COVERING LAWS; DETERMINISM; FORTUNE; PHILOSOPHY OF HISTORY.

Texts

Aristotle. *Categories and De Interpretatione.* Trans. J.L. Ackrill. Oxford: Clarendon Press, 1963.

Aron, Raymond. *Introduction to the Philosophy of History.* Boston: Beacon Press, 1961.

Boethius. *De Interpretatione* [On Interpretation]. In *Patrologiae Cursus Completus, Series Latina,* vol. 64. Ed. J.-P. Migne. Paris: Garnier, 1891.

Bury, J.B. "Cleopatra's Nose." In *Selected Essays of J.B. Bury,* ed. Harold W. Temperley. Cambridge, Eng.: Cambridge University Press, 1930.

———. *The Idea of Progress.* London: Macmillan, 1928.

Collingwood, Robin George. *The Idea of History.* New York: Oxford University Press, 1956.

Cournot, Antoine Augustin. *An Essay on the Foundations of Our Knowledge.* Trans. Merrit H. Moore. New York: Liberal Arts Press, 1956.

Dray, William H. *Philosophy of History.* Second ed. Englewood Cliffs, NJ: Prentice-Hall, 1993.

Gallie, W.B. *Philosophy and the Historical Understanding.* London: Chatto and Windus, 1964.

Leff, Gordon. *History and Social Theory.* Garden City, NJ: Doubleday, 1971.

Ockham, William of. *Predestination, God's Foreknowledge, and Future Contingents.* Trans. M.M. Adams and Norman Kretzmann. New York: Appleton-Century-Crofts, 1969.

Controversy in Historical Writing

Contrary to the view held by many specialists in the exact and natural sciences, and a fair proportion of the general public, who regard controversies as further proof that history is not a science and believe that the study of history has made little real, consolidated progress over the years, controversy is in fact an essential instrument in the development of historiography.

Controversy can be defined, in Geoffrey Elton's words, as "the sharpest manifestation of the normal dialectic of historical research—of that exchange of answers to questions by which we progress to a new and more complete understanding of problems." (Fogel and Elton, 1983, p. 104) Konrad Repgen considers that three requirements must be met for an argument among historians to warrant the description of a struggle: 1) major opposition between thesis and antithesis; 2) the subject of the dispute should be important from the point of view of content; 3) the argument should not be confined to the ivory tower of academia; it should at least partly capture the public eye. Repgen also introduces an important distinction between different types of historical controversy, between those that arise on issues of historical methodology, and those that are metamethodological (that is, concerned with the philosophy, *Weltanschauung,* or ideology of the historians involved).

On the other hand, in the context of the discussion surrounding historiographical progress, F.R. Ankersmit thinks it appropriate to reintroduce the old distinction between "historical research" and "historical writing." It is not hard to show how controversies of the former type are generally less bitter, and can be solved more easily than the latter. If we understand historical discourse to be a realist discourse, and accept the text's claim to be a realist representation of part of the past, then, as Ankersmit perceptively explains, "if we have a debate between, for example, a Marxist and a liberal historian, the debate is not merely on statements about historical reality. Rather, such a debate concerns the question what actually is the nature or essence of history" (106).

The number and intensity of controversies varies greatly according to the country and the age. Sixteenth-century Europe witnessed vigorous exchanges among historians over such issues as national descent and the antiquity of various confessional denominations. In later seventeenth-century England, historians would contest in heated terms the origins of the nation's civil wars. Various concepts such as the rise of the middle classes or the origins of the Industrial Revolution continue to stimulate strife among modern historians. In the last century, however, no country has had such continuous and intense historiographical controversies as has Germany.

What are the reasons for such differences? In Germany's case, the factors that help to account for this would appear to include: a) the interest a nation as a whole takes in a historiographical controversy is in direct proportion to its internal differences regarding its own identity; b) all retrospective nationalism is more sensitive to historical debate; c) the younger varieties of nationalism and newer nations have a greater need to "invent their past"; d) a nation's political situation helps to explain the degree and intensity of a controversy at any particular moment. The balance of this discussion will seek to illuminate the topic by examining a number of notorious German examples of historical controversy.

Among the greatest controversies in German historiography, any of which might serve as a good example of the phenomenon, one must give first place to the *Lamprechtstreit*. Karl Lamprecht (1856–1915) favored a history focusing on a generous understanding of the concept of "culture" in contrast to a history based on the actions of the state, and was especially interested in explaining the collective with the aid of the social sciences and systematic comparison. His methodological writing and his monumental *German History* (1891–1911) met with harsh opposition beginning in the 1890s from the orthodox representatives of the German historical school who, as far as academic power was concerned, won a sweeping victory and maintained their dominance over the profession until the end of the Weimar Republic.

The vigor of traditional points of view in German historiography explains why the emergence of the "Bielefeld school" in the early 1960s, spearheaded by Hans-Ulrich Wehler and Jürgen Kocka, who proposed a new form of "total history"

fashioned by dialogue with the social sciences, was to spark the second great methodological controversy of modern German historiography. And the critical and political nature of the "Bielefeld school" is itself easier to understand in the light of the first of the two controversies surrounding the direction of German history after 1945, known as the Fischer Controversy. Fritz Fischer's (b. 1908) *Griff nach der Weltmacht* [Germany's Aims in the First World War], published in 1961, triggered a bitter dispute, not only because he maintained that the German objectives in World War I were principally to prevent an internal revolution and achieve the hegemony of the *Reich* in Europe, but above all because he implicitly rejected the idea that the errors of Naziism had nothing to do with Germany itself and considered that they would not have been possible without the political and military traditions of Prussia and the German Empire.

The last of the controversies revolving around recurring historical problems in Germany, the *Historikerstreit*, focused directly on the Hitler regime: the specific question was whether, as Charles S. Maier writes, "Nazi crimes were unique, a legacy of evil in a class by themselves, irreparably burdening any concept of German nationhood, or whether they are comparable to other national atrocities, especially Stalinist terror." (p. 4) The polemic unfolded from 1986 to 1987, and made a great impact on German public opinion.

In short, as Ann Rigney states, "the debates continue, following a complicated series of checks and balances, denials, shifts of emphasis, revisions of revisions." (p. 92) In this way, history too would seem to corroborate Karl Popper's view that there are "few if any examples of a development of thought which is slow, steady and continuous, and proceeds by successive degrees of improvement rather than by trial and error and the struggle of ideologies."

Ignacio Olábarri

See also COUNTERFACTUALS; LOGIC AND HISTORICAL ENQUIRY; PHILOSOPHY OF HISTORY, ANALYTIC.

References

Ankersmit, F.R. "On Historiographical Progress." *Storia della Storiografia/History of Historiography* 22 (1992): 103–107.

Fogel, Robert W., and Geoffrey R. Elton. *Which Road to the Past? Two Views of History*. New Haven, CT: Yale University Press, 1983.

Iggers, Georg G. *The German Conception of History: The National Tradition of Historical*

Thought from Herder to the Present. Rev. ed. Middletown, CT: Wesleyan University Press, 1983.

Maier, Charles S. *The Unmasterable Past: History, Holocaust and German National Identity,* Cambridge, MA: Harvard University Press, 1988.

Popper, Karl. *Conjectures and Refutations.* London: Routledge, 1965.

Repgen, Konrad. "Methoden- oder Richtungskämpfe in der deutschen Geschichtswissenschaft seit 1945? [Methodological or Ideological Struggles in German Historical Scholarship Since 1945?]." *Geschichte in Wissenschaft und Unterricht* [History in Scholarship and Education] 30 (1979): 591–610.

Rigney, Ann. "Time for Visions and Revisions: Interpretation Conflict from a Communicative Perspective." *Storia della storiografia/ History of Historiography* 22 (1992): 85–92.

Conze, Werner (1910–1986)

German historian. Conze studied at the universities of Marburg, Leipzig, and Königsberg, obtaining his doctorate in 1934. He served in the German Wehrmacht until severely wounded in 1941. He was appointed professor of history at the universities of Posen ([Poznań] 1943–1945), Münster (1951–1957), and Heidelberg (from 1957). Between 1945 and 1951 he was an independent scholar in Göttingen. Conze was one of the most outstanding historians of modern and early-modern Europe of his generation. He largely succeeded in combining traditional methods of historical research with innovations drawn from the social sciences. Continuing 1930s work on the link between *völkische* history and sociological methods of enquiry, as first developed by Otto Brunner and others, he emphasized the importance of incorporating sociological, cultural, and economic aspects into post-1945 German historiography. With the support of several learned research institutions and scholarly journals that he established, and the assistance of a great number of students, Conze mapped a route that allowed an increasing number of German historians to move away from the study of political history and the history of ideas in their traditional forms. Beginning in the 1960s, Conze increasingly became concerned to explore the social and structural aspects of history, while also embracing the "history from below" approach that gained prominence in that decade.

Klaus Larres

Texts

Agrarverfassung und Bevölkerung in Litauen und Weissrussland [The Agrarian Structure and Population of Lithuania and White Russia]. Leipzig, Ger.: Hirzel, 1940.

Hirschenhof: Die Geschichte einer deutschen Sprachinsel in Livland [Hirschenhof: The History of a German-Speaking Community in Livonia]. Hanover: Hirschendt, 1963.

Die Strukturgeschichte des technisch-industriellen Zeitalters als Aufgabe für Forschung und Unterricht [The Structural History of the Age of Technology and Industry As a Task for Research and Teaching]. Cologne: Westdeutscher Verlag, 1957.

"Vom Pöbel zum Proletariat [From Rabble to Proletariat]." *Vierteljahreshefte für Sozial- und Wirtschaftsgeschichte* [Quarterly for Social and Economic History] 41 (1954): 333–364.

Leibniz als Historiker [Leibniz As Historian]. Berlin: De Gruyter, 1951.

References

Engelhardt, U., V. Sellin, and H. Stuke, eds. *Soziale Bewegung und politische Verfassung: Beiträge zur Geschichte der modernen Welt* [Social Movements and Political Constitutions: Contributions to the History of the Modern World]. Stuttgart: Industrielle Welt, 1976, 895–905. (Bibliography of Conze's work).

Kocka, Jürgen. "Werner Conze und die Sozialgeschichte der Bundesrepublik Deutschland [Conze and Social History in the Federal Republic of Germany]." *Geschichte in Wissenschaft und Unterricht* [History As Scholarship and Pedagogy] 37 (1986): 593–602.

Kosselleck, Reinhard. "Werner Conze: Tradition und Innovation." *Historische Zeitschrift* 245 (1987): 529–543.

Schieder, W., and V. Sellin, eds. *Sozialgeschichte in Deutschland: Entwicklungen und Perspektiven im internationalen Zusammenhang* [German Social History: Developments and Prospects in the International Context]. 4 vols. Göttingen: Vandenhoeck & Ruprecht, 1986.

Coquery-Vidrovitch, Catherine (b. 1935)

Social and economic historian of Africa. Born and educated in Paris, Coquery-Vidrovitch teaches at the Université Paris VII and directs the "Third

World, African" program within the French National Centre for Scientific Research. An early article on the "African mode of production" (1969) challenged ill-fitting European concepts for African economic and political evolution with a distinctively African model derived from Marxist insights. *Congo* (1972) remains a landmark study of how colonial capitalism affected African societies. Her vast body of work since then focuses on long-term social and economic change in the manner of the Annales school, in search of the deeper roots of Africa's current dependency and poverty.

P.S. Zachernuk

Texts

Africa: Endurance and Change South of the Sahara. Trans. David Maisel. Berkeley: University of California Press, 1988.

African Women: A Modern History. Trans. Beth Raps. Boulder, CO: Westview Press, 1997.

Le Congo au temps des grandes compagnies concessionnaires: 1898–1930 [The Congo in the Grand Concessionary Company Era]. Paris: Mouton, 1972.

Histoire des villes d'Afrique noire [Cities In Sub-Saharan African History]. Paris: Albin Michel, 1993.

"Research on an African Mode of Production." Trans. S. Sherwin. In *Perspectives on the African Past,* ed. M.A. Klein and G.W. Johnson. Boston: Little, Brown, 1972.

Correia, Gaspar (late fifteenth century–ca. 1563)

Portuguese historian. Correia traveled to the Orient in 1512 as secretary to Afonso de Albuquerque, the first great strategist for the Portuguese in the Asian seas. He remained in the Orient until he died, and his extensive personal experience, his fascination with the customs of Asian peoples, and his own interest in reading local chronicles spurred him to write a chronicle of the Portuguese in the Orient from the beginning until the mid-sixteenth century. Entitled *Lendas da Índia* [Legends of India], it was first published in 1858. Prior to this he had written a preliminary work, *Crónicas dos Reys de Portugal e Sumários das suas Virtudes* [Chronicles of the Kings of Portugal and a Summary of Their Virtues]. His keen eye, inquiring mind, and ability to portray everyday life and tradition in Asia make *Lendas da Índia* a rare instance of adaptation and acculturation to the Oriental world.

Jorge M. dos Santos Alves

Texts

Crónicas de D. Manuel e de D. João III (até 1533). Ed. José Pereira da Costa. Lisbon: Academia das Ciências de Lisboa, 1992 [i.e., 1993].

Lendas da Índia. Ed. Rodrigo José de Lima Felner, 8 parts in 4 vols. Lisbon: Academia Real das Sciencias, 1860–1866.

References

Serrão, Joaquim Veríssimo. *A Historiografia Portuguesa* [Portuguese Historiography], vol. I. Lisbon: Editorial Verbo, 1972.

Cosmas [Kosmas] of Prague (ca. 1045–1125)

Bohemian priest, dean, and chronicler. Cosmas, born into a family of the Bohemian lesser nobility, studied at Liège before returning to his native country. He served as secretary to Bishop Gebhard of Prague (1068–1089) and accompanied him to the imperial synod convened in Mainz by Emperor Henry IV in May 1085. Having earlier been married and widowed, Cosmas was not ordained priest until 1099, when he became a canon and then dean of the cathedral chapter of St. Vitus in Prague. His major historical work was the three-volume *Chronica Boemorum* [Chronicle of the Bohemians], written in Latin, which recorded Bohemian history from its beginnings to 1125, the year of Cosmas's death. It was the first such work written in that country, and although it is filled with popular tales and ethnographic descriptions borrowed from classical authors, it is generally considered a reliable record, especially in books two and three, which deal with events during Cosmas's own lifetime.

Monica Sandor

Texts

Cosmae Pragensis, chronica Boemorum. Ed. Bertold Bretholz. *Monumenta Germaniae Historica: Scriptores rerum Germanicorum,* new series, II. Berlin: Weidmannsche Verlag, 1955.

References

Bosl, Karl. *Handbuch der Geschichte böhmischen Länder* [Handbook of the History of Bohemian Lands]. Vol. I. Stuttgart: Hiersemann, 1967.

Dvornik, Francis. *The Making of Central and Eastern Europe.* London: Polish Research Centre, 1949.

Costa y Martinez, Joaquín (1846–1911)

Spanish lawyer, intellectual, and historian. Costa was born in Monzón, Huesca province. As a child, he grew up in rural poverty and paid for his education by working as a mason while he pursued his bachelor's degree, which he obtained in 1864. The government chose him to attend the 1867 Paris Universal Exposition as a pensioned worker, an experience that had a profound influence on his subsequent intellectual development because it made him aware of Spain's cultural and economic backwardness. Costa published his first book, *Ideas de la Exposición de Paris de 1867* (Ideas of the 1867 Paris Exposition) in 1868. Back in Madrid, he became a lawyer and received a Ph.D. (1872); unable to obtain a university position, he joined the Institucion Libre de Enseñanza (Free Institute of Education) in 1878. In 1881, he taught at the lawyer's college. Living in poverty, he spent his time conducting research for the works that he would eventually publish, and participating in a number of scientific congresses. In 1894, he moved to Jaen to take up a position as a notary. Costa contributed to the foundation of the *Revista de Geografía Comercial* (Journal of Commercial Geography). In 1884, he founded the Sociedad de Africanistas (Society of Africanists) and organized various scientific expeditions into Africa. He wrote extensively on numerous topics from legal studies to an analysis of Spain's social, political, and economic situation. Among his most significant works is a *Historia critica de la Revolucion española* [Critical History of the Spanish Revolution].

Carlos Pérez

Texts

Colectivismo agrario en España [Agrarian Collectivism in Spain]. 2 vols. Zaragoza: Guara, Instituto de estudios agrarios, pesqueros y alimentarios, 1983.
Historia critica de la Revolucion española. Ed. Alberto Gil Novales. Madrid: Centro de Estudios Constitucionales, 1992.
Historia politica social: Patria [Social Political History: Fatherland]. Ed. José Garcia Mercadal. Madrid: Aguilar, 1961.

References

Cheyne, George J.G. *A Bibliographical Study of the Writings of Joaquin Costa, 1846–1911*. London: Tamesis Books, 1972.
Martin-Retortillo, Cirilo. *Joaquin Costa: Propulsor de la Reconstrucion Nacional* [Joaquin Costa: Architect of National Reconstruction]. Barcelona: Editorial AEDOS, 1961.

Counterfactuals

A form of conditional statement in which the antecedent is a false past-tense subjunctive statement, for example, Had Carthage won the Punic Wars, Africa would have dominated Europe and Hebrew would have become the universal language. Hume defined causation using a counterfactual: had the cause not occurred, neither would have the effect. One of the basic problems of logic is that a material interpretation of counterfactuals leads always to a true value, irrespective of how reasonable the conditional may be, for instance, Had Genghis Khan been a pacifist, Richard Nixon would have spoken Mongolian, is true. The failure of traditional logic to deal with counterfactuals has led contemporary philosophy to analyze causality as a primitive notion.

The weighing of causes in historiography is based sometimes on counterfactuals: had a historical cause been absent, how different would the effect have been? For example, Robert Fogel used cliometric methods to measure the effect of railroad building on the growth of the American economy in the nineteenth century, concluding that it had been far less important than previously believed. The use of counterfactuals to weigh causes is particularly useful in economic historiography where the causes and effects are often quantifiable and relevant mathematical functions are available for the computation of counterfactuals. Critics have pointed out that it is very rare to find in history a closed system, within which all the historical effects of a cause can be computed; and that counterfactuals are nearly useless outside fields that have established equations. For example, who can answer, How would history have looked had Hitler never existed or had Cleopatra had a longer nose?

Aviezer Tucker

See also CAUSATION; CLIOMETRICS.

Texts

Climo, T.A., and P.G.A. Howells. "Possible Worlds in Historical Explanation." *History and Theory* 15 (1976): 1–20.
Fogel, Robert William. "Historiography and Retrospective Economics." *History and Theory* 9 (1970): 245–264.
Hurst, B.C. "A Comment on the Possible Worlds of Climo and Howells." *History and Theory* 18 (1979): 52–60.

Couto, Diogo Do (1542–1616)

Portuguese historian, satirist, and orator. Born in Lisbon, Couto was still a young man when, after entering the service of the Portuguese court, he traveled to the Orient in 1559. In 1594 he was appointed official chronicler of Portuguese Asia and head of the future central Estado da Índia Archives. Immersed in Goa's Indo-Portuguese society, curious about its past, and enjoying privileged access to official documentation, Couto continued the history of Portuguese Asia where João de Barros' *Ásia* had stopped, retaining the structure and title of the earlier work and completing it in 1615. Aware of the problems and conflicts besetting Portuguese Asia, he wrote two critical satires of his times in the form of dialogues: *O Diálogo do Soldado Prático: Observações sobre as principaes causas da decadência dos Portuguezes na Ásia* [Dialogue of the Veteran Soldier: Remarks on the Principal Causes of Portuguese Decadence in Asia] (1790) and *Diálogo do Soldado Prático, que trata dos enganos e desenganos da Índia* [Dialogue of the Veteran Soldier, Dealing with the Disappointments and Defraudments of India] (1790). His output also includes speeches and eulogies of famous families and figures of the Portuguese expansion in the Orient, the most renowned being *Vida de D. Paulo de Lima Pereira* [The Life of the Honorable Paulo de Lima Pereira] (1765).

Jorge M. dos Santos Alves

Texts

Décadas da Ásia [Decades of Asia]. 15 vols. Lisbon: Livraria Sam Carlos, 1974–1975.
O Soldado Prático, que trata dos enganos e desenganos da Índia. Ed. M. Rodrigues Lapa. Lisbon: Livraria Sá Da Costa Editora, 1980.
Diogo do Couto e a Década VIII [Diogo do Couto and the Eighth Decade]. Ed. M.A. Lima Cruz. Lisbon: Comissão Nacional para as Comemorações dos Descobrimentos Portugueses, 1993.
Vida de D. Paulo de Lima Pereira. Lisbon: J. Filippe, 1765.

References

Boxer, C.R. *Three Historians of Portuguese Asia: (Barros, Couto and Bocarro).* Macao: Imprensa Nacional, 1948.

Covering Laws

Lawlike generalizations used to provide deductive explanations about singular events. The complex debate about the Covering Law theory of historical explanation (also called the "nomological-deductive theory") began with Carl Hempel's essay, "The Function of General Laws in History" (1942). Hempel argued that an ideal historical explanation would use general laws to deduce an outcome from the initial conditions of the event. Relevant laws were invariant principles in the form of "When X occurs, the result will be Y" (for example, a metal will expand when heated under constant pressure). Presumably, historians were to apply general laws from various sciences like biology and social psychology, but Hempel was agnostic about whether historians would in fact be able to discover laws of historical change. A neo-positivist, Hempel argued that subjectivist approaches such as "emphatic understanding" would not provide satisfactory or deterministic explanations.

Numerous critics rejected or significantly modified the Hempelian approach. Advocates of humanistic historiography, such as William Dray, defended idiographic accounts based on human intentions and argued that human choices could not be reduced to deterministic laws. Some philosophers of science denied that *all* full explanations in science depend upon general laws, and many theorists questioned whether the putative laws of the so-called social sciences were dependable or universally valid. Examining Hempel's article, Karl Popper and others noted that many of Hempel's examples dealt only with the trivial, obvious aspects of events, while other examples used only generalizations of broad tendency, not universal laws.

Responding to his critics in a 1962 article entitled "Explanation in Science and History," Hempel allowed for a probabilistic-statistical form of deductive explanation: the assertion that if certain conditions are realized, then a particular occurrence will come about with such-and-such statistical probability. Most of Hempel's critics were willing to concede that historical interpretations are commonly based on generalizations of probability, although adding that these generalizations are usually imprecise and not susceptible to statistical quantification.

Thomas T. Lewis

See also DETERMINISM; PHILOSOPHY OF HISTORY—ANALYTICAL; SOCIOLOGY AND HISTORY.

Texts

Dray, William. *Laws and Explanation in History.* London: Oxford University Press, 1957.
Gardiner, Patrick. *The Nature of Historical Explanation.* London: Oxford University Press, 1952.

Hempel, Carl. *Aspects of Scientific Explanation, and Other Essays in the Philosophy of Science.* New York: Free Press, 1965.

References

Lewis, Thomas. "Karl Popper's Situational Logic and the Covering Law Model of Historical Explanation." *Clio* 10 (1981): 291–321.

Lloyd, Christopher. *Explanation in Social History.* Oxford: Basil Blackwell, 1986.

Crawfurd, John (1783–1868)

Colonial administrator and orientalist. Crawfurd studied medicine at Edinburgh University before receiving a five-year medical appointment with the British Army in India. He was then transferred to Penang where he acquainted himself with the language and people. He occupied principal government posts under T.S. Raffles during the British occupation of Java from 1811 to 1817 and went on political missions to Bali and Celebes. He would later serve as ambassador to the courts of Siam, Cochin China, and Ava, and he ran for parliament unsuccessfully on four occasions. After Java was restored to the Dutch he returned to England where he wrote his major work, the *History of the Indian Archipelago,* which describes in three volumes practically every island and people in the Archipelago. Its geographic, anthropological, and linguistic observations were marked by a belief, probably formed at Edinburgh University, that the environment determines human progress. Crawfurd graded peoples of the Archipelago from "barbaric" to "most civilized" according to criteria such as their modes of subsistence and government, which he believed were determined by factors such as terrain and climate. He advocated tax and land reforms in his *History* that partly opposed Raffle's taxation schemes and argued that they could be most effectively implemented under European occupation. Among his other principal works were *A Grammatical Dictionary of the Malay Language* (1852) and a *Descriptive Dictionary of the Indian Islands and Adjacent Countries* (1856), both of which continue his concerns with progress, hierarchy, and race.

Mary C. Quilty

Texts

A Descriptive Dictionary of the Indian Islands and Adjacent Countries. London: Frank Cass, 1967.

A Grammatical Dictionary of the Malay Language. 2 vols. Singapore and New York: Oxford University Press, 1984.

History of the Indian Archipelago Containing an Account of the Manners, Arts, Languages, Religions, Institutions and Commerce of Its Inhabitants. London: Frank Cass, 1967.

References

Bastin, John. "English Sources for the Modern Period of Indonesian History." In *An Introduction to Indonesian Historiography,* ed. Soedjatmoko et al. Ithaca, NY: Cornell University Press, 1965, 252–271.

Boon, James. *Affinities and Extremes: Criss-Crossing the Bittersweet Ethnology of East Indies History, Hindu-Balinese Culture and Indo-European Allure.* Chicago: University of Chicago Press, 1990.

Harrison, B. "English Historians of the 'Indian Archipelago': Crawfurd and St. John." In *Historians of South East Asia,* ed. D.G.E. Hall. London: Oxford University Press, 1961, 245–254.

Quilty, Mary. "Textual Empires: A Reading of Early British Histories of Southeast Asia." Ph.D. thesis, University of Melbourne, 1992.

Creighton, Donald Grant (1902–1979)

Canadian historian. Creighton was born in Toronto, Ontario, and educated at the University of Toronto (B.A. 1925) and Oxford University (B.A. 1927, M.A. 1929). He joined the history department at the University of Toronto in 1927, where he remained until retirement in 1971. Creighton initially achieved prominence for his formulation of the "Laurentian thesis," which turned Harold Adams Innis's earlier "staples thesis" into a design of national development built on the east–west axis of the St. Lawrence river system. He subsequently personified this design in an award-winning biography of Canada's first prime minister, John A.Macdonald, which also challenged historians to new levels of literary attainment. Creighton's later career was devoted to jeremiads against the twin threats to Canadian nationalism—continentalism and regionalism.

M. Brook Taylor

Texts

Canada, the Heroic Beginnings. Toronto: Macmillan, 1974.

The Commercial Empire of the St. Lawrence, 1760–1850. Toronto: Ryerson Press, 1937.

The Forked Road: Canada, 1939–1957. Toronto: McClelland and Stewart, 1976.

John A. Macdonald. 2 vols. Toronto: Macmillan, 1952–1955.

References

Berger, Carl. *The Writing of Canadian History: Aspects of English-Canadian Historical Writing since 1900.* Second ed. Toronto: University of Toronto Press, 1986.

Moir, John S., ed. *Character and Circumstance: Essays in Honour of Donald Grant Creighton.* Toronto: Macmillan 1970.

Creighton, Mandell (1843–1901)

English historian, editor, and Anglican bishop. Creighton was born in Carlisle and educated at Oxford, where he became a fellow and tutor in 1866. Ordained four years later, he left the university in 1875 for a northern parish. In 1884 he was appointed the first Dixie professor of ecclesiastical history at Cambridge, and in 1886 assumed the editorship of the newly established *English Historical Review,* placing that journal upon a sound financial footing and recruiting both professional and amateur contributors. He resigned his academic posts in 1891 when appointed bishop of Peterborough, whence he was transferred to London in 1897. Creighton's published works included a *History of the Papacy* (1882–1894), written in the scrupulous tradition of Ranke, and two works on English history, *Cardinal Wolsey* (1888) and *Queen Elizabeth* (1896). Creighton's portrayal of Elizabeth I blended admiration for her Protestant heroism and distaste for her hesitancy and lack of moral vigor. His most significant historiographical contribution was that his work wedded ecclesiastical history to the "scientific" historical methodology that had developed during the nineteenth century.

Myron C. Noonkester

Texts

Cardinal Wolsey. London and New York: Macmillan, 1888.

A History of the Papacy from the Great Schism to the Sack of Rome. 6 vols. New York: AMS Press, 1969.

Queen Elizabeth. London: Longmans, Green, 1896.

References

Creighton, Louise. *Life and Letters of Mandell Creighton.* 2 vols. London: Longmans, Green, 1904.

Kenyon, J.P. *The History Men.* London: Weidenfeld and Nicolson, 1983.

Croatian Historiography

Historical writing in the Croatian-speaking territories of the former Yugoslavia. Croatian historiography has found its rationale in the existence of the separate Croatian people, or at least in the existence of an independent Croatian state in various periods of history. The earliest forms of Croatian historical writing can be found in the Byzantine period, during which local authors wrote their historical works initially only in Latin and Italian; Croatia would produce a first-class Latin historian in Matthias Flacius, leader of the evangelical wing of the Lutheran church in the mid-sixteenth century, who headed the team of clergymen that produced *The Magdeburg Centuries,* the most famous Protestant ecclesiastical history to be produced during the European Reformation.

The beginnings of modern Croatian historical writing (as writing about the history of the Croats themselves), however, can be found in *De regno Dalmatiae et Croatiae libri sex* [Six Books on the Kingdom of Dalmatia and Croatia] (1666) by Ivan Lucius, who is sometimes called the father of Croatian historiography, and Ritter Pavao Vitezović's *Croatia rediviva* [Croatia Revived] (1700). The ideas and models of these two historians were taken up by the romantic "Illyrianist" movement in the middle of the nineteenth century. Croatian nationalist thought was further stimulated in ensuing decades by the historical thinking of the leading figures of the Croatian Party of Rights. This perspective, wherein historical writing was inseparably linked to nationalist politics, was maintained between the two world wars by the representatives of the Croatian Peasant Party.

From 1850 until the end of World War I, one can also discern the rise in Croatia of German-influenced "scientific" historiography, especially in the work of I. Kukuljević, F. Rački, T. Smičiklas, V. Klaić, and F. Šišić, in whose hands historical writing moved away from romantic traditionalism and patriotic functionalism toward a critical assessment of available sources. In the interwar period, Milan Šufflay reinterpreted the Croatian Middle Ages and the perennial question of the Croatian relationship with Albania. It was at this time, too, that pioneering research on the economic history of Croatia was initiated by R. Bičanić.

The victory of the Communist partisans in World War II, and the subsequent reestablishment of Yugoslavia under Tito, brought the Marxist paradigm to the forefront, though it was regularly contested by so-called bourgeois and nationalistic tendencies. In 1948, for example, the academician Anto Babić produced his *Istorija naroda Jugoslavije* [History of the Yugoslav Peoples], which was long neglected. During the early postwar era, official Marxist historiography concentrated on the less ideologically laden history of distant times. In 1963, however, this trend was suddenly broken by the publication of the partisan general Terzić's monograph *Jugoslavija u aprilskom ratu 1941* [Yugoslavia during the April War of 1941]. This work blamed the Croats for collaboration with the Axis powers and for the fall of the first Yugoslavia (the former Kingdom of the Serbs, Croats, and Slovenes). This provided Croatian historians with an excellent opportunity to expound their contrary views. Tito himself reacted to this controversy by condemning nationalist manifestations in historiography.

Croatian national views were once again freely expressed during the "Croatian Spring" (1967–1972). At this time, the journal *Časopis za Suvremenu Povijest* [Journal of Contemporary History] was established in Zagreb as a vehicle for the views of Croatian historians. In 1968, Jaroslav Šidak, Mirjana Gross, Igor Karaman, and Dragovan Šćepić published their interpretation of modern Croatian history in *Povijest hrvatskog naroda g. 1860–1914* [History of the Croatian People, 1860–1914]. This was criticized by official Yugoslav historians for neglecting the wider Yugoslav context. In turn, when Vladimir Dedijer and Milorad Ekmečić produced their *Istorija Jugoslavije* [History of Yugoslavia], Gross and Šidak condemned as unbalanced its treatment of Croatian and Serbian history. Croatian historians outside the academic establishment such as Vlado Gotovac and Franjo Tuđman expressed even more nationalistic views. During the suppression of this movement, Trpmir Mačan's *Povijest hrvatskog naroda* [History of the Croatian People] was even taken out of circulation. Criticism of historical orthodoxy along the unitarist line (an orthodoxy that was itself more often than not a cloak for Greater-Serbian nationalism) was now earmarked as Croatian extremism and banned.

With the fall of the Communist regime in 1991, and the breakup of Yugoslavia into its ethnic components, revisionist and nationalist trends revived within Croatian historiography. More attention has recently been given to the role of religion in history, for example in J. Krišto's *Prešučena povijest:—Katolička crkva u hrvatskoj politici, 1850–1918* [The Suppressed History: The Catholic Church in Croatian Politics, 1850–1918] (1994); similar interest is emerging in the various national figures and movements of the Croatian past. A revision of the history of the Croatian Banovina and the Independent State of Croatia just before and during World War II is also under way. Criticism of the partisan history of the war, previously found only in dissident circles, has now been officially consecrated, as may be seen in Franjo Tuđman's, *Bespuća povijesne zbiljnosti* [The Wastelands of Historic Reality] (1989). But Tuđman himself has recently recognized that this critique (for example, in its treatment of the Jasenovac question) has been somewhat overstated. It is to be hoped that this admission might prove the starting point of a more detached historiography, less subject to the changing winds of political regimes.

Robert Stallaerts

See also MAGDEBURG CENTURIATORS; SERBIAN HISTORIOGRAPHY.

Texts
Macan, Trpimir. *Povijest hrvatskoga naroda.* Zagreb, Croatia: Nakladni zavod Matice hrvatske, 1992.
Šidak, Jaroslav et al. *Povijest hrvatskog naroda g. 1860–1914.* Zagreb, Croatia: Školska knjiga, 1968.

References
Antoljak, Stjepan. *Hrvatska historiografija do 1918* [Croatian Historiography before 1918]. 2 vols. Zagreb, Croatia: Nakladni Zavod Matice hrvatske, 1992.
Banac, Ivo. "Historiography of the Countries of Eastern Europe: Yugoslavia." *American Historical Review* 97 (1992): 1084–1104.
"Govor maršala Tita na svečanom skupu Slovenačke akademije znanosti i umetnosti [Tito's Address to the Official Meeting of the Slovene Academy for Arts and Sciences]." *Istorijski Glasnik* 2 (1948): 3–9.
Krišto, Jure. "Neuspjela potraga revizionizmom [The Unsuccessful Quest for Revisionism]." *Vjesnik* 27 (1994): 14–15.
Nečak, Dušan. "Zur erforschung der Jugoslawischen Geschichte nach 1945 [Research on Yugoslav History after 1945]." *Österreichische Osthefte* 29 (1987): 92–104.
Novak, Viktor. "Jugoslovenska istoriografija izmedju dva svetska rata i njeni suvremeni zadaci [Yugoslav Historiography between the Two World Wars and Its Present Task]." *Istorijski Časopis* 1 (1948): 198–217.
Petrovich, Michael B. "Continuing Nationalism in Yugoslav Historiography." *Nationalities Papers* 6 (1978): 161–177.
———. "Croatian Humanists and the Writing of History in the Fifteenth and Sixteenth Centuries." *Slavic Review* 37 (1978): 624–639.

———. "Dalmatian Historiography in the Age of Humanism." *Medievalia et Humanistica* 12 (1958): 84–103.

Raukar, Tomislav. "Cetiri desetljeća historiografije o hrvatskom srednjovjekovlju, 1945–1985 [Forty Years of Historiography on the Croatian Middle Ages, 1945–1985]." *Historijski Zbornik* 41 (1988): 61–75.

Šidak, Jaroslav. "Hrvatska historiografija— njezin razvoj i današnje stanje (1971) [Croatian Historiography: Questions of Evolution and Status (1971)]." *Historijski Zbornik* 23–24 (1970–1971): 1–20.

Stallaerts, Robert, and Jeannine Laurens. *Historical Dictionary of the Republic of Croatia.* Metuchen, NJ: Scarecrow Press, 1995.

Tuđman, Franjo. *Bespuća povijesne zbiljnosti* [The Wastelands of Historic Reality]. Zagreb: Nakladni Zavod Matice hrvatske, 1989.

Vucinich, W.S. "Postwar Yugoslav Historiography: Bibliographical Article." *Journal of Modern History* 23 (1951): 41–47.

Croce, Benedetto (1866–1952)

Italian historian and philosopher. Croce was the most influential thinker in Italy during the first half of the twentieth century. Writing widely in the genres of history, historiography, philosophy, aesthetics, and literary criticism, his influence and legacy still shape Italian culture today. The sheer volume and range of his work has left an indelible impression on Italian intellectual life. His work guided the thinking of many other historians, such as R.G. Collingwood and even Italian Marxists such as Antonio Gramsci. Croce was shaped by, and in turn helped to shape, Neapolitan culture. Naples was to exert a critical influence on his thinking, especially the tradition of Giambattista Vico. Conversely, Croce was instrumental in bringing Neapolitan and Italian culture in touch with wider European intellectual currents. After an earthquake destroyed his home, killing his parents and sister, Croce lived for three years in Rome with the idealist philosopher Silvio Spaventa. An early study of Marxism, *Materialismo storico ed economia marxista* [Historical Materialism and Marxist Economics] (1900) lead Croce to Hegel (*Cio' che e' vivo e cio' che e' morto della filosofia di Hegel* [That Which Is Living and That Which Is Dead in the Philosophy of Hegel], 1907) and eventually to historiography, publishing *Teoria e storia della storiografia* [Theory and History of Historiography] in 1917, and, four years later, *Storia della storiografia italiana del secolo XIX* [History of Italian Historiography in the Nineteenth Century] (1921). For nearly half a century, Croce also directed journals that helped define and direct cultural debate in Italy; *La Critica* (1903–1944) and its successor *Quaderni della critica* (1944–1952). His lifelong project was elaborating a "Philosophy of the Spirit," which combined his work in history, aesthetics, and logic, and his neo-idealism directly challenged the dominant intellectual traditions of positivism and materialism.

Croce insisted on the separation of culture from politics, and his faith in "history as the story of liberty" led him to view fascism as a "parenthesis" in Italian history. After an initial period of support, he became one of the most important critics of fascism and published the famous "Manifesto of Antifascist Intellectuals" on 1 May 1925. His subtle condemnation of fascism appeared in his 1928 *Storia d'Italia dal 1871 al 1915* [History of Italy from 1871 to 1915] and his *Storia d'Europa nel secolo decimonono* [History of Europe in the Nineteenth Century], published in 1932. In 1939, he published *Storia come pensiero e come azione* [History As Thought and As Action], which turned to an examination of history as "thought and action." After the war, he was instrumental in shaping public debate about fascism and the development of Italian history.

Stanislao G. Pugliese

Texts

Autobiography. Trans. R.G. Collingwood. Oxford: Oxford University Press, 1927.

History As the Story of Liberty. Trans. Sylvia Sprigge. New York: Norton, 1941.

History: Its Theory and Practice. Trans. Douglas Ainslie. New York: Russel and Russel, 1960.

Opera complete [Complete Works]. 67 vols. Bari, Spain: Laterza, 1965.

References

Caponigri, A. Robert. *History and Liberty: The Historical Writings of Benedetto Croce.* London: Routledge & Kegan Paul, 1955.

Jacobitti, Edmund E. *Revolutionary Humanism and Historicism in Modern Italy.* New Haven, CT: Yale University Press, 1981.

Roberts, David D. *Benedetto Croce and the Uses of Historicism.* Berkeley: University of California Press, 1987.

Crusades, Historians of the

Contemporary historians of western Europe's crusades, principally in the Holy Land, but sometimes elsewhere in Europe, Asia, and Africa. The majority of crusade histories deal with expeditions in the Levant undertaken between 1096 and 1270, the classic era of the crusades, but historians were still writing about latter-day crusades well into the sixteenth century.

Writers of crusade histories assumed that God was the Divine Author of history, who called upon his chosen Christian people to perform heroic acts in his service. As God's historical agents, the crusaders were helping to realize the divine plan for humanity. Notwithstanding this shared vision, crusade accounts varied greatly due to historical situations and the various perspectives of the reporters.

Historians of the First Crusade generally emphasized the belief that the crusade's triumphant capture of Jerusalem in 1099 was accomplished by God's united people through his grace. The first complete crusade history was the anonymous *Gesta Francorum* [Deeds of the Franks], which was completed before the end of 1101. Composed in an artless style by a participant who marched with the Norman contingent from southern Italy, it served as the main source for several more "literary" histories composed by clerics who had not participated in the crusade, but who desired to place the movement into its full theological context. Because the *Gesta* dealt with a phenomenon that had no antecedents in Greco-Roman history, its author was not constrained by classical historiographical prototypes. Rather, the Bible, the rites of the Church, and vernacular knightly epics served as the *Gesta's* literary and conceptual models. Biblical and epic elements also run throughout the First Crusade's other great eyewitness histories, especially Fulcher of Chartres's *Jerusalem History*, which carried the story of the crusaders in the Holy Land down to 1127. Because he lived to witness and write about the checkered fortunes of the crusader states after 1099, Fulcher's account covers a fair number of crusader disasters, as well as triumphs.

The next several generations of Western crusade historians had to deal increasingly with setbacks and rescue missions, as resurgent Islam increasingly pressed against the crusader states. Two significant Latin historians who dealt with these troubles were the clerics Odo of Deuil and William of Tyre. Odo served as chaplain to King Louis VII during the unsuccessful Second Crusade (1146–1148), and his account, *The Journey of King Louis to the East,* highlights an increasingly important theme in crusade historiography—the perfidy of Greek Christians, whom he blamed for the crusade's failure. Called originally to rescue Eastern Christendom from the Turks, by the mid-twelfth century the crusades were a major irritant in Western–Byzantine relations. Odo, a brief visitor to the East, showed little appreciation for eastern Mediterranean culture and political realities. On his part, Archbishop William of Tyre, who was born in Jerusalem, displayed the ecumenical vision of a native Levantine. William's *Jerusalem History,* also known as *The History of Deeds Done beyond the Sea,* narrates in twenty-three books the successes and failures of the crusaders in the east down to 1184, the probable year of his death. Although his history drew deeply from earlier crusade accounts, as well as from classical models, William's work was original, as well as vast in scope. Above all else, he wrote movingly of the homeland that he loved and treated sympathetically and fairly the diverse peoples who inhabited it. At the same time, he supported the ideal of a crusader state centered on Jerusalem and wrote with melancholy foreboding of the difficulties that beset and awaited contemporary crusaders because of their moral shortcomings.

The archbishop's worst fears were realized three years after his death when Jerusalem fell to the forces of Saladin, thereby sparking the Third Crusade (1189–1192). Because it involved Europe's three most powerful monarchs, the crusade produced a large number of histories. They included: Ambroise's *History of the Holy War,* an account in French verse that presents the crusade from the perspective of Richard the Lionheart's camp; Rigord's *Deeds of Philip Augustus,* which does the same for King Philip II of France; and Ansbert's *History of the Expedition of Emperor Frederick.* All three focus as much on the central figures of their respective hero kings as they do on the crusade as a holy undertaking, suggesting that new currents were stirring in Europe.

Because the Third Crusade failed to recapture Jerusalem, another major expedition sailed from Venice in 1202, with the aim of liberating Jerusalem by way of Alexandria. The Fourth Crusade never reached Alexandria or Jerusalem, but it managed to capture Constantinople and establish the Latin empire of Constantinople (1204–1261), thereby bringing to a head the animosities recorded by Odo of Deuil, a half century earlier. This turn of events occasioned a flood of crusade accounts, the two most important of which were by Geoffrey of Villehardouin and Robert of Clari. Each composed his history in Old French prose, an historiographical novelty, and each presented the crusade from a different perspective. Villehardouin, one of the army's second-rank leaders, shows us the crusade as seen from the councils of the barons; Clari, a humble knight, serves as a counterbalance to Villehardouin's view from the top and allows us to view the crusade from the ranks and to see, close up, the face of battle.

Although lay warriors had fashioned histories of earlier crusades, beginning with the First Crusade, clerical historians had, until now, largely dominated the field and imposed their theological perspectives on the genre. With Clari and Villehardouin's vernacular military histories, the emphasis had shifted.

The West continued to launch crusades for much of the rest of the century, and even produced at least one more first-rate history by a cleric, Oliver of Paderborn's *The History of Damietta,* an account of the ill-fated Fifth Crusade (1217– 1221). But the best history of the later crusades was composed by a lay lord, Jean of Joinville. A major part of Joinville's biography of King Louis IX, which he composed in French between 1305 and 1309, relates in detail the king's six-year-long campaign in Syria-Palestine and Egypt from 1248 to 1254. The essence of Joinville's story is that his late friend, the recently canonized St. Louis, had comported himself throughout that crusade as a true knight and Christian gentleman. Miracles and other forms of divine intervention play no role in this crusade story; the saintly king, the father of his people, holds center stage. When Louis dies while on a second crusade in 1270, Joinville declares him a martyr, but he also bitterly laments that the king's taking the cross for a second time was "one of the saddest days France has ever seen." The West's historiographical vision of the crusade had thus changed substantially in the course of two centuries.

Alfred J. Andrea

Texts

Hallam, Elizabeth, ed. *Chronicles of the Crusades.* New York: Weidenfeld and Nicolson, 1989.

Krey, August C. *The First Crusade: The Accounts of Eye-Witnesses and Participants.* Princeton, NJ: Princeton University Press, 1921.

Peters, Edward, ed. *The First Crusade: The Chronicle of Fulcher of Chartres and Other Source Materials.* Philadelphia: University of Pennsylvania Press, 1971.

Peters, Edward, ed. *Christian Society and the Crusades, 1198–1229: Sources in Translation.* Philadelphia: University of Pennsylvania Press, 1971.

References

Smalley, Beryl. "Conquest and Crusade." In her *Historians of the Middle Ages.* London: Thames and Hudson, 1974, chapter 9.

Cui Shu [Ts'ui Shu] (1740–1816)

Chinese historian, principally famous for his critical examination of the classics. Born into a scholar-official family whose ancestors had often held important posts in the Hubei province, Cui received rigorous training in the classics in his childhood, acquainting himself first with unannotated texts of the classics, and then with the late commentaries, a method insisted upon by Cui's father, Cui Yuansen (1709–1771), who had become a village schoolteacher after his failure to obtain a *juren* degree. Cui succeeded in gaining his *juren* title in 1762 but failed to win the higher qualification of *jinshi.* In 1796 and again in 1802, Cui served as county magistrate in the Fujian province, but his real interest was still in scholarship. After his retirement from office, Cui returned to his hometown and devoted himself to the study of ancient classics. Cui argued that the texts that had appeared during the Qin and Han dynasties, and which were regarded as the most authentic by the School of Han Learning because of their antiquity, were in fact frequently unreliable, containing unauthorized accretions and false interpretations. The only way, he believed, to attain thoroughly authentic texts of the classics was by close study and comparison of their texts. In doing so, he found that some popular ancient emperors were actually not mentioned in the classics but were added or had their stories embellished in the literature of later periods. Cui thus resolved to write a book that could rectify these accretions and expose the fallacies in their then current interpretation. The result of his labors from 1783 to 1805 was the work entitled *Kaoxin Lu* [A Record of Beliefs Investigated]. After its completion, he continued to revise it until 1814, two years before his death. In *Kaoxin Lu,* Cui questioned the authorship of the classics such as the *Great Learning* and the *Doctrine of the Mean,* and rejected some passages in the *Analects.* His skepticism, arrogance, and overconfidence rendered him unpopular in his time, but modern scholars such as Hu Shi (1891– 1962) and Gu Jiegang (1896–1980) revered his work. Hu Shi in 1921 published a chronological biography of Cui Shu, whom he called a "scientific historian." Gu Jiegang edited Cui's other works into *Cui Dongbi yishu* [The Works Bequeathed by Cui Shu] in 1936.

Q. Edward Wang

Texts

Cui Dongbi yishu. Ed. Gu Jiegang [Ku Chieh-kang]. 2 vols. Shanghai: Shanghai guji chubanshe, 1983.

C

References

Hu Shi. "Kexue de gushijia Cui Shu [A Scientific Historian of Ancient China: Cui Shu]." In *Cui Dongbi yishu,* ed. Gu Jiegang, vol. 2, 1–176.

Schneider, Laurence. *Ku Chieh-kang and China's New History.* Berkeley: University of California Press, 1971.

Cultural History

The historical practice that incorporates cultural anthropology and literary theory in order to decode past expression of all sorts. In the late twentieth century, a new cultural history has emerged from the confluence of cultural anthropology and literary criticism. Intellectually omnivorous, it defines culture to include the most diverse aspects of past human expression. As yet a tendency rather than a full-fledged field, cultural history still lacks much institutional apparatus of its own.

Although a newcomer, cultural history has a long pedigree. The idea of past culture traces back to the Renaissance, which largely defined itself by discovering the wholeness and distinctness of classical antiquity. The Enlightenment of the eighteenth century, progressive and sometimes smug, easily saw even its recent past as having an alien spirit. In the early nineteenth century, von Ranke set a historicist paradigm, so tightly bound to primary sources as to quell investigations of culture. Nevertheless, Hegelian idealism inspired Jakob Burckhardt's *Die Cultur der Renaissance in Italien (1860)* (translated in 1929 as *The Civilization of the Renaissance in Italy*), which first defined the Renaissance as a historical period, and also treated it as a cultural whole embracing most of life. Burckhardt thus offered a pioneering model for integrating the most diverse expressions—women's costume, warfare, statecraft, manners—into a larger pattern. The later nineteenth century produced much German-language history of culture *(Kulturgeschichte)*. This work, despite Burckhardt's example, attended largely to high culture and generally assumed that past cultures posed few epistemological problems, as if *Verstehen* (understanding) could grasp past ideas directly. The same epistemological complacency infected the French Annales school of the mid-twentieth century when it espoused *mentalité,* a fuzzy concept that embraced every aspect of mental life—habits of seeing, hearing, smelling, moods, and passions, as well as thoughts—and raised the historiographical prestige of vernacular culture. In English, E.P. Thompson's *Making of the English Working Class* (1963) helped persuade Marxist historiography, traditionally contemptuous of "mere superstructure," the frothy rationalization of material reality, at last to take religion, values, and beliefs as causes of weighty effects.

Contemporary cultural history thus has many ancestors, for it traces to *mentalité* its exploration of the remote crannies of experience, to Marxism its interest in ordinary folk, to Burckhardt its goal of integration, to the Renaissance and the Enlightenment its sense of distance from the past. Nevertheless, the label now attaches largely to the radically self-skeptical historiography of recent decades.

The newer cultural history has espoused cultural anthropology and literary theory. The latter bequeaths a fascination with texts and with what words and signs mean. From the French theorists Foucault and Derrida comes the practice of deconstruction, a relentless exploration of the cognitive strategies built into language, art, and behavior. Cultural historians often share the acute epistemological self-consciousness and antipositivist skepticism of these thinkers and their followers. Like them, cultural historians often shun the canons of high culture, exploring instead the decentered, the bizarre, and the marginal. They also often try to read against the grain or to explore the boundaries of genre. So, for instance, Natalie Davis in *Fiction in the Archives* treats legal documents as art, and Roger Chartier (in "Texts, Printings, Readings," in L. Hunt, *The New Cultural History,* 124–175) investigates the interplay of literate and oral narratives. Meanwhile, with anthropology, cultural history has turned to ritualized actions of all sorts, and to the politics of manipulated meaning. Some, like Robert Darnton, adopt the structuralism of the anthropologists Claude Lévi-Strauss and Clifford Geertz, which posits underlying patterns that generate and explain a culture's myriad details. Others, like some anthropologists, denying such subterranean "structures," instead study the politics of symbolic action or deconstruct expressions into fragments of multiple, labile meaning. Thus, cultural history debates its tactics of explication.

Cultural history has both strengths and predicaments. On the positive side, it possesses openness, lively imagination, and the skill to winkle meaning out of unexpected crannies of the past. Its all-embracing populism seeks meaning in chapbooks, manners, riots, jokes, and sexual practices. Mixing the political with the expressive, the discipline handily vaults the old, sterile debate between Marx and Weber about the priority of either. Thus, to a degree, the field is integrative. On the other hand, many classical devices of intellectual integration collapse. For one, causality grows slippery. For another, epistemological indeterminacy undercuts clear criteria for explication. Thus, meaning threatens to become multiple, contradictory, and even evanescent, for deconstruction has no fast or testable rules. This method, with its denial of firm knowledge of the past, can push scholars toward solipsism. Furthermore, anticanonical habits and elusive criteria make it hard to choose between Confucius and chocolate wrappers; everything seems equally significant. Cultural history thus runs the risk of an antiquarianism that refuses to lodge matters in larger schemes. Its very eclecticism can fragment Burckhardt's or Geertz's sense of a coherent culture. The movement itself thus at present enjoys lively controversies that may well shift its practices.

Elizabeth S. Cohen and Thomas V. Cohen

See also ANTHROPOLOGY AND HISTORY; ENLIGHTENMENT HISTORIOGRAPHY; *KULTURGESCHICHTE;* LITERATURE AND HISTORY; NEW HISTORICISM.

Texts
Darnton, Robert. *The Great Cat Massacre.* New York: Basic Books, 1984.
Davis, Natalie Zemon. *Fiction in the Archives.* Stanford, CA: Stanford University Press, 1987.

References
Burke, Peter. "Reflections on the Origins of Cultural History." In *Interpretation and Cultural History,* ed. Joan H. Pittock and Andrew Wear. New York: St. Martin's Press, 1991, 5–24.
Hunt, Lynn, ed. *The New Cultural History.* Berkeley and Los Angeles: University of California Press, 1989.
Nussdorfer, Laurie. "Review Essay" on Lynn Hunt, *The New Cultural History* and on Joan H. Pittock and Andrew Wear, *Interpretation and Cultural History. History and Theory* 33 (1993): 74–83.

Cumont, Franz-Valéry-Marie (1868–1947)
Belgian epigrapher, archaeologist, and historian of Roman religion. Cumont was born in Alost to a liberal family and received a doctorate from the University of Ghent (1887). After studies in Bonn, Berlin, Vienna, and Paris, including work under Theodor Mommsen, he taught at Ghent from 1892 to 1910. Cumont also served as conservator

of Brussels's Musée du Cinquantenaire (1898–1912). After he failed to be appointed professor of Roman history, he resigned from the faculty. He thereafter lived in Rome and Paris, and engaged in research and excavations supported by his own funds. At his death, he bequeathed his library to the Academica Belgica. Cumont's research assessed the nature and influence of Roman paganism, as in his *Les religions orientales dans le paganisme romaine* [The Oriental Religions in Roman Paganism] (1907), *Astrology and Religion among the Greeks and Romans* (1912), and *After Life in Roman Paganism* (1923), the last of which would be revised as *Lux Perpetua* [Perpetual Light] (1949). Closely related was Cumont's exploration of archaeological and epigraphical monuments, including among other works, his account of excavations at Dura-Europos from 1922 to 1923 and his interdisciplinary analysis of Roman religious imagery in *Recherches sur le symbolisme funéraire des Romains* [Research on Roman Funerary Symbolism] (1942).

Bonnie Effros

Texts
After Life in Roman Paganism. New York: Dover Publications, 1959.
Astrology and Religion among the Greeks and Romans. New York: Dover Publications, 1960.
Fouilles de Doura-Europos (1922–1923). [The Excavations at Dura-Europos]. 2 vols. Paris: P. Geuthner, 1926.
Lux Perpetua. Reprint ed. New York: Garland, 1987.
The Oriental Religions in Roman Paganism. New York: Dover Publications, 1956.
Recherches sur le symbolisme funéraire des Romains. Paris: P. Geuthner, 1966.

References
De Ruyt, Franz. "Cumont, Franz." *Biographie Nationale* 39, fasc.1. Brussels: Bruylant, 1976, cols. 211–222.

Cunningham, William (1849–1919)
British economic historian and cleric. Born in Edinburgh, Cunningham attended university there and at Cambridge, in preparation for a career in the church. He became vicar of Great St. Mary's at Cambridge and was later archdeacon of Ely. He was also university lecturer in economic history (Cambridge) and later Tooke professor of statistics at King's College, London. His writing was shaped by his religion and the dual intellectual influences of T.H. Green and Arnold Toynbee.

In the 1890s, these influences came together in Cunningham's objection to orthodox economics (which then included modern economic history): that it drew universally applicable laws from an individualistic view that conceived of human economic behavior as essentially selfish. For Cunningham, such an analysis was not complete (since it ignored custom and community) and could not be applied to earlier societies. Rather, economics should be more historical and descriptive and less scientific and theoretical. The methodological dispute also assumed a personal nature with public attacks on Alfred Marshall (the leading Cambridge economist) and his conception of the discipline. When the Marshallian conception of economics as a largely deductive science became dominant, Cunningham hoped to see established a new independent university discipline of economic history. His chief historical work—*The Growth of English Industry and Commerce* (1882)—was written to fill the need for a textbook, but remains a key early work of the new subject.

Andrew J. Hull

Texts

The Growth of English Industry and Commerce. Cambridge, Eng.: Cambridge University Press, 1882.
"The Perversion of Economic History." *Economic Journal* 2 (1892): 491–506.
Politics and Economics: An Essay on the Nature of the Principles of Political Economy, Together with a Survey of Recent Legislation. London: Kean-Paul, Trench, 1885.

References

Kadish, A. *Historians, Economists and Economic History.* London and New York: Routledge, 1989.
Koot, Gerard M. *English Historical Economics, 1870–1926.* Cambridge, Eng.: Cambridge University Press, 1987.
Maloney, John. *Marshall, Orthodoxy and the Professionalisation of Economics.* Cambridge, Eng.: Cambridge University Press, 1985.
Wood, J.C. *British Economists and the Empire.* London: Croom Helm, 1983.

Curti, Merle Eugene (1897–1996)

American historian. Curti was born in the small Nebraska village of Papillion near Omaha. Educated at Harvard, he was Frederick Jackson Turner's last doctoral student. After teaching at Smith College and the Teacher's College of Co-

lumbia University, Curti joined the history faculty at the University of Wisconsin in 1942, where he spent the rest of his career until retiring in 1968. Although his interests were too broad and eclectic to tempt him to develop any "Curti school," his popularity as a teacher as well as his broader impact on the profession may be measured by his remarkable record of directing eighty-six doctoral dissertations, many of them subsequently published, during his quarter century at Wisconsin. As much as anyone of his generation, Curti laid out and developed the dimensions of the new field of American intellectual history, particularly the social uses of ideas and knowledge. His brilliant synthesis *The Growth of American Thought* (1943) won a Pulitzer Prize and was republished abroad in five other languages. In scores of books and articles he often treated subjects—for example, the peace movement, influences on education, women's history, and the American impulse to do good at home and abroad—a generation or more before such interests became fashionable. He also pioneered new methodologies, as when he demonstrated the value of quantitative analysis in his groundbreaking study of the settlement and development of Trempealeau County, Wisconsin—*The Making of an American Community: A Case Study of Democracy in a Frontier Community* (1959).

E. David Cronon

Texts

American Paradox: The Conflict of Thought and Action. New Brunswick, NJ: Rutgers University Press, 1956.
American Philanthropy Abroad: A History. New Brunswick, NJ: Rutgers University Press, 1963.
The Growth of American Thought. Third ed. New York: Harper, 1964.
The Making of an American Community: A Case Study of Democracy in a Frontier Community. Stanford, CA: Stanford University Press, 1959.

References

Cronon, E. David. "Merle Curti: An Appraisal and Bibliography of His Writings." *Wisconsin Magazine of History* 54 (1970–71): 119–135.

Curtius Rufus [Quintus Curtius] (dates unknown)

Latin historian. Nothing is known about Curtius Rufus's life, including his exact name. His ten-volume *Historiae Alexandri Magni Macedonis* is the only known book in Latin devoted to the life of Alexander the Great. The work has been dated as early as the Julio-Claudian period and as late as the reign of Severus Alexander. Books I, II, and X are lost, and there are large gaps in books V, VI, and IX. Thus his introduction, which probably included his intentions in writing the book, has been lost. Curtius was principally a biographer and rhetorician, and his selection of material was different from other historians of Alexander. As a moralizer, he tried to reconcile different views of Alexander in his sources.

Mark W. Chavalas

Texts
History of Alexander. Trans. J.C. Rolfe. 2 vols. Cambridge, MA: Harvard University Press / Loeb Classical Library, 1946.

References
Hammond, N.G.L. *Three Historians of Alexander the Great: The So-Called Vulgate Authors, Diodorus, Justin, and Curtius.* Cambridge, Eng.: Cambridge University Press, 1983.

Czech Historiography

Historical writing by and about the Czech (Bohemian and Moravian) peoples since the early Middle Ages. Czech historiography has a long tradition, originating in the early medieval period and faithfully reflecting the tumultuous and distinguished history of the Bohemian and Moravian peoples in the heart of central Europe. Several overarching themes assert themselves throughout, all of them concerning the evolving identity, and sometimes very survival, of this small nation. How to regard the close but also conflicted (at times even threatening) relationship between Czechs and Germans is one of the longest lived of these themes. A second, related theme, and perhaps the single most dominant in all Czech historiography, concerns the role of the Hussite tradition in Czech history, or, more broadly, the respective roles of Catholicism and Protestantism in shaping a Czech national tradition. The implications are enormous for questions of national character and identity; crudely stated, are Czechs more fundamentally idealistic rebels or pragmatic compromisers, and which is the surest road to national survival? A third theme is also related to the first two: what role has the Bohemian nobility played in Czech national history? Are they, as the original *natio,* the wellspring of a national culture that can rightly claim its place among the most advanced in Europe, or does the Czech-speaking peasant more appropriately represent the ethnic and linguistic nation, as well as important traditions of egalitarianism and the nobility of simple hard work? Finally, one should mention the consciousness of Czechs as a small part of a much larger and more powerful body, that of Slavdom. This last theme emerges most powerfully in Czech history and historiography in the nineteenth century as a counter to the centuries-long pressures of Germanization alluded to above.

A very basic periodization of Czech historiography would necessarily include the following: 1) early medieval (ninth and tenth centuries) legends, written in Old Church Slavonic; 2) medieval (eleventh through fourteenth centuries) legends, chronicles, and annals, written mostly in Latin, and recording the rise of the Czech kingdom to greatness under the Přemyslid, and later, Luxemburg, dynasties; 3) Hussite (fifteenth century); 4) Reformation/humanist (sixteenth century to the defeat of the Protestant estates by the Catholic Habsburgs at the Battle of White Mountain in 1620); 5) Catholic-German Baroque (mid-seventeenth to mid-eighteenth centuries); 6) national renascence (late eighteenth century to World War II); 7) Stalinist-Soviet (1948–1989); and 8) post-Soviet contemporary.

Medieval Czech historiography begins with the legends of the Sts. Cyril and Methodius (late ninth century) and the earliest legends of St. Wenceslas (tenth century) and reaches its apogee in the *Chronica Bohemorum,* written by the Canon of the Chapter of Prague, Cosmas (Kosmas, 1056–1125). This is the seminal work of not only Czech historiography, but also Czech national literature and identity in general. An extraordinary work of the fourteenth century is the *Kronika Dalimilova* (1308–1314), the first chronicle to be written in the Czech language. It strongly opposes the growing pressures of the *Drang Nach Osten,* while celebrating the Czech past and tradition as captured in the earlier work of Cosmas.

Hussite historiography of the fifteenth century reflects the times, dividing fairly neatly into radical (Taborite, peasant-oriented) and moderate (Utraquist, noble and burgher) camps. Notable works from the period include Petr of Mladoňovice's first-hand account of the teaching and martyrdom of Jan Hus; the humanist *Historia Bohemica* of Aeneas Sylvius Piccolomini (later Pope Pius II); the *Cronicon Sacerdotum Taboriensium,* a spirited defense of the Taborites; and some of the more interesting contemporary, mostly Utraquist, accounts collected and published by František Palacký in the nineteenth century as the *Staré letopisy české* (1829).

Humanist historiography further fragmented in the sixteenth century, into three camps: neo-Utraquist, Catholic, and the Unity of the Czech Brethren. The first had limited success in trying to argue that an essentially Utraquist moderation and ability to compromise characterized Czech history since the earliest times. The Catholic interpretation, best developed by an ordained priest, Vaclav Hajek (d. 1553), in the *Kronika česka,* published in 1541, represented the officially sanctioned interpretation (supporting sovereign and nobility), and dominated Czech history writing for the next two centuries, until both its methodology and conclusions were effectively demolished during the Enlightenment. The contributions of the Unity lay in their efforts to preserve archival sources (although much was lost after 1620 nonetheless) and to promote the use of the Czech language.

The single greatest exponent of the post-White Mountain period of the German-Catholic baroque was undoubtedly Bohuslav Balbín (1621–1688), who sought to synthesize all Czech history into a Catholic interpretation that rejected radical Hussitism, but lamented the contemporary decline of Czech culture and sought to lay claim to the greatness of the pre–White Mountain Czech humanist tradition. Balbín and his followers celebrated the era of Charles IV as representing the zenith of Czech achievement and contributed much to keeping alive the consciousness of a separate Czech identity through the years known by Czechs as the *Temno* (dark ages, until about 1780).

The Enlightenment challenged prevailing historical interpretations with its insistence on both greater religious toleration and new critical methodologies. In 1781, history gained a new status as an academic discipline at Prague University. The Piarist monk Gelasius Dobner (1719–1790) laid the foundation for new interpretations with his critical commentaries on the chronicles of earlier times, which fatally undermined the authority of the Hajek tradition, and opened new vistas. Among the new generation of critical historians, Josef Dobrovský (1753–1829) produced models of the new scholarship in a series of critical monographs on early medieval Czech history, as well as on the era of Charles IV. However, while much of the history writing of the Enlightenment was imbued with patriotism, and a growing sense of national identity, the critical mood of the age did not lend itself to a new synthesis of Czech history,

which had to wait until severe rationalism and methodological stringency were tempered by the more Romantic notions of the nineteenth century.

The *magnum opus* of all Czech historiography is František Palacký's (1798–1876) *Dějiny národu českého v Čechach a v Moravě* [History of the Czech Nation in the Czech and Moravian Lands], which in five volumes covered the years from the origins of the Czech nation, to the union with the Habsburg lands in 1526. This work established a new romantic philosophy of Czech history, namely that the history of the Czech people is the history of the Czech national idea and its struggle for self-determination. In Palacký's interpretation, the Hussite revolt was the supreme expression of this struggle, which pitted the ancient Slavic love of liberty and egalitarianism against Germanic authoritarianism and privilege. While Palacký's interpretation of Czech history was enormously influential in shaping the national renascence of the nineteenth century, many historians criticized Palacký's "philosophy" as romanticized, politicized, and overly idealistic.

The most influential of all of the historians of the "critical school" in the last quarter of the nineteenth century was Jaroslav Goll (1846–1929), one of the founders and first editors of the *Český casopis historický* in 1895. Goll did more than any other single historian to establish the professional discipline of Czech history, writing first-rate monographical studies himself, and training the first generation of truly professional Czech historians in the historical seminar at the Czech University. The so-called Goll school of historians dominated Czech history until the Communist takeover in 1948. Among them, Václav Novotný (1869–1932) and Josef Pekař (1870–1937) emerged to lead two divergent wings. Novotný and his followers tended toward careful study of the pre–White Mountain period, reaching conclusions that supported Tomas Garrigue Masaryk's (1850–1937) glorification of Hussitism, while Pekař and his associates concentrated on the seventeenth and eighteenth centuries, pioneering in the development of social and economic history, advancing theses highly critical of Palacký, and increasingly associating themselves with the Habsburg (conservative and Catholic) orientation.

During the years of independence between the two world wars, Czech historiography was further characterized by a movement known as the "New Pragmatism," simply stated, an effort to make historical study pragmatically useful in the education of citizens in the new Czechoslovak state. During these years some historians worked to establish a fundamental historiography for both Moravia (for example, František Hrubý [1887–1943]) and Slovakia (for example, Václav Chaloupecky [1882–1951]). In addition, economic history was greatly advanced by the work of Bedřich Mendl (1892–1940).

Nazi dismemberment of Czechoslovakia effectively brought Czech historical study to a standstill. After the war, efforts by surviving historians to reinvigorate the discipline were cut short by the Communist coup d'état of 1948. As elsewhere in Eastern Europe at this time, Stalinism meant the imposition on historians of a strict Marxist ideological conformity, marking a distinct break with earlier traditions of Czech historiography. While during the subsequent (post-Stalin) years of Soviet domination there was not insignificant ideological flux (the liberalization between 1956 and 1968 being followed by the "normalization" that accompanied the Warsaw Pact invasion of Czechoslovakia in 1968), a Marxist (and pro-Russian) historical interpretation was maintained until the end of 1989, when the system itself collapsed. During these years, the institutional bases for secondary and higher education in history were enormously expanded (especially in Slovakia), and some very useful work was accomplished in the fields of economic history, historical demographics, nationalism studies, and Reformation studies. Some completely independent (politically) studies were even undertaken by historians outside of the officially sanctioned institutions, notably by members of the *Historický Klub* of Prague.

Since 1989, Czech historians have taken advantage of their recovered freedom to explore fresh issues and problems in Czech history, as well as to revisit old ones. A new history of the Czech lands by a team of historians (*Dějiny zemí koruny české*), published in Prague in 1992, marks a new era in Czech historiography, one that seeks not so much to establish the exceptionality of the Czech nation (as so often in the past), but rather to place its history within the context of broader central European history, and to explore the nature of its relationships to other peoples (including, notably, Germans and Jews) and traditions (especially Habsburg).

Anita Shelton

Texts

Dějiny zemí Koruny české [History of the Czech Crown Lands]. Ed. Petr Čornej, Pavel Bělina, and Jiří Pokorný. 2 vols. Prague: Paseka, 1992.

Palacký, František. *Dějiny narodu českého v Čechach a na Moravě* [History of the Czech Nation in the Czech and Moravian Lands]. 5 vols. in 10. Prague: Nakl. J.G. Kalve, 1848.

References

Agnew, Hugh LeCaine. *Origins of the Czech National Renascence*. Pittsburgh, PA: University of Pittsburgh Press, 1993.

Brock, Peter, and H. Gordon Skilling, eds. *The Czech Renascence of the Nineteenth Century*. Toronto: University of Toronto Press, 1970.

Kořalka, Jiří. "Historiography of the Countries of Eastern Europe: Czechoslovakia." *American Historical Review* 97 (1992): 1026–1040.

Rossos, Andrew. "Czech Historiography, pt. 1." *Canadian Slavonic Papers* 24 (1982), no. 3: 245–260; and "Czech Historiography, pt. 2." *Canadian Slavonic Papers* 24 (1982), 3 no. 4: 59–385.

C

D

Damisch, Hubert (b. 1928)

French art historian and philosopher. Damisch teaches at the Ecole des Hautes Etudes en Sciences Sociales (Centre d'histoire et de théorie de l'art) in Paris. He is well-known in France and other Francophone countries for his critical and theoretical approach to art, which is shaped by semiotics, psychoanalysis, and structuralism. In such seminal essays as *Théorie du nuage* [Theory of Clouds] (1972) and *Fenêtre jaune cadmium: Les dessous de la peinture* [Cadmium Yellow Window: The Underside of Painting] (1984), he has developed his own theory of "painting as material thought"; according to Damisch, any individual painting, when situated within its proper historical context, raises a specific set of questions that can never be reduced to, or by, any discursive model or practice. In his most influential book, *L'Origine de la perspective* (1987), Damisch challenges the traditional conception of perspective as a method corresponding to a precise moment in history, arguing that it should instead be considered as a wider model on which not only painting but other contemporary art forms have regulated themselves.

Carol Doyon

Texts

Théorie du nuage: Pour une histoire de la peinture. Paris: Editions du Seuil, 1972.
Fenêtre jaune cadmium: Les dessous de la peinture. Paris: Seuil, 1984.
Le Jugement del Paris [The Judgment of Paris]. Paris: Flammarion, 1992.
The Origin of Perspective. Trans. John Goodman. Cambridge, MA: MIT Press, 1994.
Semiotics and Iconography. Lisse, Netherlands: Peter de Ridder, 1975.

References

Didi-Huberman, Georges. *Ce que nous voyons, ce qui nous regarde.* Paris: Éditions de Minuit, 1992.
———. *La Peinture incarnée, suivi de Le chef d'oeuvre inconnu par Honoré de Balzac.* Paris: Éditions de Minuit, 1985.

Damrong Rajanubhab, Prince (1862–1943)

Thai prince and historian. Prince Damrong had a very active public life, including periods serving as head of the Ministry of Public Instruction and later the Ministry of the Interior. After the overthrow of the absolute monarchy in 1932, he went into exile in Penang. Widely known in Thailand as the "Father of Thai History," Damrong has had an immense influence on the development of Thai historiography. As president of the Wachirayan Library (later renamed the National Library) after 1915, Damrong organized the editing and publication of an enormous amount of the kingdom's written material previously available only in manuscript form or in rare publications. These publications have subsequently become the basic source material for the writing of Thai history. Besides the scores of historical works he published on a wide range of topics, Damrong also wrote hundreds of prefaces to accompany the library's own publications of historical, literary, religious, and cultural works. Many of these prefaces remain the standard interpretations of the works with which they were published. More recently, Damrong's influence has come under attack by critics of royalist historiography.

Patrick Jory

Texts

Buddhism in Thailand. London: Royal Thai Embassy, 1963.

A History of Buddhist Monuments in Siam. Trans. S. Sivaraksa. Bangkok: Siam Society, 1962.
Journey through Burma in 1936. Bangkok: River Books, 1991.

References

Breazeale, Kennon. "A Transition in Historical Writing: The Works of Prince Damrong Rachanuphap." *Journal of the Siam Society* 59 (1971): 25–49.

Daniel, Samuel (1562–1619)

English poet, dramatist, and historian. Born in Somersetshire and educated at Oxford, Daniel made his first mark as a writer of sonnets and narrative verse. He later combined his poetic talent and historical interest to produce *The Civil Wars,* a much-revised epic poem on the Wars of the Roses told in eight books. His primary sources for this well-balanced if unexciting rendition of the Tudor myth were Raphael Holinshed and Edward Hall or Halle. In his last years he produced *The Collection of the Historie of England,* a prose history of England that was to have run from earliest times to the reign of Elizabeth, but failing health led him to end the project at Edward III. The work was the most successful and widely read summary of medieval English history through most of the seventeenth century and was reprinted in the eighteenth; it was especially remarkable for Daniel's use of primary sources, such as letters, to supplement the chronicles and for his thoughtful vision of English history as an organic unity.

Paul Budra

Texts

The Civil Wars. Ed. Laurence Michel. New Haven, CT: Yale University Press, 1958.
The Collection of the Historie of England [1618]. Delmar, NY: Scholar's Facsimiles and Reprints, 1986.

References

Tillyard, E.M.W. *The English Epic and Its Background.* London: Chatto and Windus, 1954.
Woolf, D.R. *The Idea of History in Early Stuart England.* Toronto: University of Toronto Press, 1990, chapter 3.

Dao Duy Anh (1905–1988)

Vietnamese Marxist scholar of culture, language, and history; born in Bi Kieu village, Thanh Hoa province. Dao Duy Anh was one of the first Vietnamese to introduce Marxism into Vietnam. After he became involved in the Tan Viet Cach Menh Dang (New Vietnam Revolutionary Party) in 1927, he was arrested and given a suspended prison sentence. Dao Duy Anh is widely known for his Chinese–Vietnamese and French–Vietnamese dictionaries and his book *Viet Nam van hoa su cuong* [Brief History of Vietnamese Culture] (1938). The last book argued that Vietnam's culture consisted not of elite dogmas, but of commonly shared practices and beliefs. An idiosyncratic Marxist, Dao Duy Anh emphasized the importance of culture, not economics, in Vietnam's history. In the post-1945 period, Dao Duy Anh participated in the Democratic Republic of Vietnam's project to rewrite the history of Vietnam. Despite his minor participation, with some other intellectuals, in criticizing the government (during the 1956 Nhan Van—Giai Pham literary affair), the state allowed him to continue to publish his scholarship. He continued his work into the 1980s.

Shawn McHale

Texts

Anh, Dao Duy. *Nho nghi chieu hom* [Evening Meditations]. Ho Chi Minh City: Tuoi Tre, 1989.
Thanh, Le. *Cuoc phong van cac nha van* [Interview with Writers]. Hanoi: Doi moi, 1942.

References

Marr, David. *Vietnamese Tradition on Trial, 1920–1945.* Berkeley and Los Angeles: University of California Press, 1981.

Darnton, Robert (b. 1939)

American historian specializing in the sociocultural history of *ancien régime* and revolutionary France. Professor of history at Princeton University, Robert Darnton has made significant contributions to the history of the book and has helped to integrate approaches associated with cultural anthropology through case studies in French cultural history. In the former of these two genres Darnton's *The Business of Enlightenment* was an important study of the diffusion of new ideas through European society. Widely cited by historians of the book, his essay "What Is the History of Books?" outlines a model of print distribution termed the "communications circuit," which has had a significant impact on the field's evolution. In his other cultural studies Darnton has attempted to extract the symbolic meaning of cultural episodes in French history. Much of his best work has been in the form of short interpretive articles, many of which appear in two important collections: *The Great Cat Massacre* and *The Kiss of Lamourette*.

Louis-Georges Harvey

Texts

The Business of Enlightenment: A Publishing History of the Encyclopedie, 1775–1800. Cambridge, MA: Belknap Press, 1979.
The Forbidden Bestsellers of Pre-Revolutionary France. New York: W.W. Norton, 1995.
The Great Cat Massacre and Other Episodes in French Cultural History. New York: Basic Books, 1984.
The Kiss of Lamourette: Reflections in Cultural History. New York: W.W. Norton, 1990.
The Literary Underground of the Old Regime. Cambridge, MA: Harvard University Press, 1982.
Mesmerism and the End of the Enlightenment in France. Cambridge, MA: Harvard University Press, 1968.
And Daniel Roche. *Revolution in Print: The Press in France, 1775–1800.* Berkeley: University of California Press, 1989.

Davidson, Basil Risbridger (b. 1914)

British author, journalist, and historian of Africa. A professional journalist from 1938 until 1962, service in World War II sparked Davidson's interest in African soldiers. In 1951 Davidson attended the first conference on African history organized by Roland Oliver at the School of Oriental and African Studies (SOAS), to report on it for his newspaper. He became deeply and personally interested in the work of historians in Africa and devoted much of his publishing life to the cause of making their work, often highly technical, known to a wide public. He strongly supported the movement for African self-government and was active in the anti-apartheid movement. He has held visiting fellowships in, among others, the universities of Ghana, California, and Edinburgh and in 1970 received the Haile Selassie African Research Award.

Davidson's international recognition centers around his numerous scholarly works on African history. Since 1951, when he began to devote profound research interest and personal attention to African studies, Davidson has published more than twenty-five books. His contributions to African studies rest principally on three seminal works, *Old Africa Rediscovered* (1959), *The African Past* (1964), and *Modern Africa* (1982). Deviating from the traditional Eurocentric conclusions of colonial anthropologists who insisted that Africa had no history, culture, and civilization before the arrival of the Europeans, *Old Africa* was one of the first authoritative works on precolonial Africa by a European which amply demonstrated Africa had a rich and splendid past that was worthy of recognition. Soon after its publication, this book was adopted by most African universities because not only did it "rediscover" and restore faith in African history and culture, but it also appeared, auspiciously, at the dawn of independence, when African nationalists romanticized their "glorious" past. This work has been published in more than twenty countries and in various languages worldwide. *The African Past* confronted, with numerous examples of well-ordered societies, the claims by earlier European scholars that Africa had been a land of chaos and stagnation prior to the advent of Europeans. Davidson's *Modern Africa,* which has been revised several times, surveys colonial and contemporary Africa in a unique way by correlating the fragility of many African nascent states to the arbitrariness of their creation by the departing European colonizers. But just as far-reaching was Davidson's eight-part television series on Africa in 1984, broadcast worldwide, which aimed at re-educating the world about African peoples and cultures. Although some of Davidson's readers and viewers might feel that he is somewhat eulogistic in evaluating Africa's past, seeking to redress age-old stereotypes is one of the most difficult aspects of diffusing new scholarship. Most recently, Davidson has speculated on the future course of African development in his volume *The Black Man's Burden* (1992). He remains one of the few non-African scholars whose works enjoy the confidence of Africans and serious students of African history.

Apollos O. Nwauwa

Texts

Africa in History: Themes and Outlines. Revised ed. London: Phoenix, 1992.
The African Awakening. London: Cape, 1955.
African Kingdoms. New York: Time-Life Books, 1966.
The African Past: Chronicles from Antiquity to Modern Times. New York: Grosset and Dunlap, 1967.
The Black Man's Burden: Africa and the Curse of the Nation-State. London: James Currey, 1992.
Modern Africa. London: Longman, 1983.
Old Africa Rediscovered. London: Longman, 1959.

References

Fyfe, Christopher, ed. *African Studies since 1945: A Tribute to Basil Davidson.* London: Longman, 1976.

Davis, Natalie Zemon (b. 1929)

American historian; professor, Princeton University; president of the American Historical Association (1987). Although Davis works primarily in sixteenth-century French history, her books and articles have exerted great influence on historians of other eras and areas. Davis has investigated cultural activity in the broadest sense, using insights from anthropology, psychology, and literature. Her methodology is inclusive, and her aim is to understand the reciprocal effects of social structures and individual as well as group consciousness.

Davis's best-known contributions to historical scholarship are *Society and Culture in Early Modern France* (1975), a collection of eight of her seminal essays, and *The Return of Martin Guerre* (1983). In the first, she explores the culture of ordinary people and the ways in which the collectivities to which they belonged affected their beliefs and actions. While her focus is on religious change, specifically that brought about by Calvinism, she casts her net widely, exploring topics like ritual behavior, actions of urban masses, gender roles, or the effect of the written word on popular culture. The second book examines how ordinary people constructed their identity. Working closely with sixteenth-century documents, Davis looks at an impostor who impersonated another man, and the effects of his actions on both the simple and the learned. This strange story became a successful film.

Davis's interest in self-representation continued in her *Fiction in the Archives: Pardon Tales and Their Tellers in Sixteenth-Century France* (1987), which stresses what she calls "cultural exchange" between official or learned and popular or oral culture. In almost all her work Davis has focused on the complexity of this "exchange," showing with verve and imagination that the boundaries separating the two are infinitely complex and that no simple generalizations can be made concerning them. Her most recent book is *Women on the Margins: Three Seventeenth-Century Lives* (1995).

Elisabeth G. Gleason

Texts

Fiction in the Archives: Pardon Tales and Their Tellers in Sixteenth-Century France. Stanford, CA: Stanford University Press, 1987.
The Return of Martin Guerre. Cambridge, MA: Harvard University Press, 1983.
Society and Culture in Early Modern France. Stanford, CA: Stanford University Press, 1975.

Women on the Margins: Three Seventeenth-Century Lives. Cambridge, MA: Harvard University Press, 1995.

References

"Bibliography of Natalie Zemon Davis' Works." In *Culture and Identity in Early Modern Europe (1500–1800): Essays in Honor of Natalie Zemon Davis,* ed. Barbara D. Diefendorf and Carla Hesse. Ann Arbor: University of Michigan Press, 1993.
"Interview with Natalie Zemon Davis." In *Visions of History,* ed. Marho: Radical Historians' Organization. New York: Pantheon, 1983.

Davis, Paulina Wright (1813–1876)

Historian, editor, and suffragist. Davis was born in Bloomfield, New York. Orphaned at the age of seven, she went to live with an aunt in Le Roy, New York, where she received her education. She intended to be a missionary, but her 1833 marriage to merchant Francis Wright of Utica, New York, ended that plan. For a time, she gave lectures to women's groups on anatomy and physiology, helping open the medical profession to women. In 1849, long widowed, she married future congressman Thomas Davis, of Providence, Rhode Island. There, in February of 1853, she founded the *Una,* the first newspaper specifically devoted to women's rights. Davis published for three years at her own expense, despite her critics' claims that such work was unbecoming for a woman. She continued working for women's rights, particularly suffrage, and in 1870 coordinated the meeting of the National Woman Suffrage Movement in New York City. The following year she moved to Florence, Italy, to study art. When her health failed, she returned to Rhode Island and died at her home in Providence. Davis is best known for *A History of the National Woman's Rights Movement,* first published in 1871. This remains the major work on the movement's early years.

Tina Weil Moore

Texts

A History of the National Woman's Rights Movement. New York: Source Book Press, 1970.

References

Stanton, Elizabeth Cady, Susan B. Anthony, and Matilda Joslyn Gage. *History of Woman Suffrage.* Salem, NY: Ayer Co., 1985.

Dawson, Christopher (1889–1970)

English historian and philosopher. Dawson was born in Hay Castle, Hay on Wye on the border of Breconshire and Herefordshire. In 1896 the family moved to Hartlington Hall, Skipton (Yorkshire), where his father inherited ancestral property. The Dawsons were Anglican in religion and of the military squirearchy. Dawson was educated at Winchester and Trinity Oxford where he was much influenced by the historian E.I. Watkin. In 1914, at the age of twenty-five, Dawson was received into the Roman Catholic Church; all his publications appeared after that event, and his last academic post was to the professorship of Roman Catholic studies in the Harvard Divinity School in 1958. Dawson's first book, *The Age of the Gods* (1928), although concerned with pre-Christian cultures, begins to formulate the central thesis of much of his later work, namely that religious beliefs and practices are the basis of culture. His historical reputation was greatly enhanced by his *Making of Europe* (1932), a survey of European history from A.D. 400 to 1000 that embraced every element and influence in the origins of Europe—Judeo-Christian, Greco-Roman, Byzantine, Islamic, Celtic, Teutonic, Slavic, and Nordic. His central theme is the vitality of the Christian Church in converting the "barbarian" west—a search for the soul of Europe. However, he cannot be simply categorized as a romantic medievalist. His later work is concerned with the philosophical problems of the twentieth century: a few books that indicate the sophistication of his understanding are *Progress and Religion* (1929), *Religion and Culture* (1948), *Dynamics of World History* (1956), and the *Historic Reality of Christian Culture* (1960). But perhaps the most controversial of his books was *Religion and the Rise of Western Culture* (1950). Immensely erudite, Dawson studied a wide variety of religious cultures but saw in their underlying unity the key to human progress and in religion itself the basic value in the unity of history.

J.J.N. McGurk

Texts

The Age of the Gods: A Study in the Origins of Culture in Prehistoric Europe and the Ancient East. London: J. Murray, 1928.

Dynamics of World History. New York: Sheed and Ward, 1956.

The Historic Reality of Christian Culture: A Way to the Renewal of Human Life. London: Routledge and Kegan Paul, 1960.

The Making of Europe: An Introduction to the History of European Unity. London: Sheed and Ward, 1932.

Progress and Religion: An Historical Enquiry. London: Longmans, Green, 1929.

Religion and Culture. London: Sheed and Ward, 1948.

Religion and the Rise of Western Culture. New York: Sheed and Ward, 1950.

Tradition and Inheritance. St.Paul, MN: Wanderer Press, 1970.

References

Locas, C. "Christopher Dawson, a Bibliography." *Harvard Theological Review* 66 (1973): 177–206.

Boyd, Ian, ed. *The Chesterton Review* 9 (1983): no. 2 (special issue on Dawson).

De la Vallée Poussin, Louis (1869–1938)

Belgian Sanskritist and authority on Buddhism. De la Vallée Poussin was professor of comparative grammar of Greek and Latin at the University of Ghent. His interest in Buddhism was aroused by his linguistic studies, and his main contribution came in Buddhist metaphysics and logic. He published three renowned volumes in the *Histoire du Monde* series, which covered Indian history down to the Muslim period: *Indo-Européens et Indo-Iraniens* [Indo-Europeans and Indo-Iranians] (1924), *L'Inde aux Temps des Mauryas* [India in the Time of the Mauryas] (1930), and *Dynasties et Histoire de l'Inde* [The Dynasties and History of India] (1935). Additionally, he authored more than ten other books on various aspects of Indian Buddhism. De la Vallée Poussin's approach to his subject was an intellectual one; he was said to have had no real sympathy for Buddhism, remaining a devout Catholic all his life, but his approach was extremely thorough, careful, and critical, if dry, and warmly received by scholars both in his own time and later.

Roger D. Long

Texts

The Buddhist Councils. Calcutta: K.P. Bagchi, 1976.

Dynasties et Histoire de l'Inde. Paris: E. de Boccard, 1935.

L'Inde aux Temps des Mauryas. Paris: E. de Boccard, 1930.

Indo-Européens et Indo-Iraniens. Paris: E. de Boccard, 1924.

The Way to Nirvana: Six Lectures on Ancient Buddhism As a Discipline of Salvation. Cambridge, Eng.: Cambridge University Press, 1917.

D

References

Saunders, Kenneth J. *Epochs in Buddhist History: The Haskell Lectures, 1921.* Chicago: University of Chicago Press, 1924.

De Ruggiero, Guido (1888–1948)

Italian philosopher and historian of philosophy. Working in the idealist tradition with Benedetto Croce and Giovanni Gentile, De Ruggiero gained prominence with *La filosofia contemporanea* [Contemporary Philosophy] (1912). Like Croce, he influenced non-Italian historians such as R.G. Collingwood. De Ruggiero contributed to important journals, including Giuseppe Prezzolini's *La Voce* in Florence and Piero Gobetti's *Rivoluzione liberale* in Turin. He taught at the universities of Messina and Rome until 1942 (when he was dismissed for his antifascist activities) during which time he completed a monumental ten-volume history of Western philosophy, *Storia della filosofia* (1912–1947). In 1921, he published two books, *Il pensiero politico meridionale nei secoli XVIII e XIX* [Southern Political Thought in the Eighteenth and Nineteenth Centuries] and *L'Impero britannico dopo la guerra* [The British Empire after the War]. With the advent of Fascism, De Ruggiero continued writing for newspapers and journals in support of liberal monarchy; his popular and influential work, *Storia del liberalismo italiano* [History of Italian Liberalism] appeared in 1925. This was an analysis of the crisis of liberalism in the early twentieth century and a passionate defense of liberalism, not just as a political ideology, but as an entire system of culture, ethics, beliefs, and values. Translated into many languages and reprinted in many editions, it was a powerful manifesto for European antifascists. In 1941, a new edition was released and De Ruggiero joined the Action Party; after the fall of the Fascist regime, he served as minister of education. His work retains an ideal of society where individuals are able to fully develop their potential within a context of law, freedom, and reason. De Ruggiero's own philosophical system avoided abstraction and instead sought to formulate concrete, ethical principles for living in the modern world.

Stanislao G. Pugliese

Texts

Existentialism. Ed. R. Heppenstall and trans. E.M. Cocks. London: Secker and Warburg, 1946.
The History of European Liberalism. Trans. R.G. Collingwood. Boston: Beacon Press, 1967.
Modern Philosophy. A.H. Hannay and R.G. Collingwood. New York: Macmillan, 1921.

References

Garin, Eugenio. "Guido De Ruggiero." *Belfagor* 6 (1958): 722–728.
Gily Reda, Clementina. *Guido De Ruggiero.* Naples: Società editrice napoletana, 1981.
Salvatorelli, Luigi. "Guido De Ruggiero politico." *Belfagor* 7 (1959): 670–678.

De Thou, Jacques-Auguste (1553–1617)

French historian and politician. Born in Paris into a distinguished family of royal officials, De Thou studied law at the University of Orleans and entered the high ranks of officialdom himself in 1580 as a royal councilor at the Parlement of Paris, of which he became a presiding judge in 1586. In 1603 he published the first part of his most significant work, the *Historiarum sui temporis* [History of His Own Times], of which the entire manuscript has never been published. In this multivolume book, which principally covers the French religious wars of the late sixteenth century, De Thou advanced the historiographical principles learned from historical theorists such as Jean Bodin: seek truth in evidence and balance in judgments. In company with many intellectuals of his day, he was influenced by neostoicism, asserting that the absence of passion is a fundamental condition of acceptable history writing, which is to be accomplished by maintaining an intellectual distance from historical actors. Despite such principles, De Thou's book is sympathetic to the royal cause during the wars. For this reason it was placed on the Index of Prohibited Books by the Roman Catholic Church in 1609. Despite its bias, the book was influential and was reprinted repeatedly until the nineteenth century. It inspired many similar "contemporary" histories in the seventeenth century in a number of European countries and remains a useful source for the wars of religion.

James R. Farr

Texts

Mémoires de la vie de Jacques-Auguste de Thou. Amsterdam: F. L'Honoré, 1713.
The Works of Jacques-Auguste de Thou. Ed. S. Kinser. The Hague: Martinus Nijhoff, 1967.

References

Kinser, Samuel. *The Historiography of Jacques-Auguste De Thou.* Ph.D. dissertation, Cornell University, 1960.

Ranum, Orest. *Artisans of Glory: Writers and Historical Thought in Seventeenth-Century France.* Chapel Hill: University of North Carolina Press, 1980.

Debo, Angie (1890–1988)

U.S. historian of Native Americans. Born and raised in rural Kansas and Oklahoma, Debo studied at the University of Oklahoma under E.E. Dale, who sparked her early interest and passed on the perspectives of F.J. Turner, giving her a sense of the importance of regional history. She received her Ph.D. in 1933 and published her dissertation, *The Rise and Fall of the Choctaw Republic,* a year later. Unable to find a teaching position, she turned to writing regional and Indian history. Debo is best known for her work (thirteen books and many articles) in Indian history, especially the tribes of Oklahoma. She interpreted North American history from the Indians' perspective. On occasion the non-Indian community challenged her objectivity. To Debo, Indians were active determinants in and at the center stage of U.S. history.

Russell M. Magnaghi

Texts

And Still the Waters Run. Princeton, NJ: Princeton University Press, 1940.
Geronimo: The Man, His Place, His Time. Norman: University of Oklahoma Press, 1976.
A History of the Indians of the United States. Norman: University of Oklahoma Press, 1970.
Prairie City: The Story of an American Community. Norman: University of Oklahoma Press, 1944.
The Rise and Fall of the Choctaw Republic. Second ed. Norman, OK: University of Oklahoma Press, 1961.

References

McIntosh, Kenneth. "Geronimo's Friend: Angie Debo and the New History." *Chronicles of Oklahoma* 66 (1988): 164–177.

Decline, Idea of

Historical concept, principally associated with linear and cyclical philosophies of history. The creation stories of many world cultures include an account of decline or fall, as in Genesis with the expulsion of Adam and Eve from an earthly paradise. Historians in the Western tradition developed this view as a cyclical theory of recovery and renewal, followed by decline and disintegration, to explain the rise and fall of states and civilizations. They adopted organic metaphors to elaborate the complex, but inevitable, process of cyclical change: human communities follow the same temporal progression of birth, growth, maturity, decline, and death as may be observed in plants and animals. Elements of this approach can be found in Thucydides's *Histories,* with later Greek and Roman historians applying the assumption of cyclical repetition in various forms.

Early church fathers and medieval Christian historians reoriented the classical view of history to a new religious perspective, documenting the decline of pagan Rome and the emergence of Christian culture. During the fourteenth century, Petrarch reinterpreted that tradition by portraying his immediate past as a period of *tenebrae,* or time of cultural darkness and decline. His negative assessment of the Middle Ages as the "Dark Ages" was promoted by later humanists and historians of the modern period. Four hundred years after Petrarch, Edward Gibbon, in *The History of the Decline and Fall of the Roman Empire* (1776–1788), would attribute the demise of pagan Rome primarily to the rapid spread of the Christian religion.

Renaissance and modern historians revived interest in the cyclical approach of ancient historians. Giambattista Vico, in *Scienza Nuova* [New Science] (1725), elaborated the cyclical view, with human "nations" passing through different stages of development, including decline. But the most significant popular adaptation of the cyclical theory emphasizing decline was by the German historian, Oswald Spengler. In *Der Untergang des Abendlandes* [The Decline of the West] (1918), he treated historical recurrence as a "morphological" pattern of cultural emergence and dissolution. Claiming that the cyclical process is similar in all major historical cultures, Spengler predicted that the future of the West was one of decadence and decline. The message of this prophet of doom gained a wide hearing, given the pessimistic conditions of postwar Germany. While critical of Spengler's approach, Arnold Toynbee, in *A Study of History* (1934–1954), showed how each of his twenty-one civilizations passed through similar stages of growth, decline, and dissolution, with a final stage marked by the formation of a universal state.

James V. Mehl

See also KULTURPESSIMISMUS; PHILOSOPHY OF HISTORY—SUBSTANTIVE; PROGRESS.

References

Chaunu, Pierre. *Histoire et Décadence.* Paris: Librairie Académique Perrin, 1981.

Friedlander, Saul et al. *Visions of Apocalypse: End or Rebirth?* New York: Holmes and Meier, 1985.

Herman, Arthur. *Prophets of Despair: The Idea of Decline in Western History.* New York: Free Press, 1996.

Hughes, H. Stuart. *Oswald Spengler: A Critical Reading.* New York: Scribner, 1952.

Degler, Carl Neumann (b. 1921)

American historian. Degler was born in Orange, New Jersey. He received his A.B. at Upsala College (1942) and his M.A. (1947) and Ph.D. (1952) from Columbia University. He taught at several colleges, including Vassar (1952–1968), before moving in 1968 to Stanford University, where he is currently professor emeritus (1990–). He was president of the Organization of American Historians in 1979 and 1980. Degler has won several prizes for his work, notably the Pulitzer, the National Book Award, the Beveridge, and the Bancroft for *Neither Black Nor White* (1971), an outstanding comparative study of slavery in Brazil and the United States. He has written several other books on the Old South, including *The Other South* (1974) and *Place over Time* (1977). He has been a highly versatile historian. He was one of the first historians, and one of the few men, to write on women's history in works such as *At Odds* (1980). His work on Social Darwinism, *In Search of Human Nature* (1991), is another fine example of his many fields of expertise.

Walter A. Sutton

Texts

At Odds: Women and the Family in America from the Revolution to the Present. New York: Oxford University Press, 1980.

In Search of Human Nature: The Decline and Revival of Darwinism in American Social Thought. New York: Oxford University Press, 1991.

Neither Black Nor White: Slavery and Race in Brazil and the United States. New York: Macmillan, 1971.

The Other South: Southern Dissenters in the Nineteenth Century. New York: Harper and Row, 1974.

Out of Our Past: The Forces That Shaped Modern America. Revised ed. New York: Harper and Row, 1970.

Place over Time: The Continuation of Southern Distinctiveness. Baton Rouge: Louisiana State University Press, 1977.

Delany, Martin Robinson (1812–1885)

Writer, editor, abolitionist, and black nationalist. Delany was born a free man in Charles Town, Virginia. Although prohibited by law, he received an education. At the age of nineteen, he moved to Pittsburgh where, in 1843, he began the *Mystery,* a black newspaper. Later he served for two years as assistant editor of the *North Star,* working with Frederick Douglass. He espoused emigration and spent two years in Africa just prior to the Civil War investigating the possibilities of black settlement. Commissioned as the first black major in the Army, Delany worked for three years in the Freedmen's Bureau in South Carolina, remaining there throughout Reconstruction. Ailing, he joined his family in Xenia, Ohio, where he died. While Delany published a number of books, critical attention has centered on two publications. The earliest, *The Condition, Elevation, Emigration, and Destiny of the Colored People of the United States* (1852), advocated the emigration of free blacks. The other, *Blake; or, The Huts of Africa* (1861–1862), is a novel in which a slave incites rebellion and then emigrates to Cuba. Delany received little popular attention until the rise of black nationalism in the 1960s and 1970s. It was during this period that these major works were reprinted.

Tina Weil Moore

Texts

Blake; or, The Huts of Africa. Boston: Beacon Press, 1970.

The Condition, Elevation, Emigration, and Destiny of the Colored People of the United States. New York: Arno Press, 1968.

References

Griffith, Cyril E. *The African Dream: Martin R. Delany and the Emergence of Pan-African Thought.* University Park: Pennsylvania State University Press, 1975.

Sterling, Dorothy. *The Making of an Afro-American: Martin Robinson Delany, 1812–1885.* Garden City, NY: Doubleday, 1971.

Delbrück, Hans (1848–1929)

German historian. Delbrück studied at the universities of Heidelberg, Greifswald, and Bonn, and served in the Franco-Prussian war of 1870–71. Subsequently, he obtained his Ph.D. in 1873 and was a tutor to the son of Emperor Friedrich Wilhelm (1874–1879). He lived as an independent scholar before finally obtaining a professorship in 1895, when he was chosen to succeed Heinrich von Treitschke at the University of Berlin (1896–1921). From 1883–1919 he coedited (until 1889, in collaboration with Treitschke) the influential *Preussische Jahrbücher*. He was also a member of the Prussian Parliament (1882–1885) and of the German Reichstag (1884–1890). In politics Delbrück regarded himself as an "enlightened conservative" or a "conservative social-democrat." He favored an Anglo-German rapprochement and, during World War I, advocated the pursuit of moderate German war aims as well as reforms within Prussia. Later he strongly opposed Tirpitz and Ludendorff, although he contested the war-guilt clause imposed at Versailles. Delbrück, to whom the basis of all history consisted of the polarization of opposing forces and structures, was an important yet controversial military historian. He differentiated between a "strategy of attrition" and a "strategy of annihilation," and he was the first to analyze the connection between a nation's approach to war and its economic, constitutional, cultural, and social conditions. He also proposed a new methodology by insisting that the philological analysis of ancient and medieval sources alone was insufficient. Other facts reported in these sources (for instance, the number of soldiers participating in a certain battle) also needed verification or *Sachkritik*. To facilitate this he did not hesitate to draw conclusions from the comparison of battles and war strategies that were centuries apart. He was also among the very few historians in recent times to attempt the writing of a single-authored world history, publishing in later life an influential *Weltgeschichte* that questioned many traditional historical beliefs.

Klaus Larres

Texts

Historische und politische Aufsätze [Historical and Political Essays]. Berlin: Walter & Apolant, 1887.

Leben des Feldmarschalls Grafen Neithardt von Gneisenau [The Life of Field Marshall Count von Gneisenau]. 2 vols. Berlin: G. Reimer, 1880.

Geschichte der Kriegskunst im Rahmen der politischen Geschichte [History of the Art of War in the Context of Political History]. 7 vols. Berlin: G. Stilke, 1900–1936.

Weltgeschichte [World History]. 5 vols. Berlin: O. Stollberg, 1924–1928.

References

Bruch, Rüdiger vom. *Wissenschaft, Politik und öffentliche Meinung: Gelehrtenpolitik im Wilhelminischen Deutschland 1890–1914* [Scholarship, Politics, and Public Opinion: Academics and Politics in Wilhelmian Germany, 1890–1914]. Husum, Germany: Matthiesen, 1980.

Bucholz, Arden. *Hans Delbrück and the German Military Establishment*. Iowa City: University of Iowa Press, 1985.

Christ, Karl. "Hans Delbrück." In his *Von Gibbon zu Rostovtzeff* [From Gibbon to Rostovtzeff]. Darmstadt, Germany: Wissenschaftliche Buchgesellschaft, 1989.

Hillgruber, A. "Hans Delbrück." In *Deutsche Historiker*, vol. 8, ed. H.U. Wehler. Göttingen: Vandenhoeck & Ruprecht, 1973, 416–428.

Thimme, Annelise. *Hans Delbrück als Kritiker der Wilhelminischen Epoche* [Hans Delbrück As a Critic of the Wilhelmian Era]. Düsseldorf: Droste-Verlag, 1955.

Delisle, Léopold (1826–1910)

French historian. Delisle's interests focused on the Middle Ages, especially the reign of Philip Augustus. Although he made many original contributions to his field, Delisle was perhaps best known for his work as an editor of a large number of primary sources from the thirteenth and fourteenth centuries. His first major work was *Catalogue des actes de Philippe-Auguste* [Acts of Philip Augustus] (1856), and it established his reputation as a careful scholar and editor. This was followed by the *Rouleaux des morts du XIᵉ au XVᵉ siècle* [Death Rolls from the Eleventh to the Fifteenth Centuries] (1866) and numerous other works. He edited the last two volumes of the *Recueil des historiens des Gaules et de la France* [Collection of the Historians of Gaul and France] (1904), a twenty-four-volume work that had begun in the first half of the eighteenth century, as well as *Recherches sur la librairie de Charles V* [Researches on the Library of Charles V] (1907). He was also a principal editor of the catalog of printed books of the Bibliothèque Nationale, Paris.

Mack P. Holt

Texts

Catalogue des actes de Philippe-August. Paris: A. Durand, 1856.

Recherches sur la librairie de Charles V, roi de France, 1377–1380. 2 vols. Paris: H. Champion, 1907.

References

Carbonell, Charles-Olivier. *Histoire et Historiens: Une mutation idéologique des historiens français, 1865–1885* [History and Historians: An Ideological Change, 1865–1885]. Toulouse, France: Privat, 1976.

Lacombe, Paul. *Bibliographie des travaux de M. Léopold Delisle.* 2 vols. Paris: Imprimerie nationale, 1902; Paris: H. Leclerc, 1911.

Demography—Historical

The study of population size, growth, and mobility in past times. When Joseph and Mary went up to Bethlehem, they went to be counted. People began to count themselves with their numeracy skills for much the same reasons that they used their literacy skills to classify social life into legal categories. The Roman census was a primary technology of their power in dominating subject peoples in conquered territories like Palestine. Its roots reach back to the very beginning of the republic; the first enumeration dates back to 508 B.C., but P.A. Brunt's study, *Italian Manpower, 225 B.C.14.A.D.,* of this source only covers the late republic and early empire. Leaving aside the desire to turn census figures into population counts, the basic point concerning the Roman census is that it was a recurrent mode of surveillance. Yet the Roman exercise in social self-knowledge was not in any way unique—the Old Testament mentions a variety of similar self-examinations, and among the earliest Assyrian texts is a census dating back some 2,700 years.

Ancient enumerators were inveterate census takers yet they only counted some individuals—free men who were fit for war and/or liable for taxes. This situation changed in the early Middle Ages when the family farm—called *mansus, focus, familia, casata, casa massaricia* (in Italy), *hufe* (in Germany), *hide* (in England)—had become the basic component of manorial and fiscal assessment. The most famous censuslike enumeration of the peasant families in northwestern Europe is the early-ninth-century *polyptych* (survey) made by the abbot Irminon of the lands of the Parisian monastery of St. Germain des Prés. David Herlihy's study, *Medieval Households,* pivots on his use of this source.

In a large part of the feudal heartland, *la révolution censive* obliterated the original role of the manorial system around the year 1000. England was exceptional in this regard—as in so many others—because manorial court rolls have survived in abundance. Court rolls provide unusually detailed information about the way that lords confiscated peasant wealth through annual recognitions *(tallage),* death duties *(heriot),* marriage fees *(merchet),* fines for sexual misconduct *(leyrwite),* and annual exemptions from residing on the manor *(chevage).* By linking these multiple references to discrete individuals, scholars led by J.A. Raftis have pioneered the reconstitution of thirteenth- and fourteenth-century English manorial populations. The best monograph on this subject is Zvi Razi's *Life, Marriage and Death in a Medieval Parish* (1980).

A quite different source for analyzing the social and demographic profile of medieval populations was the product of nascent state-building efforts. The Domesday Book of 1086 was created by the Norman king to gain a full appreciation of the extent of the English conquest. Similar concerns sparked the French monarchy when it organized a survey of hearths in its kingdom in 1328, the last year of Capetian rule. This scrupulously exact enquiry laid the groundwork for major innovations in financing state formation. Numbering the people was, therefore, at the heart of royal absolutism in both England and France.

Jacob Burckhardt's classic study, *The Civilization of the Renaissance in Italy* (1860), notes that Florentines employed statistical concepts in their drive to analyze social life in a systematic manner. This view of things runs through their accounting practices, their historical writing, their manuals of conduct, and their social regulations. Inspired as they were by their classical republican arguments about equality, liberty, patriotism, and enlightenment, fifteenth-century Florentines saw a direct analogy between the Roman census and their own. The most singular Renaissance text that has survived as a result of this quantitative mentality was the Florentine *catasto* of 1427; this tax register has been the primary source in David Herlihy and Christiane Klapisch-Zuber's monograph *Tuscans and Their Families.*

The Florentine *catasto* remains as a testament to administrative efficiency, but it was not without parallel elsewhere. Similar procedures were described as early as the tenth century when the Venetians were keeping lists of the inhabitants of their serene city. By the thirteenth and fourteenth centuries, the use of the technologies of numeracy and literacy to survey the communal population seems to have been common practice throughout the peninsula. This regulatory initiative combined with the imperatives of governance to keep lawyers and notaries busy tracking people, things, and the power relationships between people and things. In Renaissance Italy, then, literacy and numeracy were employed to create a grid of surveillance that was predicated on the widespread knowledge of and familiarity with written instruments. The Florentine *catasto* reflects the early modern scribal regard for information that was widely disseminated among the population by its notarial culture, abetted by the first secular educational project.

The English Domesday Book of 1086, the French Hearth Tax survey of 1328, and the 1427 Florentine *catasto* are only the most remarkable surviving examples of a massive *volonté de savoir*. In them, the collection of self-knowledge took on arithmetic shape. But below this national-level-data collection, there were many other examples of numeracy being employed in the pursuit of social self-knowledge. These local and occasional surveys have provided historians with valuable information. Perhaps the most striking example of this historical activity occurred when Peter Laslett, in the course of researching the social context within which the seventeenth-century political philosophers Robert Filmer and John Locke wrote, analyzed two small and seemingly random enumerations of the obscure English villages of Clayworth, in Nottinghamshire, and Cogenhoe, in Bedfordshire. Laslett's serendipity is now the stuff of historiographical legend: he built on it to establish the Cambridge Group for the History of Population and Social Structure when, along with his former student E.A. Wrigley, he was granted funding by the Nubar Gulbenkian Foundation in 1964. The Social Sciences Research Council took over financing their work in 1968 and, more recently, the Cambridge Group has been absorbed into the Cambridge University history faculty.

In getting the work of the Cambridge Group off the ground, Laslett employed an innovative approach to data collection: he used his connections at the British Broadcasting Corporation to appeal to amateur historians all over the country to ask them to search in their local records offices and forward copies of any relevant documents to his new population studies center. This secret army of researchers flooded the Cambridge Group with over four hundred censuses, enumerations, listings, and other relevant materials. Perhaps the most conspicuous discovery that resulted from the first phase of the Cambridge Group's study of local population listings was Laslett's assertion in *The World We Have Lost* (1965) that, contrary to conventional wisdom, early modern households were neither large nor extended but rather small and nuclear. Similarly, he argued that reference to the example of Juliet in Shakespeare's play was seriously misleading with regard to the age at first marriage for women. Laslett further questioned the value of evidence drawn from literature and "soft data." Following up the controversial argument of *The World We Have Lost,* the Cambridge Group published further volumes on household and family structures, illegitimacy, and literacy—all were based on the exploration of "hard data" and were in tune with the times in that they employed quantitative methods to explore social historical issues.

To build up their bank of "hard data," the Cambridge Group again tapped the energy of their secret research army to create a massive file of aggregated, parish-level, monthly counts of baptisms, burials, and marriages for 530 parishes. In 1981, E.A. Wrigley and R.S. Schofield published *The Population History of England and Wales, 1541–1871;* this landmark study employed the 404 best examples from this large sample of parish-level data. This evidence was aggregated to create a proxy for national totals—but unlinked at the level of individuals or families—on baptisms, burials, and marriages to trace the outlines of England's demographic evolution.

A new era in population surveillance developed in Reformation state formations that aimed to keep individual subjects in view by tracking them in parochial registers of birth/baptism, marriage, and death/burial. To be sure there are forerunners of this quantitative form that date from fifteenth-century Geneva, but the earliest, complete data-sets were brought on stream by Henry VIII's desire to police his own magisterial reformation. For some English parishes, there is a complete run of information from 1538 until 1837, the beginning of civil registration. But while the English data have the benefit of longitude, they are not particularly detailed and until E.A. Wrigley published his studies of Colyton, Devon, it was widely believed that the English parish registers were useless for demographic purposes. In the past twenty-five years, the Cambridge Group for the History of Population and Social Structure has overseen the collection of a national sample of English parish reconstitutions. They are currently in the process of completing a survey of this data from a selection of twenty-six villages.

Meticulous reconstitutions of family formations in fact began in France, with the work of Louis Henry who devised the methodology and provided the scholarly world with the first example of its value. This demographer found himself driven backward after being asked by President

D

de Gaulle to account for the failure of the French to reproduce themselves (and to provide the motherland with soldiers) with the same fervor as their German enemies who had defeated them in battle in 1870, 1914, and 1940. Henry chose to study the obscure Norman village of Crulai—some five kilometers from Camembert—which had a marvelously complete and exceptionally detailed set of parish registers. Enormous numbers of family reconstitution studies have been completed in France, mostly by master's-level students at the Institut national des études démographiques.

Building on the genealogical literature that proliferated in the nineteenth century, and developing new techniques for demographic analysis, family reconstitution studies provide a diachronic analysis that can be placed alongside the synchronic descriptions of social structure that derives from census enumerations and listings of inhabitants. While family reconstitution studies provide extremely detailed analysis and statistical results, there is a methodological problem with the process since it only takes into account the demographic product of those families who remained continuously in residence in the registration unit under observation. Obviously, therefore, those who were mobile or migrants were under-enumerated or missed altogether. While this is a deficiency, studies have shown that little bias seems to result from it. The rapid increase in lifecycle and lifetime mobility that occurred in Europe after the mid-eighteenth century means that family reconstitution studies are most valuable for the early modern period. Nevertheless, there have recently been innovative studies using modified versions of the original methodology for nineteenth-century urban populations.

The urge to quantify social relations found hospitable surroundings in northern Europe. Theoretical consideration of the stochastic laws of chance processes emerged at the same time when lotteries, tontines, and life insurance schemes quite literally bet on human lives. In this way—and quite by coincidence—astronomers and other mathematical luminaries were involved in creating a new view of social relations based on probability. Since the late seventeenth century, one of the cornerstones of modern populations has been their desire to create stochastic models for thinking about themselves. Merging concerns with social regulation with the accumulation of masses of quantitative data also laid the groundwork for the Malthusian theories that would provide inspiration for social engineers as well as Charles Darwin.

Modern governmental statistical departments can be traced to this vision of social engineering, although it must be pointed out that the first country to keep close tabs on its whole population—Sweden—did so for religious/pedagogical purposes. Notwithstanding this exception, the collection of statistical information has proceeded uninhibited in the realm of secular governance in the nineteenth century. In the modern world we are awash in this sea of data. The single most outstanding result of research into these vast banks of data has been the multination "Princeton Fertility Project" headed by Ansley J. Coale. In addition, there have been a great many studies of urban populations that have employed census enumerations to investigate the lives of otherwise obscure people. Historical demographers of the modern world are, therefore, in a very different position with regard to sources from their colleagues who study the ancient and early modern periods when data collection was less systematic and its survival was much more a matter of chance.

Perhaps the most singular characteristic of research into historical demography has been the use of modern techniques of analysis into premodern collections of data. In this regard, the urge for premodern societies to count themselves has provided researchers with an opportunity that has been exploited in a number of ingenious ways to expand our appreciation of past social formations.

David Levine
Jennifer Melville

See also FAMILY HISTORY (COMPARATIVE); FAMILY RECONSTITUTION; GENEALOGY; RURAL HISTORY; SOCIAL HISTORY.

References

Brunt. P.A. *Italian Manpower, 225 B.C.–14.A.D.* Oxford: Oxford University Press, 1972.

Burke, Peter. "Classifying the People: The Census As Collective Representation." In his *The Historical Anthropology of Early Modern Italy.* Cambridge, Eng.: Cambridge University Press, 1987, 27–39.

Coale, Ansley J., and Susan Watkins. *The Decline of Fertility in Europe.* Princeton, NJ: Princeton University Press, 1986.

Hacking, Ian. *The Emergence of Probability.* Cambridge, Eng.: Cambridge University Press, 1975.

Henry, Louis, and M. Fleury. *Des registres paroissiaux à la histoire de la population.* Paris: I.N.E.D., 1956.

Henry, Louis, and E. Gauthier. *La population de Crulai.* Paris: I.N.E.D. Cahier 33, 1958.

Herlihy, David. *Medieval Households.* Cambridge, MA: Harvard University Press, 1985.

Herlihy, David, and Christiane Klapisch-Zuber. *Tuscans and Their Families.* New Haven, CT: Yale University Press, 1985.

Kreager, Philip. "Early Modern Population Theory: A Reassessment." *Population and Development Review* 17 (1991): 207–227.

Laslett, Peter. *The World We Have Lost.* London: Methuen, 1965.

Laslett, Peter, and Richard Wall. *Household and Family in Past Times.* Cambridge, Eng.: Cambridge University Press, 1972.

Lot, F. "L'État des paroisses et des feux de 1328." *Bibliotheque de l'École des Chartes* 90 (1929): 51–107; 256–315.

Razi, Zvi. *Life, Marriage and Death in a Medieval Parish.* Cambridge, Eng.: Cambridge University Press, 1980.

Wrigley, E.A. *An Introduction to English Historical Demography.* London: Weidenfield and Nicolson, 1966.

———, and R.S. Schofield. *The Population History of England and Wales, 1541–1871.* London: Edward Arnold, 1981.

Dependency Theory

See WORLD SYSTEMS THEORY/DEPENDENCY THEORY.

Derrida, Jacques (b. 1930)

Algerian-born French philosopher. Derrida was educated in Paris and currently teaches at the École Normale Supérieure and at the University of California at Irvine. His notion of "deconstruction," first elucidated in the introduction to a translation of Husserl's *Origin of Geometry* (1962) is based on the argument that the meaning of a text often has nothing to do with an author's intentions, but rather can be best understood against the background of inherent structures of a text, for example, unconscious slips or puns, gaps, inversions, or metaphors. In *De la grammatologie* (1976), Derrida criticized the two thousand-year tradition of Western metaphysics as postulating a simple correspondence between a knowing, conscious subject and an inert, objective world. Derrida called this overestimation of reason "logocentrism." He also developed a critique of the supposed Western practice of privileging speech over writing because the former offers the illusion of fixed meaning. He called this phenomenon "phonocentrism."

In Derrida's wide-ranging philosophical expositions, the possibility of final interpretations is eschewed in favor or an open-ended process of deferred meaning, a product of endless interaction between reader and text. Derrida has argued that deconstruction has an ethics and a political orientation, but it is unclear how normative positions can ever be established that deconstruction itself cannot undermine, as Henry Gates has pointed out. Derrida's most recent book, *The Specter of Marx* (1994) represents a departure from pure theory into concrete engagement with political issues of the day, while retaining a deconstructionist reading of Marx's critics, from Max Stirner to Francis Fukuyama.

Derrida's writings have had the most impact among cultural historians, in particular the followers of Stephen Greenblatt and the New Historicists. Some critics see deconstruction as a problematic methodology for writing history because of a lack of criteria for distinguishing between fact and interpretation. (See, for instance, Joyce Oldham Appleby's remarks in the collaborative volume *Telling the Truth about History.*) Derrida's supporters argue that the selection of facts always constitutes an interpretation, and consciousness of the context of historical writing is better than pretending that pure correspondence to external reality can just be taken for granted.

For cultural historians, Derrida's philosophy offers a methodological bridge to anthropology and other disciplines that question the Western humanistic emphasis on intentionality and reason in history. Rather than seeing history as a causally linked chain of action and response, cultural historians may place the emphasis on local or "microhistories," which subvert a dominant narrative; alternatively, they may describe cultural practices as irreducible to a logical and objective description of the traditional form used by historians who feel compelled to fit all aspects of human activity into a universal narrative. Historians dealing with ethnic issues have also argued that Derrida's notion of "differed meaning" or "difference" can help reconstruct the historical experience of racial minorities and other groups excluded from a dominant European-centered chronology.

Elliot Neaman

Texts

Derrida: A Critical Reader. Ed. David Wood. Cambridge, MA: Blackwell, 1992.

A Derrida Reader: Between the Blinds. Ed. Peggy Kamuf. New York: Columbia University Press, 1991.

References

Appleby, Joyce Oldham, Lynn Hunt, and Margaret Jacob. *Telling the Truth about History.* New York: Knopf, 1994.

Bennington, Geoffrey. *Jacques Derrida.* Chicago: University of Chicago Press, 1993.

Brook, Thomas. *The New Historicism: And Other Old-Fashioned Topics.* Princeton, NJ: Princeton University Press, 1991.

Gates, Henry Louis. *"Race," Writing and Difference.* Chicago: University of Chicago Press, 1986.

Hunt, Lynn, ed. *The New Cultural History.* Berkeley: University of California Press, 1989.

Deśawarṇana

Old Javanese poem. Formerly known as the *Nāgarakṛtāgama,* this work was completed on September 30, 1365. The author, Mpu Prapanca, was superintendent of Buddhist Affairs at the court of Majapahit (located in East Java), under King Hayam Wuruk. The work is quite unique, as it supplies a description of Java at that time, including such matters as the royal family, the capital, dependencies, organization of religious domains, and clergy. Central to the work is an account of a royal tour through East Java in 1359, giving an eyewitness report on the country and including an interview with an elderly cleric, who relates the history of the dynasty from its founder Ken Angrok (Ranggah Rajasa), who seized power in 1222, down to the conquest of Bali in 1343. Descriptions of major court celebrations are also given in detail. The author's purpose in giving a "Description of the Districts" (as the title translates) is to show how prosperous and powerful Java was at that time; this condition he attributes to the qualities of his king as a living god, working for the welfare of the world. The information supplied by the text is a goldmine for historians wishing to get a picture of Java and its prominent place in Southeast Asia in the second half of the fourteenth century.

Stuart Robson

See also BABAD; BALINESE HISTORIOGRAPHY; *PARARATON.*

Texts

Mpu Prapanca. *Deśawarṇana (Nāgarakṛtāgama).* Trans. Stuart Robson. Leiden, Netherlands: KITLV Press, 1995.

Determinism

The metaphysical doctrine that all events are predetermined. Historical determinism claims that all historical events are predetermined. Some historical determinists have claimed to have developed a deterministic science of history, or at least that such a "science" can be developed.

Historical determinism has religious, speculative, or scientific contexts. Religious historical determinism holds that an extra-historical agency determines collective destiny. Fatalism holds that future history will happen irrespective of human actions and efforts. Some substantive philosophies of history posit a teleological scheme of history, moved by impersonal forces, irrespective of how historical agents perceive their actions. Historical scientific determinism holds that sufficient conditions determine historical effects. Some historiographic determinists have suggested one or few causal factors, such as climate or the means of production, as the principal determinants of history.

Coincidence, unpredictability, and free will have been at various times brought to bear as arguments against historical determinism. The course of history is, it has been put, greatly affected by coincidence. Moreover, unlike astronomical systems, historical processes are not sufficiently isolated for deterministic description. Nonhistorical factors may intervene in history. Factors external to processes studied by historians may change them. But this does not imply indeterminism, merely intersection of two or more causal chains, each of which may be deterministic. Accident is relative to a system, not indeterminist. The philosopher Maurice Mandelbaum has noted that a deterministic science is possible only in relatively "closed systems"; it has not been conclusively decided whether history or parts of it may be construed as closed systems.

Karl Popper argues that innovation in history is unpredictable. Yet, *historical* determinism (relating to events as they actually happened), as distinct from *historiographic* determinism (relating to our accounts of those events), does not imply the predictability of history. Determinism claims that there are sufficient conditions of everything, *whether or not* they are known in advance. A stronger antideterminist argument claims that history is unique and can be expressed only by concrete universals like "the Renaissance," not by abstract universals that form the language of science. The project here is to clarify both the precise meaning of the word "unique," and its implications for historical determinism. In short, history itself may be deterministic, even if no deterministic science of history is possible.

The third and most common argument against historical determinism is based on free will. Those holding that determinism and free will are incoherent are known as *incompatibalists*; their opponents are *compatibalists*. Isaiah Berlin has claimed that if determinism is true, the idea of human responsibility, expressed by guilt, blame, praise, punishment, reward, etc. makes no sense because responsibility assumes that agents control their actions and could have chosen otherwise. Compatibalists claim that free will can be described in causal terms, when agents cause their actions. Ordinary historiography offers no proof for either side of the debate on historical determinism. Causation may be compatible with indeterminism, and historians do not usually cite sufficient conditions.

Contemporary philosophers have explicated several kinds of determinism and free will, some of which are compatible with each other and some are not. On the other hand, philosophers have also lost some interest in the old debate about historical determinism (Collingwood, Popper, Berlin, E. Nagel, E.H. Carr) because science itself has been discovered in the twentieth century to be more probabilistic and chaotic than deterministic.

Aviezer Tucker

See also CAUSATION; CHAOS THEORY; LOGIC AND HISTORICAL ENQUIRY; PHILOSOPHY OF HISTORY—ANALYTICAL.

References
Dray, William H. *Philosophy of History.* Engelwood Cliffs, NJ: Prentice-Hall, 1993.

Deutscher, Isaac (1907–1967)

British historian and journalist. Deutscher was born in Cracow, Poland, and from 1924 to 1939 worked as a journalist for the Polish Press; from 1926 to 1932 he was a member of the Communist Party of Poland and edited Communist periodicals. A leading member of the anti-Stalinist opposition he was expelled for alleging that Stalin had departed from Marxism and Leninism. Subsequently he worked as proofreader, and in 1939, just before the outbreak of war, moved to London as a correspondent. Deutscher remained a confirmed Marxist throughout his life. He always believed that the Soviet Union was not a totalitarian state and that only a Marxist could understand its contemporary problems. He was convinced that most of its revolutionary tasks had yet to be completed. He also participated in the "teach-in" movement against the Vietnam War

in the United States in the mid-1960s. For several years Deutscher's growing reputation rested on his shrewd analytical writing on Russian and Eastern European affairs for *The Economist* (1942–1949) and *The Observer* (under the pseudonym Peregrine, 1942–1947). In 1949 his groundbreaking study of Stalin brought him instant fame. Deutscher's keen sense of the movement of history and his deep interest in the failures and successes of the Russian revolutionary era drew him ideologically toward Leon Trotsky's thought while not blinding him to Trotsky's mistakes. He especially revered Lenin, but his plans for a large-scale biography of the latter, and an autobiography, were cut short by his sudden death.

Klaus Larres

Texts
The Great Contest: Russia and the West. New York: Oxford University Press, 1960.
The Prophet Armed: Trotsky, 1879–1921. London: Vintage Books, 1954.
The Prophet Outcast: Trotsky, 1929–1940. London: Vintage Books, 1963.
The Prophet Unarmed: Trotsky, 1921–29. London: Vintage Books, 1959.
Russia after Stalin. London: Hamish Hamilton, 1953.
Stalin: A Political Biography. Second ed. Oxford and New York: Oxford University Press, 1949.
The Unfinished Revolution: Russia, 1917–67. New York: Oxford University Press, 1967.

References
Carr, E.H. "Isaac Deutscher: An Obituary." *Cambridge Review* 14 (Oct. 1967): 8.
Labedz, Leopold. "Deutscher As Historian and Prophet." *Survey* 8 (1962): 121–144.
———. "Deutscher As Historian and Prophet, II." *Survey* 23 (1977–1978): 146–164.

al-Dhahabī, Shams al-Dīn (1274–1348)

Historian and religious scholar active in Damascus. Al-Dhahabī is perhaps the most important figure in what has been called the Syrian school of early Mamlūk historiography. He produced a considerable body of work, not only in history but also related to traditions regarding Muḥammad. Al-Dhahabī's learning, wisdom, and other qualities were praised by his contemporaries and later biographers. His fame as a historian mainly rests on *Ta'rīkh al-Islām* [The History of Islam], which comprised seventy volumes covering the first seven

D

centuries of Islamic history; each volume contains a decade's worth of chronicles followed by the obituaries of prominent people who died during these years. Unfortunately, the manuscript of some of the middle volumes has yet to come to light. This work was subsequently continued by its author and by several other Mamlūk writers and was abridged in six different forms by al-Dhahabī himself. Of special interest are the final volumes, which contain much precious information about the early Mamlūk state as well as the Mongol invasions of the Islamic world.

Reuven Amitai-Preiss

Texts
Ta'rīkh al-Islām. Beirut: Dār al-Kitāb al-Arabī, 1988– .

References
Ben Cheneb, M., and J. de Somogyi. "Al-Dhahabī." *Encyclopaedia of Islam.* Second ed. Vol. 2. Leiden: E.J. Brill, 1960, 214–216.
Little, D.P. *An Introduction to Mamlūk Historiography.* Wiesbaden: Franz Steiner Verlag, 1970, 61–66.

Dialectic
A mode of philosophical thought strongly associated with the study of history and the search for subtle patterns of its development, the dialectic has most often (but not always) been employed by Marxists.

Dialectical thought can be traced to antiquity, including the observations of Plato and Socrates and most especially those of Heraclitus. "Contradictions," the inclusive oppositions between contending forces of nonindependent origins, can be seen to express a dynamic of natural and human affairs. The study of dialectics thus permits a view of conflicted unity and the organic tensions and their displacement (or sublation) into a higher synthesis, yielding still other levels of contradictions and syntheses.

Jakob Boehme, the Lusatian cobbler-philosopher (1557–1624) revived dialectical thought and gave it a radical-romantic edge through a mystical interpretation of both human and divine history. Essentially a way of knowing God's purpose, dialectic reconciled Evil and Good as necessary elements through the working out of mysterious processes. In the final consequence, the human creature would return to paradise and recognize the coherence and interrelation of all things.

Romantics from William Blake to Friedrich Schiller borrowed heavily from Boehme's mystical vision, but G.W.F. Hegel drew other meanings. Dialectic for Hegel became the system of grasping reason in history, at least in the history of human consciousness. Although heavily Eurocentric in its attempted incorporation of various historical themes, and despite viewing the rise of the state as a veritable culmination of historical process, Hegel's philosophical dynamic overwhelmed his own limited conclusions. Between master and slave (in the *Phenomenology of Mind*), for instance, there is no question that the latter must be the primary actor. The divine *Turba* portrayed by Boehme thus becomes in Hegel an earthly turbulence with unforeseeable consequences.

As a leftist Hegelian, the young Karl Marx, in his "Critique of Hegel's Philosophy of Right," undertook to render the "criticism of heaven . . . into the criticism of earth, the criticism of religion into the criticism of law, and the criticism of theology into the criticism of politics," and so forth. Marx's later study of political economy (especially the commodity form) and his depiction of the proletariat as a class whose socialized labor thrust upon it the option of revolutionary activity owed almost everything to the philosophical kernel of the dialectic.

From the 1890s to the 1910s, during which period the study of Marxist philosophy proceeded eclectically, near-idealistic systems of dialectical analysis took shape alongside crudely materialistic ones, using dialectics as mere trimming. The failure of revolution in the West and the subsequent consolidation of Stalinism rendered dialectics a mere formalistic claim to superior wisdom, without any meaningful historical usefulness. In the post-1956 period, especially after the diffusion of writings by the young Marx, the study of dialectics resumed its eclectic character, providing in the works of such admired Marxist scholars as C.L.R. James many unique opportunities for insights into the processes of history.

Paul M. Buhle

See also CLASS; HEGEL; MARX; MARXISM AND HISTORIOGRAPHY.

Texts
Boehme, Jakob. *Six Theosophic Points and Other Writings.* Trans. John Rolleston Earle. Ann Arbor: University of Michigan Press, 1958.
Hegel, George Wilhelm Friedrich. *The Philosophy*

of History. Trans. J. Sibree. New York: Dover, 1956.

James, C.L.R. *Notes on Dialectics.* London: Allison & Busby, 1980.

Korsch, Karl. *Marxism and Philosophy.* Trans. Fred Halliday. London: New Left Books, 1970.

References

Nicolescu, Basarab. *Science, Meaning, & Evolution: The Cosmology of Jacob Boehme.* New York: Parabola Books, 1991.

Pinkard, Terry P. *Hegel's Dialectic: The Explanation of Possibility.* Philadelphia: Temple University Press, 1988.

Smith, Tony. *Dialectical Social Theory and Its Critics: From Hegel to Analytical Marxism and Postmodernism.* Albany: State University of New York Press, 1993.

Warren, Scott. *The Emergence of Dialectical Theory: Philosophy and Political Inquiry.* Chicago: University of Chicago Press, 1984.

Diceto, Ralph de (ca. 1125–ca. 1201)

English chronicler and clergyman. Ralph de Diceto's origins are obscure. He may have been born at Diss in Norfolk, but even his nationality is disputed. A successful cleric who rose to the post of dean of St. Paul's Cathedral, Diceto wrote two major works of historical importance. The first, *Abbreviationes Chronicorum* [Epitome of Chronicles] (ca. 1188) covers world history from the creation to A.D. 1147 and was essentially a compilation of existing chronicles. His second and more significant work, the *Ymagines Historiarum,* covers the period from 1147 to 1202 (although Ralph's authorship extended only to 1199). Ralph relied heavily on the work of Robert de Monte for the earlier sections, but from about 1188 onward his accounts became more original and authoritative. His residence in London and acquaintance with many leading figures ensured that he presented a detailed and accurate description of the events of his time, in particular the controversy between Archbishop Thomas Becket and Henry II. In both of his historical works, Ralph sought to overcome the limitations of the annalistic style of writing by placing symbols in the margins to which he then assigned common themes. This method probably influenced the later chronicler Matthew Paris, who would adopt a similar system.

Keith Robinson

D

Texts

Radulfi de Diceto decani Lundoniensis opera historica: The Historical Works of Master Ralph de Diceto, Dean of London. ed. William Stubbs. 2 vols. London: Rolls Series/ Longman & Co., 1876.

References

Gransden, Antonia. *Historical Writing in England c. 550 to c. 1307.* Ithaca, NY: Cornell University Press, 1974.

Stubbs, William. "The Historical Works of Master Ralph De Diceto, Dean of London." In Stubbs, *Historical Introductions to the Rolls Series,* ed. Arthur Hassall. London: Longmans, Green and Co., 1902.

Dike, Kenneth Onwuka (1917–1983)

Nigerian historian, educator, and administrator. Dike was born in Awka, Nigeria. He attended Dennis Memorial Grammar School, Onitsha, Achimota College, Fourah Bay College, the University of Durham, the University of Aberdeen, and the University of London. His doctoral study at the University of London, which focused on trade and politics in the Niger delta, utilized oral sources and helped lead to worldwide acceptance of oral tradition as a legitimate source for scholarly historical enquiry. The resultant publication *Trade and Politics in the Niger Delta 1830–1885* (1956), examined the history of southern Nigeria in the nineteenth and twentieth centuries. Described as a tour de force, it marked a watershed in the development of modern African historiography and inspired many other historical studies of the region. Dike's *Reports on the Preservation and Administration of Historical Records in Nigeria* (1953) aided the establishment of the Nigerian National Archives in 1952. In addition to his writings, Dike was an active administrator who created the National Museum and the Institute of African Studies at Ibadan; he also developed the African history curriculum in the department of history, University College, Ibadan (renamed the University of Ibadan), at a time when the only courses taught focused on European activities in Africa. Dike's commitment to the dissemination of historical scholarship about Africa extended to such projects as the *Ibadan History Series,* the Benin Historical Research Scheme, and the establishment of the Historical Society of Nigeria and its associated periodical, *The Journal of the Historical Society of Nigeria.* Dike was both a distinguished scholar and educator, who pioneered the autonomy of modern African historiography, and an administrator, who transformed a colonial university college into a center of academic excellence in Africa.

Onaiwu Wilson Ogbomo

Texts

With J. Ade Ajayi. "African Historiography." In *International Encyclopedia of the Social Sciences,* ed. David L. Sills. 19 vols. New York: Macmillan, 1968–1991, vol. 6, 394–400.

With Felicia Ekejiuba. *The Aro of South-Eastern Nigeria, 1650–1980: A Study of Socio-Economic Formation and Transformation in Nigeria.* Ibadan, Nigeria: University Press, 1990.

Issues in African Studies and National Education: Selected works of Kenneth Onwuka Dike. Awka, Nigeria: Kenneth Onwuka Dike Centre, 1988.

The Origins of the Niger Mission 1841–1891. Ibadan, Nigeria: Ibadan University Press, 1957.

Trade and Politics in the Niger Delta, 1830–1885: An Introduction to the Economic and Political History of Nigeria. Oxford, Clarendon Press, 1956.

References

Afigbo, A.E. *K.O. Dike and the African Historical Renascence.* Owerri, Nigeria: RADA Publishing Company, 1986.

Ajayi, J.F. Ade. "History and the Social Sciences." In his *History and the Nation and Other Addresses.* Ibadan, Nigeria: Spectrum Books, 1990, 45–69

———. "Towards a More Enduring Sense of History." In his *History and the Nation and Other Addresses.* Ibadan, Nigeria: Spectrum Books, 1990, 40–44.

Dilthey, Wilhelm (1833–1911)

German philosopher and theologian. Dilthey taught at the universities of Basel, Kiel, Breslau, and, from 1882 until his death, Berlin. Dilthey was a founder of the historical school of hermeneutics, a methodology of the human sciences that distinguished sharply between the natural and the social sciences. In his early work, he argued that historical reality can only be understood by mentally reexperiencing *(nacherleben)* the intentions, thoughts, and motivations of historical actors. This psychological process he called *Verstehen* (subjective understanding). In his *Einleitung in die Geisteswissenschaften* [Introduction to the Social Sciences] (1883) Dilthey argued that *Verstehen*

is the only possible methodology for the human sciences, since in contrast to the nonhuman objects of investigation of the natural sciences, human beings are trying to understand a world whose meaning they cannot escape. The object of the historical sciences is given, for Dilthey, in the organization of the "life-world," that is, the institutions, linguistic conventions, morality, values, art, and other expressions of human meaning. Dilthey argued that the hermeneutical reconstruction of history could not be established on the basis of individual psychology, but rather had to encompass collective linguistic structures, human action and experience. In Dilthey's later work, in particular his *Aufbau der geschichtlichen Welt in den Geisteswissenschaften* [The Structure of the Historical World in the Social Sciences] (1910), he argued that *Verstehen* was not a subjective method for arriving at an understanding of historical action, but was rather a means of arriving at objective knowledge about the social structures of human life. Dilthey's work was important for the philosophy of Edmund Husserl, Hans Georg Gadamer, Martin Heidegger, and Helmut Plessner. A hermeneutical approach to history, which views the study of the past as a contribution to philosophical anthropology and seeks metaphysical answers about human existence, is still an important alternative to more positivist, empirical approaches to history, which are generally agnostic about the deeper ontological and existential significance of the practice of history.

Elliot Neaman

Texts

Gesammelte Schriften [Complete Writings]. Second ed. 12 vols. Stuttgart and Göttingen: Teubner, 1957–1960.

Introduction to the Human Sciences: An Attempt to Lay a Foundation for the Study of Society and History. Trans. Ramon J. Betanzos. Detroit: Wayne State University Press, 1988.

References

Frohman, Lawrence S. "Phenomenology; Politics and the Philosophy of History in the Work of Wilhelm Dilthey." Ph.D. thesis, University of California, Berkeley, 1992.

Makkreel, Rudolf A. *Philosopher of the Human Studies.* Princeton, NJ: Princeton University Press, 1975.

Owensby, Jacob. *Dilthey and the Narrative of History.* Ithaca, NY: Cornell University Press, 1994.

Dio [Cassius Dio Cocceianus] (ca. 164–after A.D. 229)

Roman senator and historian. Dio came from the elite of Nicaea in Bithynia. Like his father, he was a senator, provincial governor, and consul. After 218, Dio governed several provinces before his retirement to Bithynia. Dio wrote a history of Rome in eighty books from Aeneas to A.D. 229. Only about a third of his history has survived. Evidence for the lost parts of his work can be gleaned from other authors and Byzantine collections as well as epitomes made by the later scholars Xiphilinus and Zonaras. In his coverage of the early Roman Empire (a large extant portion), Dio stresses the relationship between the emperors and the senate. His rhetorical style and reproductions of speeches may influence his accuracy. His Greek style was influenced by Thucydides. Dio probably wrote most of his narrative during the 220s and may have been influenced by contemporary events. Dio is the most significant historical source for the middle Roman Empire and forms a critical bridge between the earlier writings of Tacitus and the later work of Ammianus.

R.M. Frakes

Texts
Dio's Roman History. Ed. and trans. Earnest Cary. 9 vols. Cambridge, MA: Harvard University Press/Loeb Classical Library, 1979.

References
Barnes, T.D.. "The Composition of Cassius Dio's Roman History." *Phoenix* 38 (1984): 240–255.
Millar, Fergus. *A Study of Cassius Dio.* Oxford: Clarendon Press, 1964.

Diodorus Siculus (ca. 90 B.C.–ca. 20 B.C.)

Greek Sicilian author of a world history. Born in Agyrium (north-central Sicily), he worked for thirty years in Rome. Inspired by the incorporation of western Europe and the Mediterranean into the Roman Empire, Diodorus wrote an annalistic summary in Greek covering from the fall of Troy (1184 B.C.) to 60/59 B.C., entitled *Bibliotheke Historike* [Historical Library]. This comprised forty books, of which only I–V and XI–XX survive intact. Though apparently an immediate success in the contemporary commercial book market, the *Historical Library* has left little testimony to its use by pagan readers, but it became very popular with Christian and Byzantine writers, who appreciated its convenient summary of eleven hundred years of history and its pervasive interest in moral edification. Modern scholars criticize Diodorus for being chronologically inaccurate and insufficiently analytical. Because of the loss of so many of his sources, however, Diodorus's work remains important as the only extant continuous narrative of some periods of Greek and Near Eastern history between 480 and 301 B.C.

Catherine Rubincam

Texts
Diodorus of Sicily. Trans. C.H. Oldfather et al. 12 vols. Cambridge, MA: Harvard University Press/Loeb Classical Library, 1933–1967.

References
Sacks, Kenneth S. *Diodorus Siculus and the First Century.* Princeton, NJ: Princeton University Press, 1990.

Dionysius of Halicarnassus (ca. 65 B.C.–ca. 1 B.C.)

Greek historian, rhetorician, and literary critic. Dionysius moved from his native Halicarnassus to Rome in 30 B.C., where he became a respected member of a Greco-Roman literary circle. He wrote, over a period of twenty-two years, both a *Romaike Archaiologia* [History of Archaic Rome], in twenty books and a series of rhetorical essays on literary criticism. The *History* claimed to be the first Greek work to narrate the early part of Rome's history, from the legendary beginnings to the outbreak of the First Punic War. It recommended Roman sovereignty under Augustus as the best guarantor of the survival of upper-class society in the Greek sections of the empire. Dionysius's literary critical works, the largest surviving collection by a single Greco-Roman author, were addressed to members of his circle at Rome. The literary program they recommended (the use of the best stylistic models from the classical period) went hand in hand with the political program of the *History.*

Catherine Rubincam

Texts
The Critical Essays. Trans. Stephen Usher. 2 vols. Cambridge, MA: Harvard University Press/ Loeb Classical Library, 1974–1985.
Roman Antiquities. Trans. E. Cary. 7 vols. Cambridge, MA: Harvard University Press/Loeb Classical Library, 1937–1950.

References
Gabba, Emilio. *Dionysius and the History of Archaic Rome.* Berkeley: University of California Press, 1991.

Bonner, S.F. *The Literary Treatises of Dionysius of Halicarnassus: A Study in the Development of Critical Method.* Cambridge, Eng.: Cambridge University Press, 1939.

Diplomatic
See PALEOGRAPHY AND DIPLOMATIC.

al-Djabartī [Jabarti] Abd al-Raḥmān ibn Hasan (1753–1825)

Egyptian chronicler and historian. Al-Djabartī was born in 1753 in Cairo into an affluent family from al-Djabart, a village near the port of Zayla on the Red Sea. His father, Hassan, was a wealthy businessman who had studied mathematics and astronomy, as well as Turkish and Persian. He also enjoyed a close friendship with the Ottoman authorities and the elite Mamlūk families of the country. Al-Djabartī wrote two important works: *Muzhir al-Takdīs bi-dhahāb dawlat al-Faransīs* [The Appearance of Piety in the Demise of the French Rule] and *Adjai'b al-āthār fi'l-tarādjim wa 'l -akhbār* [Wondrous Relics of Biographies and Annals]. In his first work, *Muzhir,* al-Djabartī described the most important historical events that occurred during the French occupation of Egypt from 1798 to 1801. Adopting an anti-European attitude, he denounced the French as uncivilized atheists and drunkards who had insulted Islamic values. In his second and most important work, *'Adja'ib,* however, al-Djabartī radically changed his evaluation of the French and praised them for their system of justice and scientific advances. *'Adja'ib* is considered the most important historical source for studying the history of the French occupation of Egypt.

Mehrdad Kia

Texts
Aja'ib al-Athar fi'l Tarajim wa'l-Akhbar. 4 vols. Cairo: Bulaq Press, 1879.
Bonaparte's Proclamations, As Recorded by Abd al-Rahman al-Jabarti. Trans. Martin Hinds. Cairo: Al-Arab Bookshop, 1971.
Mazhar al-taqdis bi-zawal dawlat al-Faransis. Cairo: al-Hayah al-Ammah li-Shuun al-Matabi al-Amiriyah, 1961.

References
Ayalon, David. "The Historian al-Jabarti and His Background." *Bulletin of the School of Oriental and African Studies* 23 (1960): 218–248.

Crabbs, Jack A., Jr. *The Writing of History in Nineteenth Century Egypt: A Study in National Transformation.* Cairo: American University in Cairo Press; Detroit, MI: Wayne State University Press, 1984.

Holt, P.M. "al-Jabarti's Introduction to the History of Ottoman Egypt." *Bulletin of the School of Oriental and African Studies* 25 (1962): 40–42.

Djuwaynī, 'Ala' al-Dīn 'Atā-Malik b. Muḥammad (1226–1283)

Persian historian of the Mongol conquests. Djuwaynī was born in Azadvar, in Khorasan, into a family with a long tradition of financial service to Iran's Turkish overlords. He followed his father into the service of the new Mongol conquerors in 1248, visiting the Mongol capital in Qaraqorum twice in 1249 and 1252. On his return, Djuwaynī participated in Hüle'ü's campaigns against the Isma'ili ("Assassin") sect in Alamut and the Abbasid caliph in Baghdad. He held high office until 1281, when opponents at court had him twice imprisoned. Djuwaynī was finally released but died of a stroke; shortly afterward, his enemies destroyed his family. Although Djuwaynī abandoned his masterpiece, *Ta'rīkh-i djahān-gushāy* [History of the World Conqueror], around 1260, leaving it unrevised, it supplies irreplaceable data on the Mongol conquests, and deeply influenced later Middle Eastern historians. Writing in an ornate rhetorical style, the author extolled the simplicity, hardihood, and camaraderie of the Mongol nomads, while deploring the violence of their invasion and the decadence of previous Muslim rulers that had allowed it to happen.

Christopher Pratt Atwood

Texts
History of the World Conqueror. Trans. John Andrew Boyle. 2 vols. Manchester: Manchester University Press, 1958.
The Ta'rikh-i-Jahan-gusha of Ala'u 'd-Din Ata Malik-i-Juwayni. Ed. Mirza Muḥammad ibn Abdu'l-Wahhab-i Qazwini. 3 vols. Leiden: E.J. Brill; London: Luzac & Co., 1912–1937.

References
Lewis, Bernard, and P.M. Holt, eds. *Historians of the Middle East.* London: Oxford University Press, 1962.
Rosenthal, Franz. *A History of Muslim Historiography.* Leiden: E.J. Brill, 1952.

Długosz, Jan (1415–1480)

Polish historian of the late medieval period. Długosz was one of the greatest European historians of his time as well as a prominent diplomat and politician. He was born in Brzeźnica and became an associate of Bishop (later Cardinal) Zbigniew Oleśnicki. He died in Cracow in 1480. His greatest work was *Annales seu cronicae incliti Regni Poloniea* [Annals or Chronicles of the Glorious Kingdom of Poland] in ten volumes (1455). This chronological history begins with a geographical description of Poland and an account of its legendary past, and ends in 1480. Długosz based his work on both Polish and foreign sources as well as on ancient authors, from whom he drew rhetorical patterns. Długosz's historical method is marked by a critical approach to sources (including direct comparison of contradictory versions of events), though he is also noted for his nationalist bias and tendentiousness (omitting, for instance, information unfavorable to Poland). His other works include illustrated *Banderia Pruthenorum* [The Banner of the Prussians] (prior to 1466); the first Polish list of coats-of-arms *Insignia seu clenodia Regni Poloniae* [The Coats-of-Arms of the Kingdom of Poland] (dating between 1455 and 1480); lists of real estates owned by the church; catalogs of Polish bishops; and biographies of saints.

Ewa Domańska

Texts

Roczniki czyli Kroniki Sławnego Królestwa Polskiego [History of Poland]. 11 vols. Warsaw: PWN, 1964–1985.

References

Długossiana: Studia historyczne w pięćsetlecie śmierci Jana Długosza [Dlugossiana: Historical Studies on the Five Hundredth Anniversary of the Death of Jan Długosz]. 2 vols. Cracow: Wydawnictwo Uniwersytetu Jagiellońskiego, 1980–1985.

Dobb, Maurice (1900–1967)

Economist and economic historian. Born in London, Dobb joined the Communist Party in 1921, became a lecturer in economics at Cambridge in 1924, and, during the 1920s, was the only Communist to teach at a British university. Over a career spanning forty years, Dobb made contributions to the history of economic thought and Soviet economic studies and coedited with Piero Sraffa the complete writings of David Ricardo. Dobb's major contribution to historiography consisted of *Studies in the Development of Capitalism* (1946), a Marxist analysis of the transition from feudalism to capitalism based on the most recent scholarship in economic history. The book launched an international debate in the early 1950s, recently extended in discussions of the writings of the historian Robert Brenner. In the original debate, Dobb's contention that feudalism collapsed because of inherent contradictions was challenged by the American economist Paul Sweezy who argued that feudal decline was tied to the revival of trade.

Dennis Dworkin

Texts

Studies in the Development of Capitalism. London: Routledge and Kegan Paul, 1946.

References

Hilton, Rodney, ed. *The Transition from Feudalism to Capitalism.* London: Verso, 1976.
Kaye, Harvey J. *The British Marxist Historians: An Introductory Analysis.* Cambridge, Eng.: Polity Press, 1984.

Döllinger, Johann Joseph Ignaz von (1799–1890)

German Catholic theologian and historian. Döllinger studied philosophy and theology in Würzburg and Bamberg, was ordained a priest in 1822, and taught ecclesiastical law and history at the Lyceum in Aschaffenburg (1823–1826). His first book (1826) established his scholarly reputation and led to his appointment to a chair of canon law and church history at King Ludwig I's new Catholic University in Munich. Subsequently he represented his university in the Bavarian Landtag (1845–1847), sat in the Frankfurt National Assembly as leader of the Catholic Right in 1848, and served as president of the Bavarian Academy of Sciences (1873–1890). During the first three decades of Döllinger's life in Munich he remained a staunch Roman Catholic and was even regarded by some as the epitome of the arch-ultramontane believer. His membership of the Josef Görres's circle and other personal contacts, his historical studies, and his belief in religious freedom gradually brought him into conflict with the Jesuits and the Vatican after 1860. Pope Pius IX's proclamation of the *Syllabus errorum* (1864) and the new dogma of the Immaculate Conception of Mary stood in sharp contrast to Döllinger's views. He published numerous articles and several books (under various pseudonyms) critical of

D

these neoscholastic developments, calling for unity and the pursuit of the traditional principles of Catholicism. He regarded the decision of the First Vatican Council to proclaim the infallibility of the Pope (1870) as running counter to the historical roots of Catholicism and to the Scriptures themselves. He publicly refused to accept the new dogma and the establishment, as he saw it, of a new church. As a result of his resistance, he was excommunicated in March 1871. Although initially he discouraged the setting up of a separate organization, Döllinger soon became involved in the activities of the so-called Old Catholic Church, though he did not cease working for ecumenical reunion. As a historian, Döllinger concentrated on the early history of the church; he influenced a number of later historians, most notably the Englishman Lord Acton, who studied with him in Munich for several years.

Klaus Larres

Texts

Fables Respecting the Popes in the Middle Ages. Trans. Alfred Plummer. London: Rivingtons, 1871.

The First Age of Christianity and the Church. Trans. H.N. Oxenham. Fourth ed. London: Gibbings and Co., 1906.

Hypolytus and Callistus; or, The Church of Rome in the First Half of the Third Century. Trans. Alfred Plummer. Edinburgh: T. and T. Clark, 1876.

References

Conzemius, V., ed. *Ignaz von Döllinger: Briefwechsel mit Lord Acton, 1850–90* [Döllinger: Correspondence with Lord Acton, 1850–90]. 3 vols. Munich: Beck, 1963–1971.

Kobell, L. von. *Conversations of Dr. Döllinger.* Trans. K. Gould. London: R. Bentley, 1892.

Finsterhölzl, J. *Ignaz von Döllinger.* Graz, Austria: Styria, 1969.

Friedrich, J. *Ignaz von Döllinger.* 3 vols. Munich: Beck, 1899–1901.

Domanovszky, Sándor (1877–1955)

Hungarian historian. Domanovszky studied in Budapest and taught in Pozsony (Bratislava) and Budapest. From 1914 to 1948 he was professor of cultural history at Péter Pázmány University in Budapest; during much of this period he served as editor (1913–1943) of the most important Hungarian historical journal, the *Századok* [Centuries], and as vice president (1916–1946) of the Hungarian

Historical Association. Domanovszky focused on medieval Hungarian economic and cultural history and on Habsburg political history during the late eighteenth and early nineteenth centuries. His studies of a variety of sources established his reputation as a master of historical criticism; he was also a leading figure in a variety of Hungarian economic history projects during the 1920s and 1930s.

Attila Pók

Texts

Ed. *A Budai Krónika* [The Chronicle of Buda]. Budapest: Athéneum, 1903.

Gazdaság és társadalom a középkorban [Economy and Society in the Middle Ages]. Ed. Ferenc Glatz. Budapest: Gondolat, 1979.

Die Geschichte Ungarns [History of the Hungarian People]. Munich: Rosl, 1923.

A harmincadvám eredete [The Origins of "Tricesima"]. Budapest: Magyar Tudományos Akadémia, 1916.

József nádor élete és iratai [Life and Papers of Palatine Joseph]. 4 vols. in 5 books. Budapest: Kiadja a Magyar Történelmi Társulat, 1925–1944. (Part of the series *Fontes historiae Hungaricae aevi recentoris.*)

Kézai Simon mester krónikája: Forrástanulmány [The Chronicle of Master Simon Kézai: A Source Study]. Budapest: Magyar Tudományos Akadémia, 1906.

References

Glatz, Ferenc. "Domanovszky Sándor helye a magyar történettudományban [Sándor Domanovszky's Place in Hungarian Historical Scholarship]." *Századok* [Centuries] 112 (1978): 211–234.

Donnan, Elizabeth (1883–1955)

American economic historian and text editor. Born in 1883 in Morrow County, Ohio, Donnan graduated from Cornell University in 1907 and served as White Fellow of political science at her alma mater. A professor in the economics department at Wellesley College from 1920 to 1949, Donnan compiled and edited documents in economic history. She acquired her professional reputation with the four-volume *Documents Illustrative of the Slave Trade to America* (1930–1935). *Documents,* originally conceptualized by John Franklin Jameson, her colleague at the historical division of the Carnegie Institution, depicted slave trading in the British West Indies and colonies. Donnan carefully edited ship journals, contracts, petitions, and depositions, presenting white merchants' and planters' attitudes and detailing the commercial aspects of slavery. She focused on Caribbean and South Carolinian slavery because of the predominance of trading in those areas and abundant primary sources. With these volumes Donnan corrected myths about the practice and demonstrated the economic and historical significance of slavery long before its revival as a topic of inquiry in the 1960s.

Elizabeth D. Schafer

Texts

Ed. *Documents Illustrative of the Slave Trade to America.* 4 vols. Washington, DC: Carnegie Institute of Washington Publication, no. 409, 1930–1935.

And Leo F. Stock, eds. *An Historian's World: Selections from Correspondence of John Franklin Jameson.* Philadelphia: American Philosophical Society, 1956.

Ed. *Papers of James A. Bayard 1796–1815.* New York: Da Capo Press, 1971.

References

Parish, Peter J. *Slavery: History and Historians.* New York: Harper & Row, 1989.

Dopsch, Alfons (1868–1953)

Austrian medieval economic historian. Dopsch was trained at the Institut für österreichische Geschichtsforschung and was professor at the University of Vienna from 1898 to 1936. A historian of economic and social conditions, Dopsch rejected theoretical approaches, proceeding instead through rigorous examination of early medieval documents. His conclusions emphasized continuities and gradual evolution rather than sudden and drastic change. In particular he challenged the "catastrophic theory," first formulated by the humanists of the Italian Renaissance, that Roman culture and society were destroyed by Germanic barbarians in the process of making an entirely new (and much cruder) civilization in the early Middle Ages. Rather, he argued, the German nations preserved and developed the Roman legacy right through to the age of Charlemagne. Dopsch's interpretation was challenged by Henri Pirenne, who found continuity decisively broken by the advent of Islam in the seventh century. The debate over the character and extent of continuity and change from late antiquity to the Middle Ages continues today.

Bruce L. Venarde

Texts

The Economic and Social Foundations of European Civilization. Ed. Erna Patzelt; trans. M.G. Beard and Nadine Marshall. New York: Harcourt, Brace and Co., 1937.

References

Dopsch, Alfons. "Selbstdarstellung [Autobiography]" and "Ergänzung zur Selbstdarstellung [Supplement to the Autobiography]." In *Beiträge zur Sozial- und Wirtschaftsgeschichte: Gesammelte Aufsätze, zweite Reihe* [Articles on Social and Economic History: Collected Essays, Second Series]. Vienna: L.W. Seidel & Sohn, 1938, 277–328.

Dray, William H. (b. 1921)

Analytical philosopher of history. The main proponent of the methodological autonomy of historiography against its assimilation to science (as advocated by Carl Hempel) or literature (Hayden White), Dray was born in Montreal, Canada. After serving in the Royal Canadian Air Force during World War II, he studied history in Toronto and philosophy at Oxford. He taught at the University of Toronto, Trent University, and the University of Ottawa.

Dray continued, developed, and revised, the work of R.G. Collingwood, analyzing historiography as one of the humanities. Dray stressed the role of rational reconstruction and emphatic understanding *(Verstehen)* from the "inside" in historiographic explanation. He denied that all historiographic explanation takes the shape of answering a "why question." It is possible to explain by making historical events intelligible. Dray demonstrated the "subjective" value judgments involved in how historians assign causes and distinguish causes from conditions. Dray developed much of his life's work for explicating the logic of historiographic narrative, and the perspectivity of historiography, through impressive philosophical analyses of historiographic case studies, for example, of the historiography of the origins of the American Civil War, of the English Civil War, and of the causes of World War II. This underlies Dray's conviction that analytical philosophy of history should not deal only with abstract philosophical issues but be relevant for the work, interests, and concerns of historians.

Aviezer Tucker

See also CAUSATION; COLLIGATION; COLLINGWOOD; COVERING LAWS; FACT; PHILOSOPHY OF HISTORY—ANALYTICAL.

D

Texts

History As Re-enactment: R.G. Collingwood's Idea of History. Oxford: Oxford University Press, 1995.

Laws and Explanation in History. London: Oxford University Press, 1957.

On History and Philosophers of History. Leiden, Netherlands: E.J. Brill, 1989.

Perspectives on History. London: Routledge and Kegan Paul, 1980.

Philosophy of History. Second ed. Englewood Cliffs, NJ: Prentice-Hall, 1993.

References

Van der Dussen, W.J., and Lionel Rubinoff. *Objectivity, Method and Point of View: Essays in the Philosophy of History.* Leiden, Netherlands and New York: E.J. Brill, 1991.

Drinov, Marin (1838–1906)

Bulgarian historian. Born in Panagyurishte, Drinov studied history in Kiev and Moscow during the 1860s. In 1869, he cofounded and was elected chairman of the Bulgarian Literary Society, which eventually developed into the Bulgarian Academy of Sciences. In 1873 he was appointed associate professor and in 1876 professor at the University of Kharkhov in Russia. As a member of the provisional Russian administration in 1878 and 1879, he provided Bulgaria with a national library and laid the foundations of a national education system. Drinov was mainly interested in the ethnogenesis of the Bulgarian people, in medieval and church history, in Bulgarian folklore, and in early-nineteenth-century literature. As the first influential professionally trained historian, daring to oppose the far more popular "romantic" history writing of his contemporaries, Drinov initiated the "academic school" in Bulgarian historiography.

R. Detrez

Texts

Izbrani sûchineniya [Selected works]. Ed. Ivan Duychev. 2 vols. Sofia, Bulgaria: Nauka i izkustvo, 1971.

Droysen, Johann Gustav (1808–1884)

German historian of ancient Greece and modern Prussia, theorist of historical method, and national liberal politician—identities that were inseparable in his work. Born in the Berlin suburb of Treptow, the son of a military chaplain during the wars of liberation against France, Droysen breathed the patriotic spirit of that era. He attended the University of Berlin, where he returned to finish his career after teaching at Kiel and Jena. Droysen, Heinrich von Sybel, and their younger contemporary, Heinrich von Treitschke, were the dominant figures among those who were informally known as the Prussian school of history (so-called for its contention that the Kingdom of Prussia was destined to overcome the separateness of the German states and restore their former unity). By convincing wide segments of educated Germany to accept Prussian leadership, Droysen and other Prussophile historians contributed in some measure to that outcome when the German Second Empire was established in 1871. With his background in philology and classical studies, Droysen published first on ancient Greece and Alexander the Great (1833). But even in these early writings on Greek history he found a lesson for Germans: the high cost of political disunity and the need for national union under strong authority. Droysen pursued this theme vigorously in his works on Prussia beginning in the 1850s, resulting in the monumental *History of Prussian Policy.* Based on original research in the Prussian state archives, the fourteenth and final volume appeared posthumously in 1886. Droysen's *Historik* or *Outline of the Principles of History,* drawn from his lectures of the 1850s, has proven to be of more lasting interest due to his attempt to establish the principles upon which he believed historiography to be based. Droysen responded to the growing prestige of science by making a strong case for the autonomy of history.

Thomas E. Willey

Texts

"Art and Method." In *The Varieties of History,* ed. Fritz Stern. New York: Meridian Books, 1956, 120–144.

Outline of the Principles of History. Trans. Benjamin Andrews. Boston: Ginn & Company, 1893.

Texte zur Geschichtstheorie / Johann Gustav Droysen: mit ungedruckten Materialen zur "Historik" [Texts on Historical Theory / Johann Gustav Droysen: with Unpublished Materials on the "Historik"] Ed. Günther Birtsch and Jörn Rüsen. Göttingen, Germany: Vandenhoeck and Ruprecht, 1972.

References

Gooch, G.P. *History and Historians in the Nineteenth Century.* Boston: Beacon Press, 1959.

Iggers, Georg G. *The German Conception of History: The National Tradition of Historical Thought from Herder to the Present.* Revised ed. Middletown, CT: Wesleyan University Press, 1983.

Southard, Robert. *Droysen and the Prussian School of History.* Lexington: University of Kentucky Press, 1995.

Du Bois, William Edward Burghardt (1868–1963)

African-American historian and civil rights leader. Born in Great Barrington, Massachusetts, Du Bois was educated at Fisk, Harvard, and Berlin. His approximately two-thousand publications, including dozens of books, range widely across genres and disciplines. In 1895 Du Bois became the first black person ever awarded a Harvard Ph.D. He died in Accra, Ghana, where he had lived since 1961.

Du Bois's dissertation, *The Suppression of the African Slave Trade to the United States of America 1638–1870*, was published in 1896 as the inaugural volume in Harvard's Historical Studies series. A broader work than its title implies, *Suppression* described the rise of New World slavery, detailed efforts to curb the slave trade, and demonstrated, contrary to the popular and scholarly consensus of the day, that slavery had profoundly shaped American history. Du Bois faulted the founding fathers for protecting slave property. Like Du Bois's later works, *Suppression* spotlighted "the paradox of slavery" in "'the land of the free'"—a paradox that, over half a century later, became widely recognized as a major problem for American historiography. Anticipating C.L.R. James's *The Black Jacobins* (1938), *Suppression* also linked the Haitian revolution's defeat of French forces to Napoleon's decision to sell the Louisiana Territory to Jefferson.

In the early twentieth century, when most historians thought "Africa had no history" and deemed blacks unfit for self-government, Du Bois used the highest standards of contemporary historical scholarship to prove the opposite and spearheaded the struggle to make black history a recognized field. Du Bois's *The Souls of Black Folk* (1903) included essays on Reconstruction, Southern history, and slave songs, and his biography of the abolitionist *John Brown* appeared in 1909. The *American Historical Review* published his article "Reconstruction and Its Benefits" in 1910, but not until 1979 did that journal publish another article by a black historian.

Du Bois's magnum opus, *Black Reconstruction in America 1860–1880* (1935), asserted that slavery had caused the American Civil War, that the slaves' collective actions had determined the war's outcome, and that in the postwar decade the freed people had struggled intelligently to obtain full equality as U.S. citizens. While these arguments ran counter to the then dominant historiography of the Dunning school and the Progressive historians, since 1960 they have become fundamental to newer interpretations of the Civil War era. Du Bois's final chapter, "The Propaganda of History," critiqued the racial bias of two generations of Reconstruction historiography, and Du Bois's deep interest in the philosophy of history is evident in *Black Reconstruction*'s serious and self-conscious engagement with the problem of objectivity in historical studies.

Du Bois's books on African history—*The Negro* (1915), *Black Folk Then and Now* (1939), and *The World and Africa* (1947)—long predated the modern renaissance of African history. The earliest of these, *The Negro,* one of the first serious attempts to sketch African history and cultures for American readers, was especially influential in its day. All of Du Bois's work insisted that European, world, and American history were all deeply influenced by black people as historical subjects and by conflicts over the control of Africa, its diaspora, and black labor. Hence Du Bois anticipated much of Eric Williams's thesis in *Capitalism and Slavery* (1944) and influenced subsequent studies of colonialism, slavery, and emancipation.

Mark David Higbee

Texts

Black Folk Then and Now. Ed. H. Aptheker. Millwood, NY: Kraus-Thomson, 1975.

Black Reconstruction in America 1860–1880. New York: Atheneum, 1992.

John Brown. New York: International Publishers, 1974.

The Negro. New introduction by H. Aptheker. Millwood, NY: Kraus-Thomson, 1975.

The Souls of Black Folk. New York: Penguin, 1995.

The Suppression of the African Slave Trade to the United States of America 1638–1870. Baton Rouge: Louisiana University Press, 1969.

The World and Africa. New York: International Publishers, 1965.

References

Aptheker, Herbert. *The Literary Legacy of W.E.B. Du Bois.* White Plains, NY: Kraus, 1989.

Lewis, David Levering. *W.E.B. Du Bois: Biography of a Race, 1868–1919.* New York: Henry Holt, 1993.

D

Du Cange, Charles du Fresne, Sieur (1610–1688)

French historian. Du Cange began his career engaged in his family's traditional parliamentary and judicial pursuits. In 1668, however, he moved to the Parisian parish of St. Gervais and turned to historical studies. He worked with the circle of scholars patronized by Colbert and Guillaume de Lamoignon, laboring to perfect methods of historical criticism. His primary areas of interest were the history of France, the history of his native province of Picardy, and the history of the Crusades. His major printed works in these fields were the important *Histoire de l'Empire de Constantinople sous les empereurs français jusq'à la Conquête des Turcs* [History of the Empire of Constantinople under the French Emperors until the Turkish Conquest] (1657) and the *Histoire Byzantine* [Byzantine History] (1680). He wrote numerous important manuscripts and was responsible for the printing of several medieval histories and chronicles. The rigorous, meticulous research and note-taking for which he was so well known and respected led to the publication on which his future reputation would rest, the three-volume *Glossarium ad scriptores mediae et infimae latinitatis.* A biobibliographical catalogue of some five thousand Latin authors, it was supplemented by a glossary and an essay on the coins and medals of the later empire.

Krista Kesselring

Texts

Glossarium ad scriptores mediae at infimae latinitatis. Graz, Austria: Akademische Druck, 1954.

Histoire de l'Empire de Constantinople sous les empereurs français jusq'à la Conquête des Turcs. Ed. J.A. Buchon. 2 vols. Paris: Collection des chroniques nationales françaises, 1824–1828, vols. 47–48.

References

Feugère, Leon. *Etude sur la vie et les ouvrages de Du Cange* [Study of the Life and Works of Du Cange]. Paris: P. Dupont, 1852.

Knowles, David. *Great Historical Enterprises.* London: Nelson, 1963.

Du Tillet, Jean (d. 1570)

French archival scholar. Central to establishing the archivist tradition and national institutional history in sixteenth-century France, Du Tillet inherited both the office of chief clerk *(greffier civil)* of the Parlement of Paris and the title Sieur de la Bussière. From 1521, he regularly signed legal documents and, from 1526, as *greffier.* His *Receuil des roys de France* [Collection of the Kings of France], published posthumously in 1577 and 1578, and in seven further editions before 1618, was widely regarded as the century's monumental work on French history. The *Collection* represented forty years of experience in service to crown and parlement, and informed rulers and institutional leaders of their precedents and ancient privileges. It had practical political applications in revealing the forms and ranks of historical assemblies and ceremonies where politics were conducted. Throughout his life, Du Tillet's *Collection* was classified as a state secret, and he had nearly unique access by royal command to all French archives. His documentation challenged the commonplaces among writers following the style of the *ars historica.* It showed that the Salic law was more recent than Pharamond, denied the Trojan origins of the Franks, and downscaled the splendor of many past events. He used history in his polemical writing: in two 1560 tracts that established the historical age of majority for kings of France at fifteen years, and in tracts opposing religious toleration as a departure from a thousand-year tradition that had preserved the monarchy. He should not be confused with his younger brother, also named Jean, who was bishop first of Saint Brieux and then of Meaux and the author of a universal chronicle, *De Regibus Francorum,* and studies in Roman Law and church history.

Lawrence M. Bryant

Texts

Recueil des roys de France, leurs couronne et maison. Paris: P. Mettayer, 1607.

Jean Du Tillet and the French Wars of Religion: Five Tracts, 1562–1569. Ed. Elizabeth A.R. Brown. Binghamton, NY: Binghamton University Press, 1994.

References

Hanley, Sarah. *The "Lit de Justice" of the Kings of France: Constitutional Ideology in Legend, Ritual, and Discourse.* Princeton, NJ: Princeton University Press, 1983.

Kelley, Donald R. *Foundations of Modern Historical Scholarship: Language, Law, and History in the French Renaissance.* New York: Columbia University Press, 1970.

Dubnow, Simon (1860–1941)

Russian Jewish historian and ideologue of Jewish autonomism. Reared in a religiously observant family, Dubnow became captivated by the Jewish Enlightenment and Russian radical positivism in his adolescence. Living illegally in St. Petersburg in the early 1880s, he began publishing literary criticism and other articles in the Russian-Jewish press. Dubnow settled in Odessa in the early 1890s where, influenced by the German-Jewish historian Heinrich Graetz, the English philosophers Herbert Spencer and John Stuart Mill, the Zionist ideologist Ahad Ha-Am, and also by Russian populist intellectuals, he formulated what he later called a "sociological" approach to Jewish history, which emphasized the adaptation of Jewish communal institutions to varied diaspora conditions. After 1905 he lived in St. Petersburg as a leading figure in the efflorescence of Russian-Jewish historical research and became the spokesman for a non-Marxist, non-Zionist Jewish nationalism that called for minority cultural rights for Jews and other peoples in a multinational state and a secularized Jewish community body embracing all Jewish ideologies, religious and nonreligious. Opposed to communism, he moved to Berlin in 1922. When the Nazis came to power in 1933 he took refuge in Latvia, where he was murdered during the SS extermination of the Jewish community of Riga in 1941. Dubnow wrote extensively in Russian, Hebrew, and Yiddish. Besides his overview of Jewish history and writings on Jewish nationalism, he published studies on the history of the Jews in Eastern Europe, a scholarly edition of the minutes of the Jewish council of Lithuania between 1623 and 1761 (1922), a pioneering *History of Hasidism* (revised edition, 1930–1932), and an autobiography, *Book of Life: Reminiscences and Reflections, Material for the History of My Time* (Riga, 1934–1940).

Robert M. Seltzer

Texts

History of the Jews. Trans. Moshe Spiegel. 5 vols. South Brunswick, NJ: Thomas Yoseloff, 1967–1973.

History of the Jews in Russia and Poland from the Earliest Time to the Present Day. Trans. Israel Friedlaender. 3 vols. Philadelphia: Jewish Publication Society of America, 1916–1920.

Nationalism and History: Essays on Old and New Judaism. Ed. Koppel S. Pinson. Philadelphia: Jewish Publication Society of America, 1958.

References

Dubnov-Erlich, Sophie. *The Life and Work of Simon Dubnow.* Trans. Judith Vowles; ed. Jeffrey Shandler. Bloomington: Indiana University Press, 1991.

Seltzer, Robert M. "Coming Home: The Personal Basis of Simon Dubnow's Ideology." *The Association for Jewish Studies Review* 1 (1976): 283–301.

Steinberg, Aaron, ed. *Simon Dubnow: The Man and His Work: A Memorial Volume on the Centenary of His Birth.* Paris: World Jewish Congress, 1962.

Duby, Georges (1919–1996)

French medievalist. Born in Paris but raised and educated in Mâcon and Lyon, Duby taught at the university at Lyon while working on his dissertation, which was published in 1953. He taught at Besançon and Aix before taking a chair in the history of medieval societies at the Collège de France in Paris. Heavily influenced by his study of geography and his reading of Marc Bloch's *Feudal Society,* Duby in his acclaimed dissertation examined in minute detail a small region of east-central France in the central Middle Ages. His investigation arose from the conviction that "a society, like a landscape, is a system whose structure and evolution are determined by a multiplicity of factors, related not by cause and effect but by correlation and interaction." He proposed a critical break in French history: in the years 980 to 1030, a new social system of lords and castles, knights and peasants arose in the wake of the disintegration of public power. The period from this "feudal revolution" to the reconstitution of the royal state ca. 1200 had been Duby's primary chronological focus, although he also wrote extensively on earlier and later eras. Duby was a tremendously productive polymath whose subject matter spanned a broad spectrum of topics including peasant life, mental attitudes, the roles of knights and nobles, fine arts, marriage, and women. He was one of the great and influential figures in medieval studies of the twentieth century. In 1987, he became one of a handful of academic historians ever to be elected to the Académie Française. Duby described his intellectual development and career in *History Continues,* first published in France in 1991.

Bruce L. Venarde

Texts

The Age of the Cathedrals: Art and Society, 980–1420. Trans. Eleanor Levieux and Barbara Thompson. Chicago: University of Chicago Press, 1981.

The Chivalrous Society. Trans. Cynthia Postan. Berkeley: University of California Press, 1977.

The Early Growth of the European Economy: Warriors and Peasants from the Seventh to the Twelfth Century. Trans. Howard B. Clarke. Ithaca, NY: Cornell University Press, 1974.

The Knight, the Lady, and the Priest: The Making of Modern Marriage in Medieval France. Trans. Barbara Bray. New York: Pantheon Books, 1983.

La société au XIe et XIIe siècles dans la région mâconnaise [Society in the Maconnais in the Eleventh and Twelfth Centuries]. Paris: A. Colin, 1953.

The Three Orders: Feudal Society Imagined. Trans. Arthur Goldhammer. Chicago: University of Chicago Press, 1980.

References

Duby, Georges. *History Continues.* Trans. Arthur Goldhammer. Chicago: University of Chicago Press, 1994.

Moore, R.I. "Duby's Eleventh Century." *History* 69 (1984): 36–49.

Duchesne, Louis-Marie-Olivier (1843–1922)

Historian of the early Christian church. A native of Brittany, ordained priest in 1867, Duchesne studied theology and church history in Paris and Rome. After writing a thesis on the *Liber pontificalis* [Book of Bishops], a collection of biographies of early popes which he was the first to study critically, he taught church history in Paris. From 1895 until his death he was director of the French School at Rome. An expert in paleography, epigraphy, and archaeology, Duchesne pursued the history of ancient Christian institutions with a scientific rigor that more than once brought him into conflict with ecclesiastical authorities. His three-volume masterpiece, *Histoire ancienne de l'église* (1906–1910), almost immediately translated into English as *The Early History of the Church* (1909–1914), was banned for a time from Roman Catholic institutions. In *Fastes épiscopaux de l'ancienne Gaule* [Bishop-Lists of Ancient Gaul] (1894–1915), he disposed of legends tracing the origins of Christianity in France to apostolic times. Other works deal with early Christian liturgy and the topography of Rome in the Middle Ages.

M. Vessey

Texts

Christian Worship: Its Origins and Evolution. Trans. M.L. McClure. London: SPCK, 1903.

The Early History of the Christian Church. Trans. C. Jenkins. 3 vols. London: J. Murray, 1909–1924.

Fastes épiscopaux de l'ancienne Gaule. 3 vols. Paris: Thorin et fils, 1894–1915.

Le liber pontificalis. 3 vols. Paris: E. de Boccard, 1981.

References

Hablouville, Claude d'. *Monseigneur Duchesne: biographie critique.* Paris: E. Sansot et Cie., 1911.

Waché, Brigitte. *Monseigneur Louis Duchesne (1843–1922).* Rome: École Française de Rome, 1992.

Dudo of St. Quentin (fl. late tenth century)

Latin historian of Normandy. Dudo served as sometime chancellor for early Norman dukes and was dean of St. Quentin in his native Vermandois. Dudo's *Gesta Normannorum* [Deeds of the Normans] was commissioned in 994 by Duke Richard I and completed due to the continued patronage of the ducal house. This history of the reigns of Richard I and his predecessors (also called *De moribus et actis primorum Normanniae ducum* [On the Customs and Deeds of the First Dukes of Normandy]) is written in *prosimetrum* (rhythmic prose alternating with verse) and includes extensive "invented" scenes and conversations. Dudo's narrative was extremely influential in subsequent centuries; however, a number of authors, particularly in the twentieth century, have seen Dudo as a mendacious panegyrist for the Norman dukes. Dudo may also have written the history of the monastery of Fécamp contained in the manuscript Rouen, Bibliothèque Municipale 528.

Felice Lifshitz

Texts

De moribus et actis primorum Normanniae ducum. Ed. Jules Lair. Caen, France: F. Le Blanc-Hardel, 1865.

References

Lifshitz, Felice. *The Norman Conquest of Pious Neustria.* Toronto: Pontifical Institute of Mediaeval Studies Press, 1995.

Shopkow, Leah. "The Carolingian World of Dudo of St.Quentin." *Journal of Medieval History* 15 (1989): 19–37.

Duff, James Grant (1789–1859)

Scottish historian of the Marāṭhās of India. Educated at Marischal College, Aberdeen, Duff joined the East India Company's military service in 1805. He became adjutant and interpreter for his regiment, assistant to Mountstuart Elphinstone (another colonial administrator and historian), Resident at Poona, and Resident to the princely state of Satara. He retired to Scotland and published his *History of the Mahrattas* (1826), which remained the standard work on the history of the Marāṭhās for over half a century. Almost entirely a political history, it has been reprinted numerous times, translated into Marāṭhī, and is still in print at the end of the twentieth century. Duff was encouraged to work on the Marāṭhās by his superior, Elphinstone, who handed over to him state papers and correspondence of the Marāṭhās, some of which have since been lost. At the end of the nineteenth century Duff's chronology and interpretations began to be criticized by Marāṭhā nationalists, who called for a rewriting of Marāṭhā history. Nonetheless, histories of the Marāṭhās have, until the end of the twentieth century, mainly been glosses on Duff.

Roger D. Long

Texts

History of the Mahrattas. 2 vols. New Delhi: Associated Publishing House, 1971.

References

Gordon, Stewart. *The Marathas 1600–1818.* Cambridge, Eng.: Cambridge University Press, 1993.

———. *Marathas, Marauders and State Formation in Eighteenth Century India.* Delhi: Oxford University Press, 1994.

Dugdale, Sir William (1605–1686)

Antiquary and herald. Dugdale was born at Shustake, in Warwickshire. His father belonged to the minor gentry and encouraged his son to study local history and antiquities. Dugdale's scholarly activities attracted the patronage of the antiquary Sir Henry Spelman and the courtier Sir Christopher Hatton, who supported Dugdale's researches by securing him a position in the College of Arms in 1638. During the English civil war, Dugdale supported the royalist cause and suffered persecution and exile. He resumed his heraldic duties in 1660, attaining in 1677 both the office of Garter King-of-Arms and a knighthood. Dugdale's three most important works were the *Monasticon Anglicanum* (1655–1673), *The Antiquities of Warwickshire* (1656), and *The Baronage of England* (1675–1676). All were pioneering efforts of extraordinary quality, which still retain their usefulness for modern researchers. They also all involved collaboration or at least substantial borrowings from the researches of others. The *Monasticon* was actually largely the work of Roger Dodsworth (1585–1654), Dugdale's co-author. Later Dugdale extensively utilized materials gathered by Dodsworth when he wrote the *Baronage.* Even his *Antiquities,* an outstanding contribution to local history, borrowed from the researches of others, all of which gained Dugdale the undeserved reputation as "The Grand Plagiary." In addition to his antiquarian works, he also authored a history of St. Paul's Cathedral and a *Short View* of Britain's civil wars, the latter colored by his royalist perspective.

Ronald H. Fritze

Texts

The Antiquities of Warwickshire. London: Thomas Warren, 1656.

The Baronage of England. 2 vols. London, Abel Roper et al., 1675–1676.

Monasticon Anglicanum. Ed. J. Caley, H. Ellis, and B. Bandinel. 8 vols. London: Longman, 1817–1830.

A Short View of the Late Troubles in England. Oxford: Moses Pitt, 1681.

References

Douglas, David C. *English Scholars 1660–1730.* Revised ed. London: Eyre & Spottiswoode, 1951.

Duhem, Pierre (1861–1916)

Historian and philosopher of science. Duhem was born at Paris into a bourgeois family. He attended the École Normale Supérieure where he studied physics and chemistry, taking a Ph.D. in 1888. His was a prickly and argumentative personality bristling with unfashionable ideas: atoms were figments, the republic was dangerous and ungodly, Galileo was wrong and disobedient and got what he deserved, and so on. These views arose from a staunch Catholicism and conservatism close to that of Action Française, and they ensured that in republican France he would never achieve a prestigious chair at any Parisian university; he passed his career in teaching positions at Lille, Rennes, and Bordeaux.

Duhem's early career was devoted to physical chemistry, thermodynamics, and "energetics."

Just after 1900, however, he began the series of historical studies for which he is best known, starting with a critical study of James Clerk Maxwell's electromagnetic theory, which he condemned for its dependence on mechanical modeling. He believed that physical theories could only summarize observations in conventional ways; that it was a mistake to think that such theories "represent" or faithfully picture reality; and that science could not, and should not, assert any metaphysical claims. Partly to vindicate this positivism, partly to demonstrate a thoroughgoing continuity from classical, through medieval, to early modern science, Duhem undertook a systematic study of medieval writings on physical and cosmological subjects. The "history of medieval science" is virtually his creation, starting with *Études sur Léonard de Vinci* (1906–1913) and continuing through the ten-volume *Le Système du Monde* (1913–1959). Duhem showed that a continuous tradition of cosmological speculation and criticism stretched from Plato and Aristotle to Galileo, whose own dismantling of Aristotelian physics relied (for what was sound in it) crucially upon the earlier scholastic analysis of motion by Buridan, Ockham, and the Merton school. But, according to Duhem, Galileo was mistaken in his realism, in his corpuscularianism, and in his defiance of ecclesiastical authority. Though many of Duhem's conclusions are no longer defensible, his works must still be consulted as a starting point for study of cosmology in the West. He presents a paradox; for though he embraced a nominalist view of science, he simultaneously held a realist view of history.

Stuart Pierson

Texts

The Aim and Structure of Physical Theory. Princeton, NJ: Princeton University, 1954.

Le Système du monde: Histoire des doctrines cosmologiques de Platon à Copernic. 10 vols. Paris: Hermann, 1913–1959.

To Save the Phenomena: An Essay on the Idea of Physical Theory from Plato to Galileo. Chicago: University of Chicago Press, 1969.

References

Cohen, H. Floris. *The Scientific Revolution: An Historiographical Inquiry.* Chicago: University of Chicago Press, 1993.

Jaki, Stanley L. *Uneasy Genius: The Life and Work of Pierre Duhem.* The Hague: Nijhoff, 1984.

Miller, Donald G. "Duhem." *Dictionary of Scientific Biography* 4, 225–233.

Dumézil, Georges (1898–1988)

French mythologist and linguist. Born in Paris, Dumézil was a professor of Indo-European civilization at the Collège de France and director of studies in the Section des Sciences Religieuses of the École des Hautes Études of the Sorbonne. In 1978, he was elected a member of the French Academy. Dumézil's theory of Indo-European Tripartite ideology formed the basis of almost all his work. Nineteenth-century scholars had noted similarities among many of the languages of Europe, the Middle East, and India and had posited that they all descended from a common tongue. This suggested that many of the world's societies shared a common origin. Moving beyond pure linguistic comparison, Dumézil probed into ancient myths, uncovering structural similarities and a shared ideology. The Tripartite theory stated the same three classes—the priests, the warriors, and the agricultural producers could be found in the myths of each society. Furthermore, most myths were based on the function of one of these groups. Also of considerable importance was Dumézil's methodology. He rejected correspondences as random, unless they could be organized into a system. He also cautioned against taking a selective approach in research, stating that all evidence must be gathered and taken into account before conclusions could be drawn. Dumézil's methodology and structuralist approach has influenced many twentieth-century scholars.

Keith Robinson

Texts

Archaic Roman Religion. Trans. Philip Krapp. 2 vols. Chicago: University of Chicago Press, 1970.

Camillus: A Study of Indo-European Religion As Roman History. Ed. Udo Strutynski; trans. Annette Aronowitz and Josette Bryson. Berkeley: University of California Press, 1980.

The Destiny of a King. Trans. Alf Hiltebeitel. Chicago: University of Chicago Press, 1973.

The Destiny of the Warrior. Trans. Alf Hiltebeitel. Chicago: University of Chicago Press, 1970.

From Myth to Fiction: The Saga of Hadingus. Trans. Derek Coltman. Chicago: University of Chicago Press, 1973.

Gods of the Ancient Northmen. Ed. Einar Haugen. Berkeley: University of California Press, 1973.

The Plight of a Sorcerer. Ed. Jaan Puhvel and David Weeks. Berkeley: University of California Press, 1986.

The Stakes of the Warrior. Ed. Jaan Puhvel; trans. David Weeks. Berkeley: University of California Press, 1983.

References

Belier, Wouter W. *Decayed Gods: Origin and Development of Georges Dumézil's "Idéologie Tripartie."* Leiden, Netherlands and New York: E.J. Brill, 1991.

Littleton, C. Scott. *The New Comparative Mythology: An Anthropological Assessment of the Theories of Georges Dumézil.* Third ed. Berkeley and Los Angeles: University of California Press, 1982.

Durkheim, Emile (1858–1917)

French sociologist. Durkheim was a student of the historian Fustel de Coulanges, and he retained a lifelong interest in the past, most explicit in his book on the "evolution" of French education, but implicit in his other works as well. His sociological studies—on religion, on suicide, on the division of labor—have in common an emphasis on social cohesion, on consensus, on shared attitudes, or as Durkheim called them "collective representations," thus rejecting both the individualism of Herbert Spencer and Karl Marx's emphasis on social conflict. He was also a great believer in the comparative method of social analysis. Durkheim's efforts to establish his subject as an autonomous discipline involved emphasizing its differences from history as well as from philosophy, leaving to the historians the study of "particular events" (the surface of the past according to him), while sociologists studied its deeper structures. Nevertheless, Durkheim's vision of the past attracted some French historians who refused to be confined to the study of events. Among them were a historian of China, Marcel Granet, a historian of classical Athens, Gustave Glotz; and, most important of all, Marc Bloch, whose *Feudal Society* (1939–1940) as well as his earlier *Royal Touch* (1923) are based on the comparative method and impregnated with the Durkheimian ideas of social cohesion and collective representations. Fernand Braudel's later notorious dismissal of the history of events also owes something to Durkheim's example.

Peter Burke

Texts

The Division of Labor in Society. Ed. Lewis A. Coser; trans. W.D. Halls. New York: Free Press, 1984.

Durkheim and the Law. Ed. Steven Lukes and Andrew Scull. Oxford: Martin Robertson, 1983.

Education and Sociology. Trans. Sherwood D. Fox. Glencoe, IL: Free Press, 1956.

The Elementary Forms of Religious Life. Trans. Karen E. Fields. New York: Free Press, 1995.

With Marcel Mauss. *Primitive Classification.* Ed. and trans. Rodney Needham. Chicago: University of Chicago Press, 1963.

References

Bellah, Robert N. "Durkheim and History." In *Emile Durkheim,* ed. Robert A. Nisbet. Englewood Cliffs, NJ: Spectrum, 1965.

Burke, Peter. *History and Social Theory.* Oxford: Polity, 1992.

Dutch Historiography—1500 to Present

Historical writing in the Netherlands since the Renaissance. Around 1500, humanism made its entry into Dutch historical writing. A narrative historiography came into being, following the example of the classics, closely tied to belles lettres, and specifically aimed at passing on political lessons. The new spirit is already apparent in the so-called *Divisiekroniek* [Division Chronicle] (1517) by Cornelius Aurelius (ca. 1460–1531). This cleric, a regular canon, also engendered the Batavian myth, a variant of the medieval myth about the Trojan origin: on the basis of the Roman historian Tacitus, it was assumed that the inhabitants of contemporary Holland were direct descendants of the Batavians, the brave and loyal allies of the Romans. This myth, intended to remind the contemporaries of the great origins of their *"patria,"* was widespread in the seventeenth century. At the same time, there arose a controversy about the exact location of ancient Batavia.

Besides the Batavian myth, another important historical theme, for the Renaissance writer Reinier Snoy (ca. 1477–1537), among others, was the nature of the count's authority in old Holland. Interest in this subject was provoked by the difficulties with the ruler, the Spanish king Philip II. Following the Dutch revolt against Spain, this theme played a major role in the political discussions on the bearer of sovereignty in the republic, particularly among the republican historiographers of Holland, who wished to curtail the power of the *stadtholders* (the house of Orange-Nassau) and who therefore defended the proposition that the sovereignty had always been vested in the rulers of towns and provinces (and thus not with the counts).

In the last quarter of the sixteenth century, the revolt itself at once became the center of attention for the historiographers. In a first phase, chroniclers like Emanuel van Meteren (1535–1612) and Pieter Christiaenzoon Bor (1559–1635) brought together countless documents and testimonies relating to the struggle against Spain. In its next phase, the tragedy was represented in a classical manner by the statesman and magistrate Hugo Grotius (1583–1645), also the author of a *Liber de antiquitate reipublicae Batavicae* [A Treatise of the Antiquity of the Commonwealth of the Battavers] (1610), and especially by the poet and playwright Pieter Corneliszoon Hooft (1581–1647), whose *Neederlandsche histoorien* [Histories of the Low Countries] (1642–1654) were the high point of Dutch humanist historical writing. Only the minister Gerard Brandt the elder (1626–1685), the author of a few biographies and a *Historie der reformatie* [The History of the Reformation] (1671–1704), was able to continue this tradition. Other seventeenth-century historians, such as the diplomats and political agents Lieuwe van Aitzema (1600–1669) and Abraham de Wicquefort (1606–1682), wrote cynically tinged histories of episodes from the recent past of the United Netherlands. Their work was supplemented by an abundant literature of pamphlets, clearly showing just how much history and politics were interwoven.

The strong urbanization, particularly in the western parts of the republic, also brought another historical genre into blossom, that of urban histories and topographies. These combined historical particulars with geographical and sometimes ethnographic data. The first extensive urban history, by Johannes Isacius Pontanus (1571–1639) concerns Amsterdam and dates from 1611; histories of Leiden (1614) and Deventer (1616) rapidly followed. This genre remained popular until well into the eighteenth century. Meanwhile, antiquarianism, too, had become fully grown. From the first half of the seventeenth century, and independently of narrative historical writing, there developed the critical study of physical relics of the past: inscriptions, coins, and remnants of buildings, and of textual artifacts such as medieval chronicles. The Leiden-based scholar Petrus Scriverius (1576–1660) carried out important work in the field of source criticism; Antonius Matthaeus (1635–1710), professor of law in Leiden, compiled a monumental edition of medieval historical texts. In the field of auxiliary sciences, a pioneering role was played by the French philologer Joseph Justus Scaliger (1540–1609), who also taught in Leiden, author of the important *Opus novum de emendatione temporum* [A New Work on the Emendation of Chronology]

(1583). Historical pyrrhonism, a form of extreme skepticism that in about 1700 led to a crisis in the matter of the reliability of the available historical documentation, was refuted by the classicist Jacobus Perizonius (1651–1715), professor in Franeker and Leiden and researcher of Roman legends; in the end, pyrrhonism helped to stimulate the further development of antiquarianism in the eighteenth century.

In many fields, eighteenth-century historiography displayed a substantial continuity with that of the two preceding centuries. This is demonstrated by, among others, the voluminous *Vaderlandsche historie* [National History] (1749–1759) by the Amsterdam publicist and historian Jan Wagenaar (1709–1773), the burgher who was also the author of an urban history of Amsterdam. The Dutch Enlightenment, which had strong Christian features, was much less controversial than its French counterpart. Only in *De opkomst en bloei van de Republiek der Vereenigde Nederlanden* [The Rise and Bloom of the Republic of the United Netherlands] (1774) by the physician Simon Stijl (1731–1804) was the historiographic ideal of the philosophes clearly reflected: the work was a concise narrative that aimed at phrasing moral maxims rather than adding to the knowledge of the national past. A similar pragmatism was also the driving force behind eighteenth-century statistics, the new "state science," in which the current era was analyzed in a historical manner in order to provide support for expectations with regard to the future. One of these statisticians was the Leiden professor Adriaan Kluit (1735–1807), whose fame, however, principally rests on his *Historia critica comitatus Hollandiae et Zeelandiae* [A Critical History of the Counties of Holland and Zeeland] (1777–1782), an attempt to practice medieval history in a more scholarly manner than had previously been the case.

This "scholarization" was only carried through slowly. An initiative by King William I in 1826 in this matter did have some results in the southern part of the new Kingdom (the future Belgium), but remained unsuccessful in the North. There, historical writing remained highly colored with controversies, judging in particular by the posthumously published lectures on national history by the poet Willem Bilderdijk (1756–1831), the Netherlands' only full-blooded romantic. Sixteenth- and seventeenth-century history occasioned the most heated disputes. In his *Handboek der geschiedenis van het vaderland* [Manual for the History of the Nation] (1846), the antirevolutionary statesman Guillaume Groen van Prinsterer (1801–1876) developed a Calvinist and Orangist view; on the other side, in countless essays, the head of the Public Record Office, Reinier Cornelis Bakhuizen van den Brink (1810–1865), defended a liberal and republican position. Nevertheless they, too, provided instruments for raising standards of scholarship still higher. Groen, in his capacity of keeper of the Private Royal Archives, published an important edition of source material for the period 1552–1688, the *Archives ou correspondance inédite de la maison d'Orange-Nassau* [Archives or Unpublished Correspondance of the House of Orange-Nassau] (1835–1861).

The appointment in 1860 of Robert Jacobus Fruin (1823–1899) to the then recently established chair of Dutch history at the University of Leiden reinforced the trend toward "scholarization." His ideal of impartiality became the standard of academic historical study, not only in the various universities' faculties of arts, but also in those of theology, where, notably, Johannes Gerhardus Rijk Acquoy (1829–1896) gave church history a more scholarly stature. At the same time, the historical infrastructure was being further expanded. In 1902, the Government Committee for National History was set up alongside the (Dutch) Historical Society, founded at Utrecht in 1845; its task was to coordinate the publication of source material concerning the national past. Higher education in history was modernized through the introduction of seminars based on the German model. An important role in these renewals was played by Fruin's successor in Leiden, Petrus Johannes Blok (1855–1929), who would author the work of historical synthesis that his master did not publish. This *Geschiedenis van het Nederlandsche volk* [History of the Dutch People] (1892–1908) confronted the small Netherlands with its own great past by way of encouragement. This nationalist motive had also been the mainspring for the man of letters Conrad Busken Huet (1826–1886) when he recalled the republic's golden age in his cultural history of the seventeenth century, *Het land van Rembrand* [The Land of Rembrandt] (1882–1884).

Historical writing, in the decades after 1900, was also marked by fluctuations in national consciousness and by the process of "pillarization," which divided Dutch society into four ideological compartments (Catholic, orthodox-Protestant, socialist, and liberal). On the confessional side, the apologetic commitment to the past lived on. Both the Catholic and the orthodox-Protestant pillars studied history within their own institutions. Among the Catholics, the groundwork for this historiographic "emancipation" was laid by

the physician Willem Johannes Franciscus Nuyens (1823–1894), author of *Geschiedenis der Nederlandsche beroerten in de XVIde eeuw* [History of the Dutch Turmoils in the Sixteenth Century] (1865–1870), written from a Catholic point of view. On the liberal side, a new generation of historians, born around 1870, advocated recognizing the distinctive nature of the historical discipline (as distinguished from the positivism of the natural sciences), broadening the categories of historical subject matter to embrace social, economic, and contemporary history, and openly confronting historical materialism. This generation also included Johan Huizinga (1872–1945), professor in Groningen and later in Leiden. In 1919, he published his *Herfsttij der Middeleeuwen* [The Waning of the Middle Ages], a history of mentalities of the Burgundian elite, based on literary and artistic sources and written in a grand style.

In the period between the world wars, these developments continued. On the one hand, there was a growing tendency toward scholarship and organization. Otto Alexander Oppermann (1873–1945), a professor in Utrecht, introduced modern medievalism, with its minute source criticism, from Germany. The entrepreneur Nicolaas Wilhelmus Posthumus (1880–1960), holder of the first chair in economic history in the Netherlands (in Rotterdam), saw to the foundation of historical institutions such as the International Institute of Social History (1935). On the other hand, the tone was being set by a group of historians, all born around 1890, whose works delivered various clear messages from within the national and "pillarized" framework; this group is often referred to as the "lyrical generation." Pieter Catharinus Arie Geyl (1887–1966) was the apologist of "Great-Netherlandish" historiography; Jan Marius Romein (1893–1962) committed himself to Marxism; and Ludovicus Jacobus Rogier (1894–1974) promoted the Catholic revival, for example in his *Geschiedenis van het katholicisme in Noord-Nederland in de zestiende en zeventiende eeuw* [History of Catholicism in the Northern Netherlands in the Sixteenth and Seventeenth Centuries] (1946).

World War II did not signify the end of this nationally or ideologically inspired historiography. On the contrary, the voluminous and successful *Het Koninkrijk der Nederlanden in de Tweede Wereldoorlog* [The Kingdom of the Netherlands in the Second World War] (1969–1988) by Lou de Jong (b. 1914–), the first director of the National Institute of War Records (1945), was the work of an author who was not only a historian but also a popular educator.

D

It was not until 1960 that historical writing finally broke away from the national and "pillarized" framework. Besides the practice on a small scale of committed historiography (including women's history), a new movement of "scholarization" developed, particularly in economic (agrarian) and social (demographic) history. The old colonial history was modernized, becoming a history of European expansion and of reactions to it among colonizers and colonized. At the same time, Dutch historians were attempting to connect historiography in their country with international developments. As a result, the tone was now being set by historians who adopted a terser and less emotive attitude than had their predecessors. The representatives of this "pragmatic generation" (born around 1920), such as Ernst Heinrich Kossmann (b. 1922–), had a special eye for what might be called the "plasticity" of the past. They produced their work in a period in which the professional historical enterprise was growing explosively throughout western Europe. This growth also led to fragmentation, however, as the previously integrated discipline of history fell apart into countless subfields, each with its own issues and problems demanding special attention, distinctive methodologies, and various forms of institutional support.

Jo Tollebeek

See also BELGIAN HISTORIOGRAPHY; URBAN HISTORY.

References

Duke, A.C., and C.A. Tamse, eds. *Clio's Mirror, Historiography in Britain and the Netherlands.* Zutphen, Netherlands: De Walburg Pers, 1985.

Geurts, P.A.M., and A.E.M. Janssen, eds. *Geschiedschrijving in Nederland* [Historical Writing in the Netherlands]. 2 vols. The Hague: Martinus Nijhoff, 1981.

Haitsma Mulier, E.O.G., and G.A.C. Van der Lem, eds. *Repertorium van geschiedschrijvers in Nederland 1500–1800* [Repertory of Historians in the Netherlands 1500–1800]. The Hague: Nederlands Historisch Genootschap, 1990.

Lancée, J.A.L., ed. *Mythe en werkelijkheid: Drie eeuwen vaderlandse geschiedbeoefening (1600–1900)* [Myth and Reality: Three Centuries of Dutch Historical Study (1600–1900)]. Utrecht, Netherlands: HES Publishers, 1979.

Leeb, I.L. *The Ideological Origins of the Batavian Revolution. History and Politics in the Dutch Republic 1747–1800.* The Hague: Martinus Nijhoff, 1973.

Luykx, P., and N. Bootsma, eds. *De laatste tijd: Geschiedschrijving over Nederland in de 20e eeuw* [In Recent Years: Historical Writing about the Netherlands in the Twentieth Century]. Utrecht, Netherlands: Het Spectrum, 1987.

Mijnhardt, W.W., ed. *Kantelend geschiedbeeld: Nederlandse historiografie sinds 1945* [A Tilting Image of History: Dutch Historiography since 1945]. Utrecht and Antwerp: Het Spectrum, 1983.

Roelevink, J. *Gedicteerd verleden: Het onderwijs in de algemene geschiedenis aan de Universiteit te Utrecht, 1735–1839* [The Dictated Past: The Teaching of General History at the University of Utrecht, 1735–1839]. Amsterdam: APA–Holland Universiteits Pers, 1986.

Tilmans, K. *Historiography and Humanism in Holland in the Age of Erasmus: Aurelius and the "Divisiekroniek" of 1517.* Nieuwkoop, Netherlands: De Graaf Publishers, 1992.

Tollebeek, J. *De ijkmeesters: Opstellen over de geschiedschrijving in Nederland en België* [The Gaugers: Essays on Historical Writing in the Netherlands and Belgium]. Amsterdam: Bert Bakker, 1994.

———. *De toga van Fruin: Denken over geschiedenis in Nederland sinds 1860* [Fruin's Gown: Thinking about History in the Netherlands since 1860]. Amsterdam: Wereldbibliotheek, 1996.

E

Eadmer of Canterbury (d. ca. 1130)
Anglo-Saxon biographer. A Benedictine monk of Christ Church, Canterbury, Eadmer was the first Englishman after the Norman Conquest to write contemporary history. In addition to saints' lives, Eadmer wrote two lives of his bishop, Anselm of Canterbury, both largely based on intimate first-hand information and written shortly after the events described. The *Life of St. Anselm,* written between 1093 and 1125, concerns Anselm's private life, the *Historia novorum* [History of Recent Events], his public career in its historical context. Eadmer's histories are strongly biased toward the archdiocese of Canterbury in its struggle against the northern archdiocese of York for primacy over the English church.

Maura K. Lafferty

Texts

History of Recent Events in England. Trans. G.
    Bosanquet. Philadelphia: Dufour, 1965.
The Life of St. Anselm, Archbishop of Canterbury.
    Ed. and trans. Richard W. Southern. London: T. Nelson, 1962.

References

Southern, Richard W. *Saint Anselm and His Biographer.* Cambridge, Eng.: Cambridge University Press, 1963.
Gransden, Antonia. *Historical Writing in England c. 550–1307.* London: Routledge and Kegan Paul, 1974, 129–142.

Eberhard, Wolfram (1909–1989)
Historian of China and pioneer of Chinese folklore studies. Trained in Berlin in Chinese studies and sociology, as a young scholar Eberhard pioneered the academic study of Chinese folklore in Germany while cultivating links with the folklore studies movement in China. He served as professor of Chinese in Ankara from 1937 to 1948, the year his *Chinas Geschichte* [History of China] first appeared. In the same year he moved to the sociology department at Berkeley, where for the next four decades he continued to carry out innovative research. From the 1930s onward he published prolifically on Chinese popular and local cultures and on Chinese cultural values generally. He was instrumental in rebuilding folklore studies in Taiwan in the 1950s and maintained close links with scholars there. His analyses of Chinese historical sociology combined theoretical sophistication with a firm mastery of literary and other sources. His historical works include monographs on almost all periods of the imperial era, on topics ranging from fashion and literature to class structures, social mobility, and the dynamics of dynastic transitions. An intellectual cosmopolitan, Eberhard drew with ease on Max Weber and Karl Marx as well as on comparative literary and cultural analysis. His breadth made him a notable critic of Karl Wittfogel's analysis of "Oriental despotism," while his study of guilt and sin (1967) considered affective structures in comparative terms.

G.R. Blue

Texts

Chinese Fairy Tales and Folk Tales, London:
    Kegan Paul, 1937.
*Die chinesischen Novellen des 17.–19.
    Jahrhunderts: Eine sociologische Untersuchung*
    [Chinese Stories from the Seventeenth to the Nineteenth Centuries: A Sociological Inquiry]. Ascona, Switzerland: Artibus Asiae, 1948.
Conquerors and Rulers: Social Forces in Medieval China. Leiden, Netherlands: E.J. Brill, 1965.

A Dictionary of Chinese Symbols. London: Routledge & Kegan Paul, 1986.

Guilt and Sin in Traditional China. Berkeley: University of California Press, 1967.

A History of China. Fourth ed. Berkeley: University of California Press, 1977.

Local Cultures of South and East China. Leiden, Netherlands: E.J. Brill, 1968.

Settlement and Social Change in Asia. Hong Kong: University of Hong Kong Press, 1967.

Social Mobility in Traditional China. Leiden, Netherlands: E.J. Brill, 1962.

Ecclesiastical History

Historiography recording the development of the Christian church. While at first it might seem to involve nothing more than an account of the evolution of the Christian movement and its institutions, ecclesiastical history has had a complex history because of the dual character of the church itself. Certainly the church has a tangible institutional and social dimension that reflects the influence of identifiable historical forces and circumstances. To this extent the theme of ecclesiastical history is not different from that of other forms of historical enquiry. But because its supernatural origin and transcendent destiny distinguish the church from secular organizations, historiography that confines itself to the profane events of history proper furnishes an inadequate means of recording church history. The tension between the historical and transcendent aspects of the church has shaped ecclesiastical historiography from antiquity to the modern period. Between the fourth and the eighteenth centuries, church historians simply accepted the transhistorical structure of salvation history as the context for their subject, but at times disagreed over the higher significance of this or that episode in the church's earthly history. Academic scholarship since the Enlightenment has grown so uneasy with the expression of metaphysical claims of any sort that modern church historians have more and more confined their attention to the secular development of the Christian movement.

In late antiquity Christian authors struggled to gain a synoptic view of church history in the wider context of Roman history. The sudden transformation of imperial policy toward Christians in the early fourth century inspired an initial wave of optimism followed by a more cautious reassessment of the empire's meaning. Eusebius of Caesarea viewed the Constantinian revolution as a sign that Rome had, after all, a positive role to play in Christian history. With a pious emperor presiding over a unified church, the aboriginal divine order for the world had been restored. Eusebius's *Ecclesiastical History* (ca. 325) begins with the birth of Jesus, which the bishop paired with the rise of monarchy under Augustus, and comes down to the peace of the church under Constantine. The themes he chose to follow later became canonical for ecclesiastical historians. These included the bishops of the greatest sees, the oral and written expression of the Christian revelation in each generation, heresy, the fate of the Jews, pagan attacks on the church, and the torments endured by the defenders of the faith. In a second work, called the *Chronicle* (ca. 303), Eusebius presented the Christian Roman Empire as the culmination of God's plan for world history. He followed the lead of the third-century chronicler Julianus Africanus who had prepared tables comparing Hebrew and Christian chronology with that of the Roman Empire and its Hellenistic and ancient Near Eastern predecessors. The idea of the design behind profane history, or progress in history expressed in this chronicle tradition was one of ecclesiastical history's great contributions to historiography in general.

In response to Christian optimism in the wake of the Constantinian revolution, Augustine wrote *The City of God* (425) as a warning about the danger of linking the historical fate of the church to the fortunes of any purely earthly institution, even the Roman Empire. He distinguished between God's salvific work within history, which is perfect, and mankind's understanding of that work, which is incomplete. He sketched a historical continuum in which citizens of the City of Man mingle with citizens of the City of God, the two groups being differentiated only at the end of time. Thus even the visible, institutional church comprises a mixed membership during the historical interim between the Incarnation and the Last Judgment.

Fundamental though Augustine's ideas later turned out to be for the theology of history, Eusebius's works had a more immediate impact on the actual writing of ecclesiastical history. The historical outlook of the Middle Ages revealed Eusebian parentage in its tendency to subordinate all history, whether secular or ecclesiastical, to the course of salvation history. An obvious sign of this is the emergence of a Christian system of chronology, first enunciated by Dionysius Exiguus in the sixth century and later adopted widely, which places the Incarnation at the center of time and reckons the dates of other events before or after it.

Yet the ecclesiastical history of the Middle Ages was not simply a rehearsal of the antique pattern, because medieval authors seldom had occasion to reflect on the church as an entity separate from others. Most of the themes of Eusebian ecclesiastical history appeared in one or another medieval literary form, such as saints' lives and the passions of martyrs, catalogs of heretics and catalogs of orthodox writers, Episcopal biographies, and synodal transactions. But in a church that had grown to encompass all of Western society, there was little need for a synthetic account comparable to Eusebius's *Ecclesiastical History*.

In practice medieval historians were often more concerned with natural, secondary causation and the careful use of source material than their avowed metahistorical convictions might lead one to expect. The *Ecclesiastical History of the English People* (731) of the English monk Bede is an outstanding example of a form of national ecclesiastical history common in the early Middle Ages. He recorded the mission sent to England by Pope Gregory I and the growth of the faith among this Germanic people as a part of the fulfillment of the New Testament promise to expand the church among the Gentiles before the Last Judgment.

The dispute between papacy and empire over authority within Christendom stimulated interest in the theology of history during the high Middle Ages. Most of the ecclesiastical history produced during this period remained faithful to the thought of Augustine and Eusebius. But the distressing events of their day prompted a few authors to carry apocalyptic and millenarian speculation beyond the limits charted by Augustine. Prophetic revelations inspired the Calabrian abbot Joachim of Fiore to announce that the third great period of world history was at hand. Although it had originated at the time of St. Benedict, this third stage would mature only after the current turmoil of the church had given way to a period of terrestrial peace and happiness for the elect before the end of history.

Once again it was a crisis within the Western church that produced fundamental changes in ecclesiastical history during the sixteenth century. Although the issues of contention that led to the Protestant Reformation were doctrinal and sacramental rather than historical, they were rooted in divergent views of history and the character of authentic apostolic tradition, and reflected different ways of applying the ideas of Eusebius and Augustine. Within a few years of Martin Luther's excommunication, controversy spread from theology and doctrine to historiography, and on all sides rival versions of ecclesiastical history appeared.

These conflicts attained a high level of sophistication because of the technical advances of humanism. With their interest in philology and a determination to recover original texts, humanist scholars such as Desiderius Erasmus contributed to the sources and method of ecclesiastical history. Of equal importance was the heightened awareness of the qualitative difference between various historical epochs. Lorenzo Valla's exposure of the Donation of Constantine as a forgery during the fifteenth century exemplifies a general tendency to historicize documents and sources of all kinds.

Protestant historiography expressed the reformers' conviction that a thread of continuity linked their churches with that of the New Testament. The most impressive Lutheran history was a collective undertaking known as the *Magdeburg Centuries* (1559–1574), initiated by Matthias Flacius Illyricus. Its thirteen volumes trace the corruption of the authentic Gospel teaching within the church of Rome from antiquity to 1300. Each "century" addressed the themes that had appeared in Eusebius's *Ecclesiastical History*, but with new standards of documentation and an interest in the development of ecclesiastical hierarchy and the sacraments that would have been foreign to Eusebius. A few histories, such as the *Acts and Monuments of These Latter and Perilous Days* (1563) by the Englishman John Foxe, enjoyed popular success. In this account, John Wycliffe and the Lollards preserved the spirit of primitive Christianity, just as the ancient martyrs found modern counterparts in English Protestant victims of persecution.

Sixteenth-century Catholic historians sought to show that the Roman church had continued to serve as the vessel of divine grace since ancient times. Cesare Baronio responded to the *Magdeburg Centuries* in a twelve-volume *Annales ecclesiastici* [Ecclesiastical Annals] (1588–1607), which traced the development of dogma, theology, liturgy, institutions, orders, schisms, and heresies from the foundation of the church to the accession of Pope Innocent III (1198). Like its Lutheran opposite, the *Ecclesiastical Annals* is based on documentary evidence and incorporates verbatim excerpts from the primary sources.

During the early modern period, ecclesiastical history began to yield its central place in the field of historiography to chronicles of kingdoms and states considered as entities separate from the

E

church. Even within ecclesiastical history explicit references to the transhistorical goal of the church became scarce in an era of scientific inquiry and secularization. Although assumptions about the meaning of human history that were Christian in origin persisted throughout the period, ecclesiastical history as such increasingly came to be one form of historiography among others.

On the eve of its modernization, the discipline made its greatest technical contributions to historiography at large. In his *On Diplomatics* (1681), the Benedictine scholar Jean Mabillon responded to skeptics who challenged the authenticity of many of the charters and manuscripts held in premodern archives. He proposed a variety of empirical tests meant to determine whether a particular document was spurious or genuine. While at first these technical advances were placed in the service of ecclesiastical history, Mabillon's advances in paleography and diplomatics soon proved of value in secular historiography as well.

Universities became important centers of ecclesiastical history during the eighteenth century. One of the prominent eighteenth-century Protestant church historians was Johann Lorenz von Mosheim of the University of Göttingen. His *Institutions of Ancient and Modern Ecclesiastical History* (1739) is often cited as the first modern ecclesiastical history. Mosheim reflected some of the assumptions of the Enlightenment in his effort to cultivate an impartial, nondenominational perspective and in his willingness to study the church as an institution or society no different from others. While avoiding references to salvation history and the church's transcendent end, Mosheim did accept the existence of progress within history and so could present the Reformation as a step toward modern individualism.

Ecclesiastical history benefited from the rehabilitation of medieval history brought about by romanticism and national historiography in the early nineteenth century. Important schools of ecclesiastical history appeared at the universities of Tübingen and Munich, where Johann Adam Möhler and Johann von Döllinger were notable practitioners. Although they dropped the distaste for the medieval church and traditional piety that had marred ecclesiastical history of the Enlightenment era, these scholars engaged in a scientific historiography that reflected the rationalism and secular outlook of the modern period.

This secularizing tendency has intensified during the present century even as interest in ecclesiastical history has grown. Numerous professional societies, periodicals, and reference handbooks re-

lated to or solely concerned with the subject have appeared. Ancillary fields such as hagiography, iconography, liturgics, and the history of dogma have come into their own. Since 1945 the history of Christian missions has been a prominent concern of ecclesiastical historians at all levels. Scholars such as Kenneth Scott Latourette have written synthetic histories of the church in Africa, Asia, and the New World as well as in Europe and the Mediterranean. But within academic scholarly discourse, the dominant rationalist paradigm precludes open expression of the values and beliefs that animated the work of premodern ecclesiastical historians.

David F. Appleby

See also CHRISTIANITY, VIEWS OF HISTORY IN; CHRONICLES, MEDIEVAL; HAGIOGRAPHY; MARTYROLOGY; RELIGIONS, HISTORY OF.

Texts

Baronio, Cesare [Caesar Baronius]. *Annales ecclesiastici.* 12 vols. Rome: ex typographia Vaticana, 1588–1607.

Bede. *A History of the English Church and People.* Revised ed. Trans. Leo Sherley-Price. New York: Penguin, 1968.

Eusebius. *The History of the Church from Christ to Constantine.* Trans. G.A. Williamson New York: Penguin, 1965.

Latourette, Kenneth Scott. *A History of the Expansion of Christianity.* 7 vols. New York: Harper, 1937–1945.

Mosheim, Johann Lorenz von. *An Ecclesiastical History.* Trans. Archibald Maclaine. Cincinnati, OH: Applegate, 1857.

References

Blockx, Karel. *A Bibliographical Introduction to Church History.* Louvain, Belgium: Katholieke Universiteit Leuven, 1982.

Jedin, Hubert. "General Introduction to Church History." In *History of the Church,* ed. Hubert Jedin, John Dolan, and Konrad Repgen. 10 vols. New York: Crossroad, 1965–1981, vol. 1, 1–56.

Momigliano, Arnaldo. "The Origins of Ecclesiastical Historiography." In his *The Classical Foundations of Modern Historiography.* Berkeley: University of California Press, 1990.

Nigg, Walter. *Die Kirchengeschichtsschreibung* [Ecclesiastical Historiography]. Munich: C.H. Beck, 1934.

Patrides, C.A. *The Grand Design of God.* London: Routledge and Kegan Paul, 1972.

Echard, Laurence (1670?–1730)

English historian and eclectic writer. A Suffolk native who spent much of his life in Lincolnshire, Echard wrote works of geography, travel, translation, and history. His clerical career benefited from the patronage of Archbishop William Wake, and from 1712 he was Archdeacon of Stow. He helped prepare an edition of Camden's *Britannia* (1695), wrote *The Roman History* (1695–1698), and composed a history of the early Christian church, *A General Ecclesiastical History* (1702). Echard was best known for his three-volume *History of England* (1707–1718), a moderate Whig work concerned with documenting the survival of Anglicanism in the face of Catholic and dissenting adversaries. He found much common ground with Tory depictions of King Charles I as a martyr for the Church of England. In fact, readers welcomed both the even-handedness and the attractive literary quality of his narrative compared with his immediate predecessors in the genre of general history, James Tyrrell and Robert Brady. Echard's day in the sun lasted only until 1725, when the English translation of Rapin supplanted his work as the standard history of England, although later historians such as David Hume and Catharine Macaulay continued to use him as an authority.

Philip Hicks

Texts

A General Ecclesiastical History. 2 vols. London: J. Tonson, 1702.
History of England. 3 vols. London: J. Tonson, 1707–1718.
The Roman History. 2 vols. London: M. Gillyflower et al., 1695–1698.

References

Hicks, Philip. *Neoclassical History and English Culture: From Clarendon to Hume.* Basingstoke, Eng.: Macmillan, 1996.
Stephan, Deborah. "Laurence Echard—Whig Historian." *Historical Journal* 32 (1989): 843–866.

Economic History

The study of past production, consumption, distribution, and associated institutions, which are analyzed with the aid of economic theory and its antecedent, political economy.

The intellectual antecedents of economic history in Britain and North America are found in the British tradition of political economy during the eighteenth and nineteenth centuries. Contributors to this tradition debated the economic dimensions of nation building and other public controversies with the aid of historical evidence and particular views about the nature of historical change. The view of history in Adam Smith's *The Wealth of Nations* (1776), for example, highlights the role of human self-interest, the existence and working of markets to achieve efficient outcomes, the contribution to growth of capital accumulation, and the relationship between political and economic power. Smith's conceptualization of long-term change as successive stages in the evolution of productive activity is one of the first explicit statements of economic historical change in the long run. Another landmark contribution to historical political economy was J.E. Thorold Rogers's *Six Centuries of Work and Wages* (1884). In this and other work Rogers assembled an enormous quantity of wage and price data in order to examine rural poverty under the impact of land laws and agricultural improvement.

The dramatic advance of factory production attracted a great deal of interest in nineteenth-century Britain. Studies of individual industries and industrialists were widely read. At Oxford University, Arnold Toynbee's (uncle of the more famous historian of civilizations, Arnold J. Toynbee) *Lectures on the Industrial Revolution in England* (1884) underlined the importance of industrial change and provided the first historical narrative in which economic circumstance evolved of its own internal momentum rather than being dictated by political and legal considerations. The social reform movement of the 1880s adopted Toynbee's concept of the industrial revolution in order to focus attention on the social consequences of industrialization and enclosure (related to industrialization in some accounts). Important contributions to the subsequent debates include Lawrence and Barbara Hammond's *The Village Labourer* (1911) and the great works of R.H. Tawney, including *The Agrarian Problem of the Sixteenth Century* (1912) and *Religion and the Rise of Capitalism* (1926). Of course, not all economic history may be interpreted as a response to the reform impulse; George Unwin's *Industrial Organisation in the Sixteenth and Seventeenth Centuries* (1904) provides a useful example.

University lecturing in historical political economy or economic history during the late nineteenth century quickly led to the preparation of survey texts that helped to define the field, such as W.J. Ashley's *Introduction to English Economic History and Theory* (1888) and William Cunningham's *Growth of English Industry and Commerce* (1882).

Within the university, there was some tendency to construe historical political economy as a subfield of history. At Oxford, for example, the academic home for political economy was the School of Modern History. At Cambridge, papers in economics and economic history were part of the History Tripos (final honors examination).

The emergence of the modern science of economics at the end of the nineteenth century had enormous influence over the subsequent development of historical political economy. A more theoretical approach to political economy that abstracted from historical experience and relied almost exclusively on deductive reasoning had been evolving since the publication of David Ricardo's *Principles of Political Economy and Taxation* (1817). The adoption of differential calculus and the intellectual and institutional leadership of Alfred Marshall greatly strengthened this approach. In 1903 Marshall established at Cambridge for the first time an Economics Tripos. Henceforth, economics would be studied independently of other disciplines. The History Tripos continued to include papers in economic history (and even some theory), but the new economics curriculum excluded economic history unless it was modern and immediately relevant to the study of current economic phenomena. In subsequent decades the science of economics became increasingly innocent of history and of diminishing relevance to the practicing economic historian. Sir John Clapham was more sympathetic to theory than most political economists during the 1880s and 1890s, but his "Of Empty Boxes" in the *Economic Journal* (1922) laments the failure to develop a more useful theory. Shortly thereafter Clapham published his comprehensive *Economic History of Modern Britain* (1926–1938) which made little use of economic theory beyond the basic principles of supply and demand.

Throughout most of the twentieth century British economic history has been a semiautonomous field spanning the two disciplines. From the vantage point of other historians, economic history is distinguished by the application of economic principles and quantitative techniques to institutions and activities deemed to be of economic significance. Many of the most important contributions to economic history are valued in part because they provide an economic dimension to issues of interest to some other field of history. For example, E.A. Wrigley and Roger Schofield's *Population History of England and Wales* (1981) contributes to both demographic and economic history. Charles Wilson's *History of Unilever* (1954)

is both business and economic history. Many of the essays in *The Agrarian History of England and Wales* (b. 1967–) are both agricultural and economic history.

Within economics, economic history is distinguished by its empirical examination of long-run change, the analysis of economic events in their historical and institutional context, and a willingness to investigate economic phenomena even if a comprehensive theoretical explanation is impossible because of the limitations of theory, evidence, or both. Colin Clark's *The Conditions of Economic Progress* (1940) and the many publications of Simon Kuznets, including *Modern Economic Growth* (1966), are seminal contributions using the categories of national income analysis. Important work on the British economy in this tradition includes Nick Crafts' *British Economic Growth during the Industrial Revolution* (1985) and R.C.O. Matthews, et al., *British Economic Growth, 1856–1973* (1982). The recent publication of R.C. Allen's *Enclosure and the Yeomen* (1992) and Jeffrey Williamson's *Did British Capitalism Breed Inequality?* (1985) demonstrates that new contributions to old topics continue to raise controversy.

The topic in British economic history with the most enduring appeal remains the industrial revolution. T.S. Ashton's *Iron and Steel in the Industrial Revolution* (1924) and *The Industrial Revolution* (1948) are still widely read. Scholars in other countries have made outstanding contributions, as evidenced by Paul Mantoux's *The Industrial Revolution in the Eighteenth Century* (1928) and David Landes's *The Unbound Prometheus* (1969). The topic remains important among historians in large part out of concern for the social consequences of industrialization and urbanization. Economists are fascinated by the British industrial revolution as an example of technological change apparently permitting an escape from the constraint of limited resources and leading to an acceleration of economic growth. Most recently there has been considerable debate in the pages of the *Economic History Review* about the timing and nature of the industrial revolution and the extent to which it may be regarded as an abrupt and/or profound change in the British economy.

The study of economic history in North America began at roughly the same time as in Britain, but the field has developed along somewhat different lines. W.J. Ashley took up the chair of political economy and constitutional history at the University of Toronto in 1888; four years later he accepted the first chair of economic history in the English-speaking world, at Harvard University. Issues central to the British literature including land distribution, industrialization, and poverty have attracted less attention in North America, perhaps not surprisingly on a high-income continent with easily available freehold land. Another difference arose because North American governments very early developed an ambitious state data-gathering system, which has provided ready fuel for the fires of quantitative history. A strong revival in the economic approach to economic history, or cliometrics, has been possible since the 1950s in part because historical economists have been able to use a considerable amount of quantitative evidence collected by American and Canadian governments.

A variety of organizing concepts with an economic dimension have been used to interpret North American history. Douglass North's *Economic Growth of the United States* (1961) emphasizes the role of exports. Technology is the central theme of Nathan Rosenberg's *Technology and American Growth* (1972). Harold Innis examined the interaction between technology and resources in his *Essays in Canadian Economic History* (1956), as does Sir John Habakkuk in his *American and British Technology in the Nineteenth Century* (1962). Lance Davis and Douglass North explore the interaction between institutional evolution and economic activity in *Institutional Change and American Economic Growth* (1971). The great size of the North American continent directs particular attention at transportation systems and internal trade, on which Robert Fogel's *Railroads and American Economic Growth* (1964) is a particularly important, though controversial, contribution.

The size of the North American economy also creates a natural respect for regional differentiation, first documented for the nineteenth century by Richard Easterlin in his "Interregional Differences," which appeared in the *Studies in Income and Wealth* series (1960). John McCallum's *Unequal Beginnings: Agriculture and Economic Development in Quebec and Ontario until 1870* (1980) is one of many works to argue that regional differences originate with the nature of local agriculture. Agriculture in the Southern United States was heavily influenced by the use of slave labor before the Civil War and by the subsequent adjustment to abolition. Gavin Wright's *Old South, New South* (1986), Roger Ransom and Richard Sutch's *One Kind of Freedom* (1977), and Robert Fogel's *Without Consent or Contract* (1989) are distinguished contributions to a long line of economic historical treatments of the Southern economy. Jeremy Atack and Fred Bateman's *To Their Own Soil: Agriculture*

in the Antebellum North (1987) is the most useful survey of Northern agriculture. The terms on which land was acquired are a more specialized but important topic examined in Alan Bogue's *Money at Interest* (1955), Paul Gates's *Land Policy and Tenancy* (1973), and Robert Swierenga's *Pioneers and Profits* (1968).

The single most comprehensive overview of the North American manufacturing sector remains Victor Clark's *History of Manufactures* (1929). Outstanding studies of individual industries include Phillip Scranton's *Proprietary Capitalism* (1983), from the history side of the field, and Peter Temin's *Iron and Steel in Nineteenth-Century America* (1964), from the economics side of the field. The large size of business enterprise in the United States attracts a great deal of attention; Alfred D. Chandler Jr.'s *The Visible Hand* (1977) situates the rise of American big business in the long-term evolution of management strategy, corporate structure, and technological change. F.W. Taussig's *Tariff History of the United States* (1914) and John Dales's *The Protective Tariff in Canada's Development* (1966) provide overviews of tariff development in the two countries.

Stanley Lebergott's *Manpower in Economic Growth* (1964) remains an influential monograph on employment and the labor force; Brinley Thomas's *Migration and Economic Growth* (1954) contributes an important international context. Richard Easterlin's "Population Change and Farm Settlement," published in the *Journal of Economic History* (1976), demonstrates the adaptation of demographic behavior to land availability. Women in the labor market are considered by Claudia Goldin in her *Understanding the Gender Gap* (1990). The analysis of unemployment during the Great Depression of the 1930s remains the subject of considerable debate. Milton Friedman and Anna Schwartz give a monetary view in *Monetary History of the United States* (1963); an alternative view emphasizing movements in the demand (rather than supply) for money is taken by various authors including Peter Temin in his *Did Monetary Forces Cause the Great Depression?* (1976). Continued analysis of the Great Depression and other topics in economic history is summarized in the various essays collected together in Alexander Field's *The Future of Economic History* (1987).

Kris Inwood

See also BUSINESS HISTORY; CAPITALISM; CLIOMETRICS; DEMOGRAPHY—HISTORICAL; INDUSTRIAL REVOLUTION; RURAL HISTORY; URBAN HISTORY.

Texts

Atack, Jeremy, and Peter Passell. *A New Economic View of American Life.* Second ed. New York: Norton, 1994.

Crafts, N.F.R. *British Economic Growth during the Industrial Revolution.* London: Oxford University Press, 1985.

Davis, Ralph. *The Rise of the Atlantic Economies.* London: Weidenfeld and Nicolson, 1973.

Floud, Roderick, and Donald McCloskey, eds. *The Economic History of Britain since 1700.* Second ed. Cambridge, Eng.: Cambridge University Press, 1994.

Foreman-Peck, James. *A History of the World Economy.* Second ed. Hemel Hempstead, England: Harvester Wheatsheaf, 1995.

Hughes, Jonathon, and Louis Cain. *American Economic History.* Fourth ed. New York: HarperCollins, 1994.

Matthews, R.C.O., C.H. Feinstein, and J.C. Odling-Smee. *British Economic Growth, 1856–1973.* Oxford: Oxford University Press, 1982.

Norrie, Kenneth, and Douglas Owram. *A History of the Canadian Economy.* Second ed. Toronto: Harcourt Brace, 1996.

References

Berg, Maxine. "The First Women Economic Historians." *Economic History Review* 45 (1992): 308–329.

Coleman, D.C. *History and the Economic Past.* Oxford: Clarendon Press, 1987.

Field, Alexander, ed. *The Future of Economic History.* Boston: Kluwer-Nijhof, 1987.

Fogel, Robert, and Geoffrey Elton. *Which Road to the Past?* New Haven, CT: Yale University Press, 1983.

Harte, N.B., ed. *The Study of Economic History.* London: Frank Cass, 1971.

Hartwell, R.M. "Good Old Economic History." *Journal of Economic History* 33 (1973): 28–40.

Kadish, Alon. *Historians, Economists and Economic History.* London: Routledge, 1989.

McCloskey, Donald. *Econometric History.* London, Macmillan, 1987.

Education, Modern History of

Educational history from national visions to international comparisons and a recognition of complexity. As Bernard Bailyn noted for the United States in 1960, early educational history was usually inspirational in tone. While the British waxed eloquent over the rise of England's great universities or public schools for elite boys, Americans enthused about social improvement through free, coeducational schooling for all. In former British colonies, the development of state schooling was hailed as the natural accompaniment of parliamentary democracy. Institutional histories lacked context and often ignored topics like the education of minorities or women. Exceptional studies treating the education of groups whose education was different because of their class, gender, race, religion, or ethnicity, remained uncritically optimistic: women, aboriginals, and other minorities were ennobled and enabled by an education that was always beneficial.

A more critical history of education dates from the 1960s. In Great Britain, historians began to challenge an educational history that had been complacent about class. Brian Simon, Harold Silver, Peter Searby, Lawrence Stone, and Philip Corrigan were among those who revealed an evolving national educational system that was class-biased both in intention and execution. In the United States, Carl Kaestle, Clarence Karier, Michael Katz, David Tyack, and Lawrence Veysey led revisionist historians whose work exposed class, ethnic, and racial discrimination in educational politics, showing who benefited (and who did not) from the "reform" of school systems and higher education. Critics of this work, however, accused revisionists of replacing unbounded optimism with undue pessimism about education.

Former British colonies, whose historians remained on the scholarly margins, were slower to develop critical studies. But their very marginality encouraged Canadian and Australian historians, for example, to look at different models and ask new questions. Following the work of Susan Houston and Alison Prentice on the class dynamics of nineteenth-century Upper Canadian education, Bruce Curtis wondered why Canada and Ireland were quicker to develop centralized school systems than the imperial center itself and showed how the disciplines of state schooling penetrated political consciousness and altered behavior. Paul Axelrod, Jean Barman, Nadia Fahmy-Eid, Chad Gaffield, R.D. Gidney, W.J.P. Millar, Neil Sutherland, Brian Titley, Michael Welton, and Donald Wilson were among the Canadians who participated in an international quest to integrate the history of minority, religious, private, and secondary schools, colleges, universities, professional schools, and education for adults into developing interpretive schemes, often altering these schemes in the process.

Australians, too, contributed new perspectives. While North American historians had explored the feminization of teaching, Noeline Kyle demonstrated that men retained their predominance among teachers longer in Australia. Where North American teacher associations had been seen as localized and initially rather weak, Australian Andrew Spaull told the histories of more vibrant teacher-union movements. Ian Davey explored the microhistory of working-class schooling, using methods he had developed with Michael Katz in Canada. Following Joan Burstyn, Geraldine Clifford, Patricia Palmieri, and Maxine Seller on obstacles facing British and American women in education, Ailsa Zainu'ddin, Marjorie Theobald, and Alison Mackinnon exposed forgotten women's colleges and schools, their dynamic teachers, the problems Australian women students and teachers encountered, and the connections between the higher education of women and fertility decline. Pavla Miller provided a synthesis, drawing on work in many countries, and elaborating the ways in which class, ethnicity, and gender relations were always implicated in modern, Western educational development.

European studies have been important as well. Well known beyond the borders of France were the writings of Jacques and Mona Ozouf on French teachers and primary education; the more recent work of Pierre Bourdieu on elite formation has been even more influential. Among those writing about French education in English, Patrick Harrigan and Jo Burr Margadant have contributed intriguing perspectives on mobility and elite education and the first generation of women *professeures,* respectively. Similar themes have been explored in the Swedish context by Christina Florin, in the Russian by Christine Johanson, and for German education, by Peter Lundgren and Konrad Jarusch, among others. And fascinating new work is also emerging as historians of Asia and Africa become interested in the implications of educational change in the nations and regions they study.

Once isolated from the mainstream, historians of education now strive to see the educational past more complexly. They probe the multiple identities of teachers and taught, and probe schools' relationships to families, local communities, church, and state, asking questions that are relevant to their time and place, as well as to their gender, race, ethnicity, or class. Their work often reaches beyond national and regional boundaries. The result is not necessarily agreement; it is, however, more true to life—and more interesting—than earlier histories in which the politics were largely hidden.

Alison Prentice

References

Butchart, Ronald E. "'Outthinking and Outflanking the Owners of the World': A Historiography of the African American Struggle for Education." *History of Education Quarterly* 28 (1988): 333–366.

Dumont, Micheline et Nadia Fahmy-Eid. "La pointe de l'iceberg: L'histoire de l'éducation et l'histoire de l'éducation des filles au Québec [The Tip of the Iceberg: The History of Education and the History of Girls' Education in Quebec]." *Historical Studies in Education/Revue d'histoire de l'éducation* 3 (1991): 211–236.

Gaffield, Chad. "Children, Schooling, and Family Reproduction in Nineteenth-Century Ontario." *Canadian Historical Review* 72 (1991): 157–191.

Goodenow, Ronald K., and William E. Marsden, eds. *The City and Education in Four Nations.* Cambridge, Eng.: Cambridge University Press, 1992.

Grew, Raymond, and Patrick Harrigan. *School, State, and Society: The Growth of Elementary Schooling in Nineteenth-Century France—a Quantitative Analysis.* Ann Arbor: University of Michigan Press, 1991.

Mackinnon, Alison. "Male Heads on Female Shoulders? New Questions for the History of Women's Higher Education." *History of Education Review* 19 (1990): 36–47.

Miller, Pavla. "Education and the State: The Uses of Marxist and Feminist Approaches in the Writing of Histories of Schooling." *Historical Studies in Education/revue d'histoire de l'éducation* 1 (1989): 283–306.

———. "Historiography of Compulsory Schooling: What Is the Problem?" *History of Education* 18 (1989): 123–144.

Prentice, Alison, and Marjorie R. Theobald, eds. *Women Who Taught: Perspectives on the History of Women and Teaching.* Toronto: University of Toronto Press, 1991.

Theobald, Marjorie R., and R.J.W. Selleck. *Family, School & State in Australian History.* Sydney: Allen & Unwin, 1990.

Urban, Wayne J. "New Directions in the Historical Study of Teacher Unionism." *Historical Studies in Education/Revue d'histoire de l'éducation* 2 (1990): 1–15.

Warren, Donald, ed. *American Teachers: Histories of a Profession at Work.* New York: Macmillan Publishing Company, 1989.

Wilson, J. Donald, ed. *An Imperfect Past: Education and Society in Canadian History.* Vancouver: Centre for the Study of Curriculum and Instruction, University of British Columbia, 1984.

E

Eichhorn, Karl Friedrich (1781–1854)

German legal historian. Eichhorn was born in Jena, the son of the well-known theologian and orientalist, Johann Georg Eichhorn. In 1797 he began to study law at Göttingen University, earning his doctorate in 1803 and habilitating in 1805. From 1805 he taught in Frankfurt/Oder, before moving in 1811 to the University of Berlin, which had been founded the year before. At Berlin he lectured on legal history along with Friedrich Carl von Savigny. In 1817 he returned to Göttingen, but in 1829 left the teaching profession and briefly retired. In 1831, however, he returned to the University of Berlin, where he taught state and church law. In 1834 he gave up his chair in order to devote his time to political activity as a member of the *Geheimes Obertribunal* (High Secret Tribunal) and the *Staatsrat* (Council of State), before retreating once more into private life, this time for good. Together with Savigny, Eichhorn edited the *Zeitschrift für geschichtliches Recht* [Journal for the Historical Study of Law]. Eichhorn is regarded, along with Savigny, as the founder of the "Historical school of law" that gave practical jurisprudence a historical basis. His contemporary reputation was established by three books. The *Deutsche Staats- und Rechtsgeschichte* [German Constitutional and Legal History] (1808) is now regarded as his most important work and a milestone in the development of legal history. In it he described the historical development of German constitutional law and the sources of the law, as well as civil, criminal, and procedural law. In his *Einleitung in das deutsche Privatrecht mit Einschluss des Lehenrechts* [Introduction to German Private Law, Including Feudal Law] (1823) Eichhorn attempted a scientific description of German law in its totality; venturing beyond particular legal traditions that were generally studied in isolation from one another, he tried to make connections between feudal law and other legal systems. Finally, he produced a fundamental work on ecclesiastical law in the two volumes of his *Grundsätze des Kirchenrechts* [Principles of Church Law] (1831–1835).

Thomas Fuchs

Texts

Deutsche Staats- und Rechtsgeschichte. Fourth ed. 4 vols. Göttingen: Vandenhoeck & Ruprecht, 1834–1836.
Einleitung in das deutsche Privatrecht mit Einschluss des Lehenrechts. Fifth ed. Göttingen: Vandenhoeck & Ruprecht, 1845.

Grundsätze des Kirchenrechts der Katholischen und der Evangelischen Religionspartei in Deutschland. 2 vols. Göttingen: Vandenhoeck & Ruprecht, 1831–1833.

References

Gooch, G.P. *History and Historians in the Nineteenth Century.* Third ed. New York: Peter Smith, 1949.
Jelusic, K. *Die historische Methode Karl Friedrich Eichhorns* [The Historical Method of Karl Friedrich Eichhorn]. Baden: R.M. Rohrer, 1936.

Einhard [Eginhard] (ca. 775–840)

Frankish historian and hagiographer. Born in the eastern Frankish region, Einhard was educated at the monastery of Fulda. From 794, he studied with Alcuin (d. 804) at the palace school of Charlemagne. Artistically endowed, he supervised architectural projects at the imperial court. Charlemagne also entrusted Einhard with a mission to assure papal approval of the empire's division (806). In exchange for tutoring his son Lothar, Louis the Pious (d. 840) granted Einhard monasteries in Ghent, Maastricht, Fontanelle, Paris, Pavia, and Fritzlar. After unsuccessful efforts to quell conflicts among Louis's sons, he retreated from political life and entered the monastery of Seligenstadt with his wife in 830, dying there a decade later. Einhard's religious writing included the *Translatio et Miracula SS. Marcellini et Petri* [The Translation and Miracles of Sts. Marcellinus and Peter] (ca. 830), composed on the occasion of the relics' transfer to his lands at Mülheim, where he would thereafter build a church. Sixty-six of Einhard's letters also survive. Most significant, however, was his *Vita Caroli Magni* [The Life of Charlemagne] (830s), a secular biography modeled largely on Suetonius. Einhard provided therein a firsthand and highly popular account of the emperor's accomplishments, a reign which he considered more laudable than that of Louis the Pious.

Bonnie Effros

Texts

"The Letters of Einhard," and "The Translation and Miracles of the Saints Marcellinus and Peter." In *Carolingian Civilization: A Reader*, ed. Paul Edward Dutton. Peterborough, Ontario: Broadview Press, 1993, 198–246; 283–310.
The Life of Charlemagne. Trans. Evelyn Scherabon Firchow and Edwin H. Zeydel. Coral Gables, FL: University of Miami Press, 1972.

References

Beumann, Helmut. *Ideengeschichtliche Studien zu Einhard und anderen Geschichtsschreibern des früheren Mittelalters* [Intellectual History Studies of Einhard and Other Historians of the Early Middle Ages]. Darmstadt: Wissenschaftliche Buchgesellschaft, 1962.

Ganshof, François L. "Eginhard, biographe de Charlemagne" [Einhard, Biographer of Charlemagne]. *Bibliothèque d'humanisme et Renaissance* 13 (1961): 217–230.

Eisenstein, Elizabeth Lewisohn (b. 1923–)

American historian of the development of print culture in early modern Europe. Turning from an initial interest in the French Revolution, Eisenstein devoted her research during the 1960s and 1970s to the cultural and intellectual impact of the invention of printing in western Europe. This resulted in her best-known work, *The Printing Press As an Agent of Change: Communications and Cultural Transformations in Early-Modern Europe* (1979). Maintaining that the importance of printing had been underestimated, she argued that the use of the press was a crucial agent of change in the transition from medieval to modern Western culture. She explored the revolutionary impact of the new communications technology in three areas: the Renaissance, the Reformation, and the scientific revolution. While receiving much attention from scholars and the reading public, Eisenstein's work has been criticized for its polemical tone, its excessive length, and its heavy reliance on secondary sources. It has, nevertheless, established itself as a seminal work in the history of the book and of print culture, two areas that have grown enormously in the 1980s and 1990s.

James V. Mehl

Texts

The First Professional Revolutionist: Filippo Michele Buonarroti, 1761–1837: A Biographical Essay. Cambridge, MA: Harvard University Press, 1959.

Grub Street Abroad: Aspects of the French Cosmopolitan Press from the Age of Louis XIV to the French Revolution. Oxford: Clarendon Press, 1992.

The Printing Press As an Agent of Change: Communications and Cultural Transformations in Early-Modern Europe. 2 vols. Cambridge, Eng.: Cambridge University Press, 1979.

The Printing Revolution in Early Modern Europe (abridged version of last item). Cambridge, Eng.: Cambridge University Press, 1983.

References

Who's Who in America 1997. New Providence, NJ: Reed Elsevier, 1996, vol. 2, 1200

Eliade, Mircea (1907–1986)

Romanian novelist and historian of religions. Eliade was born in Bucharest where he began his studies, and which he completed in Rome and Calcutta between 1928 and 1931. He lectured for a time at several European universities such as Bucharest, Rome, and Paris and then became, during World War II, a member of Romania's diplomatic legations in London (1940) and Lisbon (1941–1944). In 1945, he moved to Paris and then, in 1956, to the United States, where he became a professor of the history of religions at the University of Chicago. In 1959 he edited, with Ernst Jünger, the journal *Antaïos,* and in 1961 he founded a new international journal, *The History of Religions.* He was awarded honorary doctorates by several universities and was editor in chief of *The Encyclopaedia of Religion.* At the time of his death he had achieved a global reputation as a writer and an expert in religion studies. The American Academy of Religion formally declared him to have been the single most influential scholar of comparative religion in the twentieth century.

Eliade studied religious phenomena with the intention of writing an authoritative history of religions. His *Traité d'histoire des religions* (later translated as *Patterns in Comparative Religion*), first published in 1949, was both an exploratory study for this project and a pioneering work in the study of comparative religion. After making a number of further contributions to this field, he published his important synthesis of religious history, the *Histoire des croyances et des idées religieuses* (later translated as *A History of Religious Ideas*). This work had a long gestation, being the mature expression of ideas he had first developed while teaching successive courses in the history of religions at Bucharest University (1933–1938), in Paris at the École des Hautes Études (1946–1948), and, finally, at Chicago. The book is shaped by a vast erudition ordered by an encyclopedic mind. Its most important contribution lies in Eliade's ability to consider religious phenomena as an expression of the human spirit and intellect in various ages, in the perspective of the profound unity of human mind, and from this to represent the historically complex relationship between the "sacred" and the "profane." Moreover, his history stimulated interdisciplinary interest in religion, drawing as it did on anthropology, archaeology, and psychology. Eliade considered

E

himself both a historian and a phenomenologist, highly sensitive to both historical evidence and problems of hermeneutics. His corpus of works, including his fundamental study of primitive religions and outstanding monograph, *Shamanism,* unquestionably represents an important contribution toward the development of the history of religions, but its significance has been debated by scholars in the field, some of whom consider him to have been the century's greatest authority on the subject, while others deem his views to have been "antihistorical" in the sense of being insufficiently attentive to the differing social and cultural contexts within which religious beliefs occur.

S. Lemny

Texts

Autobiography. Trans. Mac Linscott Ricketts. 2 vols. San Francisco: Harper and Row, 1981–1988.

Cosmos and History: The Myth of the Eternal Return. Trans. Willard R. Trask. New York: Harper, 1959.

From Primitives to Zen: A Thematic Sourcebook of the History of Religions. New York: Harper and Row, 1967.

A History of Religious Ideas. Trans. Willard R. Trask. 3 vols. Chicago: University of Chicago Press, 1978–1985.

Patterns in Comparative Religion. London: Sheed and Ward, 1979.

The Quest: History and Meaning in Religion. Chicago: University of Chicago Press, 1984.

Shamanism: Archaic Techniques of Ecstacy. Trans. Willard R. Trask. Revised ed. London: Routledge and Kegan Paul, 1964.

References

Allen, Douglas, and Dennis Doeing. *Mircea Eliade: An Annotated Bibliography.* New York: Garland, 1980.

Altizer, Thomas J.J. *Mircea Eliade and the Dialectic of the Sacred.* Westport, CT: Greenwood Press, 1975.

Dudley, Guilford, III. *Religion on Trial: Mircea Eliade and his Critics.* Philadelphia: Temple University Press, 1977.

Ricketts, Mac Linscott. *Mircea Eliade: The Romanian roots, 1907–1945.* 2 vols. New York: Columbia University Press, 1988.

Elias, Norbert (1897–1990)

German sociologist. Elias studied medicine, philosophy, and psychology at the universities of Breslau and Heidelberg, became assistant to Karl Mannheim in Frankfurt (1930), finished his habilitation in 1933, and fled Hitler's Germany in the same year. In 1938 he moved from Paris to London. After World War II he taught at the University of Leicester (1954–1962) before becoming briefly a professor at the University of Ghana (1962–1964). He returned to Germany as a visiting professor at the Zentrum für Interdisziplinäre Forschung in Bielefeld, but lived in Amsterdam. Elias was the most influential sociologist of his generation. Influenced by Mannheim, Sigmund Freud, and Max Weber, he developed his own original theories of the interpenetration of individuals with their society known as figurational sociology. He argued that individuals have no nonsocial identity. A person's deepest emotions are influenced by the very fluid and unpredictable social figurations they establish with other people, and it is within these figurations that the increase in human knowledge takes place. Elias's reputation rests largely on his magnum opus *The Civilizing Process,* first published in German in 1939, but only widely assimilated when it was reprinted and translated into several languages thirty years later. In it Elias defined the development that led to the civilizing process as the "social constraint towards self-constraint." He claimed that minor processes like the gradual change of table manners over the centuries are in fact significant for understanding major political and social trends in the Western world. Elias was able to relate historical structures to historical processes and change, and was thus highly regarded by the historians of the Annales school.

Klaus Larres

Texts

The Civilizing Process. Trans. E. Jephcott. Oxford: Blackwell, 1994.

The Court Society. Trans. E. Jephcott. Oxford: Blackwell, 1983.

Reflections on a Life. Trans. E. Jephcott. Cambridge, Eng.: Polity Press, 1994.

What Is Sociology? Trans. Stephen Mennell and Grace Morrissey. New York: Columbia University Press, 1978.

References

Duindam, J.F.J. *Myths of Power: Norbert Elias and the Early Modern Court.* Amsterdam: Amsterdam University Press, 1995.

Gleichmann, P., ed. *Macht und Zivilisation* [Power and Civilization]. Frankfurt am Main: Suhrkamp, 1984.

———, ed. *Materialien zu Norbert Elias' Zivilisationstheorie* [Materials Concerning

Norbert Elias's Theory of Civilization].
Frankfurt am Main: Suhrkamp, 1979.

Gouldsblom, J. *Sociology in the Balance.* New York: Columbia University Press, 1977.

Mennel, S. *Norbert Elias, Civilisation and the Human Self-Image.* Oxford: Blackwell, 1989.

Rehberg, K.S. "Norbert Elias: Ein Etablierter Aussenseiter [Norbert Elias: An Establishment Outsider]" In *Merkur-Deutsche Zeitschrift für europäisches Denken* [German Journal for European Thought] 46 (1992): 348–353.

Elkins, Stanley Maurice (b. 1925)

American historian. Elkins was born in Boston, Massachusetts. After military service from 1943 to 1946, he graduated from Harvard University and Columbia (M.A. 1951, Ph.D. 1959), having studied under Richard Hoftstadter. During this period he taught at the Fieldstone School in New York City from 1951 through 1954. Elkins began his college teaching career as an assistant professor of history at the University of Chicago in 1955. He moved to Smith College in 1960 and became professor of history in 1964. In 1969, Elkins was named Syndenham Clark Parson Professor of History. He has received several fellowships from such organizations as the Rockefeller Foundation (1954–1955), the Social Science Research Council (1963–1964), the Institute for Advanced Study (1970–1971, 1976–1977), and the Guggenheim Foundation (1976–1977). He served as president of the New England American Studies Association from 1968 through 1969. Elkins's first major publication was *Slavery: A Problem in American Institutional and Intellectual Life* (1968). He has collaborated with Eric McKitrick on such works as *The Hofstadter Aegis: A Memorial* (1974) and *The Age of Federalism* (1993).

Judith Boyce DeMark

Texts

And Eric McKitrick. *The Age of Federalism.* New York: Oxford University Press, 1993.

Ed., with Eric McKitrick. *The Hofstadter Aegis: A Memorial.* New York: Knopf, 1974.

Slavery: A Problem in American Institutional and Intellectual Life. Third ed. Chicago: University of Chicago Press, 1976.

References

Novick, Peter. *That Noble Dream: The "Objectivity Question" and the American Historical Profession.* Cambridge, Eng.: Cambridge University Press, 1988.

Ellet, Elizabeth Fries Lummis (1812–1877)

American writer, poet, and historian. Elizabeth Lummis was born at Sodus Point, New York. In the mid-1830s, she married William Henry Ellet, a chemist and academician. After her marriage, she and her husband lived in South Carolina where William was a chemistry professor. During the years in the South, Elizabeth wrote and published several books, essays, and poems. Her first publication was an anonymous translation of Silvio Pellico's *Euphemio of Messina* (1834). She then published *Poems, Translated and Original* (1835). The couple moved to New York in 1848, where William Ellet worked as a chemical consultant at Manhattan Gas Company. For several years, Elizabeth Ellet contributed articles to such journals as *Saturday Evening Post* and continued writing books, including *Summer Rambles in the West* (1853) and *The Practical Housekeeper* (1857). She died of Bright's Disease in New York City in 1877. Although her earliest writings have been described as being filled with rumor and innuendo, Ellet's focus and style matured. Her greatest significance is her pioneering contribution to women's history, beginning with the three-volume *Women of the American Revolution* (1848–1850) and *Domestic History of the American Revolution* (1850). Ellet continued her study of women's history in *The Pioneer Women of the West* (1852).

Judith Boyce DeMark

Texts

Domestic History of the American Revolution. New York: Baker and Scribner, 1850.

The Eminent and Heroic Women of America. New York: Arno, 1974.

The Pioneer Women of the West. Philadelphia: H.T. Coates, 1852.

The Women of the American Revolution. 3 vols. New York: Baker and Scriber, 1848–1850.

References

Griswold, Rufus Wilmot. *The Female Poets of America.* Philadelphia: Carey and Hart, 1849.

Moss, Sidney D. *Poe's Literary Battles.* Cherry Hill, NJ: Arcturus Books Paperbacks, 1963.

Elliot, Henry Miers (1808–1853)

English civil servant, historian, editor, and translator. Elliot was educated at Winchester College from the age of ten. Nine years later, he passed an open examination for an immediate civil appointment to India. After holding a succession of minor

E

posts, Elliot became foreign secretary to the governor-general in 1847. He died on his way home, at Simon's Town, South Africa.

Elliot's reputation rests mainly on his work entitled *History of India As Told by Its Historians*. However, this work was edited by another English Orientalist, John Dowson (1820–1881), and published posthumously in eight large volumes between 1867 and 1877. These volumes, as their title indicates, were substantial translations of Arabic and Persian sources on the history of medieval India under Islamic rule. Elliot's translated extracts and annotations remained for decades a standard reference on the history of medieval India. However, they have recently come under concerted criticism by both Indian and Western scholars, for their excessive concentration on political intrigues, court policies, and factional strife. Consequently, it has been demonstrated that Elliot's purpose was to attempt to contrast the chaotic nature of political life in medieval India with that of British rule and its orderly rational character. Despite his patient labors as a meticulous scholar, Elliot had a very low opinion of his sources, so much so that he declined to style them histories or consider their authors as historians. Nevertheless, the range of Elliot's translations included the most illustrious geographers and historians of medieval Islamic civilization.

Y. Choueiri

Texts

Elliot, H.M. *The History of India As Told by Its Own Historians*. Ed. John Dowson, 8 vols. London: Trubner, 1867–1877. Second ed. Calcutta: Susil Gupta (India) Ltd., 1952.

Nizami, Khaliq Ahmed. *Supplement to Elliot and Dowson's History of India*. Vol. II, *Ghaznavids and the Ghurids*. Delhi: Idarah-1 Adabiyat-I, Delli, 1981.

References

Philips, C.H. "James Mill, Mountstuart Elphinstone, and the History of India." In *Historians of India, Pakistan and Ceylon*, ed. C.H. Philips. London: Oxford University Press, 1962, 217–229.

Elphinstone, Mountstuart (1779–1859)

British historian and administrator for the East India Company. Educated at the High School, Edinburgh, and Kensington, Elphinstone subsequently educated himself. He went to India as a "writer" in 1795, serving in Benares. In 1801 he

was sent to the Bombay province, where he became a British resident, but was then sent on a mission to Afghanistan; during this mission he wrote his *Account of the Kingdom of Caubul* (1815). He retired as governor of Bombay at the age of forty-eight in 1827 and twice turned down the office of governor-general of India. Elphinstone was the author of *History of India* (1841), which dealt with the country's past up to the British period. His *Rise of British Power in the East* was intended to replace James Mill's unsympathetic multivolume *History of India;* but Elphinstone's work was never finished, the revolt of 1857 having changed the public mood to so great a degree that a sympathetic history of India would have been unwelcome. It was, however, published posthumously in 1887.

Roger D. Long

Texts

Account of the Kingdom of Caubul. Karachi, Pakistan: Oxford University Press, 1972.
History of India. London: John Murray, 1841.
The Rise of British Power in the East. London: John Murray, 1887.

References

Choksey, R.D. *Mountstuart Elphinstone: The Indian Years, 1796–1827*. Bombay: Popular Prakashan, 1971.
Forrest, G.W. *Selections from the Minutes and Other Official Writings of the Honourable Mountstuart Elphinstone, Governor of Bombay*. London: R. Bentley, 1884.

Elton, Sir Geoffrey Rudolph (1921–1994)

Naturalized English historian. Born in Germany and educated in Prague, Elton was the son of a distinguished classical scholar, Victor Ehrenberg, who fled with his family from the Nazis in 1939. While teaching in a private school in North Wales, Elton took a University of London degree by correspondence course. After war service—during which the army made him change his name from Ehrenberg—Elton took British citizenship and researched for his doctorate under Sir John Neale at the University of London. He spent virtually his entire academic career at the University of Cambridge, becoming professor of English constitutional history in 1967 and Regius professor in 1983. He was knighted in 1986. Famous chiefly as a historian of the period of the English Reformation, Elton's first book in 1953 on Thomas Cromwell's statecraft was entitled *The Tudor Revolution in Government*. Other studies of the Cromwellian period followed—

Policy and Police (1972) and Reform and Renewal (1973)—as well as a number of successful textbooks on sixteenth-century England and Reformation Europe. Four volumes of his collected essays appeared between 1974 and 1992, and in 1986 his revisionist account of *The Parliament of England, 1559–81* attacked Neale's interpretation of that subject. Elton's interest in historiography—usually taking the form of a defense of traditional values—was expressed in such publications as *The Practice of History* (1967), *Political History: Principles and Practice* (1970), and *Return to Essentials* (1991). Elton was president of the Royal Historical Society (1972–1976) and founded for that society a series of annual bibliographies of new publications and a monograph series, *Studies in History.*

R.C. Richardson

Texts

The English. Oxford, Eng.: Blackwell, 1992.

The Parliament of England, 1559–81. Cambridge, Eng.: Cambridge University Press, 1986.

Policy and Police. Cambridge, Eng.: Cambridge University Press, 1953.

Political History: Principles and Practice. New York: Basic Books, 1970.

The Practice of History. London: Methuen, 1967.

Reform and Renewal: Thomas Cromwell and the Common Weal. Cambridge, Eng.: Cambridge University Press, 1973.

Return to Essentials. Cambridge, Eng.: Cambridge University Press, 1991.

The Tudor Constitution. Second ed. Cambridge, Eng.: Cambridge University Press, 1982.

The Tudor Revolution in Government. Cambridge, Eng.: Cambridge University Press, 1953.

References

Beer, Barrett L. "G.R. Elton: Tudor Champion." In *Recent Historians of Great Britain: Essays on the Post-1945 Generation,* ed. W.L. Arnstein. Ames: Iowa State University Press, 1990, 13–35.

Kenyon, J.P. *The History Men: The Historical Profession in England since the Renaissance.* Second ed. London: Weidenfeld, 1993.

Emili, Paolo (ca. 1460–1529)

Italian historian. Emili was born in Verona and came to Paris about 1484, where he became a leading humanist, and until his death served three kings as a confidant and official historiographer. After writing several preparatory manuscripts such as the *Gallica antiquitas* [Antiquities

of the Gauls] (1488), Emili published *De rebus gestis Francorum* [Of the Deeds of the French] (1516–1520) in nine books; a tenth book was completed by a relative and the entire work published in 1539, a decade after the author's death. Emili consciously adapted the French tradition to his Livian standards and integrated it into a broader vision of western European history, which was well received by his contemporaries and throughout the rest of the sixteenth century, as its many reprints and translations testify.

Thomas Maissen

Texts

De rebus gestis Francorum. Paris: Vascosan, 1539.

References

Cochrane, Eric. *Historians and Historiography in the Italian Renaissance.* Chicago: University of Chicago Press, 1981, 345–348.

Davies, Katharine. *Late XVth Century French Historiography, as Exemplified in...Paulus Aemilius.* Ph.D. dissertation, Edinburgh University, 1954.

Maissen, Thomas. *Von der Legende zum Modell: Das Interesse an Frankreichs Vergangenheit in der italienischen Renaissance* [From Myth to Model: The Interest in the French Past during the Italian Renaissance]. Basel, Switzerland: Helbing und Lichtenhahn, 1994, 176–210.

Encina, Francisco Antonio (1874–1965)

Chilean historian. The most prominent Chilean historian of the twentieth century, Encina was the author of a monumental history of his country, the *Historia de Chile desde la prehistoria hasta 1891* [History of Chile from Prehistory to 1891], published in twenty volumes from 1940 to 1952. Trained as a lawyer, Encina was a nonacademic historian who eschewed the liberal ideology and anti-Hispanicism of nineteenth-century Chilean historiography. He differentiated between the historical researcher and the historian proper, who, because of his intuition, was capable of writing interpretive works of historical synthesis. Despite his xenophobia and pronounced racism, Encina made a significant contribution to the understanding of Chilean history, changing the way Chileans understood their national past. The last half of the work, nearly ten volumes, deals with the rise and fall of the *estado portaliano*—the conservative regime headed by Diego Portales, which favored the oligarchical interests of the great landlords and merchants—from 1830 to 1891. It is Encina's major contribution as it offers a revisionist interpretation of nineteenth-century Chilean history. During this period, and starting with Portales, enlightened strong men had provided order and progress, making possible the improvement of administration, the development of education and public services, and significant economic gains, thereby arousing the envy of Chile's South American neighbors.

George L. Vásquez

Texts
Historia de Chile desde la prehistoria hasta 1891. 20 vols. Santiago de Chile: Editorial Nacimiento, 1950–1952.

References
Acevedo, Edberto Oscar. *Manual de historiografía hispanoamericana contemporánea* [Manual of Contemporary Latin-American Historiography]. Mendoza, Argentina: Editorial de la Facultad de Filosofía y Letras, 1992, 224–229.
Griffin, Charles C. "Francisco Encina and Revisionism in Chilean History." *Hispanic American Historical Review* 37 (1957): 1–28.

Engels, Friedrich (1820–1895)
Political publicist, philosopher, and historian. Engels was the son of a German industrialist from Barmen. He was trained as a merchant and worked for his father's firm in Manchester, where he experienced the negative effects of early capitalist production. In 1845, his most important early work appeared, *The Conditions of the Working Class in England,* in which he described the exploitation of the English proletariat. Shortly before its publication he met Karl Marx and became his lifelong friend and collaborator. Together they developed a materialist conception of history that was most clearly formulated in Marx and Engels's *German Ideology* (written in 1845–1846, but first published in 1932). Influenced by Hegel, Marx and Engels offered a theory of history from the perspective of economic forces that not only explained the course of history, but also contained within it the source of human liberation and redemption. It was seen as a criticism of the ideologically driven "bourgeois" historiography, which served to legitimize bourgeois hegemony and the oppression of the proletariat. Human history was the story of those who controlled the means of production of material life and how this conditioned social, political, and cultural spheres.

Of particular importance was Engels's *Origin of the Family, Private Property and the State* (1884), which argued that the historical development of private property under male domination spelled the end of matriarchal society and the enslavement of women. This has become an important text for contemporary feminism. On the other hand, although both Marx and Engels predicted the evolution of a higher form of family and relationship between the sexes once capitalism had been defeated, neither supported the full emancipation of women.

John R. Hinde

See also MARX, KARL; MARXISM AND HISTORIOGRAPHY.

Texts
The Marx–Engels Reader. Ed. Robert C. Tucker. New York: W.W. Norton, 1972.

References
Rigby, G.H. *Engels and the Formation of Marxism: History, Dialectics and Revolution.* Manchester, Eng.: Manchester University Press, 1992.

English Historiography—Medieval and Early Modern (to 1700)

The Middle Ages
As in most western countries, the writing of history began during the Middle Ages either as a vehicle for recording the unfolding of God's will, or as a type of record-keeping. In many cases the two functions were merged, as when monastic Easter Tables were annotated with brief remarks on a year's events, thereby becoming rudimentary "annals." Other early medieval histories had different origins and a more thematic organization. Gildas (fl. sixth century), the first major English historian of the post-Roman era, wrote his *De Excidio et Conquestu Britanniae* [The Ruin and Conquest of Britain] to record the downfall of the Britons at the hands of Saxon invaders and to commemorate divine anger with the sins of the British, which had led to their destruction. Gildas's theme of providential punishment being inflicted on an entire nation, with its echoes of Old Testament episodes of divine retribution, would become a commonplace of much later medieval and early modern historical writing.

The greatest historian of the Anglo-Saxon era was the Venerable Bede (ca. 672–735), who borrowed from Gildas as well as from the fourth-century ecclesiastical historian, Eusebius, to write his own *Historia ecclesiastica gentis Anglorum* [Ecclesiastical History of the English People]. The work, completed in 731, recounts the story of the "English" (that is, the Anglo-Saxons) as a people belonging to the broader community of Christendom but also to a distinctive *ecclesia anglicana* (English Church). It remains one of the great historical works of the early Middle Ages and is comparable to Gregory of Tours's history of the Franks and Jordanes's of the Goths, both of which had been written nearly two centuries previously. The only work to rival Bede's in importance is the *Anglo-Saxon Chronicle,* a vernacular work perhaps commissioned by King Alfred the Great in 893, and written by successive authors in different locations between the late ninth and mid-twelfth centuries. Unlike Bede, who saw English history as a unity connected by the foundation and flourishing of Christianity, the chroniclers' annals, which vary considerably in length and detail, recorded events for the most part as they occurred or shortly thereafter, thereby making the *Chronicle* especially valuable as a primary source for the era of the Viking invasions. In the hands of twelfth-century monks, it would prove an ongoing influence on subsequent medieval chronicle writing. The Anglo-Saxon period also witnessed the writing of a number of biographies, of which the anonymous *Life of St. Cuthbert* (ca. 634–687) and Asser's (d. 908/909) *Life of King Alfred* (893) are the most significant, both as sources and especially as later models for biography. Finally, the late tenth century saw the completion, in Latin, of *The Chronicle of Aethelweard,* the first work of history known to have been written by a member of the English laity.

Aethelweard's work was to remain the solitary example of lay historiography for nearly four centuries. Through most of the Middle Ages history writing was a craft left almost entirely in the hands of churchmen, and especially members of the monastic orders. This did not change at the Norman Conquest, and Anglo-Norman historians, who (like Bede) wrote in ecclesiastical Latin rather than old English or Norman French, continued to predominate. Among the outstanding historians of the High Middle Ages in England (1066–1272), Orderic Vitalis (1075–1143), William of Malmesbury (ca. 1095–1143), and, in the thirteenth century, Matthew Paris (1200–1259), deserve special mention for their ability to recount events accurately, with scrupulous evaluation both of written records and of eyewitness accounts. Most immediately influential, however, was Geoffrey of Monmouth's (ca. 1100–1153)

Historia Regum Britanniae [History of the Kings of Britain] (1135) a semifanciful recounting of the history of England beginning with the legendary discoverer of Britain, Brutus, a refugee from the fall of Troy. Although Geoffrey's veracity was doubted quite early on (for instance by the chronicler William of Newburgh [ca. 1135–ca. 1198]), his stories of an imagined remote past proved enduring and would not be widely discounted until late in the sixteenth century.

In the later Middle Ages (1272–1485), the tradition of Latin chronicle writing endured, and was carried on most vigorously at the Monastery of St. Albans in which Matthew Paris wrote; here, a long line of chroniclers such as Paris, Roger of Wendover (d. 1236), and William Rishanger (fl. early fourteenth century), continued to produce accounts of the recent and remote past, generally grafting their own annalistic record of contemporary events onto preexisting chronicles compiled in similar fashion by their monastic predecessors. The St. Albans's Chronicle, as these works are often collectively called, concluded in the early fifteenth century with Thomas of Walsingham (1345–ca. 1422); it can be viewed as a kind of English counterpart of the slightly later French *Grandes chroniques* written at St. Denis, but without that work's close and semiofficial connection to the monarchy.

By the fourteenth century, however, the social and political context of English historiography had begun subtly to shift, occasioning changes in style and subject matter and the development of an expanded audience. In the era of an expansive and aggressive late medieval kingship, and of extended foreign wars against the Scots and the French, a new group of readers emerged in the military aristocracy, whose members were becoming interested in stories from the past that told not of godliness, miracles, and saintly piety but rather of chivalry and honor. Notable chroniclers in this vein include Sir Thomas Gray (d. after 1367), whose *Scalacronica,* covering the period from the early Britons to 1363, was the first historical work to have been written by a layman since Aethelweard. But the greatest historian in this chivalric tradition was a transplanted Frenchman, Jean, or John, Froissart (ca. 1333–ca. 1410), who arrived in England in the mid-fourteenth century and spent much of his life at the English court. His *Chronicles,* written in French prose, recount the early part of the Hundred Years' War between England and France in an epic fashion emphasizing courage, nobility, and military virtue; its ancestry is traced most properly not to the monastic

E

chronicles but to earlier continental Crusade historians (such as Joinville and Villehardouin), to prose romance, and to the earlier *chansons de geste.* The success of Froissart is a mark of the gradually increasing interest in the past beyond monastic cloisters, though in fact the fully chivalric chronicle was rare in fifteenth-century England (as compared with France). The major later example was the metrical chronicle of the politically flexible Sir John Hardyng (1378–ca. 1465), whose work exists in alternative Lancastrian and Yorkist versions, both written in English.

At the same time, a very different type of chronicle writing was emerging in English towns, and especially in London. These included, first, a family of London-based, anonymous chronicles usually known simply as *The Brut,* and, secondly, a rather different type of civic chronicle that shared the *Brut's* urban origins (and influenced some of the latter's writers), though appealing to a different audience. As towns gradually acquired corporate status, and with it a sense of civic identity distinguishing them from both the aristocracy and the clergy, so there arose records of the years of office of mayors and sheriffs. Like the monastic Easter Tables centuries earlier, these annals frequently had attached to them accounts of events in the city and the wider country. In general, the tradition of civic chronicle writing was less well developed than in more highly urbanized parts of Europe, but in works such as the late-fifteenth-century *Great Chronicle of London* and the more wide-ranging *New Chronicles* by the London official Robert Fabyan (who may also have authored the *Great Chronicle*), there is firm evidence that historical interests were spreading among the urban elites. It is interesting that the growth of vernacular historiography during this period parallels almost exactly the precipitous decline of monastic historiography, though individual religious houses and, often, secular clergy like Geoffrey le Baker (fl. mid-fourteenth century), still penned Latin chronicles up to the mid-seventeenth century. The single most popular chronicle of the fifteenth century was of monastic origins, but it was very different from the sort of work written by Matthew Paris and his successors; this was the *Polychronicon* by the Chester monk Ranulf Higden. A combination of monastic chronicle and encyclopedia of natural history and geography in seven books (that is, chapters), the *Polychronicon* covered all of world history, and did not remain long the exclusive property of a monastery; over a hundred manuscripts exist, many from Higden's own lifetime. The work was translated into English

by John of Trevisa in 1387, at the request of a nobleman, and in this form it soon supplanted Bede and Geoffrey of Monmouth (neither of whom had written universal history) as a kind of historical companion on the shelves of manuscript book collectors.

The quieting down of the Anglo–French and Anglo–Scottish wars, and the onset of internal conflicts culminating in the Wars of the Roses between the rival Lancastrian and Yorkist branches of the ruling house of Plantagenet changed the ways in which history was written; and it enhanced the general trend toward lay interest in the past. A further indicator of this, and the one with greatest significance for the sixteenth and seventeenth centuries, lies in the activities of the sort of aristocratic patrons and manuscript collectors of the fifteenth century to whom Higden's *Polychronicon* appealed, such as Humfrey (or Humphrey), Duke of Gloucester (1391–1447), a younger brother of King Henry V, and John Tiptoft, earl of Worcester (1449–1470), a Lancastrian nobleman. Humfrey initiated the importation of foreign scholars, and especially Italian humanists, to England early in the century. He patronized Tito Livio Frulovisi, one of many authors to compose a Latin biography of the duke's dead royal brother, Henry V. Tiptoft similarly encouraged historical scholarship and he himself wrote a chronicle covering the period from Brutus the Trojan to 1429, which has unfortunately long been lost. A further example is provided by Sir John Fastolfe, another influential layman, who supported the antiquarian endeavors of William Worcester (1415–1482). And near the end of the century, the availability of historical works was considerably enhanced following the establishment of the first English printing press by William Caxton, who issued a number of medieval historical works in the course of his career, including the *Brut* and Trevisa's version of Higden's *Polychronicon,* with a continuation by Caxton himself. As we shall see further on, however, the advent of print had far-reaching implications for the ways in which English historians chose to write about their past, eventually sounding the death-knell of the medieval chronicle form.

The Early Modern Era, 1485–1714
Historical writing continued to develop during the Tudor period. After the first glimmers of humanism in the early to mid-fifteenth century, the reigns of Henry VII (r. 1485–1509) and Henry VIII (r. 1509–1547) witnessed a further, if still somewhat premature, period of continental-style humanist historiography exemplified in such

works as Sir Thomas More's (1477/78–1535) unfinished biography of King Richard III and Polydore Vergil's (ca. 1470–1555) much longer *Anglica Historia,* a full account in humanist Latin of English history from Roman times until Vergil's own day. Neither was as immediately influential as one might have expected. More's *Richard,* though published in two rather different Latin and English versions, was little read for several decades. Vergil, a long-time resident in England who published his work only late in life and abroad, was more widely consulted, but his foreigner's perspective infuriated English readers, including John Leland (1506–1552), one of the best scholars of his day. In the first place, Vergil began only with Julius Caesar's account of the Britons, which he regarded as the first reliable source; second, he dared to cast doubt on such time-honored fixtures, many of which derived from Geoffrey of Monmouth, as the foundation of Britain by mythical Trojan refugees such as Brutus, or the exploits of fictional or semifictional British kings, especially King Arthur. Leland, a man of humanist inclinations himself, and several other English authors took aim at Vergil and dismissed him as an insolent and ignorant Italian—later critics would go even further and charge Vergil with systematically destroying English historical documents or sending them off to his papal master! Together with More, Vergil can thus be regarded as a kind of "false start" to humanist historiography in England, with a more solidly footed tradition lying a few decades ahead, in the Elizabethan and early Stuart eras.

Meanwhile, the vernacular chronicle enjoyed a kind of "Indian summer" that lasted into the 1580s. A long line of historians sent a variety of works to press; they included Edward Hall (ca. 1497–1547), Richard Grafton (d. 1572), Raphael Holinshed (fl. 1560–1580; the organizer rather than author of the work that bears his name, which is most famous as a sourcebook for Shakespeare), and John Stow (1529–1605), the last of whom was the final great representative of the civic chronicle tradition. With the exception of Hall, who like Polydore Vergil used reigns as the basic compositional unit of his chronicle, these authors continued to organize their works largely by "annals" or years rather than by reigns. These histories found an audience interested in their accounts of English exploits abroad, and especially for the achievements of the Tudor rulers with regard to the reestablishment of a firm government and the reform of the English church.

The most influential history of the mid- to late Tudor era was, however, a very different work that harkens back to Bede and Eusebius, as well as to medieval hagiography (saints' lives): the Protestant reformer John Foxe's (1517–1587) *Acts and Monuments,* first published in English in 1563. This was a voluminous retelling of English history, within the context of the whole Christian church from patristic times to the Reformation. It was built not on annals but on biographical accounts of centuries of martyrs to "true" religion and culminated in the stories of the victims of persecution under the Catholic Queen Mary. Though large and expensive by comparison with most of the secular chronicles save Holinshed's mammoth enterprise, the "Book of Martyrs" as it was commonly called was undoubtedly the single most widely read historical book of the sixteenth and seventeenth centuries. It was reprinted several times and copies were held, by ecclesiastical order, in every cathedral and many parish churches; library lists of the period show that it appeared in private collections more often than any other historical work. Foxe's celebration of English faith under persecution and its often apocalyptic call for vigilance against the Antichrist, Rome, ensured his book's longevity well into the nineteenth century, when an oft-quoted (and textually unreliable) nineteenth-century multivolume edition appeared, as well as numerous popular abridgments. No fully adequate study exists of either the martyrologist or his work, the true complexity and sophistication of which is becoming increasingly apparent, though some recent scholarship has partially remedied this deficit; a new critical edition of the *Acts and Monuments* is currently in the planning stage.

By the end of Queen Elizabeth's (r. 1558–1603) reign, humanist scholarship and a refined style of writing modeled on Livy and especially Tacitus, and invigorated by the Florentine political thinker and historian, Machiavelli, had taken hold more securely. At almost precisely the time that the Tudor chronicles began to decline in popularity among the laity—especially among an increasingly well-educated gentry and urban mercantile elite—there appeared a radically different type of historiography often known to modern scholars as the "politic history." This was generally presented in the form of a biography, or history of the reign of a particular king, placed less emphasis on panegyric or celebration of personal military achievements, and relegated providence to the background. Instead, authors stressed character, moral virtue, and especially political prudence.

E

Often designed to fulfill Cicero's dictum that history was the "mistress of life" and "light of truth," such writings could be politically dangerous. Tudor readers often thought about the past not as cause and effect but rather, in the long-standing tradition of medieval and humanist learning, as analogy and parallel, with one historical person or event being directly comparable to another. John Hayward (ca. 1564–1627), one of the first of the politic historians, found himself in deep trouble with the Elizabethan regime when his *First Part of the Life and Raigne of King Henrie the IIII* (1599), essentially an account of the deposition of Richard II in 1399, was read by Elizabeth I and her ministers as a veiled attack on the queen and support for Hayward's patron, the earl of Essex. After the earl's rebellion two years later, Hayward narrowly escaped going to the scaffold with his master, though he survived to write several other regnal biographies during the reign of James I. In avoiding the capital penalty Hayward was more fortunate than Sir Walter Ralegh (1552–1618), whose unfinished *History of the World* (1614), though universal in scope, is less a throwback to Higden's *Polychronicon* than a peculiar but highly readable melding of Reformation providential themes with Machiavellian politics. It, too, encountered royal displeasure. Ralegh wrote his *History*—which remained very popular for the next century—while in prison under sentence of death; in it he commented that such exercises in ancient history were likely to be safer than recounting recent events: following truth "too near the heels" could result in having one's teeth struck out. A degree of such caution is evident in the most famous though not the greatest of the politic historians, Francis Bacon (1561–1626), the disgraced ex-chancellor whose *History of the Reign of King Henry the Seventh* was intended (unsuccessfully) to restore his political stature with James I and his heir, the future Charles I. A prudent objectivity can also be found in a writer who transcended the bounds of politic history, William Camden (1551–1623). In his careful *Annales* of Queen Elizabeth's reign, Camden managed to avoid most of the political and religious minefields of the day while maintaining careful, if sometimes uncritical, attention to the public documents to which James I had given him privileged access.

The politic historians remained much in demand throughout the seventeenth and early eighteenth century, when a large collected edition of their works was assembled and extended to the later seventeenth century by the bishop and scholar, White Kennett (1660–1728). In some ways the authority and accessibility of their works—all except Camden had written in English, and even he had almost immediately been translated—inhibited for nearly a century new writing about the late medieval and Tudor periods. Their most lasting effect was in effectively selling readers on the shortcomings—some of which were perceived rather than real—of their own chronicle predecessors, who were blamed for writing ungainly English or, worse, bad Latin, for being credulous toward their sources and uncritical of inherited myths such as Brutus the Trojan (Polydore Vergil's earlier criticism of Galfridian legend now, finally, receiving a favorable hearing), and for composing wayward, digressive annals that recorded information without really telling a central story. Some of this was true, but recent scholarship has shown many of the medieval and some of the Tudor chronicles, for instance Holinshed's *Chronicles,* to be far more sophisticated and skeptical than their humanist critics allowed. Nevertheless, the criticisms made by the humanists were widely accepted by seventeenth-century readers, and the day of the chronicle had finally passed. The printing press that had made it so readily available now produced works, including the politic history and the Shakespearian history play, that rendered the chronicle an historiographical dinosaur.

Yet humanist political history, the proximate ancestor of two Augustan historiographical masterpieces, Clarendon's *History of the Rebellion* (1702–1704) and Gilbert Burnet's *History of His Own Time* (1723–1734), did in fact have a more potent rival than the chronicle among genres of writing about the past, though one that for a time was not recognized as history proper. This was the antiquarian treatise, which took a variety of forms. The most important of these was the "chorography," a detailed investigation of the history of a particular county or town. Aside from one or two isolated fifteenth-century figures such as the aforementioned William Worcester, the first great representative of the antiquarian tradition was the same John Leland who had attacked Polydore Vergil over the accuracy of Geoffrey of Monmouth. Leland was a fine scholar and poet whose *Itineraries* was a record of his travels throughout England in the 1530s and 1540s, with particular emphasis given to the architectural and physical features, including ruins, of the communities that he visited. Though unpublished until the early eighteenth century, Leland's work, circulating in manuscript, was a major influence on the growth of antiquarianism during the later Tudor and early Stuart period. An equally important influence was the combination of university humanism with legal training. This flowered in the early 1600s, when scholars, such as Sir Henry Spelman (ca. 1564–1641) and John Selden (1584–1654), studied complex problems, such as the origins and character of feudal tenures and the nature of parliament.

Many antiquarian topics were discussed in the forum provided by the short-lived Society of Antiquaries that met from 1586 to 1614 (a prototype for the modern society, founded in the mid-eighteenth century and still in existence); the record of their meetings includes many short essays on artifacts such as coins, or on land-holding patterns, or archaic legal practices. Many of the society's members also engaged in chorography, the type of antiquarianism with greatest appeal to provincial gentry. Although several notable local studies of counties or even specific towns were produced, especially the lawyer William Lambarde's (1536–1601) *Perambulation of Kent* (1576) and the former chronicler John Stow's *Survey of London* (1598), the dominant work in this vein was *Britannia*, by William Camden, the future historian of Queen Elizabeth's reign. A former schoolmaster, Camden published the first edition of his work in 1586; although less detailed than either Stow's *Survey of London* or Leland's *Itineraries*, the *Britannia* was the first full-scale, county by county description of England and Scotland, ostensibly focusing on its Roman remains but in practice spanning the whole of British history. It was expanded and reprinted several times into the eighteenth century and inspired many imitators, including a large number of writers whose accounts of their own counties or parishes still remain mainly in manuscript.

Yet despite the high level of scholarship it attained, and its descent from the same continental humanist parentage as the politic histories, antiquarianism remained for a time a kind of ancillary to history, rather than history itself; even Camden did not accept that *Britannia* was a work of history though we now would regard it as such. Humanist historical theory of the day required of history that it be cast as a narrative and that it provide moral or political lessons, which most of the antiquarian works avoided doing; the kind of inclusive encyclopedism practiced by the Tudor chroniclers and their medieval predecessors was by now frowned upon, and the antiquaries had decided tendencies in that direction. In practice, however, the distinction between antiquities and history would eventually break down, as the boundaries of both became fuzzier. When the lawyer John Selden, one of the most learned scholars of the

seventeenth-century, wrote his *Historie of Tithes* (1618)—an antiquarian-style study of the origins and evolution of ecclesiastical property rights that touched off a storm of controversy—he claimed that it was, in fact a history.

The achievements of the early Stuart antiquaries would continue to influence scholarship, and the sense of what history comprised, through the rest of the century, culminating in a flurry of erudite activity in the Restoration and Augustan era (1660–1730). During this period, a variety of documents ranging from medieval chronicles (now valued as sources rather than as literary models) to royal diplomatic correspondence was edited by scholars such as Thomas Hearne (1678–1735) and Thomas Rymer (1641–1713); ecclesiastical history enjoyed a resurgence in the writings of Henry Wharton (1664–1695) and John Strype (1643–1737); interest in the early Middle Ages and especially in the culture and language of the Anglo-Saxons flourished anew; and the records of government departments were analyzed in detail, as in Thomas Madox's (1666–1727) *History and Antiquities of the Exchequer*, the work of a career bureaucrat and the first serious scholar to hold the title of Historiographer Royal, which had first been created in the 1660s.

Aside from the development of various types of antiquarian study, the mid-seventeenth century also marked, in two ways, a real watershed in the development of mainstream historical writing in England. First, the civil wars and interregnum (1642–1660) produced a flurry of uncensored political and religious history of differing ideological and confessional stripes; and second, the focus of readers' attention was shifted sharply away from the medieval and Tudor eras toward recent catastrophes. There is no space to mention all the historians who wrote on the civil wars in the half-century following the Restoration, but virtually every author who published could now expect a response either in the form of satire and published critiques, or even full-scale histories from an opposing perspective. Thus the former parliamentarian functionary John Rushworth's (1612–1690) *Historical Collections*, written from the parliamentary point of view, was mirrored by the royalist John Nalson's (ca. 1638–1696) rather misleadingly titled *Impartial Collection*. Edward Hyde, earl of Clarendon (1609–1674), the moderate adviser of both Charles I and II whose *History of the Rebellion* would eventually appeal to eighteenth-century Whig and Tory readers alike, was countered by John Oldmixon (1673–1742) and, indirectly, by Bishop Gilbert Burnet (1643–1715); Laurence Echard's (ca. 1670–1730) *History of England* from a Tory perspective similar to Clarendon's came up against the Huguenot refugee Paul de Rapin-Thoyras's (1661–1725) loudly Whiggish version; and John Walker's (1674–1747) valuable collective study of the Anglican clergy dispossessed by the Puritan regime of the 1640s and 1650s, had a nonconformist *doppelgänger* in the Dissenting scholar Edmund Calamy's (1671–1732) comparable account of Puritan clergy ejected after the Restoration. As English historiography entered the modern age, it had become a matter for vigorous public debate and a forum for contesting ideologies.

D.R. Woolf

See also CHRONICLES, MEDIEVAL; CRUSADES; ENGLISH HISTORIOGRAPHY—MODERN (SINCE 1700); LAW AND HISTORY; RENAISSANCE, HISTORIOGRAPHY DURING; SCOTTISH HISTORIOGRAPHY.

References

Butterfield, Herbert. *The Englishman and His History.* Hamden, CT: Archon Books, 1970.

Douglas, D.C. *English Scholars, 1660–1730.* Second ed. London: Eyre & Spottiswoode, 1951.

Ferguson, Arthur B. *Clio Unbound: Perceptions of the Social and Cultural Past in Renaissance England.* Durham, NC: Duke University Press, 1979.

Gransden, Antonia. *Historical Writing in England.* 2 vols. London: Routledge and Kegan Paul, 1974–1982.

Hicks, Phillip. *Neoclassical History and English Culture: from Clarendon to Hume.* New York: St. Martin's Press, 1996.

Kingsford, Charles Lethbridge. *English Historical Literature in the Fifteenth Century.* Oxford: Clarendon Press, 1913.

Levine, Joseph M. *Humanism and History.* Ithaca, NY: Cornell University Press, 1987.

Levy, F.J. *Tudor Historical Thought.* San Marino, CA: Huntington Library, 1967.

Woolf, D.R. *The Idea of History in Early Stuart England.* Toronto: University of Toronto Press, 1990.

English Historiography—Modern (since 1700)

The Eighteenth Century

By the accession of George I in 1714, the political and religious situation in England was beginning to settle, after over a century of turmoil, into a constitutional monarchy. This consisted of a king and a cabinet-style government, ruling over a new United Kingdom embracing both Scots and English, responsible to a Parliament controlled by aristocratic and gentry interests and dominated by formal parties (Whigs and Tories). In religion, the English half of the kingdom was now ministered to by an official Anglicanism seated in an established church that, in the face of an uneasy toleration of Dissent, no longer enjoyed a monopoly of faith.

Historians writing in this environment thus faced a very different set of circumstances, and historical issues, than encountered by their predecessors. At the same time, their audience had expanded enormously. The growth of literacy in the preceding hundred years had pushed public interest in history of various kinds—political, religious, local, antiquarian, biographical—into a wide public market beyond the educated elite. The word "history" soon became a kind of catchword for any "truthful" account of past events (or, in an alternative usage, for a study of physical phenomena, as in the case of "natural history")—so much so that the authors of the soon-dominant fictional form of the eighteenth and nineteenth centuries, the novel, began to employ the word "history" in their titles as a way of feigning realism. It is not going too far to say that by 1750, if not earlier, history in the broadest sense had truly become a sort of master genre. Although it was still not, of course, anything like a "discipline" in the modern academic sense, educational institutions increasingly stressed the reading of history as part of their curriculum, rather than using it simply to train pupils to write effective prose, as had been the case when Caesar and Livy were studied in Tudor Oxford.

One of the most notable features of eighteenth-century English historiography is the advent of the female reader and, to a lesser extent, writer of history. The novelist Sarah Scott (d. 1795) published histories, albeit mainly under a pseudonym, and Charlotte Cowley, about whom little is known, wrote a *Ladies' History of England.* The greatest female historian of the eighteenth century was Catharine Sawbridge Macaulay (1731–1791), the unconventional, fervent republican sympathizer whose *History of England,* essentially an account of the Stuart period, achieved both fame and notoriety for its author. Macaulay's *History,* which has only recently begun to receive the attention its author merits, became the most serious contemporary rival to David Hume's (see below) Tory interpretation of English history, and the two historians carried on a public exchange of criticism that looks relatively polite compared to the early ideological polemics of the late seventeenth century, or the vituperative ad hominem battles of the Victorian era.

Yet for every Macaulay or Cowley, there were at least ten male historians, and still many more male readers than female. Jane Austen gave up writing a history because she found it a female-unfriendly genre, and one of the characters in her novel *Northanger Abbey* regarded history as "all about popes and kings . . . and no women." History remained in the eighteenth century a game dominated by men, and gentlemen at that. Aside from a continuing tradition of detailed antiquarian and philological scholarship, beginning in the Restoration and early Georgian era (which would produce colorful scholars such as the Druid-enthusiast and archaeologist William Stukeley [1687–1765]), the prevalent forms of historical writing throughout the century remained political narrative and a resurgent religious or ecclesiastical history, the latter necessitated by doctrinal struggles within Anglicanism and between the established church and its Roman Catholic and Dissenting rivals.

This is not to suggest that the eighteenth century was a period of historiographical stasis. There *were* fresh influences blowing in from abroad, which make eighteenth-century historical works distinguishable from even Restoration examples of the genre. Just as humanism had had a leavening effect in the sixteenth century, two hundred years later the work of continental Enlightenment philosophes like Voltaire and Montesquieu began to make themselves known in historical writing in England. As it had in the 1500s, a strong tradition of intellectual xenophobia (which has never entirely dissipated) imposed some limitations on this. Indeed, the most original, thoughtful, and wide-ranging British historical works of the later eighteenth century were not English at all, but Scottish, as authors such as John Millar (1735–1801) and Adam Ferguson (1723–1816) published historical studies of laws, manners, and customs from a comparative and philosophical perspective, and William Robertson (1721–1793) wrote a brilliant history of the reign of the Emperor Charles V. David Hume (1711–1776), an admirer of Montesquieu (and best known in his own day as a historian rather than as a philosopher), wrote what would eventually become, after disconcertingly sluggish early sales, the best-selling *History of England* in the entire century; despite its Tory perspective (at a time of Whig political dominance) it would remain for many readers *the* English history, at least until the time of T.B. Macaulay (1800–1859; no relation to Hume's rival, Catharine Macaulay). Among the odd features of Hume's history, aside from the relative moderation of his partisan views

and his unmodish sympathy for Charles I, was that he wrote it backwards, beginning with the seventeenth century and only later following this with volumes on the Tudors and then the Middle Ages, which he depicted with the philosophe's characteristic distaste. He is also notable for his dismissal of scholarly research as tedious and unimportant, the true work of the historian lying in making philosophical judgments about the lessons of history.

The greatest English historian of the century, however, did not concern himself with English history at all. Edward Gibbon's (1737–1794) *Decline and Fall of the Roman Empire* is an enduring monument to Enlightenment values and the heritage of Augustan philological erudition. One of the greatest historical works ever written in any language, it was influenced at least as much by the Scottish philosophers as by the writings of modern Italian and German students of the Roman and Byzantine past. The *Decline and Fall* is less entertaining in some ways than either Hume or, in the next century, Macaulay. But it is a complex amalgam of skepticism, cold moral judgment, and intellectual aloofness glossed over with sincere admiration for the greatness of Rome and sympathy for its decline at the hands of "barbarism and religion," by which latter term Gibbon meant, in Enlightenment fashion, the spread of Christianity. Gibbon's masterpiece, probably the most studied history ever written in the English language, remains in conception, learning, and style one of the few works in the history of English historical writing that deserves the overused title of "classic."

The Victorian Era

The nineteenth century saw greater improvements in education, especially for the middle classes, some social and political reform, and the spread of popular literacy through public libraries, early workers' educational institutes, and cheaper print. History continued to rival the novel as the most popular of genres, but this was a rivalry of mutual benefit—at no other time have the relations of fiction and nonfiction been both so close and so symbiotic. As Enlightenment philosophical history gave way to revolution and romanticism in the early nineteenth century, interest rekindled in periods such as the Middle Ages (scorned as a time of superstition by the philosophes, as Hume's example abundantly shows). The popular historical imagination was strongly influenced by historical narrative painting (a weak tradition in the visual arts prior to the mid-eighteenth century)—with its depiction of great English or more properly "British" heroes and heroines, from the ancient

E

queen Boadicea to an Oliver Cromwell newly rehabilitated by authors like Thomas Carlyle. The establishment of public repositories for artifacts of the past, most notably the British Museum, and the enormous success of historical novels such as those by Sir Walter Scott also fostered public enthusiasm for history.

In this context, the "genteel" tradition of the man of letters continued, though the public spats among later Victorian historians may make the notion of "gentility" somewhat inapt. It was, however, still largely the preserve of men. The nineteenth century would witness several additional female historians emerge as heiresses, of sorts, to Catharine Macaulay. Agnes Strickland (1796–1874), with the assistance of her sister Elizabeth, authored a remarkable series of multivolume books on the lives of British queens and princesses and is perhaps the most notable among the Victorian women historians, together with Mary Anne Everett Wood Green (1818–1895), who also wrote royal lives but is best known today as an editor of several volumes of the *Calendar of State Papers* for the seventeenth century. As one recent scholar has pointed out, however, these female writers for the most part avoided imitating Mrs. Macaulay in the writing of political history, and they tried to defuse the criticisms of their male counterparts by writing "lives" instead of "histories." They were, not unreasonably, wary of acerbic critics like the antiquarians J.M. Kemble and Francis Palgrave, the latter of whom thought that ladies were better suited to "labeling pots of jam." That a tradition of female historical writing persisted at all is one of the more neglected facets of intellectual life in the nineteenth century.

For the men who dominated the mainstream, however, the nineteenth century was to prove a "golden age." The greatest era of English historical writing as high literary art began with the constitutional historian and lawyer Henry Hallam (1777–1851), the new century's first serious pretender to the mantle of Hume, and with a Roman Catholic historian, John Lingard (1771–1851), whose history was moderate enough, despite its author's work as an active polemicist for his faith, to appeal even to Protestant readers. The tradition would peak at mid-century with a colorful cast of figures as various as the politician, poet, and essayist Thomas Babington Macaulay; the short-lived but controversial student of cultural history, Henry Thomas Buckle (1821–1862); the moralizing Tudor historian, James Anthony Froude (1818–1894); and Froude's most

bitter critic, the unattractive anti-Semite Edward Augustus Freeman (1823–1892). It would come to a conclusion with the Irish politician and historian of the eighteenth century, William Edward Hartpole Lecky (1838–1903), the apologist for empire, John Robert Seeley (1834–1895), and, at the very end of the century, Macaulay's great-nephew, George Macaulay Trevelyan (1876–1962), a popularizer whose extremely long career connects the age of the Victorian masters with the mid-twentieth century.

Macaulay himself was by far the most commercially successful historian of his and perhaps any age and the only one who has achieved a literary stature equivalent to Gibbon. He was an admirer of Walter Scott and himself a public figure; his *History,* initially billed as a "supplement to Hume," quickly eclipsed Hume and all other contenders in popularity. Macaulay is also the model for the nineteenth-century gentleman of means and (despite his public activities) of relative leisure. He wrote his history beyond the groves of academe and with little thought for its concerns, but he was by no means unusual in this regard. With a few exceptions such as J.R. Seeley, the great Victorian historians did not write their works from the base of a formal university appointment. In part this reflected the fact that in the first half of the century history had not yet become a distinct discipline in the undergraduate curriculum, which in any case still tended to favor ancient history, studied under the rubric of classics. This remained true despite the fact that Oxford and Cambridge had each had, since 1724, a "Regius" chair of modern history ("modern" meaning post-Roman); the post was essentially a patronage appointment, in the hands of the government of the day, that could often go to a popular author such as Charles Kingsley (Cambridge) or Goldwin Smith (Oxford) rather than to what we would now call (a trifle anachronistically for the Victorian era) an "academic" historian.

This does not mean that good historical writing did not occur in the universities, merely that the production of successful historical works tended to center around the offices of London publishers, not in the libraries of Oxford and Cambridge colleges. By the 1860s and 1870s this was beginning to change as career clerics with historical interests and a university home rivaled affluent middle-class gentlemen as authors of history. Two of the century's most important historians, both of whom died in the same year as Queen Victoria, spent significant parts of their ecclesiastical careers at the universities. William Stubbs

(1825–1901) was the author of an influential medieval constitutional history and the indefatigable editor of a variety of medieval chronicles in the Rolls Series; he was also the Regius professor at Oxford from 1866 to 1884, when he left the university to become a bishop. Mandell Creighton, his younger contemporary (1843–1901), was Dixie professor of ecclesiastical history at Cambridge before he, like Stubbs, also became a bishop; Creighton was the most learned authority of the century on the age of the Reformation. Both men were rare among their generation in their close attachments to the university; by comparison, the outstanding political historian of the second half of the century, Samuel Rawson Gardiner (1829–1902), whose history of early seventeenth-century England has shaped research and writing on that era until well into our century, was at first kept from an Oxford or Cambridge appointment by his sectarian religious views. When he was eventually offered the Regius chair at Oxford in 1894, in succession to Froude, he turned it down, fearing that it would prove a distraction from his beloved research—not the last person to do so, as the example of F.W. Maitland at Cambridge would illustrate a decade later.

The middle years of the nineteenth century saw an enormous growth in public interest in history, represented in the many historical and antiquarian societies that sprang up, such as the Camden Society, the Surtees Society, and various local associations. Nevertheless, the day of the unaffiliated, nonacademic scholar was beginning to pass, although the research-oriented historians appointed to university chairs had a hard time influencing their college-appointed academic peers well into the early twentieth century. As John Kenyon's account of the growth of the English historical profession shows, the would-be reformers among the professoriate often encountered strenuous resistance among college tutors whose primary concern remained—quite properly for their period—teaching future civil servants and politicians rather than conducting research or training future historians. Nevertheless, the establishment of formal undergraduate degrees in history (for the first time independent of classics, law, theology, or other disciplines) at Oxford and Cambridge in the last three decades of the century, helped, as did the central place of historical studies at some of the new universities of the later Victorian era, most notably London and Manchester. At the latter institution, Bishop Stubbs's outstanding pupil, Thomas Frederick Tout (1855–1929) was one of a number of still-highly regarded medieval and Tudor historians who eschewed the comprehensive knowledge approach of the Oxford and Cambridge schools for intensive study of select periods. Even Oxford and Cambridge were not immune to change. Both Seeley, a former London classicist turned champion of beneficent imperialism, and Creighton, the scholarly early modernist, were influential in reforming the historical curriculum at Cambridge. Their work was continued by Lord Acton, a man more famous for his essays, moralizing epigrams, and vast collections of archival notes than he was for the major work that was expected of him but that he never produced. It was Acton (1834–1902) who planned the first *Cambridge Modern History*— an unfinished near-disaster at the time of his death in 1902—as a formidable collection of rigorous and erudite history accessible to both scholarly and popular readers; its successor, the *New Cambridge Modern History* was completed only in 1970.

Intellectually, it is tempting to look to the Continent once more in search of the influences behind these institutional developments. Certainly the great German seminar teachers and scholars, such as Leopold von Ranke, had their English admirers, for instance Mark Pattison (1813–1884), who became an early apostle of the idea of university research as an end in itself. Acton had trained under the formidable German ecclesiastical historian, Johann Joseph Ignaz von Döllinger, and admired Ranke's commitment to factual accuracy, but not the great German's disavowal of the historian's function as a moralizing "judge," a robe that Acton was all too happy to wear. The German-style seminar system itself, however, remained foreign to England until the twentieth century. Graduate studies in history did not catch on in England with anything like the success they enjoyed at contemporary American universities, which had been much more directly, if naively, influenced by the Rankean credo. Doctoral degrees would only be established at Oxford and Cambridge in 1917 and 1920, respectively, long after they had already become, in the United States, a mandatory training ground; even today the occasional brilliant undergraduate can slide into a college fellowship without the tiresome business of writing a dissertation. Though historians such as another Oxford ex-Stubbsian, Reginald Lane Poole (1857–1939), were able to inject principles of German *Quellenkritik* (source criticism) into the curriculum, the closest thing to a seminar system prior to World War II would be that found at the Institute of Historical Research at

London, founded in 1920 by Poole's former pupil, the Tudor historian Albert Frederick Pollard (1869–1948).

Nor, similarly, did French methodological positivism of the mid- to late-nineteenth century, as found in the *Introduction to the Study of History* by Charles-Victor Langlois and Charles Seignobos (first published in French in 1896), have much initial effect—although Seeley had inclinations in that direction, and one of his successors in the Regius chair, the ancient historian John Bagnell Bury (1861–1927), who was an admirer of Buckle, spoke in a famous address of history being "a science, nothing more and nothing less," and not a branch of literature. By and large English scholars have always preferred their own, less highly theorized form of "commonsense" empiricism, and most English historians today, whatever their rigor with sources, would prefer the philosopher and ancient historian Robin George Collingwood's (1889–1943) conception of history as an autonomous enquiry distinct in methods and goals from the sciences. Like the German historians, the French had their admirers and readers, as demonstrated by the number of English translations of foreign works; unlike the Germans, their reputation did not suffer during the prolonged period of Anglo-German enmity that set in before, during, and after the great war. On the whole, however, English historical scholarship in the late nineteenth and early twentieth centuries should not be viewed as primarily an offshoot of Continental developments; this should not, perhaps, be too surprising in an era when Britain was the dominant imperial power rather than an insular poor relation of the great early modern European monarchies as it had been from 1500 to 1700.

Further improvements to the conditions of historical writing occurred mainly in the care of and availability of documents. In this regard, the establishment of the Public Record Office, which opened its doors in Chancery Lane in 1856, was most significant, together with the reform of the British Museum's vast manuscript and print treasures and the opening of its own famous circular reading room in 1857; both institutions were in the process of moving to more modern facilities as this article was written.

A related but distinct development at mid-century was the coming of organized, and sometimes publicly funded, historical source publication and of scholarly "megaprojects," beginning with the *Rerum Britannicarum medii aevi scriptores,* better known as the "Rolls Series" of medieval chronicles (so-called because it was patronized by the then Master of the Rolls, Lord Romilly). This was a rather idiosyncratic and qualitatively uneven counterpart to the German *Monumenta Germaniae Historica.* Other sources appeared in the publications of the Camden Society, the Selden Society, and the Surtees Society, and in the transactions of numerous county historical, antiquarian, and archaeological societies. The work continued in the second half of the century with the publication of calendars, lists, and indexes of the contents of the Public Record Office. This trend would culminate, near the end of the century, in various other local record and antiquarian societies' publications of manuscript and archaeological evidence, in the Historical Manuscripts Commission's series of *Reports* on private archival holdings across the country, and in large-scale works of scholarship such as Acton's *Cambridge Modern History.* The year 1885 saw the founding of the *English Historical Review,* the country's first national periodical vehicle for historical research, which commenced publication under the editorship of Mandell Creighton and was turned into a modern scholarly journal by his former assistant, Poole, in the first two decades of the twentieth century.

Perhaps the greatest of all these publishing ventures was Leslie Stephen's *Dictionary of National Biography,* a miracle of collective authorship (a modern-day successor to which is, in 1997, well underway); the *DNB*'s hundreds of articles, which remain the first port of call for many students and scholars, were to provide useful training exercises for a whole generation of *fin de siècle* English historians such as Pollard and C.H. Firth. Finally, among "antiquarian" works whose parentage can be traced back to Camden and his late-Elizabethan contemporaries, the *Victoria History of the Counties of England* (usually known by the shorthand "VCH"), which is still unfinished after a nearly a century, aspired to provide exhaustive studies of the geography, natural history, architecture, and antiquities of individual shires. (It is worth noting that the VCH was in large measure the work of female medievalists, who contributed extensively to its essays on social and economic history, particularly in its earliest volumes.) The VCH spawned its own line of descendants, including a growing number of local historical journals, as well as the school of English Local History School established by W.G. Hoskins (1908–1992) and now based at the University of Leicester, and a modern collaborative venture, the multivolume *Agrarian History of England and Wales.*

The Twentieth Century

From the Renaissance through the late nineteenth century, it would be fair to say that literary style had always outweighed depth of research and originality of scholarship as a requirement for the historian. There had always been exceptions—John Selden in the seventeenth century had made virtually a fetish out of his combination of profound erudition and opaque, dull style—but it would be an anachronistic mistake to look too far back for the putative "scientific" history of the modern era. The Victorians had made a show of scholarship, though the most erudite and painstaking of their number, such as the medievalist Francis Palgrave (1788–1861), keeper of the queen's records (mentioned above as an opponent of women historians), had remained on the margins of historical writing and commanded relatively little public interest. In choosing among the narrative historians, too, readers showed a decided preference for the flash of a Macaulay over the solid learning of a Creighton. On the other hand, even the great literary masters knew that their histories had to be trusted, and visits to the archives or at least the British Museum, were becoming part of the historian's writing process; but research was not yet conceived of as an intellectually distinct activity to be largely completed before writing began, as illustrated by the working habits of Gardiner, who relied thoroughly on primary sources, studied in chronological order, but wrote them up as he went along, a practice from which his modern admirers have abstained.

The scholarly foundations of the nineteenth century would, however, help to support the remarkable edifice of erudition constructed by another scholar who labored outside a history department, the lawyer and constitutional expert Frederic William Maitland (1850–1906), who was Downing professor of the laws of England at Cambridge from 1888 until his ill health led first to a premature retirement and then an early death. Although he had a relatively short career, Maitland was the prolific author or editor of a great number of works, and his scrupulously careful attention to medieval legal records in the Public Record Office helped to keep medieval history on the pedestal built for it by Stubbs as the "elite" field of English historical research. Maitland also reinforced the interest of Stubbs in constitutional history while seriously revising much of what the bishop had written. Although his works are relatively dry and have never been popular favorites, Maitland is now revered as the first English historian fully to adopt the methods of Ranke and of Theodor Mommsen (the eminent German classicist), and to turn the technical knowledge of the legal historian toward the study of past society at large. G.R. Elton (1921–1994), author of a brief book about Maitland, once remarked that the latter was the only twentieth-century historian whom he completely admired.

Maitland's impact was at first indirect, since historians did not give up writing narratives in favor of his sort of intensive legal study. Victorians such as Gardiner and Creighton had their heirs in political historians such as Charles Harding Firth (1857–1936) of Oxford, who continued Gardiner's account of the seventeenth century, and A.F. Pollard, who anticipated Elton's modern vision of the sixteenth century. Maitland's methods, developed for the study of central legal records, were also to some degree better-suited to medievalists, than to scholars working on modern periods for which the font of surviving records is so vast as to be unmasterable by a single historian. Ultimately, Maitland's most enduring legacy was what he himself represented as a model of tireless research and cautious analysis.

It is impossible to summarize adequately the richness of historical scholarship in England since World War I and any attempt to do so in the space of a short article would end up as a mere list of names; a few highlights will have to suffice here. Among the political historians active in the first third of the century, perhaps the most powerful, in mind as well as personality, was Lewis Namier (1888–1960), a Jewish émigré from Polish Russia. Through his thorough exploitation of the vast archive of the dukes of Newcastle, Namier painted a picture of politics in the mid-eighteenth century that was nearly as revolutionary as Maitland's, both in its methods and in its conclusions. It was Namier who finally made the eighteenth century a legitimate field of study in its own right, and he, too, who virtually invented the technique of "prosopography," the study of institutions through a minute examination of the collective biographies of their members. Although he himself has been criticized for reducing political issues to mere partisan and family interests, devoid of principle, his methods remain in use. It was in the Namierite tradition and initially under the master's own influence that the ongoing History of Parliament project was conceived. The project, which is based in London, continues to grind out collections containing brief but definitive biographies of every person who has ever sat as a member of Parliament.

One could list many other important political historians from Namier's day to the present, but the first half of the century is also noticeable for the early growth of social history before its great breakthrough in the 1960s and 1970s. There had been hints of this before, in the Enlightenment's attention to manners and customs, in Buckle's interest in civilization and learning, in the famous chapter on English society in 1685 in Macaulay's history, and, above all, in the *Short History of the English People* (1874) by John Richard Green (1837–1883). A chronically ill parson, Green is one of the more attractive figures among the later Victorian historians but is mentioned at this stage precisely because his interest in the past lives of ordinary people made him an oddity among the Victorians; one of the most remarkable facts about him is that despite this unusual interest, he was, very strangely, befriended by the curmudgeonly Freeman, a man famous for saying that "history is past politics and politics present history."

Freeman's view of the close relation of history and politics was closer to the Victorian understanding of the scope of history than Green's popular heterodoxy. So powerful a voice as Cambridge's Seeley had denounced such exercises as Green's as a frivolous diversion from the important task of training future statesmen. Yet the commercial success of Green's work, written toward the end of a century that had seen considerable efforts to ameliorate the lot of the poor through political reform and education, showed that there was an untapped market for this sort of book. This fact was further illustrated by the later success of G.M. Trevelyan's *English Social History* (1944)—which, however, continued to define its subject negatively, as "history with the politics left out."

The pedigree of Green can be traced backward to Adam Smith and the figures of the Scottish Enlightenment; his heritage, however, led forward in two distinct directions. The first of these was economic history. Unlike social history, economic history was fairly quick to find an academic home, albeit in departments of economics and political science. Economic history owed its success in the first part of the twentieth century to the work of groundbreaking scholars like George Unwin (1870–1925), William James Ashley (1860–1927), and John Clapham (1873–1946); Ashley would help to establish economic history in the United States, where he was appointed to a Harvard chair in 1892. Economic history also attracted considerable talent from the moderate left of the political spectrum, including the Webbs, Sidney (1859–1947) and Beatrice (1858–1943); the Hammonds;

Barbara (1873–1961) and John Lawrence Le Breton (1872–1949); and Eileen Power (1889–1940). Economic history continues to be studied in Britain, although since World War II it has receded in status among economists, who have been increasingly concerned with the theoretical and mathematical aspects of their subject. Among historians, it has proved to be less attractive than social history, which necessarily includes aspects of economic history. It continues to attract distinguished female historians such as Sylvia Thrupp (b. 1903–) and Joan Thirsk (b. 1922–); but despite the considerable female contribution to the writing of economic history in the past century, women have not been well-served by appointments to senior professorships in the subfield. Eileen Power, elected to the chair of economic history at the London School of Economics in 1931, was only the second woman appointed to such a professorship; aside from Eleanora N. Carus-Wilson (1897–1977), there have been no women appointed to named chairs of economic history since.

The Hammonds's studies of the laboring poor—and their very different interpretation of the effects of industrialization on living standards from that advanced by Clapham—connect the liberal economic historians with social history proper, which dealt more directly with the daily lives and working conditions of the multitudes of the past and which was, in its non-Marxian forms, less concerned with structures and market forces than was economic history. Many historians deserve some credit for challenging the dominance of political narrative with its generally conservative leanings, for example Alice Clark (1874–1934), a suffragist and early progenitor of women's history, and Power, whose studies of *Medieval English Nunneries* (1922) and *Medieval People* (1924) were similarly pathbreaking, especially in linking the economic to the social. But the most influential founder of social history was Richard Henry Tawney (1880–1962), the Christian Socialist whose *Agrarian Problem in the Sixteenth Century* (1912) and *Religion and the Rise of Capitalism* (1926) show a considerable erudition in economic texts and documents, leavened with a sympathy toward the lot of the poor and an angry hostility to the institutions of the social elite—Tawney could be almost Actonian in his capacity to denounce past examples of capitalist excess. Living through both world wars, Tawney, in retirement, was eventually party to one of the century's most bitter historical controversies, the "storm" over the economic and social standing of the sixteenth- and early-seventeenth-century gentry, which erupted in the early 1950s and pitted him and a young Oxford historian, Lawrence Stone (b. 1919–), on the one side, against the historical essayist and political conservative Hugh Trevor-Roper (b. 1914–) on the other.

From Tawney, the road might be thought to lead more or less directly through the far Left radicalism of the post–World War II Communist Party Historians' Group, some of whose members, such as Eric Hobsbawm (b. 1917) and Christopher Hill (b. 1912), are still alive and active as of 1997; to the most gifted English social historian of the 1960s, 1970s, and 1980s, E.P. Thompson (1924–1993); and to the establishment of journals of social history such as *Past & Present* and its younger, more radical counterpart, *History Workshop*. But it is a crooked road indeed, on which we find historians of wide-ranging interests and ideological leanings. The family resemblance between Green, or even Tawney, at one end, and, at the other, Thompson or Keith Thomas (b. 1933), a historian of early modern popular culture, or the historical demographers such as E.A. Wrigley (b. 1931) and the Cambridge Group for the History of Population and Social Structure, or the oral historian Paul Thompson (b. 1935), is fairly remote, like any ancestral similarity, but it is there nonetheless. At the same time, however, modern English social history cannot be viewed, any more than political history, as a monolith, either ideologically or methodologically. It is worth noting in this connection that English historical writing in the late twentieth century remains most conservative and most impervious to theoretical developments such as postmodernism and to incursions from the social sciences, for the earlier periods (the Middle Ages and early modern eras in particular); it is rather less so for the eighteenth century and after, the period that attracted E.P. Thompson and Asa Briggs (b. 1921) and more recent students of class such as Raphael Samuel, Gareth Stedman Jones, and Patrick Joyce.

The last ten years have seen a slight cooling of interest in social history and certainly a turning away from the kind of heavily quantitative social-science-influenced work that appeared from the mid-1960s to the early 1980s, but political history has not even come close to regaining its once unshakable dominance. Although there has been a government-sponsored move in the 1990s to turn the undergraduate and school curriculum back to "essentials" like English history, there also exists vigorous resistance to that notion. The breadth of historical writing today is marked by a high degree of activity in a number of new approaches, many of which derive ultimately from postwar social history. There is, for instance, a strong interest in women's history and gender studies, which may yet redress the underrepresentation of women in the senior professional ranks. Cultural history has become a staple of seminars and monographs, especially in the early modern and modern periods. Twentieth-century studies of England and the wider world are an area of growth—both traditional political histories of parliamentary politics or the world wars (in the tradition of the controversial A.J.P. Taylor [1906–1990]), and newer types of social history that involve the use of innovative techniques such as oral history. Longer-established subdisciplines, focusing on non-European history continue to thrive, reflecting both three decades of postimperial immigration to the United Kingdom and the current political trend toward European unity and a broader "globalization"; this is manifest in the historiographical activities of institutions such as the School of Oriental and African Studies (SOAS) at the University of London, and in the continued vitality of imperial and commonwealth history. Although the production of doctorates in history has slowed since the mid-1980s owing to cutbacks in higher education in the wake of Thatcherism, the universities continue to produce high-level specialized research. The several university presses, and commercial publishers like Longman and Penguin, continue successfully to market such research to the general public. Many old issues continue to be fought, such as the nature of medieval kingship, or the origins and significance of the English civil war, but at least they are pursued with more refined scholarly methods and, on occasion, with new and imaginative insights drawn from beyond the discipline. As the millennium ends, English historiography has relinquished whatever intellectual hegemony it had in the nineteenth century, but it has not yet lost its capacity to produce work of striking originality and rigorous scholarship, nor its considerable appeal as part of the educated person's literary diet.

D.R. Woolf

See also CLASS; CULTURAL HISTORY; ENGLISH HISTORIOGRAPHY—MEDIEVAL AND EARLY MODERN (TO 1700); HISTORY WORKSHOP; IMPERIAL AND COMMONWEALTH HISTORY, BRITISH; INDUSTRIAL REVOLUTION; JOURNALS, HISTORICAL; PROFESSIONALIZATION OF HISTORY; SCOTTISH HISTORIOGRAPHY; SOCIAL HISTORY; WHIG INTERPRETATION.

E

References

Berg, Maxine. *A Woman in History: Eileen Power, 1889–1940.* Cambridge, Eng.: Cambridge University Press, 1996.

Blaas, P.B.M. *Continuity and Anachronism: Parliamentary and Constitutional Development in Whig Historiography and in the Anti-Whig Reaction Between 1890 and 1930.* The Hague and Boston: M. Nijhoff, 1978.

Burrow, J.W. *A Liberal Descent: Victorian Historians and the English Past.* Cambridge, Eng.: Cambridge University Press, 1981.

Butterfield, Herbert. *The Whig Interpretation of History.* New York: AMS Press, 1978.

Douglas, D.C. *English Scholars, 1660–1730.* Second ed. London, Eyre & Spottiswoode, 1951.

Gooch, G.P. *History and Historians in the Nineteenth Century.* London and New York: Longmans, Green, 1913.

Kaye, Harvey J. *The British Marxist Historians.* Cambridge, Eng.: Polity Press, 1984.

Kenyon, John. *The History Men: The Historical Profession in England since the Renaissance.* Second ed. London: Weidenfeld and Nicolson, 1993.

Levine, Philippa. *The Amateur and the Professional: Antiquarians, Historians, and Archaeologists in Victorian England, 1838–1886.* Cambridge, Eng.: Cambridge University Press, 1986.

Maitzen, Rohan. "'This Feminine Preserve': Historical Biographies by Victorian Women." *Victorian Studies* 35 (1995): 371–393.

Taylor, Miles. "The Beginnings of Modern British Social History." *History Workshop Journal* 43 (1997): 155–176.

Thirsk, Joan. "The History Women." In *Chattel, Servant or Citizen,* ed. Mary O'Dowd and Sabine Wichert. Belfast, N. Ireland: Institute of Irish Studies, Queen's University of Belfast, 1995, 1–11.

Woolf, D.R. "A Feminine Past? Gender, Genre, and Historical Knowledge in England, 1500–1800." *American Historical Review,* 102 (1997); 645–79.

Wormell, Deborah. *Sir John Seeley and the Uses of History.* Cambridge, Eng.: Cambridge University Press, 1980.

Enlightenment Historiography

The form of European historiography characteristic of the European Enlightenment. Not comprising all eighteenth-century historiography, this specific form combined research among archival documents and other sorts of evidence with a critical standpoint, especially along the lines of the arguments of the literary figures associated with the philosophy of the Enlightenment movement. Its proponents agreed that civilization was made up of more than just diplomacy and battles and that historiography must be more than an accumulation of facts. However, just as the Enlightenment itself was varied and the positions espoused by its exponents were often in disagreement, not just from country to country but from individual to individual, so also Enlightenment historiography varied widely. Subjects ranged from modern China (François Arouet de Voltaire) to the art of Greek antiquity (Johann Joachim Winckelmann). Chief influences ran from the seventeenth-century legal historian Arthur Duck (on Pietro Giannone) to the Enlightenment political theorist Jean-Jacques Rousseau (on Johannes Müller). Interpretations and guiding principles were often in distinct contrast. Edward Gibbon, for instance, in spite of his convictions about the role of Christianity in the fall of the Roman Empire, did not share the virulent anti-ecclesiastical attitude of Voltaire. Johann Gottfried Herder did not share Marie Jean Antoine Caritat de Condorcet's assurance about the likelihood of progress in human affairs nor Gibbon's admiration for classical culture. And along with Justus Möser, he disagreed with the rationalist faith of Gibbon and Voltaire. Furthermore, a figure like Giambattista Vico, who can scarcely be excluded from the methodological and philosophical innovativeness that were the hallmark both of the Enlightenment and its historiography, nonetheless disagreed with practically every other tenet of the movement. He insisted upon recurring cycles rather than progress, he remained aloof from any explicit criticism of existing institutions (at least in his historical work), and he deliberately undermined the validity of classical antiquity as a source of models for civil conduct.

In spite of this complexity, Enlightenment historiography may be said to have emerged fully grown in one publication: Neapolitan historian Pietro Giannone's *Storia civile del regno di Napoli* [Civil History of the Kingdom of Naples] in 1723, which combined research and social criticism in a novel way. It presented a new historiographical approach, treating cultural and social events as the bases for political ones. It drew primarily upon documents or upon sixteenth- and seventeenth-century repertories of documents rather than upon previous narratives. It investigated the origins of the problems of contemporary Naples in the feudal and ecclesiastical power exercised during the kingdom's various periods of foreign domination. And, it offered its conclusions as a model for the reforms Giannone believed were necessary in Neapolitan society.

Similarly in France, the *Le siècle de Louis XIV* [The Age of Louis XIV] (1751) of Voltaire, though far less erudite in method ("devil take the details," he once said), aimed to reconstruct an entire cultural and social epoch as a basis from which to criticize the current regime, in this case in order to propose the model of Enlightened despotism. His *Essai sur les moeurs* [Essay on Manners] (1753) served as a far more powerful indictment of contemporary institutions, aimed at opposing the providential view of history by the values of secularism, humanity, justice, and civilization. In it, Voltaire provided daring examples of comparative history (juxtaposing modern Quakers and early Christians, modern Westerners and modern Chinese), but rarely revealing his sources of information—as Gibbon later complained. Condorcet's *Esquisse d'un tableau historique des progres de l'espirit humain* [Sketch for a Historical Picture of the Progress of the Human Mind], while not a work of research, deserves mention as the mature expression of the law of progress through technological advance and instruction that was a hallmark of the French school.

The influential *Universal History* (1747–1768) of George Sale and his collaborators, including Archibald Bower, belongs to the British Enlightenment mainly for its extraordinary breadth of conception; methodologically it was not particularly innovative and the collaborative scheme prevented a unified philosophical point of view, much less a single social purpose. Such features on the other hand were present in Scottish philosopher David Hume's *History of England from the Invasion of Julius Caesar to the Revolution in 1688* (1754–1761). Based on the empirical principles of causation explained by Hume in his *Inquiry Concerning Human Understanding* (1758), this work conducted the Enlightenment battle against fanaticism and party spirit both on the Tory and the Whig sides. Nonetheless, the first in Britain to come seriously to terms with Voltaire's historical ideas was William Robertson, who, covering some of the same historical periods as Voltaire in his *History of the Reign of the Emperor Charles V* (1769), was knowledgeable enough to understand the *Essai*'s value as well as criticize its faulty scholarship. To correct this defect, he made good use of his knowledge of medieval legal and constitutional

history in a series of "proofs and illustrations" backing up his narrative and actually amounting to independent dissertations. Where he failed was to achieve a fully harmonious combination of erudite research and philosophy. Here Edward Gibbon, in his *History of the Decline and Fall of the Roman Empire* (1778–1788), succeeded more brilliantly than any other writer of the age. Far less scornful than Voltaire of late-seventeenth- and early-eighteenth-century paleography, numismatics, epigraphy, and textual criticism, he carefully mined the classical works of Jean Mabillon, Gottfried Wilhelm Leibniz, Ezechiel Spanheim, Thierry Ruinart, Richard Simon, and Ludovico Antonio Muratori. And his unsurpassed portrait of medieval life and institutions was a model for all subsequent historiography.

The new historiography received an actual (though by no means exclusive) institutional context in the newly founded University of Göttingen and in the *Allgemeine historische Bibliothek* [General Historical Library] founded in 1767 with an introduction by Johann Christoph Gatterer explaining the application of philosophical principles to universal history. The German Enlightenment historiography that emerged from this self-conscious professionalization of the discipline contributed much to the historicist movement of the following century, but was by no means identical with that movement. Justus Möser, who in his *Osnabrückische Geschichte* [History of Osnabrück] (1768) pioneered the use of statutes for tracing social history, was just as careful as Voltaire to emphasize the ethical values proven by his research, and he traced the origins of modern despotism to the decline of the medieval communes. Swiss-born and Göttingen-educated Johannes Müller wrote *Der Geschichten schweizerischer Eidgenossenschaft* [History of the Swiss Confederation] (1786) with all the passion characteristic of the Gothic revival then in progress. Like Möser, with whom he shared an admiration for Rousseau, he held up the Middle Ages as a time of now-lost spiritual profundity. To Herder fell the task of summarizing and interpreting the accomplishments of the entire school, in his *Ideen zur Philosophie der Geschichte der Menschheit* [Ideas Concerning the Philosophy of the History of Mankind] (1784–1791), where, without engaging in any sort of original research himself, he drew upon all the main contributors of the century, from Giannone to Möser to Müller, organizing his argument according to the most fundamental categories of Enlightenment thought (for example, the chapter heading: "The human race is destined to change course and culture and form, but its well-being will always be based on reason and justice.") Herder's theories about the invariability of national character and race, about the differences in the distribution of abilities from one culture to another, about cultures of particular peoples as organic wholes contributed as much to the development of historiographical thought in his own century as they did to the nationalist historiography that was to be the hallmark of the post-Enlightenment.

B. Dooley

Texts

Condorcet, Jean-Antoine-Nicolas de Caritat, Marquis de. *Sketch for a Historical Picture of the Progress of the Human Mind.* Trans. June Barraclough, with an introduction by Stuart Hampshire. London: Weidenfeld and Nicolson, 1955.

Gianonne, Pietro. *Istoria civile del Regno di Napoli.* Ed. Antonio Marongiu. 7 vols. Milan: Marzorati, 1970–1972.

Gibbon, Edward. *The History of the Decline and Fall of the Roman Empire.* Ed. J.B. Bury. 7 vols. New York: AMS Press, 1974.

Herder, Johann Gottfried. *Outlines of a Philosophy of the History of Man.* Trans. T. Churchill. New York: Bergman Publishers, 1966.

Hume, David. *The History of England from the Invasion of Julius Caesar to the Revolution in 1688.* 6 vols. Indianapolis, IN: Liberty Classics, 1983–1985.

Möser, Justus. *Sämmtliche Werke.* 14 vols. Oldenburg-Berlin: G. Stalling, 1944–1990, vols. 12–13: *Osnabruckische Geschichte.*

Müller, Johannes von. *Der Geschichten schweizerischer Eidgenossenschaft.* Ed. Friedrich Gundolf. Leipzig: H. Haessel, 1923.

Robertson, William. *The History of the Reign of the Emperor Charles V.* 2 vols. Philadelphia: Robert Bell, 1770.

Vico, Giambattista. *The New Science.* Trans. Thomas Goddard Bergin and Max Harold Fisch. Ithaca, NY: Cornell University Press, 1968.

Voltaire, François Arouet de. *The Age of Louis XIV.* Trans. Martyn P. Pollack. London: J.M. Dent, 1961.

Winckelmann, Johann Joachim. *History of Ancient Art.* New York: F. Ungar, 1968.

References

Blanke, Horst Walter. *Aufklärung und Historik: Aufsätze zur Entwicklung der Geschichtswissenschaft, Kirchengeschichte und Geschichtstheorie in der deutschen Aufklärung* [Enlightenment and History: Studies in the Development of Historical Learning, Church History, and Historical Theory in the German Enlightenment]. Waltrop, Germany: Spenner, 1991.

Fueter, Eduard. *Geschichte der neueren Historiographie* [History of Modern Historiography]. Münich: R. Oldenbourg, 1911.

Grell, Chantal. *L'histoire entre erudition et philosophie: Étude sur la connaissance historique à l'age des Lumières* [History between Erudition and Philosophy: A Study of Historical Knowledge in the Age of Enlightenment]. Paris: Presses universitaires de France, 1993.

Krieger, Leonard. "The Heavenly City of the Eighteenth-Century Historians." *Church History* 47 (1978): 279–297.

Levine, Joseph M. *Humanism and History: Origins of Modern English Historiography.* Ithaca, NY: Cornell University Press, 1987.

Momigliano, Arnaldo. "Eighteenth-Century Prelude to Mr. Gibbon." In his *Sesto contributo.* Rome: Edizione di storia letterata, 1980, 249–263.

Ennen, Edith (b. 1907)

German historian of medieval towns and of women. Ennen studied first at Freiburg and Berlin before earning her doctorate (1933) at Bonn with a study of *Die Organisation der Selbstverwaltung in den Saarstädten vom ausgehenden Mittelalter bis zur Französischen Revolution* [The Organization of Autonomy in the Saar from the End of the Middle Ages to the French Revolution]. In 1935 she qualified as an archivist in Berlin, and worked from 1936 to 1947 as an assistant at the Institut für geschichtliche Landeskunde der Rheinlande (an organization she would later direct, from 1968 to her retirement in 1974). After World War II she directed the municipal archives of Bonn. In 1961, she was appointed honorary professor at Bonn, moving to a chair in Saarbrücken in 1964. Interested in Rhenish agrarian and rural history, her principal area of activity has, however, been urban history. The author of a number of systematic and carefully researched studies, based on a profound knowledge of both literary and archival sources, Ennen has distinguished herself as one of the most widely respected of scholars working on the history of the medieval town. Her 1972 book *Die europäische Stadt des Mittelalters* [The European City in the Middle Ages] (1972) remains an important survey of that subject, and her earlier examination of urban history from the beginning of the Romano-Germanic era, *Frühgeschichte der europäischen Stadt* [Early History of the European City] (1953), is one of the best descriptions of the transition from the late Roman to the fully formed medieval town. Ennen was also a pioneering women's historian and became well known to a wider public with her book *Frauen im Mittelalter* [Women in the Middle Ages] (1984), in which are described women's conditions of life from the fifth century A.D. to the Reformation.

Thomas Fuchs

Texts

Frauen im Mittelalter. Fourth ed. Munich: C.H. Beck, 1991.
Frühgeschichte der europäischen Stadt. Third ed. Bonn: Ludwig Röhrscheid, 1981.
Gesammelte Abhandlungen zum europäischen Städtewesen und zur rheinischen Geschichte [Collected Papers on European Towns and Rhenish History]. Vol. 1. Ed. G. Droege et al.; vol. 2. Ed. D. Hörold and F. Irisigler. Bonn: Ludwig Röhrscheid, 1977–1987.
The Medieval Town. Amsterdam: North Holland Publishing, 1979.

References

"Ennen, Edith." In *Kürschners Deutscher Gelehrtenkalender 1992.* Sixteenth ed. vol. 1. Berlin: Walter de Gruyter, 1992.

Environmental History—United States

Writing in the United States concerning the North American environment and its historical development; a subfield of American history and of environmental history. U.S. environmental historiography can be loosely clustered into the following categories: the dual relationship between people and nature; the conservation and preservation movements; and the ideology of environment. The first category would include William Cronon's *Changes in the Land: Indians, Colonists, and the Ecology of New England* (1983) and Richard White's *The Roots of Dependency: Subsistence, Environment, and Social Change among the Choctaws, Pawnees, and Navajos* (1983), both of which works attempt to place humans within, interacting with, and influencing their environments.

In the second category one can place Samuel P. Hays, whose *Conservation and the Gospel of Efficiency: The Progressive Conservation Movement* (1959), written in an earlier period of political

history, focuses on historical actors with conservation concerns such as Gifford Pinchot and Theodore Roosevelt. Conversely Stephen R. Fox's study of *John Muir and His Legacy: The American Conservation Movement* (1981) focused on the battle between the preservationist John Muir and Gifford Pinchot; unlike Hays, who wrote before the high tide of environmentalism, Fox openly sides with the preservationist.

The third category includes studies such as Roderick Frazier Nash's *The Rights of Nature: A History of Environmental Ethics* (1989) and Donald Worster's *Nature's Economy: A History of Ecological Ideas* (1977); these works, by preeminent intellectual historians, methodically trace the ideology and ethics of various environmentalists in the past. This historiography has its origins in frontier history. Variously reviled, revised, and loved, Frederick Jackson Turner, the cornerstone of frontier history, unwittingly pioneered environmental history, in "The Significance of the Frontier in American History" (1893). By the 1930s, Walter Prescott Webb clearly saw himself as an environmental historian. In *The Great Plains* (1931), Webb also stressed land along with other aspects of nature, including climate, animals, and plants. Both historians developed themes prominent in the contemporary historiography. In addition, James Malin's *History and Ecology: Studies of the Grassland* (1984) was a significant contribution to the early historiography. Rachel Carson's *Silent Spring* (1962), the popular exposé of pesticides, is a rough dividing line between this pre- and post-1960s historiography.

A new environmental history is evolving in the 1980s and 1990s. Martin V. Melosi's *Garbage in the Cities: Refuse, Reform, and Environment, 1880–1930* (1981) and William Cronon's *Nature's Metropolis: Chicago and the Great West* (1991) are the foundation for a growing urban environmental history. Carolyn Merchant has written one of many histories to critique the gendered construction of the environment, with *Ecological Revolutions: Nature, Gender, and Science in New England* (1989). Jeffery K. Stine's *Mixing the Waters: Environment, Politics, and the Building of the Tennessee–Tombigbee Waterway* (1993) and Arthur F. McEvoy's *Fisherman's Problem: Ecology and the Law in the California Fisheries, 1850–1980* (1986) are emblematic of analyses of utilitarian use and exploitation of the waterways and oceans, respectively. William Cronon's *Changes in the Land* (1983) and Richard White's *The Roots of Dependency* (1983), both of which are multicultural histories, underscore the relationship between whites, Native Americans, and nature. Finally,

Alfred Crosby's *The Columbian Exchange: Biological and Cultural Consequences of 1492* (1972) and Carolyn Merchant's *The Death of Nature: Women, Ecology, and the Scientific Revolution* (1980) represent the growing field of global history.

Dianne D. Glave

See also ENVIRONMENTAL HISTORY—WORLD; WORLD HISTORY; WORLD SYSTEMS THEORY.

Texts

Cronon, William. *Changes in the Land: Indians, Colonists, and the Ecology of New England* New York: Hill and Wang, 1983.

———. *Nature's Metropolis: Chicago and the Great West.* New York: Norton, 1991.

Crosby, Alfred. *The Columbian Exchange: Biological and Cultural Consequences of 1492.* Westport, CT: Greenwood, 1972.

Fox, Stephen R. *John Muir and His Legacy: The American Conservation Movement.* Boston: Little, Brown, 1981.

Hays, Samuel P. *Conservation and the Gospel of Efficiency: The Progressive Conservation Movement.* Cambridge, MA: Harvard University Press, 1959.

Malin, James. *History and Ecology: Studies of the Grassland.* Ed. Robert P. Swierenga. Lincoln: University of Nebraska Press, 1984.

McEvoy, Arthur F. *The Fisherman's Problem: Ecology and the Law in the California Fisheries, 1850–1980.* New York: Cambridge University Press, 1986.

Melosi, Martin V. *Garbage in the Cities: Refuse, Reform, and Environment, 1880–1930.* College Station: Texas A&M University Press, 1981.

White, Richard. *The Roots of Dependency: Subsistence, Environment, and Social Change among the Choctaws, Pawnees, and Navajos.* Lincoln: University of Nebraska Press, 1983.

References

Merchant, Carolyn, ed. *Major Problems in American Environmental History.* Lexington, MA: D.C. Heath and Co., 1993.

White, Richard. "American Environmental History: The Development of a New Historical Field." *Pacific Historical Review* 54 (1985): 297–335.

Worster, Donald, et al. "A Roundtable: Environmental History." *Journal of American History* 76 (1990): 1087–1146.

Environmental History—World

As a subject, environmental history is the study of how human beings and human societies have related to the natural world through time. As a method, it is the use of ecological analysis as a means of understanding human history. Environmental historians recognize the ways in which the living and nonliving systems of the earth have influenced the course of human affairs. They also evaluate the impacts of changes caused by human agency in the natural environment. To do environmental history properly requires familiarity with ecology and other sciences, the history of science and technology, and geography and other branches of the social sciences and humanities. Indeed, much good environmental history has been written by geographers and scientists as well as historians. There are several historical fields so closely allied to environmental history that a rigid line of separation cannot be drawn. These include but are not limited to forest history, agricultural history, historical climatology, and the history of epidemics.

The emergence of environmental history as an active subdiscipline parallels the growth of environmentalism, particularly in North America and Europe, after World War II. It has roots, however, in earlier writing about relationships between nature and human history. Ancient Greek thinkers such as Herodotus, Hippocrates, and Theophrastus speculated on environmental influences. Among modern commentators, first place is often accorded to George Perkins Marsh, U.S. ambassador to Italy, whose great work, *Man and Nature,* appeared in 1864. Marsh observed that many human activities such as deforestation deplete the natural resources on which civilization depends. He suggested that this factor contributed to the downfall of the Roman Empire and other organized societies.

Initially environmental history faced a problem of acceptance in part because it was confused with environmental determinism, the doctrine that climate and other external factors control human affairs. Marsh was not a determinist, but Ellsworth Huntington did take such a position in books such as *Civilization and Climate* and had racist opinions as well. Later students of climate such as Emmanuel Le Roy Ladurie *(Times of Feast, Times of Famine)* did something to remove the stigma of determinism, but the need for careful correlation of climatic changes and historical events remained.

As part of an effort to broaden the horizon of history, the Annales school in France emphasized the importance of geographical settings and provided a formative impulse for environmental history. Lucien Febvre's *Geographical Introduction to History,* which anticipated some topics that would be explored, was published in 1924. Fernand Braudel's study, *The Mediterranean and the Mediterranean World in the Age of Philip II,* is a model work in the field.

Under the stimulus of rising environmental concern, the American Society for Environmental History (ASEH) was founded in 1976. Its journal, *Environmental Review,* subsequently retitled *Environmental History Review,* now *Environmental History,* and its biennial conferences included papers on many areas of the world. Kendall Bailes edited a collection of some of these (*Environmental History: Critical Issues in Comparative Perspective*). A European Association for Environmental History (EAEH) was later organized. The journal *Environment and History,* published in England but with a strong interest in Asia, Africa, and beyond, began in 1995. In the same year, a Belgian-produced Dutch-language journal, *Tijdschrift voor Ecologische Geschiedenis,* also commenced publication. Other periodicals that often open their pages to articles on world environmental history include *Annales: E.S.C.; Capitalism, Nature, Socialism; Écologie Politique; The Ecologist* (UK); *Environmental Ethics; Journal of World History;* and *Mountain Research and Development.* Cambridge University has a global environmental history unit in the history of science department.

Not surprisingly for so vast a topic, no adequate general study of world environmental history has appeared. A seminal collection of essays spanning the chronological sweep of human history, *Man's Role in Changing the Face of the Earth,* appeared in 1956 under the editorship of W.L. Thomas Jr. More recently, Donald Worster collected a representative series of articles. Late in his career, Arnold Toynbee took up the task of writing an environmental history of the world, but his *Mankind and Mother Earth* does not seriously address many major environmental questions. I.G. Simmons addresses these admirably, but is brief. Clive Ponting produced *A Green History of the World,* a topical treatment of environmental issues in human history that is a useful introduction, but suffers from lack of documentation. At this writing, no world history textbook does anything more than nod in the direction of environmental history, and many ignore the subject.

Chronologically, environmental historians have emphasized the last two centuries, when human-initiated processes of environmental change were rapid and noticeable, but work on earlier periods is not lacking. Clarence Glacken produced a much-admired survey of the history of pivotal environmental ideas to 1800 entitled *Traces on the Rhodian Shore* (1967), but did not complete a projected volume covering the modern Western world. The ancient Mediterranean basin is examined in Donald Hughes's *Pan's Travail,* which emphasizes Greek and Roman environmental problems. Robert Sallares wrote a detailed treatment, *The Ecology of the Ancient Greek World.* There are useful studies of Mediterranean forest history by Russell Meiggs *(Trees and Timber in the Ancient Mediterranean World)* and by J.V. Thirgood *(Man and the Mediterranean Forest).* The best treatment of cultural ecology in ancient Egypt is by the environmental archaeologist, Karl Butzer, and titled *Early Hydraulic Civilization in Egypt.*

One of the most influential articles ever published on environmental history was "The Historical Roots of Our Ecologic Crisis," by the medievalist and historian of technology, Lynn White, published in *Science* in 1967. White argued that the modern tendency to abuse the environment resulted from the Western medieval Christian tendency to devalue the natural world. Antithetically, in her book, *Christianity, Wilderness, and Wildlife,* Susan Bratton asserted that monasticism contained a strong tradition of nature appreciation. Charles Bowlus, in a collection by Lester Bilsky entitled *Historical Ecology,* tied famine and the Black Death to deforestation and environmental deterioration.

The environmental history of the modern world, however, has received by far the most attention from scholars. *The Earth as Transformed by Human Action,* edited by B.L. Turner II and others (1990), is an updated successor to Thomas's pioneering collection. In early modern environmental history, the impact of imperialism on colonial landscapes, and on colonizing societies, has received admirable treatment from Alfred Crosby in the much acclaimed *Columbian Exchange* and its wide-ranging sequel, *Ecological Imperialism.* He investigated the intrusion of European biota into formerly isolated ecosystems that did not resist them well, such as America, Australia, and many islands. Richard Grove's *Green Imperialism* concentrates on India, South Africa, and oceanic islands, showing how observation of changes in the climate and vegetation of these places stimulated the rise of modern environmentalist thought. Richard Tucker and John Richards edited a collection, *Global Deforestation and the Nineteenth-Century World Economy.*

A brief look at writing in the environmental history of major regions outside North America might begin with Europe. An excellent collection of essays in European environmental history is *The Silent Countdown,* edited by Peter Brimblecombe and Christian Pfister. There are active environmental history groups in several European nations, whose activities are chronicled in the *Environmental History Newsletter* of the EAEH. Andrew Jamison and others compiled a comparative study of environmental movements in Sweden, Denmark, and the Netherlands, entitled *The Making of the New Environmental Consciousness.* Among recent works in France are Pascal Acot's *Ecologie et environnements* and J.M. Drouin's *L'écologie et son histoire.* The environmental history of the Netherlands has several important studies, including G. van de Ven's collection, *Manmade Lowlands* (1993), covering the history of land reclamation, and a history of the conservation movement (in Dutch) by H.J. van der Windt (1995). Ernst-Eberhard Manski, of Stevoort, has begun a multilingual bibliographical database of European environmental history. John McNeill's *Mountains of the Mediterranean World* covers five representative localities and their peoples.

The environmental history of Russia is the concern of several scholars at the Institute for the History of Science and Technology of the Russian Academy of Sciences, including Yuri Chaikovsky, Anton Struchkov, and Galina Krivosheina. Douglas Weiner has produced several studies of Russian environmentalism, notably *Models of Nature.*

South Asia has a strong tradition of academic history, and environmental history there is allied with ecology and history of science. In India, due to the historical experience of the subcontinent, environmental history emphasizes forest history. Two leading researchers, Ramachandra Guha of the Nehru Memorial Museum and Library in New Delhi, and Madhav Gadgil of the Indian Institute of Science, Bangalore, coauthored *This Fissured Land,* an ecological history of India. The History of Science division of the National Institute of Science, Technology, and Development Studies, New Delhi, sponsored an impressive series of publications and conferences, forwarded by Deepak Kumar and Satpal Sangwan. A collection of important papers appeared as *Nature and the Orient,* edited by Richard Grove and others. Ajay Rawat of Kumaon University chronicled the deforestation of the Himalaya and its effect upon local people, especially women and tribes, in a number of publications including his edited *History of Forestry in India.* Ranabir Chakravarty wrote on the effects of ancient irrigation, and Subash Chandran studied ancient sacred groves that still survive today, protected by villagers.

The *Indonesian Environmental History Newsletter* is published in Leiden, the Netherlands, by an international group of scholars. Environmental scholarship in Indonesia itself is still in an early stage. On Oceania, there is a fine article by John McNeill, "Of Rats and Men," in the *Journal of World History.* John Dargavel, a forest historian, has convened conferences and edited the collection *Changing Tropical Forests: Historical Perspectives on Today's Challenges in Asia, Australasia and Oceania.*

China is a vast realm whose environmental history has barely been touched. The best study available is Yi-fu Tuan's brief *China.* Vaclav Smil's *The Bad Earth* and He Bochuan's *China on the Edge* are contemporary environmental studies with little historical depth. (The last-named work was suppressed in China.) "Ecological Crisis and Response in Ancient China" by Lester Bilsky, in his edited volume, is a valuable article. Japan is represented by T.C. Smith's *Agrarian Origins of Modern Japan* and several works by Conrad Totman, including *The Green Archipelago.*

Historians in Africa have given much attention to conservation. An important collection is *Conservation in Africa,* edited by David Anderson and Richard Grove. There are a number of important publications by H. Kjejkshus (for example, *Ecology Control and Economic Development in East African History)* and William Beinart ("Soil Erosion, Conservationism and Ideas about Development" in *Journal of Southern African Studies).* The tendency to think of conservation as a topic outside the political sphere is countered in Clark Gibson's "Killing Animals with Guns and Ballots" in *Environmental History Review.*

Works on the environmental history of Latin America have been strongly influenced by Crosby's conception of biological exchange. A good example is Elinor Melville's *Plague of Sheep,* which investigates environmental consequences of the conquest of Mexico. Warren Dean produced important studies of the destruction of Brazilian forests, such as *With Broadax and Firebrand.*

In recent years, the creation of the United Nations Environment Programme and other international agencies concerned with conservation and sustainable development has opened a new field for historians. John McCormick, *Reclaiming Paradise,* and John Young, *Sustaining the Earth,* are fine book-length studies.

Finally, no general historiography of environmental history has appeared, but William Green included a valuable chapter in his *History, Historians, and the Dynamics of Change.* Green maintains that no approach to history is more perceptive of human interconnections in the world community or of the interdependence of humans and other living beings on the planet. Environmental history, he adds, supplements traditional economic, social, and political forms of historical analysis. As Braudel once observed, the environment can no longer be seen merely as the stage setting on which human history is enacted. It is an actor; indeed, it comprises a major portion of the cast.

J. Donald Hughes

See also ANNALES SCHOOL; ENVIRONMENTAL HISTORY—UNITED STATES; WORLD HISTORY.

References

Bailes, Kendall E., ed. *Environmental History: Critical Issues in Comparative Perspective.* Lanham, MD: University Press of America, 1985.

Bilsky, Lester J., ed. *Historical Ecology: Essays on Environment and Social Change.* Port Washington, NY: Kennikat Press, 1980.

Green, William A. "Environmental History." In his *History, Historians, and the Dynamics of Change.* Westport, CT: Praeger, 1993, 167–190.

Hughes, J. Donald. "Ecology and Development As Narrative Themes of World History," *Environmental History Review* 19 (1995): 1–16.

Marsh, George Perkins. *Man and Nature.* Cambridge, MA: Harvard University Press, 1965.

Simmons, Ian Gordon. *Changing the Face of the Earth: Culture, Environment, History.* Oxford: Blackwell, 1989.

———. *Environmental History: A Concise Introduction.* Oxford, Blackwell, 1993.

Thomas, William L., Jr., ed. *Man's Role in Changing the Face of the Earth.* Chicago: University of Chicago Press, 1956.

Worster, Donald, ed. *The Ends of the Earth: Perspectives on Modern Environmental History.* Cambridge, Eng.: Cambridge University Press, 1988.

Epigraphy and Papyrology

Epigraphy is chiefly the study of the primary transmission of written materials inscribed on durable surfaces (such as metal, marble, stone, or clay). Papyrology is the study of papyrus manuscripts. The sheer volume of inscriptions (more than one million cuneiform texts have been found in Syro-Mesopotamia alone) gives epigraphy a prominence in the study of ancient history. Inscriptions in some cases are the primary source of written information in the absence of a manuscript tradition (as for the ancient Near East, Crete, and South Asia). Moreover, they add a precious supplement to the existing Greco-Roman manuscript tradition. They often afford the most direct access to understanding ancient chronology, legal institutions, public decrees, boundary and tribute information, epitaphs, sacrificial and ritual procedures, civil and federal constitutions, the functions of councils and assemblies, voting procedures, senatorial resolutions, magisterial edicts, and the study of prosopography. Furthermore, ancient authors such as Thucydides and Polybius studied and quoted epigraphic material.

Papyrology is a recent subdiscipline of epigraphy. Although papyri are normally perishable, many have been preserved because of unique climatic conditions in Egypt and nearby areas. Most of them range from the Ptolemaic to early Islamic periods (300 B.C.–A.D. 700). They were written primarily in Greek, but others have been found in ancient Egyptian, Aramaic, Hebrew, Coptic, Latin, Middle Persian, and even Arabic. Since they were not intended for preservation, papyri offer an unaltered witness of their age. They are usually subdivided into nonliterary (formal records such as land sales, mortuary and ritual texts, adoption decrees, and wills), and literary papyri (for instance, Aristotle's *Athenian Constitution* and Greek fragments of the Bible). Papyri are the main resource for reconstructing the economic and social conditions of Greco-Roman Egypt. In the present century, such important discoveries as the Dead Sea Scrolls, though not, strictly speaking, papyri, have similarly supplemented our knowledge of the ancient Middle East.

Mark W. Chavalas

See also NUMISMATICS; PALEOGRAPHY AND DIPLOMATIC.

Texts

Hunt, A.S., and C.S. Edgar. *Select Greek Papyri.* 2 vols. Cambridge, MA: Harvard University Press/Loeb Classical Library, 1932–1934.

Pritchard, J.S., ed. *Ancient Near Eastern Texts Relating to the Old Testament.* Third ed. Princeton, NJ: Princeton University Press, 1969.

References

Keppie, L. *Understanding Roman Inscriptions.* Baltimore, MD: Johns Hopkins University Press, 1992.

Turner, E.G. *Greek Papyri: An Introduction.* Oxford: Clarendon Press, 1980.

Woodhead, A.G. *The Study of Greek Inscriptions.* Second ed. Cambridge, Eng.: Cambridge University Press, 1981.

Erikson, Erik Homburger (1902–1994)

Born at Frankfurt am Main, Germany, Erikson emigrated to the United States in 1933. His work as a psychoanalyst specializing in the psychology of young people has resulted in the publication of numerous works on related topics. Of particular interest is his groundbreaking "psychohistory" of the German Reformer, *Young Man Luther*. Heralded as a radical departure in Luther biography at a time when Reformation studies were enjoying an international renaissance, *Young Man Luther* has also been pilloried as an arbitrary application of twentieth-century psychoanalytic theory to a member of a past and therefore alien culture. David Stannard attacks psychohistory in his book *Shrinking History*, taking Erikson to task for applying modern psychoanalysis to Luther. Stannard argues that there is no evidence to support Erikson's long-distance "diagnosis" of an Oedipus complex in the young Luther, or of trauma resulting from putative beatings by an overbearing father; however, Erikson's interpretation of the famous "Tower Experience" (Luther's revelation concerning justification by faith and grace, which he claimed to have had while on the toilet) helps make psychological sense of an intensely personal experience, and cannot be dismissed. Owing in part to the fierce controversy it engendered, Erikson's innovative book opened new avenues of historical dialogue and research, and enriched historical discussion with systematic (if often poorly documented) insights into the possible motives and character of historical figures. In a subsequent study, *Gandhi's Truth*, Erikson refined his analysis to explain "the origins of non-violence" in the domestic life of the Indian leader.

Andrew Colin Gow

See also PSYCHOHISTORY.

Texts

Gandhi's Truth. New York: Norton, 1969.
Life History and the Historical Moment. New York: Norton, 1975.
Young Man Luther: A Study in Psychoanalysis and History. New York: Norton, 1958.

References

Capps, D., W. Capps, and M.G. Bradford, eds. *Encounter with Erikson: Historical Interpretation and Religious Biography.* Missoula, MT: American Academy of Religion, 1977.
Stannard, David. *Shrinking History: On Freud and the Failure of Psychohistory.* Oxford: Oxford University Press, 1980.

Erslev, Kristian Sofus August (1852–1930)

Danish historian, pedagogue, and archivist. Kristian Erslev was born in Copenhagen, received his basic education at Maribo, and earned his doctorate from the University of Copenhagen in 1879. He enjoyed a long teaching career at the university, where he became a professor in the early 1880s. He also was a leader in the development of the administration of the Carlsberg Fund and served as archivist at the Royal Archives (1916–1924). Erslev was an enormously productive historian. His principal works in Danish history focused on the late medieval and early modern periods and include *Kong Valdemars Jordebog og den nyere Kritik* [King Valdemar's Farm Book and the New Criticism] (1875), *Danmarks-Norges Len og Lensmænd 1596–1600* [Denmark-Norway's Counties and County Governors, 1596–1600] (1885), *Dronning Margrethe og Kalmarunionens Grundlæggelse* [Queen Margrethe and the Founding of the Union of Kalmar] (1882), and *Aktstykker og Oplysninger till Rigsraadets og Stændermodernes Historie I–III* [Sources for the History of the Council of State and Meetings of the Estates] (1883–1890). He also contributed to the multivolume *Danmarks Riges Historie* [History of the Danish Kingdom] (1898–1905) and authored several general European medieval histories and a number of important works on historical methods including *Grundsætninger for historisk Kildekritik* [The Foundations of Historical Source Criticism] (1892). Erslev was a leader of the "critical school" of late-nineteenth-century historians in Denmark, and his scholarship and teaching always reflected his commitment to careful examination of primary sources as well as an appreciation for the importance of narrative.

Byron J. Nordstrom

Texts

Danmarks Riges Historie. Copenhagen: Nordiske forlag, 1896–1907.
Dronning Margrethe og Kalmarunionens Grundlæggelse. Copenhagen: J. Erslev, 1882.
Valby i gamle dag, og nu [Valby, Then and Now]. Copenhagen: Dansk byhistorisk forlag, 1954.
Historieskrivning: Grundlinier til nogle kapitler af historiens theori [Writing History: Basic Elements in the Theory of History]. Copenhagen: Universitetsbogtrykkeriet, 1911.

References

Bach, Erik. *Danske Historieskrivare* [Danish Historical Writing]. Copenhagen: J.H. Schultz, 1942.

Jorgensen, Ellen. *Danske Historikere fra Saxo til Kr. Erslev* [Danish Historians from Saxo to Kristian Erslev]. Copenhagen: Gyldendsal, 1923.

———. *Historiens studium i Danmark i det 19. aarhundrede, udg. af den Danske historiske forening paa Carlsbergfondets bekostning* [Historical Studies in Denmark during the Nineteenth Century]. Copenhagen: B. Lunos bogtrykkeri, 1943.

Essentialism

The belief that historical entities, including people and cultures, possess immanent and timeless characteristics in common with comparable entities, and that these "essences" transcend or override historical distinctions of time and circumstance. Philosophically, essentialism refers to the assumption that all material entities have innate qualities with which they are endowed—independent of our knowledge of them—that predetermine the nature and course of their existence: cats have a "catlike" essence, rocks are rocklike, and so on. This can be extended to human beings and historically has often been used to protect the social status quo: aristocrats being treated as inherently or essentially noble, barbarians or peasants as essentially barbarous. The long-standing debate over "nature or nurture" revolves around the degree to which persons who are born within a particular social setting and with inherited characteristics can be shaped by proper education or training into persons of different social status, moral character, or occupational interest. Essentialism has been a staple of one branch of philosophy, metaphysics, since the time of Aristotle and was an important element in medieval scholasticism, to which modern existentialism, which asserts the freedom of individuals to determine the course of their existence, in the face of an absurd (rather than providentially orderly) universe, is a radical departure.

There has always been an element of essentialism to historical writing. Most writers of history have had to assume some sort of human commonality in order to explain past behavior, even if this only takes the minimalist form of shared emotions and physical responses to similar situations. It is generally assumed, usually implicitly rather than explicitly that a military leader will wish to win battles rather than lose them, that persons facing a threat will attempt to preserve their life and well-being, or that most individuals will generally seek self-aggrandizement in the form of money, status, or sexual gratification rather than pain: in some senses, this is Bentham's principle of utility and its later descendant, behaviorism (which, however, stresses the capacity to learn different responses to situations) looked at historically, and it is a psychology that has been subject to a good deal of criticism in this century, especially since Freud.

All this being said, it is important to acknowledge that essentialism itself is not an essence: it has taken different forms at different periods. Despite the stress on rationality of Greek philosophy, essentialism does not especially mark ancient Greek historical writing—the writings of Herodotus, with their attention to the different manners and customs of the Persians and Greeks, evince an early recognition of the idea of national character (which is a lesser, nonglobal, version of essentialism); Thucydides, for his part, saw in the different regimes of Athens and Sparta the sources of those cities' respective fates in the Pelopponesian war. Because the Greeks saw the realm of the rational as lying outside the historical, they were not much given to speculations on the commonality of all past cultures. This became less true in the Hellenistic and Roman imperial eras, and Plutarch, in writing his parallel lives of famous Greeks and Romans, carried one version of essentialism to a logical conclusion, in making direct comparisons of the lives and characters of paired historical figures. The providentialism of most medieval world chronicles derived in a different way from assumptions about the unchanging, fallen quality of the human spirit and the necessity of divine redemption in the fullness of time.

Historiographically, essentialism has also come under criticism at various times, even when it appears to have been a governing assumption in historical thinking. During the Renaissance, when history, and in particular political history, was studied largely for its didactic and predictive benefits, historians commonly assumed the existence of a wide range of shared human characteristics, while nevertheless having to come to terms with alien cultures such as the Ottoman Turks and, later, natives of the New World. Some historians, indeed, were skeptical of the utility of historical example even before this: the Florentine politician and historian, Francesco Guicciardini, for instance, criticized the contemporary practice of reading about individuals or episodes from the past in order to predict the outcome of events (as represented perhaps most prominently in the writings of his friend Niccolò Machiavelli) on the grounds that no two events could ever be said to be identical. Jean Bodin and Michel de Montaigne had similar reservations, despite the former's early attempt to establish a series of laws in history. Two centuries later, the English historical philosopher and politician Henry St. John, Lord Bolingbroke, criticized those who judge the customs of other peoples by their own, which are assumed to be timeless and innately superior; David Hackett Fischer has usefully termed this particular variety of essentialism "the fallacy of ethnomorphism." Bolingbroke's views on this matter were not, however, decisive for the eighteenth century, which preferred to listen to his teachings about history as "philosophy teaching by example." Enlightenment historians and philosophers, determined to uncover the features common to past societies and to discover an overall pattern to history, promulgated an even stronger form of essentialism than had their late medieval and Renaissance predecessors. It would take the advent of romanticism, with its renewed attention to the strange, exotic, and wild quality of past cultures (evidenced, for instance, in their renewed fascination with the Middle Ages), coupled with the belief among certain German thinkers—Herder, for instance—that distinctive national characteristics make a compelling difference in the unfolding of history. This, again, was really a more limited kind of essentialism since it subsumed individuals under common social mores; it is the historical *Volk,* rather than its human members, that is truly distinctive. Nineteenth-century historicism, however, was able to build on this by reaching a balance between recognition of the uniqueness of each historical entity (be that persons, nations, or even periods) and the sense, strongest in German conservatives like Ranke and later Treitschke, that amid all this individuality, the world was still unfolding according to a plan, each part containing the image of the whole. On the Left, Marxism substituted for the essentialist constructs of intellect, national character, and nature, the different, but still deterministic concept of dialectical materialism: class supplanted national character, the mode of production displaced the "spirit" or "reason."

In the late twentieth century, essentialism has been both more clearly identified as a factor in historical writing, past and present, and more trenchantly attacked from various quarters. Most recently, feminist historians and historians of non-Western cultures have argued strongly (often against the Marxist roots from which many have derived) that intellectual, cultural, and social history need to be rethought and that assumptions about the "timeless" nature of humans and common features of civilizations need to be reexamined, if not discarded altogether. Such historians, in some ways echoing the earlier reaction of nineteenth-century historicists to Enlightenment assumptions about the "laws" of history, have similarly pressed for a history that takes greater note of individuality, cultural variation, educability, and indigenous (rather than imperialistic) social change, a history that pays attention to the margins rather than the center, to the atypical and odd rather than the "normal."

D.R. Woolf

See also ANTHROPOLOGY AND HISTORY; CULTURAL HISTORY; ENLIGHTENMENT HISTORIOGRAPHY; EUROCENTRISM; GERMAN HISTORICAL THOUGHT.

References

Fischer, David Hackett. *Historians' Fallacies: Toward a Logic of Historical Thought.* New York: Harper, 1970.

Lowenthal, David. *The Past Is a Foreign Country.* Cambridge, Eng.: Cambridge University Press, 1985.

Phillips, Mark. *Francesco Guicciardini: The Historian's Craft.* Toronto: University of Toronto Press, 1977.

White, Hayden. *Metahistory: The Historical Imagination in Nineteenth-Century Europe.* Baltimore, MD: Johns Hopkins University Press, 1973.

Estonian Historiography

Historical writing produced in Estonia, one of the three Baltic states. Before the establishment of Estonian independence in 1918, the historical works that appeared in this region were almost entirely written by Baltic Germans, who formed the ruling elites from the thirteenth to the twentieth century. This body of historical literature ranged from medieval chronicles to serious academic works produced by professional historians at the University of Tartu (German: *Dorpat*) in the nineteenth century. With the rise of an Estonian national movement in the 1860s, a historical consciousness developed among the emerging intelligentsia, but only a few historical works, written by amateur historians such as Jakob Hurt and Villem Reiman, appeared before the end of imperial Russian rule in 1917.

Beginning in 1919, the transformation of the University of Tartu into an Estonian national institution, supported by the Republic of Estonia, laid the basis for a new historiography produced by professionally trained Estonian historians.

Institutionally, the promotion of historical research was centered in the Academic Historical Society (1920–1940) and its scholarly publication, *Ajalooline Ajakiri* [Historical Journal] (1922–1940). The dominant subject matter in the historiography of the interwar era was the Swedish period—that is, the seventeenth century—of Estonian history, reflecting strong contemporary intellectual ties to Finland and Sweden. The leading Estonian historian of the 1920s and 1930s was Hans Kruus (1891–1976), whose doctoral dissertation in 1931 broke new ground by investigating the social history of the Estonian peasantry in the turbulent 1840s. His one-volume survey history of Estonia was published in German and French editions in the early 1930s, and he served as editor in chief of the major collaborative work of the interwar period, *Eesti ajalugu* [History of Estonia], of which three volumes (of the projected five) appeared between 1935 and 1940.

The forced annexation of Estonia by the Soviet Union in 1940 brought an end to the first phase of a developing native historiography. The upheavals of World War II, including the initial Sovietization in 1940–1941, the German military occupation in 1941–1944, and the Soviet reannexation in 1944, prevented any serious historical research, and following the war what remained of the Estonian historical establishment was forced to adhere to a rigid Soviet interpretation of the past. The Stalin years were a wasteland, as even Kruus, who had sought to make his peace with the new regime, was arrested in 1950. Although the situation improved in the post-Stalin decades, many subjects remained taboo, and survey histories of Estonia were distorted by the officially sanctioned need to stress an alleged "great friendship" between Estonians and Russians. In spite of these problems, some historical work of lasting value was produced during the decades of Soviet rule, especially in historical demography (Heldur Palli, Sulev Vahtre) and agrarian history (Herbert Ligi, Enn Tarvel, Juhan Kahk). During the latter part of World War II some Estonian historians fled to the West and continued their work there, most notably Arnold Soom in Sweden, who wrote on the social and economic history of the seventeenth century.

The most recent past—the glasnost years in the late 1980s and the period following the renewal of independence in 1991—witnessed the reestablishment of a native historiography in Estonia. By 1989, historical writing began to break free of Soviet-era restrictions, making increasing use of previously inaccessible archival sources and secondary literature published in the West.

The major focus of the new historical research was on subjects that had been taboo in the previous fifty years: the "blank spots" of the interwar independence era and the Stalinist period to 1953. For the first time since 1940, Estonian historians—mainly based at the Academy of Sciences' Institute of History and the University of Tartu—had open access to all sources in their homeland as well as to the external world, and scholars from abroad could freely use archives and other depositories in Estonia.

Toivo U. Raun

See also LATVIAN HISTORIOGRAPHY; LITHUANIAN HISTORIOGRAPHY; SOVIET HISTORIOGRAPHY.

References

Rauch, Georg von, ed. *Geschichte der deutschbaltischen Geschichtsschreibung* [History of Baltic German Historical Writing]. Cologne: Böhlau, 1986.

Raun, Toivo U. *Estonia and the Estonians.* Second ed. Stanford, CA: Hoover Institution Press, 1991.

Ethnicity and National Origins, Ideas of

Beliefs about the beginnings of peoples and the origins of specific nations or ethnic groups, sometimes presented as myth and legend, and at other times in more conventional historical forms. During the Middles Ages and the early modern period, chroniclers and historians often developed and propagated beliefs about national origins. One of the most common myths in France, Spain, and England, for instance, was that the people were descendants of Trojan refugees (and, thus, the nation's origin was contemporary with or even preceded Rome's founding by other Trojan exiles.) Another variant of the national-descent myth substituted the children and grandchildren of Noah for the Trojans.

Increased skepticism, philological scrutiny, and humanist attention to the state in Renaissance historiography undermined belief in founding figures like Francion (France) and Brutus (Britain) and the "pseudo-Berosus" and other supporting texts. The new, secular political theory of Jean Bodin and Thomas Hobbes was unspecific, even unconcerned, about national and ethnic origins, but it emphasized the construction of the state as a rational and practical action by human beings to improve their chances for prosperity and security. By the eighteenth century, mature Enlightenment thinkers such as Immanuel

Kant were seeking a "science" of history (to match Newton's accomplishments in cosmology) that rested on universal laws, for example, the "cosmopolitan" constitutional implications of the unsocial sociability of human nature. History was a teleological process, rooted in the nature of things whose meaning or purpose would engulf all humankind sooner or later. Where a nation or the species was going was more important than where they had been; the issue of origins faded to insignificance. In the nineteenth century G.W.F. Hegel and Karl Marx respectively attempted universal histories by replacing the root energy of human nature with the dialectical, progressive force of ideas and classes. Again, in these cosmopolitan frameworks issues of national or ethnic origins had little or no significance.

Nevertheless, attention to ethnic and national origins did not disappear completely in the eighteenth and early nineteenth centuries: it was in a recessive mode in comparison to the dominant universal aspirations of Enlightenment, philosophical historiography. Romanticism's attraction to origins, localities, Volks experience, languages, and medieval organic notions of society, however, offered an important counterpoise to Kantian and Marxian cosmopolitanism. (And, of course, current postmodern theorists often claim Johann Gottfried von Herder and other romantics as their forbears.) The nation, rather than the state, regained stature since it embodied the spirit, language, culture, and unique experience of its Volk. Thus, there is no universal community of *man;* only an array of nations or races, each with its own origins, character, and destiny. Social Darwinism, which became popular in the later decades of the nineteenth century, described the world as an arena of competing races, each with its own peculiar talents or qualities, and, consequently, a world in which some races surely were to dominate (that is, colonize) others. The Nazis managed to conjure the worst possibilities of this outlook into their perverse notion of Aryan superiority.

The Nazi debacle notwithstanding, we have witnessed in recent decades a renewal of commitment to ethnic and national identity, though often in a more critical and sometimes specifically antiracist, anti-essentialist form. Much as romantic nationalism stymied the cosmopolitan political aspirations of the Enlightenment, so the appeal of the ethnic community or nation has emerged as a powerful alternative to the tattered, mutually exclusive "universals" of the Cold War era. A new reverence for "culture" among Western intellectuals and an equally strong aversion to the mere suggestion of hegemonic intentions has yielded a generation of "alterity-preoccupied, deeply anti-imperialist" practitioners in the humanities and social sciences, according to David Hollinger. "Diversity" has replaced "unity" as the mark of respect and equality. And, serving as a balance to the anomie and rootlessness of exhausted Modernism, the "ethnos" offers "situatedness" within a bonded community of memory and anticipation.

Paralleling these developments over the last three decades, historians, historically inclined sociologists, and political scientists—John Armstrong, Leah Greenfeld, David Hollinger, Samuel P. Huntington, Michael Ignatieff, Hans Kohn, Murray G.H. Pittock, Boyd C. Shafer, and Anthony D. Smith, among others—have been reexamining the roots and sustaining power of national and ethnic "identity." On one level, the multiplicity of ethnic histories decenters any attempt at an overarching world narrative and aligns with the postmodern orientation to the past and present. The most formal postmodern student of these matters emphasizes the "curiously simultaneous solidity and insubstantiality of ethnic communities and nations" (Armstrong). Ethnicity might rest in the eye of the beholder. More conventional historical sociology reveals the changes in the meaning of "nation," from a derisive term for a group of foreigners in the ancient world to a unique and sovereign people today (Greenfeld). We are also learning that "myths" and "memories" remain a sine qua non of nation formation and for sustaining a collective sense of purpose, whether the nations are well-established or struggling to emerge.

At issue in this research is just how to explain the emergence of the "modern state." Primordialists hold that the nation is the natural, timeless unit of human association that has taken different forms in different historical settings. Modernists, by contrast, insist that the nation is the peculiar form and culture required by an industrial society. Perhaps the most heuristic approach lies somewhere in between: the nation is not timeless, but it is sustained by myth and memory; the industrial nation is unique, but it necessarily does not destroy all bonds that preceded it (Smith). Sometimes premodern cultural ties are broken by the political and industrial revolutions, but often they adapt and apotheosize. This depends as much upon "their internal proprieties as upon the uneven incidence of the modern revolutions." While objective factors such as population, resources, geography, communications, infrastructure, and the like, do distinguish particular nations, far more important are their subjective dimensions: memory, value, myth, and symbolism. These later factors, imbedded in the arts, languages, sciences, and laws of the nation "leave their imprint on the perceptions of subsequent generations and shape the structures and atmosphere of the community through the distinctive traditions they deposit."

A recent and intriguing application by Samuel P. Huntington of the subjective dimensions of national culture to the more encompassing entity, civilization, leads to new perspectives (neoromantic? neo-Darwinist?) on world politics. Civilizations, like nations, are unique and often must face irreconcilable differences among one another because of their inner dimensions of culture, history, ethnic solidarity, and religion, all of which are bound up with myth and memory.

Paul A. Fideler

See also ESSENTIALISM; EUROCENTRISM; LITERARY THEORY; MEMORY; NATIONAL CHARACTER; NATIONALISM; POSTMODERNISM.

References

Armstrong, John. *Nations before Nationalism.* Chapel Hill: University of North Carolina Press, 1982.

Greenfeld, Leah. *Nationalism: Five Roads to Modernity.* Cambridge, MA: Harvard University Press, 1992.

Hollinger, David A. *Postethnic America: Beyond Multiculturalism.* New York: Basic Books, 1995.

Huntington, Samuel P. "The Clash of Civilizations?" *Foreign Affairs* 72 (1993): 22–50

Ignatieff, Michael. *Blood and Belonging: Journeys into the New Nationalism.* New York: Viking, 1993.

Kendrick, T.D. *British Antiquity.* London: Methuen, 1950.

Kohn, Hans. *Prophets and Peoples: Studies in Nineteenth Century Nationalism.* New York: Octagon Books, 1975.

Pittock, Murray G.H. *The Invention of Scotland: The Stuart Myth and the Scottish Identity, 1638 to the Present.* London: Routledge, 1991.

Shafer, Boyd C. *Faces of Nationalism: New Realities and Old Myths.* New York: Harcourt Brace J. Jovanovich, 1972.

Smith, Anthony D. *The Ethnic Origins of Nations.* Oxford: Basil Blackwell, 1986.

———. *The Ethnic Revival.* Cambridge, Eng.: Cambridge University Press, 1981.

Ethnohistory

Methodology for studying the past that combines anthropological and historical approaches. "Ethnohistory" is a term used by anthropologists and historians to refer to the use of historical documents, sometimes in conjunction with archaeological, ethnographic, or linguistic data, to portray the past of nonliterate or non-Western peoples. While it is done in different styles, ethnohistory differs from "history" in its close association with ethnographic fieldwork carried out by anthropologists, an often explicit concern with ethnological theory, and an overriding interest in local populations—such as tribal groups or peasant communities—rather than large historical events. Doing ethnohistory entails a commitment to understanding the local peoples' points of view—which normally differ from that of the ethnohistorian—and employing them to write a culturally grounded historical narrative or ethnography. As such, ethnohistory may be further distinguished from folk history, which focuses explicitly on the actors' own concepts of time and history, and amounts to a kind of sociology of knowledge.

A loosely structured methodology and set of interests rather than a distinct discipline, ethnohistory is a hybrid endeavor which, at least ideally, attempts a synthesis of anthropological and historical approaches. The term was first used by North American anthropologists in the early twentieth century to characterize their use of documents to reconstruct the cultures of American Indians prior to European contact. Ethnohistorical research increased markedly in the United States following the creation of the Indian Claims Commission by Congress in 1946. Employed as expert witnesses by Indian tribes and the government, many anthropologists became acquainted with archival sources they had previously ignored. In the following decade the Ohio Valley Historic Indian Conference was founded partly to accommodate the interest developed among anthropologists and historians by the Indian claims cases. The group's journal, *Ethnohistory,* in 1955 proclaimed its devotion to "original research in the documentary history of the culture and movements of primitive peoples, with special emphasis on the American Indian." In 1966, the conference became the American Society for Ethnohistory and since then the term has gained wide, though by no means universal, currency among anthropologists and historians in North America, parts of Latin America (especially Mexico and Peru), Australia, and the Pacific, though it remains little used in Europe. The society holds an annual meeting and continues to sponsor *Ethnohistory.*

While never forsaking its roots in anthropology and American Indian studies, the scope of ethnohistory broadened considerably after the 1960s. In 1984, *Ethnohistory* defined its subject as "relating to the past of cultures and societies in all areas of the world, emphasizing the use of documentary and field materials and historiographic and anthropological approaches." Like most hybrid fields, however, ethnohistory is regarded in contrasting ways by different segments of its constituency. Historians tend to be more concerned with change and historical narratives, anthropologists with the construction of more synchronic historical ethnographies and questions of theory. In both disciplines, a basic dichotomy remains between those who view ethnohistory as the special (that is, ethnological) use of documentary evidence, and others who view it as the use of documentary evidence for special (for example, nonliterate, tribal) people.

In practice, however, a bi- or multicultural frame of reference is common. Most ethnohistorians study people different from themselves, frequently in colonial or frontier contexts, and the documents they use are rarely written by the subjects of study in their own language (especially prior to the twentieth century), but by conquering outsiders. While ethnohistorical work will continue to be divided along disciplinary and theoretical lines, its explicit concern with cross-cultural contexts and the methodological challenges they present for historical study are common threads that give unity to the field.

John K. Chance

See also ANTHROPOLOGY; CULTURAL HISTORY; ETHNICITY AND NATIONAL ORIGINS; INDIGENOUS HISTORIOGRAPHY.

References

DeMallie, Raymond J. "'These Have No Ears': Narrative and the Ethnohistorical Method." *Ethnohistory* 40 (1993): 515–538.

Krech, Shepard III. "The State of Ethnohistory." *Annual Review of Anthropology* 20 (1991): 345–375.

Eurocentrism in the Writing and Teaching of History

The assumption that Europe (or, by extension, the West) possesses a history and historiography superior to those of non-European (non-Western) peoples. This form of Eurocentrism manifests itself at several levels: ontology ("they do not have a history"); epistemology ("we cannot know their history"); ethics ("their history has no value"); utilitarianism ("their history is not relevant or useful"); and didactics ("their history is too difficult and too embarrassing").

During the era of Western expansion up to and including the early twentieth century, *ontological* eurocentrism (promulgated by Hegel, among others) was one of the principal justifications of intellectual imperialism. "Primitive" peoples were said to be without history because they were deemed incapable of historical action. Their past, like that of "prehistoric" peoples, was seen as a succession of barbarism, poverty, and stagnation. Only after the arrival of the whites could the indigenous peoples claim a place in history. In some territories, it was even denied that indigenous peoples had lived there before the whites arrived. Historiography of later years has adequately and extensively refuted these assumptions by revealing the richness of non-Western history. *Epistemological* Eurocentrism was the result of the primacy that for centuries had been given to the written source. Where non-Western written sources were not available, alternative sources remained unacknowledged; where they had been preserved, they were either ignored or destroyed by the colonial authorities. When combined with the ontological level, a strong and a mild version of epistemological Eurocentrism developed. The first could be worded as "we cannot know their history, therefore they do not have one," the second as "they do have a history, but we cannot know it." Gradually the definition of "source" was extended to include archaeological, iconographical, linguistic, and oral evidence. It remains a fact, however, that the history of certain periods, regions, and social strata cannot be reconstructed, or only with the greatest difficulty.

The classical form of Eurocentrism, however, is represented at the *ethical-normative* level. Until relatively recently, whenever episodes of non-Western history have been dealt with, they have been evaluated and stereotyped according to Western concepts and criteria. Non-Western societies were thus characterized by their alleged deficiencies: they had no writing, no state, no prosperity, no culture—hence their history was not considered worth studying. Great achievements contradicting this were often explained by an assumed pristine European intervention. *Utilitarian* Eurocentrism was the result of this lack of understanding. With regard to the numerous contributions to the West by non-Western peoples, it was mostly forgotten that they were contributions from elsewhere, or it was assumed that they had only been perfected by Western hands. Only gradually has the realization dawned that cultural contributions have come from everywhere, and that both comparative history and world history could not exist without non-Western components.

Finally, it should be conceded that non-Western terminology, institutions, and ways of thinking entail their own didactical problems—which is the import of *didactical* Eurocentrism. However, these problems do not necessarily lead to a confused, caricatural, or pernicious representation of history. Historical mechanisms, ideas, and evolutions can, after careful preparation, also be illustrated with the help of non-Western examples. Furthermore, it is certainly true that major parts of non-Western history tell the story of hunger, poverty, and injustice and are therefore painful episodes to deal with. The same can be said, however, about Western history. Besides, history should not be reduced to its embarrassing side. History teaching is particularly suited to put the idealized version of the Western success story in perspective and present a more balanced view of all aspects of history.

Anthropological doctrines have played a major part in both the justification and the critique of Eurocentrism. In recent times, historians from all regions have denounced Eurocentrism. In some cases the result has been an inverted ethnocentrism: the historical achievements of non-Western peoples have been exaggerated. Conversely, it has even been maintained, paradoxically, that the happiest peoples were those without history. The most penetrating question, however, in this evaluation process has been this: is historiography a Western invention? A negative answer assumed that historiography developed independently outside the West. On the other hand, a positive answer implied that the West had either a superior or a specific way of dealing with the past. The first option (superiority) distinguished between a mythical and a historiographical phase in dealing with the past, and asserted that for a long time only the West had reached the latter stage. The second option (specificity) regarded *every* way of dealing with the past as mythical, and saw historiography as the very epitome of this myth in the Western context. Neither answer denied that the West's contribution to historiography was unique.

The above question is preceded by the question of whether the substratum of historiography—historical consciousness—is universal. It is highly doubtful whether it is psychologically possible or bearable *not* to deal with one's past. Admittedly, the process of confronting the past could be termed ahistorical, certainly in earlier times, in the sense that the past was not seen as clearly separated from the present, but was assumed to continue into the present or to repeat itself in cycles. Several historians have inferred from this that historical consciousness is compatible with a linear but not with a cyclical conception of time. They concluded that the first conception is essentially Western while the second is non-Western and that the two cannot coexist. This theory condemns non-Western peoples to what has been called an "ethnographic present" and is therefore certainly not undisputed. Still, this does not alter the fact that everywhere peoples can be found who have felt less need than others, or to whom it was of less interest, to cultivate their historical consciousness. In fact, these needs (clarification of existence and identity; and a desire for continuity, didactic examples, or comfort) and interests (justification of power or the support of legal claims) do not occur equally in the West nor elsewhere, and the past is used in various degrees for their gratification. If, then, historiography is viewed as the expression of a vigorous historical consciousness and as a special, methodical form of memory, it cannot be omnipresent. Thus many "peoples without history" have existed (with a past, history, time conception, and historical consciousness, but without historiography). However, those peoples who for various reasons did develop their own historiography can be found not only in the West but everywhere. Historiographical traditions of the Near East are older than those of the West, while the Chinese tradition is both older and more continuous. All the same, Europe has had an old and strong tradition of historiography ever since the days of Herodotus in the fifth century B.C. The difficult and discordant transformation between the sixteenth and nineteenth century from this European tradition to modern historiography, based on the historical–critical method, had many causes. One of those was the confrontation with newly discovered non-Western cultures, which gave a crucial impetus to evolutionary thinking. This particular combination of causes did not occur outside Europe, although elements of methodological doubt by themselves had been employed previously and elsewhere. During and especially after the era of European exploration, document-based, written historiography achieved hegemony throughout the world, generally at the expense of non-Western types of traditional historiography. Nowadays it is undoubtedly the dominant form of historiography, having also influenced scholarship in the Third World both institutionally and intellectually. On the other hand, many of its aspects have come under attack. Several historians have called into question the claim of modern Western historical writing to be the sole scientific or socially useful form of historiography, while the advent of the "linguistic turn" has threatened to undermine some of its most cherished principles. Yet the core of modern historiography—historical criticism—has remained largely unchallenged, precisely because of its universal utility. The fact that non-Western historians can criticize the work of their Western colleagues by using Western methods suggests that these methods have developed beyond their Western roots and character. Both non-Western and Western historians have contributed to modern historiography through their innovative ideas concerning sources, concepts, subjects, and methods: not only as experts in their own history but also, and perhaps particularly, as relative outsiders to each other's history.

Antoon de Baets

See also ANTHROPOLOGY AND HISTORY; CHINESE HISTORICAL THOUGHT; ESSENTIALISM; INDIGENOUS HISTORIOGRAPHY; MEMORY AND HISTORY; MYTH AND HISTORY; ORAL TRADITION; TIME; WORLD HISTORY.

References

Barraclough, Geoffrey. *Main Trends in History.* New York and London: Holmes & Meier, 1979.

History of Humanity. Paris: Unesco and London: Routledge, 1994.

Lévi-Strauss, Claude. "Race and History." In *Race, Science and Society,* ed. L. Kuper. Paris: Unesco and London: Allen & Unwin, 1975, 95–134.

Moniot, Henri. "L'histoire des peuples sans histoire [The History of the People without History]." In *Faire de l'histoire. I. Nouveaux problèmes,* ed. Jacques Le Goff and Pierre Nora, Paris: Gallimard, 1974, 106–123.

Nandy, Ashis. "History's Forgotten Doubles." *History and Theory* 34 (1995): 44–66.

Preiswerk, Roy, and Dominique Perrot. *Ethnocentrism and History: Africa, Asia and Indian America in Western Textbooks.* New York: NOK, 1978.

Vansina, Jan. *Oral Tradition As History.* London: James Currey, 1985.

European Expansion, Chroniclers and Historians of

Historical writings by explorers, settlers, missionaries, and court historians of America and Asia between 1492 and 1720. The expansion of Europe is generally regarded as fundamental to the makeup of the modern world. Already in the middle of the sixteenth century, the Spanish chronicler Francisco López de Gómara referred to the discovery of America as "the greatest event since the creation of the world, apart from the incarnation and death of Him who created it," a claim that was echoed with even more confidence just over two centuries later, when the famous Scots economist, Adam Smith, remarked that "the discovery of America and that of a passage to the East Indies by the Cape of Good Hope are the two greatest and most important events recorded in the history of mankind."

Late-fifteenth-century Europeans were not, as is often assumed, entirely unprepared for these momentous events. Contacts with non-European cultures had been on the rise at least since the time of the crusades, and, especially after the Mongol mission in the thirteenth century, the instinctive Christian antagonism toward non-Christians had begun to dissipate.

It is important, however, to avoid the common anachronism that seeks to explain these developments from the point of view of an incipient cultural relativism. Although the interest in non-Christian cultures was genuine, the belief in the universality of human experience and in the absolute truth of the Christian faith was absolutely fundamental. Equally important was the unquestionable assumption that the classical view of the world, what was then known as the *oecumene,* was essentially correct. Only in this context is it possible to make sense of the attitudes of European historians of the non-European world in the early modern period. The descriptions of South East Asia by Portuguese writers like João de Barros or Fernão Lopes de Castanheda, for instance, are imbued with a strong sense of mission, which is based on a total acceptance of the principle of "plenitude of power," meaning papal temporal authority over both Christians and pagans. The same is true of the early European accounts of America, in which, with hindsight, one of the most striking aspects is the persistence of the conviction that the new continent was somehow part of the known world. It is well known, for instance, that Columbus died convinced that he had reached some part of Asia. Even more surprising is to find, half a century later, that the famous Dominican friar, Bartolomé de las Casas (1474–1566), deployed a very similar argument in his defense of the full humanity of the Amerindians.

Las Casas's logic is not as bizarre as it might appear at first sight. For in the context of early modern cosmology, the full humanity of the natives of America depended upon their belonging to the same world as Europeans, Asians, and Africans. To suggest otherwise, to accept that America was something wholly "new," was tantamount to denying the humanity of its native inhabitants, unless, of course, one was prepared to accept that the biblical and classical traditions could be so fundamentally mistaken.

This was one of the preoccupations at the core of the famous debate at Valladolid in 1550–1551, where Las Casas defended the Amerindians against the suggestions by historians and lawyers, like Gonzalo Fernández de Oviedo and Juan Ginés de Sepúlveda, that the natives of America were in the same state as Aristotle's "natural slaves." In practice, the debate did not need to be won too urgently; indeed, the full humanity of the Amerindians had already been accepted and defended by pope Paul III in his bull *Sublimus Deus* (1537), following the very solid philosophical and theological foundations laid by the School of Salamanca, especially the writings of Francisco de Vitoria, wherein the principle of "plenitude of power" had been shaken to its foundations. All the same, the Valladolid debate, and the arguments brought forward by both sides, highlighted how difficult it was going to be for Europeans to come to terms with the novelty of America and the challenge it posed to traditional cosmology.

Indeed, the majority of early modern historians maintained that the external world was legible *secundum scriptura,* by which they meant, in careful hierarchical order, the Bible, the fathers of the church, and a corpus of classical writers among whom Aristotle was preeminent. Consequently, the European historians of the non-European world, whose authority rested almost solely upon their status as firsthand observers, usually angled their work in ways that did not conflict with the demands of the canon. This is particularly evident in the writings of the early explorers whose observations sought to confirm traditional legends and fables. The power of classical myths and legends was so compelling that it made Europeans see exactly those things they had gone out to find: giants and wild men, pygmies, cannibals and Amazons, women whose bodies never aged, and cities paved with gold. Nevertheless, in proportion as it became increasingly evident that the world beyond

the frontiers of the *oecumene* was not merely exotic but actually quite different, every attempt to represent it inevitably came to constitute an attempt to resolve the clear tension between the appeal to experience and the demands of the canon.

One recurring difficulty was how to distance historical accounts from romances of chivalry. The problem was especially delicate because the romances always claimed to be true history. Thus historians had the twofold problem of, on the one hand, separating ancient historiography from romance and, on the other, securing the acceptance that their own accounts were exactly what the romances claimed to be, that is, true. Not surprisingly, many of the early accounts unwittingly followed the claim of the romances that the truest kind of history was the one from which the presence of the historian had been totally effaced. The text, in other words, was sufficient unto itself, since the narrative had not been made, but found.

By contrast, those who were more informed about what was at issue, and in particular about the danger of what we nowadays call "incommensurability," naturally turned away from unmediated experience and emphasized the central importance of authorial experience. In this, the aim was to offer a means of mediating between, on the one hand, the generally accepted premise that hermeneutics was inseparable from authority and, on the other, the disturbing presence of the facts. Las Casas's desperate attempt to find a place for America within the authorized canon, for instance, always leads us from the text to experience, and from experience back to the text; his attempt, in other words, was to use the facts to interpret the canon and the canon to situate the facts.

It is not difficult to see why Las Casas's method, like that of most of his contemporaries, was doomed. The mere presence of America was enough proof that the authority of the canon was dangerously fragile. Some early modern thinkers began to see the discovery of America as proof of the power of lived experience over any theoretical claim based upon exegesis. "Where experience and reason are in conflict," wrote Pomponazzi, "we should hold to experience and abandon reason."

The first great historian of America to adopt this line of enquiry was the Spanish Jesuit José de Acosta (1540–1600), whose extremely influential *Natural and Moral History of the Indies* is one of the most objective and original of early modern accounts of the cultures of the New World. Where previous authors had reverted to tradition or ancient wisdom, Acosta insisted that empirical knowledge and experience should always take precedence over the doctrines of ancient philosophers in any examination of the causes and effects of natural phenomena. The method was in perfect tune with current Jesuit missionary practice which produced its most remarkable representatives in China and India with Matteo Ricci and Roberto de Nobili. The insistence on the need to assess non-European cultures on their own terms, and the pursuit of causality and generality where previous writers had been content with mere observation and description, became characteristic of Jesuit historiography well into the early eighteenth century. The French Jesuit Joseph-François Lafitau, for instance, argued that cultures were primarily systems of symbolic representation that provide the means of communication between people in different societies.

It is no doubt this quality, which in many ways resembles the purpose and method of modern science, that won Jesuit historians the respect and admiration of the Enlightenment, and although it would be a gross anachronism to suggest that they are the direct predecessors of Voltaire and Diderot, it would be difficult to disagree with Anthony Pagden's opinion that their work, especially Acosta's, "made some kind of comparative ethnology, and ultimately some measure of historical relativism, inescapable."

Fernando Cervantes

See also ETHNOHISTORY; INDIGENOUS HISTORIOGRAPHY; LATIN AMERICAN HISTORIOGRAPHY—WRITING ON THE COLONIAL AND PRECOLONIAL PERIODS FROM THE SIXTEENTH CENTURY TO THE PRESENT DAY.

Texts

Acosta, José de. *Historia Natural y Moral de las Indias* [1590]. Ed. Edmundo O'Gorman. Mexico City: UNAM, 1962.
Las Casas, Bartolomé de. *Apologética Historia Sumaria* [1551]. Ed. Edmundo O'Gorman. 2 vols. Mexico City: UNAM, 1967.

References

D.A. Brading. *The First America: The Spanish Monarchy, Creole Patriots and the Liberal State.* Cambridge, Eng.: Cambridge University Press, 1991.
Elliott, J.H. *The Old World and the New.* Cambridge, Eng.: Cambridge University Press, 1970.
Pagden, Anthony. *European Encounters with the New World: From Renaissance to Romanticism.* New Haven, CT, and London: Yale University Press, 1993.

Eusebius of Caesarea (ca. 260–339/40)

Late Roman churchman and historian. Eusebius was born in Caesarea and was educated, according to later tradition, by the priest Pamphylius, himself a follower of Origen. During the persecution of 307 he fled to Tyre and then to the region of Thebes. He entered the entourage of Constantine, becoming the emperor's favorite and encouraging his conversion. At the time of the edict of toleration in 313, Eusebius became bishop of Caesarea and afterward participated in many church councils, generally siding with the Arians. Eusebius wrote numerous theological and scholarly works, including the *Preparation of the Gospels,* a Christian interpretation of history; the *Chronicle,* an attempt to give the dates of major events in Greek, Near Eastern, and Christian history; the panegyrical *Life of Constantine;* and the ten-book *Church History,* the first systematic history of the Christian church, written in Greek, citing numerous documents, but far from impartial.

Stephen A. Stertz

Texts

Eusebius Werke [Works]. Ed. I.A. Heikel et al. 9 vols. Leipzig-Berlin: J.C. Hinrichs, 1902–1956.
The History of the Church from Christ to Constantine. Trans. G.A. Williamson; ed. Andrew Louth. New York: Penguin, 1989.
In Praise of Constantine. Trans. and ed. H.A. Drake. Berkeley: University of California Press, 1978.

References

Barnes, T.D. *Constantine and Eusebius.* Cambridge, MA: Harvard University Press, 1981.
Grant, R.M. *Eusebius As Church Historian.* Oxford: Clarendon Press, 1980.

Eutropius (fl. fourth century A.D.)

Roman historian. Eutropius held numerous offices in the later Roman Empire, including secretary *(Magister Memoriae)* and Asian proconsul. His effusive praise of the emperor Julian the Apostate (whom he accompanied on his Persian expedition) suggests that Eutropius was a pagan. He wrote a ten-volume work entitled *Breviarium ab urbe condita* [An Abridgement of Roman History] from the foundation of the city to the accession in A.D. 364 of the emperor Valens, to whom it was dedicated. Eutropius apparently composed this epitome because the writing of Roman history had become increasingly voluminous and difficult for readers to synthesize. He evidently followed Livy as a main source, but also used a variety of other writers. The *Breviarium* occasionally fills a gap left by more authoritative historians, thereby securing its importance with modern scholars. Although there are some factual and chronological errors (compounded by the omission of many details awkward to Rome), the work has been considered fairly equitable and accurate. Eutropius's work had a great reputation with the Christian historians of the medieval period, who consulted it frequently. In the eighth century Paulus Diaconus continued the *Breviarium* to A.D. 553. Eutropius was said to have written other works, the names of which are unknown.

E

Mark W. Chavalas

Texts
Justin, Cornelius Nepos, and Eutropius. Trans. J.S. Watson. London: George Bell & Sons, 1890.

References
Breisach, Ernst. *Historiography: Ancient, Medieval, Modern.* Second ed. Chicago: University of Chicago Press, 1994.

F

Fabyan, Robert (d. 1513)

London chronicler and merchant. Fabyan was
born into a well-to-do family from Essex. After
joining the Drapers Company in London, he became active in the city's politics, serving as an al-
derman and as sheriff in 1493. During the fifteenth century, individual London merchants had
often maintained brief listings of events in manuscript for their personal use. Known as London
Chronicles, these focused mainly on contemporary
events. Fabyan's significance lies in his expansion
of his "Concordance of Histories" (better known
as *New Chronicles*) into a general history of England. In general, Fabyan confined his analytical
techniques merely to a comparison of rival historical accounts although, unlike most of his contemporaries, he would sometimes reject information
derived from earlier writers such as Geoffrey of
Monmouth. Fabyan's *New Chronicles* was first
printed in 1516 with expanded editions appearing
in 1533, 1542, and 1559. Later historians such
as Polydore Vergil and Edward Hall used the
work, which supplies some unique information
on the history of late-fifteenth-century London.
Modern scholarship also credits Fabyan with partial authorship of the anonymous *Great Chronicle
of London*.

Ronald H. Fritze

Texts

*The New Chronicles of England and France by
Robert Fabyan*. Ed. Henry Ellis. London:
Rivington, 1811.

References

Gransden, Antonia. *Historical Writing in En-
gland*. Vol. 2, *c.1307 to the Early Sixteenth
Century*. Ithaca, NY: Cornell University
Press, 1982.

Kingsford, Charles Lethbridge. *English Historical
Literature in the Fifteenth Century*. Oxford:
Clarendon Press, 1913.

Fact

(1) A situation or state of affairs that actually took
place prior to and independent of our thought
about it. (2) A true description of facts in the first
(1) sense. Fact (2) is often distinguished from
value, fiction, interpretation, and theory. Accordingly, the meaning of "historical fact" (1 and 2) is
related to the debates about historiographic objectivity and truth.

The empiricist view about facts may be summed up in the words of Henri Houssaye: "We
want nothing more to do with the approxima-
tion of hypotheses, useless systems, theories as
they are brilliant as they are deceptive, superflu-
ous moralities. Facts, facts, facts—which carry
within themselves their lesson and their philosophy. The truth, all the truth, nothing but the
truth." (Houssaye, quoted in P. Novick, *That Noble
Dream*.) A more sophisticated formulation of this
empiricist position claims that historical facts are
self-evident, prima facie elements of any series of
events. True historiographic facts (2) correspond
with historical facts (1), although the criteria of
correspondence are unstatable in any generally
applicable or agreed upon form.

The opposite position is the extreme relativist claim of Hayden White that there are no facts
(1) only "textual facts." According to White, historiography is not about a "real" past, but about
texts. Horkheimer has noted that "the very concept
of 'fact' is a product—a product of social alienation." Extreme relativism holds that it is impossible to distinguish fact (2) from fiction and value
judgment.

Perhaps most historians and philosophers of history attempt to reconstruct a new notion of "fact" (2) that avoids the extremes of naive empiricism and non-commonsensical relativism. Following the demise of the empiricist paradigm in historiography, there has been a continuous search for a new standard for historical writing. In the 1950s, Quine argued for the rejection of the clear distinction between fact (2) and interpretation and theory, and its replacement by a continuum ranging from the most theoretical abstraction to the most empirical facts (2).

From a different perspective, Herodotus wrote long ago, at the end of the first Western work of history: "These, then, are the facts, as they appear to me." Selection of facts, choice of comparison situations in causal explanations, the language of historians, choice of narrative form, use of rhetorical devices, may all reflect value judgments. All kinds of knowledge, scientific knowledge included, are used for a variety of pragmatic, rhetorical, and ideological functions. Philosophers have in recent times attempted to examine whether or not historiographic "value" statements may be distinguished from historiographic "factual" statements, and if not, whether value judgments can have an "objective" sense. If interpretation and theoretical assumptions are part of all historiographic accounts, can interpretation-free "chronicle facts" be identified and agreed on? How can historians separate factually (1) based historiography from fiction, for example, "revisionist" Nazi historiography of the Holocaust. As the century ends, it is hard to see a single, dominant, new notion of fact emerging.

Aviezer Tucker

See also CAUSATION; PHILOSOPHY OF HISTORY—ANALYTICAL; RELATIVISM; WHITE, HAYDEN

Texts

Kuzminski, Adrian. "Defending Historical Realism." *History and Theory* 18 (1979): 316–349.

Mandelbaum, Maurice. *Philosophy, History, and the Sciences: Selected Critical Essays.* Baltimore: Johns Hopkins University Press, 1984.

Novick, Peter. *The Noble Dream: The "Objectivity Question" and the American Historical Profession.* New York: Cambridge University Press, 1988.

White, Hayden. *Metahistory: The Historical Imagination in Nineteenth-Century Europe.* Baltimore, MD: Johns Hopkins University Press, 1973.

Fairbank, John King (1907–1991)

American sinologist. Born into a middle-class family in Huron, South Dakota, Fairbank received his doctorate in modern Chinese history at Oxford University. During his tenure as a professor at Harvard University (1936–1940, 1946–1977), he contributed in various capacities as a historian, educator, and program promoter. A productive scholar, the long list of his publications included works on Qing (1644–1911) diplomacy, Sino–Western relations, and the Chinese Revolution. As an expert on China, he attempted through his lectures and writings to influence the course of Sino–American relations during the Cold War years. Under his directorship, the Harvard East Asian Research Center had trained a generation of specialists who taught in over a hundred universities in America and abroad. Indefatigably, Fairbank helped raise funds and organize academic activities to promote East Asian studies. Largely through his efforts, the United States has since become the country with the largest constituency of East Asianists outside the Far East. Among his many scholarly contributions were *The United States and China* (1948), *Trade and Diplomacy on the China Coast* (1953), and *The Chinese World Order* (1968). He was one of the principal editors of *The Cambridge History of China*.

Henry Y.S. Chan

Texts

China: A New History. Cambridge, MA: Harvard University Press, 1992.

Chinabound: A Fifty-Year Memoir. New York: Harper & Row, 1982.

Ed. *The Chinese World Order.* Cambridge, MA: Harvard University Press, 1968.

The United States and China. Fourth ed. Cambridge, MA: Harvard University Press, 1979.

References

Evans, Paul M. *John King Fairbank and the American Understanding of Modern China.* Cambridge, MA: Basil Blackwell, 1988.

Family History (Comparative)

The description and analysis of historical and cross-cultural variation in family and kinship organization. Within the discipline of history, the specialized study of family life in past time is a recent phenomenon. The literature produced in its name grew so rapidly in the 1970s and early 1980s, however, that one historian called family history a "growth industry." At first, most research in this emerging field focused on family patterns in Europe and the United States. But within the last ten or fifteen years, and partly as a consequence of interdisciplinary exchanges between anthropologists, sociologists, and historians, there has been greater coordination between the study of kinship in non-Western societies and the study of family life in the West.

Family history received much of its initial impetus from social history's emphasis on the texture of everyday life and on the actions of ordinary people. One major branch of family history, variously labeled the history of sentiment or private life, explores what might be called the family's "inner face." It encompasses what contemporary Westerners think of as the domain of personal experience, including the history of sexuality and birth control, childhood and aging, and courtship and marriage. Its major contribution is to underscore that even the most intimate facets of human social relations—such as the tenor of the emotional bonds and the structures of authority that govern ties between parents and children, and husbands and wives—are not only socially deeply consequential, but subject to historical change. Even the very concepts, "family," child," and "love," for example, have not been invested with the same meaning in the past or in all cultures, nor have they referred to precisely the same set of social relations.

Historians are equally interested in the family's "outer face," the family considered as a major social institution with important bearing on economic and political life. Here, the "family strategies" approach, which stresses the ways in which different social groups actively use their family and kinship networks to meet challenges posed by changing economic, political, and cultural circumstances, has been an influential tool of analysis. For example, in many peasant societies, property-owning households are the fundamental unit of economic organization. In such settings, the decisions made by family heads concerning the allocation and coordination of the labor of coresident kin and servants have major consequences for the economy. Families may also be the basic institution for transmitting wealth and cultural capital between the generations. When this is so, family inheritance strategies heavily affect the social fates of future generations and are directly implicated in the reproduction of systems of social stratification. Similarly, negotiations among family members, especially between husbands and wives, over the allocation of family resources and labor, the timing and frequency of childbearing, and much else, are structured by, and, in turn, greatly influence the contours of gender relations in the larger society. Finally, family life shapes political

institutions. In stateless or very decentralized polities, kinship systems are a major axis of political administration and rule: kinship relations are political relations. Moreover, family life, conceived ideologically as a major source of moral order, is also an important object of public policy in state societies.

If there is one major lesson to be learned from the historical and comparative study of family organization, it is that there is no single, or universal family form prevailing across cultures or to which all societies are tending. Rather, the historical and social landscape displays a great range of family patterns adapted to a disparate array of cultural, economic, and political conditions. This variation can be dramatic, not only as between societies, but within cultures. Even as many societies, and their cultural elites, in particular, may single out ideologically a particular family type as ideal or normatively authoritative, family organization varies among classes and according to ethnicity as people adapt their family and kinship networks to differing social opportunities and constraints.

Toby L. Ditz

See also DEMOGRAPHY—HISTORICAL; FAMILY RECONSTITUTION; GENDER; GENEALOGY; KINSHIP; PUBLIC/PRIVATE; SOCIAL HISTORY.

Texts

Ariès, Philippe. *Centuries of Childhood: A Social History of Family Life.* Trans. Robert Baldick. New York: Vintage, 1962.

Gutiérrez, Ramón A. *When Jesus Came, the Corn Mothers Went Away: Marriage, Sexuality, and Power in New Mexico, 1500–1846.* Stanford, CA: Stanford University Press, 1991.

Gutman, Herbert G. *The Black Family in Slavery and Freedom, 1750–1925.* New York: Pantheon, 1976.

Rubin, Lillian Breslow. *Worlds of Pain: Life in the Working-Class Family.* New York: Basic Books, 1969.

Ryan, Mary P. *Cradle of the Middle Class: The Family in Oneida County, New York, 1790–1865.* New York: Cambridge University Press, 1981.

Stack, Carol B. *All Our Kin: Strategies for Survival in a Black Community.* New York: Harper-Colophon, 1974.

References

Ariès, Philippe, and Georges Duby, eds. *A History of Private Life.* 5 vols. Cambridge, MA: Belknap Press of Harvard University Press, 1990.

Hareven, Tamara K. "History of the Family and Complexity of Social Change." *American Historical Review* 96 (1991): 95–124.

Journal of Family History: Studies in Family, Kinship, and Demography. Minneapolis, 1976–.

Stone, Lawrence. "Family History in the 1980s." *Journal of Interdisciplinary History* 7 (1981): 51–87.

Tilly, Louise. "Individual Lives and Family Strategies in the French Proletariat." *Journal of Family History* 4 (1979): 137–152.

Family Reconstitution

Methodology sometimes used in Family History. Family reconstitution is a technique for extracting information about the life histories of individuals from ecclesiastical sources (parish registers) of the precensus period and for merging these individual histories into a general history of the family unit to which those individuals belonged. In most localities the registers of births, marriages, and deaths were separate (frequently book-length) documents, so that fragments of information about an individual (for instance, a woman's birth date, the date of her marriage, the dates of her first and subsequent children, the date of her death), and about all individuals in a given family unit, tended to be located in different volumes and scattered over a long period of time. The technique is said to be fully successful if it produces all life history information about all individuals of a given conjugal family unit—husband, wife, and all offspring—from their births to their deaths; and for a substantial proportion of the families that resided in a particular locality. Partial information, however—for example, the birth and marriage dates of two individuals—can also be useful.

Simply stated, the purpose of the family reconstitution technique is to enable researchers to make sound generalizations about the timing of certain crucial family-related events in a locality on the basis of as large a number of such events as the sources will yield. Experience has shown that the complete reconstitution of all family units that ever lived in a locality is not possible, because of in- and out-migration of individuals and entire family units and because of discontinuities in the registers. On the basis of an assembled data base, the researcher can study in detail the timing of such crucial sociodemographic variables as the age of menarche, the age at first marriage, the age difference between husband and wife, premarital conception, the spacing of births, and remarriage; and at a higher level of concern general fertility, marital fertility, age-specific fertility, mortality, and nuptiality. If a sufficiently large number of families in a given locality (or from a number of similar localities) are reconstituted, comparative analysis becomes possible by social class (or estate), occupation, and other sociogeographic variables.

The technique was given currency in historical demography by the French demographer Louis Henry during the late 1950s in his research on Genevan bourgeois families. About a decade later it was refined and applied to a large sample of English populations by the work of the Cambridge Group for the History of Population and Social Structure. In these decades, the transfer of information from registers to "family reconstitution forms," as well as the linking of individual forms to each other, was accomplished manually; but in subsequent decades various computer programs have made these tasks less labor-intensive.

Andrejs Plakans

See also DEMOGRAPHY, HISTORICAL; FAMILY HISTORY (COMPARATIVE); GENEALOGY.

References

Macfarlane, Alan, with Sarah Harrison and Charles Jardine. *Reconstructing Historical Communities.* Cambridge, Eng.: Cambridge University Press, 1977.

Willigan, J. Dennis, and Katherine A. Lynch. *Sources and Methods of Historical Demography.* New York: Academic Press, 1982.

Wrigley, E. Anthony. *An Introduction to English Historical Demography.* New York: Basic Books, 1966.

Fan Wenlan [Fan Wen-lan] (1893–1969)

Marxist historian of modern China. Fan's *Zhongguo tongshi* [General History of China] is considered a milestone among Chinese Marxist studies of the country's history written for the general reader. Born into a small landlord family, he attended a modern Shanghai middle school directed by educator and reformer, Huang Yanpei, and graduated from Beijing University in 1917. While teaching at Nankai University in Tianjin, Fan supported the radical May Thirtieth movement (1925), joining the Communist Party the next year. After the Japanese invasion, Fan left his professorship at Henan University to join the Communist New Fourth Army. In 1940, Liu Shaoqi sent him to Yan'an where he studied at the Marxism–Leninism Academy, talking frequently with Mao Zedong. While teaching at the Central Party School he began to organize and write the multivolume general history, which became his life work. This history, widely used in middle schools and universities, follows the model of several earlier non-Marxist Chinese general histories. His analysis reflects the work of many other non-Marxist and Marxist historians from Liang Qichao to Guo Moruo, with whose periodization he differed. After 1949 Fan became director of the Institute of Modern History.

Mary G. Mazur

Texts

Zhongguo tongshi. 5 vols. Beijing: People's Press, 1978.

References

Feuerwerker, Albert, ed. *History in Communist China.* Cambridge, MA: MIT Press, 1968.

Fan Ye [Fan Yeh] (398–445)

Author of *Hou-Han shu* [Later or Eastern Han History]. Born into a family of several generations of officials, Fan Ye himself began his official career, which saw him occupy a succession of different posts, at the age of seventeen. During the Liu-Song dynasty (420–479), he plotted with others to replace Emperor Wen with the emperor's younger brother. The conspiracy was exposed and consequently Fan was executed. Prior to Fan's *Hou-Han shu,* there were at least eighteen histories written on the Later Han, but Fan was satisfied with none of them. On the basis of these early works, he began to write his own history, which was designed to include ten imperial annals, ninety biographies, and ten treatises. At the time of his execution, however, he had completed only the annals and the biographies. Later, Liu Zhao of the Liang dynasty (502–556) supplemented Fan's history with the eight treatises from Sima Biao's *Xu Hanshu* [Sequel to Han History]. Fan's history superseded all its predecessors and by the seventh century it became the definitive history of the Later Han.

Yuet Keung Lo

Texts

Hou-Han shu. 18 vols. Beijing: Zhonghua shuju, 1965.

References

Li Zongye. *Zhongguo lishi yaoji jieshao* [Introduction to Major Works of Chinese History]. Shanghai: Shanghai Guji chubanshe, 1982.
Shen Yue. "Biography of Fan Ye." In *Songshu* [Song History]. 8 vols. Beijing: Zhonghua shuju, 1974.

Fang Hsüan-ling

See FANG XUANLING.

Fang Xuanling [Fang Hsüan-ling] (578–648)

Chinese historian and administrator. A native of Linzi in Shandong, Fang was a Sui (581–618) official who joined Tang Taizong's (r. 626–649) retinue after the Taiyuan uprising (617). He took part in the Xuanwu Gate incident (626) and was awarded leading ministerial positions in the imperial government when Taizong ascended the throne. Fang played a key role in formulating the policies that contributed to the prosperity of the early Tang. He also participated in the dynasty's historiographical projects. In 629 Taizong appointed Fang and Wei Zheng [Wei Cheng] (580–643) to supervise the compilation of the histories of the six dynasties preceding the Tang (618–907). In addition he was the chief compiler of the *Jinshu* [Chin-shu; History of the Jin] covering the period 265–420. Under imperial commission, Fang collaborated with a board of historians to write a standard history to replace the earlier works. The *Jinshu* is noteworthy as the first of the Chinese histories which was written by committee.

Henry Y.S. Chan

Texts

Jinshu. Beijing: Zhonghua shuju, 1974.

References

Twitchett, Denis. *The Writing of Official History under the T'ang.* Cambridge, Eng.: Cambridge University Press, 1992.
Wechsler, Howard J. *Mirror to the Son of Heaven.* New Haven, CT: Yale University Press, 1974, chap. 4–5.

Faqih, Yakhshī (fl. late fourteenth–early fifteenth century)

Ottoman historian. Son of an imam (prayer leader) who lived in Bursa, capital of the Ottoman Empire before the conquest of Constantinople, Faqih is generally considered to be the author of one of the earliest accounts of Ottoman history, *Menāqib-i āl-i ʿOsmān* [Legends of the House of Osman]. This work, based on the observations of Faqih and his father, Ilyas, chronicles the rise of the Ottomans to ca. 1402 and the dynastic struggles between Sultan Mehmed I and his brother Suleiman. Although Faqih's chronicle has not survived, it is generally considered to be one of the main sources used by other early Ottoman historians. The Ottoman historian, Aşikpaşazade (b. 1400), for example, obtained important material for his *Tevārīkh-i āl-i 'Osmān* [Histories of the House of Osman] from Faqih while recuperating from an illness in his home in 1413.

Corinne Blake

Texts
The chronicle is not extant.

References
Inalcik, Halil. "The Rise of Ottoman Historiography." In *Historians of the Middle East,* ed. B. Lewis and P.M. Holt. London: Oxford University Press, 1973, 152–167.

Febvre, Lucien (1878–1956)
French historian. Febvre was born in Nancy and educated at the École Normale. His doctoral thesis, *Philippe II et la Franche-Comté* (1912) immediately established his reputation. It was not a conventional study of the policies of Philip II in this region, but a study of the geography, social structure, and social history of the region that shaped Philip's policies. At the University of Strasbourg, Febvre met his colleague and long-time collaborator, Marc Bloch, with whom he founded the journal *Annales* in 1929. He published a number of seminal articles between the wars on the French Reformation, all of which exhibited Febvre's devotion to what he called "a new kind of history." His last major book was a 1942 study of religious mentality in sixteenth-century Europe, later translated as *The Problem of Unbelief in the Sixteenth Century: The Religion of Rabelais*; in this Febvre argued that Rabelais could not be an atheist, since no one in the sixteenth century had the mental or linguistic categories to conceive of a world without a God. This thesis has been much criticized by later students of early modern belief and of popular mentalities, but the book remains a seminal work in the area today. With Henri-Jean Martin, Febvre also wrote *L'Apparition du Livre* (1958; translated in 1976 as *The Coming of the Book*), an important early entry into discussions of the advent of print culture in early modern Europe.

Mack P. Holt

Texts
And Henri-Jean Martin. *The Coming of the Book: The Impact of Printing 1450–1800.* Trans. David Gerard; ed. Geoffrey Nowell-Smith and David Wootton. London: New Left Books, 1976.

Martin Luther: A Destiny. Trans. Roberts Tapley. London: J.M. Dent, 1930.
A New Kind of History and Other Essays. Ed. Peter Burke; trans. K. Folca. London: Routledge and Kegan Paul, 1973.
Philippe II et la Franche-Comté. Paris: H. Champion, 1911.
The Problem of Unbelief in the Sixteenth Century: The Religion of Rabelais. Trans. Beatrice Gottlieb. Cambridge, MA: Harvard University Press, 1982.
La terre et l'evolution humaine: Introduction géographique à l'histoire [The Earth and Human Evolution: A Geographical Introduction to History]. Paris: Renaissance du livre, 1922.

References
Burke, Peter. *The French Historical Revolution: The Annales School, 1929–1989.* Stanford, CA: Stanford University Press, 1990.
Mann, Hans Dieter. *Lucien Febvre: La pensee vivante d'un historien* [Lucien Febvre: The Living Thought of a Historian]. Paris: A. Colin, 1971.

Fejérpataky, Lászlo (1857–1923)
Hungarian historian and archivist. Born in Prešov in then upper Hungary, modern Slovakia, he was a descendant of a lower noble family from Liptov county. He studied at the gymnasium and university in Budapest and at the Historical Institute in Vienna. He taught prospective secondary school teachers until 1880 when he joined the manuscript division of the university library in Budapest. In 1895 he became an archivist at the Hungarian National Museum and was named a director of the Royal Szechenyi Library and professor at the University in Budapest in 1895. In 1930 he was appointed director of the Hungarian National Museum. He died shortly after being named the deputy state secretary of the Ministry of Culture and Education in 1923. Fejérpataky served as the secretary and vice president of the Hungarian Society for Heraldry and Genealogy and edited its yearbook. He conducted research at archives throughout Europe and prepared critical editions of documents that contributed to the development of Hungarian historiography, heraldry, genealogy, and numismatics. His most important works were the history of the royal chancellery of the Arpáds, the papal tithe in Hungary, and editions of medieval city books from the towns of upper Hungary.

David P. Daniel

Texts

Irodalmunk az Árpádok korában [Our Literature in the Time of the Arpáds]. Budapest: Rudnynászky, 1878.

A királyi kancellária az Árpádok korában [The Royal Chancellery during the Time of the Arpáds]. Budapest: Magyar Tudományos Akadémia, 1885.

Magyar czímeres emlékek [Monuments of Hungarian Heraldry]. 2 vols. Budapest: Kiadja a Magyar Heraldikai es Genealogiai Társasag, 1901–1926.

Magyarországi városok régi számadás könyvei [Old Registers of the Hungarian Royal Cities]. Budapest: Magyar Tudományos Akadémia, 1885.

Monumenta Vaticana. Rationes collectorum pontificiorum in hungaria 1281–1375 [Vatican Documents. Registers of the Collection of the Papal Tithe in Hungary, 1291–1375]. Budapest: Franklin, 1887.

Monumenta Vaticana historiam regni Hungariae illustrantia [Vatican Documents Illustrating the Kingdom of Hungary]. Budapest: Franklin, 1885.

References

Gulyás, Pál. *Fejérpataky Lászlo*. Budapest: Orszagos Széchenyi Könyvtár, 1923.

Feminism

A social movement and a body of theory committed to identifying, explaining, and challenging the subordination of women in the past and the present. Feminism encompasses several theoretical positions, each differing in its analysis of the causes of women's oppression.

Feminist historical scholarship of the late 1960s and early 1970s set out to recover the experiences of women neglected by conventional historical accounts. A liberal feminist perspective is evident in those works that emphasized the legal and customary restraints faced by women as they struggled to attain equal rights with men in the public sphere. At the same time, research on women's relationships among themselves and the creation of a specific female culture recognized women's potential for agency in the face of oppressive social and economic conditions.

A major focus of feminist research has been the examination of the endurance of varying modes of patriarchy, or the systems through which male dominance is perpetuated in society as a whole. Sexual politics, the relations of power between men and women, are understood as fundamental to the overall social organization of power, shaping political institutions and economic organization as well as the social and cultural institutions of family, religion, and education. As part of this broader project, theorists of patriarchy have directed attention to the ways in which men have attempted to appropriate women's sexuality and reproductive capacities. In a radical feminist approach, sexuality is given priority in structuring the relationships between men and women in society. The term patriarchy has, however, been criticized for its ahistoricity by some feminist scholars, who object to its connotations of unchanging, universal male and female essential natures.

These critiques, together with a dissatisfaction with Marxism's failure adequately to account for gender inequalities, have prompted a more nuanced consideration of the divergent interests existing among women and their relation to broader social and economic forces. A socialist–feminist analysis seeks to retain an emphasis on historical materialism while incorporating gender as one of the key axes of power in society. Rather than viewing women's position and experience solely in terms of changes in the social relations of production, dual systems theorists insist on the independent analytical status of the sex–gender system. Patriarchy and capitalism, gender and class relations, are accorded equal weight in explanations of women's oppression.

Given the difficulties of understanding gender inequalities within existing frameworks of social history, many feminist historians have turned to the analytical possibilities offered by postmodernism. Associated with poststructuralist literary theory, this variant of feminist history is primarily concerned with the social and cultural construction of gender identities and hierarchies, with a particular emphasis on language and systems of meaning. In this approach, gender is understood not only as an element of the social relations between men and women, shaping social norms, institutions and identities, but as a means of signifying and legitimating power. As a system of meaning, gender informs perceptions of all social life, thus offering new perspectives on the more established fields of political and economic history. Feminist scholars continue to debate the value of postmodernist theory for feminist history, many voicing skepticism concerning its apparent denial of the material foundations of women's past experience. The postmodern critique of a universal category of woman (or man) is viewed as politically and intellectually paralyzing by some

F

scholars. For others, the renewed attention to difference and diversity among women holds the promise of a more thoroughgoing analysis of complex relations of power between women and men and among women themselves. The ongoing critique of dominant explanatory models is evident in the challenge to move beyond the confines of a Eurocentric feminism in order to address the experiences of black and non-Western women, and explore fully the intersections of race, class, and gender in the past.

Susan E. Brown

See also CLASS; EUROCENTRISM; GENDER; PATRIARCHY; POSTMODERNISM; PUBLIC/PRIVATE; WOMEN'S HISTORY.

References

Bennett, Judith M. "Feminism and History." *Gender & History* 1 (1989): 251–272.

"Common Grounds and Crossroads: Race, Ethnicity and Class in Women's Lives." *Signs* 14 (1989): Special Issue.

Fox-Genovese, Elizabeth. "Socialist-Feminist American Women's History." *Journal of Women's History* 1 (1990): 181–210.

Kelly, Joan. *Women, History, Theory.* Chicago: University of Chicago Press, 1984.

Kerber, Linda K. "Separate Spheres, Female Worlds, Woman's Place: The Rhetoric of Women's History." *Journal of American History* 75 (1988): 9–39.

Lewis, Jane. "The Debate on Sex and Class." *New Left Review* 149 (1985): 108–120.

Nicholson, Linda J. *Gender and History: The Limits of Social Theory in the Age of the Family.* New York: Columbia University Press, 1986.

Rowbotham, Sheila. *Hidden from History.* New York: Pantheon, 1974.

Scott, Joan W. ed. *Feminism and History.* Oxford, Eng.: Oxford University Press, 1996.

Scott, Joan W. *Gender and the Politics of History.* New York: Columbia University Press, 1988.

Smith-Rosenberg, Carroll. "The Female World of Love and Ritual: Relations between Women in Nineteenth-Century America." *Signs* 1 (1975–1976): 1–29.

Stansell, Christine. "A Response to Joan Scott." *International Labor and Working-Class History* 31 (1987): 24–29.

Vicinus, Martha. *A Widening Sphere.* Bloomington: Indiana University Press, 1977.

Feminist History

See FEMINISM; PATRIARCHY

Feng Yulan [Fung Yu-lan] (1895–1990)

Historian of Chinese philosophy. Born to a scholar–gentry family in Henan province, Feng Yulan studied Chinese philosophy at Beijing University from 1915 to 1918. He left China for America in 1919 and entered Columbia University, where he studied philosophy. Feng received his Ph.D. in 1921 and published his dissertation, *A Comparative Study of Life Ideals,* in 1924. Returning to China, Feng taught Chinese philosophy at Yanjing University and Qinghua University. Employing Western philosophical categories and following the Western model of comparative philosophy, Feng wrote his major study, the *Zhongguo zhexue shi* [History of Chinese Philosophy] in 1933. Feng's book was the first of its kind to analyze systematically the evolution of Chinese philosophy. Although Feng did not think all Chinese modes of thought were philosophical, he argued that some of them were undoubtedly so and ought to be valued as such. Feng taught in America from 1946 to 1947 and published *A Short History of Chinese Philosophy* in 1948.

Tze-ki Hon

Texts

Aids to the Study of Chinese Philosophy. Ed. and trans. Lucius Chapin Porter. Beijing: n.p., 1934.

Chuang Tzu: A New Selected Translation with an Exposition of the Philosophy of Kuo Hsiang. Shanghai: The Commercial Press, 1933.

A Comparative Study of Life Ideals: The Way of Decrease and Increase with Interpretations and Illustrations from the Philosophies of the East and the West. Shanghai: The Commercial Press, 1924.

A History of Chinese Philosophy. Trans. Derk Bodde. 2 vols. Princeton, NJ: Princeton University Press, 1952.

The Spirit of Chinese Philosophy. Trans. E.R. Hughes. Boston: Beacon Press, 1962.

References

Masson, Michel C. *Philosophy and Tradition: The Interpretation of China's Philosophic Past: Fung Yu-lan, 1939–1949.* Taibei: Institut Ricci, 1985.

Ferguson, Adam (1723–1816)

Scottish historian and philosopher. A Highlander and a Gaelic speaker, Adam Ferguson was born in 1723 at Logierait, Perthshire, and was educated at Perth grammar school, the University of St. Andrews, and Edinburgh University. In 1757 he succeeded David Hume as librarian of the Advocates' Library in Edinburgh. He later held in succession the chairs of natural philosophy, pneumatics and moral philosophy, and mathematics at Edinburgh University, with brief absences in Europe as tutor to the third earl of Chesterfield; in North America as secretary to the Carlyle Peace Commission; and in Germany and Italy, researching Roman history. He died in St. Andrews. Ferguson's major work, *An Essay on the History of Civil Society* (1767), is a natural history of the evolution of humanity from the "rude" to the "polished" state, inflected by Machiavellian moralizing against the dangers of the political and social corruption and overspecialization that accompany the otherwise "civilizing" effects of commercial society. Ferguson has been seen as a progenitor of modern sociology. For Marx, he was "the master of Adam Smith"; others have seen him as the master of Marx himself. His *History of the Progress and Termination of the Roman Republic* (1783) was less original than the *Essay,* but remained influential throughout Europe well into the nineteenth century.

David Armitage

Texts

The Correspondence of Adam Ferguson. Ed. Vincenzo Merolle. 2 vols. Brookfield, VT: William Pickering, 1995.
An Essay on the History of Civil Society. Ed. Fania Oz-Salzberger. Cambridge, Eng.: Cambridge University Press, 1996.
The History of the Progress and Termination of the Roman Republic. 3 vols. London: Price, Whitestone, et al., 1783.

References

Kettler, David. *The Social and Political Thought of Adam Ferguson.* Columbus: Ohio State University Press, 1965.
Lehmann, William C. *Adam Ferguson and the Beginnings of Modern Sociology.* New York: Columbia University Press, 1930.

Ferguson, Wallace Klippert (1902–1983)

Canadian historian of the Renaissance. Born in Ontario, Ferguson received his B.A. from the University of Western Ontario in 1924 and Ph.D. from Cornell University in 1927 as a student of Preserved Smith. Ferguson taught at New York University from 1928 to 1956 and at the University of Western Ontario from 1956 until retirement. He was the author of a critical edition of Erasmus's *Opuscula* and three widely used European history

textbooks. Ferguson's most famous book, however, was *The Renaissance in Historical Thought,* which analyzes the concept of the Renaissance from its origins. Francesco Petrarca (or Petrarch) (1304–1374) invented the notion of the Renaissance by dividing history into three ages: the ancient world, the "dark" Middle Ages, and a new age of rebirth ("renaissance") in the fourteenth century. Ferguson explains how the idea of the Renaissance took hold in the fifteenth and sixteenth centuries. He then follows its interpretation through the European Enlightenment, Jacob Burckhardt's view of the Renaissance as the beginning of the modern world (1860), and the anti-Renaissance reaction of twentieth-century medieval scholars. Written with clarity, impartiality, and occasional wit, the book is the fundamental history of the concept of Renaissance and a classic of historiography.

Paul F. Grendler

Texts

Ed. *Erasmi Opuscula, a Supplement to the Opera Omnia.* The Hague: M. Nijhoff, 1933.
The Renaissance in Historical Thought: Five Centuries of Interpretation. Boston: Houghton Mifflin, 1948.
Renaissance Studies. New York: Harper & Row, 1970.
And Geoffrey Bruun. *A Survey of European Civilization.* Fourth ed. Boston: Houghton Mifflin, 1969.

Fernández de Piedrahita, Lucas (1624–1688)

Spanish Jesuit historian. Fernández de Piedrahita was born in Santa Fe de Bogota on March 6, 1624. He was educated by the Jesuits in the College of San Bartolomé and rose rapidly in the church hierarchy, obtaining a series of appointments. Summoned to defend himself before the Council of the Indies in Spain, he remained there for six years. In 1669, after winning his case, Fernández de Piedrahita returned to the Americas as the bishop of Santa Marta. In 1676, after being named the bishop of Panama, he was captured by pirates who subsequently released him in Panama. During his stay in Spain in the 1660s, he wrote the *Historia General de las Conquistas del Nuevo Reino de Granada* [General History of the Conquest of the New Kingdom of Granada], a history of the conquest of Colombia. It is not an original work, but a rewriting of the various manuscripts about New Granada that he had consulted. This was first published in Antwerp in 1688, the year of his death.

Carlos Pérez

Texts

Historia General de las Conquistas del Neuvo Reyno de Granada, published as *Noticia historial de las conquistas del Nuevo Reino de Granada* [Historical News of the Conquest of the New Kingdom of Granada]. Ed. Sergio Elias Ortiz. 2 vols. Bogota: Editorial Kelly, 1973.

References

Laverde Amay, Isidoro. *Ojeada historico-critico sobre los origines de la literatura Columbiana* [Historical-Critical Survey of the Origins of Colombian Literature]. Bogota: Banco de la Republica Biblioteca Luis Angel Arango, 1963.

Otero Munoz, Gustavo. *La literatura colonial de Colombia* [Colonial Literature of Colombia]. La Paz, Colombia: Imp. artistico, 1928.

Ferrand, Paul Gabriel Joseph (1864–1935)

French arabist. Born in Marseille, Ferrand received his diploma from l'École des Langues Orientales in Malayan studies. He entered the diplomatic corps in the Ministry of Foreign Affairs and was sent to Madagascar in 1887. His first work was published in 1891, entitled *Les Musulmans à Madagascar et aux Iles Comores.* Ferrand collected and worked with Arabic and Malagasy manuscripts; ten years' service in Madagascar gave him mastery of Malagasy and allowed him to make comparisons between Malagasy and Malayan. After serving for a time in Iran, he was transferred to Paris where he worked as the *attaché commercial,* dealing with Germany, Belgium, the Netherlands and Switzerland. During this time, he published and defended his *thèse de Lettres* under the title *Essai de phonétique comparée du malais et des dialectes malgaches.* Ferrand was posted to New Orleans in 1914 and remained there until the end of World War I. During this period, he wrote numerous articles for *Journal Asiatique,* primarily on portions of insular Southeast Asia. These articles include: *Voyages des Javanais à Madagascar* (1910); *Malaka, le Malayu et Malayur* (1918); *Le k'ouen louen et les anciennes navigatios interoceaniques dans les mers du Sud* (1919); and *L'Empire Sumatranais de Çrivijaya* (1922). Ferrand's work with ancient documents related as much to linguistics as to ethnology and history. He confirmed that the Sumatrans had arrived in Madagascar in the ninth century and that there were successive waves of arrivals of other Malayans. Among his works, he published a list of those ancient authors who supported the idea of the aboriginal ancestry of the Malagasan people; Ferrand himself believed that the Malagasans, together with Africans and Malayans, composed the primitive peoples of Madagascar.

Damon L. Woods

Texts

L'empire Sumatranais de Çrivijaya [The Sumatran Empire of Çrivijaya]. Paris: Imprimerie nationale, 1922.

Ed. and trans. *Instructions nautiques et routiers arabes et portugais des XVᵉ et XVIᵉ siècles* [Nautical and Road Instructions of the Arabs and Portuguese in the Fifteenth and Sixteenth Centuries]. 3 vols. Paris: Geuthner, 1921–1928.

Les poids, mesures et monnaies des mers du Sud aux XVIᵉ et XVIIᵉ siècles [Weights, Measures and Moneys in the South Seas during the Sixteenth and Seventeenth Centuries]. Paris: Imprimerie nationale, 1921.

Relations de voyages et textes géographiques arabes, persans et turks relatifs à L'Extrème Orient du XVIIᵉ et XVIIIᵉ siècles [Relations of the Voyages and Geographic Texts of the Arabs, Persians, and Turks Relating to the Far East in the Seventeenth and Eighteenth Centuries]. 2 vols. Paris: E. Leroux, 1913–1914.

Voyage du marchand arabe Sulayman en Inde et en Chine, rédigé en 851, suivi de remarques par Abu Zayd Hasan [Voyage of the Arab Merchant Suleiman in India and Chine, Written in 851, with Remarks by Abu Zayd Hasan]. Translation, introduction, glossary and index by Ferrand. Paris: Editions Bossard, 1922.

Ferrari, Giuseppe (1811–1876)

Italian historian and philosopher of history. Ferrari abandoned his law practice, after obtaining a degree at the University of Pavia (1832), in order to study the Neapolitan philosopher Giambattista Vico. His work on Vico, published in France, gained him status as a brilliant thinker and a post at the University of Strasbourg. In the 1850s, he published several further works. *Filosofia della rivoluzione* [Philosophy of the Revolution] (1851) was an examination of the French Revolution as the key event in modern history, ushering in the promise of a secular culture and social justice, while *La federazione republicana* [The Republican Federation] (1851) turned to the 1848 revolutions in Italy. After the unification of Italy, he served as a deputy in the new parliament. In his last years,

Ferrari returned to Vico and formulated a theory of historical evolution in his *Teoria dei periodi politici* [Theory of Political Periods] (1874) and *L'aritmetica della storia* [The Arithmetic of History] (1875) which proposed the use of mathematical laws to understand the cyclical nature of history.

Stanislao G. Pugliese

Texts

Essai sur le principe et les limites de la philosophie de l'histoire [Essay on the Principal and Limits of the Philosophy of History]. Paris: Didier, 1843.

Histoire des revolutions d'Italie [History of the Revolutions in Italy]. Paris: Didier, 1858.

Histoire de la raison d'Etat [History of Reason of State]. Paris: Editions Kime, 1992.

References

Lovett, Clara Maria. *Giuseppe Ferrari and the Italian Revolution.* Chapel Hill: University of North Carolina Press, 1979.

Film and History

The use of film as a source for historical research and as a vehicle for historical education. Concerned that written documentation—long the bedrock of historical inquiry—has rendered a largely elitist view of the past, historians are searching for ways to rescue the largely ignored or forgotten voices, thoughts, and imagination of common people, meaning the vast majority of humankind. Their quest has led them to innovative possibilities: tapestries, paintings, photographs, clothing and jewelry, oral traditions including myths, comic books and tombstones, both planned and spontaneous processions, games, rituals, festivals—the list of wondrous options goes on and on—and, of course, includes the communications product of our times, motion pictures.

Historians now tend to approach film in three ways: 1) as the re-creation of a historical event; 2) as a stepping stone to ponder and discuss historical happenings and processes; 3) as a reflection of the society that produced the film. Of these, the third route has proved to be the most interesting and challenging (and controversial), if only because filmmakers insist upon their right to alter and arrange data in the name of "artistic" or "dramatic license" and rarely aspire to re-create history in the sense of the professional historian. So while a popular movie like *Bonnie and Clyde* (1967) may not tell us much about those desperadoes who rampaged in America's Midwest during the 1930s, nor reveal anything meaningful about the Great Depression, it may well mirror the tastes, manners, fantasies, and goals of audiences in the late 1960s. About the same time, *The Graduate* (1967), which opened slowly, but soon gained enormous popularity through word of mouth, seems to have done the same, as did *The Sound of Music* (1965), based on a failed musical play and sneered at by most potential producers, a motion picture that still stands as one of the great money grossers of all time. Historians want to know why. What sensibilities in audiences did these movies touch?

For evidence of a society's changing mores and values (meaning culture), historians also track films over time. In the United States, for example, they may trace the changing (disintegrating?) relationship between American children and their parents through *A Tree Grows in Brooklyn* (1945) to *East of Eden* (1954), then *Splendor in the Grass* (1961), and on to *Easy Rider* (1969). Or, they may examine the concept of American rugged individualism through the depictions of and relationships between heroes, villains, and society embedded in the Western film genre. They look at the portrayal of technology in *2001: A Space Odyssey* in 1968 and compare it with that of *Star Wars* a decade later. Why is the linkage between humanity and technology so disdained in the first film (remember the computer Hal) and embraced in its successor (Luke and the robots are each other's salvation)? Historians are weighing the answer in the contexts of those respective times. They are doing the same with the spate of apocalyptic films that appeared in the 1970s. Shifting (and nonshifting) racial attitudes along with those concerning women and gays have been among those most studied and analyzed through film by social and cultural historians.

Virtually all of these studies are fueled by the hypothesis that theatrical motion pictures are best seen as commercial products of multinational corporations whose portfolios go far beyond the entertainment industry. The premise is that, by and large, movies, including so-called documentaries, are crafted and shaped (some would prefer manipulated) to make a profit—that investors demand a healthy return. Although the great majority of films lose money, investors seem willing (although increasingly less so) to gamble that *their* motion picture project will become a lucrative blockbuster. Those movies which do so, runs the argument, must please audiences and therefore reflect their feelings, or at least how audiences want to feel about themselves. In fact, most screen plays are written, edited, and processed by committees with an eye toward potential wide audience appeal. As a result, controversial material is muted and certain themes omitted altogether.

Because historians understand that subject matter is deliberately skewed in the endeavor to create a pleasing product, the most revealing studies of movies have been tied to the cinema industry itself. Research into company production, financial, and legal files (when permitted) has proved to be exceedingly fruitful. Presidential papers have exposed the political ties between the government and Hollywood. More challenging has been the attempt to gauge systematically audience reaction; box office receipts may not be the best (and certainly are not the only) way to measure public appeal. The emphasis on movies as the business of capitalism along with the attempts to get inside the heads of audiences, has not dampened the scholar's ambition to dissect the picture per se. Toward this end, they have used traditional and postmodern techniques usually reserved for literature. Findings and conclusions have aroused impassioned debate and scorching criticism. In fact, the study of film as a cultural artifact has only received lukewarm acceptance in academic circles as a legitimate scholarly endeavor. There are, however, signs of breakthrough, if only because humanities classes need enrollment, and publishers tend to solicit manuscripts that have broad public appeal.

Historians recognize that one generalizes about film at great peril. They appreciate that many creative filmmakers have never had a reasonable opportunity to display their motion pictures because distribution companies see no commercial potential in their work. Michael Parenti has heatedly attacked the industry and its "prejudiced products" in *Make-Believe Media: The Politics of Entertainment* (1992) and *Inventing Reality: The Politics of the News Media* (1993). Although the industry is worldwide, most scholarly investigation of movies as a cultural artifact has been limited to American popular films in theaters and on television, which is not meant to exclude stimulating cultural studies of movies made in Great Britain, France, Germany, Italy, Japan, and India. Regardless of the place of production, historians know that their findings only "suggest" certain things about culture. Larger claims invite just criticism.

Because the methodological approach to historical film study is in its infancy and highly controversial, serious books and scholarly articles on the topic are limited and of uneven quality. Nonetheless, there are some good places for students of the subject to start. The best scholarly journal

in the area is *Film & History*, published quarterly by the history department of the University of Florida. Special numbers have been devoted to issues such as the depictions of American Indians in movies. *The American Historical Review* annually publishes suggestive film reviews written by historians that cover worldwide cinema.

Paul J. Vanderwood

See also PHOTOGRAPHS—HISTORICAL ANALYSIS OF.

References

Bergman, Andrew. *We're in the Money: Depression America and Its Films.* New York: Harper and Row, 1971.

Carnes, Mark C., ed. *Past Imperfect: History According to the Movies.* New York: Henry Holt, 1995.

Ferro, Marc. *Cinema and History.* Detroit: Wayne State University Press, 1988.

Hellmann, John. *American Myth and the Legacy of Vietnam.* New York: Columbia University Press, 1986.

O'Connor, John E., ed. *Image As Artifact: The Historical Analysis of Film and Television.* Melbourne, FL: Kriegar, 1990.

———, and Martin A. Jackson. *American History/American Film: Interpreting the Hollywood Image.* New York: Frederick Ungar, 1979.

——— and Martin A. Jackson *Teaching History with Film.* Washington, D.C.: Discussion on Teaching, American Historical Association, 1974.

Parenti, Michael. *Inventing Reality: The Politics of the News Media.* New York: St. Martins Press, 1993.

———. *Make-Believe Media: The Politics of Entertainment.* New York: St. Martin's Press, 1992.

Rollins, Peter C., ed. *Hollywood As Historian: American Film in Cultural Context.* Lexington: University of Kentucky Press, 1983.

Rosenstone, Robert A. *Revisioning History: Film and the Construction of a New Past.* Princeton, NJ: Princeton University Press, 1995.

Short, K.R.M. *Feature Film As History.* Knoxville: University of Tennessee Press, 1981.

Sklar, Robert, and Charles Mussar, eds. *Resisting Images: Essays on Cinema and History.* Philadelphia: Temple University Press, 1990.

Sorlin, Pierre. *The Film in History: Restaging the Past.* Totowa, NJ: Barnes and Noble, 1980.

Vidal, Gore. *Screening History.* Cambridge, MA: Harvard University Press, 1992.

Finley, Sir Moses I. (1912–1986)

American (later British) ancient historian. Born Moses Finkelstein (a name he retained until the early 1940s), Finley studied at Syracuse and Columbia universities and taught at Columbia and the City College of New York. From 1937 to 1939 he worked for the Institute of Social Research, a broadly Marxist organization that had moved from Hitler's Germany to New York. After working for American relief agencies during the war, he held posts at Rutgers University, but was dismissed for political reasons in the McCarthy purges of 1952. He moved in 1954 to England and became a British subject in 1962. At Cambridge he became fellow of Jesus College (1955), professor of ancient history (1970–1979), and master of Darwin College (1976–1982). He was knighted in 1979. Finley made his reputation with two books, *Studies in Land and Credit in Ancient Athens, 500–200 B.C.* (1952) and *The World of Odysseus* (1954), but his most important work was on ancient slavery and economics. In *The Ancient Economy* (1973) he denied the significance of the "profit-motive" in ancient decision-making. His "minimalist" position is increasingly regarded as too extreme, but was important in correcting anachronistic approaches. Here and elsewhere, for example in *Ancient Slavery and Modern Ideology* (1980), Finley postulated a spectrum of different statuses rather than a polar opposition between slave and free. *Ancient History: Evidence and Models* (1985), and the collection of essays, *The Use and Abuse of History* (1975), well illustrate his wide-ranging, "holistic" methods, concerned with creating models rather than accumulating undigested data—the "antiquarianism" about which he was so scathing.

Richard Fowler

Texts

The Ancient Economy. Second ed. London: Hogarth Press, 1985.

Ancient History: Evidence and Models. London: Chatto and Windus, 1985.

Politics in the Ancient World. Cambridge, Eng.: Cambridge University Press, 1983.

Studies in Land and Credit in Ancient Athens, 500–200 B.C.: The Horos-Inscriptions. New Brunswick, NJ: Rutgers University Press, 1952.

The Use and Abuse of History. Corrected ed. London: Hogarth Press, 1986.

The World of Odysseus. New York: Viking Press, 1954.

Finnish Historiography

Historical writing in Finland, principally in Finnish and Swedish. The earliest examples of the recording of history in Finland took the form of epic poetry, legends, and stories going back to the pagan era as an oral tradition. They were followed by annals and chronicles of the medieval Christian period, many of which were shared with Sweden. The annals were written in Latin while Swedish was generally used in the chronicles, which often served the purposes of political propaganda and were polemical in tone and content.

The Lutheran Reformation brought some limited historical writing in Finnish. The earliest examples were composed by clerics. By the turn of the sixteenth to the seventeenth century, the contributions to political history by an educated nobleman, Claes Hermansson Fleming, had broadened its scope. With the establishment of the University of Turku (1640), the base for Finnish historiography improved with the beginning of academic study of and research into history in Finland. Its purpose was to discover, and if necessary create, an illustrious past for the fatherland. But it also produced useful information about the physical and human environment of the country, including its geography, culture, languages, customs, administration, and economy.

The eighteenth-century Enlightenment ushered in a more critical approach to sources. The subjects and topics of historical study expanded beyond the history of the fatherland itself, while at the same time local history was cultivated. Algoth Scarin and Henrik Gabriel Porthan, two professors of the University of Turku, were the most influential historians of the century.

Finnish historiography expanded still further, while increasing in complexity, during the nineteenth century. First, coming under the influence of romanticism and idealistic nationalism, it made an important contribution to nation building in the autonomous Finnish state that emerged in association with Russia after 1809. Adolf Ivar Arwidsson, Zacharias Topelius, and Yrjö Sakari Yrjö-Koskinen were key figures in this process. During the second half of the century historical works written in Finnish emerged parallel to those written in Swedish and soon surpassed them in volume.

Around the end of the nineteenth century, Finnish historiography began to be differentiated into many subfields. Cultural, economic, and social history became fashionable, but political and legal history remained at the forefront, in the context of polemics with Russian nationalist historians about Finnish autonomy. Besides pursuing the study of Finnish history, many scholars looked beyond their national frontiers to investigate the history of medieval and early modern Europe. The achievement of national independence (1917), however, caused historians once again to concentrate on Finnish and political history. The study of history continued during this period to shape Finnish national identity. Reflecting the dual ethnolinguistic background and composition of the nation, two broad major lines of interpretations, advanced respectively by Finnish- and Swedish-speaking scholars, offered competing views of many aspects and events of the past. Sometimes leading to heated historical debates, this dual approach nevertheless stimulated much research and a wider popular interest in history.

During the decades following World War II, nationalistic historiography declined in influence. An approach that was at once broader and more professional came into its own, and historians also became once more interested in topics other than Finnish history. Various subfields—including family and women's history—began to multiply, reflecting general trends in the study of history elsewhere. Ambitious and extensive projects, investigated by teams of historians, have also become fashionable, often generously financed through public funding and offering employment to greater numbers of historians.

Pekka Kalevi Hämäläinen

See also SCANDINAVIAN HISTORIOGRAPHY.

References

Tommila, Päiviö. *Studies in the History of Society in Finland before World War Two*. Jyväskylä, Finland: Studia Historica Jyväskylensia, 1981.

———. *Suomen historiankirjoitus: Tutkimuksen historia*. [Historical Writing in Finland: A History of Research]. Helsinki: WSOY, 1989.

Salokangas, Raimo, and Päiviö Tommila. *Press History Studies in Finland—Past and Present*. Jyväskylä, Finland: Studia Historica Jyväskylensia, 1982.

Firth, Sir Charles Harding (1857–1936)

English historian. Firth came from a prominent and wealthy family of Sheffield metalsmiths and was educated at Oxford University where he spent virtually his entire academic career. He became Regius professor of history in 1904 and held the appointment until his retirement in 1925. He was knighted in 1922. Though never taught by Samuel

Rawson Gardiner, Firth was a great admirer of his work and continued Gardiner's great narrative history of the seventeenth century down to 1658, the year of Oliver Cromwell's death, in his *Last Years of the Protectorate* (1909). His earliest publications were editions of texts—the contemporary lives of Colonel John Hutchinson by his wife, Lucy; of the duke of Newcastle by his wife, Margaret Cavendish; and of the republican Edmund Ludlow. He also edited the Clarke papers (which he discovered) relating to army politics in the 1640s and 1650s. In addition, he wrote no less than 225 articles for the *Dictionary of National Biography*. Thereafter, Firth brought out studies of *Oliver Cromwell and the Rule of the Puritans in England* (1900), *Cromwell's Army* (1902), and of *The House of Lords during the Civil War* (1910). Dedicating himself at Oxford (amidst much opposition) to reforming the teaching of his subject, Firth paid great attention to the importance of source criticism and historiography. One such course of lectures was posthumously published in 1938 as *A Commentary on Macaulay's History of England*.

R.C. Richardson

Texts

A Commentary on Macaulay's History of England. New York: Barnes and Noble, 1965.

Cromwell's Army. London: Methuen, 1902.

Essays Historical and Literary. Oxford: Clarendon Press, 1938.

The House of Lords during the Civil War. Totowa, NJ: Rowman and Littlefield, 1974.

The Last Years of the Protectorate. London and New York: Longmans, Green, 1909.

References

Kenyon, J.P. "Sir Charles Firth and the Oxford School of Modern History, 1892–1925." In *Clio's Mirror: Historiography in Britain and the Netherlands*, ed. A.C. Duke and C.A. Tamse. Zutphen, Netherlands: De Warburg Pers, 1985, 163–184.

Richardson, R.C. *The Debate on the English Revolution Revisited*. London: Routledge, 1988.

Fischer, Fritz (b. 1908)

German historian. The occupant of a chair in history at the University of Hamburg from 1942 to 1973, Fischer's work concentrated on political and religious history of Germany. After 1945, like many of his generation, he repudiated the views he had previously held during the Third Reich. While relying on traditional methods of textual criticism of documents of politics and state, Fischer's work was less innovative in the field of methodology than in the global interpretation of twentieth-century German history. His major book *Griff nach der Weltmacht* (1961) [Germany's Aims in the First World War], provoked a sharp controversy in the German historical community. The "Fischer controversy" rested on his basic assumptions about Germany's responsibility for the outbreak of the war. In contrast to the moderate conservative consensus among German historians, Fischer concluded that the German imperial government had actively prepared for an international conflict and that extensive annexationist ambitions were supported by a broad consensus of public opinion. Fischer directly attacked those viewpoints that continued to insist on the basically defensive character of German policy. He challenged the notion that all European nations equally shared hegemonic ambitions, and that the quest for an international balance of power had provoked the war. While reversing the "primacy of foreign policy," Fischer's assumptions rested on the "primacy of domestic policy," according to which the sources of German expansionism were not to be found in Germany's geopolitical position but in the economic, social, and political structures of the country. The same thesis was worked out in *Krieg der Illusionen* (1969; translated as *War of Illusions* in 1975). As in his later book *Bündnis der Eliten* (1979; translated as *From Kaiserreich to Third Reich* in 1986), Fischer strongly emphasized the basic continuity between German policies through the Wilhelmine empire and the Third Reich. In so doing, he refuted the thesis maintained by conservative historians, like Friedrich Meinecke, Gerhard Ritter, and Hans Rothfels, that the Nazi experience had marked a fundamental break with Prussian-German traditions.

The Fischer controversy reflected the growing split between the classical paradigm of documentary research, and a more complex methodology of social analysis. Fischer's approach inspired a younger generation of German historians who increasingly started to investigate the interrelations between economic interests, social structures, and politics in German history, as well as their impact on the German *Sonderweg* ("special path"), now predominantly described in negative terms as the fateful course of Germany in the twentieth century. The controversy is now generally regarded as a turning point in the general reorientation of German historiography.

Georgi Verbeeck

Texts

From Kaiserreich to Third Reich: Elements of Continuity in German History, 1871–1945. Trans. Roger Fletcher. London: Allen & Unwin, 1986.

Germany's Aims in the First World War. New York: Norton, 1967.

War of Illusions: German Policies from 1911 to 1914. Trans. Marian Jackson. London: Chatto and Windus, 1975.

References

Iggers, Georg G. *New Directions in European Historiography*. Middletown, CT: Wesleyan University Press, 1975.

———, ed. *The Social History of Politics: Critical Perspectives in West German Historical Writing since 1945*. Leamington Spa, Eng.: Berg Publishers, 1985.

Moses, John A. *The Politics of Illusion. The Fischer Controversy in German Historiography*. London: Prior, 1975.

Fisher, Herbert Albert Laurens (1865–1940)

English historian of Europe. One of the most widely read English historians of his day, Fisher attended Winchester and Oxford as a classics scholar before embarking on a political career. As president of the Board of Education in the Lloyd George ministry he instituted several important educational reforms. Fisher afterward served as warden of New College, Oxford. Fisher's monograph, *Napoleonic Statesmanship: Germany* (1903) emphasized the paradox between the exalted principles professed by Napoleon's statecraft and the ignoble aspects of its application. His *Bonapartism* (1908) and *Napoleon* (1913) briefly but brilliantly charted the elements of contradiction in the empire as both a product of and a reaction against the tradition of the French Revolution. But Fisher's masterpiece was *The History of Europe* (1935) which, despite its numerous controversial interpretations, achieved excellence in synthesis, balance, and insight. In the preface to this work, Fisher remarked that the only pattern he could discern in history was the march of events as unique contingencies shaping human destinies. The hallmarks of Fisher's writings are his vivid prose and fresh analogies, his agnosticism, and his liberal humanism.

Pradip Bhaumik

Texts

Bonapartism: Six Lectures Delivered in the University of London. Oxford: Clarendon Press, 1908.

The History of England, from the Accession of Henry VII to the Death of Henry VIII, 1485–1547. London and New York: Longmans, Green, 1906.

The History of Europe. 3 vols. Boston and New York: Houghton Mifflin, 1935–1936.

Napoleon. London: Oxford University Press, 1964.

References

Ogg, David. *Herbert Fisher, 1865–1940.* London: Edward Arnold, 1947.

Flacius Illyricus, Mathias

See MAGDEBURG CENTURIATORS.

Flexner, Eleanor (b. 1908)

Historian of U.S. women. In the mid-1950s Flexner, a nonacademic feminist, researched and wrote *Century of Struggle,* a history of the long campaign to win American women the vote. The book begins by explaining the ways in which industrialism and the frontier undermined traditional roles for women and opened the way to their greater participation in public life. The abolitionist movement is treated as a place where women learned organizational skills and first engaged in public speaking. The movements for higher education for women and their entry into the professions in the nineteenth and early twentieth centuries are explored. Flexner is careful to distinguish between various movements and initiatives for women's rights, not all of which centered on gaining the vote. The book provides a very thorough analysis of the various suffrage organizations, their leadership, tactics, ideologies, and conflicts. The book contains numerous biographical sketches of women's rights advocates and unlike many other early works in women's history does not slight the roles of black or working-class women. Despite the fact that this book was written well before the renewed interest in women's rights in the 1960s and the academic interest in women's history, it remains a pioneering work and a valuable source of information.

Barbara A. McGowan

Texts

Flexner, Eleanor. *Century of Struggle: The Woman's Rights Movement in the United States.* Revised ed. Cambridge, MA, and London: Belknap Press, 1975.

Flodoard of Rheims (ca. 893–966)

Frankish chronicler. Flodoard was educated at Rheims, entering the clergy and holding a benefice there for most of his life. Although he wrote a number of religious works in Latin verse and a history of the diocese of Rheims, his reputation as a historian rests on his *Annales,* a chronicle of France from the year 919. Diplomatic roles gave him entrée to political matters. His work is indispensable for the later Carolingian period despite a lack of discrimination that borders on credulity.

Kerry E. Spiers

Texts

Annales. Ed. P. Lauer. Paris: A. Picard et fils, 1905.

References

Smalley, Beryl. *Historians in the Middle Ages.* London: Thames and Hudson, 1974.

Sot, Michel. *Un historien et son eglise au Xe siecle: Flodoard de Reims* [A Historian and His Church in the Tenth Century: Flodoard of Rheims]. Paris: Fayard, 1993.

Florus, Lucius Ann[a]eus (fl. early second century A.D.)

Roman historian, rhetor, and poet. This Florus is probably the Florus of a partially extant dialogue about Vergil, which states that he was born in Africa, lived in Spain, and returned to Rome under Hadrian. In addition to some minor works, he is most familiar as the author of an *Epitome bellorum omnium DCC* [Summary of All Wars for 700 Years], a brief history of Rome's wars up to 27 B.C. This was a much-used text during the Renaissance. More than simply an epitome, it periodized Roman history through the metaphor of a human life, from birth and childhood (under kings), through adolescence and youth (the republic), into maturity and then decline (the empire).

Stephen A. Stertz

Texts

Epitome. Ed. E.S. Forster. London: Heinemann/ Loeb Classical Library, 1929.

References

Bessone, Luigi. "Floro: Un retore storico e poeta [Florus: A Rhetor, Historian, and Poet]." In *Aufstieg und Niedergang der Römischen Welt* [Rise and Decline of the Roman World]. Second series, vol. 34, part 1. Berlin: de Gruyter, Walter & Co., 1993.

———. *La Tradizione Liviana* [The Livian Tradition]. Bologna, Italy: Patron, 1977.

Focillon, Henri (1881–1943)

French art historian and critic. Focillon, who succeeded Emile Mâle at the Sorbonne in 1925, was the principal advocate of formalism in France. His theory, though akin to those of Alois Riegl and Heinrich Wölfflin, owes much to the Bergsonian *"élan vital"* and is more dynamic and complex than his German counterparts. His intimate knowledge of artistic production as a critic and his wide-ranging experience as a historian (from the Middle Ages to the twentieth century) provided the grounds on which he developed his own method in his most influential book, *The Life of Forms in Art* (1934). For Focillon, if a work of art has to be examined in its own materiality and space, it can only be understood in its historical context where it is a unique development in a series of possible formal experiments *(métamorphoses)*. His essays on medieval architecture and sculpture are the best examples of his anti-iconographical approach.

Carol Doyon

Texts

L'Art des sculpteurs romans: Recherches sur l'histoire des formes [The Art of the Roman Sculptors: Researches on the History of Forms]. Paris: E. Leroux, 1931.

The Art of the West in the Middle Ages. Ed. Jean Bony; trans. Donald King. 2 vols. Ithaca, NY: Cornell University Press, 1980.

The Life of Forms in Art. Trans. Charles B. Hogan and George Kubler. New York: Zone Books, 1989.

La peinture au XIXᵉ siècle [Painting in the Nineteenth Century]. Paris: Renouard, 1927.

The Year 1000. Trans. F.D. Wieck. New York: F. Ungar, 1971.

References

Bonnet, Jacques, ed. *Pour un temps: Henri Focillon* [For a Time: Henri Focillon]. Paris: Centre Georges Pompidou, 1986.

Kubler, George. *The Shape of Time: Remarks on the History of Things.* New Haven, CT: Yale University Press, 1962.

Salvini, Roberto. *Pure visibilité et formalisme dans la critique au début du XXᵉ siècle* [Pure Visibility and Formalism in Criticism at the Beginning of the Twentieth Century]. Paris: Klincksieck, 1988.

Fogel, Robert William (b. 1926)

American economist and economic historian. After earning his M.A. at Columbia University and Ph.D. at the Johns Hopkins University, Fogel began teaching at Johns Hopkins; he later moved to Rochester and then, in 1962, to the University of Chicago; he has supervised doctoral dissertations at Brandeis, Chicago, Harvard, Princeton, Rochester, and Texas.

Fogel's early research examined railroads in the American economy. In *Railroads and American Economic Growth* (1964) he used quantitative evidence; the concept of "social savings," combined with the counterfactual method suggests in this book that without railroads the American economy in 1890 would have been only slightly smaller than its actual size. Hence, Fogel argues, railroads were not indispensable to American economic growth. In *Time on the Cross* (1974) Fogel and coauthor Stanley Engerman explored the reasons why the oppressive institution of slavery had flourished in the antebellum South. Fogel and Engerman argued that the ownership of slaves was profitable because the intensive use of slave labor in large work groups permitted economies of large-scale production and plantation profitability. Fogel and Engerman conclude that slavery, although immoral, made a strong contribution to antebellum economic growth. Fogel later returned to the topic in his important work *Without Consent or Contract: The Rise and Fall of American Slavery* (1989). Fogel's latest and largest research program examines the relationship between economic circumstances and indicators of physical health. Evidence is being collected from many periods and countries about weight, height, and other physical characteristics. Fogel and collaborators explore the relationship among biological characteristics, economic resources (such as income and nutrition) and demographic outcomes (such as mortality). In 1993 Fogel shared the Nobel Prize for economics with Douglass North, another economic historian. The Nobel Committee singled out *Railroads and American Economic Growth* and Fogel's powerful influence on the evolution of cliometrics or quantitative economic history in North America. Fogel's exchange of opinion with Geoffrey Elton in *Which Road to the Past?* summarizes his views on the use of economic theory and quantitative methods in the development of historical knowledge.

Kris Inwood

Texts

Railroads and American Economic Growth: Essays in Econometric History. Baltimore, MD: Johns Hopkins University Press, 1964.

"Second Thoughts on the European Escape from Hunger." In *Nutrition and Poverty,* ed. S.R. Osmani. Oxford: Clarendon Press, 1992, 243–286.

And Stanley Engerman. *Time on the Cross: The Economics of American Negro Slavery.* Boston: Little, Brown, 1974.

And G.R. Elton. *Which Road to the Past? Two Views of History.* New Haven, CT: Yale University Press, 1983.

Without Consent or Contract: The Rise and Fall of American Slavery. New York: Norton, 1989.

References

David, Paul A., ed. *Reckoning with Slavery: A Critical Study in the Quantitative History of American Negro Slavery.* New York: Oxford University Press, 1976.

Goldin, Claudia. "Cliometrics and the Nobel." *Journal of Economic Perspectives* 9 (1995): 191–208.

Gutman, Herbert George. *Slavery and the Numbers Game: A Critique of Time on the Cross.* Urbana: University of Illinois Press, 1975.

McClelland, Peter D. *Causal Explanation and Model Building in History: Economics and the New Economic History.* Ithaca, NY: Cornell University Press, 1975.

Foner, Eric (b. 1943)

American historian of the nineteenth-century United States. Foner was born in New York City and received B.A. degrees from both Columbia University and Oxford University. After completing his graduate work at Columbia, he began teaching there in 1969. In 1973, he accepted a position at City College, New York, but returned to Columbia in 1982, where he has since remained. Foner has published numerous books and articles in American history, including biographies of Thomas Paine and Nat Turner. His main areas of specialization are the periods preceding and following the American Civil War. Unlike many of his contemporaries, Foner does not place great value on the use by historians of statistics and computers. "Great issues are not susceptible to analysis by the numbers," he has argued. His pioneering study of the ideology of the antebellum Republican party stressed its antislavery core. Its leaders, he contended, were convinced that Northern society, based on free labor and open opportunity, was irreversibly in conflict with the slave-based society of the South. Although some critics have questioned whether the views of antebellum Republican lead-

ers were very widely shared by the party rank and file, Foner's interpretation has remained a major contribution to American political history. His extensive research on developments after the Civil War has forced a reconsideration of topics long considered controversial. Emphasizing the essential radicalism of Reconstruction programs, Foner has produced a distinguished new synthesis on that era.

Kevin J. O'Keefe

Texts

America's Reconstruction. New York: Harper Collins, 1995.

Free Soil, Free Labor, Free Men: The Ideology of the Republican Party before the Civil War. New York: Oxford University Press, 1975.

Nothing but Freedom: Emancipation and Its Legacy. Baton Rouge: Louisiana State University Press, 1983.

Politics and Ideology in the Age of the Civil War. New York: Oxford University Press, 1980.

Forner, Juan Pablo (1754–1797)

Spanish Crown official and writer. Forner was the author of *Reflexiones sobre el modo de escribir la historia de España* [Reflections on the Method of Writing the History of Spain], written in 1788 but not published until 1816. This book set down guidelines for historical writing that greatly influenced nineteenth-century Spanish historiography. The *Reflexiones* argued the need for unearthing original documents and verifying facts. Forner also explained that the mission of the historian was to "relive past events." This, he believed, could best be done by single individuals—hence his unsuccessful lobbying efforts to restore the post of royal chronicler, which had been eliminated earlier in the century. Forner attacked the writing of "traditional" history, which concentrated too heavily on politics and warfare, ignoring those factors that constituted "internal history." His approach was both innovative and unorthodox, insisting, for example, that Spanish historians study the expulsion of the Jews and Moriscos with an eye to explaining the decline of Spain's agriculture and commerce in the late sixteenth and early seventeenth centuries.

George L. Vásquez

Texts

Discurso sobre el modo de escribir y majorar las historia de España. In *La crisis universitaria: La historia de España: Dos discursos* [The University Crisis: The History of Spain: Two

Treatises], ed. François Lopez. Barcelona: Textos Hispánicos Modernos, Editorial Labor, S.A., 1973. (This contains a modern ed. of Forner's *Reflexiones.*)

References

Vásquez, George L. "Juan Pablo Forner and the Formation of the 'New History' in Spain." *Iberian Studies* 7 (1978): 75–80.

Fortune

A concept popular from antiquity to the Renaissance, used to denote a superior, external, force shaping human affairs. Deriving from an association with the Roman goddess Fortuna, who was originally worshiped as a beneficent deity bringing abundance, Fortune emerged from the earlier Greek concept of Tyche. In his *Histories,* the Greek historian Polybius (ca. 200– ca. 118 B.C.) considered Tyche as an ultimately benign force in history. Adopting the premises of Aristotelian natural philosophy, he perceived a pattern of growth and decay among political states, with Tyche participating in a causal role. He argued that it was the historian's duty to trace her overall designs in order to explain the apparent randomness of history, thereby himself explaining the rise of Rome and the demise of Greek city-states. In the late Republic, the concept was thoroughly Romanized. Livy and Plutarch attributed much of the Roman success to the causal and beneficent role of Fortune. The first-century B.C. dictator Lucius Cornelius Sulla called himself Felix (the happy, fortunate) and justified his own ascendancy as following from the favors of Fortune, as did Julius Caesar in his *Civil War.*

The impact of Stoic philosophy in the second and third centuries provoked a close association with the concepts of Fate and Chance. In the fifth century, Boethius grafted a Judeo-Christian framework onto prevailing pagan beliefs. In his *Consolation of Philosophy,* he adopted the Augustinian linear time scheme and Fortune was made subservient to Providence, God's governance of the world. Thus Fortune might be irrational according to human understanding, but she was only an instrument in a divine order itself incomprehensible to man. Following Boethius, Fortune as a capricious figure drawing the wheel of time came to prominence; this is the image that figures most commonly in medieval considerations of Fortune. Ptolemaic cosmology, with its formula of immutable heavens governing a sublunar sphere existing in time, supported a continuing view of the direct, causal role of Fortune in human affairs.

During the Renaissance, Fortune's role as agent was hotly debated by humanists such as Coluccio Salutati, and in the early sixteenth century Machiavelli forcefully revived the Polybian cyclical view of history. Invoking natural analogies, Machiavelli argued that Fortune was a force that could be harnessed, most famously comparing it to a woman, in *The Prince,* his influential political manual. Historical examples were culled to support his points; the study of Fortune's effects thus became a major component of historical knowledge. Later writers hesitated to go as far in this direction as Machiavelli, and with the triumph of the seventeenth-century scientific revolution, natural explanations of historical events were increasingly preferred to extranatural ones. But Fortune persisted as an explanation for the unaccountable, surviving within Christian literary culture as well as having parallels in other traditions of historiography.

Adriana A.N. McCrea

References

Frakes, Jerold C. *The Fate of Fortune in the Early Middle Ages.* Leiden, Netherlands, and New York: E.J. Brill, 1988.

Pitkin, H.F. *Fortune Is a Woman.* Berkeley: University of California Press, 1984.

Pocock, J.G.A. *The Machiavellian Moment: Florentine Political Thought and the Atlantic Republican Tradition.* Princeton, NJ: Princeton University Press, 1975.

Foucault, Michel (1926–1984)

French historian and cultural critic. Foucault is renowned for his innovative histories of the rhetorical strategies that have shaped attitudes toward a range of human behaviors, particularly those on the boundaries of public acceptance (such as insanity, criminality, sexual promiscuity). His work is loosely associated with the historiography of collective mentalities, but is of signal importance for having introduced the deconstructionist method of poststructuralist philosophy into historical scholarship.

Foucault's academic training was in philosophy and psychology. His major philosophical work, *The Order of Things* (1966), analyzed the changing vocabularies in which knowledge was reconstituted between the sixteenth and eighteenth centuries. More appealing to historians, however, were his studies of the historical elaboration of discourse about asylums: madhouses (1961), hospitals (1963), and prisons (1975). Paying little attention to the institutional development of the asylums themselves, he focused on the proliferating discourse about their purposes during the modern era.

Historians have found Foucault's work thought-provoking, less for his documentation of the rise of the asylum, more for his consideration of that documentation itself as a reality worthy of the historian's analysis. The discursive practices that attended the rise of modern asylums, he argued, were not mere reflections of popular attitudes about human behavior but rather constituent elements of strategies calculated to mold them. The study of such discourse, he contended, enables the historian to understand the way power shapes knowledge, for the power to speak with authority implies the power to define licit and illicit behaviors. In this shift of emphasis—from the history of ideas considered as expressions of cultural values toward the history of rhetorical forms conceived as instruments for constructing social identity—Foucault redirected historians' attention from the content of ideas to the mode in which they are proffered for public acceptance. His histories describe the myriad of rhetorical techniques devised to manage ("police") modern society.

Foucault's interest in the "policing" powers of rhetoric eventually led him to the history of discourse about sexuality, a realm of human experience highly resistant to public management. His first volume on the subject interpreted the "sexual revolution" of the twentieth century as a burgeoning discourse about deviant sexual behavior that narrowed the accepted boundaries of normality. In subsequent volumes he turned to discourse about sex in classical antiquity, a counterpoint to the morality of denial of the modern age in its formulation of a more permissive "economy of pleasure."

On one level, Foucault's last, unfinished project on the history of techniques of the self developed out of his research on sexual identity. But on another it was a reprise of his sustained interest in the policing process, considered this time not in light of the techniques by which society manages individuals but of those by which individuals manage themselves. In effect, he repudiated Sigmund Freud's search for hidden self-knowledge by locating his psychoanalytic method within the historical context of a discourse dating from antiquity about techniques of self-care.

For many historians, Foucault remains a controversial figure. But from an historiographical standpoint, his work was crucial in acquainting them with poststructuralist notions about the rhetorically constructed nature of human culture.

Recent historical studies of discursive practices, the politics of memory, and the construction of social identity draw heavily upon his conceptual formulations. Because of Foucault's usage, such notions as "archaeology" (the study of the reuse of discarded conventions of language), "genealogy" (historical links in discourse traced from the present backward), "monuments" (the investment of evidence with commemorative meaning), and "economy" (the definition of boundaries within particular spheres of interactive human behavior) have acquired evocative new meanings for historians and suggest the extent of his diffuse influence on historical scholarship in the late twentieth century beyond the work of his students and admirers.

Patrick Hutton

Texts

The Archaeology of Knowledge. Trans. A.M. Sheridan Smith. New York: Harper and Row, 1972.
The Birth of the Clinic. Trans. A.M. Sheridan Smith. New York: Random House, 1973.
Discipline and Punish. Trans. Alan Sheridan. New York: Random House, 1977.
A History of Sexuality. Trans. Robert Hurley. 3 vols. New York: Random House, 1978–1986.
Madness and Civilization. Trans. Richard Howard. New York: Random House, 1973.
The Order of Things. Trans. Alan Sheridan. New York: Random House, 1970.

References

Bernauer, James, and David Rasmussen, eds. *The Final Foucault.* Cambridge, MA: MIT Press, 1988.

Four Empires

A prophetic interpretation of world history based mainly on the Old Testament Book of Daniel. A key pillar of the premodern Western tradition of providential history, this view coexisted with others, such as the six-age theory based on the creation week, and the Pauline division of ages before the law, under the law, and under grace. These and related schemes all conceived of history as a preordained, universal pattern.

Although the idea of history as a succession or "translation" of empires went back to Persian and Greek sources, its key formulations came in Daniel 2 and 7. In chapter 2, Daniel interprets King Nebuchadnezzar's dream—a statue with a head of gold, chest and arms of silver, belly and thighs of bronze, and legs and feet of iron mixed with clay—as a prophecy of world empires. In chapter 7, Daniel similarly explains his own dream of four beasts arising from the sea. The ten horns of the dread fourth beast, like the toes of the statue, indicate a division of the final empire. A "little horn" arises to pluck out three of the ten horns; this is an evil ruler who will wreak havoc before the end. The overall image is suggestive of world historical decline, ending only with the coming of God's eternal kingdom.

Under Roman rule, interpreters came to view the four empires as Babylonia, Persia, Greece, and Rome. Among early Christians, Rome was generally identified with the terrible fourth beast of Daniel 7. While medieval world chronicles tended to favor the six-age scheme used by Augustine of Hippo, the four-empire motif persisted through the influence of works such as Jerome's *Commentary on Daniel*. The idea saw more intensive use in the ideologically charged late-medieval and Renaissance periods. It was especially influential in Germany, partly because of the belief that the final *Imperium* had passed to the Holy Roman Empire. Many Protestant thinkers applied the conception, often to show the nearness of the Last Judgment. World histories based at least partly on this pattern remained common into the seventeenth century. The notion was famously invoked by the "Fifth Monarchy Men" of the English civil war era, revolutionaries who looked to a final, godly kingdom (see Daniel 2:44).

This framework had already begun to crack with the humanist division into ancient, medieval, and modern, a pattern based on entirely different premises. In the later sixteenth century the French jurist Jean Bodin mounted a heavy attack on the four-empires scheme. The Enlightenment era brought a widespread abandonment of the whole idea of providential history. Even so, in the nineteenth century the four-empires view was still far from dead among educated Westerners. In our time it remains important to some biblically inspired interpreters.

Robin B. Barnes

See also CHRISTIANITY, VIEWS OF HISTORY IN; JUDAISM, VIEWS OF HISTORY IN (ANTIQUITY TO 1500); PERIODIZATION; RENAISSANCE, HISTORIOGRAPHY DURING.

References

Collins, John J. *Daniel: A Commentary on the Book of Daniel*. Minneapolis, MN: Fortress Press, 1993.
Rowley, H.H. *Darius the Mede and the Four World Empires in the Book of Daniel*. Cardiff: University Press of Wales, 1935.

Swain, Joseph Ward. "The Theory of the Four Monarchies: Opposition History under the Roman Empire." *Classical Philology* 35 (1940): 1–21.

Fox-Genovese, Elizabeth (b. 1941)

Economic and social historian of eighteenth-century France and the southern United States. Born in Boston, Fox-Genovese received a Ph.D. (1974) from Harvard University. Before joining the faculty of Emory University in Atlanta in 1986, she taught at the University of Rochester (1973–1980) and the State University of New York at Binghamton (1980–1986). With Eugene Genovese, she founded the journal, *Marxist Perspectives* (1978–1980). At Emory she organized the university's Institute for Women's Studies, which she headed until 1992, and became Eleonore Raoul professor of humanities (1988). One of relatively few historians in the United States who works in several fields, Fox-Genovese's *Origins of Physiocracy* (1976) connects the thinking of eighteenth-century French physiocrats to their economic and social contexts. Her and Eugene Genovese's *Fruits of Merchant Capital* (1983) analyzes the relationship of the plantation system to the evolution of early modern capitalism in the West. In *Within the Plantation Household: Black and White Women of the Old South* (1988), she describes the plantation South as precapitalist. Fox-Genovese illustrates this conclusion by re-creating the world of women within selected patriarchal households, a world not bound by bourgeois values. *Feminism without Illusions* (1991), a book of essays, critically examines the relationship between feminism and individualism.

Ellen Nore

Texts

Feminism without Illusions: A Critique of Individualism. Chapel Hill: University of North Carolina Press, 1991.
Fruits of Merchant Capital: Slavery and Bourgeois Property in the Rise and Expansion of Capitalism. New York: Oxford University Press, 1983.
"Introduction." In *French Women in the Age of the Enlightenment*, ed. S.I. Spencer. Bloomington: Indiana University Press, 1984.
The Origins of Physiocracy: Economic Revolution and Social Order in Eighteenth-Century France. Ithaca, NY: Cornell University Press, 1976.
Within the Plantation Household: Black and White Women of the Old South. Chapel Hill: University of North Carolina Press, 1988.

F

References

Grossman, Ron. "Mainstream Marxist." *Chicago Tribune* (24 Nov. 1993): sec. 5, p. 1.

Wyatt-Brown, Bertram. "Matrons and Mammies." *Reviews in American History* 17 (1989): 219–224.

Foxe, John (1517–1587)

English Protestant martyrologist and historian. Born in Lincolnshire, England, Foxe fled to Europe during the Marian reign and produced, with the support of the Protestant community, a Lollard martyrology, *Commentarii rerum in ecclesia gestarum* (1554), and an expanded martyrology, *Rerum in ecclesia gestarum* (1559). After returning to England, Foxe translated and supplemented *Rerum* to produce *Acts and Monuments,* a history of the English and Roman churches to the Reformation (1563), which was further revised and expanded several more times during his life. The book soon became known simply as "The Book of Martyrs" and a 1570 order in Convocation commanded that a copy of it be kept chained in Cathedral churches. Many parish libraries acquired editions of it also, and in the seventeenth century it proved to be one of the most commonly owned books in households that had few books, despite its size and relative expense. Foxe advanced the use of primary and oral sources, providing documentary ground for later histories. His most significant accomplishment was to historicize the earlier writer John Bale's apocalyptic vision. Abridged and reissued on various occasions up to the present, *Acts and Monuments* has substantially influenced English religious and national identity, a role intended for it from the first. A nineteenth-century edition by S.R. Cattley has been reprinted but should be used with caution, and a project is now (1997) underway to provide a modern critical edition of Foxe's text.

Devorah Greenberg

Texts

Acts and Monuments. Ed. G. Townsend. New York: AMS Press, 1965.

References

Collinson, Patrick. "Truth and Veracity: The Legend of John Foxe's Book of Martyrs." In *Clio's Mirror: Historiography in Britain and the Netherlands: Papers Delivered to the Eighth Anglo-Dutch Historical Conference,* ed. A.C. Duke and C.A. Tamse. Zutphen, Netherlands: De Walburg Pers, 1985, 31–54.

Haller, William. *Foxe's Book of Martyrs and the Elect Nation.* London: J. Cape, 1963.

Mozley, J.F. *John Foxe and His Book.* New York: Macmillan, 1940.

Wooden, Warren. *John Foxe.* Boston: Twayne, 1983.

Francastel, Pierre (1900–1970)

French art historian and sociologist. Francastel is seen in the field of art history as the instigator of a special blend of the sociology of art; he is also considered by practitioners of the *Nouvelle Histoire* in France as a pioneer of the history of mentalities and of the "imaginary." His practice of sociology must be differentiated both from Pierre Bourdieu's dynamic theory of the field and from the Marxist social history of art. In order to distance himself from traditional empirical art history, Francastel developed a theory in which he argued that architecture, sculpture, and painting constitute specific forms of knowledge. In his wide-ranging essays (covering topics from the Middle Ages to l'École de Paris) he analyzed the structures and the functioning of this "plastic or aesthetic thought" embodied in different figurative systems. In his view, art articulates and restructures in the field of the "imaginary" the organization of social space.

Carol Doyon

Texts

Art et technique aux XIXe et XXe siècles [Art and Technique in the Ninteenth and Twentieth Centuries]. Paris: Denoel/Gonthier, 1972.

La figure et le lieu: L'ordre visuel du Quattrocento [The Figure and the Place: Visual Order in the Quattrocento]. Paris: Gallimard, 1967.

Medieval Painting. Ed. Hans L.C. Jaffe; trans. Robert Erich Wolf. New York: Dell, 1967.

Peinture et société: Naissance et destruction d'un espace plastique de la Renaissance au Cubisme [Painting and Society: The Birth and Destruction of Plastic Space from the Renaissance to Cubism]. Lyons: Audin, 1951.

La realité figurative: Éléments structurels de sociologie de l'art [Figurative Reality: Structural Elements in the Sociology of Art]. Paris: Gonthier, 1965.

References

La Sociologie de l'art et sa vocation interdisciplinaire: L'oeuvre et l'influence de Pierre Francastel [The Sociology of Art and Its Interdisciplinary Calling: The Work and Influence of Pierre Francastel]. Paris: Éditions Denoël/Gonthier, 1976.

Frank, Tenney (1876–1939)

Classicist, epigrapher, and historian. Born near Clay Center, Kansas, and educated at the universities of Kansas, Chicago, Berlin, and Göttingen, Frank taught at the University of Chicago, Bryn Mawr College, and at Johns Hopkins University. Frank's publications include, among other works: *Roman Imperialism* (1914), *An Economic History of Rome to the End of the Republic* (1920), *Vergil: A Biography* (1922), *A History of Rome* (1923), *Roman Buildings of the Republic* (1924), and *Aspects of Social Behaviour in Ancient Rome* (1932). From 1932, he supervised the five-volume *Economic Survey of Ancient Rome,* of which he himself wrote the first and last volumes on Rome and Italy (1933 and 1940). Frank was also a distinguished contributor to the *Cambridge Ancient History.* Frank's originality as a historian lay in his employment of nonliterary and archaeological evidence for the study of the Roman economy, his placement of Roman literary figures within an overall historical context, and his use of mineralogical research for the dating of Roman buildings.

Lionel J. Sanders

Texts

Aspects of Social Behaviour in Ancient Rome. Cambridge, MA: Harvard University Press, 1932.

An Economic History of Rome to the End of the Republic. Second ed. Baltimore, MD: Johns Hopkins University Press, 1927.

A History of Rome. New York: Holt, 1923.

Roman Buildings of the Republic. Rome: American Academy in Rome, 1924.

Roman Imperialism. New York: Cooper Square, 1972.

References

Broughton, T. Robert S. "Frank, Tenney." In *Classical Scholarship: A Biographical Encyclopedia,* ed. W.W. Briggs and William M. Calder III. New York and London: Garland, 1990, 68–76.

Franklin, John Hope (b. 1915)

Distinguished U.S. historian and the major African-American historian of the past half-century. Before breaking the "color line" by accepting tenure at Brooklyn College (1956), Franklin could only teach in black colleges despite his Harvard doctorate. He subsequently held endowed chairs at the University of Chicago and Duke University, presided over major historical associations, held distinguished lectureships abroad, and received nearly one hundred honorary degrees.

Franklin's field is Southern history, focusing on race relations. His voluminous work confronts the dilemma of a minority historian: becoming professionally marginal by studying one's own group or conforming to their neglect by mainstream historians (which rests on the misconception that "equal" means "identical"). His comprehensive and balanced textbook, *From Slavery to Freedom,* has been a standard work of reference in African-American history since 1947. His 1948 review, "Whither Reconstruction Historiography?" challenged prevailing racial bias. Franklin sought scholarly objectivity in his publications while participating, as a scholar, in the struggle for equality in America, a position criticized in both aspects by younger Afrocentrists. By restricting interpretation, "objectivity" flaws his biography of pioneer African-American historian George Washington Williams. A recognized leader of his profession, Franklin maximizes warmth and dignity as a historian.

Robin Brooks

Texts

The Free Negro in North Carolina, 1790–1860. Chapel Hill: University of North Carolina Press, 1943.

From Slavery to Freedom: A History of African Americans. New York: Alfred A. Knopf, 1947. (Note: the last two of seven editions of this work were coauthored with Alfred A. Moss Jr.)

George Washington Williams: A Biography. Chicago: University of Chicago Press, 1985.

The Militant South, 1800–1861. Revised ed. Cambridge, MA: Harvard University Press, 1970.

"Whither Reconstruction History?" In his *Race and History: Selected Essays, 1938–1988.* Baton Rouge and London: Louisiana State University Press, 1989 (Note: this volume also contains autobiographical material.)

References

Anderson, Eric, and Alfred A. Moss Jr., eds. *The Facts of Reconstruction: Essays in Honor of John Hope Franklin.* Baton Rouge: Louisiana State University Press, 1991.

Novick, Peter. *That Noble Dream: The "Objectivity Question" and the American Historical Profession.* Cambridge, Eng.: Cambridge University Press, 1988, 349; 350; 472–473; 476; 507–508.

Star, Jack. "Above All, a Scholar." *Change* (February 1977): 27–33.

Freeman, Edward Augustus (1823–1892)

Medieval historian and politician. Born in Staffordshire, Freeman graduated from Oxford University and returned there in 1884 to assume the Regius professorship of modern history. In his early years as a High Churchman he wrote several studies of Gothic architecture. He also unsuccessfully contested parliamentary elections as a Liberal, challenged Anthony Trollope's views on the cruelty of fox hunting, led an agitation against the Turks, and actively supported Gladstone's Home Rule legislation for Ireland. A racialist and nationalist, Freeman believed that English liberties had been born in Teutonic forests, as became evident in his *History of the Norman Conquest* (1867–1879), but he also displayed an interest in federalism and democracy in such works as his *History of Federal Government* (1863) and *History of Sicily* (1891–1892). Critics questioned his reliance upon printed sources and his pedantic terminology, but he initiated important discussions regarding the consequences of the Norman Conquest and the relationship between history and politics in the development of European civilization.

Myron C. Noonkester

Texts

Historical Essays. London: Macmillan, 1871.
History of Federal Government. Second ed. London and New York: Macmillan, 1893.
The History of Sicily from the Earliest Times. 4 vols. Oxford: Clarendon Press, 1891–1894.
The History of the Norman Conquest of England. 5 vols. New York: AMS Press, 1977.

References

Burrow, John W. *A Liberal Descent: Victorian Historians and the English Past.* Cambridge, Eng.: Cambridge University Press, 1981.
Gooch, G.P. *History and Historians in the Nineteenth Century.* London: Longmans, 1913.
Kenyon, J.P. *The History Men.* London: Weidenfeld and Nicolson, 1983.

French Historiography

Historical writing and thought in France from the Middle Ages to the late twentieth century.

Medieval

The first historian of post-Roman Gaul was Bishop Gregory of Tours (ca. 539–594), who recounted the bloody deeds of the Merovingian kings until 591. His *Decem libri historiarum,* generally known as the *History of the Franks,* was continued by the monk Fredegar to 642. It was Fredegar who launched the legend of the Trojan origin of the Franks. In the ninth century the greatest ruler of the Carolingian dynasty, Charlemagne, was the subject of a biography by Einhard (or Eginhard, ca. 775–836), who participated in the revival of learning at the court of the emperor and of his son and successor, Louis I. Thereafter, apart from a few chronicles, little history was written in France until the time of the Crusades. The soldier and diplomat Geoffroi (or Geoffrey) de Villehardouin (ca. 1150–1212) composed a graphic account of the crusaders' diversionary attack upon Constantinople in 1204, a campaign in which he played a major organizing role. Another crusader, Jean de Joinville, seneschal of Champagne (ca. 1225–1318), wrote about Louis IX's crusade in the middle of the thirteenth century. His informal *Histoire de Saint Louis* [History or Life of Saint Louis] contained many tall stories of the marvels of Egypt and Palestine, as well as details of the battles in which he participated. He recorded personal conversations with the king, in which his own down-to-earth comments contrasted with his sovereign's exalted views.

In 1274 the monk Primat of Saint-Denis presented Philip III, the successor of Saint Louis, with a French translation of the Latin *Grandes Chroniques de France* [Great Chronicles of France]. This collaborative enterprise, covering the known and imagined history of France from the earliest years, was centered on the seventh-century abbey of Saint-Denis, which became the burial place of the French kings. It incorporated such works as the biographies of Louis VI and Louis VII by Abbot Suger (1081–1151). The first half of the Hundred Years War was related in chivalric terms by Jean Froissart (ca. 1337–1410), who made use of an earlier narrative by Jean le Bel (ca. 1290–1370). Froissart's own work was continued to 1444 by Enguerrand de Monstrelet, and to 1461 by Mathieu d'Escouchi. A very different note was struck by Philippe de Commynes (ca. 1446–1511), who deserted Charles the Bold of Burgundy to become a leading counselor to his enemy, Louis XI of France. Commynes's *Memoirs* show appreciation of the craft and cruelty of Louis XI, while paying lip service to moral precepts and divine providence. The work was cited as a source of exemplary statecraft and, equally, of archetypal tyranny, by many succeeding generations. Events were depicted from the Burgundian viewpoint, and in less realistic terms, by the poet-rhetoricians Georges Chastellain (1405–1475) and Olivier de la Marche (ca. 1425–1502). The Norman bishop Thomas Basin (1412–1490) provided a passionate indictment of Louis XI, using Roman historical models acquired through his contacts with Italian humanists such as Poggio Bracciolini (1380–1459). At the end of the century another *rhétoriqueur,* Jean Lemaire de Belges (ca.1453–1525), composed a poetic account of such legends as the Trojan origin of the French in his *Illustrations of Gaul.*

Early Modern

Humanist models of historiography from classical antiquity, with their emphasis upon style, their obsession with moral precepts, and their penchant for invented speeches, appeared in French historical writing in the late fifteenth century. An early French humanist work was the *Compendium de origine et gestis Francorum* [Summary or Compendium on the Origin and the History of the Franks] by Robert Gaguin (1433–1501). Gaguin drew much from the *Grandes Chroniques,* but showed some skepticism about Trojan origins while accepting accounts of the supposititious early Frankish king, Pharamond. Paolo Emili or Emili (ca. 1460–1529) was imported from Verona by Louis XII to write another *De rebus gestis Francorum* [Deeds of the Franks], and he expressed more forthright doubts about patriotic myths. Emili found the Franks to be German, an opinion endorsed in the next generation by François Hotman (1524–1590) and others. Those favoring Celtic origins declared the Franks to be Gauls who had wandered east of the Rhine and returned in the last years of the Roman Empire.

The most scholarly influence upon French historiography came from the Italian school of legal humanists, whose first followers in France were Guillaume Budé (1468–1540), Andrea Alciato (1492–1550), and Jacques Cujas (1520–1590). Their concern was the elucidation of contradictions in Roman law and their textual method involved a relativism that saw various accretions, consolidated in Justinian's sixth-century codification, to have been added in different ages to serve the varying needs of the Roman republic and empire. The possibilities in this approach were best exemplified in a work by François Baudouin (1520–1573), *De institutione historiae uniuersae et eius cum iurisprudentia coniunctione* [On the Institution of Universal History and Its Conjunction with Jurisprudence]. One of the greatest historians of law, Charles Dumoulin (1500–1566), used history to show the independence of the Gallican church from Rome, the decay of feudalism, and the consonance of provincial French custom with natural right. The historical approach contrasted with the theoretical exercises of jurists who preferred abstract reasoning to philology and textual scholarship, but these Bartolists, as they were called after Bartolus of Sassoferato, a fourteenth-century systematizer, at times used comparativist methods that could be applied to historical interpretation. Such was the case with the *Methodus ad facilem historiarum cognitionem* [Method for the Easy Comprehension of History], published in 1566 by Jean Bodin (1530–1596).

Later in the sixteenth century, legal humanist history and philology were combined with archival expertise. Jean du Tillet (d. 1570), the registrar of the Parlement of Paris, not only studied the high court's records dating back to the thirteenth century but also received a commission to organize the archives of even earlier governmental institutions, collectively known as "the treasury of charters" *(trésor des chartes).* His work was continued by Pierre Pithou (1539–1596), Claude Fauchet (1544–1593), Etienne Pasquier (1529–1615), and other antiquaries. Pasquier's *Recherches de la France* [Researches on France] took the form of a vast compendium of separate essays dealing with institutions, ethnography, political history, linguistics, religion, culture, and social traditions. Despite their erudition, the antiquaries at times displayed bias, especially in defense of the Gallican church.

There were many contemporary accounts of the wars of religion, most of them written for polemical purposes. Two that stand out for their fair-mindedness and shrewd appraisal of motives were the *Historiarum sui temporis* [History of His Own Time] by the learned magistrate Jacques-Auguste de Thou (1553–1617) and the *Historia delle guerre civile di Francia* [The History of the Civil Wars of France] by an Italian page at the Valois court, Enrico (or Arrigo Caterino) Davila (1576–1631). Two other dispassionate accounts were composed by the royal historiographer Bernard de Girard, sieur du Haillan (1535–1610), and Henri Lancelot de Voisin, sieur de la Popelinière (1540–1608), who aspired, unsuccessfully, to the same office. Du Haillan was notable for his critical use of sources and his humanist style, La Popelinière for his history of historiography and his attempt to define the perfect form for the genre. A generation earlier some striking reflections on the nature of history had been offered by Louis le Roy (1510–1577), best known for his commentary on Aristotle's *Politics.* His *De la vicissitude ou varieté des choses en l'univers* [On the Vicissitude or Variety of Things in the Universe] stressed the mutability of human affairs and suggested that disorder and decay were intrinsic to the natural world.

F

At the beginning of the seventeenth century, Joseph Justus Scaliger (1540–1609) and Isaac Casaubon (1559–1614) were commonly acknowledged as among the most erudite of European scholars. Scaliger revised ancient chronology, while Casaubon provided Protestant revisions to the Catholic version of Christian history set out in the *Annales Ecclesiastici* [Ecclesiastical Annals] of Cesare Baronio (1538–1607). In the age that followed, history suffered from the criticism of freethinking *libertins* such as François de la Mothe le Vayer (1588–1672), who pointed to its unreliability, and of the philosopher René Descartes (1596–1650), who denied it the possibility of deductive reasoning. At the same time critical standards for evaluating historical testimony were developed by the Jesuit Bollandists in their project to set the lives of the saints upon a firm historical basis. Later the Benedictine monks of Saint-Maur developed criteria for the editing of medieval documents. Their most famous scholar, Jean Mabillon (1632–1707), provided a handbook of scholarly techniques in his *De re diplomatica* (1681). Charles du Fresne, sieur du Cange (1610–1688), produced a vast dictionary of medieval Latin associated with the Maurists. He also edited the works of Villehardouin and Joinville.

The two most enduring histories of France written under Louis XIV were by François Eudes de Mézerai (or Mézeray) (1610–1683) and Fr. Gabriel Daniel (1649–1728). Mézerai completed the first version of his book during the rebellion of the Fronde, with which he had some sympathy. He displayed wit, elegance, and independent judgment and resented the later endeavors of the king's minister, Colbert, to censor some of his views. Writing at the end of the reign, Daniel, on the other hand, subscribed to the common practice of adulating the sun king. This was also the tenor of *Histoire de Louis XIV* [The History of Louis XIV] by Paul Pellisson-Fontanier (1624–1693), who assisted in the writing of the royal memoirs. Earlier, Hardouin de Péréfixe (1605–1671), who acted as a tutor to the young Louis XIV, wrote a life of his royal pupil's grandfather, Henri IV, in heroic terms. Memoirs and biographies became fashionable genres at this time. Among the most piquant sets of personal recollections were the memoirs of Cardinal de Retz (1614–1679), who described his role as an agitator during the Fronde with dissimulated candor.

The great apologist for the policies of Louis XIV was Bishop Jacques-Bénigne Bossuet (1627–1704), who composed for the king's guidance a *Discours sur l'Histoire Universelle depuis la Création du Monde*

jusqu'à Charlemagne [Discourse on Universal History from the Creation to Charlemagne], tracing the march of divine providence from the beginning of the world to the early ninth century A.D. Some of Louis's despotic interventions in religious matters had historiographic repercussions. The king's persecution of the Huguenots, for instance, provoked the pastor Pierre Jurieu (1637–1714) to write his *Histoire du Calvinisme et celle du Papisme mises en parallèle* [The History of Calvinism and That of Papism Set in Parallel]. Bossuet replied to this and similar works with the *Histoire des Variations des Églises protestantes* [History of the Differences among the Protestant Churches]. Standing on different ground in these polemics was the pyrrhonist (skeptic) and Protestant exile Pierre Bayle (1647–1706). Bayle's great *Dictionnaire historique et critique* [Historical and Critical Dictionary] (1695–1697) provided a mass of historical data on religious and philosophical issues, and accompanied each entry with detailed source notes in which he set one opinion against another, and left the reader to judge. The *Dictionnaire* has justly been called "the Bible of the Enlightenment." Not all history at this time, however, was a matter of controversy. The Jansenist Sébastien Le Nain de Tillemont (1637–1698) wrote on the early Christian church and the Roman Empire with an erudition that defied criticism.

The Eighteenth Century

In the eighteenth century the Enlightenment's confidence in the power of human reason and its questioning of religious dogmatism produced new kinds of history. At the same time the scholarly editing of historical texts by the Maurists continued, culminating in the *Recueil des historiens des Gaules et de la France* [Collection of the Historians of Gaul and of France], supervised by Dom Martin Bouquet (1685–1754). Among the most popular general histories of France were those by Charles-Jean-François Hénault (1685–1770), a magistrate and frequenter of the *salons* of the Enlightenment, and Louis-Pierre Anquetil (1723–1806), a clergyman whose histories of the troubles of the sixteenth and seventeenth centuries were much superior to his more general work, written after the Revolution. To judge from the number of editions in which it was issued, the most read history in the generation before the Revolution was the *Histoire philosophique et politique des etablissemens & du commerce des européens dans les deux Indes* [The Philosophical and Political History of the Settlements and Trade of the Europeans in the Two Indies] by Abbot Guillaume-Thomas

Raynal (1713–1796). This vast study of the expansion of European influence throughout the world was infused with the principles of the Enlightenment, and Denis Diderot (1713–1784), the editor of the movement's compendium of knowledge, the *Encyclopédie,* contributed to it.

A common stance of Enlightenment historians was to judge the past in terms of the moral and material improvement they perceived in their own age. The most eloquent spokesmen for the idea of progress were Anne-Robert-Jacques Turgot, baron de l'Aulne (1727–1781), the economist and reforming minister of Louis XVI, and his disciple, Marie Jean Antoine-Nicolas de Caritat, Marquis de Condorcet (1743–1794). Progress was not envisaged, however, as a steady advance. Philosopher-historians tended to disparage the Middle Ages as dark, barbarous, and superstitious. Others could see history as discontinuous without judging the past in terms of the present. Near the beginning of the century Abbot René Aubert de Vertot composed political histories as series of revolutions within states, as in his *Histoire des révolutions arrivées dans le gouvernement de la republique romaine* [History of the Revolutions in the Government of the Roman Republic]. Later a powerful factor in revolutionary ideology was *Observations sur l'histoire de France* [Observations on the History of France] by Gabriel Bonnot de Mably (1709–1789), who distinguished many separate regimes in the French past, some superior to others.

Mably made one of the last prerevolutionary contributions to a long-standing historical controversy that took race and class as controlling elements in history. At the start of the century Henri de Boulainvilliers tried to reclaim a positive role for the traditional nobility by asserting that they were descended from the Franks, who had practiced liberty and egalitarianism among themselves, whereas the third estate were the heirs to the conquered Gauls. In response, Abbot Jean-Baptiste Dubos (1670–1742) sustained the cause of authoritarian monarchy by depicting the Frankish kings as the allies of the Roman Empire in defending Gaul against other Teutonic peoples, and hence having the same absolute authority as the emperors. In his *L'Esprit des lois* [Spirit of the Laws] (1748), the great constitutionalist Charles de Secondat, baron de Montesquieu (1689–1755), sought social and political balance by standing midway between these opinions. During the conflicts between the ministers of Louis XV and the high courts or parlements, some extreme defenders of the rights of the judiciary to an independent role in government used history to defend the argument that the crown had betrayed a pristine Frankish constitution guaranteeing rights to the citizen. This unhistorical fundamentalism was countered in kind by defenders of royal authority. Jacob-Nicolas Moreau (1717–1804) orchestrated the efforts of a team of antiquaries to edit the texts of royal ordinances through the ages, and published *Leçons de morale, de politique et de droit public, puisées dans l'histoire de notre monarchie* [Lessons in Morals, Politics and Public Law Drawn from the History of Our Monarchy]. In the course of this project one of the editors, Louis de Bréquigny (1714–1794), advanced the theory of the gradual enfranchisement of the third estate from the twelfth century, and its alliance with the crown to destroy the usurped authority of the feudal aristocracy. Such a doctrine could support belief in the coexistence of royal autocracy and democratic liberty, as it did in *Considérations sur le gouvernement ancien et présent de la France* [Considerations on the Ancient and Present Government of France] by Louis XV's minister René-Louis de Voyer, marquis d'Argenson (1694–1757), or an argument for popular rights and representative participation, as it did with Mably.

The best-remembered historian of the age, Voltaire (François-Marie Arouet, 1694–1778), was not, of course, himself immune from controversy. While he used history in the cause of liberty, he supported the crown against the parlements. Among his many historical works, his *Siècle de Louis XIV* [Century of Louis XIV], covered cultural history and the history of science as well as politics and allowed his skeptical vein to emerge in his treatment of the religious problems of the age of the sun king. His *Essai sur les Moeurs* [Essay on Customs] treated the medieval centuries from the time of Charlemagne, where Bossuet had left off, but human endeavor, rather than divine providence, was the motif. At the same time his prejudice against medieval themes was patent. Nor did he have the analytic skill in discerning cause and effect displayed by Montesquieu in the latter's *Considérations sur les causes de la grandeur des Romains et de leur décadence* [Considerations on the Causes of the Greatness of the Romans and Their Decline]. Voltaire preferred individual motives to social generalizations, and slipped into witticisms at the expense of deeper judgments. For all this, Voltaire's style and command of sources earned him a reputation as a historian that has lasted longer than his purely literary achievements.

F

Nineteenth Century

History was never more popular than in the aftermath of the French Revolution. A desire to explain the cataclysm, a need to relate new social and political forms to the past, and a nostalgia for much that had disappeared, produced an unquenchable appetite for historical works, as well as for historical novels and historical drama. The fiction of the British novelist Sir Walter Scott, the rehabilitation of medieval Christianity by René de Chateaubriand (1768–1848), and the popularizing of German literature and idealist philosophy by Germaine de Staël (1766–1817), contributed to the romantic movement. In history the rationalism of the Enlightenment was replaced by an attempt to make the past come alive by the re-creation of atmosphere and local color. This did not prevent the historians of the time from using new types of explanatory analysis; nor did it mean that imagination substituted for scholarly documentation. The archivist and professor at the Collège de France, Pierre-Claude-François Daunou (1761–1840), published twenty volumes of his lectures, in which attention to method and sources was paramount. This was also an age in which published memoirs and sets of documents proliferated.

The most fervent promoter of the new kind of history was Augustin Thierry (1795–1856), who published a series of articles denouncing old-style history as anachronistic, inaccurate, and concerned with the great instead of the common people. He was more concerned with the conquered than the conquerors, and his *Histoire de la conquête de l'Angleterre par les normands* [History of the Conquest of England by the Normans] reflected his views on the Franks and the Gauls, which revived the eighteenth-century theme of the rise of the third estate against their feudal exploiters. Later Thierry published tales from Merovingian times extracted from Gregory of Tours. In this he identified himself with the narrative historians of the new school. It was the contention of Prosper Brugière, baron de Barante (1782–1866), who wrote a history of the fifteenth-century dukes of Burgundy, that the historian should let the sources speak for themselves, and withhold his own judgment.

The so-called philosophical historians looked for underlying social causes. François-Auguste Mignet (1796–1884) composed a succinct history of the French Revolution from a social-determinist viewpoint. His friend, the future statesman Adolphe Thiers (1797–1877), wrote on the same subject and with the same assumptions, but in much more diffuse terms. Both justified the Revolution while deploring its excesses. This was also the approach of the greatest historian of this group, and the future political rival to Thiers, François Guizot (1787–1874). The more conservative Guizot used a broader canvas than Mignet and Thiers and merged philosophy and literature with his interpretation of the inevitable triumph of the middle class as holding the balance between absolute monarchy and dangerous democratic tendencies. After early essays on the Middle Ages and the history of representative government, he concentrated upon the English civil wars of the seventeenth century, and lectured generally upon the nature of civilization.

Two friends who drifted apart in later life but typified the romantic movement in mid-century were Edgar Quinet (1803–1875) and Jules Michelet (1798–1874). Early in their careers both came under the influence of past philosophers of history: Quinet with Johann Gottfried Herder and German idealism, Michelet with Giambattista Vico and his adage that "man makes himself." Quinet wrote on revolutions in Italy and Germany, and, late in life, composed a history of the French Revolution. Michelet's evocative, and at times declamatory, *Histoire de France* [History of France] reached the late fifteenth century in the mid-1840s, before he adopted a more radical stance and wrote a long history of the French Revolution. He then returned to his general history, but showed less sympathy for the Middle Ages and a greater desire to depict the suffering of the common people. His empathetic approach and his remarkable style have remained an inspiration to French historians to the present day. Another historian who has continued to attract admiration was Alexis de Tocqueville (1805–1859), whose *De la démocratie en Amérique* [Democracy in America] saw democratic equality not just as the product of a new society but as the inevitable trend of history. His *L'Ancien Régime et la révolution* [The Old Regime and the Revolution] studied the causes of the French Revolution and found popular liberty sacrificed to equality. This book stressed continuity and undercut assumptions about climactic change in French society.

Two historians who set the tone for the later nineteenth century were Ernest Renan (1823–1892) and Hippolyte Taine (1828–1893). Renan was a philologist and Hebrew scholar who wrote about the origins of Christianity. While he lost his faith and became a scientific materialist, he contrived to retain imaginative and spiritual elements. Taine was a man of extraordinary breadth who specialized in the history of art and of literature.

He sought constantly to blend the physical and the psychological and devised a scientific method to integrate cultural creativity with social developments. A belief in the scientific nature of history also informed a historian of a more traditional type, Numa-Denis Fustel de Coulanges (1830–1889), whose best-known work was *La cité antique* [The Ancient City]. Fustel de Coulanges had more to say about religion and morality than about politics, but it was in the area of political history that his emphasis upon accuracy and detachment came most into play. This trend culminated at the end of the century when Charles Seignobos (1854–1942) and Charles-Victor Langlois (1863–1929) produced their celebrated text, *Introduction aux études historiques* [Introduction to Historical Studies]. Strict attention to documentary methods had been supported by a variety of institutions throughout the century. The École Nationale des Chartes was established in 1821, and the Société de l'Histoire de France was founded by Guizot in 1833. The graduate research center, L'École pratique des Hautes Études, came into being in 1884, while Gabriel Monod started the professional journal, *Revue Historique* in 1876.

Twentieth Century

A narrow concentration on political and diplomatic history that was closely based upon documentary sources continued to prevail in the early twentieth century. It was evident, although not dominant, in two multivolume general histories of France edited, respectively, by Ernest Lavisse (1842–1922) in the first decade and Gabriel Hanotaux (1853–1944) in the third. However, reaction against this narrow regimen soon occurred, as a movement began to integrate history with newer social sciences. Among supporters of such an association were the economist François Simiand (1873–1935), the geographer Paul Vidal de la Blache (1843–1918), and the philosopher Henri Berr (1863–1954), who founded the journal *Revue de Synthèse Historique* in 1900. The economic historians Henri Sée (1864–1936) and Henri Hauser (1866–1946) also wrote other kinds of history. Meanwhile a succession of eminent scholars of the French Revolution, such as Alphonse Aulard (1849–1928), Albert Mathiez (1874–1932), Georges Lefebvre (1874–1959), and Albert Soboul (1914–1982), developed schools of interpretation favoring radical republican or, as with the last three historians, Marxist models. Another Marxist, Ernest Labrousse (1895–1986), explained the Revolution with quantitative studies of economic statistics.

After World War I Marc Bloch (1886–1944) and Lucien Febvre (1878–1956) renewed the reaction against narrative political history and founded the school associated with the journal at first titled *Annales d'histoire économique et sociale*. Their interdisciplinary approach was analytic and problem-oriented. Bloch was a medievalist who wrote on rural history and feudal society and was influenced by the sociologist Emile Durkheim (1858–1917), a trenchant critic of event-centered history. One of Bloch's most admired works examined early modern belief in the magical healing powers attributed to consecrated kings. This book, *Les rois thaumaturges* (1924) (best known through its English translation, entitled *The Royal Touch*), became a model for the study of mentalities, a later fashion among *annaliste* historians. Most of Febvre's published work dealt with the early modern period and concentrated on the history of religious belief. He was an admirer of Michelet, and also of Jean Jaurès, the politician and author of *Histoire socialiste de la Révolution française* [Socialist History of the French Revolution]. Febvre's student, Robert Mandrou (1921–1984), used his master's notes to write *Introduction à la France moderne, 1500–1640: Essai de psychologie historique* (1961), later translated as *An Introduction to Modern France: An Essay in Historical Psychology, 1500–1640*.

After World War II, the *annaliste* movement took over the French historical establishment. The sixth section of the École pratique des Hautes Études, devoted to the social sciences, was created with Febvre as its director. The greatest name among the *annalistes,* Fernand Braudel (1902–1985), was associated with Febvre in the control of a subbranch known as the Centre des Recherches historiques. Braudel's *La Méditerranée et le monde méditerranéen à l'époque de Philippe II,* later translated into English as *The Mediterranean and the Mediterranean World under Philip II,* was organized according to three distinct kinds of time: the geographic (or *longue durée*) where human history was immobile, the conjunctural where social and economic trends intersected, and the eventual where individual human actions were apparent. His *Civilisation matérielle, économie et capitalisme, XVᵉ-XVIIIᵉ siècle* (translated as *Civilization and Capitalism, 15th–18th Century*) was intended to historicize the conditions of everyday life. Braudel expressed contempt for the superficiality of narrative history and had little sympathy for the study of mentality or for serial quantitative history, although he paid tribute to the statistical work of his student Pierre Chaunu (b. 1923) on the Atlantic trade. Braudel founded the Maison des Sciences de l'Homme, and on his retirement handed over the sixth section to the medievalist Jacques Le Goff (b. 1924).

The most prominent historian in the third generation of the *annalistes* is Emmanuel Le Roy Ladurie (b. 1929), who completed his vast study of the peasantry of Languedoc over the centuries under Braudel. From 1969, when Le Roy Ladurie and Le Goff joined the board of *Annales,* the movement has diversified. Among many who have made significant contributions in a variety of fields are Pierre Goubert (b. 1915), Georges Duby (1919–1996), François Furet (b. 1927), Michel Vovelle (b. 1933), and Roger Chartier (b. 1945). Cultural studies are now, perhaps, the most popular area of historical enterprise for the annalists, and while this seems to link them with Bloch and Febvre, it must be said that the movement as a whole has lost coherence. It has been, nonetheless, the most influential source of new ideas in history in this century. There are others, of course, who, although not associated with the Annales school, will remain celebrated in French historiography, notably the institutional historian Roland Mousnier (1907–1993) and the eccentric philosopher, Michel Foucault (1926–1984).

J.H.M. Salmon

See also ANNALES SCHOOL; ANTIQUARIANISM; BOLLANDISTS AND MAURISTS; CHRONICLES, MEDIEVAL; ECCLESIASTICAL HISTORY; ENLIGHTENMENT HISTORIOGRAPHY; FRENCH REVOLUTION; HAGIOGRAPHY; LAW AND HISTORY; *MOS GALLICUS* AND *MOS ITALICUS;* PHILOLOGY; ROMANTICISM; SERIAL HISTORY; STRUCTURALISM.

References

Archambault, Paul. *Seven French Chroniclers: Witnesses to History.* Syracuse, NY: Syracuse University Press, 1974.

Bédarida, François et al. (eds.) *L'histoire et le metier d'historien en France 1945–1995* [History and the Historical Profession in France, 1945–1995]. Paris: Editions de la maison des sciences de l'homme, 1995.

Burke, Peter. *The French Historical Revolution: The Annales School, 1929–1989.* Stanford, CA: Stanford University Press, 1990.

Coornaert, Emile. *Destins de Clio en France depuis 1800: Essai* [The Destinies of Clio in France since 1800: Essays]. Paris: Editions Ouvrières, 1977.

Dubois, Claude-Gilbert. *La Conception de l'histoire en France au XVIᵉ siècle* [The Idea of History in Sixteenth-Century France]. Paris: Nizet, 1977.

Guenée, Bernard. *Histoire et culture historique dans l'Occident mediéval* [History and Historical Culture in the Medieval West]. Paris: Aubier, 1980.

Kelley, Donald R. *The Foundations of Modern Historical Scholarship.* New York: Columbia University Press, 1970.

Ranum, Orest. *Artisans of Glory: Writers and Historical Thought in Seventeenth-Century France.* Chapel Hill: University of North Carolina Press, 1980.

Revel, Jacques, and Lynn Hunt (eds.) *Histories: French Reconstructions of the Past.* Trans. Arthur Goldhammer et al. New York: New Press, 1995.

Walch, Jean. *Les Maîtres de l'histoire, 1815–1850* [The Masters of History, 1815–1850]. Geneva: Slatkine, 1986.

French Revolution

The French Revolution of 1789 to 1799 deserves special attention in a book of this kind because for over two hundred years it has been a field in which the major approaches to history and the principal ideological interpretations of history have fought for supremacy. Control over the interpretation of this particular upheaval has been considered critical because many people have considered it the event that in some way or another ushered in the modern age.

In the past century successive interpretations have dominated for a generation or two, each in turn giving way to a successor without any lasting consensus being reached. At first a predominantly political interpretation of the Revolution prevailed, although from the time of the event itself there arose Leftist analyses that emphasized its social dimensions. As republicans solidified their control over France under the Third Republic after 1870, the republican interpretation of the event enjoyed wide support. Alphonse Aulard, the author of many books, typified these historians. Their analysis of the Revolution served their program of a strong republic, wide male suffrage, separation of church and state, and state-controlled secular education. In describing the great *journées* of the Revolution, when mass insurrection changed the course of events, republicans were vague in their description of "the people" who rose up, purposely glossing over divisions in the populace because republicans wanted to emphasize how the Republic embraced and united all classes.

In the wake of the Russian Revolution and the Depression of the 1930s, the Marxists tended to take over, turning the Sorbonne into a kind of Vatican for their movement. Albert Mathiez,

Georges Lefebvre, and Albert Soboul in turn provided leadership in reinterpreting the Revolution and in obtaining disciples around the world. For them, class warfare was the key to understanding the Revolution, and they expected that such understanding would help the cause of socialism or communism in France and elsewhere. For these Marxist historians, the basic cause of the Revolution was the clash of a rising bourgeoisie with a resurgent nobility just at the time that bankruptcy had weakened the monarchy. The bourgeoisie destroyed the remnants of feudalism and allegedly opened the way for nineteenth-century capitalism. Although the bourgeoisie used the discontent of the lower classes to move the Revolution along, they always kept their own interests foremost in their minds. In the end, they betrayed the popular forces and unwittingly weakened the First Republic. The lesson was supposed to be clear: never trust the bourgeoisie; put your faith in the workers and socialism.

Despite their political agenda, the Marxist school included very able historians who greatly enriched our understanding of the Revolution and its dynamic. Because of their interest in writing history "from the bottom up," they probed the conditions among the peasants, the small shopkeepers and artisans, and the participants in revolutionary crowds. They investigated the cost of living and the recurrent food scarcities that lay behind popular unrest. The crowd took on real faces.

By the time of Soboul's death in 1982, however, the Marxist school had long been on the defensive. The critique was led by English-speaking historians following the famous lectures by Alfred Cobban on the "myth" of the French Revolution, by which he meant the notion of a rising bourgeoisie clashing with an ambitious aristocracy. Accumulating empirical evidence, some of it garnered by Marxist historians themselves, had undermined the Marxist theory. It turned out on close examination that the upper bourgeoisie and the nobility appeared not to be two distinct classes, but a single privileged elite—they shared the same types of real property, similar investments in land and government bonds, enjoyed similar tax exemptions, and held common values. They went to classical colleges together, read the same books, saw the same plays, and sometimes intermarried. Moreover, Marxist evidence for class warfare between the so-called Girondists and the Montagnards in the first nine months of the Convention was unconvincing. So, too, was their claim that the "Federalist" revolt of 1793 had been largely based on different classes. Finally, the evidence suggested that the Terror was an intraclass rather than an interclass conflict.

There were, however, problems with the revisionist critique. George Taylor, whose research suggested that there was only one elite in Old Regime France, seemed to share the Marxist assumption that property and investment determine class. He underemphasized the fact that there was a juridical line between nobles and even the wealthiest commoners. This line was a legal division rather than a social one, but a division with important social and political consequences nonetheless. Not only did nobles have the right to distinctive attire and privileged access to court, they also monopolized virtually all the top offices in the government, army, and church. If the upper bourgeoisie were very like the nobles above them, but the nobles enjoyed greater prestige and power, was that not a possible reason for resentment? Revisionists such as William Doyle seem to have real difficulty in explaining the bitter disputes between the nobles and the leaders of the Third Estate, the commoners, at the beginning of the Revolution.

Above all, if class and economic interest did not drive the Revolution forward, what then was the Revolution all about? In the late 1970s and 1980s, some revisionists such as Lynn Hunt came up with an apparent answer: it was about the emergence of a new political culture, the antecedent of modern liberal republican political culture. At the same time, the advent of modern literary criticism provided an explanation for the dynamism of the Revolution, once attributed to class conflict and popular unrest: the driving force became *discours*. Keith Baker argued that preparation for the Revolution involved the invention of new discourses, one of which eventually triumphed, a discourse centered on the idea of the general will and national sovereignty. And according to François Furet, the leading French exponent of this interpretation, those revolutionaries such as Robespierre who were most skilled in exploiting this discourse were able to dominate up until the end of the Terror. In this view, the Revolution becomes a linguistic event.

This latter-day version of revisionism also seems unsatisfactory. It minimizes the role of the conditions among the lower classes that the Marxists brought to our attention a generation ago. It ignores the fact that the beginning of the organized Terror in September 1793 was precipitated by mob pressure from the *sans-culottes* of the sections of Paris, not by the rhetoric of members of the Committee of Public Safety and the Convention.

F

Inflation, food scarcity, and wartime conditions need once again to be integrated into the analysis of the upheaval. Moreover, the antirevolutionary attitudes of peasants in various parts of France seems better explained by lack of economic gains, resentment at being pressed into the army, and disruption of their traditional religious practices than by rhetoric.

Other approaches have still not been fully integrated into an overall synthesis. The work of historians of women has been very important, making up for the Marxist emphasis on class rather than gender. Darline Levy, Harriet Applewhite, Joan Landes, Olwen Hufton, and others, have shown that, despite their exclusion from voting and representation in the government, women did participate in insurrections, took part in food riots, swore civic oaths, and attended political clubs. They even had women's clubs until the government closed them down in 1793. Most women, however, held a highly gendered view of society, one in which women normally were excluded from political life. Studies by such scholars as Emmett Kennedy, Warren Roberts, James Leith, Mona Ozouf, Laura Mason, and Hugh Gough, of the attempt by the revolutionaries to mobilize the various media of the period—theater, art, architecture, festivals, music, and the press—in order to mold a new citizenry have, similarly, not yet been well integrated into general histories of the upheaval. Moreover, the portrayal of the Revolution as the birth-time of a modern liberal political culture needs to be qualified by acknowledgment of the illiberal features of the decade—the idea of sovereignty as singular, intolerance of political parties, rejection of legitimate opposition, constant calls for some kind of tutelary dictatorship, the actual dictatorship of the Committee of Public Safety, and attempts to regiment culture. These, too, form part of the legacy of this epochal event.

Finally, there is an interpretation that goes back to Alexis de Tocqueville in the early nineteenth century: that the Revolution was a stage in the rise of the centralized modern state, whether or not it was one in the rise of the bourgeoisie. Theda Skocpol and others have argued that the streamlining, bureaucratization, and centralization of the state has to be seen in light of France's competition with other powers. There is a useful discussion of the impact of the Revolution on the state in John Bosher's general history of the event.

James A. Leith

References

Bosher, J.F. *The French Revolution.* New York: W.W. Norton, 1988.

Doyle, William. *The Oxford History of the French Revolution.* Oxford: Clarendon Press, 1989.

Furet, François, and Mona Ozouf. *A Critical Dictionary of the French Revolution.* Trans. Arthur Goldhammer. Cambridge, MA: Harvard University Press, 1989.

Kennedy, Emmet. *A Cultural History of the French Revolution.* New Haven, CT, and London: Yale University Press, 1989.

Freyre, Gilberto (1900–1987)

Brazilian historian and sociologist. Freyre studied at Columbia University, where he was influenced by Franz Boas's attack on "scientific racism." Freyre's groundbreaking study of racial amalgamation in colonial Brazil, *Casa grande e senzala* [Masters and Slaves] (1933), was the most influential work in twentieth-century Brazilian historiography. Freyre's basic message, that a new race and a new culture evolved during the era of colonial Brazil, was nothing short of revolutionary. This was particularly so as Brazilians had been taught that a tropical, hybrid society was by definition inferior. It constituted the first volume of a trilogy that presented a new scheme for the periodization of Brazilian history, pegged to the rise and fall of "the patriarchal economy." One novel aspect of Freyre's periodization was the concept that the transition from one period to another did not always take place in the same way nor at the same speed within the different regions of Brazil. Also important was the emphasis Freyre placed on cultural elements in his studies, often eschewing traditional historical materials.

George L. Vásquez

Texts

The Masters and Slaves: A Study in the Development of Brazilian Civilization. Trans. Samuel Putnam. New York: Knopf, 1956.

References

Carvalho, Joaquim. *Entrevista con Gilberto Freyre* [Interview with Gilberto Freyre]. Mexico City: Frente de Afirmación Hispánica, 1975.

Chacon, Varmireh. *Gilberto Freyre: Uma biografia intelectual* [Gilberto Freyre: An Intellectual Biography]. São Paulo, Brazil: Companhia Editorial Nacional, 1993.

Ferrer, Ada. "Gilberto Freyre: A Problem in the Historiography of Brazilian Slavery." *Inter-American Review of Bibliography* 38 (1988): 196–211.

Frobenius, Leo (1873–1938)

German ethnographer and archaeologist. Frobenius made twelve trips to widely scattered parts of Africa between 1904 and 1935, but he is particularly associated with his excavations at Ife in Nigeria in 1912. By discerning Mediterranean influences in the artifacts he found at this undoubtedly ancient site, he was able to use the results of his work to support his theory of *Kulturkreis* (culture circles). He eventually went even further, postulating that the Yoruba were the last carriers of the culture of Atlantis. However bizarre, these theories, seemingly supported by archaeological evidence and conjuring up a homogeneous African culture, proved popular into the 1970s. Influenced by Heinrich Schliemann, Frobenius took myth literally, which led him to perform a valuable service in collecting enormous amounts of oral tradition at an early stage in its study. However, his wild speculations regarding the origins of African cultures, combined with his strident advocacy of diffusionism, meant that his theories could find little evidentiary support. Moreover, many of his trips were little more than foraging expeditions on behalf of various museums, in which thousands of pieces of art were removed from their natural environment, never to be returned.

David Henige

Texts

African Genesis. New York: Stackpole, 1937.
Afrika. Leipzig: F. Brandstetter, 1904.
The Childhood of Man: A Popular Account of the Lives, Customs and Thoughts of the Primitive Races. Trans. A.H. Keane. London: Seeley, 1909.
Kulturgeschichte Afrikas [Cultural History of Africa]. Zurich: Phaidon-Verlag, 1933.
Leo Frobenius 1873–1973: An Anthology. Ed. Eike Haberland; trans. Patricia Crampton. Wiesbaden, Ger.: F. Steiner, 1973.
Peuples et sociétés traditionelles du Nord-Cameroun [Peoples and Traditional Societies in North Cameroon]. Trans. Eldridge Mohammadou (into French). Stuttgart, Ger.: F. Steiner Verlag, 1987.

References

Jahn, Janheinz. *Leo Frobenius, the Demonic Child.* Austin, TX: African and Afro-American Studies Research Center, 1974.

Froissart, Jean (ca. 1333–ca. 1410)

Chronicler and poet from the county of Hainault in the Low Countries. Froissart was born in Valenciennes into a merchant family of modest means. He began his writing career as a poet around the year 1361, when he joined the household of Philippa of Hainault, wife of King Edward III of England. Throughout his life he composed several dozen ballads and songs in rhymed verse, among which the most popular was the romance *Meliador* in thirty thousand lines. As early as 1361, however, Froissart had also turned his hand to the writing of history, and it is for his work in this genre that he became famous in his own day and renowned in subsequent centuries.

Froissart's *Chronicles,* written in vernacular French prose style, has been held by many to be the greatest of all fourteenth-century historical works, surpassing those of other English and French writers. It describes in minute and altogether convincing detail the complex events of the Hundred Years War, in which England and France fought for hegemony in western Europe. Book I, which treats the years 1325 to 1378, underwent at least five major revisions and occupied the author for most of his adult life; the final recension, dated ca. 1400, runs to a quarter of a million words. It draws heavily, and in some cases exclusively, on an earlier chronicle written by Jean le Bel. But beginning with the events of the year 1362, when le Bel's account ends, Froissart's writing reveals the originality that was to earn him such widespread popularity. Books II, III, and IV are based almost entirely on oral testimony, meticulously collected by the author on his travels through England, Scotland, the Low Countries, Brittany, southern France, and Italy. Froissart has been criticized for his unwillingness to verify the accuracy of his informants' stories by consulting written documents (including the *Grandes Chroniques de France* [Great Chronicles of France]), to which he undoubtedly had access, and for treating his patrons and his heroes, especially King Edward III and the Black Prince, with unabashed admiration. But he himself made it clear that his intention was to relate the "great feats of arms" that occurred during the conflict between England and France so as to instruct the young fighting men of his age in the proper conduct of chivalric war. The tremendous success of his endeavor was attested to as early as the fifteenth century, when over a hundred manuscripts of the *Chronicles,* some richly illuminated, others inexpensive copies, circulated on the Continent and in England. Later medieval writers, notably Philippe de Commynes and Jean de Wavrin, made free use of the work.

Froissart's history was one of the first chronicles to be printed, translated, and widely disseminated in the sixteenth century, and it remained the standard reference for the history of the fourteenth century until well into the period of the Enlightenment. In the 1870s, the *Chronicles* came under the scrutiny of textual scholars, and Froissart's methods of assembling, collating, and editing his information were roundly condemned. More recently, his reputation as a chronicler has been rehabilitated. Historians now urge that his account of crucial events in the Hundred Years War be supplemented with other written primary source materials, but all argue that, within its genre, the *Chronicles* remains of inestimable value in its ability to convey the breadth and depth of fourteenth-century chivalric society.

Cynthia J. Neville

Texts

Chronicles. Ed. and trans. Geoffrey Brereton. Baltimore, MD: Penguin, 1968.

References

Palmer, J.N.N., ed. *Froissart: Historian.* Woodbridge, Eng.: Boydell Press, 1981.
Shears, F.S. *Froissart Chronicler and Poet.* London: George Routledge & Sons, 1930.

Frontier Thesis

See TURNER, FREDERICK JACKSON.

Froude, James Anthony (1818–1894)

English historian, biographer, and editor. The brother of Richard Hurrell Froude, one of the leaders of the Tractarian movement at Oxford, Froude recounted his own loss of faith in an autobiographical novel, *The Nemesis of Faith.* As the editor of *Fraser's Magazine,* he became a biographer of Thomas Carlyle and Erasmus, wrote books on Ireland and the West Indies, and contributed essays to literary reviews on subjects ranging from English seamen to biblical criticism. His *History of England* (1870) investigated the period from the death of Cardinal Wolsey to the defeat of the Spanish Armada. In recognition of his scholarly labors he was appointed to the Regius professorship at Oxford. Although Froude was among the first English historians to investigate the archives at Simancas, Paris, and Vienna, reviewers questioned his accuracy, while liberals and Catholics reacted uneasily to his favorable treatment of Henry VIII and his portrayal of the English Reformation as an early triumph of Protestant imperialism.

Myron C. Noonkester

Texts

History of England, from the Fall of Cardinal Wolsey to the Death of Elizabeth. 12 vols. New York: AMS Press, 1969.

References

Burrow, John W. *A Liberal Descent: Victorian Historians and the English Past.* Cambridge, Eng.: Cambridge University Press, 1981.
Dunn, W.H. *James Anthony Froude: A Biography.* 2 vols. Oxford: Clarendon Press, 1961–1963.

Fruin, Robert Jacobus (1823–1899)

Dutch historian. Fruin was born in Rotterdam. After completing his studies and taking his doctoral degree, he became a teacher at the Gymnasium in Leiden. In those years, he was also politically active in liberal circles. In 1860, he became professor of Dutch history at the University of Leiden. He held this position until he was given emeritus status in 1894. He died in Leiden. During his years as a teacher, Fruin published two monographs on the Dutch Revolt, the *Tien jaren* [Ten Years] (1857–1858) and *Het voorspel van den Tachtigjarigen oorlog* [The Prelude to the Eighty Years War] (1859–1860). In these he clarified the image of the revolt as it had been painted, among others, by John Lothrop Motley. During his professorship, Fruin did not write studies of any magnitude. He did, however, publish countless articles in which he proved himself to be a master of historical criticism and in which he attempted to achieve his own ideal of historical impartiality. This earned him the name of the "Dutch Ranke." Fruin's historical work favored political pacification and national conciliation.

Jo Tollebeek

Texts

Geschiedenis der staatsinstellingen in Nederland tot den val der Republiek [History of the Constitutional Bodies in the Netherlands up to the Fall of the Republic]. Ed. H.Th. Colenbrander. The Hague: Martinus Nijhoff, 1980.
Tien jaren uit de Tachtigjarige oorlog 1588–1598 [Ten Years from the Eighty Years War 1588–1598]. Utrecht and Antwerp: Het Spectrum, 1959.
Verspreide geschriften [Scattered Writings]. Ed. P.J. Blok et al. 10 vols. The Hague: Martinus Nijhoff, 1900–1905.

References

Smit, J.W. *Fruin en de partijen tijdens de Republiek* [Fruin and the Parties under the Republic]. Groningen, Neth.: Wolters, 1958.

Tollebeek, J. *De toga van Fruin: Denken over geschiedenis in Nederland sinds 1860* [Fruin's Gown: Thinking about History in the Netherlands since 1860]. Amsterdam: Wereldbibliotheek, 1996.

Fu I-ling

See FU YILING.

Fu Yiling [Fu I-ling] (1911–1988)

Chinese economic historian. Born in Fuzhou, Fujian province, Fu received his bachelor degree from Xiamen University in 1934, and then went to Japan, where he studied sociology. After returning to China, Fu worked at the Institute of Social Sciences at the Fujian Academy until 1949. During the period of the People's Republic of China (PRC) he was the professor of history at Xiamen University, also serving as chair of the history department and head of the university's History Institute. Near the end of his career he was appointed president of the university. Through much of this period, he was also a research fellow at the History Institute of the Social Science Academy in Beijing. Fu was a renowned historian in the PRC, specializing in studies of Chinese socioeconomic history in the Ming and Qing dynasties. His research was based firmly on primary sources. He examined, for instance, a great number of tenancy contracts (collected mostly in southern China) and investigated the relationship between landlords and tenant peasants in order to see the nature of Chinese feudal society of the late imperial period. In the 1950s, Fu participated in discussions of whether the "sprouts of capitalism" had emerged in dynastic China, arguing that although China before the nineteenth century was by and large a feudal society, it nevertheless displayed sporadic capitalist features, especially in southern China. Fu provided ample evidence in his work to prove the existence of various workshops and factories, mainly in the textile industry but also in other sectors of the economy in many provinces; the size of these and their levels of production, he contended, were similar to those in Europe during its early stages of capitalism. Although the scholarly discussion of this matter was interrupted by the Cultural Revolution, Fu continued his studies of China's rural economy and produced a number of significant works.

Q. Edward Wang

Texts

Fu Yiling zhishi wushinian wenbian [Anthology of Fu Yiling's Works]. Fuzhou, China: Xiamen daxue chubanshe, 1989.

Ming Qing fengjian tudi suoyouzhi lungang [An Outline of the History of Feudal Landownership in the Ming and Qing Dynasties]. Shanghai: Shanghai renmin chubanshe, 1992.

Ming Qing Fujian shehui yu xiangcun jingji [Society and Rural Economy in Fujian Province during the Ming and Qing Dynasties]. Fuzhou, China: Xiamen daxue chubanshe, 1987.

Ming Qing nongcun shehui jingji [Rural Society and Economy in the Ming and Qing Dynasties]. Beijing: Sanlian shudian, 1961.

Ming Qing shehui jingji bianqian Lun [A Study of Socio-Economic Changes in the Ming and Qing Dynasties]. Beijing: Renmin chubanshe, 1987.

Ming Qing shehui jingjishi lunwenji [Anthology of Studies of Socio-Economic History in the Ming and Qing Dynasties]. Beijing: Renmin chubanshe, 1982.

Ming Qing shidai shangren ji shangye ziben [Merchants and Merchant Capital in the Ming and Qing Dynasties]. Beijing: Sanlian shudian, 1956.

References

Dirlik, Arif. *Revolution and History: Origins of Marxist Historiography in China, 1919–1937*. Berkeley: University of California Press, 1978.

Feuerwerker, Albert, ed. *History in Communist China*. Cambridge, MA: MIT Press, 1968.

Fujita Yūkoku (1774–1826)

Japanese historian, philosopher, and politician of the Mito school. Born as Fujita Kumonosuke (also known as Fujita Jirōzaemon) into a textile trader's family, he was identified at a young age as inclined to learning and was sent to the Mito domainal school. At fifteen he was employed as an editor on the *Dai Nihon shi* [History of Great Japan] project and obtained samurai status for his efforts. In 1807, at the age of thirty-four, his efforts and talents were further recognized when he was made the director of the Shōkōkan, the institutional home of the *Dai Nihon shi* project and the Mito school. He was a prolific writer and was widely praised for his works on public policies and on agronomy. He was the father of Fujita

Tōko and the teacher of Aizawa Seishisai and others who were instrumental in the restructuring of the Tokugawa (1603–1868) political order and the establishment of the Meiji regime (1868–1912). His work was praised by shogunal adviser Matsudaira Sadanobu and eventually earned him the Upper Fourth rank at the imperial court. His greatest contribution, however, was in continuing the *Dai Nihon shi* project, which had been begun in 1657 by Tokugawa Mitsukuni. Although not completed until 1906, the greater part of this 243-volume work was published in 1697. The project was terminated after Mitsukuni's death in 1720 until the Mito domain revived the project and, under Yūkoku's supervision, published a new edition in 1810. This work treats the fifty imperial reigns from Emperor Kammu (eighth century) through Emperor Gokomatsu (fifteenth century). The work proceeds chronologically with a list of consulted sources appended to each entry. Rather than being a comprehensive work of historical analysis, the *Dai Nihon shi* is best known as an ethical treatment of individuals in society.

James Edward Ketelaar

Text

Yūkoko zenshū [Complete Works]. Ed. Kikuchi Kanjirō. Tokyo, 1935.

References

Koschmann, J. Victor. *The Mito Ideology: Discourse, Reform, and Insurrection in Late Tokugawa Japan, 1790–1864.* Berkeley and Los Angeles: University of California Press, 1987.

Wakabayashi, Bob Tadashi. *Anti-Foreignism and Western Learning in Early Modern Japan: The* New Theses *of 1825.* Cambridge, MA: Harvard University Press, 1991.

Fukuda Tokuzō (1874–1930)

Japanese economist and historian. Fukuda is now best known for his introduction of neoclassical economics, but he began his career as a historian, influenced by German historical thought and scholarship. Born in Tokyo, he studied at Tokyo Higher Commercial School before going to Germany to study historical economics under the direction of Lujo Brentano; he was awarded his doctorate (1900) for a thesis in which he tried to prove that the "law of history" applied equally to Western and Japanese societies. After returning to Japan, he wrote many papers on neoclassical and Marxist economics. He was supportive of the former and critical of the latter, but is honored for his pioneering work in introducing both fields into Japan and for his perceptive analysis.

Takashi Fujii

Texts

Fukuda Tokuzō Keizaigaku Zenshū [Collected Works]. Tokyo: Dōbunkan, 1924–1927.

References

Morris-Suzuki, Tessa. *A History of Japanese Economic Thought.* London and New York: Routledge, 1989.

Fukuzawa Yukichi (1835–1901)

Japanese Enlightenment intellectual, political philosopher, and educator. Born the second son to a samurai stationed in Osaka but later adopted into another family (Nakamura), he retained his original name throughout his life. He began studying Chinese texts as a teenager; he traveled to Nagasaki in 1854 to begin study of the Dutch language and thought and continued his work in Osaka through 1855. By order of his domain in 1855 he returned to Edo (Tokyo) and opened a Dutch Studies academy; this academy was the foundation for one of contemporary Japan's leading private universities, Keio. In 1856 he abandoned Dutch as useless for true international communication and concentrated on English. In 1860 he joined the Japanese embassy to the United States for ratification of the 1858 treaty on trade. In 1861 he traveled to Europe and in 1866 he again toured America. His observations abroad were published in 1866 in *Seiyō jijō* [Conditions of the West], which quickly sold 250,000 copies and established him as a major figure of the Enlightenment. He followed this with two other bestsellers *Bummeiron no gairyaku* [Outline of a Theory of Civilization] (1875) and *Gakumon no susume* [An Encouragement of Learning, finished in 1876]. His *Fukuōjiden* [Autobiography] (1899), another bestseller, is a dramatic record of the Meiji era transition. Crediting Berkeley, Guizot, Spencer, Tocqueville, and others as his inspiration, Fukuzawa was active in the people's rights movement, the formation of a national assembly, popular education, and international cosmopolitanism. In recognition of his stature his visage was selected to adorn the ten-thousand-yen bill.

James Edward Ketelaar

Texts

The Autobiography of Yukichi Fukuzawa. Ed. and trans. Eiichi Kiyooka. New York: Columbia University Press, 1966.

An Encouragement of Learning. Ed. and trans. David Dilworth and Umeyo Hirano. Tokyo: Sophia University Press, 1969.

References

Ienaga Saburō. *Fukuzawa Yukichi.* Tokyo: Chikuma Shobō, 1963.

Fulcher of Chartres (ca. 1057–1127)

Chaplain and crusade chronicler. Fulcher studied for the priesthood at Chartres (France), and was probably already in holy orders when Pope Urban II preached the first crusade at the famous Council of Clermont in 1095. Though it cannot be demonstrated that Fulcher was present at the council, he responded to the appeal and joined the party of Stephen, count of Blois, probably serving as his chaplain. He took part in the initial battles such as that of Dorylaeum (1097), and after Jerusalem fell to the crusaders he remained in the East. There he became a canon of the Church of the Holy Sepulchre and served as chaplain to King Baldwin I of Jerusalem. His *Historia Hierosolymitana* [History of Jerusalem], begun in 1101 and covering the years 1095 to 1127, is one of the best sources available on the first crusade. His report of the pope's sermon at Clermont presents the pontiff's intention as one of peacemaking on behalf of Christians in the Middle East. After recounting the crusade campaigns and battles, which he presents as miraculous works of God, Fulcher proceeds to describe the acculturation of the Western settlers in the crusader states. Indeed he observes that "we who were occidentals have now become orientals" in matters of dress and manners. His history would have a great deal of influence on subsequent crusade chroniclers such as William of Tyre.

Monica Sandor

Texts

Fulcheri Carnotensis Historia Hierosolymitana. Ed. Henrich Hagenmeyer. Heidelberg: Carl Winters Universitätsbuchhandlung, 1913.

A History of the Expedition to Jerusalem, 1095–1127. Ed. Harold S. Fink; trans. F.R. Ryan. Knoxville: University of Tennessee Press, 1969.

References

Epp, Verena. *Fulcher von Chartres, Studien zur Geschichtsschreibung des ersten Kreuzzuges* [Fulcher of Chartres, Studies toward a Historiography of the First Crusade]. Düsseldorf: Droste, 1990.

Giese, W. "Untersuchungen zur Historia Hierosolymitana des Fulcher von Chartres [Inquiries into the History of Jerusalem of Fulcher of Chartres]." *Archiv für Kulturgeschichte* [Archive for Cultural History] 69 (1987): 62–115.

Munro, Dana C. "A Crusader." *Speculum* 7 (1932): 321–335.

Fung Yu-lan

See FENG YULAN.

Furet, François (b. 1927)

Historian of the French Revolution. Furet was trained among the *annalistes* of the sixth section of the École Pratique des Hautes Études (of which Furet later became president). A former member of the Communist Party, Furet's most important work constitutes an attack on the Marxist historiography of the Revolution.

Furet's debt to the *Annales* is most evident in his *Reading and Writing* (1977), which deals with literacy in the *longue durée* from the Reformation to the late nineteenth century. Most of Furet's work, however, has concentrated on the politics and ideology of the Revolution.

In *The French Revolution,* first published in 1965, Furet asserted that the events of 1789 were neither a social nor a bourgeois revolution. Furet's reinterpretation of the Revolution as an ideological and political, rather than social, rupture remains crucial to his research on the political culture of the Revolution. His *Critical Dictionary of the French Revolution* contains extensive essays on ideological issues but very little material on social change. In addition, Furet has turned his attention to nineteenth-century writers on the Revolution such as Alexis de Tocqueville and Augustin Cochin, whose discussions of the Revolution were likewise political and ideological (*Interpreting the French Revolution,* 1978).

Furet's scholarship has also been deeply concerned with interpretations of the Terror. *The French Revolution* argued that the Terror represented the Revolution skidding off course. More recently Furet has revised this opinion, and in *Interpreting the French Revolution* he maintains that the Terror was inherent in revolutionary democracy from the beginning.

Carol E. Harrison

Texts

And Mona Ozouf, eds. *Critical Dictionary of the French Revolution.* Trans. A. Goldhammer. Cambridge, MA: Belknap Press, 1989.

And Denis Richet. *The French Revolution.* Trans. S. Hardman. New York: Macmillan, 1970.

In the Workshop of History. Trans. J. Mandelbaum. Chicago: University of Chicago Press, 1984.

Interpreting the French Revolution. Trans. E. Forster. Cambridge, Eng.: Cambridge University Press, 1981.

Marx and the French Revolution. Trans. D.K. Furet. Chicago: University of Chicago Press, 1988.

Le passé d'une illusion: Essai sur l'idée communiste au XXᵉ siècle [The Past of an Illusion: Essay on the Communist Ideal in the Twentieth Century]. Paris: Calmann-Lévy, 1995.

And Jacques Ozouf. *Reading and Writing: Literacy in France from Calvin to Jules Ferry.* Cambridge, Eng.: Cambridge University Press, 1982.

Revolutionary France, 1770–1880. Trans. A. Nevill. Oxford: Blackwell, 1992.

References

Dosse, François. *New History in France: The Triumph of the Annales.* Trans. P.V. Conroy. Urbana and Chicago: University of Illinois Press, 1994.

"François Furet's Interpretation of the French Revolution." Forum with articles by C. Langlois, D. Bien, D. Sutherland, F. Furet. *French Historical Studies* 16 (1990): 766–802.

Furnivall, John Sydenham (1878–1960)

English scholar and public servant. Born in Essex, Furnivall graduated from Cambridge University. He served as an Indian Civil Service officer in Burma from 1902 to 1923, during which time he founded the Burma Research Society (1910); he would later found the Burma Book Club and Burma Education Extension Association (1928). He served as a planning adviser to the U Nu government after the independence of Burma. In 1960 he left Burma and returned to England, dying later that year. Furnivall was one of the first Western scholars to develop a theory for understanding Asian colonial societies. His "plural society" theory was developed in the 1930s and expressed in *Netherlands India* (1939) and numerous other writings. The theory dealt with the question of the relation between economic process and sociocultural integration among the different ethnic components of a society. The concept of plural society was used extensively in writings on Southeast Asian countries during the 1960s and 1970s and has also been employed in Caribbean and African studies.

Teruko Saito

Texts

Colonial Policy and Practice: A Comparative Study of Burma and Netherlands India. New York: New York University Press, 1956.

Netherlands India: A Study of Plural Economy. New York: Macmillan, 1944.

References

Evers, Hans D., ed. *Sociology of Southeast Asia: Readings on Social Change and Development.* Kuala Lumpur and New York: Oxford University Press, 1980.

Fustel De Coulanges, Numa-Denis (1830–1889)

French historian of antiquity and of medieval France. Fustel de Coulanges was born in Paris and entered the École Normale Supérieure in 1850. He then worked at the École française d'Athènes until poor health forced him to leave (1855). When Fustel de Coulanges received his doctorate in 1858, he was named to the lycée Saint-Louis. In 1860, he joined the faculty of history at Strasbourg, after which he returned to Paris to teach at the École Normale Supérieure (1870). In 1875, Fustel de Coulanges became a member of the Institut de France and taught ancient history at the Sorbonne. From 1878, he was professor of medieval history, and he directed the École Normale Supérieure from 1880 to 1883. In 1881, he became an officer of the Legion of Honor. In his research, Fustel de Coulanges looked solely to primary evidence, giving little credence to secondary material or romantic ideology. In *La cité antique* [The Ancient City] (1864), he utilized classical sources to formulate a broad discussion of preurban social institutions. Despite its universal acclaim, Fustel de Coulanges was criticized by scientific historians who found his interpretation too imaginative. Following the Franco-Prussian War and the Commune of Paris (1870–1871), Fustel de Coulanges wrote a number of pieces on the war. His subsequent work on early medieval history, such as *Histoire des institutions politiques de l'ancienne France* [History of the Political Institutions of Ancient France] (1874), defended Roman aspects of the French legal tradition after the Germanic migrations. He outlined his methodology of detailed, interdisciplinary analysis in: "De l'analyse des textes historiques" [On the Analysis of Historical Texts] (1886).

Bonnie Effros

Texts

L'Alsace est-elle allemande ou française? [Is Alsace German or French?]. Paris: E. Dentu, 1870.

The Ancient City. Baltimore, MD: Johns Hopkins University Press, 1980.

"De l'analyse des textes historiques." *Revue des Questions historiques* 2 (1886): 259–290; 349–358.

Histoire des institutions politiques de l'ancienne France, ed. Camille Julian. 6 vols. Brussels: Culture et Civilisation, 1964.

References

Hartog, François. *Le XIXᵉ siècle et l'histoire: Le cas Fustel de Coulanges* [The Nineteenth Century and History: The Case of Fustel de Coulanges]. Paris: Presses Universitaires de France, 1988.

Herrick, Jane. *The Historical Thought of Fustel de Coulanges.* Washington, DC: Catholic University of America Press, 1954.

Momigliano, Arnaldo. "From Mommsen to Max Weber." *History and Theory* 21 (1982): 16–32.

F

G

Gadamer, Hans-Georg (b. 1900)

German philosopher of hermeneutics, widely influential in methodological discussions of the interpretation of historical texts. Gadamer, who spent most of his professional life in Heidelberg, was a student of Martin Heidegger, but made his own indelible mark with the publication of *Wahrheit und Methode* (later translated into English as *Truth and Method*). The modern discipline of hermeneutics begins with Friedrich Schleiermacher (1768–1834), and Gadamer's *magnum opus* is the single most important treatment of the interpretation of texts since then. In a word, Gadamer reminds scholars that all human understanding occurs only within a given language and tradition, and that we can never understand anything that we do not in some sense already know. In a potent phrase, Gadamer likens the act of understanding to the fusion of two horizons: the historical text with the consciousness of the present, a dialectic wherein unity and difference are mediated in their distinction. According to Gadamer's younger critic, Jürgen Habermas, we are all still "young Hegelians" and, in *Truth and Method,* Gadamer indeed takes up the intrinsic antagonism between G.W.F. Hegel (1770–1831) and Schleiermacher, who had been colleagues and rivals at the University of Berlin. Schleiermacher's hermeneutics sought to overcome the "consciousness of loss and estrangement" by reconstruction (that is, reproducing "in the understanding the original purpose" of a text). Hegel, by contrast, believed that we are able only to proceed by a dialectic of integration, whereby there is an "interior recollection" of the text, in which the human spirit is conscious of itself. Schleiermacher's efforts to reproduce the original purpose of a text were countered by Hegel's sense that we only have the fruits torn from the living tree of tradition. Gadamer, in our century, has reaffirmed that the historical task is not the restoration of a forever elusive past, but its speculative "mediation with contemporary life."

Thomas H. Curran

Texts

Truth and Method. Second rev. ed. Trans. rev. by Joel Weinsheimer and Donald G. Marshall. New York: Crossroad, 1989.

References

Derksen, L.D. *On Universal Hermeneutics: A Study in the Philosophy of Hans-Georg Gadamer.* Amsterdam: VU Boekhandel/ Uitgeverij, 1983.

Michelfelder, Diane P., and Richard E. Palmer, eds. *Dialogue and Deconstruction: The Gadamer-Derrida Encounter.* Albany: State University of New York Press, 1989.

Misgeld, Dieter, and Graeme Nicholson, eds. *Hans-Georg Gadamer on Education, Poetry, and History: Applied Hermeneutics.* Trans. Lawrence Schmidt and Monica Reuss. Albany: State University of New York Press, 1992.

Gaguin, Robert (1433–1501)

French historian, clergyman, and scholar. Born in Calonne-sur-la-Lys, he became a prominent figure in Parisian literary circles and on occasion a servant to the king. A poet, moralist, and orator, he wrote, without official support, a French history, *Compendium de origine et gestis Francorum* [Summary on the Origin and the History of the French] (1495). This work was intended to revise French historiography according to humanist literary rules. It praises, in refined Latin, the French and their kings, in keeping with French historiographical traditions. Frequently published before 1600 and translated into French (1514), it remained influential throughout the sixteenth century.

Franck Collard

Texts

Compendium Roberti Gaguini super Francorum gestis. Paris: T. Kerver et al., 1500/1501.

References

Schmidt-Chazan, Mireille. "Histoire et sentiment national chez Robert Gaguin" [History and National Feeling in Robert Gaguin]. In *Le métier d'historien au Moyen Age* [The Work of the Historian in the Middle Ages], ed. Bernard Guenée. Paris: Sorbonne, 1977, 233–301.

Gairdner, James (1828–1912)

Scottish archivist, editor, and historian. Gairdner was born in Edinburgh, where his father worked as a physician. Raised a Presbyterian, Gairdner never attended university but instead moved to London where he took up employment in the Public Record Office in 1846 at the age of eighteen. He became an assistant keeper in 1859, and retired in 1893. Gairdner's greatest contributions to scholarship lay in editing and calendaring historical documents, especially the massive *Letters and Papers, Foreign and Domestic, of the Reign of Henry VIII* (1862–1910), which was completed in partial collaboration with J.S. Brewer and R.H. Brodie. This remains today a basic source for early Tudor history, its fuller summaries of documents held not only in the Public Record Office, but also in the British Museum (as it then was), and elsewhere rendering it superior as a research tool to the comparable calendars of Elizabethan and early Stuart state papers. Gairdner's other important editorial projects included *Memorials of King Henry the Seventh* (1858), *Letters and Papers Illustrative of the Reigns of Richard III and Henry VII* (1861–1863), and *The Paston Letters* (1872–1875 and 1896). Gairdner also wrote several historical monographs including *The English Church in the Sixteenth Century* (1902) and *Lollardy and the Reformation in England* (1908–1913). Both works display strong Anglo-Catholic sentiments of sympathy to the pre-Reformation church and criticism of the Protestant Reformation.

Ronald H. Fritze

Texts

The English Church in the Sixteenth Century from the Accession of Henry VIII to the Death of Mary. New York: AMS Press, 1971.

Ed. with J.S. Brewer and R.H. Brodie. *Letters and Papers, Foreign and Domestic, of the Reign of Henry VIII.* 21 volumes. London: HMSO/Public Record Office, 1862–1910.

Lollardy and the Reformation in England: An Historical Survey. 4 vols. London and New York: Macmillan, 1908–1913.

References

Hunt, William. "Preface." In Gairdner's *Lollardy and the Reformation in England,* vol. 4. London: Macmillan, 1913.

Ganshof, François Louis (1895–1980)

Belgian medievalist. Ganshof obtained doctoral degrees in both law and history from the University of Ghent. Under the supervision of Henri Pirenne, he produced a Ph.D. thesis on the *ministeriales* of medieval Germany Ganshof succeeded Pirenne as professor of medieval history at Ghent and held this position until his retirement in 1961. Over the course of his career he produced a prodigious ten books and 197 articles, the majority of which focused on the history of Carolingian law and institutions. Two of his better-known works remain *Qu'est-ce que la feodalite?* (1944, later translated into English as *Feudalism*) and his magisterial analysis of the nature, growth, and impact of Frankish legislation: *Wat warren de capitularia?* [What Were the Capitularies] (1955). Ganshof earned an international reputation not for striking originality or creativity, but for immense erudition, meticulous scholarship, and precise, thoughtful analyses.

Krista Kesselring

Texts

The Carolingians and the Frankish Monarchy: Studies in Carolingian History. Ithaca, NY: Cornell University Press, 1971.

Feudalism. Third English ed. New York: Harper, 1964.

Frankish Institutions under Charlemagne. Providence, RI: Brown University Press, 1968.

Wat warren de capitularia? Brussels: Palais du Académie, 1955.

References

Bibliographie des travaux historiques de Francois-Louis Ganshof. Wetteren, Belgium: Imprimerie De Meester, 1943.

Garcilaso de la Vega, El Inca (1539–1616)

Mestizo chronicler and literary stylist. Garcilaso was the son of a Spanish conquistador and an Inca princess. He served as his father's amanuensis when the latter was *corregidor* of Cuzco. At the age of twenty he traveled to Spain where he served in the Castilian army, reaching the rank of captain. Later he moved to Córdoba and took minor religious orders. In 1605 he published *La Florida del Inca* [The Florida of the Inca], a dramatic account of Hernando de Soto's ill-fated attempt to conquer Florida. Four years later he published *Comentarios reales de los Incas* [Royal Commentaries of the Incas], a eulogy of the Inca Empire, which he referred to as "the other Rome." It was a conscientious attempt to correct the false image of Peru presented by the early Spanish chroniclers. The second part of his history, *Historia general del Perú* [General History of Peru], was published posthumously in 1617. This work, banned in 1782 by the Spanish authorities because of its nascent Peruvian nationalism, described the Spanish conquest and revealed Garcilaso's divided loyalties as he refused to condemn the *encomienda* and other onerous aspects of Spanish rule.

George L. Vásquez

Texts

The Florida of the Inca: A History of the Adelantado, Hernando de Soto, Governor and Captain General of the Kingdom of Florida, and of Other Heroic Spanish and Indian Cavaliers. Ed. and trans. John Grier Varner and Jeannett Johnson Varner. Austin: University of Texas Press, 1951.
Royal Commentaries of the Incas and General History of Peru. Trans. Harold V. Livermore. Austin: University of Texas Press, 1987.

References

Brading, D.A. "Inca Humanist." In his *The First America: The Spanish Monarchy, Creole Patriots, and the Liberal State, 1492–1867.* Cambridge, Eng: Cambridge University Press, 1991, 255–272.
————. "The Incas and the Renaissance: The Royal Commentaries of Inca Garcilaso de la Vega." *Journal of Latin American Studies* 18 (1985): 1–23.
Miró Quesada, Aurelio. *El Inca Garcilaso.* Lima: Pontificia Universidad Católica del Perú, Fondo Editorial, 1994.

Gardiner, Dorothy Kempe (1873–1957)

English local historian and amateur archaeologist. The daughter of Sir John Kempe, Gardiner spent much of her long life in Canterbury. Her keen interest in local history manifested itself in her life's work. At the time of her death she was the chair of the Canterbury Archaeological Society and served on the council of the Kent Archaeological Society. In addition to a number of books on the history of both the city of Canterbury and Canterbury Cathedral, Gardiner published *Companion into Kent* (1934) and *Companion into Dorset* (1937). Drawing upon the work of previous historians and topographers, these local guidebooks were for the most part concerned with the historical and literary associations of sites. In 1929, her *English Girlhood at School* appeared. Although other studies of the history of female education in England had been published before, Gardiner's work was unique in that it focused primarily on the educational practices of the sixteenth to eighteenth centuries, rather than on the extensive reforms of the nineteenth century. Her authoritative editorial work in *The Oxinden Letters, 1607–1642* (1933) and the succeeding volume *The Oxinden and Peyton Letters, 1642–1670* (1937) also met with critical acclaim.

Jennifer A. Morawiecki

Texts

Companion into Dorset. London: Methuen, 1937.
Companion into Kent. London: Methuen, 1934.
English Girlhood at School: A Study of Women's Education through Twelve Centuries. Oxford: Oxford University Press, 1929.
Ed. *The Oxinden and Peyton Letters, 1642–1670: Being the Correspondence of Henry Oxinden of Barham, Sir Thomas Peyton of Knowlton and Their Circle.* London: Sheldon Press, 1937.
Ed. *The Oxinden Letters, 1607–1642: Being the Correspondence of Henry Oxinden of Barham and His Circle.* London: Constable, 1933.

References

"The Education of Girls." Review of *English Girlhood at School. Times Literary Supplement.* London, England. August 1, 1929.
"Mrs. D. Gardiner: Archaeology in Kent." Obituary. *The Times.* London, England. January 25, 1957, 10.

Gardiner, Samuel Rawson (1829–1902)

English historian. Born in Hampshire, Gardiner was educated at Winchester College and at Christ Church, Oxford, but his conversion to the Irvingite Catholic Apostolic Church blocked him from beginning an academic career in the still firmly Anglican ancient university. Instead he taught in London—a situation that proved ideal for his research at the Public Record Office—at Bedford College, and at King's College. Although he was a popular lecturer who produced school textbooks and edited a well-known edition of *Constitutional Documents of the Puritan Revolution* (1889), he was above all a researcher and made a major contribution to the establishment in England of the rigorous methodology of the emergent discipline of history. Scholarly recognition was slow to come. Gardiner was director of the research-based Camden Society from 1869 to 1897, and he edited twelve volumes of documents for that body. For ten years after 1891 he was editor of the recently founded *English Historical Review,* the principal organ of the English historical profession. The first installment of Gardiner's multivolume epic *History of England* in the seventeenth century appeared in 1863. Thereafter he soldiered on in a rigidly chronological fashion and had reached 1656 by the time of his death; the work was continued by his admirer, Sir Charles Firth. Studies of *Oliver Cromwell's Place in History* and of *Oliver Cromwell* appeared in 1897 and 1901, respectively. Gardiner's *History* has been challenged on many points of fact, but his close attention to sources analyzed according to a strict chronology has given the work longevity, and in recent years it has been frequently cited with admiration by modern revisionist seventeenth-century historians.

R.C. Richardson

Texts

Ed. *Constitutional Documents of the Puritan Revolution.* Third ed. Oxford: Clarendon Press, 1906.
Cromwell's Place in History. Freeport, NY: Books for Libraries Press, 1969.
History of England from the Accession of James I to the Outbreak of the Civil War, 1603– 1642. 10 vols. New York: AMS Press, 1965.

References

Adamson, J.S.A. "Eminent Victorians: S.R. Gardiner and the Liberal As Hero." *Historical Journal* 33 (1990): 641–657.
Kenyon, J.P. *The History Men: The Historical Profession in England since the Renaissance.* Second ed. London: Weidenfeld, 1993.
Lang, T. *The Victorians and the Stuart Heritage.* Cambridge, Eng.: Cambridge University Press, 1994.
Richardson, R.C. *The Debate on the English Revolution Revisited.* London: Routledge, 1988.

Garneau, François-Xavier (1809–1866)

French Canadian historian, poet, and author of travel literature. Garneau was born in Quebec City and spent virtually his entire life there. Raised in modest circumstances, he obtained his education largely through his innate abilities and diligence. He became a notary in 1830, but spent little time practicing that profession. From June 1831 until June 1833 he lived in London, England, employed as secretary to an envoy of the *Chambre d'Assemblée du Bas-Canada* (the Quebec legislative body) on a mission to the British government. During this period he also visited Paris, taking advantage of every opportunity to broaden his understanding of political realities. After returning to Quebec City he assumed a variety of positions, including those of bank teller and translator. Although remaining a certified notary, he published poetry and founded two short-lived cultural magazines. The unrest associated with the revolt of the *Patriotes* in 1837 spurred him to write history: after the rebellion failed and the Act of Union was used to suppress the French Canadian faction, he resolved to turn his pen to the defense of his nationality. In 1845 he published the first volume of his monumental work, *L'Histoire du Canada depuis sa découverte jusqu'à nos jours* [The History of Canada from Its Discovery until the Present]. The initial volume dealt with the seventeenth century; two subsequent volumes, published consecutively, brought the account to 1840. For French Canada, the appearance of this opus constituted the most significant literary, and indeed ideological, event of the nineteenth century. Garneau, influenced by Augustin Thierry's *La Conquête de l'Angleterre par les Normands* [The Norman Conquest of England], saw as the mainspring of French-Canadian history the French colonists' struggles, first, against the Amerindians and, later, against the British—the latter conflict having been initiated on the battlefield and then prolonged, after 1763, in the political arena. Although clerical leaders viewed Garneau's liberal ideas with alarm, his *Histoire* constituted French Canada's finest "national" history until World War II. Garneau also inspired a whole body of patriotic literature produced by novelists, poets, and public figures who drew upon his narratives for epic tales and portrayals of great heroes. His history went through nine printings, the last edition appearing in 1969. Only Lionel Groulx's twentieth-century work can be said to have had comparable influence.

Pierre Savard

Texts

Histoire du Canada. Eighth ed. 9 vols. Montreal: Editions de l'arbre, 1944–1946.

Histoire du Canada Français. 6 vols. Montreal: Amis de l'histoire, 1969.

References

Bergeron, Gérard. *Lire François-Xavier Garneau, 1809–1866: Historien national* [Reading Garneau: The National Historian]. Quebec City: Institut québécois de recherche sur la culture, 1984.

Gagnon, Serge. *Quebec and Its Historians, Vol. I: 1840–1920.* Trans. Yves Brunelle. Montreal: Harvest House, 1982.

Gatterer, Johann Christoph (1727–1799)

German historian. Gatterer was appointed to the chair of history at the University of Göttingen in 1759. He was one of Germany's most important historians of the late Enlightenment and the Göttingen school. Besides writing numerous universal histories, he edited historical journals and actively promoted the auxiliary disciplines. Gatterer sought to revitalize the study of history and to raise it to an autonomous academic discipline through the development of a form of Universal History that would go beyond the mere compilation of facts and capture the inner connectedness of events. To this end, he maintained that history was a rational, dynamic process that could be revealed only through a sound theory of historical knowledge and methods of research based on the critical examination of source material. Gatterer's work therefore represents a transitional stage between the traditional historiography of the Enlightenment and the modern research practices of Ranke and German historicism.

John R. Hinde

Texts

Ioh. Christophori Gattereri . . . Elementa artis diplomaticae universalis [Gatterer's Elements of the Art of Diplomatic]. Göttingen: Van den Hoeck, 1765.

Handbuch der neuesten Genealogie und Heraldik [Handbook of Genealogy and Heraldry]. Nuremberg: Raspischen, 1759–1772.

References

P.H. Reill. *The German Enlightenment and the Rise of Historicism.* Berkeley: University of California Press, 1975.

Gaubil, Antoine (1689–1759)

French Jesuit missionary to and historian of China. Arriving in China in 1722, Gaubil encountered the increasing hostility of the Qing court to missionary endeavor. But that did not prevent him from continuing the Jesuit strategy of placing their expertise at the service of the dynasty. He eventually became the official interpreter for foreigners and head of the imperial school, which trained Manchu diplomats for their dealings with foreigners, largely Orthodox Russians whom the Jesuits favored at the expense of the Protestant Dutch. This orientation might have helped secure his membership in the Russian Imperial Academy. But the kind of erudition that brought him membership in the Royal Society and Académie des Inscriptions et Belles Lettres also entered into the matter. It also won him the friendship of the sinophile G.W. von Leibnitz (*Novissimo Sinica,* 1697). Gaubil's *Histoire de Gentchiscan* (1739) was the first Western biography of Genghis Khan to draw upon Asian sources. His translation of the ancient *Shujing* [Book of History] (1771), to which was appended a *Traité de la chronologie chinoise* [Treatise of Chinese Chronology], which helped fuel the debate that pitted Chinese chronology against that of the Bible.

John F. Laffey

Texts

Histoire de Gentchiscan et toute le dinastie des Mongolls ses successeurs conquéran de la Chine. Trans. R.P. Gaubil. Paris: Briasson, 1739.

Traité de la chronologie chinoise. Ed. M. Silvestre de Sacy. Paris: Treuttel et Würtz, 1814.

References

Allan, C.W. *Jesuits at the Court of Peking.* Arlington, VA: University Publications of America, 1975.

Rowbotham, A.H. *Missionary and Mandarin: The Jesuits at the Court of China.* New York: Russell & Russell, 1966.

Gay, Peter (b. 1923)

German-born U.S. historian of European culture. Born in Berlin, Gay emigrated to the United States in 1941 and received his Ph.D. from Columbia University (1951), where he became a professor in 1962. In 1970 he moved to Yale University, where he is now Sterling professor of history (emeritus). Gay is a historian of the human experience in its individual and collective elements. His reappraisals of the Enlightenment, in a series of books, have become classics. Since their publication, he has continued to contribute important biographies and studies of eighteenth- and nineteenth-century intellectuals, including Voltaire, Locke, Rousseau, Ranke, and, above all, Freud. As an orthodox Freudian, Gay places psychohistorical methods at the center of historical inquiry. He has also investigated the emotional, social, and gender-specific dimensions of the nineteenth-century *bourgeoisie,* and written a defense of Freud and Freudian ideas directed at historians, who have generally been unreceptive to them. Gay's writing is characteristically witty and incisive, and as erudite studies, his works are based on an extensive use of primary sources and a sensitivity to social, political, and intellectual factors.

John B. Roney

Texts

The Bourgeois Experience. Vol. 1, *Education of the Senses.* New York: Oxford University Press, 1984; Vol. 2, *Tender Passions.* New York: Oxford University Press, 1986; Vol. 3, *Cultivation of Hatred.* New York: Norton, 1993.

The Enlightenment: An Interpretation. 2 vols. New York: Norton, 1977.

Freud for Historians. New York: Oxford University Press, 1985.

Style in History. New York: Basic Books, 1974.

Gay and Lesbian History

See SEXUALITY.

Geertz, Clifford (b. 1926)

American cultural anthropologist of Java, Bali, and Morocco. Geertz received his Ph.D. from Harvard and has taught at Berkeley, Chicago, and the Institute for Advanced Study in Princeton. His historical work grows out of his central concern with the concept of culture. For him, culture is a system of symbols through which human beings give meaning to complex reality. It pervades all human conduct, including politics and the marketplace, rather than being a distinct domain, such as art or religion. Culture refers to patterned behavior and meaningful action and not to brute motion. Thus two instances of the same physiological movement may be distinguished at the level of cultural meaning: for instance a wink versus a tick.

In *Negara,* his study of state power in Bali, Geertz concentrates more on symbols and meanings than on the ways in which people use power to further their ambitions. In the introduction to this book he argues for a developmental approach to history. He studies patterns and processes as they unfold in time rather than arranging events and periods in their chronological sequence. In his view, ethnographic method is ideally suited to delineate the patterns of systems and processes that comprise the developmental approach.

His affinity for developmental studies more broadly reflects his hermeneutic or interpretative approach to social analysis. He is concerned more with meaningful action than with particular action as such. All human conduct is mediated or shaped by culture, and different cultures (including different historical periods) must be understood in relation to their own assumptions and not ours. Culture matters because all human beings orient their conduct to their perceptions of reality. Culture in this sense is not a distinct level of analysis, but an approach to all areas of human life from religion and science, through common sense and law, to the Moroccan market and the Balinese state. It encompasses not only ideas but also patterned ways of behaving and arranging material things.

It would be difficult to exaggerate Geertz's broad influence on the human sciences from literary studies and history to political theory and psychology. Within history, his work has been particularly influential among social historians.

Renato Rosaldo

Texts

After the Fact: Two Countries, Four Decades, One Anthropologist. Cambridge, MA: Harvard University Press, 1995.

"History and Anthropology." *New Literary History* 21 (1990): 321–335.

The Interpretation of Cultures: Selected Essays. London: Fontana, 1993.

Negara: The Theater State in Nineteenth-Century Bali. Princeton, NJ: Princeton University Press, 1980.

The Social History of an Indonesian Town. Cambridge, MA: MIT Press, 1961.

References

Burke, Peter. *History and Social Theory.* Cambridge, Eng.: Polity, 1992.

Geijer, Erik Gustaf (1783–1847)

Swedish historian, lyricist, and political activist. Geijer, one of Sweden's principal intellectual leaders in the early nineteenth century, was born in the small iron foundry community of Ransäter.

Educated at Uppsala University, he became a professor of history there in 1817 and established a place as one of its most popular and widely heard lecturers. Traditionally, it has long been argued that he was a conservative romantic until 1838, when he openly began to argue and support liberal views. More recent scholarship rejects this break-with-the-past interpretation, given his lifelong interest in social problems, especially among the rural poor. As a historian, Geijer is important for reviving scholarly interest, raising the quality of narrative, and insisting on high standards of scholarship. He was a historicist and romantic, and his works, such as *Svea rikes häfder* [Chronicles of the Swedish State] (1825) and three-volume *Svenska folkets historia* [A History of the Swedish People] (1832–1836), reflect his search for the threads of continuity in the past and his love of tradition and the common folk.

Byron J. Nordstrom

Texts

History of the Swedes. Trans. J.H. Turner. London: Whittaker & Company, 1845.

The Poor Laws in Their Bearing on Society: A Series of Political and Historical Essays. Stockholm: L.J. Hierta, 1840.

Svenska folkets historia. Stockholm: Norstedt, 1876.

Ur Erik Gustaf Geijers historiska föreläsningar [Selections from the Historical Lectures of Erik Gustaf Geijer]. Uppsala, Sweden: Lundequistska bokhandeln, 1947.

References

Algulin, Ingemar. *A History of Swedish Literature.* Stockholm: The Swedish Institute, 1989.

Scott, Franklin J. *Sweden: The Nation's History.* Carbondale: Southern Illinois University Press, 1988.

Gender

Initially referring to feminine and masculine forms within language, feminists have extended this term to refer also to socially learned behavior and expectations that distinguish between masculinity and femininity. While biological sex is identified by genetic and anatomical characteristics, socially learned gender is an acquired identity. We learn, through culturally and historically specific socialization, how to behave as women or men. This socialization can override biological sex identity, assigning genetically female bodies a masculine identity and vice versa. While the specific attributes of females and males may vary dramatically over time and across cultures, as well as by class, race, or other divisions, the relationship between females and males has frequently been defined in oppositional terms, with masculine traits receiving more value than feminine traits. Gender analysis thus reminds us that women and men are not independent categories; they are constructed in relation to each other and must be understood and analyzed with that in mind.

The second wave of feminist activism and scholarship, which emerged in the 1960s, gave little time to gender as a category of analysis. Feminist historians focused on the need to retrieve, validate, and make visible the experiences and the history of women. Whether trying to understand and improve women's position, or seeking to integrate women into the materialist and class analysis of the Marxist framework, this scholarship remained explicitly focused on women. A mushrooming literature testified to the complex, rich history of women from all walks of life. While disproportionately concerned with white middle-class women in Europe and North America, the history of women of other races and classes, and women in other parts of the world, began to be written as well. Meanwhile, journals and conferences devoted solely to women's history established its legitimacy, if not primacy, in the historical profession.

In the 1970s, some feminist scholars began to define the parameters of this exclusive focus on women. They argued that the intractable nature of women's subordination could not be understood without a better understanding of male–female relations and the sex/gender systems that defined and maintained the hierarchy of differences between women and men. However, while these differences were seen as socially constructed and historically specific, the biological definition of the bodies on which these differences were inscribed continued to be treated as a given. Gender was introduced to supplement sex, not to replace it.

These debates over gender and sex/gender systems had already begun to filter into historical practice. In 1976, for example, Natalie Zemon Davis's widely circulated call for historical analysis of both sexes rather than just women was published. While acknowledging the socially constructed nature of men and women, however, she questioned neither the biological definition of gendered bodies, nor the historical preference for empirical analysis. Her approach appealed to some historians, who saw it as a way to adopt a less provocative and more inclusive approach to the study of women and men. Others embraced the study of gender relations in institutions such as the family. More recently, historians like Linda Gordon and Ava Baron have offered insights into the underlying factors that construct and maintain gender inequities in key political, social, and economic institutions and relationships.

The search for more profound explanations of gender relations has led some historians to adopt a more explicitly theoretical approach to the history of gender. While some, like Judith Bennett, have drawn on radical feminist theories of patriarchy, others have sought to add gender to the Marxist or socialist feminist analysis of class and power. More recently, scholars such as Joan Scott have drawn on poststructuralist thinking about the relationship between language/discourse, power, and identity, to argue for an approach that pays attention to the way language and symbolic representations construct male and female identities, and the way these identities are used to signify relationships of power. The utility of this perspective continues to be a matter of heated debate. Some historians remain unconvinced, particularly in Britain and Europe. Others, such as Lynn Hunt and Thomas Laqueur, and historians interested in difference, race, and colonial/postcolonial history find some elements useful if combined with historical concern for specificity and change over time. Whatever the theoretical and methodological perspective, the central role of gender in women's (and men's) lives is no longer a matter of dispute.

Jane L. Parpart

See also ESSENTIALISM; FEMINISM; PATRIARCHY; POSTMODERNISM; SEXUALITY; WOMEN'S HISTORY.

Texts

Baron, Ava. "Gender and Labor History: Learning from the Past, Looking to the Future." In her *Work Engendered: Toward a New History of American Labor.* Ithaca, NY: Cornell University Press, 1991.

References

Bock, Gisela. "Women's History and Gender History: Aspects of an International Debate." *Gender and History* 1 (1989): 7–30.

Canning, Kathleen. "German Particularities in Women's History/Gender History." *Journal of Women's History* 5 (1993): 102–114.

Davis, Natalie Zemon. "'Women's History' in Transition: The European Case." *Feminist Studies* 3 (1976): 83–103.

Hunt, Nancy Rose. "Placing African Women's History and Locating Gender." *Social History* 14 (1989): 359–379.

Nicholson, Linda. "Interpreting Gender." *SIGNS* 20 (1994): 79–105.

Rose, Sonya. "Gender History/Women's History: Is Feminist Scholarship Losing Its Critical Edge?" *Journal of Women's History* 5 (1993): 89–101.

Scott, Joan W. *Gender and the Politics of History.* New York: Columbia University Press, 1988.

Genealogy

(1) The study of family descents, often expressed through pedigrees or family trees, and thereby an ancillary discipline to historical research; (2) a simple form of historical writing organizing the past according to dynastic lines of descent. Genealogy, or the recording and reconstruction of family ancestry (above definition 1), has always had a close relation with historical studies. The earliest forms of chronicles in the ancient near east (above definition 2) were essentially king-lists tracing the lineage of authority (sometimes back to a deity), and the historical sections of the Old Testament are of course a record of lines of descent. The Greeks, too, paid attention to descent, usually from a god or demigod: Homeric heroes frequently refer to their genealogies, and about 500 B.C. Hecataeus of Miletus declared a family tree going back sixteen generations; the famous tombstone of Heropythos of Chios (mid-fifth century B.C.) lists his progenitors back through fourteen generations. Among the most complete early genealogies is that of the Philaid line, mentioned in Thucydides, though it, too, includes legendary as well as historical ancestors, a general problem with early genealogies that occasioned great suspicion of their reliability among some later ancient historians such as Polybius.

In non-Western cultures, oral tradition has sometimes been used to memorialize the genealogies of particular families, while elsewhere such records of ancestry have been committed to writing, albeit in a different format than in Europe. The genealogies compiled by the inhabitants of precolonial Sulawesi, for instance, were intended principally for the purposes of marriage alliances. The *Purāṇas* of early India were constructed, first by poets and bards, then by the priestly *brāhmaṇas,* to legitimize various Indian dynasties and record their rulers, as for instance in the *Viṣṇu Purāṇa,* which was composed in the mid-first millennium A.D. The Incas, whose ancestral myths are now known to us principally through the work of sixteenth-century Europeans, combined memorized traditions with the keeping of numerical records in the form of knotted cords or *quipus.*

A concern for the preservation and transmission of genealogical records has been a hallmark of highly stratified, hierarchical societies in which personal status is determined by paternal or maternal descent. On the other hand, challenges to that stratification can also produce genealogical interest. The so-called pedigree craze in late sixteenth-century England may be seen, for example, as a direct consequence of the increased social mobility of the mid-1500s, and of the rapid rise of new families into the gentry or even the peerage—the newer the family, often the keener its members were to establish a glorious ancestry, or at the least a long-standing residency in their counties. Late medieval and Renaissance Italian families, to give another example, paid careful attention to recording not only descents but other details of family members in private records known as *ricordanze*. Record-keeping practices could vary widely within particular societies at a particular time, and most early genealogical records in the West emphasize male rather than female descent. In most European cultures female names have tended to disappear from the genealogical record, though they are often preserved in the form of memories and oral traditions. There is considerable evidence of this, for instance, in early modern England, where genealogy was traced almost exclusively through male descent (with women appearing not in their own right but only as they married into the male line) but where women appear to have commemorated the past privately and informally, paying greater attention to their female ancestors. It is important to recognize that the patrilineal quality of Western genealogy is not universally practiced. In some Asian areas, indeed, patrilineal genealogies were the exception rather than the rule. In general, the Sulawesi genealogies mentioned above recorded the transmission of status through the female line.

As a tool or ancillary discipline in aid of historical research, genealogy came into its own during the early modern era. In Britain, for example, heralds and antiquaries studied the descents of particular noble and gentle families intensively, while registration of pedigrees (the characteristic tree-shaped chart giving descents and often dates of birth and marriage) were required to be submitted to the heralds, as agents of the College of Arms, to ensure that those claiming gentility had legitimate title to such honor. In more rigidly stratified parts of Europe, for instance Venice (the most socially exclusive of the Italian aristocracies, which kept a "Golden Book" listing those families included in the patriciate), France, and Spain, genealogy was used in a negative way to maintain the integrity of the nobility. Offices analogous to the English College of Arms evolved in other countries, though the English system of visitations appears to have been unique in its systematic approach to the inspection of genealogical evidence. The use of genealogy as a social tool is, again, far from being an exclusively European phenomenon: in colonial and postcolonial societies, genealogy can often provide a link between an individual and his or her remote ancestors in the parent country. The Mormon Church, for instance, maintains an extensive "International Genealogical Index," originally conceived of as an aid to the church's adherents, but containing an extraordinarily rich collection of information useful to amateur and professional genealogists.

Because its principles are relatively easy to grasp, in comparison with epigraphy or paleography, genealogy has acquired a popular status that eludes most other parahistorical disciplines. Local archives throughout Europe and North America, because they hold family and official records (such as English parish records, or modern British and American census data) are frequently visited by persons wishing either to trace a particular ancestor's life, or to construct a family tree. But the same records have become increasingly indispensable to a number of varieties of academic historiography. Scholars in the heraldic tradition, such as Sir Anthony Wagner, have continued to hone genealogy into a useful and semiscientific tool. Meanwhile, social history, which in recent years has focused increasingly on local studies (for example in "microhistory," or in the "family reconstitution" work of the Cambridge Group for the History of Population and Social Structure) has availed itself of both the records and the tools of the genealogists' trade, and have thereby gone some distance toward a reintegration of genealogy into history proper. Cultural historians have reaped similar benefits: manuals of heraldry and records of descent can be used, for example, by historians of the book and of readership to trace the provenance and ownership of personal libraries.

D.R. Woolf

See also BUGIS AND MAKASSAR (IN SULAWESI) HISTORIOGRAPHY; FAMILY RECONSTITUTION; LOCAL HISTORY; MICROHISTORY; SOCIAL HISTORY.

References

Bizzocchi, Roberto. *Genealogie incredibili* [Incredible Genealogies]. Bologna, Italy: Società editrice il Mulino, 1995.

Brown, Donald. *Hierarchy, History, and Human Nature: The Social Origins of Historical Consciousness*. Tucson: University of Arizona Press, 1988.

Fox-Davies, Arthur Charles. *A Complete Guide to Heraldry*. London: Bracken Books, 1993.

Hamilton-Edwards, G. *In Search of Ancestry*. Chichester, England: Phillimore, 1974.

Hey, David, ed. *The Oxford Companion to Local and Family History*. Oxford, Eng.: Oxford University Press, 1996.

Kent, F.W. *Household and Lineage in Renaissance Florence*. Princeton, NJ: Princeton University Press, 1977.

Round, J.H. *Family Origins and Other Studies*. London: Constable, 1930.

Thapar, Romila. "Genealogical Patterns As Perceptions of the Past." *Studies in History* 7 (1991): 1–36.

Thomas, Rosalind. *Oral Tradition and Written Record in Classical Athens*. Cambridge, Eng.: Cambridge University Press, 1989, 155–195.

Urton, Gary. *The History of a Myth: Pacariqtambo and the Origin of the Inkas*. Austin: University of Texas Press, 1990.

Wagner, Anthony. *English Genealogy*. Second ed. Oxford: Clarendon Press, 1972.

Genovese, Eugene D. (b. 1930)

American Marxist historian of the United States. Born in Brooklyn, Genovese earned his B.A. from Brooklyn College (1953), where he became intrigued by Southern history while studying with Arthur C. Cole, and his M.A. and Ph.D. (1959) from Columbia University. Genovese taught at Polytechnic Institute of Brooklyn (1958–1963), Rutgers University (1963–1967), Sir George Williams University (1967–1969), and the University of Rochester (1969–1990). Since 1990 he has served as distinguished scholar in residence at the University Center in Georgia. A leading historian of the Old South, Genovese's works have appeared in five languages. Writing from a Marxist perspective, Genovese defined slaveholders as a prebourgeois class and examined comparative slavery in *The Political Economy of Slavery* (1965), *In Red and Black* (1968), and *The World the Slaveholders Made* (1969). In *Roll, Jordan, Roll* (1974), Genovese identified planter paternalism, black cultural expression, and resistance as central to the slave experience. In *From Rebellion to Revolution* (1979) he explained the shift in slave uprisings in the Americas "from attempts to secure freedom from slavery to attempts to overthrow slavery as a social system." Genovese underscored the tensions between slavery and bourgeois property in *Fruits of Merchant Capital* (1983) (with Elizabeth Fox-Genovese). Genovese's current research focuses on the cultural and intellectual lives of the master class, 1790–1861, a topic he introduced in *The Slaveholders' Dilemma* (1992).

John David Smith

Texts

From Rebellion to Revolution: Afro-American Slave Revolts in the Making of the Modern World. Baton Rouge: Lousiana University Press, 1979.

The Fruits of Merchant Capital: Slavery and Bourgeois Property in the Rise and Expansion of Capitalism. Oxford, Eng.: Oxford University Press, 1983.

In Red and Black: Marxian Explorations in Southern and Afro-American History. New York: Pantheon, 1971.

The Political Economy of Slavery. New York: Pantheon, 1965.

Roll, Jordan, Roll. New York: Pantheon, 1974.

The Slaveholders' Dilemma: Freedom and Progress in Southern Conservative Thought, 1820–1860. Columbia: University of South Carolina Press, 1992.

The World the Slaveholders Made. New York: Pantheon, 1969.

References

Meier, August, and Elliott Rudwick. *Black History and the Historical Profession, 1915–1980*. Urbana: University of Illinois Press, 1986.

Parish, Peter J. *Slavery: History and Historians*. New York: Harper & Row, 1989.

Roper, John Herbert. "Marxing through Georgia: Eugene Genovese and Radical Historiography for the Region." *Georgia Historical Quarterly* 80 (1996): 77–92.

Surowiecki, James. "Genovese's March." *Lingua Franca* 7 (December/January 1997): 36–52.

Gentry Controversy

Debate in English historiography, principally held in the 1950s and 1960s, concerning the wealth of the early modern gentry and its implications for political and social history, especially the English civil wars, 1642 to 1660. The controversy, often referred to as the "storm over the gentry," centers in the alleged rise of the gentry (in English society, the elite rank immediately below the titled peerage) during the period 1540 to 1640. At issue was a social explanation of the English civil wars (or English Revolution as it was then often called). R.H. Tawney had explained the revolution by positing a shift in the balance of landownership and power caused by class dispositions toward estate management, inflation, new agricultural technology, and wealth disbursed by the court to the new predatory middling class of gentry. Lawrence Stone gave the controversy impetus in his study of the debt crisis of the aristocracy. H.R. Trevor-Roper then anatomized Stone's statistical methods and handling of documents, causing Stone to retreat on some fronts while refining an argument based on the counting of manors (units of property held by the land-owning classes). Trevor-Roper enlarged his attack, arguing that the "mere" gentry living on small estates were indeed declining while a minority of others who had tapped the largesse of the crown were prospering. J.P. Cooper weighed in with a detailed examination of the statistical problems involved in counting manors as an index of social and political change. The American historian J.H. Hexter declared war on all parties, arguing that the "storm over the gentry" was a misplaced attempt to revive the Marxist theory of the transition from feudalism to capitalism in which the agents were the rising gentry rather than urban elites. According to Hexter, this theory sold at a discount the great religious and political struggles of the age. On another front, the medievalist J.S. Roskell pleaded that the chronology was errant, as the gentry had risen to prominence in the Commons in the later medieval parliaments.

In the 1960s historians began to study in detail, and from new archival evidence, local patterns of landownership, office holding, agrarian improvement, and the distribution of wealth. As their work took hold the controversy played out because they had established new data on key points: (1) upward mobility in rural society had been steady over four centuries and had accelerated as land-labor dynamics altered in the period spanning the Black Death and the Dissolution of the Monasteries; (2) court gentry did in fact get some favorable leases and grants from the crown, often working with London syndicates, but most lands went at market prices; (3) the gentry were a tiny part of society, varying above and below 1 percent of the whole adult male population of England; (4) postmortems and subsidy assessments showed aggregate wealth among knights, esquires, and gentlemen was very uneven and did not coordinate with trends in their religious and political loyalties; (5) the gentry owned a smaller share of the wealth of their communities than they did of the landed wealth; (6) gentry religion and politics

were best understood in terms of local dynamics and magnate affinities; and, finally, (7) gentry sons at all levels were crowding into Cambridge, Oxford, and the Inns of Court as education became crucial to success in service to the crown at all levels.

Arthur J. Slavin

References

Coleman, D.C. "The Gentry Controversy and the Aristocracy in Crisis, 1558–1641." *History* 51 (1966): 165–178.

Cooper, J.P. "The Counting of Manors," *Economic History Review,* Second Series 8 (1956): 377–389.

Cornwall, J. "English Population in the Sixteenth Century." *Economic History Review,* Second Series 23 (1970): 32–44.

Hexter, J.H. "The Storm over the Gentry." In his *Reappraisals in History.* Second ed. Chicago: University of Chicago Press, 1979.

Prest, W. "The Legal Education of the Gentry at the Inns of Court, 1540–1640." *Past and Present* 38 (1967): 20–39.

Stone, Lawrence. "The Anatomy of the Elizabethan Aristocracy." *Economic History Review* 18 (1948): 1–41.

Tawney, R.H. "The Rise of the Gentry, 1558–1640." *Economic History Review* 11 (1941): 1–38.

Trevor-Roper, H.R. "The Elizabethan Aristocracy: An Anatomy Anatomised." *Economic History Review,* Second Series 3 (1951): 279–298.

———. *The Gentry, 1540–1640.* London: Cambridge University Press for the Economic History Society, 1953.

Geoffrey of Monmouth (ca. 1100–1155)

Medieval monk and author of a largely fictional, but highly influential, history of ancient Britain. Geoffrey's precise origins are unknown, but he may have been born in Brittany and moved as a child to Wales. As a churchman, Geoffrey was prior of Monmouth Abbey; Augustinian canon at St. George's, Oxford; and finally, bishop of St. Asaph, Wales. Geoffrey's *Prophecies of Merlin* purports to be Merlin's collected prophecies but most are probably Geoffrey's invention and were later incorporated into his *History.* They were consulted as serious prophecies for centuries. The *Historia Regum Britanniae* [History of the Kings of Britain] (1135) is primarily secular, relating the rise and fall of the British from their legendary king, Brutus, to Cadwallader. It includes much Arthurian material.

Geoffrey claimed that he was translating an old British book, but he seems to have invented much, perhaps as deliberate parody of contemporary history and society. The most popular and influential history of the twelfth century, Geoffrey's work challenged the insular notions of contemporary historians, who had stressed Anglo-Saxon dominance. Its truthfulness was contested by contemporary historians, among them William of Newburgh, and by later foreign humanist scholars such as Polydore Vergil, but it continued to be generally accepted and often vigorously defended, especially in Wales, until near the end of the sixteenth century.

Maura K. Lafferty

Texts

The History of the Kings of Britain. Trans. Lewis
     Thorpe. Harmondsworth, Eng.: Penguin,
     1966.

References

Hanning, Robert W. *The Vision of History in
     Early Britain.* New York: Columbia University Press, 1966, 121–169.
Leckie, R. William Jr. *The Passage of Dominion:
     Geoffrey of Monmouth and the Periodization
     of Insular History in the Twelfth Century.*
     Toronto: University of Toronto Press, 1981.
Taylor, Rupert. *The Political Prophecy in England.*
     New York: Columbia University Press, 1911.

Geography—Historical

The study of the interactions of people, environments, and locations in the past. With distant origins in the writings of classical authorities (Strabo and Hippocrates), Enlightenment scholars (Alexander von Humboldt and Carl Ritter), and modern historians in the effervescence of European geographical scholarship between 1870 and 1920, historical geography has accented two perspectives—the environmental and the locational—and four thematic lines of enquiry: (1) environment as constraint; (2) environmental malleability; (3) locational geopolitics; and (4) regional identity. The first pair of these may be traced to the German geographer Friedrich Ratzel, the second pair to the British geographer and politician Halford Mackinder.

Historical geography's dual environmental perspectives have their roots in the writings of Ratzel (1844–1904). Making liberal use of historical evidence, Ratzel delineated three themes for geographical research: (1) environmental constraints on human affairs; (2) humanity's capacity for transforming environments and landscapes; and (3) the mobility of people and ideas. Unfortunately the scope of Ratzel's ideas was diminished by the monocausal environmental determinism of his foremost American disciple, Ellen Churchill Semple. Semple's most famous work, *American History and Its Geographic Conditions* (1903), papered over ambiguities in the American past with formulaic pronouncements on nature's power, e.g., in blocking western expansion with the Appalachians or causing great cities to arise on the fall line.

In response to these excesses, environmentalism took a new turn when the French geographer Paul Vidal de la Blache presented the alternative of "possibilism." In this more supple version of nature–society relations, Vidal maintained that the power of environmental constraints depended less on nature than on cultural values and the technical sophistication of livelihood systems. As American historical geographers adopted Vidal's position, Semple's determinism soon gave way. In the 1920s, Harlin Barrows and Carl Sauer spoke respectively of humanity's long history of adjustment to nature's vicissitudes and, more radically, of human agency and culture as the dynamic elements in landscape transformation. Vidal's possibilism also proved attractive to his colleagues, the French historians Marc Bloch and Lucien Febvre, who regarded *géohistoire* as the keystone for the social and economic histories of their Annales school.

Running alongside environmentalism, however, was a rather different perspective on historical geography, one that accented location (space), region, and place and that emerged most clearly in the geopolitics of Halford Mackinder (1861–1947). Mackinder's justly famous "heartland" thesis premised a macroscale geopolitics on location, region, state formation, and evolution. Rejecting Ratzel's organismic theory of the state (and of *lebensraum*), Mackinder's locational theory depicted a tripartite geography of Eurasian power relations in which interior continental regimes (the heartland) and peripheral maritime locations contested over the "geographical pivot" (eastern Europe) of history. When, after 1914, events tended to affirm Mackinder's thesis, his historical geography was pressed into service, first by Allied diplomats charged with redrafting the map of Europe along historical–geographical lines, and second by scholars interested in reconstructing the key role of core regions in the rise of European nation-states (historical geographers Derwent Whittlesey and Norman Pounds), exploring the contentious intranational divisions between maritime- and land-based regional regimes (historian Edward Fox), and, eventually, formulating macrogeographic interpretations of imperialism (historical geographer Donald Meinig) and the world system (sociologist Immanuel Wallerstein).

From geopolitics it was but a short step to a second line of locational enquiry dealing with the constituents of Mackinder's thesis—the historical geographies of regions and nations. In this endeavor, one of Germany's leading geographers, Alfred Hettner, took the lead. Having been affiliated with Max Weber's multidisciplinary research project *(Outlines of Social Economics),* Hettner's definition of geography as the description of area and the identification of regional character afforded historical processes an ample role—a role that was all but eliminated by his American disciple Richard Hartshorne who favored ahistorical regional descriptions frozen in time (usually the present). In consequence, when in the 1940s and 1950s, American regional geographers invoked history—as they almost invariably did—they felt an abiding sense of guilt that lasted until the 1960s when Andrew Clark effected a rapprochement of historical and geographical analyses.

These four lines of historical–geographical research were further differentiated during and after the interwar years. The environmentalists, having abandoned Semple's determinism, consolidated around Sauer and the Berkeley school of cultural–historical geography and Bloch and Febvre's Annales school of *géohistoire.* These two schools shared an inclusivist mode of enquiry, and little else. Sauer's agenda (and his students') focused on the power of human agency in changing the face of the earth, embraced all of human time, deployed the perspectives of anthropology, archaeology, and history; and delineated certain enduring themes: agricultural origins and diffusion; livelihood evolution and landscape change; and the effects of pre-Columbian demography and the European encounter of the New World. The Annales school, meanwhile, nurtured the alternative view of environmental constraint. Particularly in the works of Fernand Braudel, these constraints constituted a deep history conferring upon regions a unity and coherence that endured over the *longue dureé* of structural time, seldom to be effaced by episodic events or cycles of events.

Simultaneously, proponents of the regional-locational perspective pursued two lines of inquiry: (1) the geopolitics of Whittlesey, Pounds, Fox, Meinig, and Wallerstein; and (2) the socioeconomic regional geographies of Andrew Clark and H.C. Darby and their prolific students. Both blurred the lines between historical geography and its cognate disciplines, the former with historical social science, the latter with historians specializing in particular regions and nations—a blurring that has continued with historical geography's recent accommodation of structurationism, humanism, Marxism, and deconstruction.

In sum, historical geography in the 1990s reflects a legacy of multidisciplinary scholarship embracing the effects of environmental constraints, human agency, geopolitics, and regional identity on the interactions of people, environments, and locations over all of human time.

Carville Earle

See also ANNALES SCHOOL; ATLASES—HISTORICAL; ENVIRONMENTAL HISTORY—WORLD; WORLD HISTORY.

References

Earle, Carville, et al. "Historical Geography." In *Geography in America,* ed. Gaile, Gary L. and Cort J. Willmott. Columbus, Ohio: Merrill Publishing, 1989, 156–191.

Martin, Geoffrey J., and Preston E. James. *All Possible Worlds: A History of Geographical Ideas,* Third ed. New York: John Wiley, 1993.

Gerald of Wales [Giraldus Cambrensis, Gerald De Barri] (1146–1223)

Medieval Latin historian, naturalist, and ethnographer of the British Isles. Gerald, of Welsh and Norman heritage, was born in Wales. He studied law in Paris and entered royal service during the conquest of Wales and Ireland by the Angevin monarchs of England. In 1198, he launched an ecclesiastical career as archdeacon of Brecon, yet failed to achieve the bishopric of St. David's. In 1203, he retired to a scholarly community gathered at Lincoln. There he wrote prolifically, making multiple recensions both of new works and of works originally composed in royal and ecclesiastical service. Both the patronage that he received and the official rewards to which he aspired drove Gerald's output in all three phases of his career. His earliest works, written in royal service, have remained popular and influential (although controversial) for eight hundred years, having been repeatedly epitomized or translated into English and Welsh: *Topographia Hiberniae* [The Topography of Ireland] (1187 to 1188), *Expugnatio Hibernica* [The Conquest of Ireland] (1188), *Itinerarium Kambriae* [A Journey through Wales] (1191), and *Descriptio Kambriae* [The Description of Wales] (1194) describe the

G

"primitive" Celtic cultures of the British Isles with a view toward facilitating the Angevin royal conquest.

Felice Lifshitz

Texts

The History and Topography of Ireland. Trans. John J. O'Meara. Atlantic Highlands, NJ: Humanities 1982.

The Journey through Wales and the Description of Wales. Trans. L. Thorpe. Harmondsworth: Penguin, 1978.

The Life of St. Hugh of Avalon, Bishop of Lincoln 1186–1200. Ed. and trans. Richard M. Loomis. New York: Garland, 1985.

References

Bartlett, Robert. *Gerald of Wales.* Oxford: Clarendon Press, 1982.

Richter, Michael. *Giraldus Cambrensis: The Growth of the Welsh Nation.* Revised ed. Aberystwyth: National Library of Wales, 1976.

German Historical Thought, 1500 to Present

Philosophical thought and writing about history by German-speaking authors.

I. The Reformation and Seventeenth Century

At the dawn of the German Reformation, three forms of historical narrative existed—the local and regional chronicle, the world chronicle, and church history. The northern German historians in 1500, influenced by Italian humanists and especially by the Dutch humanist Erasmus, brought new critical tools to the fashioning of these narrative forms—source criticism, philology, and interpretation. Johannes Naucler's *Chronicon* (1516) is an example of this new scholarship at work within the older tradition of the world chronicle. German historians exercised the new critical history primarily in the search for the origins of their national identity, a project in almost every northern European nation in 1500. Conrad Celtis (1459–1508) edited Tacitus's *Germania* in 1500, a step in determining an accurate German past. Jakob Wimpheling (1450–1528), Johannes Aventinus (1477–1534), and Heinrich Bebel (1472–1518) brought a passion to the search for a Germanic past, which was balanced by the more careful scholarship of Beatus Rhenanus (1485–1547). The former scholars accepted any mythic or legendary material favorable to the nobility of Germanic origins—for example, the account in

the Pseudo-Berosus of Tuisco, a son of Noah, who was reputed to have founded the German nation. Rhenanus based his facts primarily upon Tacitus, bringing out separate editions of his works in 1519, 1533, and 1544.

Rhenanus brought to historical thought a notion of cultural change over time that would be seminal for the historicism of later German historiography. His investigations into the migration of Germanic tribes led him to the realization that a "people" can disappear as well as emerge over the course of centuries. This sense of change in time helped Rhenanus maintain a cosmopolitan balance in relation to the search for nation. The German past was a question of "antiquity" for him, not an issue of the present. This set Rhenanus apart from his fellow German humanists, for whom the German past was a living thread for their immediate identity. This difference in conception—whether the past is a "dead object" or part of the flux of the present—recurs throughout German historical thought from Rhenanus to the contemporary age. Most recently, Jürgen Habermas has stressed the temporal and rational boundary between the present and the past in his debate with Hans-Georg Gadamer, for whom the past continues as an essential dimension of one's existence. The majority of German thinkers since 1500 have favored a notion that the past is an integral, "alive" presence in one's contemporary experience—a cultural conception that differs from the empiricist perspective of English and French historical thought.

Ulrich von Hutten (1488–1523) and Martin Luther (1483–1546) brought to the historical thought of their time a view of the singular moment in which individuals affect the course of history. The complexity, singularity, and effectiveness of human intentions in history became with these men a hallmark of German historical thought until the present. Hutten's dialogue *Arminius* was based upon Tacitus's story of the Germanic hero's conflict with the Romans. Many commentators believe Hutten saw the Emperor Maximilian as a potential Arminius of his time in relation to the Roman Church. Luther shared with the majority of German humanists the view that the past was not dead, rather that it had to be seen as a pragmatic link with the present. He held that the "hero" in history penetrated to the hidden significance that was God's plan, using the knowledge of past and present to effect change for the better.

Luther's historical methodology was on a par with that of the best northern humanists. He used source criticism and stressed the empirical facts of particular situations to support the notion of institutional change in his church history. Luther, in fact, is paradigmatic of German historical thought in every characteristic salient since his lifetime. His notion of a hidden authority in history whose purpose was within each human event, but required interpretation by the historical agent (as well as by the historical commentator) is replicated even among secular historians, and can be identified in the philosophical and social-psychological interests of contemporary German historical thinkers. German historical thought differs from other European models in its stress on an overarching "formal cause" (an Aristotelian concept), whose pattern informs the particular event and whose manifestation can be found in each particular moment. Luther typifies the German historical thinker in his philological precision and general interest in manifestations of language and its artifacts, his focus upon human motivation and intention, his sense of cultural change, his premise that each event is wholly singular in its character (even when it is a manifestation of an idea or principle), and his belief that history is a living dimension of contemporary thought. Luther's historical judgment also carried a sense of "necessary truth." His church history was programmatic in its implications: it was intended for institutional change, and its historical artistry lay in the power of the syntheses. This is a characteristic of subsequent German histories where even the "neutral" vision of *wie es eigentlich gewesen* [the past as it essentially/actually happened] imparts in the *eigentlich* a division of truth from falsehood, and suggests the principles that necessarily have led to this state of affairs. Luther would prove to be typical as well in that he was not chiefly a historian, for in Germany nonhistorians have contributed many of the major ideas that have shaped historical thought.

The seventeenth century brought the next major augmentation in German historical thought with the emerging concept of natural law. The Dutch humanist, Hugo Grotius (1583–1645), was to be as influential upon German thinkers in the 1600s as his compatriot Erasmus had been at the inception of the Reformation. Grotius's *De Jure Belli ac Pacis* [Of the Law of War and Peace] (1625) grounded the historical thinking of Gottfried Wilhelm Leibniz (1646–1716) and Samuel Pufendorf (1632–1694) in contrasting ways within natural law principles. Leibniz focused upon the principles of human nature, which underpinned any comprehension of human events. In *Codex Iuris Gentium* (1693) he wrote that there are two rules for writing histories that expressed, respectively, the public and the private dimensions of

being human. Leibniz's attention to public records for the former history established precedents for archival research; his arguments for the significance of personal motivation in historical judgments raised anecdote, letter, and memoir to a legitimate dimension of historical narrative. Leibniz provided a logical basis for a historicist view of history by viewing historical events as a form of calculus initiated by God. Change in the historical order is constant, but can be conceived as an incremental continuity.

Pufendorf provided a counterweight to continuity thinking in his extrapolation of natural law. Changes within and between generations in the historical experience of nations could be analyzed according to natural causal categories: there were "permanent" factors of geography, resources, and popular disposition, and "transitory" factors of the changing situation and strength of neighbor, particularly measured by the actual authority and policies of their rulers. However, each generation had no necessary connection to the experience of the preceding one. Pufendorf thus sketched the program for later German historicism that recognized cultural relativity, but eschewed the teleological principles that assured the incremental continuity.

Pufendorf was more secular in determining the principles of historical cause than Leibniz. Historical cause for Leibniz was the historical agent moved by divine imperatives that were subjectively experienced—the individual moral conscience in its exercise of "right reason." The guiding aegis for Pufendorf was "reason of state." His *Constitution of the German Empire* (1667) placed national history in the service of political doctrine.

II. The Enlightenment

The century that followed—the Enlightenment—evidenced an increasing tension between the aristocratic authorities and the middle classes who sought, under the aegis of law, changes in the political and economic structure. As capitalistic forms of economy emerged, the industrial revolution began and republican ideas were disseminated, German thinkers from the middle classes contributed new philosophical schemas and a new form of narrative to historical thought. Justus Möser's (1720–1794) *History of Osnabrück* (1768) was introduced by a short essay that divided previous German history into four periods that differed in their political, social, legal, and economic bases. The form of the essay was what Nietzsche would later call "critical history"—it compared and contrasted events within the framework of an interpretative idea. A strong subtext was the dispossession of the common classes from their original rights and authority. Historical narratives before this work lacked the consistent and coherent counterpoint of argument and evidence. Gotthold Ephraim Lessing's (1729–1781) *Education of the Human Race* (1780) created the schema of historical "progress" in its account of the development of human moral consciousness. The schema of progress in law appeared in Immanuel Kant's (1724–1804) *Idea for a Universal History from a Cosmopolitan Point of View* (1784). Kant did not see progress as inevitable, however. He challenged Leibniz's notion of the continuity in natural history; in human history he saw the presence of "pathological" choice as a hallmark of regressive cultural periods.

Jean-Jacques Rousseau's publication of *Emile* in 1762 and the republication of Leibniz's *New Essays* in 1768 profoundly influenced German historical and literary thought: the closing decades of the eighteenth century and the initial decade of the nineteenth witnessed a clearer focus upon individual differences among persons and nations, and the idea of stages of maturation in cultural as well as personal development. Johann Gottfried Herder (1744–1803) coined the concept of *Einfühlung* (empathy), which was to be brought into historical interpretation, and the notion of differing *Volkgeister* (national spirits) and their developmental maturation according to a genetic principle of stages of human life. Most important, perhaps, is Herder's seminal introduction of the notion of dialectical relationships between events that generate this development, a notion to be perfected in the next century by the Hegelians. The most comprehensive example of Herder's historical thought is *Ideas for the Philosophy of the History of Mankind* (1784–1791). Johann Wolfgang von Goethe (1749–1832) in his essay *Winckelmann und sein Jahrhundert* [Winckelmann and His Century] (1805), and the appendix outline to his translation of Benevenuto Cellini's *Autobiography* (1795–1798), brought this individualizing perspective into the relationship between persons and their cultural milieu. Goethe's biographical studies initiated a form of critical history in which the development of the personality was understood against the cultural generation that nourished it.

Johann Gottlieb Fichte (1762–1814), Friedrich Wilhelm Joseph Schelling (1775–1854), and Georg Wilhelm Friedrich Hegel (1770–1831) developed more systematically and with greater specificity the historicist principles of Leibniz, Herder, Lessing, and Kant. History for these German idealists was a continuum of stages and periods of the absolute spirit (God). Each phase was separate and distinct, yet dialectically related. An individual brought forward the past into the present as a living continuity through an act of reasoned will. An inner logic lay within the individual and behind interpersonal events; this logic imparted an a priori order that guided events in time. To find accord with this order made one a moral cocreator of this necessary reality. One spirit permeated the arts, sciences, and other cultural processes and products of age. The German idealists began the study of cultural expressions such as myth, religion, and the art of particular ages in order to demonstrate the notion of a cultural totality.

The greatest difference between German idealist thought and the Enlightenment thinking of Lessing, Herder, and Kant lay in the experience of the French Revolution and Napoleon, which brought the import of the political nation more saliently into historical judgment. Fichte's "Addresses to the German Nation" (1807–1808) typified this political–philosophical historiography: freedom was the final and formal cause of history. But freedom was not solely an individual matter; true freedom was realized only when the individual was able to find an integration of personal will and the will of the nation. This congruence of the individual and the nation reflected a break to some degree with natural law principles as the basis for comprehending the individual in history. Enlightenment thinkers had sought anthropological evidence to define the discrete human being, the consequence of which was to give the individual priority over the social contract, which was but a contingent ramification of these separate individual wills. Fichte, Schelling, and Hegel saw society existing as a corporate being chronologically prior to any social contract, and existing also prior to discrete individuality. The state was an ethical principle in itself that necessarily subsumed individuals. Historical laws were to be found only in the qualitative particularity of events among nations. Each nation had its ethnologically distinct spirit and its singular destiny.

III. The Advent of Historicism

The teleological continuity of the German idealists was countered in the same generation by the "historism" (as the German form of historicism is often called) of Wilhelm von Humboldt (1767–1835). As with the historicizing idealists, history was to be studied through the particular enactments of individuals; however, the unique individuality of each person and event disallowed establishing the totalities that permitted one to speak of progressive continuums. History was irrational; in order to comprehend the singularity of history one must bring broad learning and accurate empathy, or *Verstehen,* to one's study of human relationships. Although natural law principles existed as an ideal background of cause in history, the necessity of temporal–spatial contingency qualified their application. The Roman historian, B.G. Niebuhr (1776–1831), and the jurist who began the Historical School of Law, Friedrich Karl von Savigny (1779–1861), shared with Humboldt the historicism that held each past age and culture to be unique, developing from the heterogeneity of its people and their folkways with no necessary relation or inherent teleology toward the present. For each of these thinkers, the influence of past culture lived on within the inherited customs and norms that persisted over ages. Yet, there was no compelling truth in the persistence of past culture. Historical understanding made it possible to modify, even to discontinue the force of this heritage through a critical understanding both of it and of one's present cultural needs. Niebuhr and Savigny rejected the use of natural law principles in comprehending historical actuality. Emphasis upon accurate sources and textual analysis enabled the historian or jurist to determine sequences and influences of historical cause that were rooted in the ethnological singularity of a culture.

Leopold von Ranke (1795–1886) was educated within the "historism" of Niebuhr and Savigny. To write history *wie es eigentlich gewesen* is to allow the events of a historical milieu to signal the character of that milieu without the interjection of the historian's cultural values. This tempered the German propensity to use the past as a helpmate for guiding the present. Ranke did recognize an implicit, tranquil progress in history within "dominant trends" that could be identified, and, thereby, a "continuity." Ranke reflected the attention given to the power of the nation-state by the other historians of his generation in his focus upon political and diplomatic records as the best source of historical reality. The influence of his "objective" thoroughness persisted well into the twentieth century in Western historical scholarship.

Ranke's identification with the conservative authorities of Prussia in the post-Napoleonic years may be seen as a contributing factor in his nonjudgmental history. The liberal, bourgeois historians, exemplified by Johann Gustav Droysen (1808–1884), were less satisfied with their historical position in the pre- and post-1848 years of aristocratic restoration, and they viewed historical science as an instrument for cultural change. Values were central to historical judgment because they enabled the historical interpreter to see which events in the past supported historical progress. Droysen's *Outline of the Principles of History* (1858) is his thorough exposition of these ideas. One of the central lines of historical–cultural development for Droysen and the other German liberal historians was that of constitutional law. Yet, the German liberal historians' stress upon the executive and military authority of the ruler distinguished their constitutionalism from the English tradition of Locke, Burke, and Mill. Droysen, the founder of the Prussian school of historians, supported the Prussian state as a necessary channel for a *Rechtsstaat,* a state based on law. His belief that only a strong leader and a powerful state can generate historical progress is reflected in his early works *History of Alexander the Great* (1833) and the two-volume *History of Hellenism* (1836–1843), as well as his unfinished *History of Prussian Politics,* begun in 1855.

Karl Marx (1818–1883) was an exception to pre- and post-1848 German historical thought in his location of historical agency within social classes rather than the state. The young Marx was influenced by the Hegelian notion of the human spirit developing its potential in history through a dialectical interplay of opposing ideas. Marx relocated the source of this historical movement from the absolute spirit to the elements of human nature. The economic plane of daily survival, together with its attendant technologies and divisions of labor, was in particular viewed as the channel and source of historical cause and effect. Marx's ontological definition of the human being as a "work animal" brought a reformulated natural law foundation into a historicist framework, one that encouraged research in the new social sciences to support its theses. Culture was the outcome of meeting ontological needs, and thus the foundation for an improved development of human potential. Yet, the cultural systems could in themselves alienate their members from that potential if these systems no longer proved adequate for species maturation. The science of history was the most significant science because it tracked and examined the changes in the material systems of culture. In the *German Ideology* (1846) Marx first clarified this process of human self-alienation within historical forms of culture. In *The Class Struggles in France 1848–1850* and *The Eighteenth of Brumaire of Louis Bonaparte,*

G

Marx wrote the critical history of a particular set of events that illustrated his theses.

Jacob Burckhardt (1818–1897), who came to maturity in the same generation as Droysen and Marx, also viewed historical science as a method for changing the existing culture. Burckhardt conceived history morphologically—the birth, development, and death of historical values and norms. A rebirth of these values was possible in a creative culture, but only through a radical transformation of existing institutions. Burckhardt employed a paradigm of historism to challenge the historicist sense of linear or dialectical progress over generations. Recognition of the morphological diversity of historical periods taught the present that change in cultural direction was possible. His historical works focused upon ages that exemplified cultural renewal—*The Time of Constantine the Great* (1853) and *The Civilization of the Renaissance in Italy* (1860).

The increasing conflict between the aristocratic, republican, democratic, and socialistic orientations to culture in the closing decades of the nineteenth century brought with it competing value positions in historical judgment. Bismarck's political success in uniting Germany was achieved in part by subsuming the conflict among these diverse values to the cooperative support of the new German state. Historians and cultural analysts who saw in the outcome of Bismarck's *Realpolitik* (politics of realism) a renewal of German culture became more value neutral in their historical judgment. Heinrich von Treitschke (1834–1896), who succeeded Ranke as the official historiographer of Prussia (1886), reflected the Social Darwinism that emerged in the Bismarck era. While before 1871 Treitschke had been a constitutional liberal, as was his mentor Droysen, Bismarck's success shifted Treitschke's interpretation of historical reality to the salience of the powerful state as the self-justifying modus vivendi of history. The *Machtstaat* (the state based on power) was a reality above the competing values of individuals and social interests, and its maintenance and survival could not be judged in terms of the ethics of individuals. Treitschke's multivolume *German History in the Nineteenth Century* (1879–1894) had a profound influence upon a wide reading public and helped foster sentiment that supported German imperialism. Value neutrality in the wake of the imposed unity of the new German state was fecund as well for a neo-Rankean school of historians. Max Lenz (1850–1932) and Erich Marcks (1861–1938) refocused historical scholarship upon the singular events among world powers that were the compass of history for all in a nation regardless of their subjective differences. Lenz's collection of essays, *From Luther to Bismarck* (1900), and Marcks's Bismarck biographies typify the Rankean emphasis upon the role of the authoritative leader in initiating and guiding these singular events.

Karl Lamprecht (1856–1945) conducted a *Methodenstreit*, a debate on historical method, with the neo-Rankean school. Lamprecht held that objective history must take into account the competing values and the consequent social tensions of a historical period, which could only be understood with the help of auxiliary disciplines in the social sciences. History was a collective phenomenon, not one of singular events and great individuals. His twelve-volume *German History* (1891), which evidenced his interdisciplinary palette as well as his view of human development through stages of history, recalled the late Enlightenment cultural history of Herder and Lessing.

The attempts of Treitschke and the neo-Rankeans to preserve objective history by rising above the competing realities of different value positions, or that of Lamprecht by a positivistic account of the social-psychological complexity of cultural milieus, were seriously challenged by a new historical point of view that questioned the epistemological bases of ascertaining historical objectivity. Ernst Mach (1838–1916) cast in doubt the historicist faith in the objective progress of the human and natural sciences by questioning the effectiveness of language as a medium of historical interpretation. His studies in the history of physics and optics undercut the notion of materialist objectivity apart from language and perception. He demonstrated how a change in concept opened up new kinds of evidence and produced new forms of research. He called for a reformulation of scientific conceptions with every generation.

Wilhelm Dilthey (1833–1911) also sought a firmer basis for historical objectivity through a concern with the language and the underlying consciousness of the historical judgment. The locus of historical objectivity was to be found in the initiating intention of the historical act. A new heuristic of historical interpretation must be developed, Dilthey suggested, to penetrate the intentions of historical agents, and how these intentions were affected by their milieu. Dilthey's focus upon intentionality was paralleled in German philosophy by the rigorous phenomenology of Franz Brentano (1838–1917) and Edmund Husserl (1859–1938) that analyzed the grammar and imagery of immediate judgments. Phenomenological analysis would become a twentieth-century auxiliary science for historical study in the microsociological history of the Frankfurt school, and in the various schools of psychohistory. Dilthey believed that the discipline of history must derive its tools from the many human sciences that explored the complexity of consciousness and its manifestations. The study of nonhuman nature through the natural sciences posed a totally different set of problems to be solved with other empirical and rational methodologies. Dilthey outlined the differences in his *Introduction to the Human Sciences* (1883).

IV. The Twentieth Century

Between World War I and World War II German historians worked within the disciplinary paradigms that had emerged since 1871. The content of their concerns was greatly influenced by the political and social travail in the wake of Germany's defeat. Works that focused upon the reemergence of Germany after the defeat by Napoleon, and upon the Bismarck era, reminded them of what was potential in the German character even in the face of their present situation. The historical thought of Friedrich Meinecke (1862–1954), editor of the *Historische Zeitschrift* [Historical Journal] from 1896 to 1935, was indicative of the continuities in values and methodology brought by the historicist thinkers of the Bismarckian and Wilhelmian eras to the Weimar Republic. For Meinecke, the most significant dimension of historical understanding lay in comprehending the cultural role of the nation-state, which was conceived in the tradition of Hegel and Ranke as a collective "individual" that subsumed the separate and conflicting interests of its populace in its own rationale. Meinecke viewed German history in the tradition of Droysen and Treitschke: Germany's unification and growth as a nation had required a *Sonderweg*, a "special path," that necessitated state authority in contrast to the popular, democratic development of other Western nations. Only the strong role of the Prussian *Machtstaat* had enabled the separate regions, and divisive religious and class interests, to form a unity. In *Machiavellism: The Doctrine of Raison d'Etat* (1924) he examined significant political thinkers and personalities from Machiavelli to Frederick the Great in their struggle in the service of the state to integrate the dual, indeed antithetical poles of force in the name of physical necessity and ethical action. Besides its relevance for reflecting upon Weimar state policy, this study of a concept in its development within the changing circumstances of European history helped establish the history of ideas as a new avenue of historicist scholarship.

In the interwar years, a reemergence of social history with the enhanced tools of the social sciences challenged the Rankean tradition Meinecke represented. The Frankfurt school of Marxist cultural analysis—Max Horkheimer (1895–1973), Herbert Marcuse (1898–1979), and Theodor Adorno (1903–1969)—deepened a historical interpretation that grounded historical cause within the productive conditions of a culture with a phenomenological dissection of the effect of these conditions upon the immediate judgment and intentions of individuals. Sigmund Freud (1856–1939), the founder of psychoanalysis and a student of Franz Brentano, used phenomenological analysis of the artifacts of culture to develop a notion of pathological, historical cultures, which was adapted by the Frankfurt school in their augmentation of Marx's concept of the historical alienation of social milieus. Otto Hintze (1861–1940) and Eckart Kehr (1902–1933), a student of Meinecke, countered the traditional historicist methodology of the political biography in comprehending the dynamics of history with critical social history. Internal politics which reflected the tensions of competing social milieus were depicted through a careful, document-based analysis. Kehr's work on the German naval buildup of 1894–1901, and a subsequent study of economic actualities of the German Reform period of 1806 to 1815, would be seminal for post–World War II historians.

The majority of German historians during the Nazi era maintained the vision and methodologies of the historicist political history, which supported the *Machtstaat* and *Sonderweg* tradition. They were not replaced in the universities by Nazi ideologues because of the tacit support of the expansion of the German state endemic to that tradition. Meinecke was asked to step down as the editor of the *Historische Zeitschrift,* but his replacement, Karl Alexander von Müller, continued the historicist methodological orthodoxy, represented by Müller's biographical series entitled "Political Masters."

In its effort to comprehend its own immediate Nazi past, post–World War II historical science moved away from the Rankean paradigm of biographical political history, or that of the value-neutral history of ideas begun by Meinecke. The political state and the ideas salient in any era were conceived as expressions of complex and conflicting socioeconomic milieus rather than supraindividual essences. Ernst Nolte's *The Epoch of Fascism* employed a phenomenological analysis of fascist ideation rooted in the social fabric that was its matrix. While he sought the singular

G

characteristics of an idea as it was expressed by a distinct cultural milieu, his interpretative stance opened toward comparative history. For example, Germany's destruction of the Jews, Slavs, gypsies, and others was one form of population extermination whose idea and practice could be found in other centuries and in other countries. Nolte's cross-cultural interpretation of the causes of the Holocaust helped initiate the 1986 *Historikerstreit* (controversy among historians). Perhaps the most profound mirror of the changes and continuities in historiographical orthodoxy in Germany since 1945 can be found in this prolonged debate. The *Historikerstreit* not only probed the matrix of the Holocaust, but also used this set of events to debate how German history in the past and the present was to be conceived.

Nolte's interpretation was questioned by historians who employed the historicist traditional emphasis on the singularity of historical causation within a specific time and place. Christian Meier and Jürgen Kocka felt that Nolte's comparative analysis, which focused upon universally shared inhumane ideas that generated Holocaustlike phenomena in other countries, failed to focus upon the particularities of Germany from 1933 to 1945. The inattention to the political and institutional problems that gave rise to the Nazi state was viewed as a weakness in historical method, but, even worse, as a means of deflecting examination into causes that either still existed or were potential in the culture.

The debate over the historical image of Germany evidenced an effort by Michael Stürmer, Klaus Hildebrand, and Andreas Hillgruber to resurrect the historicist tradition of the *Machtstaat,* which had fallen into disrepute after 1945. In this neoconservative approach to the Holocaust, the state was seen as a supraindividual entity with its own necessary policies. The defense of eastern Europe in the closing year of the war, which permitted the Holocaust to be extended, was a tragic but necessary policy in the face of German social and geopolitical interests. Germany in the present needed to reestablish itself as a European state with distinct continental interests. Jürgen Habermas, Hans Mommsen, Wolfgang Mommsen, and Jürgen Kocka attacked this traditional view by conceiving the state as a changing amalgam of conflicting sociopolitical interests rather than a supraindividual entity. Germany in the Nazi era grew out of the structural expressions of Weimar's social and political realities, which still must be investigated. The present state had its own sociopolitical matrices, but ones that were never other than the people themselves.

Mark E. Blum

See also ESSENTIALISM; *KULTURPESSIMISMUS;* MARXISM AND HISTORIOGRAPHY; NATIONALISM; PHILOSOPHY OF HISTORY—SUBSTANTIVE.

References

Iggers, Georg G. *The German Conception of History: The National Tradition of Historical Thought from Herder to the Present.* Revised ed. Middletown, CT: Wesleyan Unversity Press, 1983.

Joachimsen, Paul. *Geschichtsauffassung und Geschichtsschreibung in Deutschland unter dem Einfluss des Humanismus* [Historical Interpretation and Historical Writing in Germany under the Influence of Humanism]. Aalen, Germany: Scientia, 1968.

Wehler, Hans-Ulrich, ed. *Deutsche Historiker* [German Historians]. 5 vols. Göttingen: Vandenhoeck & Ruprecht, 1971.

Gerretson, Frederik Carel (1884–1958)

Dutch historian and politician. Gerretson had a wide-ranging early career as a reserve officer in the Dutch army, Latin teacher in El Paso, Texas, journalist, poet, supporter of Flemish self-determination within Belgium, and an official in the Netherlands Ministry of Colonies. He obtained his doctorate in 1917 in Heidelberg and worked for the Dutch oil company BPM (now Royal Dutch Shell) until 1925, when he was appointed to the University of Utrecht as professor and head of a new faculty of Indology, pejoratively called the "oil and sugar faculty" because it was believed to train future Indies civil servants to favor Dutch commercial interests in the colony. His major work was a history of Royal Dutch Shell, but he wrote also on the period of Dutch political unity with Belgium (1815–1830) and the development of Dutch Protestantism. His main impact, however, was in his training of younger historians at Utrecht (notably W.P. Coolhaas and A. Alberts) and in his polemical writings supporting Pan-Netherlandic nationalism and opposing concessions to Indonesian nationalism, especially after World War II.

Robert Cribb

Texts

History of the Royal Dutch. 4 vols. Leiden, Netherlands: E.J. Brill, 1953–1957.

References

Henssen, Emile. *Gerretson en Indië.* Groningen, Netherlands: Wolters-Noordhoff-Bouwma, 1983.

Gervinus, Georg Gottfried (1805–1871)

German historian. Gervinus was professor of history in Göttingen before being dismissed for his criticism of the Hanoverian crown in 1837. He later taught in Heidelberg. A committed democrat, and an opponent of absolutism and Bismarck's *Realpolitik,* he was sharply criticized by the nationalist historians of the Prussian school. Because of his political activities he was prosecuted for treason by officials in Baden, although the charges were eventually dropped. Gervinus is best known for his work on the literary history of Germany, *Geschichte der poetischen National-Literatur der Deutschen* [History of German Poetry] (1835–1842), in which he attempted to combine political and cultural history, and his *Geschichte des neunzehnten Jahrhunderts* [History of the Nineteenth Century] (1855–1866). Gervinus was, in many respects, an outsider. Although his work is similar to that of other nineteenth-century historicists who attempted to combine historical objectivity with active political engagement, he also shared with Enlightenment historians the belief that history was part of the universal process of emancipation.

John R. Hinde

Texts

Geschichte der Florentinischen Historiografie bis zum sechzehnten Jahrhundert [History of Florentine Historical Writing up to the Sixteenth Century]. Frankfurt am Main: F. Varrentrapp, 1833.
Geschichte der poetischen National-Literatur der Deutschen. 5 vols. Leipzig: W. Englemann, 1835–1842.
Geschichte des neunzehnten Jahrhunderts [History of the Nineteenth Century]. 8 vols. Leipzig: W. Englemann, 1855–1866.

References

Hübinger, Gangolf. *Georg Gottfried Gervinus.* Göttingen: Vandenhoeck & Ruprecht, 1984.

Geyl, Pieter Catharinus Arie (1887–1966)

Dutch historian. Geyl was born in Dordrecht. Initially the London correspondent for a Dutch newspaper, he became professor of Dutch history at University College, London, and in 1936 he was appointed to the chair of modern history at Utrecht, in which city he died. Geyl advocated a national history that would not take the existing states of the Netherlands and Belgium as a point of departure, but the unity of the Dutch-speaking people in the Netherlands and Flanders. This so-called Great-Netherlandish perspective dominates his unfinished principal work, the *Geschiedenis van de Nederlandsche stam* [History of the Dutch Race] (1930–1937). At the same time, he criticized the Orangist and Calvinist traditions in Dutch historical writing. After World War II, he became internationally known for his historiographical essays and his polemical writings, directed against all forms of philosophical–historical speculation (by Arnold Toynbee, among others) as well as the prophecies of doom with regard to Western culture.

Jo Tollebeek

Texts

Debates with Historians. New York: Meridian, 1962.
The Netherlands in the Seventeenth Century. 2 vols. London: Benn; New York: Barnes and Noble, 1961–1964.
Orange and Stuart, 1641–1672. Trans. A.J. Pomerans. London: Weidenfeld and Nicolson, 1968.
The Revolt of the Netherlands, 1555–1609. London: Benn; New York: Barnes and Noble, 1966.

References

von der Dunk, H.W. "Pieter Geyl. History As a Form of Self-Expression." In *Clio's Mirror: Historiography in Britain and the Netherlands,* ed. A.C. Duke and C.A. Tamse. Zutphen, Netherlands: De Walburg Pers, 1985, 185–214.
Tollebeek, J. *De toga van Fruin: Denken over geschiedenis in Nederland sinds 1860* [Fruin's Gown: Thinking about History in the Netherlands since 1860]. Amsterdam: Wereldbibliotheek, 1996.

Giannone, Pietro (1676–1748)

Italian historian and jurist. Born in Ischitella and educated at the University of Naples, Giannone began his career in law as an associate of the Neapolitan reforming jurists involved in the antifeudal battle against the local nobility and the jurisdictional battle with Rome. His historical ideas developed from this experience, which he evaluated in the light of the English civil lawyer Arthur Duck's (1580–1648) history of Roman law in Europe. However, the resulting masterwork, his *Civil History of the Kingdom of Naples,* was a self-consciously innovative combination of legal history, cultural history, and social history. Conceived over a period of some twenty years and published in 1723, it aimed to combine erudition (often borrowed from sixteenth- and seventeenth-century authors possessing first-hand experience with the documents) and a philosophical outlook in harmony with the virulent antiecclesiastical program characteristic of the Enlightenment in order to provide the new Austrian rulers of Naples with a basis for correcting the social and political problems caused by the excessive influence of Rome and the Catholic Church in Neapolitan civic affairs. Enemies of Giannone's ideas managed to chase him all the way to Vienna, where he worked on an unfinished history of the origins of civilization (the *Triregno*); and in trying to repatriate, he was captured in 1736 in Piedmont, where he remained in prison to the end of his life and, among other works, wrote a vivid and detailed account of his intellectual development.

B. Dooley

Texts

Istoria civile del Regno di Napoli [Civil History of the Kingdom of Naples]. Ed. Antonio Marongiu. 7 vols. Milan: Marzorati, 1970–1972.
Vita scritta da lui medesimo [Autobiography]. Ed. Sergio Bertelli. Milan: Feltrinelli, 1960.

References

Ricuperati, Giuseppe. *L'esperienza civile e religiosa di Pietro Giannone* [The Civil and Religious Experience of Pietro Giannone]. Milan and Naples: R. Ricciardi, 1970.

Gibbon, Edward (1737–1794)

English historian of Rome and memorialist. Born into a family of politically active Hampshire gentry, Gibbon converted to Roman Catholicism while at Oxford in 1753. His father responded by sending him to Lausanne, Switzerland, where a strict regimen under the supervision of a Calvinist tutor reclaimed him for the Protestantism of his country. In subsequent years, Gibbon published his *Essay on the Study of Literature* (1761) in French and toured the European continent. He served as captain of the Hampshire Grenadiers during the Seven Years War and, in 1774, became a member of Parliament for the borough of Liskeard, later obtaining office in Lord North's administration. In February 1776 the first volume of the *Decline and Fall of the Roman Empire* struck the English-speaking literary world with unexpected force. Its virtues of narration and research were immediately evident and Horace Walpole pronounced it a "classic work." Clergymen, however, expressed shock at the sneering irony with which chapters 15 and 16 treated early Christianity. Additional installments of the *Decline and Fall* appeared in 1781 and 1788, as Gibbon extended his account to the fall of Constantinople in 1453. Gibbon's other great work, his *Memoirs,* was a posthumous redaction of six uncompleted drafts, which were extant at the time of his death. In it Gibbon created his own authorial persona, portraying himself as the "historian of the Roman Empire."

Analyses of Gibbon's work have spanned several disciplines. The *Decline and Fall* has attracted attention from literary scholars eager to analyze its narrative strategies and to place it in the autobiographical context provided by the *Memoirs.* Gibbon's insistence that religious history be free of dogmatic fetters long ago insured that the *Decline and Fall* would form a landmark in the historiography of Christianity. Extensively debated from the start, Gibbon's five causes for the triumph of the Christian religion within the Roman Empire represented a groundbreaking attempt to analyze Christianity as a social movement. Although Gibbon's treatment of Byzantines, Germans, Mongols, and Muslims has subsequently come to seem unsympathetic, his work provides a point of departure for ethnography.

The *Decline and Fall* may be read with equal insight as an exemplar of the eighteenth-century Enlightenment or the culmination of a humanistic tradition stretching back through the Renaissance to the Greek and Latin classics. Drawing upon influences that ranged from Tacitus to Reformation-era polemicists and compilers, Gibbon's work confronted a question of momentous concern to his century: why had Rome declined, and was it possible that European civilization might once again succumb to barbarism and superstition? Gibbon's suggestion that barbarian invasions and otherworldly enthusiasm overwhelmed an empire strained by "immoderate greatness" implied that moderation, taste, and cultivation of the arts and sciences might offer a preservative against the distempers that threaten all civilizations. In methodology, the *Decline and Fall* brilliantly combined the erudite and philosophical approaches to history that were prevalent in France during the eighteenth century, but it also owed much to the example provided by Gibbon's Scottish contemporaries, David Hume and William Robertson. Both a beginning and an end, the *Decline and Fall* represents the supreme demonstration of scholarship and imagination in eighteenth-century historiography.

Myron C. Noonkester

Texts

The Decline and Fall of the Roman Empire. Ed. David Womersley. 3 vols. New York: Viking Penguin, 1995.

Memoirs of My Life. Ed. Betty Radice. Harmondsworth: Penguin, 1984.

References

Burrow, John W. *Gibbon.* Oxford: Oxford University Press, 1985.

Craddock, Patricia. *Edward Gibbon: A Reference Guide.* Boston: G.K. Hall, 1987.

———. *Edward Gibbon, Luminous Historian, 1772–1794.* Baltimore, MD: Johns Hopkins University Press, 1989.

Porter, Roy. *Gibbon: Making History.* New York: St. Martin's, 1988.

Womersley, David. *The Transformation of the Decline and Fall of the Roman Empire.* Cambridge, Eng.: Cambridge University Press, 1988.

Giesebrecht, Wilhelm von (1814–1889)

German historian. Giesebrecht was one of Leopold von Ranke's students and a firm adherent of his ideas. He taught at a gymnasium in Berlin before becoming professor in Königsberg in 1857 and in Munich in 1862. Although largely forgotten today, Giesebrecht was an extremely popular historian during his lifetime. His work was admired by scholars, but was designed to be accessible to the general reading public. He gained a solid reputation for his narrative skill and mastery of style, as well as for his critical examination of documents. Giesebrecht was also popular because he wrote patriotic history that glorified the German past and promoted German nationalism. His most important work, *Geschichte der deutschen Kaiserzeit* [History of the German Imperial Era] (1855–1895), which went through many editions and was only published in its entirety after Giesebrecht's death, celebrated the universalism of the medieval German monarchs. He glorified the empire of the eleventh century, arguing that it was a high point in German history, a time when the people were united under a strong emperor who dominated the West.

John R. Hinde

Texts

Ed. *Annales altahenses maiores.* Hanover: Hahn, 1891.

Geschichte der deutschen Kaiserzeit. Ed. W. Schild. 6 vols. Brunswick, Germany: C.A. Schwetschke, 1873–1895.

References

Thompson, J.W. *A History of Historical Writing.* 2 vols. New York: MacMillan, 1942.

Gilbert, Felix (1905–1991)

German-American historian. Gilbert was born in Baden-Baden, Germany. He studied at the University of Heidelberg and received his Ph.D. from the University of Berlin in 1931. He immigrated to the United States in 1936 and was naturalized in 1943. During World War II he was a research assistant for the Office of Strategic Services (1943–1945) and later worked for the Department of State (1945–1946). In 1946 he became professor of history at Bryn Mawr College, leaving there in 1962 to begin his long service in the School of Historical Studies at the Institute for Advanced Study in Princeton, New Jersey. At his death he was professor emeritus at the Institute. Gilbert wrote about a variety of subjects, including World War II, in *Hitler Directs His War* (1950); Renaissance Italy, in *Machiavelli and Guicciardini* (1965), as well as numerous articles on Machiavelli and Renaissance Florence generally; and European historiography, in *History, Politics and Culture* (1990). His *End of the European Era* (1970) is an outstanding textbook. *To the Farewell Address* (1962) received the Bancroft Prize. Acknowledged as a superb teacher and scholar, in 1985 Gilbert received the American Historical Association's first Award for Scholarly Distinction, recognition of his masterful scholarship in several fields.

Walter A. Sutton

Texts

With David Clay Large. *The End of the European Era.* Fourth ed. New York: Norton, 1991.

History: Choice and Commitment. Cambridge, MA: Belknap Press of Harvard University Press, 1977.

History: Politics, or Culture? Reflections on Ranke and Burckhardt. Princeton, NJ: Princeton University Press, 1990.

Hitler Directs His War. New York: Oxford University Press, 1950.

Machiavelli and Guicciardini: Politics and History in Sixteenth-Century Florence. Princeton, NJ: Princeton University Press, 1965.

To the Farewell Address: Ideas of Early American Foreign Policy. Princeton, NJ: Princeton University Press, 1961.

G

Gildas (fl. sixth century)

British ecclesiastic and chronicler. Born in the year of the battle of Mount Badon (ca. 500), Gildas studied in Wales, under St. Illtud, and probably also on the Continent. He was reputed to have founded the monastery of St. Gildas at Ruys and was revered as a saint in both Britain and Brittany. Although his name was subsequently assigned to histories now attributed to Nennius, his *De Excidio et Conquestu Britanniae* [The Ruin and Conquest of Britain] is his only extant work and the only surviving British tract of its era. The *De Excidio* was an important source for Bede, who used it when writing his *Historia Ecclesiastica* [Ecclesiastical History]. Gildas describes the last years of Romano-British ascendancy, the invasions of the Saxons, a brief British recovery under Ambrosius Aurelianus, and the subsequent decline of British morals and military might. Gildas's main purpose in writing his work was to chronicle the sins of the British. His focus is frustrating for the modern historian, because he names few personages before his own contemporaries. Gildas was aware of his work's shortcomings and blamed them on his own poor sources.

Ruth McClelland-Nugent

Texts

The Ruin of Britain, and Other Works. Ed. and trans. Michael Winterbottom. London: Phillimore, 1978.

References

Higham, N.J. *The English Conquest: Gildas and Britain in the Fifth Century.* Manchester: Manchester University Press, 1994.

O'Sullivan, Thomas D. *The De Excidio of Gildas: Its Authenticity and Date.* Leiden, Netherlands: E.J. Brill, 1978.

Gilson, Etienne Henry (1884–1978)

French philosopher, historian, and university professor. Educated at the Sorbonne, where he received his doctorate in 1913, Gilson taught medieval philosophy at the Sorbonne, the École Pratique des Hautes Études, and the Collège de France and held the chair in history of spirituality at the Institut Catholique de Paris from 1943. He was instrumental in founding and taught for many years at the Pontifical Institute of Mediaeval Studies in Toronto. Though trained in Cartesian philosophy, he devoted much of his career to revitalizing the historical study of medieval thought. In the scholastic thinkers he found an authentic "Christian philosophy," which he insisted was as important to current philosophical thinking as to a proper historical appreciation of the medieval mind. His main interest was the thought of Thomas Aquinas, but he also published major studies of thinkers such as Augustine, Bernard of Clairvaux, Dante, and Duns Scotus. Many of his magisterial works on medieval thought have become standard texts, notably *The Spirit of Mediaeval Philosophy* (1932) and *Reason and Revelation in the Middle Ages* (1938). His approach to the Middle Ages reflected the humanism he delighted to find in Aquinas, of whom he once observed: "beyond the humanism of the letter and the form, there is a humanism of the spirit, with all that it implies about confidence in the stability, value, and efficacy of nature and of man."

Monica Sandor

Texts

The Christian Philosophy of Thomas Aquinas. Trans. Laurence K. Shook. New York: Random House, 1956.

A Gilson Reader: Selected Writings. Ed. Anton C. Pegis. Garden City, NY: Hanover House, 1957.

History of Christian Philosophy in the Middle Ages. New York: Random House, 1955.

Reason and Revelation in the Middle Ages. New York: Scribner's Sons, 1938.

The Spirit of Mediaeval Philosophy. Trans. A.H.C. Downes. London: Sheed and Ward, 1936.

References

Echauri, Raul. *El pensamiento de Etienne Gilson* [The Thought of Etienne Gilson]. Baranain (Pamplona), Spain: Ediciones Universidad de Navarra, 1980.

Maritain, Jacques, ed. *Etienne Gilson: Philosophe de la chrétienté* [Etienne Gilson: Philosopher of Christendom]. Paris: Cerf, 1949.

McGrath, Margaret. *Etienne Gilson: A Bibliography.* Toronto: Pontifical Institute of Mediaeval Studies, 1982.

Pegis, Anton C. "Gilson and Thomism." *Thought* 211 (1946): 435–454.

Shook, Laurence K. *Etienne Gilson.* Toronto: Pontifical Institute of Mediaeval Studies, 1984.

Ginzburg, Carlo (b. 1939)

Italian pioneer of microhistory, specializing in the culture of subaltern classes in early modern Europe. Born in Turin, Ginzburg grew up in a family of scholars, writers, and leftist political activists. After studies at Pisa with the great Reformation scholar, Delio Cantimori, he taught first at Rome and then, from 1970, at Bologna. In 1962, he began to explore Inquisition records at Udine, in the Italian northeast, not only as records of persecution but also as sources for forgotten popular beliefs and practices. A sojourn at the Warburg Institute in London in 1964 led him also into art historical writing (*The Enigma of Piero della Francesca*) and into speculations on sleuthing as a historical method. His subsequent appointment in 1988 to the University of California at Los Angeles, where he remains, forged North American alliances.

Much of Ginzburg's scholarship has centered on the religion and culture of late medieval and early modern Italy, especially on heresy and witchcraft. Reading Antonio Gramsci, the intellectual godfather of Italian leftism, not only reinforced Ginzburg's populist sympathies, but also inspired an enduring interest in the tense dialogue between a hegemonic high culture and an embattled, but resilient, popular tradition. For example, his early book, *I Benendanti* (1966; later translated as *Night Battles*) traces how inquisitors persuaded a rural fertility cult who had believed they waged nocturnal battles against sorcerers to see themselves as witches. In *Il Formaggio e i vermi* (1976; translated as *The Cheese and the Worms*), Ginzburg explores the cosmology of a rural miller, a self-made heretic, to reconstruct the lens through which he refracted elite culture. Ginzburg's later work on witchcraft, particularly *Storia notturna* (1989; translated as *Ecstasies*), ranges ambitiously over classical mythology and Eurasian folklore.

Ginzburg has innovated in microhistory and in exploring the role of hidden and ambiguous clues in historical detective work. His eclecticism and daring have found few imitators and some detractors, who charge him with privileging the marginal or with flimsy conjectures. At the same time, his work has helped turn scholarship toward a much more sophisticated reading of judicial records in a campaign to resurrect subaltern worlds. The translation of many of his works has brought these important developments in Italian postwar historiography to the English-speaking world.

Elizabeth S. Cohen and Thomas V. Cohen

Texts

The Cheese and the Worms: The Cosmos of a Sixteenth-Century Miller. Trans. John Tedeschi and Ann Tedeschi. Baltimore, MD, and London: Johns Hopkins University Press, 1980.
Clues, Myths and the Historical Method. Trans. John Tedeschi and Ann Tedeschi. Baltimore, MD: Johns Hopkins University Press, 1989.

Ecstasies: Deciphering the Witches' Sabbath. Trans. R.R. Rosenthal. Harmondsworth: Penguin, 1991.
The Enigma of Piero della Francesca: The Baptism, The Arezzo Cycle, The Flagellation. Trans. Martin Ryle and Kate Soper. London: Verso, 1985.
Il Nicodemismo: Simulazione e dissimulazione religiosa nell' Europa del '500 [Nicodemism: Religious Simulation and Dissimulation in Sixteenth-Century Europe]. Turin, Italy: Einaudi, 1970.
Night Battles: Witchcraft and Agrarian Cults in the Sixteenth and Seventeenth Centuries. Trans. John Tedeschi and Ann Tedeschi. London: Routledge and Kegan Paul; Baltimore, MD: Johns Hopkins University Press, 1983.

References

Muir, Edward. "Introduction: Observing Trifles." In *Microhistory and the Lost Peoples of Europe,* ed. Edward Muir and Guido Ruggiero. Baltimore: Johns Hopkins University Press, 1991, vii–xxviii.
Schutte, Ann. "Review Article: Carlo Ginzburg." *Journal of Modern History* 48 (1976): 296–315.

Giovio, Paolo (1483/86–1552)

Italian churchman, historian, and biographer. A native of Como, he was educated as a doctor but abandoned medicine for a career in the church. Eventually appointed bishop of Nocera, he gathered his material while resident at Rome from 1512 to 1549, much of that time in the Vatican. His personal friendships with many of the protagonists of his history facilitated his practice of eyewitness history but led to accusations of partiality, despite his willingness to tell his patrons "bitter truths." Giovio's *Sui temporis historiarum libri* [History of His Own Times], a history of the entire Mediterranean world from 1483 to 1544, was the last major work in the humanist historical tradition and the only one, after Flavio Biondo's *Decades,* to aspire to universal history. Giovio was well-informed on Ottoman history, and his narrative of the struggle against the Turks in Hungary is fundamental. He is also important for a military history of Italy. Like Guicciardini, he believed that foreign domination of Italy was brought on by the excessive ambitions of the Italian princes and by their internecine struggles, but, despite his admiration for Polybius, his analyses of diplomacy were limited by the conventions of Renaissance Latin historiography. His historical biographies

G

of Leo X, Adrian VI, Gonzalo de Córdoba, Pompeo Colonna, Alfonso d'Este, and Ferdinando d'Avalos are also important.

T.C. Price Zimmermann

Texts

Pauli Iovii opera. 11 vols. (8 published to date). Rome: Istituto poligrafico dello stato, 1956– .

References

Cochrane, Eric. *Historians and Historiography in the Italian Renaissance.* Chicago: University of Chicago Press, 1981, 366–376.

Zimmermann, T.C. Price. *Paolo Giovio: The Historian and the Crisis of Sixteenth-Century Italy.* Princeton, NJ: Princeton University Press, 1995.

Godechot, Jacques (1907–1989)

Historian of the French and "Atlantic" revolutions. Godechot was born in Lorraine, in 1907, into a Jewish middle-class family. After beginning his professional training at Nancy, he completed his doctorate at the Sorbonne (1938). He accepted an appointment at the University of Toulouse in 1945 and remained there for the rest of his career, as an extraordinarily active teacher, administrator, and scholar. A prolific and fiercely independent historian, it is difficult to identify Godechot with a single historiographical trend or school. Imbued from his earliest days with a respect for the Revolution that had accorded civic rights to Jews, Godechot shared the sympathies of the socialist historians at the Sorbonne. Nevertheless, his thesis on *Les commissaires aux armées sous le Directoire* [Army Superintendents under the Directory] (1937) extended his interests beyond the borders of France from the very beginning, and he was encouraged to perceive the French Revolution in the context of a broader "Atlantic" or "Western" revolution. First suggested in his *Histoire de l'Atlantique* [History of the Atlantic] (1947) and subsequently developed in collaboration with Robert R. Palmer in a conference paper at Rome in 1955, the idea of the "Atlantic Revolution" underpinned many of Godechot's books, notably *La Grande Nation* [The Great Nation] (1956), *France and the Atlantic Revolution of the Eighteenth Century* (1965), and *L'Europe et l'Amérique à l'époque napoléonienne* [Europe and America in the Napoleonic Age] (1967). This was not a thesis that won immediate acceptance, being objected to by historians who saw it as a product of Cold War politics or as part of an effort to deny the specificity and uniqueness of the French Revolution.

Ian Germani

Texts

Les Commissaires aux armées sous le Directoire: Contribution à l'étude des rapports entre les pouvoirs civils et militaires. Paris: Fustier, 1941.

France and the Atlantic Revolution of the Eighteenth Century, 1770–1799. Trans. Herbert H. Rowen. New York: Free Press, 1965.

La grande nation. Second ed. Paris: Aubier Montaigne, 1983.

References

Forster, Robert et al. "American Historians Remember Jacques Godechot." *French Historical Studies* 16 (1990): 879–892.

"Numéro spécial: Hommage à Jacques Godechot (1907–1989)." *Annales Historiques de la Révolution Française* 281 (1990): 304–344.

Góis, Damião de (1502–1574)

Portuguese historian, diplomat, humanist, and traveler. Born in Alenquer, Góis joined the court of King Manuel I as a boy. In 1523 he joined the European circuit along which spices and news about the Portuguese discoveries were distributed. Initially he was employed as an ambassador (until 1532) and then as a scholar and intellectual (until 1545). Divided between propaganda about the military and missionary deeds of the Portuguese in the Orient and geographical news of Asia, Góis's works enjoyed wide circulation in Europe. On returning to Portugal he was appointed head of the Archives of the Realm *(Torre do Tombo)* (1548), and he wrote two chronicles of the Portuguese royal family: *Crónica do Felicissimo Rei D. Manuel* [Chronicle of the Most Fortunate King Manuel] (1566) and *Crónica do Príncipe Dom João o Segundo do Nome* [Chronicle of Prince John the Second of the Name] (1567). His interest in and eventual conversion to Lutheranism led to his arrest by the Holy Inquisition in 1571. Sentenced to life imprisonment, he died three years later.

Jorge M. dos Santos Alves

Texts

Crónica do Felicissimo Rei D. Manuel. 4 vols. Coimbra: Imprensa da Universidade, 1949–1955.

References

Hirsch, Elisabeth Feist. *Damião de Góis: The Life and Thought of a Portuguese Humanist, 1502–1574.* The Hague: M. Nijhoff, 1967.

Goll, Jaroslav (1846–1929)

Founder of modern Czech historiography and architect of its Europeanization. Through his experiences at various European universities, Goll had become an ardent adherent of historical positivism and succeeded in making it a guiding principle of Czech historiography in the closing decades of the nineteenth century. He was convinced that much of human past can be positively ascertained through a strict attention to the content of surviving documents and the circumstances under which they had been created. He also insisted on the study of Czech history within the closely examined contexts of European history and historiography. To accomplish these goals, he founded a modern historical seminar at the University of Prague and a truly professional historical journal, *Český časopis historický* [Czech Historical Journal] (both in collaboration with Antonín Rezek), and held his students to high standards in research and writing. He gave them exemplary demonstrations of this in his own works, which, although not very numerous, excelled as models of meticulous scholarship and brilliant presentation.

Goll's works included two masterpieces on the role of the Czech lands in the history of central Europe, *Čechy a Prusy ve středověku* [Czech Lands and Prussia in the Middle Ages] (1897); and *Válka o země Koruny české, 1740–1742* [War for the Lands of the Bohemian Crown, 1740–1742] (1915). In the field of domestic Czech history, he made a decisive contribution to the exposure, as Romantic forgeries, of the purported medieval poems, *Historický rozbor básní Rukopisu královédvorského* [Historical Analysis of the Poems of the Manuscript of Dvůr Králové] (1886); and to the illumination of the origins of an early Reformation sect, Jednota Českých bratří [Unity of the Czech Brethren] in a synthesis and modification of several earlier works, *Chelčický a Jednota v 15. století* [Chelčický and the Unity in the Fifteenth Century] (1916).

Josef Anderle

Texts

Čechy a Prusy ve středověku. Prague: Bursík & Kohout, 1897.
Chelčický a Jednota v 15. století. Prague: Historický klub, 1916.
Historický rozbor básní Rukopisu královédvorského. Prague: E. Valečka, 1886.
Válka o země Koruny české, 1740–1742. Prague: Česká akademie věd a umění, 1915.

References

František Kutnar. "Jaroslav Goll." In his *Přehledné dějiny českého a slovenského dějepisectví*

[General History of Czech and Slovak Historiography]. Prague: Státní pedagogické nakladatelství, 1977, vol. 2, 21–35.
Kazbunda, Karel. *Stolice dějin na pražské universitě* [The Chair of Czech History at Prague University]. Vol. III. Prague: Universita Karlova, 1968, vol. 3, 48–63; 161–173, et passim.
Marek, Jaroslav. *Jaroslav Goll.* Prague: Melantrich, 1991.

Gombrich, Sir Ernst Hans Josef (b. 1909)

Austrian-born British art historian. Gombrich was born and educated in Vienna, at the Theresianum, and then at the University of Vienna (Ph.D. 1933), where his most influential teachers were Emanuel Loewy, Julius von Schlosser, and Ernst Kris. In 1936, Gombrich emigrated to Great Britain, where he joined the staff of the Warburg Institute in London. From 1959 until 1976, when he retired, he was professor of the history of the classical tradition at the University of London and director of the Warburg Institute. He has held numerous visiting professorships. Gombrich's major publications include *The Story of Art* (1950), *Art and Illusion* (1960), and *Norm and Form* (1966). Taking a psychoanalytic approach to art Gombrich has worked on the two fronts of the theory of art and of its practice, arguing that the two are inseparable. He makes little distinction between prehistoric and contemporary art asserting the common nature of all creativity. In *Tributes: Interpreters of Our Cultural Tradition* (1984) Gombrich honors friends and scholars who have influenced him. *Sight and Insight: Essays on Art and Culture in Honour of E.H. Gombrich at 85* (1994) is a festschrift that reflects the wide range of his interests and also the extent of his influence, which has been felt among mainstream historians, for whom Gombrich's work has often provided the link between their work and that of art historians.

Elvy Setterqvist O'Brien

Texts

Art and Illusion: A Study in the Psychology of Pictorial Representation. Fifth ed. London: Phaidon, 1977.
Norm and Form: Studies in the Art of the Renaissance. Fourth ed. Chicago: University of Chicago, 1985.
The Story of Art. Fifteenth ed. London: Phaidon, 1989.

References

Kultermann, Udo. *The History of Art History.* Pleasantville, NY: Abaris Books, 1993.

Gong Zizhen [Kung Tzu-chen] (1792–1841)

Chinese historian, reformist thinker, poet, and scholar. A native of Hangzhou in Zhejiang province in the south, Gong's career in the bureaucracy was singularly unsuccessful. In 1829 he passed the metropolitan examinations after five failed attempts, but never did well in the bureaucracy. As a historian, Gong was an important exponent of the *Gongyang zhuan* [The Commentary of Master Gongyang], one of the three main commentaries on the *Chunqiu* [Spring and Autumn Annals], itself the main historical ancient classic of China. Beginning in 1815, he wrote a series of articles on Chinese history and his own times based largely on two concepts in the Gongyang Commentary, namely *bian* (change or reform) and *zhi* (statecraft). This led him to emphasize the processes of change in history and his own time. He advocated major government reform, the banning of opium, and abolition of the binding of women's feet. Such revolutionary ideas made him enemies in powerful places in his own time, but exercised great influence on later reformers.

Colin Mackerras

Texts

Gong Zizhen quanji [The Complete Works of Gong Zizhen]. Ed. Wang Peizheng [Wang P'ei-cheng]. Beijing: Zhonghua shuju, 1959.

References

Wong, Shirleen S. *Kung Tzu-chen.* Boston: Twayne, 1975.

González de Mendoza, Juan (1545–1615)

Spanish historian of China. The leading European commentator on China in the sixteenth century, González de Mendoza was born in Castile. Ordained as an Augustinian friar in Mexico, he hoped to participate in Spanish efforts to convert (and perhaps to conquer) a China upon which he would never set sight. Returned to Europe, he was commissioned by Pope Gregory XIII to compile a compendium of what was then known of the Middle Kingdom. His *Historia de las casas mas notables, ritos y costumbres del gran Reyno de la China* [History of the Most Notable Houses, Rites, and Customs of the Great Kingdom of China] appeared in 1585 and by the end of the century had gone through numerous editions and had been translated into all the major European languages. It drew upon sometimes unacknowledged Portuguese and Spanish sources—printed, manuscript, and oral—and was structured along the lines pioneered by Spanish historians of Mexico. While paying some attention to neighboring regions, González de Mendoza's presentation of the *gran Reyno* emphasized its geographical extent, multitudinous and industrious population, wealth, and the relative rationality of Ming political structures and social practices. The apparent achievements of a non-Christian people unsettled some Europeans and led to accusations of exaggeration, if not fabrication, but they also roused the interest and the approval of such humanists as Giovanni Botero and Michel de Montaigne.

John F. Laffey

Texts

Historia de las cosas mas notables, ritos y costumbres del gran reyno de la China. Anvers, Belgium: Pedro Bellero, 1596.
The Historie of the Great and Mightie Kingdome of China, and the Situation Thereof: Togither with the Great Riches, Huge Citties, Politike Gouernement, and Rare Inuentions in the Same. Facsimile reprint. New York: Da Capo Press, 1973.

References

Lach, Donald F. *Asia in the Making of Europe.* Vols. 1 and 2. Chicago: University of Chicago Press, 1965, 1977.

Gooch, George Peabody (1873–1968)

English diplomatic historian. A product of Eton and Cambridge, Gooch was a Liberal parliamentarian, a social worker, and a long-serving editor of the *Contemporary Review.* Gooch's *History and Historians in the Nineteenth Century* (1913) is regarded as his most significant contribution to historical scholarship, but he went on to write or edit a number of other works. His preoccupation with the cause of a stable international peace after World War I led him to edit and contribute to the *Cambridge History of British Foreign Policy* (1922–1923), and coedit the multivolume *British Documents on the Origins of the War* (1926–1938). Gooch viewed the drift of his country into that war as a corollary of its entente diplomacy. He depreciated the *realpolitik* of the antebellum European statesmen and the harshness of the Versailles peace and consistently denounced the Nazi regime. Later, Gooch produced some excellent short biographical sketches of such eighteenth-century European rulers as *Frederick the Great* (1947). A balanced, dispassionate scholar, Gooch rejected deterministic or didactic history, and his works are stamped with genuine erudition, integrity, and tolerance.

Pradip Bhaumik

Texts

English Democratic Ideas in the Seventeenth Century. Second ed. New York: Harper, 1959.

Frederick the Great. New York: Knopf, 1947.

History and Historians in the Nineteenth Century. London: Longmans, Green, 1913.

References

Eyck, Frank. *G.P. Gooch.* London: Macmillan, 1982.

Gordon, Linda (b. 1940)

American social historian. Gordon earned an M.A. and Ph.D from Yale University and currently teaches at the University of Wisconsin. In her first book, an edited collection of primary material on American working-women's history, Gordon described writing history as a political act and characterized herself as a feminist and a socialist. Her second book, *Woman's Body, Woman's Right* (1976), was a social history of birth control in America focusing on the point of view of women seeking sexual and reproductive self-determination. In Gordon's view, birth control is the single most important material factor in ensuring the emancipation of women. She stresses throughout her history that politics, not technology, has determined the development and availability of safe methods of birth control. Gordon then wrote *Heroes of Their Own Lives* (1988), a discussion of the history and politics of family violence in the United States. This work argues that family violence was defined and treated differently in various eras of American history. In periods of conservative ascendancy, the violence was attributed to psychological problems while in reform epochs such as the Progressive era there was more emphasis on social causes and government regulation. Gordon's most recent work is a history of single mothers and the welfare system, *Pitied but Not Entitled,* which explains the ways in which aid to single mothers has been stigmatized much more than forms of government help to other groups, such as unemployed male wage-earners.

Barbara A. McGowan

Texts

America's Working Women: A Documentary History, 1600 to the Present. Ed. Rosalyn Baxandall, Linda Gordon, and Susan Reverby. New York: Random House, 1995.

Heroes of Their Own Lives: The Politics and History of Family Violence 1880–1960. New York: Viking, 1988.

Pitied but Not Entitled. New York: Free Press, 1994.

Woman's Body, Woman's Right: A Social History of Birth Control in America. New York: Penguin, 1976.

Goubert, Pierre (b. 1915)

French social historian. Goubert, a native of Saumur, is one of the most visible and respected members of the second generation of the Annales school of historians in Paris. He taught at a variety of French institutions before taking up a position at the Centre National de la Recherche Scientifique in 1951. He subsequently held positions in the École des Hautes Études en Sciences Sociales and at the universities of Rennes, Nanterre, and the Sorbonne. Goubert had studied with Marc Bloch, and his teacher's mastery of French rural history was evident in his doctoral thesis, the first of the great regional theses to come out of the École des Hautes Études, entitled *Beauvais et le Beauvaisis de 1600 à 1700.* Goubert divided his work into two parts: structures, focusing on demographic pressures in the region of Beauvais in the seventeenth century, and conjunctures, a general social and economic history of the region. He made a clear case for studying the common people rather than kings and princes, a theme he tried to reinforce in his *Louis XIV and Twenty Million Frenchmen,* one of the first revisions of the reign of the Sun King. Here Goubert pointed out that economic stagnation, combined with the finite tax resources of his subjects, significantly limited Louis's absolute monarchy.

Mack P. Holt

Texts

Beauvais et le Beauvaisis de 1600 à 1730: Contribution de l'histoire sociale de la France du XVIIᵉ siècle [Beauvais and the Beauvaisis from 1600 to 1730: A Contribution to the Social History of France in the Seventeenth Century]. 2 vols. Paris: École des Hautes Études en Sciences Sociales, 1960.

Louis XIV and Twenty Million Frenchmen. Trans. Anne Carter. New York: Vintage Books, 1970.

References

Burke, Peter. *The French Historical Revolution: The Annales School, 1929–1989.* Stanford, CA: Stanford University Press, 1990.

Graetz, Heinrich (1817–1891)

German Jewish historian. Born in Xions, Prussia, Graetz received a traditional Jewish education but privately pursued the study of classical and modern literature. He received his doctorate in 1845 for a thesis on Gnosticism and Judaism, and, a year later, published *The Construction of Jewish History*, which applied a Hegelian-influenced perspective to the unfolding of Judaism. In 1853 he was appointed to the faculty of the Jewish Theological Seminary of Breslau, a leading institution of the "Positive-Historical School" of nineteenth-century German Jewry that rejected radical reform of Judaism but was sympathetic to modernizing Judaism and respectful of the pursuit of Jewish historical knowledge according to scientific methods *(Wissenschaft des Judentums)*. Between 1853 and 1876 Graetz published his greatest work, *Geschichte der Juden*, an eleven-volume narrative of the *History of the Jews* emphasizing the vibrancy of Judaism not only in its ancient period but also in the Middle Ages and modern times. Contrary to the Jewish Reformers of his day, who tended to insist that modern Judaism was divesting itself of its ethnic character, for Graetz the Jewish people was a "living folk," with a distinct religious destiny as a spiritual nation and a messianic role in world history. A supporter of Jewish emancipation, his criticisms of German culture aroused the ire of the anti-Semitic Prussian historian Heinrich von Treitschke in 1879–1880. A meticulous scholar with a passionate, opinionated, dramatic style, Graetz also published works on the Hebrew Bible and on the significance of Judaism in modern times. His *History of the Jews* had considerable impact on the modern Jewish historical consciousness.

Robert M. Seltzer

Texts

History of the Jews. Abrid. and trans. Bella Loewy. 6 vols. Philadelphia: The Jewish Publication Society of America, 1891–1898.

The Structure of Jewish History and Other Essays. Ed. and trans. Ismar Schorsch. New York: Jewish Theological Seminary of America, 1975.

References

Baron, Salo. "Heinrich (Hirsch) Graetz: A Biographical Study" and "Graetz and Ranke: A Methodological Study." In *History and Jewish Historians: Essays and Addresses*, ed. Arthur Hertzberg and Leon A. Feldman. Philadelphia: Jewish Publication Society of America, 1964, 263–275.

Kochan, Lionel. "The Messiah As the Spirit of History: Krochmal and Graetz." In his *The Jew and His History*. New York: Schocken Books, 1977, 69–87.

Seltzer, Robert M. "Graetz, Dubnow, Baron." *Jewish Book Annual* 48 (1990–1991): (5751), 169–182.

Gramsci, Antonio (1891–1937)

Italian politician and Marxist theoretician. Gramsci was born in Ales on the Italian isle of Sardinia and began his scholarly career in 1911 at the University of Turin, where he joined the Socialist labor movement. In the aftermath of World War I, he formed a Leftist radical faction, which ultimately evolved into the Italian Communist Party in 1921. After his stay in the Soviet Union as a functionary of the Communist International (Comintern), he became the head of his party and was elected a member of Parliament. Under the law banning the Communist Party imposed by Mussolini's Fascist regime, Gramsci was arrested and imprisoned in 1926. After eleven years of imprisonment he was finally released because of poor health, but died soon thereafter in a Roman hospital.

It was during his imprisonment that Gramsci turned from revolutionary action to philosophical study. His work would be published posthumously after World War II. From his famous "Prison Notebooks" editors extracted "books" by grouping together fragments on related topics. Gramsci's ideas greatly influenced the further development of Italian communism in particular and the Western reorientation of Marxist theory in general. At the center of Gramsci's thinking was the need for a new synthesis between vulgar materialism and neo-Hegelian idealism. In his insistence that man was a product of history, and not merely of physical nature, he generally showed more consideration than conventional Marxists for the conditions of human creativity and freedom. Gramsci restored the relevance of political institutions and culture as driving forces in the historical process. Rejecting economic reductionism, he considered moral and intellectual reform, and the creation of a dominant culture as the essence of revolution and historical progress. Intellectual and cultural "hegemony," not economic determinism or the use of naked force, ultimately regulates society in Gramsci's theory. Stressing the relative independence of both politics and culture from material factors such as the structures of production, Gramsci paved the way for a general reorientation in Marxist historical writing about bourgeois society and fascism.

Georgi Verbeeck

Texts

Letters from Prison. Ed. Lynne Lawner. London: Cape, 1975.

Opere di Antonio Gramsci [Works of Antonio Gramsci]. 12 vols. Turin, Italy: Einaudi, 1947–1972 (Includes *Lettere del Carcere* [Letters from Prison], *Quaderni del Carcere* [Prison Notebooks], and other political studies).

Selections from the Prison Notebooks of Antonio Gramsci. Ed. Quintin Hoare and Geoffrey Nowell Smith. London: Lawrence and Wishart, 1971.

References

Boggs, Carl. *The Two Revolutions: Antonio Gramsci and the Dilemmas of Western Marxism.* Boston: South End Press, 1984.

Davidson, Alastair. *Antonio Gramsci: Towards an Intellectual Biography.* London: Merlin, 1977.

Mouffe, Chantal, ed. *Gramsci and Marxist Theory.* London: Routledge and Kegan Paul, 1979.

Sassoon, Anne Showstack, ed. *Approaches to Gramsci.* London: Writers and Readers, 1982.

Grandes Chroniques de France.

French chronicles, compiled between the thirteenth and fifteenth centuries A.D. The *Grandes chroniques* is considered as the near-official history of the French monarchy in the late Middle Ages. It was written in Saint-Denis abbey, where monks had been collecting Latin chronicles about the French kings since the twelfth century. Based on these texts, a collection and translation into French, the *Roman des Rois* (1274), was prepared for King Louis IX; this evolved into the *Grandes chroniques*. The work would be augmented during the reign of every sovereign, at Saint-Denis or in other places, until 1461. The *Grandes chroniques* was published in 1477, after which its readership expanded beyond the northern French nobility. Although a heterogeneous collection of successive texts, the *Grandes chroniques* praises continuously, from beginning to end, the Frankish monarchs and people. They thus played an important role in the late medieval construction of the French nation and its sense of history.

Franck Collard

Texts

France before Charlemagne: A Translation from the Grandes chroniques. Trans. Robert Levine. Lewiston, NY: Edwin Mellen Press, 1990.

Grandes chroniques de France, Ed. J. Viard. Paris: Société de l'histoire de France, 1920–1953. [This edition stops in 1328.]

References

Guenée, B. "Les 'Grandes chroniques de France,' 1274–1518." In *Les lieux de mémoire.* vol. II, *La Nation,* part one, ed. P. Nora, Paris: Gallimard, 1986, 189–215.

Spiegel, G. *The Chronicle Tradition of Saint-Denis, a Survey.* Brookline, MA: Classical Folia Editions, 1978.

Greek Historiography—Ancient

From the classical to the Roman period, limited to traditional forms of history writing. Herodotus may not have been the first Greek we can properly call a historian (Hecataeus of Miletus has supporters for that claim), but all concede that he is the first who counts. Writing during the second and third quarters of the fifth century, Herodotus was ultimately driven by two purposes: to describe the extent and diversity of the Persian Empire and its subject peoples, and to determine how several small, disunited Greek states were able to thwart a massive invasion by the Persian king and his armies. For the former purpose, he drew inspiration from ethnographies and mythologies, including the work of his older contemporary, Hecataeus, and sources as far back as Homer's *Odyssey.* For the second purpose, of describing the Persian wars, he both continued and broke with tradition. Since Homer, war had been the prescribed subject of epic. Herodotus accepted this tradition and even supplied his own epic style and grandeur. But writing in a highly rationalistic age, Herodotus relied substantially on human causality to frame his narrative. Moreover, because he lived within a generation of the events he chronicled, he gathered his evidence by asking questions of participants and eyewitnesses. In privileging the oral component of historical tradition and in submitting that tradition to critical scrutiny, he created a work that survives as a watershed in the history of ideas.

Thucydides, who may well have heard Herodotus recite parts of the Persian wars in Athens, ridiculed the romance in that work yet failed to escape its essential influence: war, too, would be his subject. But in excluding romance, Thucydides excluded almost everything else. Focusing narrowly on the Peloponnesian War, fought between Athens and Sparta and their allies during the last third of the fifth century, he reveals almost nothing of Greek social life or cultural values. The factual recitation of warfare is relentless. The reader is spared only by the soaring, though difficult, set speeches, created by Thucydides and placed in the mouths of generals and politicians, and by occasional powerful analysis (the description of the Great Plague at Athens, for example, has become a trope throughout the ages). His brilliance is beyond dispute, and his authority rests not only on the quality of his historical narrative, but on the fact that he himself participated in the war. He established forever the importance of chronicling contemporary history and of imposing on the narrative the highest standards of precision and accuracy.

Herodotus and Thucydides stand as twin towers of Greek history writing, eclipsing completely the thousands of other authors by whom only a handful of works are extant today. This is no mere accident. Herodotus and Thucydides lived during a period of astonishing cultural achievement, and their writings are connected intellectually and spiritually with those of Pindar, Aeschylus, Sophocles, Euripides, Aristophanes, and Plato. What later writer would dare contend with them in covering the same material? With almost no competitors, their works became essential for understanding that remarkable age. Their writings were more in demand and far more widely disseminated than those of any other ancient history writer, so that the destruction of individual libraries or centers of learning could not threaten their existence. And, as founding members of the classical canon, read throughout the ages equally for literary inspiration, their historical insights and practices have become commensurately influential.

The epigoni of Herodotus and Thucydides, then, suffer greatly by comparison. Xenophon had the temerity to try to succeed Thucydides. His *Hellenica* began where Thucydides stopped, covering the next half century. The work is reasonably accurate, but, as it proceeds beyond the first two books, superficial and uninspired. Yet unlike Herodotus and Thucydides, Xenophon was an author of multiple works and displayed great boldness in exploring several different genres. His life of the Spartan king, Agesilaus, is the first standalone political biography that survives from antiquity, and, if the *Cyropaedia,* his highly moralizing work on the education and values of the Persian monarch Cyrus, departs at convenient moments from historical fact, it nevertheless influenced the likes of Cicero several centuries later. Xenophon also tried his hand at, among other things, an essay on Athenian revenues, an investigation into the Spartan constitution, and several works on Socrates.

The diversity of Xenophon's literary activity proved far more typical of later historians than did the single contributions of Herodotus and Thucydides. History writing was never, in antiquity, viewed as an independent profession. A list from second-century B.C. Alexandria that details the intellectual professions does not include historians. And in fact, most appear to have survived by being independently wealthy, enjoying the patronage of the powerful, or teaching practical skills, especially rhetoric. Any of these strategies will affect the outcome of an individual historical work as well as the overall career of the historian. Herodotus, who had some financial resources but who seems also to have sung for his supper in Athens, made that city central to his work. Thucydides, who certainly enjoyed independent means, viewed Athenian democracy with an aristocratic eye. Posidonius wrote an influential history in the first century B.C. in which his interpretation of Rome's role was colored by his far more important philosophical teachings. Posidonius's experience was probably the more common, as historians taught and wrote on a variety of subjects in order to make a living. History writing in antiquity never became a unified and independent craft.

The major competitors to Xenophon in the fourth century were Ephorus and Theopompus. Like Xenophon (and a lesser-known author, Cratippus), Theopompus began one of his historical works precisely where Thucydides had left off. In so doing the tradition of historical continuity was established. The practice continued informally throughout antiquity (for example, the successive works of Timaeus, Polybius, Posidonius, and Strabo acknowledged their predecessors). But historians rarely attempted to improve upon earlier works by exploring new bodies of knowledge or different approaches. Posidonius's ethnographic appreciation of Rome's subjects is fundamentally different from Polybius's interpretation of Roman rule based on military and diplomatic accomplishments. But rather than starting anew and giving a different portrait of Rome's earlier hegemony, Posidonius accepted the Polybian account and began his work where the earlier history ends.

Indeed, any attempt to go over earlier ground generally produced sterile narrative. Diodorus compiled a thousand-year history down to his own time by following previous individual narratives closely; Arrian, living half a millennium after the events, wrote a history of Alexander's campaigns by synthesizing what he thought were the most accurate accounts; and Plutarch created his biographies of Greeks and Romans by selecting material from earlier histories that best illuminated his moral insights. Thucydides had made the point that original history was contemporary history, and thus investigations into the distant past generally consisted of rationalizing and reconciling established accounts rather than attempting to uncover new evidence. Nevertheless, the challenge to continue or to reinterpret the past produced a historical consciousness that spread beyond its practitioners to include the broader public through the awareness of history in ritual, literature, and the plastic arts. Although historians did not have a clearly demarcated place among the ancient professions, history and historical works were highly prized. One need only read the letters of Cicero to appreciate the centrality of history to rhetoric, philosophy, politics, and the living of the good life.

History's ambiguous status as a profession and as a craft, then, remained unresolved. The Greek society that developed for humankind theater and political oratory was predominantly oral in expression, and history never completely broke from the performing arts. Aeschylus's tragic play, *The Persians,* presents some essential factual evidence, while its "historical" counterpart, Herodotus's *Persian Wars,* at times abandons historical principles to achieve romantic and tragic effect. It is little wonder that Lucian in his didactic tract, *How to Write History,* eleven times refers to listeners of historical works and only twice refers to readers. Political and forensic oratory, although not generally included within the historical genre, also provide essential historical information. Orators frequently based their arguments on history and even created history of their own. They often rewrote their speeches precisely with the intention that they be understood by later generations as testimony to their actions. The line between historical exposition and oral display was quite thin.

Ephorus and Theopompus, trained in history by the orator Isocrates (so at least tradition claims), produced works heavily laden with rhetorical devices. Most conspicuous among them were speeches purportedly spoken by historical characters and moral judgments rendered by the historian. Herodotus had included speeches in his work, but Thucydides lifted the practice to a high art form. He experimented with several different types of oratory, all brilliantly executed, and these provide the reader with respite from the narrative and extraordinary insight into policy and human motivation. But Thucydides worried openly that the speeches were at least in part his own creation rather than the actual words spoken, and no one in antiquity ever satisfactorily resolved that problem. Indeed, later historians usually created speeches of greater style than substance, so that what was gained was not even historical insight but merely dramatic effect. Similarly, moral judgments of historical characters

entertained as much as they educated. These moral judgments were designed, at least in theory, to spur on the reader to emulate the best and avoid the worst actions of that individual. When offered by Polybius, these judgments had utility, because he suggested significant correctives to a character's political or military decisions. In the hands of more rhetorically minded authors, the judgments could be pompous, scandalous, or mendacious. But then again, as a genre without a firm place within the academic disciplines, history needed to be entertaining. Polybius railed against sensationalism, yet a century later Dionysius of Halicarnassus, who knew quite a bit about style, testified that almost no one read Polybius anymore.

History, in fact, never convincingly established that its purpose was to discover and preserve the truth. That might have been the claim of Thucydides and Polybius, but other writers openly embraced different intentions, such as moral education, political propaganda, or simple entertainment. A later writer refers to novels as "historical works" *(historikoi),* and, indeed, many ancient novels did use historical figures as central characters. Again, its intersection with rhetoric and lack of formal recognition within the academy probably did most to obfuscate history's purpose.

Beginning with the works of Theopompus and Ephorus, histories grew in size. Physically, there was enormous inflation and some were as much as ten times longer than those of Herodotus and Thucydides. Some of the added bulk might have been due to the use of rhetorical devices in the narrative, but changing conditions in publishing, distributing, and purchasing that can no longer be identified might also have been responsible.

What is most readily apparent, however, is that historians now tended to deal with larger subjects. The narrowly focused monograph continued to be popular throughout antiquity. We know the titles—but often not much more—of thousands of smaller works on such subjects as chronology, ritual, ethnography, geography, and especially local history. The related genre of biography also grew significantly, as powerful people wanted their stories told. Beginning in the fourth century, however, pride of place went to narratives that addressed the actions and intersections of multiple Greek states and even non-Greek lands. The archaic poet, Hesiod, had already divided world history into successive stages, and Herodotus had somewhat unsystematically covered Persian expansion. But the forcible unification of Greece under Philip of Macedon, the conquest of the East by his son Alexander, and the integration of the Mediterranean by Rome successively demanded broader synthesis. Universal histories, as they were called, became the final product of this process of integration. The philosophical unity of humanity, understood by the Stoics in the Hellenistic period, could be viewed through Rome's political unity (for example as by Diodorus and Posidonius, although very differently). And that, in turn, provided a model for a spiritual unity proposed by St. Augustine and other Christian authors.

Greek history writing, multifarious and ambiguous in design and aim, profoundly influenced the literatures of all peoples with whom the Greeks had contact. It can be traced in Rome from Fabius Pictor, who even chose to write in Greek, to Sallust and Tacitus who fell under the spell of Thucydides. In Jewish literature, Jason of Cyrene (the original author of Maccabees II), Josephus, and a full range of intertestamental authors clearly reflect Greek methods. The historical fragments of the works of the Egyptian Manetho and Berossus of Babylonia also reveal the penetration of Hellenistic history writing. In the New Testament, Luke and Acts especially bear such influence, while Christian hagiography developed from the Greek biographical tradition.

As Greece is central to Western tradition, Greek historical writers naturally claim special authority in our craft. Ranke's famous insistence on factually driven narratives derives from acknowledged emulation of Thucydides's similar obsession, and the opening of Macaulay's *History of England* is in direct imitation of Thucydides's initial justification of his own subject. In this century, however, Herodotean approaches are in ascendancy, reflected in current interest in social history and in the application of anthropology to history writing.

Kenneth S. Sacks

See also BIOGRAPHY; BYZANTINE HISTORIOGRAPHY; GREEK HISTORIOGRAPHY—MODERN; HAGIOGRAPHY; ROMAN HISTORIOGRAPHY—ANCIENT.

Texts

Jacoby, F. *Die Fragmente der griechishen Historiker* [Fragments of the Greek Historians]. Leiden: Brill, 1923–.

References

Fornara, C. *The Nature of History in Ancient Greece and Rome.* Berkeley: University of California Press, 1983.

Momigliano, Arnaldo. *The Classical Foundations of Modern Historiography.* Berkeley: University of California Press, 1990.

———. *Contributo alla storia degli studi classici e del mondo antico* [Contribution to the History of Classical Studies and of the Ancient World]. Rome: Edizioni di storia e letteratura, 1955–1992 (9 *Contributi* in 12 vols.).

———. "Greek Historiography." *History and Theory* 17 (1978): 1–28.

Walbank, F. *Selected Papers.* Cambridge, Eng.: Cambridge University, 1985.

Greek Historiography—Modern

Historical writing in Greece from ca. 1500 to the present. The fall of Constantinople in 1453 interrupted an evolving tradition of Byzantine humanism, whose greatest representative in historiography was Laonikos Chalkokondyles. Other Greek humanists of the period took refuge in Italy and were integrated into the culture of the Renaissance. Greek culture during the sixteenth century proved rather poor in historical writing. Two versions of a chronicle dating from this period, the *Istoria patriarchiki Constantinoupoleos* [Patriarchal History of Constantinople] (1454–1578), compiled by Manuel Malaxos and the *Istoria politiki Constantinoupoleos* [Political History of Constantinople] (1391–1578), compiled by Theodosios Zygomalas, both adaptations of earlier chronographic sources, were published by Martinus Crusius in his *Turcograicia* in 1586.

A distinct Byzantine tradition that survived in the bosom of Greek culture under Ottoman rule was the genre of Christian chronicles, narrating the history of the world since the creation. A characteristic example of this genre was the *Vivlion Istorikon* [Historical Book], also known as *Chronographos* [Chronographer], pseudonymously attributed to Dorotheos, nonexistent bishop of Monemvasia. The work was first published in 1631, although the text also survives in several sixteenth-century manuscripts. This became the most popular Greek historical work in the Ottoman period, appearing in at least eighteen editions up to 1818. A more learned version of the Christian chronicle was the *Epitomi ierokosmikis istorias* [Epitome of Universal History] by Nektarios, Patriarch of Jerusalem, first published in 1677 and reprinted six times before 1805. A third example of chronicle writing was the work of an eighteenth-century author, Athanasios Komninos Ypsilantis entitled *Ekklesiastikon kai politikon vivlia dodeka* [Twelve Books on Ecclesiastical and Political Affairs], covering events from Julius Caesar to 1789; this work was published only in part in 1870. Another eighteenth-century author, the prolific

Caesarios Dapontes, recorded contemporary events in a number of chronicles, which remained unpublished during his lifetime.

The earliest form of learned historiography in Greek culture was—predictably for a society deprived of its own state and organized around its church—ecclesiastical history. Two patriarchs of Jerusalem pioneered the genre: Dositheos Notaras wrote an *Istoria peri ton en Ierosolymois patriarchefsanton* [History of the Patriarchs of Jerusalem], posthumously published in 1715, while his nephew and successor Chrysanthos Notaras wrote an *Istoria kai perigraphi tis Agias Gis kai tis Agias poleos Ierousalim* [History of the Holy Land and of the Holy City of Jerusalem] (1728). Chrysanthos, an accomplished geographer and astronomer with wide interests, also wrote a history of China from 1368 to 1680, which he completed in Moscow in 1694 but left unpublished. Another prelate with geographical interests, Meletios Mitrou, Archbishop of Athens, composed both a *Geographia palaia kai nea* [Geography Old and New] (1728) and a general *Ekklisiastiki Istoria* [Ecclesiastical History]; the latter book was published in three volumes in 1783, seventy years after the author's death.

A major turning point in the emergence of secular historiography was the Greek translation in sixteen volumes of Charles Rollin's *Histoire ancienne* [Ancient History] (1750). The publication of this work was a clear sign of a new curiosity in the Greeks' pagan ancient past, which had been submerged during the Christian Middle Ages. The new interest in classical history was a clear sign of the outlook of the Enlightenment that had begun to be felt in Greek culture during this period. From the middle of the eighteenth century to the Greek War of Independence in 1821, Greek historiography revealed the impact of Enlightenment thought in two characteristic ways. One was an increasing interest in ancient Greek history and culture, reflected notably in works by G. Sakellarios (1796), V. Papaefthimiou (1807), Gregorios Palliouritis (1815), and A. Stageiritis (1815–1820), and in translations of well-known works of Enlightenment classicism such as those by the Abbés Jean-Jacques Barthélemy and Claude François Xavier Millot, as well as works by Oliver Goldsmith and Louis Domairon. The same interest also motivated the publication of new editions of Thucydides in 1799, 1802, and 1805.

A parallel development was an expanding curiosity about contemporary international relations and conflicts and the history of faraway lands. This new awareness of a broader world was registered in the inauguration in 1759 of a project on "world history" whose original intention was, according to the editor, G. Constantinou, to produce a volume on every kingdom in the world. Two volumes eventually appeared, on Russia (1759) and China (1763). William Robertson's four-volume *History of America* was translated and published by Georgios Vendotis in Vienna (1792–1794). Greek fascination with the progress of Russia, combined with the instigation of Russian propaganda, produced two biographies of Peter the Great, one originally composed in Italian by Antonios Katiphoros (1736), and subsequently translated in Greek, and a second by Athanasios Skiadas (1737). The Russo-Turkish wars of the eighteenth century stimulated a Greek edition of a major six-volume work published anonymously in Italian by Domenico Caminer and translated in Greek by Spyridon Papadopoulos (1770–1773). Along the same lines, Agapios Loverdos published a compilation drawing on the Italian annual register of world events, *Storia dell' anno,* under the title *Istoria ton dyo eton 1787–1788* [History of the Two Years 1787–1788] (1791). All of these works were printed at the Greek presses operating in Venice.

It was also at Venice in 1788 that there appeared perhaps the most original historiographical attempt of the Greek Enlightenment, the *Istoria chronologiki tis nisou Kyprou* [Chronological History of the Island of Cyprus] by the Archimandrite Kyprianos. Whereas most secular historiography up to 1821 consisted of translations and adaptations, Kyprianos, although he drew on a variety of sources, attempted to write his own history of his native island and to explain the collective predicament of the Greeks under Ottoman rule by considering social, cultural, and material causes. The culmination of the Greek historiographical Enlightenment can be seen in the twelve-volume work of Constantinos Koumas, who wrote a world history drawing on contemporary German historians, especially on the *Weltgeschichte* by Karl Friedrich Becker (1830–1832). Finally under this rubric, of special interest in this period are works that highlight the "Balkan dimension" of the Greek Enlightenment, such as Triandaphyllos Doukas's versified *Istoria ton Slavenoservon* [History of the Slaveno-Serbs] (1807), which narrates the outbreak of the Serbian uprising in 1803, Daniel Philippides' *Istoria tis Rumunias* [History of Romania] (1816), in which the name "Romania" is used for the first time to describe as one unity the three principalities of Wallachia, Moldavia, and Transylvania, and Dionysios Photeinos's three-volume *Istoria tis palai Dakias* [History of Dacia] (1818–1819).

G

The Greek War of Independence and the emergence of Greece as an independent nation in 1830 established an entirely new context for Greek historical writing. The decades after independence were marked by a prolific literature of memoirs and historical accounts of the war of liberation. Among the latter category, works by Spyridon Trikoupis (1853) and Ioannis Philimon (1859–1861) are the most notable. What also appears clearly during this period is a pronounced interest in the philosophy of history, motivated by a quest for the deeper meaning of Greek collective destinies. The most characteristic statements of this interest were the works of Georgios Kozakis-Typaldos (1839) and Markos Renieris (1841).

The challenge represented by Jacob Philipp Fallmerayer's argument that the modern Greeks were the progeny not of classical Hellenes but of the Slavic tribes that had settled in Greece in the Middle Ages, posed with great urgency the problem of continuity in Greek history. This motivated serious reflection about the medieval conditions of the Greek people and a reawakened interest in Byzantium, which the Enlightenment had largely written off as a period of decline and obscurantism. These new interests are best reflected in the work of Spyridon Zambelios. Building to some extent on Zambelios, Constantinos Paparrigopoulos constructed his own imposing synthesis of the history of the Greek nation, in which medieval Byzantium was rehabilitated as an integral component of Greek historical continuity. Paparrigopoulos's contemporary and rival, Constantinos Sathas, who was thwarted in his ambitions for an academic career, produced important editions of medieval and early modern source material, which are still of value today.

In about the same period and spanning the early part of the twentieth century, two other editors of primary material, Manuel I. Gedoon (1851–1943) and Athanasios Papadopoulos Kerameus (1856–1912), produced massive and truly invaluable editions of medieval and early modern sources, focusing on the history of the Orthodox Church and Greek cultural life outside Greece, especially in the jurisdictions of the patriarchates of Constantinople and Jerusalem, respectively.

Paparrigopoulos's successors at the University of Athens in the nineteenth and twentieth centuries, Paul Karolides, Spyridon Lambros, Socratis Kougeas, Constantinos Amantos, and Dionysios Zakithinos, pursued the study of Byzantine history, thus cementing the theory of the continuity of the Greek nation.

The twentieth century saw the further evolution of Greek academic historiography within the same framework. Original research focused increasingly on the publication of manuscript sources, and historical writing remained analytical, veering away from the task of synthesis. Renewal came invariably from outside the history faculties and even from outside the universities. During the interwar period Andreas Andreades inaugurated economic history in the law school at Athens. A major challenge to conventional historiography came from a tradition of Marxist writers, often writing from prison, including G. Skliros, Yiannis Kordatos, and S. Maximos. A final challenge to academic historiography has been the work of C.Th. [Constantinos] Dimaras (1904–1992) in literary and intellectual history. Writing in conscious opposition to academic conventions, and focusing on the rise and failure of the Enlightenment in Greek thought, Dimaras extended from outside the universities a serious invitation to his countrymen to undertake a rewriting of the history of modern Greek culture and ideology.

Since the collapse in 1974 of the seven-year military dictatorship, Greek historical writing has experienced a new efflorescence, especially through a reorientation in the direction of economic and, to a lesser extent, social history. This is obviously a conscious reaction to the nationalist "idealism" of earlier academic historiography. Conventional and novel approaches are incorporated side-by-side in the collective fifteen-volume *Istoria tou ellinikou ethnous* [History of the Greek Nation] (1970–1978), which constitutes a mirror of Greek historical scholarship in the second half of the twentieth century. By its very title and overall structure and approach, this work nevertheless indicates the continuing weight of Paparrigopoulos's conceptualization in the historical self-understanding of contemporary Greece.

Paschalis M. Kitromilides

See also BYZANTINE HISTORIOGRAPHY; ECCLESIASTICAL HISTORY; GREEK HISTORIOGRAPHY—ANCIENT.

References

Kitroeff, Al. "Continuity and Change in Contemporary Greek Historiography." *European History Quarterly* 19 (1989): 269–298.

Kitromilides, P.M. *Enlightenment, Nationalism, Orthodoxy: Studies in the Culture and Political Thought of Southeastern Europe.* London: Variorum, 1994, chaps. 1, 2, 11, 12.

———. "Ideologikes epiloges kai istoriographiki praxi [Ideological Options and Historiographical Practice]." *Thesaurismata* 20 (1990): 500–517.

Patrinelis, C.G. *Proimi neoelliniki istoriographia (1453–1821)* [Early Modern Greek Historiography (1453–1821)]. Thessaloniki: Aristotle University of Thessaloniki, 1990.

Stassinopoulou, M.A. *Weltgeschichte im Denken eines griechischen Aufklärers: Konstantinos Michail Koumas als Historiograph* [World History in the Thought of a Greek Enlightener: Konstantinos Michail Koumas As Historian]. Frankfurt am Main: Peter Lang, 1992.

Zakythinos, D.A. "Metavyzantini kai neotera elliniki istoriographia [Post-Byzantine and Modern Greek Historiography]." *Praktika tis Akadimias Athinon* 49 (1974): 57–103.

Green, John Richard (1837–1883)

English historian. Born in Oxford, Green grew up in straitened circumstances, and delicate health, in a staunchly Anglican household. He rebelled by adopting liberal political viewpoints that resulted in his expulsion from Magdalen College School. Securing a scholarship to Jesus College, Oxford, he quickly became disillusioned and contented himself with a pass degree in 1859. Inspired to enter the Anglican priesthood in 1860, Green spent the next decade working in the most impoverished parishes of East London, exacerbating the tubercular condition that ultimately claimed his life. He also struggled to liberalize the Church of England, hoping to bring its doctrines into line with modern science and historical criticism. During these years, he became a writer for the *Saturday Review* and a close friend of the historian Edward Augustus Freeman. Physically exhausted and embittered by the church's muzzling of liberal clergy, Green left his clerical post in 1869, determined to make his mark as a historian. His *Short History of the English People* (1874), proved enormously and enduringly popular. An expanded version of it appeared three years later. In an attempt to leave behind a reputation for more scholarly work, he published, in the last two years of his short life, *The Making of England* and *The Conquest of England*. In these final works, he was assisted considerably by his wife, Alice Stopford Green, whom he married in 1877 and who later became a notable historian of Ireland. Green's reputation now rests almost entirely on the *Short History of the English People,* a book that was extremely influential in the United States as well as throughout the British Empire. Shaped by a disdain for traditional political and military narratives and a reverence for the common people, the *Short History* encouraged the writing of social and cultural history. At the same time, however, Green's literary flair, popular tone, and neglect of archival sources made him suspect to the emerging historical professionals, who emphasized heavily documented monographs intended for fellow specialists. Critics tended to castigate him as one of the "Whig" historians, and to link him with Freeman and William Stubbs as part of the "Oxford school," but recent work in Victorian historiography makes his distinctiveness clear.

Anthony Brundage

Texts

The Conquest of England. London: Macmillan, 1882.

Historical Studies. Ed. Alice Stopford Green. London: Macmillan, 1903.

History of the English People. 4 vols. London: Macmillan, 1877–1880.

Letters of John Richard Green. Ed. Leslie Stephen. London: Macmillan, 1901.

The Making of England. London: Macmillan, 1882.

Short History of the English People. London: Macmillan, 1874.

References

Brundage, Anthony. *The People's Historian: John Richard Green and the Writing of History in Victorian England.* Westport, CT: Greenwood Press, 1994.

Jann, Rosemary. *The Art and Science of Victorian History.* Columbus: Ohio University Press, 1985.

Schuyler, Robert Livingstone. "John Richard Green and His Short History." *Political Science Quarterly* 64 (1949): 321–354.

Green, Mary Anne Everett (née Wood) (1818–1895)

English historian and editor of (mainly seventeenth-century) historical documents. Born in Sheffield into a prominent Methodist family, Green moved to London and embarked upon an independent scholarly career as the editor of the *Letters of Royal and Illustrious Ladies of Great Britain* (1846) and the author of the *Lives of the Princesses of England, from the Norman Conquest* (1849–1855). In 1853 she was nominated as an editor of the *Calendar of State Papers: Domestic Series.* She devoted the remainder of her career to this task, supplying the volumes for the reigns of James I and Charles II, and the Commonwealth. Green was a meticulous

G

and productive historian who enjoyed a secure position in the scholarly community of her day. Her authorial personality is most clearly revealed in her only narrative history, the *Lives of the Princesses of England,* a lively work, which expresses an admiration for tactful, clever, influential, and, above all, staunchly Protestant women in history.

Karen O'Brien

Texts

Elizabeth, Electress Palatine and Queen of Bohemia. Ed. S.C. Lomas. London: Methuen, 1909.

Ed. *Letters of Henrietta Maria.* London: R. Bentley, 1857.

As Mary Anne Wood. *Letters of Royal and Illustrious Ladies of Great Britain.* 3 vols. London: H. Colburn, 1846.

Lives of the Princesses of England, from the Norman Conquest. 6 vols. London: H. Colburn, 1849–1855.

Grégoire, Henri (1881–1964)

Belgian Byzantine historian. Grégoire was born in Huy, Belgium, and studied at the University of Liège, where he obtained his doctorate (1902). He was engaged in an inquiry regarding Leopold II's misgovernment of the Congo, and was obliged to leave the kingdom for Athens and the Near East. He returned in 1909, and taught at the Free University of Brussels. Among his many accomplishments, he founded the journal *Byzantion* (1924) and founded and edited the intellectual magazine *Le Flambeau* [The Flame] (at first an organ of the resistance to Germany in World War I). His greatest achievements came as an epigrapher, but he was also active as a translator, as well as an archaeologist, hagiographer, and Byzantinist. Most of his publications were in the form of articles or archaeological reports.

Stephen A. Stertz

Texts

Autour de l'épopée byzantine [Concerning the Byzantine Epic]. (Reprinted scholarly articles and papers.) London: Variorum, 1975.

With P. Orgels, J. Moreau, and A. Maricq. *Les persecutions dans l'empire romain.* Second ed. Brussels: Palais des Academies, 1964.

Recueil des inscriptions grecques-chrètiennes d'asie mineure [Collection of the Greco-Christian Inscriptions of Asia Minor]. Amsterdam: A. Hakkert, 1968.

References

Mavris, N.G. "La carrière d'Henri Grégoire [The Career of Henri Grégoire]." *Byzantion* 35 (1965): vi–xiv. [Reprint with additions to article first appearing in *Byzantina-Metabyzantina* 1 (1946).]

Gregorovius, Ferdinand Adolf (1821–1891)

German ancient and medieval historian. Gregorovius was born in Neidenburg in East Prussia and studied theology at the University of Königsberg, although his doctoral dissertation was on Plotinus. After working as a private tutor and journalist he went in 1852 to Rome, where he conceived and wrote his masterpiece on the history of that city during the Middle Ages. In 1874 he settled in Munich, although he continued to visit Rome and toured Greece and western Asia. Gregorovius is most famous for his monumental, eight-volume *Geschichte der Stadt Rom im Mittelalter* [History of the City of Rome in the Middle Ages] (1859–1872), a work criticized by contemporary academics but eventually appreciated as a classic account and still of value today. Besides travel writings, journals, and poetry, he produced other historical works, notably *Geschichte des römischen Kaisers Hadrian und seiner Zeit* [History of the Roman Emperor Hadrian and His Times] (1851), *Lucrezia Borgia* (1874), and a two-volume *Geschichte der Stadt Athen im Mittelalter* [History of the City of Athens in the Middle Ages] (1889).

Richard Fowler

Texts

Geschichte der Stadt Athen im Mittelalter: Von der Zeit Justinians bis zur turkischen Eroberung [History of the City of Athens in the Middle Ages: From the Time of Justinian to the Turkish Conquest]. Munich: Deutscher Taschenbuch Verlag, 1980.

Geschichte des römischen Kaisers Hadrian und seiner Zeit. Konigsberg: J.H. Bon, 1851.

History of the City of Rome in the Middle Ages. Trans. Mrs. Gustavus W. Hamilton (from the fourth German ed.). 8 vols. in 13. New York: AMS Press, 1967.

Lucretia Borgia, According to Original Documents and Correspondence of Her Day. Trans. John Leslie Garner. New York: D. Appleton, 1904.

Rome and Medieval Culture: Selections from the History of the City of Rome in the Middle Ages. Trans. Mrs. G.W. Hamilton; ed. K.F. Morrison. Chicago: University of Chicago Press, 1971.

References

Hönig, J., *Ferdinand Gregorovius: Eine Biographie* [Ferdinand Gregorovius: A Biography]. Stuttgart: Cotta'sche Buchhandlung, 1944.

Kruft, Hanno-Walter. *Der Historiker als Dichter: Zum 100. Todestag von Ferdinand Gregorovius* [The Historian As Poet: On the Centenary of the Death of Ferdinand Gregorovius]. Munich: Verlag der Bayerischen Akademie der Wissenschaften (In Kommission bei C.H. Beck), 1992.

Gregory of Tours (ca. 539–594)

Historian and hagiographer of the Franks. Born in Clermont to a Roman senatorial family, Gregory was raised by his uncle Gallus, bishop of Clermont. He received his education from his great uncle Nicetius, bishop of Lyon. In 563 Gregory became a deacon and made pilgrimage to the shrine of Martin of Tours. Consecrated bishop there in 573, he entered into the fray among the various Merovingian political factions. In addition to his activities as an administrator, evangelist, and promoter of the cult of Martin, Gregory devoted himself to hagiographical and historical writing until his death. Considered the principal hagiographer of the sixth century, Gregory wrote in simple and "barbarous" Latin. Central among his compositions were the miracles of Julian (580s) and Martin (593), and his *Liber vitae patrum* [Life of the Fathers] (ca.592), in which he focused on significant Gallo-Roman bishops, especially those of Clermont and Tours. Like his *Liber in gloria confessorum* [Glory of the Confessors] (ca. 587–588) and *Liber in gloria martyrum* [Glory of the Martyrs] (590s), these texts served a pastoral function. In contrast, Gregory's *Decem libri historiarum* [Ten Books of the Histories] (573–594) explained the universal role of saints from the time of creation. Gregory thereby promoted Catholic achievements while at the same time denigrating the Goths, who subscribed to the heresy of Arianism.

Bonnie Effros

Texts

Glory of the Confessors. Trans. Raymond Van Dam. Liverpool: Liverpool University Press, 1988.

Glory of the Martyrs. Trans. Raymond Van Dam. Liverpool: Liverpool University Press, 1988.

The History of the Franks. Trans. Lewis Thorpe. Harmondsworth: Penguin, 1974.

Life of the Fathers. Trans. Edward James. Liverpool: Liverpool University Press, 1985.

Saints and Their Miracles in Late Antique Gaul. Ed. and trans. Raymond van Dam. Princeton, NJ: Princeton University Press, 1993. (Translated extracts from Gregory.)

References

Goffart, Walter. *The Narrators of Barbarian History* (A.D. *550–800): Jordanes, Gregory of Tours, Bede and Paul the Deacon.* Princeton, NJ: Princeton University Press, 1988.

Heinzelmann, Martin. *Gregor von Tours: Zehn Bücher Geschichte* [Gregory of Tours: Ten Books of History]. Sigmaringen, Germany: Jan Thorbeke Verlag, 1994.

Wallace-Hadrill, J.M. "The Work of Gregory of Tours in the Light of Modern Research." In his *The Long-Haired Kings.* Toronto: University of Toronto Press, 1962, 49–70.

Grote, George (1794–1871)

English banker, politician, and historian. Born in Beckenham, Kent, and educated at the Charterhouse, he worked in the bank founded thirty years earlier by his German grandfather first (1810) as a clerk and later as a governor (1830–1843). He also served from 1832 to 1841 as member of Parliament for the city of London, campaigning vigorously, but unsuccessfully, for the adoption of the ballot. He retired from both politics and banking in 1841 and devoted the rest of his life to writing. He contributed largely to the organization of University College, London, with which he remained associated from its foundation (1828) to his death. He was buried in Westminster Abbey. Grote's fame is based on his twelve-volume *History of Greece* (1846–1856), although he also wrote supplementary works on ancient and modern philosophical subjects. His scrupulous evaluation of historical evidence made him unusually skeptical about the mythical period, while his liberal principles led to an unusually favorable judgment on Athenian democracy.

Catherine Rubincam

Texts

A History of Greece from the Earliest Period to the Close of the Generation Contemporary with Alexander. 10 vols. London: John Murray. 1888.

References

Clarke, M.L. *George Grote: A Biography.* London: Athlone Press, 1962.

Momigliano, Arnaldo. *George Grote and the Study of Greek History: An Inaugural Lecture Delivered at University College, London.* London: University of London, 1952.

Groulx, Lionel (1878–1967)

French Canadian historian, novelist, and essayist. Groulx was born in Vaudreuil, near Montreal. Ordained a Catholic priest in 1903, he taught history and literature in a classical college. He later completed graduate theological studies in Rome and studied literature in Switzerland. From 1915 to 1949 he taught Canadian history at the University of Montreal. During this period he also served as director of a patriotic journal; published novels, essays, and his first historical works; and was a popular speaker. In the 1920s and 1930s he was at the height of his influence as an ideologist of French Canadian nationalism. Perceived as French Canada's principal historian, he commanded a large audience. His nationalistic ideas, however, met with opposition in clerical and political circles. With the exception of a brief period of sympathy for the concept of a sovereign Quebec, Groulx's activities were dedicated to the defense of French Canadian rights within the Canadian Confederation. As a historian, he exalted the deeds and accomplishments of French Canadian heroes, from explorer Jacques Cartier to Premier Honoré Mercier, who defended Quebec's constitutional rights in the late nineteenth century. Groulx's most ambitious work was the four-volume *L'Histoire du Canada français depuis la découverte* [History of French Canada since Its Discovery] (1950–1952). Self-educated in history, he was anxious that Quebec historians receive quality training and that they be enabled to meet and exchange ideas in appropriate venues. In 1946 he founded l'Institut d'histoire de l'Amérique française, which was to become the leading learned society dedicated to the study of Quebec's past. The following year he launched the *Revue d'histoire de l'Amérique française* [Historical Journal of French America], which was soon recognized as Quebec's most notable historical journal. With the emergence of a secular and more progressive Quebec, neonationalism and the development of a historiography less centered on the survival of French Canada (at both Laval University and the University of Montreal, for example), Groulx's works became seriously outdated. After his death a college and a Montreal subway station were named in his honor. His memoirs and the early years of his personal diary

were published in four volumes. A team of scholars is currently preparing an edition of his voluminous correspondence.

Pierre Savard

Texts

Abbé Groulx: Variations on a Nationalist Theme. Ed. Susan M. Trofimenkoff; trans. Joanne L'Heureux and Susan M. Trofimenkoff. Vancouver: Copp Clarke, 1973.

La découverte du Canada: Jacques Cartier [The Discovery of Canada: Jacques Cartier]. Second ed. Montreal: Fides, 1966.

Histoire du Canada français depuis la découverte [History of French Canada since Its Discovery]. 4 vols. Montreal: L'action nationale, 1950–1952.

La Naissance d'une race [Birth of a Race]. Montreal: Librairie Granger Frères, 1938.

Notre grande aventure: L'empire français en Amérique du Nord (1535–1760) [Our Great Adventure: The French Empire in North America (1535–1760)]. Montreal and Paris: Fides, 1958.

Notre maître le passé [Our Teacher, the Past]. 3 vols. Montreal: Granger, 1936–1944.

References

Ferretti, Lucia. *Lionel Groulx, la Voix d'une époque* [Lionel Groulx, Voice of an Era]. Montreal: L'Agence du livre, 1983.

Gaboury, Jean-Pierre. *Le Nationalisme de Lionel Groulx: Aspects idéologiques* [The Nationalism of Lionel Groulx: Ideological Aspects]. Ottawa: University of Ottawa Press, 1970.

Gagnon, Serge. *Quebec and Its Historians.* Vol I, *1840–1920.* Trans. Yves Brunelle. Montreal: Harvest House, 1982.

———. *Quebec and Its Historians.* Vol. II, *The Twentieth Century.* Trans. Jane Brierley. Montreal: Harvest House, 1985.

Gu Jiegang [Ku Chieh-kang] (1893–1980)

Modern historian of ancient China, ethnographer, and historical geographer. Born to a Suzhou scholar-gentry family, Gu Jiegang received a traditional education. While studying at Beijing University in the late 1910s, he was drawn to Hu Shi's "scientific reorganization of Chinese history." Gu made his fame by editing the first few volumes of *Gushi bian* [Discussions of Ancient History] (1927–1941). He shocked the academic community by promoting a "stratification theory" in studying Chinese history. He also argued that the received picture of China's past was the result of generations of reconstructions and fabrications. In the 1920s, Gu also wrote on folklore, folk songs, and pilgrim organizations, and is now considered to have been one of the founders of modern Chinese ethnography. In the 1930s, Gu turned his attentions to historical geography by editing the *Yu Gong* bimonthly. After 1949, Gu concentrated on the *Shangshu* [Book of Documents], which he believed to be the most reliable source for a true account of early China.

Tze-ki Hon

Texts
The Autobiography of a Chinese Historian. Trans. Arthur W. Hummel. Leiden: E.J. Brill, 1931.
Ed. *Gushi bian.* Vols. 1, 2, 3, and 5. Beijing: Pu she, 1927–1935.

References
Schneider, Laurence. *Ku Chieh-kang and China's New History: Nationalism and the Quest for Alternative Traditions.* Berkeley: University of California Press, 1971.

Gu Yanwu (Ku Yen-wu) (1613–1682)

Leading Chinese scholar, phonetician, geographer, and historian. Gu came from Kunshan, very near modern Shanghai, and spent the first part of his life in southern China. However, as a result of a personal feud against him, he left in 1657 for northern China where he lived almost all the rest of his life. The Manchus, who founded the Qing dynasty in 1644, seized Kunshan the next year. Gu was bitterly anti-Manchu all his life, and as a result of this he never sought or gained high office. Gu's views on historical and other research emerge in his slogan, borrowed from Confucius, that one should "base scholarship on the widest range of texts" *(bo xue yu wen)*. He opposed the notion of intuitive knowledge, common in his time, and emphasized the need for creating new hypotheses and testing them through evidence derived from as many sources as possible. He founded the "School of Han Learning" *(Han xue pai)*, the chief feature of which was its appeal to the inductive method of scholarship called "examining evidence."

Colin Mackerras

Texts
Gu Tinglin shiwen ji [Collection of Gu Yanwu's Poetry and Prose]. Hong Kong: Zhonghua shuju, 1976.

References
Balazs, Etienne. *Political Theory and Administrative Reality in Traditional China.* London: School of Oriental and African Studies, 1965.
Hagman, Jan. *Bibliographic Notes on Ku Yen-wu (1613–1682).* Stockholm: Föreningen för orientaliska studier, 1973.

Gu Yingtai [Ku Ying-t'ai] (1620–1690)

Chinese historian active during early Qing period. As Educational Commissioner in Zhejiang for two years from 1656, Gu collected material for his *Mingshi jishi benmo* [History of the Ming Dynasty]. This work, organized in annals to which the author adds his own evaluation, contains eighty chapters, each of which treats a separate subject or event during the preceding Ming dynasty. In a six-chapter addendum, Gu discusses the battles leading up to the defeat of the Ming regime by its Manchu conquerors. Several other scholars assisted Gu in his compilation of this work. Gu, who was representative of the historiographical traditions of his society, omits mention of the spectacular overseas voyages of the 1420s and 1430s, uses material more suited for historical fiction than objective history in describing the fate of the Jianwen emperor, and generally employs his material in the praise–blame paradigm of traditional Chinese historiography. Unlike many contemporary historians, he aimed, not at eulogizing the past dynasty, but at producing a work that would be of assistance to the Qing as a guide to the past. Gu published the work extremely early in the Qing in 1658 and had access to sources unavailable to later historians. The book's value lies in its reproduction of rare original source material, often from the court gazette, much of which is no longer extant elsewhere. It is especially rich for the history of the last decades of the Ming. After the *Ming shi,* it is probably the most useful work on Ming history.

Carney T. Fisher

Texts
Mingshi jishi benmo. 4 vols. Beijing: Zhonghua shuju, 1977.

References
Hummel, Arthur W., ed. *Eminent Chinese of the Ch'ing Period.* New York: Paragon Book Gallery, 1970.

Guamán [Huamán] Poma de Ayala, Felipe (ca. 1530–1615)

Inca interpreter and secretary for various colonial officials, Guamán Poma became a lay preacher and writer. His *Nueva corónica y buen gobierno* [The New Chronicle and Good Government] was probably finished in 1615 when he was eighty or more years old. Belonging to the first generation of indigenous New World historians, he questioned Spain's right to empire. According to Guamán's chronology, the Andean peoples had been Christianized long before the arrival of the Spaniards, thus obviating the need for forceful evangelization. He also condemned Inca rule, which had subjected the Indian population to superstitious religious practices and idolatry. He sought to create an Andean kingdom as part of a universal Christian empire under Spanish rule. The most original aspect of his work is the four hundred illustrations that depict every aspect of Inca life. Guamán's manuscript, addressed to King Philip III, never reached the Spanish ruler; in fact, it would not be unearthed until 1908, when it was discovered by a German scholar researching in the Royal Collection in Copenhagen. A facsimile copy was made available only in 1936 by the Ethnography Institute in Paris.

George L. Vásquez

Texts

Letter to a King: A Peruvian Chief's Account of Life under the Incas and under Spanish Rule. Ed. and trans. Christopher Dilke. New York: E.P. Dutton, 1978.

References

Adorno, Rolena. *Guamán Poma: Writing and Resistance in Colonial Peru.* Austin: University of Texas Press, 1986.
Padilla Bendezu, Abraham. *Huamán Poma, El indio cronista dibujante.* Mexico City: Fondo de Cultura Económica, 1979.

Guha, Ranajit (b. 1923)

Indian historian and the leading figure of the Subalternist Group, which analyzes the resistance from below to British colonialism in India. In these studies the focus is on what Antonio Gramsci termed the "subaltern classes" rather than on the elite leaders of society who have traditionally been considered pivotal in political action. Guha edited the first six volumes of *Subaltern Studies: Writings on South Asian History and Society* (1982–1989). His "Prose of Counter-Insurgency" in

volume 2 (1983) is the classic statement of the school; it is reproduced in *Selected Subaltern Studies* (1988), which also contains other articles analyzing the Subaltern school group. He is the author of several works on Bengal but his three influential lectures at the Center for Studies in Social Sciences, Calcutta (1987), where he argued for an "autonomous" Indian history of India as an alternative to the British-influenced views of the history of the subcontinent, were published as *An Indian Historiography of India: A Nineteenth-Century Agenda and Its Implications* (1988).

Roger D. Long

Texts

Elementary Aspects of Peasant Insurgency in Colonial India. Delhi: Oxford University Press, 1983.
An Indian Historiography of India: A Nineteenth-Century Agenda and Its Implications. Calcutta: K.P. Bagchi, 1988.
Selected Subaltern Studies. New York: Oxford University Press, 1988.
Subaltern Studies: Writings on South Asian History and Society. Delhi: Oxford University Press, 1982–1989.

References

Chakrabarty, Dipesh. "Trafficking in History and Theory: Subaltern Studies." In *Beyond the Disciplines: The New Humanities,* ed. K.K. Ruthven. Canberra: Australian Academy of the Humanities, 1992.
Prakash, Gyan. "Subaltern Studies As Postcolonial Criticism." *American Historical Review* 99 (1994): 1475–1490. (*AHR* "Forum" on Guha and the Subaltern School.)

Guibert of Nogent (ca. 1064–ca. 1125)

French historian of the First Crusade and autobiographer. The youngest son of a noble family of Clermont-en-Beauvaisis, Guibert entered the Benedictine abbey of Saint-Germer-de-Fly at the age of thirteen. His most important works appeared after 1104 when he became abbot of Nogent-sous-Coucy. In a history called *Gesta Dei per Francos* [The Deeds of God as Performed by the Franks] (1108), Guibert traced the First Crusade from the Council of Clermont to the fall of Jerusalem. He later added an appendix covering the years from 1101 to 1104. While the work exhibits its author's unusually keen awareness of the limitations of sources, it does not reflect the rationalism that has at times been imputed to

Guibert, and it is not superior to other records of the First Crusade either in the range or the accuracy of its contents. Guibert's well-known memoirs (ca. 1115) are patterned after the *Confessions* of St. Augustine and have been central in modern discussions of the medieval understanding of the individual. The third book of the memoirs includes a valuable account of the communal rising against the bishop of Laon in 1112.

David F. Appleby

Texts

Gesta Dei per Francos. Ed. D. Bongarsius. In *Recueil des historiens des croisades: Historiens occidentaux.* 5 vols. Paris: Imprimerie Nationale, 1844–1895, vol. 4 (1879): 113–263.

References

Archambault, Paul J., ed. and trans. *A Monk's Confession: The Memoirs of Guibert of Nogent.* University Park: Pennsylvania State University Press, 1996.

Guicciardini, Francesco (1483–1540)

Florentine statesman and historian. Guicciardini's *Storia d'Italia* [History of Italy] (1494–1534), a milestone in historiography, originated in his desire to comprehend the origin of the Italian wars (1494–1559) and the loss of Italian liberty. A Florentine patrician, he held important offices under the Medici popes culminating in the lieutenant-generalship of the papal army in 1526 and 1527. Discussions with Machiavelli sharpened his insights into political behavior. Writing in Italian rather than Latin enabled him to discard previous conventions of humanist historiography and to develop "pragmatic" analyses of motive based on the sort of assumptions about human behavior that appear in his *Ricordi.* He used documentary sources extensively. His theory that the ambitions and divisions of the Italian princes were responsible for attracting the foreigner into Italy reflected his understanding of the human causes of history, despite the undeniable power of chance, whether termed Fortune, Destiny, or Providence. His useful *Storie fiorentine* [Florentine Histories] are also important.

T.C. Price Zimmermann

Texts

The History of Florence. Trans. Mario Domandi. New York: Harper and Row, 1970.
The History of Italy. Abrid. and trans. S. Alexander. New York: Macmillan, 1969.

Maxims and Reflections of a Renaissance Statesman. Trans. Mario Domandi. New York: Harper and Row, 1965.

References

Bondanella, P.E. *Francesco Guicciardini.* Boston: Twayne, 1976.
Phillips, Mark. *Francesco Guicciardini: The Historian's Craft.* Toronto: University of Toronto Press, 1977.
Ridolfi, Roberto. *The Life of Francesco Guicciardini.* Trans. Cecil Grayson. London: Routledge and Kegan Paul, 1967.

Guizot, François Pierre Guillaume (1787–1874)

French liberal historian and politician. Guizot was born in Nîmes, and in 1798 his family moved to Geneva after his father was killed in the Terror of 1793. In 1805 he studied law in Paris, but decided to pursue the humanities. In 1812, at the youthful age of twenty-five, he became professor of modern history at the Sorbonne. Guizot rescued historical study from the antirevolutionary conservatives. As a liberal he used history to demonstrate that revolutions developed out of natural progressions and that, like the English revolution, the French would find success. Like his contemporaries, Victor Cousin, Prosper de Barante, and Charles de Rémusat, Guizot embodied the liberal—and doctrinaire—bourgeois character that wanted to balance the older traditions with new revolutionary ideas. His lectures at the Sorbonne (1828–1830) proved very popular and set a new course for liberal and romantic studies. In 1828 he published one of the first histories of civilization in *General History of European Civilization.* He highlighted the growth of the bourgeois, middle class, representative government, and the guiding hand of providence, symbolized in liberty. The 1830 revolution gave power to the liberals and between 1830 and 1848 Guizot held important political posts under King Louis Philippe, including the ministries of education, internal, and external affairs. His influence during the July Monarchy, official and scholarly, was immense. He helped to advance French scholarship as a whole by organizing the collection, editing, and publication of the sources of French history and by founding the *Société de l'histoire de France* (1833) and the *Collection de documents inédits sur l'histoire de France* [Collection of the Unpublished Sources of French History] (1836). After his fall from power in the revolution of 1848, Guizot turned back to scholarship in retirement and completed his study of the seventeenth-century English "revolution"; he was the first historian to use that word to describe the conflict between Charles I and Parliament.

Guizot used history to teach unity among all classes: in his view, all men must submit to the development of liberty, the nation, and the moral citizen, yet he also believed that only the educated and propertied could govern. At the same time, however, individual conscience was for him the source and guardian of civilization. At a time of heightened politicization of history, Guizot postponed judgment in his narrative of European civilization. He believed that two historical elements work in harmony: intuition is developed through reason, and these human elements cooperate with the unseen work of divine providence.

John B. Roney

Texts

Histoire de la Révolution d'angleterre depuis l'avènement de Charles Ier jusqu'à sa mort [History of the English Revolution from the Accession of Charles I to his Death]. Fourth ed. Paris: Victor Masson, 1850.

Historical Essays and Lectures. Ed. Stanley Mellon. Chicago: University of Chicago Press, 1972.

History of France from the Earliest Times to the Year Eighteen Forty-Eight. Trans. Robert Black. 8 vols. Chicago: Hooper, Clarke, 1869–1898.

References

De Broglie, Gabriel. *Guizot.* Paris: Perrin, 1990.

Johnson, Douglas. *Guizot: Aspects of French History, 1787–1874.* London: Routledge, 1963.

Mellon, Stanley. *The Political Uses of History.* Stanford, CA: Stanford University Press, 1958.

Rosanvallon, Pierre. *Le moment Guizot.* Paris: Gallimard, 1985.

Guo Songtao [Kuo Sung-tao] (1818–1891)

Chinese statesman, diplomat, and writer. After studying as a young man in the Yuelu Academy, Guo passed the civil service exam and became *Jinshi* in 1847, whereupon he was appointed to the Hanlin Academy. After working with Zeng Guofan (1811–1872) to organize a volunteer force to defeat the Taiping rebels, Guo's career began to prosper. He received appointments in the provincial governments of the Guangdong and Fujian

provinces and in 1875, he became the deputy defense minister. His appointment as minister to Great Britain made him the first Chinese official in modern times to be stationed in a Western country. In 1878 Guo also served concurrently as his country's minister to France, but was ordered back to China at the end of the same year. Guo kept a diary, which commenced at his trip to Beijing for the civil service examination until his death. Portions of the diary were published during his lifetime as the *Shixi Jixing* [Records of My Trip to the West]; this was well received since it was one of the earliest books to provide an eyewitness account of Western culture and society to a turn-of-the-century Chinese readership. In 1981 and 1983 the Hunan People's Press in China published the most complete version of Guo's diary to appear to date; this is based on sixty-one handwritten books and is entitled *Guo Songtao riji* [Guo Songtao's Diary]. The *Diary* begins in 1855 and ends in 1891, a day before Guo's death. It covers a variety of subjects, ranging from court politics and diplomacy, to social environment, public opinion, intellectual trends, and education. It is thus an invaluable primary source for students of modern Chinese history.

Q. Edward Wang

Texts

Guo Songtao riji. 4 vols. Changsha: Hunan renmin chubanshe, 1981–1983.

Guo Songtao shiwenji [Guo Songtao's Poems and Essays]. Changsha: Yuelu shushe, 1984.

Guo Songtao zougao [Guo Songtao's Memorials]. Changsha: Yuelu shushe, 1983.

References

Frodsham, J.D., ed. *The First Chinese Embassy to the West: The Journals of Kuo Sung-tao, Liu Hsi-hung, and Chang Te-yi.* Oxford: Clarendon Press, 1974.

Zeng Yongling. *Guo Songtao dazhuan* [A Great Biography of Guo Songtao]. Shenyang: Liaoning renmin chubanshe, 1989.

Gupta, Rajanikanta (1849–1900)

Indian historian. Gupta was born in a village in present-day Bangladesh, but he lived and worked in Calcutta. A childhood illness impaired his hearing, and he was unable to complete his formal education; but he studied privately and supported himself through writing, mainly in Bengali. Gupta's interests included nationalism, the lives of great men, literature, and history. Inspired by the works of Bankim Chandra Chatterjee (1838–1894), Gupta recognized that "nationalism" in India needed a nationalist interpretation of history. He was, however, also influenced by European positivism, and in one of his writings on historiography (1898), he pleaded for research into and the preservation of historical records such as old Bengali manuscripts. It was he, in fact, who would initiate the famous archive of Bengali manuscripts at the Bangiya Sahitya Parishad (Bengali Literary Society).

Gupta wrote a number of textbooks on history, but he is principally remembered as the first professional historian of Bengal, a claim that rests on his *Sipahi Yuddhera Itihasa* [History of the Sepoy War] (1879–1900). It was written in five volumes and took twenty-one years to complete (the fifth and final volume was published after his death). Gupta researched his topic thoroughly, reading all the materials available in English and in printed media including newspapers, public records, official letters, and histories related to the events of 1857. Although he relied heavily on the English sources and his narrative follows the earlier work of Sir John Kaye, Gupta provided the first Indian interpretation of the Great Revolt of 1857.

S.N. Mukherjee

Texts

Sipahi Yuddhera Itihasa. 5 vols. Calcutta: Nabapatra Prakasana, 1981–1983.

References

Bandyopadhaya [Banerjee], Brajendranath, et al., eds. *Sahitya Sadhak Charitmala.* 12 vols. Calcutta: Bangiya-Sahitya-Parishat, 1943–1977, vol. 6.

Sengupta, Kiranasankara, and Jyotsna Simharaya, eds. *Rajanikanta Gupta: Byatiktba O Manisha.* Calcutta: Lekhaka Samabaya Samiti, 1976.

Gutman, Herbert George (1928–1985)

American historian and educator. Gutman was born in New York City. Following undergraduate study at Queens College and graduate work at Columbia University, he completed his Ph.D. in history at the University of Wisconsin, Madison, in 1959. After serving on the faculty of several universities, he joined the City University of New York in 1972 and taught at the Graduate Center, where he directed the American Working-Class History project. He died in New York City. Believing that ordinary people merited examination, Gutman became a leading advocate of the culturalist approach espoused by British historian E.P. Thompson in *The Making of the English Working Class* (1963). Through detailed research, Gutman demonstrated that the working class has a rich tradition that warrants discussion. As such, the new labor history in North America has continued to be molded by Gutman's scholarship and counsel. His critique of Robert Fogel and Stanley Engerman's cliometric exploration of slavery, *Time on the Cross,* proved to be one of the most serious attacks on that work, while he himself contributed to African-American history in *The Black Family in Slavery and Freedom, 1750–1925.*

William E. Fischer Jr.

Texts

The Black Family in Slavery and Freedom, 1750–1925. New York: Pantheon, 1976.

Slavery and the Numbers Game: A Critique of "Time on the Cross." Champaign and Urbana: University of Illinois Press, 1975.

Work, Culture, and Society in Industrializing America. New York: Knopf, 1976.

References

American Social History Project Staff. *Who Built America?* New York: Pantheon, 1992.

Berlin, Ira, ed. *Power and Culture: Essays on the American Working Class.* New York: Pantheon, 1987.

"Interview with Herbert Gutman." In *Visions of History,* ed. Marho: Radical Historians' Organization. New York: Pantheon, 1983.

G

H

Habakkuk, Sir Hrothgar John (b. 1915)
British historian of population, landownership, and technology of modern Britain and America. Habakkuk taught at Cambridge University (1938–1950) before becoming Chichele professor of economic history at Oxford University in 1950. Serving in numerous administrative and professional capacities, including vice-chancellor of the university (1973–1977) and president of the Royal Historical Society (1976–1980), he was knighted in 1976. With M.M. Postan he edited both *The Cambridge Economic History* series and the *Economic History Review* (1950–1960). Since a seminal first article appeared in the latter journal in 1940, his analysis of British landownership and the increasing possibilities for commercial investment on the eve of the industrial revolution has been debated, revised, and often reconfirmed. He argues that after 1690 it was the older aristocracy that consolidated and "improved" its underdeveloped holdings, largely through enclosure, by utilizing capital generated from nonagricultural sources. The newer, gentry landowners who achieved great gains in the preceding period, however, made few investments, usually purchasing land to acquire rent income, and for the higher social status property conveyed. Habakkuk's subsequent research has continued in this vein but centered more on how the Malthusian checks on population were breached through technological breakthroughs and the greater capitalization of agriculture. Habakkuk's work has thus contributed substantially to current understanding of British social and demographic patterns before and during the first wave of industrialization.

Ben Lowe

Texts
American and British Technology in the Nineteenth Century: The Search for Labour-Saving Inventions. Cambridge: Cambridge University Press, 1962.
Marriage, Debt, and the Estates System: English Landownership, 1650–1950. Oxford: Clarendon Press, 1994.
Population Growth and Economic Development since 1750. New York: Humanities Press, 1971.

References
Rotberg, Robert I., and Theodore K. Rabb, eds. *Population and Economy: Population and History from the Traditional to the Modern World.* Cambridge, Eng., and New York: Cambridge University Press, 1986.
Thompson, F.M.L., ed. *Landowners, Capitalists, and Entrepreneurs: Essays for Sir John Habakkuk.* Oxford: Clarendon Press, 1994.

Habib, Mohammad (1894–1971)
Indian medieval historian. Habib read modern history at New College, Oxford, and in 1922 joined the Muslim University, Aligarh, India, becoming one of its most prominent and influential members. In 1927 he published his two principal monographs, *Sultan Muhmud of Ghaznin* and *Hazrat Amir Khusran of Delhi.* His best-known work was his joint editing with K.A. Nizami of a volume of the *Comprehensive History of India* on the period of the Delhi Sultanate. The latter work was published in 1970 under the auspices of the Indian History Congress, and underlines the preeminence of the "Aligarh school" in Indian historiography. Later, Habib's colleague Nizami edited a new collection of his unpublished essays, which were published posthumously as *Politics and Society during the Early Medieval Period.*

Emma C. Alexander

Texts

Comprehensive History of India. Vol. 5, *The Delhi Sultanate.* Delhi: People's Publishing House, 1970.

Hazrat Amir Khusrau of Delhi. Bombay: D.B. Taraporevala, 1927.

Politics and Society during the Early Medieval Period. Ed. K.A. Nizami. Delhi: People's Publishing House, 1974.

Sultan Mahmud of Ghaznin. Bombay: Aligarh Muslim University Publications, 1927.

References

Hardy, Peter. *Historians of Medieval India: Studies in Indo-Muslim Historical Writing.* London: Luzac, 1960.

Hagiography

The literature of the Christian cult of the saints from late antiquity to the Reformation. The term "hagiography" derives from the Greek *hagios,* "holy" (corresponding to the Latin *sanctus*) and *graphe,* "writing." In current use, it refers both to the literary documents of the medieval saints' cult and to the modern scientific study of those documents. In the former sense, it applies to all "writings inspired by religious devotion to the saints and intended to increase that devotion" (Delehaye). These include accounts of the trials and deaths of martyrs; biographies or "lives" of holy men and women *(vitae sanctorum),* stories of miracles attributed to the saints, of the discovery of their mortal remains, and of the transfer ("translation") of relics from one place to another; sermons, hymns, and poems in honor of the saints; prayers addressed to the saints; catalogs of saints arranged by the date of their "birthdays" (i.e., the days on which they died and were born into eternal life).

In medieval Christianity, the saint was a person whose posthumous example edified the faithful and who, as one of the blessed, was held to be a source of spiritual power. The title was conferred by Christian communities on those whose heavenly patronage they wished to secure, often on the basis of a real or supposed local connection with the departed. The devotional, especially liturgical, life of the church is the usual context for hagiography in the Middle Ages. (The process by which saints of the Western church were formally "canonized" by the pope did not begin to evolve until the tenth century, and only became systematic in the seventeenth.) The first class of persons from the post-apostolic era to be distinguished in this way were the martyrs who died in the Roman persecutions.

Early accounts of their heroism ("Acts of the Martyrs") combine reliable historical information with pious fiction in variable proportions and set the tone for later narratives. After the end of the persecutions, the martyr's place was taken by ascetics like St. Antony the hermit (d. 356), whose *Life* (attributed to Athanasius of Alexandria) inaugurated a long tradition of monastic hagiography. From the late fourth century onward, the lives of eminent bishops were also regularly commemorated in writing, while Latin poets such as Pope Damasus, Ambrose of Milan, and Prudentius began the practice of turning earlier martyr stories into verse. Compendia containing "lives" or anecdotes of more than one saint are attested from the time of Eusebius of Caesarea; notable literary examples include the *Lausiac History* of Palladius (ca. 419), the *Religious History* of Theodoret of Cyrrhus, and the *Dialogues* of Pope Gregory the Great. Hagiography in all its kinds proliferated throughout the Middle Ages in Greek, Latin, the languages of oriental Christianity, and increasingly in the vernaculars of western Europe as well. Selected narratives designed for liturgical and other formal readings were gathered into legendaries, the English word "legend" deriving from the Latin *legenda,* meaning saints' lives that were "to be read." The *Golden Legend* of Jacobus de Voragine (fl. thirteenth century) condensed much of this material into a form that proved both popular and influential.

Christian humanists of the Renaissance adapted many of the traditional devices of medieval hagiography in composing "lives" of important literary figures of their own epoch (for instance, the *Life of Petrarch* by the late-fifteenth-century German humanist Rudolph Agricola). At the same time, reforming scholars like Erasmus sought to strip away the fictional accretions of previous writing on the saints; his *Life of St. Jerome* provided the model for a new kind of Christian historical biography. Though hostile to the Roman Catholic saints' cult, Protestants could still exploit the hagiographic genres, as the Englishman John Foxe did in his *Acts and Monuments,* dubbed the "Book of Martyrs." On the Catholic side, the work of the Jesuit scholars H. Rosweyde and J. van Bolland in the early seventeenth century led to the publication of the *Acta Sanctorum* [Acts (i.e., Records) of the Saints] by the Belgian society of Bollandists. This comprehensive critical survey (still in progress) of the documents relating to individual saints in the order of their appearance in the Roman Church calendar is one of the foundations of modern "scientific" hagiography.

M. Vessey

See also BIOGRAPHY; BOLLANDISTS AND MAURISTS; MARTYROLOGY.

Texts

The Acts of the Christian Martyrs. Trans. H. Musurillo. Oxford: Clarendon Press, 1972.

Early Christian Biographies. Trans. R.J. Deferrari. New York: Fathers of the Church, 1952.

Golden Legend: Readings on the Saints. Trans. W.G. Ryan. 2 vols. Princeton, NJ: Princeton University Press, 1993.

Soldiers of Christ: Saints' Lives from Late Antiquity and the Early Middle Ages. Ed. T.F.X. Noble and T. Head. University Park, PA: Pennsylvania State University Press, 1995.

References

Brown, Peter. *The Cult of the Saints: Its Rise and Function in Latin Christianity.* Chicago: University of Chicago Press, 1981.

Delehaye, H. *The Legends of the Saints.* Trans. D. Attwater. New York: Fordham University Press, 1962.

Dubois, Jacques, and Jean-Loup Lemaitre. *Sources et méthodes de l'hagiographie médiévale* [Sources and Methods of Medieval Hagiography]. Paris: Cerf, 1993.

Farmer, David, ed. *The Oxford Dictionary of Saints.* Revised ed. Oxford: Clarendon Press, 1992.

Knowles, David. "The Bollandists." In his *Great Historical Enterprises.* London: Thomas Nelson, 1963, 3–32.

Wilson, Stephen, ed. *Saints and Their Cults: Studies in Religious Sociology, Folklore and History.* Cambridge, Eng.: Cambridge University Press, 1983, 309–417 [annotated bibliography].

on seventeenth- and nineteenth-century Hungarian political history and wrote extensively on the history of modern industrial technology, drawing creatively on the works of German sociologists such as Hans Freyer and Alfred Vierkandt.

Attila Pók

Texts

A Batthány-kormány külpolitikája [Foreign Policy of the Batthány-Government]. Budapest: Akadémiai Kiadó, 1957.

L'enseignment de l'écriture aux universités médiévales [The Discovery of Writing in the Medieval Universities]. Budapest: Academia Scientiarum Hungarica, 1954.

Esterházy Miklós nádor iratai: Az 1642 évi meghiúsult országgyülés időszaka [The Papers of Palatine Miklós Esterházy: The Period of the Failed Diet of 1642]. Budapest: Magyar Tudományos Akadémia, 1929.

A Kossuth-emigráció Törökországban [The Kossuth Emigration in Turkey]. Budapest: Magyar Történelmi Társulat, 1927.

Az újkor története [The History of the Modern Age]. Budapest: Magyar Szemle Társaság, 1936.

Vergleichende Schriftproben zur Entwicklung und Verbreitung der Schrift im 12–13 Jahrhundert [A Comparative Investigation into the Development and Spread of Writing in the Twelfth and Thirteenth Centuries]. Budapest: Verlag Danubia, 1943.

References

Glatz, Ferenc, ed. *Hajnal István: Technika, müvelődés* [Istvan Hajnal: Technics and Culture]. Budapest: História-MTA Történettudományi Intézete, 1993.

Hajnal, Istvån (1892–1955)

Hungarian historian. Hajnal studied in Budapest, Leipzig, and Vienna. He began his career as an archivist on the staff of the Hungarian National Archives and National Museum (1922–1930) and became private archivist to Duke Pál Esterházy from 1930 to 1949. He held the chair of modern world history at Péter Pázmány University in Budapest and from 1931 to 1943 was coeditor of *Századok* [Centuries], the most important Hungarian historical journal. One of the most original of modern Hungarian historians, Hajnal studied medieval diplomatics and conducted comparative paleographical investigations that led him to wide-ranging conclusions concerning the character of medieval European culture. He also published sources and monographs

Halecki, Oskar (1881–1973)

Polish historian. Halecki was born in Vienna and from 1918 to 1939 was a professor at Warsaw University. After World War II he went into exile in the United States, where he was professor and chairman in the department of Eastern European history at Fordham University, New York (1944–1961). He was the founder and director of the Polish Institute of Arts and Sciences of America in New York (1942–1962). One of the key figures in Polish émigré circles hostile to the communist regime in Poland and to the USSR, he was criticized in Poland (particularly by Władysław Gomułka) and none of his works was published there before 1991. He died in White Plains, New York. Halecki was a well-known historian, specializing in the history of Poland of the Jagiellonian period; his *Dzieje Unii Jagiellońskiej* [History of the Jagiellonian Union] appeared in two volumes in 1919 and 1920. He was one of the first historians in this century to conduct research into the history of Byzantium, and he also authored *Historia Polski* [A History of Poland], which has been translated into many foreign languages. Halecki emphasized the role of Catholicism and the Catholic Church in the history of Poland as the gateway to the West and Christendom. In his *Limits and Divisions of European History* (1950), he divided European history into three periods: Mediterranean, European, and Atlantic.

Ewa Domańska

Texts
A History of Poland. London: Routledge and Kegan Paul, 1978.
Jadwiga of Anjou and the Rise of East Central Europe. Ed. T.V. Gromada. Atlantic Studies on Society in Change, 73. New York: Distributed by Columbia University Press, 1991.
The Limits and Divisions of European History. London: Sheed and Ward, 1950.

References
Pajewski, Janusz. "Oskar Halecki." *Kwartalnik Historyczny* 4 (1975): 915–916.

Halévy, Elie (1870–1937)
French historian of Britain. Halévy was born at Etretat and received his education at the Lycée Condorcet and the École Normale Supérieure, emerging well versed in philosophy and history. For many years he was a professor at the École Libre des Sciences Politiques. After visiting England in the early 1890s, he set about to explain its peaceful development. Certain that the effects of religion, and especially of Methodism, were responsible for English social and political stability (a contentious idea), he produced a groundbreaking work on English utilitarianism, *The Origins of Philosophic Radicalism* (1901–1904). He also wrote a magisterial, though incomplete, multivolume treatment of the nineteenth and early twentieth centuries, *A History of the English People in the Nineteenth Century* (first published in French, 1913–1947). Both these works are better known in their English translations than in the original French. He died at Saucy-et-Brie before he could finish his projected volumes on the period 1841 to 1895. Halévy's French perspective illuminated his subjects, and today his works are considered historical classics.

Walter A. Sutton

Texts
The Era of Tyrannies: Essays on Socialism and War. Trans. R.K. Webb. Garden City, NY: Anchor Books, 1965.
The Growth of Philosophic Radicalism. Trans. Mary Morris. 3 vols. Boston: Beacon Press, 1955.
A History of the English People in the Nineteenth Century. Trans. E.I. Watkin. 4 vols. [vol. 4 completed by R.B. McCallum]. London: Ernest Benn, 1949–1951.

References
Ausubel, Herman, J.B. Brebner, and E.M. Hunt, eds. *Some Modern Historians of Britain.* New York: The Dryden Press, 1951.

Hall [Halle], Edward (ca. 1497–1547)
English common lawyer and chronicler. Hall's parents lived at Northall, Shropshire, and were early adherents of the Reformed religion. After graduating from King's College, Cambridge, in 1518, Hall studied the common law at Gray's Inn, London. He was elected to Parliament by Bridgnorth in 1542 although he had probably also sat in earlier parliaments. He died in London. Throughout his political and legal career, Hall staunchly supported the Tudor dynasty, and his chronicle *The Union of the Two Noble and Illustre Famelies York and Lancaster* (1548) heaped praise on Henry VIII while it also revealed a muted Protestant sympathy. The work of his predecessor, the Italian humanist Polydore Vergil, guided Hall's approach to history, especially the idea of seeing themes or meanings in dynastic, political history. For Hall, the theme of English history was the search for order, which Henry VII had restored and the firm rule of Henry VIII preserved. Succeeding Tudor historians, such as Richard Grafton, John Stow, and Raphael Holinshed copied Hall's *Union* extensively.

Ronald H. Fritze

Texts
Hall's Chronicle: Containing the History of England. Ed. H. Ellis. London: J. Johnson, 1809.

References
Levy, F.J. *Tudor Historical Thought.* San Marino, CA: Huntington Library, 1967.

Hallam, Henry (1777–1859)
English historian. Hallam was born at Windsor, the only son of John Hallam, canon of Windsor, and received his education at Eton and Christ

Church, Oxford. Family wealth and his appointment as commissioner of stamps afforded him the leisure to pursue a studious life devoted to history. Although a thorough Whig, he was not active in politics. He died in Penhurst, Kent. Over a period of nearly thirty years he produced in succession three major works upon which rests his reputation as a historian: *A View of the State of Europe during the Middle Ages* (1818), *The Constitutional History of England from the Accession of Henry VII to the Death of George II* (1827), and *An Introduction to the Literature of Europe during the Fifteenth, Sixteenth and Seventeenth Centuries* (1837–1839). A meticulous researcher, Hallam tried to limit his observations to what an unbiased reading of the primary documents would reveal. And by the standards of the time his works do stand out as being eminently fair and balanced, in particular his constitutional history. Hallam also recognized the complexity of history, urging that all historical subjects need to be examined in their numerous relations with one another.

Richard A. Voeltz

Texts

The Constitutional History of England from the Accession of Henry VII to the Death of George II. Buffalo, NY: W.S. Hein, 1989.
An Introduction to the Literature of Europe during the Fifteenth, Sixteenth and Seventeenth Centuries. London: Johnson, 1970.
A View of the State of Europe during the Middle Ages. Philadelphia: P. Dobson and Son, 1872.

References

Ausubel, Herman, J.B. Brebner, and E.M. Hunt, eds. *Some Modern Historians of Britain.* New York: I. Washburn, 1951.
Hale, J.R. *The Evolution of British Historiography.* London: Macmillan, 1967.
Peardon, Thomas P. *The Transition in English Historical Writing 1760–1830.* New York: Columbia University Press, 1933.

Hamilton, Earl Jefferson (1899–1989)

Historical economist. Born in Houlka, Mississippi, Hamilton graduated from Mississippi State University and received his Ph.D. from Harvard (1929). He taught at Duke, Northwestern, the University of Chicago, and State University of New York, Binghamton. Following in the tradition of J.E. Thorold Rogers, William Beveridge, and the Vicomte d'Avenel, Hamilton pressed the quantity theory of money in his work, to which he brought a knowledge of six languages. The so-called Hamilton thesis argues that it was Spanish bullion imported from the New World that triggered the price revolution, or great inflation, of the sixteenth century. While historical demographers insist population increase set off the price/wage spiral, Hamilton's massive data described Spanish wages and prices for the International Committee of Price History. In his final years, he was at work studying the early quantity theories of John Law.

A.J. Carlson

Texts

American Treasure and the Price Revolution in Spain, 1501–1650. Cambridge, MA: Harvard University Press, 1934.
"The History of Prices before 1750." In *XIe Congrès International des Sciences Historiques.* Stockholm: Almquist & Wiksell, 1960.
Money, Prices, and Wages in Valencia, Aragon, and Navarre, 1351–1500. Cambridge, MA: Harvard University Press, 1936.
War and Peace in Spain, 1651–1800. Cambridge, MA.: Harvard University Press, 1947.

References

W.C. Robinson, "Money, Population and Economic Change in Late Medieval Europe." *The Economic History Review,* 2d ser. 12 (1959): 63–76. (See also M.M. Postan's reply: "Note," Ibid., 77–82).

Hamitic Hypothesis

Concept relating to the colonial historiography of Africa. The term "Hamites" derives from early European ethnography which, on biblical authority, divided human types into the families of Noah's three sons: Shem, Japhet, and Ham. Africans were the children of Ham. But this distant African connection to Christian history was challenged after about 1800. European ethnography, powered by attitudes of racial and historical superiority and shaped by evolutionary theory, reduced Africans to the status of isolated primitives with little historical accomplishment or innate ability. Ancient Egypt, however, was excepted; it was deemed a great civilization antecedent to modern Europe. The Hamites—variously defined by linguistic, cultural, and physical criteria—were then pictured as a non-African race linked with ancient Egypt but not with the rest of ancient Africa. Attempts to sketch sub-Saharan African history in the later nineteenth and early twentieth centuries, in keeping with these assumptions, credited any progressive change to "Hamitic" influences from the direction of Egypt, or to similar outside causes. Thus Johnston's widely read *History of the Colonization of Africa by Alien Races* (1899) theorized that the great empires of medieval West Africa were created by conquerors crossing the Sahara Desert, and the imposing stone structures of Great Zimbabwe (in modern Zimbabwe) were built by Phoenician colonizers. Immigrations and external influences— collectively termed the "Hamitic Hypothesis" by later critics—were entrenched as the determinant historical dynamics throughout sub-Saharan Africa in Seligman's *Races of Africa* (1930). Early African and African-American writers developed alternative Hamitic hypotheses more in the spirit of the biblical model. Blyden, for example, in "The Negro in Ancient History" (1869), asserted that all Africans descended from Ham, the ancient Egyptians included. Although he identified Hamitic migrations as the agents of change in sub-Saharan Africa, Blyden understood these as black Africans uplifting the mass of Africans, not as whiter races conquering darker ones. Hamitic models were challenged on a number of fronts through the 1950s and 1960s, as colonial power declined. New archaeological and linguistic evidence revealed long-standing patterns of change within Africa, which could not be explained by foreign disruptions. Further, efforts to refute the prejudices of Johnston's era and establish that Africa indeed had a history inspired the scrutiny of assumptions behind the Hamitic hypothesis and the generation of more satisfactory accounts of Africa's distant past. The Hamitic hypothesis is now widely rejected; foreign influences are treated as one of many causes of development rooted in Africa's regional dynamics.

P.S. Zachernuk

See also AFRICAN HISTORIOGRAPHY

Texts

Blyden, Edward W. "The Negro in Ancient History." *Methodist Quarterly Review* 51 (1869): 71–93.

Johnston, Harry H. *A History of the Colonization of Africa by Alien Races.* Second ed. Cambridge, Eng.: Cambridge University Press, 1913.

Seligman, C.G. *Races of Africa.* Fourth ed. London: Oxford University Press, 1966.

References

Horton, Robin. "Stateless Societies in the History of West Africa." In *History of West Africa,* third edition, ed. J.F.A. Ajayi and M. Crowder. Longman: New York, 1985, vol. 1, 87–128.

Sanders, E.R. "The Hamitic Hypothesis: Its Origin and Function in Time Perspective." *Journal of African History* 10 (1969): 521–532.

Han Ch'iyun (1765–1814)

Korean historian and scholar. A brief sojourn in China encouraged Han to take a more objective view of Korean history than was then the practice among his compatriots and may also have been responsible for his urging the need for cultural exchanges among China, Korea, and Japan; on the other hand, he saw Korea as providing the focus and center of any such exchange rather than as an equal partner. In *Haedong Yŏksa* [History of Korea] (1823), his only surviving work, Han used the best sources then available, including more than five hundred foreign documents and numerous domestic records. His collection and organization of these materials was his principal contribution to Korean historiography. He was the first Korean scholar to recognize the importance of Japanese sources for the investigation of Korean history. In an effort to ensure "objectivity," his work tended merely to recount historical facts rather than set forth commentaries on or evaluations of them. The book also includes passages on lower-class culture, ancient customs, dialects, rare surnames, coins, various products of Korea, and so on; and his collections under these rubrics would provide valuable information to later historians.

Minjae Kim

Texts

Haedong Yŏksa. 2 vols. Seoul: Ryŏkang Press, 1987.

References

Hwang Wŏn-gu and Yi T'ae-jin. "Haedong Yŏksaŭi Jonghapjŏk Gŏmto" [Comprehensive Studies on Haedong Yŏksa]. *Chindan Hakpo* 53–54 (1982): 231–249.

Han Yu (768–824)

Chinese writer, poet, and historian. Han was an influential figure in Chinese literature whose poetry had a great impact on the culture of the Song dynasty. He was also known for his advocacy of the *guwen* (ancient style) movement, in which Han called for a return to a simple style in essay writing. Successful in the civil service examination, Han entered officialdom in his early years and held various posts, including being the official historian. He left a history called *Shunzong shilu* [Veritable Records of the Emperor Shunzong], in which he aimed to provide a complete and accurate historical account of the brief reign of the emperor Shunzong in 805. Han's book is the earliest surviving *shilu* or "veritable record" in China, recording the emperor's deeds and words, upon which official historians wrote the court chronicle, known as the "basic annals" in the Standard Histories.

Q. Edward Wang

See also CHINESE HISTORIOGRAPHY—STANDARD HISTORIES.

Texts

Changli Xiansheng quanji [Complete Works of Han Yu]. China: Yuan Hai Tang, 1620–1644.

Shunzong shilu [The Veritable Records of the Emperor Shunzong, 28 February, 805–831; August, 805]. Ed. and trans. Bernard S. Solomon. Cambridge, MA: Harvard University Press, 1955.

References

Hartman, Charles. *Han Yu and the Tang Search for Unity.* Princeton, NJ: Princeton University Press, 1986.

Lu Dafang et al. *Han Yu nianpu* [Han Yu's Chronological Biography]. Beijing: Zhonghua Shuju, 1991.

Pulleyblank, E.G. "The *Shun-tsung Shih-lu.*" *Bulletin of the School of Oriental and African Studies* 19 (1957): 336–344.

Twitchett, Denis. *The Writing of Official History under the T'ang.* Cambridge, Eng.: Cambridge University Press, 1992.

Hancock, Sir William Keith (1898–1988)

Australian, British, and Commonwealth historian and environmentalist. Born in Melbourne, Hancock was the son of an Anglican minister. His upward academic trajectory throughout life remained constant and relatively unimpeded. Winning scholarships to Melbourne Grammar School and the University of Melbourne (1917–1920), he graduated to an assistant lectureship in history at the University of Western Australia before becoming a Rhodes scholar at Balliol College, Oxford, where he studied the decline of the Italian Risorgimento. This was followed by several years residence in Tuscany while he examined Italian land use and became, in his own words, a "blundering disciple" of Benedetto Croce. Returning to Australia in 1926, he assumed the chair of history at Adelaide University, a post he held until 1930. It was in this period that he produced, at the suggestion of his Balliol acquaintance H.A.L. Fisher, his seminal work, *Australia* (1930). For several generations of Australian historians, *Australia* would remain an unfailing beacon, illuminating a set path through the national historical terrain from which few were prepared to stray. Very much a distillation of then dominant liberal perceptions, the book was an expertly written synoptic essay, linking political and economic history with national culture. Innocent of theoretical input and averse to class analysis, the study emphasized British imperial virtues, transmitted through an antipodean, rural setting to create the embryonic characteristics of "independent Austral-Britons."

Following this triumph, Hancock held a series of chairs at Birmingham, Oxford, and London universities, during which time he produced the admirable *Survey of British Commonwealth Affairs* (1937–1940) and *The British War Economy* (1949). He was knighted for his efforts in editing the official British World War II history project. Returning to the Australian National University in 1956 to head the research school of social science, he continued to publish widely. An early biography, *Country and Calling* appeared in 1954 and *Professing History* in 1976. Two other works, *Discovering Monaro* (1972) and *Battle of Black Mountain* (1974) give evidence of Hancock's profound commitment to the Australian homeland and to local environmental struggles. Yet it is for his "young man's cheeky book," *Australia* that he will be principally remembered.

Raymond Evans

Texts

Australia. London: Ernest Benn, 1930.

The Battle of Black Mountain: An Episode of Canberra's Environmental History. Canberra: Department of Economic History, Research School of Social Sciences, Australian National University, 1974.

And M.M. Gowing. *The British War Economy.* London: HMSO, 1949.

Country and Calling. London: Faber and Faber, 1954.

Professing History. Sydney: Sydney University Press, 1976.

Ricasoli and the Risorgimento in Tuscany. London: Faber and Gwyer, 1926.

Smuts. 2 vols. Cambridge, Eng.: Cambridge University Press, 1962–1968.

Survey of British Commonwealth Affairs. 2 vols. London: Oxford University Press, 1937–1942.

References

Rowse, T., *Australian Liberalism and National Character*. Melbourne: Kibble Books, 1978.

Hang Shih-chün

See HANG SHIJUN.

Hang Shijun [Hang Shih-chün] (1696–1773)

Chinese historian. Born in Hangzhou in Zhejiang province, the precocious Hang Shijun attracted the notice of scholars while still young. Recommended to compete in a special imperial examination in 1736, Hang was appointed a compiler of the Hanlin Academy, where he worked as a collator for the imperial editions of *Shisan jing* [Thirteen Classics] and *Ershi'er shi* [Twenty-Two Dynastic Histories], serving meanwhile as the editor for the compilation of *Sanli yishu* [Exegesis of the Three Rites]. In 1743, when he took the examination for the post of censor, his papers commented on state affairs and offended the emperor. As a result Hang was dismissed and returned to the south, where he taught at various academies until his death. Hang labored enthusiastically in the study of Confucian classics and of history. His chief production in pursuing historical research was his study of a number of Standard Histories, including *Shiji* [Records of the Historian], *Hanshu* [History of the Former Han], *Hou Hanshu* [History of the Later Han], *Sanguo zhi* [Records of the Three Kingdoms], *Jin shu* [History of the Jin], and *Jin shi* [History of the Jin Dynasty]. These studies are notable for their author's breadth of information and vast capacity for assimilating data.

Shao Dongfang

Texts

Daogu tang waiji [Collected Essays from the Hall of Enumerating Antiquities]. Ed. Wang Zengwei. Qiantang, China: Zhenqi tan, 1888.
Sanguo zhi buzhu [Supplementary Commentary to the *Records of the Three Kingdoms*]. Taibei, Taiwan: Taiwan shangwu yinshuguan, 1983.
Zhushi yiran [Study of the Errors in the Standard Histories]. Taibei, Taiwan: Yinwen yinshuguan, 1966.

References

Elman, Benjamin A. *From Philosophy to Philology: Intellectual and Social Aspects of Change in Late Imperial China*. Cambridge, MA: Harvard University Press, 1984.

Liang Chi-chao. *Intellectual Trends in the Ch'ing Period*. Trans. Immanuel C.Y. Hsu. Cambridge, MA: Harvard University Press, 1959.

Hani Gorō (1901–1983)

Historian of Japan. Born in Kiryū, Gunma prefecture, Hani studied history at Tokyo University and philosophy in Heidelberg. Hani was a leading academic figure in the Kōza wing of the Japanese capitalism debate, and made a major contribution to Marxist historical scholarship. After 1945 he was associated with Tokyo and Nihon universities, and became a member of the House of Councilors. Within the Kōza faction, Hani emphasised Japan's incorporation into world capitalist markets as a cause of economic and political change, whereas Hattori Shisō stressed indigenous capitalist development. Hani also argued that Asiatic features contributed to the peculiar form of Japanese feudalism, and left a legacy that hindered completion of an indigenous bourgeois-democratic revolution. Hani's most significant articles were published in Iwanami's *Nihon Shihonshugi Hattatsu-shi Kōza* [Lectures on the History of the Development of Capitalism in Japan] and brought together in his collected works, *Hani Gorō Rekishiron Chosakushū* [Collected Historical Writings of Hani Gorō] and *Meiji Ishin-shi Kenkyū* [Studies on the History of the Meiji Restoration].

Janet E. Hunter

Texts

Hani Gorō Rekishiron Chosakushū. 4 vols. Tokyo: Aoki Shoten, 1967.
Meiji Ishin-shi Kenkyū. Tokyo: Iwanami Shoten, 1978.

References

Beasley, W.G., and E.G. Pulleyblank, eds. *Historians of China and Japan*. London: Oxford University Press, 1961.
Hoston, Germaine A. *Marxism and the Crisis of Development in Prewar Japan*. Princeton, NJ: Princeton University Press, 1986.

Hanotaux, Gabriel (1853–1944)

French politician, diplomat, and historian. Hanotaux studied in Paris at the École des Hautes Études and the École des Chartes. He began his career as an archivist in the foreign ministry under the Third Republic and quickly won promotion in the diplomatic corps. In 1894 Hanotaux was named foreign minister (the youngest man to have held that post in France). A strong supporter of French colonial expansion, he fell from power over the Anglo-French colonial rivalry at the time of the Fashoda affair (1898). He spent the rest of his life lecturing and publishing both history and pro-colonial tracts.

Hanotaux wrote unapologetically republican and patriotic history. His initial interest focused on Cardinal Richelieu, whom he saw as a statesman in a tradition of French *grandeur* stretching from Philip the Fair to the Revolution. The *Histoire du cardinal de Richelieu* won Hanotaux membership in the Academie Française in 1897. Hanotaux is best known today for his four-volume *Contemporary France* (first published from 1903 to 1908), which narrates the early years of the Third Republic from 1871 to 1900. *Contemporary France* is an extremely personal history, colored by Hanotaux's own experiences at the center of the events he describes. Today, *Contemporary France* is more useful as a source on, rather than an analysis of, the politics of the Third Republic.

Carol E. Harrison

Texts

Contemporary France. Trans. J.C. Tarver. 4 vols. New York: G.P. Putnam's Sons, 1903.

Histoire du cardinal de Richelieu. 6 vols. Paris: Societé de l'histoire nationale/Librairie Plon, 1932–1947.

References

Heggoy, A.A. *The African Policies of Gabriel Hanotaux (1894–98).* Athens: University of Georgia Press, 1972.

Vetter, V.S. "Gabriel Hanotaux." In *Classic European Historians,* ed. S.W. Halperin. Chicago: University of Chicago Press, 1970.

Harnack, Adolf von (1851–1930)

German theologian and church historian. Harnack (von Harnack after 1914) studied theology in Dorpat and Leipzig from 1869 to 1872. In 1873 he earned his doctorate, habilitating at Leipzig in the following year with a study on the history of the Gnostics. In 1879 he became professor of church history at the University of Giessen, moving in 1886 to a similar position at Marburg. In 1888 he was appointed to a chair at Berlin, where he taught until his retirement in 1921, remaining professor emeritus there until his death. Harnack is regarded as the most important church historian of the nineteenth and early

twentieth centuries, and he achieved a great deal, also, as an organizer of scholarly endeavors. In this secondary occupation he was the director between 1905 and 1921 of the Königliche Bibliothek (Royal Library) in Berlin, which was later renamed the Preussische Staatsbibliothek (Prussian State Library). From 1911 until his death, he was the president of the Kaiser-Wilhelm-Gesellschaft zur Förderung der Wissenschaften (The Emperor Wilhelm Society for the Advancement of Knowledge), which he had founded. Before World War I, Harnack's political thought made him a resolute supporter of the empire and an opponent of the reformist challenge represented by social democracy; it was in this context that he led the "Evangelisch-Sozialer Kongress" of 1903 to 1911. After the war he became a strong supporter of the Weimar Republic. In 1890, Harnack became a member the Prussian Academy of Sciences, in which capacity he directed the edition of the *Griechischen christlichen Schriftsteller der drei ersten Jahrhunderte* [Greek Church Fathers of the First Three Centuries]. To provide a foundation for this project he wrote the two-volume *Geschichte der altchristlichen Literatur bis Eusebius* [The History of Early Christian Literature before Eusebius] (1893–1904). On the occasion of the centennial of the academy he published his *Geschichte der Königlich Preussischen Akademie der Wissenschaften zu Berlin* [History of the Royal Prussian Academy of Sciences of Berlin] in three volumes (1900), an important summary of research into the history of scientific organizations. Among his many historical works, two in particular must be mentioned: the *Entstehung und Entwicklung der Kirchenverfassung und des Kirchenrechts in den ersten zwei Jahrhunderten* [Origins and Development of the Constitution and Law of the Church in the First Two Centuries] (1910) and *Mission und Ausbreitung des Christentums in den ersten drei Jahrhunderten* [The Missions and Expansion of Christianity in the First Three Centuries] (1902). His monograph *Marcion* (1921) confused the public because of the statements made therein about the importance of the Old Testament. The *Lehrbuch der Dogmengeschichte* [Handbook on the History of Dogma] (1886–1890) is now regarded as Harnack's most important work. It was in this three-volume study that he first advanced the seminal concept of the history of dogma, described the origins and development of Christian teachings, and interpreted the dogma as the Hellenization of the Gospel.

Thomas Fuchs

Texts

The Constitution and Law of the Church in the First Two Centuries. Ed. H.D.A. Major; trans. F.L. Pogson. London: Williams and Norgate, 1910.

Geschichte der Königlich Preussischen Akademie der Wissenschaften zu Berlin. 3 vols. Berlin: Reichsdruckerei, 1900.

History of Dogma. Trans. N. Buchanan from the third German ed. 7 vols. New York: Russell and Russell, 1958.

The Mission and Expansion of Christianity in the First Three Centuries. Trans. J. Moffat. Second ed. 2 vols. London: Williams and Norgate, 1904–1905.

References

Glick, G.W. *The Reality of Christianity: A Study of Adolf von Harnack As Historian and Theologian.* New York: Harper and Row, 1967.

Pauck, W. *Harnack and Troeltsch: Two Historical Theologians.* New York: Oxford University Press, 1968.

Texts

American History Atlas. Chicago: Denoyer-Geppart, 1930.

American History Told by Contemporaries. 5 vols. New York: Macmillan, 1897–1929.

The Foundations of American Foreign Policy. New York: Da Capo Press, 1970.

Guide to the Study and Reading of American History. Boston and London: Ginn and Company, 1912.

Slavery and Abolition, 1831–1841. New York and London: Harper & Brothers, 1906.

References

Morison, Samuel E. "Albert Bushnell Hart." Massachusetts Historical Society, *Proceedings* 67 (1966): 28–52.

Novick, Peter. *That Noble Dream: The "Objectivity Question" and the American Historical Profession.* Cambridge, Eng., and New York: Cambridge University Press, 1988.

Whelan, Michael. "Albert Bushnell Hart and History Education, 1854–1907." Ph.D. dissertation, Columbia Teachers College, 1989.

Hart, Albert Bushnell (1854–1943)

Historian of the United States and editor. Born to wealth in Cleveland, Ohio, Hart graduated from Harvard (1880) and completed a Ph.D. at the University of Freiburg in Baden, Germany (1883), where he studied with Hermann von Holst, a distinguished scholar of the American Constitution. Hired by Harvard in 1883, he remained there until retiring in 1926. As one of the first generation of professional historians in the United States, he served as president of both the American Historical Association (1909) and the American Political Science Association (1912) and as editor of *The American Historical Review* (1895–1909). Emphasizing constitutional and political change and foreign policy, Hart contributed to American historiography primarily by editing serial volumes, guidebooks, and documents for wide audiences. He oversaw the publication of and contributed a volume, *Slavery and Abolition* (1906), to the first American Nation series (1904–1907), twenty-five chronological and topical books presenting a version of American history that stressed Hart's own interests. Parts of his multivolume documentary collection, *American History Told by Contemporaries* (1897–1929), remain in print. He also published historical maps, anticipating later historical atlases.

Ellen Nore

Hartz, Louis (1919–1986)

American historian and political theorist. As a Harvard political scientist, Hartz became a household name among historians with the publication of his *Liberal Tradition in America* (1955). This work appeared to contradict a book Hartz had published in 1948 (*Economic Policy and Democratic Thought: Pennsylvania, 1776–1860*) in which he had argued, contrary to the conventional wisdom, that laissez-faire had been honored more in the breach than the observance. *The Liberal Tradition in America,* in contrast, contended that a specter was haunting America—that of the seventeenth-century English philosopher John Locke. Ordinary Americans were, Hartz argued, fundamentally Lockean even if they had never read Locke. Hartz insisted that Lockean values held sway largely because of the absence of a feudal heritage, which suggests that he was far from being the intellectual determinist that some of his critics held him to be. In Hartz's account, the pervasiveness of individualistic beliefs explained not only the irrelevance of a George Fitzhugh in the South and the egalitarian rhetoric of business conservatism in the North but also pragmatic philosophy and the nonideological character of the New Deal. This thesis was cold comfort to the radical and reactionary alike. Hartz's study epitomized what has come to be called consensus historiography. He and other scholars took sharp issue with an earlier generation of historians such as Charles Beard and Vernon Parrington. Though he is often lumped with Daniel Boorstin, Hartz was hardly a celebrant of the consensus he depicted. He firmly believed that as long as Americans remained in the grip of Lockean absolutes they would never be able to come to terms with the Third World. In the 1960s, Hartz published *The Founding of New Societies,* a comparative history that expanded upon many of his earlier observations. At the time of his death he was at work on a grand synthesis of world history—an attempt to place the liberal, Lockean tradition within an even larger context.

Barry Riccio

Texts

Economic Policy and Democratic Thought: Pennsylvania, 1776–1860. Cambridge, MA: Harvard University Press, 1948.

The Founding of New Societies: Studies in the History of the United States, Latin America, South Africa, and Australia. New York: Harcourt, Brace, 1964.

The Liberal Tradition in America. New York: Harcourt, Brace, 1955.

References

Morton, Marion J. *The Terrors of Ideological Politics: Liberal Historians in a Conservative Mood.* Cleveland, OH: Case Western Reserve Press, 1972.

Pells, Richard H. *The Liberal Mind in a Conservative Age: American Intellectuals in the 1940s and 1950s.* New York: Harper and Row, 1985.

Sternsher, Bernard. *Consensus, Conflict, and American Historians.* Bloomington: Indiana University Press, 1975.

Haskell, Francis James Herbert (b. 1928)

Art historian. Educated at Eton and King's College, Cambridge, Haskell is professor of the history of art at Oxford University. He has served as a trustee of the Wallace Collection and was named a fellow of the British Academy in 1971. His *Patrons and Painters* of 1963 examined the relationship between art and society in seventeenth- and eighteenth-century Italy. From there he moved to explore changes in taste; generally, in *Rediscoveries in Art,* and (with Nicholas Penny) specifically, in *Taste and the Antique.* His most recent book, *History and Its Images,* investigates the role of images in the historical enterprise from the antiquarians

of the sixteenth and seventeenth centuries through nineteenth- and twentieth-century historians like Jules Michelet and Johan Huizinga. Although he has tackled broad subjects, Haskell's scholarship is marked by his attention to archival detail and his empiricism.

Sheila ffolliott

Texts

The Age of the Grand Tour. New York: Crown, 1967.

History and Its Images: Art and the Interpretation of the Past. New Haven, CT, and London: Yale University Press, 1993.

Patrons and Painters: A Study in the Relations between Italian Art and Society in the Age of the Baroque. Second ed. New Haven, CT, and London: Yale University Press, 1980.

Rediscoveries in Art: Some Aspects of Taste, Fashion and Collecting in England and France. Ithaca, NY: Cornell University Press, 1976.

With Nicholas Penny. *Taste and the Antique: The Lure of Classical Sculpture, 1500–1900.* New Haven, CT, and London: Yale University Press, 1981.

Haskins, Charles Homer (1870–1937)

American medieval historian. Haskins was born in Pennsylvania and educated at Johns Hopkins University; he taught at Johns Hopkins and then at the University of Wisconsin, where he was made full professor at the age of 22, and finally at Harvard, where he was Henry Charles Lea professor from 1928 to 1931. He served on the American delegation to the Paris peace conference in 1918 and 1919. Haskins was undoubtedly the most important American medieval historian of his time and was a founder of the Medieval Academy. Although his earliest works were on Norman institutions, his major studies were devoted to the intellectual history, education, and science of the Middle Ages. His histories of medieval universities and of science set the groundwork for all subsequent work in these areas and remain valuable tools today. It was Haskins who first posed the question, much debated since, whether the cultural flowering in twelfth-century Europe could be called a "renaissance." In his classic book on *The Renaissance of the Twelfth Century* (1927) he argued against the prevailing view of the Middle Ages as an "epoch of ignorance, stagnation, and gloom . . . in sharpest contrast to the light and progress and freedom of the Italian Renaissance which followed"; he suggested, to the contrary, that the twelfth century showed true intellectual, literary, and scientific creativity and a renewed interest in the Latin classics comparable to later Renaissance humanism.

Monica Sandor

Texts

Norman Institutions. Cambridge, MA: Harvard University Press, 1918.
The Normans in European History. Boston and New York: Houghton Mifflin, 1915.
The Renaissance of the Twelfth Century. Cambridge, MA: Harvard University Press, 1927.
The Rise of Universities. New York: Henry Holt, 1923.
Studies in Mediaeval Culture. Oxford: Clarendon Press, 1929.
Studies in the History of Mediaeval Science. Cambridge, MA: Harvard University Press, 1924.

References

Benson, Robert L., and Giles Constable, eds. *Renaissance and Renewal in the Twelfth Century.* Oxford: Clarendon Press, 1982, xvii–xxx.
Taylor, Charles H., ed. *Haskins Anniversary Essays in Mediaeval History.* Boston: Houghton Mifflin, 1929, 389–398.

Hattori Shisō (1901–1956)

Historian of Japan. Born in Shimane, Hattori studied sociology at Tokyo University, eventually becoming professor at Tōyō University. Hattori's writings on the 1868 Meiji Restoration became a focal part of the debate on the nature of Japanese capitalism that occupied Japanese Marxists in the interwar years and had a lasting influence on interpretations of Japanese history. Hattori's *Meiji Ishinshi* [History of the Meiji Restoration] (1928–1929) became a key text for the Kōza faction in the debate, which argued for a two-stage revolution in Japan. His articles in the early 1930s emphasized the existence of "capitalist" characteristics in pre-Meiji Japan and became the starting point for the "manufacture controversy," a major subset of the capitalism debate. The articles containing Hattori's views on manufacture were initially published in the journal *Rekishi Kagaku* [Historical Science] and the volume *Ishinshi no Hōhōron* [Methodology of the History of the Restoration] and were subsequently brought together under the title *Meiji Ishinshi Kenkyū* [Studies on the Meiji Restoration] (1955). His collected works were published in 1955 as *Hattori Shisō Chosaku Shū.*

Janet E. Hunter

Texts

Hattori Shisō Chosaku Shū. 7 vols. Tokyo: Rironsha, 1955.
Ishinshi no Hōhōron. Tokyo: Hakuyōsha, 1933.
Meiji Ishinshi. Tokyo: Sanryū Shobō, 1948.
Meiji Ishinshi Kenkyū. Tokyo: Sanwa Shoten, 1947; Kureha Shoten, 1948.

References

Hoston, Germaine A. *Marxism and the Crisis of Development in Prewar Japan.* Princeton, NJ: Princeton University Press, 1986.
Sumiya, Mikio, and Koji Taira, eds. *An Outline of Japanese Economic History 1603–1940.* Tokyo: Tokyo University Press, 1979.

Hayashi Razan (1583–1657)

Japanese Confucian philosopher and bureaucrat. Born in Kyoto as Hayashi Nobukatsu (and also known as Hayashi Matasaburō), he began his education at the Buddhist temple Kenninji, but soon left Buddhism to study under a student of the polymath Fujiwara Seika. He was said to have had a flawless and comprehensive memory. He received a minor appointment in the Tokugawa government in 1605 and wrote a series of papers on ceremonies, rituals, and regulations. The pinnacle of his official career was reached the year before his death, when he lectured before the shōgun on a Confucian classic. His heirs followed him as heads of the academy begun by him and continued instruction of the Zhu Xi [Chu Hsi] style of Confucian thought with extensive use of Han and Tang dynasty texts as a basis for Japanese learning. He wrote more than 150 works, including several collections of essays and poetry. The focus of his work was on the metaphysical basis of an individual's place in society, and the practical moral concerns for the individual in society. To this end, he on the one hand attacked Buddhism as other-worldly, amoral, and asocial and, on the other, promoted the unity of native divinities *(kami)* and Confucian principles. Much of his fame is due to later interventions, such as the posthumous biography written by his sons, which seeks to credit him with founding a Confucian political orthodoxy central to the ruling government. His actual accomplishments were more modest.

James Edward Ketelaar

Texts

Hōncho tsugan [History of the Nation]. Ed. Hayashi Shunshai. 18 vols. Tokyo: Kokusho Kankōkai, 1918–1920.

References

Nosco, Peter, ed. *Confucianism and Tokugawa Culture.* Princeton, NJ: Princeton University Press, 1984.

Ooms, Herman. *Tokugawa Ideology: Early Constructs, 1570–1680.* Princeton, NJ: Princeton University Press, 1985.

Hayes, Carlton Joseph Huntley (1882–1964)

American historian. A noted teacher and historian of modern western Europe at Columbia University, Hayes is associated with James Harvey Robinson and the New History movement at the beginning of the twentieth century. Between 1942 and 1945 Hayes served as the American ambassador to Spain. In addition to his studies on modern nationalism—*Essays on Nationalism* (1926) and *The Historical Evolution of Modern Nationalism* (1931), Hayes was a prominent author of textbooks on modern European history. These included *A Political and Cultural History of Modern Europe* (1916), *A Generation of Materialism, 1871–1900* (part of the Rise of Modern Europe series edited by William L. Langer), and a two-volume set, *Modern Europe to 1870* and *Contemporary Europe since 1870* (1953). He preferred a biographical approach in his teaching and writing and has been compared in terms of style and interests to his German contemporary, Friedrich Meinecke.

James V. Mehl

Texts

Contemporary Europe since 1870. Revised ed. New York: Macmillan 1958.

Essays on Nationalism. New York: Macmillan, 1926.

A Generation of Materialism, 1871–1900. Westport, CT: Greenwood Press, 1983.

The Historical Evolution of Modern Nationalism. New York: Russell & Russell, 1968.

Modern Europe to 1870. New York: Macmillan, 1961.

A Political and Cultural History of Modern Europe. 2 vols. New York: Macmillan, 1932–1936.

References

Directory of American Scholars. Third ed. New York: R.R. Bowker, 1957, 323–324.

Earle, Edward Mead, ed. *Nationalism and Internationalism: Essays Inscribed to Carlton J.H. Hayes.* New York: Columbia University Press, 1950, introduction.

Hayward, Sir John (ca. 1564–1627)

English historian and civil lawyer. Hayward was born in Suffolk and attended Cambridge University, where he earned an LL.D. in 1591. Practicing as a civil lawyer in the courts of Arches and Admiralty, he became a Master in Chancery in 1616 and was knighted in 1619. Hayward maintained a strong interest in history throughout his life, and in his own writings he attempted to follow the precepts of humanism in general and of Machiavelli and Tacitus in particular. His historical interpretations also bear the imprint of his training in civil law. During the 1590s he entered the circle of the ill-fated Robert Devereux, earl of Essex. He published *The First Part of the Life and Raigne of King Henrie the IIII* in 1599 and dedicated it to Essex. After the earl's abortive coup in 1601, the Privy Council examined and imprisoned Hayward because of his history's suspect treatment of the deposition of Richard II. Hayward, however, was no revolutionary propagandist, as is evident from his later writings, which all supported the Jacobean political and religious establishment. These works include: *The Lives of the III Normans, Kings of England* (1613); *The Life, and Raigne of Edward the Sixt* (1630); the *Annals of the First Four Years of Queen Elizabeth* (first published in the nineteenth century); and a manuscript continuation of the history of Henry IV (first published in 1991).

Ronald H. Fritze

Texts

Annals of the First Four Years of the Reign of Queen Elizabeth. Ed. J. Bruce. London: J.B. Nichols, 1840 (Camden Society, original series, vol. 7).

The First and Second Parts of John Hayward's "The Life and Raigne of King Henrie III." Ed. John. J. Manning. London: Royal Historical Society, 1991 (Camden Society, fourth series, vol. 42).

The Life and Raigne of King Edward the Sixth. Ed. Barrett L. Beer. Kent, OH: Kent State University Press, 1993.

References

Levy, F.J. *Tudor Historical Thought.* San Marino, CA: Huntington Library, 1967.

Woolf, D.R. *The Idea of History in Early Stuart England.* Toronto: University of Toronto Press, 1990.

Heckscher, Eli Filip (1879–1952)

Swedish economist and historian. Heckscher was the son of banker and philanthropist Edvard Heckscher. He was educated at Uppsala University and received his doctorate in economics in 1907. Two years later he was appointed professor at the Stockholm School of Economics (Handelshögskolan). He was an advocate of classical economic liberalism, and during the 1920s and 1930s his income from teaching activities was regularly supplemented by his appointment to government commissions and committees. By the late 1920s, Heckscher's scholarly attention had shifted almost entirely to Swedish economic history. In over a dozen books and countless articles he sought to define the basic aspects of Sweden's economy at various times in the past and to identify elements of continuity in the country's economic history. At the same time, he nurtured a generation of young scholars in the field. These achievements explain why he is considered the father of modern economic history in Sweden. The *Scandinavian Economic History Review* was established in Heckscher's memory and to continue his legacy.

Byron J. Nordstrom

Texts

The Continental System. Oxford: Clarendon Press, 1922.
An Economic History of Sweden. Trans. Göran Ohlin. Cambridge, MA: Harvard University Press, 1954.
Mercantilism. Second ed. London: Allen & Unwin; New York: Macmillan, 1955.

References

Scott, Franklin J. *Sweden: The Nation's History.* Carbondale: Southern Illinois University Press, 1988.
Söderlund, E. "Eli F. Heckscher." *Scandinavian Economic History Review* 1 (1953): 137–140.

Heer, Friedrich (1916–1983)

Austrian historian and cultural critic. Heer was born in Vienna and completed his dissertation in 1938. He was active in the resistance against national socialism in the period up to and including World War II, and from 1949 to 1961 he worked as a journalist for various newspapers and journals. Most importantly, he was the editor of *Die Furche* [The Furrow], an important literary and political journal, and was a copublisher of *Der Neue Forum* [New Forum], a voice of Leftist Catholicism in postwar Austria. Beginning in 1961 he was dramatic manager of the Vienna Burgtheater as well as lecturer in occidental history at the University of Vienna. Despite the fact that he possessed a universal grasp of history and published a steady stream of important and best-selling books, he was never awarded the professorship he coveted at the University of Vienna. Possibly his scholarship was deemed too popular for the rigid academic tastes of the time, or his politics were too liberal for the conservative establishment. Heer's works cover a wide range of European intellectual and cultural history, from ancient to modern times. Though Heer espoused a traditional methodology of *Geistesgeschichte,* using summaries, historical background, and critical reflection, his research is useful for obtaining broad, panoptic surveys of important European thinkers, works of art, religion, and cultural institutions.

Elliot Neaman

Texts

Europe, Mother of Revolutions. Trans. Charles Kessler and J. Adcock. New York: Praeger, 1972.
God's First Love: Christians and Jews over Two Thousand Years. Trans. Geoffrey Skelton. New York: Weybright and Talley, 1970.
The Intellectual History of Europe. Trans. Jonathan Steinberg. Cleveland: World Publishers, 1966.

Hegel, Georg Wilhelm Friedrich (1770–1831)

German idealist philosopher, and the most influential continental philosopher after Kant. Born in Stuttgart, Hegel studied at Tübingen and taught at the universities of Jena, Heidelberg, and Berlin (1818–1831). Owing to Napoleon's victory at Jena in 1806 (of which Hegel approved), he was obliged to seek employment for several years as an editor and later head of a school before returning to university life as professor at Heidelberg in 1816. Two years later he moved to Berlin, where he spent the remainder of his life.

In philosophy, Hegel has influenced the Young Hegelians, Karl Marx, the British idealists, Benedetto Croce, contemporary French philosophy, and, most recently, Francis Fukuyama. Hegel's historicism and historical dialectics, partly mediated through Marx, has also had an enduring, if controversial, influence on historiography.

Hegel attempted to unite Immanuel Kant's *ding an sich* (the thing in itself) with "things as they are for us." Kant had concluded that we can never know the world as it is, independent of us; we can know only the conceptual framework through which we necessarily understand the world. Hegel attempted to unify the world through monistic idealism and variously called his unified ideal spiritual reality "mind," "reason," and "the spirit," *(Geist)*. The spirit is self-moving and free; its realization in space is nature, and its realization in time is history. The direction and meaning of history is increased freedom for the spirit to become self-conscious, aware of the historical process and its direction. The creative acts of the spirit in its historical development lead to contradictions in alienation *(Entfremdung, Entäusserung),* when the creative act gives what it creates independent existence, while wishing to unite it with creative subjectivity. History develops, like the history of philosophy, through contradictions leading not to the victory of one side, but to the overcoming of any contradiction in a third "higher" position. Hegel expressed these historical–spiritual contradictions in the term "dialectics" (which Marx interpreted in materialistic-class terms) when a *thesis* and an *anti-thesis* clash and are overcome by a *synthesis.*

World history is the self-realization of the world spirit *(Weltgeist),* using the various national spirits *(volkgeist)* as developing facets of the world spirit. National spirits unify all their manifestations: philosophy, religion, art, political and social structure, etc. This historicist understanding of all the cultural expressions of an era as representing a *Zeitgeist* (spirit of the age) contributed much to historiography. Once a national spirit makes its contribution to the realization of the world spirit, it is overcome by a new synthesis.

The cunning of wisdom (the spirit), uses irrational motives or vices of individuals or nations for its ends. For example, Alexander the Great, Julius Caesar, and Napoleon, were used by the spirit for its own purposes and were discarded when these were achieved. Historical actors do not understand the historical process they take part in until it is over: "the owl of Minerva flies at dusk"— that is, wisdom and understanding appear only at the end of the day. No historically limited morality can condemn the cunning of wisdom; history is its own justification. Hegel conflated mystical statism with philosophy of history. Only the state has history and consciousness. Freedom for the individual is following the law. Much of later totalitarianism was based on this aspect of Hegelianism.

The most important national spirits in the development of the spirit toward increasing freedom, self-consciousness, and rationality are the Oriental, Greek, Roman, and German spirits. The Oriental spirit, in itself composed of Chinese, Indian, Persian, and Judaic spirits, is marked by despotism, limited liberty, and unity of state and religion; lack of individuality, self-consciousness, concept of soul, and history. Yet, the Jewish God is already purely spiritual. Creation *ex-nihilo* by the word emphasizes the rational creativeness of the Jewish God.

Greece was a spiritual and individualistic civilization, in which Nature was interpreted intellectually and spiritually, *Physis* and *Cosmos* expressing order and intelligibility. Greek creative art is *subjective* (nature and the body being expressions of the spirit); *objective* (expressing religiosity in the shape of the individual and beautiful Greek Gods); and *political* (as it represents the polis, democracy, rational morality, and law). In Hegel's view, individualistic subjective moralism destroyed Greek civilization.

Roman imperial spirituality represented a gap between "internal" and "external" morality, leading to philosophies seeking to overcome the world through pleasure or indifference. Christianity separated an internal spiritual world from an external evil world. The German (that is, European) spirit overcame this distinction in self-conscious freedom. The Reformation united the internal and external. The spiritual world, the church, became secular; the secular world became spiritual through science, art, and national consciousness. New subjectivism and spirituality perceive the world as spiritual. Kepler and Newton discovered that a human type of wisdom rules the universe, and the world became home. Morality is based on free will rather than on scriptures and traditional holy rights, leading to a conflict between the two, the French Revolution. In the post-Napoleonic era, wisdom progressed to rule the modern state, the real realization of the rational.

Aviezer Tucker

See also CROCE, BENEDETTO; DIALECTIC; GERMAN HISTORICAL THOUGHT; HISTORICISM; MARX; MARXISM AND HISTORIOGRAPHY; PHILOSOPHY OF HISTORY—SUBSTANTIVE; ROMANTICISM; *ZEITGEIST.*

Texts

Lectures on the Philosophy of World History, Introduction: Reason in History. Ed. Johannes Hoffmeister, trans. H.B. Nisbet. Cambridge, Eng.: Cambridge University Press, 1975.
The Philosophy of History. Trans. J. Sibree. Magnolia, MA: Peter Smith, 1970.

References

Perkins, Robert L., ed. *History and System: Hegel's Philosophy of History.* Albany, NY: SUNY Press, 1984.

Wilkins, Burleigh Taylor. *Hegel's Philosophy of History*. Ithaca, NY: Cornell University Press, 1974.

Heidegger, Martin (1889–1976)

German philosopher, connected with phenomenology and existentialism. A student and academic successor of Edmund Husserl at the University of Freiburg, Heidegger supported the Nazis both as rector of the university and as a party member. He had a decisive influence over the development of philosophy in continental Europe, but has been reviled in analytical philosophy.

Heidegger's main concern was the question of "being." What does it mean, he asked, for something to "be"? Heidegger's historicist insight was that "to be" has different meanings in different historical epochs. The history of being records the changes in how everything appeared to be. What does not come under an epochal perception of being, of what *is,* will not be revealed in that epoch, just as a color-blind person is unable to perceive certain colors. Other historical changes are but reflections of the metaphysical changes in the history of being. *Truth* is "unconcealment." But every "unconcealment" also conceals, whenever some entities appear as *being* according to a certain metaphysics, other things are excluded from *being.* According to Heidegger, the history of being since Plato is a devolutionary one, gradually distancing us further and further from truth as uncovered by the pre-Socratic philosophers. Modern being is technological. Everything, including "human resources," stands in reserve as a raw material. This involuntary metaphysical process is responsible for the disasters of modernity (including Heidegger's own Nazism), for the predominance of Nietzschean nihilism, and for the "will to power," which is a will toward greater accumulation of raw materials. Heidegger longed for a posttechnological, postmetaphysical, poetical age that would let things *be,* without fitting them into a metaphysical scheme of being; on the other hand, he also held that the history of being toys with men who cannot affect it, and that "only a God can save us now."

Aviezer Tucker

Texts

The Basic Problems of Phenomenology. Trans. Albert Hofstadter. Bloomington: Indiana University Press, 1982.
Being and Time. Trans. John MacQuarrie and Edward Robinson. London, SCM Press, 1962.

References

Barash, Jeffrey Andrew. *Martin Heidegger and the Problem of Historical Meaning.* Dordrecht and Boston: Martinus Nijhoff, 1985.
Caputo, John D. "Demythologizing Heidegger: *Aletheia* and the History of Being." *The Review of Metaphysics* 41 (1988): 519–546.

Helmold of Bosau (ca. 1125–ca. 1178)

German chronicler. Details of Helmold's life are sketchy. Ordained a deacon in 1150, he became a priest at Bosau by or before 1163. Interest in missions led him to chronicle the history and movements of the Slavs (called "Wends" by the Germans). His account, somewhat sympathetic to the Slavs and less so to the Danes, seems to rest on good sources. The chronicle was continued by Arnold of Lübeck.

Kerry E. Spiers

Texts

Chronicle of the Slavs. Trans. F. Tschan. New York: Columbia University Press, 1935.
Helmoldi presbyteri Bozoviensis cronica Slavorum. Ed. B. Schmeidler. Hanover and Leipzig: Hahn, 1909.

References

Smalley, Beryl. *Historians in the Middle Ages.* London: Thames and Hudson, 1974.

Henry of Huntingdon (ca. 1080–ca. 1155)

Medieval English chronicler. The son of an archdeacon, Henry himself became archdeacon of Huntingdon and Hertford in 1110. While holding this office he was encouraged by his bishop to write the *Historia Anglorum* [History of the English], which he completed in ten books. Published gradually in five different versions between 1129 and 1154, the *Historia* was an unusual project, which linked contemporary and more remote English history, drawing for its sources on both ancient historians and earlier English chroniclers. In addition to the history of his own country, Henry included genealogies, a treatise on the contempt of the world, and a book of miracles. The work, influential in England and Normandy, was designed to amuse but also to teach the reader the consequences of sin and to despise the transient goods of the world. Its number of surviving manuscripts suggests that it was widely read in the twelfth century and after.

Maura K. Lafferty

Texts

The Chronicle of Henry of Huntingdon. Ed. and trans. T. Forester. London: H.G. Bohn, 1853.

References

Gransden, Antonia. *Historical Writing in England c. 550 to c. 1307.* London: Routledge and Kegan Paul, 1974, 193–201.

Partner, Nancy. *Serious Entertainments: The Writing of History in Twelfth-Century England.* Chicago: University of Chicago, 1976, 11–48.

Herculano de Carvalho Araújo, Alexandre (1810–1877)

Portuguese historian. Herculano is considered to be the founding father of modern Portuguese historiography. He did not have a university education but took classes in "Aula do Comércio," and in paleography in the Torre do Tombo National Archive. An opponent of absolutism, he went into exile in France, from there traveling to England and to the Azores, from whence he returned to mainland Portugal in the Liberal Army. A man of many talents—librarian, journalist, poet, novelist, politician, pedagogue, and historian—he was also a public figure, who took part in all the great discussions of the time in Portugal, in the area of political ideology particularly but not exclusively as a partisan of secularization against the supporters of Catholic ecclesiastical power. He argued for a political theory that he considered Portuguese in origin, one based upon the power of local councils. A man of consistent ethical principals, he finally turned away from politics and died in Vale de Lobos, a farm near Santarém, where he had retired to live as a writer and a farmer. To understand Herculano as a historian, one needs to know the complex web of his life and his personality, as indeed one must with Thierry, Guizot, or Michelet, his great French contemporaries who were also, to some degree, his models. In 1842 he published *Cartas sobre a História de Portugal* [Letters on Portuguese History], the first systematic reflection on a new way to "make history" with a "social" and "secular" approach. His *História de Portugal* (1846–1853) is considered a masterpiece, although it does not proceed beyond the thirteenth century. As a romantic, the Middle Ages were dear to him, and as a historical novelist he frequently chose medieval themes. Another of his books, equally famous but generally taken to be less accurate—it must be read in the context of his po-

lemics against the clergy—was *História da origem e do estabelecimento da Inquisição em Portugal* [History of the Origins and Establishment of the Inquisition in Portugal] (1854–1859). Finally, it must be pointed out that quite aside from his historiographical works, Herculano collected numerous documents scattered through the country, and published the resulting, vast collection of sources under the title of *Portugaliae Monumenta Historica.*

Luís Reis Torgal

Texts

Antologia da Historiografia portuguesa—vol. II. Ed. A.H. de Oliveira Marques. Lisbon: Europa-América, 1975.

História da origem e estabelecimento da Inquisição em Portugal. Ed. Jorge Borges de Macedo and Vitorino Nemésio. Lisbon: Bertrand, 1975–1976.

História de Portugal. Ed. José Mattoso. Lisbon: Bertrand, 1980–1981.

References

Serrão, Joaquim Veríssimo. *História Breve da Historiografia portuguesa.* Lisbon: Editorial Verbo, 1962.

Torgal, Luís Reis, J.M. Amado Mendes, and Fernando Catroga. *História da História em Portugal.* Lisbon: Círculo de Leitores, 1996.

Herder, Johann Gottfried (1744–1803)

German philosopher and man of letters. Herder was born of poor parents at Mohrungen in Prussia and educated for the church. He became a court preacher and vice president of the consistory to the duke of Saxe-Weimar. Particularly influential are his critique of Enlightenment ideas and his philosophy of history, presented in *Ideen zur Philosophie der Geschichte der Menschheit* [Ideas on the Philosophy of the History of Humanity] (1784–1791). Herder denied the Enlightenment conviction that there is an unchanging human nature, reflected in history. In his view, circumstances of geography and climate, social organization, and national character influence human nature and history; he did not, however, clarify the relationship between natural circumstances and national spirits *(Volksgeist).* Herder is held to have been one of the fathers of modern nationalism because of his assumption that nations and their spirits, encompassing all the facets of a civilization, are the basic analytical units of historiography. Each nation goes through an organic cycle, contributing to history its distinct spirit and values, and then dying. Despite his historicist relativism, which denied the possibility of comparison between cultures, Herder had a teleological and progressive scheme of history, leading to the realization of humanity *(Humanität)* and the triumph of reason and justice.

Aviezer Tucker

Texts
J.G. Herder on Social and Political Culture. Ed. F.M. Bernard. Cambridge, Eng.: Cambridge University Press, 1969.

References
Berlin, Isaiah. *Vico and Herder.* London: Hogarth Press, 1976.
Iggers, Georg G. *The German Conception of History: The National Tradition of Historical Thought from Herder to the Present.* Revised ed. Middletown, CT: Wesleyan University Press, 1983.

Herlihy, David (1930–1991)
American historian of medieval and Renaissance Italy. After receiving his doctorate from Yale University (1956), Herlihy taught at Bryn Mawr College (1955–1964), the University of Wisconsin (1964–1973), and Harvard University (1973–86), where he was named Henry Charles Lea professor of history, before becoming Barnaby and Mary Critchfield Keeney professor at Brown University (1986–1991). Herlihy held several professional offices including president of the Medieval Academy (1982–1983) and president of the American Historical Association (1990–1991). His innovative approaches to social history and the urban context of the Italian Renaissance first appeared in his published dissertation, *Pisa in the Early Renaissance: A Study of Urban Growth* (1958). By analyzing closely the effects of late-medieval demographic crises on Tuscan households and their implications for social and intellectual change within the commune, Herlihy offered penetrating and original interpretations of early Renaissance culture, founded more in social history than in independent intellectual developments. His and Christiane Klapisch-Zuber's 1978 (English trans., 1985) quantitative study of the 1427 census in Florence is a superb and enduring monument to this type of scholarship. Recognizing the role of women and families in medieval and Renaissance societies, Herlihy inspired and mentored numerous scholars who continue to make further significant contributions in this field.

Ben Lowe

Texts
Medieval and Renaissance Pistoia: The Social History of an Italian Town, 1200–1430. New Haven, CT: Yale University Press, 1967.
Medieval Households. Cambridge, MA: Harvard University Press, 1985.
Opera Muliebria: Women and Work in Medieval Europe. Philadelphia: Temple University Press, 1990.
Pisa in the Early Renaissance: A Study of Urban Growth. New Haven, CT: Yale University Press, 1958.
And Christiane Klapisch-Zuber. *Tuscans and Their Families: A Study of the Florentine Catasto of 1427.* New Haven, CT: Yale University Press, 1985. (Originally published in French in 1978.)

References
Howell, Martha C. *Women, Production and Patriarchy in Late Medieval Cities.* Chicago: University of Chicago Press, 1986.
Klapisch-Zuber, Christiane. *Women, Family and Ritual in Renaissance Italy.* Chicago: University of Chicago Press, 1985.

Herodotus (ca. 484–420 b.c.)
Greek historian. Herodotus was born in Halicarnassus, a Greek city in what is now southwestern Turkey. He came from a prominent family, but spent his early life in exile. He traveled widely in the East Mediterranean, visiting Egypt, Babylon, Phoenicia, and the Black Sea area. He settled for a while in Athens. He is said to have given a public reading of part of his *History* there in 446 and to have been rewarded from the public treasury. He later became a citizen in the Greek colony at Thurii in Italy, where he died. We know of only one work, a *History* of the wars between the Greeks and the Persians in 490–479 b.c. He refers to other "Assyrian stories," but if he did write these, we know nothing about them.

The English word "history" comes from Herodotus's opening sentence: "This is the setting forth of the *historia* of Herodotus of Halicarnassus." In Greek, however, *historia* meant simply "enquiry," and as a genre it blurred the forms of writing that we separate as ethnography, folklore, geography, and history. Herodotus's conception of *historia* had strong links with the older genre of heroic epic; like Homer, Herodotus's aim was to keep alive the memory of famous deeds, and he freely invented speeches in which his key characters explained events.

Unlike Homer, though, Herodotus did not give the gods the main causal role in events, although he was unwilling to deny their importance either. For instance, he accepted that various gods had intervened in the war on the Greek side, and that they were behind the Persian king Xerxes's decision to invade Greece in 480 B.C.; but he explained the Greek victories primarily in human terms. He was often criticized in antiquity for his gullibility, but he nevertheless distinguished sharply between what it was possible to know about and what was mythical, arguing that while the origins of the wars between Greeks and Orientals might go back to the heroic age, king Croesus of Lydia was the first man whom he *knew* to have wronged the Greeks.

He argued that the Greeks won the wars because they were a hard, pure, simple, free, and poor people. In the time of the founder of their empire, King Cyrus, the Persians had been very similar; but by 480, Herodotus believed, they had become soft and decadent, and were guilty of hubris. He attached great importance to geography, seeing climate as explaining many differences in national character. He made lengthy digressions on geography and local customs, with the whole of Book 2 being devoted to Egypt. He argued that the Greeks had borrowed much of their culture from the Egyptians in the distant past. Because of this some ancient writers called him a "foreigner-lover" *(philobarbaros)*. At some points he did take a relativist position, suggesting that everyone thinks their own customs are best; but ultimately he believed that the Greeks were morally superior. He praised the contributions of the Spartans to the war, but honored the Athenians as the real saviors of Greece.

Herodotus has been called both "the father of history" and "the father of liars." Judgments depend upon the viewer's vantage point. Compared with some later historians, particularly Thucydides, he seems amiable, discursive, and perhaps gullible, with a casual attitude toward source criticism; but seen in his setting, he did much to create the context for true historical enquiry.

Ian Morris

See also GREEK HISTORIOGRAPHY—ANCIENT; THUCYDIDES.

Texts

The History: Herodotus. Trans. David Grene. Chicago: University of Chicago Press, 1987.

References

Dewald, Caroline, and John Marincola, eds. *Herodotus and the Invention of History.* Arethusa, vol. 20, Buffalo: State University of New York Press, 1987.
Lateiner, David. *The Historical Method of Herodotus.* Toronto: University of Toronto Press, 1989.

Herrad of Landsberg [Herrad of Hohenburg] (ca. 1125–1195)

Abbess of Hohenburg, and early female student of the past. Details of Herrad's life are sketchy, but she appears to have been born at or near the castle of Landsberg. In 1167 she became abbess of the monastery of Hohenburg and achieved a reputation as great leader of the house in matters both spiritual and secular. Beginning in as early as 1159, Herrad compiled material for the *Hortus Deliciarum* [Garden of Delights], a work of spiritual devotion made up of numerous painted miniatures punctuated by scripture, prose, poetry, and even music. The true quality and breadth of the work can only be imagined as, tragically, both the original and the only known complete copies were destroyed at Strasbourg in 1870 during the Franco-Prussian War. Only incomplete copies remain. That Herrad was well-read can be established because she frequently cited her sources, who ranged from St. Jerome to contemporaries such as Peter Lombard. Apparently created by several different hands, the miniatures of the *Hortus Deliciarum* were extremely detailed and well crafted; like many medieval artists, those that illustrated the *Hortus* lacked a sense of anachronism, depicting Old Testament warriors as knights clad in chain-mail. Although a number of contemporary scenes were depicted, many others were based on the Bible— the preeminent source of sacred history in the Middle Ages—and thus can be considered a variety of historical writing. The *Hortus* is significant for its many examples of the values, customs, and costumes of the twelfth century and for its use of early sources in a careful manner by a female scholar.

Keith Robinson

Texts

Hortus Deliciarum [Garden of Delights]. Ed. Roslie Green. 2 vols. London: Warburg Institute, 1979.

References

Cames, Gérard. *Allegories et symboles dans l'Hortus deliciarum* [Allegories and Symbols in the Hortus]. Leiden, Netherlands: E.J. Brill, 1971.

Gillen, Otto. *Ikonographische Studien zum Hortus deliciarum der Herrad von Landsberg* [Iconographic Studies on the Hortus]. Berlin: Deutscher Kunstverlag, 1931.

Hexter, Jack H. (1910–1996)

American historian. Born in Memphis, Tennessee, he was educated at the University of Cincinnati and Harvard (Ph.D., 1937). A demanding teacher, many of whose students recall his "marine corps version of graduate school," Hexter's scholarly career spanned over fifty years, during which he taught at several universities, with an interruption for military service, before becoming professor of history at Washington University, St. Louis (1957–1964) and then Stille professor at Yale (1964–1978). He returned to Washington University as "distinguished historian" (1978–1986), also serving as director of the Center for the History of Freedom (1985–1989; director emeritus from 1990 until his death). An early modern European specialist, Hexter both "did history" and "talked" about it. Hexter's earliest book, *The Reign of King Pym* (1941) and his last published essay, "Parliament, Liberty, and Freedom of Elections" (1992), illustrate the imaginative use of sources the historian must employ as "men of letters seeking to render what happened intelligible." Developing what one critic calls "apperceptive mass," Hexter was highly critical of overspecialization, or "tunnel history," that separates and isolates from one another such approaches as political, ecclesiastical, or intellectual history. Thus his fundamental work on *More's Utopia, the Biography of an Idea* (1952) sought to appreciate More's thought within its chronological context. Urging the removal of "the blinders of taxonomy" implicit in Marxist class history or in historical relativism, Hexter's later works, *The History Primer* (1971) and *Doing History* (1971) urge a precise use of language that should "focus on human decision." Noted for a witty and amusing style, Hexter also drew attention to the "lumpers" and "splitters," historians who, respectively, seek common elements in phenomena while ignoring telling distinctions, or insist on overrefining categories and finding differences without being able to generalize.

A.J. Carlson

Texts

And E. Surtz, eds. *The Complete Works of Thomas More.* Vol. 4, *Utopia.* New Haven, CT: Yale University Press, 1965.

Ed. *Parliament and Liberty, from the Reign of Elizabeth to the English Civil War.* Stanford, CA: Stanford University Press, 1992.
Reappraisals in History. Evanston, IL: Northwestern University Press, 1961.
The Reign of King Pym. Cambridge, MA: Harvard University Press, 1941.

References

Mink, Louis O. "The Theory of Practice: Hexter's Historiography." In *After the Reformation: Essays in Honor of J.H. Hexter,* ed. Barbara C. Malament. Philadelphia: University of Pennsylvania Press, 1980.

Higden, Ranulf (ca. 1280–ca. 1363)

English Benedictine monk and chronicler. Higden joined the Chester Abbey of St. Werburgh and took vows in 1299. To write his *Polychronicon,* a well-known chronicle of world history from Creation to 1340, Higden consulted chronicles by Josephus, Suetonius, Eusebius, Bede, and Geoffrey of Monmouth, as well as saints' lives. The work contains a world geography, an Old Testament narrative, and the myths and history of Greece and Rome. He describes Christianity's spread and chronicles British history, including Arthurian legends, the Anglo-Saxon invasions, and Augustine's mission. Besides anecdotes, the *Polychronicon* includes a famous map of the medieval view of the world and information on language, placenames, and science. Used by many later writers, the *Polychronicon* remained a standard source of world history until the seventeenth century.

Christopher M. Bellitto

Texts

Polychronicon. C. Babington and J.R. Lumby, eds. 9 vols. Rolls Series, vol. 41. London: Longman, 1865–1886.

References

Gransden, Antonia. Historical Writing in England. 2 vols. London: Routledge and Kegan Paul, 1974–1982.
Taylor, John. *The Universal Chronicle of Ranulf Higden.* Oxford: Clarendon Press, 1966.

Hill, (John Edward) Christopher (b. 1912)

English historian. Born in York, Hill was educated at Balliol College, Oxford, and, except for a two-year period as a lecturer at University College Cardiff (1936–1938) spent virtually the whole of his subsequent academic career there. He served as master of Balliol College from 1965 until his retirement in 1978. Apart from an early book on Lenin, Hill's prolific output as a historian has been centered on the "English revolution" of the seventeenth century and has been typified by a Marxist perspective, a concern with the social and economic ramifications of Puritanism, with the interface between literature and politics, and with the popular, democratic revolution of the 1640s and 1650s that failed. Hill's earliest articles appeared in the 1930s, and in 1940 he edited *The English Revolution 1640,* a Marxist textbook. Since 1956 and the publication of *Economic Problems of the Church from Archbishop Whitgift to the Long Parliament,* a steady stream of research works has come from his pen, the most recent of them being *The English Bible and the Seventeenth-Century Revolution* (1993). *The World Turned Upside Down* (1972) was his major contribution to "history from below." He has produced biographical studies of Cromwell, Milton, and Bunyan; two textbooks, *The Century of Revolution* (1961) and *Reformation to Industrial Revolution* (1967); and six volumes of essays. There has sometimes been intemperate criticism—from revisionists and others—of his assumptions, historical methods, and conclusions.

R.C. Richardson

Texts

The Century of Revolution. London: Thomas Nelson, 1961.

Economic Problems of the Church from Archbishop Whitgift to the Long Parliament. Oxford: Oxford University Press, 1956.

The English Bible and the Seventeenth-Century Revolution. London: Penguin, 1994.

Milton and the English Revolution. London: Faber and Faber, 1977.

Society and Puritanism in Pre-Revolutionary England. London: Secker and Warburg, 1964.

The World Turned Upside Down. London: Maurice Temple Smith, 1972.

References

Eley, Geoff, and William Hunt, eds. *Reviving the English Revolution: Reflections and Elaborations on the Work of Christopher Hill.* London: Verso, 1988.

Hexter, J.H. *On Historians.* London: Collins, 1979.

Kaye, Harvey J. *The British Marxist Historians.* Cambridge, Eng.: Polity Press, 1984.

Pennington, D.H., and K.V. Thomas, eds. *Puritans and Revolutionaries: Essays in Seventeenth-Century History Presented to Christopher Hill.* Oxford: Clarendon Press, 1978.

Richardson, R.C. *The Debate on the English Revolution Revisited.* London: Routledge, 1988.

Hilton, Rodney Howard (b. 1916)

English historian. Hilton was born in Middleton, near Manchester. He attended Manchester Grammar School and then Oxford University, completing his Ph.D. research before serving in the British army in World War II. Later, he was appointed a lecturer at the school of history at the University of Birmingham and then professor of medieval Social History until his retirement in 1982. A founding member of the Communist Party Historians' Group (1946–1956), he and several others in the group founded the independent journal, *Past & Present* (1952). A pioneer in the development of peasant studies, "history from the bottom up," and class-struggle analysis, Hilton was a major participant in the international debate on the transition from feudalism to capitalism. Feudalism in medieval Europe had long been understood narrowly in terms of the lord-vassal relationship; Hilton, however, insisted on a more socioeconomic and dynamic approach emphasizing the relations of production and conflict between seigneurial lords and exploited peasants. His most recent research has been on urban-class conflicts and the place of towns in medieval society.

Harvey J. Kaye

Texts

Bond Men Made Free: Medieval Peasant Movements and the English Rising of 1381. London: Temple Smith, 1973.

Class Conflict and the Crisis of Feudalism. Second ed. New York: Verso, 1990.

The Decline of Serfdom in Medieval England. Second ed. London: Macmillan, 1983.

The Economic Development of Some Leicestershire Estates in the Fourteenth and Fifteenth Centuries. London: Oxford University Press, 1947.

English and French Towns in Feudal Society. Cambridge, Eng.: Cambridge University Press, 1992.

The English Peasantry in the Later Middle Ages. Oxford: Clarendon Press, 1975.

And H. Fagan. *The English Rising of 1381.* London: Lawrence and Wishart, 1950.

A Medieval Society: The West Midlands at the End of the Thirteenth Century. Cambridge, Eng.: Cambridge University Press, 1966.

References

Aston, T.H., P.R. Coss, C. Dyer, and J. Thirsk, eds. *Social Relations and Ideas: Essays in Honour of R.H. Hilton.* Cambridge, Eng.: Cambridge University Press, 1983.

Hilton, R.H., ed. *The Transition from Feudalism to Capitalism.* London: Verso, 1976.

Kaye, Harvey J. *The British Marxist Historians.* Cambridge, Eng.: Polity Press, 1984.

———. *The Education of Desire: Marxists and the Writing of History.* New York: Routledge, 1992.

Hintze, Otto (1861–1940)

German historian. Beginning in 1878, Hintze studied history and philosophy at Greifswald and Berlin. In 1884 he earned his doctorate under the direction of Julius Weizsäcker, habilitating in 1895 under Heinrich von Treitschke and Gustav von Schmoller. In 1899 he became professor extraordinarius and in 1902 he attained a chair in Berlin. Hintze is regarded as one of the most important historians of the twentieth century and among the first scholars to use social and economic analysis as a tool for the study of administrative history. Well acquainted with Prussian political history, he derived from Schmoller (under whom he had worked from 1888 on the *Acta Borussica*) the impetus toward social and economic history. Hintze edited and published the archives of the Prussian silk industry and wrote a study of this topic. His introduction to his edition of the historical sources for Prussian administrative organization is acclaimed even today as an exemplary survey of its subject. In 1915, Hintze was commissioned to write a history of Prussia, *Die Hohenzollern und ihr Werk* [The Hohenzollern and Their Accomplishments], which was to become a standard work. After World War I he retired but continued to do research, which now focused more on the pre-absolutist epoch and led to three remarkable essays: *Wesen und Verbreitung des Feudalismus* [The Nature and Spread of Feudalism](1929), *Typologie der ständischen Verfassungen des Abendlandes* [A Typology of the Constitution of Society in the West] (1930) and *Weltgeschichtliche Bedingungen der Repräsentativverfassungen* [World Historical Conditions for Representative Constitutions] (1931). Throughout his work, Hintze emphasized a sociological interpretation of the state and provided an important analysis of the work of Max Weber. In his politics, Hintze supported the liberal-conservative position of the Wilhelmian state and was hostile toward democracy, but he remained neutral toward the Weimar Republic.

Thomas Fuchs

Texts

Gesammelte Abhandlungen [Complete Works]. Ed. G. Oestreich. Second ed. 3 vols. Göttingen: Vandenhoeck & Ruprecht, 1964–1970.

The Historical Essays of Otto Hintze. Ed. F. Gilbert. New York: Oxford University Press, 1975.

References

Gerhard, D. "Otto Hintze: His Work and His Significance in Historiography." *Central European History* 3 (1970): 17–48.

Iggers, Georg G. *The German Conception of History: The National Tradition of Historical Thought from Herder to the Present.* Second ed. Middletown, CT: Wesleyan University Press, 1983.

Historia

Classical term for "history." *Historia* is the term used by Herodotus ("father of history," as Cicero called him) in the very first line of his seminal work, making "enquiry" into the memorable events of the conflicts between Greeks and barbarians in the sixth and fifth centuries B.C., although such "history" could be directed at nature, as Plato suggested, as well as at the human past. (The root was the Greek term *histor,* which first appeared in Homer, *Iliad* 499–501, to designate the arbiter of a dispute.) From fifth-century Greek usage the word passed into Latin and the European vernaculars, including English, and enjoyed a rich and complex semantic career down to the present. In the wake of Herodotus, Thucydides, and their successors *historia* came to refer to a literary genre in which the writer of history *(historiographos)* treated (according to Polybius) "the history of past events" in the known world.

In Latin *historia* followed Greek precedent, referring sometimes to the knowledge of facts but, more usually, to written narrative of such facts. Grammar was divided into "history" and "method," illustrating the tendency down to the time of Bacon and beyond to contrast historical material with conceptual ordering. As narrative, *historia* was distinguished from bare annals and from childish fables. "History is an account of things done, remote from the memory of our age," declared Cicero, who later gave the most famous of all definitions of the nature and purpose of history by the rhetorical formula representing it as "the witness of time, the light of truth, the life of memory, the mistress of life, and the messenger of antiquity." It was Cicero, too, who gave a more formal definition by laying down the two "laws" of history, that one should not dare to say what is false and that he must say only what is true; and for centuries these criteria served to distinguish history also from the sister arts of poetry and rhetoric and to suggest its special role in explaining the causes and revealing the meaning of political and social events.

Classical usages were preserved by Christian authors, but increasingly "historia" referred to the actual events of the past, especially the biblical past, with Jerome writing of the "order of history" *(historiae ordo)* and Augustine of the "truth of history" *(veritas historiae).* The term was also applied to the literary sense of a text *(sensus historicus* or *secundum historiam)* as distinguished from various figurative meanings. Most fundamental was the separation between profane and sacred or divine history—in Augustinian terms the city of man and the city of God—the former designating the secular history of the gentile nations *(historia gentium)* and the latter Scriptures and the privileged story of the Judeo-Christian tradition.

In the Middle Ages, *historia* had a kaleidoscopic career, along with agnate terms such as *chronica, gesta, biblia, exemplum, vita,* and *officium,* and in pictorial, musical, and liturgical, as well as literary contexts. Medieval "history" was universal as well as local, sacred as well as profane, and the term appeared in almost one hundred titles from the ninth to the fourteenth centuries in one guise or another (including *historie, historje, histori, historii, history, histoire, hestoria, istoria, estoria, storia, hystoria, hystori, hystorie, hystory, hijstori, ystoria,* and *ystorje*). The standard definition of the term was that given by Isidore of Seville—"History is the narration of deeds by which things done in the past are known."

History in this sense was central to the Renaissance obsession with classical and Christian antiquity not only as one of the humanities *(studia humanitatis)* but also as the method required for an understanding of this remote past, which was separated from modern times by a millennium of darkness in which the sense of history was lost and barbarism returned. Humanists affected to restore the theory as well as the practice of history in a classical sense in a wide range of narrative and antiquarian works devoted to the recovery of ancient (and eventually medieval) culture and, in the case of rhetoricians like Lorenzo Valla, to the proposition that history was, because of its vitality and utility, superior to philosophy

and other sciences. *Historia* was given definition, or rather its classical definition was restored, in dozens of treatises devoted to the "art of history" *(ars historica),* in which, as Jean Bodin argued in his *Method for the Easy Comprehension of History* (1566), history was itself promoted from the level of art to that of science.

In modern times, the semantic history of the term *historia* (and its vernacular progeny) has been extraordinarily rich and varied. From its earlier rhetorical meanings—history as the substance and then the narration of things done—the term was employed in the contexts of logic, psychology, and natural philosophy to refer to apprehension of particulars, experience, and probable as distinguished from the allegedly certain knowledge of natural science. Yet there always remained the larger implication that history was a form of wisdom—"the knowledge of things divine and human"—and above all of self-understanding that was essential to the human condition; and out of this implication emerged later, often metahistorical, conceptions of the "philosophy of history," a phrase popularized in the eighteenth century by Voltaire and Herder and elaborated on in the nineteenth and twentieth centuries.

From the beginning *historia* had, at least implicitly, a threefold meaning: first, as investigation, the investigations undertaken by Herodotus, and the questions asked by any historian; second, as the knowledge acquired from such investigations, the answers to the questions posed; and third, as the formulation of this knowledge, as in the text of Herodotus, at least as it was known by later editors and readers. It was in the last connection that history in all of its national contexts overlapped with literature, joining imagination with memory and reason in reconstructing the past, bringing history under the jurisdiction of rhetoric, and allowing passage across the boundaries between history and fiction. All of this seems in keeping with the original enterprise of the father of history.

Donald R. Kelley

References

Acton, John Emerich Edward (Dalberg-Acton). "The Study of History." In *Selected Writings of Lord Acton,* ed. J. Rufus Fears. Vol. II, *Essays in the Study and Writing of History.* Indianapolis, IN: Liberty Classics, 1985, 504–552.
Kelley, Donald R. "Humanism and History." In *Renaissance Humanism: Foundations, Forms, and Legacy.* Vol. III, *Humanism and the Disciplines,* ed. Albert Rabil Jr. Philadelphia: University of Pennsylvania Press, 1988, 236–270.

H

Keuck, Karl. *Historia: Geschichte des Wortes und seines Bedeutung in den Antike und in dem romanischen Sprachen* [Historia: The Historia of the Word and Its Significance in the Classical and Romance Languages]. Emsdetten, Ger.: Doctoral thesis, University of Münster, 1934.

Knape, Joachim. *Historie in Mitteralter und früher Neuzeit: Begriffs- und gattungsgeschichtliche Untersuchungen im interdisziplinären Kontext* [Historia in the Middle Ages and Early Modern Era: An Examination of the Idea in an Interdisciplinary Context]. Baden-Baden: Verlag Valentin Koerner, 1984.

Koselleck, Reinhard. "Geschichte, Historie." In *Geschichtliche Grundbegriffe* [Historical Foundations], ed. Otto Brunner, Werner Conze, and Reinhard Koselleck, vol. II. Stuttgart: Ernst Klett Verlag, 1975, 593–717.

Seifert, Arno. *Cognitio Historica* [Historical Understanding]. Berlin: Duncker und Humblot, 1976.

Historia Augusta (written fourth–fifth centuries A.D.)

Collection of biographies of Roman emperors. The "Augustan History" (so named by Isaac Casaubon in his edition of 1603) contains a series of circumstantial and often fanciful accounts of the careers and characters of Roman emperors (Augusti) and usurpers, from the time of Hadrian to that of Carinus and Numerianus (late third century). Modeled on Suetonius's *Lives of the Twelve Caesars,* it purports to be the work of six authors living in the reigns of Diocletian and Constantine (late third–early fourth centuries), named as Aelius Spartianus, Julius Capitolinus, Vulcacius Gallicanus, Aelius Lampridius, Trebellius Pollo, and Flavius Vopiscus. The obvious inauthenticity of many of the documents cited in the text has prompted modern scholars to doubt these attributions. Following recent studies by Ronald Syme and others, the *Historia Augusta* is now widely thought to have been compiled toward the end of the fourth century, probably by a single person. The work was used by Montesquieu and, mistrustfully, by Edward Gibbon.

M. Vessey

Texts

Lives of the Later Caesars. Trans. A.R. Birley. Harmondsworth, Eng.: Penguin, 1976.

Scriptores Historiae Augustae. Trans. D. Magie. 3 vols. Cambridge, MA: Harvard University Press, 1921–1932.

References

Syme, Ronald. *Ammianus and the Historia Augusta.* Oxford: Clarendon Press, 1968.

———. *Emperors and Biography: Studies in the Historia Augusta.* Oxford: Clarendon Press, 1971.

Historical Anthropology

See ANTHROPOLOGY AND HISTORY.

Historical Atlases

See ATLASES, HISTORICAL.

Historical Demography

See DEMOGRAPHY—HISTORICAL.

Historicism

The application of what is taken to be historical understanding and method to all phenomena; in particular (in Maurice Mandelbaum's words), "the belief that an adequate understanding of the nature of any phenomenon and an adequate assessment of its value are to be gained through considering it in terms of the place which it occupied and the role which it played within a process of development." "Development" is change in a specific direction. Historicist phenomena are unfolding, developing processes whose ends are encoded in, and explained by, their beginnings. This definition includes several different and even mutually incompatible "historicist" doctrines and methods. The first of these consists of an "organismic" understanding of phenomena as aspects of larger developing processes. The second consists in understanding things in their unique, concrete, particularity, ideographically. The third, Karl Popper's definition, is that "Historicism is an approach to the social sciences which assumes that *historical prediction* is their principal aim and which assumes this aim is attainable by discovering the 'rhythms' or the 'patterns', the 'laws' or the 'trends' that underlie the evolution of history."

In its extreme form, the first version of historicism holds that all knowledge and values *express* the perspective of a tradition or historical context rather than *represent* the world. All knowledge and values are relative to their historical context. Intellectual expressions are understood through the reconstruction of purposes, functions, and contexts. This pure type of historicism has to treat itself, moreover, as bounded by interests, assumptions, and context. The self-reflection of pure historicism shows it to be relative as well, unless universal claims are *constitutive* of parts of the world rather than *representing* it. Much discussion of historicism is of these relativistic repercussions. Ultimately, historicism under this definition abolishes the distinctions between science and ideology, knowledge and opinion.

The second, individualizing, kind of historicism is, on the face of it, incompatible with the first. While historicism of the first kind seeks to understand each phenomenon as expressing something common to several phenomena, the second kind seeks to understand phenomena in their unique particularity. Attempts to combine the two concentrate on interpreting historical individuality as a historical epoch, national spirit, state, race, etc. Thus history becomes a succession of historicist units with no universal standards of evaluation.

Popper, to take the third form, uses the word "historicism" as a blanket term, conflating many negatively evaluated positions, associated loosely with some historicist positions. As J.A. Passmore has suggested in summarizing Popper, "In consequence he often writes as if he had overthrown position A when in fact his argument is only directed against position B, which although occasionally associated with position A by no means entails it." Instead of prediction, Popper actually discussed large-scale unconditional prophecies. Popper referred to historicism as "well-considered and close-knit philosophy," as "a doctrine of method," and as "a method," although he treated historicism as a doctrine of the methods of the social sciences. Finally, Popper actually attacked different positions from those that he had previously defined as historicist.

Until World War I, historicism had mainly negative connotations arising from the misapplication of the historical method to areas where it is inappropriate, similar to "scientism" or "psychologism," and associated with historical relativism and the uncritical acceptance of appearances. After the war, advocates of historicism began to define their position, as a worldview, advocating the liberation of man and the ushering in of a new historicist age through the understanding of the historicity of all knowledge and established beliefs.

Following the German defeat in World War I, Ernst Troeltsch suggested that historicism was the characteristic modern world view, entailing an understanding of all knowledge and experience in developmental historical terms. Historicism had led, in Troeltsch's view, to the crisis of modernity, to moral and intellectual relativism. Troeltsch sought to solve this crisis by discovering that absolute and universal values are not transcendental, but can be found *within* history. Karl Mannheim, on the other hand, viewed historicism as finally liberating the modern world from the absolutist theological worldview of the Middle Ages, preserved by the Enlightenment; in his view, Vico and Hegel should replace Herder, Goethe, and Ranke as its founders. Mannheim held that moral skepticism does not follow historicist moral relativism because values may be rooted in specific sociohistorical contexts. Karl Heussi would continue this tradition of historicism, further tracing its historical roots.

Friedrich Meinecke stressed, more than his predecessors, the developing unique, concrete, individuality of every historical phenomenon as the defining characteristic of historicism. Accordingly, Meinecke traced the historical roots of historicism back along a different path than that followed by Mannheim and Heussi, going back to the seventeenth century but focusing on the eighteenth-century German national antithesis to natural law, enlightenment, French, cosmopolitan, and western European traditions. Meinecke identified Goethe and Ranke, not Hegel and Marx, among the founding fathers of historicism. Although Meinecke conceived historicism as the worldview of the modern world, he upheld contextually based absolute values, refusing to concede the existence of a crisis of historicist relativism.

Benedetto Croce's historicism was distinctly Hegelian in thrust. In Croce's view, everything is history, the developing epochal manifestations of rational spirit. Each historical epoch is an "individual which is rationalized and, only by virtue of the universal, historically individualized." Croce's historicism is not relativistic, however, because history is absolutely rational.

After World War II the identification by some historicist thinkers of the basic units of history with states, nations, races, and classes was held responsible respectively for antidemocratic authoritarianism, (Fascist) nationalism, (Nazi) racism, and Stalinist Marxism. This led to antihistoricist criticism by liberal philosophers such as F.A. Hayek, Karl Popper, Karl Löwith, and Claude Lévi-Strauss. Historicism has, however, been revived in recent times in the form of Heideggerian-influenced postmodernism.

Aviezer Tucker

See also NEW HISTORICISM.

Texts

Croce, Benedetto. *History: Its Theory and Practice.* Trans. D. Ainslie. New York: Russell & Russell, 1960.

Heussi, Karl. *Die Krisis des Historismus.* Tübingen, Germany: Mohr 1932.

Mannheim, Karl. *Essays on the Sociology of Knowledge.* Ed. and trans. Paul Kecskemeti. London: Oxford University Press, 1952.

Meinecke, Friedrich. *Historicism: The Rise of a New Historical Outlook.* Trans. J.E. Anderson. New York: Herder & Herder, 1972.

Popper, Karl. *The Poverty of Historicism.* London: Routledge & Kegan Paul, 1957.

Troeltsch, Ernst. *Der Historismus und Seine Probleme.* Tübingen, Germany: Mohr 1922.

References

D'Amico, Robert. *Historicism and Knowledge.* New York: Routledge, 1988.

Essays in Historicism: History and Theory. Beiheft 14. Middletown, CT: Wesleyan University Press, 1975.

Iggers, Georg G. *The German Conception of History.* Middletown CT: Wesleyan University Press, 1968.

———. "Historicism: The History and Meaning of the Term." *Journal of the History of Ideas* 56 (1995): 129–152.

Mandelbaum, Maurice. *History, Man, and Reason.* Baltimore, MD: Johns Hopkins University Press, 1971.

History and Culture of the Indian People, The (1953–1977)

An eleven-volume encyclopedic work, conceived in 1944 by K.M. Munshi, a nationalist politician who founded the Bharatiya Vidya Bhavan, an education society, in Bombay in 1938. It was the first important general history of India to be produced in India after independence, and aimed to be a history of India and its people, rather than a history of those who have invaded it from time to time. The chief editor of the series was the renowned historian R.C. Majumdar, and Munshi himself wrote introductions to the first four volumes. The eleven volumes contain some nine thousand pages, written by about seventy-five contributors, and lavishly illustrated with 283 plates and twenty maps. While the volumes are sometimes densely written and present a mass of information, they are useful as a source on Indian history and culture and, perhaps more important, as an example of the views, interests, and manner of writing history of a generation of Indian historians who had lived through, and sometimes taken part, in the nationalist struggle. They were anxious that India's past might be described by sons, and also that the world might catch a glimpse of India's soul as Indians see it.

Roger D. Long

Texts

The History and Culture of the Indian People. Vol. 1, *The Vedic Age* (1951); Vol. 2, *The Age of Imperial Unity* (1951); Vol 3, *The Classical Age* (1954); Vol. 4, *The Age of Imperial Kanauj* (1955); Vol. 5, *The Struggle for Empire* (1957); Vol. 6, *The Delhi Sultanate* (1960); Vol. 7, *The Mughal Empire* (1974); Vol. 8, *The Maratha Supremacy* (1977); Vol. 9, *British Paramountcy and Indian Renaissance,* Part 1 (1963); Vol. 10, *British Paramountcy and Indian Renaissance,* Part II (1965); and Vol. 11, *Struggle for Freedom* (1969). Bombay: Bharatiya Vidya Bhavan, 1951–1977.

History Workshop

British and European historical movement and, since 1976, an associated left-leaning historical journal. History Workshop was begun in 1967 by left-wing workers and tutors, many of them associated with Ruskin College in Oxford. Then and now, the purpose of History Workshop has been to democratize the practice of history and to provide a forum in which everyone—not just the professional scholar—can participate in the study of the past. In its methodological purview, History Workshop seeks to expand disciplinary boundaries and the ways and means by which historians perform their craft, giving special attention to oral history as an essential tool for the preservation and analysis of popular memory and workers' experiences. As a movement the Workshop draws its impetus from libertarian ideals, shop-floor militancy, and the educational requirements of adult learners, but its most enduring and dynamic enquiry in recent years has involved women's and feminist history, with special attention being devoted to the relationship between feminist and socialist historiography. The talks and papers at the Workshop's silver anniversary conference in 1991 demonstrate that the Workshop movement has sought to include discussion of national identity, racism, women and technology, and green history, as well as the vexed question of "what is left of the Left?" While the recent perils of the Left have generated much interest within the Workshop movement, they have in no way threatened the movement's existence, chiefly because History Workshop has always proven adaptive and responsive, studying past and present together while avoiding orthodoxies and theories that might restrict its mandates, constituencies, and subject matter. Besides its regional, national, and international assemblies and conferences, History Workshop also has its own journal. This began in 1976 with the subtitle "a journal of socialist historians," revised in 1981 to "'a journal of socialist and feminist historians," and in 1995 dropped altogether as a sign of welcome to "newer radicalisms" such as gay and lesbian history, postcolonial history, and the politics of the environment. The Workshop *Journal* is a scholarly publication with a world-wide following, and at the same time it attempts to serve as a record and organ of History Workshop *the movement,* containing notes, queries, and comments on regional and international activities by Workshop groups in Britain, Europe, and North America.

Ian Dyck

See also Marxism and Historiography; Public History; Radical History (United States); Sexuality.

Texts

Samuel, Raphael, ed. *History Workshop: A Collectanea, 1967–1991.* London: History Workshop, 1991.

History Workshop: A Journal of Socialist and Feminist Historians. London: Routledge, 1976–1989; Oxford: Oxford University Press, 1989–.

Hjärne, Harald Gabriel (1848–1922)

Swedish historian. Hjärne was educated at Uppsala University and became a professor of history there in 1885. His professional career, however, extended beyond the university, and he was active in the political arguments of the period, serving as a member of the Swedish parliament on two occasions in the early twentieth century. During the first of these he was influential in shaping the official reactions to Norway's bid for independence in 1905. He may have been the most broadly educated of the Swedish historians of his generation. He advocated careful source criticism and comparative approaches, but was also guided by intense religious and ethical views, which shaped his work. For example, he considered seventeenth-century Sweden to have been a major bulwark against the rise of a barbarian Russia. These views are especially clear in *Gustaf Adolf: Protestanismens förkämpe*

[Gustavus Adolphus: Defender of Protestantism] (1901) or *Karl XII: Omstörtningen i östeuropa 1697–1703* [Charles XII and Disorder in Eastern Europe] (1902). His broad interests made him a "universalist," and his scholarship reflects a wide range of chronological and thematic focuses.

Byron J. Nordstrom

Texts

Engelsk imperialism och parlamentarism [English Imperialism and Parliamentarianism]. Stockholm: Bonnier, 1940.

Gustaf Adolf: Protestanismens förkämpe: Några synpunkter. Stockholm: n.p. 1901.

Karl XII: Omstörtningen i östeuropa 1697–1703. Stockholm: Ljus Forlag, 1982.

Reformationsriksdagen i Västerås [The Reformation Riksdag in Västerås]. Stockholm: Hokerberg, 1893.

Revolutionen och Napoleon: Några drag och synpunkter [The Revolution and Napoleon: Issues and Perspectives]. Stockholm, 1911.

Unionskrisen. Uppsala: Almqvist & Wiksells, 1895.

References

Scott, Franklin J. *Sweden: The Nation's History.* Carbondale: Southern Illinois University Press, 1988.

Torstendahl, Rolf. *Källkritik och vetenskapssyn i svensk historisk forskning, 1820–1920* [Source Criticism and Scholarly Methods in Swedish Historical Research]. Stockholm: Svenska bokförlaget, 1964.

Hmannan Mahayazawindawgyi [The Great Royal Chronicle of the Glass Palace]

Burmese chronicle. *Hmannan Mahayazawindawgyi* was compiled by the Monywe Sayadaw and a committee of scholars in 1829 by order of King Bagyidaw of the Konbaung dynasty of Burma. The committee was composed of learned ministers, monks, and brahmins knowledgeable about history, literature, and religion. Their charge was to write a history of the kings of Burma (*yazawin,* literally "genealogy of kings"). The stated purpose of the endeavor was to establish a "standard . . . for all duties of the king, for all affairs of state, for all matters of religion, and not a thing full of conflicting and false statements . . . ." Its title derives from the fact that it was written in the *hmannan,* or "palace of glass," one of the buildings in the main palace.

"In the Burmese year 1229 (A.D. 1867), on the third day of the waxing moon of the month of Tawthalin" (September–October), King Mindon, a successor of King Bagyidaw who had commissioned the *Hmannan,* commanded another group of scholars to write the "Second Chronicle," *Dutiya Yazawindawgyi,* suggesting that the *Hmannan* was then known to the court as *Pahthama Yazawindawgyi* or the "First Royal Chronicle." The first part of the *Dutiya Yazawindawgyi,* in seven volumes, ended with the year 1854, and the second, in three volumes, with 1869. After the British formally annexed Burma in 1886, another small group of scholars from the now extinct court continued the narrative of the "Second Chronicle" to the year 1885 when Mandalay fell to the British. This third segment, along with another written in 1922 by U Tin, a minister of the Burmese court who was part of the group that wrote the third segment, brought the narrative up to 1916 when the last king of Burma, Thibaw, died while under British-forced exile in India. This was published as *Konbaungset Mahayazawindawgyi* [The Great Royal Chronicle of the Konbaung Dynasty], which began the narrative in 1752 when the Konbaung dynasty was founded.

In reality, the *Hmannan* is not the first chronicle written in Burma, since a number of other chronicles preceded it by several centuries. But because these had been written by private individuals, and not by a committee commissioned by the state, one could say that the *Hmannan* was the first state-sponsored history of Burma. But in terms of content, subject matter, organizational schema, worldview, and other matters, the *Hmannan* is a virtual copy of the *Mahayazawingyi* [The Great Chronicle of Kings] written by one U Kala, probably in 1720 or 1721. And although it is not known for certain whether King Taninganwe (r. 1714–1733), who reigned at the time U Kala was writing his history, actually commissioned him to write this history, the author clearly expressed his loyalty to the king in his work. On the other hand, U Kala leaves out an important word in his title, *daw,* a word denoting royalty, included by the *Hmannan.* In any case, most scholars are agreed that the *Hmannan* is essentially a larger and updated version of the *Mahayazawingyi,* despite the claim by its authors that theirs was meant to "correct the errors" in U Kala's work. Nevertheless, for the historian of Burma concerned primarily with events and chronology, the *Hmannan's* narrative from 1720 (or 1721) to 1821 remains indispensable.

The *Hmannan* has been published in Burmese by different presses at different times during the course of the twentieth century. No English translation of the complete text exists today, although in 1923 the third, fourth, and fifth parts of the Mandalay edition of 1907 were translated into English by Pe Maung Tin as *The Glass Palace Chronicle of the Kings of Burma.* The translation covers only the period from the beginning of the founding of Tagaung—with which the Burmese people associate their origins—to the death of King Narathihapade and the "fall" of Pagan in 1287, considered erroneously to be the last king of that dynasty. This translated portion has often been cited, also erroneously, as the *Hmannan,* when in fact it represents only about a fifth of the whole work. Another partial translation, by Phraison Salarak, also exists: this focuses on the relations between Siam and Burma as described in the *Hmannan,* and is presented as a series of long articles in the *Journal of the Siam Society.*

Michael Arthur Aung-Thwin

See also BURMESE HISTORIOGRAPHY—CHRONICLES.

Texts

The Glass Palace Chronicle of the Kings of Burma. Trans. Pe Maung Tin. Rangoon: Rangoon University Press, 1923, introduction.

Hmannan Mahayazawindawgyi [The Great Royal Chronicle of the Glass Palace]. Ed. Daw Pwa Khin and U Hla Maung. 3 vols. Rangoon: Pyi Kyi Mandaing Press, 1967.

U Kala. *Mahayazawingyi* [The Great Chronicle of Kings]. Ed. Saya Pwa. 3 vols. Rangoon: Hanthawaddy Press, 1960.

Konbaungset Mahayazawindawgyi [The Great Royal Chronicle of the Konbaung Dynasty]. Ed. U Maung Maung Tin. 3 vols. Rangoon: Laytimandaing Press, 1968.

References

Aung-Thwin, Michael. "Burma before Pagan: Status of Archaeology Today." *Asian Perspectives* 25 (1982–1983) [published 1987]: 1–21.

———. *Pagan: The Origins of Modern Burma.* Honolulu: University of Hawaii Press, 1985.

———. "Prophecies, Omens, and Dialogue, Tools of the Trade in Burmese Historiography." In *Moral Order and the Question of Change: Essays on Southeast Asian Thought,* ed. David K. Wyatt and Alexander Woodside. Southeast Asia Studies Monograph Series, no. 24. New Haven, CT: Yale University Southeast Asia Program, 1982, 78–103.

Luce, G.H. *Phases of Pre-Pagan Burma: Languages and History.* Oxford: Oxford University Press, 1985, vol. 1.

Phraison Salarak. "Intercourse between Burma and Siam: As Recorded in *Hmannan Yazawindawgyi.*" *Journal of the Siam Society* 5.1 (1908): 1–82; 8.2 (1911): 1–119; 11.3 (1914–1915): 1–67; 12.2 (1918): 1–48; and 13.1 (1919): 1–65.

Stargardt, Janice. *The Ancient Pyu of Burma.* Cambridge and Singapore: Publications on Ancient Civilization in South East Asia and Institute of Southeast Asian Studies, 1990.

U Tet Htoot. "The Nature of the Burmese Chronicles." In *Historians of South East Asia,* ed. D.G.E. Hall. London: Oxford University Press, 1962, 50–62.

Hobsbawm, Eric (b. 1917)

Social and cultural historian. From a British and Austrian Jewish background, Hobsbawm grew up in Vienna and Berlin before moving to England in the 1930s. A lifelong Communist, he has been a leading advocate of a unified and pluralist Left in British politics. He spent most of his academic career at Birkbeck College, University of London, where he remains an emeritus professor. Hobsbawm has made major contributions to economic, social, and cultural history. His work on the early English working class and primitive forms of rebellions, notably banditry, helped to create "history from below." His multivolume history of Europe and the world in the nineteenth and twentieth century, beginning with *The Age of Revolution, 1789–1914* (1962) and ending with *The Age of Extremes, 1914–91* (1994), represents a complex Marxist interpretation that treats the modern world as a coherent whole. In the 1980s, Hobsbawm developed a highly influential approach to late nineteenth-century nationalism, viewing it as an "invented" response to modernization, population shifts, and mass mobilization.

Dennis Dworkin

Texts

The Age of Empire. New York: Pantheon Books, 1987.

Labouring Men. London: Weidenfeld and Nicolson, 1964.

Primitive Rebels. New York: W.W. Norton and Co., 1965.

References

Kaye, Harvey J. *The British Marxist Historians: An Introductory Analysis.* Cambridge, Eng.: Polity Press, 1984.

Hodgson, Marshall G.S. (1922–1968)

Historian of Islam. A student of Gustave Edmund von Grunebaum (1909–1972), Hodgson was trained and eventually taught at the University of Chicago. At the time of his premature death he was professor of history and chairman of the Committee on Social Thought. In his brief career Hodgson made two principal contributions to the field. The first was in Shi'ism. In addition to his monograph on the Nizārī Ismâîlîs, Hodgson wrote several articles, among which is his seminal essay "How Did the Early Shi'a Become Sectarian?" But it is for his massive—and massively ambitious—*The Venture of Islam,* published posthumously, that Hodgson is primarily known. The *Venture* is a textbook that seeks to introduce and survey Islamic history from its origins to modernity, as well as a manifesto that sets out Hodgson's iconoclastic views. Deeply critical of the Euro- and Arabocentrism that characterized much writing on Islam, and keen to locate Islamic history within world history, Hodgson proposed new terminology (for example "Islamicate"); a wider geographic and cultural focus; and, in a series of biographical and textual studies, a vision of the articulation and transformation of a single (but not monolithic) "Islamicate" civilization. He also set out the position of this civilization within the broader context of world history, and his views on world history in general, in several articles.

Chase F. Robinson

Texts

"How Did the Early Shi'a Become Sectarian?" *Journal of the American Oriental Society* 75 (1955): 1–13.

The Order of Assassins: The Struggle of the Early Nizârî Ismâîlîs against the Islamic World. The Hague: Mouton, 1955.

The Venture of Islam: Conscience and History in a World Civilization. Chicago: University of Chicago, 1974.

Rethinking World History: Essays on Europe, Islam, and World History. Ed. E. Burke III. Cambridge, Eng.: Cambridge University Press, 1993.

Hofstadter, Richard (1916–1970)

American historian. Born in Buffalo, New York, Hofstadter received his undergraduate degree from the University of Buffalo and his doctorate from Columbia University. He spent his career at Columbia, writing a number of books on American politics, education, reform movements, and intellectual life. His first book, *Social Darwinism in American Thought,* traced the impact of Darwinian thought on American social ideas in the Gilded Age and the Progressive Era. His second work was among his most ambitious and important. *The American Political Tradition* described the political ideas and careers of important political figures from the founding fathers to Franklin Roosevelt. Hofstadter argued that political ideas in America were mainly built around the support of a developing industrial capitalism and that differences between political parties were often relatively minor. Hofstadter was also interested in the role of intellectuals in American life, and he wrote about academic freedom and its opponents. In 1955, *The Age of Reform,* Hofstadter's critical analysis of populism, progressivism, and the New Deal, won the Pulitzer prize. Hofstadter was sometimes criticized for being "elitist" and for being a "consensus" historian who downplayed the role of ideological conflict in American life, but he was more often appreciated for his extremely sophisticated discussion of American institutions and ideas.

Barbara A. McGowan

Texts

The Age of Reform. New York: Knopf, 1955.
The American Political Tradition and the Men Who Made It. New York: Knopf, 1948.
Anti-Intellectualism in American Life. New York: Knopf, 1963.
The Idea of a Party System. Berkeley: University of California Press, 1969.
The Paranoid Style in American Politics and Other Essays. New York: Knopf, 1965.
The Progressive Historians. New York: Knopf, 1968.

References

Elkins, Stanley, and Eric McKitrick, eds. *The Hofstadter Aegis.* New York: Knopf, 1974.
Novick, Peter. *That Noble Dream: The "Objectivity Question" and the American Historical Profession.* Cambridge, Eng.: Cambridge University Press, 1988.

Holanda, Sérgio Buarque de (1902–1982)

Brazilian historian. Holanda spent a year in Weimar Germany where he attended Friedrich Meinecke's lectures. At the University of São Paulo he became the first director of the multidisciplinary Institute of Brazilian Studies (1962–1964). His first and most popular historical work, *Raízes do Brasil* [The Roots of Brazil], appeared in 1936. Holanda interpreted the Brazil of the 1930s through an analysis of the Portuguese colonial legacy. He also offered a new periodization that divided Brazilian history into two epochs—rural and urban—with 1888 as the dividing point. Later works examined various aspects of Brazilian colonial history ignored by previous scholars. Between 1966 and 1972 he edited a collaborative survey of Brazilian history, *História Geral da Civilização Brasileira,* of which he authored volume 7. Holanda's only work available in English is his essay "Historical Thought in Twentieth-Century Brazil" published in E. Bradford Burns's *Perspectives on Brazilian History* (1967). Holanda led his generation in emphasizing the importance of the social sciences, the need to shift from expository to interpretive history, and the integration of the Brazilian historical experience into Western civilization.

George L. Vásquez

Texts

"Historical Thought in Twentieth-Century Brazil." In *Perspectives on Brazilian History,* ed. E. Bradford Burns. New York: Columbia University Press, 1967.
Moncoes. Third expanded ed. São Paulo: Editora Brasiliense, 1990.
Raízes do Brasil. Rio de Janeiro: J. Olympio, 1936.

References

Barbosa, Francisco de Assis, ed. *Raízes de Sérgio Buarque de Holanda* [The Roots of Sérgio Buarque de Holanda]. Rio de Janeiro: Rocco, 1989.
Graham, Richard. "Interview with Sérgio Buarque de Holanda." *Hispanic American Historical Review* 62 (1982): 3–17.

Holinshed, Raphael (fl. 1560–1580)

English historian. Although his pedigree cannot be traced authoritatively, he is probably the Holinshed who matriculated at Christ's College, Cambridge, in 1544. He was employed as a translator in the London printing office of Reginald Wolfe at the beginning of Elizabeth's reign. Holinshed also worked under Wolfe's direction on a large universal history and cosmography that was later taken over by John Stow but never published. Holinshed's major work was *The Chronicles of England, Scotlande, and Irelande* (1577). The most elaborate and objective history published in England thus far, this two-volume chronicle was dedicated to William Cecil, Lord Burghley, and included the history of Scotland to 1571, the history of Ireland to 1547, and the history of England to 1575.

Holinshed's translation of the twelfth-century chronicle of Florence of Worcester has survived in Harleian Manuscript 563 at the British Library. He was dead when the greatly enlarged second edition of his chronicle was published in 1587. The second edition was a collaborative effort produced by Abraham Fleming, John Hooker, alias Vowell, Francis Thynne, John Stow, and others. This edition was used by Shakespeare and became the most influential English chronicle of the sixteenth century. The first issue of the second edition was heavily censored by the government to guarantee political correctness, but a complete reprint of the original version was published in 1807 and 1808.

Barrett L. Beer

Texts

The First and Second Volumes of Chronicles. Ed. J. Vowell et al. Second ed. 3 vols. London: J. Harison et al., 1587.

References

Levy, F.J. *Tudor Historical Thought.* San Marino, CA: Huntington Library, 1967.

Patterson, Annabel. *Reading Holinshed's Chronicles.* Chicago: University of Chicago Press, 1994.

Holocaust, Historiography of the

"Holocaust" is the term widely used in North America since the 1960s to refer to the persecution and murder of two-thirds of European Jewry, about six million people, by the Nazi regime during the Second World War. Although broadly accepted, this usage is not without challenges from certain quarters. Preferring the Hebrew "Shoah," or even "Judeocide," a few writers object to "Holocaust," seeing the original Greek meaning of "a sacrifice totally consumed by fire" as singularly inappropriate for mass murder without any sacrificial meaning and having nothing necessarily to do with fire. A minority have also challenged the exclusive focus on Jews—seeking to include the Sinti and Roma (Gypsies) and disabled persons as particularly victimized by Nazism, for example, or extending to the murderous assault on some East European nationalities. They would use the term for all victims of Nazi wartime atrocities. Still others consider "holocaust" (with a lowercase *h*) in a generic sense as denoting any large-scale massacre, without any necessary reference to Nazis or Jews. However, despite some terminological imprecisions or inaccuracies associated with the word's origins, most historians accept the focus as we have

understood it here, accepting that there were important elements of uniqueness in the motivation and the scale of the Nazis' victimization of European Jewry. At the same time, historians commonly seek connections both with other victims of Nazism and with other episodes of mass killing in history.

The historiography of the Holocaust parallels that of Nazi Germany in many respects. As with the history of the Third Reich, there is disagreement over many matters, including origins. To be sure, no one denies the great importance of anti-Semitism in Hitler's own ideology—to the point that many see it at the core of his worldview. And few would dispute its importance in the policies of the regime. Historians have charted the intense, brutal campaign against the Jews of Germany from the moment that Hitler became chancellor in 1933, examining the series of laws and decrees that gradually isolated the 525,000 Jews in German society, stripped them of their rights, removed them from their employment, robbed them of their property, and subjected them to random acts of terror. Historians have tracked the Jews' turning to emigration as their last resort, seeing the flow of Jews abroad intensifying particularly after the *Kristallnacht* riots against them by SA (precursor of the "SS") and party activists in November 1938. And they have also noted how, just as this flow of refugees increased, new barriers to immigration were being raised everywhere, both in Europe and in North and South America.

But scholars differ considerably in their understanding of how persecution and expulsion led to Europeanwide mass murder, notably the deportation of many hundreds of thousands of Jews to death camps in Poland where they were killed, many by poison gas. While there is widespread agreement that Hitler had a key role in Jewish matters, scholars disagree on how closely he followed events and the extent to which he directed Nazi Jewish policy. Those historians usually referred to as intentionalists—one thinks of Lucy Dawidowicz, Gerald Fleming, or Richard Breitman—see both Hitler's ideas about the Jews and the Nazis' anti-Jewish program of the mid-1930s as pointing directly to the genocidal outcome during the Second World War. War, these writers feel, gave the Führer the pretext to carry out a predetermined, murderous objective on a grand scale. Other scholars, known as functionalists—a group including Hans Mommsen, Uwe Dietrich Adam, and Christopher Browning—stress the evolution of Nazi policy toward the Jews, contending that mass murder only emerged as a realistic option during the course

H

of the war itself, specifically, the ideologically charged Barbarossa campaign against the Soviet Union. They see the Nazis as groping toward a "solution" of the "Jewish problem" that they had defined, opting for a comprehensive strategy of mass murder only when other options were blocked and when, through trial and error, they developed techniques by which an entire people could be destroyed. Among functionalists, some consider that Hitler made a decision for the Final Solution during the summer of 1941, in the euphoria of victory during the first stages of the Russian campaign; others see Nazi policy crossing the line to Europeanwide killing somewhat later, in the autumn of that year, when Hitler and his military leadership realized that they would not achieve an early victory over the Soviets.

Following Raul Hilberg's groundbreaking *Destruction of the European Jews* (1961), perhaps the most important single work ever written on the subject, some scholars have been more interested in the "how" than the "why" of the Holocaust; they explore the mechanisms by which it was possible to murder such a vast number of people by drawing heavily on the resources of the modern state. Historians who investigate such questions point to the vast scale and extent of the murderous enterprise, carried out across an entire continent and administered by large bureaucracies and branches of the German civil service. For some, the most recent of whom is Zygmunt Bauman, the key lies in the "modernity" of the process—the use of the most up-to-date bureaucratic, scientific, and technological methods. For others, the key element has much more continuity with the past—the demonic force of anti-Semitism, linked in the views of some to a Christian past, energized by a victorious Nazi state, driven by a fanatic leader, supported by a thoroughly indoctrinated German population, and assisted by eager collaborators both inside and outside the Reich. For still others what counts is a pseudoscientific orientation— the Nazi obsession with a racial utopia, rooted in Darwinian thought and extending considerably beyond a fixation with Jews.

In her 1961 reportage on the trial of Adolf Eichmann in Jerusalem, Hannah Arendt popularized the notion of the "banality of evil" as a vehicle for understanding lower- and middle-ranking perpetrators—a theme picked up in a study of mass murders committed by one police battalion in a book by Christopher Browning entitled, appropriately enough, *Ordinary Men* (1992). This understanding of the perpetrators contrasts with approaches that stress the high de-gree of ideological motivation of the killers and the intense hatred of Jews in the societies from which they came. At issue here is an understanding not only of the relatively small numbers of those who did the actual killing, but also the great army of "desk murderers" and other workers who took charge of transportation, scheduling, construction, disposing of the Jews' former property, and so on.

Some have argued that the murders would never have reached the scale that they did had bystanders not attended the process with indifference and even hostility toward the victims. Historians have sought to define the limits of complicity inside Nazi Europe, examining the roles of concentration camp personnel, police, the *Wehrmacht,* and others, down to ordinary civilians. Another line of enquiry has focused on societies drawn into the orbit of the Third Reich, either as allies, collaborators, occupied populations, or neutrals. One viewpoint, associated in particular with the earliest wave of writing on bystanders, tends to be highly judgmental—holding contemporary actors to standards of conduct, which in fact were defined much later, often by the Holocaust itself. Now, just past the fiftieth anniversary of the end of the Second World War, historical writing tends to be more balanced, with important new research being brought to bear on all of these subjects. And finally, some historians have recently turned to the study of rescue—a theme popularized by the Hollywood film, *Schindler's List* (1994)—in an attempt to comprehend the historical dynamics of altruism.

Another focus of attention and field of historiographical dispute is the comportment of the Jews themselves. Prompted in part by some passages in Arendt's *Eichmann in Jerusalem* (1963) and Hilberg's *Destruction of the European Jews,* some historians took up the charge, originally made by young Jewish resistance fighters in the ghettos of eastern Europe, that European Jews went to their deaths "like sheep to the slaughter." Arendt's focus was really on the complicity of the *Judenräte,* the Nazi-imposed Jewish councils set up by the Nazis across Europe; Hilberg's charge was that traditional patterns of Jewish behavior militated against open resistance. Since the 1960s historians interested in this issue—many of them from Israel, in particular Israel Gutman and Yehuda Bauer— have heavily criticized this point of view. In addition, we now have the magisterial work of Isaiah Trunk on the *Judenräte* of occupied Poland, with a far more learned and balanced view than those referred to above, together with numerous monographic studies of particular ghettos under Nazi rule. Finally, it should be noted that historians in recent decades have researched and debated the phenomenon of Jewish resistance—both in western and central Europe, where underground activity was mainly devoted to rescue; and also in eastern Europe, where in addition to dangerous strategies for survival there were underground urban fighting organizations, partisan bands, a few ghetto revolts, and even uprisings in camps.

Michael R. Marrus

References

Bauer, Yehuda. *The Holocaust in Historical Perspective.* Seattle: University of Washington Press, 1978.

Bauman, Zygmunt. *Modernity and the Holocaust.* Ithaca, NY: Cornell University Press, 1989.

Browning, Christopher. *Ordinary Men: Reserve Police Battalion 101 and the Final Solution in Poland.* New York: HarperCollins, 1992.

———. *The Path to Genocide: Essays on Launching the Final Solution.* New York: Cambridge University Press, 1992.

Burleigh, Michael, and Wolfgang Wippermann. *The Racial State: Germany 1933–1945.* New York: Cambridge University Press, 1991.

Dawidowicz, Lucy S. *The Holocaust and the Historians.* Cambridge, MA: Harvard University Press, 1981.

Gutman, Israel, ed. *Encyclopedia of the Holocaust.* 4 vols. New York: Macmillan, 1990.

———, and Gideon Greif, eds. *The Historiography of the Holocaust Period: Proceedings of the Fifth Yad Vashem International Historical Conference, Jerusalem, March 1983.* Jerusalem: Yad Vashem, 1988.

Hilberg, Raul. *The Destruction of the European Jews.* Revised ed. 3 vols. New York: Holmes & Meier, 1985.

Marrus, Michael R. *The Holocaust in History.* New York: New American Library, 1987.

Trunk, Isaiah. *Judenrat: The Jewish Councils in Eastern Europe under Nazi Occupation.* New York: Macmillan, 1972.

Yahil, Leni. *The Holocaust: The Fate of European Jewry, 1932–1945.* New York: Oxford University Press, 1990.

Hong Liangji [Hung Liang-chi] (1746–1809)

Chinese historical geographer. A native of Jiangsu, Hong Liangji began his official career in 1790, upon succeeding in the metropolitan civil service examination, but retired after a brief exile to Xinjiang in 1799. An avid traveler, Hong left behind numerous travelogs. His writings on the journey to and stay in Xinjiang are especially valuable for the insight into the conditions of the region. His works on historical geography include studies of the boundaries of the Three Kingdoms (220–280), Sixteen Kingdoms (304–439), and Eastern Jin (317–420), as well as contributions to the gazetteers of a number of localities in Henan, Anhui, and Shaanxi.

John Lee

Texts

Hong Beijiang Xiansheng yiji (Hung Pei-chiang Hsien-sheng i-chi). [Collected Works of Master Hong Liangji]. 84 vols. Hubei, China: Hubei Kanshuchu, 1889.

References

Waley-Cohen, Joanna. *Exile in Mid-Qing China: Banishment to Xinjiang, 1758–1820.* New Haven, CT, and London: Yale University Press, 1991.

Honjō Eijirō (1888–1973)

Japanese socioeconomic historian. Active mainly from the 1920s to the first half of the 1940s, Honjō was a professor in the faculty of economics of Kyoto University. He was born at Nishijin in Kyoto to a silk-weaving family. When he graduated from Kyoto University in 1913, he wrote *Nishijin no kenkyū* [A Study of the Nishijin Silk Industry] (1914). He gained his doctorate in economics through his thesis: *Tokugawa Bakufu no Beika Chōsetsu* [The Rice Price Policies of the Tokugawa Shogunate] (1923)—later published under the title of *Edo–jidai no Beika Chōsetsu* (1924). The Edo era was his main field of study. He was well known as a member of the Japanese historical school. Although the Marxist school was ascendant in the 1920s and the 1930s, he disputed their findings and tried to establish the school of positivism. While encouraging many younger scholars who would later have distinguished careers (Horie Yasuzō and Miyamoto Mataji were among his students), he also established the Institute of Japanese Economic History. After World War II, he was elected a member of the Japan Academy.

Takashi Fujii

Texts

Honjō Eijirō Chosakushū [The Collected Works of Honjō Eijirō]. Osaka: Seibundōshuppan, 1971–1973.

References

Nagahara, K., and M. Kano. *Nippon no Rekishi– ka* [Japanese Historians]. Tokyo: Nipponhyōronsha, 1976.

Hooft, Pieter Corneliszoon (1581–1647)

Dutch poet, playwright, and historian. Hooft was born in Amsterdam. After a long tour through France, Italy, and Germany and a period studying law and humanities at the University of Leiden, he became bailiff of Muiden and Gooiland in 1609. In those functions, he turned the Muider castle into an intellectual center of the Dutch republic. He died in The Hague. After having published a biography of Henri IV of France in 1626, Hooft worked until his death on his *Neederlandsche histoorien* [Histories of the Low Countries] (1642 and posthumously 1654), a chronologically organized account of the Dutch Revolt, written in the style of Tacitus and with specific attention to the political lessons that could be drawn from the narrated events. In addition, he also wrote *Rampsaligheden der verheffinge van den huize van Medicis* [Miseries of the Grandeur of the House of Medici] (published posthumously in 1649), a chronicle of the Florentine family dynasty running to the end of the sixteenth century.

Jo Tollebeek

Texts

Alle de gedrukte werken 1611–1738 [The Complete Printed Works 1611–1738]. Ed. W. Hellinga and P. Tuynman. 9 vols. Amsterdam: University Press Amsterdam, 1972.

De briefwisseling van Pieter Corneliszoon Hooft [The Correspondance of Pieter Corneliszoon Hooft]. Ed. H.W. van Tricht et al. 3 vols. Culemborg, Netherlands: Tjeenk Willink and Noorduijn, 1976–1979.

References

Groenveld, S. *Hooft als historieschrijver: Twee studies* [Hooft as a Historiographer: Two Studies]. Weesp, Netherlands: Heureka, 1981.

Haitsma Mulier, E.O.G. "Grotius, Hooft and the Writing of History in the Dutch Republic." In *Clio's Mirror: Historiography in Britain and the Netherlands,* ed. A.C. Duke and C.A. Tamse. Zutphen, Netherlands: De Walburg Pers, 1985, 55–72.

Horváth, Mihály (1809–1878)

Hungarian historian, politician, and bishop. Horváth studied at Pest University and the Catholic priest's seminary in Vác. From 1832 to 1844 he served as both a priest and family tutor in various private households throughout Hungary. In 1844 he moved to Vienna and taught there for four years. An active participant in the 1848–1849 Hungarian revolution, he was in that year appointed bishop of Csanád. He served briefly as minister of public education during the summer of 1849 before going into exile later that year in Belgium, France, Italy, and Switzerland. He returned to Hungary in 1867 and for the next ten years served as vice president and finally (1877–1878) president of the Hungarian Historical Association. He was a member of the Hungarian parliament from 1868 to 1873 and again from 1876 to 1878, the year of his death. One of the principal founders of modern professional historical scholarship in Hungary, he was greatly influenced by contemporary German liberal historians (for instance Wachsmuth and Heeren). He was also the first scholar to deal with Hungary's economic and social past, presenting a critical picture of Hungarian feudalism and Habsburg policies in the country that had paved the way toward its transformation into a bourgeois society. His most influential and enduring works, however, focused on the period of his own early life, especially the period from 1825 to 1849.

Attila Pók

Texts

Az ipar és a kereskedelem története Magyarországban a három utolsó század alatt [The History of Industry and Trade in Hungary during the Last Three Centuries]. Buda: Egyetemi Nyomda, 1840.

Az ipar és kereskedés története Magyarországban a XVI. század elejéig [The History of Industry and Trade in Hungary to the Early Sixteenth Century]. Buda: Egyetemi Nyomda, 1842.

Horváth Mihály Polgárosodás, liberalizmus, függetlenségi harc [Horváth Mihály: Embourgeoisment, Liberalism, and the Struggle for Independence]. Ed. Lajos Pál. Budapest: Gondolat, 1986.

Huszonöt év Magyarország történetéből [Twenty-Five Years in the History of Hungary, 1823–1848]. 2 vols. Geneva: Puky Miklós, 1864.

Magyarország függetlenségi harczának története 1848–ban és 1849–ben [The History of Hungary's Struggle for Independence in 1848 and 1849]. Second ed. 3 vols. Pest: Bath, 1871–1872.

Magyarország történelme [The History of Hungary]. 6 vols. Pest: Heckenast Gusztáv Tulajdona, 1860–1863.

References

Pamlényi, Ervin. *Horváth Mihály.* Budapest: Mûvelt Nép Könyvkiadó, 1954.

Hoskins, William George (1908–1992)

English historian. Hoskins, who was born and educated in Exeter, claimed descent from generations of farmers and bakers in Devon, and his own strong local roots in both countryside and town helped shape his later academic specialism. He became the foremost English local historian of his generation and, more than any other practitioner, raised its status from antiquarianism to that of a rigorous, yet accessible, academic discipline. Although from Devon, Hoskin's principal laboratory for the study of local history became Leicestershire as a result of his appointment in 1931 to the small university college in that county. He remained at Leicester until 1951—when he moved to Oxford—but returned to his former base from 1965 to 1968 as Hatton professor of English local history. He published numerous articles on Leicestershire history in the *Transactions* of the county's learned society, and it was Leicestershire that provided the subject for his outstanding study of *The Midland Peasant: The Economic and Social History of a Leicestershire Village* (1957). Hoskins also wrote groundbreaking, provocative articles on rural rebuilding and on English harvests, but his most enduring achievement was his book *The Making of the English Landscape* (1955). Here Hoskins's skills and sensitivities as historian, poet, and visionary were revealed at their best. In it he provided a helpful blend of historiography and practical guidelines. Hoskins was an inspiring teacher who urged generations of students to prize walking boots no less than books. It has been justly said of him (by Phythian-Adams, 1992, p. 143) that "he revolutionized the historical perceptions of his fellow countrymen."

R.C. Richardson

Texts

English Local History, the Past and the Future. Leicester: University of Leicester, 1966.
Fieldwork in Local History. Second ed. London: Faber and Faber, 1982.
Leicestershire: An Illustrated Essay on the History of the Landscape. London: Hodder and Stoughton, 1957.
Local History in England. Third ed. London and New York: Longman, 1984.
The Making of the English Landscape. Ed. C. Taylor. London: Hodder and Stoughton, 1988.

References

Chalklin, C.W., and M.A. Havinden, eds. *Rural Change and Urban Growth: Essays in Regional History in Honour of W.G. Hoskins.* London: Longmans, 1974.
Phythian-Adams, Charles. "Hoskins' England. A Local Historian of Genius and the Realisation of His Theme." *Leicestershire Archaeological and Historical Society Transactions* 66 (1992): 143–159.
Thirsk, Joan. "William George Hoskins, 1908–1992." *Proceedings of the British Academy* 87 (1995): 339–354.

Hotman [Hotoman], François (1524–1590)

French jurist, historian, and religious polemicist. Hotman is best remembered for his theory of the ancient constitution set forth in *Francogallia* (1573). In 1548, after an education in the law at the University of Orleans and a period as a lecturer in Paris, he reacted against his staunchly Catholic father, a magistrate in the parlement of Paris, by escaping to Geneva, where he became a leading figure in the Calvinist movement. He returned to France as a celebrated professor of Roman law, but continued to defend the Protestant cause and in 1560 denounced the ultra-Catholic Cardinal of Lorraine in his anonymous *Letter to the Tiger of France.* In 1567 Hotman began to compose *Francogallia,* which was originally intended as an impartial treatise on the constitution, to accompany another work written at this time, *Antitribonian,* which advocated the substitution of French public law for Roman law in legal education. *Francogallia* began to reflect theories of constitutional opposition to the crown in the civil wars of the late 1560s, and it sounded a yet more radical note by being published in the aftermath of the massacre of St. Bartholomew's Night. It remained, however, primarily historical in tone. It argued in terms of an ancient constitution founded by the liberty-loving Franks in the fifth century. It advocated a return to the pristine model, regarding change as a process of corruption. The essential element in the mixed constitution was the representative public council, or estates general, which had elected and deposed kings and made other major governmental decisions. This ancient mode was supposed to have been undermined by the early Capetians, subverted by the ambitions of the judicial parlements, and finally betrayed by Louis XI. This thesis was illustrated by hundreds of historical references, selected often out of context to prove the point. *Francogallia* nearly doubled in size in the second and third Latin editions of 1576 and 1586. Its argument was first intensified and then subtly modified to accommodate the fact that the Huguenot leader, Henry of Navarre, had become heir presumptive to the French crown in 1584. However, Hotman never departed from his stress upon the role of the estates general. In his last years he wrote against papal pretensions in the Bourbon cause. His work remained influential long after his death. In late-seventeenth-century England *Francogallia* was invoked by English Whigs to support the theory of the Gothic constitution. A preface provided in 1711 by its translator, Viscount Molesworth, was separately entitled *The Principles of a Real Whig*.

J.H.M. Salmon

Texts

Francogallia by François Hotman. Ed. Ralph E. Giesey; trans. J.H.M. Salmon. Cambridge, Eng.: Cambridge University Press, 1972.

References

Donald R. Kelley. *Foundations of Modern Historical Scholarship.* New York: Columbia University Press, 1970.

———. *François Hotman, a Revolutionary's Ordeal.* Princeton, NJ: Princeton University Press, 1973.

Hou Wailu [Hou Wai-lu] (1903–1987)

Chinese Marxist intellectual historian. Hou was born in rural Shandong, where he attended a traditional primary school. After studying history at Beijing Normal School, in 1927 he went to France where he studied Marxist philosophy and political economy at the University of Paris and joined the Chinese Communist Party. Upon returning to China, he taught at the Beijing University Law Academy. In the 1930s he translated Marx's *Das Kapital* and later was associated with the Sino–Soviet Cultural Association. After the anti-Japanese War (1937–1945) he edited the weekly supplement, "New Thought Tide," in the Shanghai newspaper, *Wenhui*. Following the establishment of the People's Republic of China, he was appointed to several academic administrative posts and in 1980 became the director of the History Institute of the Academy of Social Science. Hou was the author of several widely read works that analyzed Chinese

thought and actively reappraised neo-Confucianism from the orthodox Marxist perspective.

Mary G. Mazur

Texts

With Chang Chichih, et al. *A Short History of Chinese Philosophy.* Trans. Wang Chengchung. Beijing: Foreign Languages Press, 1959.

Zhongguo jindai zhexue shi [History of Modern Chinese Philosophy]. Beijing: People's Press, 1978.

Zhongguo sixiang tongshi [General History of Chinese Thought]. 5 vols. Beijing: Renmin chubanshe, 1957–1960.

References

Feuerwerker, Albert, ed. *History in Communist China.* Cambridge, MA: MIT Press, 1968.

Hourani, Albert Habib (1915–1993)

British historian of Arab thought and culture. Hourani was born in Manchester in 1915, the son of Lebanese immigrants. He was educated at Mill Hill School in London, and Magdalen College, Oxford, whence he graduated in 1936 with first class honors in politics, philosophy, and economics. The direction of Hourani's professional life changed profoundly after visiting Lebanon, before the outbreak of World War II. While in Beirut, he taught at the American University for two years. He then spent the war years working in Cairo as a political researcher in the office of the British Minister of State. After the war, he became an active member of the Arab Bureau in Jerusalem defending the rights of the Palestinian people. It was after his return to London in 1947 that he met and assisted Arnold Toynbee in his work at the Institute of International Affairs. Between 1951 and 1979, Hourani held the post of Lecturer in the History of the Middle East at Oxford, an appointment that took up most of his energies with teaching, supervising, and guiding both students and colleagues.

Hourani's reputation as a scholar rests on two major books: *Arabic Thought in the Liberal Age 1798–1939* (1962) and *A History of the Arab Peoples* (1991). The first work is primarily concerned with the manner in which Arab intellectuals adopted and reworked European ideas of progress, nationalism, civilization, and the state. The latter was composed with the aim of studying deeper social changes and urban developments within the context of a cultural perspective that treats Arab civilization as an indigenous movement.

Y. Choueiri

Texts

Arabic Thought in the Liberal Age, 1798–1939. Cambridge, Eng.: Cambridge University Press, 1994.

A History of the Arab Peoples. Cambridge, MA: Harvard University Press, 1991.

References

Reid, Donald M. "*Arabic Thought in the Liberal Age* Twenty Years After." *International Journal of Middle East Studies* 14 (1982): 541–557.

Howard, Sir Michael Eliot (b. 1922)

British military historian. Howard was born in London and educated at Wellington College and Christ Church, Oxford. During World War II he served as a captain in the Coldstream Guards. He began his academic career at King's College, London in 1947. He became reader in war studies at the University of London (1953–1963) and then professor of war studies (1963–1968). In 1968 Howard became fellow of higher defense studies at Oxford (1968–1977), then Chichele professor of the history of war (1977–1980), and finally Regius professor of modern history (1980–1989). After his retirement from Oxford in 1989 he was appointed Robert A. Lovett professor of military and naval history at Yale University. Howard's works cover the period from the Renaissance to the present. His early studies include *Soldiers and Governments* (1957) and *Disengagement in Europe* (1958). In the 1960s, Howard established himself as one of the most profound of English military writers. His *Franco-Prussian War* (1961), a classic, was followed by *The Theory and Practice of War* (1965). He also wrote *Grand Strategy,* the fourth volume in the United Kingdom History of the Second World War (1972), and *The Continental Commitment* (1973). His *War in European History* (1976) enlarged Cyril Falls's, *The Art of War from the Age of Napoleon to the Present Day* and clearly demonstrated his comprehension and historical range in military history. In 1976 Howard, with Peter Paret, translated Clausewitz's, *On War.* This was followed by several other books including *War and Liberal Conscience* (1978), *Restraints on War* (1979), *The Causes of War* (1983), *Clausewitz* (1983), *Strategic Deception: British Intelligence in the Second World War (1990),* and *The Lessons of History* (1991).

Norman Tobias

Texts

The Causes of War and Other Essays. Cambridge, MA: Harvard University Press, 1983.

The Franco-Prussian War. New York: Macmillan, 1961.

The Lessons of History. New Haven, CT, and London: Yale University Press, 1991.

Soldiers and Governments. London: Eyre and Spottiswoode, 1957.

War and the Liberal Conscience. New Brunswick, NJ: Rutgers University Press, 1978.

References

Lider, Julian, *British Military Thought after World War II.* Aldershot, Eng.: Gower Publishing House, 1985.

Paret, Peter, with Gordon A. Craig and Felix Gilbert, ed. *The Makers of Modern Strategy.* Princeton, NJ: Princeton University Press, 1986.

Hrushevsky, Mykhailo (1864–1934)

Ukrainian historian. The preeminent historian of Ukraine and a political and civic leader from 1894 to 1913, Hrushevsky held the chair of Ukrainian history at Lviv University where he developed a school of Ukrainian history. He was imprisoned by the Russians in 1914 and would die in exile in Russia twenty years later. Initially at least, Hrushevsky's approach to history was populist, stressing social and popular interests over those of the state. The most influential of his numerous writings was a nine-volume *Istoriia Ukrainy-Rus* [Ukrainian-Russian History] (1898–1937), the first major synthesis of Ukrainian history. He also contributed substantially to cultural and archaeological studies, consistently arguing that Ukraine is distinct from Russia in origin and in political, economic, and cultural development. In 1917, having been released from prison, he chaired Ukraine's Central Rada and led the newly independent government. After several years in the West, he returned to Ukraine in 1924. Increasingly, the USSR disparaged his "nationalistic" approach and, after 1930, suppressed much of his work.

Elizabeth V. Haigh

Texts

A History of Ukraine. Ed. O.J. Frederiksen. New Haven, CT: Yale University Press, 1941.

References

Prymak, T. *Mykhailo Hrushevsky and the Politics of National Culture.* Toronto: University of Toronto Press, 1987.

Hsiao I-shan
See Xiao Yishan.

Hsiao Kung-ch'üan
See Xiao Gongquan.

Hsiao Tzu-hsien
See Xiao Zixian.

Hsun Yüeh
See Xun Yue.

Hu Shi [Hu Shih] (1891–1962)
Chinese historian, and a pioneer of Western historical method in China. Having recently returned from studies in America, Hu Shi was a leader of the May Fourth New Culture movement in the late 1910s and an advocate of "scientific reorganization of Chinese history" in the 1920s. He helped to establish a new style of history, which stressed evidential proof, logical argument, and historical context. In his *Zhongguo zhexueshi dagang, shangchuan* [An Outline of the History of Chinese Philosophy, Vol. One] (1919), Hu Shi revolutionized the Chinese view of the ancient period by seeing it as a process of evolution rather than the golden age for all generations. By publishing his Columbia University dissertation *The Development of the Logical Method in Ancient China* (1922), and by republishing the works of Cui Shu (1740–1816), Hu Shi proved to his countrymen that learning the Western historical method would not be difficult because ample precedents for it already existed in Chinese culture. A leader in literary studies himself, Hu Shi broadened the scope of history through his analysis of literature, and in particular of novels written in the vernacular.

Tze-ki Hon

Texts
China's Own Critics: A Selection of Essays by Hu Shih and Lin Yu-Tang, with Commentaries by Wang Ching-Wei. Beijing: China United Press, 1931.
The Chinese Renaissance. Second ed. New York: Paragon, 1963.
The Development of the Logical Method in Ancient China. Shanghai: Oriental Book Co., 1922.
Zhongguo zhexueshi dagang shangchuan. 2 vols. Taibei: Yuanliu chupan shiye gufen youxian gongsi, 1986.

References
Grieder, Jerome B. *Hu Shih and the Chinese Renaissance: Liberalism in the Chinese Revolution, 1917–1937.* Cambridge, MA: Harvard University Press, 1970.
———. *Intellectuals and the State in Modern China: A Narrative History.* New York: Free Press; London: Collier Macmillan, 1981.

Huang Tsung-hsi
See Huang Zongxi.

Huang Zongxi [Huang Tsung-hsi] (1610–1695)
Chinese historian and philosopher. Son of a late Ming (1368–1644) scholar-official, Huang Zongxi witnessed the decline and fall of the dynasty. After the establishment of the Qing (1644–1911) dynasty, he lived in seclusion at his hometown in Zhejiang and devoted himself wholly to academic studies. A prolific writer, Huang is best known for two works. The *Mingyi daifang lu* [Plan for the Prince] is a critical study of the political system of his time. Huang's *Mingru xuean* [Records of Ming Scholars], a compendium of Ming thought, remains invaluable for the study of Chinese and intellectual history. But he did not live to complete the *Song Yuan xuean* [Records of the Song (960–1279) and Yuan (1279–1368) Scholars]. He is generally regarded as the founder of the Eastern Zhejiang school. His critical approach in historical studies had influenced generations of Qing scholars. Among the famous historians of this school were Wan Sitong [Wan Ssu-t'ung] (1638–1702), Quan Zuwang [Ch'uan Tsu-wang] (1705–1755), and Zhang Xuecheng [Chang Hsüeh-ch'eng] (1738–1801).

Henry Y.S. Chan

Texts
Huang Tsung-hsi. *The Records of Ming Scholars.* Trans. Julia Ching and Fang Chao-ying. Honolulu: University of Hawaii Press, 1987.

References
Struve, Lynn A. "Huang Zongxi in Context: A Reappraisal of His Major Writings." *Journal of Asian Studies* 47 (1988): 474–502.

Hugh of Fleury (d. after 1119)
French ecclesiastical historian and hagiographer. Hugh was a monk of the Benedictine monastery at Fleury-sur-Loire who presented works to several

descendants of William the Conqueror. He dedicated his *Ecclesiastical History* (ca. 1110) to Countess Adèle of Blois-Chartres, daughter of the Conqueror. Although modern scholars find the work unoriginal, medieval readers valued it as a digest of events between the time of Ninus of Nineveh and the Carolingians. In about 1115 Hugh presented a history of the modern kings of France to Matilda, daughter of Henry I of England and wife of the German Emperor Henry V. For the monks of Sarlat, he rewrote an earlier *Life of St. Sacerdos,* an eighth-century bishop of Limoges. Going beyond literary revision of his text, Hugh improved the accuracy of the *Life* by comparing it with other written sources so as to elucidate the bishop's career and its historical context. He later abridged the *Ecclesiastical History* to facilitate use of the *Life.* Hugh's critical approach to written sources illustrates one of the important developments in twelfth-century historical thought.

David F. Appleby

Texts

Hugonis Floriacensis opera historica [Historical Works]. Ed. Georg Waitz. *Monumenta Germaniae Historica, Scriptorum tomus IX.* Stuttgart: Anton Hiersemann, 1983, 337–406.

Vita sancti Sacerdotis. Ed. J.-P. Migne. *Patrologiae cursus completus, Series latina.* vol. 163, Paris: J.-P. Migne, 1854, cols. 979–1004.

References

Head, Thomas. *Hagiography and the Cult of Saints: The Diocese of Orléans, 800–1200.* Cambridge, Eng.: Cambridge University Press, 1990.

Hugh of St. Victor (d. 1141)

Augustinian canon at St. Victor, Paris, biblical scholar, and theologian. Hugh follows Augustine in his philosophy of history, and he gives primary importance to sacred history. In his works, Hugh repeatedly attempts to place the subjects of his discussion into their historical context. His *Didascalicon* (late 1120s), a treatise on the liberal arts, for example, places their development into a progressive historical framework. This historically oriented methodology reveals more of Hugh as a historian than do his explicit statements about history or his *Chronicle.* In the *Didascalicon,* Hugh argues that *historia,* which he sees as meaning both the literal significance of scripture and as historical events, has a fundamental role in sacred learning, for history is the foundation for allegorical and moral interpretations of the Bible. The student of the Bible must know important persons, affairs, times, and places of history, and Hugh's *Chronicle* outlines those that a beginner should learn.

Maura K. Lafferty

Texts

"The Didascalicon": A Medieval Guide to the Arts. Trans. Jerome Taylor. New York: Columbia University Press, 1961.

References

Smalley, Beryl. *The Study of the Bible in the Middle Ages.* Third ed. Oxford: Blackwell, 1983.

Southern, Richard W. "Aspects of the European Tradition of Historical Writing: Hugh of St. Victor and the Idea of Historical Development." *Transactions of the Royal Historical Society,* Fifth series, 21 (1971): 159–179.

Huizinga, Johan (1872–1945)

Dutch historian and theorist of culture. After graduating from the University of Groningen in philosophy and history, Huizinga briefly studied Indo-Germanic linguistics at the University of Leipzig, before taking his Ph.D. at Groningen in 1897. From 1905 to 1915 he was a professor of history there. Thereafter he taught at the University of Leiden until it was closed by the Germans in the 1940s. He was imprisoned as a leader of the resistance movement and was not released until 1942, dying shortly before the 1945 liberation. Huizinga believed that a cultural historian should portray the patterns of culture, and in *Homo Ludens* (1938) made one of the first efforts to explore seriously the element of play in history. His earlier work, *The Waning of the Middle Ages,* was written in the aftermath of World War I and brought the profound pessimism of that era to bear on an earlier period. The result was a brilliant cultural study of the relations between literature, art, and religion in Europe during the fourteenth and fifteenth centuries. It remains a classic in cultural historiography after over seventy years.

Thomas F. Mayer

Texts

The Autumn of the Middle Ages. Trans. Rodney J. Payton and Ulrich Mammitzsch. Chicago: University of Chicago Press, 1996. (A rev. trans. with some significant changes.)

Erasmus and the Age of Reformation. Trans. F. Hopman. New York: Harper, 1957.

Homo Ludens: A Study of the Play Element in Culture. London: Routledge and Kegan Paul, 1938.

H

The Waning of the Middle Ages: A Study of the Forms of Life, Thought and Art in France and the Netherlands in the XIVth and XVth Centuries. Trans. F. Hopman. London: Edward Arnold, 1924.

References

Weintraub, Karl. *Visions of Culture.* Chicago: University of Chicago Press, 1966, 208–246.

Humanism and History

See RENAISSANCE, HISTORIOGRAPHY DURING.

Humboldt, Wilhelm von (1767–1835)

German statesman and scholar. Humboldt studied law from 1787 to 1790 in Frankfurt/Oder and Göttingen, but he felt attracted to languages. As early as 1791 he left the Prussian civil service after just one year and lived in Jena from 1794 to 1797 in the circle of Schiller and Goethe. During the period 1797–1801 he lived in Paris, from whence he also traveled extensively through Spain. While resident at the Vatican he developed a picture of the ancient world, which he took as a model for the reconstruction of the Prussian state, especially as far as the reorganization of its educational system was concerned. After 1810 he was active in the diplomatic service, participating, for instance, at the Congress of Vienna. As a result of his demands for a more liberal system of government he was dismissed in 1819, after the Karlsbad Decrees, and retired to private life in 1820. Humboldt exerted a great influence on German intellectual history of the nineteenth century. The foundation of the University in Berlin took place during his tenure in the Ministry of Culture from 1809 to 1819, and it was established in accordance with his ideas about education. Following the epistemology of idealism he emphasized the liberty of the institution, the unity of research and teaching, and the community of teachers and students. Along with his political writings and comparative language studies written mostly after 1820, the most important of his works for historiography is his lecture *Über die Aufgaben des Geschichtsschreibers* [On the Historian's Tasks] (1821) at the Academy in Berlin. The ideas in this lecture are now regarded as having been programmatic for historicism.

Thomas Fuchs

Texts

Gesammelte Werke [Complete Works]. 7 vols. Berlin: G. Reimer, 1841.

Humanist without Portfolio: An Anthology of the Writings of Wilhelm von Humboldt. Trans. Marianne Cowan. Detroit: Wayne State University Press, 1963.
The Limits of State Action. Ed. J.W. Burrow. Cambridge, Eng.: Cambridge University Press, 1969.
"On the Historian's Task." *History and Theory* 6 (1967): 57–71.

References

Sweet, P.R. *Wilhelm von Humboldt: A Biography.* 2 vols. Columbus: Ohio State University Press, 1978.

Hume, David (1711–1776)

Scottish philosopher and historian. Educated in Edinburgh, Hume spent much of the period from 1734 to 1749 on the mainland of Enlightenment Europe, and it is to these years that much of his philosophical writing belongs. His appointment in 1752 as keeper of the Library of Advocates in Edinburgh was a turning point in his career, since it gave him the base from which to write his projected *History of England.* Like other Enlightenment writers Hume saw history as an extension of philosophy, and he denounced the antiquarianism and Whig partisanship that he believed previous historians of England—such as the Huguenot exile Paul de Rapin-Thoyras (1661–1725)—had displayed. Hume began with the seventeenth century and published his findings in 1754. The choice of starting point was significant; it enabled Hume to refute Whig notions of the "ancient constitution," to portray Parliament as the aggressor, to indulge his Enlightenment dislike of Puritanism, and "to shed [as he himself put it] a generous tear for the fate of Charles I." Despite initially disappointing sales in London and a chorus of opposition, Hume's project soon prospered, and he sold the copyright for a new complete edition in 1763 for three thousand pounds. A civil list pension came his way in the same year. Although not a "Tory" historian by design, this was the reputation that Hume rapidly acquired, and once so designated the label stuck. He resisted invitations to continue his history into the eighteenth century; "I am too old, too fat, too lazy, and too rich," he said, and reconsidered his plan to settle permanently in London. He returned to his native Edinburgh in 1769, and it was there seven years later that he died.

R.C. Richardson

Texts

The History of England: From the Invasion of Julius Caesar to the Revolution in 1688. Abridged by R.W. Kilcup. Chicago: University of Chicago Press, 1975.

History of Great Britain: The Reigns of James I and Charles I. Ed. D. Forbes. Harmondsworth, Eng.: Penguin, 1970.

References

Black, J.B. *The Art of History.* London: Methuen, 1926.

Mossner, E.C. *The Life of David Hume.* Oxford: Clarendon Press, 1954.

Wexler, E.E. *David Hume and the History of England.* Philadelphia: American Philosophical Society, 1979.

Hung Liang-chi

See HONG LIANGJI.

Hungarian Historiography

Historical writing by Hungarian authors from the Middle Ages to the present day. Historical writing in Hungary, as elsewhere in Europe, emerged as a modern discipline by about the middle of the nineteenth century. Its early origins, again as in western Europe and also as in the case of other central European peoples (Poles, Czechs, Croats), go back to medieval legends, annals, *gesta,* and chronicles dealing with the origins of the Magyar people and the Hungarian state. The adoption of Christianity (integrating Hungary into the western cultural sphere) was a most important topic for these works and contemporary dynastic and political conflicts are echoed in them also (for instance in Simon Kézai's *Gesta Hungarorum* of ca. 1283 and János Thuróczy's *Chronica Hungarorum* of 1488—the latter a "standard" work until the early eighteenth century).

In accordance with the demands of a new secular culture under the impact of humanism, Antonio Bonfini, an Italian scholar at King Mathias Corvinus's (r. 1458–1490) lavish Renaissance court, wrote in classical Latin a new synthesis, the *Rerum Ungaricarum Decades Quattuor et Dimidia* [Four and a Half Books on Hungarian History] during the late 1480s and early 1490s. With the medieval Hungarian empire falling victim to Ottoman expansion by the middle of the sixteenth century, the two greatest Hungarian representatives of humanist historiography worked in politically separated territories. István Szamosközy (1570–1612) wrote in semi-independent Transylvania mainly about his own times, whereas Miklós Istvánffy (1538–1615) produced—as a sequel to Bonfini's work—his *Historiarum de Rebus Ungaricis Libri XXXIV* [Thirty-Four Books on Hungarian Affairs], covering the period 1490–1606 in the Habsburg-controlled part of Hungary. Under the impact of baroque culture a great number of memoirs, valuable both from a historical and a literary point of view, were written, such as the Transylvanian prince János Kemény's (1607–1662) *Önéletírás* [Autobiography] and the analogous *Önéletírás* by the Transylvanian chancellor Miklós Bethlen (1642–1716).

The ideas of the Enlightenment initiated a critical approach to earlier descriptions and interpretations of Hungarian history in an effort to broaden the scope of historical investigations and include the history of the *entire* nation. Mátyás Bél (or Matthias Bél, 1684–1749), a great polymath, started a systematic collection of Hungarian historical sources. Though this project, the *Adparatus ad Historiam Hungariae* [Introduction to Hungarian History] (1735–1746) remained incomplete, like his attempt at the historical–geographic description of the whole country (*Notitia Hungariae Noavae Historico-Geographica* [New Historical and Geographical Notes on Hungary] 1735–1742), Bél's scholarly production earned him great prestige throughout Europe. A group of Jesuit scholars continued the Protestant Bél's systematic source-collecting activity. The leading figure of this group, György Pray (1723–1801) is generally considered to be the first truly critical Hungarian historian. His numerous works include a Hungarian church history entitled *Specimen Hierarchiae Hungaricae* [Sources on the Hungarian Hierarchy] (1776–1779) and a five-volume synthesis of Hungarian history from the beginnings to 1564, the *Annales Regum Hungariae* [Annals of the Kings of Hungary] (1763–1770). A colleague of his, István Katona (1732–1811) is best known for his forty-two-volume *Historia Critica Regum Hungariae* [Critical History of the Kings of Hungary] (1779–1817); a collection of sources, this was primarily used by the great-synthesis writers of the nineteenth century, who were able to make good use of its materials.

These writers increasingly wrote in the vernacular or in Western languages such as German instead of the Latin of the earlier era. Among their publications, Ignácz Aurél Fessler's (1765–1839) ten-volume German-language *Die Geschichte der Ungern und ihrer Landsassen* [The History of Hungary and Its Citizens] (1815–1825) and János

Engel's (1770–1814) *Geschichte des Ungrischen Reiches* [History of the Hungarian Empire] (1813–1814) proved the most popular. Romantic nationalism also left its trace on Hungarian historiography: István Horvát's (1784–1846) *Rajzolatok a magyar nemzet legrégibb történeteiböl* [Sketches on the Most Ancient History of the Hungarian Nation] (1825), replete with fantasies about the distinguished but fictitious ancestors of the Hungarians, is the best-known example of that genre.

Modern Hungarian historiography was born in the aftermath of the 1848–1849 Habsburg–Hungarian conflict. As elsewhere in an era of strong nationalist sentiments, historical writing was charged with the important function of strengthening the defeated nation's identity, and historians themselves were often caught up in the turmoil—the two leading figures of the National Liberal School, Mihály Horváth and Làszlö Szalay, spent some of their most creative years in exile. Certain important events, such as the foundation of the Historical Commission of the Hungarian Academy of Sciences in 1854, or the initiation of the huge source-publication series *Monumenta Hungariae Historica* [Monuments of Hungarian History] in 1857 preceded the Habsburg-Hungarian Compromise of 1867 (which resulted in greater economic development and a measure of political stability). The first generation of positivist historians, whose intellectual horizons stretched beyond Hungary to a wider Europe, and especially to Germany, emerged only in the 1880s. Gyula Pauler (1841–1903), who established and organized the Hungarian National Archives in the late 1870s, and Sándor Szilágyi (1827–1889), the editor of an impressive (and widely read) ten-volume history of Hungary (1895–1898), each helped to strengthen contemporary Hungarian national identity. The founders of the Hungarian Historical Association in 1867 (including Mihály Horváth, Imre Mikó, Arnold Ipolyi, and others) were not yet "professionals" from the point of view of the German or French university system, however. Most of them had degrees in theology or law, and it was only in 1885 that a National Congress of Historians was held, out of which emerged plans for the systematic training of historians in newer critical–philological methodology. By then, a number of Hungarian historians—for instance Henrik Marczali (1856–1940), Dávid Angyal (1857–1943), Károly Tagányi (1858–1924), László Fejérpataky (1857–1923), Árpád Károlyi (1853–1940), Lajos Thallóczy (1854–1916)—had studied in Paris at the École des Chartes, in Berlin at the lectures and seminars of Ranke and Wattenbach, or Vienna (Sickel's Institut für Österreichische Geschichtsforschung). Their research interests focused on various aspects of the history of the Hungarian state, although economic and cultural history found some institutional support as well, the former in Károly Tagányi's journal, the *Magyar Gazdaságtörténelmi Szemle* [Hungarian Economic History Review], which was published between 1894 and 1906, and the latter in Remig Békefi's chair of Hungarian civilization at the University of Budapest (1899–1911). It was primarily Marczali and Fejérpataky—both of whom were appointed to professorships at Budapest University in 1895—and Károlyi and Thallóczy, at the Vienna State Archives (the most important repository of sources for Habsburg-ruled Hungary), who trained the leading figures of the next generation, scholars such as Sándor Domanovszky (1877–1955), Gyula Szekfű (1883–1955), Bálint Hóman (1885–1953), Ferenc Eckhart (1885–1957), István Hajnal (1892–1955), and Elemér Mályusz (1898–1989). This younger generation that came to maturity during and after World War I had to work, however, under completely new circumstances. In 1918, the victorious entente powers reduced Hungary to a third of its former territory. In the aftermath of this political disaster, scholarship continued nonetheless. The chairman of the Hungarian Historical Association, Kuno Klebelsberg, who also served as Minister of Culture from 1922 to 1931, initiated a new source-publication series, the *Fontes Historiae Hungaricae Aevi Recentoris* [Sources for Modern Hungarian History]). In spite of the trying economic hardships of the day, it seemed both a political and scholarly necessity that research be undertaken on the historical causes of Hungary's tragedy. Enormous volumes would be published on the problems of national minorities (Slovaks, Serbs, Croats), on the history of the revolution and war of independence in 1848 and 1849, on the great reformer of the first half of the nineteenth century, István Széchenyi, and on two Habsburg princes of the late eighteenth and early nineteenth centuries, the archdukes Alexander Leopold and Joseph.

The most ideologically, politically, and socially influential works of the interwar period emerged from the *Geistesgeschichte* (intellectual history) school of historiography, which focused on identifying the basic cultural trends in historical developments, and attempted to capture the intellectual direction and emotional tenor of the ages under investigation. The most representative work from this group of historians is Bálint Hóman's and Gyula Szekfű's *Magyar történet*

[Hungarian History], first published in seven volumes from 1927 to 1934. Sándor Domanovszky, Elemér Mályusz, and István Hajnal, whose interests centered primarily around social and economic developments, were the most important historians of the interwar period to emerge in opposition to the *Geistesgeschichte* school.

The Communist takeover of 1948 in the aftermath of World War II proved another turning point in Hungarian historiography. Marxism–Leninism in a greatly distorted form was made the ideological basis for historical scholarship, which now took place in a highly centralized institutional setting. Yet despite the political attempts to impose the pattern of class-struggles and other axioms of historical materialism as key concepts on historiography, impressive results were produced. Marxism provided an impetus to social and economic history (Erik Molnár's works on mediaeval Hungarian society are a good example); and the tightly controlled but secure and relatively well-funded new research institutes offered good opportunities to pursue long-term projects. Until the late 1950s, however, contacts with the main trends of international scholarship were very limited, and "bourgeois" (that is, noncommunist) historians like Domanovszky, Hajnal, Mályusz, and some of their students were pushed into the background. From the early 1960s on—in parallel with the coming of limited detente—Hungarian historiography started a most productive and internationally renowned period with research interests covering more fields than ever before. Regional, pan-European, and even broader comparative investigations were undertaken by Elemér Mályusz, György Győrffy, Jenő Szűcs, András Kubinyi, and Pál Engel in medieval economic, social, and intellectual history; by Zsigmond Pál Pach and Ferenc Szakály in early modern economic, social, and political history; by Kálmán Benda, Éva H. Balázs, and Domokos Kosáry in eighteenth-century studies; and by Iván T. Berend and György Ránki in the social and economic history of the nineteenth and twentieth centuries. Endre Arató and Emil Niederhauser produced important research in modern East European social, economic, and intellectual history, as did István Diöszegi and Emil Palotás in modern European diplomatic history, and Péter Hanák on the social, economic, and cultural history of the Austro-Hungarian monarchys. In twentieth-century social, political, and intellectual history, the names of Magda Ådám, Ferenc Glatz, Tibor Hajdu, Gyula Juhász, Mária Ormos, Zsuzsa L. Nagy, Péter Sipos, and Loránt Tilkovszky are most familiar outside Hungary.

A peculiar feature of Hungarian historiography that should not be overlooked in this necessarily brief summary is represented by the activity of historians concerned with the ethnic minority of approximately three million Hungarians living in neighboring countries: Zsigmond Jakó and Samu Benkö from Transylvania (in Romania) are perhaps the best known among these. Finally, Hungarian historians in western Europe and the United States (István Deák, Peter Sugar, Ferenc Fejtö to mention only three of the most prominent), most of them first-generation immigrants whose works are written mainly in Western languages, continue to do much to introduce Hungarian history to the world.

Attila Pók

References

Deák, István. "Historiographies of the Countries of Eastern Europe: Hungary." *American Historical Review* 97 (1992): 1041–1063.

Glatz, Ferenc. *Történetiró és politika: Szekfü, Steier, Thim és Miskolczy nemzetröl és államról* [Historians and Politics: Szekfű, Steier, Thim and Miskolczy on Nation and State]. Budapest: Akadémiai Kiadó, 1980.

Léderer, Emma. *A magyar polgári történetirás rövid története* [A Short History of Hungarian Bourgeois Historiography]. Budapest: Kossuth Könyvkiadó, 1969.

R. Várkonyi, Ågnes. *A pozitivista történetszemlélet a magyar történetirásban* [The Positivist View of History in Hungarian Historiography]. 2 vols. Budapest: Akadémiai Kiadó, 1973.

Várdy, Steven Béla. *Modern Hungarian Historiography.* Special issue of *East European Quarterly,* vol. 17. Boulder, CO: East European Monographs, 1976.

Hutchinson, Lucy (née Apsley) (1620–after 1675)

English Puritan biographer and translator. As a young woman, Hutchinson read widely in classics, patristics, and history. In 1638 she married a Nottinghamshire gentleman who became a parliamentarian army officer and a minor Commonwealth politician. (Colonel John Hutchinson would escape punishment as a regicide at the Restoration in 1660, but he was later suspected of plotting and died in prison in 1664.) Hutchinson's fame as a historian rests on her biography of her husband, written between his death and 1671, but first published only in 1806. She claimed to write for private consolation. But the *Life* accounts for Colonel Hutchinson's public actions and extended "digressions" justify Puritan and republican revolution in the wake of defeat. Its style and argument combine both Puritan and classical elements. Although often animated against her husband's opponents, Hutchinson draws Plutarchian characters with both faults and virtues. The characterizations also owe much to a Puritan (she was a Baptist) search for the workings of providence in mundane existence. Hutchinson details political debates at all social levels of revolutionary society and the familial and neighborly wounds of civil war Nottingham. Like her contemporary, Margaret Cavendish, Hutchinson's *Life* transcends the private sphere of much seventeenth-century biography and amounts in places to a history of the civil wars. Though Hutchinson casts herself as one submissive to patriarchy, her audacious enterprise threatens set gender roles. Her brief and incomplete autobiography sketches England's history and reveals a view of English providentialism influenced by the earlier martyrologist, John Foxe.

Newton E. Key

Texts

Memoirs of the Life of Colonel Hutchinson; with the Fragment of an Autobiography of Mrs. Hutchinson. Ed. James Sutherland. London: Oxford University Press, 1973.

References

Keeble, N.H. "'The Colonel's Shadow': Lucy Hutchinson, Women's Writing and the Civil War." In *Literature and the English Civil War,* ed. Thomas Healy and Jonathan Sawday. Cambridge, Eng.: Cambridge University Press, 1990, 227–247.

I

Ibn 'Abd al-Ḥakam (798/99–870)

'Abd al Raḥmān b. 'Abdallāh b. 'Abd al-Ḥakam
b. Aᶜyan, Abū 'l-Qāsim, belonged to a celebrated
Egyptian non-Arab Muslim family of legal scholars
and historians. Although Ibn 'abd al-Raḥmān
himself was interested in Islamic jurisprudence, his
main interests were in *ḥadīth* (the traditions of the
Prophet Muḥammad and his friends) and history.
He is the earliest Arabic historian of Egypt whose
work has survived. His most important book is
Futūḥ Miṣr wa-'l-Maghrib wa-'l-Andalus [The Conquests of Egypt, North Africa and Spain]. It concentrates primarily on the early history of Egypt until
c. 663, the death of 'Amr b. al-'Āṣ (the conqueror
and governor of Egypt), and provides very valuable
information regarding the conquest of Egypt by the
Arabs and the settlement of the Arab tribes in al-
Fusṭāṭ (old Cairo). It also recounts the conquests of
North Africa and Spain. This book was extensively
used and quoted by medieval historians of Egypt.

Amikam Elad

Texts

'Āmir, 'Abd al-Munᶜim. *Futūḥ Miṣr wa-'l-
Maghrib li-Ibn 'Abd al-Ḥakam 275H.:871.*
Cairo: Lajnat al-Bayān al-'Arabī, 1961.
*The History of the Conquests of Egypt, North Af-
rica and Spain, Known as Futūḥ Miṣr of Ibn
'Abd al-Ḥakam.* Ed. Charles Torrey. New
Haven, CT: Yale University Press, 1922.

References

Brunschvig, R. "Ibn 'Abda'lhakam et la Conquête
de l'Afrique." *Annales de l'Institut d'Études
Orientales* 6 (1942–1947), 108–155.
Guest, R., ed. *The Governors and Judges of Egypt of
al-Kindī. E.J.W. Gibb Memorial Series.* Vol. 19.
Leiden: E.J. Brill; London: Luzac and Co.,
1912.

Ibrāhīm Aḥmad al-'Adawī. *Ibn 'Abd al-Ḥakam
Rā'id al-Mu'arrikhīn al-'Arab.* Cairo:
Maktabat al-Anglū al-Miṣriyya, 1963.
Rosenthal, F. "Ibn 'Abd al-Ḥakam."
Encyclopaedia of Islam. Second ed. Leiden,
Netherlands: E.J. Brill, 1960– , vol. 3,
674–675.
Torrey, C.C. "Ibn 'Abd al-Ḥakam."
Encyclopaedia of Islam. First ed. 4 vols. in
7. Leiden: E.J. Brill, 1913–1936, vol. 2,
353.

Ibn 'Abd al-Ẓāhir, Muḥyī al-Dīn (1223–1292)

Egyptian official and historian, famous for both
his Arabic prose and his biographies of Mamlūk
sultans. He served as head of chancery and as
private secretary to the Sultan Baybars (1260–
1277) and was commissioned by the latter to
compose a royal biography. Although this work
suffers from an overly partisan approach, and
indeed was read to and approved by the sultan
himself, it is a mine of information about the
early Mamlūk state and its relations with the
Mongols and crusaders and incorporates many
documents *in extenso.* Ibn 'Abd al-Ẓāhir later
wrote a biography of Sultan Qalawun (1279–
1290) and left an unfinished life of Sultan al-
Ashraf Khalīl.

Reuven Amitai-Preiss

Texts

Al-Rawḍ al-zāhir fī sīrat al-malik al-zāhir. Ed.
'A-'A. al-Khuwayṭir. Riyad: n.p., 1976.
Partial ed. and trans. in F. Sadeque,
Baybars I of Egypt. Dacca: n.p., 1956.
*Tashrīf al-ayyām wa'l-'uṣūr fī sīrat al-malik
al-manṣūr.* Ed. M. Kāmil. Cairo: n.p.,
1961.

References

Holt, P.M. "Three Biographies of al-Ẓāhir Baybars." In *Medieval Historical Writing in the Christian and Islamic Worlds,* ed. D.O. Morgan. London: School of Oriental and African Studies, 1982, 19–29.

Khowaiter, Abdul-Aziz. *Baibars the First.* London: The Green Mountain Press, 1978, 144–166.

Pedersen, J. "Ibn 'Abd al-Ẓāhir." *Encyclopaedia of Islam.* Second ed. Leiden, Netherlands: E.J. Brill, 1960– , Vol. 3, 679 and 680.

Ibn 'Ā'idh, Muḥammad (767– ca. 848)

Muḥammad b. 'Ā'idh b. 'Abd al-Raḥmān [or Sa'īd or Aḥmad] b. 'Ubaydallāh Abū 'Abdallāh [or Abū Aḥmad], al-Qaurshī (that is from the tribe of Quraysh), al Dimashqī. Ibn 'Ā'idh was a *muftī* in Damascus and, although he held the views of the *Mu'tazila* and scholars of different religious sects, and did not usually rely on the work of anyone other than coreligionists, he was generally regarded as a reliable transmitter of *ḥadīth* (the traditions of the Prophet Muḥammad) by his contemporaries as well as by later scholars. He served in the 'Abbāsid administration in Damascus and was in charge of the Bureau of Land Taxes of the Ghūṭa region during the reign of the 'Abbāsid Caliph al-Ma'mūn (813–833). Ibn 'Ā'idh adheres to the school of the Syrian scholars of *ḥadīth* and historians who lived from the middle of the eighth to the middle of the ninth centuries. He wrote several works, none of which survived, although small segments can be found in some of the printed Arabic works from the Muslim period. Five of his works are mentioned in contemporary or later sources. Three are usually mentioned together and were quoted by later Muslim scholars as well as modern scholars: (1) *Kitāb al-Maghāzī* [The Book of Military Expeditions of the Prophet Muḥammad]; (2) *Kitāb al Futūḥ* [The Book of the (Islamic) Conquests]; (3) *Kitāb al-Ṣawā'if* [The Book of Summer Military Expeditions]. For these books Ibn 'Ā'idh used material from the *Maghāzī* of his teacher, the well-known Damascene jurist and historian, al-Walīd b. Muslim (d. ca. 810) in addition to material from much earlier compositions on the Arab conquests, such as the (lost and unknown) treatise of Yazīd b. 'Abīda (mid- to end of the seventh century), transmitted to him by one of his teachers, 'Abd al-A'lā b. Mushir (757/58–833), who was also a well-known scholar from Damascus. This transmission proves that books on the Arab conquests were composed at a very early date, almost immediately after the conquests. The other two less well-known books

are (4) *Kitāb al-Siyar* [Book on the Laws of War] and (5) *Kitāb Mulaḥ al-Nawādir* [Book of Anecdotes of the Curiosities].

Amikam Elad

Texts

Ibn 'Asākir, Abū 'l-Qāsim 'Alī b. al-Ḥasan. *Ta'rīkh Madīnat Dimashq* [a facsimile copy of al-Ẓāhiriyya MS]. Amman: Dār al-Bashīr li-'l-Nashr wa-'l-Tawzī', 1989. Vol. 15, 486–489.

al-Dhahabī, Muḥammad b. Aḥmad b. 'Uthmān. *Siyar A'lām al-Nubalā'.* Beirut: Mu'assasat al-Risāla, 1982. Vol. 11, 104–108.

References

Rosenthal, F. "Ibn 'Ā'idh." *Encyclopaedia of Islam.* Second ed. Leiden: E.J. Brill, 1960–, Vol. 3, 698.

Sukayna al-Shihābī. "Ta'rīkh Madīnat Dimashq: Maṣdar lam Yudarras wa-Ahamiyyatuhu fī Ta'rīkh Ṣadr al-Islām." Ed. M.'A. al-Bakhīt. *Bilād al-Shā m fī Ṣadr al-Islām: al-Mu'tamar al-Duwalī al-Rābi' li-Ta'rīkh Bilād al-Shām.* Amman: Maṭba'at al-Jāmi'a al-Urduniyya, 1987. Vol. 1, 359–367.

Ibn al-'Adīm, Kamāl al-Dīn (1192–1262)

North Syrian official, judge, and author. Ibn al-'Adīm composed two works that are important sources for the history of Syria in the Ayyubid period: a large, but only partially extant, biographical dictionary *(Bughyat al-ṭalab)* of people connected to his hometown, Aleppo (Ḥalab); and a chronicle *(Zubdat al-ḥalab),* centered around the history of the city from earliest times up to 1243.

Reuven Amitai-Preiss

Texts

Bughyat al-ṭalab fī ta'rīkh ḥalab. Ed. S. Zakkār. 11 vols. Damascus: n.p., 1988–1989.

Selections trans. into French in *Recueil des historiens des croisades: Historiens orientaux.* 5 vols. Paris: Imprimerie Nationale, 1872–1906. Vol. 3. (1884), 695–732.

Zubdat al-ḥalab min ta'rīkh ḥalab. Ed. S. Dahhān. 3 vols. Damascus, 1951–1968; trans. into French as *Histoire d'Alep,* ed. S. Dahan. 2 vols. Damascus: Institut français de Damas, 1951.

References

Lewis, B. "Ibn al-'Adīm." *Encyclopaedia of Islam.* Second ed. Leiden, Netherlands: E.J. Brill, 1960–. Vol. 3, 693–694.

Morray, D.W. *An Ayyubid Notable and His World.* Leiden, Netherlands: E.J. Brill, 1994.

Ibn al-Athīr ['Izz al-Dīn 'Alī ibn Muḥammad] (1160–1233)

Muslim historian. An important chronicler primarily active in Mosul (where he died), Ibn al-Athīr came from a family prominent in both administrative and scholarly affairs in the area. He studied in Baghdad, traveled to Syria where for a while he accompanied Saladin's army, and lived for a short period in Aleppo and Damascus. Ibn al-Athīr's fame primarily rests on his multivolume chronicle *al-Kāmil fī al-ta'rīkh* [The Completion of History], which begins with the antecedents of Islam from the creation onward, and, from the appearance of the prophet Muḥammad, concentrates on the history of the Muslims. While the larger part of the book is mainly derivative from earlier works, Ibn al-Athīr inserts much material on his own times, gathered from eyewitness accounts as well as his personal observations. His treatment of Saladin is not always positive, which is not surprising given his and his family's ties with the Zengids (about whom he composed a separate history, the *Bāhir*), whose fortunes had greatly suffered as a result of the activities of the famous Ayyubid leader. Ibn al-Athīr is a particularly important source for the relations of the Muslim world with the Crusaders as well as the history of the first Mongol invasion of the Islamic world (1219–1223).

Reuven Amitai-Preiss

Texts

Al-Kāmil fī al-ta'rīkh, published under the title *Chronicon quod perfectissimum inscribitur.* Ed. C.J. Tornberg. 13 vols. Leiden: E.J. Brill, 1867–1876; reprinted Beirut: Dar Sader, 1965–1967.

Al-Ta'rīkh al-bāhir fī al-dawlat al-atābakiyya [History of the Atabegs]. Ed. 'A.'A. Ṭulaymāt. Cairo: Dār al-Kutub al-Ḥadītha, 1963.

Selections relevant to Crusades trans. into French in *Recueil des historiens des croisades. Historiens orientaux.* 2 vols. Paris: Imprimerie Nationale, 1872–1906.

References

Richards, D.S. "Ibn al-Athīr and the Later Parts of the *Kāmil:* A Study of Aims and Methods." In *Medieval Historical Writing in the Christian and Islamic Worlds,* ed. D.O. Morgan. London: School of Oriental and African Studies, 1982, 76–108.

Rosenthal, F. "Ibn al-Athīr." *Encyclopaedia of Islam.* Second ed. Leiden, Netherlands: E.J. Brill, 1960–. Vol. 3, 723–725.

Ibn al-Furāt, Nāṣir al-Dīn (1334–1405)

Egyptian historian known for his voluminous chronicle, *Ta'rīkh al-duwal wa'l-mulūk* [The History of Dynasties and Kings]. This was envisioned as a universal chronicle, but Ibn al-Furāt only completed the volumes for the years after 1006, not all of which have survived. His work is a mine for modern historians because it incorporates long passages from now-lost compositions. Ibn al-Furāt, who was generally scrupulous in citing the names of his sources and quoted them accurately (making it clear when he was summarizing), often presents several versions of the same event. Until recently, he has been eclipsed by the slightly later al-Maqrīzī, which is certainly unjustified given the latter's penchant for summarizing Ibn al-Furāt, invariably without attribution and often in an inexact manner.

Reuven Amitai-Preiss

Texts

Ayyubids, Mamlukes and Crusaders. Ed. and trans. U. and M.C. Lyons, with introduction and notes by J. Riley-Smith. Cambridge, Eng.: Heffer, 1971. Selections for the years 1244–1277.

Ta'rīkh [al-duwal wa'l-mulūk]. Ed. C. Zurayk and N. Izzedin. 4 vols. Beirut: al-Maṭba`ah al-Amirkāniyya, 1936–1942; ed. H.M. al-Shammā`. 3 vols. Basra: Maṭba'at Ḥaddād, 1967–1970.

References

Ashtor, E. "Some Unpublished Sources for the Bahri Period." In *Studies in Islamic History and Civilization* ("Scripta Hierosolymitana," vol. IX), ed. U. Heyd. Jerusalem: Hebrew University, 1961, 11–30.

Cahen, Claude. "Ibn al-Furāt." *Encyclopaedia of Islam.* Second ed. Leiden, Netherlands: E.J. Brill, 1960–. Vol. 3, 768–769.

Ibn al-'Ibrī [Bar Hebraeus], Abu'l Faradj (1226–1286)

Christian Jacobite (Monophysite) bishop and author of histories in both Syriac and Arabic. Ibn al-'Ibrī was born in Malatya, in Asia Minor, and educated at Antioch and Tripoli. He was a polymath who wrote not only on history but also on philosophy, science, and literature and mastered Syriac, Arabic, and Hebrew. In 1264, he was appointed head of the eastern Jacobite church, a position that brought him into close contact with the political leaders of his turbulent age, including the dreaded Mongols. He is best known for his

Chronography in Syriac and its abridgment, *Ta'rīkh Mukhtaṣar al-duwal,* in Arabic. These are universal chronicles that record history from the creation to the author's own days. They exemplify a tradition of oriental Christian historiography written under, and sometimes at the request of, Arabic-Islamic rulers, and their chief interest is the manner in which they act as intermediaries between the Greek or Syriac Christian historical tradition on the one hand and the Arabic-Islamic on the other. As a historian, Ibn al-'Ibri displays a notable interest in science, medicine, and theology and his coverage of western Mongol affairs is particularly authoritative.

Tarif Khalidi

Texts

The Chronography of Gregory Abu'l-Faraj the Son of Aaron, the Hebrew Physician, Commonly Known as Bar Hebraeus; Being the First Part of His Political History of the World. Ed. and trans. E.A.W. Budge. London: Oxford University Press/H. Milford, 1932.

Tarikh Mukhtasar al-Duwal. Ed. A. Salihani. Beirut: Imprimerie Catholique, 1890.

References

Lewis, Bernard, and P.M. Holt, eds. *Historians of the Middle East.* London: Oxford University Press, 1962.

Noldeke, Theodore. *Sketches from Eastern History.* Trans. John Sutherland Black. London and Edinburgh: Adam and Charles Black, 1892.

Ibn al-Ḳalānisī, Abū Ya'lā Ḥamza Ibn Asad al-Tamīmī (1073–1160)

Mayor of Damascus and the first Arab chronicler of the Crusades. Ibn al-Ḳalānisī, a member of an established and respected Damascene family, was well-educated in literature, theology, and law. He served as secretary in *Diwan al-Rasa'il* (the Chancery Department), eventually becoming its head. He was twice the mayor of Damascus. Ibn al-Ḳalānisī's work *Dhayl Ta'rīkh Dimashk* [Continuation of the Chronicle of Damascus] is indispensable for the study of the early Crusades in the Levant even though it was intended to be a chronicle of Damascus. He depended on written documents and oral accounts taken from actual participants; more than two thirds of the book provides eyewitness accounts of the first and second Crusades. Covering the period of the lifetime of the author and his father, it served as the primary source for subsequent Arab historians.

Mahmood Ibrahim

Texts

The Damascus Chronicle of the Crusades [Abridged]. Trans. H.A.R. Gibb. University of London Historical Series, no. 5. London: Luzac, 1932.

References

Arab Historians of the Crusades. Ed. and trans. into Italian Franceso Gabrieli; trans. into English E.J. Costello. Berkeley and Los Angeles: University of California Press, 1969.

Ma'aluf, Amin. *The Crusades through Arab Eyes.* Trans. Jon Rothschild. New York: Schocken Books, 1985.

Ibn al-Qilai [Jibra'il ibn al-Qilai] (d. 1516)

Maronite historian and poet. Ibn al-Qilai was born in Mount Lebanon, but nothing further is known about his date of birth or his childhood. In 1470, a Franciscan friar recruited Ibn al-Qilai into that religious order and sent him to study in Rome. In 1493, he returned to Mount Lebanon as a Catholic missionary and was appointed as the resident adviser to the Maronite patriarch. Sometime later, Ibn al-Qilai was appointed bishop of the Maronite community of Nicosia, Cyprus, where he remained until his death. He was the author of *Midihah 'ala Jabal Lubnan* [A Hymn on Mount Lebanon], an epic poem written in Arabic. *Midihah* is considered the first attempt by a Maronite to present a history of his community. Ibn al-Qilai used the work to present a glorified version of Maronite history, in order to generate unity and solidarity among his people. He asserted that in defending themselves against the threat of Islam, the Maronite community had always maintained its internal unity; this had been shattered, however, when Maronites began to join heretical Christian sects such as the Melchites and Jacobites. These heresies needed to be purged, Ibn al-Qilai concluded, in order to restore such unity.

Mehrdad Kia

Texts

Madihah 'ala Jaba Lubnan. In Bulus Qar'ali. *Hurub al Muḳaddamin: 1075–1450.* Lebanon: Bayt Shabab, 1937.

References

Harik, Iliya F. *Politics and Change in a Traditional Society: Lebanon, 1711–1845.* Princeton, NJ: Princeton University Press, 1968.

Salibi, Kamal S. *A House of Many Mansions: The History of Lebanon Reconsidered.* London: I.B. Tauris, 1985.

———. *Maronite Historians of Medieval Lebanon.* Beirut: American University of Beirut,
1959.

Ibn Baṭṭūṭa (1304–1368/9 or possibly 1377)

Shams al-Dīn, Abū ʿAbdallāh Muḥammad b.
ʿAbdallāh al-Lawātī al-Tanjī, known as Ibn
Baṭṭūṭa, was the greatest traveler of the Middle
Ages. His travels extended over a period of thirty
years and covered almost all the lands under Muslim rule in his time, more territory and more countries than those of Marco Polo. The description of
his travels, entitled *Tuḥfat al Nuẓẓār fī Gharāʾib
al-Amṣār wa-ʿAjāʾib al-Asfār* (more commonly
known as *Riḥlat Ibn Baṭṭūṭa*), is one of the most
interesting and important sources for the political and social history of the Muslim world during the second quarter of the fourteenth century.
Although in some cases, his testimony forms an incidental, unimportant source, no more than background information, in others they represent one
of the major sources if not the only one available.
Even though his descriptions and reports are not
consistent, it is impossible to ignore him as a witness to events of the time. It is likely that Ibn
Baṭṭūṭa did not keep written records and the fact
that he relied solely upon his memory explains, in
the opinion of most scholars, the many inaccuracies found therein, such as incorrect names and
historical data, and inaccurate (indeed impossible)
chronology. In addition, Ibn Juzayy, one of the
chief secretaries to the vizier of the Sultan of Morocco, was commissioned by the sultan to assemble
the passages dictated by Ibn Baṭṭūṭa into one composition. Consequently, the book is the product of
Ibn Juzayy's editing. These shortcomings do not
undermine the general credibility of the work,
and it is generally agreed (with certain exceptions)
that his work is reliable, providing a wealth of
important detail, as well as descriptions and fine
distinctions relating to many aspects of Islamic
civilization.

Amikam Elad

Texts

Voyages d'Ibn Battoutah. Ed. and trans. (into
French) C. Defrémery and B.R.
Sanguinetti. Paris: L'Imprimerie Nationale,
1893. Trans. (into English) H.A.R. Gibb
(vols. 1 and 2) and C.F. Beckingham (vol.
3) as *The Travels of Ibn Baṭṭūṭa, A.D. 1325–
1354.* 3 vols. Cambridge, Eng.: Cambridge
University Press for the Hakluyt Society,
1958–1962.

References

Dunn, R.E. *The Adventures of Ibn Baṭṭūṭa: A
Muslim Traveler of the Fourteenth Century.*
Berkeley and Los Angeles: University of
California Press, 1989.
Elad, A. "The Description of the Travels of Ibn
Baṭṭūṭa in Palestine: Is It Original?" *Journal
of the Royal Asiatic Society* (1987): 256–272.
Hrbek, I. "The Chronology of Ibn Baṭṭūṭa's
Travels." *Archiv Orientalni* 30 (1962):
409–489.
Janssens, H.F. *Ibn Batouta "Le voyageur de l'Islam"
(1304–1369)* [Ibn Baṭṭūṭa, the Traveler of
Islam]. Brussels: Office de la Publicité,
1948.
Miquel, A. "Ibn Baṭṭūṭa." *Encyclopaedia of Islam.*
Second ed. Leiden, Netherlands: E.J. Brill,
1960–. Vol. 3, 735–736.

Ibn Isḥāḳ, Muḥammad [ibn Isḥāḳ ibn Yasār ibn Khiyār] (d. 761)

Arabic-Islamic historian and author of the earliest
surviving and complete biography of the prophet
Muḥammad. He belonged to a family that had once
been enslaved but had embraced Islam, become free,
and engaged in scholarship. Born in Medina in the
early eighth century, he studied there and in Egypt
but eventually settled in Baghdad, where he was
patronized by the ruling ʿAbbāsid dynasty. His *Sīra*
[Life of Muḥammad], part of a larger work on world
history from the creation onward, has remained,
from his age to ours, the single most important
source for the prophet's life. Ibn Isḥāḳ brought to
his biography an immense store of knowledge on
Christian, Jewish, and Arabian antiquities, enabling
him to place that biography in a broad prophetic
context. No mere transmitter, he was a careful and
critical arranger of historical materials. While preserving legendary materials about the prophet, he
nevertheless aimed to reconstruct his life with as
much chronological and geographical accuracy as
was possible in his day and age. His work had a complex history. Edited by Ibn Hishām (d. 833), the
biography came to acquire two authors. Only recently has the original work of Ibn Isḥāḳ been recovered, allowing us to form a more accurate judgment of its pristine shape and value.

Tarif Khalidi

Texts

Sīra. Ed. M. Hamidullah. Rabat: Maʿhad al-
Dirasat waʾl Abhath liʾl Taʿrib, 1976.
Sīra. [Ibn Isḥāḳ/Ibn Hishām]. Ed. M. Saqqa et
al. Cairo: Mustafa al-Babi al-Halabi, 1935–

1936; trans. A. Guillaume as *The Life of Muhammad*. London: Oxford University Press, 1955.

References

Duri, A.A. *The Rise of Historical Writing among the Arabs*. Ed. and trans. Lawrence I. Conrad. Princeton, NJ: Princeton University Press, 1983.

Khalidi, Tarif. *Arabic Historical Thought in the Classical Period*. Cambridge, Eng.: Cambridge University Press, 1994.

Rosenthal, Franz. *A History of Muslim Historiography*. Second ed. Leiden: E.J. Brill, 1968.

Ibn Iyās [Abuʾl-Barakāt al-Nasseri Muḥammad ibn Aḥmad ibn Iyās al-Ḥanafī] (1448–1524)

Egyptian historian and chronicler. Ibn Iyās was born in Cairo in 1448. His great-grandfather, grandfather, and father had held important posts in Mamlūk officialdom and enjoyed close relationships with Mamlūk dignitaries. Ibn Iyās studied under the Egyptian scholar and chronicler, al-Suyuti, and the Egyptian historian and jurist Abd al-Basit ibn Khalil al-Ḥanafī. Ibn Iyās wrote several historical tracts. His most important historical work was *Badāʾi ʿal-zuhūr fi waḳāʾi ʿal-duhūr* [Marvels Blossoming among Incidents of the Epochs]. This book covered the history of Egypt from the pre-Islamic period down to the end of the Mamlūk dynasty. The significance of *Badāʾi* lay in the fact that it provided historians with a firsthand, eyewitness account of the last fifty-five years of the Mamlūk rule in Egypt. The book is also the only extant historical account of the reign of Ḳānṣawh al-Ghawrī (1501–1516), during which the power of the Mamlūk state began to disintegrate. *Badāʾi* is therefore an essential source for understanding the causes for the fall of the Mamlūks and the conquest of Egypt by the Ottoman ruler Sultan Selim I in 1517.

Mehrdad Kia

Texts

Badaʾi al-zuhur fi waqaʾi al-duhur. Ed. Mohamed Mostafa. 3 vols. Wiesbaden: Franz Steiner Verlag GMBH (Bibliotheca Islamica), 1975.

References

Petry, Carl. *Twilight of Majesty: The Reigns of the Mamluk Sultans, Ashraf Qaytbay and Qanshu al-Ghawri in Egypt*. Seattle: University of Washington Press, 1993.

Winter, Michael. *Society and Religion in Early Ottoman Egypt: Studies in the Writings of Abd al-Wahhab al-Shaʿrani*. New Brunswick, NJ: Transaction Books, 1982.

Ibn Khaldūn [Walī al-Dīn Abu Zayd ʿAbd al-Raḥhmān ibn Muḥammad ibn Muḥammad Abī Bakr Muḥammad ibn al-Ḥasan] (1332–1406)

Muslim historian, sociologist, and philosopher. Ibn Khaldūn was born in Tunis in 1332. There, he received a traditional Islamic education, studying the Quran, the Hadīth (tradition), and Islamic law. At the age of seventeen, Ibn Khaldūn lost his parents to the Black Death, a traumatic event that left a profound impact on his personal and intellectual development. He held various governmental posts under the rulers of Maghreb and in Granada, Spain. He also traveled extensively in North Africa and southern Spain. On several occasions, he was arrested for involvement in political intrigues. Increasingly concerned with the unstable political situation in Maghreb, Ibn Khaldūn finally left Tunis for Cairo, Egypt, in 1382. In Egypt, he was appointed the chief magistrate of the Maliki Muslims. He died in Cairo in 1406.

Ibn Khaldūn has been called the "first sociologist of history." He discussed his philosophy of history in *Mukaddima (Muqaddimah)* and in the introduction to his universal history, *Kitāb al-ʿIbar wa Diwan al-Mubtadaʾ wa al-Khabar* [Universal History of the World]. In *Muqaddimah,* Ibn Khaldūn attempted to develop a theory of historical change. He criticized the traditional annalistic method of past historians for failing to demonstrate a genuine curiosity for their subject. Ibn Khaldūn wished to transcend the traditionalist approach and develop a new methodology through which the historian could examine the actual causes of the rise and fall of power structures. In articulating his theory, he took into consideration the impact of geography, climate, and religion in the shaping of historical events. He defined history as a study of the totality of human past, including politics, culture, and economics. The central concept in his philosophy of history was that of *asabiyya,* or group spirit. Ibn Khaldūn maintained that individuals, groups, and tribes who seized power possessed social cohesion and group spirit. After they consolidated their power and they felt secure in their position, however, they began to lose their vigor and cohesion. Contending factions began to emerge, and fighting ensued over political power and the financial resources of the state. Aside from factionalism and internal struggles, the contending factions refused to implement governmental reforms because they viewed change as a threat to their privileged status. Factionalized from within, and resistant to reform, the ruling group created the necessary preconditions for its own destruction by a new group that enjoyed cohesion and group spirit.

Mehrdad Kia

Texts

An Arab Philosophy of History: Selections from the Prolegomena of Ibn Khaldun of Tunis. Ed. and trans. Charles Issawi. London: Murray, 1950.

The Muqaddimah: An Introduction to History. Trans. Franz Rosenthal. 3 vols. New York: Pantheon Books, 1958.

References

Azmah, Aziz. *Ibn Khaldun: An Essay in Reinterpretation.* London and Totowa, NJ: Frank Cass, 1982.

Baali, Fuad. *Society, State, and Urbanism: Ibn Khaldun's Sociological Thought.* Albany: State University of New York Press, 1988.

Rosenthal, Erwin I.J. *Political Thought in Medieval Islam: An Introductory Outline.* Cambridge, Eng.: Cambridge University Press, 1958.

Rosenthal, Franz. *A History of Muslim Historiography.* Leiden: E.J. Brill, 1952.

Ibn Khallikān, Shams al-Dīn Aḥmad (1211–1282)

Arabic-Islamic biographer and author of one of the most celebrated biographical dictionaries of premodern Islamic civilization. Ibn Khallikān was born in Irbil, in northern Iraq, to an aristocratic family, and was educated in Aleppo. In 1261, He was appointed chief judge of Damascus, a post he held with some interruptions until his death. His dictionary, entitled *Wafayāt al-A`yān* [Obituaries of Notables], includes famous figures from Arabic-Islamic history as well as contemporaries of the author. There are 855 carefully chosen, alphabetically arranged entries, drawn mostly from the world of scholarship. Ibn Khallikān's dictionary was destined to become a model of its genre for later dictionaries. The author claimed to have observed utmost accuracy in the collection and assessment of dates and facts. Based upon a wide range of written and oral sources, the dictionary is often the first source that needs to be consulted on the lives of prominent premodern Islamic scholars. Of equal value is the place that this dictionary occupies in the history of Arabic Islamic historiography for it helped to entrench the view that history was synonymous with biography. The entries are structured with great skill and exclude the lives of the earliest Muslims, ostensibly because these are too well known but perhaps also in order to avoid hagiography.

Tarif Khalidi

Texts

*Wafayat al-A`yan.* Ed. I. `Abbas. Beirut, 1968–1972; trans. M. de Slane as *Ibn Khallikan's Biographical Dictionary.* 4 vols. Paris and London: Oriental Translation Fund of Great Britain and Ireland, 1842–1871.

References

Fahndrich, Helmut E. "The *Wafayat al-A`yan* of Ibn Khallikan: A New Approach." *Journal of the American Oriental Society* 93 (1973): 432–445.

Khalidi, Tarif. *Arabic Historical Thought in the Classical Period.* Cambridge, Eng.: Cambridge University Press, 1994.

Ibn Miskawayh, Abu `Ali Ahmad Ibn Muḥammad (d. 1030)

Arabic Islamic philosopher and historian. Miskawayh was born in Rayy, near Tehran, around the year 935. He is a notable example of the scholar-bureaucrat of the mid-`Abbasid period, acting for many years as royal librarian and passing much of his life in the company of viziers and high state officials, as well as the intellectual luminaries of his age. He possessed wide literary and philosophical interests, was a distinguished stylist and accomplished poet, and had a particular interest in psychology and ethics. As a historian, his reputation rests upon his *Tadjārib al-umam* [Experiences of the Nations], a political history pruned of all divine or prophetic elements so as to turn it into a usable "manual of political conduct" for statesmen and political or military leaders. Of central importance is his concept of *tadbīr,* by which he meant the proper management or direction of public affairs. Miskawayh intended his *Tadjārib* to be illustrative of how leaders past and present were able to anticipate or control events and prepare the necessary resources to deal with the emergencies of government. Hence, much of it is divided into subheadings entitled, for instance, "an act of cunning," "an act of deception," "a good counsel," "a plot," and so forth. Government is an art requiring financial competence, military skill, and the ability to judge the patterns and motives of human action, and history for Miskawayh exemplified that art.

Tarif Khalidi

Texts

Tajarib al-umam. In *The Eclipse of the 'Abbasid Caliphate: Original Chronicles of the Fourth Islamic Century*, ed. and trans. H.F. Amedroz and D.S. Margoliouth. 7 vols. Oxford: B. Blackwell, 1920–1921.

References

Arkoun, Mohammed. *Contribution à l'étude de l'humanisme Arabe au IVᵉ/Xᵉ siècle* [Contribution to the Study of Arab Humanism in the Fourth/Tenth Century]. Paris: J. Vrin, 1970.

Khalidi, Tarif. *Arabic Historical Thought in the Classical Period.* Cambridge, Eng.: Cambridge University Press, 1994.

Ibn Taghrī Birdī, Abū Al-Maḥāsin (1409/10?–1470)

Egyptian historian and courtier. Ibn Taghrī Birdī, who knew the Turkish spoken by the Mamlūk military class (his father had been an important Mamlūk officer), was well acquainted with the sultanate's military and political elite. His main works were a large biographical dictionary *(al-Manhal al-ṣāfī),* and the chronicle *al-Nujūm al-zāhira,* a history of Egypt from 641 to his own times. This latter work incorporated many passages from now-lost books of earlier historians. He also composed *Ḥawādith al-duhūr,* a continuation of al-Maqrīzī's *Sulūk.* In his annals for contemporary events, Ibn Taghrī Birdī at times expresses himself strongly on the current state of Egypt's affairs.

Reuven Amitai-Preiss

Texts

Al-Manhal al-ṣāfī wa'l-musawfī ba'd al-wāfī. Ed. M.M. Amīn. 7 vols. Cairo: Al-Hay'a al-Miṣriyya al-'Āmma lil-Kitāb, 1984–1894.

Al-Nujūm al-zāhira fī mulūk miṣr wa'l-qāhira. Cairo: Dār al-Kutūb al-Miṣriyya, 1930–1956.

Les Biographies du Manhal Safi. [Summary]. Trans. G. Wiet. Cairo: Imprimerie de l'Institut français d'archeologie orientale, 1932.

Extracts from Abū 'l-Maḥāsin ibn Taghrī Birdī's Chronicle Ḥawādith al-Duhūr. Ed. William Popper. 4 vols. Berkeley: University of California Press, 1930–1942.

History of Egypt, 1382–1469 A.D. Partial trans. William Popper. New York: AMS Press, 1976.

References

Popper, W. "Abū 'l-Maḥāsin . . . b. Taghrībirdī." *Encyclopaedia of Islam.* Second ed. Leiden, Netherlands: E.J. Brill, 1960–. Vol. 1, 238.

Wiet, G. "L'Historien Abul Mahasin [The Historian Abul Mahasin]." *Bulletin de l'Institut d'Égypte* 12 (1929–1930): 89–105.

Ideas, History of

Mode of historical enquiry concerned with the history and development of thought. The "history of ideas" is associated, in the United States, with the work of Arthur O. Lovejoy and his followers, but in fact it is a field that has a much longer history. The phrase itself was first employed by Giambattista Vico, who (alluding to J.J. Brucker's survey of the history of Platonic ideas, the *Historia doctrina de ideis* of 1723) designated his "new science," in one of its principal aspects, as "the history of ideas" *(la storia delle idee).* For Vico this history "took its start not when the philosophers began to reflect *[riflettere]* on human ideas" but rather when the first men began to think humanly *(umanamente pensare),* that is, not with Plato but with myth and poetry; and in later generations, too, the history of ideas has ventured far beyond the jurisdiction of formal philosophy.

The view that ideas represented a matter not just for philosophical speculation or psychological analysis but also for historical investigation was pursued by many later authors. In being assimilated to history, however, ideas were reduced to opinion, argued Thomas Reid, so that "The idea of Aristotle, or of Epicurus, signify the opinions of these philosophers," recalling that "Bruckerus, a learned German, wrote a whole book giving the history of ideas." This line was also pursued by philosophers in the tradition of philosophical idealism and philosophical psychology. Friedrich August Carus, for example, recalled the old eclectic assumption that the study of history must consider error as well as wisdom, logic, and "pure ideas" *(reine Ideen);* and Wilhelm von Humboldt associated this subject with the "task of the historian," who "has all the strands of temporal activity and all the expressions of eternal ideas as his province."

The history of ideas found another champion in Victor Cousin, founder of French Eclectic philosophy in the early nineteenth century. In his "spiritualist" fashion Cousin celebrated a long tradition of the "history of ideas," going back especially to the earlier school of German Eclecticism and to the monumental history of Brucker, whom Cousin honored as "the father of the history of philosophy." According to Eugène Lerminier, another eclectic of that period devoted to the history of ideas, "From one century to another ideas prolong their relevance; and the more they are powerful and accepted in one particular period, the slower they will be to die and give way to others which they have produced." Lerminier made this comment in connection with what he called "the history of one of the essential ideas of humanity," namely, the influence of the social ideas of the Enlightenment on legal and social Restoration France.

In Germany the counterpart of old-fashioned history of ideas was the sort of *Ideengeschichte* practiced by Friedrich Meinecke and reinforced by the efforts of Wilhelm Dilthey, Ernst Cassirer, and other post-Kantian philosophers to establish foundations for the human sciences *(Geisteswissenschaften)*, although a closer parallel these days is the new school of *Begriffsgeschichte,* which is much more concerned with social and political context. The history of ideas as such has also been taught, for example, in France (Jean Starobinski and Michel Foucault), in Spanish-speaking countries, in Romania, and in Sweden—at the University of Uppsala, where John Nordstrom was an early pioneer in this field.

In the United States the connections with philosophy were from the beginning remarkably close, as reflected, for example, in the essays published by the collected *Studies in the History of Ideas* published by the Columbia University philosophy department (1918, 1925, 1935) in order "to encourage research and the exercise of historical imagination" in "a larger field of inquiry [than philosophy] . . . , in which it appears that ideas have a history." These volumes included scholarly contributions by John Dewey, F.J.E. Woodbridge, John Herman Randall Jr., Herbert Schneider, Sidney Hook, Ernest Nagel, and Richard McKeon. Another American center was the "History of Ideas Club" of the Johns Hopkins University, which began meeting in 1923 and which over the next thirty years featured among its speakers (to give a long and only partial list) Arthur Lovejoy, George Boas, Gilbert Chinard, Marjorie Nicolson, Dumas Malone, Tenney Frank, Stephen D'Irsay, Harold Cherniss, Charles Beard, Theodor Mommsen, Niels Bohr, Carl Becker, William Albright, Leo Spitzer, John von Neumann, Hans Baron, Owen Lattimore, Elio Gianturco,

Lionello Venturi, Friedrich Engels-Janosi, Samuel E. Morison, Ludwig Edelstein, Américo Castro, Charles Singleton, Hajo Holborn, Don Cameron Allen, René Wellek, Erich Auerbach, Basil Willey, Alexandre Koyré, Eric Voegelin, and many others (down in fact to the present day).

The moving spirit of the history of ideas in this century has unquestionably been Lovejoy, whose *Great Chain of Being* (1936) was not only the model for the tracing of a single "unit-idea" (in Lovejoy's terminology) but also a manifesto for the history of ideas in general. Lovejoy was also, with Philip Wiener, a founder of what became and remains the major vehicle of the inter- or pandisciplinary field envisioned by him, the *Journal of the History of Ideas (JHI),* founded in 1940. Both in his classic book and in the first issue of this journal, Lovejoy offered prescriptions for this field, arguing that it touches on at least a dozen areas of study, including the history of philosophy, science, language, religion, literature, the arts, education, and sociology; political, social, and economic history; and folklore and ethnology. For Lovejoy the fundamental elements of the history of ideas were not merely doctrinal "isms" but rather unconscious mental habits, dialectical motives, or methodological assumptions, different kinds of quasi-aesthetic "metaphysical pathos," philosophical semantics (the keywords of an "idea-cluster"), and more explicit principles; and these elements were to be traced through all disciplines and in collective as well as individual thought. Nor was Lovejoy unaware of the excesses and confusions to which his project was subject. Still, he believed that the history of ideas had important contributions to make not only to scholarship but also to our understanding of the human condition in a century torn by much greater excesses and confusions.

The history of ideas was to begin with almost a monopoly of historians of philosophy, and its methodology reflected this bias, which Vico had noted over two centuries before. "Hence," wrote George Boas, a close colleague of Lovejoy at Hopkins, "it is clear that before one can write the history of an idea one must disentangle it from all the ambiguities that it has acquired in the course of time." This sort of decontextualization— "thin" rather than "thick description" as David Hollinger has put it—has been criticized especially by historians and literary scholars, who doubted the historical value of isolating "unit-ideas." For Leo Spitzer, for example, the Lovejoyian history of ideas recalled the idealist *Geistesgeschichte,* which likewise had neglected the emotional, cultural, and especially linguistic dimensions of thought, while others have inclined toward what Peter Gay has called "the social history of ideas," which emphasized correlations and connections between social and intellectual structures.

The idealist implications of Lovejoy's program have continued to provoke objections, and the phrase "intellectual history" has largely replaced that of "history of ideas" among scholars, including philosophers. Yet such critiques of Lovejoy's approach were in part a product not only of new fashions in philosophy, but also of the very interdisciplinarity that he had recommended and the rivalry of methods among the humanistic disciplines. And the field itself, as reflected not only in the *JHI* but also in many books that were conscious contributions to the history of ideas, was cultivated by practitioners of a wide range of disciplines. More recently these disciplines, including the history of philosophy, science, literature, and the arts have become more specialized and have established their own journals; and as a result the *JHI* has been increasingly concerned with the interstices between the older disciplines and unconventional questions arising in these contested border areas and in areas of cultural history in general.

Lovejoy's own presence is very much with us, as is his agenda, although in a modified form and in a very different "climate of opinion" (to employ one of his favorite expressions). Among the differences the most important are perhaps the so-called linguistic turn, which has posed the question of distinct and disparate languages, or idioms, even within a single discourse and which has "problematized" (to employ an expression of which he would surely have disapproved) the very idea of "idea"; the shift of emphasis from author to reader, from creation to reception; critical questions of "canon-formation," which undermine assumptions about the classic status or historical significance of texts; controversial issues of context, in terms of cultural as well as socioeconomic and political categories; and employment of the new technology of electronic texts and databases. As Lovejoy and Boas well realized, however, ideas change; and these phenomena, too, are part of the process that the history of ideas continues to explore.

Donald R. Kelley

See also BEGRIFFSGESCHICHTE; CULTURAL HISTORY; KULTURGESCHICHTE; MENTALITIES.

References

Kelley, Donald R., ed. *The History of Ideas: Canon and Variations.* Rochester, NY: University of Rochester Press, 1990.

LaCapra, Dominick, and Stephen L. Kaplan, eds. *Modern European Intellectual History: Reappraisals and New Perspectives.* Ithaca, NY: Cornell University Press, 1982.

Lovejoy, Arthur O. *The Great Chain of Being: A Study of the History of an Idea.* Cambridge, MA: Harvard University Press, 1950.

Tobey, Jeremy L. *The History of Ideas: A Bibliographical Introduction.* 2 vols. Santa Barbara, CA: Clio Books, 1975–1977.

Vovelle, Michel. *Ideologies and Mentalities.* Trans. Eamon O'Flaherty. Chicago: University of Chicago Press, 1990.

Wiener, Philip P., ed. *Dictionary of the History of Ideas.* 5 vols. New York: Scribner's, 1968.

Ienaga Saburō (b. 1913)

Japanese historian. Born in Aichi prefecture, Ienaga attended Tokyo Normal High School and graduated from Tokyo Imperial University with a concentration in Japanese intellectual history in 1937. In 1940 he published his first book, *Nihon ni okeru hitei no ronri no hattatsu* [The Development of the Theory of Negation in Japan], and began a series of publications on ancient and medieval Japanese Buddhist history. During the Pacific War he taught high school in Niigata and in Tokyo. In 1949 he became a professor at Tokyo Kyōiku University and at Chūo University, and he was awarded his Ph.D. in 1950. In the early 1950s his work took two new directions: first, he focused on modern Japanese cultural and political history; second, he began work on history textbook production for the public schools. In 1963 his high school textbook *Shin Nihon shi* [New History of Japan] was censored by the Ministry of Education's textbook examiners and Ienaga began a legal battle questioning the constitutional legality of such textbook screening. He filed suits against the state in 1965 (seeking damages for suffering during the ministry's investigation), in 1966 (seeking revocation of changes in the textbook demanded by the ministry), and in 1984 (claiming a fundamental, and thus illegal, bias to ministry-approved textbooks). These issues centered on Article 21 of the Constitution, which guarantees freedom of expression and prohibits censorship, Article 23, which guarantees academic freedom, and Article X of the Fundamental Law of Education, which prohibits the unreasonable control of education. While initial rulings (in 1970 and 1974) on the first two suits were in Ienaga's favor, in 1982 the Supreme Court ruled on the issue by claiming that since the Ministry of Education's textbook screening system had been extensively revised since the 1960s (when the charge was filed) the suit was no longer valid. Appeals still continue.

James Edward Ketelaar

Texts

History of Japan. Tokyo: Japan Travel Bureau, 1954.
Japanese Art. New York: Weatherhill, 1979.
The Pacific War: 1931–1945. New York: Random House, 1978.

References

Horio Teruhisa. *Educational Thought and Ideology in Modern Japan: State Authority and Intellectual Freedom.* Ed. and trans. Steven Platzer. Tokyo: University of Tokyo Press, 1988.

Ikeuchi Hiroshi (1878–1952)

Japanese scholar of Korean and Manchurian history. Ikeuchi studied history at Tokyo Imperial University, from which he graduated in 1904, thereafter joining the department of academic investigation of the Manchurian Railway Company in 1909. He studied the history and geography of Korea and Manchuria under the guidance of Shiratori Kurakichi, working closely with his colleagues, Tsuda Sayukichi (or Sōkichi) and Inaba Iwakichi. In 1913, he was appointed lecturer at the college of literature at his alma mater and was promoted in 1916 to assistant professor to teach Korean history. In 1922 he received a doctorate upon completion of his dissertation, "Relationships between Jürched and the Northeastern Border of Early Chosŏn Dynasty Korea." He became professor in 1925 and was admitted to the prestigious Imperial Academy of Japan *(tēkoku gakushiin)* in 1937. He retired from Tokyo Imperial University in 1939. His research was based on the thesis that Korean history was an integral part of Manchurian-Korean history (*Mansŏnsa* or *Mansenshi*). His major research interest was in the field of political and military history during the region's premodern period, and he guided a number of students in this field. His methodology, as the noted Japanese historian Hatada Takashi has observed, characteristically examined historical evidence critically in order to arrive at the most logical conclusion. His major publications include *Bun'eki ke{- ab}chō no eki* [The Wars of 1592 and 1597] (1914–1936) and *Genkō no shinkenkyū* [A New Study of the Mongol Invasions] (1947).

His numerous articles are assembled in *Mansenshi kenkyū* [A Study of Manchurian-Korean History], divided into a volume on the medieval period (chūsē hen), published in 1937, and one on antiquity (jōsei hen) that appeared in 1951.

Fujiya Kawashima

Texts

Genkō no shinkenkyū. Tokyo: Toyo Bunko, 1931.

References

Itō Abito, Ōmura Masuo, Kajimura Hideki, and Takeda Sachio, eds. *Chōsen o Shiru Jiten* [Dictionary of Information about Korea]. Tokyo: Heibonsha, 1986, 10.
Kyōdai Tōyōshi jiten, (ed.). *Sinhen Tōyōshi Jiten* [New Dictionary of East Asian History]. Tokyo: Tokyo Sōgensha, 1980, 43.

Ilyŏn

See IRYŎN.

'Imād al-Dīn, al-Kātib al-Isfahānī (1125–1201)

Medieval Muslim writer and historian. 'Imād al-Dīn served as an official to several rulers, most notably to Saladin (d. 1193). He is best known for his highly stylized accounts of Saladin's wars against the Crusaders, which include many of the diplomatic letters that he himself composed.

Reuven Amitai-Preiss

Texts

Al-Barq al-Shāmī. Ed M. al-Ḥayyārī (Amman, 1986), vol. III; ed. F.S. Ḥusayn (Amman, 1986), vol. V; ed. R. Sheshen [Şeşen] (Istanbul, 1979), vol. V.
Kitāb al-fatḥ al-qussī fī al-fatḥ al-qudsī. Ed. C. de Landerg. Leiden: E.J. Brill, 1888. Trans. H. Massé into French as *Conquête de la Syrie et de la Palestine par Saladin* [The Conquest of Syria and Palestine by Saladin]. Paris: Librairie orientaliste Paul Geuthner, 1972.

References

Massé, H. "'Imād al-Dīn." *Encyclopaedia of Islam.* Second ed. Vol. 3, 1157–1158.
Richards, D.S. "'Imād al-Dīn al-Isfahānī: Administrator, Littérateur and Historian." In *Crusaders and Muslims in Twelfth-Century Syria,* ed. M. Shatzmiller. Leiden: E.J. Brill, 1993, 133–146.

Imanishi Ryū (1875–1932)

Japanese historian of Korea. Born in Ikeda, Gifu prefecture, Imanishi graduated from Tokyo University in 1903 and first visited Korea in 1906. As assistant professor at Kyoto University from 1914, and then professor, he became Japan's leading authority on the archaeology and history of ancient Korea. In 1925 he became a member of the official history committee of the Japanese colonial government in Korea, and the following year became professor at the new Seijō (Seoul) University, while continuing to hold his post at Kyoto. In this capacity he undertook excavations and contributed to officially sponsored publications on archaeological findings and early Korean history. He also studied in China, 1923 to 1925, in France, and in the United Kingdom. Imanishi was the author of many essays and books on Korean history and archaeology, including the Government General of Korea's 1916 and 1917 reports on Korean archaeological findings. His major findings were published by his students after his death as *Shiragi-shi Kenkyū* [Studies on the History of Silla], *Kudara-shi Kenkyū* [Studies on the History of Paekche], and *Chōsen-shi no Shiori* [Guidebook to Korean History].

Janet E. Hunter

Texts

Chōsen-shi no Shiori. Seoul: Chikazawa Shoten, 1935.
Kudara-shi Kenkyū. Seoul: Chikazawa Shoten, 1934.
Shiragi-shi Kenkyū. Seoul: Chikazawa Shoten, 1933.

References

Heibonsha. *Ajia Rekishi Jiten* [Dictionary of Asian History] (1959).

Immigration, Historiography of—United States

Historical writing principally concerning immigration to the United States. Humans have always been migratory, and much of the task of history consists of reconstructing and making sense of their treks and migrations. The largest of these in recent history is the exodus of some sixty million Europeans to other continents over the last four centuries. Most headed for a "New World" in the Americas or the Pacific, but some went to India, southern Africa, or China. This vast movement of Europeans, in turn, helped increase the geographic mobility of the peoples they settled among, so that, by the nineteenth century, Asians and Pacific Islanders were heading to North America and Indians were relocating in east and south Africa. In large measure, the history of the world over the last half millennium is the story of population movements.

By far the most studied of these is the migration from Europe to North America. Early students tended to fall into two camps: concerned Americans worried that a deluge of immigrants might dilute the native stock; and concerned European officials worried that emigration would deplete their own population. Some of these governmental studies have proven highly useful since they meticulously documented the names, ages, places of birth, occupations, and other biographical details of the emigrants along with descriptions of the local conditions, the so-called push factors, which impelled their nationals to leave. An influential monograph drawing upon these data is Kristian Hvidt, *Flight to America: The Social Background of 300,000 Danish Emigrants* (1975). In similar fashion, some of the U.S. studies inspired by nativist concerns—the forty-one-volume *Reports of the (Dillingham) Immigration Commission* of 1911 is a leading example—also contain highly useful data about emigrants and the conditions they encountered in their new homes. These data, however, were often tabulated in highly misleading ways, most notoriously as a series of invidious comparisons between so-called old (from northern and western Europe) and new (from southern and eastern Europe) immigrations.

Modern scholarship on European immigration to North America largely began with Marcus Lee Hansen's posthumously published *Atlantic Migration, 1607–1860,* edited by Arthur M. Schlesinger Sr. (1940) and Oscar Handlin's *Boston Immigrants, 1790–1880* (1941). It is no accident that the two appeared within a year of each other and from the same press. Handlin's study was his dissertation, prepared under Schlesinger's direction, and he and Hansen corresponded at length about their researches.

Hansen, in addition to dissolving the largely honorific distinction between colonist and immigrant, set the migration to North America in the context of broader population movements within as well as without Europe. Brinley Thomas gave this approach a sophisticated economic emphasis in *Migration and Economic Growth: A Study of Great Britain and the Atlantic Economy* (1954). Frank Thistlewaite, in an enormously influential 1960 article on "Migration from Europe Overseas in the Nineteenth and Twentieth Centuries," suggested that population movements for all of Europe correlated with the demand for labor in an increasingly integrated international economy. Walter Nugent's *Crossing: The Great Transatlantic Migrations, 1870–1914* (1992) is a remarkably concise and useful recent application of the Hansen–Thomas–Thistlewaite approach. Other important works in this tradition have been contributed by Hans Norman and Harald Runblom, Ewa Morawska, and Michael J. Piore. Important collections of essays are those edited by Rudolph J. Vecoli and Suzanne M. Sinke, *A Century of European Migrations, 1830–1930* (1991); Julianna Puskás, *Overseas Migration from East-Central and Southeastern Europe, 1880–1940* (1990); Ida Altman and James Horn, *"To Make America": European Emigration in the Early Modern Period* (1991); Dirk Hoerder and Horst Rössler, *Distant Magnets: Expectations and Realities in the Immigrant Experience, 1840–1930* (1993); and the special issue, edited by Dirk Hoerder, of the *Journal of American Ethnic History,* 13 (Fall 1993), on European ports of emigration. Hoerder also edited *Labor Migration in the Atlantic Economies: The European and North American Working Classes during the Period of Industrialization* (1985) and has done more than any scholar, aside from Harald Runblom, director of the Multiethnic Research Center of Uppsala University, to bring together European and American students of immigration.

Lucie Cheng and Edna Bonacich have collected studies exploring the links in what we might call the "Pacific economy," which explain *Labor Immigration under Capitalism: Asian Workers in the United States before World War II* (1984). In this same tradition is Yasuo Wakatsuki, "The Japanese Emigration to the United States, 1866–1924: A Monograph," (*Perspectives in American History* 10 [1979], 389–516), while Magnus Mörner with Harold Sims studied migration in Latin America in a 1985 work jointly published by UNESCO and the University of Pittsburgh Press, *Adventurers and Proletarians: The Story of Migrants in Latin America.* Philip Curtin pioneered the study of slavery as a component of the "Atlantic economy" with *The Atlantic Slave Trade: A Census* (1969). So it is fair to say that the "Hansen" approach to the study of migration continues to expand and flourish.

The same is true of the "Handlin" approach, the intensive study of particular nationality groups in particular settings. Some of the best early works were by Handlin students such as Moses Rischin, *The Promised City: New York's Jews, 1870–1914* (1962). In 1964, Rudolph Vecoli published an influential critique of Handlin, "Contadini in Chicago: A Critique of *The Uprooted.*" This emphasized the degree to which immigrants were successful in adapting to their new surroundings while holding on to their cultures. Even so, *Boston's Immigrants* has remained a model for two generations of scholars. Handlin's use of census and other quantitative materials has proved especially influential. Important studies in this vein include Josef J. Barton, *Peasants and Strangers: Italians, Rumanians, and Slovaks in an American City, 1890–1950* (1975); Dino Cinel, *From Italy to San Francisco* (1982); Kathleen Neils Conzen, *Immigrant Milwaukee: Accommodation and Community in a Frontier City* (1976); Jon Gjerde, *From Peasants to Farmers: The Migration from Balestrand, Norway, to the Upper Middle West* (1985); and Ewa Morawska, *From Bread and Butter: The Life Worlds of East Central Europeans in Johnstown, Pennsylvania, 1890–1940* (1985).

As the number of such monographs grows, so does the sense in the profession that there are no safe generalizations one can make about the experiences of any immigrant population based upon its experiences in any single setting. This has not slowed the torrent of case studies and, unfortunately, it has not led their authors to compare systematically their findings with those of their colleagues either, despite the example of David Ward, whose 1971 study of *Cities and Immigrants: A Geography of Change in Nineteenth Century America* is a suggestive analysis of the ways in which successive waves of immigrants fit into a rapidly urbanizing United States. As a result, cries for synthesis mount. Partial answers, for at least one nationality group, are offered by Kerby Miller, *Emigrants and Exiles: Ireland and the Irish Exodus to North America* (1985), and Hasia Diner, *Erin's Daughters in America* (1983). Susan A. Glenn, *Daughters of the Shtetl: Life and Labor in the Immigrant Generation* (1990) brings together the scholarship on Jewish immigrant women from eastern Europe.

Exemplary as several of these studies are, they do not claim to provide the synthesis immigration historians so crave. On the other hand, there are several excellent surveys of the literature including Thomas J. Archdeacon, *Becoming America: An Ethnic History* (1983); John Bodnar, *The Transplanted: A History of Immigrants in Urban America* (1985); Roger Daniels, *Coming to America: A History of Immigration and Ethnicity in American Life* (1990); and James Stuart Olson, *The Ethnic Dimension in American History* (second ed., 1994). An excellent overview of recent immigration to the United States is Reed Ueda, *Postwar Immigrant America: A Social History* (1994). For studies of migration as a worldwide phenomenon one must turn to the *International Migration Review,* the one indispensable journal in the field.

John F. McClymer

See also ATLASES—HISTORICAL; DEMOGRAPHY—HISTORICAL; SOCIAL HISTORY; URBAN HISTORY.

References

Altman, Ida, and James Horn, eds. *"To Make America": European Emigration in the Early Modern Period.* Berkeley: University of California Press, 1991.

Archdeacon Thomas J. *Becoming America: An Ethnic History.* New York: The Free Press, 1983.

Daniels, Roger. *Coming to America: A History of Immigration and Ethnicity in American Life.* New York: HarperCollins, 1990.

Handlin, Oscar. *Boston Immigrants, 1790–1880.* Cambridge, MA: Harvard University Press, 1941.

Hansen, Marcus Lee. *The Atlantic Migration, 1607–1860.* Cambridge, MA: Harvard University Press, 1940.

Hoerder, Dirk, and Horst Rössler, eds. *Distant Magnets: Expectations and Realities in the Immigrant Experience, 1840–1930.* New York: Holmes & Meier, 1993.

Nugent, Walter. *Crossing: The Great Transatlantic Migrations, 1870–1914.* Bloomington: University of Indiana Press, 1992.

Piore, Michael J. *Birds of Passage: Migrant Labor in Industrial Societies.* Cambridge, Eng.: Cambridge University Press, 1979.

Puskás, Julianna, ed. *Overseas Migration from East-Central and Southeastern Europe, 1880–1940.* Budapest: Akadémiai kiadó, 1990.

Thistlewaite, Frank. "Migration from Europe Overseas in the Nineteenth and Twentieth Centuries." *Rapports* of the *XIᵉ Congrès International des Sciences Historiques.* Stockholm: International Congress of Historical Sciences, 1960.

Thomas, Brinley. *Migration and Economic Growth: A Study of Great Britain and the Atlantic Economy.* Cambridge, Eng.: Cambridge University Press, 1954.

Vecoli, Rudolph. "Contadini in Chicago: A Critique of *The Uprooted.*" *Journal of American History* 51 (1964): 404–417.

Vecoli, Rudolph J., and Suzanne M. Sinke, eds. *A Century of European Migrations, 1830–1930.* Urbana: University of Illinois Press, 1991.

Ward, David. *Cities and Immigrants: A Geography of Change in Nineteenth Century America.* New York: Oxford University Press, 1971.

Imperial and Commonwealth History, British

Imperial history as a historical speciality had its beginnings in a series of lectures presented by J.R. Seeley, Regius professor of history at Cambridge University, in the early 1880s. These lectures were later published as *The Expansion of England* (1883), a classic and comprehensive, if Eurocentric, political account of the creation of what Seeley saw as a British "World State." Such a vision of empire with all its costs and benefits dominated studies such as the multivolume *Cambridge History of the British Empire* (1929–1959), and it is not absent from relatively recent studies such as A.P. Thornton's *The Imperial Idea and Its Enemies* (1959), Paul Knaplund's *The British Empire 1815–1939,* and Nicholas Mansergh's *The Commonwealth Experience* (1969). And as late as 1984, T.O. Lloyd's *The British Empire 1558–1983* still had a Seeley-like focus upon the actions of the British state and its constitutional offspring.

But today such Eurocentric and London-based histories seem increasingly old fashioned and even parochial. Indeed imperial and commonwealth history as a distinct field of historical enquiry has profoundly changed in the last thirty years. It has splintered into what Dane Kennedy (1987) has termed " . . . a multitude of specialized, autonomous research fields separated by geographical, temporal, and methodological boundaries, not to mention by the altered ideological agenda of ex-imperial powers and new nation states." The British historian David Fieldhouse has written that there was indeed a "great fall and many doubted whether the bits, could, or even should, be put together again." The old paradigm of imperial history based on beliefs in the fulfillment of some sort of imperial destiny has lost its support and consequently it is fading in historical and pedagogical terms, in some cases even being forcibly eliminated from university curricula by irate Africanists. The days when history departments would hire someone with an exclusively British imperial background to teach African history are long over. When a historical field loses its cohesive meaning, fragmentation will inevitably result. While not necessarily a negative development, the shattering of imperial history is also indicative of the pervasive trend toward greater compartmentalization in history.

Imperial or commonwealth history, as a meaningful field is not, however, totally moribund, for as Fieldhouse has remarked, it " . . . survives in new and still evolving forms because if it did not exist it would have to be invented." Many of the recent debates over imperial history have taken place in the pages of the *Journal of Imperial and Commonwealth History,* including that over Ronald Hyam's controversial ideas concerning sexuality and empire. Fieldhouse himself has made a substantial contribution in the area of imperial business history with *Merchant Capital and Economic Decolonization: The United Africa Company, 1929–1987* (1995). He makes no claim to be writing African history; rather, he presents the history of a European trading company that never made huge profits. It actually made more of its money in Europe than in Africa, and it made that money from buying commissions, suppliers' bonuses, freight rebates, interest charges on loans to overseas companies, and markups. The function of the African trading networks was to realize the profits made by the company in Europe. P.J. Cain and A.G. Hopkins in two volumes, *British Imperialism: Innovation and Expansion 1688–1914* (1993) and *British Imperialism: Crisis and Destruction 1914–1990* (1993), challenge the long-accepted explanation of Britain's rise to international greatness and it's subsequent decline. The engine that drove the British Empire was not proconsuls or the "man on the spot," nor was it the trade in manufactured goods and the industrial revolution. Instead, Cain and Hopkins point to the banks and to the network of commercial, shipping, insurance, and other financial services centered in London. The empire reflected Britain's financial and commercial primacy and not its early lead in manufacturing. The interests of bondholders became the fly-wheel of empire. The text in both volumes is rooted in economics, and one finds little room for the dreamers, ideologues, and movers of empire, but this is a significant study that ranges well beyond the traditional boundaries of imperial historiography. More conventionally, the American-based historian William Roger Louis is acting as general editor of a new multivolume *Oxford History of the British Empire,* which, when completed, should provide a synthesis of new and old approaches to imperial history; volume 5 of this work will include an extensive survey of the historiography of the empire.

In the areas of economics and culture the new imperial historiography challenges the old assumptions and breaks new ground. The above studies show the economic and political impact of empire, but one of the still evolving forms is the study of gender and empire. Recent scholarship by Helen Callaway, *Gender, Culture and Empire* (1987), Claudia Knapman, *White Women in Fiji,* *1835–1930* (1986), Margaret Strobel, *European Women and the Second British Empire* (1991), and Anne McClintock, *Imperial Leather: Race, Gender, and Sexuality in the Colonial Context* (1995) have altered long-standing assumptions about imperial history being a masculine domain with European women viewed as an intrusive and destructive element.

Imperial history has thus now fragmented into areas such as women's history, family history, social history, "new nations" history, the history of decolonization, and cultural studies. All of this is to acknowledge that the cultural impact, and even the persistence of European imperialism in such areas as literature and education, is equally as important as any political or economic aspects. This notion has helped spawn a new academic subculture of postcolonial studies, including the pioneering and seminal study of *Orientalism* (1978) by Edward Said, and that author's more recent book, *Culture and Imperialism* (1993). McClintock's *Imperial Leather,* for instance, uses feminist, postcolonial, psychoanalytic, and socialist theories to argue that the categories of gender, race, and class do not exist in isolation, but emerge in intimate relation to one another. Drawing on diverse cultural forms—novels, advertising, diaries, poetry, oral history, and mass commodity spectacle—McClintock examines imperialism not only as a poetics of ambivalence, but also as a politics of violence. Rejecting traditional binaries of self/other, man/woman, colonizer/colonized, McClintock calls instead for a more complex and nuanced understanding of categories of social power and identity.

Richard A. Voeltz

See also AFRICAN HISTORIOGRAPHY; GENDER; IMPERIALISM; ORIENTALISM; POSTMODERNISM; WOMEN'S HISTORY—INDIA AND PAKISTAN.

Texts

Berger, M., "Imperialism and Sexual Exploitation: A Review Article," and Ronald Hyam, "A Reply." *Journal of Imperial and Commonwealth History* 17 (1988): 83–98.

Cain, P.J., and A.J. Hopkins. *British Imperialism: Crisis and Destruction 1914–1990.* White Plains, NY: Longman, 1993.

———. *British Imperialism: Innovation and Expansion, 1688–1914.* White Plains, NY: Longman, 1993.

Callaway, Helen. *Gender, Culture, and Empire.* Urbana and Chicago: University of Illinois Press, 1987.

Cambridge History of the British Empire. 9 vols. New York and London: Cambridge University Press, 1929–1959.

Fieldhouse, D.K. *Merchant Capital and Economic Decolonization: The United Africa Company, 1929–1987.* New York and London: Oxford University Press, 1995.

Hyam, Ronald. *Empire and Sexuality.* Manchester and New York: Manchester University Press, 1991.

Knapland, Paul. *The British Empire 1815–1939.* New York: Howard Fertig, 1969.

Knapman, Claudia. *White Women in Fiji 1835–1930.* London: Allen and Unwin, 1986.

Lloyd, T.O. *The British Empire 1558–1983.* London and New York: Oxford University Press, 1984.

Louis, William Roger. *The British Empire in the Middle East, 1945–1951: Arab Nationalism, the United States, and Postwar Imperialism.* Oxford: Clarendon Press, 1984.

———, ed. *Imperialism: The Robinson and Gallagher Controversy.* New York: New Viewpoints, 1976.

Mansergh, Nicholas. *The Commonwealth Experience.* New York: Frederick A. Praeger, 1969.

McClintock, Anne. *Imperial Leather: Race, Gender and Sexuality in the Colonial Contest,* New York: Routledge, 1995.

Robinson, Ronald and John Gallagher. *Africa and the Victorians: the Official Mind of Imperialism.* London: Macmillan, 1961.

Said, Edward. *Culture and Imperialism.* New York: Knopf, 1993.

———. *Orientalism.* New York: Pantheon Books, 1978.

Seeley, J.R. *The Expansion of England.* Chicago: University of Chicago Press, 1971.

Strobel, Margaret. *European Women and the Second British Empire.* Bloomington: Indiana University Press, 1991.

Thornton, A.P. *The Imperial Idea and Its Enemies: A Study in British Power.* London: Macmillan, 1959.

References

Adas, Michael. *"High" Imperialism and the "New" History.* Washington, DC: American Historical Association, 1994.

Fieldhouse, D.K. "Can Humpty-Dumpty Be Put Together Again? Imperial History in the 1980s." *Journal of Imperial and Commonwealth History* 12 (1984): 9–23.

Kennedy, Dane. "The Expansion of Europe." *Journal of Modern History* 59 (1987): 331–343.

Mullet, Charles F. *The British Commonwealth.* Washington, DC: American Historical Association, 1961.

Strobel, Margaret. *Gender, Sex, and Empire.* Washington, DC: American Historical Association, 1994.

Winks, Robin, ed. *British Imperialism: Gold, God, Glory.* Hinsdale, IL: D.C. Heath, 1963.

Imperial School of American History

A reinterpretation of American colonial history and the American Revolution that became dominant from the beginning of the twentieth century to World War II. The leading historians responding to the nationalist school of the nineteenth century were Herbert Levi Osgood, Charles McLean Andrews, and George Louis Beer. Their revisionism, resting on institutional history, was presented in the setting of England's commercial and colonial expansion, thus highlighting the European roots of colonial America. It was a sympathetic scrutiny of the British colonial system that minimized the unfavorable effects of imperial policy on colonial economic life. Although their critics argued that they undermined the fundamental continuity of American history and rendered an inaccurate evaluation of the impact of English rule on the colonial economy, the thought of the imperial school was generally accepted by the 1930s and incorporated into textbooks. Herbert L. Osgood (1855–1918), who taught American and European history at Columbia University, published *The American Colonies in the Seventeenth Century,* subtitled *The Chartered Colonies: Beginnings of Self-Government* (vols. 1 and 2, 1904). He argued that the colonial era and the American Revolution were but aspects of the English imperial system. The first historian to pay close attention to the period between 1690 to 1760, he thought that inquiring into the tensions developing between two different and diverging political societies was important to an understanding of the American Revolution. Osgood's third volume in the series on the seventeenth century, entitled *Imperial Control: Beginnings of the System of Royal Provinces* (1907) suggested that to understand colonial history required a comprehension of British imperial policy. Continuing his work in this field, the subject of his manuscript, *The American Colonies in the Eighteenth Century,* nearly complete at the time of his death (posthumously published in four volumes in 1924) was the British colonial system of control and colonial resistance, up to 1763.

Charles McLean Andrews (1863–1943), a professor of American history at Yale University, followed up Osgood's pioneering efforts. Andrews methodically researched in the British archives, independently reaching similar conclusions. He published *The Colonial Background of the American Revolution: Four Essays in American Colonial History* (1924, revised edition)—a misleading title—pushing the reassessment of the years from 1607 to 1783 the furthest. He rejected as simplistic the notion that Britain's tyrannical rule caused the American Revolution, arguing that it was chiefly the political and constitutional effort by the colonial assemblies directed against the aristocratic British Parliament that explained the making of the conflict. Like Osgood, who acclaimed his work, Andrews considered the period from 1690 to the middle of the eighteenth century the most acute in colonial history and urged its study. Andrews's major, massive work, *The Colonial Period of American History: The Settlements* (1934–1937), was a reassertion of his views. In a fourth volume, subtitled *England's Commercial and Colonial Policy* (1938), Andrews described the efforts between 1660 and 1696 to enforce the Navigation Acts.

George Louis Beer (1872–1920), a younger contemporary of Osgood and Andrews who was influenced by the former, made the British Empire his central concern. He published his master's thesis, *The Commercial Policy of England toward the American Colonies* (1893), a short book on a then largely unexplored topic. Exceeding Osgood in viewing colonial history from Britain's perspective, he argued that the mercantilist system had imposed restrictions on colonial manufactures. Writing on the eighteenth century first, Beer's *British Colonial Policy, 1754–1765* (1907) contributed significantly to the reappraisal of the American Revolution. In *The Origins of the British Colonial System, 1578–1660* (1908) and *The Old Colonial System, 1660–1754* (1912), Beer expanded on the effects of the British acts of trade and navigation on the colonies.

Bernard Hirschhorn

Texts

Andrews, Charles M. "The American Revolution: An Interpretation." *American Historical Review* 31 (1926): 218–232.

———. *The Colonial Background of the American Revolution: Four Essays in American Colonial History.* New Haven, CT: Yale University Press, 1924.

———. *The Colonial Period of American History: The Settlements* (1934–1938). 4 vols. New Haven, CT: Yale University Press, 1934.

Beer, George Louis. *The Commercial Policy of England toward the American Colonies.* New York: Columbia College, 1893.

———. *The Origins of the British Colonial System, 1578–1660.* New York: Macmillan, 1908.

Osgood, Herbert Levi. *The American Colonies in the Seventeenth Century.* 3 vols. New York: Macmillan, 1904–1907.

The American Colonies in the Eighteenth Century. 4 vols. New York: Columbia University Press, 1924–1925.

References

Kraus, Michael. *A History of American History.* New York: Farrar and Rinehart, 1937, 400–438.

———. *The Writing of American History.* Norman: University of Oklahoma Press, 1953, 242–270.

Imperialism

Historical interpretations of the reasons for and the impact of European imperialism from the turn of the twentieth century to the present. The concept of imperialism was used in France from about the 1830s but gained greater currency in Europe after the 1870s and was popularized in journalistic writings in the 1890s following the European partition of the African continent. It became an analytical category with the publication of J.A. Hobson's detailed study in 1902 of the late-nineteenth-century European scramble for colonies. The imperial expansion of Europe, particularly in the period after 1870, he argued, was primarily guided by the need of organized industrial and financial interests in Europe for worldwide markets for goods and capital. The publication in 1916 of V.I. Lenin's study of imperialism furthered scholarly interest in the subject. Unlike Hobson, for whom the European powers had the choice of avoiding the imperialist solution to national economic problems, Lenin focused more sharply on the inevitability of imperialism. Imperialism, he argued, was intrinsically linked to the capitalist mode of production and was therefore a political imperative at "the highest [or latest] stage of capitalism," that is, in the period of finance capitalism, leading to the territorial division of the world among a handful of European nations, all of which were competing capitalist powers.

This enormously influential theory of imperialism opened up a whole new field of historical enquiry among adherents and critics alike.

Some empirical investigations, particularly those by Marxist scholars such as Maurice Dobb, confirmed that economic considerations formed the foundational basis of imperialism. Economic historians like Patrick O'Brien, who have taken the "balance sheet" approach to empire, however, deny that Europe benefited from its empire as much as has been asserted, and even those historians (Paul Bairoch, for example) who do admit that colonial economies were profoundly transformed by imperialist exploitation deny the significance of the benefits derived by European imperialist nations from colonies. The most persuasive critiques have come from economic historians who have challenged Lenin's primary formulation that imperialism is inevitable at the stage of finance-capitalism by demonstrating that European capital flowed primarily to independent states in Europe, North and South America, South Africa, and Australasia rather than to the colonies in Asia and Africa, although without denying Europe's relentless search for expanded markets for its manufactures. Other critics of the economic basis of imperialism have attempted to show that strategic rather than economic considerations lay at the root of empire, particularly in the late nineteenth century when British expansion in Africa, for instance, was guided more by the need to defend and safeguard interests in India.

Nevertheless, Marxist interpretations of imperialism continue to be influential even today (as in Eric Hobsbawm's 1989 study), particularly among historians of the newly independent nations. The primacy accorded to economic theories of imperialism was also extended to analyses of the phenomenon of fascism, which Leon Trotsky understood as resulting from a conjunctural crisis of advanced capitalism, in which latecomers to industrialization such as Germany and Italy were drawn to imperial war-mongering in Europe and elsewhere in order to extend their dominions for definite commercial and industrial purposes. Conversely, there are some historians such as D.K. Fieldhouse who have argued that national mass hysteria climaxed in imperialism, and that even the scramble for Africa must be interpreted as a primarily political phenomenon rather than an economic one.

The emergence of independent nation-states in Asia and Africa after 1947 formed the background against which the enduring influence of economic theories of imperialism was increasingly challenged and revised. Using the partition of Africa in the late nineteenth century as an example, John Gallagher and Ronald Robinson argued for accrding a centrality to politics in any understanding of imperialism. They portrayed the European powers as only reluctantly shouldering the burdens of imperial rule: thus the pragmatics of imperial rule amounted to "trade with informal control if possible, trade with rule when necessary." More important, imperialism was discussed as a mode of collaborating with indigenous elites to the mutual benefit of the two, thereby making nationalism, in Robinson's words, "the continuation of imperialism by other means." This perspective of the Cambridge school of historiography was pushed in new directions by historians such as Anil Seal who demonstrated that "colonial nationalism" emerged from the gradual disillusion of the indigenous elite with their foreign collaborators. Other historians (J.F.A. Ajayi, for instance) focused on the continuities rather than the disjunctures of colonial rule, to demonstrate that imperialism was merely one of several similar historical episodes.

Contrary to leftist-nationalist histories of imperialism that emphasized the drain of wealth from the colonies, this historiography argued that imperialism, far from distorting capitalist development in various parts of the world, in fact became part of a process that was already under way in the colonies. Finally, the Cambridge school of historiography highlighted the strategic and pragmatic reasons for "decolonization" thereby denying the role of nationalist movements in the liberation of colonies, and in the process, effacing the effects of colonialism itself.

In the 1960s, the experience of Latin American underdevelopment prompted a fresh emphasis by André Gunder Frank, among others, on the economic basis of imperialism, one that understood capitalism as "a world system" that developed the European metropolis at the expense of "peripheral" Third World economies. European history was reinterpreted from this perspective by Immanuel Wallerstein, and in turn encouraged a range of historical investigations, particularly of the erstwhile colonies, which explored the effects of a capitalist world system on the "peripheries."

Without minimizing or ignoring the material basis and consequences of imperialism on colonies, a fresh focus was developed in the late 1950s, particularly by scholars from Francophone Africa, on the cultural and psychological effects of imperialism, which has influenced historical writing. Frantz Fanon used Marxist insights to discuss the psychological domination of the colonized mind, and analyzed the process by which the colonized peoples' consciousness of their history and culture was destroyed by imperialism. Fanon and others such as Amilcar Cabral argued that this produced contradictory consequences, often causing the colonized person to identify with colonial stereotypes, while making a "return to the source" the only viable response in the struggle against cultural domination. Within the domain of psychology, there have also been attempts, such as that by Ashis Nandy, to chart the complex and deleterious effects of colonization on the psyche of colonizing people themselves and the ways in which this determined forms of resistance to cultural domination. But by far the most influential recent work on the cultural aspects of imperialism has been Edward Said's *Orientalism,* which reemphasizes the ways in which imperial powers produced new knowledges of the societies they ruled with enduring material as well as ideological consequences. Said's insights have inspired a large number of recent historical projects, although many have indirectly minimized or ignored questions relating to the economics of empire.

Some recent historical studies, such as those in a collection edited by John Mackenzie, have focused on the development of an "imperial culture" within Britain itself, tracing the ways in which a sense of pride, and even a sense of responsibility, was assiduously cultivated among the British people through the construction and circulation of images of empire in a variety of popular genres such as films, fiction, painting, and the music hall tradition. Such work has emphasized that the ideological work of empire building was by no means marginal to the enterprise of empire. On the other hand, social and cultural historians have argued that the development of an imperial culture within the colonies necessarily involved the reinvention of certain symbols that evoked precolonial forms of power and authority instead of replacing them entirely, most evident in the recasting of spectacular rituals (Bernard Cohn), law, or architecture.

Europe's subjugation of and control over large areas of the world required the deployment of new technologies on a vast scale, whether in weaponry, communications, or disease control, which some scholars have seen as both accounting for, and emanating from, imperial power. The major epistemological shift engendered by imperialism was among the most long-lasting of its effects, a process by which indigenous scientific knowledges were systematically discredited and displaced in order to establish the hegemony of Western science and technology, as Michael Adas suggests. Since the nineteenth and twentieth centuries also witnessed momentous changes in the spread, identification, and control of disease resulting from the colonial encounter, the history of imperial health and medicine has assumed importance not only because of its demographic impact, but also as it led to the establishment and consolidation of European power worldwide.

An understanding of the relations of power that underwrote sexual encounters between the imperialists and the colonized people has more recently engaged historical interest. In such works as Kenneth Ballhatchet's 1980 study, sexuality becomes a critical site on which the rule of racial, and class, difference was played out, and further, a site that reveals the complicity between contending patriarchies, whether of the imperialist and nationalist kind, in controlling female sexuality, as analyzed by Susan Pedersen.

The challenges posed by feminist theories to the discipline of history have engendered fresh perspectives on the nature and impact of imperialism. Historical reconstructions of the roles played by women in the empire not only as wives and mistresses but also as missionaries, teachers, and doctors have given way to more nuanced understandings of the gendered division of labor in the imperial hierarchy that accorded specific roles to European men and women, who together constituted the face of empire in the colonies. The sexual economy of "difference" between ruler and ruled that formed the basis of imperial rule led to a range of gendered identities in the colonies; on the other hand, the links between imperialism and metropolitan feminism frequently undermined the possibility of international feminist solidarities.

The decisive shift of the mantle of global domination from western Europe to the United States, particularly in the post-1945 period, has encouraged research on the history of American imperialism. Two important historiographical strands may be distinguished. One strand, represented by J.W. Pratt, considers the American imperial effort as a brief interlude that led to the Spanish–American War of 1898 and was quickly abandoned thereafter. The other strand that has developed, under the influence of Charles Beard, in works such as those by William A. Williams, views the United States as inherently imperialist right from its origins—that is, from the conquest and settlement of North America to the cold war politics of the post-1945 phase. More recent scholarship also emphasizes the long reach of American cultural imperialism particularly in the field of contemporary mass culture.

Janaki Nair

See also FEMINISM; GENDER; IMPERIAL AND COM-
MONWEALTH HISTORY, BRITISH; INDIAN HISTO-
RIOGRAPHY—POSTCOLONIAL; MODERNIZATION
THEORY; NATIONALISM; ORIENTALISM; WORLD
SYSTEMS THEORY.

References

Adas, Michael. *Machines As the Measure of Men:
Science, Technology and the Ideologies of Western
Dominance.* Ithaca, NY: Cornell University
Press, 1989.

Ajayi, J.F.A. "The Continuity of African Institutions
under Colonialism." In *Emerging Themes of
African History,* ed. Terence Ranger. Nairobi:
East Africa Publishing House, 1968.

Arnold, David, ed. *Imperial Medicine and Indigenous Societies.* Delhi: Oxford University
Press, 1989.

Bairoch, Paul. "Historical Roots of Economic
Underdevelopment: Myths and Realities."
In *Imperialism and After: Continuities and
Discontinuities,* ed. Wolfgang J. Mommsen
and Jurgen Osterhammel. London: Allen
and Unwin, 1986, 191–216.

Ballhatchet, Kenneth. *Race, Sex and Class under
the Raj: Imperial Attitudes and Policies and
Their Critics, 1793–1905.* London:
Weidenfeld and Nicolson, 1980.

Bayly, C.A. *Rulers, Townsmen and Bazaars:
North Indian Society in the Age of British
Expansion 1770–1870.* Cambridge, Eng.:
Cambridge University Press, 1983.

Cabral, Amilcar. *Return to the Source.* New York:
Monthly Review Press, 1973.

Callaway, Helen. *Gender, Culture and Empire:
European Women in Colonial Nigeria.*
Houndmills: Macmillan Press, 1987.

Cohn, Bernard. "Representing Authority in Victorian India." In *The Invention of Tradition,*
ed. E.J. Hobsbawm and T.O. Ranger. Cambridge, Eng.: Cambridge University Press,
1989, 165–210.

Dobb, Maurice. *Studies in the Development of
Capitalism.* Revised ed. London: Routledge
and Kegan Paul, 1972.

Fanon, Frantz. *Black Skin, White Masks.* Trans.
C.L. Markmann. London: MacGibbon and
Kee, 1968.

Fieldhouse, D.K. "Imperialism: A Historiographical Revision." *Economic History Review,* Second Series 14 (1961): 187–209.

Frank, André Gunder. *Capitalism and Underdevelopment in Latin America: Historical Studies of
Chile and Brazil.* Harmondsworth: Penguin,
1971.

Gallagher, John, and Ronald Robinson. "The
Imperialism of Free Trade." *Economic History Review,* Second Series 6 (1953): 1–15.

Headrick, Daniel. *The Tools of Empire: Technology
and European Imperialism in the Nineteenth
Century.* New York: Oxford University Press,
1981.

Hobsbawm, Eric J. *The Age of Empire: 1875–
1914.* New York: Vintage, 1989.

Hobson, J.A. *Imperialism: A Study.* London:
Unwin Hyman, 1988.

Lenin, Vladimir Ilyich. *Imperialism, the Highest
Stage of Capitalism.* Moscow: Progress Publishers, 1970.

Mackenzie, John, ed. *Imperialism and Popular
Culture.* Manchester: Manchester University Press, 1986.

Nandy, Ashis. *The Intimate Enemy: Loss and Recovery of Self under Colonialism.* Delhi: Oxford University Press, 1983.

O'Brien, Patrick. "The Costs and Benefits of
British Imperialism, 1846–1914." *Past
and Present* 120 (1988): 163–200.

Pedersen, Susan. "National Bodies, Unspeakable Acts:
The Sexual Politics of Colonial Policy Making."
Journal of Modern History 63 (1991), 647–680.

Pratt, J.W. *America's Colonial Experiment: How the
US Gained, Governed, and in Part Gave Away
a Colonial Empire.* New York: Prentice-Hall,
1950.

Robinson, Ronald. "Non-European Founda-
tions of European Imperialism: Sketch for a
Theory of Collaboration." In *Studies in the
Theory of Imperialism.,* ed. R. Owen and B.
Sutcliffe. London: Longman, 1972.

Said, Edward. *Orientalism.* London: Routledge
and Kegan Paul, 1978.

Seal, Anil. *The Emergence of Indian Nationalism:
Competition and Collaboration in the Later
Nineteenth Century.* Cambridge, Eng.:
Cambridge University Press, 1971.

Stoler, Ann. "Sexual Affronts and Racial Fron-
tiers: European Identities and the Cultural
Politics of exclusion in Colonial Southeast
Asia." *Comparative Studies in Society and
History* 34 (1992): 514–551.

Trotsky, Leon. *The Struggle against Fascism in
Germany.* Harmondsworth: Penguin, 1975.

Wallerstein, Immanuel. *The Modern World System.*
Vol. II. New York: Academic Press, 1980.

Williams, William Appleman. *Empire As a Way
of Life: An Essay on the Causes and Character
of America's Present Predicament along with a
Few Thoughts about an Alternative.* New
York: Oxford University Press, 1980.

Inalcik, Halil (b. 1916)

Turkish historian. Born in Istanbul, Inalcik earned his Ph.D. in 1942 from the University of Ankara. After teaching in Ankara and at various American universities, he moved to the United States in 1972, where he became a professor at the University of Chicago until his retirement in 1986. Inalcik's extensive and wide-ranging publications, based on archival sources such as law court records *(sicillat)* and cadastral surveys *(tahrir),* brought new perspectives to Ottoman social and economic history. His work on Ottoman administration in the fifteenth and sixteenth centuries, for example, revealed the structure of the Ottoman land tenure and taxation systems; his work on Ottoman administration in the Balkans demonstrated that many Christian landowners kept their land after the Ottoman conquests. Inalcik has also played an active and important role in preserving, collecting, and publishing Ottoman documents.

Corinne Blake

Texts

The Middle East and Balkans under the Ottoman Empire. Bloomington: Indiana University Press, 1992.

The Ottoman Empire: Conquest, Organization and Economy. London: Variorum Reprints, 1978.

The Ottoman Empire: The Classical Age, 1300–1600. London: Praeger, 1973.

Studies in Ottoman Social and Economic History. London: Variorum Reprints, 1985.

References

Naff, Thomas, ed. *Paths to the Middle East: Ten Scholars Look Back.* Albany, NY: SUNY Press, 1993.

Indian Historiography—Ancient

Historical writings on the Indian subcontinent during the precolonial period. The search for histories of early India by modern scholars began in the eighteenth century. European scholars, specifically seeking histories, found it difficult to locate such texts from the Sanskrit tradition. Indian culture, and particularly the Sanskrit articulation of Indian culture, came to be defined, therefore, as ahistorical. It was stated that the only exception was the *Rājataraṅginī* of Kalhaṇa, a twelfth-century history of Kashmir, regarded as atypical in Sanskrit literature. This axiomatic statement has only recently come to be questioned. Much of the problem was that the historical concerns of early India were not the same as those of post-Enlightenment Europe.

Two terms in Sanskrit, *itihāsa* and *purāṇa* are associated either separately or conjointly with traditions relating to the past. The literal meaning of *itihāsa* is "thus it was" and has come to be used now to mean history, but earlier it was not history in any modern sense of the term. *Purāṇa* means that which belongs to ancient times and includes events and stories believed to go back to early periods. A text on political economy, the *Arthaśāstra,* provides a wide-ranging definition of *itihāsa-purāṇa.* Later, by the mid-first-millennium A.D., the name *Purāṇa* was applied to specific texts, generally linked to emerging socioreligious sects and what has been called Puranic Hinduism. *Itihāsa-Purāṇa* was regarded as a source for the tradition of the ruling clans, the *kṣatriyas.* From the perspective of the orthodox Vedic Brahmanism, it tended initially to be seen as second-order knowledge, perhaps because it did not incorporate ritual and normative texts. Doubtless this ambiguity about the importance of the *itihāsa-purāṇa* tradition also contributed to the impression that a concern with the past was alien to Indian civilization.

It has been argued that a historical tradition in early India did exist but that it was a weak tradition, its weakness being attributed to the decentralized nature of political institutions, to the role of the priestly elite in fabricating genealogies for rulers of low caste whose status could not be openly proclaimed, and to the exclusive control by scribes and *brāhmaṇas* over the transmission of the tradition and from whom a critical assessment could not be expected. The cyclical concept of time was also seen as obstructing a sense of history. But these views have little support in recent studies of ancient Indian historiography.

It would be pertinent to analyze the forms in which Indian society has chosen to record its past. This is likely to tell us more about the community that endorses these versions as perspectives on the past. Thus some predictable features of the *itihāsa-purāṇa* tradition would be the legitimization of the ruling caste in the context of caste-based society, and the transformation of pre-state systems into monarchies and of these into more complex forms. Every society has many pasts, and this is especially so in a society constituted of multiple social segments. The records of these many pasts would be varied and a comparative analysis of variant forms might further clarify the perceptions of the past.

Such perceptions were in part embedded within the larger structure of texts with other functions and therefore requiring to be prized out. These were origin myths, compositions in praise of heroes, or narratives interspersed in what are said to be the genealogies of ancient descent groups. In as much as myths and legends encapsulate social assumptions, they are significant to the recollection of the past. Other texts had a more externalized historical form in that they were biographies of rulers and those in authority, or were chronicles available both as texts and inscriptions, and written in a recognizable format. These more familiar forms of historical records seem to coincide with the strengthening of the monarchical state as the ultimate form of political authority and high culture.

The embedded forms tend to be scattered. The earliest are the *dāna-stutis* of the *Ṛgveda,* hymns in praise of gift-giving where the more generous heroes were lauded as model patrons, providing evidence of their identity to later generations. The *ākhyānas,* often recited as part of the elaborate sacrificial rituals, are narratives of ancient heroes. Their inclusion in the sacrificial ritual gave them greater credence as well as ensuring continuity. Some of these narratives were modified, elaborated upon, and reconstructed to suit the requirements of later times. Not least of these are the variants as found in the epics, the *Mahābhārata* and the *Rāmāyaṇa.* Variant versions introduce new features into the story, for the appeal to the past can also be to fix a precedent for action in the present.

The keepers of the tradition, originally oral, were the *sūta* and the *māgadha,* the poets and bards, whose status was gradually lowered when priestly *brāhmaṇas* began taking over the tradition. Records at the royal courts were maintained, it is said, by scribes and others. Structuring the past was recognized as a source of power. Thus the encapsulation of the past drew on the varied genealogical patterns in the early *Purāṇas,* but also reformulated this material. The bifurcation of the bard and the *brāhmaṇa* created a parallel tradition that continues to this day. The bards maintain the genealogies of tribal chiefs and the lesser aristocracy. In the absence of royal courts, the patrons of the *brāhmaṇas* are the dominant castes.

The perception of the past from the Puranic perspective can perhaps be best illustrated by reference to the chapter on succession, the *vaṃśānucarita* of the *Viṣṇu Purāṇa,* dated to the mid-first-millennium A.D. (The term *vaṃśa* literally refers to the bamboo plant, appropriate to a genealogy, as each segment grows out of a node.) The initial section, relating the story of the various Manus who ruled in remote antiquity, is mythological and is associated with enormous cycles of time. In one of these cycles there occurs the Flood, which also acts as a time marker. The ruling Manu

is saved in the fashion of the Mesopotamian version. He becomes the progenitor of the descent groups to which the various heroes of the ruling clans belong. His eldest son is the ancestor of the Sūryavaṃśa or Solar lineage and the younger, androgynous child is ancestress to the Candravaṃsa or Lunar lineage. The symbolism is replete with many layers of meaning. Interestingly, the *Rāmāyaṇa* and *Mahābhārata* are narratives of the last few generations of these lineages. In the succession of heroes and ruling clans, reckoning is by generations and therefore time is linear although within the framework of the overall cyclic ages—the *yugas.* Social relations take different patterns suggesting that these were being registered and were important to the way in which the past was seen. The function of genealogies was as a source of presumed identity. The second time marker was the great war described in the *Mahābhārata* in which nearly all the clans are said to participate and meet their end. It is as the texts say, the end of the age of the *kṣatriya* heroes.

Subsequent to this, the text changes from the past to the future tense and claims to be predicting the events that are described. Lineages give way to dynasties, and generalized time reckoning by generation gives way to regnal years. Most of the dynasties, historically attested to from other sources, are known to have ruled from about the fourth century B.C. to the fourth century A.D. This is a very different past from that of the heroes, for now royal families rule monarchical states. It is emphasized that this is the age of the upstart, low-caste families and foreign "degenerate" *kṣatriyas.* It is in some ways quite remarkable that through the idiom of genealogical patterns there is so much that relates to how the past was perceived.

Another category of texts grew out of the courtly ambiance and looked briefly back at the past. These are biographies of kings, which become a significant genre of literature in the period after the seventh century A.D. and interestingly after the termination of the Puranic genealogies. The seminal forms of royal biographies are to be found in earlier official inscriptions. The first historical biography, reflective of this new genre, was Bāṇabhaṭṭa's *Harṣacarita,* in the seventh century. A spate of biographies were written from the tenth to the thirteenth centuries, among them Vākpatirāja's *Gauḍavaho,* Bilhaṇa's *Vikramāṅkadevacarita,* and Sandhyākaranandin's *Rāmacarita.* Occasionally the biography was of a minister, such as the *Kīrtikaumudī.*

The biographies were generally contemporary with the rulers, but each carried a sketch of the dynasty and then proceeded to record the important events of the patron's life. A brief history of the author's family provided the appropriate credentials. Although couched in the literary style of court poetry and referred to as *kāvyas,* indulging in poetic license, nevertheless the biography often centered on actual events crucial to the political authority of the patron, such as Harṣa establishing himself as the king of Kannauj in the *Harṣacarita* or the Pāla king defeating the Kaivarta revolt in the *Rāmacarita.* Contested succession occasionally required legitimization through supernatural intervention, and the biography justified the patron's right to rule.

This was also the period that saw the composition of a large number of *vaṃśāvalis* or chronicles of ruling families. The *vaṃśāvali* is literally the path to succession. These can be narratives of a dynasty, maintained by a family of court poets, or else in summary form, where they often occur as royal inscriptions. The chronicles are charters of validation of the family and of the region constituting the kingdom. Inscriptions came to be engraved after the family had established itself; such inscriptions, being official statements, were regarded as a mark of authority, were precisely dated in regnal years (or in one of the many current eras), and drew to some extent on the archives said to be maintained at the court. An example of this would be the Dhaṅga inscription of the Candella dynasty composed in the tenth century A.D. It briefly mentions the previous seven rulers and their contribution to establishing the dynasty. The ruling king's father is eulogized as is the king himself who was the patron of the temple where the inscription is located. Temples when built and endowed by royalty or by the elite, were symbols of power and frequently the location of inscriptions. Families of obscure origin such as the Candellas required origin myths invoking divine connections. Status was recognized when a marriage alliance with an established *kṣatriya* family was mentioned. Campaigns and battles are referred to, as are generous endowments to *brāhmaṇas,* gifts that ensured the fabrication of genealogies for such ruling families, frequently linking them to the earlier Solar or Lunar line and endorsing the origin myth. Occasionally there are other documents from other ruling families or even from the popular tradition of oral epics that do not endorse the official version of events as related in inscriptions or in the chronicles of a particular dynasty. These are in effect debates between factions about the identity and authority of those in power.

The longer *vaṃśāvalis,* or chronicles, maintained by bards and court poets often set the history of the dynasty in the context of the region. These were written in various parts of the subcontinent—Nepal (for example, the *Gopālarāja-vaṃśāvali),* Kashmir (the *Rājataraṅgiṇī* and its sequels), Chamba, Gujerat, Sind, Malabar (the *Mūṣakavaṃśa* of Atula on the Ay kingdom), Assam (the *buranjis*), to mention just a few—and many were strikingly similar in format and purpose. The compositions as we have them date to the early second millennium A.D. but obviously they drew on earlier sources, both oral and written. The chronicle of the kingdom of Chamba in the northern Himalayas weaves a narrative from which it is possible to observe the gradual transformation of clan territories into a kingdom. Early rulers are linked to the heroes of the Puranic genealogies, providing the appropriate status. Connections with the neighboring kingdom of Kashmir introduce the ancestors of later ruling families. The genealogy of rulers appears to be a seamless construction but in effect there are major changes recorded in variant family names and the locating of families in a dispersed geography. The expansion moves from a small, high valley to a larger valley to a bigger territory. The descendants of lesser chiefs begin to take royal titles indicative of a change in the nature of authority. A capital is established as the royal center. Roving religious teachers and ascetics of earlier times yield place to recognized Vaiṣṇava religious sects, and temples adorn the capital. At this point marriage alliances become important to status, and there is also much mention of campaigns and endowments. The chronicles become parallel statements to the inscriptions.

Kalhaṇa's *Rājataraṅgiṇī* is the most sophisticated and consciously historical of such chronicles. This is largely because of the author's awareness of the need to use, after critical examination, a variety of sources on the past, which he lists as the statements of earlier kings, inscriptions, coins, texts pertaining to the history of religious centers—the *mahātmyas,* and texts with other information, as well as the oral tradition remembered by his peers. This chronicle is quite extraordinary in its detail and its perception of the importance of history.

The *itihāsa-purāṇa* tradition, in its various forms and written in Sanskrit, came to constitute the core of one kind of historical thinking. There were other traditions reflecting a historical consciousness but taking a different form. One example was that of the Buddhist monastic chronicles from Sri Lanka, written in Pāli. Drawing on various oral traditions and focusing on the history of the *saṅgha* (the Buddhist Order) or of a *vihāra* (monastery), they inevitably included a substantial segment of secular history where it impinged on that of the religious institution. Thus the first two chronicles from Sri Lanka, the *Dīpavaṃsa* and the *Mahāvaṃsa,* were both composed in the mid-first-millennium A.D. but included events from an earlier period, some of which doubtless came through the oral tradition. They are written as histories of Sri Lanka, which it is stated is predestined for the coming of Buddhism and, in the case of the *Mahāvaṃsa,* the history of the Mahāvihāra monastery is intertwined with that of the Sri Lankan kingdom. There is some borrowing from the *itihāsa-purāṇa* tradition, since early Sri Lankan history is tied into early Indian history.

Similar to the focus of Buddhist historical narrative but more influenced in style by the court literature in Sanskrit, were the texts of the Jainas. These were mainly narrations of the biographies of their teachers and of their royal patrons, where either the latter were introduced to ensure historicity for the former, or else the narrative was a perception of historical events from the Jaina perspective. This activity coincides with the ascendancy of Jainism in western India, starting with the ninth century *Ādi Purāṇa* and becoming established in the twelfth to the fourteenth centuries with works such as Hemacandra's *Pariśiṣṭaparvan,* Merutuṅga's *Prabandhacintāmaṇi,* and the *Prabhāvakacarita* of Prabhācandra.

Monasteries, as the institutional centers for preserving the Buddhist and Jaina historical tradition, maintained chronicles of monastic and sectarian activities. These texts have been said to carry a more evident historical perspective which differs from the *itihāsa-purāṇa* tradition. Among the reasons for this would be the historicity of the founders, the breaking away from what has been regarded as orthodoxy and orthopraxy, and the importance of an eschatology more conducive to a historical worldview. History supported the mission of the founders. Equally significant was the social background of the patrons of these sects and the urban and literate milieu of the early teaching. With the institutionalization of the sects as orders, the need developed to maintain versions of sectarian conflicts among these orders, as well as their property relations and the interplay between religious orders and political power.

Common to all these traditions was a broad-based eschatology bounded by the immense cycle of time—the *mahāyuga*—with utopian conditions at its start, gradually declining toward its end. Within the cycle, the constituents of history observed a linear form. The dichotomy between cyclical and linear is not very apposite since the two, and possibly other intervening forms, coexisted. The decline was ultimately stemmed by the coming of a messianic or a millenarian figure and although a new cycle was initiated, it is not visualized as merely a repetition of the present cycle. The immensity of the cycle did not require a further eschatology.

The arrival of the Arabs, Turks, Afghans, and Mughals did not bring to a close the importance of the *itihāsa-purāṇa* tradition. Although no longer dominant at the capitals of the major kingdoms, it was still fostered in those where legitimization from the past was culled from earlier historical traditions. The introduction of European concepts of historical writing marked the termination of earlier traditions.

Romila Thapar

See also INDIAN HISTORIOGRAPHY—COLONIAL PERIOD; MARĀṬHĀ HISTORIOGRAPHY; NEPALI HISTORIOGRAPHY; SINHALESE HISTORIOGRAPHY; TIME.

References

Pathak, V.S. *Ancient Historians of India.* Bombay: Asia Publishing House, 1966.

Philips, C.H., ed. *Historians of India, Pakistan and Ceylon.* London: Oxford University Press, 1961.

Thapar, Romila. "Genealogical Patterns As Perceptions of the Past." *Studies in History* 7 (1991): 1–36.

———. *Interpreting Early India.* New Delhi: Oxford University Press, 1993.

———. *Time as a Metaphor of History: Early India.* New Delhi: Oxford University Press, 1996.

Warder, A.K. *An Introduction to Indian Historiography.* Bombay: Popular Prakashan, 1972.

Indian Historiography—Colonial Period

Contemporary and later writing about the history of South Asia during the period of British rule, ca. 1800–1947. The first historians of colonial India were scholar-officials, servants of the English East India Company and later of the crown, who found time outside their administrative work to explore the origins and growth of Britain's Oriental empire. James Mill, author of *The History of British India* (1818), perhaps the earliest of the genre, was chief examiner of correspondence at the company's headquarters in London; Sir Alfred Lyall, author of *The Rise and Expansion of the*

British Dominion in India (1893), was successively resident in Rajputana and foreign secretary of the government of India. Thus they were able to cite and quote from archival sources then closed to the public. Yet this freedom was compromised by their official ties and by a natural desire to justify the imperial system, which had given them employment. Indeed, the general tenor of this school of writing became, if anything, more hyperbolic as the twentieth-century progressed: as one can see by comparing Vincent A. Smith (1919) with H.G. Rawlinson's *British Achievement in India* (1948). Under threat, the raj called up history to offer moral support.

Yet the British did not have this propaganda game all to themselves. As the discipline of history in the Western mode became established in the subcontinent's schools and universities, nationalistic-minded Indians too found ammunition in history for their cause. Between 1901 and 1903, a retired Indian Civil Service officer, Romesh Chandra Dutt, published his *Economic History of India,* a work which can be said to have founded the serious study of the evolution of the Indian economy under colonialism. This was followed, after some indifferent efforts in the 1920s and 1930s, by Jawaharlal Nehru's *The Discovery of India* (1944), written in Alipore jail, and by A.R. Desai's Marxist expose, *Social Background of Indian Nationalism* (1948). In this counterhistoriography, the raj was represented as an essentially malign force, exploitative, oppressive, and resistant to change. However the main focus here was on Indian agency, on Indians making their own history independently of government; and particularly on the metanarrative of the "freedom struggle."

Down to the transfer of power in 1947, therefore, the historiography of colonial India remained to a large extent the monopoly of insiders with an axe to grind. And this tendency persisted even into the early postcolonial era, fueled by patronage from the newly established Congress government in New Delhi that in 1952 set up a board to oversee the writing of a series of "official" history texts. Indeed the last of the British "official" histories, ex-Reforms Commissioner H.V. Hodson's account of partition, *The Great Divide,* appeared as late as 1969. True, Indian history by this stage had begun to find a place in the halls of academe, particularly in India itself. But the lack of archival sources and the sense that the colonial period was too recent and the memories too fresh to allow for objective judgment, constrained the amount of professional writing on modern (as opposed to ancient and "medieval") themes. Moreover the output was uneven. Most overseas work produced during this time, such as C.H. Philips's *The East India Company 1784–1834* (1940) dealt with the foundations of British power rather than with the high noon of colonialism in the late nineteenth century; and where scholars did engage with the latter period, they rarely moved outside the existing conceptual frameworks. Thus, studies of British policy and ideology, while increasingly well documented and philosophically sophisticated— Eric Stokes's *English Utilitarians and India* (1959) being in this respect, a landmark—remained anchored at the level of high officialdom and of all India. Similarly, studies of nationalism continued to focus on elite leaders like Gandhi. What is more, there was a strong sense of positivism about this writing—Marxist-influenced works, such as B.B. Misra's *The Indian Middle Classes: Their Growth in Modern Times* (1961), not excepted. There was a consensus that the story of colonialism was one of (albeit harsh) transformation by means of British governmental power.

In the 1960s, however, this picture changed dramatically as the U.S. cold war–inspired "area studies" programs on Asia began to bear fruit, and South Asian studies spread to places like Australasia and Canada. As of 1960, less than a hundred scholarly monographs had been published on colonial India; over the next two decades over five hundred appeared, as well as a clutch of new scholarly journals devoted largely to this field, such as the *Indian Economic and Social History Review* (1963), *Modern Asian Studies* (1967), and *South Asia* (1971). But the core of this "industrial revolution," as it has been called, was an eruption of new ways of thinking about colonial India. First, borrowing from the fieldwork studies of anthropologists and political scientists, historians started to dig downward, a shift exemplified by R.E. Frykenberg's *Guntur District* (1965). Second, South Asian economic historians discovered the technique of quantification and utilized it to produce detailed studies of demographic and economic change under colonialism, as in Dharma Kumar's *Land and Caste in South India* (1965). Third, scholars in Cambridge associated with John Gallagher and Anil Seal applied Namierite statistical methods and Pareto's theory of "elite circulation" to the study of the nationalist movement and its relations with the government, most ambitiously in Seal's *Emergence of Indian Nationalism* (1968). In the process the metanarrative of modernization under the aegis of British rule dissolved. The raj was reenvisioned as a bumbling, parasitic institution heavily dependent on Indian "collaborators," Indian nationalism as a deeply fractured movement driven by self-interest rather than by patriotism and more interested in supplanting the raj than in destroying it.

More recent historiography has further muddied the waters. First, there was a predictable reaction. During the 1970s the "Cambridge school" came in for vehement criticism for its structuralist rigidity and for its neglect of ideas, while the quantifiers were attacked both for getting the figures wrong and for placing too much faith in statistics. Then came a push, initially from Marxist historians but later from scholars influenced by Antonio Gramsci and E.P. Thompson, for a new kind of Indian history "from below" which would give recognition both to the autonomy of "subaltern" groups and to their capacity, in resisting the domination of elites, to shape the course of events. The most conspicuous outcomes of this initiative have been the *Subaltern Studies* edited by Ranajit Guha, the first of which appeared in 1982. But a notable precursor was the symposium edited by D.A. Low, *Congress and the Raj* (1977), in which contributors drew upon Eric Wolf's theory of "middle" peasant militancy to construct a convincing explanation of why Congress was able, in the 1930s, to capture the countryside. Since then, the field of enquiry has widened to include other neglected areas: domestic life, particularly as it affected women, as in Meredith Borthwick's *The Changing Role of Women in Bengal* (1984); Hindu–Muslim conflict, as in Sandria Freitag's *Collective Action and Community* (1989); public health and disease, as in David Arnold's *Colonizing the Body* (1993); and the impact of Western aesthetics on Indian culture, as in Partha Mitter's *Art and Nationalism in Colonial India* (1994). However the price of all this enrichment has been a loss of coherence. The story of colonial India has been so deconstructed as to be no longer easily capable of narrative treatment, at least within the old overarching frameworks. The time is ripe for a new synthesis.

Ian Copland

See also IMPERIALISM; INDIAN HISTORIOGRAPHY—ANCIENT; INDIAN HISTORIOGRAPHY—POST-COLONIAL.

Texts

Borthwick, Meredith. *The Changing Role of Women in Bengal, 1849–1905*. Princeton, NJ: Princeton University Press, 1984.

Desai, A.R. *Social Background of Indian Nationalism*. Bombay: Popular Book Depot, 1960.

Freitag, Sandria B. *Collective Action and Community: Public Arenas and the Emergence of Communalism in North India*. Berkeley: University of California Press, 1989.

Frykenberg, Robert Eric. *Guntur District 1788–1848: A History of Local Influence and Central Authority in South India*. Oxford: Clarendon Press, 1965.

Guha, Ranajit, ed. *Subaltern Studies Vol. 1*. Delhi: Oxford University Press, 1982.

Hodson, H.V. *The Great Divide: Britain, India, Pakistan*. London: Hutchinson, 1969.

Kumar, Dharma. *Land and Caste in South India: Agricultural Labour in the Madras Presidency during the Nineteenth Century*. Cambridge, Eng.: Cambridge University Press, 1965.

Low, D.A., ed. *Congress and the Raj: Facets of the Indian Struggle, 1917–47*. London: Heinemann, 1977.

Lyall, Sir Alfred Comyne. *The Rise and Expansion of the British Dominion in India*. Fifth ed. London: John Murray, 1911.

Mill, James. *The History of British India* (abrid., in one volume). Ed. William Thomas. Chicago: Chicago University Press, 1975.

Misra, B.B. *The Indian Middle Classes: Their Growth in Modern Times*. London: Oxford University Press, 1961.

Mitter, Partha. *Art and Nationalism in Colonial India, 1850–1922*. Cambridge, Eng.: Cambridge University Press, 1994.

Nehru, Jawaharlal. *The Discovery of India*. Ed. R.I. Crane. Garden City, NY: Anchor Books, 1960.

Philips, C.H. *The East India Company, 1784–1834*. Delhi: Oxford University Press, 1961.

Seal, Anil. *The Emergence of Indian Nationalism: Competition and Collaboration in the Later Nineteenth Century*. Cambridge, Eng.: Cambridge University Press, 1968.

Stokes, Eric. *The English Utilitarians and India*. Oxford: Clarendon Press, 1959.

References

Bayly, C.A. "English Language Historiography on British Expansion and Indian Reactions since 1940." In *Reappraisals in Overseas History*, ed. P.C. Emmer and H.L. Wesseling. Leiden, Netherlands: E.J. Brill, 1979, 21–53.

Guha, Ranajit. *An Indian Historiography of India: A Nineteenth Century Agenda and Its Implications*. Calcutta: K.P. Bagchi, 1988.

Philips, C.H., ed. *Historians of India, Pakistan and Ceylon*. London: Oxford University Press, 1961.

Ray, Sibnarayan. "India: After Independence (Contemporary Indian Historiography)." *The Journal of Contemporary History* 2 (1967): 125–140.

Spodek, Howard. "Pluralist Politics in Modern India: The Cambridge Cluster of Historians of Modern India." *American Historical Review* 84 (1979): 688–707.

Indian Historiography—Postcolonial

Historical writings about the Indian subcontinent written after the achievement of independence in 1947. The term loosely covers a range of historians who have published mainly from the 1980s and who have been influenced by contemporary intellectual debate.

The phase "postcolonial" can be used to indicate a locus in time for the historian, or a philosophical position informing the historian's text. It may be presented as a matter of location: the author (and the subject?) exist in, and are defined by, position in a historical time that is after or following colonialism. By extension the historian is one who bears the marks of that colonialism and is constructed by it—even if merely by inhabiting a space free from colonialism. Alternatively, postcolonial historiography constitutes a critique of the colonial/Enlightenment project of European imperialism prior to the mid-twentieth century, and becomes in itself a counterdiscourse to the "civilizing" values of modernity and to the liberal humanist discourse of western Europe. In practice both strands often interweave—even within the same text—so the distinction becomes blurred. In theory, however, their implications diverge. The first implies a relationship with the imperial center in that it accepts the imperium as *post facto* arbiter of significance; the second denies such relevance by establishing not merely noncolonial agency in the past, or many such agencies, but equally the existence of counternarratives and countersignifications. There is no clear pattern as to how postcolonial historians approach the inherent issues, since the terminology necessarily contains within itself an element of diffuseness and ambiguity.

Intimations of the postcolonial historiographical project insofar as India is concerned appeared after independence in 1947 in writings on the nationalist movement and the mass campaigns prominently guided by Mohandas Gandhi ("the Mahatma"). They presented the autonomy of Indian action and privileged Indian identity in contradistinction to the pervasive presence of the imperium. The approach was subsequently attacked by the "subalterns," a group of Indian, British, and Australian historians led by Ranajit Guha, who was based at the Australian National University. Guha argued that such nationalist stories denied the agency of suppressed groups within Indian society, denied their voice in resisting domination, and privileged elites rather than the suppressed. Deriving inspiration from Karl Marx's reference to subalterns marching down through history as refracted through Antonio Gramsci's notions of hegemony, the group has published nine volumes of papers under the continuing title of *Subaltern Studies*. From the first volume in 1982 the emphasis has been upon relationships of subordination and resistance, not on categories determined by modes of production. The volumes presented case studies of tribes (or tribals as they are known in India), peasants, agricultural workers, urban working-class laborers—all in situations of conflict and resistance; other papers delineated populist perceptions of Mahatma Gandhi or traced the *mentalité* of tribals in relation to alcohol or peasants caught in famine. Though not unique among their contemporary historians in the focus on underclasses and resistance, the subaltern group most prominently gave voice to people hitherto denied agency, and in doing so reflected the radical intellectual concerns of the late 1960s and 1970s. In consequence of the underlying political agenda the early papers tended to reify the subaltern as a category rather than as individual(s).

The theoretical basis of the subaltern enterprise was posed by Guha in the first volume, and further implications were examined in detail by Partha Chatterjee while others like Gyanendra Pandey, Shahid Amin, David Hardiman, Dipesh Chakrabarty, and David Arnold developed the methodology in their topical accounts. The inclusion in the fourth volume (1985) of Bernard S. Cohn and Gayatri Spivak from American academia signaled changes in orientation. Cohn's focus on the formation of knowledge and the imposition of language under the British raj reaffirmed the structure of relationships under colonial rule. Spivak brought to the group a rigorous analytic derived from her familiarity with Jacques Derrida and other postmodernist theorists. In reemphasizing the need to allow suppressed voices to be heard, and then withdrawing from the postulate that *only* suppressed voices should be heard, and heard without the intermediating influence of the historian, she linked the subaltern project with other writings in the postmodern mode. She also defined a location for the historian in contemporary India, a location echoed by anthropologist Veena Das in volume 6: " . . . the consciousness of ourselves as colonial subjects is itself modified by our own experience and the relation we establish to our intellectual traditions." The project, always political in underlying agenda, moved to encompass autobiography—but of the historian/author as much as the historical subject.

Other contemporaneous exercises in the postcolonial history of the subcontinent derived from the theoretical insights of poststructuralism, deconstruction, representation, and postmodernism as represented in a variety of disciplines. The paradigms presented in Roland Barthes's sign-as-symbol, Foucault's Knowledge/Power, and Lacan's "Other" guided one trend in postcolonial historiography, that of colonial subjectivities and discourse. Frantz Fanon provided an interrogation of colonialism's subordinated subject as against the autonomy of that subject. Edward Said's *Orientalism* showed how Europeans constructed knowledge to create a subordinated Asia based on polarities of "otherness"; Enlightenment criteria of rationality hence resulted in a racialized and alien Asian "other." Ronald Inden applied the approach in *Imagining India* to his analysis of the way belief systems mediated knowledge of the colonial subject, paralleling Partha Mitter's earlier (but less conceptual) treatment of visual representations of Indian otherness in *Much Maligned Monsters*. A summation of research into the Oriental discourse and its formation of knowledge about South Asia appears in Breckenridge and van der Veer's edited volume, *Orientalism and the Postcolonial Predicament*.

Other writers, led by Chicago's B.S. Cohn, critiqued notions of progress and emancipation in imperial constructions of knowledge. They include Gyan Prakash, and historian-anthropologists such as Nicholas Dirks and Arjun Appadurai. The work of Gauri Vishwanathan demonstrates a reverse trend—the impact of what happened in India on Britain—and delineates how the Enlightenment literary text masked the material purposes of colonization. On the other hand, Aijaz Ahmad uses literature, theory and political writing to interrogate the direction of such studies.

Another strand of postcolonial historiography focused not on colonial discourses of knowledge and power but on the fragmentary and multiple pasts of India and on its many suppressed voices. The most prominent and initial exponents, Homi K. Bhabha and Gayatri Spivak, did so in journal articles subsequently gathered together in equally influential volumes questioning agency in the postcolonial and postmodern. Bhabha's article

"Signs Taken for Wonders" analyzed the reception to a specific example of the discourse of colonial power/knowledge and gave primacy to that reception. Spivak noted the appearance of the Rani of Sirmur in official records only when it suited the needs of the East India Company. Later, in *Outside in the Teaching Machine* (p. 241), she highlighted the point: "When the very well-known face is brought out, remember the face that you have not seen, the face that has disappeared from view." In another brilliant essay she explored the relevance of gender to subordination and argued the subaltern could not speak, here counterpointing Lata Mani's analysis of the discourses and representations surrounding *sati* (the burning of widows) in the early nineteenth century. Mrinalini Sinha's account of Bengal later in the century examined gender stereotypes as constructions of imperial discourse and the extent of their internalization by colonized populations.

Using similar technologies Gyanendra Pandey probed the outburst of communal violence in the 1990s by focusing on colonial discourses about religious groupings to explain the internalization of communal categories in his contemporaneous situation. He was not alone. Other historians, less influenced by current theoretical discourse, but equally concerned with the outbreak of Hindu fundamentalism, have used the colonial past partly to illuminate their present. Their work appears in volumes edited by K.N. Panikkar and S. Gopal as well as in the "After Ayodhya" special issue of *South Asia*.

The issues that had surfaced in regard to subjugated identities, subordinated pasts and significance continue to produce variant solutions. Dipesh Chakrabarty has argued that a different kind of history is being created, one sensitive to pasts previously excluded, less linear and more diffuse and fragmented. Partha Chatterjee has attempted overarching interpretations and extended the theoretics needed to handle those pasts within postcolonial agendas. In *The Nation and Its Fragments,* he ambitiously sets a program that focuses on anticolonial nationalists in colonial times who in setting up their own spheres of sovereignty equally marginalized other groups.

The postcolonial historian, then, is concerned with two discourses of power, the imperium and colonial indigenous elites within that imperium, all signified by what has occurred after colonialism. Theoretics, epistemological enquiry, and a concern for the self of the historian located in a postcolonial present all conjoin to establish bodies of writings that explicate the present by using a past that is fragmented and has plurality.

Postulating alternative criteria to the European imperium and establishing India's pasts as having integrity and meaning in their own right, India's postcolonial historiography locates the historian in a present that is defined by its pasts.

Jim Masselos

See also GENDER; IMPERIALISM; INDIAN HISTORIOGRAPHY—COLONIAL PERIOD; ORIENTALISM; POSTMODERNISM.

Texts

"After Ayodhya." Special Issue of *South Asia,* New Series 17 (1994).

Ahmad, Aijaz. *In Theory: Classes, Nations, Literatures.* London and New York: Verso, 1992.

Bhabha, Homi K. "Signs Taken for Wonders: Questions of Ambivalence and Authority under a Tree Outside Delhi, May 1817." In *The Location of Culture.* London and New York: Routledge, 1994, 102–122.

Breckenridge, Carol A., and Peter van der Veer, eds. *Orientalism and the Postcolonial Predicament: Perspectives on South Asia.* Philadelphia: University of Pennsylvania Press, 1993.

Chakrabarty, Dipesh. "Postcoloniality and the Artifice of History: Who Speaks for the 'Indian' Pasts." *Representations* 37 (1992): 1–26.

Chatterjee, Partha. *Nationalist Thought and the Colonial World: A Derivative Discourse?* London: Zed Books, 1986.

Chatterjee, Partha. *The Nation and Its Fragments: Colonial and Postcolonial Histories.* Princeton, NJ: Princeton University Press, 1993.

Gopal, S., ed. *Anatomy of a Confrontation: The Babri-Masjid-Ram Janmabhoomi Issue.* New Delhi and New York: Viking, 1991.

Guha, Ranajit, ed. *Subaltern Studies I: Writings on South Asian History and Society.* Delhi: Oxford University Press, 1982.

Inden, Ronald. *Imagining India.* Oxford: Blackwell, 1990.

Mani, Lata. "Contentious Traditions: The Debate on *Sati* in Colonial India." In *Recasting Women: Essays in Colonial History,* ed. Kumkum Sangari and Sudesh Vaid. New Delhi: Kali for Women, 1989, 88–126.

Pandey, Gyanendra, ed. *Hindus and Others: The Question of Identity in India Today.* New Delhi: Viking, 1993.

Pandey, Gyanendra. *The Construction of Communalism in Colonial North India.* Delhi: Oxford University Press, 1990.

Panikkar, K.N. ed. *Communalism in India: History, Politics, and Culture.* Delhi: Manohar, 1991.

Sinha, Mrinalini. *Colonial Masculinity: The 'Manly Englishman' and the 'Effeminate Bengali' in the Late Nineteenth Century.* Manchester and New York: Manchester University Press, 1995.

Spivak, Gayatri Chakravorty. "Can the Subaltern Speak?" In *Marxism and the Interpretation of Culture,* ed. C. Nelson and L. Grossberg. Basingstoke: Macmillan, 1988, 271–313.

———. *In Other Worlds: Essays in Cultural Politics.* New York and London: Methuen, 1987.

———. *Outside in the Teaching Machine.* New York and London: Routledge, 1993.

Vishwanathan, Gauri. *Masks of Conquest: Literary Study and British Rule in India.* London: Faber and Faber, 1989.

References

Das, Veena. "Discussion: Subaltern As Perspective." In *Subaltern Studies VI: Writings on South Asian History and Society,* ed. Ranajit Guha. Delhi: Oxford University Press, 1989, 310–324.

Masselos, Jim. "The Dis/appearance of Subalterns: A Reading of a Decade of Subaltern Studies." *South Asia,* New Series 15 (1992): 105–126.

O'Hanlon, Rosalind. "Recovering the Subject: *Subaltern Studies* and Histories of Resistance in Colonial South Asia." *Modern Asian Studies* 22 (1988): 189–224.

Indigenous Historiography

The recovery of the past of indigenous peoples worldwide, through compilation and study of oral testimony, artifacts, custom and ritual, and written accounts by the peoples themselves and by observers from other cultures.

The recovery and comprehensive study of the indigenous past is a very new field. Key aspects of the endeavor are in the process of definition. Not even the United Nations has established a comprehensive list of the peoples who can claim the title "indigenous." Anthropologists, historians, and literary critics from the traditionally dominant cultures have evaluated the wide range of possible sources in different ways. The peoples themselves make preemptive claims to tell their own history and reject all but the most recent narratives from the "settler" cultures, whether by popular or academic authors.

The formal written history of "indigenous" cultures begins with the Spanish conquest of the Americas and the studies done by sixteenth-century churchmen like Fray Bernardino de Sahagún (*General History of the Things of New Spain/Florentine Codex),* the memories of soldiers like Bernal Díaz del Castillo (*The History of the Conquest of Mexico,* 1632), or of assimilated members of the subject peoples like Garcilaso de la Vega, El Inca (*Royal Commentaries of the Incas,* 1609; *General History of Peru,* 1617).

Indigenous peoples, however, have always found such written records suspect, the perspective of the dominant culture, of the conqueror. Their voice and their memory, they would explain, have been preserved in codices and oral narratives, in the customs and rituals of each community, in the contours and seasons of their traditional lands. To them the life of the peoples is continuous and communal, not broken like that of Europeans into individual lives with pasts, presents, and futures.

Twentieth-century anthropologists such as Franz Boas from the United States and Bronislaw Malinowski from Great Britain were the first to try to capture this indigenous perspective. With cameras, tape recorders, and notebooks they and their students tried to preserve what they deemed the essentials of the specific indigenous cultures they studied. Subsequent generations of anthropologists in the United States in collaboration with the leaders of indigenous groups created "ethnohistory," the melding of anthropological insights with the written records favored by historians.

The creation of the U.S. government Indian Land Claims Commission in 1946 gave impetus to this collaboration. Anthropologists, historians, and tribal leaders worked to validate legal rights to ancestral territories based on indigenous oral narrative and tribal custom with the extant written sources. This legal use of a variety of sources and disciplines has continued into the 1990s, particularly in Southeast Asia and Amazonia where no treaties exist and where indigenous land claims have again been threatened or ignored.

The result of these collaborations is a rich array of histories: reference works such as the Smithsonian multivolume *Handbook of North and American Indians* and Alvin Josephy's *The Indian Heritage of America* (1991 ed.); narratives of conquest and resistance by indigenous historians, like Vine Deloria Jr. (*Custer Died for Your Sins,* 1970) and nonindigenous scholars such as Angie Debo (*And Still the Waters Run,* 1966), Francis Paul Prucha (*The Great Father: The United States Government and the American Indians,* 1984),

and John Hemming (*Amazon Frontier: The Defeat of the Brazilian Indians,* 1987); and specialized studies such as Inga Clendinnen's *Aztecs: An Interpretation* (1991). All to some extent or another utilize history, anthropology, and archaeology to recover the indigenous history of the Americas.

The written history of indigenous peoples has always had a political component, either to justify subordination when written by representatives from the "settler" cultures, or more recently to chronicle and justify resistance. Recent acknowledgment and study of these political uses has added new dimensions to the field. For example, North American literary critics like Brian Swann and Arnold Krupat, have set new standards for the reading and use of indigenous autobiographies. They have studied the interplay between cultures evident in the "telling" of one's own life but in a manner acceptable to the dominant culture. Others have been encouraged to find a wider range of voices like Roger Moody in *The Indigenous Voice* (2 vols., 1988), or to preserve the original voice more exactly. In *Life Lived Like a Story: Life Stories of Three Yukon Elders* (1990), Julie Cruikshank gives some stories printed so as to convey the oral rhythms and pauses of the indigenous languages. Marjorie Shostak, in *Nisa, the Life and Words of a !Kung Woman* (1981), arranged the interviews into a continuous narrative, but also oversaw the making of a film in which Nisa spoke for herself.

The writings of anthropologists like Clifford Geertz (*Interpretation of Cultures,* 1973) and James Clifford and George E. Marcus (*Writing Culture: The Poetics and Politics of Ethnography,* 1986) have made scholars more aware of the significance of perspective in writings about "the other." Even an observer is in fact a participant. Cultures construct historical memory in different ways and for different purposes. This has led to yet another group of studies, of the first encounters between indigenous and European cultures. For example, Marshall Sahlins in his essays on the Pacific Islands (*Islands of History,* 1985), used indigenous traditional beliefs, oral memory, and the full range of European sources to demonstrate the effects of different cultural and social structures on encounters between peoples and on the construction and uses of the memory of those encounters.

The critical approach of "Subaltern Studies," the avowedly political history formulated by a group of South Asian scholars led by Ranajit Guha of India, offers new techniques for the reconstruction and translation of the combination of indigenous memory and European records into history. Subaltern Studies both validate indigenous skepticism of previous written histories and provide methods for analyzing these sources from dominant cultures in unorthodox ways. These historians, like North American indigenous activists, see history as power—yet another means by which the conquered have been made inferior, silenced, and denied agency. Subaltern Studies popularized the concept of "reading against the grain," that is, reading traditional sources in new ways for what they do not say as well as what they do say. For example, Annie E. Coombes in *Reinventing Africa: Museums, Material Culture and Popular Imagination in Late Victorian and Edwardian England* (1994) and Elizabeth Edwards in *Anthropology and Photography, 1860–1920* (1992) take apart the information collected about indigenous and other subjugated peoples to demonstrate that these artifacts tell as much about the collectors as they do about the people from whom they were collected.

Judith P. Zinsser

See also ANTHROPOLOGY AND HISTORY; ETHNOHISTORY; ORAL HISTORY; ORAL TRADITION.

References

Clifford, James. *The Predicament of Culture.* Cambridge, MA: Harvard University Press, 1986.

Krupat, Arnold. *For Those Who Came After: A Study of North American Autobiography.* Berkeley: University of California Press, 1985.

Prakash, Gyan, Florencia E. Mallon, and Frederick Cooper. "AHR Forum on Subaltern Studies." *American Historical Review* 99 (1994): 1475–1546.

Schwartz, Stuart B., ed. *Implicit Understandings: Observing, Reporting, and Reflecting on the Encounters between Europeans and Other Peoples in the Early Modern Era.* New York: Cambridge University Press, 1994.

Indonesian Historiography—Modern

The builders of Indonesian national identity in the twentieth century were heirs to a diversity of literary and historiographical traditions. Indian, Persian, and Islamic elements had been adapted into verse epics, genealogies, chronicles, and court diaries in the Malay, Javanese, Balinese, Sundanese, Bugis, Makassar, Aceh, and Minangkabau languages, while many other peoples had handed down oral traditions of considerable depth. For

the Dutch-created urban intellectuals who created modern Indonesian historiography, however, Dutch histories of the Netherlands East Indies had been a more influential model. In Dutch schools of the period 1910–1940 they had discovered the splendors of the Hindu–Buddhist kingdoms of Java and Sumatra, while subsequent history had chiefly been about the rise of Dutch power over the whole archipelago. By turning the perspective of colonial writers like Frederik Wilhelm Stapel, Willemine Fruin-Mees, and Nicolaas Johannes Krom upside down, they developed a modern historiography that took the national unity of Indonesia as its endpoint.

Muhammad Yamin (1903–1962), a lawyer from Minangkabau (Central Sumatra) who spent his adult life in Java, was the most enterprising of the early nationalist amateur historians. In the early 1920s he had written enthusiastically about Malay and Sumatran history, but by 1928 had moved, like many of his contemporaries, to an Indonesian national perspective, which accepted the central position of Java. He was secretary of the 1928 Indonesian Youth Congress, which issued the celebrated declaration: "Indonesia: one people [race], one language, one motherland." Yamin not only gave the keynote speech to this assembly, but also wrote a historical play performed for delegates on the manner in which a Javanese peasant, Ken Arok, had been able to rise to become king and unify Java. During the Japanese occupation he produced further books about Javanese heroes—the fourteenth century chancellor of Majapahit, Gajah Mada, *Hero of Archipelago Unity,* and the leader of the anti-Dutch rebellion of the 1820s, Diponegoro, *Hero of Indonesian Independence.* A 1951 book, *Six Thousand Years of the Red-White Flag,* traced the unity of Indonesia back to prehistoric times, while his most scholarly work (published posthumously in 1962) was a three-volume study of the government of precolonial Majapahit.

As minister of information in the Guided Democracy period of President Sukarno, Yamin was in a good position to popularize his perception of national history. He had a powerful ally in the president himself, moreover, for Sukarno had spent a period of his youth teaching history in a private nationalist school and was always convinced of the power of historical imagery to inspire nationalist commitment. By 1930, Sukarno had developed his influential trichotomy—"glorious past; dark present; glittering future." During the dark colonial present, chief attention was given by the nationalists to the colonial causes of economic stagnation and exploitation, and to the series of "rebels" whom colonial textbooks had portrayed as the last obstacles to the rise of Dutch power. By the 1940s the anti-Dutch leaders of the final stages of the three great colonial wars of the nineteenth century—Pangeran Diponegoro in Java, Tuanku Imam Bonjol in Minangkabau, and Teuku Umar in Aceh—had become established as the three principal heroes of nationalist struggle, recognized everywhere in the street names that replaced Dutch names.

The Japanese occupation of Indonesia (1942–1945) was brief but critical. Dutch books and usages were banned with an immediacy the nationalists themselves could not have contemplated, and new histories in the national language—Bahasa Indonesia, based on Malay—had to be written hurriedly. The most influential of these was the first major national history, *Sedjarah Indonesia,* by the established Sumatran author and playwright Sanusi Pane. Predominantly political in emphasis, this laid the foundation for the way national history would be taught in independent Indonesia, with roughly equal emphasis to four periods—the Hindu–Buddhist past, principally in Java before 1500; the Islamic kingdoms and conflict with the VOC (Dutch United East India Company) from about 1500 to 1800; the nineteenth century focusing on anticolonial wars and rebellions; and the rise of nationalism in the twentieth century.

The first twenty years of Indonesian independence (1945–1965) were marked by controversy and conflict in ideas as in politics. While the nationalist format was undoubtedly dominant, it was strongly challenged by Muslims who emphasized the sultanates of the sixteenth and seventeenth centuries and the Islamic modernist revival of the nineteenth century rather than Java's Hindu heritage; by Marxist writers who saw nothing worthy of emulation in Indonesia's "feudal" past; and by liberals like Soedjatmoko who sought a broadly humanist understanding of nationalism.

Since the establishment of the New Order government of President Suharto in 1966 there has been a steady consolidation of an official nationalist history for the purposes of nation building through the school system, while at the same time Indonesia's proliferating universities and research institutes harbored a growing number of professional historians who participate in many international trends of contemporary historiography.

Working in tandem with the military, the government was able to establish the nationalist concepts of the Sukarno period, suppress the rival concepts of the Marxists, and marginalize explic-

itly Muslim formulations to a religious domain where they did not challenge nationalism. The chief instruments of this pattern were the centralized national school system, a cult of officially sanctioned heroes celebrated each "Heroes' Day" (November 10), courses in the national "Pancasila" ideology for all officials and university students, and the museums and monuments built to commemorate the past.

A key figure in the development of this official history was (Brigadier General) Dr. Nugroho Notosusanto, a capable professional historian who for many years headed the military history section of the armed forces as well as teaching at the University of Indonesia. As minister of education in the 1980s he ensured not only that the obligatory history subject in all schools served the objective of national unity, but also that an additional compulsory subject, "History of National Struggle" was added in 1985—although removed ten years later after Nugroho's death. Together these two compulsory subjects represented a larger share of the primary and secondary curriculum than any other subject. Dr. Nugroho also had a hand in the design of graphic depictions in the National Monument Museum and the Armed Forces Museum of the struggle of Indonesia, defined in essentially military terms, to become a free and united nation.

The cult of heroes was institutionalized in a number of decrees by President Sukarno from 1957 to 1963, which laid down the procedure for declaring national heroes who had outstandingly resisted colonialism, served the cause of independence, or otherwise contributed to Indonesian national development, as well as the remuneration for their descendants and the manner of commemorating them. Ninety-four heroes (including twenty-three post-1945 military officers, but only nine women) were declared between 1959 and 1992, although the two communists among them were removed from the list after the change of direction in 1965 and 1966. Under President Suharto the process of lobbying for heroes to be declared has become preeminently a means of legitimizing the role of regions, ethnic groups, and other social formations within the overall nationalist format.

The professional historians who began to emerge in the 1960s were cautiously critical of this official history. Their intellectual leader was Professor Sartono Kartodirdjo (b. 1921) of Gadjah Mada University in Yogyakarta, who established an international reputation for his work on peasant revolts, and in retirement produced a sociologically informed *Pengantar Sejarah Indonesia*

Baru [Guide to Modern Indonesian History] in two volumes (1987–1993). His students, such as Taufik Abdullah (Minangkabau, Islamic, and theoretical), A.B. Lapian (maritime and early modern), Abdurrahman Surjomihardjo (intellectual) and Ibrahim Alfian (Aceh) became the most influential historians of the 1980s and 1990s.

Tension between this group of professionals and the politically connected historians in Jakarta led by Nugroho came to the surface over the preparation of a "standard" Indonesian national history intended to replace the work of foreigners and provide the basis for all teaching in schools. All the professional historians were brought into this ambitious project under the overall editorship of both Nugroho and Sartono. Disagreements had not been resolved, however, when the six volumes were rushed into print in 1977, and Professor Sartono made known his misgivings over Nugroho's high-handedness in dealing especially with the twentieth-century volumes. Nevertheless these volumes represent the most substantial collective expression of an Indonesian national history to date.

Anthony Reid

References

Reid, Anthony, and David Marr, eds. *Perceptions of the Past in Southeast Asia.* Singapore: Heinemann, 1979.

Schreiner, Klaus. *Politischer Heldenkult in Indonesien* [Political Hero-Cults in Indonesia]. Hamburg: Dietrich Reimer Verlag, 1995.

Kartodirdjo, Sartono, Marwati Djoened Poesponegoro, and Nugroho Notosusanto, eds. *Sejarah Nasional Indonesia.* 6 vols. Jakarta: Balai Pustaka, 1977.

Soedjatmoko, ed. *An Introduction to Indonesian Historiography.* Ithaca, NY: Cornell University Press, 1965.

Industrial Revolution

Usually, the first phase of British industrialization starting in the late eighteenth century, but sometimes more generally, any case of industrialization. Its precise definition, however, is persistently plastic; its cause and effects, timing and pace remain highly controversial.

French authors in the 1820s started to draw parallels between their own political revolution and Britain's "révolution industrielle," typically identifying it with the steam engine and mechanization of the cotton industry. The concept assumed greater significance, however, for German radicals such as Friedrich Engels. In 1845, he theorized that from the factories of the Industrial Revolution, which had destroyed the rural idyll of feudal England, would arise the revolutionary proletariat which would in turn overthrow capitalist society. Amplified by Marx in *Das Kapital* (1867), this concept of the Industrial Revolution as a major historical turning point only began to influence British socialists in the 1880s. Yet it was Arnold Toynbee, nonsocialist reformer and Oxford historian, who introduced the wider British public to the Industrial Revolution. In his repeatedly reissued *Lectures on the Industrial Revolution in England* (1884), Toynbee delineated a social catastrophe: "the steam engine, the spinning-jenny, the power loom" had uprooted a stable, rural population and catapulted it into the mercilessly competitive free market, with disastrous consequences—pauperism, urban squalor, and class conflict.

The first generation of professional economic historians took its cue from Toynbee's cataclysmic pessimism, enshrining it in the subject's founding textbooks. Not until the interwar period was this orthodoxy seriously challenged. Scarcely using the term "industrial revolution," J.H. Clapham's *An Economic History of Modern Britain* (1926–1938) described a more gradual, evolutionary process of change, less detrimental to working people. But the short, fast Industrial Revolution resurfaced, although this time on a vigorous tide of postwar optimism. T.S. Ashton's *Industrial Revolution* (1948) heralded a new interpretation that celebrated the origins of sustained economic growth in the late eighteenth century, a view subsequently bolstered by the groundbreaking statistics produced by Phyllis Deane and W.A. Cole in 1962. W.W. Rostow made explicit the economic historian's new mission—to demonstrate the route to global development. His *Stages of Economic Growth: A Non-Communist Manifesto* (1960) offered a model for growth, a capitalist stage theory that paralleled Marx's and pivoted on an even faster Industrial Revolution or "take-off" (only nineteen years in Britain); other countries had already followed, or could in future follow, the same path to prosperity.

While Marxist historians, such as Eric Hobsbawm and E.P. Thompson, still disputed the social costs of early industrialization with "the optimists," attention was refocused in the 1970s on the speed and timing of change. Recalculations of national income and occupational data have revived the perception of British industrialization as protracted and evolutionary, starting long before 1760, but far from complete by 1830; economic growth accelerated only gently. Dismissed is the idea of a sharp break meriting the term "industrial revolution." The case for a major discontinuity is not, however, dead. From the regional perspective, favored by proponents of protoindustrialization theory, it is contested that, for example, Lancashire, if not Britain as a whole, had experienced dramatic change by 1830.

The 1980s witnessed some radically new interpretations. E.A. Wrigley recast the Industrial Revolution as two overlapping phenomena: in the second, Britain's massive coal reserves and technologies fortuitously rescued it, ca. 1830, from the resource exhaustion implicit in its earlier, "traditional" phase of economic growth based on textiles, trade, and commercial agriculture. E.L. Jones, however, perceived modern industrialization as merely a special case of per capita ("real") growth, rare but not unique in history—a less insular perspective through which to view the Industrial Revolution.

Christine MacLeod

Texts

Ashton, T.S. *The Industrial Revolution: 1760–1830.* London: Oxford Paperbacks, 1968.

Clapham, J.H. *An Economic History of Modern Britain.* 3 vols. Cambridge, Eng.: Cambridge University Press, 1926–1938.

Deane, Phyllis, and W.A. Cole. *British Economic Growth, 1688–1959: Trends and Structure.* Second ed. Cambridge, Eng.: Cambridge University Press, 1967.

Engels, Friedrich. *The Condition of the Working Class in England.* Ed. David McLellan. Oxford: Oxford University Press, 1993.

Jones, E.L. *Growth Recurring: Economic Change in World History.* Oxford: Clarendon Press, 1988.

Marx, Karl. *Capital: A Critique of Political Economy,* volume 1, with introduction by Ernest Mandel. Trans. Ben Fowkes. Harmondsworth: Penguin, 1976.

Rostow, W.W. *The Stages of Economic Growth: A Non-Communist Manifesto.* Third ed. Cambridge, Eng.: Cambridge University Press, 1990.

Toynbee, Arnold. *Lectures on the Industrial Revolution in England.* London: Rivingtons, 1884.

Wrigley, E.A. *Continuity, Chance and Change: The Character of the Industrial Revolution in England.* Cambridge, Eng.: Cambridge University Press, 1988.

References

Cannadine, David. "The Present and the Past in the English Industrial Revolution 1880–1980." *Past and Present* 103 (1984): 131–172.

Coleman, D.C. *Myth, History, and the Industrial Revolution.* London and Rio Grande: Hambledon Press, 1992.

Innis, Harold Adams (1894–1952)

Canadian political economist, historian, and pioneer in communication studies. Innis was born on a farm near Otterville, Ontario, and educated at McMaster University, then at Toronto (B.A., 1916; M.A., 1918), and at the University of Chicago (Ph.D., 1920). He joined the department of political economy at the University of Toronto in 1920, and was its head from 1937 until his death. Innis's reputation rests primarily on his formulation of the staples thesis, an analytic method that stressed the importance of export commodities as an explanation of colonial development. In the Canadian context, the successive pursuit of such staples as fish, fur, timber, and wheat suggested that the nation "emerged not in spite of geography but because of it." Innis's interest in the technological determinants of economic change subsequently led him to more controversial reflections on the role of communications in shaping culture.

M. Brook Taylor

Texts

The Bias of Communication. Ed. P. Heyer and D. Crowley. Toronto: University of Toronto Press, 1991.

The Fur Trade in Canada: An Introduction to Canadian Economic History. Rev. ed. Toronto: University of Toronto Press, 1970.

A History of the Canadian Pacific Railway. Toronto: McClelland and Stewart, 1923.

Staples, Markets, and Cultural Change: Selected Essays of Harold Innis. Ed. D. Drache. Montreal: McGill-Queen's University Press, 1995.

References

Berger, Carl. *The Writing of Canadian History: Aspects of English-Canadian Historical Writing since 1900.* Second ed. Toronto: University of Toronto Press, 1986.

Neill, Robin. *A New Theory of Value: The Canadian Economics of H.A. Innis.* Toronto: University of Toronto Press, 1972.

Inoue Kiyoshi (b. 1913)

Japanese historian. Born in Kochi prefecture, Inoue graduated from Tokyo Imperial University with a concentration in modern Japanese history in 1936.

He was a student of the Kōza faction Marxist Hani Gorō. During the Pacific War he worked in the ministry of education, on an editorial board with a focus on the history of the Meiji Restoration (mid-nineteenth century), and on the *Gakushiin* [Peer's Academy] editorial board for a history of the Japanese imperial household. In 1946 Inoue published *Tennōsei no rekishi* [History of the Imperial System], a polemical tract critical of the emperor and the imperial system. In the postwar period he became a leading figure in academia, founder and first head of the Rekishigaku kenkyū kai (Historical Research Association). He joined the Institute for Humanistic Research at Kyoto University in 1954 and was made full professor in 1961. He was active in protests and lawsuits directed against the government regarding issues of academic freedom and the control of information. In 1951 he published *Gendai Nihon shi* [History of Modern Japan], focusing on the colonies, aggressions, and oppressive nature of the Japanese state. In 1957 he made an extensive critique of his own work, was critical of the Japanese Communist Party, and sought to promote friendship between Japan and China. He was very active in the 1950s and 1960s in campaigns for popular rights and *burakumin* issues.

James Edward Ketelaar

Texts
Tennō no sensō sekinin [The Emperor's War Responsibility]. Tokyo: Iwanami shoten, 1991.

References
Fujiwara Akira. *Ronshō gendaishi* [Essays on Modern History]. Tokyo: Chikuma Shobō, 1976.

Intellectual History
See CULTURAL HISTORY; IDEAS, HISTORY OF; KULTURGESCHICHTE.

Interdisciplinary History
Simply defined, interdisciplinary history is any study of the past that relies to some degree on the techniques and approaches of another discipline. Thus, an account of climatic patterns and their effects during the Middle Ages might depend on dendochronology, the analysis of tree rings. A discussion of political attitudes in the early American republic might draw on literary theory as a means of exploring published tracts.

One could argue that the writing of history has been interdisciplinary from its earliest days.

Herodotus was as much an anthropologist, a geographer, a student of myth, and an archaeologist as he was a historian. In the nineteenth century, as the modern historical profession coalesced, Jacob Burckhardt set a standard for combining different ways of looking at an earlier civilization that has rarely been equaled. In addition to the close reading of evidence, largely textual, that had long been the bread and butter of the historian, Burckhardt turned to art, philosophy, the sociology of the family, the elucidation of ritual, and much more in order to create a profound and nuanced understanding of his subject.

For nearly a century after the 1860 publication of Burckhardt's masterpiece, *The Civilization of the Renaissance in Italy,* there were few who followed his example. The one major area of interaction, largely because of the influence of Karl Marx, was with economics. Already significant in the late nineteenth century, thanks to the Marxists and their critics, but gathering strength and prominence between the two world wars, the application of economic analysis to history became a subfield within the profession, prompting the creation of specialized academic departments, the founding of new journals such as *The Economic History Review,* and the publication, beginning in 1941, of the multivolume *Cambridge Economic History.* Although the growing discipline of sociology also drew attention from historians, especially in response to the work of Max Weber, until World War II the chief arena of interdisciplinary research was in economic history. Its leading exponents, including Marc Bloch in France, John Clapham in Britain, Eli Heckscher in Sweden, and Charles Beard in the United States, demonstrated the significance of economic institutions and their influence on human history, and thus helped reshape our understanding of the past and of the way it has to be investigated.

During the three decades following World War II, the spectrum of interactions broadened beyond recognition. Quantitative techniques, for example, which hitherto had been the province primarily of economic historians, began to invade such disparate areas of study as politics, agriculture, and even family life. In some specialties, statistical sophistication came to be the equivalent of language mastery as a qualification for advanced research. Both in the Soviet Union and in the West, there was increased resort to computers and the high-speed functions they could perform. More generally, the openness to the theories and approaches of other disciplines set in motion a transformation of virtually every field of enquiry. Exemplary was the new attention given to demography, to psychology, and to anthropology.

The appeal of population studies and family reconstitution techniques was that they brought to descriptions of marriage, childbearing, and mortality patterns over the past five hundred years a level of precision they had previously lacked. In France, Britain, and the United States, in particular, historical demography became a major enterprise in the 1950s and 1960s, with its own scholarly organizations and publications. Among the pioneers in the field, Louis Henry and Pierre Goubert in France, E.A. Wrigley and Roger Schofield in Britain, and Ansley Coale and Etienne van de Walle in the United States used the tools of the demographer to fashion new frameworks for understanding such topics as the duration of marriages, changes in life expectancy and fertility, migration, and population growth. These findings, in turn, added important dimensions to social and economic history, and cast new light on such subjects as the youthfulness of political and artistic leaders during various periods.

The encounter with psychology was also largely a post–World War II development. Sigmund Freud himself, in studies of Moses and Leonardo da Vinci, had suggested the appropriateness of his ideas to the writing of history, but that enterprise took shape only in the work of one of his disciples, Erik H. Erikson. In controversial but widely influential biographies of Martin Luther (1962) and Mahatma Gandhi (1969), Erikson helped to launch a new field of interdisciplinary endeavor, soon to be called psychohistory. Beyond its usefulness for biographies of individuals, this approach was also applied to mass phenomena such as heresy prosecutions and fascist youth organizations. As it lost the reputation of being an unfamiliar, highly technical, and hermetic subspecialty, psychohistory, like historical demography, developed into an almost conventional weapon in the historian's armory.

A similar integration, following a widely discussed pioneering stage, took place in the application of anthropology to history. Taking their lead especially from anthropologists like Clifford Geertz and Mary Douglas, who were noted for their close examination of symbolic meanings and the coherences of traditional societies, a number of scholars found original ways of interpreting historical evidence. Even in the absence of field studies, it proved possible to illuminate anew such topics as magical beliefs, religious ritual, and gender relations. Keith Thomas's *Religion and the Decline of Magic* (1971), for instance, was but the most monumental of a succession of investigations into the nature of witchcraft, all of which were shaped by the anthropologist's nonjudgmental use of evidence and sensitivity to cultural assumptions.

The proliferation of interdisciplinary work in the 1960s and 1970s encouraged an unprecedented self-consciousness about method among historians, and served as a central inspiration for the founding of *The Journal of Interdisciplinary History* in 1970. Created explicitly to encourage these interactions, the journal helped to extend them into new areas by sponsoring conferences that explored the links between history and a wide variety of scholarly disciplines, from climatology and nutrition to religion and art. By the 1990s it had become clear that this exchange across traditional boundaries was no longer exceptional, but rather one of the defining characteristics of late-twentieth-century historical research. Thus had the profession as a whole taken on the coloration that had been foreshadowed by Herodotus and Burckhardt.

Theodore K. Rabb

See also ANTHROPOLOGY AND HISTORY; CLIOMETRICS; CULTURAL HISTORY; FAMILY HISTORY; PSYCHOHISTORY.

Texts

Thomas, Keith. *Religion and the Decline of Magic.* London: Weidenfeld, 1971.

References

Aydelotte, William O., Allan G. Bogue, and Robert William Fogel, eds. *The Dimensions of Quantitative Research in History.* Princeton, NJ: Princeton University Press, 1972.
Brown, JoAnne, and David K. van Keuren, eds. *The Estate of Social Knowledge.* Baltimore, MD: Johns Hopkins University Press, 1991.
The Journal of Interdisciplinary History. Vols. 1–. Cambridge, MA: MIT Press, 1970–.

Iorga, Nicolae (1871–1940)

Romanian historian, statesman, and educator. Nicolae Iorga was born in Botaşani and graduated from the University of Iasi. He continued his studies in Paris and at the University of Leipzig, earning his doctorate under the supervision of Karl Lamprecht in 1893. Upon returning to Romania he took up the chair of world history at the University of Bucharest, holding it from 1894 until his death nearly a half century later. Astoundingly prolific (his bibliography runs more than five hundred pages), Iorga was first nominated to the

Romanian Academy at the unprecedented age of only twenty-seven. Rising to the position of rector of the University of Bucharest in 1929, he also found the time to establish a cultural summer school in Vălenii-de-Munte and to cofound the Institute for Southeast European Studies. Elected to Parliament in 1907, Iorga joined the notorious anti-Semite A.C. Cuza to begin the National-Democratic Party. In the 1930s Iorga's political career brought him the posts of prime minister and minister of public education and worship. As a result of his conflicts with the fascist Iron Guard and his hostility toward the German domination of Romania, he was murdered in November 1940 by the Legionary Police of the Capitol. Iorga's publications covered topics in European history from the Byzantine Empire to modern Romanian foreign policy. Extremely sensitive to the fragility of the enlarged Romania created after World War I, he championed a nationalism that not only influenced his writing of history, but led him into a somewhat genteel, if no less xenophobic, antagonism toward minorities. He was, however, quite correctly cited in U.S. diplomatic dispatches as the "foremost figure in the educational and literary world of Romania."

William O. Oldson

Texts

Ed. and trans., with Septime Gorceix. *Anthologie de la littérature roumaine des origines au XXᵉ siècle* [Anthology of Romanian Literature from Its Origins to the Twentieth Century]. Paris: Delagrave, 1920.

Brève histoire des croisades: Et de leurs fondations en Terre Sainte [A Brief History of the Crusades and Their Foundations in the Holy Land]. Paris: J. Gamber, 1924.

Considerazioni generali sugli studi storici [General Considerations on the Study of History]. Ed. Bianca Valota Cavallotti. Milan: Unicopli, 1990.

Etudes byzantines [Byzantine Studies]. 2 vols. Bucharest: Institut d'études byzantines, 1939–1940.

A History of Roumania: Land, People, Civilisation. Trans. Joseph McCabe. London: T.F. Unwin, 1925.

Istoria poporului românesc. Bucharest: Editura ştiinţifică şi Enciclopedică, 1985.

References

Oldson, William O. *The Historical and Nationalistic Thought of Nicolae Iorga.* Boulder, CO: East European Monographs; New York, Columbia University Press, 1973.

Iranian Historiography

See PERSIAN HISTORIOGRAPHY.

Irish Historiography

Historical writing on Ireland since the Middle Ages. A survey of Irish historical writing can usefully begin with two influential texts produced in the twelfth century, a period of great political and cultural change, including the arrival of the Anglo-Normans and church reform. The *Leabhar Gabhála Éirinn* [The Book of the Taking of Ireland] was a monastic compilation of much earlier Gaelic lore and legend about Ireland, which used a biblical chronology and told the story of the successive peoples who had colonized the island down to the mid-twelfth century. *The History and Topography of Ireland* by Gerald of Wales (Giraldus Cambrensis), was an account of Ireland and its history by a member of the Fitzgerald family who were among the first Anglo-Normans to acquire lands in Ireland. Gerald's portrayal of the Irish as barbaric became the standard English interpretation down to the nineteenth century when refutations of him still featured in the work of Irish historians.

Following the Renaissance, histories were written in the narrative style, although the medieval annalistic approach continued in the Gaelic literary tradition. Its last and perhaps most famous manifestation was the seventeenth century *Annála Ríoghachta Éireann* [Annals of the Kingdom of Ireland], which updated the existing annals to 1616. A renewed interest in the past coincided with a period of intense recolonization from Britain, and historical works reflected the profound transformation of Irish society and culture. Sir John Davies's *Discoverie of the True Causes Why Ireland Was Never Entirely Subdued* (1612) was a landmark in colonist perspectives on the difficulties in properly controlling Ireland, based on chancery and exchequer sources, as well as on consideration of Gaelic culture and especially Gaelic law. Geoffrey Keating's *Foras Feasa ar Éirinn* [literally, Basis for Knowledge about Ireland] (c. 1634) was significant as the first narrative history to be written in Gaelic and as an influence on later nationalist historians. Keating was of Anglo-Norman descent and sought to legitimize his ancestors' conquest of Ireland. As a Counter-Reformation priest, he also aimed to provide a history of the Catholic people of the island. From this time on, history was written largely from a sectarian viewpoint.

This was particularly the case in the eighteenth century, but Enlightenment concerns were also evident. The most important Catholic historian and Gaelic scholar, Charles O'Conor, in his *Dissertations on the History of Ireland* (1766), depicted precolonial Ireland as a golden age of civility and learning, in part to refute allegations of native Irish barbarism and also to argue for an end to the stringent penal laws against Catholics. Protestant partisan histories, most notably Edward Ledwich's *Antiquities of Ireland* (1790), masked their sectarianism with a skepticism directed at Catholic accounts and at the Gaelic sources, such as the *Leabhar Gabhála,* on which they were partly based. In contrast, Thomas Leland's *History of Ireland* (1773) adopted a "philosophical" approach to the past and attempted, albeit unsuccessfully, to move beyond a religious partisanship, which was felt to be out of keeping with the times. Leland's work was noteworthy in being the first detailed examination of the colonial period and is still of use to medievalists today. The late-eighteenth-century interest in antiquarianism and history, sometimes called the first Celtic revival, was a casualty of the bloody rebellion of 1798. In its immediate aftermath, history was considered dangerously political and learned societies foundered for lack of elite support. However, there was a revival of interest from the 1830s involving a group of scholars who worked on the major cartographical project, the Ordnance Survey of Ireland. Among these were John O'Donovan and Eugene O'Curry, the foremost Gaelic scholars of the period, whose English translations of important Gaelic manuscripts such as *Annála Ríoghachta Éireann* (1848–1851) and *Ancient Laws of Ireland* (1865–1901), laid the foundation for modern research into medieval Ireland.

In the 1860s a Public Records Act was passed, making official sources available to the historian. The first to consult these was J.P. Prendergast whose major work, *The Cromwellian Settlement of Ireland* (1865), emphasized the growing importance of the themes of conquest and colonization, as well as reflecting contemporary concerns about the land system in Ireland. Most of the significant works in this period were direct responses to contemporary politics; none more so than J.A. Froude's *English in Ireland in the Eighteenth Century* (1872–1874). Although based on considerable archival research, this was mainly an attack on contemporary Liberal policy toward Ireland. Despite this, Froude's portrayal of English government mismanagement and of the social and economic deprivation and political dangers that

resulted became the standard nationalist interpretation until the 1960s. Perhaps the greatest single work on Irish history was written partly to refute many of Froude's more overtly racist allegations. W.E.H. Lecky's *History of Ireland in the Eighteenth Century* (1892) was noteworthy for its breadth and insight and for its conscious effort to conform to the new historiographical standards of scientific objectivity and respect for sources. It remains the classic work on the period.

In the first decades of this century major progress was made in the field of early Irish history, based on the work of O'Donovan and O'Curry and also on the pioneering philological researches of German Celtic scholars. Eoin MacNeill, the first professor of early and medieval Irish history at University College Dublin, published important studies, albeit in a popular vein, of early Irish society and law, *Phases of Irish History* (1919) and *Celtic Ireland* (1921). The latter appeared in the year in which the Union between Great Britain and Ireland was dissolved and the island was partitioned, the smaller part, Northern Ireland, remaining within the United Kingdom and the larger, the Irish Free State and later Éire or the Republic of Ireland, becoming an independent state under the gradually emerging Commonwealth. MacNeill was a nationalist and prominent in the independence movement and his histories were in part designed to commemorate and celebrate an immemorial Irish nation that was poised to regain its independence.

In the earliest years of the new state historical writing was characterized mainly by this type of Whig-nationalist thesis. This changed in the 1930s, when two young historians, T.W. Moody and R.D. Edwards, who had done postgraduate work in the University of London, returned with the aim of establishing Irish academic research on the relatively new principles of European, and more particularly English, academic practice. This involved extensive and painstaking archival research, written up in detailed monographs such as those produced by Edwards, *Church and State in Tudor Ireland* (1935), and Moody, *The Londonderry Plantation, 1609–41* (1939). In 1938, the journal *Irish Historical Studies* was founded as a showcase for this new scholarly approach. A major aim was to move away from the dominant one-dimensional nationalist narratives, and this was assisted by the growing diversity and complexity of approaches within the discipline itself.

From the 1950s some of the most significant work was done in the fields of economic and social history. Foremost here were K.H. Connell for his work on demography, *The Population of Ireland, 1750–1845* (1950), and L.M. Cullen who produced the first economic history survey since that of the nationalist, George O'Brien, in 1919. Cullen's *Economic History of Ireland since 1660* (1972) marked the definitive break from the pattern of reading the Irish economy in terms of political developments instead of economic indices. Cullen also produced the first Annales-style history, *The Emergence of Modern Ireland, 1600–1900* (1981), a study of the underlying structures of Irish society over a three-hundred-year period. Recently, J.G.A. Pocock's proposal of a "British history" has resulted in a number of medieval and early modern studies situating Ireland within a "British Isles" (or "two islands") context. Such attempts to view Irish history in a British or, more rarely, European context are welcome, but will neither easily nor quickly replace a national approach, particularly given how much basic research remains to be done on so many facets of the Irish past.

Clare O'Halloran

Texts

Davies John. *A Discovery of the True Causes Why Ireland Was Never Entirely Subdued.* [London, 1612]. Shannon, Ireland: Irish University Press, 1969.
Four Masters. *Annals of the Kingdom of Ireland.* Ed. and trans. John O'Donovan. Third ed. 7 vols. Dublin: De Búrca Rare Books, 1990.
Keating Geoffrey. *Foras Feasa ar Éirinn: The History of Ireland.* Ed. and trans. David Comyn and P.S. Dineen. 4 vols. 1902–1914. Reprint, with preface by Breandán Ó Buachalla. Dublin: Irish Texts Society, 1987.
Lebor Gabála Érenn: The Book of the Taking of Ireland. Ed. and trans. R.A.S. Macalister. 5 vols. Dublin: Irish Texts Society, 1938–1956.

References

Brady, Ciaran, ed. *Interpreting Irish History: The Debate on Historical Revisionism, 1938–94.* Dublin: Irish Academic Press, 1994.
Lee Joseph, ed. *Irish Historiography, 1970–1979.* Cork: Cork University Press, 1981.
Leerssen Joseph Th. *Mere Irish and Fíor-Ghael: Studies in the Idea of Irish Nationality.* Amsterdam and Philadelphia: John Benjamins, 1986.
Moody T.W. ed. *Irish Historiography, 1936–70.* Dublin: Irish Committee of Historical Sciences, 1971.

Iryŏn [Ilyŏn] (1206–1289)

Korean Buddhist monk and historian. To Iryŏn, about whose life little is known, Buddhism was the core of the national spirit; he also considered irrational factors as among the moving forces of history. *Samguk Yusa* [Heritage of the Three Kingdoms] (ca. 1281), his principal work, is probably one of the two most important books for the study of Korea's early history. It provides a unique source for ancient folklore, mythology, and poetry.

Minjae Kim

Texts

Samguk Yusa. Trans. Ha Tae-Hŭng and Grafton K. Mintz. Seoul: Yonsei University Press, 1972.

References

Academy of Korean Studies. *Samguk Yusaŭi Chonghapjŏk Kŏmt'o* [A Comprehensive Examination of *Samguk Yusa*]. Seoul: Academy of Korean Studies, 1987.

Ishimoda Shō (1912–1986)

Historian of medieval Japan. Ishimoda was born in Sapporo (Hokkaido), and graduated in history from Tokyo University in 1937. Having joined a socialist study association at school, historical materialism remained the basic analytical framework for all his writings. Ishimoda worked in publishing before becoming professor at Hōsei University in 1948. Ishimoda's reputation rests both on his work on ancient and medieval Japan and on his leading position in the "people's history" *(minshūshi)* movement. His reputation was established by his *Chūseiteki Sekai no Keisei* [Formation of the Medieval World] (1946), which used contemporary estate documents to analyze village collectives and class conflict in the medieval world. Further groundbreaking works explored medieval cultural and literary developments and the origins of the Japanese state, and included *Nihon no Kodai Kokka* [The Ancient Japanese State] (1971) and *Nihon no Kodai Kokkaron* [Theory of the Ancient Japanese State] (1973).

Janet E. Hunter

Texts

Chūseiteki Sekai no Keisei. Tokyo: Tokyo Daigaku Shuppankai, 1957.
Nihon no Kodai Kokka. Tokyo: Iwanami Shoten, 1971.
Nihon no Kodai Kokkaron. Tokyo: Iwanami Shoten, 1973.

References

Tonomura, H. *Community and Commerce in Late Medieval Japan.* Stanford, CA: Stanford University Press, 1992.

Iskandar Beg al-Shahīr bi-Munshī (ca. 1560–ca. 1632)

Persian historian of the reign of Shah 'Abbās of the Safavid dynasty. Iskandar Beg began his professional career as an accountant but soon joined the royal secretariat at the court of the Safawid king Shah 'Abbās, rising to the rank of Munshī Bashi, or head secretary, in 1592. He is best known as the author of *Tā'rīkh-i 'Ālam-ārā-yi 'Abbāsī,* the single most important primary source on the history of the Safavids. His official position at the court provided him with firsthand information and allowed him personally to witness many of the events described in the book. A short introduction provides valuable information on the origin of the Safavids and the history of the dynasty before Shah 'Abbās I. The main body of the work deals with the reign of 'Abbās I and describes the major events of each year. The bulk of the work was completed by 1616, with an additional section completed in 1629, when Shah 'Abbās died. After the death of 'Abbās I, Iskandar Beg began a history of his successor, Shah Ṣafī, known as *Dhayl-i Tā'rīkh-i 'Ālam-ārā-yi 'Abbāsī,* but he was only able to cover the first four years of Ṣafī's reign before dying.

Hootan Shambayati

Texts

History of Shah Abbas the Great (Ta'rikh-e alam ara-ye Abaassi). Trans. Roger Savory. 3 vols. Boulder, CO: Westview Press, 1978–1986.

References

Rosenthal, Franz. *A History of Muslim Historiography.* Second ed. Leiden: E.J. Brill, 1968.

Italian Historiography

Historical writing from the Italian peninsula since the Middle Ages. "Italy" as a nation-state did not exist until the second half of the nineteenth century, yet long before there arose a recognizable "Italian" school of historiography informed by humanism and the concern with local or regional history.

Medieval historiography was dominated by the chronicle tradition but there were some important exceptions. Dante Alighieri (1265–1321), in his *De vulgari eloquentia*—though not strictly a work of historiography—posed the "language question" in its most succinct form, foreshadowing the humanist concern with philology. Antonio Pierozzi (1349–1459), the Dominican bishop of Florence for the last fourteen years of his life, authored a *Chronicon* that appeared posthumously in 1485 and that provided an appropriate conclusion to his lifelong study of St. Thomas Aquinas. Also important were Giovanni Cavalcanti (1381–1450) and Alamanno Rinuccini (1419–1499). Although composed in the later fifteenth century, Vespasiano da Bisticci's (1421–1498) *Le vite* [The Lives of Renaissance Princes, Popes, and Prelates] belongs to the older tradition of medieval compilations of famous lives rather than to the emerging humanist style of biography that appeared in the sixteenth century.

A new historiography flourished during the Renaissance (1350–1600). Emerging from the humanist literary tradition that was being revived in the city-states, it eventually replaced the tradition of the medieval chronicle. The importance of rhetoric and philology was stressed in this newer historiography, reflecting the use of ancient historians rather than medieval chroniclers as models. Renaissance historians insisted that history was not merely chronicle but could fulfill aesthetic, didactic, utilitarian, political, and scientific principles. An early example is Petrarch's (1304–1374) study of a fourteenth-century rebel, *The Revolution of Cola di Rienzo.* Petrarch's *Lives of Illustrious Men* was virtually a history of Rome from Romulus to Titus. Deeply influenced by Livy's *History of Rome* and Thucydides' *History of the Peloponnesian War,* the Florentine chancellor and scholar Leonardo Bruni (1366–1444) completed his *Historium Florentini Populi* [History of the Florentine People] in 1449. An earlier work, based on a second-century Greek model praising Athens and written to instill pride, was the *Laudatio Florentinae Urbis* (1403–1404) [Panegyric to the City of Florence]. The importance of philology was demonstrated by Lorenzo Valla (1407–1457), who remains best known for proving the falsity of the so-called Donation of Constantine (a medieval forgery long believed to prove papal suzerainty over western Europe) in his *De falso creditia et ementia Constantini donatione declamatio* [On the False Donation of Constantine] (1440); through his close attention to language and its change over time, Valla thus initiated the work of modern textual criticism.

Niccolò Machiavelli (1469–1527) gained immortal notoriety for his *Prince* of 1513, but his *Discorsi sopra la prima deca di Tito Livio* [Discourse on the First Ten Books of Titus Livy] (1513–1517) provides a better indication of his republican sentiments. His last major work, which culminated a lifetime of learning and reading and incorporated his experiences as officeholder, political philosopher, and exile, was the *Istorie fiorentine* [Florentine Histories] of 1520–1525, which covers the great city from 375 until 1492. Machiavelli's younger contemporary, Francesco Guicciardini (1483–1540), a Florentine diplomat and sometime papal official, is best known for his *Storia d'Italia* [History of Italy], one of the first attempts by an Italian at a narrative, national history of a brief period. Guicciardini's work, which covers the period from 1492 to 1534, situates Italian history as tragedy (as Thucydides had done for ancient Athens) since the obsession with local independence prevented the formation of a modern nation-state. Elsewhere on the peninsula, the Venetian government employed a number of scholars to write histories of the maritime republic. Among others, the government commissioned Marc'Antonio Coccio, better known as Sabellico (1436–1506) to write *Rerum Venetarum* [History of Venice] (1487). Of fundamental importance are the *Relazioni* of the Venetian diplomatic corps in describing the workings of the "Serene Republic."

A different approach to the problem of Italian history is represented by Paolo Giovio (1486–1552), who came from the northern city of Como, studied philosophy at Padua, and taught in Rome. Well known for his biographies of illustrious men and his stress on contemporary history, his *Sui Temporis Historiae* [History of His Time] which appeared between 1550 and 1552, was an often imitated work of "universal" history. Giovio insisted on a larger canvas, incorporating the French, Spaniards, and Germans as well as the Russians, Hungarians, and Turks into his portrait of the age.

Among biographical writers, Giorgio Vasari (1511–1574) stands out. Vasari was a student of Michelangelo, who convinced his pupil that he was a better writer than painter. Vasari's *Vite de' più eccellenti pittori, scultori e architettori* [Lives of the Most Eminent Painters, Sculptors, and Architects] (1550) moved easily between biography and history; indeed, it is widely considered the first work of art history. It is also important for its concept of the artist as "genius" and the creation of the "divine" Michelangelo as cultural icon and representative of the tormented artist who suffers for his art.

Ecclesiastical history was virtually a distinct branch of the genre at this time, represented by such authors as Cesare Baronio (1538–1607), a Vatican librarian who wrote a voluminous history in defense of the Roman Catholic interpretation of history. Perhaps the most important ecclesiastical historian of the later Renaissance was the Venetian Paolo Sarpi (1562–1623). Deeply religious and shaped by the spirit of the Counter Reformation, Sarpi undertook the task of writing the history of the Council of Trent (1545–1563). A history of the council would be, according to Sarpi, "the Illiad of our times." The result was his famous *Istoria del Concilio tridentino* [History of the Council of Trent]; because Venice then had poor relations with the papacy (attempts had been made by Rome to assassinate Sarpi), and because his history proved critical of the council and of the popes, his history first appeared under a pseudonym in London in 1619.

On a more theoretical level, sixteenth-century Italian historiography was dominated by the *ars historica* debate, which insisted on the importance of rhetoric in the writing of history. These scholars (Sperone Speroni, Francesco Robortello, Francesco Patrizi, Alessandro Sardi, Giovanni Viperano, and Uberto Foglietta) recognized that the historian must pick and choose those events that make their way into the narrative, that the writing of history was a continual process and that consequently, those narratives could not be "true" *(verum)* but only "truthful" *(verax),* thus anticipating the eighteenth-century Neapolitan, Giambattista Vico (1668–1744), and more modern conceptions of historiography.

Enlightenment historiography in Italy at the time of Vico was marked, as in the rest of Europe, by conceptions of progress and faith in reason. One of the exemplars of this tradition was Pietro Giannone of Naples. His *Storia civile del regno di Napoli* [Civil History of the Kingdom of Naples] appeared in 1723. Ludovico Antonio Muratori (1672–1750) published the *Rerum Italicarum scriptores* [Writers on Italian Affairs] and the *Antiquitates Italie Medii Aevii* [Antiquities of Medieval Italy], both of which were collections of documents; and the *Annali d'Italia* [Annals of Italy], a documentary history. Cesare Beccaria (1738–1794) almost single-handedly revolutionized Europe's conception of crime and punishment with his *Dei delitti e delle pene* [On Crime and Punishment] (1764), which was not only a review of the history of ecclesiastical control of courts and prisons, but also a manifesto on reform. Pietro Verri (1728–1797), who, along with his brother Alessandro edited the Milanese journal *Il Caffè,* was a contemporary of Cesare Beccaria and wrote his own denunciation of judicial history.

The most influential eighteenth-century Italian scholar was Vico himself, who was, ironically, critical of the assumptions of Enlightenment thought. A philosopher, philologist, and historian, Vico published his *De Nostri Temporis Studiorum Ratione* [On the Study Methods of Our Time] in 1709; his *De Antiquissima Italorum Sapientia* [On the Most Ancient Knowledge of the Italians] followed a year later. Most importantly, Vico's *Scienza nuova* [New Science] (third ed. 1744) challenged Enlightenment assumptions concerning epistemology and historiography and was to influence thinkers outside of Italy as well.

During the first half of the nineteenth century, Italian historiography was marked by the movement for national unification, the Risorgimento. Bringing together the currents of nationalism, liberalism, and romanticism unleashed by the French Revolution, historical writing was harnessed for the cause of unification. Consequently, some of the best historical writing was done by novelists such as Alessandro Manzoni *(I promessi sposi)* and the poet Leopardi. In addition there was a Catholic-Liberal historical school represented by Manzoni, Gino Capponi (1793–1876), Cesare Balbo (1789–1853), Cesare Cantù (1804–1895), Carlo Troya (1785–1858), and Luigi Tosti (1811–1897). The Count Capponi wrote a history of his native Florence, while Troya and Tosti turned their attention to documents in the archives of the monastery of Monte Cassino. Balbo argued strongly for independence in his work; Cantù wrote both a "universal" history and a national history, which were read by generations of Italians. The Catholic-Liberal school sought a confederate Italy unified under the papacy. Their underlying assumption was that political liberty was the prerequisite for cultural vitality.

Other nineteenth-century historians were the "dissidents" of the Risorgimento: Carlo Cattaneo (1801–1869), Giuseppe Ferrari (1811–1876), and Carlo Pisacane (1818–1857). Cattaneo's *Dell'insurrezione di Milano del 1848* [The Insurrection of Milan of 1848] (1848) and Pisacane's *La rivoluzione in Italia* [The Revolution in Italy] (1851) both dealt with the armed struggle to secure national independence. Ferrari's *Essai sur le principe et les limites de la philosophie de l'histoire* [Essay on the Principle and Limits of a Philosophy of History] (1843) offered a more theoretical reflection on historiography. Francesco Siliprandi (1816–1892) examined the neglected role of the peasants during the struggle for unification in his *La rivoluzione dei contadini* [The Revolution of the Peasants] of 1884. A curious example of "prophetic historiography" was Giuseppe Ricciardi's *Storia d'Italia dal 1850 al 1900* (published at Paris in 1842), in which the author projected the future history of Italy from 1850 to 1900.

Historical writing in Liberal Italy (1861–1922) was marked by two competing tendencies: one saw the Risorgimento as a success; the other believed that there were fundamental flaws in the new state because of the deficiencies of the process of unification. Common themes—which would carry over into twentieth-century historiography—included political corruption, the place of Italy in European affairs, and perhaps most importantly, the "Southern Question," which addressed the political, social, cultural, and economic division between northern and southern Italy.

A dominant figure of the late nineteenth and early twentieth century was Pasquale Villari (1827–1917). After producing biographies of the religious reformer Girolamo Savonarola and Niccolò Machiavelli, he published *I primi due secoli della storia di Firenze* [The First Two Centuries of Florentine History] (1893); his major work on historiography was *L'origine e il progresso della filosofia della storia* [The Origin and Progress of the Philosophy of History] of 1859.

Around the turn of the nineteenth century, Italian historiography was strongly influenced by positivism, as the eclecticism and literary flair of the earlier generation of historians gave way to a "scientific" examination of documents and a narrower scope. This trend was reinforced by the influence of two major journals, the *Archivio Storico Italiano* (est. 1842) and the *Rivista Storica Italiana* (est. 1884). Countering this tendency was Guglielmo Ferrero (1871–1942) whose five-volume *Greatness and Decline of Rome* was widely read by the public, even if criticized by philologists and traditional historians. His work dealt with the last years of the Roman republic, and his criticism of dictatorship would cause him problems with the Fascist regime late in life.

As the example of Ferrero illustrates, positivism achieved less strong a position in Italy than it acquired in some other European countries. Twentieth-century Italian historiography has been dominated by the imposing figure of Benedetto Croce (1866–1952). It was Croce, along with Bertrando Spaventa (1817–1883) and Giovanni Gentile (1875–1944), who countered positivism by resurrecting the tradition of idealism in Italy. Croce himself was a philosopher, literary and aesthetic critic, and historian. Following Vico and the older tradition of *artes historicae,* Croce insisted that history could never be a science; rather, it was an art. As an art, it was inseparable from philosophy; indeed, they were virtually the same thing for Croce. In addition, he argued that all history is refracted through present concerns; hence his famous dictum that "all history is contemporary history." Among his voluminous writings are several major works of historiography, including *Teoria e storia della storiografia* [Theory and History of Historiography] (1917); *Storia dell storiografia italiana del secolo XIX* [History of Nineteenth Century Italian Historiography] (1921); and *Storia come pensiero e azione* [History As Thought and Action] (1939).

Historiography during Mussolini's regime (1922–1943/45) was subservient to Fascist ideology. Gentile's "actual idealism" provided the prescribed framework for a figure like Gioacchino Volpe (1876–1971) the "official" historian of the regime. An early work by Volpe on the Middle Ages had a strong influence on medieval historiography, while his *L'Italia in cammino* [Italy on the March] (1927) and *Storia del movimento fascista* [History of the Fascist Movement] (1939) were sanctioned by Fascist officials. Two major undertakings of the Fascist regime were the publication of the *Enciclopedia Italiana* under the direction of Gentile and the publication of a projected thirty-volume history of Rome. Interestingly, both projects also employed nonfascist scholars.

Postwar Italian historiography has been radically altered by the publication of Antonio Gramsci's (1891–1937) *Prison Notebooks*. His critique of the Risorgimento, attention to the "Southern Question," and reexamination of literature, dialect, and popular culture have led to fertile new explorations. Gramsci's theories challenged the dominance of Crocean idealism while retaining aspects of that idealism and provided the matrix for a twentieth-century humanistic Marxism.

Another important figure was Gaetano Salvemini (1873–1957) whose early studies of medieval Florence, the French Revolution, and Mazzini were influential. Salvemini devoted himself to the antifascist struggle, teaching at Harvard during his exile from Italy. His essays on history and historiography, delivered at the University of Chicago, were published as *Historian and Scientist* (1939). The most important contemporary Italian historian of the Enlightenment has been Franco Venturi (1914–1994) whose *Italy and the Enlightenment* (1972) is considered a classic in its field. Two figures principally important for introducing modern German historicism into Italy were Carlo Antoni, author of *Dall storicismo alla sociologia* [From Historicism to Sociology] and

Pietro Rossi, who wrote *Lo storicismo tedesco contemporaneo* [Contemporary German Historicism] (1956); Rossi has also edited *La storiografia contemporanea* [Contemporary Historiography] (1987).

Among contemporary historians, Arnaldo Momigliano (1908–1987) was a prolific writer on ancient, medieval, and modern historiography. Among his works, many of which are available in English translations, are *Studies in Historiography* (1969), *Essays in Ancient and Modern Historiography* (1977), *Tra storia e storicismo* [Between History and Historicism] (1985), and *The Classical Foundation of Modern Historiography* (1990).

Giuseppe Galasso's *Croce, Gramsci e altri storici* [Croce, Gramsci and Other Historians] (1969) is a dated, but still valuable, work. More recent is Leo Valiani's *Fra Croce e Omodeo: Storia e storiografia nella lotta per la libertà* [Between Croce and Omodeo: History and Historiography in the Struggle for Liberty] (1984). Federico Chabod, a student of Croce, published his *Italia contemporanea* [Contemporary Italy] in 1961. A study in the Marxist vein is Ernesto Ragionieri's (1926–1975) *Storiografia in cammino* [Historiography on the March] (1987). Also important is Giuliano Procacci's popular *Storia degli italiani* [History of the Italians] (1987). *Labirinto italiano* [Italian Labyrinth] (1989) by Nicola Tranfaglia is a study of fascism, antifascism, and historiography. Norberto Bobbio's *Profilo ideologico del novecento italiano* [Ideological Profile of Twentieth-Century Italy] (1986) is an invaluable introduction to the major philosophical and historiographical schools. Innovative work has been done by Giorgio Candeloro, Delio Cantimori, and Carlo Ginzburg, whose *The Cheese and the Worms* (1989) is a much-read example of *microstoria* (microhistory), which has strong Italian roots.

Studies of the fascist and post–World War II periods continue to be important. Renzo De Felice is considered one of the most important historians working today. After works on the Jacobins and a history of Italian Jews, he has turned his attention to a multivolume biography of Mussolini, which has generated considerable controversy, including charges that the author is seeking to "rehabilitate" the Fascist dictator. The relationship between fascism and history is explored by Giuseppe Quazza et al. in *Storiografia e fascismo* [Historiography and Fascism] (1985), by Jader Jacobelli in *Il fascismo e gli storici oggi* [Fascism and Historians Today] (1988), and by Angelo Del Boca *Il regime fascista: Storia e storiografia* [The Fascist Regime: History and Historiography] (1995). The Armed Resistance has been reexamined with Claudio Pavone's *Una guerra civile: Saggio storico sulla moralità della Resistenza* [A Civil War: A Historical Essay on the Morality of the Resistance] (1991). Also worthy of note is Fulvio Di Giorgi's *La storiografia di tendenze marxista e la storia locale in Italia nel dopoguerra* [Marxist Historiography and Local History in Post-War Italy] and *La storiografia italiana degli ultimi trent'anni* [Italian Historiography of the Last Thirty Years] both published in 1989. Finally, the Turin publisher Einaudi has embarked on the most ambitious project of current Italian historiography, a multivolume *Storia d'Italia* [History of Italy].

Stanislao G. Pugliese

See also CHRONICLES, MEDIEVAL; ENLIGHTENMENT HISTORIOGRAPHY; MICROHISTORY; RENAISSANCE, HISTORIOGRAPHY DURING.

References

Antoni, Carlo. *From History to Sociology.* Trans. Hayden White. Detroit: Wayne State University Press, 1959.

Bobbio, Norberto. *Ideological Profile of Twentieth-Century Italy.* Trans. Lydia G. Cochrane. Princeton, NJ: Princeton University Press, 1995.

Cantimori, Delio. *Storici e storia.* Turin: Einaudi, 1971.

Chabod, Federico. *Italia contemporaneo.* Turin: Einuadi, 1961.

Croce, Benedetto. *History: Its Theory and Practice.* Trans. Douglas Ainslie. New York: Russell and Russell, 1960.

———. *History As the Story of Liberty.* Trans. Sylvia Sprigge. New York: Norton, 1941.

Del Boca, Angelo. *Il regime fascista: Storia e storiografia.* Rome and Bari: Laterza, 1995.

Di Giorgi, Fulvio. *La storiografia di tendenze marxista e la storiografia locale in Italia nel dopoguerra.* Milan: Vita e pensiero, 1989.

Ferrari, Giuseppe. *Essai sur le principe et les limites de la philosophie de l'histoire.* Paris: Joubert, 1843.

Galasso, Giuseppe. *Croce, Gramsci e altri storici* [Croce, Gramsci and Other Historians]. Milan: Mondadori, 1969.

Giannone, Pietro. *Storia civile del regno di Napoli.* Ed. Antonio Marongiu. Milan: Marzorati, 1970–1972.

Gramsci, Antonio. *Prison Notebooks.* Ed. Quintin Hoare and Geoffrey Nowell Smith. New York: International Publishers, 1971.

Jacobelli, Jader, ed. *Il fascismo e gli storici oggi.* Rome: Laterza, 1988.

Momigliano, Arnaldo Dante. *The Classical Foundations of Modern Historiography.* Berkeley: University of California Press, 1990.

———. *Studies in Historiography.* London: Weidenfeld & Nicholson, 1969.

Pavone, Claudio. *Una guerra civile: Saggio storico sulla moralità della Resistenza.* Turin: Bollati Boringhieri, 1991.

Procacci, Giuliano. *Storia degli italiani.* Rome, Bari: Laterza, 1987.

Quazza, Giuseppe et al. *Storiografia e fascismo.* Milan: Franco Angeli, 1985.

Ragionieri, Ernesto. *Storiografia in cammino.* Rome: Riuniti, 1987.

Ricciardi, Giuseppe. *Storia d'Italia dal 1850 al 1900.* Paris: Lacombe, 1842.

Rossi, Pietro. *Lo storicismo tedesco contemporaneo.* Turin: Einaudi, 1956.

Salvemini, Gaetano. *Historian and Scientist.* Cambridge, MA: Harvard University Press, 1939.

Tranfaglia, Nicola. *Labirinto italiano.* Florence: La Nuova Italia, 1989.

Valiani, Leo. *Fra Croce e Omodeo: Storia e storiografia nella lotta per la libertà.* Florence: Le Monnier, 1984.

Venturi, Franco. *Italy and the Enlightenment.* New York: New York University Press, 1972.

Volpe, Gioacchino. *L'Italia in cammino.* Rome: Editori Laterzi, 1991.

J

Jacoby, Felix (1876–1959)

Classical philologist and historiographer. Born in Magdeburg, Germany, Jacoby's first major work was his dissertation on the chronicle of Apollodoros (1902). There followed an edition of the *Marmor Parium,* a chronographic inscription, and numerous articles for the authoritative encyclopedia on antiquity, A.F. von Pauly's *Realencyclopädie der klassischen Altertumswissenschaft,* including major studies of Herodotus and Hellanicus. At the same time Jacoby began to collect and edit the fragments of the Greek historians (quotations from lost works in extant sources), and the first volume of this monumental work appeared in 1923. Forced to leave Germany in 1939, Jacoby continued his work in Oxford, where he remained until his return to Germany in 1956. Jacoby's other works included numerous articles on a variety of subjects ranging from Latin elegy to Hesiod, and a massive work on the local historians of Athens, or Atthidographers *(Atthis).* Jacoby did not live to complete his collection of fragments, and the commentary on the ethnographical writers has now been undertaken by Charles W. Fornara.

Loren J. Samons II

Texts

Apollodors Chronik. Eine Sammlung der Fragmente [Apollodoros' Chronicle: A Collection of the Fragments]. Berlin: Weidmann, 1902.
Atthis: The Local Chronicles of Ancient Athens. Oxford: Oxford University Press, 1949.
Die Fragmente der griechischen Historiker [The Fragments of the Greek Historians]. Berlin and Leiden: E.J. Brill, 1923–1958; subsequent fascicles by Charles W. Fornara et al.
Griechische Historiker [Greek Historians]. Stuttgart: Druckenmüller, 1956 (a reprint of *Realencyclopädie* articles).
Das Marmor Parium. Berlin: Weidmann, 1904.

References

Chambers, M. "Felix Jacoby." In *Classical Scholarship: A Biographical Encyclopedia.* ed. W.W. Briggs and W.M. Calder III. New York: Garland, 1990, 205–210.
Fornara, C. *Die Fragmente der griechischen Historiker,* IIIc, fasc. 1. Leiden: Brill, 1994.

Jacques de Vitry (1160/70–1240)

French preacher, bishop, and historian. Jacques de Vitry, probably a native of Champagne, entered religious life in the diocese of Liège around 1210 after studies at Paris. He had been drawn to the Low Countries by their apostolic movements, whose early members he documented in the biography of the laywoman Marie d'Oignies. He soon made his name as a lively preacher and, after retirement, would compile a collection of more than four hundred sermons. Around 1213 he was charged with preaching the Fifth Crusade, and was consecrated bishop of Acre in 1216. He traveled to his diocese and was present at the siege of Damietta (1218–1219). Unhappy in his troubled see, he resigned it in 1228 and retired to Rome, where he was made a cardinal. It was probably in the Middle East that Jacques began his two great histories, the *Historia Orientalis* [History of the East] and the *Historia Occidentalis* [History of the West], completed by around 1223. The former relies partly on earlier crusade chronicles such as that of William of Tyre, but includes an account of the campaign at Damietta and a description of the customs of the various peoples of the Middle East. The second book is not a chronological history but a critical study of the various groups within the Western church and society. Its aim is polemical, intended to point out the failings specific to each group and call for reform.

Monica Sandor

Texts

The Historia Occidentalis of Jacques de Vitry. Ed. J.F. Hinnebusch. Fribourg, Switzerland: Fribourg University Press, 1972.

Les Lettres de Jacques de Vitry [Letters of Jacques de Vitry]. Ed. R.B.C. Huygens. Leiden: E.J. Brill, 1960.

Libri duo quorum prior orientalis sive Hierosolimitanae alter occidentalis historiae nomine inscribitur [Two books, of Which the First Is Known as the History of the East, or of Jerusalem, and the Second as the History of the West]. Ed. Franciscus Moschus. Douai: B. Bellerus, 1597.

The Life of Marie d'Oignies by Jacques de Vitry. Trans. Margot King. Toronto: Peregrina, 1987.

Vita Mariae Oigniacensis [Life of Marie of Oignies]. Ed. D. Papebroek. *Acta Sanctorum* (June), vol. V. Paris: Palmé, 1867, cols. 547–572.

References

Cannuyer, Christian. "La date de rédaction de l'*Historia orientalis* de Jacques de Vitry (1160/70–1240), évêque d'Acre [The Date of Composition of the *Historia orientalis* of Jacques de Vitry]." *Revue d'Histoire Ecclésiastique* 78 (1983): 65–72.

———. "Sur une reprise de l'*Historia orientalis* de Jacques de Vitry [A Review of the *Historia orientalis* of Jacques de Vitry]." *Revue d'Histoire des Religions* 200 (1983): 407–410.

Funk, Philipp. *Jakob von Vitry, Leben und Werke* [Jacques de Vitry, Life and Works]. Leipzig: B.G. Teubner, 1909.

Quaglia, A. "Sulla datazione e il valore della *Historia occidentalis* di Giacomo da Vitry [On the dating and the value of the *Historia occidentalis* of Jacques de Vitry]." *Miscellanea francescana* 83 (1983): 177–192.

James, Cyril Lionel Robert (1901–1989)

Historian of slavery. The first notable scholar of New World slave revolt, a Pan-Africanist activist, and historian of modern sport, C.L.R. James was the son of a humble Trinidadian schoolmaster. He spent most of his adult life in Britain and the United States as a political philosopher and activist. James wrote short stories and a novel about Trinidadian popular life before leaving for England in 1933. While there, he prepared the autobiography of a prominent cricketer, wrote an important pamphlet for West Indian self-government, and served as cricket correspondent to the *Manchester Guardian;* during the same period,

he also agitated for African independence and compiled his epic volume of the historic Haitian uprising, *The Black Jacobins.* He left London for New York in 1939 to work as a political leader of the Trotskyist movement. He soon became deeply involved in African-American history and culture, writing many political documents and organizing among the sharecroppers of Missouri. Expelled from the United States during the McCarthy Era, James spent most of the 1950s and 1960s in the United Kingdom and Trinidad. His *Beyond a Boundary,* formally a history of cricket, was a sweeping interpretation of modern sports and their role in world culture. He also critically examined the failings of the nationalist revolutions, especially those led by his former political protégés, Kwame Nkrumah of Ghana and Eric Williams of Trinidad. Returning to the United States in 1969, James lectured widely, attaining historical status as the éminence grise of Pan-African aspirations.

Paul M. Buhle

Texts

Beyond a Boundary. New York: Pantheon, 1983.

The Black Jacobins: Toussaint L'Ouverture and the San Domingo Revolution. New York: Vintage, 1963.

The C.L.R. James Reader. Ed. Anna Grimshaw. Oxford: Blackwell, 1993.

A History of the Pan African Revolt. Chicago: Charles H. Kerr Company, 1994.

Nkrumah and the Ghana Revolution. London: Allison & Busby, 1977.

References

Buhle, Paul, ed. *C.L.R. James: His Life and Work.* London: Allison & Busby, 1986.

———. *C.L.R. James: The Artist As Revolutionary.* London: Verso, 1988.

Henry, Paget, and Paul Buhle, eds. *C.L.R. James's Caribbean.* Durham, NC: Duke University Press, 1992.

Jameson, Anna (née Murphy) (1794–1860)

Anglo-Irish critic, historian, and art historian. Jameson was born in Dublin; her English mother and Irish father Denis Murphy, a painter of miniatures, emigrated to England in 1798. Self-educated, Anna Murphy worked as a governess before marrying Robert Jameson, a barrister, in 1825. They separated after he became vice-chancellor of Upper Canada in 1837. Precariously independent, Anna Jameson supported her parents and unmarried sisters to the end of an arduous working life that was also marked by durable friendships. Jameson's fields of interest initially consisted of travel writing, literary and art criticism, cross-cultural comparison, and history treated biographically for a female readership as in *Memoirs of Celebrated Female Sovereigns* (1831). Her pioneering contributions to British art history emerged especially in catalogues of London collections published in 1842 and 1844, and in *Sacred and Legendary Art* (1848–1864), a series of studies emphasizing the pertinence of popular traditions to Christian iconography.

Adele Ernstrom

Texts

Completed by Elizabeth Eastlake. *The History of Our Lord As Exemplified in Works of Art.* 2 vols. London: Longman, Brown, Green, and Longman, 1864.

Letters of Anna Jameson to Ottilie von Goethe. Ed. G.H. Needler. London: Oxford University Press, 1939.

Memoirs and Essays Illustrative of Art, Literature, and Social Morals. New York: Wiley and Putnam, 1846.

Memoirs of Celebrated Female Sovereigns. New York: J. and J. Harper, 1832.

Memoirs of the Early Italian Painters. 2 vols. London: C. Knight, 1845.

Sacred and Legendary Art. Series title, comprising (in chronological order):
———*The Poetry of Sacred and Legendary Art.* 2 vols. London: Longman, Brown, Green, and Longman, 1848.
———*Legends of the Monastic Orders, As Represented in the Fine Arts.* London: Longman, Brown, Green, and Longman, 1850.
———*Legends of the Madonna, As Represented in the Fine Arts.* London: Longman, Brown, Green and Longman, 1852.

References

Holcomb, Adele M. "Anna Jameson: The First Professional English Art Historian." *Art History* 6 (1983): 171–187.

Thomas, Clara. *Love and Work Enough: The Life of Anna Jameson.* Toronto: University of Toronto Press, 1967.

Janssen, Johannes (1829–1891)

Historian of the German people and contributor to *Kulturgeschichte.* Janssen is best known for his *Geschichte des deutschen Volkes seit dem Ausgang des Mittelalters* [History of the German People since the Close of the Middle Ages] (1876–1894), an eight-volume cultural history from the fifteenth century to the beginning of the Thirty Years' War. Inspired by patriotic and nationalistic sentiments and by his own Catholic faith, Janssen focused his research on the cultural development of Germany from the late fifteenth century. In the first volume, Janssen portrayed a Germany renewed by a flowering of intellectual and spiritual life on the eve of the Reformation. In later volumes, he interpreted the evangelical reform as a "deformation" or decline from the vibrant Catholic culture of the previous century. While his multivolume history appealed to a wide readership (with its eighteen editions, as well as English and French translations), recent historians, such as Joseph Lortz, have criticized Janssen for overlooking the many corruptions and abuses in the pre-Reformation church. At the same time, Bernd Moeller and other scholars have emphasized many of the same positive religious impulses in the church that Janssen had discussed.

James V. Mehl

Texts

History of the German People since the Close of the Middle Ages. Trans. M.A. Mitchell and A.M. Christie. 17 vols. New York: AMS Press, 1966.

Schiller als Historiker [Schiller As Historian]. Freiburg im Breisgau: Herder'sche Verlagshandlung, 1863.

References

Ozment, Stephen. *The Reformation in the Cities.* New Haven, CT: Yale University Press, 1975, 15–18.

Pastor, Ludwig von. *Aus dem leben des Geschichtschreiber Johannes Janssen* [On the Life of the Historian Johannes Janssen]. Cologne: J.P. Bachem, 1929.

Japanese Historiography—to 1900

Historical writing in Japan from earliest times to the beginning of the twentieth century. Reflections on the past are found in virtually every period of Japanese history. These reflections have been recorded in an impressive variety of forms dating from the very earliest writings composed in the archipelago during the seventh century through the establishment of modern historical writing in the Meiji period (1868–1912). While late nineteenth-century historical writing in Japan is often divided into the three major divisions of

Japanese national history *(Kokushi)*, East Asian history *(Tōyōshi)*, and Western history *(Seiyōshi)* [with these latter two occasionally conjoined as World history *(Seikaishi)*], the histories of the earlier periods are almost exclusively concerned with domestic issues. There are four major periods of historical writing in Japan prior to the twentieth century: (1) the earliest national histories; (2) medieval historical tales or chronicles; (3) early-modern domainal-based histories; and (4) modern "scientific" histories.

National Histories

The first historical works were compiled in the early seventh century under the auspices of the imperial prince Shōtoku. Three such works seem to have been composed: the Record of the Emperors *(Tennōki)*, the Fundamental Records *(Hongi)*, and the National Record *(Kokki)*. The first two of these were destroyed by fire in the *coup d'etat* of 645 and the latter, while rescued from the flames that consumed the other works, was subsequently lost. Many of the great houses of the day also kept historical records, most likely genealogical records, but none of these is extant.

The earliest extant writings found in the Japanese archipelago are in fact historical writings: the *Kojiki,* or Record of Ancient Matters, completed in A.D. 712, and the *Nihonshoki,* or Documentary Record of Japan *(Nihon),* completed in A.D. 720. These works were both imperially commissioned, the former by Empress Gemmei in 711 (probably a continuation of a project initiated by her uncle and father-in-law, Emperor Temmu ca. 680), and the latter by Emperor Temmu in 682. Thus both works were planned and completed almost at the same time and often treat many of the same events. They both begin their accounts with the primordial creation of the world and all things contained therein and, most important for later chapters, the subsequent establishment of the imperial lineage as directly descended from the creator deities themselves. In relating these divine beginnings, both texts draw extensively upon earlier oral traditions, popular legends, traditions held by some of the noble families, and from foreign (Korean and Chinese) sources. Both texts purported to correct mistakes and resolve confusions found in competing records of the past as held by the various noble families, and thus both claimed a final, imperial authority for the composition of a true "mirror," or reflection of the past. There are also several important differences between these two works in terms of content and structure. The *Kojiki* concludes its

coverage in A.D. 641 while the *Nihonshoki* chronicles events as late as A.D. 697. The *Nihonshoki* is often regarded as the more "accurate" of the two works for discussion of this period crucial to the formation of the early Japanese state. Yet even the chronological proximity of events does not prevent the composers of the *Nihonshoki* from lifting numerous quotes verbatim from Continental sources and representing them as speeches made by Japanese emperors and empresses. Moreover, at many crucial points the two texts diverge in nomenclature and interpretation and thus provide numerous opportunities for analysis and speculation regarding early language use and historical contestations. The *Nihonshoki* is also composed in a manner that may be jarring to modern readers. While the *Kojiki* recounts events with a single narrative voice and proceeds in a clearly chronological fashion, the *Nihonshoki,* primarily in the early chapters, clusters together numerous alternative versions for each event, which are loosely connected by the phrase "another account states . . . " One purpose of this method seems to have been to include all acceptable versions of the past in a narrative united and dominated by the ruling imperial families. Finally, the language of composition of these two works also differs significantly. The *Nihonshoki* was composed almost exclusively in Chinese, most likely to have it stand on par with the great dynastic histories of China, which were very clearly models for this work. The *Kojiki,* on the other hand, was composed in a complex admixture of styles: sometimes in Chinese, sometimes in Japanese with Chinese characters used exclusively for their phonetic value, and sometimes in a combination of these two styles. One consequence of this complex method of writing was that the *Kojiki* was virtually ignored until its rediscovery in the eighteenth century, while the *Nihonshoki* continued to serve as one of the "official" records of the early imperial state.

The *Nihonshoki* became the paradigm of early historical writing. Five other imperially commissioned works were completed between the eighth and early tenth centuries. These works, together with the *Nihonshoki,* are called the *Rikkokushi* [Six National Histories]; they were all composed in classical Chinese, were document based, were compiled by an imperially sponsored team of scholars and bureaucrats, and were accepted as authoritative works containing the absolute truth about the past. The other five national histories are the *Shoku Nihongi* [Chronicles of Japan, Continued], completed in 797 and covering nine imperial reigns from 697 to 791; the *Nihon kōki* [Later

Chronicles of Japan], completed in 840 and covering four reigns from 792 to 832; the *Shoku Nihon kōki* [Later Chronicles of Japan, Continued], completed in 869 and covering the single reign of Emperor Nimmyō from 832 to 850; the *Nihon Montoku Tennō Jitsuroku* [True Records of Emperor Montoku of Japan], compiled in 879 and covering the single reign of Emperor Montoku from 850 to 858; and the *Nihon Sandai Jitsuroku* [True Records of Three Reigns of Japan], compiled in 901 and covering three reigns from 858 to 887. While other imperially sponsored historical projects were initiated after these six, the results were fragmented and later dispersed. The power of the central government was also significantly challenged in the tenth century, and this first form of centralized historical production drew to a close.

Historical Tales

The earliest, largely annalistic historical writings in Japan, were centered on and sponsored by the emerging political order of the imperial court. By the fourteenth century, however, profound fractures in the aristocratic system and the emergence of numerous increasingly enfranchised and militarily powerful clans had resulted in many uprisings and several full-scale wars. Together with these dramatic social changes there occurred a rethinking of the social order itself. Not surprisingly, reflections on the recent and more distant past also underwent significant changes during this period. Later students of the period have grouped the romantic, dramatic, and unabashedly didactic writings on the past that were composed from the eleventh century onward into a genre called *rekishi monogatari* [Historical Tales]. These tales were written by independent, that is, not imperially sponsored, scholars and thinkers, who drew freely on the extensive oral literary materials of the day as well as on diaries and other personal accounts to present events from the legendary founding of the Yamato state in 660 B.C. through the execution of the Kamakura political order and the creation of the northern and southern courts in 1333. While these tales did use certain aspects of the earlier national histories, such as employing imperial reigns for their narrative structures, they also represent significant departures from this earlier mode. They were written in Japanese, not the classical Chinese favored by the court histories; at least one, the *Eiga Monogatari* [Tales of Flowering Fortunes] (ca. 1100), was written by a woman; they eschewed mere recitation of major court events in favor of extensive discussions of particular individuals and their motivations, as well as multiple interpretations of complex events (violent or otherwise); and they were all generally far more concerned with the details of material life than their textual ancestors. This model of historical writing is often compared to the biographical-records *(kiden)* style begun in China, the *locus classicus* of which is Sima Qian's [Ssu-ma Ch'ien] *Shiji* or *Shih chi* [Historical Records] (ca. 75 B.C.). The historical usefulness of these works has been criticized by questioning their accuracy. Indeed, each of these tales is known to contain numerous minor errors in such matters as the dates of events or the anachronistic use of ranks and titles. Moreover, because of their didactic intent they all also engage in greater or lesser degrees of distortion for dramatic effect. More importantly, however, these tales are also seen to represent a new age of historical speculation and interpretation.

There are many examples of this genre and conflicting definitions as to which works are to be included as historical tales. Many tales that deal explicitly with warfare, for example, are often grouped into their own category, *Gunki monogatari* [War Tales] and some later historical works are excluded as sui generis. In brief, the most widely read and paradigmatic works of medieval historical writing are the *Okagami* [Great Mirror], composed between 1025 and 1125 and covering the years from 850 to 1025; the above-mentioned *Eiga Monogatari,* composed roughly simultaneously to the *Okagami* and covering the years from 946 to 1092; the *Gukanshō* [Miscellany of Foolish Views] composed ca. 1220 by the Tendai priest Jien and covering the entire range of Japanese imperial history until the date of composition; and the *Jinnō Shōtōki* [Chronicles of Gods and Sovereigns], composed in 1339 and claiming the same comprehensiveness as the *Gukanshō*. These first two texts, and other examples of the genre written during the eleventh and twelfth centuries, tend to concentrate on biographical descriptions with limited theoretical analysis of the operation of history per se. The latter two works, in contrast, expand upon the tale genre by including Buddhist and Shinto analytical strategies in their interpretation of the past and in their prognostications for the future.

Early Modern Histories

In the long history of sustained, critical reflections on the past, the seventeenth and eighteenth centuries in Japan are perhaps the most active. The Tokugawa political order (1603–1868) sought to establish its place in the records of the archipelago and, much like its imperial predecessor, was actively engaged in the production of official records of the past. There are several examples of this genre and the most elaborate project of this sort was carried out in the Mito domain and begun in 1657. This project, which was to continue off and on until 1906, was an early modern attempt to continue the work begun in the Six National Histories. It was written in Chinese, followed the imperial reigns, and concentrated upon court and central government affairs. The work also included, however, extensive biographical sections and numerous tables and chronicles in addition to extended historiographical essays. The work was also based upon significant research and the documents used were footnoted at the end of each section. Another example of official Tokugawa historical writing was produced by Arai Hakuseki (1657–1725), shogunal adviser and prominent official. While a prolific writer on the past, perhaps his most enduring work was the *Tokushi yoron* [Essays on History], first compiled in 1712. These essays were originally lectures delivered to the shogun with the intent, in the best Confucian tradition, of instructing the ruler, through extensive examples drawn from the past, in the arts of diplomacy, politics, and history. Arai used many sources and was particularly indebted to the *Jinnō shōtōki* and the national histories as he constructed a sweeping periodization of the past that demonstrated the dynamic nature of history, the power of human agency, and the historical inevitability of the formation of the Tokugawa order. Such politicized histories continue into the nineteenth century with the Hayashi school producing the *Tokugawa jikki* [True Record of the Tokugawa] and its supplement by the end of the Tokugawa period.

In contrast to these officially sponsored historical productions there were dozens of scholars who were engaged in the interpretation of the past and were profoundly concerned with problems of interpretation. Some of the preeminent writers are, among the Nativist *(Kokugaku)* scholars, Motoori Norinaga (1730–1861) and Hirata Atsutane (1776–1843); among Confucianists, Itō Jinsai (1627–1705) and Ogyū Sorai (1666–1728); and, among the Buddhists, Tenkai (1536–1643) and Tetsugen (1630–1681). Finally, the work of Tominaga Nakamoto (1715–1746), which was critical of all the preceding traditions, is perhaps the most far-reaching of all eighteenth-century works. Relying, as he did, upon the purely rational and its rejection of the past as a necessary absolute, Tominaga created an entirely new way of understanding the past.

Tominaga's emphasis upon the lacquerlike layers *(kajō)* of past events as the constituents of history and his suggesting of the precise means by which historical change and development occurred, opened the door to modern analytical enquiry.

Scientific Histories

During the Meiji Era (1868–1912), historical writing in Japan was transformed into a modern and "scientific" discipline. This, however, was not without a significant look to earlier styles. In 1869 Sanjō Sanetomi (1837–1891) was ordered by the government to create a Chinese-style history of the nation. The Historical Compilation Office *(Dajōkan shūshikyoku)* was established in 1875 to carry out this task, and Shigeno Yasutsugu (1827–1910) was made its director. Research on the *Dai Nippon Hennenshi* [Annals of Great Japan], as the work was called, was terminated by Inoue Kaoru, the minister of education, while still incomplete. The annals were seen to be already out of date and something of a political liability. Shigeno was instrumental in bringing a disciple of Leopold von Ranke, Ludwig Riess, to Japan in 1887 in order to teach at Tokyo Imperial University. Riess's emphasis was upon the techniques used to produce a document-based, factual history. When these methods were directed toward the earlier sources relied upon for the production of these Annals, much of the imperially based histories came under significant, and politically undesirable, scrutiny. Shigeno's student, Kume Kunitake (1839–1931), for example, noted that the *Dai Nihon Shi* was in fact heavily indebted to the medieval war tale, the *Taiheiki*, a work he described as pure fiction worthless for historical enquiry. For this and other public attacks on the received national history, Kume's position at Tokyo Imperial University was terminated and his writings were confiscated. Kume's dismissal and the cancellation of the *Dai Nippon Hennenshi* both occurred in 1892. The relation between history and the state in Japan is a long and complex one that has never resolved itself into a clear separation of those who write of the past and those who rule the present. The political and analytical tensions between the earlier writings on the past and modern historical methods continued unabated throughout the Meiji period and on into the twentieth century.

James Edward Ketelaar

See also JAPANESE HISTORIOGRAPHY—TWENTIETH CENTURY; *REKISHI MONOGATARI*.

Texts

The Future and the Past: A Translation and Study of the Gukanshō. Ed. and trans. Delmer M. Brown and Ichiro Ishida. Berkeley: University of California Press, 1979.

Kojiki. Trans. Donald Philippi. Tokyo and Princeton, NJ: University of Tokyo Press and Princeton University Press, 1969.

Lessons from History: The Tokushi Yoron by Arai Hakuseki. Trans. Joyce Ackroyd. St. Lucia: University of Queensland Press, 1982.

Nihongi: Chronicles of Japan from the Earliest Times to 697. Trans. W.G. Aston. London: George Allen & Unwin, Ltd., 1956.

Okagami: The Great Mirror, Fujiwara Michinaga (966–1027) and His Times. Trans. Helen Craig McCullough. Princeton, NJ: Princeton University Press, 1980.

A Tale of Flowering Fortunes: Annals of Japanese Aristocratic Life in the Heian Period. Ed. and trans. William H. and Helen Craig McCullough. 2 vols. Stanford, CA: Stanford University Press, 1980.

Tominaga Nakamoto. *Emerging from Meditation.* Ed. and trans. Michael Pye. Honolulu: University of Hawaii Press, 1990.

References

Brownlee, John S. *Political Thought in Japanese Historical Writing.* Waterloo, Ont.: Wilfrid Laurier University Press, 1991.

Harootunian, H.D. *Things Seen and Unseen: Discourse and Ideology in Tokugawa Nativism.* Chicago: University of Chicago Press, 1988.

Sakai Naoki. *Voices of the Past: The Status of Language in Eighteenth-Century Japanese Discourse.* Ithaca, NY: Cornell University Press, 1991.

Sakamoto Tarō. *The Six National Histories of Japan.* Trans. John Brownlee. Vancouver and Tokyo: UBC Press and University of Tokyo Press, 1991.

Japanese Historiography—Twentieth Century

Professional historiography in modern Japan begins in the Rankean nineteenth century; and it begins with the Meiji state, which both underwrote historical study and served as its primary object. Positivism and empiricism in Japanese historiography have, in other words, been bound up with the nation and national identity. The specificity of *twentieth-century* Japanese historiography, in turn, lies in its tangled relations with official Japanese nationalism, and in the successive transformations of world perspective that marked the rise and fall of Japanese imperialism. Indeed, the professionalization of the discipline and the defining of fields for historical research and teaching at all levels coincided with the establishment of the Japanese Empire itself. From the late 1890s onward, Japanese historians worked within or across a formally defined "trinity" of fields: national or Japanese history *(kokushi, Nihonshi)*, Western history *(Seiyōshi)*, and East Asian history *(Tōyōshi)*.

The application of what one might call "national empiricism" to ever-wider areas of the world called forth a response that defines the characteristic feature of twentieth-century historical writing in Japan. For while the professional "mainstream" may be Rankean, it has been accompanied, challenged, even at some points overturned by a series of overlapping, sometimes mutually contradictory, contestations. Between the 1910s and the 1930s the center of historical inquiry in Japan moved from narrowly political matters to broader social, economic, and cultural issues, along with serious undertakings in comparative economic history. We might describe the overall trend as post-Rankean, as long as this term is understood to mean that "fact"-and-document-based historiography as such was never rejected outright so much as relocated in a field traversed by a number of "strong" interpretive lines.

Yet what determined these extensions and contestations? First, we must consider the tension inherent in the relationship between empiricism and nationalism itself. The interest of the modern Japanese state in history lay in its attempt to tie itself back to a supposedly unbroken imperial line by means of materials collected from the early nineteenth century onward by Hanawa Hoki'ichi and his successors under the title of *Dai Nihon shiryō* [Historical Materials of Great Japan], which the Historiographical Institute at Tokyo Imperial University was charged with maintaining and collating. This was the documentary basis for an officially sanctioned "imperial view of history" *(kōkoku shikan)*. Beginning in the 1890s, and with dreary regularity over the decades between then and 1945, the *kōkoku shikan* functioned as an ideological throttle for even the most "disinterested" research on historical matters pertaining to the imperial institution. In the prototypical case, Kume Kunitake (1839–1931), a member of the first generation of German-trained historians, was compelled to resign his post in 1892 after publishing an article (influenced by then current studies in anthropology and comparative religion) in which he declared Shintō to be a "vestige of sky-worship." So, too, in 1910 the prestigious authors of a school history textbook submitted to the ministry of education, who had treated the two rival imperial courts of the fourteenth century together rather than condemning the eventual loser as traitorous. None of these authors was a radical innovator in methodology, let alone subversive. Their suppression cast a chill over any political history that touched on the imperial institution. The effect was felt strongly in historical education and especially in the schools.

Special mention must be made in this connection of Tsuda Sōkichi (1873–1961), whose meticulous studies of the ancient imperial court revealed the highly political character of the earliest official myth-histories of Japan. Tsuda was concerned far more with the "bearers" of Japan's emerging national culture in a given epoch, than with legitimating or refuting official claims about the imperial lineage. In the process of publishing his work (between 1916 and 1932), Tsuda had planted ideological land mines that were triggered only later, when the liberalizing trends of the World War I era had given way to a suffocating ideological conformism underwritten by military dominance. In 1939, Tsuda was charged with "desecrating the national polity," for work he had written years earlier, and went to trial along with his publisher.

The interest of the Tsuda case is as much historiographical as political. Tsuda's was only one instance of a trend toward works giving sustained critical attention to the character and quality of "real life" and people in Japanese history that took hold in the World War I era and afterward, in a context of accelerating industrialization, imperial expansion, rapid growth of the working and middle classes, and political, economic, and social "democratization." Works such as Tsuda's or the pioneering survey of the "social problem in Japanese history" by Miura Hiroyuki, studies in Japanese economic history by Honjō Eijirō (1888–1973), while certainly not all "popular" in style, were produced largely outside the context of Tokyo Imperial University, either at Kyoto Imperial, with its distinct anti-Tokyo (meaning antibureaucratic and antiempiricist) ethos; or at private universities such as Waseda, which were noticeably more congenial places for the production of adventurous scholarship. Local history was given strong impetus by the pioneering ethnography of Yanagita Kunio (1875–1962); while the anarchist and feminist Takamure Itsue, writing in isolation, produced significant work on the history of mar-riage. The latter half of the 1920s also saw the publication of massive collections of documents on Tokugawa and Meiji history, among them the *Nihon keizai taiten* [The Canon of the Japanese Economy], compiled by Takimoto Sei'ichi (1928–1930) and the *Meiji bunka zenshū* [Compendium of Meiji Culture], compiled by Yoshino Sakuzō (1925). Just as the mild liberalism typical of the period sought to bring about "government for the people," the new trend in social and cultural history strove to create a "history for the people."

This trend was extended and transformed by the rise of Marxism. Beginning after World War I, the social science "movement" intensified over the course of the 1920s and early 1930s, running headlong into the Great Depression and the lurch to the Right that followed. Its effects were startlingly apparent, beginning with an upsurge in studies of economic and social history, but extending to all fields of historiography and far beyond it. The distinctive Marxist concerns with methodological correctness (textual fidelity to the founders' teachings) and political practice combined to produce the first real analyses undertaken of Japan's capitalist development: the multivolume *Nihon shihonshugi hattatsushi kōza* [Lectures on the History of the Development of Japanese Capitalism] (1932–1933) remains a landmark of historiography and social analysis. Its arguments produced heated counterarguments: the so-called Debate on Japanese Capitalism, in which disputants sought to place the Meiji Restoration in the framework of late development and hence find historical keys to political practice, continued through much of the 1930s and in some respects has not yet concluded even today. The same period also saw the establishment of the historiographical profession's most important "Protestant" body, the Marxist Rekishigaku Kenkyūkai (Society for Historical Study) or Rekken, founded in 1933, and revived in 1945 after wartime suppression.

The maturation of generations of professional historians in the context of Japan's expanding world role after 1918 brought the production of original work by Japanese scholars working on both Western and East Asian history. Within the "trinity" of fields mentioned earlier, Western history was probably more prestigious than East Asian history but less so than that of Japan. With a few exceptions, however, that scholarship has remained a closed book to the historiographical world outside Japan. The "language barrier" (which has never prevented Japanese scholars from doing original work in Western languages) is only part of the reason. Cultural prejudices on the part of

Western scholars and undue methodological timidity on the part of Japanese also had a role. The fact was that by the 1930s three generations of scholars had been trained in Europe or by Europeans. Mitsukuri Genpachi, a Rankean of liberal sentiments, wrote prolifically on the *ancien régime,* revolution, and Napoleonic era in France, including a history of the socialist movement. Miura Shinshichi, who studied with Karl Lamprecht, was a pioneer in comparative cultural history on a grand scale. The inauguration by Takagi Yasaka of American history as a serious field dates from these years. Finally, what might be called the transwar generation, represented by Ōtsuka Hisao (b. 1907), Matsuda Tomoo, Takahashi Kōhachirō, and others were making their first forays into comparative economic history by the mid-1930s. A medievalist of the same generation, Uehara Senroku, exemplifies in two ways the best of the profession: the strong drive to master original documents, while also seeking (after 1945) to push Japanese historical scholarship beyond its formal "trinity" to a genuine "world history" *(sekaishi).*

In the long run, however, apart from the historiography of Japan itself, Japanese scholarship on East Asia has been of greater significance than that on Western history. The reasons are obvious: a shared written language; a millennium of cultural relations, albeit transformed by Japan's unprecedented thrust onto the continent; and access to sites and materials underwritten by military and political force. Beginning in the decade after the Russo–Japanese War of 1904 and 1905, Japanese historians of China such as Naitō Konan (1866–1934) and Shiratori Kurakichi were building upon ethnographic surveys of Japan's new sphere of influence—those undertaken by the South Manchurian Railroad were decisively important—to establish a body of historical scholarship on China and Korea. Naitō in particular generated a number of long-influential theses concerning the periodization of Chinese social history; and in general, Japanese standards of textual study as well as the vast quantity of materials, systematically collected and "canonized" over the course of the Japanese Empire's eight decades assured Japanese scholarship pride of place.

For Japanese historians, regardless of field, the war years were a virtually unmitigated catastrophe; the official "Nipponism" of the New Order was profoundly hostile to any critical enterprise. The sustained repression of the Left had silenced Marxists or driven them to some degree of cooperation with the wartime state. Although some excellent work was in fact carried out—by Ōtsuka and Maruyama Masao (b. 1914) for example—

the social sciences as a whole were not ennobled by their work in this period; and it is the paradox of Marxism that because of its insistence on the unity of theory and practice, many scholars who wrote under its inspiration felt compelled to remain close to the field of political action rather than take refuge in "pure" scholarship, even at the price of an intellectual degradation they would later come to repent. As a result, the liberal humanists among the historians probably emerged with their scholarly consciences less shredded by their experience.

The end of the war in 1945 did represent a new beginning: the taboos placed on historical scholarship by the occupation pale in comparison to those that were removed. Marxism entered its heyday with the return to prominence of organizations such as Rekken. But in some ways, the most notable feature of the first postwar decade is the serious debate among contending schools—especially Marxist and Weberian—and the de facto "united front" across ideological lines. The wholesale reconsideration of prewar society, extending far back into the ancient period, occupied much of the first postwar decades, and resulted in a huge body of work. Prewar figures such as Hattori Shisō (1901–1956) and Hani Gorō (1901–1983) combined efforts with younger scholars—Tōyama Shigeki (b. 1913), Ishimoda Shō (1912–1986), Maruyama Masao, Ōtsuka Hisao, and others—to redirect the energies of the profession toward democratization as a scholarly and political goal. As exemplified in Maruyama's powerful 1946 analysis of "ultranationalism," the historiographical task of these years was to root out the "backwardness" that supported the imperial system of modern times. Probably no historian, no matter how conservative politically, could have emerged from this time without a decent knowledge of Marxism and a complex object lesson in the relation of politics and scholarship. It is worth noting, in this connection, the vigorous growth of works on Russian economic and intellectual history, reflecting, perhaps, the strong and understandable interest among Japanese in the complex links between late-developing capitalism and socialism. Of even greater significance was the rise in status enjoyed by Chinese history in Japan as Mao's victory approached. Maeda Naonori's clarion call in 1948 for a sweeping reconsideration of China's social history set the agenda for a new generation and a new epoch; indeed the founding of the People's Republic seemed to have redeemed the profession, throwing the onus of imperialism—including cultural imperialism—onto the United States.

The incarnation of the cold war in Japan, followed by economic recovery, brought to prominence an American-inspired "modernization" approach whose centerpiece was a positive reassessment of the Tokugawa "legacy" to modern Japan: the anti-Marxist intent was, in certain cases, quite clear, but should not blind us to those truly distinguished works that emerged at this juncture. For nearly a generation, marked by the Hakone Conference of 1960 and successor meetings through the early 1970s, increasing numbers of Japanese and American historians worked through the interpretive and ideological ramifications of this reconsideration, never fully agreeing on its purpose or direction. Japanese scholars tended to keep up their critical guard *or* give in to a neo-exceptionalism that was underwritten by official attempts to whitewash Japan's modern role in continental Asia; while Americans, less immediately vested, could play the mediating role. But in an important sense, the "paradigm" crashed and burned in Vietnam, with the Americans learning what Japanese of the Co-Prosperity Sphere generation perhaps already knew.

Many historians writing after the mid-1960s questioned both the elitism and Eurocentrism of the would-be democratic enlighteners—their teachers—and moved the profession toward a new "people's history." *Minshūshi,* while hardly a uniform approach, in fact embodied a triple reaction against the elitism of the early postwar "enlighteners," formulaic Marxism, and the triumphalism that emerged in the wake of the 1964 Olympics and Meiji centenary celebrations of 1968. Positively put, it attempted to discover the roots of an indigenous democracy (or more broadly a decent society) in pre- and post-Restoration Japan. This quest led a number of major practitioners, such as Irokawa Daikichi, Kano Masanao, Yasumaru Yoshio, and Haga Noboru, to "unearth" a vast and rich body of historical material, and (as with Irokawa) to reconnect methodologically with the work of prewar ethnographers, especially Yanagita Kunio. The years since the 1970s, in Japan as elsewhere, have seen an accelerating pluralization and deepening of fields and approaches. Medieval history, represented by Amino Yoshihiko, has been an area of genuine interest and intellectual energy. In some ways, the healthiest aspect of recent decades has been the emergence of a new style of work between Japanese and American and European historians, toward greater equality and mutual engagement with both documentary evidence and interpretations, rather than a division of labor in which "their" data was organized and interpreted by "our" theory. At the same time, the growing presence of other Asian scholars working with Japanese historians, and a willingness on the part of both to confront the modern history of the region, including a consideration of the legacy of Japanese colonialism that goes beyond blanket denunciation, is also appearing. But the future of these developments is not assured as long as official attitudes in Japan toward modern history continue to partake of the politics of denial that have marked them for so long.

Andrew E. Barshay

See also JAPANESE HISTORIOGRAPHY—TO 1900; *REKISHI MONOGATARI.*

References

Beasley, W.G., and E.J. Pulleyblank, eds. *Historians of China and Japan.* Oxford: Oxford University Press, 1961.

Bosworth, R.J.B. *Explaining Auschwitz and Hiroshima: History Writing and the Second World War, 1945–1990.* London and New York: Routledge, 1993, chap. 8.

Gluck, Carol. "The People in History: Recent Trends in Japanese Historiography." *Journal of Asian Studies* 38 (1978): 25–50.

Kano Masanao. "The Changing Concept of Modernization: From a Historian's Viewpoint." *Japan Quarterly* 32 (1976): 28–35.

Sumiya, Mikio, and Koji Taira. *An Outline of Japanese Economic History: Major Works and Research Findings.* Tokyo: University of Tokyo Press, 1979.

Tanaka, Stefan. *Japan's Orient: Rendering Pasts into History.* Berkeley and Los Angeles: University of California Press, 1993.

Jaurès, Jean (1859–1914)

French socialist historian. By vocation a politician and journalist, Jaurès turned to historical writing only late in his career. Born at Castres (Tarn) into a bourgeois family, he early on displayed intellectual brilliance. He studied philosophy at the École Normale Supérieure, then entered the teaching profession before embarking on a political career. As a socialist he was repeatedly elected to the Chamber of Deputies between 1885 and his assassination on the eve of World War I. After an electoral defeat returned him to private life between 1898 and 1902, Jaurès undertook a multivolume "socialist" history of France. He both edited the collection and contributed four volumes that treated the Revolutionary period down to 1794. Based on original research, his work demonstrated that the Revolution originated in a struggle between the aristocracy and bourgeoisie, with the latter striving to secure political power to match its economic strength. But Jaurès also stressed the efforts that the laboring classes and peasantry made to attain political and social equality. He drew vivid portraits of all major Revolutionary leaders and carefully scrutinized their ideas. His work strongly influenced succeeding generations of French historians.

James Friguglietti

Texts

Histoire socialiste de la Révolution française [Socialist History of the French Revolution]. 7 vols. Paris: Editions Sociales, 1968–1973.

References

Goldberg, Harvey. *The Life of Jean Jaurès.* Madison: University of Wisconsin Press, 1962.

Jewish Historiography—Modern (since A.D. 1500)

The expulsions from Spain in 1492 and from Portugal in 1496 led to a burst of Jewish historical writing unprecedented since biblical times. Solomon ibn Verga of Seville's *Shevet Yehudah* [Staff of Judah] (first published in Adrianople in 1553), despite its pietistic orientation, includes a realistic analysis of the political causes of the traumatic events and the problematic place of Jews in non-Jewish society. Samuel Usque's *Consolations for the Tribulations of Israel* (written in Portuguese and published at Ferrara in 1553) gives an account, in the form of a pastoral dialogue, of ancient Jewish history and later persecutions and sufferings, with the apologetic aim of demonstrating that God has not abandoned the Jewish people and that Marranos should return to Judaism. Several other Hebrew chronicles on France, Turkey, Italy, and central Europe were also produced by sixteenth-century Jews, but historical writing, despite the stimulus of the invention of printing, remained a peripheral interest of Jewish intellectuals during the early modern period. Unique among Renaissance figures was Azariah dei Rossi, whose daring *Me'or Einayim* [Enlightener of the Eyes], published at Mantua in 1573, pioneered the critical use of non-Jewish classical and secular writings to complement biblical and rabbinic sources. More a foundation than a historical reconstruction as such, dei Rossi's book met with considerable opposition from traditional authorities and its groundbreaking character was acknowledged only in the nineteenth

century. The massacres of the Jews in the Ukraine during 1648 and 1649 resulted in a number of chronicles mixing traditional themes with remarks on the social conditions of the day, the most valuable being Nathan Nata Hannover's *Yeven Mezulah* [Abyss of Despair] (Venice, 1653).

The first comprehensive modern Jewish historian was Isaac Marcus Jost of Frankfurt, an early supporter of German Reform Judaism who applied the canons of eighteenth-century Enlightenment rationalism to Judaism. His *History of the Jews* was published between 1820 and 1829; a later work by him, published in the late 1850s, was able to make use of the remarkable efflorescence of research into the Jewish past that had appeared, mainly in Germany, in the interim. The turning point in modern Jewish historiography was the formation in 1822 of the short-lived *Verein für Cultur und Wissenshaft des Judentums* [Society for the Cultural and Scientific Study of Judaism] by a group of young German Jewish intellectuals, including Leopold Zunz, whose *Sermons of the Jews* on the *midrash,* the ancient homiletic literature, became a landmark in the modern Jewish historical consciousness. For the founders of the *Wissenschaft des Judentums,* the treatment of Judaism as *Wissenschaft* (that is, as involving the analysis of the historic totality of Judaism, as it was then understood, with the meticulous systematic procedures that were applied to both the humanities and natural sciences) led to the reconstruction and reinterpretation of the Jewish past with far-ranging implications. Concerned to defend the acceptability of Judaism and the emancipation of Jews as full citizens of the lands in which they lived, the nineteenth-century champions of *Wissenschaft des Judentums* emphasized the recovery of lost or ignored religious and literary works (especially medieval Jewish philosophy, poetry, historiography, and law), the continual intellectual vitality of Judaism through the Middle Ages (although Heinrich Graetz and others were critical of the supposed obscurantism of Jewish mystics), and a certain preoccupation with the persecutions and massacres of Jews in Europe. An outstanding historiographical achievement of this phase was Graetz's *Geschichte der Juden* [History of the Jews] from the biblical period to the nineteenth century, which was translated into many languages, including Hebrew and English. Besides his own research, Graetz was able to draw on the growing body of work by bibliographers, philologists, and investigators in the archives of Europe to construct a passionate but intellectually rigorous account of the entirety of Jewish history up to his own day.

By the end of the nineteenth century, Jewish historians in Russia and Poland began to focus on the social, economic, and political factors shaping Jewish life in the diaspora and a far greater appreciation of the Yiddish culture and other distinctive features of the Eastern European Ashkenazic world. In the turn from a German-Jewish historiography influenced by philosophical idealism to one shaped by positivism, sociology, and secularism, an influential figure was Simon Dubnow, who called for the collection of primary sources on the Jews of Eastern Europe and himself published studies of the Jews of Poland and Lithuania, a history of the origins of eighteenth-century Hasidism, and a multivolume *World History of the Jewish People.* The first two decades of the twentieth century saw the emergence of Russian Jewish scholarly journals and historical publications at the level of methodological sophistication that had been attained in Western countries in the preceding century. After the Russian Revolution a number of scholarly institutes published works with an orientation that the Communist Party considered politically reliable, mainly of a Marxist nature; "bourgeois" and then all original Jewish scholarship in the Soviet Union largely came to an end by the late 1930s and has only begun to reappear in the 1990s.

The Jewish national revival and the influence of general historiographical trends lent a new richness and complexity to twentieth-century Jewish historical studies in European countries up to the Holocaust. Most European Jewish scholars were associated either with modern rabbinic seminaries in Breslau, Berlin, and elsewhere, or with institutes for Jewish studies in the various European countries. From the mid-1920s, the Hebrew University of Jerusalem became a center for Jewish historical research. It attracted eminent scholars trained in European universities in various fields of Judaica, for example, Gershom Scholem, a German Jewish intellectual who became the leading authority in the history of Jewish mysticism, and Yitzhak Baer, known for his work in the history of the Jews of Spain and on topics in late antiquity and the Middle Ages. Other European scholars who emigrated to Palestine found positions in secondary schools, teachers' colleges, and other institutions. After Israel became independent in 1948, new universities in Tel Aviv, Haifa, and Beersheva trained Israeli-born historians who have come to professional maturity since the 1960s.

Before the 1960s, most American scholarship on Jewish history was done under the auspices of rabbinical seminaries. One notable exception was Salo W. Baron, at Columbia University, who produced a massive *Social and Religious History of the Jews* (second ed., 1952–1983, in eighteen volumes covering up to 1650). Since then, Jewish history has become recognized in the curriculum of most American institutions of higher learning, and new journals and many publication series have appeared.

Because Jewish history overlaps with every area of western Asia, North Africa, Europe, the Americas, and other regions, and because it embraces the history of a social group (one whose composition has changed in the course of time) and a cultural tradition (ranging from folk traditions and magic to sophisticated metaphysical and juridical systems of thought), it has lent itself to a broad range of interdisciplinary approaches. Historians of Jewish subjects specialize in interconnections with ancient Near Eastern civilizations (via the Hebrew Bible), the classical cultures of the Mediterranean (in Hellenistic Judaism and the various sects and movements of Judaism in Palestine in late antiquity), the origins of Christianity and Islam and subsequent entanglements with Christendom and the Islamic world (from China and Central Asia to North Africa and the Iberian peninsula to medieval Europe north of the Alps), the early modern communications and trade network from the Caribbean and North Atlantic to eastern Poland and the Balkans, and more. Modern Jewish history has become a distinct area of study, concerned with local and interregional history, migration and demography, economic change, the secularization of religious groups, political integration, social and cultural rejection, persecution and genocide, changing gender roles, acculturation and assimilation, and movements for cultural renascence and national independence. Jewish history has become, therefore, multidimensional and multicultural, paradigmatic for minority groups living in diasporas and also for ancient religious traditions coping with the impact of the scientific and industrial revolutions and other features of modernity. As a result of modern historical study, Jewish philosophies of history, therefore, must now confront a multiplicity of Jewish identities within the context of a continuous, ever-changing whole of a problematic and challenging nature.

Robert M. Seltzer

See also CHRISTIANITY, VIEWS OF HISTORY IN; HOLOCAUST; JUDAISM, VIEWS OF HISTORY IN (ANTIQUITY TO 1500).

References

Baron, Salo W. *History and Jewish Historians: Essays and Addresses.* Ed. Arthur Hertzberg and Leon A. Feldman. Philadelphia: Jewish Publication Society of America, 1964.

Glatzer, Nahum N. "The Beginnings of Modern Jewish Studies." In *Essays in Jewish Thought.* University: University of Alabama Press, 1978, 149–165.

Kochan, Lionel. *The Jew and His History.* New York: Schocken Books, 1974.

Kozodoy, Neal, ed. "What Is the Use of Jewish History?" In *What Is the Use of Jewish History? Essays by Lucy S. Dawidowicz.* New York: Schocken Books, 1992, 3–19.

Meyer, Michael A., ed. *Ideas of Jewish History.* New York: Behrman House, 1974.

Rotenstreich, Nathan. *Tradition and Reality: The Impact of History on Modern Jewish Thought.* New York: Random House, 1972.

Schorsch, Ismar. *From Text to Context: The Turn to History in Modern Judaism.* Hanover, NH: University Press of New England, 1994.

Seltzer, Robert M. "From Graetz to Dubnow: The Impact of the East European Milieu on the Writing of Jewish History." In *The Legacy of Jewish Migration,* ed. David Berger. Social Science Monographs. New York: Brooklyn College Press, 1983, 49–60.

Yerushalmi, Josef Hayim. *Zakhor: Jewish History and Jewish Memory.* Seattle: University of Washington Press, 1982.

Jien [Fujiwara Jichin] (1155–1225)

Japanese Tendai Buddhist priest. Son of an imperial regent and member of the Fujiwara clan; he was also known by his posthumous name (given by Emperor Shijo in 1237), Fujiwara Jichin. He began his monastic training at eleven and took the tonsure at the Tendai main temple Enryakuji at age thirteen. After holding a series of appointments in the Tendai organization he became head abbot (*zasu*) of the Enryakuji for the first time in 1192. (He was also made *zasu* in 1201, 1212, and 1214.) His reputation is based mainly upon his *Gukanshō* [Miscellany of Foolish Views, ca. 1220], a seven-volume national political history based upon the imperial reigns. By focusing on various historical "principles" (*dōri*) derived from Buddhist theology he attempted to reconcile the crisis between the imperial court and the rising powers of the great military clans. While recognizing an inevitable trajectory of historical decay he also asserted the possibility of limited human agency in affecting temporary change.

James Edward Ketelaar

Texts

The Future and the Past: A Translation and Study of the Gukanshō. Ed. and trans. Delmer M. Brown and Ichiro Ishida. Berkeley: University of California Press, 1979.

References

Taga Munehaya. *Jien.* In *Jimbutso sōsho,* vol. 15. Tokyo: Yoshikawa Kobunkan, 1961.

Joachim of Fiore (c. 1135–1202)

Calabrian abbot and apocalyptic thinker. Joachim of Fiore developed an apocalyptic vision of world history that had critical importance for subsequent Western thought. Joachim's main writings were the *Liber de concordia novi ac veteris testamenti* [Book of the Concordance of the New and Old Testaments], the *Expositio in apocalypsim* [Exposition on the Apocalypse], and the *Psalterium decem chordarum* [Ten Books on the Psalter] (all ca. 1180–1190). The most influential idea arising from these works was the interpretation of world history as a progressive unfolding of three stages, each of which was ruled over by one person of the Trinity. The Age of the Father had been a time of subjection to the Law; it had ended with the advent of Christ. The Age of the Son was the current time of faith under the Gospel. It would be followed in turn by the Age of the Holy Spirit, when spiritual freedom and love would come to final fulfillment. Joachim believed that this third and final historical stage was already dawning in the era around 1200 and would soon be fully realized. This scenario marked a fundamental break from the prevailing Augustinian view, which had discouraged eschatological visions of either progress or decay. Joachim's ideas, often twisted and applied in ways of which he would not have approved, played a basic role in late-medieval and early-modern conceptions of prophetic history; their echoes reach into modern times in a wide array of forms, including various ideologies of revolution as well as hopes for historical progress or a "New Age."

Robin B. Barnes

Texts

Apocalyptic Spirituality: Treatises and Letters of Lactantius, Adso of Montier-en-Der, Joachim of Fiore, the Franciscan Spirituals, Savonarola. Ed. and trans. Bernard McGinn. New York: Paulist Press, 1979.

Liber de concordia Novi ac Veteris Testamenti. Ed. E. Randolph Daniel. Transactions of the

American Philosophical Society, vol. 38, pt. 8. Philadelphia: American Philosophical Society, 1983.

McGinn, Bernard. *Visions of the End: Apocalyptic Traditions in the Middle Ages.* New York: Columbia University Press, 1979 (includes selections from Joachim in translation).

References

McGinn, Bernard. *The Calabrian Abbot: Joachim of Fiore in the History of Western Thought.* New York: MacMillan, 1985.

Reeves, Marjorie. *The Influence of Prophecy in the Later Middle Ages: A Study in Joachimism.* Oxford: Oxford University Press, 1969.

———. *Joachim of Fiore and the Prophetic Future.* New York: Harper and Row, 1976.

John of Thurócz [János Thuróczi] (ca. 1435–ca. 1490)

Medieval Hungarian chronicler and annalist. Descended from a noble family from Hont county in Upper Hungary, John was probably educated by the religious order of the Premonstratensians in Šahy where he later became a notary of the document depository (1470–1475) and subsequently served in two official positions, as a notary for Stephen Báthory and Thomas Draghy, and as pronotary of Mathias "Corvinus" Hunyadi. In 1488 he completed his *Chronica Hungarorum* [Hungarian Chronicle], which was printed that year in illustrated editions in Augsburg and Brno. The first three parts dealing with the origins of the Hungarians, which he erroneously viewed as descendants of the Huns, up to the reign of Sigismund Luxembourg, were based largely upon older chronicles by monastics. The final section, from the reign of Sigismund until the victory of Mathias Corvinus over the Archbishop of Esztergom (1471) was based upon his own investigations and conversations with notables. The focus of his work was not just the ruling dynasty but also the nobility, which he considered to have a distinct mission as bearers of Hungarian statehood. This first secular chronicle marks the transition from medieval clerical chronicles to early humanist historiography and was used as a basic handbook in the Hungarian kingdom until the mid-eighteenth century.

David P. Daniel

Texts

Chronica Hungarorum [Hungarian Chronicle]. Budapest: Helikon, Kossuth ny, 1985.

References

Mályusz, Elemér. *A Thuróczy-krónika és forrásai* [The Thuróczy Chronicle and Its Sources]. Budapest: Akadémiai Kiadó, 1967.

———. *Thuróczy János krónikája* [The Chronicle of János Thuróczy]. Budapest: Magyar Tudományos Akadémiai, 1944.

Marsina. Richard. "Uhorské kroniky a kronikari" [Hungarian Chronicles and Chroniclers]. *Historický časopis* 16 (1968): 430–431.

Johnson, Samuel (1846–1901)

Yoruba historian. Johnson was born of parents who had been liberated from slavery and settled in Sierra Leone under a scheme designed by British philanthropists to initiate a Christian African society. Like many Yoruba from this community, Johnson returned to his parents' homeland in modern-day western Nigeria as a missionary. His life's work involved efforts both to evangelize and to end the wars that raged among the Yoruba in the nineteenth century. His single historical work, completed by 1897 but published under his younger brother's editorial hand in 1921, was shaped by both concerns. Johnson used oral court traditions, eyewitness accounts, and his own involvement as a British diplomatic agent to compile a unique and richly detailed account of the wars, Yoruba culture, and early history. His presentation of the internal dynamics of African history and his concern to create a common Yoruba identity both presage later colonial nationalist historiography. His monumental work remains the reference point for any treatment of Yoruba history.

P.S. Zachernuk

Texts

The History of the Yorubas: From the Earliest Times to the Beginning of the British Protectorate. Ed. O. Johnson. London: Routledge and Kegan Paul, 1921.

References

Falola, Toyin, ed. *Pioneer, Patriot and Patriarch: Samuel Johnson and the Yoruba People.* Madison: African Studies Program, University of Wisconsin–Madison, 1993.

Johnston, Sir Harry Hamilton, (1858–1927)

British explorer, naturalist, and colonial administrator. Johnston was born in London and educated at King's College, London. From 1879 he served in various colonial posts and participated in the scramble, partitioning, and colonization of Africa. Johnston was widely traveled and spoke many African languages. His African enterprise began in 1882 with an expedition through southern Angola. From 1884 to 1901, he served as British consul in many African territories including Cameroon, Nigeria, Nyasaland, and Uganda. Knighted in 1896, he negotiated the famous Buganda Agreement of 1900 on behalf of Britain. Outside his official work, Johnston pursued studies in the geography and ethnology of African peoples, mainly during the period 1899–1901. His reputation came from his writings on broad African subjects. Johnston published about forty books, most of which focus on African-related topics. His penchant for scholarly enquiry and writing set him apart from other equally prominent colonial administrators. Among his works on Africa, two can be considered as crucial: *The Opening Up of Africa* (1911) and *A Comparative Study of the Bantu and Semi-Bantu Languages* (2 vols., 1919–1922). The first of these, as its title implies, describes the process of European exploration and subsequent partitioning of Africa. It emphasizes the role of Europeans not only in "opening up" the "dark continent" of Africa to the outside world, but also in initiating civilization among the African people. The *Comparative Study,* which focuses on African linguistic classifications, attempts to correlate the dominant "Negro" Bantu languages with those of the Semi-Bantu. In this work, Johnston ascribes the origins of the African Bantu languages to the Hamites (supposedly early Caucasian immigrants of northeastern African). Written in an era when Europeans strove to justify colonialism as a "civilizing mission" and the "White Man's Burden," it was only logical that Johnston's works would give little or no credit to African innovations or achievements. It is hardly surprising that most of his works on Africa later came under severe attack by modern Africanists who tend to dismiss them as catering to imperialism and "scientific racism." Nevertheless, Johnston was one of the first to perceive the complex relationships between the Bantu family of languages, and to suggest that something could be said about the long history of Bantu expansion by close study and comparison of these languages. Interestingly enough it was Johnston's modern biographer, Roland Oliver, who would become the pioneer interpreter of Bantu expansion in Africa, using archaeological, documentary, biological, and above all linguistic evidence.

Apollos O. Nwauwa

Texts

A Comparative Study of the Bantu and Semi-Bantu Languages. 2 vols. New York: AMS Press, 1977.

A History of the Colonization of Africa by Alien Races. Cambridge, Eng.: Cambridge University Press, 1905.

The Opening Up of Africa. London: William Norgate, 1911.

Pioneers in West Africa. London: Blackie and Son, 1912.

References

Oliver, Roland. *Sir Harry Johnston and the Scramble for Africa.* London: Chatto and Windus, 1957.

Joinville, Jean, Sire de (1224/1225–1317)

Thirteenth-century chronicler, principally known for his biography of Louis IX of France, which epitomizes feudal kingship and knightly service. Louis was the model king because of personal integrity and principled rule. Joinville's *Histoire de Saint Louis* concentrates on the years 1248–1254 when both men were engaged in Louis's crusade in the Near East. While serving at Acre, Joinville had composed a meditation on the Apostle's Creed to demonstrate the primacy of faith and the duty of expressing it in action. The *Histoire,* dictated in Joinville's old age (1305–1309) to instruct Louis's heirs, likewise has two parts: Louis's precepts and his deeds. Joinville promoted the sanctification of the king; but he was no sycophant. As hereditary seneschal of Champagne he had refused to follow the king on his second crusade to Tunis (1270) because of his prior duty to his own family and feudal dependents. Enshrining Louis's respect for the rights of others while demanding his own, Joinville's *Histoire* contributed to the identification of the French crown with the French people.

C.M.D. Crowder

Texts

Histoire de Saint Louis, Texte originale ramené à l'orthographe des chartes. Ed. Natalis de Wailly. New ed. Paris: Librairie Hachette, 1906.

The Life of St. Louis. Trans. René Hague (from de Wailly's French ed). London: Sheed and Ward, 1955.

References

De Wailly, Natalis. "Préface" to his edition of the *Histoire de Saint Louis.* Paris: Librairie Hachette, 1906.

Hague, René. "Introduction." In his translation of *The Life of St. Louis*. London: Sheed and Ward, 1955.

Jones, Arnold Hugh Martin (1904–1970)

English ancient historian. "Hugo" Jones was born at Birkenhead and went to New College, Oxford, in 1922. After winning a fellowship at All Souls College, Oxford, he held posts at Cairo and Wadham College, Oxford. During World War II he worked at the Ministry of Labor and in Intelligence, but afterward became professor of ancient history, first at University College, London, then at Cambridge. While at Oxford he wrote *The Cities of the Eastern Roman Provinces* (1937) and *The Greek City from Alexander to Justinian* (1940), both concerned with the development of Greek cities in western Asia. At Cambridge Jones realized his massive long-term project, *The Later Roman Empire 284–602* (1964), in two parts, a "Narrative" and a "Descriptive," with an additional volume of notes. He also coedited *The Prosopography of the Later Roman Empire* (1971–1980), and produced numerous shorter works, such as *The Herods of Judaea* (1938), *Athenian Democracy* (1957), and *The Decline of the Ancient World* (1966). His views on the ancient economy were influential on, among others, Sir Moses Finley.

Richard Fowler

Texts

The Cities of the Eastern Roman Provinces. Second ed., revised by M. Avi-Yonah et al. Oxford: Clarendon Press, 1971.
The Greek City from Alexander to Justinian. Oxford: Clarendon Press, 1940.
The Later Roman Empire 284–602. 3 vols. Oxford: Basil Blackwell, 1964.

Jordanes [or Jornandes] (d. ca. 552)

Gothic historian writing in Latin. Jordanes, notary to the Gothic chief Gunthigis-Baza, was partly Gothic in origin. Resigning as notary, he may have converted from Arian to Orthodox Christianity. In about 551, Jordanes wrote the *Getica*, a history of the Goths up to that year, in bad Latin and derived largely from lost works of Cassiodorus and other earlier works. Written from the Byzantine viewpoint, the *Getica* is a major source for the history and culture of the barbarian invaders, including the Huns. Jordanes also wrote a history of Rome (extant) and a now-lost universal chronicle.

Stephen A. Stertz

Texts

The Gothic History of Jordanes. Trans. C. Mierow. Princeton, NJ: Princeton University Press, 1915.
Opera. Ed. T. Mommsen. In *Monumenta Germaniae Historiae, Auctores Antiquissimi* Vol. 5, part 1. Berlin: Weidmann, 1882.

References

Goffart, Walter. *The Narrators of Barbarian History (A.D. 550–800)*. Princeton, NJ: Princeton University Press, 1988.

Josephus, Flavius (37/8–100)

Jewish politician, soldier, and historian. Born of a priestly family in Jerusalem, Josephus participated in the first Jewish revolt against Rome and later attached himself to the Roman cause. He authored four works in Greek: *History of the Jewish War, Antiquities of the Jews, Against Apion,* and *The Life*. His *History of the Jewish War,* an account of the Jewish revolt, stressed the invincibility of the Roman legions and the futility of Jewish resistance. In the *Antiquities,* Josephus attempted to make earlier Jewish history appeal to a Hellenistic audience by removing biblical history of its supernatural elements. The *Life* was an apology for his conduct in the Jewish war, rather than a true autobiography, while *Against Apion* was a rejoinder to anti-Semitic charges and an effort to show the superior ethics of the Jews. Although Josephus had flaws (for example, falsifying data, and having personal biases), he saw himself as a historian in the tradition of Thucydides. He was generally ignored by both Greco-Roman and Hebrew authors, but was preserved by the church fathers, who were interested in his writings because of the historical context that they provided for early Christianity.

Mark W. Chavalas

Texts

Josephus. Ed. H. St. J. Thackeray et al. 9 Vols. Cambridge, MA: Harvard University Press/ Loeb Classical Library, 1926–1965.

References

Rajak, T. *Josephus: The Historian and His Society.* London: Duckworth, 1983.

Journals, Historical

Periodicals (publications that are issued regularly and for an indeterminate duration) with historical subjects as the exclusive focus. Although publications with some of these characteristics existed earlier, historical journals proper only appeared a few decades after Leopold von Ranke's *Geschichtswissenschaft* had been established at German universities. The growing body of professional scholars delivered the needed critical mass of authors and readers who shared a systematic methodology and view of history. In 1859, Heinrich von Sybel created the *Historische Zeitschrift* as the prototypical historical journal for the growing community of historical scholars. While Ranke's *Historisch-Politische Zeitschrift* (1832–1836) had carried eclectic works of historical scholarship (with a clear political purpose), the *Historische Zeitschrift* expressed the historical methodology and interpretation of the historicism of the Ranke school. However, extrascholarly motivations also moved the scholars connected with the *Historische Zeitschrift,* who on the whole were sympathetic to the Prussian-*kleindeutsch* approach to German unification. The delay in the appearance of counterparts to the *Historische Zeitschrift* in other nations reflected the different pace in the professionalization of historiography. In France, where the German type of historiography made headway only in the course of educational reforms after 1871, historians had available at first only the *Revue critique d'histoire et de la littérature* (1866), which offered only reviews, and the *Revue des questions historiques* (1866), which was more attuned to rigorous scholarship, although from the outset it had conservative Catholic tendencies. In that climate, still lacking the critical mass of an academic historical establishment, Gabriel Monod created the *Revue Historique* (1876) in order to further the development of just such an establishment. While the review had no declared political preference, the underlying philosophy of history was that of the ideology of the French Revolution, carried on by the Republican party. The emergence of the *English Historical Review* (1886) reflected the gradual—but in England particularly slow—detachment of historiography from literature. Historical essays of excellent quality had appeared primarily in such literary vehicles as the *Edinburgh Review* and *Quarterly Review* and in Lord Acton's *North British Review.* As in the case of other historical journals, an undeclared philosophy of history did color the editorial policies of the *English Historical Review:* the strong focus on English history in its Whig interpretation. In the United States, the German model for the training of historians sponsored the growth of a body of professional scholars. That and the presence of an increasingly influential organization of historians (American Historical Association, 1884) facilitated the founding of the *American Historical Review* (1895), a journal that in turn saw as a major objective the professionalization of history. Eventually the *American Historical Review* became the organ of the American Historical Association. While the *AHR* from the beginning rejected a purely American focus, its philosophy of history accorded well with the American sense of history: progressive, liberal, democratic, and emancipatory. No clear connection can be observed between the national context and the universality of a journal's content, as imperial England's *English Historical Review* was less universal in scope than the isolationist U.S. *AHR.* As a rule, the new national historical journals eschewed open partisanship since they all followed varieties of the positivist philosophy of history, that is to let facts guide the representation of the past. They served their clientele—mostly academic historians—well by (1) speedily communicating research results and new interpretations through articles; (2) informing scholars about new publication through critical book reviews; (3) printing sets of documents (soon abandoned as a regular feature); and (4) furthering the cohesion of the profession through personnel information, notices of meetings, and news concerning historical associations. While widely copied in their format, these pioneering professional journals lost some of their overpowering position primarily due to the successful development and maturation of the discipline to which they had contributed so much. The denser the network of enquiry grew, the greater became the urge to specialization according to region and research focus among historical journals. An additional push toward specialization came from profound disagreements on the theory and philosophy of history. Here figured the extension of historical investigation to ever new aspects of life but also the hope to discover history's governing forces (economic, social, demographic, geographic). Yet specialization also resulted from the desire of groups to build or strengthen their identity and cohesion as well as foster pride in it (such as the *Journal of Negro History* [1916], the *Catholic Historical Review* [1915], and the many regional, state, and local journals). Finally, external developments, such as the emergence of the new world order after 1945 pushed new areas into the spotlight of research. Thus, of the major English-language journals on Africa 85 percent, and on Asia (including the Mid-East) 76 percent, were founded after 1945. In practice, the motives for founding journals have, of course, not been as clearly separated as can be revealed from such an analysis. A case in point was the *Mississippi Valley Historical Review* (1914; from 1964 *Journal of American History),* a journal that resulted from dissatisfactions with the *AHR* springing from feelings of regional neglect; a sense that the American Historical Association held (for a while) too rigid a view of professionalism; a belief that there existed sufficient room for a second American historical journal; and the efforts of individual persons with a strong sense of entrepreneurship. Eventually, however, specialization met its counterforce in the wish to create an all-encompassing "New History," inclusive with regard to the world, aspects of life, and all related disciplines that studied culture.

Already in 1900, the search for a New History led, in direct opposition to the founding journals with their emphasis on matters of state, to Henri Berr's founding the *Revue de Synthèse historique* (1900). In 1929, Marc Bloch and Lucien Febvre founded the most important organ on behalf of an encompassing historiography, the *Annales d'histoire économique et sociale* (after 1945, *Annales: Economies, Sociétés, Civilisations*). While the journal eventually benefited from being seen as part of the post-1945 regeneration of France, its remarkable influence on historians came through its affirmation by outstanding scholars of a cultural historiography closely linked to the social sciences and psychology. Other periodicals that would build on this view are the British journal *Past & Present* (established 1952) and later the *Journal of Interdisciplinary History* (established 1970).

One cannot overlook the fact that all of these extensions did not include the encompassing of a single readership both for the whole historical profession and for those among the general public interested in history. The price of greater specialization was generally the opposite, with decisive implications for the readership of historical journals.

The wealth of material offered by the historical journals soon needed instruments to help scholars in finding articles and book reviews they needed in their work—technically called access tools or bibliographic control. Such bibliographic control was offered through citation indices and publications of abstracts (such as *Historical Abstracts*). In the electronic age these indices have become databases, which, beneficial as they are, point to an uncertainty in the world of historical journals about the future role of electronic publishing.

Ernst Breisach

See also ANNALES SCHOOL; BIBLIOGRAPHY—HISTORICAL; COMPUTERS AND HISTORIOGRAPHY; HISTORY WORKSHOP; PROFESSIONALIZATION OF HISTORY.

References

Boehm, Eric H., et al., eds. *Historical Periodicals Directory.* 2 vols. Santa Barbara, CA: Clio Press, 1981.

Fyfe, Janet. *Historical Journals and Serials: An Analytical Guide.* Westport, CT: Greenwood Press, 1986.

Stieg, Margaret F. *The Origin and Development of Scholarly Historical Periodicals.* University: University of Alabama Press, 1986.

Jovanović, Slobodan (1869–1958)

Serbian politician and historian. Born in Novi Sad (Vojvodina), Jovanović studied law in Geneva and became a professor at the University of Belgrade. In April 1941, he became vice president in the government of Dušan Simović, and fled with it to London. Here he became president of the government-in-exile and showed himself a strong supporter of Draža Mihailovich. Jovanović produced a basic survey of the history of Serbia from 1838 to 1903 in eight volumes. In the first of these, covering the period from 1838 to 1858, he describes the actions of the so-called Defenders of the Constitution against the Obrenović dynasty and under Prince Alexander Karadjordjević. The second volume is devoted to the restoration of the Obrenović dynasty and the second reign of Prince Miloš and his son Michael (1858–1868). The following three volumes cover the reign of Milan Obrenović (1868–1889), including the war with the Turks and the proclamation of the Serbian kingdom in 1882. The last three volumes take up the reign of Milan's son Alexander, from the regency during his youth to the assassination of the king and the extinction of the Obrenović dynasty in 1903.

Robert Stallaerts

Texts

"Izvestaj Slobodana Jovanovića o poseti sprkim konsulatama u Turskoj iz 1894. godine." [Report of Slobodan Jovanović on His Visit to the Serbian Consulates in Turkey in the Year 1894]. Ed. Radoš Ljusić. *Istorijski Glasnik* 1–2 (1987): 193–215.

Sabrana Dela [Collected Works]. Ed. Ž. Stojković and R. Samardžić. Belgrade: Prosveta and Beogradski Grafički Zavod, 1990.

"Serbia in the Early Seventies." *The Slavonic Review* 4 (1925–1926): 384–395.

References

Auty, Phyllis. "Slobodan Jovanović As a Historian." *The Slavonic and East European Review* 38 (1960): 515–529.

Djordjević, Dimitrije. "Historians in Politics: Slobodan Jovanović." *Journal of Contemporary History* 8 (1973): 21–40.

Petrović, Michael Boro. "Slobodan Jovanović (1869–1958): The Career and Fate of a Serbian Historian." *Serbian Studies* 3 (1984): 3–25.

Judaism, Views of History in (Antiquity to 1500)

The Hebrew view of history in the pre-Exilic biblical period was attached to the memory of a single event, namely the divine act of deliverance from Egypt in the Exodus (cf. Deuteronomy 26:5–9). The anonymous writer(s) of the Pentateuch (first five books of the Hebrew Bible), as well as the Deuteronomist (the hypothetical author of Joshua–2 Kings) made this their primary historical theme. Unlike the cyclical views of history of their neighbors, the Hebrew writers saw history as the history of salvation, moving in linear fashion toward a set goal. They were likely the first to see their history in the context of universal history. Israel's success and prosperity depended upon their obedience to Yahweh. Although the writers of the books from Genesis to 2 Kings had no critical apparatus with which to verify their accounts by objective criteria, they had genuine antiquarian concerns. Moreover, although they were theologically motivated, they meant to convey to the reader an allegedly accurate record of Israelite history. In fact, they did not write pure history, but cultic reflections on Israel's history. The Hebrew historians were also able to distinguish between mundane causation and divine interference. History could have a political motivation, but the Hebrew God, similar to the Hellenistic concept of Fortune, was always the manipulating force behind it.

One of the intentions of First and Second Kings was to explain how the Exile (586 B.C.) came about and to express the idea that God had adequate reasons for judgment. With the destruction of Jerusalem and the monarchy, and the subsequent deportation, it appeared that God was powerless to deal with the nations encircling Israel. However, by employing a legal motif following the fracture of covenant law (cf. 2 Kings 17:20–23), the writer of Kings brought forward an explanation of history that showed that their tragedy was a product of God's judgment, not frailty. Thus, the course of Israelite history led to the execution of the prophetic word of judgment (2 Kings 2:19–22; 13:14–19).

The post-Exilic author of First and Second Chronicles (c. 450 B.C.) exalted and idealized Israelite history and viewed God as acting directly in his people's lives. Jewish historiography was now influenced by Persia and characterized by extensive usage and precise quoting of official documents (for instance in Ezra and Nehemiah). After a historical blank of three centuries (ca. 425–167 B.C.), some authors, such as Daniel, sought refuge in apocalyptic messianism, giving a new interpretation of past history, which was now placed entirely in the supernatural world. The writer of 1 Maccabees (ca. 100 B.C.), who recorded the Maccabean struggle for liberation against the Seleucids, exhibited a decisive Hellenistic influence, although keeping a biblical theological base. Apparently originally composed in Hebrew, the surviving copy of 1 Maccabees is in Greek. The writer of 2 Maccabees created an epitome of Jason of Cyrene's five-volume history of the Maccabean revolt. Like 1 Maccabees, it was clearly Hellenized, but with a biblical base, adding many supernatural encounters, and showing little influence of Greek historians; First and Second Maccabees were not, however, absorbed into the Jewish tradition until the Renaissance. Showing a more decided Hellenistic influence was the Jewish thinker Philo (ca. A.D. 20), who wrote historical monographs on contemporary events in Alexandria. His philosophy of history reflects the Stoic concept of cosmic cyclical history, tempered with a belief in biblical providence. Josephus (A.D. 75–95), who wrote on the Jewish revolt against Rome and on early Jewish history, was a Jew who wrote essentially as a Greek historian, appealing to a Hellenistic audience by rationalizing supernatural phenomena in his writings. In this period, history writing was seen by most Jews to be a Greek enterprise, not easily distinguished from paganism. Thus, Jewish-Greek historiography was never assimilated into Judaism. Maccabees, Philo, Josephus, and other works in Greek were virtually ignored by the Jews until the early modern era, but were included within the Christian tradition. The rare cases of Jewish historiography in Hebrew in this period dealt with themes of the remote past. For example, Yose ben Halafta, in the *Seder Olam Rabbah* (ca. A.D. 150), established a chronological framework for biblical history without even acknowledging Josephus.

The Jews became to some extent indifferent to historiography after the end of Jewish nationalism in the late second century A.D. The biblical and rabbinic traditions became suprahistorical, transcending historical boundaries. There was, however, a modest revival of Jewish studies in Italy, which culminated in the tenth-century attempt by a certain Joseph b. Goryon to present the historical writings of Josephus in Hebrew. Entitled the *Book of Josippon,* it was read with great interest by late medieval Jewry for information concerning events of the Second Temple and influenced the twelfth-century world chronicle of Jerahmeel b. Solomon from northern Italy. Arguably, the most important Italian Jewish historiographic work was by Ahimaaz b. Paltiel, who wrote a family *Chronicle of Ahimaaz* that preserved many fanciful legends and gave a clear picture of contemporary Jewish life. There was likewise a revival of Jewish historiography (in the form of martyrology) in northern Europe after the First Crusade. Eliezer b. Nathan of Mainz and Solomon b. Simeon wrote chronicles of the Rhineland massacres, while Ephraim b. Jacob of Bonn chronicled the massacres of Jews during the Second and Third Crusades. Conversely, Mesopotamian and Iberian Jewries were influenced by Arabic historiography. An apologetic letter by Rabbi Sherira b. Hanina (906–1006) gave a composite account of rabbinic tradition to his own day. His chronicle served as a model for later historical researches. Abraham ibn Daud of Toledo (1110–1180) wrote short histories of the Second Temple period and, like Sherira, wrote a chronicle of rabbinic learning, the *Sefer ha-Kabbalah.* His goal, however, was simply to utilize history to defend his arguments, rather than to study it for its own sake. The revival of Greek philosophy during the Renaissance encouraged a further revival of Jewish historiography, culminating in the writings of Spinoza in the seventeenth century.

Mark W. Chavalas

See also CHRISTIANITY, VIEWS OF HISTORY IN; HOLOCAUST; JEWISH HISTORIOGRAPHY—MODERN (SINCE A.D. 1500).

References

Baron, S.W. *History and Jewish Historians.* Philadelphia: Jewish Publication Society of America, 1964.
Halpern, B. *The First Historians: The Hebrew Bible and History.* San Francisco: Harper and Row, 1988.
Van Seters, J. *In Search of History: Historiography in the Ancient World and the Origins of Biblical History.* New Haven, CT: Yale University Press, 1983.

Judson, Margaret Atwood (1899–1991)

Women's educator and historian of seventeenth-century England. A graduate of Mount Holyoke College and a student of C.H. McIlwain of Harvard, Judson received her Ph.D. in 1933. Always a strong proponent of women's education, she was an active member and officer of the Berkshire Conference of Women Historians. She made her professional career at the New Jersey College for Women (now Douglass College, Rutgers University): she served as chair of the history department (1955–1963) and as acting dean of the college (1966–1967). She received the American Historical Association Award for Scholarly Distinction (1990). A leading authority on the constitutional issues of the English civil war, Judson's *Crisis of the Constitution* (1949) remained the definitive work on the theoretical and legal arguments of the English civil war into the 1990s. Its analysis of early-seventeenth-century political thinking anticipated many of the "revisionist" arguments of the origins of the English civil war.

Judith P. Zinsser

Texts

Breaking the Barrier: A Professional Autobiography by a Woman Educator and Historian before the Women's Movement. New Brunswick, NJ: Rutgers University Press, 1984.
The Crisis of the Constitution. New Brunswick, NJ: Rutgers University Press, 1949; reprint: New York: Octagon, 1976.
"Henry Parker and the Theory of Parliamentary Sovereignty, 1640–49." In *Essays in Historical and Political Theory in Honor of Charles Howard McIlwain.* Cambridge, MA: Harvard University Press, 1936.
The Political Thought of Sir Henry Vane the Younger. Philadelphia: University of Pennsylvania Press, 1969.

References

Cogswell, Thomas. "Review Article: Coping with Revisionism in Early Stuart History." *Journal of Modern History* 62 (1990): 549.

Juvayni

See DJUWAYNĪ